Organizational Theory, Design, and Change

SEVENTH EDITION

Gareth R. Jones
Texas A&M University

PEARSON

Boston Columbus Indianapolis New York San Francisco Upper Saddle River
Amsterdam Cape Town Dubai London Madrid Milan Munich Paris Montréal Toronto
Delhi Mexico City Sao Paulo Sydney Hong Kong Seoul Singapore Taipei Tokyo

Editorial Director: Sally Yagan
Acquisitions Editor: Brian Mickelson
Director of Editorial Services: Ashley Santora
Editorial Project Manager: Sarah Holle
Director of Marketing: Maggie Moylan
Senior Marketing Manager: Nikki Ayana Jones
Marketing Assistant: Ian Gold
Senior Managing Editor: Judy Leale
Production Project Manager: Ilene Kahn
Senior Operations Supervisor: Arnold Vila
Operations Specialist: Cathleen Petersen
Creative Director: Blair Brown
Sr. Art Director/Design Supervisor: Janet Slowik
Art Director: Steve Frim
Cover and Interior Designer: Joseph DePinho
Cover Photo: F.C.G./Shutterstock.com
Full-Service Project Management and Composition: Integra
Printer/Binder: RR Donnelley
Cover Printer: Lehigh-Phoenix Color/Hagerstown
Text Font: Times Ten Roman 10/12

Credits and acknowledgments borrowed from other sources and reproduced, with permission, in this textbook appear on the appropriate page within text with the exception of the icons appearing with the boxed features which are from Shutterstock.com.

Library of Congress Cataloging-in-Publication Data
Jones, Gareth R.
Organizational theory, design, and change / Gareth R. Jones.—7th ed.
p. cm.
ISBN-13: 978-0-13-272994-9
ISBN-10: 0-13-272994-6
1. Organizational behavior. 2. Organizational behavior—Case studies. I. Title.
HD58.7.J62 2013
302.3'5—dc23

2011036274

10 9 8 7 6 5 4 3 2

ISBN 10: 0-13-272994-6
ISBN 13: 978-0-13-272994-9

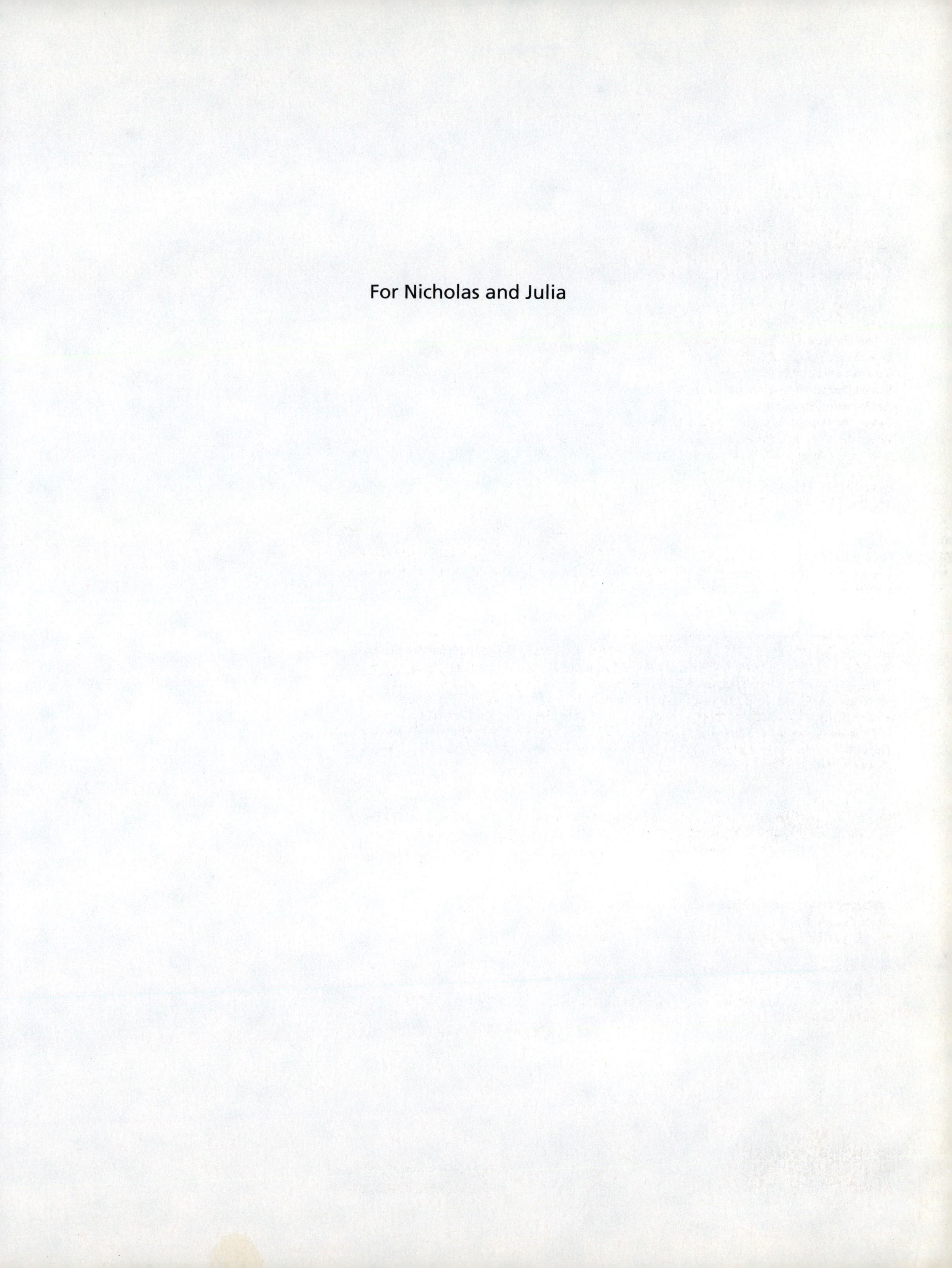

For Nicholas and Julia

Brief Contents

Preface xvii

Part 1 The Organization and Its Environment 1

Chapter 1 Organizations and Organizational Effectiveness 1
Chapter 2 Stakeholders, Managers, and Ethics 28
Chapter 3 Organizing in a Changing Global Environment 59

Part 2 Organizational Design 92

Chapter 4 Basic Challenges of Organizational Design 92
Chapter 5 Designing Organizational Structure: Authority and Control 121
Chapter 6 Designing Organizational Structure: Specialization and Coordination 148
Chapter 7 Creating and Managing Organizational Culture 179
Chapter 8 Organizational Design and Strategy in a Changing Global Environment 207
Chapter 9 Organizational Design, Competences, and Technology 240

Part 3 Organizational Change 273

Chapter 10 Types and Forms of Organizational Change 273
Chapter 11 Organizational Transformations: Birth, Growth, Decline, and Death 305
Chapter 12 Decision Making, Learning, Knowledge Management, and Information Technology 334
Chapter 13 Innovation, Intrapreneurship, and Creativity 366
Chapter 14 Managing Conflict, Power, and Politics 391

Case Studies 417
Company Index 480
Name Index 483
Subject Index 485

Contents

Preface xvii

Part 1 The Organization and Its Environment 1

Chapter 1 Organizations and Organizational Effectiveness 1

What Is an Organization? 1
How Does an Organization Create Value? 3

Why Do Organizations Exist? 5
To Increase Specialization and the Division of Labor 5
To Use Large-Scale Technology 6
To Manage the Organizational Environment 6
To Economize on Transaction Costs 6
To Exert Power and Control 7

Organizational Theory, Design, and Change 8
Organizational Structure 8
Organizational Culture 9
Organizational Design and Change 9
The Importance of Organizational Design and Change 11
Dealing with Contingencies 11
Gaining Competitive Advantage 12
Managing Diversity 14
The Consequences of Poor Organizational Design 14

How Do Managers Measure Organizational Effectiveness? 16
The External Resource Approach: Control 17
The Internal Systems Approach: Innovation 17
The Technical Approach: Efficiency 18
Measuring Effectiveness: Organizational Goals 19

The Plan of This Book 20
Organizational Design 22
Organizational Change 22

Summary 23 • Discussion Questions 23
Organizational Theory in Action: Practicing Organizational Theory 24
Open Systems Dynamics 24
The Ethical Dimension #1 24
Making the Connection #1 24
Analyzing the Organization: Design Module #1 24
Assignment 25

Chapter 2 Stakeholders, Managers, and Ethics 28

Organizational Stakeholders 28
Inside Stakeholders 28
Outside Stakeholders 30

Organizational Effectiveness: Satisfying Stakeholders' Goals and Interests 34
Competing Goals 35
Allocating Rewards 36

Top Managers and Organizational Authority 37
The Chief Executive Officer 39
The Top-Management Team 40
Other Managers 41
An Agency Theory Perspective 41
The Moral Hazard Problem 41
Solving the Agency Problem 42
Top Managers and Organizational Ethics 43
Ethics and the Law 44
Ethics and Organizational Stakeholders 45
Sources of Organizational Ethics 47
Why Do Ethical Rules Develop? 49
Why Does Unethical Behavior Occur? 51
Creating an Ethical Organization 52
Designing an Ethical Structure and Control System 53
Creating an Ethical Culture 53
Supporting the Interests of Stakeholder Groups 53
Summary 54 • Discussion Questions 55 • Organizational Theory in Action: Practicing Organizational Theory 55
Creating a Code of Ethics 55
The Ethical Dimension #2 55
Making the Connection #2 55
Analyzing the Organization: Design Module #2 55
Assignment 55

Chapter 3 Organizing in a Changing Global Environment 59
What Is the Organizational Environment? 59
The Specific Environment 61
The General Environment 63
Sources of Uncertainty in the Organizational Environment 65
Resource Dependence Theory 69
Interorganizational Strategies for Managing Resource Dependencies 70
Strategies for Managing Symbiotic Resource Interdependencies 71
Developing a Good Reputation 71
Cooptation 72
Strategic Alliances 72
Joint Venture 75
Merger and Takeover 76
Strategies for Managing Competitive Resource Interdependencies 76
Collusion and Cartels 77
Third-Party Linkage Mechanisms 78
Strategic Alliances 78
Merger and Takeover 78
Transaction Cost Theory 79
Sources of Transaction Costs 80
Transaction Costs and Linkage Mechanisms 81
Bureaucratic Costs 82
Using Transaction Cost Theory to Choose an Interorganizational Strategy 82
Summary 86 • Discussion Questions 87 • Organizational Theory in Action: Practicing Organizational Theory 87
Protecting Your Domain 87
The Ethical Dimension #3 87
Making the Connection #3 88
Analyzing the Organization: Design Module #3 88
Assignment 88

Part 2 Organizational Design 92

Chapter 4 Basic Challenges of Organizational Design 92

Differentiation 92
Organizational Roles 94
Subunits: Functions and Divisions 95
Differentiation at the B.A.R. and Grille 96
Vertical and Horizontal Differentiation 97
Organizational Design Challenges 97

Balancing Differentiation and Integration 99
Integration and Integrating Mechanisms 99
Differentiation versus Integration 102

Balancing Centralization and Decentralization 103
Centralization versus Decentralization of Authority 103

Balancing Standardization and Mutual Adjustment 106
Formalization: Written Rules 106
Socialization: Understood Norms 107
Standardization versus Mutual Adjustment 108

Mechanistic and Organic Organizational Structures 109
Mechanistic Structures 110
Organic Structures 110
The Contingency Approach to Organizational Design 112
Lawrence and Lorsch on Differentiation, Integration, and the Environment 112
Burns and Stalker on Organic versus Mechanistic Structures and the Environment 115

Summary 116 • Discussion Questions 117 • Organizational Theory in Action: Practicing Organizational Theory 117
Growing Pains 117
Making the Connection #4 117
The Ethical Dimension #4 117
Analyzing the Organization: Design Module #4 117
Assignment 118

Chapter 5 Designing Organizational Structure: Authority and Control 121

Authority: How and Why Vertical Differentiation Occurs 121
The Emergence of the Hierarchy 121
Size and Height Limitations 122
Problems with Tall Hierarchies 124
The Parkinson's Law Problem 127
The Ideal Number of Hierarchical Levels: The Minimum Chain of Command 127
Span of Control 128

Control: Factors Affecting the Shape of the Hierarchy 130
Horizontal Differentiation 130
Centralization 132
Standardization 133

The Principles of Bureaucracy 134
The Advantages of Bureaucracy 137
Management by Objectives 139

The Influence of the Informal Organization 140

IT, Empowerment, and Self-Managed Teams 141

Summary 143 • Discussion Questions 143 • Organizational Theory in Action: Practicing Organizational Theory 144
How to Design a Hierarchy 144
The Ethical Dimension #5 144

Making the Connection #5 144
Analyzing the Organization: Design Module #5 144
Assignment 144

Chapter 6 Designing Organizational Structure: Specialization and Coordination 148

Functional Structure 148
Advantages of a Functional Structure 150
Control Problems in a Functional Structure 150
Solving Control Problems in a Functional Structure 151

From Functional Structure to Divisional Structure 152
Moving to a Divisional Structure 154

Divisional Structure I: Three Kinds of Product Structure 154
Product Division Structure 154
Multidivisional Structure 156
Product Team Structure 161

Divisional Structure II: Geographic Structure 163

Divisional Structure III: Market Structure 164

Matrix Structure 166
Advantages of a Matrix Structure 167
Disadvantages of a Matrix Structure 167
The Multidivisional Matrix Structure 168
Hybrid Structure 170

Network Structure and the Boundaryless Organization 171
Advantages of Network Structures 171
Disadvantages of Network Structures 172
The Boundaryless Organization 172
E-Commerce 173

Summary 174 • Discussion Questions 175 • Organizational Theory in Action: Practicing Organizational Theory 175
Which New Organizational Structure? 175
The Ethical Dimension #6 175
Making the Connection #6 175
Analyzing the Organization: Design Module #6 175
Assignment 175

Chapter 7 Creating and Managing Organizational Culture 179

What Is Organizational Culture? 179
Differences in Global Values and Norms 182

How Is an Organization's Culture Transmitted to Its Members? 184
Socialization and Socialization Tactics 184
Stories, Ceremonies, and Organizational Language 187

Where Does Organizational Culture Come From? 189
Characteristics of People within the Organization 189
Organizational Ethics 191
Property Rights 193
Organizational Structure 196

Can Organizational Culture Be Managed? 197

Social Responsibility 199
Approaches to Social Responsibility 199
Why Be Socially Responsible? 200

Summary 202 • Discussion Questions 203 • Organizational Theory in Action: Practicing Organizational Theory 203
Developing a Service Culture 203
The Ethical Dimension #7 203

Making the Connection #7 *204*
Analyzing the Organization: Design Module #7 *204*
Assignment *204*

Chapter 8 Organizational Design and Strategy in a Changing Global Environment 207

Strategy and the Environment 207
Sources of Core Competences 208
Global Expansion and Core Competences 210
Four Levels of Strategy 211

Functional-Level Strategy 213
Strategies to Lower Costs or Differentiate Products 213
Functional-Level Strategy and Structure 215
Functional-Level Strategy and Culture 216

Business-Level Strategy 217
Strategies to Lower Costs or Differentiate Products 218
Focus Strategy 219
Business-Level Strategy and Structure 219
Business-Level Strategy and Culture 222

Corporate-Level Strategy 224
Vertical Integration 225
Related Diversification 226
Unrelated Diversification 226
Corporate-Level Strategy and Structure 227
Corporate-Level Strategy and Culture 229

Implementing Strategy across Countries 230
Implementing a Multidomestic Strategy 232
Implementing International Strategy 232
Implementing Global Strategy 233
Implementing Transnational Strategy 234

Summary 235 • Discussion Questions 236 • Organizational Theory in Action: Practicing Organizational Theory 236
What Kind of Supermarket? *236*
The Ethical Dimension #8 *236*
Making the Connection #8 *236*
Analyzing the Organization: Design Module #8 *237*
Assignment *237*

Chapter 9 Organizational Design, Competences, and Technology 240

What Is Technology? 240

Technology and Organizational Effectiveness 242

Technical Complexity: The Theory of Joan Woodward 244
Small-Batch and Unit Technology 244
Large-Batch and Mass Production Technology 247
Continuous-Process Technology 248
Technical Complexity and Organizational Structure 248
The Technological Imperative 250

Routine Tasks and Complex Tasks: The Theory of Charles Perrow 250
Task Variability and Task Analyzability 251
Four Types of Technology 252
Routine Technology and Organizational Structure 253
Nonroutine Technology and Organizational Structure 255

Task Interdependence: The Theory of James D. Thompson 255
Mediating Technology and Pooled Interdependence 256
Long-Linked Technology and Sequential Interdependence 258
Intensive Technology and Reciprocal Interdependence 259

From Mass Production to Advanced Manufacturing Technology 261

Advanced Manufacturing Technology: Innovations in Materials Technology 263

Computer-Aided Design 264

Computer-Aided Materials Management 264

Just-in-Time Inventory Systems 265

Flexible Manufacturing Technology and Computer-Integrated Manufacturing 266

Summary 267 • Discussion Questions 268 • Organizational Theory in Action: Practicing Organizational Theory 268

Choosing a Technology 268

The Ethical Dimension #9 269

Making the Connection #9 269

Analyzing the Organization: Design Module #9 269

Assignment 269

Part 3 Organizational Change 273

Chapter 10 Types and Forms of Organizational Change 273

What Is Organizational Change? 273

Targets of Change 274

Forces for and Resistance to Organizational Change 275

Forces for Change 275

Resistances to Change 278

Organization-Level Resistance to Change 278

Group-Level Resistance to Change 279

Individual-Level Resistance to Change 280

Lewin's Force-Field Theory of Change 280

Evolutionary and Revolutionary Change in Organizations 281

Developments in Evolutionary Change: Sociotechnical Systems Theory 281

Total Quality Management 282

Flexible Workers and Flexible Work Teams 285

Developments in Revolutionary Change: Reengineering 285

E-Engineering 290

Restructuring 290

Innovation 291

Managing Change: Action Research 291

Diagnosing the Organization 292

Determining the Desired Future State 292

Implementing Action 293

Evaluating the Action 294

Institutionalizing Action Research 294

Organizational Development 295

OD Techniques to Deal with Resistance to Change 295

OD Techniques to Promote Change 297

Summary 299 • Discussion Questions 300 • Organizational Theory in Action: Practicing Organizational Theory 300

Managing Change 300

Making the Connection #10 301

The Ethical Dimension #10 301

Analyzing the Organization: Design Module #10 301

Chapter 11 Organizational Transformations: Birth, Growth, Decline, and Death 305

The Organizational Life Cycle 305

Organizational Birth 306

Developing a Plan for a New Business 307

A Population Ecology Model of Organizational Birth 309
Number of Births 310
Survival Strategies 311
The Process of Natural Selection 312
The Institutional Theory of Organizational Growth 314
Organizational Isomorphism 315
Disadvantages of Isomorphism 316
Greiner's Model of Organizational Growth 316
Stage 1: Growth through Creativity 317
Stage 2: Growth through Direction 318
Stage 3: Growth through Delegation 318
Stage 4: Growth through Coordination 319
Stage 5: Growth through Collaboration 320
Organizational Decline and Death 321
Effectiveness and Profitability 321
Organizational Inertia 323
Changes in the Environment 324
Weitzel and Jonsson's Model of Organizational Decline 325
Summary 328 • Discussion Questions 329 • Organizational Theory in Action: Practicing Organizational Theory 329
Growing Pains 329
Making the Connection #11 329
The Ethical Dimension #11 329
Analyzing the Organization: Design Module #11 330
Assignment 330

Chapter 12 Decision Making, Learning, Knowledge Management, and Information Technology 334
Organizational Decision Making 334
Models of Organizational Decision Making 335
The Rational Model 335
The Carnegie Model 337
The Incrementalist Model 339
The Unstructured Model 339
The Garbage-Can Model 340
The Nature of Organizational Learning 342
Types of Organizational Learning 342
Levels of Organizational Learning 343
Knowledge Management and Information Technology 347
Factors Affecting Organizational Learning 349
Organizational Learning and Cognitive Structures 350
Types of Cognitive Biases 350
Cognitive Dissonance 350
Illusion of Control 351
Frequency and Representativeness 351
Projection and Ego-Defensiveness 352
Escalation of Commitment 352
Improving Decision Making and Learning 353
Strategies for Organizational Learning 353
Using Game Theory 354
Nature of the Top-Management Team 356
Devil's Advocacy and Dialectical Inquiry 357
Collateral Organizational Structure 358
Summary 359 • Discussion Questions 360 • Organizational Theory in Action: Practicing Organizational Theory 360

Store Learning 360
Making the Connection #12 360
The Ethical Dimension #12 360
Analyzing the Organization: Design Module #12 360
Assignment 361

Chapter 13 Innovation, Intrapreneurship, and Creativity 366

Innovation and Technological Change 366
Two Types of Innovation 366
Protecting Innovation through Property Rights 368

Innovation, Intrapreneurship, and Creativity 370
Entrepreneurship as "Creative Destruction" 371
Innovation and the Product Life Cycle 372

Managing the Innovation Process 374
Project Management 374
Stage-Gate Development Funnel 376
Using Cross-Functional Teams and a Product Team Structure 377
Team Leadership 379
Skunk Works and New Venture Divisions 380
Joint Ventures 381
Creating a Culture for Innovation 381

Innovation and Information Technology 383

Innovation and Information Synergies 384
IT and Organizational Structure and Culture 385

Summary 386 • Discussion Questions 387 • Organizational Theory in Action: Practicing Organizational Theory 387
Managing Innovation 387
The Ethical Dimension #13 387
Making the Connection #13 388
Analyzing the Organization: Design Module #13 388

Chapter 14 Managing Conflict, Power, and Politics 391

What Is Organizational Conflict? 391

Pondy's Model of Organizational Conflict 394
Stage 1: Latent Conflict 394
Stage 2: Perceived Conflict 396
Stage 3: Felt Conflict 397
Stage 4: Manifest Conflict 397
Stage 5: Conflict Aftermath 398

Managing Conflict: Conflict Resolution Strategies 399
Acting at the Level of Structure 399
Acting at the Level of Attitudes and Individuals 400

What Is Organizational Power? 401

Sources of Organizational Power 402
Authority 402
Control over Resources 403
Control over Information 404
Nonsubstitutability 404
Centrality 405
Control over Uncertainty 406
Unobtrusive Power: Controlling the Premises of Decision Making 406

Using Power: Organizational Politics 407
Tactics for Playing Politics 407
The Costs and Benefits of Organizational Politics 409

Summary 412 • Discussion Questions 412 • Organizational Theory in Action: Practicing Organizational Theory 413

Managing Conflict 413

The Ethical Dimension #14 413

Making the Connection #14 413

Analyzing the Organization: Design Module #14 413

Assignment 413

Case Studies 417

Supplemental Case Map 417

Case 1 United Products, Inc. 419
Jeffrey C. Shuman

Case 2 The Paradoxical Twins: Acme and Omega Electronics 428
John F. Veiga

Case 3 How SAP's Business Model and Strategies Made It the Global Business Software Leader 431
Gareth R. Jones

Case 4 The Scaffold Plank Incident 439
Stewart C. Malone and Brad Brown

Case 5 Beer and Wine Industries: Bartles & Jaymes 441
Per V. Jenster

Case 6 Bennett's Machine Shop, Inc. 447
Arthur Sharplin

Case 7 Southwest Airlines 459

Case 8 The Rise and Fall of Eastman Kodak: How Long Will It Survive Beyond 2011? 463
Gareth R. Jones

Case 9 Philips NV 474
Charles W. L. Hill

Case 10 "Ramrod" Stockwell 476
Charles Perrow

Company Index 480

Name Index 483

Subject Index 485

Preface

In the seventh edition of *Organizational Theory, Design, and Change*, I have kept to my theme of providing students with the most contemporary and up-to-date account of how the changing environment affects the way managers design and change organizational structure to increase organizational effectiveness. In revising my book, I have continued to focus on making the text relevant and interesting to students so it engages and encourages them to make the effort necessary to assimilate the text material—material being used every day by managers and consultants who are working to improve organizational performance. I have continued to mirror the changes taking place in the way organizations deal with their environments, such as the increasing use of outsourcing and the use of information technology, by incorporating recent developments in organizational theory and research into the text. Also, I have worked to provide vivid, current examples of the way managers of companies large and small have responded to such changes.

New to This Edition

- Over 65% of the in-chapter boxes and 90% of the closing cases are new and the rest have been updated.
- New material on the changing nature of problems involved in managing functional, product, and divisional structures and ways IT can be used to improve their performance.
- New material on the strategy–structure relationship, and new coverage about the reasons companies need to continuously examine and change their global strategies and structures.
- New material on online software development and craftswork technology and its importance in the growing services area.
- Expanded discussion of how to manage technology to create successful virtual organizational structures, such as those used by Accenture and PeopleSoft.
- A major focus is the recent ongoing changes in the mobile computing, smartphone, and software applications and the consequent effects on the changes in the competitive environment and the way companies have been changing their structures and control systems to manage these issues.
- Increased coverage of ethical issues involved in the stakeholder approach to organizations and their implications for organizational effectiveness, such as new "green" environmental coverage, and new coverage of disasters such as the BP oil spill, ethics in health care, and fraud in disguising the quality and price of goods and services.
- Explanations of the most recent developments in organizational structure, such as the product team structure, outsourcing, and network organizations because of advancements in IT.

The number and complexity of the strategic and organizational challenges confronting managers because of the changing global environment has continued to increase in the 2000s. In most companies, managers at all levels are playing catch-up as they work toward meeting these challenges by implementing new forms of organizational structure and by changing their existing structures, using the techniques and practices described in this book. Today, relatively small differences in performance between companies—the speed at which they can bring new products to market, for example, or in the way they choose to motivate their employees to find ways to increase effectiveness—can give one organization a significant competitive advantage over another. Managers and companies that use established organizational theory and design principles to change the way they operate can increase their effectiveness over time.

This is clearly evident by the way companies are continuously changing and reorganizing how they operate—at the functional, divisional, organizational, and global levels—to better compete and manage the ever-changing environment in the 2010s. Of course, the recession that began in the later 2000s, as well as continuously changing technological and economic conditions, offer new opportunities for agile companies that can adapt to meet these challenges while threatening the survival of those that cannot. Nowhere is this clearer than in the developing markets for mobile computing devices such as smartphones and tablet computers, where the performance of some companies like Apple and Samsung have soared, while those of others such as Motorola, Blackberry, and Dell have plunged.

Across all functions and levels, managers and employees must continuously search out ways to change organizational design to "work smarter" and increase performance. The challenges facing managers continue to mount as changing global forces such as increasing global outsourcing, rising commodity prices, and the emergence of new low-cost overseas competitors impact organizations large and small. Moreover, the revolution in information technology (IT) has transformed the way managers make decisions across all levels of an organization's hierarchy and across all of its functions and global divisions—and the rate of change in IT is accelerating.

The accelerated change in IT is changing the way organizations operate from top to bottom, a theme that has been extended and updated in the seventh edition. In today's world of video downloading, streaming media, text messaging, and tweeting without the use of any one type of mobile computing device, there is a need to understand how this affects organizational structure. The new edition offers up-to-date coverage of these issues throughout, peppered with examples that highlight the significant ways that advances in IT affect organizational decision making, change, and structure. For example, one issue covered in more depth is the pros and cons of global outsourcing and the new organizational problems that emerge when thousands of functional jobs in IT, customer service, and manufacturing are now being performed in countries overseas.

Encouraged by the increasing number of instructors and students who are using *Organizational Theory* with each new edition, and based on the reactions and suggestions of both users and reviewers, I have revised and updated the text in the following ways. First, just as pertinent new research concepts have been added to each chapter, outdated ideas and concepts have been omitted. As usual, my goal is to streamline the text content so students can avoid having to assimilate excessive material. Second, I am happy that the current content and arrangement of the chapters continues to be favorably received by its users. The organization of the book offers instructors many more hands-on ways in which they can help students to appreciate the power that people have over organizations to increase their effectiveness. As one student from New York City informed me in an email, "The book has given me a new vocabulary to understand the organization I work for and provided the conceptual tools needed to analyze and change it."

By bringing a discussion of organizational change and renewal to the center stage of organizational theory and design, this book stands alone. The organizational theory concepts the text describes are the same ones that firms of management consultants, chief operating officers, and the increasing number of managers responsible for organizational design and change use as they perform their roles and jobs.

Seventh Edition Content

The organization of the chapters in this edition is unchanged. Many textbooks lack a tight, integrated flow of topics from chapter to chapter. In this book, students will see beginning in Chapter 1 how the book's topics are related to one another. Integration has been achieved by organizing the material so that each chapter builds on the material of the previous chapters in a logical fashion. I also accomplish integration by focusing on one company, Amazon.com, and in several of the book's chapters I use boxed examples of this company, all of which have been updated, to illustrate organizational design and change issues.

Chapter 2, "Stakeholders, Managers, and Ethics," has proved to be popular, highlighting as it does the ethical issues that confront managers who seek to serve the interests of multiple stakeholders. I have expanded coverage of ethical issues in this edition in many chapters, offering more discussion and examples of all kinds of organizations—for-profit and nonprofit—that have benefited by the increased use of control systems to monitor their managers and their decision making. "The Ethical Dimension" exercise added to the "Organizational Theory in Action" section at the end of each chapter has also proved to be popular. Today, as corporate scandals proliferate, particularly insider trading and organizations created to defraud customers in the 2010s, it is important to ask students to think about and debate the ethical issues involved in organizational design and change.

A Focus on Managers

The managerial implications of organizational design and change are clearly articulated for the needs of students. Each chapter has one or more managerial summaries, in which the practical implications of organizational theories and concepts are clearly outlined. In addition, each chapter has several "Organizational Insight" boxes in which the experiences of a real company are tied to the chapter content to highlight the implications of the material. Each chapter also features two closing cases that allow a hands-on analysis by students.

Learning Features and Support Material

Each chapter ends with a section entitled "Organizational Theory in Action," which includes the following hands-on learning exercises/assignments:

- "Practicing Organizational Theory," which is an experiential exercise designed to give students hands-on experience doing organizational theory. Each exercise takes about 20 minutes of class time. The exercises have been class tested and work very well. Further details on how to use them can be found in the instructor's manual.
- An "Ethical Dimension" feature, where students individually or in groups can debate the ethical dilemmas that confront managers during the process of organizational design and change.
- A "Making the Connection" feature, where students collect examples of companies to illustrate organizational design and change issues.
- An ongoing "Analyzing the Organization" feature, where students select an organization to study and then complete chapter assignments that lead to an organizational theory analysis and a written case study of their organization. This case study is then presented to the class at the end of the semester. Complete details concerning the use of this and the other learning features are in the instructor's manual.
- A closing "Case for Analysis" with questions, which provides an opportunity for a short class discussion of a chapter-related theme.

In addition to these hands-on learning exercises, I have refined or added to the other learning features developed for previous editions of the book:

- Cases. At the end of the book are numerous cases to be used in conjunction with the book's chapters to enrich students' understanding of organizational theory concepts. Most cases are classical, in the sense that the issues they raise are always pertinent and provide a good learning experience for students. To preserve the teaching value of these cases, they should *not* be used for student write-ups; their value lies in the in-class discussion they generate. I have written detailed instructor notes for these cases to show how I use them in my course in organizational theory. These notes are found in the Instructor's Manual.
- "Organizational Insight" boxes relate directly to core chapter concepts.
- Chapter objectives and key terms are clearly defined and listed to aid learning.

- "Managerial Implications" sections provide students with lessons from organizational theory.
- Detailed end-of-chapter summaries facilitate learning.

Instructor Supplements

Instructors can access downloadable supplemental resources by signing in to the Instructor Resource Center at http://www.pearsonhighered.com/educator.

It gets better. Once you register, you will not have additional forms to fill out or multiple user names and passwords to remember to access new titles and/or editions. As a registered faculty member, you can log in directly to download resource files and receive immediate access and instructions for installing Course Management content to your campus server.

Need help? Our dedicated Technical Support team is ready to assist instructors with questions about the media supplements that accompany this text. Visit http://247pearsoned.custhelp.com/ for answers to frequently asked questions and toll-free user support phone numbers. The following supplements are available to adopting instructors.

PowerPoints: This presentation includes basic outlines and key points from each chapter. It includes figures from the text but no forms of rich media, which makes the file size manageable and easier to share online or via email. This set was also designed for the professor who prefers to customize PowerPoints and who wants to be spared from having to strip out animation, embedded files, and other media-rich features.

Instructor's Manual: Includes Teaching Objectives, Chapter Summaries, Outlines, Discussion Questions and Answers, Organizational Theory in Action, Cases for Analysis, Analyzing the Organization and Teaching Suggestions, and Ethical Dimensions.

Test Bank: Contains a detailed and comprehensive set of at least 60 multiple-choice questions and 15 true/false questions together with three short-answer and essay questions for each chapter.

Students Supplements

CourseSmart eTextbooks

Developed for students who want to save on required or recommended textbooks, CourseSmart eTextbooks online save students money off the suggested list prices of the print text. Students simply select their eText by title or author and purchase immediate access to the content for the duration of the course using any major credit card. With a CourseSmart eText, students can search for specific keywords or page numbers, make notes online, print out reading assignments that incorporate lecture notes, and bookmark important passages for later review. For more information or to purchase a CourseSmart eTextbook, visit www.coursesmart.com.

Acknowledgments

Finding a way to coordinate and integrate the rich and diverse organizational theory literature is challenging. Nor is it easy to present the material in a way that students can readily understand. Across the last editions of *Organizational Theory*, I have been fortunate to have the assistance of several people who contributed greatly to the book's final form. My developmental editor, Jane Tufts, helped me decide how to present the material in the chapters on structure and culture, which was my most difficult task. Her efforts can be seen in the integrated flow of material both within and between the book's chapters. Brian Mickelson, my Pearson editor, provided me with timely feedback and information from professors and reviewers, which has allowed me to shape the book to meet the needs of its intended market. Ilene Kahn ably coordinated the book's progress through production. Their efforts can be seen in the comprehensiveness of the package of materials that constitutes *Organizational Theory.* I am also grateful to the following reviewers and colleagues who provided me with detailed feedback on the chapters in this and previous editions of the book:

Reviewers

Sonny Ariss, Janet Barnard, Nate Bennett, Ken Bettenhausen, Alan Bluedorn, Karen Dill Bowerman, Tony Buono, John Butler, Marian Clark, Paul Collins, Ed Conlon, Tina Dacin, Parthiban David, Gordon Dehler, Richard Deluca, Leonidas Doty, Allen Engle, Steven Farner, Pat Feltes, Robert Figler, Steven Floyd, Linda Fried, Lawrence Gales, Deborah Gibbons, Richard Goodman, Charles Hill, Renata Jaworski, Bruce H. Johnson, Sara Keck, Leslie A. Korb, Robert M. Krug, Nancy Kucinski, Arie Lewin, Ronald Locke, David Loree, Karl Magnusen, Judi McLean-Parus, Frances Milliken, Dennis Mott, Pracheta Mukherjee, Ann Marie Nagye, Janet Near, Jeffrey R. Nystrom, Kaviraj Parboteeah, Dane Partridge, Dave Partridge, Richard Paulson, Janita Rawls, Greg Saltzman, Mary Jane Saxton, John Schaubroeck, John A. Seeger, James Segouis, Jim Sena, Dayle Smith, George Strauss, Dan Svyantek, Paul W. Swierez, Filiz Tabak, Louise Tourigny, and Carolyn Youssef.

Gareth R. Jones
College Station, Texas

Part 1
The Organization
and Its Environment

CHAPTER 1

Organizations and Organizational Effectiveness

Learning Objectives

Organizations exist in uncertain, changing environments and continually confront new challenges and problems. Managers must find solutions to these challenges and problems if organizations are to survive, prosper, and perform effectively.

After studying this chapter you should be able to:

1. Explain why organizations exist and the purposes they serve.
2. Describe the relationship between organizational theory and organizational design and change and differentiate between organizational structure and culture.
3. Understand how managers can utilize the principles of organizational theory to design and change their organizations to increase organizational effectiveness.
4. Identify the three principal ways in which managers assess and measure organizational effectiveness.
5. Appreciate the way in which several contingency factors influence the design of organizations.

What Is an Organization?

Few things in today's world are as important or as taken for granted as organizations. Although we routinely enjoy the goods and services that organizations provide, we rarely bother to wonder about how these goods and services are produced. We see online videos of manufacturing production lines churning out automobiles, PCs, or smartphones, and we watch on a local TV channel how our schools or hospitals are striving to use advances in new kinds of computer hardware and software, such as online learning programs, to help students improve their performance. Yet we rarely question how or why these organizations go about their business. Most often, we think about organizations only when they fail us in some way—for example, when we are forced to wait two hours in the emergency room to see a doctor, when our new smartphone crashes, or when we are at the end of a long line in a bank on a Friday afternoon. When such events happen, we wonder why the bank did not anticipate the rush of people and put on more tellers, why the hospital made us spend 30 minutes filling out paperwork in order to obtain service and then kept us waiting for an hour and a half, or why wireless phone companies don't insist on higher-quality hardware and bug-free software from their smartphone suppliers.

People have a casual attitude toward organizations because organizations are *intangible*. Even though most people in the world today are born, work, and die in organizations, nobody has ever seen or touched an organization. We see the products or services that an organization provides, and sometimes we see the people the organization employs, for example, as we go into a FedEx Kinko's store or doctor's office. But the reason an organization, such as FedEx Kinko's, is motivated to provide goods and services, and the way it controls and influences its members so that it can provide them, are not apparent to most people outside the organization. Nevertheless, grouping people and other resources to produce goods and services is the essence of organizing and of what an organization does.[1]

Organization
A tool people use to coordinate their actions to obtain something they desire or value.

An **organization** is a tool people use to coordinate their actions to obtain something they desire or value—that is, to achieve their goals. People who value security create an organization called a police force, an army, or a bank. People who value entertainment create organizations such as the Walt Disney Company, CBS, or a local club. People who desire spiritual or emotional support create churches, social service organizations, or charities. An organization is a response to and a means of satisfying some human need. New organizations are spawned when new technologies become available and new needs are discovered—such as social networking sites like Facebook—and organizations die or are transformed when the needs they satisfied are no longer important—such as video rental stores like Blockbuster. The need to invent improved drugs, for example, led to the creation of Amgen, Genentech, and other biotech companies. The need to handle increasing amounts of information and emerging new computer technologies led to the rise of IBM, Apple, Microsoft, Google, and other high-tech companies and the decline and failure of companies whose technology had become outdated, such as the typewriter company Smith Corona. Retail stores such as Walmart, Target, the Gap, and Sears are continually being transformed—not always successfully—as they seek to respond to the changing tastes and needs of consumers.

Who creates the organizations that arise to satisfy people's needs? Sometimes an individual or a few people believe they possess the necessary skills and knowledge and set up an organization to produce goods and services. In this way organizations like sandwich shops, Google, and software design studios are created. Sometimes several people form a group to respond to a perceived need by creating an organization. People with a lot of money may invest jointly to build a vacation resort. A group of people with similar beliefs may form a new church, or a nation's citizens may move to establish a new political party. In general, **entrepreneurship** is the term used to describe the process by which people recognize opportunities to satisfy needs and then gather and use resources to meet those needs.[2]

Entrepreneurship
The process by which people recognize opportunities to satisfy needs and then gather and use resources to meet those needs.

Today, many organizations being founded, and particularly those experiencing the fastest growth, are producing goods and services related in some way to new information

ifong/Shutterstock.com

Most of us don't think about the organizations that produce the products we use until we have a problem with those products.

technology (IT). The increasing use of mobile computing devices such as laptops, smartphones, and tablet computers linked to the World Wide Web (WWW) through wireless broadband connections are revolutionizing the way all organizations operate. This book examines this crucial issue by focusing on one company, Amazon.com, that has achieved explosive growth because of its development of IT products and services such as its Kindle book reader. In nine chapters of this book the story of this company is used to illustrate the many ways in which the IT revolution is improving the way organizations operate and create value today. We begin this analysis here by examining why and how Amazon.com was founded, which is discussed in the Focus on New Information Technology box.[3]

How Does an Organization Create Value?

The way in which an organization creates value is depicted in Figure 1.1. Value creation takes place at three stages: input, conversion, and output. Each stage is affected by the environment in which the organization operates. The **organizational environment** is the set of forces and conditions that operate beyond an organization's boundaries but affect its ability to acquire and use resources to create value.

Organizational environment The set of forces and conditions that operate beyond an organization's boundaries but affect its ability to acquire and use resources to create value.

Inputs include resources such as raw materials, machinery, information and knowledge, human resources, and money and capital. The way an organization chooses and obtains from its environment the inputs it needs to produce goods and services determines how much value the organization creates at the input stage. For example, Jeff Bezos chose to design software to make Amazon.com's website as simple and user friendly as he possibly could, and he only recruited people who could provide high-quality,

Figure 1.1 How an Organization Creates Value

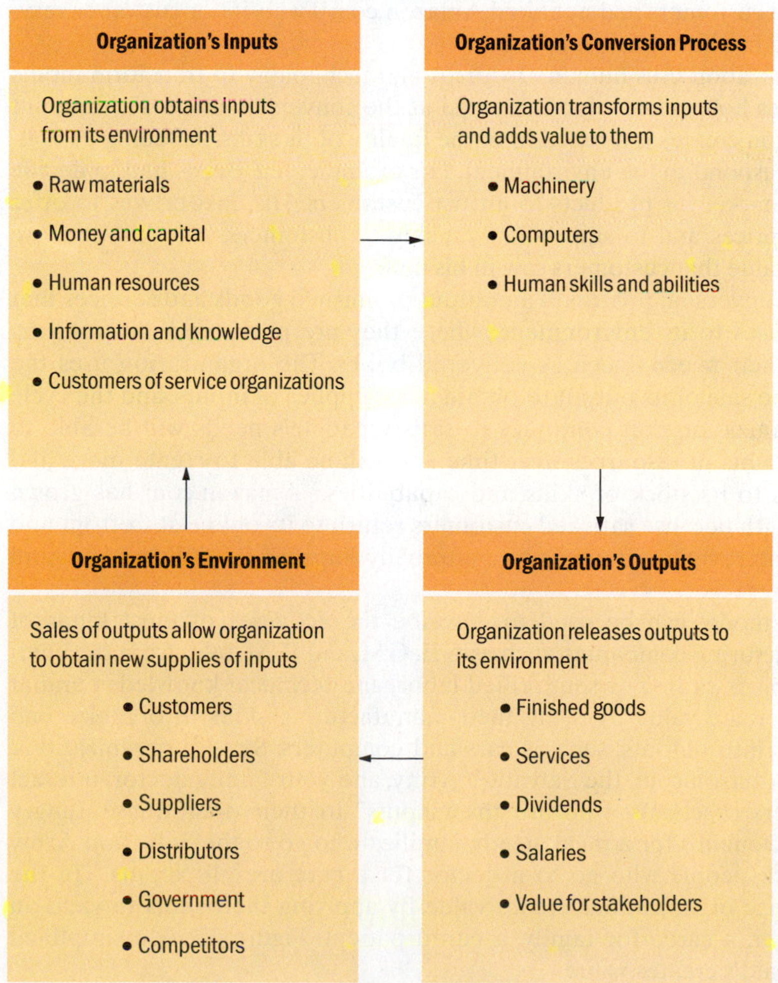

Organization's Inputs
Organization obtains inputs from its environment
• Raw materials
• Money and capital
• Human resources
• Information and knowledge
• Customers of service organizations
Organization's Conversion Process
Organization transforms inputs and adds value to them
• Machinery
• Computers
• Human skills and abilities
Organization's Environment
Sales of outputs allow organization to obtain new supplies of inputs
• Customers
• Shareholders
• Suppliers
• Distributors
• Government
• Competitors
Organization's Outputs
Organization releases outputs to its environment
• Finished goods
• Services
• Dividends
• Salaries
• Value for stakeholders

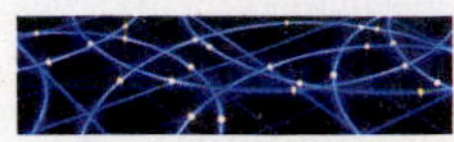

Focus on New Information Technology

Amazon.com, Part 1

In 1994, Jeffrey Bezos, a computer science and electrical engineering graduate from Princeton University, was growing weary of working for a Wall Street investment bank. With his computer science background prompting him, he saw an entrepreneurial opportunity in the fact that use of the Internet was growing at over 2,300% a year as more and more people were becoming aware of its information advantages.

Searching for an opportunity to take advantage of his skills in the new electronic virtual marketplace, he concluded that the bookselling market would be a good place to invest his personal resources. Deciding to make a break, he packed up his belongings and drove to the West Coast, deciding en route that Seattle, Washington, a new mecca for high-tech software developers and the hometown of Starbucks coffee shops, would be an ideal place to begin his venture.

What was his vision for his new venture? To build an online bookstore that would be customer friendly, easy to navigate, and would offer the broadest possible selection of books. Bezos's mission? "To use the Internet to offer products that would educate, inform and inspire."[4] Bezos realized that compared to a real bricks-and-mortar bookstore, an online bookstore would be able to offer a much larger and more diverse selection of books. Moreover, online customers would be able to search easily for any book in print on a computerized online catalog, browse different subject areas, read reviews of books, and even ask other shoppers for online recommendations—something most people would hesitate to do in a regular bookstore.

With a handful of employees and operating from his garage in Seattle, Bezos launched his venture online in July 1995 with $7 million in borrowed capital. Word of his venture spread like wildfire across the Internet and book sales quickly picked up as satisfied customers spread the good word. Within weeks Bezos was forced to relocate to new larger premises and to hire new employees as book sales soared. Bezos's new venture seemed to be poised for success.

customer-friendly service that would most appeal to his Internet customers. If he had made poor choices and customers had not liked Amazon.com's website or customer service, his company would not have been successful.

The way the organization uses human resources and technology to transform inputs into outputs determines how much value is created at the conversion stage. The amount of value the organization creates is a function of the quality of its skills, including its ability to learn from and respond to the environment. For example, Jeff Bezos had to decide how best to sell and market his products to attract customers. His answer was to offer wide choice and low prices and to ship books quickly to customers. His skill at these activities created the value that customers saw in his concept.

The result of the conversion process is an output of finished goods and services that the organization releases to its environment, where they are purchased and used by customers to satisfy their needs—such as delivered books. The organization uses the money earned from the sale of its output to obtain new supplies of inputs, and the cycle begins again. An organization that continues to satisfy people's needs will be able to obtain increasing amounts of resources over time and will be able to create more and more value as it adds to its stock of skills and capabilities.[5] Amazon.com has grown from strength to strength because satisfied customers return to its online storefront and continue to provide the revenues it needs to continually improve its skills and expand its operations.

A value-creation model can be used to describe the activities of most kinds of organizations. Manufacturing companies, such as GE, GM, and IBM, take from the environment component parts, skilled or semiskilled labor, and technical knowledge and at the conversion stage create value by using their manufacturing skills to organize and assemble those inputs into outputs, such as cars and computers. Service organizations, such as McDonald's, Amazon.com, the Salvation Army, and your family doctor, interact directly with customers or clients, who are the "inputs" to their operations. Hungry people who go to McDonald's for a meal, needy families who go to the Salvation Army for assistance, and sick people who go to a doctor for a cure are all "inputs." In the conversion stage, service organizations create value by applying their skills to yield an output: satisfied hunger, a cared-for family, a cured patient. Figure 1.2 is a simplified model of how McDonald's creates value.

Figure 1.2 How McDonald's Creates Value

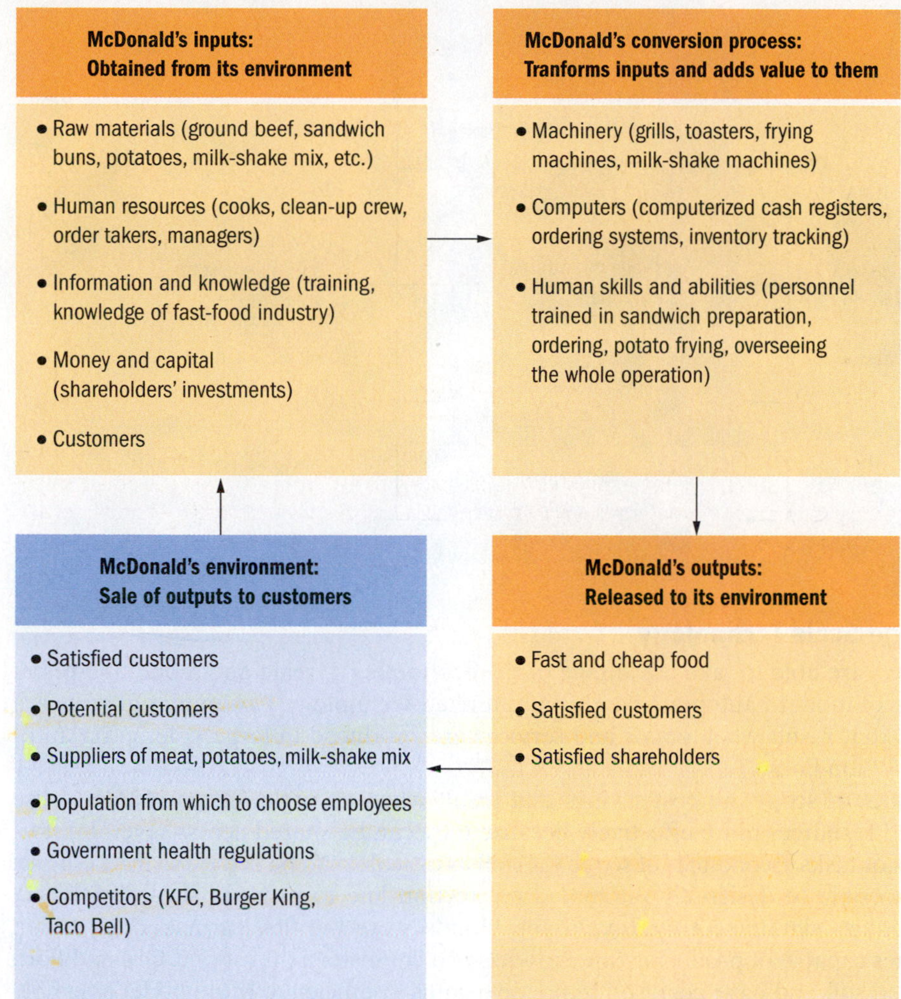

McDonald's inputs:
Obtained from its environment
• Raw materials (ground beef, sandwich buns, potatoes, milk-shake mix, etc.)
• Human resources (cooks, clean-up crew, order takers, managers)
• Information and knowledge (training, knowledge of fast-food industry)
• Money and capital (shareholders' investments)
• Customers
McDonald's conversion process:
Tranforms inputs and adds value to them
• Machinery (grills, toasters, frying machines, milk-shake machines)
• Computers (computerized cash registers, ordering systems, inventory tracking)
• Human skills and abilities (personnel trained in sandwich preparation, ordering, potato frying, overseeing the whole operation)
McDonald's environment:
Sale of outputs to customers
• Satisfied customers
• Potential customers
• Suppliers of meat, potatoes, milk-shake mix
• Population from which to choose employees
• Government health regulations
• Competitors (KFC, Burger King, Taco Bell)
McDonald's outputs:
Released to its environment
• Fast and cheap food
• Satisfied customers
• Satisfied shareholders

Why Do Organizations Exist?

The production of goods and services most often takes place in an organizational setting because people working together to produce goods and services usually can create more value than people working separately. Figure 1.3 summarizes five reasons for the existence of organizations.

To Increase Specialization and the Division of Labor

People who work in organizations may become more productive and efficient at what they do than people who work alone. For many kinds of productive work the use of an organization allows the development of specialization and a division of labor. The collective nature of organizations allows individuals to focus on a narrow area of expertise, which allows them to become more skilled or specialized at what they do. For example, engineers working in the engineering design department of a large car manufacturer like GM or Toyota might specialize in improving the design of fuel injection systems or other engine components. An engineer working for a small car manufacturer might be responsible for designing the whole engine. Because the engineer in the small company must perform many more tasks than the engineer in the large company, the degree of specialization in the small company is lower; there is less chance of discovering what makes for a great carburetor and thus creating more value for someone who desires high speed.

Figure 1.3 Why Organizations Exist

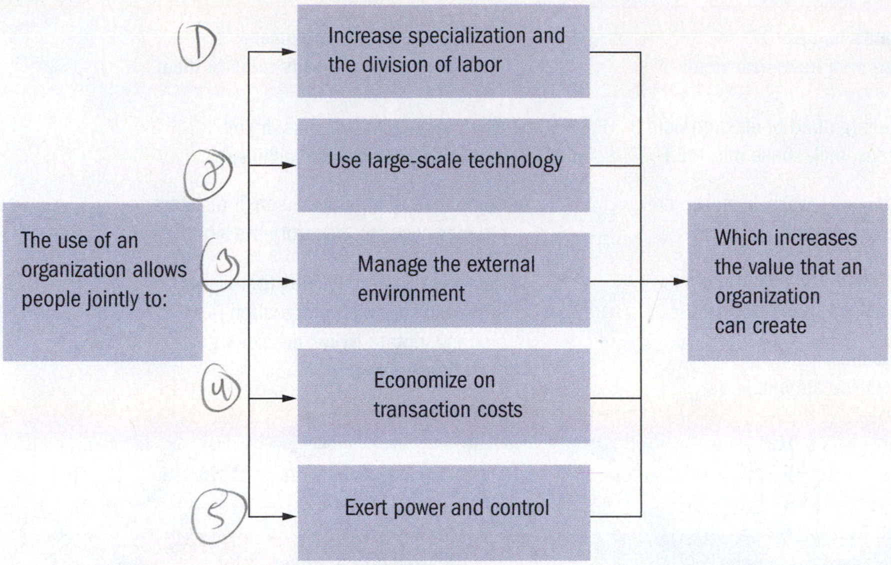

The use of an organization allows people jointly to:

- Increase specialization and the division of labor
- Use large-scale technology
- Manage the external environment
- Economize on transaction costs
- Exert power and control

Which increases the value that an organization can create

To Use Large-Scale Technology

Economies of scale Cost savings that result when goods and services are produced in large volume on automated production lines.

Economies of scope Cost savings that result when an organization is able to use underutilized resources more effectively because they can be shared across different products or tasks.

Organizations are able to take advantage of the economies of scale and scope that result from the use of modern automated and computerized technology. **Economies of scale** are cost savings that result when goods and services are produced in large volume on automated production lines.

Economies of scope are cost savings that result when an organization is able to use underutilized resources more effectively because they can be shared across several different products or tasks. Economies of scope (as well as of scale) can be achieved, for example, when it is possible to design an automated production line to produce several different types of products simultaneously. Toyota and Honda were the first carmakers to design assembly lines capable of producing three models of a car instead of just one. GM and Ford have followed suit and have achieved impressive gains in efficiency. Multimodel assembly lines give car companies lower manufacturing costs and greater flexibility to change quickly from making one model to another to meet varying customer needs.

To Manage the Organizational Environment

Pressures from the organizational environment in which they operate also make organizations the favored mode for transforming inputs into outputs. An organization's environment is the source of valuable input resources and is the marketplace into which it releases outputs. It is also the source of economic, social, and political pressures that affect an organization's ability to obtain these resources. Managing complex environments is a task beyond the abilities of most individuals, but an organization has the resources to develop specialists to anticipate or attempt to influence the many pressures from the environment. This specialization allows the organization to create more value for the organization, its members, and its customers. Large companies like IBM, AT&T, and Ford have whole departments of corporate executives who are responsible for monitoring, responding to, and attempting to manage the external environment, but those activities are just as important for small organizations. Although local stores and restaurants do not have whole departments to scan the environment, their owners and managers need to spot emerging trends and changes so that they can respond to changing customer needs, just as Jeff Bezos did; otherwise they will not survive.

To Economize on Transaction Costs

When people cooperate to produce goods and services, certain problems arise. As they learn what to do and how to work with others to perform a task effectively, people jointly have to decide who will do which tasks (the division of labor), who will get paid what amounts, and how to decide if each coworker is doing his or her share of the work. The costs associated with negotiating, monitoring, and governing exchanges between people to solve these kinds of transaction difficulties are called **transaction costs.** Organizations' ability to control the exchanges between people reduces the transaction costs associated with these exchanges. Suppose Intel bought the services of its scientists daily and thousands of scientists had to spend time every day discussing what to do and who should work with whom. Such a work system would be very costly and would waste valuable time and money. The structure and coordination imposed by the Intel organization, however, lets managers hire scientists on a long-term basis, assign them to specific tasks and work teams, and gives Intel the right to monitor their performance. The resulting stability reduces transaction costs and increases productivity.

Transaction costs
The costs associated with negotiating, monitoring, and governing exchanges between people.

To Exert Power and Control

Organizations can exert great pressure on individuals to conform to task and production requirements in order to increase production efficiency.[6] To get a job done efficiently, people must come to work in a predictable fashion, behave in the interests of the organization, and accept the authority of the organization and its managers. All these requirements make production less costly and more efficient but put a burden on individuals who must conform to organizational requirements. When individuals work for themselves, they need to address only their own needs. When they work for an organization, however, they must pay attention to the organization's needs as well as their own. Organizations can discipline or fire workers who fail to conform and can reward good performance with promotion and increased rewards. Because employment, promotion, and increased rewards are important and often scarce, organizations can use them to exert power over individuals.

Taken together, these five factors help explain why often more value can be created when people work together, coordinating their actions in an organized setting, than when they work alone. Over time, the stability created by an organization provides a setting in which the organization and its members can increase their skills and capabilities, and the ability of the organization to create value increases by leaps and bounds. By 2011, for example, Google grew to become the most valuable Internet software company in the world because Larry Page and Sergey Brin, its founders, created an organizational setting in which people are given freedom to develop their skills and capabilities to create innovative new products. In contrast, in the last decade other software companies like WordPerfect, Lotus, Novell, and even Microsoft have experienced major problems because they have not been able to create the Internet software customers want. Why does Google's organization allow it to create more and more value while these other organizations have actually reduced the value they can create? Before we can answer this question, we need to take a close look at organizational theory, design, and change.

Annette Shaff/Shutterstock.com

Giving the company's workers the freedom to innovate has helped Google stay ahead of its competition.

Organizational Theory, Design, and Change

Organizational theory The study of how organizations function and how they affect and are affected by the environment in which they operate.

Organizational theory is the study of how organizations function and how they affect and are affected by the environment in which they operate. In this book, we examine the principles that underlie the design, operation, change, and redesign of organizations to maintain and increase their effectiveness. Understanding how organizations operate, however, is only the first step in learning how to control and change organizations so that they can create wealth and resources effectively. Thus the second aim of this book is to equip you with the conceptual tools to influence organizational situations in which you find yourself. The lessons of organizational design and change are as important at the level of first-line supervisor as they are at the level of chief executive officer, in small or large organizations, and in settings as diverse as the not-for-profit organization or the assembly line of a manufacturing company.

People and managers knowledgeable about organizational design and change are able to analyze the structure and culture of the organization for which they work (or which they wish to help, such as a charity or church), diagnose problems, and make adjustments that help the organization achieve its goals. Figure 1.4 outlines the relationship among organizational theory, structure, culture, design, and change.

Organizational Structure

Organizational structure The formal system of task and authority relationships that control how people coordinate their actions and use resources to achieve organizational goals.

Once a group of people has established an organization to accomplish collective goals, organizational structure evolves to increase the effectiveness of the organization's control of the activities necessary to achieve its goals. **Organizational structure** is the formal system of task and authority relationships that control how people coordinate their actions and use resources to achieve organizational goals.[7] The principal purpose of organizational structure is one of control: to control the way people *coordinate* their actions

Figure 1.4 The Relationship among Organizational Theory and Organizational Structure, Culture, and Design, and Change

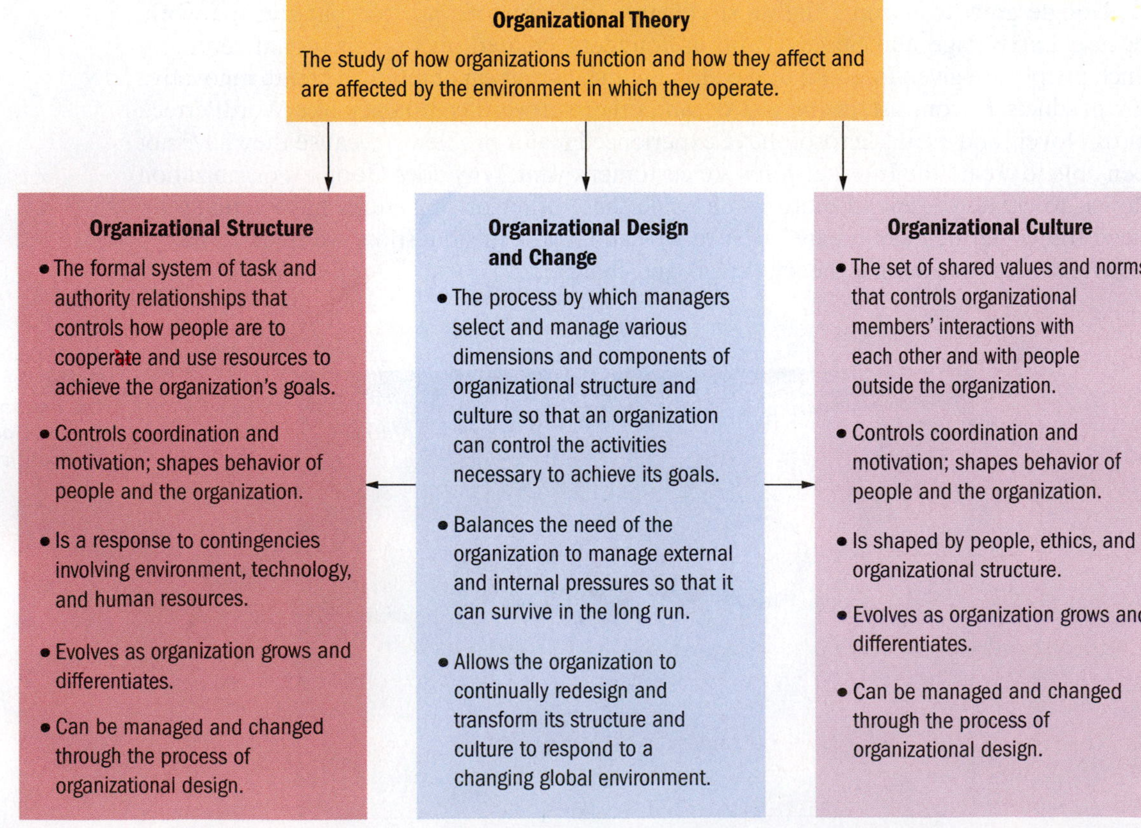

to achieve organizational goals and to control the means used to *motivate* people to achieve these goals. At Google, for example, the control problems facing Larry Page and Sergey Brin were how to coordinate their IT engineers' activities to make the best use of their talents, and how to reward them when they developed innovative products. Their solution was to place scientists in small self-contained teams and to reward them with stock in Google based on individual and team performance.

For any organization, an appropriate structure is one that facilitates effective responses to problems of coordination and motivation—problems that can arise for any number of environmental, technological, or human reasons.[8] As organizations grow and differentiate, the structure likewise evolves. Organizational structure can be managed through the process of organizational design and change.

Organizational Culture

At the same time that organizational structure is evolving, so is organizational culture. **Organizational culture** is the set of shared values and norms that controls organizational members' interactions with each other and with suppliers, customers, and other people outside the organization. An organization's culture is shaped by the people inside the organization, by the ethics of the organization, by the employment rights given to employees, and by the type of structure used by the organization. Like organizational structure, organizational culture shapes and controls behavior within the organization. It influences how people respond to a situation and how they interpret the environment surrounding the organization. At Google, Page and Brin attempted to create values that encouraged entrepreneurship and risk taking to build an organizational culture in which innovation was a valued activity. The small-team structure was helpful because scientists were continually meeting face to face to coordinate their activities and to learn from one another, which encouraged them to experiment and to find new ways of solving problems.

Organizational culture
The set of shared values and norms that controls organizational members' interactions with each other and with suppliers, customers, and other people outside the organization.

The cultures of organizations that provide essentially the same goods and services can be very different. For example, Coca-Cola and PepsiCo are the two largest and most successful companies in the soft drinks industry.[9] Because they sell similar products and face similar environments, we might expect their cultures to be similar. But they are not. Coca-Cola takes pride in its long-term commitment to employees; its loyal managers, many of whom spend their entire careers with the organization; and its cautious and cooperative approach to planning. By contrast, PepsiCo has a highly political and competitive culture in which conflicts over decision making cause frequent disputes, and often turnover, among top managers. Like organizational structure, organizational culture evolves and can be managed through organizational design and change.

Organizational Design and Change

Organizational design is the process by which managers select and manage aspects of structure and culture so an organization can control the activities necessary to achieve its goals. Organizational structure and culture are the *means* the organization uses to achieve its goals; organizational design is about how and why various means are chosen. An organization's behavior is the result of its design and the principles behind its operation. It is a task that requires managers to strike a balance between external pressures from the organization's environment and internal pressures from, for example, its choice of technology. Looking outward, the design can cause organizational members to view and respond to the environment in different ways. Looking inward, an organization's design puts pressure on work groups and individuals to behave in certain ways.

Organizational design
The process by which managers select and manage aspects of structure and culture so that an organization can control the activities necessary to achieve its goals.

Achieving the proper balance helps ensure that the organization will survive in the long run. The theories, concepts, and techniques covered in this book are intended to provide you with working models you can use to analyze organizational situations and to propose and implement suitable solutions to change an organization and increase its effectiveness.

High-tech organizations like Google, Apple, and Intel need to be flexible and capable of quick responses to the competitive moves of their rivals—Facebook, Samsung, and ARM—as they innovate new technology and introduce new products. At the same time, such organizations must have stable task relationships that allow their members to work together to create value, solve problems, and accomplish organizational objectives. In contrast, organizations like Nucor and Alcoa, which produce sheet steel and aluminium, respectively, face relatively stable environments in which customer needs are more predictable and technology changes more slowly. Consequently, their organizational design choices are likely to reflect the need for a structure and culture that reduces production costs rather than a structure and culture that promotes flexibility. In Chapters 4, 5, 6, and 7, we discuss the organizational structures and cultures that managers can design to help ensure their organizations' survival.

Organizational change
The process by which organizations redesign their structures and cultures to move from their present state to some desired future state to increase their effectiveness.

Organizational change is the process by which organizations move from their present state to some desired future state to increase their effectiveness. The goal of organizational change is to find new or improved ways of using resources and capabilities to increase an organization's ability to create value, and hence its performance.[10] Once again, organizational structure and culture are a principal means or fulcrum that managers use to change the organization so it can achieve its future desired state.

Organizational design and change are thus highly interrelated. Indeed, organizational change can be understood as the process of organizational redesign and transformation. As we discuss in later chapters, as organizations grow, their structure and culture is constantly evolving, changing, and becoming more complex. A large organization faces a different set of design and redesign problems than a small organization because its structure and culture are different from a small organization's. Managers need to recognize that their initial design choices will have important ramifications in the future as their organizations grow; indeed, it has been argued that initial choices are an important determinant of differences in long-run performance. For an example, consider how the way Steve Jobs designed the structure and culture of Apple changed over the years as he learned the principles behind organizational design, as illustrated in Organizational Insight 1.1.

Organizational Insight 1.1

How Steve Jobs Learned How to Organize and Control Apple

In 1976 Steven P. Jobs sold his Volkswagen van, and his partner Steven Wozniak sold his two programmable calculators, and they used the proceeds of $1,350 to build a circuit board in Jobs's garage. So popular was the circuit board, which developed into the Apple II personal computer (PC), that in 1977 Jobs and Wozniak founded Apple Computer to make and sell it. By 1985 Apple's sales had exploded to almost $2 billion, but in the same year Jobs was forced out of the company he founded. Jobs's approach to organizing was a big part of the reason he lost control of Apple.

Jobs saw his main task as designing the organizational structure in ways that would lead to the rapid development of new and improved PCs, but his personal style was often arbitrary and overbearing. For example, Jobs often played favorites among the many different project teams he created that caused many conflicts and led to fierce competition, many misunderstandings, and growing distrust among members of the different teams. Jobs's abrasive management style also brought him into conflict with John Sculley, Apple's CEO. Employees became unsure whether Jobs (the chairman) or Sculley was in control of the company. Both managers were so busy fighting for control of Apple that the task of ensuring its resources were being used efficiently was neglected. Apple's costs soared, and its performance and profits fell.

Apple's directors became convinced Jobs's style was the heart of the problem and asked him to resign. After he left Apple, Jobs started new ventures. First he founded PC maker NEXT to develop a powerful new PC that would outperform Apple's PCs. Then he founded Pixar, a computer animation company, which become a huge success after it made blockbuster movies such as *Toy Story* and *Finding Nemo,* both distributed by Walt Disney, and Pixar was eventually sold to Disney.

In both these companies Jobs organizing approach changed. He built strong management teams to lead the project teams developing the new PCs and movies and kept his distance. Jobs saw his main task as organizing the companies' future product development strategies and he left the actual tasks of organizing and controlling to the managers who reported to him. He gave them the autonomy to put his vision into practice and in both companies he worked to create a culture based on values and norms of collaboration and creative thinking to promote innovation.

Meanwhile Apple was struggling to compete against Dell's low-cost PCs loaded with Microsoft's Windows software; its performance was plummeting and its future looked in doubt. To help the company he founded survive, in 1996 Jobs convinced Apple to buy NEXT for $400 million and use its powerful operating system in a new line of new Apple Mac PCs. Jobs worked inside Apple to lead its turnaround and he was so successful that in 1997 he was asked to become its new CEO.

His first step was to create a clear vision and goals to energize and motivate Apple employees. Jobs decided that Apple had to introduce state-of-the art, stylish PCs and related digital equipment. He created a team structure that allowed programmers and engineers to pool their

iStockphoto.com/Justin Sullivan

skills to develop new PCs. He delegated considerable authority to the teams, but he also established strict timetables and challenging "stretch" goals, such as bringing new products to market as quickly as possible, for these groups. One result of these efforts was Apple's sleek new line of iMac PCs, which were quickly followed by a wide range of futuristic PC-related products.[11]

In 2003 Jobs announced that Apple was starting a new service called iTunes, an online music store from which people could download songs for 99 cents. At the same time Apple introduced its iPod music player, which can store thousands of downloaded songs, and it quickly became a runaway success. Apple continually introduced new generations of the iPod, each more compact, powerful, and versatile than previous models. By 2006 Apple had gained control of 70% of the digital music player market and 80% of the online music download business, and its stock price soared to a new record level.

The next milestone in Jobs's managerial history came in 2007 when he announced that Apple would introduce the iPhone to compete directly with the popular Blackberry. Once again he organized Apple's engineers into teams, not only to develop the new phone but to create an online iPhone applications platform where users would be able to download iPhone applications—such as to interact with their friends—to make their phones more useful. By 2010 over two million iPhone applications had been developed, over two billion applications had been downloaded by iPhone users, and Apple was the leader in the smartphone market.

In 2010 Jobs announced that Apple planned to introduce its new iPad tablet computer, which he claimed would be the best way to experience the Web, email, and photos and would also have a wireless reading function to compete directly against Amazon.com's successful Kindle wireless reader.[12] As before, Jobs organized a new engineering unit to pioneer the development of applications for its new iPad, and after the iPad was released in spring 2010 analysts and customers swarmed to buy it, its stock rose to a high of $219. By 2011, Apple's stock had soared to over $350 as its product teams continuously brought out new and improved versions of its iPod, iPhone, and iPad and many analysts thought the company's stock would become the most valuable in the world.

As the example of the way Steve Jobs had changed his approach to organizing people and resources suggests, people who start new organizations may initially lack the kinds of skills or knowledge to manage an organization's structure and culture effectively but many of them can develop these skills over time. An understanding of the principles behind organizational design and change helps to speed this learning process and deepens appreciation for the many subtle technical and social processes that determine how organizations operate.

The Importance of Organizational Design and Change

Because of increased global competitive pressures and the increasing use of advanced IT, organizational design has become one of management's top priorities. Today, as never before, managers are searching for new and better ways to coordinate and motivate their employees to increase the value their organizations can create. There are several specific reasons why designing an organization's structure and culture, and changing them to increase its effectiveness, are such important tasks. Organizational design and change have important implications for a company's ability to deal with contingencies, achieve a competitive advantage, manage diversity effectively, and increase its efficiency and ability to innovate.

Dealing with Contingencies

A **contingency** is an event that might occur and must be planned for, such as a changing environment pressure like rising gas prices or the emergence of a new competitor like

Contingency
An event that might occur and must be planned for.

Amazon.com that decides to use new technology in an innovative way. The design of an organization determines how effectively an organization is able to respond to various pressures in its environment and so obtain scarce resources. For example, an organization's ability to attract skilled employees, loyal customers, or government contracts is a function of the degree to which the way it is designed gives it control over those three environmental factors.

An organization can design its structure in many ways to increase control over its environment. An organization might change employee task relationships so that employees are more aware of the environment, or it might change the way the organization relates to other organizations by establishing new contracts or joint ventures. For example, when Microsoft wanted to attract new customers for its Windows software in the United States and globally, it recruited large numbers of customer service representatives and created a new department to allow them to better meet customers' needs. The strategy was very successful, and the Windows platform is still used on over 90% of all desktop PCs globally.

As pressures from competitors, consumers, and the government increase, the environment facing all organizations is becoming increasingly complex and difficult to respond to, and more effective types of structure and culture are continually being developed and tried. We discuss how the changing nature of the environment affects organizations in Chapter 3 and how organizations can influence and control their environments in Chapter 8.

One part of the organizational environment that is becoming more important and more complex is the global environment. In the 2000s U.S. companies like Apple, IBM, and Walmart are constantly under pressure to expand their global presence and produce and sell more of their products in markets overseas to reduce costs, increase efficiency, and survive. Organizational design is important in a global context because to become a global competitor, a company often needs to create a new structure and culture. Chapter 8 also looks at the structures and cultures that a company can adopt as it engages in different kinds of global activities.

Changing technology is another contingency to which organizations must respond. Today, the Internet and other advanced IT have become one of the principal methods that organizations use to manage relationships with their employees, customers, and suppliers. The growing use of IT is fundamentally changing the design of organizational structure and has led to a huge round of organizational change as organizations have redesigned their structures to make most effective use of IT. We examine the effects of IT on organizational design and change in almost all the chapters of this book but particularly in Chapter 12.

In particular, a theme throughout the book is to examine how IT is changing the nature of the boundary of the organization, and the specific ways organizations coordinate people and tasks. The growth of outsourcing and the global network organizations whose members are linked primarily through electronic means has changed the way organizations operate in many ways. The pros and cons of this change in organizing—as organizations seek to increase their effectiveness and gain a competitive advantage—are discussed in depth in later chapters.

Gaining Competitive Advantage

Increasingly, organizations are discovering that organizational design, change, and redesign are a source of sustained competitive advantage. **Competitive advantage** is the ability of one company to outperform another because its managers are able to create more value from the resources at their disposal. Competitive advantage springs from **core competences,** managers' skills and abilities in value-creation activities such as manufacturing, R&D, managing new technology, or organizational design and change. Core competences allow a company to develop a strategy to outperform competitors and produce better products, or produce the same products but at a lower cost. **Strategy** is the specific pattern of decisions and actions that managers take to use core competences to achieve a competitive advantage and outperform competitors. Consider the way in which Groupon, profiled in Organizational Insight 1.2, has been rushing to develop its strategy to capture customers and keep its competitive advantage.

Competitive advantage
The ability of one company to outperform another because its managers are able to create more value from the resources at their disposal.

Core competences
Managers' skills and abilities in value-creating activities.

Strategy
The specific pattern of decisions and actions that managers take to use core competences to achieve a competitive advantage and outperform competitors.

The *way* managers design and change organizational structure is an important determinant of how much value the organization creates because this affects how it

Organizational Insight 1.2

Groupon Forges Ahead

iStockphoto.com/Christian Rummel

In 2010, Google offered to buy Groupon, the online "daily deal" newcomer, for $6 billion as it became obvious that Internet users liked the idea of online, continually changing coupons that offered them good deals by location. Groupon grew out of a website called The Point. Founded by Andrew Mason in 2007, it was designed to allow a sufficient number of people to get together online and participate as members in a joint endeavor, so that a "tipping point" was reached that allowed them to act as a *group* to take advantage of an opportunity that could not be obtained by any one individual. As Mason said in a letter to prospective investors in 2011, "I started The Point to empower the little guy and solve the world's unsolvable problems."[13]

Mason transformed The Point into Groupon, and began hiring employees who shared his collective vision, and by 2009 it launched its online coupon service. As Mason wrote, "As an antidote to a common ailment for us city-dwellers: there's so much cool stuff to do, but the choice can be overwhelming. With so many options, sometimes the easiest thing is to go to a familiar restaurant, or just stay at home and watch a movie. As a result, we miss out on trying all the cool things our cities have to offer."[14] Mason's idea was that by focusing on one specific good or service each day in a specific geographic location, Groupon could leverage its members' collective buying power to obtain deals from companies supplying goods and services that were hard to resist. Moreover, to protect its users, Groupon promises that because nothing is more important than treating customers well, if customers feel Groupon has let them down, all they have to do is call Groupon to get a refund.

Spearheaded by Mason's vision, Groupon has built a company that saw its revenues increase by 15 times between 2010 and 2011 and has successfully managed its explosive growth. Mason took advantage of the concept of online coupons to its full effect. In fact, while global sales were nonexistent in March 2010, they were 53% of its revenues by March 2011. Indeed, to grow his company so fast, Mason has taken major risks as he has invested all the money raised from private investors, and from its growing revenues, into aggressive expansion to stay ahead of competitors—including Google and LivingSocial, which also rushed to expand their own online coupon services.

After all, any new startup can easily imitate Groupon's strategy, but being the first mover is a major advantage. Hence Mason believes that pouring money into sales and marketing to make Groupon the global leader is worth it—in the same way that eBay and Amazon.com spent billions to become the online retail portals of choice and are currently reaping the benefits of their innovative strategies. However, Groupon still faces the prospect of cutthroat competition from giants like Google. For example, in 2011 Google announced the launch of an online coupon service that will offer discounts from restaurants and other merchants if enough people agree to buy the coupons. The service, called "Google Offers" is similar to the daily deals offered by Groupon. Google is testing its new online coupon service in Portland, Oregon, and will then rapidly expand it to large cities such as New York and San Francisco as a part of a new mobile payment service Google also unveiled recently that allows users to pay for products directly through their smartphones. So, only the future will tell if Groupon can maintain its leadership over this niche of the online market or will be crushed by Google, as well as Yahoo, AOL, and Facebook (which also announced its own coupon service for its 500,000 million users in 2011).

Despite these concerns and the fact in June 2011 Groupon had only 50 million users, its initial stock offering valued the company at $30 billion—a value higher than Google's when it went public! Only time will tell if Groupon can develop the organizational structure and culture it needs to control its explosive growth; so far it is succeeding as its laid-back founder has recruited people committed to following Mason's vision and making Groupon a force in which individuals can obtain the bargaining power they need to deal with large companies.

implements strategy. Many sources of competitive advantage, such as skills in research and development that result in novel product features or state-of-the-art technology, evaporate because they are relatively easy for competitors to imitate. It is much more difficult to imitate good organizational design and carefully managed change that brings into being a successful organizational structure and culture. Such imitation is difficult because structure and culture are embedded in the way people in an organization interact and coordinate their actions to get a job done. Moreover, because successful structures and cultures form early, as at Dell and Apple, and take a long time to establish and develop, companies that possess them can have a long-term competitive advantage.

An organization's strategy is always changing in response to changes in the environment; organizational design must be a continuously evolving managerial activity for a company to stay ahead of the competition. There is never a single optimal or "perfect" design to fit an organization's needs. Managers must constantly evaluate how well their organization's structure and culture work, and they should change and redesign them continually to improve them. In Chapter 8 we consider how organizations create value by means of their strategy.

Managing Diversity

Differences in the race, gender, and national origin of organizational members have important implications for the values of an organization's culture and for organizational effectiveness. The quality of organizational decision making, for example, is a function of the diversity of the viewpoints that get considered and of the kind of analysis that takes place. Similarly, in many organizations a large part of the workforce are minority employees whose needs and preferences must be taken into consideration. Also, changes in the characteristics of the workforce, such as an influx of immigrant workers or the aging of the current workforce, require attention and advance planning. An organization needs to design a structure and control system to make optimal use of the talents of a diverse workforce and to develop an organizational culture that encourages employees to work together. An organization's structure and culture determine how effectively managers are able to coordinate and motivate workers. Today, as companies increasingly operate in countries with widely disparate cultures around the globe, organizational design becomes even more important to harmonize national with organizational culture. Organizational Insight 1.3 discusses how the use of diverse—in this case female—manufacturing managers can promote high performance.

PROMOTING EFFICIENCY, SPEED, AND INNOVATION Organizations exist to produce goods and services that people value. The better that organizations function, the more value, in the form of more or better goods and services, they create. Historically, the capacity of organizations to create value has increased enormously as organizations have introduced better ways of producing and distributing goods and services. Earlier we discussed the importance of the division of labor and the use of modern technology in reducing costs, speeding work processes, and increasing efficiency. The design and use of new and more efficient organizational structures is equally important. In today's global environment, for example, competition from countries with low labor costs is pressuring companies all over the world to become more efficient in order to reduce costs or increase quality.

The ability of companies to compete successfully in today's competitive environment is increasingly a function of how well they innovate and how quickly they can introduce new technologies. Organizational design plays an important role in innovation. For example, the way an organization's structure links people in different specializations, such as research and marketing, determines how fast the organization can introduce new products. Similarly, an organization's culture can affect people's desire to be innovative. A culture based on entrepreneurial norms and values is more likely to encourage innovation than a culture that is conservative and bureaucratic because entrepreneurial values encourage people to learn how to respond and adapt to a changing situation.

Organizational design involves a constant search for new or better ways of coordinating and motivating employees. Different structures and cultures cause employees to behave in different ways. We consider structures that encourage efficiency and innovation in Chapters 4, 5, and 6 and cultures that do so in Chapter 7.

The Consequences of Poor Organizational Design

Many management teams fail to understand the important effects that organizational design and change can have on their company's performance and effectiveness. Although organizational structure and culture control behavior, managers are often unaware of the many factors that affect this relationship, paying scant attention to the way employees behave and their role in the organization—until something happens.

Ford, Sears, and Kodak have all experienced enormous problems in the last decade adjusting to the reality of modern global competition and have seen their sales and

Organizational Insight 1.3

How Diverse Manufacturing Managers Can Help Increase Product Quality

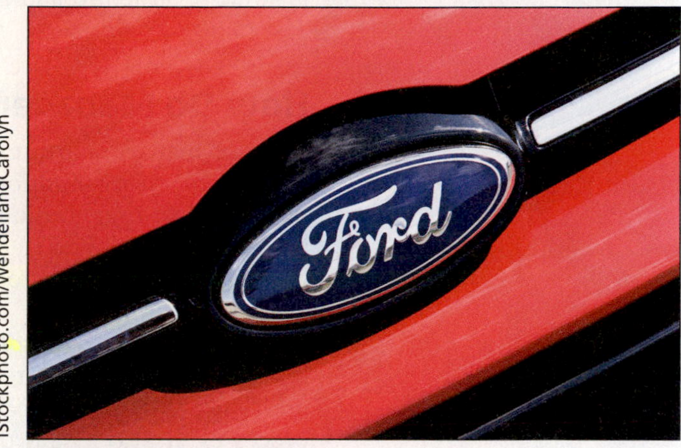

iStockphoto.com/WendellandCarolyn

Building cars remains primarily a male occupation; in 2011 roughly three out of four automotive manufacturing jobs are held by men, and women still number less than 20% of automotive manufacturing managers. Today, however, more women than men are buying new vehicles, and that shift, together with an increasing concern for diversity, has prompted major carmakers to promote more women into key management positions.[15] However, few women enroll in automotive and mechanical engineering programs because assembly plants have a reputation of being unpleasant, dirty, noisy places to work.

At Ford Motors, however, two of its female plant managers, Gloria Georger and Jan Allman, provide good examples of women who accepted the challenge of entering the manufacturing world. They embraced the opportunities such a job offers, and developed the skills that have allowed them to rise to become plant managers responsible for organizing and controlling billion-dollar manufacturing plants that employ thousands of employees.

Gloria Georger had no plans to pursue a manufacturing job and majored in accounting, but one recruiter commented on her outgoing personality and suggested she consider manufacturing where her interpersonal skills might be valuable—and manufacturing paid better than accounting. She took a job at U.S. Steel's plant in Gary, Indiana, and sure enough, her ability to motivate and work smoothly with employees led her to be promoted to production supervisor. Moreover, she claims the job helped develop the skills she needed to manage the unexpected contingencies that always arise on a fast-paced assembly line. She moved to Ford in 1986 when few women worked in manufacturing, but she quickly demonstrated the willingness to learn the cultural values and norms of its manufacturing operations and her personality allowed her to embrace and succeed in handling challenges from her mainly male colleagues and subordinates. She came to be regarded as a competent team leader and she steadily worked her way up the hierarchy of Ford's manufacturing function in different Ford plants until being promoted to her current position as the head manager of Ford's stamping plant in Chicago Heights, Illinois.[16]

Jan Allman is in charge of Ford's Torrence Avenue assembly plant, where in 2011 two-shifts of 2500 assembly line workers produce the new generation Ford Taurus, Lincoln MKS, and Explorer SUV. The parts produced by Georger's plant are assembled into the final vehicle at the Torrence Avenue plant, so close cooperation between the two plant managers is essential. Allman joined Ford in 1986 as a line engineer of an engine plant after receiving an engineering degree; she was one of two women out of 100 engineers Ford selected as interns to evaluate their performance before making hiring decisions. Allman rose to become the manufacturing engineering manager in charge of the engine plant, a position rarely held by a woman. Her hands-on organizing approach under difficult conditions impressed her colleagues, who noted her attention to detail of every aspect of the assembly process and the agreeable way in which she treated—and was treated by—employees. Hence, her promotion to become the manager of one of Ford's major assembly plants.

Both Allman and Georger agree that the growing number of women Ford has recruited into manufacturing over time has helped change the values and norms of its manufacturing culture.[17] Not only has it reduced the level of conflict between managers and workers, it has promoted cooperation and helped to promote Ford's focus on increasing product quality that is one of its major competitive advantages in the tough game of carmaking today. In 2011, for example, Ford reported its highest profits in 20 years and the company's new vehicles are increasingly ranked for their high quality.

profits fall dramatically. In response, they have slashed their workforces, reduced the number of products they make, and even reduced their investment in R&D. Why did the performance of these blue-chip companies deteriorate to such a degree? A major reason is that managers lost control of their organizational structures and cultures. These companies became so big and bureaucratic that their managers and employees were unable to change and adapt to changing conditions.

The consequence of poor organizational design or lack of attention to organizational design is the decline of the organization. Talented employees leave to take positions in strong growing companies. Resources become harder and harder to acquire, and the whole process of value creation slows down. Neglecting organizational design until crisis threatens forces managers to make changes in organizational structure and culture that derail the company's strategy. In the last decade, one major development at large companies has been the appointment of chief operating officers (COOs), who are made responsible for overseeing organizational structure and culture. COOs create and oversee teams of experienced senior managers who are responsible for organizational design and for orchestrating not only small and incremental but also organization-wide changes in strategy, structure, and culture.

How Do Managers Measure Organizational Effectiveness?

Because managers are responsible for utilizing organizational resources in a way that maximizes an organization's ability to create value, it is important to understand how they evaluate organizational performance. Researchers analyzing what CEOs and managers do have pointed to control, innovation, and efficiency as the three most important processes managers use to assess and measure how effective they, and their organizations, are at creating value.[18]

In this context, *control* means having control over the external environment and having the ability to attract resources and customers. *Innovation* means developing an organization's skills and capabilities so the organization can discover new products and processes. It also means designing and creating new organizational structures and cultures that enhance a company's ability to change, adapt, and improve the way it functions.[19] *Efficiency* means developing modern production facilities using new information technologies that can produce and distribute a company's products in a timely and cost-effective manner. It also means introducing techniques like Internet-based information systems, total quality management, and just-in-time inventory systems (discussed in Chapter 9) to improve productivity.

To evaluate the effectiveness with which an organization confronts each of these three challenges, managers can take one of three approaches (see Table 1.1). An organization is effective if it can (1) secure scarce and valued skills and resources from outside the organization (external resource approach); (2) coordinate resources with employee skills creatively to innovate products and adapt to changing customer needs (internal systems approach); and (3) convert skills and resources efficiently into finished goods and services (technical approach).

TABLE 1.1 Approaches to Measuring Organizational Effectiveness

Approach	Description	Goals to Set to Measure Effectiveness
External resource approach	Evaluates the organization's ability to secure, manage, and control scarce and valued skills and resources	• Lower costs of inputs • Obtain high-quality inputs of raw materials and employees • Increase market share • Increase stock price • Gain support of stakeholders such as government or environmentalists
Internal systems approach	Evaluates the organization's ability to be innovative and function quickly and responsively	• Cut decision-making time • Increase rate of product innovation • Increase coordination and motivation of employees • Reduce conflict • Reduce time to market
Technical approach	Evaluates the organization's ability to convert skills and resources into goods and services efficiently	• Increase product quality • Reduce number of defects • Reduce production costs • Improve customer service • Reduce delivery time to customer

The External Resource Approach: Control

The **external resource approach** allows managers to evaluate how effectively an organization manages and controls its external environment. For example, the organization's ability to influence stakeholders' perceptions in its favor and to receive a positive evaluation by external stakeholders is very important to managers and the organization's survival.[20] Similarly, an organization's ability to utilize its environment and to secure scarce and valuable resources is another indication of its control over the environment.[21]

External resource approach A method managers use to evaluate how effectively an organization manages and controls its external environment.

To measure the effectiveness of their control over the environment, managers use indicators such as stock price, profitability, and return on investment, which compare the performance of their organization with the performance of other organizations.[22] Top managers watch the price of their company's stock very closely because of the impact it has on shareholder expectations. Similarly, in their attempt to attract customers and gauge the performance of their organization, managers gather information on the quality of their company's products as compared with their competitors' products.

Top management's ability to perceive and respond to changes in the environment or to initiate change and be first to take advantage of a new opportunity is another indicator of an organization's ability to influence and control its environment. For instance, the ability and willingness of the Walt Disney Company to manage its environment by seizing any chance to use its reputation and brand name to develop new products that exploit market opportunities—such as when it bought Pixar from Steve Jobs—are well known. Similarly, CEO Larry Page has stated that his goal is to be at the forefront of new developments in mobile computing software and hardware to increase Google's competitive advantage. By their competitive attitude, these companies signify that they intend to stay in control of their environment so they can continue to obtain scarce and valued resources such as customers and markets. Managers know that the organization's aggressiveness, entrepreneurial nature, and reputation are all criteria by which stakeholders (especially shareholders) judge how well a company's management is controlling its environment.

In fast-changing environments where customers' needs change and evolve and where new groups of customers emerge as new technologies result in new kinds of products and services, companies must learn to define and redefine their businesses to satisfy those needs. Companies have to listen closely to their customers and decide how best to meet their changing needs and preferences.

The Internal Systems Approach: Innovation

The **internal systems approach** allows managers to evaluate how effectively an organization functions and operates. To be effective, an organization needs a structure and a culture that foster adaptability and quick responses to changing conditions in the environment. The organization also needs to be flexible so it can speed up decision making and create products and services rapidly. Measures of an organization's capacity for innovation include the length of time needed to make a decision, the amount of time needed to get new products to market, and the amount of time spent coordinating the activities of different departments.[23] These factors can often be measured objectively. For example, in the spring of 2011 Netflix announced that its rapid moves to negotiate agreements with major movie studios to speed the launch of its new online movie streaming service had led to a record increase in the number of its customers—and its stock price soared. Similarly, Apple was able to announce record shipments of the new models of its iPhone and iPad in 2011 as a result of its ability to redesign and improve its products much more quickly than its rivals.

Internal systems approach A method that allows managers to evaluate how effectively an organization functions and resources operate.

Improvements to internal systems that influence employee coordination or motivation have a direct impact on an organization's ability to respond to its environment. The reduction in product development time has allowed companies like Netflix and Apple to blow away competitors like Blockbuster, Comcast, and Blackberry and HP. The improved ability to get a product to market makes a company more attractive to customers who always want the product that contains the most recent technology available, such as the most advanced Intel chips, or software applications such as those in Apple's App Store.

The Technical Approach: Efficiency

Technical approach A method managers use to evaluate how efficiently an organization can convert some fixed amount of organizational resources into finished goods and services.

The **technical approach** allows managers to evaluate how efficiently an organization can convert some fixed amount of organizational skills and resources into finished goods and services. Technical effectiveness is measured in terms of productivity and efficiency (the ratio of outputs to inputs).[24] Thus, for example, an increase in the number of units produced without the use of additional labor indicates a gain in productivity, and so does a reduction in the cost of labor or materials required to produce each unit of output.

Productivity measures are objective indicators of the effectiveness of an organization's production operations. Thus it is common for production line managers to measure productivity at all stages of the production process using indicators such as number of defective products or wasted material. When they find ways to increase productivity, they are then rewarded for reducing costs. In service organizations, where no tangible good is produced, line managers measure productivity using indicators such as amount of sales per employee or the ratio of goods sold to goods returned to judge employee productivity. For most work activities, no matter how complex, a way can be found to measure productivity or performance. In many settings the rewards offered to both employees and managers are closely linked to improvements in productivity, and it is critical to select the right measures to evaluate effectiveness.[25] Employee attitude and motivation and a desire to cooperate are also important factors influencing productivity and efficiency.[26]

The importance of continuously improving efficiency is very clear in the airline business. During the recent financial crisis, most major airlines were reporting billions of dollars in losses as a result of rising fuel prices, but one airline, Southwest Airlines, was only reporting *lower* profits. In fact, Southwest has long been the most profitable U.S. airline, even though its fares in the past have been 25% or more *below* those of its rivals. The major reason for its high performance is its never-ending quest to increase operating efficiency.[27]

From the beginning, under the direction of its founder, Herb Kelleher, the airline focused on developing an operating structure that lowers the cost of inputs and the cost of converting inputs into outputs, which are on-time flights that satisfy customers.

How does it do it? First, Southwest carefully selects its human resource inputs; only 3% of those who are interviewed each year are hired, and its existing employees are the ones who do the hiring—to make certain the new person fits in and is a team player with the right attitude. This is a vital strategy because employees are expected to have a positive, helping attitude not only toward passengers but also toward each other. To increase efficiency, all of Southwest's employees are expected to help each other out whenever needed to do everything necessary to speed the departure of its planes. Efficiency in the airline business is measured by the time each plane spends in the air, not stuck at the gate, and Southwest can turn a plane around and put it back in the air in 30 to 45 minutes—way ahead of its rivals. The bottom line is that Southwest needs fewer employees than other airlines to run its fleet of planes efficiently, which translates into major cost savings.

It also uses other inputs efficiently; for example, it only flies one kind of plane, the Boeing 737, which means that far less pilot training is required and maintenance costs are reduced. It also only flies mainly into low-cost airports, not the main city airports where landing charges and traffic congestion are usually much higher and plane turnaround much slower. It also operates what is called a "hub-and-spoke" network, meaning its planes typically touch down at least once before they reach the final destination, which allows it to fill its planes more easily and so make better use of its resources. Finally, Southwest never offered passengers meals and other free perks, a policy that all airlines have now copied to reduce costs as fuel prices soar. And, although it has experimented with assigned seating, boarding is on a first-come, first-served basis, which again simplifies its procedures.

In essence, Southwest tries to streamline and simplify all of its operating procedures to improve efficiency. Only the coordination between its employees makes it possible for its lean and simplified procedures to work, however. And as we discussed earlier, for its operating structure to work efficiently, coordination is not enough; employees must also be motivated to work hard and cooperate. From the beginning Southwest motivated employees with a generous profit-sharing plan whereby employees receive stock in the company as a function of how well the company performs. Because today employees own over 20% of Southwest's stock, this is a clear indicator that its continuous concern to design an operating structure that improves efficiency has paid off. In 2011, Southwest bought AirTran, its closest low-cost competitor, to expand its national route structure. Today Southwest's low-cost rival is JetBlue, which followed Southest's strategy and both these airlines are consistently rated as the highest in customer satisfaction.[28]

Another example of an airline that competes by improving efficiency in the global package shipping business is First Global Xpress, discussed in Organizational Insight 1.4.

Official goals
Guiding principles that the organization formally states in its annual report and in other public documents.

Mission
Goals that explain why the organization exists and what it should be doing.

Measuring Effectiveness: Organizational Goals

Managers create goals that they use to assess how well the organization is performing. Two types of goals used to evaluate organizational effectiveness are official goals and operative goals. **Official goals** are guiding principles that the organization formally states in its annual report and in other public documents. Usually these goals lay out the **mission** of the organization: They explain why the organization exists and what it should be doing.

Organizational Insight 1.4

First Global Xpress Delivers Packages Faster, Cheaper, and Greener

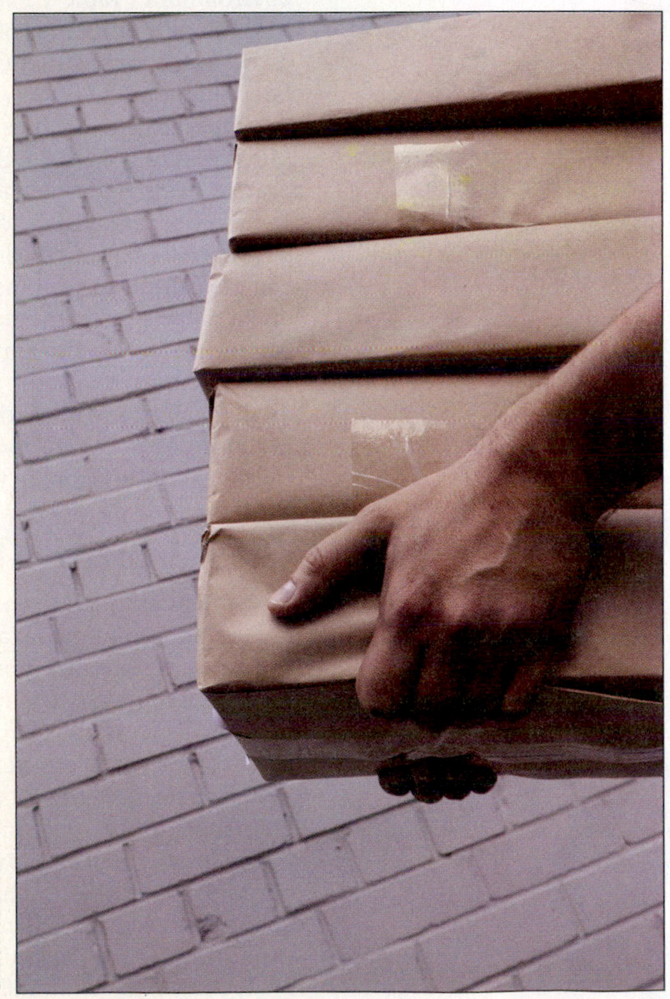

© Maurus/Dreamstime.com

First Global Xpress (FGX) is a small, $10 million global package shipping company that claims it can ship packages from the 12 largest U.S. cities on the East Coast anywhere around the globe 24 hours faster and more reliably (its package loss rate is 1% to compared to the industry average of over 8%) than large competitors such as FedEx and UPS. Also, FGX claims it can ship its over 400 customers' packages at a 20% lower cost than its large rivals and in a "greener way" because it uses less fuel oil with a 30% savings in CO_2 emissions.[29] How has it been able to do become so efficient?

First, large shipping companies like FedEx and DHL rely on a "hub-and-spoke" package distribution system so that no matter where a package is collected or its destination, it has to go through a central hub first, where packages from all over the United States are sorted for shipment to their final destination. This means that a customer's shipment, say from New York to London, has to take two different flights—one to get to a hub, such as FedEx's hub in Memphis, Tennessee, and then another to get to England. FGX does not own aircraft; it has been rapidly forming alliances with over 100 different global airlines that can ship its customers' packages directly from city to city—from New York to London, for example—which saves time and money. Of course commercial airlines charge a fee for this service, but when demand for global air travel is declining and fuel costs are rising, forming an alliance with FGX is profitable for their bottom lines. As a result, airlines such as Continental, Virgin Atlantic, and Air France are willing to work closely with FGX to ensure that its packages are shipped directly and reliably to their destination cities. Because its flights are direct, FGX can also claim that it is providing this service "in a more socially responsible, greener way."

FGX hopes to grow quickly and offer its service from other large U.S. cities such as Chicago, Houston, and Los Angeles. And its CEO claims, "Over the next five years FGX plans to keep growing, replicating its model for clients worldwide. Every day, FGX offers you the chance to save money, cut time off of your deliveries, and reduce your carbon footprint—all through the simple solution of shipping direct." The challenge facing its managers is to keep its value chain operations lean and efficient—just as Southwest does in the passenger segment of the airline business.[30]

TABLE 1.2 Amazon.com's Mission and Goals, 1998–2011

Where We Started

Amazon.com strives to be Earth's most customer-centric company where people can find and discover virtually anything they want to buy online. By giving customers more of what they want—low prices, vast selection, and convenience—Amazon.com continues to grow and evolve as a world-class e-commerce platform.

Where We Are Today

We seek to be Earth's most customer-centric company for three primary customer sets: consumer customers, seller customers and developer customers. . . . It is by design that technological innovation drives the growth of Amazon.com to offer customers more types of products, more conveniently, and at even lower prices.

Official goals include being a leading producer of a product, demonstrating an overriding concern for public safety, and so forth. Official goals are meant to legitimize the organization and its activities, to allow it to obtain resources and the support of its stakeholders.[31] Consider the way the mission and goals of Amazon.com have changed during the period 1998 to 2008 as its managers have changed its business activities to better manage its environment (Table 1.2). As these changes suggest, today Amazon.com serves the needs of three different kinds of customers because of the way it has grown and developed, and its organizational structure has become much more complex as a result, as we discuss in later chapters.

Operative goals
Specific long-term and short-term goals that guide managers and employees as they perform the work of the organization.

Operative goals are specific long- and short-term goals that guide managers and employees as they perform the work of the organization. The goals listed in Table 1.1 are operative goals that managers can use to evaluate organizational effectiveness. Managers can use operative goals to measure how well they are managing the environment. Is market share increasing or decreasing? Is the cost of inputs rising or falling? Similarly, they can measure how well the organization is functioning by measuring how long it takes to make a decision or the degree of conflict between organizational members. Finally, they can measure how efficient they are by creating operative goals that allow them to benchmark themselves against their competitors—that is, compare their competitors' cost and quality achievements with their own. UPS, FedEx, and First Global Xpress, for example, monitor one another's package delivery times and lost shipment rates to try to find ways to continuously improve their performance.

The Plan of This Book

To understand how to manage organizational design and change, it is first necessary to understand how organizations affect, and are affected by, their environments. Then the principles of organizational design and change that managers use to improve the match or fit of an organization with its environment can be better understood. To facilitate this learning process, the chapters in this book are organized so each builds on the ones that have come before. Figure 1.5 shows how the various chapters fit together and provides a model of the components involved in organizational design and change.

The number of major companies (e.g., Enron, Broadcom, and Computer Associates) whose top executives have engaged in unethical and often illegal kinds of corporate behavior, such as stock option backdating and "cooking the books," continues to increase. So it is more important than ever before that a clear link is made between ethics and organizational effectiveness because managers are responsible for protecting organizational resources and using them effectively. Chapter 2 examines the roles top managers perform in an organization, examines the claims and obligations of different organizational stakeholder groups, and examines the many ethical issues that managers face in dealing with the claims of these different groups.

The environment in which an organization operates is a principal source of uncertainty. If customers withdraw their support, if suppliers withhold inputs, if a global recession occurs, considerable uncertainty is created. Thus the organization must design its

Figure 1.5 Components of Organizational Theory, Design, and Change

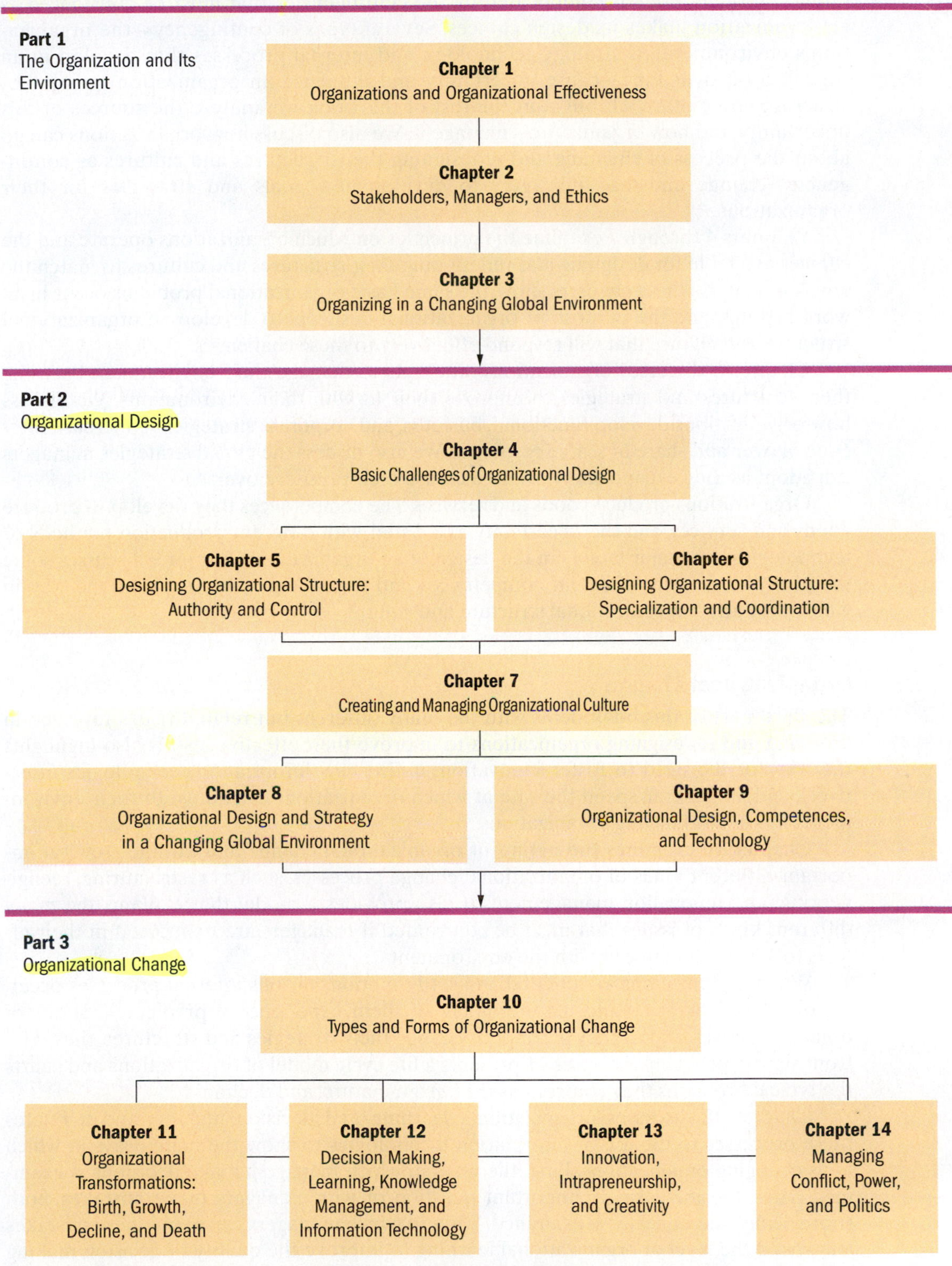

structure to manage adequately the contingencies it faces in the external environment. Chapter 3 presents models that reveal why the environment is a source of uncertainty and theories about how and why organizations act to meet uncertainties in the environment. Resource dependence theory examines how organizations attempt to gain control over scarce resources. Transaction cost theory examines how organizations manage environmental relations to reduce transaction costs.

Organizational Design

Organizational design is complicated by the contingencies that must be considered as an organization makes its design choices. Several types of contingency—the organization's environment, its strategy, technology, and internal processes that develop in an organization over time—cause uncertainty and influence an organization's choice of structure and culture. Throughout the rest of this book we analyze the sources of this uncertainty and how organizations manage it. We also discuss how organizations can go about the process of changing and redesigning their structures and cultures as contingencies change and lead managers to develop new goals and strategies for their organizations.

Chapters 4 through 7 examine the principles on which organizations operate and the choices available for designing and redesigning their structures and cultures to match the environment. As these chapters show, the same basic organizational problems occur in all work settings, and the purpose of organizational design is to develop an organizational structure and culture that will respond effectively to these challenges.

Chapter 8 discusses organizations' attempts to manage their environment by using their structures and strategies to improve their fit with their environments. We discuss how organizations develop functional, business, and corporate strategies to increase their control over and share of scarce resources. We also discuss the global strategies managers can adopt as they expand and work to increase their presence overseas.

Organizations produce goods and services. The competences they develop to produce goods and services, and the uncertainty associated with different production methods or technologies, are major factors in the design of an organization. Chapter 9 discusses some theories that describe different competences and technologies, and explains the way in which they affect organizational structure and culture.

Organizational Change

The third part of this book deals with the many different but related issues involved in changing and redesigning organizations to improve their effectiveness. It also highlights the way for the need to foster innovation, utilize new information technologies effectively, and, in general, speed the rate at which organizations can adjust to their environments has been changing organizations.

Chapter 10 examines the nature of organizational change and outlines several important different kinds of organizational change processes, such as restructuring, reengineering, and innovation management. It also provides a model that explains the many different kinds of issues that must be confronted if managers are to succeed in their efforts to achieve a better fit with the environment.

When organizations are created and set in motion, various internal processes occur. As organizations grow and mature, many of them experience a predictable series of organizing crises, and as they attempt to change their strategies and structures, they confront similar problems. Chapter 11 presents a life cycle model of organizations and charts the typical problems they confront as they grow, mature, and decline.

Chapter 12 discusses organizational learning and decision making, and it relates these processes to the use of information technologies to show the many ways in which IT is changing organizations. First, the ways in which managers make decisions is examined. Then the increasingly important question of why managers make mistakes, both strategically and ethically, is examined. Ways in which managers can avoid these mistakes and speed the level of organizational learning to improve the quality of decision making is then described. Finally, we look at how new innovations in information technology, including the Internet, have been affecting organizations and changing organizational structure and culture.

Chapters 13 looks at the related issues of innovation and project management in organizations. Project management focuses on how project managers can use various techniques to speed and promote the development of new and improved goods and services. How to foster innovation and manage research and development is a pressing problem, particularly for organizations competing globally.

Finally, Chapter 14 covers problems of politics and conflict that arise as managers attempt to change and redesign organizational structure and culture. These chapters highlight the complex social and organizational processes that must be managed if an organization is to be able to manage the change process successfully and increase its effectiveness.

Summary

We have examined what organizations are, why they exist, the purpose of organizational theory, design, and change, and the different ways in which they can be evaluated. Organizations play a vital role in increasing the wealth of a society, and the purpose of managing organizational design and change is to enhance their ability to create value and thus organizational effectiveness. Chapter 1 has made the following main points:

1. An organization is a tool that people use to coordinate their actions to obtain something they desire or value—to achieve their goals.
2. Organizations are value-creation systems that take inputs from the environment and use skills and knowledge to transform these inputs into finished goods and services.
3. The use of an organization allows people jointly to increase specialization and the division of labor, use large-scale technology, manage the organizational environment, economize on transaction costs, and exert power and control—all of which increase the value the organization can create.
4. Organizational theory is the study of how organizations function and how they affect and are affected by the environment in which they operate.
5. Organizational structure is the formal system of task and authority relationships that control how people coordinate their actions and use resources to achieve an organization's goals.
6. Organizational culture is the set of shared values and norms that control organizational members' interactions with each other and with suppliers, customers, and other people outside the organization.
7. Organizational design is the process by which managers select and manage aspects of structure and culture so an organization can control the activities necessary to achieve its goals. Organizational design has important implications for a company's competitive advantage, its ability to deal with contingencies and manage diversity, its efficiency, its ability to generate new goods and services, its control of the environment, its coordination and motivation of employees, and its development and implementation of strategy.
8. Organizational change is the process by which organizations redesign and transform their structures and cultures to move from their present state to some desired future state to increase their effectiveness. The goal of organizational change is to find new or improved ways of using resources and capabilities to increase an organization's ability to create value and hence performance.
9. Managers can use three approaches to evaluate organizational effectiveness: the external resource approach, the internal systems approach, and the technical approach. Each approach is associated with a set of criteria that can be used to measure effectiveness and a set of organizational goals.

Discussion Questions

1. How do organizations create value? What is the role of entrepreneurship in this process?
2. What is the relationship among organizational theory, design, change, and organizational structure and culture?
3. What is organizational effectiveness? Discuss three approaches to evaluating effectiveness and the problems associated with each approach.
4. Draw up a list of effectiveness goals you would use to measure the performance of (a) a fast-food restaurant and (b) a school of business.

Organizational Theory in Action

Practicing Organizational Theory

Open Systems Dynamics

Form groups of three to five people and discuss the following scenario:

Think of an organization you are all familiar with, such as a local restaurant, store, or bank. Once you have chosen an organization, model it from an open systems perspective. For example, identify its input, conversion, and output processes.

1. Identify the specific forces in the environment that have the greatest opportunity to help or hurt this organization's ability to obtain resources and dispose of its goods or services.
2. Using the three views of effectiveness discussed in the chapter, discuss which specific measures are most useful to managers in evaluating this organization's effectiveness.

The Ethical Dimension #1

An ethical exercise is present in every chapter to help you understand the many ways in which organizations can help or harm the people and groups in their environments, especially when they are managed in ways that are unethical. This exercise can be done alone or in a small group.

Think of some examples of ways in which a hospital, and the doctors and nurses who work there, could act unethically toward patients. Also, think about behaviors that demonstrate a hospital has high ethical standards.

1. List examples of these ethical and unethical behaviors.
2. How do these behaviors relate to the attempts of doctors and nurses to increase organizational effectiveness in the ways discussed in the chapter? Or to attempts to pursue their own self-interest?

Making the Connection #1

At the end of every chapter you will find an exercise that requires you to search newspapers or magazines for an example of a real company that is dealing with some of the issues, concepts, challenges, questions, and problems discussed in the chapter.

Find an example of a company that is seeking to improve its effectiveness in some way. What dimension of effectiveness (control, innovation, or efficiency) is it seeking to improve? What changes is it making to address the issue?

Analyzing the Organization: Design Module #1

To give you insight into the way real-world organizations work, at the end of every chapter there is an organizational design module for which you must collect and analyze information about an organization you will select now and study all semester. You will write up the information you collect into a report to be presented to the class at the end of the semester.

Suppose you select General Motors. You will collect the information specified in each organizational design module, present and summarize your findings on GM for your class, and then produce a written report. Your instructor will provide the details of what will be required of you—for example, how long the presentation or report should be and whether you will work in a group or by yourself to complete the assignment. By the end of the semester, by completing each module, you will have a clear picture of how organizations operate and how they deal with problems and contingencies they face.

There are two approaches to selecting an organization. One is to choose a well-known organization about which a lot has been written. Large companies like IBM, Apple Computer, and Procter & Gamble receive extensive coverage in business periodicals such as *Fortune* and *Bloomberg/Business Week.* Every year, for example, in one of its April issues, *Fortune* magazine publishes a list of the Fortune 500 manufacturing companies, and in one of its May issues it publishes a list of the Fortune 500 service companies, the biggest companies in the United States. If you choose a company on the Fortune lists, you can be sure that considerable information is published about it.

The best sources of information are business periodicals and newspapers such as *Fortune*, *Business Week*, *Forbes,* the *Wall Street Journal*, *F&S Predicasts, Value Line Investment Survey,* and *Moody's Manuals on Investment*, and many other publications summarize articles written about a particular company. In addition, you should check industry and trade publications.

Finally, be sure to take advantage of the Internet and explore the Web to find information on your company. Most large companies have detailed websites that provide a considerable amount of information. You can find these websites using a search engine such as Yahoo or AltaVista and then download the information you need.

If you consult these sources, you will obtain a lot of information you can use to complete the design modules. You may not get all the specific information you need, but you will have enough to answer many of the design module questions.

The second approach to selecting an organization is to choose one located in your city or town—for example, a large department store, manufacturing company, hotel, or nonprofit organization (such as a hospital or school) where you or somebody you know works. You could contact the owners or managers of the organization and ask whether they would be willing to talk to you about the way they operate and how they design and manage their company.

Each approach to selecting a company has advantages and disadvantages. The advantage of selecting a local company and doing your own information gathering is that in face-to-face interviews you can ask for detailed information that may be unavailable from published sources. You will gain an especially rich picture of the way a company operates by doing your research personally. The problem is that the local organization you choose has to be big enough to offer you insight into the way organizations work. In general, it should employ at least 20 people and have at least three levels in its hierarchy.

If you use written sources to study a very large organization, you will get a lot of interesting information that relates to organizational theory because the organization is large and complex and is confronting many of the problems discussed in this book. But you may not be able to obtain all the detailed information you want.

Whichever selection approach you use, be sure you have access to enough interesting information to complete the majority of the organizational design modules. One module, for example, asks about the international or global dimension of your organization's strategy and structure. If you pick a local company that does not have an international dimension, you will be unable to complete that assignment. However, to compensate for this lack of information, you might have very detailed information about the company's structure or product lines. The issue is to make sure you can gain access to enough information to write an interesting report.

Assignment

Choose a company to study, and answer the following questions about it.

1. What is the name of the organization? Give a short account of the history of the company. Describe the way it has grown and developed.
2. What does the organization do? What goods and services does it produce/provide? What kind of value does it create? If the company has an annual report, what does the report describe as the company's organizational mission?
3. Draw a model of the way the organization creates value. Briefly describe its inputs, throughputs, outputs, and environment.
4. Do an initial analysis of the organization's major problems or issues. What challenges confront the organization today—for example, in its efforts to attract customers, to lower costs, to increase operating efficiency? How does its organizational design relate to these problems?
5. Read its annual report and determine which kinds of goals, standards, or targets the organization is using to evaluate performance. How well is the organization doing when judged by the criteria of control, innovation, and efficiency?

CASE FOR ANALYSIS

How Joe Coulombe Made Trader Joe's a Success Story

Trader Joe's, an upscale specialty supermarket chain, was founded in 1967 by Joe Coulombe, who then owned a few convenience stores that were fighting an uphill battle against the growing 7-11 chain. 7-11 offered customers a wider selection of lower-priced products and Coulombe could not compete. For his small business to survive, Coulombe decided to change his strategy and supply upscale specialty products such as wine, drinks, and gourmet foods to customers. Coulombe changed the name of his stores to Trader Joe's and stocked them with every variety and brand of California wine that was then being produced. He also began to offer fine foods like bread, crackers, cheese, fruits, and vegetables to complement and encourage wine sales. His planning paid off; customers loved his new upscale supermarket concept and the premium products he chose to stock sold quickly—and they were more profitable to sell.

From the beginning Coulombe realized that finding a new niche in the supermarket business was only the first step to help his small, growing company succeed. He knew that to encourage customers to visit his stores and buy more expensive gourmet products he needed to provide them with excellent customer service. So, he had to find ways to motivate his salespeople to perform at a high level. His approach to organizing was to decentralize authority and empower salespeople to take responsibility for meeting customer needs. Rather than instructing employees to follow strict operating rules and to get the approval of their supervisor before making customer-specific decisions, employees were given autonomy to make their own decisions and provide personalized customer service. Coulombe's approach led employees to feel they "owned" their supermarkets, and he worked to develop a culture based on values and norms about providing excellent customer service and developing personalized relationships with customers, who are often on first-name terms.

Coulombe led by example and created a store environment in which employees were treated as individuals and felt valued as people. For example, the theme behind the design of his stores was to create the feeling of a Hawaiian resort: employees wear loud Hawaiian shirts, store managers are called captains, and the store décor uses lots of wood and contains tiki huts, where employees provide customers with food and drink samples and interact with them. Once again, this helped to create strong values and norms that emphasize personalized customer service.

Finally, Joe Coulombe's approach was strongly influenced by the way he went about controlling salespeople. From the outset he created a policy of promotion from within the company so that the highest-performing salespeople could rise to become store captains and beyond in the organization. And, from the beginning, he recognized the need to treat employees in a fair and equitable way to encourage them to develop the customer-oriented values and norms needed to provide personalized customer service. He decided that full-time employees should earn at least the median household income for their communities, which averaged $7,000 a year in the 1960s and is $48,000 today—an astonishingly high amount compared to the pay of employees of regular supermarkets such as Kroger's and Safeway. Moreover, store captains, who are vital in helping create and reinforce Trader Joe's store culture, are rewarded with salaries and bonuses that can exceed $100,000 a year. And all salespeople know that as the store chain expands they may also be promoted to this level. In sum, Coulombe's approach to developing the right way to organize his small business created a solid foundation on which this upscale specialty supermarket has grown and prospered.[32]

Discussion Questions

1. What was Joe Coulombe's approach to organizational design?
2. What specific decisions did he make to create Trader Joe's organizational structure and culture?
3. Go online and see how Trader Joe's is performing today. What new problems of organizing has it been facing as it has grown?

References

1 A. W. Gouldner, "Organizational Analysis," in R. K. Merton, ed., *Sociology Today* (New York: Basic Books, 1959); A. Etzioni, *Comparative Analysis of Complex Organizations* (New York: Free Press, 1961).

2 I. M. Kirzner, *Competition and Entrepreneurship* (Chicago: University of Chicago Press, 1973).

3 www.amazon.com, 2011.

4 www.amazon.com, "About Amazon.com," 2011.

5 P. M. Blau, "A Formal Theory of Differentiation in Organizations," *American Sociological Review* 35 (1970), 201–218; D. S. Pugh and D. J. Hickson, "The Comparative Study of Organizations," in G. Salaman and K. Thompson, eds., *People and Organizations* (London: Penguin, 1977), pp. 43–55.

6 P. M. Blau, *Exchange and Power in Social Life* (New York: Wiley, 1964); P. M. Blau and W. R. Scott, *Formal Organizations* (San Francisco: Chandler, 1962).

7 C. I. Barnard, *The Functions of the Executive* (Cambridge, MA: Harvard University Press, 1948); A. Etzioni, *Modern Organizations* (Englewood Cliffs, NJ: Prentice Hall, 1964).

8 P. R. Lawrence and J. W. Lorsch, *Organization and Environment* (Boston: Graduate School of Business Administration, Harvard University, 1967); W. R. Scott, *Organizations: Rational, Natural, and Open Systems* (Englewood Cliffs, NJ: Prentice Hall, 1981).

9 www.cocacola.com, 2008; www.pepsico, 2008.

10 M. Beer, *Organizational Change and Development* (Santa Monica, CA: Goodyear, 1980); J. I. Porras and R. C. Silvers, "Organization Development and Transformation," *Annual Review of Psychology*, *42* (1991), 51–78.

11 www.apple.com, 2011.

12 Ibid.

13 www.groupon.com, 2011.

14 Ibid.

15 www.ford.com, 2011.

16 Wernau, J. "Women Leave Their Stamp on Manufacturing," chicagotribune.com, May 30, 2010.

17 www.ford.com, 2011.

18 L. Galambos, "What Have CEOs Been Doing?" *Journal of Economic History* 18 (1988), pp. 243–258.

19 Ibid., p. 253.

20 Campbell, "On the Nature of Organizational Effectiveness."

21 F. Friedlander and H. Pickle, "Components of Effectiveness in Small Organizations," *Administrative Science Quarterly* 13 (1968), pp. 289–304; Miles, *Macro Organizational Behavior.*

22 Campbell, "On the Nature of Organizational Effectiveness."

23 www. netflix.com, 2011.

24 J. D. Thompson, *Organizations in Action* (New York: McGraw-Hill, 1967).

25 R. M. Steers, *Organizational Effectiveness: A Behavioral View* (Santa Monica, CA: Goodyear, 1977).

26 D. E. Bowen and G. R. Jones, "Transaction Cost Analysis of Customer-Service Organization Exchange," *Academy of Management Review* 11 (1986), pp. 428–441.

27 www.southwest.com, 2011.

28 www.consumerreports.com, May 2011.

29 www.fgx.com, 2011.

30 www.fgx.com, company overview, 2011.

31 T. M. Jones, "Instrumental Stakeholder Theory: A Synthesis of Ethics and Economics," *Academy of Management Review* 20 (1995), pp. 404–437.

32 www.traderjoes.com, 2011.

CHAPTER 2

Stakeholders, Managers, and Ethics

Learning Objectives

Organizations exist to create valuable goods and services that people need or desire. But who decides which goods and services an organization should provide or how to divide the value that an organization creates among different groups of people, such as employees, customers, or shareholders? If people behave self-interestedly, what mechanisms or procedures govern the way an organization uses its resources, and what is to stop the different groups from trying to maximize their share of the value created? In an age when the issue of corporate ethics, insider trading, and top-management greed has come under intense scrutiny, we must deal with these questions before we can address the issue of designing an organization to increase its effectiveness.

After studying this chapter you should be able to:

1. Identify the various stakeholder groups and their interests or claims on an organization.
2. Understand the choices and problems inherent in distributing the value an organization creates.
3. Appreciate who has authority and responsibility at the top of an organization, and distinguish between different levels of management.
4. Describe the agency problem that exists in all authority relationships and the various mechanisms, such as the board of directors and stock options, which can be used to help control illegal and unethical managerial behavior.
5. Discuss the vital role that ethics plays in constraining managers and employees to pursue the goals that lead to long-run organizational effectiveness.

Organizational Stakeholders

Organizations exist because of their ability to create value and acceptable outcomes for various groups of **stakeholders,** people who have an interest, claim, or stake in an organization, in what it does, and in how well it performs.[1] In general, stakeholders are motivated to participate in an organization if they receive inducements that exceed the value of the contributions they are required to make.[2] **Inducements** include rewards such as money, power, and organizational status. **Contributions** include the skills, knowledge, and expertise that organizations require of their members during task performance.

Stakeholders
People who have an interest, claim, or stake in an organization, in what it does, and in how well it performs.

Inducements
Rewards such as money, power, and organizational status.

Contributions
The skills, knowledge, and expertise that organizations require of their members during task performance.

The two main groups of organizational stakeholders are inside stakeholders and outside stakeholders. Table 2.1 summarizes the inducements and contributions of each group.[3]

Inside Stakeholders

Inside stakeholders are people who are closest to an organization and have the strongest or most direct claim on organizational resources: shareholders, managers, and the workforce.

TABLE 2.1 Inducements and Contributions of Organizational Stakeholders

Stakeholder	Contribution to the Organization	Inducement to Contribute
Inside		
Shareholders	Money and capital	Dividends and stock appreciation
Managers	Skills and expertise	Salaries, bonuses, status, and power
Workforce	Skills and expertise	Wages, bonuses, stable employment, and promotion
Outside		
Customers	Revenue from purchase of goods and services	Quality and price of goods and services
Suppliers	High-quality inputs	Revenue from purchase of inputs
Government	Rules governing good business practice	Fair and free competition
Unions	Free and fair collective bargaining	Equitable share of inducements
Community	Social and economic infrastructure	Revenue, taxes, and employment
General public	Customer loyalty and reputation	National pride

SHAREHOLDERS Shareholders are the owners of the organization, and, as such, their claim on organizational resources is often considered superior to the claims of other inside stakeholders. The shareholders' contribution to the organization is to invest money in it by buying the organization's shares or stock. The shareholders' inducement to invest is the prospective money they can earn on their investment in the form of dividends and increases in the price of stock. Investment in stock is risky, however, because there is no guarantee of a return. Shareholders who do not believe the inducement (the possible return on their investment) is enough to warrant their contribution (the money they have invested) sell their shares and withdraw their support from the organization.

During the recent recession that resulted because of the sub-prime mortgage problem, the resulting financial crisis led to a meltdown in the stock market during which most investors lost 40% or more of the value of their stock investments. As a result, more and more shareholders, who are most commonly mutual fund investors, are relying increasingly on the government and on large institutional investment companies to protect their interests and to increase their collective power to influence top managers. Large mutual fund companies like Fidelity or TIAA/CREF realize they have an increasing responsibility to their investors who lost billions in their pension funds as a result of the subprime crisis, as well as the earlier dot.com meltdown.[4] Also, mutual fund managers realize they have an increasing responsibility to monitor the performance of top managers to prevent the kinds of unethical and illegal behaviors that caused the collapse of Lehman brothers, Enron, Tyco, and many other companies whose dubious accounting practices led to a collapse in their stock price. If mutual fund companies are to protect the interests of their shareholders, they need to monitor and influence the behavior of the companies they invest in, to make sure the top managers pursue actions that do not threaten shareholders' interests while enhancing their own.

As a result of this concern for shareholders, mutual fund companies have become more vocal in trying to influence top managers. For example, they have sought to get companies to remove so-called poison pills, which are antitakeover provisions that make it much more difficult and expensive for another company to acquire it. Top managers like poison pills because it helps them protect their jobs, huge salaries, and other perks. Mutual fund companies are also showing increasing interest in controlling the huge salaries and bonuses that top managers give themselves that have reached record levels in recent years. They have also reacted to the accounting scandals that have led to the collapse of Enron and the poor performance of other companies such as Computer Associates by demanding that companies clarify their accounting procedures. And they have successfully lobbied for Congress to pass new laws such as the Sarbanes/Oxley and Dodd-Frank Acts, and to increase the power of government agencies such as the Federal Trade Commission (FTC) to regulate banks and other financial institutions. These moves have made it much more difficult for companies to hide unfair, unethical, or illegal transactions that might benefit managers but hurt other stakeholders, especially customers.

MANAGERS Managers are the employees responsible for coordinating organizational resources and ensuring that an organization's goals are met successfully. Top managers are responsible for investing shareholder money in resources to maximize the value of an organization's future output of goods and services. In effect, managers are the agents or employees of shareholders; they are appointed indirectly by shareholders through an organization's board of directors that shareholders elect to oversee managers' performance.

Managers' contributions are the skills and knowledge they use to plan and direct the organization's response to pressures from the organizational environment, and to design its structure and culture. For example, a manager's skills at opening up global markets, identifying new product markets, or solving transaction cost and technological problems can greatly facilitate the achievement of organizational goals.

Various types of rewards induce managers to perform their activities well: monetary compensation (in the form of salaries, bonuses, and stock options) and the psychological satisfaction they get from controlling the corporation, exercising power, or taking risks with other people's money. Managers who do not believe that the inducements meet or exceed their contributions are likely to withdraw their support by leaving the organization. Thus top managers move from one organization to another to obtain greater rewards for their contributions.

THE WORKFORCE An organization's workforce consists of all nonmanagerial employees. Members of the workforce have task responsibilities and duties (usually outlined in a job description) that they are accountable for performing at the required level. Employees' contribution to the organization is to use their skills and knowledge to perform required duties and responsibilities at a high level. However, how well an employee performs, in some measure, is within the employee's control. Indeed, an employee's motivation to perform well is often a function of the inducements (rewards and punishments) that the organization uses to influence job performance. Employees who do not believe that these inducements meet or exceed their contributions are likely to withdraw their support for the organization by reducing the level of their performance or by leaving the organization.

Outside Stakeholders

Outside stakeholders are people who do not own the organization and are not employed by it, but they do have some claim on or interest in it. Customers, suppliers, the government, trade unions, local communities, and the general public are types of individuals and groups that are outside stakeholders.

CUSTOMERS Customers are usually an organization's largest outside stakeholder group. Customers are induced to select a particular product (and thus a specific organization) from alternative products by their estimation of the value of what they receive from it relative to what they have to pay for it. The money they pay for the product is their contribution to the organization (its sales revenue) and reflects the value they believe they receive from the organization. As long as the organization produces a product whose price is equal to or less than the value customers feel they are getting, they will continue to buy the product and support the organization.[5] If customers refuse to pay the price the organization is asking, they withdraw their support, and the organization loses a vital stakeholder. Southwest Airlines, which as we noted in Chapter 1 focuses on increasing its efficiency to offer lower airfares, is an example of one company that strives to offer customers a lot of value, and the result is their loyal support.

Former CEO Herb Kelleher attributes his airline's success to its policy of "dignifying the customer."[6] Southwest sends birthday cards to its frequent fliers, responds personally to the thousands of customer letters it receives each week, and regularly obtains feedback from customers on ways to improve service. Such personal attention makes customers feel valued and inclined to fly Southwest, and customer support has made it one of the faster growing and the most profitable U.S. airline company for over a decade.

Moreover, Southwest believes that if management fails to treat employees right, employees will not treat customers right. And, as we also noted, Southwest's employees own 20% of the airline's stock, which increases their motivation to contribute to the organization and improve customer service.[7] One stakeholder group (employees) thus helps another (customers). One example of a company whose top managers had no concern for the well-being of its customers or employees is profiled in Organizational Insight 2.1.

Organizational Insight 2.1

Unethical Managers at a Peanut Company

Peanut Corporation of America's (PCA) president, Stewart Parnell, was fond of telling his friends and clients in his hometown of Lynchburg, Virginia, just how good things were in his commercial peanut butter processing business, which operated three plants in Virginia, Georgia, and Texas. The company produced industrial-sized containers of peanut butter that were included as an ingredient in more than 3,900 products: cakes, candies, cookies, peanut crackers, ice cream, snack mixes, and pet food made by over 200 different companies, including Kellogg's and Nestle. Also, the peanut butter was shipped to school systems and food outlets around the United States, where it was used to make millions of peanut butter and jelly sandwiches.

Parnell had a reputation as an upstanding businessman and a generous donor to many worthy causes, so it came as a shock to his friends and customers when in 2009 a major nationwide outbreak of salmonella poisoning was traced by the Food and Drug Administration (FDA) to the peanut butter produced at his plant in Blakely, Georgia. PCA's contaminated peanut butter had caused over 600 illnesses and nine deaths across the United States. The 200 food makers who used or sold Parnell's products were forced to recall more than 1,900 different peanut butter products. This was one of the nation's largest food recalls even though PCA accounted for only 2% of the nation's supply of peanut butter. In the immediate aftermath of the nationwide outbreak, peanut butter sales plummeted 24% across the board, and total industry losses amounted to over $1 billion. How could this tragedy and disaster have occurred?

Jiri Hera/Shutterstock.com

Apparently, the major cause of the disaster was the unethical and illegal actions of owner and manager Parnell. The FDA investigation that took place at the PCA Georgia plant in 2009 revealed serious problems with food safety at that plant and inadequate cleaning and sanitary procedures. The investigation also revealed internal company documents that showed at least 12 instances in which the company's own tests of its products found they were contaminated by salmonella. Previous inspections of the plant had found dirty surfaces, grease residue, dirt buildup throughout the plant, gaps in warehouse doors large enough for rodents to enter, and major problems with the plant's routine cleaning procedures that still existed in 2009. But PCA managers had taken no steps to clean up operations or protect food safety. In fact, Parnell's poor attention to food safety was traced back to 1990, when inspectors found toxic mold in products produced in PCA's

Virginia plant; the mold forced food recalls, and Parnell settled privately with the two companies whose products were affected.

After interviewing employees, FDA investigators found that this long-term inattention to food safety had arisen inside PCA's processing plants because Parnell was worried about maximizing his profits, especially when prices of peanut products had started to fall. To reduce operating costs, Parnell ordered a plant manager to ship products that had already been identified as contaminated and had pleaded with health inspectors to let him "turn the raw peanuts on our floor into money." Parnell complained to his managers that the salmonella tests were costing him business, and somehow the Georgia plant received information about the dates on which the plant would be inspected—so on those days the plant was scrubbed clean.

After the problems with the Georgia plant were discovered, it was shut down and the other PCA plants were inspected closely. In 2009 Texas health officials told Parnell to close his plant there and ordered a recall of all its products after salmonella was discovered, along with "dead rodents, rodent excrement, and bird feathers." The PCA Virginia plant was also shut down. After hundreds of lawsuits were filed against the company because of the deaths and illnesses caused by its contaminated products, PCA was forced to seek protection under the U.S. bankruptcy code. The company is now defunct; its unethical and illegal management practices put it out of business. In spring 2011 criminal charges had still not been filed against Stewart Parnell, although a federal investigation was under way. However, in 2010, 123 victims and surviving relatives and the bankruptcy court in charge of PCA agreed to a $12 million settlement—the money coming from PCA's insurance policies because the Parnell family lost nearly everything it owned.

After being criticized for the length of time it took the FDA to finally close down PCA's operations, FDA officials responded that the agency doesn't have the personnel or funding to regulate the millions of shipments made within the food industry every week. In large part, the FDA and the U.S. public must rely on the basic integrity, ethics, and honesty of food industry managers to make food that is safe to eat.

SUPPLIERS Suppliers, another important outside stakeholder group, contribute to the organization by providing reliable raw materials and component parts that allow the organization to reduce uncertainty in its technical or production operations and thus reduce production costs. Suppliers have a direct effect on the organization's efficiency and an indirect effect on its ability to attract customers. An organization that has high-quality inputs can make high-quality products and attract customers. In turn, as demand for its products increases, the organization demands greater quantities of high-quality inputs from its suppliers.

One of the reasons why Japanese cars remain so popular with U.S. consumers is that they still require fewer repairs than the average U.S.-made vehicle. This reliability is a result of the use of component parts that meet stringent quality control standards. In addition, Japanese parts suppliers are constantly improving their efficiency.[8] The close relationship between the large Japanese automakers and their suppliers is a stakeholder relationship that pays long-term dividends for both parties. Realizing this, in the 2000s U.S. car manufacturers moved to establish strong relationships with their suppliers to increase quality, and the reliability of their vehicles has increased as a result. Ford, in particular, has achieved major improvements in quality as a result, and it reported record earnings in 2011.

THE GOVERNMENT The government has several claims on an organization. It wants companies to compete in a fair manner and obey the rules of free competition. It also wants companies to obey agreed-on rules and laws concerning the payment and treatment of employees, workers' health and workplace safety, nondiscriminatory hiring practices, and other social and economic issues about which Congress has enacted legislation. The government makes a contribution to the organization by standardizing regulations so they apply to all companies and no company can obtain an unfair competitive advantage. The government controls the rules of good business practice and has the power to punish any company that breaks these rules by taking legal action against it. Because of the ongoing corporate scandals of the 2000s, many analysts have argued that more stringent rules are needed to govern many aspects of the way organizations function. Some lawmakers wanted to control the relationship between a company and the accounting firm that audits its books by limiting the number of years such a relationship can endure. Lobbying by accountancy companies eventually led to the passing of a law that only limits the length of time one of their partners can oversee a particular account. The account is then passed to another partner in the same company, not to a new accounting company, which is clearly a much weaker oversight rule. In 2011 the Dodd-Frank Act, which established a powerful government agency to protect customers from unfair ATM and interest rate charges from banks and credit card companies, was under attack from financial lobbyists who wished to weaken its power to regulate financial institutions.

TRADE UNIONS The relationship between a trade union and an organization can be one of conflict or cooperation. The nature of the relationship has a direct effect on the productivity and effectiveness of the organization and the union. Cooperation between managers and the union can lead to positive long-term outcomes if both parties agree on an equitable division of the gains from an improvement in a company's fortunes. Managers and the union might agree, for example, to share the gains from cost savings owing to productivity improvements that resulted from a flexible work schedule. Traditionally, however, the management–union relationship has been antagonistic because unions' demands for increased benefits conflict directly with shareholders' demands for greater company profits and thus greater returns on their investments.

LOCAL COMMUNITIES Local communities have a stake in the performance of organizations because employment, housing, and the general economic well-being of a community are strongly affected by the success or failure of local businesses. The fortunes of Seattle, for example, are closely tied to the fortunes of the Boeing Corporation, and Austin to those of Dell and other computer companies. Houston and the whole of the Gulf Coast have been affected by the activities of BP, for example, as discussed in Organizational Insight 2.2.

Organizational Insight 2.2

BP Has Problems Protecting Its Stakeholders

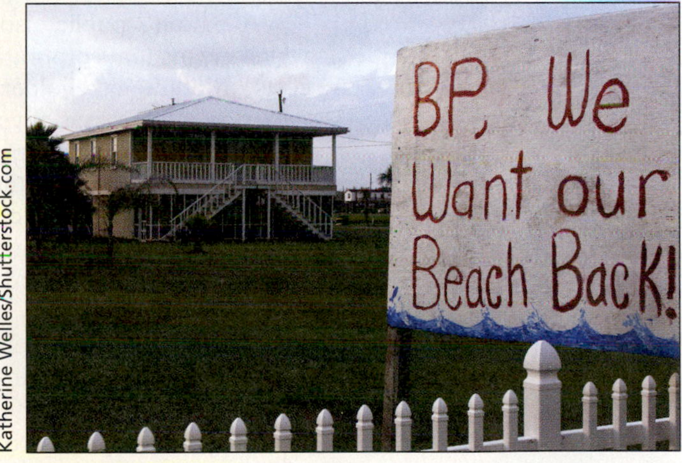

Katherine Welles/Shutterstock.com

In 2009 a U.S. judge finally approved British Petroleum's (BP) plea agreement to pay $50 million—the largest U.S. criminal environmental fine ever—after pleading guilty to charges stemming from a 2005 explosion that killed 15 workers and injured 180 workers at BP's Texas City oil refinery, the third largest in the United States, situated 40 miles from Houston. The explosion was the third largest ever in the United States and the fifth largest globally. "We deeply regret the harm that was caused by this terrible tragedy. We take very seriously the commitments we've made as part of the plea agreement," said BP spokesman Daren Beaudo.

An investigation revealed that the 2005 explosion occurred because BP had relaxed safety procedures at its Texas City refinery to reduce operating costs. The U.S. Occupational Health and Safety Association (OSHA) decided the 2005 explosion was caused by defective pressure relief systems and by poor safety management programs. Consequently, in 2007 OSHA issued its largest fine up to that date, $21 million, against BP for the lapses that led to the refinery explosion because BP sacrificed safety at the refinery to cut costs. The judgment also required the U.S. unit of London-based BP to serve three years on probation while the company tried to solve more than 500 serious safety violations that had been discovered during the investigation.

Beyond the formal fines, however, BP faced hundreds of lawsuits stemming from the explosion from workers and their families and the people and organizations that had been affected by the blast, which was felt miles from the refinery. It is estimated that BP spent over $2 billion to settle these claims, most of which were settled privately outside the courts. After paying so much in legal costs and fines, and given the bad publicity it experienced globally, you might think a company like BP would immediately move to improve its safety procedures. However, while it paid these costs, it also earned $21 billion in profit during the same year; so how did its top management respond?

Not in a highly responsive way. In 2009 OSHA issued a new record $87 million fine against the oil giant for failing to correct the safety violations identified after the 2005 explosion. The 2007 agreement between BP and OSHA included a detailed list of ways in which BP should improve safety procedures at the plant—something its managers vowed to do. But a six-month inspection revealed hundreds of violations of the 2007 agreement to repair hazards at the refinery, and OSHA decided BP had failed to live up to the terms of its commitment to protect employees and that another catastrophe was possible because BP had a major safety problem in the "culture" of this refinery.

BP responded strongly to these accusations, arguing that it had spent hundreds of millions of dollars to correct the safety problems. BP also said that after it reviewed safety procedures at its four U.S. refineries and found that its Cherry Point refinery had the best process safety culture, the head of that refinery had been promoted to oversee better implementation of process safety across BP's U.S. operations. In 2007, however, another serious incident occurred when 10 workers claimed they were injured when a toxic substance was released at the Texas City plant, which BP denied. (A jury subsequently decided in favor of these workers, who were awarded over $200 million in punitive damages in 2009.)

In any event, BP's board of directors decided to move quickly; they fired the CEO and many other top managers and appointed a new CEO, who was instructed to make global refinery safety a key organizational priority. The board also decided to make a substantial portion of the future stock bonuses for the CEO and other top managers dependent on BP's future safety record. And the board committed over $5 billion to improving safety across the company's global operations.

BP's new approach seem to be working as no more refinery accidents occurred. Then in April 2010 the Deepwater Horizon oil-drilling platform that BP had leased from its U.S.-based owner Transocean exploded, killing 11 employees, and the fractured oil pipe began to release millions of barrels of oil in to the Gulf of Mexico. Despite all of BP's attempts to use its expertise to stop the oil gushing from the pipe a mile below the sea, oil continued to flow into the gulf until the pipe was finally declared "effectively dead" on September 19, 2010. By the summer of 2011 the disaster had cost BP almost $50 billion and it was suing both Transocean and Halliburton, the rig's concrete contractor, for many billions, claiming that they were the parties mainly responsible for the rig's explosion. Litigation is expected to go on for years.

THE GENERAL PUBLIC The public is happy when organizations compete effectively against overseas rivals. This is hardly surprising, given that the present and future wealth of a nation is closely related to the success of its business organizations and economic institutions. The French and Italians, for example, prefer domestically produced cars and other products, even when foreign products are clearly superior. To some degree, they are induced by pride in their country to contribute to their country's organizations by buying their products. Typically, U.S. consumers do not support their companies in the same way. They prefer competition to loyalty as the means to ensure the future health of U.S. businesses.

A nation's public also wants its corporations to act in a socially responsible way, which means that corporations refrain from taking any actions that may injure or impose costs on other stakeholders. In the 1990s, for example, a scandal rocked United Way of America after it was revealed that its president, William Aramony, had misused the agency's funds for lavish personal expenditures. To encourage past contributors, including large donors like Xerox and General Electric, not to withhold contributions, United Way appointed Elaine L. Chao, the former head of the Peace Corps and an experienced investment banker, as the new president of the organization. She quickly introduced strict new financial controls and staved off a serious decline in public contributions. Within a few years the scandal was forgotten and contributions had returned to their former levels. The Red Cross faced similar problems after Hurricane Katrina devastated New Orleans after the inefficient way in which its managers had used its resources was revealed. That organization too has gone through a major restructuring to increase its effectiveness. Nowadays, finding ways to monitor not-for-profits to ensure that their managers are behaving ethically has become a major issue.

Organizational Effectiveness: Satisfying Stakeholders' Goals and Interests

An organization is used simultaneously by different groups of stakeholders to accomplish their goals. The contributions of all stakeholders are needed for an organization to be viable and to accomplish its mission of producing goods and services. Each stakeholder group is motivated to contribute to the organization by its own set of goals, and each group evaluates the effectiveness of the organization by judging how well it meets the group's specific goals.[9]

Shareholders evaluate an organization by the return they receive on their investment; customers, by the reliability and value of its products relative to their price; and managers and employees, by their salaries, stock options, conditions of employment, and career prospects. Often these goals conflict, and stakeholder groups must bargain over the appropriate balance between the inducements they should receive and the contributions they should make. For this reason, organizations are often regarded as alliances or coalitions of stakeholder groups that directly (and indirectly) bargain with each other and use their power and influence to alter the balance of inducements and contributions in their favor.[10] An organization is viable as long as a dominant coalition of stakeholders has control over sufficient inducements so that it can obtain the contributions it needs from other stakeholder groups. Companies like Enron and WorldCom collapsed when their illegal actions became public and their stakeholders refused to contribute; shareholders sold their stock, banks refused to lend money, and debtors called in their loans.

There is no reason to assume, however, that all stakeholders will be equally satisfied with the balance between inducements and contributions. Indeed, the implication of the coalition view of organizations is that some stakeholder groups have priority over others. To be effective, however, an organization must at least *minimally satisfy* the interests of all the groups that have a stake in the organization.[11] The claims of each group must be addressed; otherwise, a group might withdraw its support and injure the future performance of the organization, such as when banks refuse to lend money to a company or a group of employees goes out on strike. When all stakeholder interests are minimally satisfied, the relative power of a stakeholder group to control the distribution of inducements determines how an organization will attempt to satisfy different stakeholder goals and what criteria stakeholders will use to judge its effectiveness.

Problems that an organization faces as it tries to win stakeholders' approval include choosing which stakeholder goals to satisfy, deciding how to allocate organizational rewards to different stakeholder groups, and balancing short-term and long-term goals.

Competing Goals

Organizations exist to satisfy stakeholders' goals, but who decides which goals to strive for and which goals are most important? An organization's choice of goals has political and social implications. In a capitalistic country like the United States, it is taken for granted that shareholders who are the owners of an organization's accumulated wealth or capital—its machines, buildings, land, and goodwill—have first claim on the value it creates. According to this view, the job of managers is to maximize shareholder wealth, and the best way to do this is to maximize the organization's return on the resources and capital invested in the business (a good measure of an organization's effectiveness relative to other organizations).

Is maximizing shareholder wealth always management's primary goal? According to one argument, it is not. When shareholders delegate to managers the right to coordinate and use organizational skills and resources, a divorce of ownership and control occurs.[12] Although in theory managers are the employees of shareholders, in practice because managers have control over organizational resources, they have real control over the company even though shareholders own it. The result is that managers may follow goals that promote their own interests and not the interests of shareholders.[13]

An attempt to maximize stockholder wealth, for example, may involve taking risks into uncharted territory and making capital investments in R&D that may bear fruit only in the long term as new inventions and discoveries generate new products and a stream of new revenues. Managers, however, may prefer to maximize short-term profits because that is the goal on which they are evaluated by their peers and by stock market analysts who do not take the long-term view.[14]

Another view is that managers prefer a quiet life in which risks are small and they have no incentive to be entrepreneurial because they control their own salaries. Moreover, because managers' salaries are closely correlated with organizational size, managers may prefer to pursue low-risk strategies even though these may not maximize return on invested capital. For these reasons the goals of managers and shareholders may be incompatible, but because managers are in the organizational driver's seat, shareholder goals are not the ones most likely to be followed.

But even if all stakeholders agreed on which goals an organization should follow, selecting goals that will enhance an organization's chances of survival and future prosperity is no easy task. Suppose managers decide to pursue the primary goal of maximizing shareholder wealth. How should they strive to achieve this goal? Should managers try to increase efficiency and reduce costs to improve profitability or improve quality? Should they increase the organization's ability to influence its outside stakeholders and invest billions to become a global company? Should they invest organizational resources in new R&D projects that will increase its competences in innovation, something vital in high-tech industries? An organization's managers could take any of these actions to achieve the goal of maximizing shareholder wealth.

As you can see, there are no easy rules to follow. And, in many ways, being effective means making more right choices than wrong choices. One thing is certain, however: An organization that does not pay attention to its stakeholders and does not attempt at least minimally to satisfy their interests will lose legitimacy in their eyes and be doomed to failure. The importance of using organizational ethics to avoid this outcome is taken up later in the chapter.

Allocating Rewards

Another major problem that an organization has to face is how to allocate the profits it earns as a result of being effective among the various stakeholder groups. That is, managers must decide which inducements or rewards each group should receive. An organization needs to minimally satisfy the expectation of each group. But when rewards are more than enough to meet each group's minimum need, how should the "extra" rewards be allocated? How much should the workforce or managers receive relative to shareholders? What determines the appropriate reward for managers? Most people answer that managerial rewards should be determined by the organization's effectiveness. But this answer raises another question: What are the best indicators of effectiveness on which to base managerial rewards? Short-term profit? Long-term wealth maximization? Organizational growth? The choice of different criteria leads to different answers to the question.

Indeed, in the 1980s, a CEO's average salary was about 40 times greater than the average worker; by 2010, CEO salary was *600* times greater and was even greater in 2011 despite the recent financial crisis! Can this kind of huge increase be justified? More and more, given the many examples of corporate greed, analysts are saying no, and some have called for boards of directors and Congress to find ways to rein in CEO salaries.

The same kinds of consideration are true for other organizational members. What are the appropriate rewards for a middle manager who invents a new process that earns the organization millions of dollars a year or for the workforce as a whole when the company is making record profits? Should they be given company stock or short-term bonuses? Should an organization guarantee long-term or lifetime employment as the ultimate inducement for good performance? Similarly, should shareholders receive regular dividend payments, or should all profits be reinvested in a company to increase its skills and resources?

The way in which these goals can come into conflict is highlighted by the issue of whether doctors should own stock in the hospitals they practice in. In the last decades, medical doctors have increasingly become stockholders in the hospitals and clinics in which they work. Sometimes teams of doctors in a particular area join to open their own clinic. Other times, large hospital chains give doctors stock in the hospital. Such a trend has the potential to cause a major conflict of interest between doctors and their patients. Take the case of the Columbia/HCA hospital chain, which began to offer doctors a financial stake in the organization in order to encourage doctors to send their patients to a Columbia hospital for treatment.[15] Other HMOs then followed, but in the 2000s doctors have increasingly joined to form physician-owned hospitals of which they are the major stockholders and to which they send their patients.

When they become owners, however, doctors might then have the incentive to give their patients minimum standards of care to cut costs and increase the hospital's bottom line or, more likely, to overcharge patients for their services and reap extra profits that way. In addition, the financial link between doctors and hospitals means that these doctors will not use independent hospitals that may have better records at minimizing post-operative infections or providing better patient care.

Clearly the potentially competing goals of doctors and patients when doctors are shareholders has important implications for managing stakeholder interests. Indeed, there has been some support for banning doctors from holding a financial stake in their

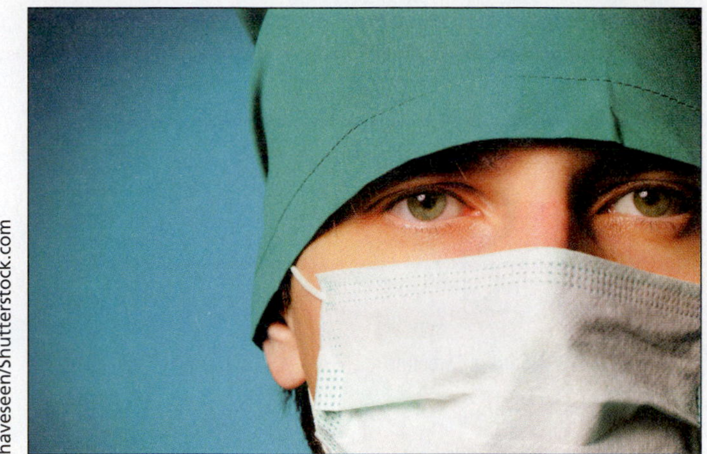

haveseen/Shutterstock.com

Do doctors face conflicting incentives when they become shareholders in the hospitals and clinics in which they work? Some experts think so.

own clinics and hospitals. However, doctors claim they are in the same situation as lawyers or accountants, and there is no more reason to suppose they will take advantage of their patients than lawyers will find ways to inflate the bills of their clients.

The allocation of rewards, or inducements, is an important component of organizational effectiveness because the inducements offered to stakeholders now determine their motivation—that is, the form and level of their contributions—in the future. Stakeholders' future investment decisions depend on the return they expect from their investments, whether the returns are in the form of dividends, stock options, bonuses, or wages. It is in this context that the roles of top managers and the board of directors become important because they are the stakeholder groups that possess the power that determines the level of reward or inducements each group—including themselves—will ultimately receive. As the employees and shareholders of Enron who lost almost all the value of their pensions and shares found out, directors and top managers often do not perform their roles well.

Top Managers and Organizational Authority

Because top management is the stakeholder group that has the ultimate responsibility for setting company goals and objectives, and for allocating organizational resources to achieve these objectives, it is useful to take a closer look at these top managers. Who are they, what roles and functions do they perform, and how do managers cooperate to run a company's business?

Authority is the power to hold people accountable for their actions and to influence directly what they do and how they do it. The stakeholder group with ultimate authority over the use of a corporation's resources is shareholders. Legally, they own the company and exercise control over it through their representatives, the board of directors. Through the board, shareholders delegate to managers the legal authority and responsibility to use the organization's resources to create value and to meet goals (see Figure 2.1). Accepting this authority and responsibility from shareholders and the board of directors makes corporate managers accountable for the way they use resources and for how much value the organization creates.

Authority
The power to hold people accountable for their actions and to make decisions concerning the use of organizational resources.

The board of directors monitors corporate managers' activities and rewards corporate managers who pursue activities that satisfy stakeholder goals. The board has the legal authority to hire, fire, and discipline corporate management. The chair of the board of directors is the principal representative of the shareholders and, as such, has the most authority in an organization. Through the executive committee, which consists of the organization's most important directors and top managers, the chair has the responsibility for monitoring and evaluating the way corporate managers use organizational resources. The position of the chair and the other directors is one of trusteeship: They act as trustees to protect the interests of shareholders and other stakeholders. The salary committee sets the salaries and terms of employment for corporate managers.

Figure 2.1 The Top-Management Hierarchy

This chart shows the ranking of the positions in the hierarchy, not necessarily the typical reporting relationships.

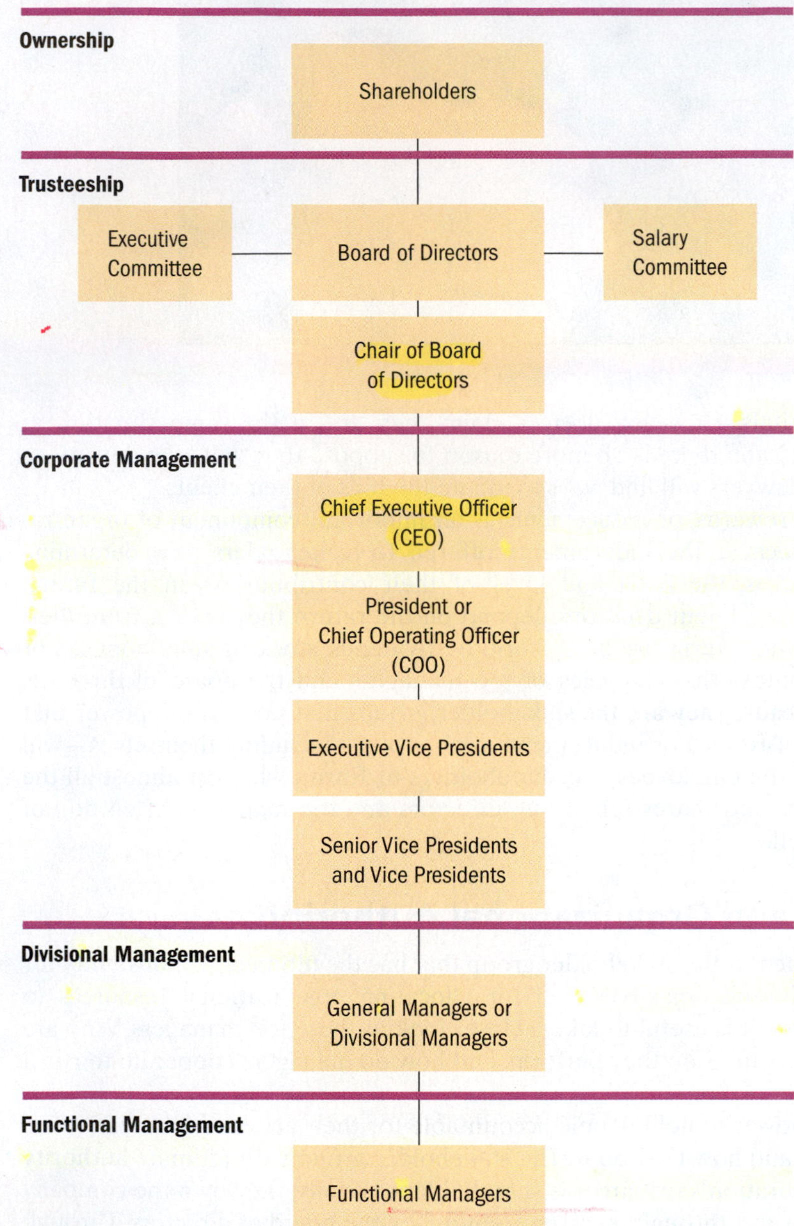

There are two kinds of directors: inside directors and outside directors. Inside directors are directors who also hold offices in a company's formal hierarchy; they are full-time employees of the corporation. Outside directors are not employees of the company; many are professional directors who hold positions on the board of many companies, or they are executives of other companies who sit on other companies' boards. The goal of having outside directors is to bring objectivity to a company's decision making and to balance the power of inside directors, who obviously side with an organization's management. In practice, however, inside directors tend to dominate boards because these people have access to the most information about the company, and they can use that information to influence decision making in management's favor. Moreover, many outside directors tend to be passive and serve as a rubber stamp for management's decisions. It has been claimed that many of the problems that have arisen, and still are arising, in companies such as Computer Associates, Walt Disney, Bank of America, HP, and other companies are the result of passive or captive directors, appointed by the CEO, who failed to exercise adequate supervision. Directors of some companies have been sued for their failure to do so and paid millions in fines.[16]

Corporate-level management is the inside stakeholder group that has the ultimate responsibility for setting company goals and objectives, for allocating organizational resources to achieve objectives, and for designing the organization's structure. Who are these corporate managers? What exactly do they do, and what roles do they play? Figure 2.1 shows the typical hierarchy of management titles and the **chain of command,** that is, the system of hierarchical reporting relationships of a large corporation. A **hierarchy** is a vertical ordering of organizational roles according to their relative authority.

Chain of command
The system of hierarchical reporting relationships in an organization.

Hierarchy
A classification of people according to authority and rank.

The Chief Executive Officer

The CEO is the person ultimately responsible for setting organizational strategy and policy. Even though the CEO reports to the chair of the board (who has the most legal authority), in a real sense the CEO is the most powerful person in the corporation because he or she controls the allocation of resources. The board of directors gives the CEO the power to set the organization's strategy and use its resources to create value. Often the same person is *both* chief executive officer and chair of the board. A person who occupies both positions wields considerable power and directly links the board to corporate management.

How does a CEO actually affect the way an organization operates? A CEO can influence organizational effectiveness and decision making in five principal ways.[17]

1. ***The CEO is responsible for setting the organization's goals and designing its structure.*** The CEO allocates authority and task responsibilities so that all an organization's employees are coordinated and motivated to achieve organizational goals. Different organizational structures promote different methods of coordinating and motivating employees at all levels.
2. ***The CEO selects key executives to occupy the topmost levels of the managerial hierarchy.*** The decision of which managers to promote to the top of the organizational hierarchy is a vital part of the CEO's job because the quality of decision making is directly affected by the abilities of an organization's top managers. The CEO of General Electric, for example, personally selects and promotes GE's 100 top managers and approves the promotions of 600 other executives.[18] By choosing key personnel, the CEO determines the values, norms, and culture that emerge in the organization. The culture determines the way organization members approach problems and make decisions: Are they entrepreneurial or are they conservative?
3. ***The CEO determines top management's rewards and incentives.*** The CEO influences the motivation of top managers to pursue organizational goals effectively. Even though they knew Enron was collapsing, in the days before, its top managers decided to award themselves over $80 million in compensation for their "work." One of the reasons Netflix has become so successful and is now the market leader in movie and TV programming rental and streaming with one in eight Americans signed up for its service is because of its way of compensating managers. Managers decide *each month* what proportion of their compensation they wish to take in the form of actual salary or stock options linked to the company's future performance. The result has been a team of committed managers devoted to maximizing the company's future potential.[19]
4. ***The CEO controls the allocation of scarce resources such as money and decision-making power among the organization's functional areas or business divisions.*** This control gives the CEO enormous power to influence the direction of the organization's future value creation activities—the kinds of products the company will make, the markets in which it will compete, and so on. Henry Ford III regained the CEO's job at Ford in the late 1990s after its former CEO, Jacques Nasser, came under criticism after spending tens of billions on countless global projects that had done little to increase the company's profitability. Ford's philosophy was that his

managers must prove their projects will make money before he would allow funds to be invested to develop new cars. CEO Ford was no more successful than former CEOs. The company's global car sales continued to drop, so in 2005 Ford decided to give up control of the company to a new CEO, Alan Mulally, who by 2011 transformed the company using his skills to make the best use of Ford's resources. In the summer of 2011, although he was now 65 years old, Mulally said he had no plans to retire, and Henry Ford joked that he hoped Mulally would be around until 2025!

5. ***The CEO's actions and reputation have a major impact on inside and outside stakeholders' views of the organization and affect the organization's ability to attract resources from its environment.*** A CEO's personality and charisma can influence an organization's ability to obtain money from banks and shareholders and influence customers' desire to buy a company's products. So can a reputation for honesty and integrity and a track record of making sound, ethical business decisions.

The ability to influence organizational decision making and managerial behavior gives the CEO enormous power to directly influence organizational effectiveness. This power is also indirect because CEOs influence decision making through the people they appoint or the organizational structure or culture they create and leave behind them as their legacy. Thus the top-management team that the CEO creates is critical to the organization's success not only in the present, but in the future.

The Top-Management Team

After the chair and CEO, the chief operating officer (COO), who is next in line for the CEO's job, or president, who may or may not be the CEO's successor, is the next most important executive. The COO or president reports directly to the CEO, and together they share the principal responsibility for managing the business. In most organizations, a division of labor takes place at the top between these two roles. Normally, the CEO has primary responsibility for managing the organization's relationship with external stakeholders and for planning the long-term strategic objectives of the organization as a whole and all its business divisions. The COO or president has primary responsibility for managing the organization's internal operations to make sure they conform to the organization's strategic objectives. In a large company the COO also oversees the operation of a company's most important business divisions and units.

At the next level of top management are the executive vice presidents. People with this title have responsibility for overseeing and managing a company's most significant line and staff responsibilities. A **line role** is held by managers who have direct responsibility for the production of goods and services. An executive vice president, for example, might have overall responsibility for overseeing the performance of all 200 of a company's chemical divisions or all of a company's international divisions. A **staff role** is held by managers who are in charge of a specific organizational function such as sales or R&D. For example, the executive vice president for finance manages an organization's overall financial activities, and the executive vice president for R&D oversees a company's research operations. Staff roles are advisory only; they have no direct production responsibilities, but their occupants possess enormous influence on decision making.

Line role
Managers who have direct responsibility for the production of goods and services.

Staff role
Managers who are in charge of a specific organizational function such as sales or R&D.

Top-management team
A group of managers who report to the CEO and COO and help the CEO set the company's strategy and its long-term goals and objectives.

Corporate managers
The members of the top-management team whose responsibility is to set strategy for the corporation as a whole.

The CEO, COO, and the executive vice presidents are at the top of an organization's chain of command. Collectively, managers in these positions form a company's **top-management team,** the group of managers who report to the CEO and COO and help the CEO set the company's strategy and its long-term goals and objectives.[20] All the members of the top-management team are **corporate managers,** whose responsibility is to set strategy for the corporation as a whole.

The way the CEO handles the top-management team and appoints people to it is a vital part of the CEO's task. For example, when the CEO appoints the COO, he or she is sending a clear signal to the top-management team about the kinds of issues and events that are of most importance to the organization. Often, for example, an organization picks a new CEO or appoints a COO who has the functional and managerial background that can deal with the most pressing issues facing a corporation. Many companies carefully select a successor to the CEO who will be able to take over and improve upon the long-term approach that will make the best use of a company's resources. Obviously, appointment to the top-management team is the first step in this process of developing the future CEO.[21] More and more the composition of the top-management team is becoming one of the main priorities of the CEO and of a company's board of directors, and the stock price of a company is often tied to a CEO's future performance. Apple investors became worried in 2011 as the health problems of Apple's Steve Jobs caused him again to take a leave of absence, and Google's investors became concerned when founder Larry Page took over as CEO from Eric Schmidt, who had led the company during its meteoric rise to fame in the 2000s.

Other Managers

At the next level of management are a company's senior vice presidents and vice presidents, senior corporate-level managers in both line and staff functions. Large companies such as Time Warner, Ford, and Microsoft have many hundreds or thousands of corporate-level managers. Also, at this level are those managers who head one of a company's many operating companies or divisions and who are known as general managers. In practice, general managers of the divisions commonly have the title of CEO of their divisions because they have direct line responsibility for *their* division's performance and normally report to the corporate CEO or COO. However, they set policy only for the division they head, not for the whole corporation, and thus are **divisional managers,** not corporate managers. Inside Ford, for example, are the divisional managers responsible for the operation of each of its carmaking divisions or units.

Divisional mangers
Managers who set policy only for the division they head.

An organization or a division of an organization also has functional managers with titles such as marketing manager or production manager. **Functional managers** are responsible for developing the functional skills and capabilities that collectively provide the core competences that give the organization its competitive advantage. Each division, for example, has a set of functional managers who report to the general or divisional manager.

Functional managers
Managers who are responsible for developing the functional skills and capabilities that collectively provide the core competences that give the organization its competitive advantage.

An Agency Theory Perspective

Agency theory offers a useful way of understanding the complex authority relationship between top management and the board of directors. An agency relation arises whenever one person (the principal) delegates decision-making authority or control over resources to another (the agent). Starting at the top of a company's hierarchy of authority, shareholders are the principals; members of top management are their agents, appointed by shareholders to use organizational resources most effectively. The average shareholder, for example, has no in-depth knowledge of a particular industry or how to run a company. They appoint experts in the industry—managers—to perform this work for them. However, in delegating authority to managers, an **agency problem**—a problem in determining managerial accountability—arises. This is because if you employ an expert manager, by definition that person must know more than you; how then can you question the decisions of the expert and the way managers are running the company? Moreover, the results of managers' performance can be evaluated only after considerable time has elapsed. Consequently, it is very difficult to hold managers accountable for what they do. Most often shareholders don't until it is too late—when the company suffers billion-dollar losses. In delegating authority, to a large extent shareholders lose their ability to influence managerial decision making in a significant way.

Agency problem
A problem in determining managerial accountability that arises when delegating authority to managers.

The problem is that shareholders or principals are at an *information disadvantage* compared with top managers. It is very difficult for them to judge the effectiveness of a top-management team's actions when it can often only be judged over several years. Moreover, as noted earlier, the goals and interests of managers and shareholders may diverge. Managers may prefer to pursue courses of action that lead to short-term profits, or short-term control over the market, whereas shareholders might prefer actions that lead to long-term profitability such as increased efficiency and long-term innovation.

The Moral Hazard Problem

When these two conditions exist and (1) a principal finds it very difficult to evaluate how well the agent has performed because the agent possesses an information advantage, and (2) the agent has an incentive to pursue goals and objectives that are different from the principal's, a *moral hazard* problem exists. Here, agents have the opportunity and incentive to pursue their own interests. For example, in the 2000s entertainment giant Time Warner came under attack because its top managers had made many acquisitions such as AOL that had *lowered* innovation, efficiency, and profits. Shareholders felt Time Warner's top-management team was pursuing the wrong strategies to increase the company's profitability; for example, they demanded the company divest AOL and its TV cable business. To make top managers confront the hard issues, shareholders demanded (1) a change in the direction and goals of the company, and (2) more financial information they could use to reduce their information disadvantage. In short, they wanted more control over the company's strategy to overcome the agency problem. As Time Warner's stock price continued to decline their power increased and the company was broken up; in 2008 it first spun off the cable division and then in 2009 it spun off AOL, both of which became independent companies with their own CEOs.

Other, more specific examples of moral hazard are regularly reported in the press, such as in May 2011 when billionaire hedge fund manager Raj Rajaratham was found guilty on all 14 counts of securities fraud for his role in a huge insider trading securities scandal. Rajaratham paid senior managers of chip companies AMD and Intel for information about upcoming changes in their strategy that allowed him to make almost $64 million by trading the stock of these companies before these changes were announced. In 2011, another 15 cases of insider trading were being prosecuted by the government in its attempt to eliminate the use of secret information to make money off ordinary stockholders. Clearly, top managers have enormous opportunities to pursue their own interests at the expense of other stakeholders.

Self-dealing
Managers who take advantage of their position in an organization to act in ways to further their own self-interest.

Self-dealing is the term used to describe the conduct of corporate managers who take advantage of their position in an organization to act in their own interests rather than in the interests of other stakeholders, such as taking advantage of opportunities to misappropriate corporate resources—including secret information.

Solving the Agency Problem

Governance mechanisms
The forms of control that align the interests of principal and agent so both parties have the incentive to work together to maximize organizational effectiveness.

In agency theory, the central issue is to overcome the agency problem by using **governance mechanisms,** or forms of control that align the interests of principal and agent so both parties have the incentive to work together to maximize organizational effectiveness. There are many different kinds of governance mechanisms.

First, the principal role of the board of directors is to monitor top managers' activities, question their decision making and strategies, and intervene when necessary. Some have argued for a clear separation between the role of CEO and chair to curb the CEO's power, arguing that the huge increase in CEO pay is evidence of the need to prevent abuses of power. Another vital task here is to reinforce and develop the organization's code of ethics, as discussed later.

The next step in solving the agency problem is to find the right set of incentives to align the interests of managers and shareholders. Recall that it is very difficult for shareholders to monitor and evaluate the effectiveness of managers' decisions because the results of these can only be assessed after several years have elapsed. Thus basing rewards on decisions is often not an effective alignment strategy. The most effective way of aligning interests between management and shareholders is to make managers' rewards contingent on the outcomes of their decisions, that is, contingent on organizational performance. There are several ways of doing this, and each has advantages and disadvantages.

Stock-based compensation schemes
Monetary rewards in the form of stocks or stock options that are linked to the company's performance.

STOCK-BASED COMPENSATION SCHEMES **Stock-based compensation schemes** are one way of achieving this. Managers receive a large part of their monetary reward in the form of stocks or stock options that are linked to the company's performance. If the company does well, then the value of their stock options and monetary compensation is much enhanced. Effectively, interests are aligned because managers become stockholders. This strategy has been used in some companies like GM and IBM, where traditionally top managers had very low stock ownership in the corporation. The board of directors insisted that top managers purchase stock in the companies, and they awarded stock options as a means of increasing top managers' stake in the company's long-term performance.

PROMOTION TOURNAMENTS AND CAREER PATHS Incentives can also take other forms. One way of linking rewards to performance over the long term is by developing organizational career paths that allow managers to rise to the top of the organization. The power of the CEO role is something to which many top managers aspire. For example, a board of directors by demoting some top executives and promoting or hiring new ones, often from the outside, can send a clear signal to top managers about what kinds of behaviors would be rewarded in the future. All organizations have "promotion tournaments" where executives compete for limited promotion opportunities by displaying their superior skills and competences. By directly linking promotion to performance, the board of directors can send out a clear signal about future managerial behaviors that would lead to promotion—and make managers focus on long-term, not short-term, objectives.

The reward from promotion to the top is not just the long-term monetary package that goes with promotion but also the opportunity to exercise power over resources, and the prestige, status, and intrinsic satisfaction that accompany the journey to the top of the organization.

The issue of designing corporate governance mechanisms to ensure long-term effectiveness is complex and one that is currently stirring enormous debate.[22] Congress has enacted some new governance mechanisms and more are planned. For example, the Sarbanes-Oxley Act introduced a new requirement that CEOs, COOs, and the chief financial officer sign off on their company's balance statements so they can be held personally and legally liable for accidental or deliberate mistakes found later. This requirement has led organizations to disclose their financial results more fully. Similarly, as noted, new rules for governing relations between companies and their accountants have been developed, and new regulations are in place that force companies to show shareholders exactly what kinds of benefit and perks CEOs and other top executives receive in addition to their salaries, such as stock options, pensions, use of company jets, and so on.

Indeed, the issue of stockholders rights has become an increasingly important issue in the 2000s as company after company admitted that they broke business laws and regulations. For example, Salomon Smith Barney agreed to pay a $5 million fine to settle charges that one of their star brokers was promoting a stock to investors even though internal emails suggested the stock was a dog. Brokers at Merrill Lynch, now part of Bank of America, were found to have acted in a similar way, privately laughing about the poor prospects of companies whose stocks they nevertheless continued to recommend to their thousands of investors. Many major mutual fund companies admitted they had allowed their fund managers and large investors to use secret information to make stock market trades that made them millions of dollars but hurt millions of small investors. Similarly, many large insurance companies admitted they had paid kickbacks to brokers to obtain their business, something that artificially raised the cost of insurance policies to customers. All these companies have paid hundreds of millions in fines to settle these charges, and their top managers, many of whom possessed enormous influence in their industries, have been fired. To learn more about Amazon's approach to Corporate Governance, visit the company website's Investor Relations section and view the Corporate Governance Guidelines.

Top Managers and Organizational Ethics

A very important mechanism of corporate governance, which has become increasingly important for a board of directors to emphasize after the recent corporate scandals, is to insist that managers follow ethical guidelines in their decision making when confronted with an ethical dilemma. An **ethical dilemma** is the quandary people find themselves in when they have to decide if they should act in a way that might help another person or group and is the "right" thing to do, even though doing so might go against their own self-interest. A dilemma may also arise when a person has to decide between two different courses of action, knowing that whichever course he or she chooses will result in harm to one person or group even while it may benefit another. The ethical dilemma here is to decide which course of action is the lesser of two evils.

Ethical dilemma
The quandary people experience when they must decide whether or not they should act in a way that benefits someone else, even if it harms others and isn't in their own interest.

People often know they are confronting an ethical dilemma when their moral scruples come into play and cause them to hesitate, debate, and reflect on the "rightness" or "goodness" of a course of action. Moral scruples are thoughts and feelings that tell a person what is right or wrong; they are a part of a person's ethics. **Ethics** are the inner-guiding moral principles, values, and beliefs that people use to analyze or interpret a situation and then decide what is the "right" or appropriate way to behave. At the same time, ethics also indicate what inappropriate behavior is and how a person should behave to avoid doing harm to another person.

Ethics
Moral principles or beliefs about what is right or wrong.

The essential problem in dealing with ethical issues, and thus solving moral dilemmas, is that no absolute or indisputable rules or principles can be developed to decide if an action is ethical or unethical. Put simply, different people or groups may dispute which actions are ethical or unethical depending on their own personal self-interest and specific attitudes, beliefs, and values. How, therefore, are we and companies and their managers to decide what is ethical and so act appropriately toward other people and groups?

Ethics and the Law

The first answer to this question is that society as a whole, using the political and legal process, can lobby for and pass laws that specify what people and organizations can and cannot do. For example, many different kinds of laws exist to govern business, such as antitrust law and employment law. Laws also specify what sanctions or punishments will follow if those laws are broken. Different groups in society lobby for which laws should be passed based on their own personal interests and beliefs with regard to what is right or wrong. The group that can summon most support is able to pass the laws that most closely align with its interests and beliefs. Once a law is passed, a decision about what the appropriate behavior is with regard to a person or situation is taken from the personally determined ethical realm to the societally determined legal realm. If you do not conform to the law, you can be prosecuted; and if you are found guilty of breaking the law, you can be punished.

In studying the relationship between ethics and law, it is important to understand that *neither laws nor ethics are fixed principles*, cast in stone, which do not change over time. Ethical beliefs alter and change as time passes, and as they do so, laws change to reflect the changing ethical beliefs of a society. There are many types of behavior—such as theft, industrial espionage, the sale of unsafe products, and insider trading—that most, if not all, people currently believe are totally unacceptable and unethical and should therefore be illegal. But the ethical nature of many other kinds of actions and behaviors is open to dispute. Some people might believe that a particular behavior—for example, top managers receiving stock options and bonuses worth hundreds of millions or outsourcing millions of jobs to lower cost locations abroad—is unethical and so should be made illegal. Others might argue that it is up to a company's board of directors to decide if such behaviors are ethical or not and thus whether a particular behavior should remain legal.

Whereas ethical beliefs lead to the development of laws and regulations to prevent certain behaviors or encourage others, laws themselves can and do change and disappear as ethical beliefs change. Thus both ethical and legal rules are *relative:* No absolute or unvarying standards exist to determine how we should behave, and people are caught up in moral dilemmas all the time. Because of this we have to make ethical choices.

The preceding discussion highlights an important issue in understanding the relationship among ethics, law, and business. In the 2000s, many scandals have plagued major companies; managers in some of these companies clearly broke the law and used illegal means to defraud investors; in others they acted unethically. In some cases, top managers encouraged members of their company's board of directors to behave unethically by offering them unethical and often illegal rewards for such behavior in return for their support of the CEO. For example, CEOs often use their positions to place longtime friends on their board of directors; although this is not illegal, obviously these people will vote in favor of the CEO at board meetings. In one classic example of such unethical behavior, directors of WorldCom granted its former CEO, Bernie Ebbers, huge stock options and a personal loan of over $150 million and in return they were well rewarded for being directors. For example, Ebbers allowed them to use WorldCom's corporate jets for a minimal cost, something that saved them hundreds of thousands of dollars a year, and gave them other perks amounting to millions of dollars.

In the light of these events some people said, "Well, what these people did was not illegal," implying that because such behavior was not illegal it was also not unethical. However, because behavior may not be illegal does *not* mean it is ethical; such behavior is clearly unethical. In many cases laws are passed *later* to close the loopholes and prevent unethical people such as Ebbers from behaving in this way. In any event, Ebbers was found guilty of fraud and sentenced to 20 years in jail, and many other executives from companies have received similar sentences and so will those convicted of insider trading. Like ordinary people, managers must confront the need to decide what is appropriate and inappropriate as they use organizational resources to create products customers want to buy.

Ethics and Organizational Stakeholders

As just noted, ethics are moral principles or beliefs about what is right or wrong. These beliefs guide individuals in their dealings with other individuals and groups (stakeholders) and provide a basis for deciding whether a particular decision or behavior is right and proper.[23] Ethics help people determine moral responses to situations in which the best course of action is unclear. Ethics guide managers in their decisions about what to do in various situations. Ethics also help managers decide how best to respond to the interests of various organizational stakeholders.

As we discussed earlier, in guiding a company's business, its dealings with both outside and inside stakeholders, top managers are constantly making choices about what is the right or appropriate way to deal with these stakeholders. For example, a company might wonder whether it should give advance notice to its employees and middle managers about big impending layoffs or plant closings, whether it should issue a recall of its cars because of a known defect that may cause harm or injury to passengers, or whether it should allow its managers to pay bribes to government officials in foreign countries where corruption is the accepted way of doing business. In all these situations managers are in a difficult situation because they have to balance their interests and the interests of the "organization" against the interests of other stakeholder groups. Essentially, they have to decide how to apportion the "helps and harms" that arise from an organization's actions between stakeholder groups. Sometimes, making a decision is easy because some obvious standard, value, or norm of behavior applies. In other cases, managers have trouble deciding what to do and experience an ethical dilemma when weighing or comparing the competing claims or rights of various stakeholder groups.[24]

Philosophers have debated for centuries about the specific criteria that should be used to determine whether decisions are ethical or unethical. Table 2.2 summarizes the three models of what determines whether a decision is ethical: the utilitarian, moral rights, and justice models.[25]

In theory, each model offers a different and complementary way of determining whether a decision or behavior is ethical, and all three models should be used to sort out the ethics of a particular course of action. Ethical issues, however, are seldom clear cut, and the interests of different stakeholders often conflict, so it is frequently very difficult for a decision maker to use these models to ascertain the most ethical course of action. For this reason many experts on ethics propose this practical guide to determine whether a decision or behavior is ethical.[26] A decision is probably acceptable on ethical grounds if a manager can answer "yes" to each of these questions:

1. Does my decision fall within the accepted values or standards that typically apply in the organizational environment?
2. Am I willing to see the decision communicated to all stakeholders affected by it—for example, by having it reported in newspapers or on television?
3. Would the people with whom I have a significant personal relationship, such as family members, friends, or even managers in other organizations, approve of the decision?

From a management perspective, an ethical decision is a decision that reasonable or typical stakeholders would find acceptable because it aids stakeholders, the organization,

TABLE 2.2 Utilitarian, Moral Rights, and Justice Models of Ethics

Utilitarian model. An ethical decision is one that produces the greatest good for the greatest number of people.

- **Managerial implications.** Managers should compare and contrast alternative courses of action based on the benefits and costs of these alternatives for different organizational stakeholder groups. They should choose the course of action that provides the most benefits to stakeholders. For example, managers should locate a new manufacturing plant at the place that will most benefit its stakeholders.
- **Problems for managers.** How do managers decide on the relative importance of each stakeholder group? How are managers to measure precisely the benefits and harms to each stakeholder group? For example, how do managers choose among the interests of stockholders, workers, and customers?

Moral rights model. An ethical decision is a decision that best maintains and protects the fundamental rights and privileges of the people affected by it. For example, ethical decisions protect people's rights to freedom, life and safety, privacy, free speech, and freedom of conscience.

- **Managerial implications.** Managers should compare and contrast alternative courses of action based on the effect of these alternatives on stakeholders' rights. They should choose the course of action that best protects stakeholders' rights. For example, decisions that would involve significant harm to the safety or health of employees or customers are unethical.
- **Problems for managers.** If a decision will protect the rights of some stakeholders and hurt the rights of others, how do managers choose which stakeholder rights to protect? For example, in deciding whether it is ethical to snoop on an employee, does an employee's right to privacy outweigh an organization's right to protect its property or the safety of other employees?

Justice model. An ethical decision is a decision that distributes benefits and harms among stakeholders in a fair, equitable, or impartial way.

- **Managerial implications.** Managers should compare and contrast alternative courses of action based on the degree to which the action will promote a fair distribution of outcomes. For example, employees who are similar in their level of skill, performance, or responsibility should receive the same kind of pay. The allocation of outcomes should not be based on arbitrary differences such as gender, race, or religion.
- **Problems for managers.** Managers must learn not to discriminate against people because of observable differences in their appearance or behavior. Managers must also learn how to use fair procedures to determine how to distribute outcomes to organizational members. For example, managers must not give people they like bigger raises than they give to people they do not like or bend the rules to help their favorites.

or society. By contrast, an unethical decision is a decision a manager would prefer to disguise or hide from other people because it enables a company or a particular individual to gain at the expense of society or other stakeholders. How ethical problems arise, and how different companies respond to them is made clear by the complex ethical issues involved in animal testing.

Along with other large cosmetics companies, Gillette, the well-known maker of razors and shaving-related products, came under increasing attack for its use of animals in product testing to determine the safety and long-term effects of new product formulations. Gillette's managers received hundreds of letters from angry adults and children who object to the use of animals in cosmetics testing because they regard such testing as cruel and unethical. Managers at several other companies have tried to avoid addressing this ethical issue but Gillette's managers approached the problem head on. Gillette's ethical stance is that the health of people is more important than the health of animals, and no other reliable method that would be accepted by a court of law exists to test the properties of new formulations. Thus if the company is to protect the interests of its stakeholders and develop new safe products that customers want to buy, it must conduct animal testing.

Gillette's managers responded to each letter protesting this policy, and often telephoned children at home to explain their ethical position—they use animals only when necessary.[27] Other cosmetics companies such as the Body Shop do not test their products on animals, however, and their managers are equally willing to explain their ethical stance to the general public: They think animal testing is unethical. However, even though the Body Shop does not directly test its products on animals, many of the ingredients used in their products were tested on animals by Gillette and other companies to ensure their safety.

Clearly, the ethics of animal testing is a difficult issue, as are most other ethical questions. The view of the typical stakeholder at present seems to be that animal testing is an acceptable practice as long as it can be justified in terms of benefits to people. At the same time, most stakeholders believe such testing should minimize the harm done to animals and be used only when necessary.

Ethical rules develop over time through negotiation, compromise, and bargaining among stakeholders. Ethical rules also can evolve from outright conflict and competition between different stakeholder groups where the ability of one group to impose their solution on another group decides which ethical rules will be followed. For example, employees might exert moral pressure on management to improve their working conditions or to give them warning of possible layoffs. Shareholders might demand that top management not invest their capital in countries that practice racism or that employ children in factories under conditions close to slavery.[28] Over time, many ethical rules and values are codified into the law of a society, and from that point on, unethical behavior becomes illegal behavior. Individuals and organizations are required to obey these legal rules and can be punished for not doing so.

Sources of Organizational Ethics

To understand the nature of an organization's ethical values, it is useful to discuss the sources of ethics. The three principal sources of ethical values that influence organizational ethics are societal, group or professional, and individual.

SOCIETAL ETHICS One important determinant of organizational ethics is societal ethics. Societal ethics are codified in a society's legal system, in its customs and practices, and in the unwritten norms and values that people use to interact with each other. Many ethical norms and values are followed automatically by people in a society because people have internalized society's values and made them part of their own. These internalized norms and values, in turn, reinforce what is taken as custom and practice in a society in people's dealings with one another. For example, ethics concerning the inalienable rights of the individual are the result of decisions made by members of a society about how they want to be treated by others. Ethics governing the use of bribery and corruption, or the general standards of doing business in a society, are the result of decisions made and enforced by people deciding what is appropriate in a society. These standards differ by society, and ethical values accepted in the United States are not accepted in other countries. For example, if I buy a pound of rice in India, I can expect that about 6–8% of that rice will be dust; moreover, I know that the more I pay for the rice the less dust I can expect. It is the custom and practice in India. In the United States, by contrast, many complex rules govern the purity of foodstuffs that companies are required to follow by law—although the peanut company discussed earlier did not follow them. Although many U.S. organizations voluntarily provide layoff benefits, many do not. In general, the poorer a country, the more likely are employees to be treated with little regard. One issue of particular ethical concern on a global level is whether it is ethical to use child labor, as discussed in Organizational Insight 2.3.

One recent attempt to do this is through the Fair Factories Clearinghouse, a joint effort launched in 2006 by companies such as L.L. Bean, Reebok, and Timberland to pool the information they collect about the work practices of the factories with which they have contracted to make their products. The aim is to create a single set of labor code standards that plants the world over must comply with if they are to be certified as ethical suppliers—or else they will be axed by all reputable companies.

When societal ethics are codified into law, then judged by the ethical standards of a society, all illegal behavior may be regarded as unethical behavior. An organization and its managers are legally required to follow all the laws of a society and to behave toward individuals and stakeholders according to the law. It is one of top management's main responsibilities to ensure that managers and employees below them in the organization are obeying the law, for top managers can be held accountable in certain situations for the performance of their subordinates. However, not all organizations behave according to the law. The typical kinds of crimes that these organizations commit are not only illegal: They may be also regarded as unethical to the extent they harm other stakeholder groups.

Organizational Insight 2.3

Is It Right to Use Child Labor?

In recent years, the number of U.S. companies that buy their inputs from low-cost foreign suppliers has been growing, and concern about the ethics associated with employing young children in factories has been increasing. In Pakistan, children as young as age 6 work long hours in deplorable conditions to make rugs and carpets for export to Western countries. Children in poor countries throughout Africa, Asia, and South America work in similar conditions. Is it ethical to employ children in factories, and should U.S. companies buy and sell products made by these children?

Opinions about the ethics of child labor vary widely. Robert Reich, an economist and secretary of labor in the first Clinton administration, believes that the practice is totally reprehensible and should be outlawed on a global level. Another view, championed by the *Economist* magazine, is that, although nobody wants to see children employed in factories, citizens of rich countries need to recognize that in poor countries children are often a family's only breadwinners. Thus, denying children employment would cause whole families to suffer, and one wrong (child labor) might produce a greater wrong (poverty). Instead, the *Economist* favors regulating the conditions under which children are employed and hopes that over time, as poor countries become richer, the need for child employment will disappear.

Many U.S. retailers typically buy their clothing from low-cost foreign suppliers, and managers in these companies have had to take their own ethical stance on child labor. Managers in Walmart, Target, JCPenney, and Kmart have followed U.S. standards and rules and have policies that dictate their foreign suppliers not employ child labor; they also vow to sever ties with any foreign supplier found to be in violation of this standard.

Apparently, however, retailers differ widely in the way they choose to enforce this policy. Walmart and some others take a tough stance and immediately sever links with suppliers who break this rule. But it has been estimated, for example, that more than 300,000 children under age 14 are being employed in garment factories in Guatemala, a popular low-cost location for clothing manufacturers that supply the U.S. market.[29] These children frequently work more than 60 hours a week and often are paid less than $2.80 a day, the minimum wage in Guatemala. Many U.S. retailers do not check up on their foreign suppliers. Clearly, if U.S. retailers are to be true to their ethical stance on this troubling issue, they cannot ignore the fact that they are buying clothing made by children, and they must do more to regulate the conditions under which these children work.

PROFESSIONAL ETHICS Professional ethics are the moral rules and values that a group of people uses to control the way they perform a task or use resources. For example, medical ethics control the way that doctors and nurses are expected to perform their tasks and help patients. Doctors are expected not to perform unnecessary medical procedures, to exercise due diligence, and to act in the patient's interest, not in their own. Scientific and technical researchers are expected to behave ethically in preparing and presenting their results to ensure the validity of their conclusions. As with society, most professional groups can enforce the ethics of their profession. For example, doctors and lawyers can be disbarred should they break the rules and put their own interests first.

In an organization, there are many groups of employees whose behavior is governed by professional ethics, such as lawyers, researchers, and accountants. These cause them to follow certain principles in deciding how to act in the organization. People internalize the rules and values of their profession, just as they do those of society, and they follow these principles automatically in deciding how to behave. On the other hand, customers often expect certain kinds of "professionals" such as people who repair cars and roofs or who provide services such as taxi transport to take advantage of them, as Organizational Insight 2.4 suggests.

INDIVIDUAL ETHICS Individual ethics are the personal and moral standards used by individuals to structure their interactions with other people. Based on these ethics, a person may or may not perform certain actions or make certain decisions. Many behaviors that one person may find unethical another person may find ethical. If those behaviors are not illegal, individuals may agree to disagree about their ethical beliefs or they may try to impose those beliefs on other people and try to make their ethical beliefs the law. If personal ethics conflict with law, a person may be subject to legal sanction. Many personal ethics follow society's ethics and have their origin in law. Personal ethics are also the result of a person's upbringing and may stem from family, friends, religious membership, or other significant social institution. Personal ethics influence how a person acts in an organization. For example, managers' behavior toward other managers and subordinates depends on the personal values and beliefs they hold.

Organizational Insight 2.4

Always Ask for an Estimate from a Cab Driver

In 2009 the New York City taxi commission, which regulates cab fares, began an investigation after it found that one cab driver from Brooklyn, Wasim Khalid Cheema, overcharged 574 passengers in just one month. The taxi drivers' scheme, the commission said, involved 1.8 million rides and cost passengers an average of $4–5 extra per trip. The drivers pressed a button on the taxi's payment meter that categorized the fare as a Code No. 4, which is charged for trips outside the city to Nassau or Westchester and is twice the rate of Code No. 1, which is charged for rides within New York City limits. Passengers can see which rate is being charged by looking at the meter, but few bother to do so; they rely on the cab driver's honesty.

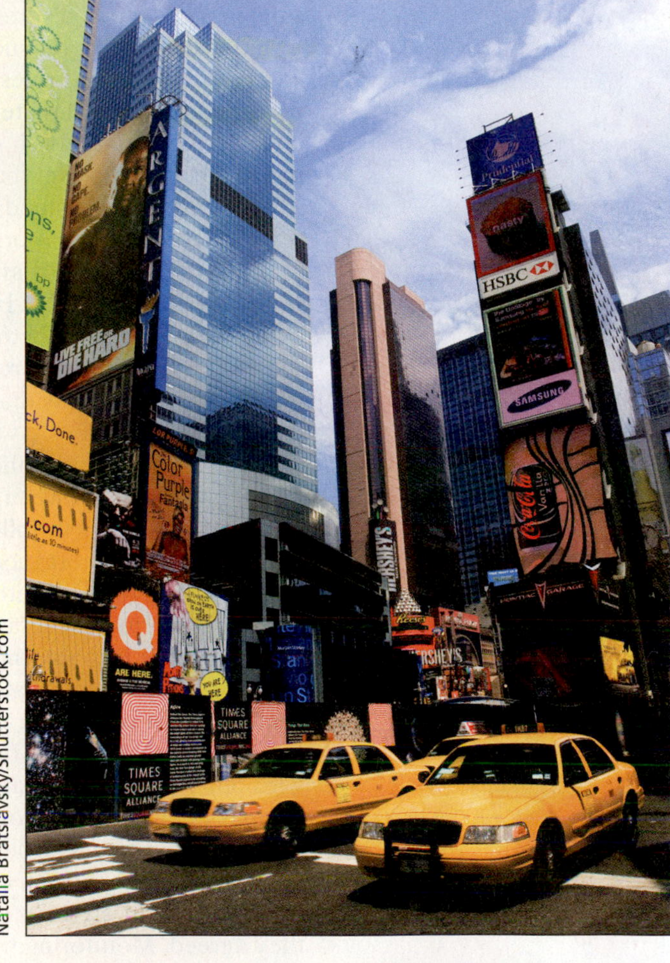

Natalia Bratslavsky/Shutterstock.com

After the commission discovered the fraud, it used GPS data, collected in every cab, to review millions of trips within New York City and found that in 36,000 cabs the higher rates were improperly activated at least once; in each of about 3,000 cabs it was done more than 100 times; and 35,558 of the city's roughly 48,000 drivers had applied the higher rate. This scheme cost New York City riders more than $8 million plus all the higher tips they paid as a result of the excess charges. The fraud ranks as one of the biggest in the taxi industry's history, and New York City Mayor Michael R. Bloomberg said criminal charges could be brought against cab drivers.

The commission also demanded that in the future a new digital metering system be introduced to alert passengers, who would have to acknowledge that they accepted the higher rate charge. Also, officials said taxi companies would eventually be forced to use meters based on a GPS system that would automatically set the charge based on the location of the cab, and drivers would no longer be able to manually activate the higher rate—and cheat their customers. In 2011, New York City signed a $1 billion contract with Nissan to supply the next generation of yellow cabs that will be used over the next decade. Each of these cabs will be equipped with the latest GPS tracking and monitoring systems that will make such unethical behavior virtually impossible; in addition they will also be continually upgraded with the latest hybrid or electric technology to increase gas mileage, which will also keep fares down.

These three sources of ethics collectively influence the ethics that develop inside an organization, or organizational ethics, which may be defined as the rules or standards used by an organization and its members in their dealings with other stakeholders groups. Each organization has a set of ethics; some of these are unique to an organization and are an important aspect of its culture, a topic discussed in detail in Chapter 7. However, many ethical rules go beyond the boundaries of any individual company. Companies, collectively, are expected to follow ethical and legal rules because of the advantages that are produced for a society and its members when its organizations and institutions behave ethically.

Why Do Ethical Rules Develop?

One of the most important reasons why ethical rules governing action develop is to slow down or temper the pursuit of self-interest. One of the best ways of understanding the self-interest issue is to discuss the "tragedy of the commons" problem. When common

land—that is, land owned by everyone—exists, it is rational for every person to maximize their use of it because it is a free resource. So everybody grazes their cattle on the land to promote their individual interests. But if everybody does this, what happens to the land, the common resource? It is destroyed by erosion because overgrazing leaves it defenseless to the effects of wind and rain. Thus the rational pursuit of individual self-interest results in a collective disaster. The same is true in many organized situations: Left to their own devices, people pursue their own goals at the expense of collective goals.

Ethical laws and rules emerge to control self-interested behavior by individuals and organizations that threatens society's collective interests. For example, the reason why laws develop to establish what is good or appropriate business practice is because they provide benefits to everybody. Free and fair competition among organizations is only possible when rules and standards exist that constrain the actions people can take in a certain situation. As a businessperson, it is ethical for me to compete with a rival and maybe drive that person out of business if I do so by legal means such as by producing a cheaper, better, or more reliable product. However, it is not ethical for me to do so by shooting that person or by blowing up his factory. Competition by quality or price creates value for the consumer; competition by force results in monopoly and hurts the customer and the public interest. This is not to say that nobody gets hurt—the rival I force out of business gets hurt—but the harm I do him has to be weighed against the gain to consumers and to myself.

Ethical issues are inherently complex ones where the problem is to distribute the helps and harms between different stakeholders. The issue is to try to act as people of goodwill and to try to follow the moral principles that seem to produce the most good. Ethical rules and moral codes develop to increase the value that can be produced by people when they interact with each other. They protect people. Without these rules, free and fair competition degenerates into conflict and warfare, and everybody loses. Another way of putting this is to say that ethical rules reduce the costs people have to bear to decide what is right or appropriate. Following an ethical rule avoids expending time and effort in deciding what is the right thing to do. In other words, ethical rules reduce *transaction costs* between people, that is, the costs of monitoring, negotiating, and enforcing agreements with other people. Transaction costs can be enormous when strangers meet to engage in business. For example, how do I trust the other person to behave ethically when I don't know that person? It is here again that the power of ethics in establishing the rules to be followed is so important. For if I can rely on the other person to follow the rules, I do not need to expend effort in monitoring the other person to make sure they do perform as they agreed. Monitoring wastes my time and effort and is largely unproductive. So when people share common ethics, it helps reduce transaction costs.

Behavior that follows accepted ethical rules confers a *reputation effect* on an individual or an organization that also reduces transaction costs. If an organization over time is known for engaging in illegal acts, how will people view that organization? Most likely with suspicion and hostility. However, suppose an organization always follows the rules and is known for its ethical business practices over and above strict legal requirements. It will have gained a reputation, which is valuable because people will want to deal with it. Unethical organizations over time are therefore penalized as people refuse to deal with them, so there are constraints on organizations beyond those of the law.

Reputation effects also help explain why managers and employees who work in organizations also follow ethical rules. Suppose an organization behaves unethically; what will be the position of its employees? To outsiders, employees come to be branded with the same reputation as the unethical organization because they are assumed to have performed according to its code of ethics. Even if the organization's unethical behavior was the product of a few self-seeking individuals, it will affect and harm all employees. For example, in Japan in the stock crash of the 1990s, many brokerage firms went bankrupt with irate clients suing these firms for disguising the real risks associated with investment in the inflated stock market. Employees of these firms found it very difficult to obtain jobs in other organizations because they were branded with the "shame" of having worked for these companies. Thus employees have the incentive for their firm to behave ethically because their fortunes are tied up with the organization's—an organization's bad reputation will hurt their reputation too.[30]

One intangible reward that comes from behaving ethically is feeling good about one's behavior and enjoying the good conscience that comes with acting within the rules of the game. Success by stealth and deceit does not provide the same intangible reward as success from following the rules simply because it is not a fair test of ability or personal qualities. Personal reputation is the outcome of behaving ethically, and the esteem or respect of one's peers has always been a reward that people desire.

In sum, acting ethically promotes the good of a society and the well-being of its members. More value is created in societies where people follow ethical rules, and where criminal and unethical behavior are prevented by law and by custom and practice from emerging. Nevertheless, individuals and organizations do perform unethical and illegal acts.

Why Does Unethical Behavior Occur?

Although there are good reasons for individuals and organizations to behave ethically, there are also many reasons why unethical behavior takes place.

PERSONAL ETHICS In theory, people learn ethical principles and moral codes as they mature as individuals in a society. Ethics are obtained from such sources as family and friends, places of worship, education, professional training, and organizations of all kinds. From these, people learn to differentiate right from wrong in a society or in a social group. However, suppose you are the son or daughter of a mobster or an enormously wealthy landed family, and your upbringing and education takes place in such a context. You may come to believe it is ethical to do anything and perform any act, up to and including murder, if it benefits your family's interests. These are your ethics. These are obviously not the ethics of the wider society and as such are subject to sanction, but in a similar way managers in an organization may come to believe any actions that promote or protect the organization are more important than any harm the organization does to others.

SELF-INTEREST We normally confront ethical issues when we are weighing our personal interests against the effects of our actions on others. Suppose you know you will get a promotion to vice president of your company if you can secure a $100 million contract, but you know to get the contract you must bribe the contract giver with $1 million. What would you do? Your career and future seems to be assured by performing this act, and what harm would it do? Bribery is common anyway, and if you don't pay the million, you can be sure that somebody else will. So what do you do? Research seems to suggest that people who realize they have most at stake in a career sense or a monetary sense are the ones most likely to act unethically. Similarly, it has been shown that organizations that are doing badly in an economic sense and are struggling to survive are the ones most likely to commit unethical and illegal acts such as collusion, price fixing, or bribery.

OUTSIDE PRESSURE Many studies have shown that the likelihood of a person's engaging in unethical or criminal behavior is much greater when outside pressure exists for that person to do so. In some organizations, for example, top managers' desires to increase performance lead them to create reward systems that have the intentional or unintentional effect of making employees act unethically and overcharge consumers. Top managers may feel that they are under similar pressures from shareholders if company performance is deteriorating and so they start to cut corners and make unethical decisions to keep their jobs. If all these pressures work in the same direction, we can easily understand how unethical organizational cultures develop as managers buy into the idea that "the end justifies the means."

The temptation for organizations collectively to engage in unethical and illegal anti-competitive behavior is very great. Industry competitors can see quite clearly the advantages to acting together to raise prices because of the extra profits they will earn. The harm they inflict is much more difficult to see because their customers may number in the millions, and each is affected in such a small way that from the perspective of the companies they are hardly hurt at all. For example, over the last few years, to retain customer goodwill, many companies have adopted the strategy of shrinking the weight of the contents of their products rather than raising their prices, because many customers do not bother to check the "price per ounce" that supermarkets are required to report.

The social costs of unethical behavior are very hard to measure. But they can be easily seen over the long run in the form of mismanaged, top-heavy, bureaucratized organizations that become less innovative and spend less and less on research and development and more and more on advertising or managerial salaries. When the environment changes and new aggressive competitors arrive the mismanaged company starts to crumble and all stakeholders lose.

Creating an Ethical Organization

In what ways can ethical behavior be promoted so that, at the very least, organizational members are able to resist any temptation to engage in illegal acts that promote personal or organizational interests at the expense of society's interests? Ultimately, an organization is ethical if the people inside it are ethical. How can people judge if they are making ethical decisions and thus acting ethically? The first way is to use the rule discussed earlier concerning a person's willingness to have his or her action or decision shared with other people.

Beyond personal considerations, an organization can encourage people to act ethically by putting in place incentives for ethical behavior and disincentives to punish those who behave unethically. Because the board and top managers have the ultimate responsibility for setting policy, they establish the ethical culture of the organization. There are many ways in which they can influence organizational ethics. For example, a manager or board member outlining a company's position on business ethics acts as a figurehead and personifies the organization's ethical position. As a leader, a manager can promote moral values that result in the specific ethical rules and norms that people use to make decisions. Outside the organization, as a liaison or spokesperson, a manager can inform prospective customers and other stakeholders about the organization's ethical values and demonstrate those values through behavior toward stakeholders—such as by being honest and acknowledging errors. A manager also sets employees' incentives to behave ethically and can develop rules and norms that state the organization's ethical position. Finally, a manager can make decisions to allocate organizational resources and pursue policies based on the organization's ethical position, as discussed in Organizational Insight 2.5.

Organizational Insight 2.5

John Mackey and the Whole Foods Ethical Code

The Whole Foods Market supermarket chain was founded by two hippies in Austin, Texas, in 1978 as a natural counterculture food store. Today, it is the world's leading retailer of natural and organic foods, with over 270 stores in North America and the United Kingdom. Whole Foods specializes in the sale of chemical- and drug-free meat, poultry, and produce; its products are the purest possible, meaning it selects the ones least adulterated by artificial additives, colorings, and preservatives. Despite the fact that it charges high prices for its pure produce, sales per store are growing fast, and the company had 299 in operation globally in 2011.[31] Why has Whole Foods been so successful? Because, says founder and co-CEO John Mackey, of the principles he established to manage his company since its beginning—principles founded on the need to behave in an ethical manner toward everybody affected by its business.

iStockphoto.com/ivanastar

Mackey says he started his business for three reasons—to have fun, to make money, and to contribute to the well-being of other people.[32] The company's mission is based on its members' collective responsibility to the well-being of the people and groups it affects, its *stakeholders;* in order of priority, at Whole Foods these are customers, team members, investors, suppliers, community, and the natural environment. Mackey measures his company's success on how well it satisfies the needs of these stakeholders. His ethical stance toward customers is that they are guaranteed that Whole Foods products are 100% organic, hormone free, or as represented. To help achieve this promise, Whole Foods insists that its suppliers also behave in an ethical way so that it knows, for example, that the beef it sells comes from cows pastured on grass—not corn fed in feed lots—and the chicken it sells is from free-range hens—and not from hens that have been confined in tiny cages that even prevent movement.

His management approach toward "team members," as Whole Foods employees are called, is also based on a well-defined ethical position. Mackey says, "We put great emphasis at Whole Foods on the 'Whole People' part of the company mission. We believe in helping support our team members to grow as individuals—to become 'Whole People.' We allow tremendous individual initiative at Whole Foods and that's why our company is so innovative and creative."[33] Mackey claims that each supermarket in the chain is unique because in each one, team members are constantly experimenting with new and better ways to serve customers and improve their well-being. As team members learn, they become "self-actualized" or self-fulfilled, and this increase in their well-being translates into a desire to increase the well-being of other stakeholders.

Finally, Mackey's strong views on ethics and social responsibility also serve shareholders. Mackey does not believe the object of being in business is primarily to maximize profits for shareholders; he puts customers first. He believes, however, that companies that behave ethically, and strive to satisfy the needs of customers and employees, simultaneously satisfy the needs of investors because high profits are the result of loyal customers and committed employees. Indeed, since Whole Foods issued shares to the public in 1992, the value of those shares has increased 20 times.[34] Clearly, taking a strong position on ethics has worked so far at Whole Foods.

Designing an Ethical Structure and Control System

Ethics influence the choice of the structure and culture that coordinate resources and motivate employees.[35] Managers can design an organizational structure that reduces the incentives for people to behave unethically. The creation of authority relationships and rules that promote ethical behavior and punish unethical acts, for example, encourages members to behave in a socially responsible way. The federal government continually tries to improve the set of standards of conduct for employees of the executive branch. Standards cover ethical issues such as giving and receiving gifts, impartiality in government work and the assignment of contracts, conflicting financial interests, and outside work activities. These regulations affect approximately five million federal workers.[36] An organization often uses its mission statement to guide employees in making ethical decisions.[37]

Whistle-blowing occurs when an employee informs an outside person or agency, such as a government agency, a newspaper, or television reporter, about an organization's (its managers') illegal or immoral behavior. Employees typically become whistle-blowers when they feel powerless to prevent an organization from committing an unethical act or when they fear retribution from the company if they voice their concerns. However, an organization can take steps to make whistle-blowing an acceptable and rewarded activity.[38] Procedures that allow subordinates access to upper-level managers to voice concerns about unethical organizational behavior can be set up. The position of ethics officer can be established to investigate claims of unethical behavior, and ethics committees can make formal ethical judgments. Ten percent of Fortune 500 companies have ethics officers who are responsible for keeping employees informed about organizational ethics, for training employees, and for investigating breaches of ethical conduct. Ethical values flow down from the top of the organization but are strengthened or weakened by the design of the organizational structure.

Creating an Ethical Culture

The values, rules, and norms that define an organization's ethical position are part of culture. The behavior of top managers strongly influences organizational culture. An ethical culture is most likely to emerge if top managers are ethical, and an unethical culture can become an ethical one if the top-management team is changed. This transformation occurred at General Dynamics and other defense contracting firms, in which corruption was common at all levels and overbilling and cheating the government had become a popular managerial sport. But neither culture nor structure can make an organization ethical if its top managers are not ethical. The creation of an ethical corporate culture requires commitment at all levels of an organization, from the top down.[39]

Supporting the Interests of Stakeholder Groups

Shareholders are the owners of an organization. Through the board of directors they have the power to hire and fire top management, and thus in theory they can discipline managers who engage in unethical behavior. Shareholders want higher profits, but do they want them to be gained by unethical behavior? In general, the answer is no because unethical behavior makes a company a riskier investment. If an organization loses its reputation, the value of its shares will be lower than the value of shares offered by firms that behave ethically. In addition, many shareholders do not want to hold stock in companies that engage in socially questionable activities. To learn more about Amazon's approach to Corporate Social Responsibility, visit the company website's Investor Relations Section and view the Corporate Governance Guidelines.

Pressure from outside stakeholders has become increasingly important in promoting ethical organizational behavior.[40] The government and its agencies, industry councils and regulatory bodies, and consumer watchdog groups all play a role in establishing the ethical rules that organizations should follow when doing business. Outside regulation sets the rules of the competitive game and, as noted earlier, plays an important part in creating and sustaining ethics in society.

Large organizations possess enormous power to benefit and harm society. But if corporations act to harm society and their own stakeholders, society will move to regulate and control business to minimize its ability to inflict harm. Societies, however, differ in the extent to which they are willing to impose regulations on organizations. In general, poor countries have the least restrictive regulations. In many countries, people pay large bribes to government officials to get permission to start a company; once in business, they operate unfettered by any regulations pertaining to child labor, minimum wages, or employee health and safety. In contrast, Americans take ethical behavior on these fronts for granted because laws as well as custom and practice discourage child labor, slave wages, and unsafe working conditions.

Summary

Organizations are embedded in a complex social context that is driven by the needs and desires of its stakeholders. The interests of all stakeholders have to be considered when designing an organizational structure and culture that promotes effectiveness and curtails the ability of managers and employees to use organizational resources for their own ends or which damages the interests of other stakeholders. Creating an ethical culture, and making sure organizational members use ethical rules in their decision making, is a vital task for all those who have authority over organizational resources. The chapter has made the following main points:

1. Organizations exist because of their ability to create value and acceptable outcomes for stakeholders. The two main groups of stakeholders are inside stakeholders and outside stakeholders. Effective organizations satisfy, at least minimally, the interests of all stakeholder groups.
2. Problems that an organization faces as it tries to win stakeholders' approval include choosing which stakeholder goals to satisfy, deciding how to allocate organizational rewards to different stakeholder groups, and balancing short- and long-term goals.
3. Shareholders delegate authority to managers to use organizational resources effectively. The CEO, COO, and top-management team have ultimate responsibility for the use of those resources effectively.
4. The agency problem and moral hazard arise when shareholders delegate authority to managers, and governance mechanisms must be created to align the interests of shareholders and managers to ensure managers behave in the interests of all stakeholders.
5. Ethics are the moral values, beliefs, and rules that establish the right or appropriate ways in which one person or stakeholder group should interact and deal with another. Organizational ethics are a product of societal, professional, and individual ethics.
6. The board of directors and top managers can create an ethical organization by designing an ethical structure and control system, creating an ethical culture, and supporting the interests of stakeholder groups.

Discussion Questions

1. Give some examples of how the interests of different stakeholder groups may conflict.
2. What is the role of the top-management team?
3. What is the agency problem? What steps can be taken to solve it?
4. Why is it important for managers and organizations to behave ethically?
5. Ask a manager to describe both an instance of ethical behavior and an instance of unethical behavior that she or he observed. What caused these behaviors, and what were the outcomes?
6. Search business magazines such as *Fortune* or *Bloomberg/BusinessWeek* for an example of ethical or unethical behavior, and use the material in this chapter to analyze it.

Organizational Theory in Action

Practicing Organizational Theory

Creating a Code of Ethics

Form groups of three to five people, and appoint one group member as the spokesperson who will communicate your findings to the class when called on by the instructor. Then discuss the following scenario.

You are the managers of the functions of a large chain of supermarkets, and you have been charged with the responsibility for developing a code of ethics to guide the members of your organization in their dealings with stakeholders. To guide you in creating the ethical code, do the following:

1. Discuss the various kinds of ethical dilemmas that supermarket employees—checkers, pharmacists, stockers, butchers—may encounter in their dealings with stakeholders such as customers or suppliers.
2. Identify a specific behavior that the kinds of employees mentioned in item 1 might exhibit, and characterize it as ethical or unethical.
3. Based on this discussion, identify three standards or values that you will incorporate into the supermarket's ethical code to help determine whether a behavior is ethical or unethical.

The Ethical Dimension #2

Think about the last time that a person treated you unethically or you observed someone else being treated unethically, and then answer these questions:

1. What was the issue? Why do you think that person acted unethically?
2. What prompted them to behave in an unethical fashion?
3. Was the decision maker aware that he or she was acting unethically?
4. What was the outcome?

Making the Connection #2

Identify an organization whose managers have been involved in unethical actions toward one or more stakeholder groups or who have pursued their own self-interest at the expense of other stakeholders. What did they do? Who was harmed? What was the outcome of the incident?

Analyzing the Organization: Design Module #2

In this model you will identify your organization's major stakeholders, analyze the top-management structure, investigate its code of ethics, and try to uncover its ethical stance.

Assignment

1. Draw a stakeholder map that identifies your organization's major stakeholder groups. What kinds of conflicts between its stakeholder groups would you expect to occur the most?

2. Using information on the company's website, draw a picture of its hierarchy of authority. Try to identify the members of the top-management team. Is the CEO also the chair of the board of directors?
3. Does the company have divisional managers? What functional managers seem to be most important to the organization in achieving a competitive advantage? What is the functional background of the top-management team?
4. Does the organization have a published code of ethics or ethical stance? What kinds of issues does it raise in this statement?
5. Search for information about your organization concerning the ethical or unethical behavior of its managers. What does this tell you about its ethical stance?

CASE FOR ANALYSIS

How Westland/Hallmark Put Profit above Safety

By all appearances the Westland/Hallmark Meat Co., based in Chico, California, and owned by its CEO Steven Mendell, was one the most efficient, sanitary, and state-of-the-art meatpacking plants in the United States. The meatpacking plant, which regularly passed inspections by the U.S. Department of Agriculture (USDA), employed over 200 workers who slaughtered and then prepared the beef for shipment to fast-food restaurants such as Burger King and Taco Bell. Most of the millions of pounds of meat the plant prepared yearly, however, were delivered under contract to one of the federal government's most coveted accounts: the National School Lunch Program, which named the plant supplier of the year in 2005.[41]

So at the end of 2007 when the Humane Society turned over a videotape, secretly filmed by one of its investigators who had taken a job as a plant employee, to the San Bernardino County district attorney that showed major violations of safety procedures, it caused an uproar. The videotape showed two workers dragging sick cows up the ramp that led to the slaughterhouse using metal chains and forklifts, shocking them with electric prods, and shooting streams of water in their noses and faces. Not only did the tape show inhumane treatment of animals, it also provided evidence that the company was flaunting the ban on allowing sick animals to enter the food supply chain, something that federal regulations explicitly outlawed for fear of human health and disease issues.

By 2008, the USDA, concerned that contaminated beef had entered the supply chain, especially the one leading to the nation's schools, issued a notice for the recall of 143 million pounds of beef processed in the plant over the last two years, the largest recall in history. In addition, the plant was shut down as the investigation proceeded. In 2008, when CEO Steven Mendell was subpoenaed to appear before the House Panel Energy and Commerce Committee, he denied these violations had taken place and that any diseased cows had entered the food chain. When panel members demanded that he view the videotape, he claimed he had not seen it, even though it was widely available, and he was forced to acknowledge that "two cows" had in fact entered the plant and that inhumane treatment of animals had taken place.[42]

Moreover, federal investigators turned up evidence that as early as 1996 the plant has been cited for overuse of electric prods to speed cattle through the plant and had been cited for other violations since, suggesting these abuses had been going on for a long period. This view gained strength when one of the workers shown in the videotape claimed that supervisors were pressuring workers to ensure 500 cows a day were slaughtered and processed so the plant could meet its quota and make the high profits the meatpacking business provides—and that he and other workers had no say in the matter: They were just "following orders from the supervisor."

These unethical and illegal work practices led investigators to fear that over the years, thousands of sick cows had been allowed to enter the food chain. Most of the 143 million pounds of beef recalled had already been consumed anyway. Not only customers, and especially schoolchildren, have been harmed by the company's illegal actions, however. It seems likely that the plant will be permanently shut down and all 220 workers will lose their jobs. Indeed, the employees directly implicated by the video have already been prosecuted and one, who pleaded guilty to animal abuse, was convicted and sentenced to six months of imprisonment in 2008.[43]

Whether or not the company's managers will experience the same fate remains to be seen, but clearly all stakeholders have been hurt by the unethical, inhumane, and illegal actions by managers that, as the Humane Society had suspected for years, were commonplace in the plant.

Discussion Questions

1. In your opinion, why did the managers and employees of the meat packing plant behave in the way they did?
2. Outline a series of steps the plant's managers should have taken to prevent this problem from occurring.

References

1 T. Donaldson and L. E. Preston, "The Stakeholder Theory of the Corporation: Concepts, Evidence, and Implications," *Academy of Management Review* 20 (1995), pp. 65–91.

2 J. G. March and H. Simon, *Organizations* (New York: Wiley, 1958).

3 Ibid.; J. A. Pearce, "The Company Mission as a Strategic Tool," *Sloan Management Review* (Spring 1982), 15–24.

4 www.TIAACREF.com, 2011; www.fidelity.com, 2011.

5 C. W. L. Hill and G. R. Jones, *Strategic Management: An Integrated Approach,* 7th ed. (Boston: Houghton Mifflin, 2010).

6 B. O'Reilly, "Where Service Flies Right," *Fortune,* August 24, 1992, pp. 115–116.

7 K. Cleland, "Southwest Tries Online Ticketing," *Advertising Age* 67 (1996), 39.

8 J. P. Womack, D. T. Jones, D. Roos, and D. Sammons Carpenter, *The Machine That Changed the World* (New York: Macmillan, 1990).

9 R. F. Zammuto, "A Comparison of Multiple Constituency Models of Organizational Effectiveness," *Academy of Management Review* 9 (1984), pp. 606–616; K. S. Cameron, "Critical Questions in Assessing Organizational Effectiveness," *Organizational Dynamics* 9 (1989), pp. 66–80.

10 R. M. Cyert and J. G. March, *A Behavioral Theory of the Firm* (Englewood Cliffs, NJ: Prentice Hall, 1963).

11 R. H. Miles, *Macro Organizational Behavior* (Santa Monica, CA: Goodyear, 1980), p. 375.

12 A. A. Berle and G. C. Means, *The Modern Corporation and Private Property* (New York: Commerce Clearing House, 1932).

13 Hill and Jones, *Strategic Management,* Ch. 2.

14 G. R. Jones and J. E. Butler, "Managing Internal Corporate Entrepreneurship: An Agency Perspective," *Journal of Management* 18 (1994), pp. 733–749.

15 C. Yang, "Money and Medicine: Physician Disentangle Thyself," *Academic Universe,* April 21, 1997, p. 34.

16 W. Zeller, "The Fall of Enron," *Business Week,* December 17, 2001, pp. 30–40.

17 A. K. Gupta, "Contingency Perspectives on Strategic Leadership," in D. C. Hambrick, ed., *The Executive Effect: Concepts and Methods for Studying Top Managers* (Greenwich, CT: JAI Press, 1988), pp. 147–178.

18 Ibid., p. 155.

19 www.netflix.com, 2011.

20 D. C. Ancona, "Top-Management Teams: Preparing for the Revolution," in J. S. Carroll, ed., *Applied Social Psychology in Organizational Settings* (Hillsdale, NJ: Erlbaum, 1990), pp. 99–128.

21 R. F. Vancil, *Passing the Baton* (Boston: Harvard Business School Press, 1987).

22 Hill and Jones, *Strategic Management,* Ch. 11.

23 T. L. Beauchamp and N. E. Bowie, eds., *Ethical Theory and Business* (Englewood Cliffs, NJ: Prentice Hall, 1979); A. MacIntyre, *After Virtue* (South Bend, IN: University of Notre Dame Press, 1981).

24 R. E. Goodin, "How to Determine Who Should Get What," *Ethics* (July 1975), 310–321.

25 T. M. Jones, "Ethical Decision Making by Individuals in Organizations: An Issue Contingent Model," *Academy of Management Journal, 16* (1991), pp. 366–395; G. F. Cavanaugh, D. J. Moberg, and M. Velasquez, "The Ethics of Organizational Politics," *Academy of Management Review, 6* (1981), pp. 363–374.

26 L. K. Trevino, "Ethical Decision Making in Organizations: A Person–Situation Interactionist Model," *Academy of Management Review, 11* (1986), pp. 601–617; W. H. Shaw and V. Barry, *Moral Issues in Business,* 6th ed. (Belmont, CA: Wadsworth, 1995).

27 B. Carton, "Gillette Faces Wrath of Children in Testing on Rats and Rabbits," *Wall Street Journal,* September 5, 1995, p. A1.

[28] W. H. Shaw and V. Barry, *Moral Issues in Business.*

[29] B. Ortega, "Broken Rules: Conduct Codes Garner Goodwill for Retailers But Violations Go On," *Wall Street Journal,* July 3, 1995, pp. A1, A4.

[30] "Why Honesty Is the Best Policy," *The Economist,* March 9, 2002, p. 23.

[31] www.wholefoodsmarket.com, 2011.

[32] John Mackey's Blog: "20 Questions with Sunni's Salon," www.wholefoodsmarket.com, 2011.

[33] Ibid.

[34] "The Green Machine," *Newsweek,* March 21, 2005, pp. E8–E10.

[35] P. E. Murphy, "Implementing Business Ethics," *Journal of Business Ethics, 7* (1988), pp. 907–915.

[36] "Ethics Office Approves Executive-Branch Rules," *Wall Street Journal,* August 7, 1992, p. A14.

[37] P. E. Murphy, "Creating Ethical Corporate Structure," *Sloan Management Review* (Winter 1989), 81–87.

[38] J. B. Dozier and M. P. Miceli, "Potential Predictors of Whistle-Blowing: A Prosocial Behavior Perspective," *Academy of Management Review, 10* (1985), pp. 823–836; J. P. Near and M. P. Miceli, "Retaliation Against Whistle-Blowers: Predictors and Effects," *Journal of Applied Psychology, 71* (1986), pp. 137–145.

[39] J. A. Byrne, "The Best-Laid Ethics Programs..." *Business Week,* March 9, 1992, pp. 67–69.

[40] D. Collins, "Organizational Harm, Legal Consequences and Stakeholder Retaliation," *Journal of Business Ethics, 8* (1988), pp. 1–13.

[41] E. Werner, "Slaughterhouse Owner Acknowledges Abuse," www.pasadenastarnews.com, March 13, 2008.

[42] D. Bunnies and N. Luna, "Sick Cows Never Made Food Supply, Meat Plant Owner Says," www.ocregister.com, March 12, 2008.

[43] "Worker Sentenced in Slaughterhouse Abuse," www.yahoo.com, March 22, 2008.

CHAPTER 3

Organizing in a Changing Global Environment

Learning Objectives

An organization's environment is the complex network of changing pressures and forces that affect the way it operates. The environment is a major contingency for which an organization must plan and to which it must adapt. Furthermore, it is the primary source of uncertainty that an organization must try to control. This chapter examines the forces that make organizing in a global environment an uncertain, complex process.

After reading this chapter you should be able to:

1. List the forces in an organization's specific and general environment that give rise to opportunities and threats.
2. Identify why uncertainty exists in the environment.
3. Describe how and why an organization seeks to adapt to and control these forces to reduce uncertainty.
4. Understand how resource dependence theory and transaction cost explain why organizations choose different kinds of interorganizational strategies to manage their environments to gain the resources they need to achieve their goals and create value for their stakeholders.

What Is the Organizational Environment?

The **environment** is the set of pressures and forces surrounding an organization that have the potential to affect the way it operates and its ability to acquire scarce resources. Scarce resources include the raw materials and skilled employees an organization needs to produce goods and services; the information it needs to improve its technology or decide on its competitive strategy; and the support of outside stakeholders, such as customers who buy its goods and services, and banks and financial institutions that supply the capital that sustains it. Forces in the environment that affect an organization's ability to secure these scarce resources include competition from rivals for customers; rapid changes in technology that might erode its competitive advantage; and an increase in the price of important inputs that raises operating costs.

Environment
The set of forces surrounding an organization that have the potential to affect the way it operates and its access to scarce resources.

In the global environment, U.S. companies have been heavily involved in international trade since colonial days when they shipped their stocks of tobacco and sugar to Europe in return for manufactured products. Throughout the 20th century, GM, Heinz, IBM, Campbell's, Procter & Gamble, and thousands of other U.S. companies established overseas divisions to which they transferred their domestic skills and competences in order to produce goods and services valued by customers abroad. Indeed, U.S. companies have been established in overseas countries for so long that people there often treat them as domestic companies. People in Britain, for example, regard Heinz, Hoover, and Ford as British companies, often forgetting their U.S. origins. Similarly, the fact that Britain is the biggest overseas investor in the United States and that British companies own or have owned such "American" institutions as Burger King, Howard Johnson's, and Ben & Jerry's ice cream is not generally known by Americans.

An organization attempts to manage the forces in its environment to obtain the resources necessary to produce goods and services for customers and clients (see Figure 3.1). The term **organizational domain** refers to the particular range of goods and services that the organization produces, and the customers and other stakeholders it serves.[1] An organization establishes its domain by deciding how to manage the forces in its environment to maximize its ability to secure important resources. To obtain inputs, for example, an organization has to decide which suppliers to deal with from the range of possible suppliers and how to manage its relationships with its chosen suppliers. To obtain money, an organization has to decide which bank to deal with and how to manage its relationship with the bank so that the bank will be inclined to authorize a loan. To obtain customers, a company has to decide which set of customers it is going to serve and then how to satisfy their needs.

Organizational domain
The particular range of goods and services that the organization produces and the customers and other stakeholders it serves.

An organization attempts to structure its transactions with the environment to protect and enlarge its domain so that it can increase its ability to create value for customers, shareholders, employees, and other stakeholders. For example, McDonald's domain is a wide range of burgers, fries, coffees and fruit drinks, and other kinds of fast-food products that the company makes to satisfy the needs of its customers.[2] McDonald's structures transactions with its environment—that is, with suppliers, bankers, customers, and other stakeholders—to obtain the resources it needs to protect and enlarge its domain.

One major way in which an organization can enlarge and protect its domain is to expand internationally. Global expansion allows an organization to seek new opportunities and take advantage of its core competences to create value for stakeholders. Before discussing the specific ways in which organizations manage their environment to protect and enlarge their domain, we must understand in detail which forces in the environment affect organizations. The concepts of specific environment and general environment provide a useful basis for analysis.[3]

Figure 3.1 The Organizational Environment

In the specific environment are forces that directly affect an organization's ability to obtain resources. In the general environment are forces that shape the specific environments of all organizations.

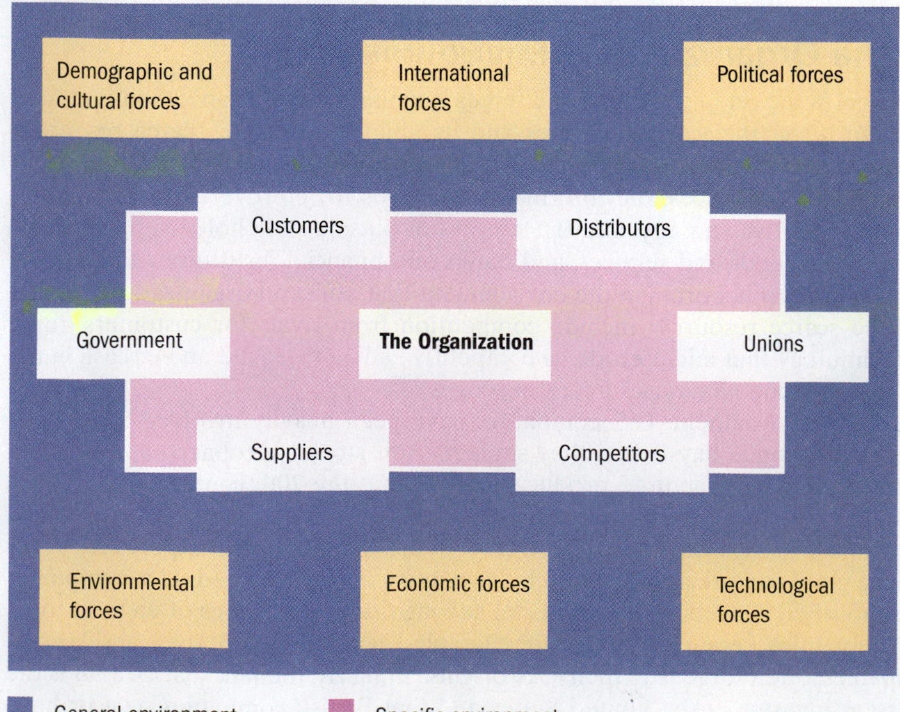

The Specific Environment

The **specific environment** consists of forces from outside stakeholder groups that directly affect an organization's ability to secure resources.[4] Customers, distributors, unions, competitors, suppliers, and the government are all important outside stakeholders that can influence and pressure organizations to act in certain ways (see Figure 3.1).

Specific environment The forces from outside stakeholder groups that directly affect an organization's ability to secure resources.

For fast-food maker McDonald's, competitors such as Burger King, Subway, and Taco Bell are an important force that affects the organization's ability to attract resources: customer revenue. Competition makes resources scarce and valuable because the greater the competition for resources, the more difficult they are to obtain. Competitors can be domestic or international. Each type has different implications for a company's ability to obtain resources. Overseas competitors have not been as important a force in the fast-food industry as they have been in the U.S. car industry, where they have reduced the ability of U.S. car companies to attract resources.

In the United States, Sony, Toyota, Samsung, BMW, and a multitude of other overseas companies compete against U.S. companies to attract American customers. Abroad, U.S. companies face competition from organizations both inside and outside the countries in which they operate. The European divisions of GM and Ford, for example, compete not only with European car companies such as Fiat, Peugeot, and BMW but also with Japanese companies such as Toyota and Honda. Indeed, in the 2000s, Japanese car companies operating in Europe established plants with the capacity to produce 750,000 new cars a year and have threatened the prosperity of Volkswagen, Ford, and Fiat.

Changes in the number and types of customers, and in customer tastes, are another force that affects an organization. An organization must have a strategy to manage its relationship with customers and attract their support—and the strategy must change over time as customer needs change. In the global environment, satisfying customer needs presents new challenges because customers differ from country to country. For example, customers in Europe—unlike Americans—typically do not like their cereal sweetened, so Kellogg and General Mills modify their products to suit local European tastes. An organization must be willing and able to tailor or customize its products to suit the tastes and preferences of different consumers if it expects to attract their business.

Besides responding to the needs of customers, organizations must decide how to manage relationships with suppliers and distributors to obtain access to the resources they provide. **Global supply chain management** is the process of planning and controlling supply/distribution activities such as acquiring and storing raw materials and semifinished products, controlling work-in-process inventory, and moving finished goods from point of manufacture to point of sale as efficiently as possible. An organization has to make many choices concerning how to manage these activities in order to secure most effectively a stable supply of inputs or dispose of its products in a timely manner. For example, should McDonald's buy or make its inputs? Should it raise cattle and chickens and vegetables and fruits? Should it make its own fast-food containers? Or should it buy all of these inputs from global suppliers? The safety of fast food is a vital issue; can input suppliers be trusted to ensure product quality and safety—such as the peanut plant discussed in Chapter 2? What is the best way for McDonald's to distribute its products to franchisees to ensure their quality? Should McDonald's own its own fleet of vehicles to supply its franchisees or should it contract with national trucking companies to distribute inputs to its restaurants?

Global supply chain management The coordination of the flow of raw materials, components, semifinished goods, and finished products around the world.

In the global environment, supplies of inputs can be obtained not just from domestic sources but from any country in the world. If U.S. companies had not used outsourcing as a means to lower the cost of their inputs by buying from overseas suppliers, they would have lost their competitive advantage to overseas competitors that did pursue outsourcing. Apple, for example, could only compete with Sony and Panasonic for the lucrative MP3 player market when it started to buy and assemble the inputs for its iPod player abroad. Apple iPod components are made in countries such as Taiwan, China, and Hong Kong, and access to low-cost global input suppliers has allowed Apple to continuously reduce the cost of making its iPod so that it now dominates the MP3 music player market. Its expertise in finding ways to buy inputs at lower cost also allows it to reduce the cost of making each new model of its iPhone and iPad so it continues to attract more customers and dominate the global environment.

The challenges associated with distributing and marketing products increase in the global environment. Because the tastes of customers vary from country to country, many advertising and marketing campaigns are country specific, and many products are customized to overseas customers' preferences. Moreover, in many countries abroad, such as Japan and India, domestic producers tightly control distribution systems, and that arrangement makes it very hard for U.S. companies to enter the market and sell their products. Global distribution also becomes difficult when an organization's products are complex and customers need a lot of information to operate or use them successfully. All of these factors mean that an organization has to consider carefully how to handle the global distribution of its products to attract customers. Should the organization handle overseas sales and distribution itself? Should it sell its products through a wholesaler in the overseas market? Should it enter into an alliance with an organization in a particular country and allow that company to market and distribute its products? Organizations operating in many countries must weigh all these options, as shown in Organizational Insight 3.1, which discusses the choices Nokia has made.

Organizational Insight 3.1

Why Nokia Opens New Plants around the Globe

Nokia is still the world's largest cellphone maker, although it has been fighting hard to maintain its lead as the popularity of smartphones has soared, and companies like Apple, Blackberry, Samsung, and now Google and Microsoft are competing for the lucrative smartphone segment of the market. While these other companies outsource their cellphone production to Asian companies, Nokia does not. Indeed, one reason for Nokia's continuing dominance in cellphones is its skills in global supply chain management, which allow it to provide low-cost phones that are customized to the needs of customers in different world regions. To achieve this, Nokia's global strategy is to make its phones in the world region where they are to be sold. Thus Nokia has built state-of-the-art factories in Germany, Brazil, China, and India, and in 2008 it opened a new plant in Romania to make phones for the expanding Eastern European and Russian market.

A major reason for beginning operations in Romania is low labor costs. Skilled Romanian engineers can be hired for a quarter of what they would earn in Finland or Germany, and production line employees can expect to earn about $450 a month—a fraction of what Nokia's German employees earn. In fact, once Nokia's Romanian factory was running, Nokia closed its factory in Bochum, Germany, in 2008 because it was too expensive to operate in a highly competitive global environment.

Opening a new factory in a new country is a complex process; and to increase the chances its new factory would operate efficiently, Nokia's managers adopted several strategies. First they worked to create a culture in the factory that is attractive to its new Romanian employees so they will stay with the company and learn the skills required to make it operate more efficiently over time. For example, the factory's cafeteria offers free food, and there are gyms, sports facilities, and (of course) a Finnish sauna. In addition, although managers from other countries run the plant at present, Nokia hopes that within a few years most of the factory's managers and supervisors will be Romanian. Its goal is to create a career ladder that will motivate employees to perform at a high level and so be promoted.

© Norebbo/Dreamstime.com

At the same time, Nokia is hardheaded about how efficiently it expects its Romanian factory to operate because all its factories are required to operate at the same level of efficiency that its most efficient global factory has achieved. Thus Nokia has created a compensation plan for factory managers based on the collective performance of all its factories. This means managers in all its factories will see their bonuses reduced if just one factory in any country performs below expectations. This is a tough approach, but its purpose is to encourage all managers to develop more efficient manufacturing techniques, which, when learned in one factory, must be shared with all other factories around the world for managers to obtain their bonuses. Nokia's goal is that efficiency will improve constantly over time as managers are encouraged to find better ways to operate and then share this knowledge across the company.

Just six months after it opened in June 2008 the Romanian plant reached the milestone of one million handsets produced. The plant's efficiency has exceeded Nokia's expectations—so much so that Nokia opened a new cellphone accessory factory next to the plant and has hired hundreds of new workers, who received a 9% salary increase in 2010 because of their high productivity. Nokia contemplated opening a new plant in Argentina to serve the booming South American market, but it eventually decided to outsource the making of its cellphones to an Argentinean supplier and decided in 2011 to open its newest plant in Brazil, the largest market in South America.[5]

Other outside stakeholders include the government, unions, and consumer interest groups. Various government agencies are interested in McDonald's policies concerning equal employment opportunity, food preparation and content, and health and safety standards, and these agencies pressure the organization to make sure it follows legal rules. Unions pressure McDonald's to increase its wages and benefits. Consumer interest groups pressure McDonald's to make its foods less fattening to prevent the growing obesity of U.S. customers.

An organization that establishes global operations has to forge good working relationships with its new employees and with any unions that represent them. If a Japanese manufacturer opens a new U.S. plant, its Japanese management team has to understand the expectations of their American employees—that is, their attitudes toward pay, seniority, and other conditions of employment. A global organization has to adapt its management style to fit the expectations of the local workforce while still working to achieve its goals, as Nokia does.

Finally, each country has its own system of government and its own laws and regulations that control the way business is conducted. A U.S. company that enters a new country must conform to the host country's institutional and legal system. Sometimes, as in the European Union (EU), the rules governing business conduct are standardized across many countries. Although this can make it easier for U.S. companies to operate across countries, it also makes it easier for these countries to protect their own home-based, domestic companies. Boeing, for example, complains that subsidies from European taxpayers have allowed Airbus Industries to undercut the price of Boeing's airplanes and develop new planes such as Airbus's new super "jumbo" at artificially reduced prices. Similarly, U.S. farmers complain that European tariffs protect inefficient European farmers and close the market to the products of more efficient U.S. producers. Often, domestic competitors lobby their home governments to combat "unfair" global competition. Japan is well known for the many ways in which it attempts to restrict the entry of overseas competitors or lessen their impact on Japanese firms. Japan has come under intense pressure to relax and abolish such regulations, as Organizational Insight 3.2 suggests.

An organization must engage in transactions with each of the forces in its specific environment if it is to obtain the resources it requires to survive and to protect and enhance its domain. Over time, the size and scope of its domain will change as those transactions change. For example, an organization that decides to expand its domain to satisfy the needs of new sets of customers by producing new kinds of products will encounter new sets of forces and may need to engage in a different set of transactions with the environment to gain resources.

The General Environment

General environment
The forces that shape the specific environment and affect the ability of all organizations in a particular environment to obtain resources.

The **general environment** consists of forces that shape the specific environment and affect the ability of all organizations in a particular environment to obtain resources (see Figure 3.1). *Economic forces*, such as interest rates, the state of the economy, and the unemployment rate, determine the level of demand for products and the price of inputs. National differences in interest rates, exchange rates, wage levels, gross domestic product, and per capita income have a dramatic effect on the way organizations operate internationally. Generally, organizations attempt to obtain their inputs or to manufacture their products in the country with the lowest labor or raw-materials costs. Sony, GE, and GM have closed many of their U.S. manufacturing plants and moved their operations to Mexico because doing so has enabled them to match the low costs of overseas competitors that outsource production to China and Malaysia. Obviously, overseas competitors operating from countries with low wages have a competitive advantage that may be crucial in the battle for the price-conscious U.S. consumer. So many U.S. companies have been forced to move their operations abroad or outsource production to compete. Levi Strauss, for example, closed the last of its U.S. factories in the 2000s and moved jeans production to Mexico and the Dominican Republic to reduce production costs. (Chapter 8 looks specifically at how an organization manages global expansion.)

Organizational Insight 3.2

American Rice Invades Japan

Fanfo/Shutterstock.com

The Japanese rice market, similar to many other Japanese markets, was closed to overseas competitors until 1993 to protect Japan's thousands of high-cost, low-output rice farmers. Rice cultivation is expensive in Japan because of the country's mountainous terrain, so Japanese consumers have always paid high prices for rice. Under overseas pressure, the Japanese government opened the market, and overseas competitors are now allowed to export to Japan 8% of its annual rice consumption. Despite the still-present hefty overseas tariff on rice—$2.33 per 2.2 pounds—U.S. rice sells for $14 dollars per pound bag, while Japanese rice sells for about $19. With the recent recession affecting Japan, price-conscious consumers are turning to overseas rice, which has hurt domestic farmers.

In the 2000s, however, an alliance between organic rice grower Lundberg Family Farms of California and the Nippon Restaurant Enterprise Co. found a new way to break into the Japanese rice market. Because there is no tariff on rice used in processed foods, Nippon takes the U.S. organic rice and converts it into "O-bento," an organic hot boxed lunch packed with rice, vegetables, chicken, beef, and salmon, all imported from the United States. The new lunches, which cost about $4 compared to a Japanese rice bento that costs about $9, are sold at railway stations and other outlets throughout Japan. They are proving to be very popular and are creating a storm of protest from Japanese rice farmers, who already have been forced to leave 37% of their rice fields idle and grow less profitable crops because of the entry of U.S. rice growers. Japanese and overseas companies are increasingly forming alliances to find new ways to break into the high-priced Japanese market, and, little by little, Japan's restrictive trade practices are being whittled away.

Technological forces, such as the development of new production techniques and new information-processing equipment, influence many aspects of organizations' operations. The use of computerized manufacturing technology can increase productivity. Similarly, investment in advanced research and development activities influences how organizations interact with each other and how they design their structures. (Chapter 9 further examines the role of technology.)

The international transfer of technology has important implications for an organization's competitive advantage. Organizations must be able to learn about and have access to technological developments abroad that might provide a low-cost or differentiation advantage. Traditionally, the U.S. has exported its technology and overseas companies have been eager to use it, but in some industries U.S. companies have been slow to take advantage of overseas technological developments. Critics charge that global learning has often been one way—from the United States to the rest of the world—to the detriment of U.S. competitiveness. It has been estimated that after World War II Japanese companies paid U.S. companies $100 million for the rights to license certain technologies and in return gained over $100 billion in sales revenue from U.S. consumers. Today, U.S. companies are anxious and willing to learn from overseas competitors to close the technological gap. Such technological learning allows an organization to develop its core competences and apply them around the world to create value, as Amazon.com has done.

Political, ethical, and environmental forces influence government policy toward organizations and their stakeholders. For example, laws that favor particular business interests, such as a tariff on imported cars, influence organizations' customers and competitors. Pressure from environmentalists, for example, to reduce air pollution or to decrease the nation's level of solid waste, affects organizations' production costs. Environmentally friendly product design and packaging may alter organizations' relationships with competitors, customers, and suppliers. Toyota pioneered the development of gas-saving hybrid vehicles such as the Prius, for example, and licensed this technology to GM and Ford in 2005. In 2009, Honda introduced a new hybrid vehicle to compete with the Prius just as Toyota introduced its next-generation Prius model, so the contest is on to see which company will be most successful. Globally, countries that do little to protect the environment see an influx of companies that take advantage of lax regulations to set up low-cost operations there. The result can be increased pollution and mounting environmental problems such as what happened in many Eastern European and Asian countries.

Demographic, cultural, and social forces—such as the age, education, lifestyle, norms, values, and customs of a nation's people—shape organizations' customers, managers, and employees. The demand for baby products, for example, is linked to national birthrates and age distributions. Demographic, cultural, and social forces are important sources of uncertainty in a global environment because they directly affect the tastes and needs of a nation's customers. Cultural and social values affect a country's attitudes toward both domestic and overseas products and companies. Customers in France and Italy, for example, generally prefer domestically produced cars even though overseas products are superior in quality and value.

A U.S. company establishing operations in a country overseas must be attuned to the host country's business methods and practices. Countries differ in how they do business and in the nature of their business institutions. They also differ in their attitudes toward union–management relationships, in their ethical standards, and in their accounting and financial practices. In some countries, bribery and corruption are acceptable business practices. As noted earlier, laws in Japan protect home-based companies that seek to prevent the entry of more efficient overseas competitors. However, the laws are changing and companies like Walmart now operate in Japan.

Sources of Uncertainty in the Organizational Environment

An organization likes to have a steady and abundant supply of resources so it can easily manage its domain and satisfy stakeholders. All the forces just discussed cause uncertainty for organizations, however, and make it more difficult for managers to control the

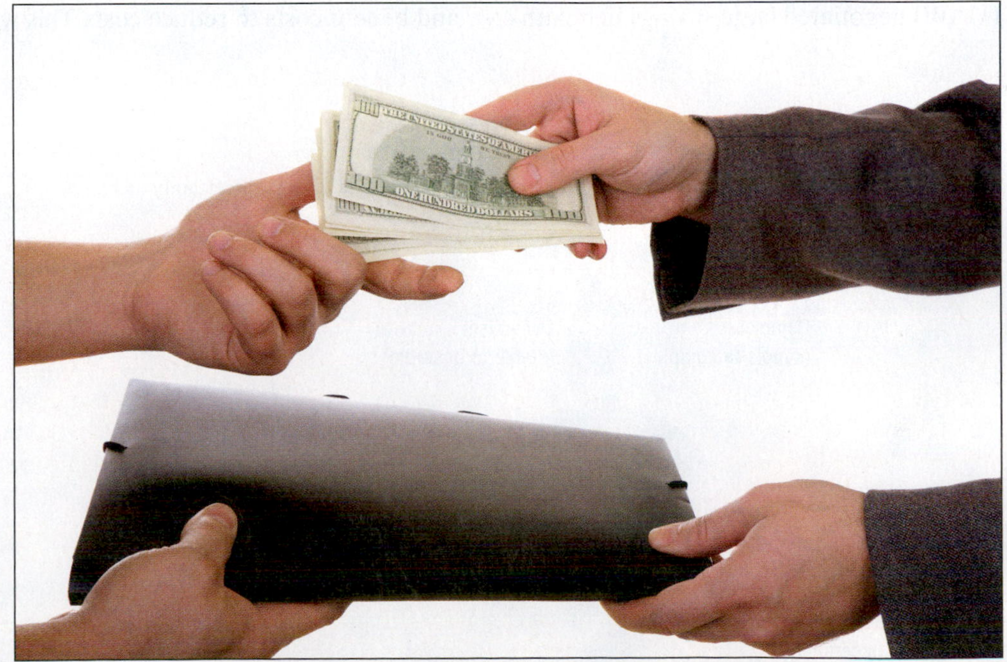

Serg Zastavkin/Shutterstock.com

In some countries, companies are expected to pay bribes if they want to do business there.

flow of resources they need to protect and enlarge their organizational domains. The set of forces that cause these problems can be looked at in another way: in terms of how they cause uncertainty because they affect the complexity, dynamism, and richness of the environment. As these forces cause the environment to become more complex, less stable, and poorer, the level of uncertainty increases (see Figure 3.2).

Environmental complexity The strength, number, and interconnectedness of the specific and general forces that an organization has to manage.

ENVIRONMENTAL COMPLEXITY **Environmental complexity** is a function of the strength, number, and interconnectedness of the specific and general forces that an organization has to manage.[6] The greater the number, and the greater the differences between them, the more complex and uncertain is the environment and the more difficult to predict and control. Ford, for example, used to obtain inputs from over 3,000 different suppliers. To reduce the uncertainty that resulted from dealing with so many suppliers, Ford embarked on a program to reduce their number—and thus the complexity of its environment. Now Ford deals with fewer than 500 suppliers; acquiring the information needed to manage its relationships with them is much easier than acquiring information to manage ten times that number.

Complexity also increases if, over time, a company produces a wider variety of products for different groups of customers. For example, if a company like McDonald's suddenly decided to enter the insurance and banking businesses, it would need a massive infusion of information to reduce the uncertainty surrounding the new transactions.

Complexity can increase greatly when specific and general forces in the environment become interconnected—that is, when forces begin to interact so their effects on the organization become unpredictable.[7] The more interconnected the forces in an organization's specific and general environments, the more uncertainty the organization faces. Suppose a major breakthrough in carmaking technology makes existing factories obsolete. This general force will cause the price of a carmaker's stock (like Ford's) to fluctuate wildly and will send financial markets into turmoil. Car manufacturers will be unsure how the breakthrough will affect their business, competition between rivals will increase (a specific force), and both management and unions will be uncertain of the effect on jobs and the future of the organization. If customers then stop buying cars (another specific force) until new models made with the new technology come out, the result may be layoffs and further decreases in the price of car company stocks.

This happened in the 2000s when GM, Chrysler, and Ford all began to lose billions of dollars because they could not reduce their costs or innovate vehicles that matched those of their Japanese competitors. To survive, these carmakers and the United Auto Workers (UAW) negotiated large savings in health care and benefit costs to reduce costs. This was

Figure 3.2 Three Factors Causing Uncertainty

As the environment becomes more complex, less stable, and poorer, the level of uncertainty increases.

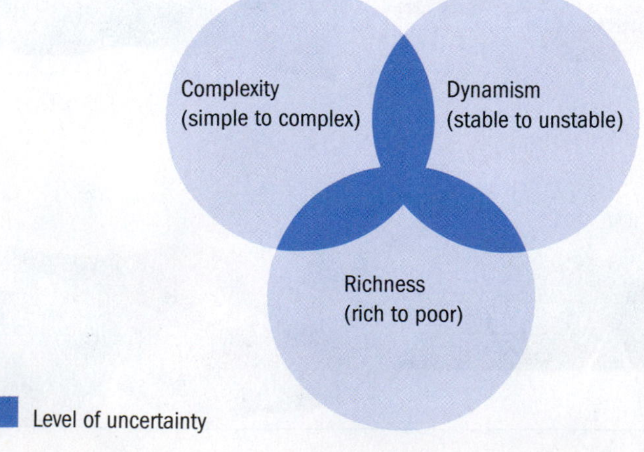

still not enough for GM and Chrysler, whose high costs forced them into bankruptcy in 2009, which allowed them to end expensive contracts with unions and car dealers. However, since they emerged from bankruptcy they, like Ford, have worked hard to make new kinds of high-quality vehicles in flexible factories that U.S. customers want, such as gas-saving hybrids, and by 2011 they were profitable once again.

The more complex an organization's environment, the greater the uncertainty about that environment. Predicting and controlling the flow of resources becomes extremely difficult, and problems associated with managing transactions with the environment increase. GM and Ford face a highly challenging future because both Honda and Toyota introduced new advanced hybrid and electric cars in 2011. But they have fought back with models of their own, such as the Chevrolet Volt, and competition is fierce to attract the hundreds of thousands of customers who wanted to buy fuel-efficient cars given the fast-rising price of gas in 2011.

ENVIRONMENTAL DYNAMISM **Environmental dynamism** is a function of how much and how quickly forces in the specific and general environments change over time and thus increase the uncertainty an organization faces.[8] An environment is stable if forces affect the supply of resources in a predictable way. An environment is unstable and dynamic if an organization cannot predict the way in which the forces will change over time. If technology, for example, changes rapidly as it does in the computer industry, the environment is very dynamic. An organization in a dynamic, unstable environment will seek ways to make it more predictable and so lessen the uncertainty it faces. Later in the chapter, we discuss strategies for managing potentially dynamic parts of the environment, including long-term contracts and vertical integration.

Environmental dynamism The degree to which forces in the specific and general environments change quickly over time and thus contribute to the uncertainty an organization faces.

Today, the existence of large new global markets for companies to enter, such as in China, India, and Eastern Europe, and the possibility of gaining access to new global resources and core competences, provide opportunities for an organization to enlarge its domain and create more value for stakeholders. However, as companies compete both at home and abroad, the environment becomes increasingly complex (greater numbers of forces must be managed, and the forces are interconnected) and increasingly dynamic (the forces change rapidly). Consequently, global expansion makes the environment more difficult to predict and control.

ENVIRONMENTAL RICHNESS **Environmental richness** is a function of the amount of resources available to support an organization's domain.[9] In rich environments, uncertainty is low because resources are plentiful and so organizations need not compete for them. Biotechnology companies in Boston, for example, have a large pool of high-quality scientists to choose from because of the presence of so many universities in the area (MIT, Harvard, Boston University, Boston College, Tufts, and Brandeis, among others). In poor environments, uncertainty is high because resources are scarce and organizations do have to compete for them. The supply of high-quality scientists in Alaska, for example, is limited, and meeting the demand for them is expensive.

Environmental richness The amount of resources available to support an organization's domain.

Environments may be poor for two reasons: (1) An organization is located in a poor country or poor region of a country; and (2) there is a high level of competition and organizations are fighting over available resources.[10] In poor environments, the greater the problems organizations face in managing resource transactions. Organizations have to battle to attract customers or to obtain the best inputs or the latest technology. These battles result in uncertainty for an organization.

In an environment that is poor, unstable, and complex, resources are especially hard to obtain and organizations face the greatest uncertainty. By contrast, in a rich, stable, and simple environment, resources are easy to come by and uncertainty is low. U.S. airlines such as American, United/Continental, and Delta have experienced a highly uncertain environment over the last decade. Low-cost airlines such as Southwest that have expanded nationally over the last decade have increased the level of industry competition and the environment has become poorer as airlines fight for customers (a resource) and must offer lower prices to attract them. The airline industry environment is complex because competing airlines (part of each airline's specific environment) are very interconnected: If one airline reduces prices, they all must reduce prices to protect their domains, but the effect is to increase uncertainty further. Finally, the high price of oil, increasing competition from airlines overseas, and the changing state of the economy are all interconnected in the airlines' environment—and change over time—making it difficult to predict or plan for contingencies, and most airlines experienced huge losses during the recent recession as a result.

In contrast, the environment of the pharmaceutical industry is relatively certain. Merck, Bristol-Myers Squibb, Pfizer, and other large companies that invent drugs receive patents and are the sole providers of their respective new drugs for 17 years. During this period, the patent-owning company can charge a high price for its drug because it faces no competition and customers have no option but to buy the drug from it. Organizations in the pharmaceutical industry exist in a stable, rich environment: Competition is low and no change occurs until patents expire or better drugs are invented. Because of a huge increase in the price of drugs during the 2000s, however, health-care providers such as HMOs and the U.S. government have used their bargaining power to force these companies to reduce drug prices. This has increased the complexity of the environment and thus uncertainty for pharmaceutical companies, which have also experienced problems innovating new blockbuster drugs. To manage complexity and slow the pace of change, the industry heavily lobbies Congress to safeguard its interests; pharmaceutical companies donate tens of millions to political parties and members of the House and the Senate. Throughout the rest of this chapter we examine in detail the strategies that organizations pursue to manage their environments. First, however, it is useful to examine the nature of the environment that confronted Jeff Bezos after he founded Amazon.com[11] (see Focus on New Information Technology, Part 2).

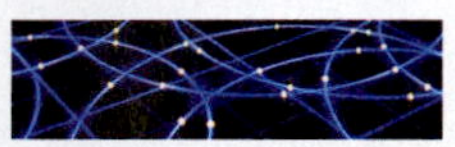

Focus on New Information Technology

Amazon.com, Part 2

The book distribution and book-selling industry was changed forever in July 1995 when Jeff Bezos brought virtual bookseller Amazon.com online. His new company's strategy revolutionized the nature of the environment. Previously, book publishers had sold their books either indirectly to book wholesalers who supplied small bookstores or directly to large book chains like Barnes & Noble or Borders or to book-of-the-month clubs. With so many book publishers and book sellers, the industry was relatively stable, with both large and small bookstores enjoying a comfortable niche in the market. In this relatively stable, simple, rich environment, uncertainty was low and all companies enjoyed good revenues and profits.

Amazon.com's virtual approach to buying and selling books changed all this. First, because it was able to offer customers quick access to all the over 1.5 million books in print and offer customers discounted book prices, this raised the level of industry competition and made the book-selling environment poorer. Second, because Amazon.com also negotiated directly with large book publishers over price and supply because it wanted to get books quickly to its customers, it led to an increase in the complexity of the environment: All players—book publishers, wholesalers, stores, and customers—became more closely linked. Third, these factors, combined with continuing changes in information technology, made the environment more unstable, and resources (customers) became harder to attract.

How has this increase in uncertainty in the environment changed the book-selling business? First, these changes quickly threatened the prosperity of small bookstores, thousands of which soon closed their doors and left the business because they were unable to compete with online bookstores. Second, large booksellers like Barnes & Noble and Borders started their own online stores to compete with Amazon.com but failed; for example, Borders was forced to close its stores in 2011 after going bankrupt. Third, Amazon.com and these new online bookstores engaged in a price war and the prices of books were further discounted. This resulted in an even more competitive, uncertain, and poorer environment.

IT is not specialized to any one country or world region. Access to the Internet and the WWW enables any online company to sell to customers around the world, providing of course that its products can be customized to the needs of overseas customers. Jeff Bezos was quick to realize that U.S.-based Amazon.com's IT could be profitably transferred to other countries to sell books. However, his ability to enter new overseas markets was limited by one major factor: Amazon.com offers its customers the biggest selection of books written in the English language; he had to find overseas customers who could read English. Where to locate then?

An obvious first choice would be the United Kingdom because its population speaks English, then other English-speaking nations such as Canada, Australia, New Zealand, and Germany. Germany? Of probably of any nation in the world, Germany has the highest proportion of English-as-a-second-language speakers because English is taught in all its high schools.

So Bezos decided to replicate Amazon.com's value-creation functions and customize its IT for other nations. First, in the United Kingdom it bought the company Bookpages, installed its proprietary technology, and renamed it Amazon.co.uk in 1996. In Germany, it acquired a small online bookseller and created Amazon.de in 1998.[12] Since then Amazon.com has also established online stores in Canada, Italy, France, Japan, and China. And, in addition, customers anywhere in the world can buy its books from one of these online stores and Amazon will ship its books to customers almost anywhere in the world.

Managerial Implications

Analyzing the Environment

1. Managers at all levels and in all functions should analyze the organizational environment periodically and identify sources of uncertainty.
2. To manage transactions with the organizational environment effectively, managers should chart the forces in the organization's specific and general environments, noting (a) the number of forces that will affect the organization, (b) the pattern of interconnectedness or linkages between these forces, (c) how rapidly these forces change, and (d) the extent and nature of competition, which affects how rich or poor the environment is.
3. Taking that analysis, managers should plan how to deal with contingencies. Designing interorganizational strategies to control and secure access to scarce and valuable resources in the environment in which they operate is the first stage in this process.

Resource Dependence Theory

Organizations depend on their environment for the resources they need to survive and grow. The supply of resources, however, depends on the complexity, dynamism, and richness of the environment. If an environment becomes poorer because important customers are lost or new competitors enter the market, resources become scarce and more valuable and uncertainty increases. Organizations attempt to manage their transactions with the environment to ensure access to the resources they depend on. They want their access to resources to be as predictable as possible because it simplifies managing their domains and promotes survival.

According to **resource dependence theory,** the goal of an organization is to minimize its dependence on other organizations for the supply of scarce resources in its environment and to find ways to influence them to secure needed resources.[13] Thus an organization must simultaneously manage two aspects of its resource dependence: (1) It has to exert influence over other organizations so it can obtain resources, and (2) it must respond to the needs and demands of the other organizations in its environment.[14]

Resource dependence theory
A theory that argues the goal of an organization is to minimize its dependence on other organizations for the supply of scarce resources in its environment and to find ways of influencing them to make resources available.

The strength of one organization's dependence on another for a particular resource is a function of two factors. The first one is how vital the resource is to the organization's survival. Scarce and valuable inputs (such as component parts and raw materials) and resources (such as customers and distribution outlets) are very important to an organization's survival.[15] The other factor is the extent to which other organizations control the resource. Crown Cork & Seal and other can manufacturers, for example, need aluminum to produce cans, but for many years the supply of aluminum was controlled by Alcoa, which had a virtual monopoly and thus could charge high prices for its aluminum.

The PC industry illustrates the operation of both factors. PC makers such as HP, Acer, Lenovo, and Dell depend on organizations such as Samsung, Nvidia, and Intel, which supply memory chips and microprocessors. They also depend on chains of electronics retailers such as Best Buy and online companies such as Amazon.com that stock their products, and on school systems and corporate customers that buy large quantities of their PCs. When there are few suppliers of a resource such as memory chips, or few organizations that distribute and sell a product, companies become highly dependent on the ones that do exist. Intel, for example, makes many of the most advanced microchips and has considerable power over PC makers who need its newest chips to compete successfully. The greater the dependence of one organization on another, the weaker it is, and the more powerful company can threaten or take advantage of the dependent organization if it chooses to do so by, for example, raising its prices.

To manage their resource dependence and control their access to scarce resources, organizations develop various strategies.[16] Just as nations craft international policies to try to increase their ability to influence world affairs, so organizations try to find ways of

Organizational Insight 3.3

Costco Takes on Powerful Distributors

Valentyn Volkov/Shutterstock.com

One of the reasons Prohibition came into being in the United States was that many bars were owned by brewers of alcoholic beverages, and it was thought that this could lead to abuse because brewers would use their power over retailing to raise prices. To separate the makers of alcoholic drinks such as beer and wine from alcohol retailers, most states adopted a three-tier distribution system that required manufacturers to sell to large distributors or wholesalers, which in turn would sell to retailers—bars, liquor stores, and today supermarkets and chain stores. It is estimated that this three-tier distribution system results in wholesalers adding a markup of about 25% to alcoholic beverages, which means customers pay 25% more than they need to pay and wholesalers are making huge profits.

In 2006 Costco, the large warehouse store chain, won an antitrust lawsuit challenging its home state's three-tier system. As its CEO James Sinegal said of alcohol wholesalers, "I would like to have a business where everybody had to buy from me," and he estimated Costco could sell beer and wine for at least 10–20% less if retailers like Costco—or Walmart or Kroger's—could buy directly from the makers of alcoholic products, many of which are abroad. Chain stores' great buying power would allow them to demand large price discounts from sellers, as has happened for other products such as soap and detergent and canned goods.

The state of Washington appealed, however, arguing that the 21st Amendment ending Prohibition gave states the authority to control alcohol regulation, including distribution. Washington was supported by 30 other states for an important reason: Sales of alcohol generate billions of dollars in state revenues—and it is much easier for states to collect that money when wholesalers distribute alcohol. In 2008 the U.S. Ninth Circuit Court of Appeals ruled largely in favor of Washington State, agreeing it had the right to decide if the three-tier system was appropriate. However, it also agreed with Costco that an important distribution rule, called a post-and-hold requirement, requiring every beer or wine distributor to file with the Liquor Control Board its wholesale prices and then maintain those prices for at least 30 days, was illegal and anticompetitive because it gave large wholesalers the information they needed to keep prices high. Costco's recent lawsuit means that U.S. lawmakers will be rethinking the regulation of alcohol sales in order to recoup the greatest profit for the states and to avoid wholesalers gobbling it up.

Despite the fact that Costco lost the appeal, the lawsuit showed how much profit goes to wholesalers, and it has led many lawmakers to think about how to change the whole distribution system so that each state—not the wholesalers—receives the high profits or taxes from the sale of alcohol. Thus while consumers might gain some relief if prices were lowered, each state would receive billions of dollars more in revenue and, moreover, could decide how high to set the sales taxes on alcohol to discourage its use. In Sweden, for example, taxes on alcohol are 300–400%; the cheapest bottle of liquor costs over $100 because that country wishes to reduce the amount of alcohol its citizens consume.

Costco has continued its efforts to reduce the power of wholesalers. Although it failed in the polls with "Initiative 1100" in 2010 that sought changes in Washington State's liquor distribution laws, its actions have led to new initiatives in the state legislature to find ways to allow both the state and large liquor distributors like Costco to benefit at the expense of distributors.

increasing their influence over the global environment. The way Costco has worked to challenge the power of liquor distributors offers a good example of the management of the environment to control resource dependence (see Organizational Insight 3.3).

Interorganizational Strategies for Managing Resource Dependencies

As the Costco example suggests, obtaining access to resources is uncertain and problematic; customers, for example, are notoriously fickle and switch to competitors' products. To reduce uncertainty, an organization needs to devise interorganizational strategies to manage the resource interdependencies in its specific and general environment. Managing these interdependencies allows organizations to protect and enlarge their domain. In the specific environment, organizations need to manage their relationships with forces such as suppliers, unions, and consumer interest groups. If they restrict access to resources, they can increase uncertainty.

In the specific environment, two basic types of interdependencies cause uncertainty: symbiotic and competitive.[17] Interdependencies are symbiotic when the outputs of one organization are inputs for another; thus **symbiotic interdependencies** generally exist between an organization and its suppliers and distributors. Intel and PC makers like HP and Dell have a symbiotic interdependency. **Competitive interdependencies** exist among organizations that compete for scarce inputs and outputs.[18] HP and Dell are in competition for customers for their laptops, tablet computers, and for inputs such as Intel's newest microchips.

Symbiotic interdependencies Interdependencies that exist between an organization and its suppliers and distributors.

Competitive interdependencies Interdependencies that exist among organizations that compete for scarce inputs and outputs.

Organizations can use various linkage mechanisms to control symbiotic and competitive interdependencies.[19] The use of these mechanisms, however, requires the actions and decisions of the linked organizations to be coordinated. This need for coordination reduces each organization's freedom to act independently and often in its own best interests. Suppose that HP, to protect its future supply of chips, signs a contract with Intel agreeing to use only Intel chips. But then a new chip manufacturer comes along with a less expensive chip. The contract with Intel obliges HP to pay Intel's higher prices even though doing so is not in HP's best interests.

Whenever an organization involves itself in an interorganizational linkage, it must balance its need to reduce resource dependence against the loss in autonomy or freedom of choice that will result from the linkage.[20] *In general, an organization aims to choose the interorganizational strategy that offers the most reduction in uncertainty for the least loss of control.*[21]

In the next sections we examine the interorganizational strategies that organizations can use to manage symbiotic interdependencies and competitive interdependencies. A linkage is formal when two or more organizations agree to coordinate their interdependencies directly to reduce uncertainty. The more *formal* a linkage, the greater are both the direct coordination and the likelihood that coordination is based on an explicit written agreement or involves some common ownership between organizations. The more *informal* a linkage, the more indirect or loose is the method of coordination and the more likely is the coordination to be based on an implicit or unspoken agreement.

Strategies for Managing Symbiotic Resource Interdependencies

To manage symbiotic interdependencies, organizations have a range of strategies from which to choose. Figure 3.3 indicates the relative degree of formality of four strategies. The more formal a strategy, the greater is the prescribed area of cooperation between organizations.

Developing a Good Reputation

The least formal, least direct way to manage symbiotic interdependencies with suppliers and customers is to develop a **reputation,** a state in which an organization is held in high regard and trusted by other parties because of its fair and honest business practices. For

Reputation A state in which an organization is held in high regard and trusted by other parties because of its fair and honest business practices.

Figure 3.3 Interorganizational Strategies for Managing Symbiotic Interdependencies

Symbiotic interdependencies generally exist between an organization and its suppliers and distributors. The more formal a strategy is, the greater the cooperation between organizations.

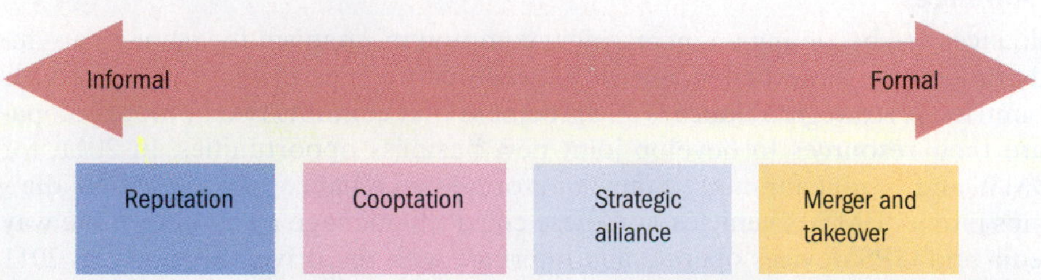

example, paying bills on time and providing high-quality goods and services lead to a good reputation and trust on the part of suppliers and customers. If a car repair shop has a reputation for excellent repair work and fair prices for parts and labor, customers return to the shop whenever their cars need servicing, and the organization is managing its linkages with customers successfully.

The DeBeers diamond cartel uses trust and reputation to manage its linkages with suppliers and customers. DeBeers customers are a select group of the world's biggest diamond merchants. When these merchants buy from DeBeers, they ask for a certain quantity of diamonds—say, $10 million worth. DeBeers then selects an assortment of diamonds that it values at $10 million. Customers have no opportunity to bargain with DeBeers over the price or quality of the diamonds. They can buy or not buy, but they always buy because they know DeBeers will not cheat them. The organization's reputation and survival depend on maintaining customers' goodwill.

Reputation and trust are probably the most common linkage mechanisms for managing symbiotic interdependencies. Over the long run, companies that behave dishonestly are likely to be unsuccessful; thus organizations as a group tend to become more honest over time.[22] Acting honestly, however, does not rule out active bargaining and negotiating over the price and quality of inputs and outputs. Every organization wants to strike the deal that best suits it and therefore attempts to negotiate terms in its favor.

Cooptation

Cooptation
A strategy that manages symbiotic interdependencies by neutralizing problematic forces in the specific environment.

Cooptation is a strategy that manages symbiotic interdependencies by neutralizing problematic forces in the specific environment.[23] An organization that wants to bring opponents over to its side gives them a stake in or claim on what it does and tries to satisfy their interests. Pharmaceutical companies coopt physicians by sponsoring medical conferences, giving away free samples of drugs, and advertising extensively in medical journals. Physicians become sympathetic to the interests of the pharmaceutical companies, which bring them onto the "team" and tell them that they and the companies have interests in common. Cooptation is an important political tool.

A common way to coopt problematic forces such as customers, suppliers, or other important outside stakeholders is to bring them within the organization and, in effect, make them inside stakeholders. If some stakeholder group does not like the way things are being done, an organization coopts the group by giving it a role in changing the way things are. All kinds of organizations use this strategy. Local schools, for example, attempt to coopt parents by inviting them to become members of school boards or by establishing teacher-parent committees. In such an exchange, the organization gives up some control but usually gains more than it loses.

Interlocking directorate
A linkage that results when a director from one company sits on the board of another company.

Outsiders can be brought inside an organization through bribery, a practice widespread in many countries but illegal in the United States. They can also be brought inside through the use of an **interlocking directorate**—a linkage that results when a director from one company sits on the board of another company. An organization that uses an interlocking directorate as a linkage mechanism invites members of powerful and significant stakeholder groups in its specific environment to sit on its board of directors.[24] An organization might invite the financial institution from which it borrows most of its money to send someone to sit on the organization's board of directors. Outside directors interact with an organization's top-management team, ensuring supplies of scarce capital, exchanging information, and strengthening ties between organizations.

Strategic Alliances

Strategic alliance
An agreement that commits two or more companies to share their resources to develop a new joint business opportunity.

Strategic alliances are becoming an increasingly common mechanism for managing symbiotic (and competitive) interdependencies between companies inside one country or between countries. A **strategic alliance** is an agreement that commits two or more companies to share their resources to develop joint new business opportunities. In 2011, for example, BMW and Nvidia announced they had formed an alliance to integrate Nvidia's graphics chips into all BMW's vehicles, and these chips will manage all aspects of the way BMW's media and GPS devices operate and interface with the driver. Similarly, in 2011

Figure 3.4 Types of Strategic Alliance

Companies linked by a strategic alliance share resources to develop joint new business opportunities. The more formal an alliance, the stronger the link between allied organizations.

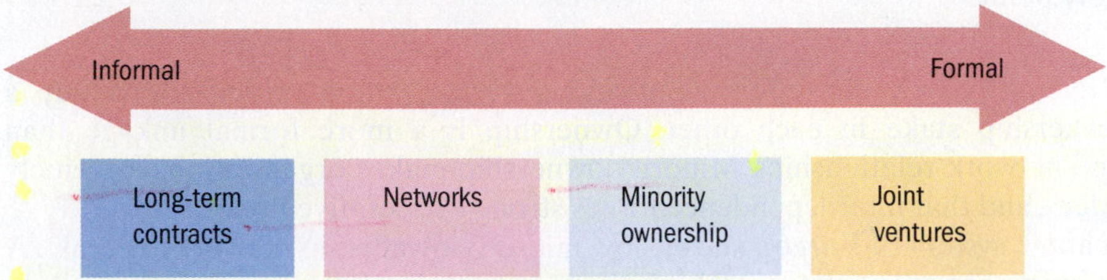

Microsoft and Nokia announced that in future Nokia's smartphones would use Microsoft's mobile phone platform and they would cooperate and use their strategic partnership to create "a new global mobile ecosystem."[25]

There are several types of strategic alliance. Figure 3.4 indicates the relative degree of formality of long-term contracts, networks, minority ownership, and joint ventures. The more formal an arrangement, the stronger and more prescribed the linkage and the tighter the control of the joint activities. In general, as uncertainty increases, organizations choose a more formal alliance to protect their access to resources.

LONG-TERM CONTRACTS At the informal end of the continuum shown in Figure 3.4 are alliances spelled out in long-term contracts between two or more organizations. The purpose of these contracts is usually to reduce costs by sharing resources or by sharing the risk of research and development, marketing, construction, and other activities. Contracts are the least formal type of alliance because no ties link the organizations apart from the agreement set forth in the contract. For example, to reduce financial risk, Bechtel Corp. and Willbros Group Inc., two leading multinational construction companies, agreed to pool their resources to construct an $850-million oil pipeline in the Caspian Sea.[26] J. B. Hunt Transport, a trucking company, formed an alliance with Santa Fe Pacific Corporation, a railroad company. Santa Fe agreed to carry Hunt's trailers across the country on railroad cars. At the end of the trip, the trains were met by Hunt's trucks, which transported the trailers to their final destination. This arrangement lowered Hunt's costs while increasing Santa Fe's revenues.

Contracts can be oral or written, casual, shared, or implicit. The CEOs or top managers of two companies might agree over lunch to meet regularly to share information and ideas on some business activity, such as standardizing computer systems or changing customer needs. Some organizations, in contrast, develop written contracts to specify procedures for sharing resources or information and for using the benefits that result from such agreements. Kellogg, the breakfast cereal manufacturer, enters into written contracts with the farmers who supply the corn and rice it needs. Kellogg agrees to pay a certain price for their produce regardless of the market rate prevailing when the produce is harvested. Both parties gain because a major source of unpredictability (fluctuations in corn and rice prices) is eliminated from their environments.

NETWORKS A **network** or network structure is a cluster of different organizations whose actions are coordinated by contracts and agreements rather than through a formal hierarchy of authority. Members of a network work closely to support and complement one another's activities. The alliance resulting from a network is more formal than the alliance resulting from a contract because more ties link member organizations and there is greater formal coordination of activities.[27] Nike and other organizations establish networks to build long-term relationships with suppliers, distributors, and customers to prevent the "core" organization from becoming too large or bureaucratic.

Network
A cluster of different organizations whose actions are coordinated by contracts and agreements rather than through a formal hierarchy of authority.

The goal of the organization that created the network is to share its manufacturing, marketing, or R&D skills with its partners to allow them to become more efficient and help it to reduce its costs or increase product quality. For example, AT&T created a network organization and linked its partners so it could produce digital answering machines at low cost. AT&T electronically sends designs for new component parts and assembly instructions for new products to its network partners, who coordinate their activities to produce the components in the desired quantities and then ship them to the final assembly point.[28]

MINORITY OWNERSHIP A more formal alliance emerges when organizations buy a minority ownership stake in each other. Ownership is a more formal linkage than contracts and network relationships. Minority ownership makes organizations extremely interdependent, and that interdependence forges strong cooperative bonds.

Keiretsu
A group of organizations, each of which owns shares in the other organizations in the group, that work together to further the group's interests.

The Japanese system of *keiretsu* shows how minority ownership networks operate. A **keiretsu** is a group of organizations, each of which owns shares in the other organizations in the group, and all of which work together to further the group's interests. Japanese companies employ two basic forms of keiretsu. Capital keiretsu are used to manage input and output linkages. Financial keiretsu are used to manage linkages among many diverse companies and usually have at their center a large bank.[29]

A particularly good example of the way a capital keiretsu network can benefit all the companies in it, but particularly the dominant ones, comes from the Japanese car industry.[30] Toyota is the most profitable car company in the world. Its vehicles are consistently ranked among the most reliable, and the company enjoys strong customer loyalty. Interdependencies with its customers are not problematic because Toyota has a good reputation. One of the reasons for this good reputation is the way Toyota controls its input interdependencies.

Because a car's reliability depends on the quality of its inputs, managing this crucial linkage is vital for success today in the global car market. To control its inputs, Toyota owns a minority stake, often as much as 40%, in many of its largest suppliers. Because of these formal ownership ties, Toyota can exercise control over the prices that suppliers charge for their components. An even more important result of this formal alliance is that it allows Toyota and its suppliers to work together to improve product quality and reliability and share the benefits. Toyota is not afraid to share proprietary information with its suppliers because of its ownership stake. As a result, parts suppliers *participate* significantly in the car design process, which often leads to the discovery of new ways to improve the quality and reduce the cost of components. Both Toyota and its suppliers share the benefits that accrue from this close cooperation.

Over time these alliances have given Toyota a global competitive advantage, which translates into control over important environmental interdependencies. Note also that Toyota's position as a shareholder in its suppliers' businesses means there is no reason for Toyota to take advantage of them by demanding lower and lower prices from them. All partners benefit from the sharing of activities. These close linkages continuously pay off when Toyota introduces the latest model of each of its vehicles, such as the Camry sedan. By taking advantage of the skills in its network, Toyota was able to engineer $1,700 in cost savings in the latest model and to introduce it at a price below that of the old model. For the same reasons, its new-model hybrid Prius will only be $1,500 more expensive than the non-hybrid version, compared to the $3,000 difference in its earlier model.

A financial keiretsu, which is dominated by a large bank, functions like a giant interlocking directorate. The dominant members of the financial keiretsu, normally drawn from diverse companies, sit on the board of directors of the bank and often on the boards of each other's companies. The companies are linked by substantial long-term stockholdings managed by the bank at the center of the keiretsu. Member companies are able to trade proprietary information and knowledge that benefits them collectively. Indeed, one of the benefits that comes from a financial keiretsu is the way businesses can transfer and exchange managers to strengthen the network.

Figure 3.5 shows the Fuyo keiretsu, which centers on Fuji Bank. Its members include Nissan, NKK, Hitachi, and Canon. The directors of Fuji Bank link all the largest and most significant keiretsu members. Each large member company has its own set of satellite companies. For example, Nissan has a minority ownership stake in many of the suppliers that provide inputs for its auto operations.

Figure 3.5 The Fuyo Keiretsu

A financial keiretsu centered around Fuji Bank in which organizations in the keiretsu are linked by minority share ownership in each other.

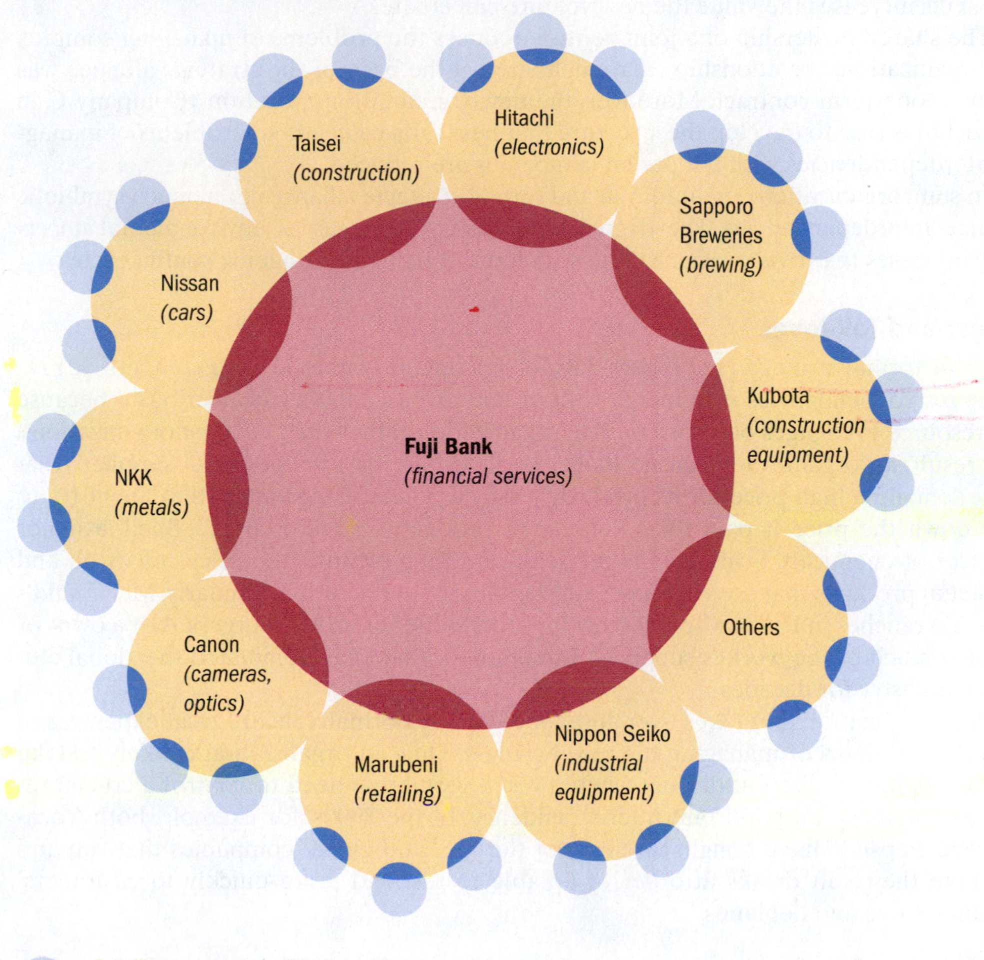

Joint Venture

A **joint venture** is a strategic alliance among two or more organizations that agree to establish and share the ownership of a new business.[31] Joint ventures are the most formal of the strategic alliances because the participants are bound by a formal legal agreement that spells out their mutual rights and responsibilities. For example, Company A and Company B agree to set up a new organization, Company C, and then cooperate to select its top-management team and design its organizational structure (see Figure 3.6). Company A and B both send executives to manage Company C and also provide the

Joint venture
A strategic alliance among two or more organizations that agree to jointly establish and share the ownership of a new business.

Figure 3.6 Joint Venture Formation

Two separate organizations pool resources to create a third organization. A formal legal document specifies the terms of this type of strategic alliance.

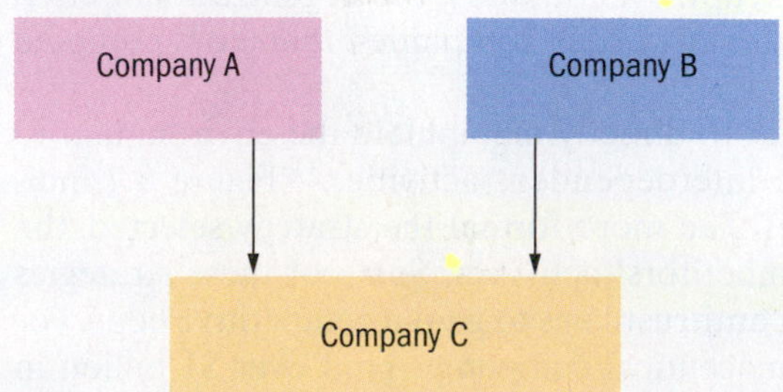

resources needed for it to grow and prosper. Participants in a joint venture often pool their distinctive competences. For example, one contributes expert knowledge on efficient production techniques and the other its competencies in R&D, and the pooling of their skills increases the value the new venture can create.

The shared ownership of a joint venture reduces the problems of managing complex interorganizational relationships that might arise if the basis of the strategic alliance was simply a long-term contract. Moreover, the newly created organization (Company C in Figure 3.6) is free to develop the structure that best suits its needs so problems of managing interdependencies with the parent companies are reduced.

In sum, organizations use informal and formal strategic alliances to manage symbiotic resource interdependencies. The degree of formality increases as environmental uncertainty increases to provide organizations with more control over ongoing contingencies.

Merger and Takeover

The most formal strategy (see Figure 3.4) for managing symbiotic (and competitive) resource interdependencies is to merge with or take over a supplier or distributor because now resource exchanges occur *within* one organization rather than *between* organizations. As a result, an organization can no longer be held hostage by a powerful supplier (that might demand a high price for its products) or by a powerful customer (that might try to drive down the price it pays for a company's products).[32] For example, Shell, a major producer of chemicals, owns several oil fields and thus controls the prices of its oil and petroleum products that are vital inputs in chemical manufacturing. Similarly, McDonald's owns vast ranches in Brazil where it rears low-cost cattle for its hamburgers. Alcoa owns or manages much of the world's supply of aluminum ore and has dominated the global aluminum industry for decades.

An organization that takes over another company normally incurs great expense and faces the problems of managing the new business. Thus an organization is likely to take over a supplier or distributor only when it has a very great need to control a crucial resource or manage an important interdependency. In the 2000s, for example, both Coca-Cola and PepsiCo have bought up many of the U.S. and global companies that can and distribute their soft drinks in order to be able to respond more quickly to customers' changing tastes and demands.

Strategies for Managing Competitive Resource Interdependencies

Organizations do not like competition. Competition threatens the supply of scarce resources and increases the uncertainty of the specific environment. Intense competition can threaten the very survival of an organization as product prices fall to attract customers and the environment becomes poorer and poorer. For example, in the last decade, landline telephone providers have been forced to slash the price of long-distance services from 20 cents a minute, to 10 cents, to 5 cents and today offer unlimited monthly service for one low price to compete with their wireless cellphone rivals. Wireless companies such as AT&T and Sprint in turn have continued to reduce their prices to attract customers who are increasingly ending their landline phone service and signing up for smartphone wireless contracts that also give them access to the Internet. The higher the level of competition, the more likely some companies in an industry are to be taken over or to go bankrupt.[33] Ultimately, the organizational environment is controlled by the handful of the strongest companies that now compete head to head for resources.

Organizations use a variety of techniques to directly manipulate the environment to reduce the uncertainty of their competitive interdependent activities.[34] Figure 3.7 indicates the relative formality of four strategies. The more formal the strategy selected, the more explicit the attempt to coordinate competitors' activities. Some of these strategies are illegal, but unethical organizations break antitrust laws to gain a competitive edge. For example, in 2003, several major Swiss pharmaceutical companies paid over $1 billion in

Figure 3.7 Interorganizational Strategies for Managing Competitive Interdependencies

Competitive interdependencies exist between an organization and its rivals. The more formal a strategy, the more explicit the attempt to coordinate competitors' activities.

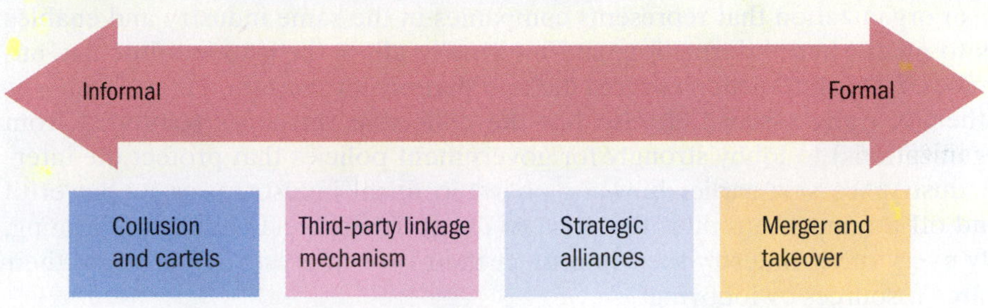

fines to settle charges they had artificially inflated the cost of vitamins to consumers, and in 2007, Samsung, Infineon, and other flash memory chip makers admitted the same thing and were fined over $700 million dollars. In 2009, LCD makers LG, Sharp, and Chunghwa pleaded guilty to conspiring to raise the price of LCD displays bought by Apple, Dell, and Motorola and were fined over $585 million. The readiness of companies to behave illegally in order to pursue their own interests must be recognized; and safeguards—laws and regulations—must be put in place to prevent this from happening.

Collusion and Cartels

A **collusion** is a secret agreement among competitors to share information for a deceitful or illegal purpose, such as keeping prices high as in the flash memory chip industry. Organizations collude to reduce the competitive uncertainty they experience. A **cartel** is an association of firms that explicitly agree to coordinate their activities as Samsung and other chip makers did.[35] Cartels and collusion increase the stability and richness of an organization's environment and reduce the complexity of relations among competitors. Both of them are illegal in the United States.

Collusion
A secret agreement among competitors to share information for a deceitful or illegal purpose.

Cartel
An association of firms that explicitly agree to coordinate their activities.

Sometimes competitors in an industry can collude by establishing industry standards.[36] Industry standards function like rules of conduct that tell competitors, for example, what prices they should charge, what their product specifications should be, or what a product's profit markup should be. Industry standards may result from price leadership. The strongest company, like Samsung in memory chips, is likely to be the price leader. It sets the prices for its products, and then the weaker organizations charge prices similar to the price leader's. In this way, industry prices are fixed at an artificially high level. Organizations can always make more profit if they collectively coordinate their activities than if they compete. Customers lose because they must pay the inflated prices.

Organizations can also collude and form a cartel without formal written agreement by signaling their intentions to each other by public announcements about their future strategy. For example, they can announce price increases they are contemplating and see whether their rivals will match those increases. This is common in the airline industry when one airline announces a price hike or a new charge for a second checked bag or a fuel surcharge, and then it waits to see how the other airlines respond. Often other airlines respond in kind and ticket prices rise, sometimes an airline like Southwest refuses to play along and so prices fall back to their original level. Organizations in an industry can try to discipline companies that break informal competitive industry rules. Some large companies have a reputation for ruthlessly going after competitors that break their industry's informal pricing rules. For example, Walmart is always ready to match any price decreases announced by Costco or Target so these companies have come to realize they will gain no advantage by lowering prices. But they can compete in other ways. Target and Costco have worked hard to develop stores that are more customer-friendly and attractive and that offer more upscale products than Walmart's, for example.

Third-Party Linkage Mechanisms

Third-party linkage mechanism
A regulatory body that allows organizations to share information and regulate the way they compete.

A more formal but still indirect way for competing organizations to coordinate their activities is through a **third-party linkage mechanism**—a regulatory body that allows organizations to share information and regulate the way they compete.[37] An example is a trade association, an organization that represents companies in the same industry and enables competitors to meet, share information, and informally allow them to monitor one another's activities.[38] This interaction reduces the fear that one organization may deceive or outwit another. A trade association also has the collective resources (obtained from member organizations) to lobby strongly for government policies that protect the interests of its industry. We saw earlier how the pharmaceutical industry uses its powerful lobby to fend off attempts to reduce the price of drugs. The cable TV, defense, farming, and virtually every other industry seek to protect their own interests and increase their access to scarce resources by lobbying.

Other examples of third-party linkage mechanisms include agencies such as the Chicago Board of Trade, stock markets, the National Collegiate Athletic Association (NCAA), and any other organization that is set up to regulate competitive interdependencies. Third-party linkage mechanisms provide rules and standards that regulate and stabilize industry competition and so reduce the complexity of the environment and thus increase its richness. Also, by increasing the flow of information, linkage mechanisms enable organizations to react more easily to change or to the dynamism of the environment. In short, third-party linkage mechanisms provide a way for competitors to manage resource interdependencies and reduce uncertainty.

Organizations that use a third-party linkage mechanism coopt themselves and jointly receive the benefits of the coordination that they obtain from the third-party linkage mechanism. The number of U.S. research and development cooperatives formed by competitors to fund joint research interests is rapidly increasing as global competition increases. Japan is the model for such third-party linkage mechanisms. Its Ministry of International Trade and Industry (MITI) has a long history of promoting industry cooperation among domestic rivals to foster joint technical developments that help Japanese companies achieve global leadership in some industries.

Strategic Alliances

Strategic alliances can be used to manage not only symbiotic interdependencies but competitive interdependencies.[39] Competitors can cooperate and form a joint venture to develop common technology that will save them all a lot of money, even though they may be in competition for customers when their final products hit the market. In 2011, for example, Ford formed a long-term joint venture with OAO Sollers, the second largest Russian carmaker, to assemble and distribute its vehicles in Russia. Also, in 2011, Groupon and Live Nation Entertainment announced they had formed a joint venture to develop a new online ticketing deals channel, GrouponLive.

Although the kinds of joint ventures just described are not anticompetitive, organizations sometimes use joint ventures to deter new entrants or harm existing competitors. Philips and Bang & Olufsen, two leading consumer electronics companies, signed an agreement to share their production and design skills, respectively, to compete with Japanese giants Sony and Panasonic.[40] Organizations can also form a joint venture to develop a new technology that they can then protect from other rivals by obtaining and defending patents. The use of strategic alliances to manage competitive interdependencies is limited only by the imagination of rival companies.

Merger and Takeover

The ultimate weapon in an organization's armory for managing problematic competitive (and symbiotic) interdependencies is to merge with, or take over, a competing organization.[41] Mergers and takeovers can improve a company's competitive position by allowing the company to strengthen and enlarge its domain and increase its ability to produce a wider range of products to better serve more customers. For example, NationsBank bought up smaller banks at a very fast rate, and in 1998 it merged with Bank of America to become the biggest bank in the United States. Everything was going well for a decade until the recent financial crisis when Bank of America bought Merrill Lynch and Countrywide Mortgage, both of which proved to be disastrous investments that might have led to its bankruptcy except for government intervention.

Many organizations might like to use mergers to become a monopoly, the sole player in the marketplace. Fortunately for consumers, and for organizations themselves, monopolies are illegal in the United States and in most other developed countries. So, if an organization becomes too strong and dominant, an accusation leveled at both Microsoft and Google, they are prevented by antitrust law from taking over other companies to become even more powerful.[42] Nevertheless, cartels, collusion, and other anticompetitive practices can ultimately be bad for organizations themselves. In the long run, as a result of changes in technology, cheap sources of labor, changes in government policy, and so forth, new entrants will be able to enter an industry, and existing companies that have reduced competition among themselves will then find themselves ineffective competitors. Protected from competition in an environment where uncertainty has been low, these monopoly-like organizations have become large top-heavy bureaucracies unable to meet the challenges of a rapidly changing environment. GM, IBM, and Kodak are organizations that controlled their competitive environments for a very long time and suffered greatly when it changed—and allowed more agile competitors to enter their markets and beat these established companies at their own game. Compared with Nokia, discussed earlier, GE had to learn the hard way how to do it right in Hungary, as discussed in Organizational Insight 3.4.

Transaction Cost Theory

In Chapter 1, we defined **transaction costs** as the costs of negotiating, monitoring, and governing exchanges between people. Whenever people work together, there are costs—transaction costs—associated with controlling their activities.[44] Transaction costs also arise when organizations exchange resources or information. Organizations interact with other organizations to get the resources they require, and they have to control those symbiotic and competitive interdependencies. According to resource dependence theory,

Transaction costs
The costs of negotiating, monitoring, and governing exchanges between people.

Organizational Insight 3.4

Don't Buy a Burnt Out Light Bulb Company

Seeking to expand globally, General Electric (GE) agreed to acquire 51% of Tungsram, a maker of lighting products and widely regarded as one of Hungary's best companies, at a cost of $150 million. GE was attracted to Tungsram because of Hungary's low wage rates and the possibility of using the company as a base from which to export lighting products to Western Europe. At the time, many analysts believed that GE would show other Western companies how to turn organizations once run by Communist Party officials into capitalist moneymakers. GE transferred some of its best managers to Tungsram and waited for the miracle to happen. It took a long time, for several reasons.

One of the problems resulted from major misunderstandings between the American managers and the Hungarian workers. The Americans complained that the Hungarians were lazy; the Hungarians thought the Americans were pushy. GE's management system depends on extensive communication between workers and managers, a practice uncommon in the previously communist country. Changing behavior at Tungsram proved to be difficult. The Americans wanted strong sales and marketing functions that would pamper customers; in Hungary's former planned economy, these were unnecessary. In addition, Hungarians expected GE to deliver Western-style wages; but GE came to Hungary to take advantage of the country's low-wage structure.[43]

As Tungsram's losses mounted, GE learned what happens when grand expectations collide with the grim reality of inefficiency and indifference toward customers and quality. Looking back, GE managers admit that, because of differences in basic attitudes between countries, they had underestimated the difficulties they would face in turning Tungsram around. To improve performance, GE laid off half of Tungsram's employees, including two out of every three managers. It invested over $1 billion in a new plant and equipment and in retraining the remaining employees and managers to help them learn the work attitudes and behaviors that a company needs to survive in a competitive global environment. In the 2000s, its Hungarian operation has become one of the most efficient in Europe; the plant exports its light bulbs all over the European Union, and GE has invested hundreds of millions more to expand its capabilities.

Managerial Implications

Resource Dependence Theory

1. To maintain an adequate supply of scarce resources, study each resource transaction individually to decide how to manage it.
2. Study the benefits and costs associated with an interorganizational strategy before using it.
3. To maximize the organization's freedom of action, always prefer an informal to a formal linkage mechanism. Use a more formal mechanism only when the uncertainty of the situation warrants it.
4. When entering into strategic alliances with other organizations, be careful to identify the purpose of the alliance and future problems that might arise between organizations, to decide whether an informal or a formal linkage mechanism is most appropriate. Once again, choose an informal rather than a formal alliance whenever possible.
5. Use transaction cost theory (see later) to identify the benefits and costs associated with the use of different linkage mechanisms to manage particular interdependencies.

Transaction cost theory A theory that states the goal of an organization is to minimize the costs of exchanging resources in the environment and the costs of managing exchanges inside the organization.

organizations attempt to gain control of resources and minimize their dependence on other organizations. According to **transaction cost theory,** the goal of the organization is to minimize the costs of exchanging resources in the environment and the costs of managing exchanges inside the organization.[45] Every dollar or hour of a manager's time spent in negotiating or monitoring exchanges with other organizations, or with managers inside one organization, is a dollar or hour that is not being used to create value. Organizations try to minimize transaction costs and bureaucratic costs because they siphon off productive capacity. Organizations try to find mechanisms that make interorganizational transactions relatively more efficient.

Health care provides a dramatic example of just how large transaction costs can be and why reducing them is so important. It is estimated that over 40% of the U.S. health-care budget is spent handling exchanges (such as bills and insurance claims) between doctors, hospitals, the government, insurance companies, and other parties.[46] Clearly, any improvements that reduce transaction costs would result in a major saving of resources. The desire to reduce transaction costs was the impetus for the formation of health maintenance organizations (HMOs) and other networks of health-care providers. HMO providers agree to reduce their costs in return for a more certain flow of patients, among other things. This trade-off reduces the uncertainty they experience.

Sources of Transaction Costs

Transaction costs result from a combination of human and environmental factors.[47] (See Figure 3.8.)

ENVIRONMENTAL UNCERTAINTY AND BOUNDED RATIONALITY The environment is characterized by considerable uncertainty and complexity. People, however, have only a limited ability to process information and to understand the environment surrounding them.[48]

Figure 3.8 Sources of Transaction Costs

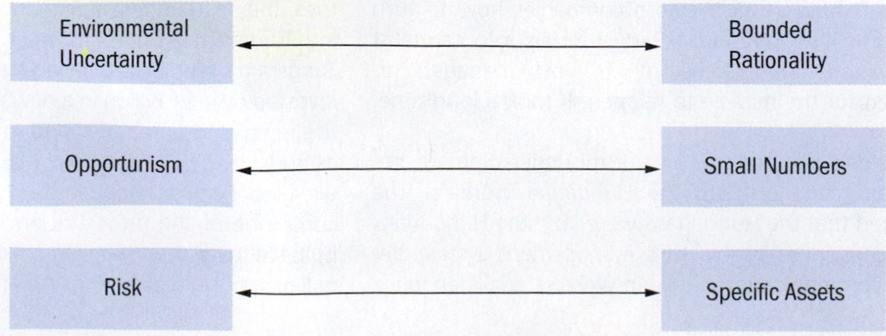

Because of this limited ability, or bounded rationality, the higher the level of uncertainty in an environment, the greater the difficulty of managing transactions between organizations.

Suppose Organization A wants to license a technology developed by Organization B. The two organizations could sign a contract. Considerable uncertainty, however, would surround this contract. For example, Organization B might want to find new ways of using the technology to make new products for itself. Given bounded rationality, it would be difficult and prohibitively expensive to try to write a contract that not only protected Organization B, which developed the technology, but also spelled out how the two organizations might jointly share in the future benefits from the technology. In this situation, the developing company (Organization B) might prefer to proceed alone and not exchange resources with Organization A, even though it knows it could create more value by engaging in the exchange. Thus, because of bounded rationality and the high transaction costs of drawing up a contract, potential value that could have been created is lost. Environmental uncertainty may make the cost of negotiating, monitoring, and governing agreements so high that organizations resort to more formal linkage mechanisms—such as strategic alliances, minority ownership, or even mergers—to lower transaction costs.

OPPORTUNISM AND SMALL NUMBERS Most people and organizations behave honestly and reputably most of the time, but some always behave opportunistically—that is, they cheat or otherwise attempt to exploit other forces or stakeholders in the environment.[49] For example, an organization contracts for component parts of a particular quality. To reduce costs and save money, the supplier deliberately substitutes inferior materials but bills for the more expensive, higher-quality parts. Individuals, too, act opportunistically: Managers pad their expense reports or exploit customers by manufacturing inferior products.

When an organization is dependent on one supplier or on a small number of trading partners, the potential for opportunism is great. The organization has no choice but to transact business with the supplier, and the supplier, knowing this, might choose to supply inferior inputs to reduce costs and increase profit.

When the prospect for opportunism is high because of the small number of suppliers to which an organization can go for resources, the organization has to expend resources to negotiate, monitor, and enforce agreements with its suppliers to protect itself. For example, the U.S. government spends billions of dollars a year to protect itself from being exploited by defense contractors such as Boeing and General Dynamics, which have been known to take advantage of their ability to exploit the government because they have so few competitors for defense-related work.

RISK AND SPECIFIC ASSETS **Specific assets** are investments—in skills, machinery, knowledge, and information—that create value in one particular exchange relationship but have no value in any other exchange relationship. A company that invests $100 million in a machine that makes microchips for IBM machines has only made a very specific investment in a very specific asset. An organization's decision to invest money to develop specific assets for a specific relationship with another organization in its environment involves a high level of risk. Once the investment is made, the organization is locked into it. If the other party tries to exploit the relationship by saying, for example, "We will not buy your product unless you sell it to us for $10 less per unit than you're charging now," the organization is in a very difficult situation. This tactic is akin to blackmail.

Specific assets
Investments—in skills, machinery, knowledge, and information—that create value in one particular exchange relationship but have no value in any other exchange relationship.

An organization that sees any prospect of being trapped or blackmailed will judge the investment in specific assets to be too risky. The transaction costs associated with the investment become too high, and value that could have been created is lost.[50]

Transaction Costs and Linkage Mechanisms

Organizations base their choice of interorganizational linkage mechanisms on the level of transaction costs involved in an exchange relationship. Transaction costs are low when these conditions exist:

1. Organizations are exchanging nonspecific goods and services.
2. Uncertainty is low.
3. There are many possible exchange partners.

In these environmental conditions, it is easy for organizations to negotiate and monitor interorganizational behavior. Thus, in a low-transaction-cost environment, organizations can use relatively informal linkage mechanisms, such as reputation and unwritten, word-of-mouth contracts.

Transaction costs increase when these conditions exist:

1. Organizations begin to exchange more specific goods and services.
2. Uncertainty increases.
3. The number of possible exchange partners falls.

In this kind of environment, an organization will begin to feel it cannot afford to trust other organizations, and it will start to monitor and use more formal linkages, such as long-term contracts, to govern its exchanges. Contracts, however, cannot cover every situation that might arise. If something unexpected happens, what will the other party to the exchange do? It has a perfect right to act in the way that most benefits itself, even though its actions are harmful to the other organization.

How does an organization act in a high-transaction-cost situation? According to transaction cost theory, an organization should choose a more formal linkage mechanism to manage exchanges as transaction costs increase. The more formal the mechanism used, the more control organizations have over each other's behavior. Formal mechanisms include strategic alliances (joint ventures), merger, and takeover, all of which internalize the transaction and its cost. In a joint venture, two organizations establish a third organization to handle their joint transactions. Establishing a new entity that both organizations own equally reduces each organization's incentives to cheat the other and provides incentives for them to do things (e.g., invest in specific assets) that will create value for them both. With mergers, the same arguments hold because one organization now owns the other.

From a transaction cost perspective, the movement from less formal to more formal linkage mechanisms (see Figures 3.3, 3.4, and 3.7) occurs because of an organization's need to reduce the transaction costs of its exchanges with other organizations. Formal mechanisms minimize the transaction costs associated with reducing uncertainty, opportunism, and risk.

Bureaucratic Costs

If formal linkage mechanisms are such an efficient way to minimize the transaction costs of exchanges with the environment, why do organizations not use these mechanisms all the time? Why do they ever use an informal linkage mechanism such as a contract if a joint venture or a merger gives them better control of their environment? The answer is that bringing the transactions inside the organization minimizes but does not eliminate the costs of managing transactions.[51] Managers must still negotiate, monitor, and govern exchanges between people inside the organization. Internal transaction costs are called bureaucratic costs to distinguish them from the transaction costs of exchanges between organizations in the environment.[52] We saw in Chapter 2 how difficult communication and integration between functions and divisions are. Now we see that integration and communication are not only difficult to achieve but cost money because managers have to spend their time in meetings rather than creating value.[53] Thus managing an organization's structure is a complex and expensive problem that becomes much more expensive and complex as the organization grows—as GM, Kodak, and IBM discovered.

Using Transaction Cost Theory to Choose an Interorganizational Strategy

Transaction cost theory can help managers choose an interorganizational strategy by enabling them to weigh the savings in transaction costs achieved from using a particular linkage mechanism against the bureaucratic costs of operating the linkage mechanism.[54] Because transaction cost theory brings into focus the costs associated with different linkage mechanisms to reduce uncertainty, it is able to make better predictions than is resource dependence theory about why and when a company will choose a certain interorganizational strategy. Managers deciding which strategy to pursue must take the following steps:

1. Locate the sources of transaction costs that may affect an exchange relationship and decide how high the transaction costs are likely to be.
2. Estimate the transaction cost savings from using different linkage mechanisms.
3. Estimate the bureaucratic costs of operating the linkage mechanism.
4. Choose the linkage mechanism that gives the most transaction cost savings at the lowest bureaucratic cost.

The experience of the Ekco Group of Nashua, New Hampshire, offers an interesting example of how a supplier can use a linkage mechanism to reduce transaction costs for customers to gain their support. Ekco makes a wide range of bakeware products, kitchen tools and equipment, household plastic products (such as laundry baskets), and pest-control devices.[55] It produces thousands of nonelectric consumer and office products that require no assembly and are replaced rather than repaired when they wear out. Ekco's wide product range reflects the needs of retail customers like Walmart and Kmart, which are continually trying to reduce the transaction costs associated with obtaining products. Obtaining a wide range of products from one supplier reduces the transaction costs associated with building many supplier relationships. By offering a broad range of products that Kmart, Walmart, and others are interested in carrying, Ekco helps the retailers minimize the number of companies they must go to for the products they want to carry. In this way, Ekco is implicitly inviting customers to increase their links with Ekco.

To foster long-term commitment and trust with its customers, Ekco installed a state-of-the-art $4 million data-processing system (a specific asset) that allows it to provide a just-in-time inventory service to retailers who supply the company with data. This system simplifies retailers' ordering and tracking of their inventory. By managing customers' transactions at no cost to them, the system further reduces the retailers' transaction costs with Ekco and strengthens their perception that it is a good company to do business with. Ekco's attempt to develop informal linkage mechanisms with its customers paid off, and sales to its major customers increase every year.[56] Ekco and its customers jointly benefit from close personal ties, and there is no need for formal and expensive mechanisms to coordinate their interorganizational exchanges.

The implication of a transaction cost view is that a formal linkage mechanism should be used only when transaction costs are high enough to warrant it. An organization should take over and merge with its suppliers or distributors, for example, only if the saving in transaction costs outweighs the costs of managing the new acquisition.[57] Otherwise, like Ekco and its customers, the organization should rely on less formal mechanisms, such as strategic alliances and long-term contracts, to handle exchange relationships. The relatively informal linkage mechanisms avoid the need for an organization to incur bureaucratic costs. Three linkage mechanisms that help organizations to avoid bureaucratic costs while still minimizing transaction costs are keiretsu, franchising, and outsourcing.

KEIRETSU The Japanese system of keiretsu can be seen as a mechanism for achieving the benefits of a formal linkage mechanism without incurring its costs.[58] The policy of owning a minority stake in its suppliers' companies gives Toyota substantial control over the exchange relationship and allows it to avoid problems of opportunism and uncertainty with its suppliers. Toyota also avoids the bureaucratic costs of actually owning and managing its suppliers. Indeed, keiretsu was developed to provide the benefits of full ownership without the costs.

In contrast, until 2005, GM used to own more suppliers than any other car manufacturer, and as a result it paid more for its inputs than the other car companies paid for theirs. These high costs arose because GM's internal suppliers were in a protected situation; GM was a captive buyer, so its supplying divisions had no incentive to be efficient and thus behave opportunistically.[59]

So what should GM do to reduce input costs? One course of action would be to divest its inefficient suppliers and then establish strategic alliances or long-term contracts with them to encourage them to lower their costs and increase their efficiency. If they cannot improve their cost or quality, GM would form new alliances with new suppliers. GM did exactly that when it spun off its Delco electronics parts subsidiary into an independent operating company; it also spun off other divisions such as its gear and axle division.[60] GM's goal is to obtain the benefits that Toyota has achieved from its strategy of minority ownership. Conversely, if GM were to experience problems with obtaining the benefits from a strategic alliance with an independent parts supplier (if, for example, its partner were acting opportunistically), it should then move to a more formal linkage mechanism and buy and merge with its suppliers.

FRANCHISING A franchise is a business authorized to sell a company's products in a certain area. The franchiser sells the right to use its resources (e.g., its name or operating system) to a person or group (the franchisee) in return for a flat fee or a share of the profits. Normally, the franchiser provides the inputs used by the franchisee, who deals directly with the customer. The relationship between franchiser and franchisee is symbiotic. The transaction cost approach offers an interesting insight into why interorganizational strategies such as franchising emerge.[61]

Consider the operational differences between McDonald's and Burger King. A very large proportion of McDonald's restaurants is owned by franchisees, but most Burger King restaurants are owned by the company. Why doesn't McDonald's own its restaurants? Why is McDonald's willing to make its franchisees millionaires instead of enriching its stockholders? From a transaction cost point of view, the answer lies in the bureaucratic costs that McDonald's would incur if it attempted to manage all its own restaurants.

The single biggest challenge for a restaurant is to maintain the quality of its food and customer service. Suppose McDonald's employed managers to run all its company-owned restaurants. Would those managers have the same incentive to maintain as high a quality of customer service as franchisees who own and so directly benefit from a high-performing restaurant? McDonald's believes that if it owned and operated all its restaurants—that is, if it used a formal linkage mechanism—the bureaucratic costs incurred to maintain the quality and consistency of the restaurants would exceed any extra value the organization and its shareholders would obtain from full ownership. Thus McDonald's generally owns only those restaurants that are located in big cities or near highways. In big cities, it can spread the costs of employing a management team over many restaurants and reduce bureaucratic costs. On interstate highways, McDonald's believes, franchisees realize they are unlikely to see the same travelers ever again and have no incentive to maintain standards.

The same issue arises on the output side when an organization is choosing how to distribute its products. Should an organization own its distribution outlets? Should it sell directly to customers? Should it sell only to franchised dealers? Again the answer depends on the transaction cost problems the organization can expect in dealing with the needs of its customers. Generally, the more complex the products are and the more information customers need about how they work or how to repair them, the greater the likelihood that organizations have formal hierarchical control over their distributors and franchisees or own their own distribution outlets.[62]

Cars are typically sold through franchised dealers because of the need to provide customers with reliable car repair. Also, because cars are complicated products and customers need a lot of information before they buy one, it is effective for manufacturers to have some control over their distributors. Thus car manufacturers have considerable control over their dealerships and monitor and enforce the service that dealerships give to customers. Toyota, for example, closely monitors the number of customer complaints against a dealership. If the number of complaints gets too high, it punishes the dealership by restricting its supply of new cars. As a result, dealers have strong incentives to give customers good service. In contrast, the transaction costs involved in handling simple products like clothes or food are low. Thus few clothing or food companies choose to use formal linkages to control the distribution of their products. Less formal mechanisms such as contracts with wholesalers or with large retail store chains become the preferred distribution strategy.

OUTSOURCING Another strategy for managing interdependencies is **outsourcing,** moving a value creation activity that was performed inside an organization to outside, where it is done by another company. An example of outsourcing would be a company hiring another company to manage its computer network or to distribute its products instead of performing the activity itself. Increasingly, organizations are turning to specialized companies to manage their information processing needs. Dell, HP, and IBM, for example, have set up divisions that supply this specialized service to companies in their environments.

Outsourcing
The process of moving a value creation activity that was performed inside an organization to outside where it is done by another company.

What prompts an organization to outsource a function is the same calculation that determines whether an organization makes or buys inputs. Does the extra value that the organization obtains from performing its own marketing or information processing exceed the extra bureaucratic costs of managing such functions? If the answer is yes, the organization develops its own function. If it is no, the organization outsources the activity.[63] This decision is likely to change over time. Perhaps in 2001 it was best to have an information-processing department inside the organization. By 2011, however, if specialized organizations are able to process information more cheaply, outsourcing this function will result in major cost savings. Outsourcing within networks, such as the one established by Nike, is another example of how outsourcing helps hold down the bureaucratic costs of managing exchanges inside an organization. Global supply chain management offers another example of how companies can reduce transaction costs and avoid bureaucratic costs, as discussed in Organizational Insight 3.5.

The specific method a company adopts to manage the outsourcing process will be the one that most effectively reduces the uncertainty involved in the exchange—to ensure a stable supply of inexpensive components, to improve quality, or to protect valuable proprietary technology. For example, in terms of the different kinds of strategic alliances presented in Figure 3.4, when uncertainty is relatively low, companies can choose to create long-term contracts with many low-cost overseas suppliers. As uncertainty increases, a company might develop a network to manage interdependencies between these suppliers

Organizational Insight 3.5

Li & Fung's Global Supply Chain Management

Finding the overseas suppliers that offer the lowest-priced and highest-quality products is an important task facing the managers of global organizations. Because these suppliers are located in thousands of cities in many countries around the world, finding them is a difficult business. Global companies often use the services of overseas intermediaries or brokers, located near these suppliers, to find the one that best meets their input requirements. Li & Fung, now run by brothers Victor and William Fung, is one of these brokers that has helped hundreds of global companies to locate suitable overseas suppliers, especially suppliers in mainland China.[64]

In the 2000s, however, managing global companies' supply chains has become a more complicated task. To reduce costs, overseas suppliers are increasingly specializing in just one part of the task of producing a product. For example, in the past, a company such as Target might have negotiated with an overseas supplier to manufacture a million units of some particular shirt at a certain cost per unit. But with specialization, Target might find it can reduce the costs of producing the shirt even further by splitting apart the operations involved in producing the shirt and having different overseas suppliers, often in different countries, perform each operation. For example, to get the lowest cost per unit, rather than just negotiate with a overseas supplier over the price of making a particular shirt, Target might first negotiate with a yarn manufacturer in Vietnam to make the yarn, then ship the yarn to a Chinese supplier to weave it into cloth, and then ship to several different factories in Malaysia and the Philippines to cut the cloth and sew the shirts. Then, another overseas company might take responsibility for packaging and shipping the shirts to wherever in the world they are required. Because a company such as Target has thousands of different clothing products under production, and these change all the time, the problems of managing such a supply chain to get the full cost savings from global expansion are clear.

Li & Fung has capitalized on this opportunity. Realizing that many global companies do not have the time or expertise to find such specialized low-price suppliers, they moved quickly to provide such a service. Li & Fung employs 3,600 agents who travel across 37 countries to find new suppliers and inspect existing suppliers to find new ways to help their global clients get lower prices or higher-quality products. Global companies are happy to outsource their supply chain management to Li & Fung because they realize significant cost savings. Even though they pay a hefty fee to Li & Fung, they avoid the costs of employing their own agents. As the complexity of supply chain management continues to increase, more and more companies like Li & Fung are appearing.

and global manufacturers and distributors, or it might take a minority ownership interest in these global companies to gain legal control over the transaction. Finally, when uncertainty is high, a company might decide to form a joint venture to control all aspects of the value-creation activity.

A transaction cost approach sheds light on why and how organizations choose different linkage mechanisms to manage their interdependencies. It improves our ability to understand the process that organizations use to manage their environments to enhance their chances for growth and survival. The solutions that exist for managing uncertain resource exchanges and organizational interdependencies range from less formal mechanisms like contracts to more formal mechanisms like ownership. The best mechanism for an organization is one that minimizes transaction and bureaucratic costs.

Summary

Managing the organizational environment is a crucial task for an organization. The first step is identifying sources of uncertainty and examining the sources of complexity, how rapidly it is changing, and how rich or poor it is. An organization then needs to evaluate the benefits and costs of different interorganizational strategies and choose the one that best allows it to secure valuable resources. Resource dependence theory weighs the benefit of securing scarce resources against the cost of a loss of autonomy. Transaction cost theory weighs the benefit of reducing transaction costs against the cost of increasing bureaucratic costs. An organization must examine the whole array of its exchanges with its environment to devise the combination of linkage mechanisms that will maximize its ability to create value. Chapter 3 has made the following main points:

1. The organizational environment is the set of forces in the changing global environment that affect the way an organization operates and its ability to gain access to scarce resources.
2. The organizational domain is the range of goods and services that the organization produces and the clients that it serves in the countries in which it operates. An organization devises interorganizational strategies to protect and enlarge its domain.
3. The specific environment consists of forces that most directly affect an organization's ability to secure resources. The general environment consists of forces that shape the specific environments of all organizations.
4. Uncertainty in the environment is a function of the complexity, dynamism, and richness of the environment.
5. Resource dependence theory argues that the goal of an organization is to minimize its dependence on other organizations for the supply of scarce resources and to find ways of influencing them to make resources available.
6. Organizations have to manage two kinds of resource interdependencies: symbiotic interdependencies with suppliers and customers and competitive interdependencies with rivals.
7. The main interorganizational strategies for managing symbiotic relationships are the development of a good reputation, cooptation, strategic alliances, and merger and takeover. The main interorganizational strategies for managing competitive relationships are collusion and cartels, third-party linkage mechanisms, strategic alliances, and merger and takeover.
8. Transaction costs are the costs of negotiating, monitoring, and governing exchanges between people and organizations. There are three sources of transaction costs: (a) the combination of uncertainty and bounded rationality, (b) opportunism and small numbers, and (c) specific assets and risk.
9. Transaction cost theory argues that the goal of organizations is to minimize the costs of exchanging resources in the environment and the costs of managing exchanges inside the organization. Organizations try to choose interorganizational strategies that minimize transaction costs and bureaucratic costs.

10. Interorganizational linkage mechanisms range from informal types such as contracts and reputation to formal types such as strategic alliances and ownership strategies such as merger and takeover.

Discussion Questions

1. Pick an organization, such as a local travel agency or supermarket. Describe its organizational domain, then draw a map of the forces in its general and specific environments that affect the way it operates.
2. What are the major sources of uncertainty in an environment? Discuss how these sources of uncertainty affect a small biotechnology company and a large carmaker.
3. According to resource dependence theory, what motivates organizations to form interorganizational linkages? What is the advantage of strategic alliances as a way of exchanging resources?
4. According to transaction cost theory, what motivates organizations to form interorganizational linkages? Under what conditions would a company prefer a more formal linkage mechanism to a less formal one?
5. What interorganizational strategies might work most successfully as a company expands globally? Why?

Organizational Theory in Action

Practicing Organizational Theory

Protecting Your Domain

Break up into groups of three to five people and discuss the following scenario:

You are a group of entrepreneurs who have recently launched a new kind of root beer, made from exotic herbs and spices, that has quickly obtained a loyal following in a large southwestern city. Inspired by your success, you have decided to increase production of your root beer to serve a wider geographic area, with the eventual goal of serving all of the United States and Canada.

The problem you have is deciding the best way to secure your domain and manage the environment as you grow. On one hand, both the ingredients in your root beer and your method of making it are secret, so you have to protect it from potential imitators at all costs—large soda companies will quickly copy it if they have a chance. On the other hand, you lack the funds for quick expansion, and finding a partner who can help you grow quickly and establish a brand-name reputation would be an enormous advantage.

1. Analyze the pros and cons of each of the types of strategic alliances (long-term contracts, networks, minority ownership, and joint ventures) as your means of managing the environment.
2. Based on this analysis, which one would you choose to maximize your chance of securing a stable niche in the soda market?

The Ethical Dimension #3

In their search to reduce costs, many global companies are buying products from suppliers in overseas countries that are made in sweatshops by women and children who work long hours for a few dollars a day. Complex arguments surround this issue. From an ethical perspective, discuss:

1. When and under what conditions is it right for companies to buy their inputs from suppliers that do employ women and children?
2. What kinds of interorganizational strategies could U.S. companies use to enforce any ethical codes they develop?

Making the Connection #3

Find an example of a company that is using a specific interorganizational strategy, such as a joint venture or a long-term contract. What linkage mechanism is it using? Use resource dependence theory or transaction cost theory to explain why the organization might have chosen that type of mechanism.

Analyzing the Organization: Design Module #3

This module and the modules in the next two chapters allow you to analyze the environment of your organization and to understand how the organization tries to manage its environment to control and obtain the resources it needs to protect its domain.

Assignment

1. Draw a chart of your organization's domain. List the organization's products and customers and the forces in the specific and general environments that have an effect on it. Which are the most important forces that the organization has to deal with?
2. Analyze the effect of the forces on the complexity, dynamism, and richness of the environment. From this analysis, how would you characterize the level of uncertainty in your organization's environment?
3. Draw a chart of the main interorganizational linkage mechanisms (e.g., long-term contracts, strategic alliances, mergers) that your organization uses to manage its symbiotic resource interdependencies. Using resource dependence theory and transaction cost theory, discuss why the organization chose to manage its interdependencies in this way. Do you think the organization has selected the most appropriate linkage mechanisms? Why or why not?
4. Draw a chart of the main interorganizational linkage mechanisms (e.g., collusion, third-party linkage mechanisms, strategic alliances) that your organization uses to manage its competitive resource interdependencies. Using resource dependence theory or transaction cost theory, discuss why the organization chose to manage its interdependencies in this way. Do you think the organization has selected the most appropriate linkage mechanisms? Why or why not?
5. In view of the analysis you have just made, do you think your organization is doing a good or a not-so-good job of managing its environment? What recommendations would you make to improve its ability to obtain resources?

CASE FOR ANALYSIS

How IKEA Manages the Global Environment

IKEA is the largest furniture chain in the world, and in 2011 the Swedish company operated over 270 stores in 25 countries. In 2011 IKEA sales soared to over $35 billion, or over 20% of the global furniture market; but to its managers and employees this was just the tip of the iceberg. They believed IKEA was poised for massive growth throughout the world in the coming decade because it could provide what the average customer wanted: well-designed and well-made contemporary furniture at an affordable price. IKEA's ability to provide customers with affordable furniture is the result of the way it expands globally and operates its global store empire. In a nutshell, IKEA's global approach focuses on simplicity, attention to detail, cost consciousness, and responsiveness in every aspect of its operations and behavior.

IKEA's global approach derives from the personal values and beliefs of its founder, Ingvar Kamprad, about how companies should treat their employees and customers. Kamprad, who is in his early 80s (and in 2010 ranked as the 11th-richest person in the world), was born in Smaland, a poor Swedish province whose citizens are known for being entrepreneurial, frugal, and hardworking. Kamprad definitely absorbed these values—when he entered the furniture business, he made them the core of his management approach. He teaches store managers and employees his values; his beliefs about the need to operate in a no-frills, cost-conscious way; and his view that they are all in business "together," by which he means that every person who works in his global empire plays an essential role and has an obligation to everyone else.

What does Kamprad's approach mean in practice? All IKEA employees fly coach class on business trips, stay in inexpensive hotels, and keep traveling expenses to a minimum. And IKEA stores operate on the simplest rules and procedures possible, with employees expected to cooperate to solve problems and get the job done. Many famous stories circulate about the frugal Kamprad, such as that even he always flies coach class and that when he takes a soda can from the minibar in a hotel room, he replaces it with one bought in a store—despite the fact that he is a multibillionaire.

IKEA's employees see what Kamprad's global approach means as soon as they are recruited to work in a store in one of the many countries in which the company operates. They start learning about IKEA's global corporate culture by performing jobs at the bottom of the ladder, and they are quickly trained to perform all the various jobs involved in store operations. During this process they internalize IKEA's global values and norms, which center on the importance the company attaches to their taking the initiative and responsibility for solving problems and for focusing on customers. Employees are rotated between departments and sometimes stores, and rapid promotion is possible for those who demonstrate the enthusiasm and togetherness that show they have bought into IKEA's global culture.

Most of IKEA's top managers rose from its ranks, and the company holds "breaking the bureaucracy weeks" in which managers are required to work in stores and warehouses for a week each year to make sure they and all employees stay committed to IKEA's global values. No matter which country they operate in, all employees wear informal clothes to work at IKEA—Kamprad has always worn an open-neck shirt—and there are no marks of status such as executive dining rooms or private parking places. Employees believe that if they buy into IKEA's work values, behave in ways that keep its growing global operations streamlined and efficient, and focus on being one step ahead of potential problems, they will share in its success. Promotion, training, above-average pay, a generous store bonus system, and the personal well-being that comes from working in a company where people feel valued are some of the rewards that Kamprad pioneered to build and strengthen IKEA's global approach.

Whenever IKEA enters a new country, it sends its most experienced store managers to establish its global approach in its new stores. When IKEA first entered the United States, the attitude of U.S. employees puzzled its managers. Despite their obvious drive to succeed and good education, employees seemed reluctant to take initiative and assume responsibility. IKEA's managers discovered that their U.S. employees were afraid mistakes would result in the loss of their jobs, so the managers strove to teach employees the "IKEA way." The approach paid off: The United States has become the company's second best country market, and IKEA plans to open many more U.S. stores, as well as stores around the world, over the next decade.

Discussion Questions

1. List the various ways in which IKEA has managed the global environment over time.
2. How would you explain the rationale behind the success of IKEA's approach to managing its environment?

References

[1] J. D. Thompson, *Organizations in Action* (New York: McGraw-Hill, 1967).
[2] www.mcdonalds.com, 2011.
[3] R. H. Hall, *Organizations: Structure and Process* (Englewood Cliffs, NJ: Prentice-Hall, 1972).
[4] R. H. Miles, Macro *Organizational Behavior* (Santa Monica, CA: Goodyear, 1980).
[5] www.nokia.com, 2011.
[6] J. Child, "Organizational Structure, Environment, and Performance: The Role of Strategic Choice," *Sociology* 6 (1972), 1–22; G. G. Dess and D. W. Beard, "Dimensions of Organizational Task Environments," *Administrative Science Quarterly* 29 (1984), 52–73.
[7] F. E. Emery and E. L. Trist, "The Causal Texture of Organizational Environments," *Human Relations* 18 (1965), 21–32.
[8] H. Aldrich, *Organizations and Environments* (Englewood Cliffs, NJ: Prentice-Hall, 1979).
[9] W. H. Starbuck, "Organizations and Their Environments," in M. D. Dunnette, ed., *Handbook of Industrial Psychology* (Chicago: Rand McNally, 1976), pp. 1069–1123; Dess and Beard, "Dimensions of Organizational Task Environments."

10 Aldrich, *Organizations and Environments.*
11 www.amazon.com, 2011.
12 Ibid.
13 J. Pfeffer and G. R. Salancik, *The External Control of Organizations* (New York: Harper & Row, 1978).
14 Pfeffer, *Organizations and Organizational Theory,* p. 193.
15 Pfeffer and Salancik, *The External Control of Organizations,* pp. 45–46.
16 D. Miller and J. Shamsie, "The Resource-Based View of the Firm in Two Environments: The Hollywood Film Studios from 1936–1965," *Academy of Management Journal* 39 (1996), 519–543.
17 Pfeffer and Salancik, *The External Control of Organizations,* p. 114.
18 H. R. Greve, "Patterns of Competition: The Diffusion of Market Position in Radio Broadcasting," *Administrative Science Quarterly, 41* (1996), 29–60.
19 J. M. Pennings, "Strategically Interdependent Organizations," in J. Nystrom and W. Starbuck, eds., *Handbook of Organizational Design* (New York: Oxford University Press, 1981), pp. 433–455.
20 J. Galaskeiwicz, "Interorganizational Relations," *Annual Review of Sociology, 11* (1985), 281–304.
21 G. R. Jones and M. W. Pustay, "Interorganizational Coordination in the Airline Industry, 1925–1938: A Transaction Cost Approach," *Journal of Management* 14 (1988), 529–546.
22 C. W. L. Hill, "Cooperation, Opportunism, and the Invisible Hand," *Academy of Management Review* 15 (1990), 500–513.
23 P. Selznick, *TVA and the Grassroots* (New York: Harper & Row, 1949).
24 J. Pfeffer, "Size and Composition of Corporate Boards of Directors," *Administrative Science Quarterly* 17 (1972), pp. 218–228; R. D. Burt, "Co-optive Corporate Actor Networks: A Reconsideration of Interlocking Directorates Involving American Manufacturing," *Administrative Science Quarterly* 25 (1980), 557–581.
25 www.microsoft.com, 2011; www.nokia.com, 2011.
26 "Bechtel, Willbros to Build Pipeline at Caspian Sea," *Wall Street Journal,* October 26, 1992, p. A3.
27 W. W. Powell, K. W. Kogut, and L. Smith-Deorr, "Interorganizational Collaboration and the Locus of Innovation: Networks of Learning in Biotechnology," *Administrative Science Quarterly* 41 (1996), 116–145.
28 R. Miles and C. Snow, "Causes of Failure in Network Organizations," *California Management Review* 4 (1992), 13–32.
29 M. Aoki, *Information, Incentives, and Bargaining in the Japanese Economy* (New York: Cambridge University Press, 1988).
30 D. Roos, D. T. Jones, and J. P. Womack, *The Machine That Changed the World* (New York: Macmillan, 1990).
31 B. Kogut, "Joint Ventures: Theoretical and Empirical Perspectives," *Strategic Management Journal* 9 (1988), pp. 319–333.
32 J. Pfeffer, "Merger as a Response to Organizational Interdependence," *Administrative Science Quarterly* 17 (1972), pp. 382–394.
33 F. M. Scherer, *Industrial Market Structure and Economic Performance,* 2nd ed. (Boston: Houghton Mifflin, 1980).
34 A. Phillips, "A Theory of Interfirm Competition," *Quarterly Journal of Economics* 74 (1960), pp. 602–613; J. K. Benson, "The Interorganizational Network as a Political Economy," *Administrative Science Quarterly* 20 (1975), pp. 229–250.
35 D. W. Carlton and J. M. Perloff, *Modern Industrial Organization* (Glenview, IL: Scott, Foresman, 1990).
36 K. G. Provan, J. M. Beyer, and C. Kruytbosch, "Environmental Linkages and Power in Resource Dependence Relations Between Organizations," *Administrative Science Quarterly* 25 (1980), 200–225.
37 H. Leblebichi and G. R. Salancik, "Stability in Interorganizational Exchanges: Rule-making Processes in the Chicago Board of Trade," *Administrative Science Quarterly* 27 (1982), 227–242; A. Phillips, "A Theory of Interfirm Organization."
38 M. Olson, *The Logic of Collective Action* (Cambridge, MA: Harvard University Press, 1965).
39 B. Kogut, "Joint Ventures: Theoretical and Empirical Perspectives," *Strategic Management Journal* 9 (1988), 319–332.
40 www.phillips.com, 2011.

41 Scherer, *Industrial Market Structure and Economic Performance.*
42 J. Cook, "When 2 + 2 = 5," *Forbes,* June 8, 1992, pp. 128–129.
43 J. Perez, "GE Finds Tough Going in Hungary," *New York Times,* July 25, 1994, pp. C1, C3.
44 A. Alchian and H. Demsetz, "Production, Information Costs, and Economic Organization," *American Economic Review* 62 (1972), 777–795.
45 O. E. Williamson, *Markets and Hierarchies* (New York: The Free Press, 1975); O. E. Williamson, "The Governance of Contractual Relationships," *Journal of Law and Economics* 22 (1979), 232–261.
46 www.msnbc.com, 2011.
47 Williamson, *Markets and Hierarchies.*
48 H. A. Simon, *Models of Man* (New York: Wiley, 1957).
49 Williamson, *Markets and Hierarchies.*
50 B. Klein, R. Crawford, and A. Alchian, "Vertical Integration: Appropriable Rents and the Competitive Contracting Process," *Journal of Law and Economics* 21 (1978), 297–326.
51 R. H. Coase, "The Nature of the Firm," *Economica N.S.* 4 (1937), 386–405.
52 G. R. Jones, "Transaction Costs, Property Rights, and Organizational Culture: An Exchange Perspective," *Administrative Science Quarterly* 28 (1983), 454–467.
53 R. A. D'Aveni and D. J. Ravenscraft, "Economies of Integration Versus Bureaucracy Costs: Does Vertical Integration Improve Performance?" *Academy of Management Journal* 37 (1994), 1167–1206.
54 G. R. Jones and C. W. L. Hill, "Transaction Cost Analysis of Strategy-Structure Choice," *Strategic Management Journal* 9 (1988), 159–172.
55 "Ekco Group," *Fortune,* September 21, 1992, p. 87.
56 "CCPC Acquisition Corp. Completes Acquisition of EKCP Group Inc.," company press release, 1999.
57 G. Walker and D. Weber, "A Transaction Cost Approach to Make or Buy Decisions," *Administrative Science Quarterly* 29 (1984), 373–391.
58 J. F. Hennart, "A Transaction Cost Theory of Equity Joint Ventures," *Strategic Management Journal* 9 (1988), 361–374.
59 K. G. Provan and S. J. Skinner, "Interorganizational Dependence and Control as Predictors of Opportunism in Dealer-Supplier Relations," *Academy of Management Journal* 32 (1989), 202–212.
60 www.gm.com, 2011.
61 S. A. Shane, "Hybrid Organizational Arrangements and Their Implications for Firm Growth and Survival: A Study of New Franchisors," *Academy of Management Journal* 39 (1996), 216–234.
62 D. E. Bowen and G. R. Jones, "Transaction Cost Analysis of Service Organization-Customer Exchange," *Academy of Management Review* 11 (1986), 428–441.
63 E. Anderson and D. C. Schmittlein, "Integration of the Sales Force: An Empirical Examination," *Rand Journal of Economics* 26 (1984), 65–79.
64 "Business: Link in the Global Chain," *Economist,* June 2, 2001, pp. 62–63.

CHAPTER 4

Basic Challenges of Organizational Design

Learning Objectives

If an organization is to remain effective as it changes and grows with its environment, managers must continuously evaluate the way their organizations are designed: for example, the way work is divided among people and departments, and the way it utilizes its human, financial, and physical resources. Organizational design involves difficult choices about how to control—that is, coordinate organizational tasks and motivate the people who perform them—to maximize an organization's ability to create value. This chapter examines the challenges of designing an organizational structure so that it achieves stakeholder objectives.

After studying this chapter you should be able to:

1. Describe the four basic organizational design challenges confronting managers and consultants.
2. Discuss the way in which these challenges must be addressed simultaneously if a high-performing organizational structure is to be created.
3. Distinguish among the design choices that underlie the creation of either a mechanistic or an organic structure.
4. Recognize how to use contingency theory to design a structure that fits an organization's environment.

Differentiation

Differentiation
The process by which an organization allocates people and resources to organizational tasks and establishes the task and authority relationships that allow the organization to achieve its goals.

Division of labor
The process of establishing and controlling the degree of specialization in the organization.

As organizations grow, managers must decide how to control and coordinate the activities that are required for the organization to create value. The principal design challenge is how to manage differentiation to achieve organizational goals. **Differentiation** is the process by which an organization allocates people and resources to organizational tasks and establishes the task and authority relationships that allow the organization to achieve its goals.[1] In short, it is the process of establishing and controlling the **division of labor,** or degree of specialization, in the organization.

An easy way to examine why differentiation occurs and why it poses a design challenge is to examine an organization and chart the problems it faces as it attempts to achieve its goals (see Figure 4.1). In a *simple* organization, differentiation is low because the division of labor is low. Typically, one person or a few people perform all organizational tasks, so there are few problems with coordinating who does what, for whom, and when. With growth, however, comes complexity. In a *complex* organization, both the division of labor and differentiation are high. In Organizational Insight 4.1, the story of how the B.A.R. and Grille restaurant grew illustrates the problems and challenges that organizational design must address. As the B.A.R. and Grille changed, its owners had to find new ways to control the activities necessary to meet their goal of providing customers with a satisfying dining experience.

The basic design challenge facing the owners of the B.A.R. and Grille was managing the increasing complexity of the organization's activities. At first, Bob and Amanda performed all the major organizational tasks themselves, and the division of labor was

Figure 4.1 **Design Challenge**

Differentiation at the B.A.R. and Grille.

A. Bob and Amanda, the owners, cook and wait tables as needed. They employ one additional server. (3 individuals in the organization)

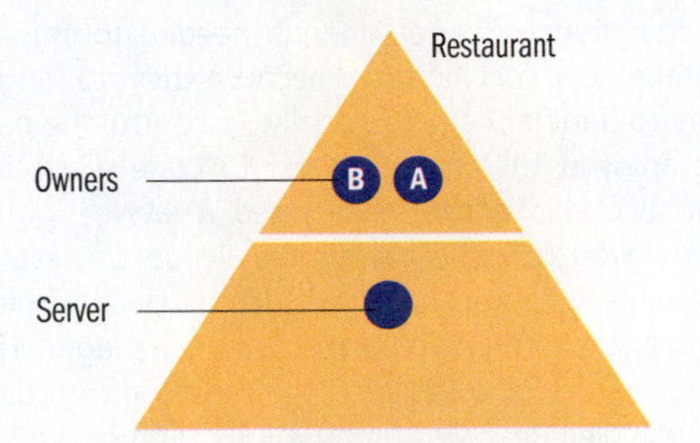

B. Bob and Amanda work in the kitchen full time. They hire servers, bussers, and kitchen staff. (22 individuals in the organization)

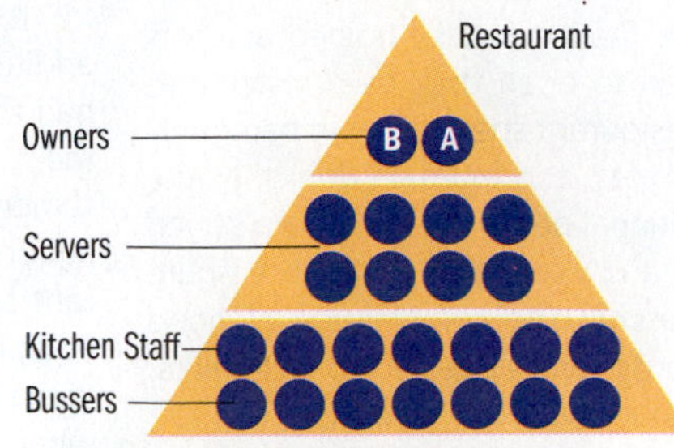

C. Unable to manage both the kitchen and the dining room, they divide tasks into two functions, kitchen and dining room, and specialize. Bob runs the kitchen, and Amanda runs the dining room. They also add more staff. (29 individuals in the organization)

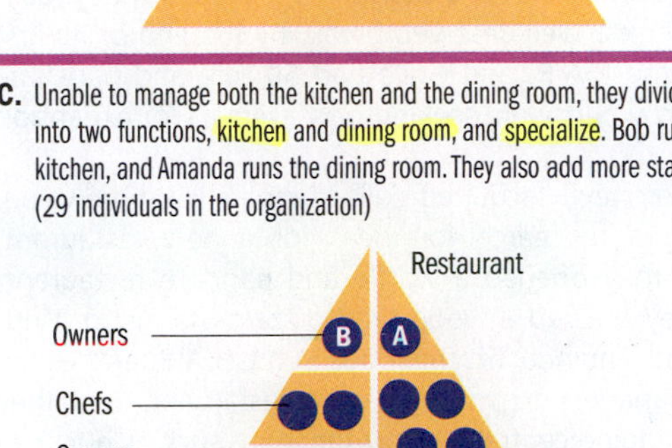

D. The business continues to prosper. Bob and Amanda create new tasks and functions and hire people to manage the functions. (52 individuals in the organization)

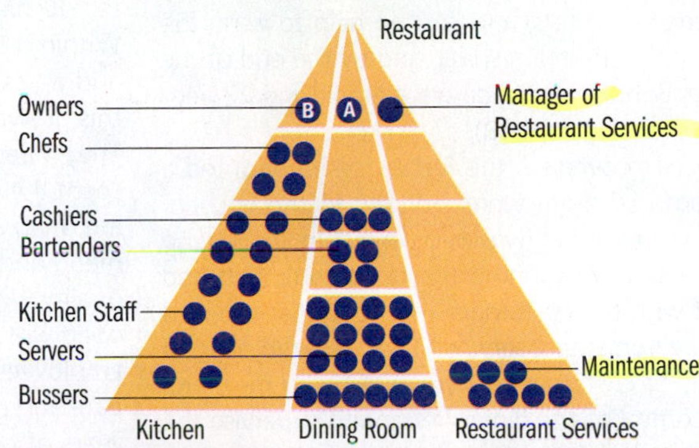

E. The Richardses see new opportunities to apply their core competences in new restaurant ventures. They open new restaurants, put support functions like purchasing and marketing under their direct control, and hire shift managers to manage the kitchen and dining room in each restaurant. (150 individuals in the organization)

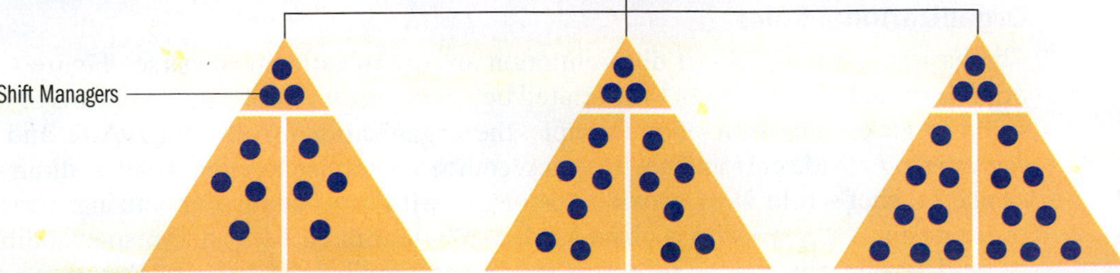

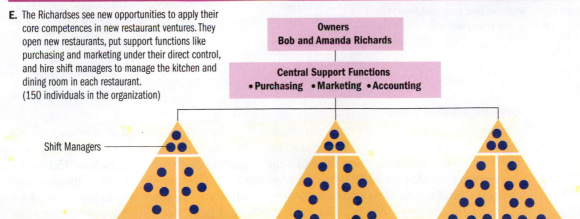

low. As the volume of business grew, the owners needed to increase the division of labor and decide which people would do which jobs. In other words, they had to differentiate the organization and allocate people and resources to organizational tasks.

Design Challenge 1

People in this organization take on new tasks as the need arises, and it's very unclear who is responsible for what, and who is supposed to report to whom. This makes it difficult to know who to call on when the need arises and difficult to coordinate people's activities so they work together as a team.

Organizational Insight 4.1

B.A.R. and Grille Restaurant

In 2004, Bob and Amanda Richards (hence B.A.R.) trained as chefs and obtained the capital they needed to open their own restaurant, the B.A.R. and Grille, a 1950s-style restaurant specializing in hamburgers, hot dogs, french fries, fresh fruit pies, and fountain drinks. At the beginning, with the help of one additional person hired to be a server, Bob and Amanda took turns cooking and waiting on tables (see Figure 4.1A). The venture was wildly successful. The combination of good food, served in a "Happy Days" atmosphere, appealed to customers, who swamped the restaurant at lunchtime and every night.

Right away Bob and Amanda were overloaded. They worked from dawn to midnight to cope with all the jobs that needed to be done: buying supplies, preparing the food, maintaining the property, taking in money, and figuring the accounts. It was soon clear that both Bob and Amanda were needed in the kitchen and that they needed additional help. They hired servers, bussers, and kitchen help to wash the mountains of dishes. The staff worked in shifts, and by the end of the third month of operations, Bob and Amanda were employing 22 people on a full- or part-time basis (Figure 4.1B).

With 22 staff members to oversee, the Richardses confronted a new problem. Because both of them were working in the kitchen, they had little time to oversee what was happening in the dining room. The servers, in effect, were running the restaurant. Bob and Amanda had lost contact with the customers and no longer received their comments about the food and service. They realized that to make sure their standards of customer service were being met, one of them needed to take control of the dining room and supervise the servers and bussers while the other took control of the kitchen. Amanda took over the dining room, and she and Bob hired two chefs to replace her in the kitchen. Bob oversaw the kitchen and continued to cook. The business continued to do well, so they increased the size of the dining room and hired additional servers and bussers (Figure 4.1C).

It soon became clear that Bob and Amanda needed to employ additional people to take over specific tasks because they no longer had the time or energy to handle them personally. To control the payment system, they employed full-time cashiers. To cope with customers' demands for alcoholic drinks, they hired a lawyer, got a liquor license, and employed full-time bartenders. To obtain restaurant supplies and manage restaurant services such as cleaning and equipment maintenance, they employed a restaurant manager. The manager was also responsible for overseeing the restaurant on days when the owners took a well-deserved break. By the end of its first year of operation, the B.A.R. and Grille had 50 full- and part-time employees, and the owners were seeking new avenues for expansion (Figure 4.1D).

Eager to use their newly acquired skills to create yet more value, the Richardses began to search for ideas for a new restaurant. Within 18 months they opened a waffle and pancake restaurant, and a year later they opened a wood-fired pizza/pasta bistro. With this growth, Bob and Amanda left their jobs in the B.A.R. and Grille. They hired shift managers to manage each restaurant, and they spent their time managing central support functions such as purchasing, marketing, and accounting, training new chefs, and developing menu and marketing plans (Figure 4.1E). To ensure that service and quality were uniformly excellent at all three restaurants, they developed written rules and procedures that told chefs, servers, and other employees what was expected of them—for example, how to prepare and present food and how to behave with customers. After five years of operation, they employed more than 150 full- or part-time people in their three restaurants, and their sales volume was over $5 million a year and a few years later, it was over $8 million.

Organizational Roles

Organizational role
The set of task-related behaviors required of a person by his or her position in an organization.

The basic building blocks of differentiation are organizational roles (see Figure 4.2). An **organizational role** is a set of task-related behaviors required of a person by his or her position in an organization.[2] For example, the organizational role of a B.A.R. and Grille server is to provide customers with quick, courteous service to enhance their dining experience. A chef's role is to provide customers with high-quality, appetizing, cooked-to-order meals. A person who is given a role with identifiable tasks and responsibilities can be held accountable for the resources used to accomplish the duties of that position. Bob and Amanda held the server responsible for satisfying the dining needs of customers, the restaurant's crucial stakeholder group. The chef was accountable for providing high-quality meals to customers consistently and speedily.

As the division of labor increases in an organization, managers specialize in some roles and hire people to specialize in others. Specialization allows people to develop their individual abilities and knowledge, which are the ultimate source of an organization's core competences. At the B.A.R. and Grille, for example, the owners identified various tasks to be done, such as cooking, bookkeeping, and purchasing, and they hired people with the appropriate abilities and knowledge to do them.

Organizational structure is based on a system of interlocking roles, and the relationship of one role to another is defined by task-related behaviors. Some roles require people

Figure 4.2 Building Blocks of Differentiation

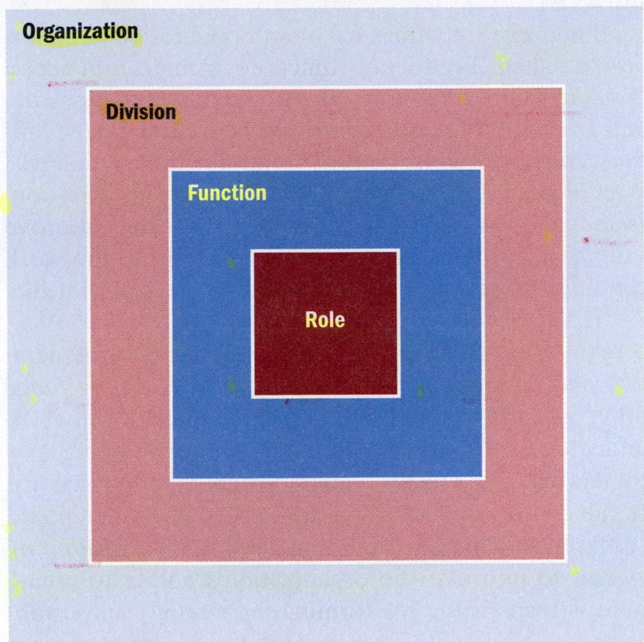

to oversee the behavior of others: Shift managers at the B.A.R. and Grille oversee the servers and bussers. A person who can hold another person accountable for his or her performance possesses authority over the other person. **Authority** is the power to hold people accountable for their actions and to make decisions about how to invest and use organizational resources.[3] The differentiation of an organization into individual organizational roles results in clear authority and responsibility requirements for each role in the system. When an individual clearly understands the responsibilities of his or her role and what a superior can require of a person in that role, the result within the organization is **control**—the ability to coordinate and motivate people to work in the organization's interests.

Authority
The power to hold people accountable for their actions and to make decisions concerning the use of organizational resources.

Control
The ability to coordinate and motivate people to work in the organization's interests.

Subunits: Functions and Divisions

In most organizations, people with similar and related roles are grouped into a subunit. The main subunits that develop in organizations are functions (or departments) and divisions. A **function** is a subunit composed of a group of people, working together, who possess similar skills or use the same kind of knowledge, tools, or techniques to perform their jobs. For example, in the B.A.R. and Grille, chefs are grouped together as the kitchen function, and servers grouped together as the dining room function. A **division** is a subunit that consists of a collection of functions or departments that share responsibility for producing a particular good or service. Take another look at Figure 4.1E. Each restaurant is a division composed of just two functions—dining room and kitchen—which are responsible for the restaurant's activities. Large companies like GE and Procter & Gamble have dozens of separate divisions, each one responsible for producing a particular product. In addition, these companies face the problem of how to organize these divisions' activities on a global level so they can create the most value, an issue discussed in detail in Chapter 8.

Function
A subunit composed of a group of people, working together, who possess similar skills or use the same kind of knowledge, tools, or techniques to perform their jobs.

Division
A subunit that consists of a collection of functions or departments that share responsibility for producing a particular good or service.

The number of different functions and divisions that an organization possesses is a measure of the organization's complexity—its degree of differentiation. Differentiation into functions and divisions increases an organization's control over its activities and allows the organization to accomplish its tasks more effectively.

As organizations grow in size, they differentiate into five different kinds of functions.[4] **Support functions** facilitate an organization's control of its relations with its environment and its stakeholders. Support functions include *purchasing*, to handle the acquisition of inputs; *sales and marketing*, to handle the disposal of outputs; and *public relations and legal affairs*, to respond to the needs of outside stakeholders. Bob and Amanda

Support functions
Functions that facilitate an organization's control of its relations with its environment and its stakeholders.

Richards hired a manager to oversee purchasing for all three restaurants and an accountant to manage the books (see Figure 4.1E).

Production functions Functions that manage and improve the efficiency of an organization's conversion processes so more value is created.

Maintenance functions Functions that enable an organization to keep its departments in operation.

Adaptive functions Functions that allow an organization to adjust to changes in the environment.

Managerial functions Functions that facilitate the control and coordination of activities within and among departments.

Production functions manage and improve the efficiency of an organization's conversion processes so that more value is created. Production functions include *production operations*, *production control*, and *quality control*. At Ford, the production operations department controls the manufacturing process, production control decides on the most efficient way to produce cars at the lowest cost, and quality control monitors product quality.

Maintenance functions enable an organization to keep its departments in operation. Maintenance functions include *personnel*, to recruit and train employees and improve skills; *engineering*, to repair broken machinery; and *janitorial services*, to keep the work environment safe and healthy—conditions that are very important to a restaurant like the B.A.R. and Grille.

Adaptive functions allow an organization to adjust to changes in the environment. Adaptive functions include *research and development*, *market research*, and *long-range planning*, which allow an organization to learn from and attempt to manage its environment and thus increase its core competences. At the B.A.R. and Grille, developing new menu choices to keep up with customers' changing tastes is an important adaptive activity.

Managerial functions facilitate the control and coordination of activities within and among departments. Managers at different organizational levels direct the *acquisition of, investment in, and control of resources* to improve the organization's ability to create value. Top management, for example, is responsible for formulating strategy and establishing the policies the organization uses to control its environment. Middle managers are responsible for managing the organization's resources to meet its goals. Lower-level managers oversee and direct the activities of the workforce.

Differentiation at the B.A.R. and Grille

In the B.A.R. and Grille, differentiation at first was minimal. The owners, with the help of one other person, did all the work. But with unexpected success came the need to differentiate activities into separate organizational roles and functions, with Bob managing the kitchen and Amanda the dining room. As the restaurant continued to grow, Bob and Amanda were confronted with the need to develop skills and capabilities in the five functional areas. For the support role, they hired a restaurant services manager to take charge of purchasing supplies and local advertising. To handle the production role, they increased the division of labor in the kitchen and dining room. They hired cleaning staff, cashiers, and an external accountant for maintenance tasks. They themselves handled the adaptive role of ensuring that the organization served customer needs. Finally, Bob and Amanda took on the managerial role of establishing the pattern of task and functional relationships that most effectively accomplished the restaurant's overall task of serving customers good food. Collectively, the five functions constituted the B.A.R. and Grille and gave it the ability to create value.

As soon as the owners decided to open new kinds of restaurants and expand the size of their organization, they faced the challenge of differentiating into divisions, to control the operation of three restaurants simultaneously. The organization grew to three divisions, each of which made use of support functions centralized at the top of the organization (see Figure 4.1E). In large organizations each division is likely to have its own set of the five basic functions and is thus a *self-contained division*.

As Chapter 1 discusses, functional skills and abilities are the source of an organization's *core competences*, the set of unique skills and capabilities that give it a competitive advantage.[5] An organization's competitive advantage may lie in any or all of an organization's functions. An organization could have superior low-cost production, exceptional managerial talent, or a leading R&D department.[6] A core competence of the B.A.R. and Grille was the way Bob and Amanda took control of the differentiation of their restaurant and increased its ability to attract customers who appreciated the good food and good service they received. In short, they created a core competence that gave their restaurant a competitive advantage over other restaurants. In turn, this competitive advantage gave them access to resources that allowed them to expand by opening new restaurants.

Figure 4.3 **Organizational Chart of the B.A.R. and Grille**

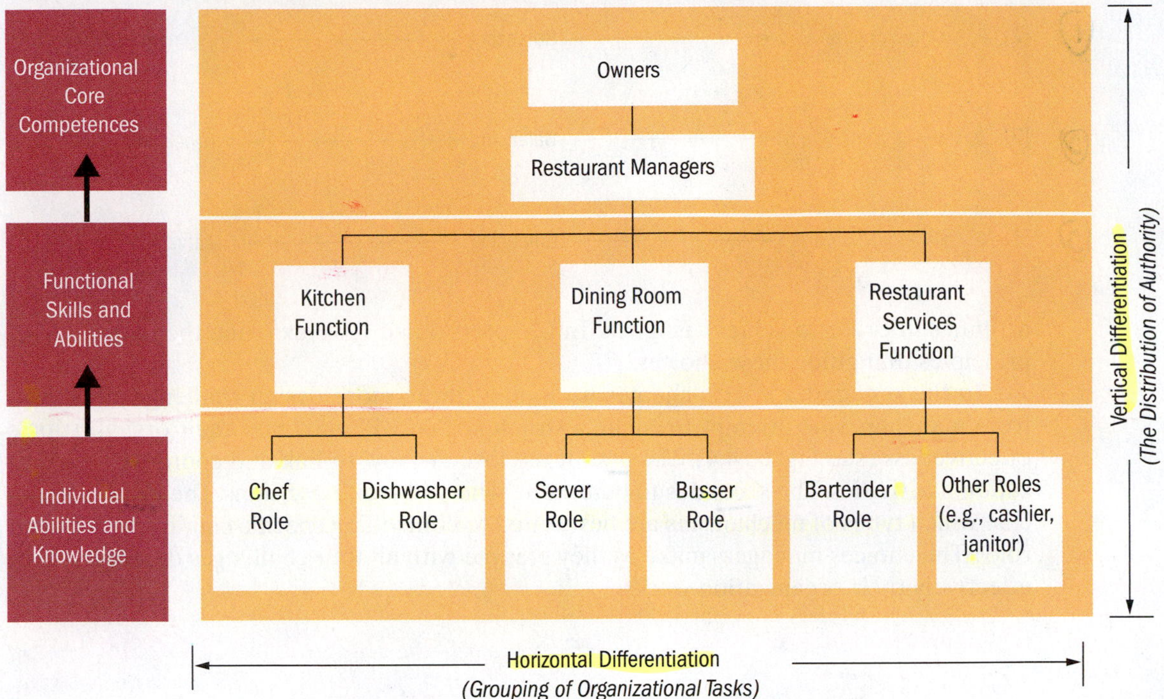

Vertical and Horizontal Differentiation

Figure 4.3 shows the organizational chart that emerged in the B.A.R. and Grille as differentiation unfolded. An organizational chart is a drawing that shows the end result of organizational differentiation. Each box on the chart represents a role or function in the organization. Each role has a vertical and a horizontal dimension.

The organizational chart *vertically* differentiates organizational roles in terms of the amount of authority that goes with each role. A classification of people according to their relative authority and rank is called a **hierarchy.** Roles at the top of an organization's hierarchy possess more authority and responsibility than do roles farther down in the hierarchy; each lower role is under the control or supervision of a higher one. Managers designing an organization have to make decisions about how much vertical differentiation to have in the organization—that is, how many levels should there be from top to bottom. To maintain control over the various functions in the restaurant, for example, Bob and Amanda realized that they needed to create the role of restaurant manager. Because the restaurant manager would report to them and would supervise lower-level employees, this new role added a level to the hierarchy. **Vertical differentiation** refers to the way an organization designs its hierarchy of authority and creates reporting relationships to link organizational roles and subunits.[7] Vertical differentiation establishes the distribution of authority between levels to give the organization more control over its activities and increase its ability to create value.

Hierarchy
A classification of people according to authority and rank.

Vertical differentiation
The way an organization designs its hierarchy of authority and creates reporting relationships to link organizational roles and subunits.

The organizational chart *horizontally* differentiates roles according to their main task responsibilities. For example, when Bob and Amanda realized that a more complex division of tasks would increase restaurant effectiveness, they created new organizational roles—such as restaurant manager, cashier, bartender, and busser—and grouped these roles into functions. **Horizontal differentiation** refers to the way an organization groups organizational tasks into roles and roles into subunits (functions and divisions).[8] Horizontal differentiation establishes the division of labor that enables people in an organization to become more specialized and productive and increases its ability to create value.

Horizontal differentiation
The way an organization groups organizational tasks into roles and roles into subunits (functions and divisions).

Organizational Design Challenges

We have seen that the principal design challenge facing an organization is to choose the levels of vertical and horizontal differentiation that allow the organization to control its

Figure 4.4 Organizational Design Challenges

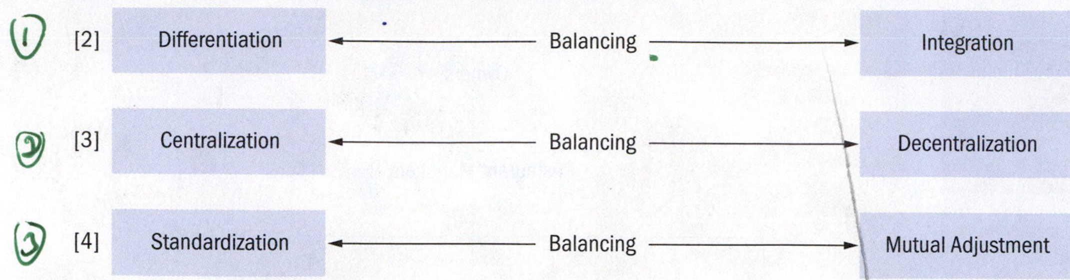

activities in order to achieve its goals. In Chapters 5 and 6 we examine the major design principles that guide these choices.

In the remainder of this chapter we look at three more design challenges that confront managers who attempt to create a structure that will maximize their organization's effectiveness (see Figure 4.4). The first of the three is how to link and coordinate organizational activities. The second is to determine who will make decisions. The third is to decide which types of mechanisms are best suited to controlling specific employee tasks and roles. The choices managers make as they grapple with all four challenges determine how effectively their organization works.

Managerial Implications

Differentiation

1. No matter what your position in an organization, draw an organizational chart so you can identify the distribution of authority and the division of labor.
2. No matter how few or how many people you work with or supervise, analyze each person's role and the relationships among roles to make sure the division of labor is best for the task being performed. If it is not, redefine role relationships and responsibilities.
3. If you supervise more than one function or department, analyze relationships among departments to make sure the division of labor best suits the organization's mission: the creation of value for stakeholders.

Mediolmages/Photodisc/Thinkstock

IT solutions such as enterprise management systems and mobile computing applications are help ing organizations promote cooperation and communication among their subunits in real time.

Balancing Differentiation and Integration

Horizontal differentiation is supposed to enable people to specialize and thus become more productive. However, companies have often found that specialization limits communication between subunits and prevents them from learning from one another. As a result of horizontal differentiation, the members of different functions or divisions develop a **subunit orientation**—a tendency to view one's role in the organization strictly from the perspective of the time frame, goals, and interpersonal orientations of one's subunit.[9] For example, the production department is most concerned with reducing costs and increasing quality; thus it tends to have a short-term outlook because cost and quality are production goals that must be met daily. In R&D, in contrast, innovations to the production process may take years to come to fruition; thus R&D employees usually have a longer term outlook. When different functions see things differently, communication fails and coordination becomes difficult, if not impossible.

Subunit orientation
A tendency to view one's role in the organization strictly from the perspective of the time frame, goals, and interpersonal orientations of one's subunit.

To avoid the communication problems that can arise from horizontal differentiation, organizations try to find new or better ways to integrate functions—that is, to promote cooperation, coordination, and communication among separate subunits. Most large companies today use advanced forms of IT that allow different functions or divisions to share databases, memos, and reports, often on a real-time basis. Increasingly, companies are using electronic means of communication like email, teleconferencing, and enterprise management systems to bring different functions together. For example, buyers at Walmart's home office use television linkups to show each individual store the appropriate way to display products for sale. Nestlé uses advanced enterprise management systems that supply all functions with detailed information about the ongoing activities of other functions.

Integration and Integrating Mechanisms

How to facilitate communication and coordination among subunits is a major challenge for managers. One reason for problems on this front is the development of subunit orientations that makes communication difficult and complex. Another reason for lack of coordination and communication is that managers often fail to use the appropriate mechanisms and techniques to integrate organizational subunits. **Integration** is the process of coordinating various tasks, functions, and divisions so they work together, not at cross purposes. Table 4.1 lists seven integrating mechanisms or techniques that managers can use as their organization's level of differentiation increases.[10] The simplest mechanism is a hierarchy of authority; the most complex is a department created specifically to coordinate the activities of diverse functions or divisions. The table includes examples of how a company like Johnson & Johnson might use all seven types of integration mechanisms as it goes about managing one major product line—disposable diapers. We examine each mechanism separately.

Integration
The process of coordinating various tasks, functions, and divisions so that they work together and not at cross purposes.

HIERARCHY OF AUTHORITY The simplest integrating technique is the organization's hierarchy of authority, which differentiates people by the amount of authority they possess. Because the hierarchy dictates who reports to whom, it coordinates various organizational roles. Managers must carefully divide and allocate authority within a function and between one function and others to promote coordination. For example, at Becton Dickinson, a high-tech medical instrument maker, the marketing and engineering departments were frequently squabbling over product specifications. Marketing argued that the company's products needed more features to please customers. Engineering wanted to simplify product design to reduce costs.[11] The two departments could not resolve their differences because the head of marketing reported to the head of engineering. To resolve this conflict, Becton Dickinson reorganized its hierarchy so that both marketing and engineering reported to the head of the Instrument Product Division.

Design Challenge 2

We can't get people to communicate and coordinate in this organization. Specifying tasks and roles is supposed to help coordinate the work process, but here it builds barriers between people and functions.

TABLE 4.1 Types and Examples of Integrating Mechanisms

Integration Mechanism (In Order of Increasing Complexity)	Description	Example (e.g., in Johnson & Johnson)
Hierarchy of authority	A ranking of employees integrates by specifying who reports to whom.	Salesperson reports to Diaper Division sales manager.
Direct contact	Managers meet face to face to coordinate activities.	Diaper Division sales and manufacturing managers meet to discuss scheduling.
Liaison role	A specific manager is given responsibility for coordinating with managers from other subunits on behalf of his or her subunit.	A person from each of J&J's production, marketing, and research and development departments is given responsibility for coordinating with the other departments.
Task force	Managers meet in temporary committees to coordinate cross-functional activities.	A committee is formed to find new ways to recycle diapers.
Team	Managers meet regularly in permanent committees to coordinate activities.	A permanent J&J committee is established to promote new-product development in the Diaper Division.
Integrating role	A new role is established to coordinate the activities of two or more functions or divisions.	One manager takes responsibility for coordinating Diaper and Baby Soap divisions to enhance their marketing activities.
Integrating department	A new department is created to coordinate the activities of functions or divisions.	A team of managers is created to take responsibility for coordinating J&J's centralization program to allow divisions to share skills and resources.

The head of the division was an impartial third party who had the authority to listen to both managers' cases and make the decision that was best for the organization as a whole.

DIRECT CONTACT Direct contact between people in different subunits is a second integrating mechanism; there are often more problems associated with using it effectively than with the hierarchy of authority. The principal problem with integration across functions is that a manager in one function has *no authority* over a manager in another. Only the CEO or some other top manager above the functional level has power to intervene if two functions come into conflict. Consequently, establishing personal relationships and professional contacts between people at all levels in different functions is a crucial step to overcome the problems that arise because subunit orientations differ. Managers from different functions who have the ability to make direct contact with one another can then work together to solve common problems—and prevent them from arising in the first place. If disputes still occur, however, it is important for both parties to be able to appeal to a common superior who is not far removed from the scene of the problem.

LIAISON ROLES As the need for communication between two subunits becomes increasingly important, often because of a rapidly changing environment, one or a few members from each subunit are often given the primary responsibility to work together to coordinate subunit activities. The people who hold these connecting, or liaison, roles are able to develop in-depth relations with people in other subunits. This interaction helps overcome barriers between subunits. Over time, as the people in liaison roles learn to cooperate, they can become increasingly flexible in accommodating other subunits' requests. Figure 4.5A illustrates a liaison role.

Task force
A temporary committee set up to handle a specific problem.

TASK FORCES As an organization increases in size and complexity, more than two subunits may need to work together to solve common problems. Increasing an organization's ability to serve its customers effectively, for example, may require input from production, marketing, engineering, and R&D. The solution commonly takes the form of a **task force,** a temporary committee set up to handle a specific problem (Figure 4.5B). One or a few members of each function join a task force that meets regularly until a solution to the problem is found. Task force members are then responsible for taking the solution back to their functions to gain

Figure 4.5 Integrating Mechanisms

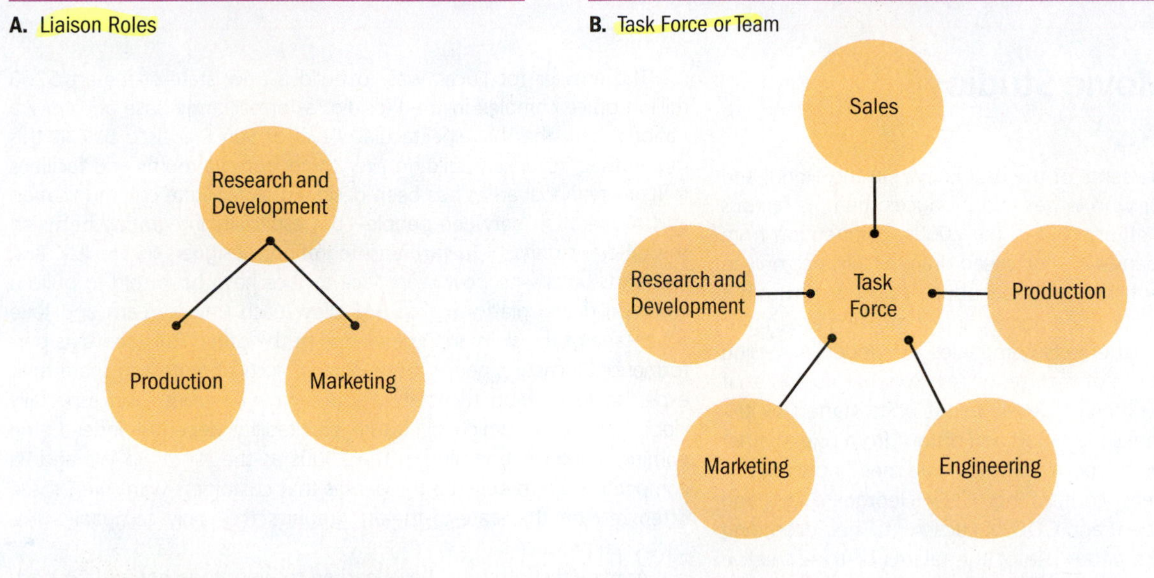

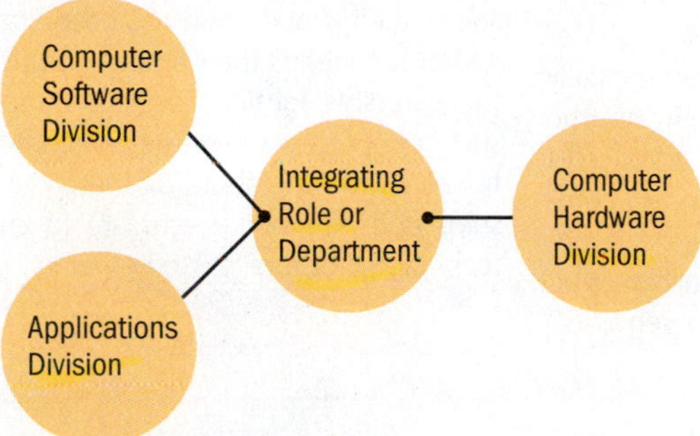

• Indicates managers with responsibility for integration between subunits.

their input and approval. To increase the effectiveness of task forces, a senior manager who is not a member of any of the functions involved usually chairs the meetings.

TEAMS When the issue a task force is dealing with becomes an ongoing strategic or administrative issue, the task force becomes permanent. A *team* is a permanent task force or committee. Most companies today, for example, have formed product development and customer-contact teams to monitor and respond to the ongoing challenges of increased competition in a global market. As discussed in Organizational Insight 4.2, LucasArts, one of the most successful movie studios, moved to a team-based organization to make the most of the talents of its creative designers.

Managers spend about 70% of their time in committee meetings.[14] Teams provide the opportunity for the face-to-face contact and continual adjustment that managers need to deal effectively with ongoing complex issues. As they set up a team structure, managers face the ongoing challenge of creating a committee system that gives them effective control over organizational activities. Sometimes teams become ineffective over time because the problems facing the organization change but team membership and structure remains unchanged. People often fight to stay on a committee, or protect their team, because team membership gives a person power in the organization. But this power does not necessarily promote organizational goals. At Whirlpool, the appliance maker, its then CEO David Whitwam pioneered the establishment of hundreds of mini-management teams throughout the company to bring about change, improve quality control, and streamline production. Whitwam's goal? To use teams to change patterns of authority and decision making to increase interaction and promote creativity among managers.[15]

Organizational Insight 4.2

Integrating a Movie Studio

The Star Wars movies are some of the best known in the world, and George Lucas, the director who writes and produces them, is famous for his pioneering special effects. But in the 2000s, competition from other special effects companies has increased dramatically, not only in the development of state-of-the-art special effects for new movies but also in the production of new video games, a fast-growing and highly profitable market. All special effects companies are under increasing pressure to make the best use of their resources. So what do you do if your company has many different development units staffed by talented engineers but that are so far apart and distant from one another that they have no incentive to cooperate and share their knowledge?

This was the problem confronting CEO George Lucas and Micheline Chau, the president and COO of LucasArts. Their overriding problem was how to make better use of the talents of their creative digital artists and engineers who worked in a very autonomous way—often working independently and connected to their coworkers mainly by video conferencing systems that allow them to share their ideas.[12]

By 2008 Lucas and Chau realized they had to find a way to integrate the activities of designers in the various groups; they especially needed to make more use of its Industrial Light & Magic Group, the unit responsible for the special effects behind the Star Wars movies and that also creates the special effects for many other movie companies. How do you encourage different groups to cooperate, especially when each contains hundreds of talented design artists who value their own autonomy and are proud of their own achievements?

The answer for Lucas was to build a new state-of-the-art $250 million office complex in the Presidio, a former army base and now a national park that has spectacular views of San Francisco Bay. In this modernistic, futuristic building everything from its rooms and facilities to its recreational areas has been designed to facilitate communication and cooperation between people—but especially integration between the different units.[13] To further integration, designers in the ILM and LucasArts units who now work face to face have been told to build a common digital platform that will allow each unit to learn and take advantage of the skills and knowledge of the other. To increase its performance, LucasArts needs these experts to collaborate and share their expertise to develop the state-of-the-art new movies, and especially video games, on which its future profitability depends. Indeed, the gaming market is booming in the 2000s as the Nintendo Wii and its competitors vie to develop the games that customers want, and these often rely on the state-of-the-art graphics that only companies like Lucas can produce.

Apparently both units have learned to work together and take advantage of the open inviting lounges and work areas where designers can meet personally to share their skills and knowledge. One recent result of their cooperation has been Star Wars: The Force Unleashed. The ILM group credits the gaming groups for providing the technology for the incredible lighting, facial, and movement effects that have made it such a popular video game. Who knows what might be in store in the future as the members of these units develop the personal relationships and networks necessary to create the next generation digital technology for movies and gaming.

INTEGRATING ROLES OR DEPARTMENTS As organizations become large and complex, communication barriers between functions and divisions are likely to increase. Managers in divisions making different products, for example, may never meet one another. Coordinating subunits is especially difficult in organizations that employ many thousands of people. One way to overcome these barriers is to create integrating roles that coordinate subunits. An **integrating role** is a *full-time* managerial position established specifically to improve communication between divisions. (A liaison role, by contrast, is just one of the tasks involved in a person's full-time job.) Figure 4.5C shows an integrating role that might exist in a large computer company like Dell or Apple.

Integrating role
A full-time position established specifically to improve communication between divisions.

The purpose of an integrating role is to promote the sharing of information and knowledge to better pursue organizational goals such as product innovation, increased flexibility, and improved customer service. People in integrating roles are often senior managers who have decided to give up authority in a specific function and focus on company-wide integration. They often chair important task forces and teams and report back directly to top management.

When a company has many employees in integrating roles, it creates an integrating department that coordinates the activities of all subunits. Du Pont, the chemical maker, has a department that employs over 200 people in integrating roles; so do Microsoft and IBM. In general, the more complex and highly differentiated an organization, the more complex are the integration mechanisms it needs to overcome communication and coordination barriers between functions and divisions.

Differentiation versus Integration

The design issue facing managers is to establish a level of integration that matches the organization's level of differentiation. Managers must achieve an appropriate *balance* between differentiation and integration. A complex organization that is highly differentiated needs a high level of integration to coordinate its activities effectively. By contrast, when an organization has a relatively simple, clearly defined role structure, it normally needs to use only simple integrating mechanisms. Its managers may find that the hierarchy of authority provides all the control and coordination they need to achieve organizational goals.

At all costs, managers need to be sure they do not differentiate or integrate their organization too much. Differentiation and integration are both expensive in terms of the number of managers employed and the amount of managerial time spent on coordinating organizational activities. For example, every hour that employees spend on committees that are not really needed costs the organization thousands of dollars because these employees are not being put to their most productive use.

Managers facing the challenge of deciding how and how much to differentiate and integrate must do two things: (1) carefully guide the process of differentiation so an organization builds the core competences that give it a competitive advantage; and (2) carefully integrate the organization by choosing appropriate coordinating mechanisms that allow subunits to cooperate and work together to strengthen its core competences.[16]

Balancing Centralization and Decentralization

In discussing vertical differentiation, we note that establishing a hierarchy of authority is supposed to improve the way an organization functions because people can be held accountable for their actions: The hierarchy defines the area of each person's authority within the organization. Many companies, however, complain that when a hierarchy exists, employees are constantly looking to their superiors for direction.[17] When some new or unusual issue arises, they prefer not to deal with it, or they pass it on to their superior, rather than assume responsibility and the risk of dealing with it. As responsibility and risk taking decline so does organizational performance, because its members do not take advantage of new opportunities for using its core competences. When nobody is willing to take responsibility, decision making becomes slow and the organization becomes inflexible—that is, unable to change and adapt to new developments.

At Levi Strauss, for example, employees often told former CEO Roger Sant that they felt they couldn't do something because "*They* wouldn't like it." When asked who "they" were, employees had a hard time saying; nevertheless, the employees felt they did not have the authority or responsibility to initiate changes. Sant started a "Theybusters" campaign to renegotiate authority and responsibility relationships so employees could take on new responsibilities.[18] The solution involved decentralizing authority; that is, employees at lower levels in the hierarchy were given the authority to decide how to handle problems and issues that arose while they performed their jobs. The issues of how much to centralize or decentralize the authority to make decisions offers a basic design challenge for all organizations.

Centralization versus Decentralization of Authority

Authority gives one person the power to hold other people accountable for their actions and the right to make decisions about the use of organizational resources. As we saw in the B.A.R. and Grille example, vertical differentiation involves choices about how to distribute authority. But even when a hierarchy of authority exists, the problem of how much decision-making authority to delegate to each level must be solved.

It is possible to design an organization in which managers at the top of the hierarchy have all power to make important decisions. Subordinates take orders from the top, are accountable for how well they obey those orders, and have no authority to initiate new actions or use resources for purposes that they believe are important. When the authority

Design Challenge 3

People in this organization don't take responsibility or risks. They are always looking to the boss for direction and supervision. As a result, decision making is slow and cumbersome, and we miss out on a lot of opportunities to create value.

to make important decisions is retained by managers at the top of the hierarchy, authority is said to be highly **centralized.**[19] By contrast, when the authority to make important decisions about organizational resources and to initiate new projects is delegated to managers at all levels in the hierarchy, authority is highly **decentralized.**

Centralized
Organizational setup in which the authority to make important decisions is retained by managers at the top of the hierarchy.

Decentralized
An organizational setup in which the authority to make important decisions about organizational resources and to initiate new projects is delegated to managers at all levels in the hierarchy.

Each alternative has certain advantages and disadvantages. The advantage of centralization is that it lets top managers coordinate organizational activities and keep the organization focused on its goals. Centralization becomes a problem, however, when top managers become overloaded and immersed in operational decision making about day-to-day resource issues (such as hiring people and obtaining inputs). When this happens they have little time to spend on long-term strategic decision making, and planning crucial future organizational activities, such as deciding on the best strategy to compete globally, is neglected.

Organizational Insight 4.3

To Decentralize or Centralize Are Important Choices at Union Pacific and Yahoo!

Union Pacific (UP), one of the biggest railroad freight carriers in the United States, faced a crisis when an economic boom in the early 2000s led to a record increase in the amount of freight the railroad had to transport—but at the same time the railroad was experiencing record delays in moving this freight. UP's customers complained bitterly about the problem, and the delays cost the company tens of millions of dollars in penalty payments. Why the problem? UP's top managers decided to centralize authority high in the organization and to standardize operations to cut operating costs. All scheduling and route planning were handled centrally at headquarters to increase efficiency. The job of regional managers was largely to ensure the smooth flow of freight through their regions.

Recognizing that efficiency had to be balanced by the need to be responsive to customers, UP announced a sweeping reorganization. Regional managers would have the authority to make everyday operational decisions; they could alter scheduling and routing to accommodate customer requests even if it raised costs. UP's goal was to "return to excellent performance by simplifying our processes and becoming easier to deal with." In deciding to decentralize authority, UP was following the lead of its competitors that had already decentralized their operations. Its managers would continue to "decentralize decision making into the field, while fostering improved customer responsiveness, operational excellence, and personal accountability." The result has been continued success for the company; in fact, in 2011 several large companies recognized Union Pacific as the top railroad in on-time service performance and customer service.[20]

Yahoo! has been forced by circumstances to pursue a different approach to decentralization. In 2009, after Microsoft failed to take over Yahoo! because of the resistance of Jerry Wang, a company founder, the company's stock price plunged. Wang, who had come under intense criticism for preventing the merger, resigned as CEO and was replaced by Carol Bartz, who had a long history of success in managing online companies. Bartz moved quickly to find ways to reduce Yahoo!'s cost structure and simplify its operations to maintain its strong online brand identity. Intense competition from the growing popularity of online companies such as Google, Facebook, and Twitter also threatened its popularity.

Bartz decided the best way to restructure Yahoo! was to recentralize authority. To gain more control over its different business units and reduce operating costs, she decided to centralize functions that had

StonePhotos/Shutterstock.com

© Danieloizo/Dreamstime.com

previously been performed by Yahoo!'s different business units, such as product development and marketing activities.[21] For example, all the company's publishing and advertising functions were centralized and put under the control of a single executive. Yahoo!'s European, Asian, and emerging markets divisions were centralized, and another top executive took control. Bartz's goal was to find out how she could make the company's resources perform better. While she was centralizing authority she was also holding many "town hall" meetings asking Yahoo! employees from all functions, "What would you do if you were me?" Even as she centralized authority to help Yahoo! recover its dominant industry position, she was looking for the input of employees at every level in the hierarchy.

Nevertheless, in 2011 Yahoo! was still in a precarious position. It had signed a search agreement with Microsoft to use the latter's search technology, Bing; Bartz had focused on selling off Yahoo!'s noncore business assets to reduce costs and gain the money for strategic acquisitions. But the company was still in an intense battle with other dot-coms that had more resources, such as Google and Facebook, and in 2011 Bartz made it clear the company was still for sale—at the right price.[22]

The advantage of decentralization is that it promotes flexibility and responsiveness by allowing lower-level managers to make on-the-spot decisions. Managers remain accountable for their actions but have the opportunity to assume greater responsibilities and take potentially successful risks. Also, when authority is decentralized managers can make important decisions that allow them to demonstrate their personal skills and competences and may be more motivated to perform well for the organization. The downside of decentralization is that if so much authority is delegated that managers at all levels can make their own decisions, planning and coordination become very difficult. Thus too much decentralization may lead an organization to lose control of its decision-making process! Organizational Insight 4.3 reveals many of the issues surrounding this design choice.

As these examples suggest, the design challenge for managers is to decide on the correct balance between centralization and decentralization of decision making in an organization. If authority is too decentralized, managers have so much freedom that they can pursue their own functional goals and objectives at the expense of organizational goals. In contrast, if authority is too centralized and top management makes all important decisions, managers lower down in the hierarchy become afraid to make new moves and lack the freedom to respond to problems as they arise in their own groups and departments.

The ideal situation is a balance between centralization and decentralization of authority so that middle and lower managers who are at the scene of the action are allowed to make important decisions, and top managers' primary responsibility becomes managing long-term strategic decision making. The result is a good balance between long-term strategy making and short-term flexibility and innovation as lower-level managers respond quickly to problems and changes in the environment as they occur.

Why were the Levi Strauss managers so reluctant to take on new responsibilities and assume extra authority? A previous management team had centralized authority so that it could retain day-to-day control over important decision making. The company's performance suffered, however, because in spending all their time on day-to-day operations, top managers lost sight of changing customer needs and evolving trends in the clothing industry. The new top management team that took over recognized the need to delegate authority for operational decision making to lower-level managers so that they could concentrate on long-term strategic decision making. Consequently, top management decentralized authority until they believed they had achieved the correct balance.

As noted earlier, the way managers and employees behave in an organization is a direct result of managers' decisions about how the organization is to operate. Managers who want to discourage risk taking and to maximize control over subordinates' performance centralize authority. Managers who want to encourage risk taking and innovation decentralize authority. In the army, for example, the top brass generally wishes to discourage lower-level officers from acting on their own initiative, for if they did, the power of centralized command would be gone and the army would splinter. Consequently, the army has a highly centralized decision-making system that operates by strict rules and with a well-defined hierarchy of authority. By contrast, at Amgen and

Becton Dickson, a medical equipment maker, authority is decentralized and employees are provided with a broad framework within which they are free to make their own decisions and take risks, as long as these are consistent with the company's master plan. In general, high-tech companies decentralize authority because this encourages innovation and risk taking.

Decisions about how to distribute decision-making authority in an organization change as an organization changes—that is, as it grows and differentiates. How to balance authority is not a design decision that can be made once and forgotten; it must be made on an ongoing basis and is an essential part of the managerial task. We examine this issue in detail in Chapters 5 and 6.

Balancing Standardization and Mutual Adjustment

Written rules and standard operating procedures (SOPs) and unwritten values and norms are important forms of behavior control in organizations. They specify *how* employees are to perform their organizational roles, and they set forth the tasks and responsibilities associated with each role. Many companies, however, complain that employees tend to follow written and unwritten guidelines too rigidly instead of adapting them to the needs of a particular situation. Strictly following rules may stifle innovation; detailed rules specifying how decisions are to be made leave no room for creativity and imaginative responses to unusual circumstances. As a result, decision making becomes inflexible and organizational performance suffers.

Dell, for example, was well known as a company that strived to be close to its customers and responsive to their needs. But as Dell grew in the 2000s it developed a standardized response to customers' requests; it only offered customers a limited range of PCs and a limited number of options to keep its costs low. Standardizing operations to reduce costs had become more important than giving customers what they wanted, for example, more powerful laptops that came in a range of colors—something that was driving increasing sales at Apple and HP. In addition, its rapid growth led to internal communication problems among Dell's different functions; increasingly communication took place through formal rules and by committee, and this slowed product development and reduced Dell's ability to offer customers new PCs that had the design and features that could compete with Apple and HP. Dell has still not recovered from this problem. In 2011 its new lines of computers still were not attracting enough customers and it was losing market share to Apple, which seemed to be able to anticipate what customers wanted from new computing devices, such as tablet computers. Apple moves quickly to design new models because a focused team of employees was in charge of each of its different products lines, for example, iPhones and iPads, and were continually searching for ways to improve their performance.

Standardization
Conformity to specific models or examples—defined by sets of rules and norms—that are considered proper in a given situation.

Mutual adjustment
The compromise that emerges when decision making and coordination are evolutionary processes and people use their judgment rather than standardized rules to address a problem.

The challenge facing all organizations, large and small, is to design a structure that achieves the right balance between standardization and mutual adjustment. **Standardization** is conformity to specific models or examples—defined by well-established sets of rules and norms—that are considered proper in a given situation. Standardized decision-making and coordination through rules and procedures make people's actions routine and predictable.[23] **Mutual adjustment,** on the other hand, is the evolving process through which people use their current best judgment of events rather than standardized rules to address problems, guide decision making, and promote coordination. The right balance makes many actions predictable so that ongoing organizational tasks and goals are achieved, yet it gives employees the freedom to behave flexibly so they can respond to new and changing situations creatively.

Formalization
The use of written rules and procedures to standardize operations.

Rules
Formal written statements that specify the appropriate means for reaching desired goals.

Formalization: Written Rules

Formalization is the use of written rules and procedures to standardize operations.[24] **Rules** are formal written statements that specify the appropriate means for reaching desired goals. When people follow rules, they behave in accordance with certain specified principles. In an organization in which formalization and standardization are extensive—for example, the military, FedEx, or UPS—everything is done by the book. There is no room for mutual adjustment; rules specify how people are to perform their roles and how decisions are to be made, and employees are accountable for following the rules. Moreover, employees have no authority to break the rules.

A high level of formalization typically implies centralization of authority. A low level of formalization implies that coordination is the product of mutual adjustment among people across organizational functions and that decision making is a dynamic process in which employees apply their skills and abilities to respond to change and solve problems. Mutual adjustment typically implies decentralization of authority because employees must have the authority to commit the organization to certain actions when they make decisions.

Socialization: Understood Norms

Norms
Standards or styles of behavior that are considered acceptable or typical for a group of people.

Norms are standards or styles of behavior that are considered typical or representative of a certain group of people and which also regulate and govern their behavior. Members of the group follow a norm because it is a generally agreed-upon standard for behavior. Many norms arise informally as people work together over time. In some organizations it is the norm that people take an hour and a quarter for lunch, despite a formally specified one-hour lunch break; in others it is the norm that no one leaves until 6:30 pm—or before the boss. Over time, norms influence and control the way people and groups view and respond to a particular event or situation.

Although many organizational norms—such as always behaving courteously to customers and leaving the work area clean—promote organizational effectiveness, many do not. Studies have shown that groups of employees can develop norms that reduce performance. Several studies have found that work groups can directly control the pace or speed at which work is performed by imposing informal sanctions on employees who break the informal norms governing behavior in a work group. An employee who works too quickly (above group productivity norms) is called a "ratebuster," and an employee who works too slowly (below group norms) is called a "chiseler."[25] Having established a group norm, employees actively enforce it by physically and emotionally punishing violators.

This process occurs at all levels in the organization. Suppose a group of middle managers has adopted the norm of not rocking the organizational boat by changing outdated work rules, even if this will increase efficiency. A new manager who enters the picture will soon learn from the others that rocking the boat does not pay as other managers find ways to punish the new person for violating this norm, even if a little shaking up is what the organization really needs. Even a new manager who is high in the hierarchy will have difficulty changing the informal norms of the organization.

The taken-for-granted way in which norms affect behavior has another consequence for organizational effectiveness. We noted in the Levi Strauss example that even when an organization changes formal work rules, the behavior of people does not change quickly. Why is behavior rigid when rules change? The reason is that rules come to be internalized, that is, they become part of a person's psychological makeup so that *external* rules become *internalized* norms. When this happens, it is very difficult for people to break a familiar rule and follow a new rule; also they will slip back into the old way of behaving. Consider, for example, how difficult it is to keep new resolutions and break bad habits.[26]

Paradoxically, an organization often wants members to buy into a particular set of corporate norms and values. Apple, Google, and Intel, for example, cultivate technical and professional norms and values as a means of controlling and standardizing the behavior of

Design Challenge 4

People in this organization pay too much attention to the rules. Whenever I need somebody to satisfy an unusual customer request or need real quick service from another function, I can't get it because no one is willing to bend or break the rules.

highly skilled organizational members. However, once these norms are established they are very difficult to change. And when an organization wants to pursue new goals and foster new norms, people find it difficult to alter their behavior. There is no easy solution to this problem. Organizational members often have to go through a major period of relearning before they understand that they do not need to apply the old set of internalized norms to new situations. Many companies, such as Ford and IBM, have undergone major upheavals to force their members to "unlearn" outdated norms and to internalize new norms, such as ones that encourage innovation and responsiveness to customers.

The name given to the process by which organizational members learn the norms of an organization and internalize these unwritten rules of conduct is **socialization.**[27] In general, organizations can encourage the development of *standardized* responses or *innovative* ones. Chapter 7 examines these issues in more detail.

Socialization
The process by which organizational members learn the norms of an organization and internalize these unwritten rules of conduct.

Standardization versus Mutual Adjustment

The design challenge facing managers is to find the best ways to use rules and norms to standardize behavior while, at the same time, allowing for mutual adjustment to provide employees with the opportunity to discover new and better ways of achieving organizational goals. Managers facing the challenge of balancing the need for standardization against the need for mutual adjustment need to keep in mind that people at higher levels in the hierarchy and in functions that perform complex, uncertain tasks rely more on mutual adjustment than on standardization to coordinate their actions. For example, an organization wants its accountants to follow standard practices in performing their tasks, but in R&D the organization wants to encourage creative behavior that leads to innovation. Many of the integrating mechanisms discussed earlier, such as task forces and teams, can increase mutual adjustment by providing an opportunity for people to meet and work out improved ways of doing things. In addition, an organization can emphasize, as Levi Strauss did, that rules are not set in stone but are just convenient guidelines for getting work done. Managers can also promote norms and values that emphasize change rather than stability. For all organizational roles, however, the appropriate balance between these two variables is one that promotes creative and responsible employee behavior as well as organizational effectiveness, as Focus on Information Technology, Part 3, discusses.

Focus on New Information Technology

Amazon.com, Part 3

How did Jeff Bezos address these design challenges given his need to create a structure to manage an online bookstore that operated through the Internet and never saw its customers, but whose mission was to provide customers a great selection at low prices? Because the success of his venture depended on providing customers with an informative, easy-to-use online storefront, it was vital that customers found Amazon.com's 1-Click checkout system easy and convenient to use and reliable. So, Bezos's design choices were driven by the need to ensure Amazon's software platform linked customers to the organization most effectively.

First, he quickly realized that customer support was the most vital link between customer and organization, so to ensure good customer service he decentralized control and empowered his employees to find ways to meet customer needs quickly. Second, realizing that customers wanted the book quickly, he moved rapidly to develop an efficient distribution and shipping system. Essentially, his main problem was handling inputs into the system (customer requests) and outputs (delivered books). So he developed IT to standardize the work or throughput process to increase efficiency, but he also encouraged mutual adjustment at the input or customer end to improve customers' responsiveness—employees were able to manage exceptions such as lost orders or confused customers as the need arose. (Note that Amazon's IT is also the most important means it uses to integrate cross-functional activities in the organization; IT is the backbone of the company's value-creation activities). Third, because Amazon.com then employed a relatively small number of people—about 2,500 worldwide—Bezos was able to make great use of socialization to coordinate and motivate his employees. Amazon.com employees were carefully selected and socialized by the other members of their functions to help them quickly learn their organizational roles and—most important—Amazon's important norm of providing excellent quality customer service. Finally, to ensure Amazon.com's employees were motivated to provide the best possible customer service, Bezos gives all employees stock in the company. Employees currently own over 10% of their company. Amazon.com's rapid growth suggests that Bezos designed an effective organizational structure.

Managerial Implications

The Design Challenges

1. To see whether there is enough integration between your department and the departments that you interact with the most, create a map of the principal integrating mechanisms in use. If there is not enough integration, develop new integrating mechanisms that will provide the extra coordination needed to improve performance.
2. Determine which levels in the managerial hierarchy have responsibility for approving which decisions. Use your findings to decide how centralized or decentralized decision making is in your organization. Discuss your conclusions with your peers, subordinates, and superior to ascertain whether the distribution of authority best suits the needs of your organization.
3. Make a list of your principal tasks and role responsibilities, and then list the rules and SOPs that specify how you are to perform your duties. Using this information, determine the appropriateness of the rules and SOPs, and suggest ways of changing them so you can perform more effectively. If you are a manager, perform this analysis for your department to improve its effectiveness and to make sure the rules are necessary and efficient.
4. Be aware of the informal norms and values that influence the way members of your work group or department behave. Try to account for the origin of these norms and values and the way they affect behavior. Examine whether they fulfill a useful function in your organization. If they do, try to reinforce them. If they do not, develop a plan for creating new norms and values that will enhance effectiveness.

Mechanistic and Organic Organizational Structures

Each design challenge has implications for how an organization as a whole and the people in the organization behave and perform.

Two useful concepts for understanding how managers manipulate all these challenges collectively to influence the way an organizational structure works are the concepts of mechanistic structure and organic structure.[28] The design choices that produce mechanistic and organic structures are contrasted in Figure 4.6 and discussed below.

Figure 4.6 How the Design Challenges Result in Mechanistic or Organic Structures

Mechanistic structures result when an organization makes these choices.	Organic structures result when an organization makes these choices.
• Individual Specialization Employees work separately and specialize in one clearly defined task.	• Joint Specialization Employees work together and coordinate their actions to find the best way of performing a task.
• Simple Integrating Mechanisms Hierarchy of authority is clearly defined and is the major integrating mechanism.	• Complex Integrating Mechanisms Task forces and teams are the major integrating mechanisms.
• Centralization Authority to control tasks is kept at the top of the organization. Most communication is vertical.	• Decentralization Authority to control tasks is delegated to people at all levels in the organization. Most communication is lateral.
• Standardization Extensive use is made of rules and SOPs to coordinate tasks, and work process is predictable.	• Mutual Adjustment Extensive use is made of face-to-face contact to coordinate tasks, and work process is relatively unpredictable.

Mechanistic Structures

Mechanistic structures Structures that are designed to induce people to behave in predictable, accountable ways.

Mechanistic structures are designed to induce people to behave in predictable, accountable ways. Decision-making authority is centralized, subordinates are closely supervised, and information flows mainly in a vertical direction down a clearly defined hierarchy. In a mechanistic structure, the tasks associated with a role are also clearly defined. There is usually a one-to-one correspondence between a person and a task. Figure 4.7A depicts this situation. Each person is individually specialized and knows exactly what he or she is responsible for, and behavior inappropriate to the role is discouraged or prohibited.

At the functional level, each function is separate, and communication and cooperation among functions are the responsibility of someone at the top of the hierarchy. Thus, in a mechanistic structure, the hierarchy is the principal integrating mechanism both within and between functions. Because tasks are organized to prevent miscommunication, the organization does not need to use complex integrating mechanisms. Tasks and roles are coordinated primarily through standardization, and formal written rules and procedures specify role responsibilities. Standardization, together with the hierarchy, are the main means of organizational control.

Given this emphasis on the vertical command structure, the organization is very status conscious, and norms of "protecting one's turf" are common. Promotion is normally slow, steady, and tied to performance, and each employee's progress in the organization can be charted for years to come. Because of its rigidity, a mechanistic structure is best suited to organizations that face stable environments.

Organic Structures

Organic structures Structures that promote flexibility, so people initiate change and can adapt quickly to changing conditions.

Organic structures are at the opposite end of the organizational design spectrum from mechanistic structures. **Organic structures** promote flexibility, so people initiate change and can adapt quickly to changing conditions.

Organic structures are decentralized so that decision-making authority is distributed throughout the hierarchy; people assume the authority to make decisions as organizational needs dictate. Roles are loosely defined and people continually develop new kinds of job skills to perform continually changing tasks. Figure 4.7B depicts this situation. Each person performs all three tasks, and the result is joint specialization and increased productivity. Employees from different functions work together to solve problems; they become involved in one another's activities. As a result, a high level of integration is needed so that employees can share information and overcome problems caused by differences in subunit orientation. The integration of functions is achieved by means of complex mechanisms like task forces and teams (see Figure 4.6). Coordination is achieved through mutual adjustment as people and functions negotiate role definitions and responsibilities, and informal rules and norms emerge from the ongoing interaction of organizational members.

Figure 4.7 Task and Role Relationships

A. Individual Specialization in a Mechanistic Structure. A person in a role specializes in a specific task or set of tasks.

A B C

X Y Z

B. Joint Specialization in an Organic Structure. A person in a role is assigned to a specific task or set of tasks. However, the person is able to learn new tasks and develop new skills and capabilities.

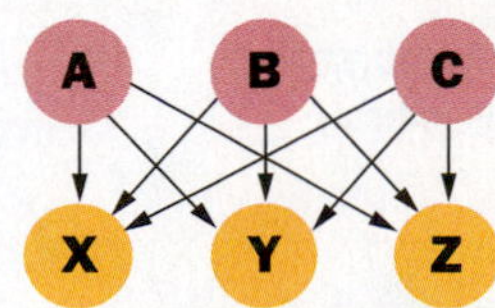

Roles

Tasks

This organic approach to decision making is very different from a mechanistic one. For example, in the IBM of the 1990s, its centralized and standardized product development system meant that getting a decision made was, according to one engineer, "like wading through a tub of peanut butter." But as Google has grown quickly in the 2000s there have been complaints that its organic approach that relied heavily on mutual adjustment is being threatened by the increasing number of rules and committees now used to evaluate new product ideas and innovations. As a result, Google has been trying to find new techniques to retain its organic approach and avoid the "peanut butter" problem.

In an organic structure specific norms and values develop that emphasize personal competence, expertise, and the freedom to act in innovative ways. Status is conferred by the ability to provide creative leadership, not by any formal position in the hierarchy and approach encouraged at Google, Netflix, and Apple. Many organizations such as IBM and Ford whose mechanistic structure made job grade, seniority, and loyalty the foundation of their norms and values have suffered in the past because the result is slow and ponderous decision making, and managers who are afraid to rock the boat—but all this has changed in the last several years as their new CEOs have championed an organic approach.

Clearly, organic and mechanistic structures have very different implications for the way people behave. Is an organic structure better than a mechanistic structure? It seems to encourage the kinds of innovative behaviors that are considered desirable: teamwork and self-management to improve quality, customer service, and reduce the time needed to get new products to market. However, would you want to use an organic structure to coordinate the armed forces? Probably not, because of the many authority and status problems that would arise in getting the army, air force, marines, and navy to cooperate. Would you want an organic structure in a nuclear power plant? Probably not, if employees adopt a creative, novel response in an emergency situation or simply make mistakes through human error that may result in a catastrophe. Would you even want an organic structure in a restaurant, in which chefs take the roles of servers and servers take the roles of chefs, and authority and power relationships are worked out on an ongoing basis? Probably not, because the one-to-one correspondence of person and role allows each restaurant employee to perform his or her role in the most effective manner. Conversely, would you want to use a mechanistic structure in a high-tech company like Apple or Google where innovation is a function of the skills and abilities of teams of creative software engineers working jointly on a project? Organizational Insight 4.4 describes how Google has been forced to manage this difficult balancing act as it has grown over the last several years.

Organizational Insight 4.4

Google Has a Social Networking Problem

Google founders Larry Page and Sergey Brin went to great lengths to create and design an organizational culture for their company that emphasizes innovation—and they still do (see Chapter 7). However, the company's rapid rate of growth added over 80,000 employees in the last three years, and by 2011 it employed over 136,000 people. Google's rapid growth that resulted from its entry into an increasing number of different product markets, such as smartphone software and social networking, led many analysts to claim that Google, despite being entrepreneurial at the level of the product group, had become too bureaucratic at the level of the whole organization.

The issue facing Google was that its product groups had split apart and were now pursuing their own interests. While this had resulted in many major gains, such as its Android software, chrome browser, and ever advancing search and online advertising competences, it was also making many mistakes because overall company goals were not being achieved. This was because the different product groups' activities were often incompatible and at cross-purposes. However, crucially, it was also because each group's relentless attempt to pursue its own interests resulted in the company's attempts to increase its strength in online social networking, such as through its "Google Wave" initiative to compete with Facebook, had all failed.

After Larry Page took over as CEO from Eric Schmidt in 2011, Schmidt admitted that his biggest mistake as CEO was that he had not recognized the major challenge posed by social networking sites such as

Sergej Khakimullin/Shutterstock.com

Twitter and in particular Facebook, whose user base had grown from 40 million users in 2007 to 500,000 million by 2011. Google's search technology cannot search within Facebook's pages, so while Facebook could build up a huge library of specific details about the interests of its members to sell to online advertisers, Google was unable to tap into this goldmine. Why is this so important? Because targeted online advertising is the key to earning higher sales revenues and by 2010 Facebook's own targeted advertising program to its 500 million users was earning it billions of dollars. It seemed that Facebook's rapid growth into online advertising would choke off Google's attempts to remain the leader so they would become fierce competitors in the online advertising market.

So in 2011 the issue facing Larry Page and his top management team was to find ways to reduce bureaucracy at the top in Google to rapidly advance its competence in social networking—it had to find ways to integrate the actions of all its different product groups to promote its competence in social networking. Page created a new top management committee—all the heads of Google's product groups are now required to meet once a week with Page to further integration and mutual adjustment to keep the company on track to succeed in social networking. As Vic Gundotra, who is in charge of Google's secret project to combat the social network Facebook commented, "We needed to get these different product leaders together to find time to talk through all the integration. Every time we increase the size of the company, we need to keep things going to make sure we keep our speed, pace, and passion."[29]

Page's task is not easy because each of Google's product groups are led by strong, charismatic leaders who aggressively pursue their own agendas and the problem is how to get these managers to work together. For example, the Android group must find ways to cooperate with the Chrome group to further social networking, and the search group has to coordinate with the advertising group to find ways to target customers at the city level, like Groupon.

In 2011 this was Google's central challenge. Page made clear how important he views this challenge by linking a substantial part of each top manager's, and the members of each product group's, annual bonus and stock options, worth tens or hundreds of millions of dollars, to how well the company performs in its online social networking initiatives in the future.

Page achieved his goal when at lightning speed Google+ was introduced in the summer of 2011 and had signed up 40 million members by October. Google is doing all it can to respond to the Facebook challenge.

The Contingency Approach to Organizational Design

Contingency approach A management approach in which the design of an organization's structure is tailored to the sources of uncertainty facing an organization.

The decision about whether to design an organic or a mechanistic structure depends on the *particular context or situation an organization faces*: the environment it confronts, its technology and the complexity of the tasks it performs, and the skills of the people it employs—and how fast these are changing. In general, the contingencies or sources of uncertainty facing an organization shape the organization's design. The **contingency approach** to organizational design tailors organizational structure to the sources of uncertainty facing an organization.[30] The structure is designed to respond to various contingencies—things or changes that might happen and therefore must be planned for. One of the most important of these is the nature of the environment.

According to contingency theory, in order to manage its environment effectively, an organization should design its structure to fit with the environment in which the organization operates.[31] In other words, an organization must design its *internal* structure to control the *external* environment (see Figure 4.8). A poor fit between structure and environment leads to failure; a close fit leads to success. Support for contingency theory comes from two studies of the relationship between structure and the environment. These studies, conducted by Paul Lawrence and Jay Lorsch, and by Tom Burns and G. M. Stalker, are examined next.

Lawrence and Lorsch on Differentiation, Integration, and the Environment

The strength and complexity of the forces in the general and specific environments have a direct effect on the extent of differentiation inside an organization.[32] The number and size of an organization's functions mirror the organization's needs to manage exchanges

Figure 4.8 The Fit between the Organization and Its Environment

A poor fit leads to failure; a close fit leads to success.

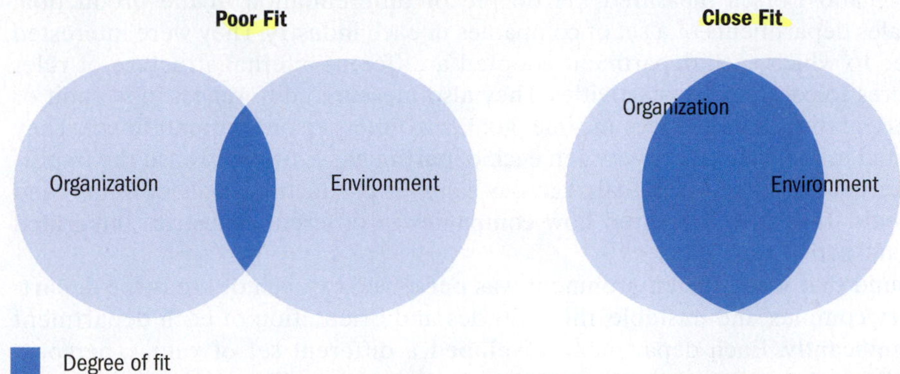

with forces in its environment (see Figure 4.9). Which function handles exchanges with suppliers and distributors? Materials management does. Which function handles exchanges with customers? Sales and marketing. With the government and consumer organizations? Legal and public relations. A functional structure emerges, in part, to deal with the complexity of environmental demands.

Paul Lawrence and Jay Lorsch investigated how companies in different industries differentiate and integrate their structures to fit the characteristics of the industry environment in which they compete.[33] They selected three industries that, they argued, experienced different levels of uncertainty as measured by variables such as rate of change (dynamism) of the environment. The three industries were (1) the plastics industry, which they said experienced the greatest level of uncertainty; (2) the food-processing industry; and (3) the container or can-manufacturing industry, which they said experienced the least uncertainty. Uncertainty was highest in plastics because of the rapid pace of technological and product change. It was lowest in containers, where organizations produce a standard array of products that change little from year to year. Food-processing companies were in

Figure 4.9 Functional Differentiation and Environmental Demands

A functional structure emerges in part to deal with the complexity of demands from the environment.

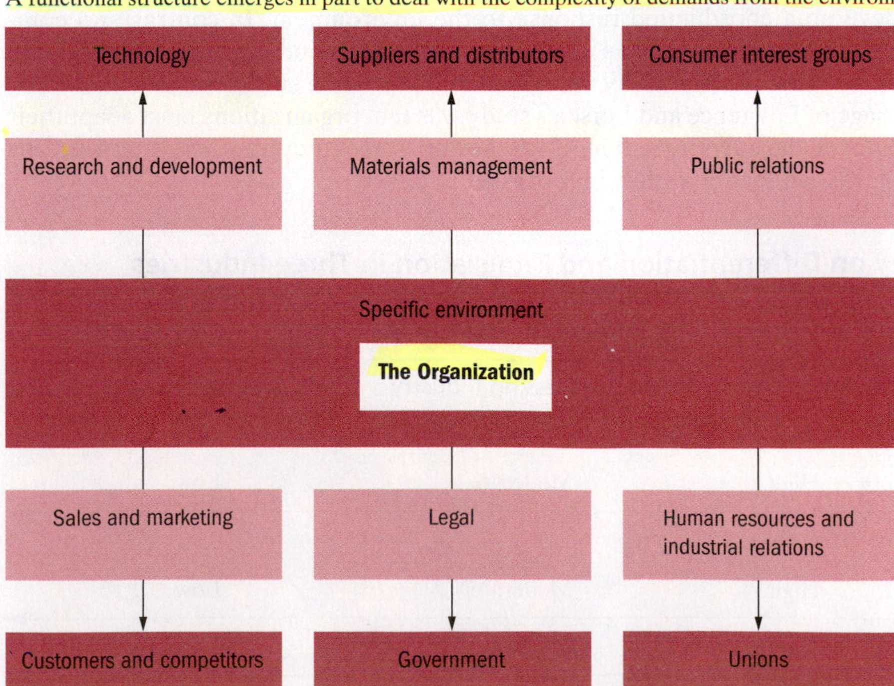

between because, although they introduce new products frequently, production technology is quite stable.

Lawrence and Lorsch measured the degree of differentiation in the production, R&D, and sales departments of a set of companies in each industry. They were interested in the degree to which each department adopted a different internal structure of rules and procedures to coordinate its activities. They also measured differences in subunit or functional orientations (differences in time, goal, and interpersonal orientations). They were interested in the differences between each department's attitude toward the importance of different organizational goals, such as sales or production goals or short- and long-term goals. They also measured how companies in different industries integrated their functional activities.

They found that when the environment was perceived by each of the three departments as very complex and unstable, the attitudes and orientation of each department diverged significantly. Each department developed a different set of values, perspectives, and way of doing things that suited the part of the specific environment it was dealing with. Thus the extent of differentiation between departments was greater in companies that faced an uncertain environment than in companies that were in stable environments.

Lawrence and Lorsch also found that when the environment is perceived as unstable and uncertain, organizations are more effective if they are less formalized, more decentralized, and more reliant on mutual adjustment. When the environment is perceived as relatively stable and certain, organizations are more effective if they have a more centralized, formalized, and standardized structure. Moreover, they found that effective companies in different industries had levels of integration that matched their levels of differentiation. In the uncertain plastics industry, highly effective organizations were highly differentiated but were also highly integrated. In the relatively stable container industry, highly effective companies had a low level of differentiation, which was matched by a low level of integration. Companies in the moderately uncertain food-processing industry had levels of differentiation and integration in between the other two. Table 4.2 summarizes these relationships.

As Table 4.2 shows, a complex, uncertain environment (such as the plastics industry) requires that different departments develop different orientations toward their tasks (a high level of differentiation) so that they can deal with the complexity of their specific environment. As a result of this high degree of differentiation, such organizations require more coordination (a high level of integration). They make greater use of integrating roles between departments to transfer information so the organization as a whole can develop a coordinated response to the environment. In contrast, no complex integrating mechanisms such as integrating roles are found in companies in stable environments because the hierarchy, rules, and SOPs provide sufficient coordination.

The message of Lawrence and Lorsch's study was that organizations must adapt their structures to match the environment in which they operate if they are to be effective. This conclusion reinforced that of a study by Burns and Stalker.

TABLE 4.2 The Effect of Uncertainty on Differentiation and Integration in Three Industries

	Degree of Uncertainty		
Variable	Plastics Industry	Food-Processing Industry	Container Industry
Environmental Variable			
Uncertainty (complexity dynamism, richness)	High	Moderate	Low
Structural Variables			
Departmental differentiation	High	Moderate	Low
Cross-functional integration	High	Moderate	Low

Burns and Stalker on Organic versus Mechanistic Structures and the Environment

Tom Burns and G. M. Stalker also found that organizations need different kinds of structure to control activities when they need to adapt and respond to change in the environment.[34] Specifically, they found that companies with an organic structure were more effective in unstable, changing environments than were companies with a mechanistic structure. The reverse was true in a stable environment: There, the centralized, formalized, and standardized way of coordinating and motivating people that is characteristic of a mechanistic structure worked better than the decentralized team approach that is characteristic of an organic structure.

What is the reason for those results? When the environment is rapidly changing and on-the-spot decisions have to be made, lower-level employees need to have the authority to make important decisions—in other words, they need to be empowered. Moreover, in complex environments, rapid communication and information sharing are often necessary to respond to customer needs and develop new products.[35] When the environment is stable, in contrast, there is no need for complex decision-making systems. Managing resource transactions is easy, and better performance can be obtained by keeping authority centralized in the top-management team and using top-down decision making. Burns and Stalker's conclusion was that organizations should design their structure to match the dynamism and uncertainty of their environment. Figure 4.10 summarizes the conclusions from Burns and Stalker's and Lawrence and Lorsch's contingency studies.

Later chapters examine in detail how to choose the appropriate organizational structure to meet different strategic and technological contingencies. For now, it is important to realize that mechanistic and organic structures are ideals: They are useful for examining how organizational structure affects behavior, but they probably do not exist in a pure form in any real-life organization. Most organizations are a mixture of the two types. Indeed, according to one increasingly influential view organizational design, the most successful organizations are those that have achieved a balance between the two, so that they are simultaneously mechanistic and organic.

An organization may tend more in one direction than in the other, but it needs to be able to act in both ways to be effective. The army, for example, is well known for having a mechanistic structure in which hierarchical reporting relationships are clearly specified. However, in wartime, this mechanistic command structure allows the army to become organic and flexible as it responds to the uncertainties of the quickly changing battlefield.

Figure 4.10 The Relationship between Environmental Uncertainty and Organizational Structure

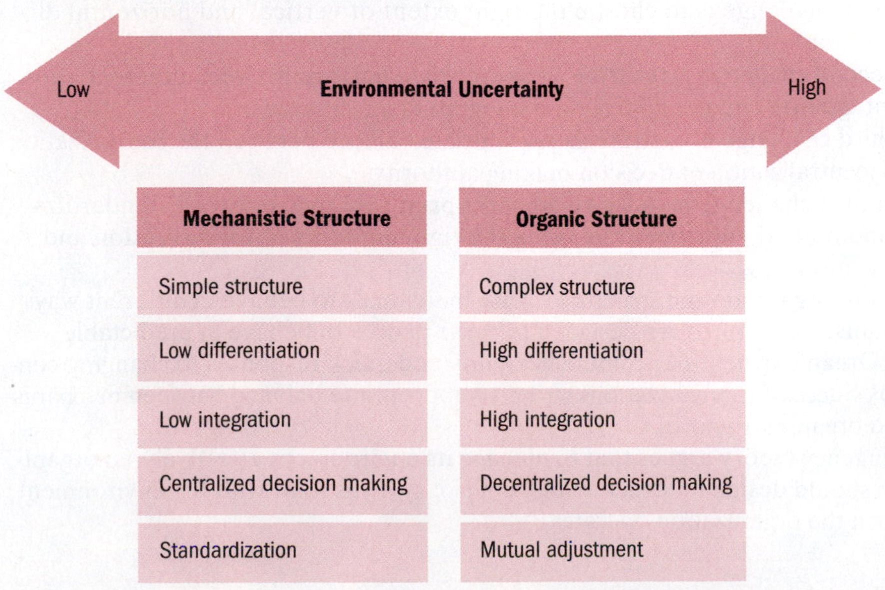

Low
Environmental Uncertainty
High
Mechanistic Structure
Simple structure
Low differentiation
Low integration
Centralized decision making
Standardization
Organic Structure
Complex structure
High differentiation
High integration
Decentralized decision making
Mutual adjustment

Similarly, an organization may design its structure so that some functions (such as manufacturing and accounting) act in a mechanistic way and others (marketing or R&D) develop a more organic approach to their tasks. To achieve the difficult balancing act of being simultaneously mechanistic and organic, organizations need to make appropriate choices (see Figure 4.6). In the next three chapters we look in more detail at the issues involved in designing organizational structure and culture to improve organizational effectiveness.

Studies by Lawrence and Lorsch and by Burns and Stalker indicate that organizations should adapt their structure to reflect the degree of uncertainty in their environment. Companies with a mechanistic structure tend to fare best in a stable environment. Those with an organic structure tend to fare best in an unstable, changing environment.

Summary

This chapter has analyzed how managers' responses to several organizational design challenges affect the way employees behave and interact and how they respond to the organization. We have analyzed how differentiation occurs and examined three other challenges that managers confront as they try to structure their organization to achieve organizational goals. Chapter 4 has made the following main points:

1. Differentiation is the process by which organizations evolve into complex systems as they allocate people and resources to organizational tasks and assign people different levels of authority.
2. Organizations develop five functions to accomplish their goals and objectives: support, production, maintenance, adaptive, and managerial.
3. An organizational role is a set of task-related behaviors required of an employee. An organization is composed of interlocking roles that are differentiated by task responsibilities and task authority.
4. Differentiation has a vertical and a horizontal dimension. Vertical differentiation refers to the way an organization designs its hierarchy of authority. Horizontal differentiation refers to the way an organization groups roles into subunits (functions and divisions).
5. Managers confront five design challenges as they coordinate organizational activities. The choices they make are interrelated and collectively determine how effectively an organization operates.
6. The first challenge is to choose the right extent of vertical and horizontal differentiation.
7. The second challenge is to strike an appropriate balance between differentiation and integration and use appropriate integrating mechanisms.
8. The third challenge is to strike an appropriate balance between the centralization and decentralization of decision-making authority.
9. The fourth challenge is to strike an appropriate balance between standardization and mutual adjustment by using the right amounts of formalization and socialization.
10. Different organizational structures cause individuals to behave in different ways. Mechanistic structures are designed to cause people to behave in predictable ways. Organic structures promote flexibility and quick responses to changing conditions. Successful organizations strike an appropriate balance between mechanistic and organic structures.
11. Contingency theory argues that to manage its environment effectively, an organization should design its structure and control systems to fit with the environment in which the organization operates.

Discussion Questions

1. Why does differentiation occur in an organization? Distinguish between vertical and horizontal differentiation.
2. Draw an organizational chart of the business school or college that you attend. Outline its major roles and functions. How differentiated is it? Do you think the distribution of authority and division of labor are appropriate?
3. When does an organization need to use complex integrating mechanisms? Why?
4. What factors determine the balance between centralization and decentralization, and between standardization and mutual adjustment?
5. Under what conditions is an organization likely to prefer (a) a mechanistic structure, (b) an organic structure, or (c) elements of both?

Organizational Theory in Action

Practicing Organizational Theory

Growing Pains

Form groups of three to five people and discuss the following scenario:

You are the founding entrepreneurs of Zylon Corporation, a fast-growing Internet software company that specializes in electronic banking. Customer demand to license your software has boomed so much that in just two years you have added over 50 new software programmers to help develop a new range of software products. The growth of your company has been so swift that you still operate informally with a loose and flexible arrangement of roles, and programmers are encouraged to find solutions to problems as they go along. Although this structure has worked well, signs indicate that problems are arising.

There have been increasing complaints from employees that good performance is not being recognized in the organization and that they do not feel equitably treated. Moreover, there have been complaints about getting managers to listen to their new ideas and to act on them. A bad atmosphere seems to be developing in the company, and recently several talented employees left. You are meeting to discuss these problems.

1. Examine your organizational structure to see what might be causing these problems.
2. What kinds of design choices do you need to make to solve them?

Making the Connection #4

Find an example of a company that has been facing one of the design challenges discussed in this chapter. What problem has the company been experiencing? How has it attempted to deal with the problem?

The Ethical Dimension #4

The way an organizational structure is designed affects the way its members behave. Rules can be applied so strictly and punitively that they harm employees, for example by increasing the stress of the job. Inappropriate norms can develop that might reduce employee incentive to work or cause employees to abuse their peers. Similarly, in some organizations, superiors use their authority to abuse and harangue employees. Think about the ethical implications of the design challenges discussed in this chapter.

1. Using the design challenges, design an organization that you think would result in highly ethical decision making; then design one that would lead to the opposite. Why the difference?
2. Do you think ethical behavior is more likely in a mechanistic or an organic structure?

Analyzing the Organization: Design Module #4

This module attempts to get at some of the basic operating principles that your organization uses to perform its tasks. From the information you have been able to obtain, describe the aspects of your organization's structure in the assignment below.

Assignment

1. How differentiated is your organization? Is it simple or complex? List the major roles, functions, or departments in your organization. Does your organization have many divisions? If your organization engages in many businesses, list the major divisions in the company.
2. What core competences make your organization unique or different from other organizations? What are the sources of the core competences? How difficult do you think it would be for other organizations to imitate these distinctive competences?
3. How has your organization responded to the design challenges? (a) Is it centralized or decentralized? How do you know? (b) Is it highly differentiated? Can you identify any integrating mechanisms used by your organization? What is the match between the complexity of differentiation and the complexity of the integrating mechanisms that are used? (c) Is behavior in the organization very standardized, or does mutual adjustment play an important role in coordinating people and activities? What can you tell about the level of formalization by looking at the number and kinds of rules the organization uses? How important is socialization in your organization?
4. Does your analysis in item 3 lead you to think that your organization conforms more to the organic or to the mechanistic model of organizational structure? Briefly explain why you think it is organic or mechanistic.
5. From your analysis so far, what do you think could be done to improve the way your organization operates?

CASE FOR ANALYSIS

Sony's "Gaijin" CEO is Reorganizing the Company

Sony, the famous Japanese electronics maker, was renowned in the 1990s for using its engineering prowess to develop blockbuster new products such as the Walkman, Trinitron TV, and PlayStation. Its engineers churned out an average of four new product ideas every day, something attributed to its culture, called the "Sony Way," which emphasized communication, cooperation, and harmony among its company-wide product engineering teams.[36] Sony's engineers were empowered to pursue their own ideas, and the leaders of its different divisions, and hundreds of product teams were allowed to pursue their own innovations—no matter what the cost. While this approach to leadership worked so long as Sony could churn out blockbuster products, it did not work in the 2000s as agile global competitors from Taiwan, Korea, and the United States innovated new technologies and products that began to beat Sony at its own game.

Companies such as LG, Samsung, and Apple innovated new technologies such as advanced LCD flat-screens, flash memory, touch-screen commands, mobile digital music, video, and GPS positioning devices, and 3D displays that made many of Sony's technologies, such as its Trinitron TVs and Walkmans obsolete. For example, products such as Apple's iPod and iPhone and Nintendo's Wii game console better met customer needs than Sony's out-of-date and expensive products. Why did Sony lose its leading competitive position?

One reason was that Sony's organizing approach no longer worked in its favor because the leaders of its different product divisions worked to protect their own personal empires and divisions' goals and not those of the whole company. Sony's leaders were slow to recognize the speed at which technology was changing and as each division's performance fell, their leaders felt threatened and competition between them increased as they sought to protect their own empires. The result was slower decision making and increased operating costs as the leaders of each division competed to obtain the funding necessary to develop successful new products.

By 2005 Sony was in big trouble; and at this crucial point in their company's history, Sony's top managers turned to a *gaijin,* or non-Japanese, executive to lead their company. Their choice was Sir Howard Stringer, a Welshman, who as the head of Sony's U.S. operations had been instrumental in cutting costs and increasing profits. Stringer's was known to be a directive but participative leader; although he was closely involved in all U.S. top management decisions he nevertheless then gave his top executives the authority to develop successful strategies to implement these decisions.

When he became Sony's CEO in 2005 Stringer faced the immediate problem of reducing operating costs that were *double* those of its competitors because the leaders of its divisions had essentially seized control of Sony's top-level decision-making authority. Stringer immediately recognized how the extensive power struggles among the leaders of Sony's different product divisions were hurting the company. So, adopting a directive, command-and-control leadership approach, he made it clear that this had to stop and that they needed to work quickly to reduce costs—but he also urged them to cooperate to speed product development across divisions. By 2007 it was clear that many of Sony's most important divisional leaders were still pursuing their own goals and were ignoring Stringer's orders.

By 2008 Stringer had replaced all the divisional leaders who resisted his orders, and he worked steadily to downsize Sony's bloated corporate headquarters staff and replace the leaders of functions who also put their own interests first. He promoted younger managers to lead its divisions and functions—managers who would obey his orders and focus on the company's performance because as Stringer said over time the culture or business of Sony had been management—not making new products.

To turn around Sony's still declining performance, Stringer had to adopt an even more directive approach. In 2009 Stringer announced he would take charge of the Japanese company's struggling core electronics group and would add the title of president to his existing roles as chairman and CEO as he reorganized Sony's divisions. He also replaced four more of its most important leaders with managers who had held positions outside Japan and were "familiar with the digital world." In the future, he also told managers to prioritize new products and invest only in those with the greatest chance of success so Sony could reduce its out-of-control R&D costs.

By 2010 Sony's financial results suggested that Stringer's initiatives were finally paying off; he had stemmed Sony's huge losses, its products were selling better, and Stringer hoped Sony would become profitable by the end of 2011. To help ensure this Stringer also took charge of a newly created networked products and services group that included its Vaio computers, Walkman digital media players, PlayStation gaming console, and the software and online services to support these products. Stringer's organizing approach was still focused on helping Sony regain its global leadership in electronic products.[37]

In January 2011 Stringer announced that Sony's performance had increased so much that it would be profitable in the second half of 2011. Then within months came the news that hackers had invaded Sony's Playstation website and stolen the private information of millions of its users. Sony was forced to shut down its Playstation website for weeks and compensate users, and together it expects the losses from this debacle to exceed $1 billion as well as the cost to its brand name. In addition, it also became clear that customers were not buying its expensive new 3D flatscreen TVs and that its revenues from consumer products would be lower than expected because of intense competition from companies like Samsung. In June 2011 Stringer reported that now the company expected to make a record loss in 2011, so his turnaround efforts have been foiled so far.

Discussion Questions

1. What pressures and forces from the environment led Stringer to change the balance between centralizing and decentralizing authority at Sony?
2. How would you describe Stringer's approach to organizing? Is he seeking to create a more mechanistic or organic structure, or what kind of balance between them?

References

1 T. Parsons, *Structure and Process in Modern Societies* (Glencoe, IL: Free Press, 1960); J. Child, *Organization: A Guide for Managers and Administrators* (New York: Harper & Row, 1977).

2 R. K. Merton, *Social Theory and Social Structure*, 2nd ed. (Glencoe, IL: Free Press, 1957).

3 D. Katz and R. L. Kahn, *The Social Psychology of Organizing* (New York: Wiley, 1966).

4 Ibid., pp. 39–47.

5 P. Selznick, "An Approach to a Theory of Bureaucracy," *American Sociological Review* 8 (1943), 47–54.

6 M. E. Porter, *Competitive Strategy* (New York: Free Press, 1980).

7 R. H. Miles, *Macro Organizational Behavior* (Santa Monica, CA: Goodyear, 1980), pp. 19–20.

8 Child, *Organization*.

[9] P. R. Lawrence and J. W. Lorsch, *Organization and Environment* (Boston: Graduate School of Business Administration, Harvard University, 1967).
[10] J. R. Galbraith, *Designing Complex Organizations* (Reading, MA: Addison-Wesley, 1973).
[11] B. Dumaine, "The Bureaucracy Busters," *Fortune*, June 7, 1991, p. 42.
[12] www.lucasarts.com, 2011.
[13] B. Hindo, "The Empire Strikes at Silos," www.businessweek.com, August 20, 2007.
[14] H. Mintzberg, *The Nature of Managerial Work* (Englewood Cliffs, NJ: Prentice-Hall, 1973).
[15] www.whirlpool.com, 2011.
[16] P. P. Gupta, M. D. Dirsmith, and T. J. Fogarty, "Coordination and Control in a Government Agency: Contingency and Institutional Theory Perspectives on GAO Audits," *Administrative Science Quarterly* 39 (1994), 264–284.
[17] A detailed critique of the workings of bureaucracy in practice is offered in P. M. Blau, *The Dynamics of Bureaucracy* (Chicago: University of Chicago Press, 1955).
[18] Dumaine, "The Bureaucracy Busters," pp. 36–50.
[19] D. S. Pugh, D. J. Hickson, C. R. Hinings, and C. Turner, "Dimensions of Organizational Structure," *Administrative Science Quarterly* 13 (1968), 65–91; D. S. Pugh and D. J. Hickson, "The Comparative Study of Organizations," in G. Salaman and K. Thompson, eds., *People and Organizations* (London: Longman, 1973), pp. 50–66.
[20] www.up.com, 2011.
[21] www.yahoo.com, 2011.
[22] Ibid.
[23] See H. Mintzberg, *The Structuring of Organizational Structures* (Englewood Cliffs, NJ: Prentice-Hall, 1979), for an in-depth treatment of standardization and mutual adjustment.
[24] Pugh and Hickson, "The Comparative Study of Organizations."
[25] M. Dalton, "The Industrial Ratebuster: A Characterization," *Applied Anthropology* 7 (1948), 5–18.
[26] J. Van Mannen and E. H. Schein, "Towards a Theory of Organizational Socialization," in B. M. Staw, ed., *Research in Organizational Behavior*, vol. 1 (Greenwich, CT: JAI Press, 1979), pp. 209–264.
[27] G. R. Jones, "Socialization Tactics, Self-Efficacy, and Newcomers' Adjustments to Organizations," *Academy of Management Journal* 29 (1986), 262–279; Van Maanen and Schein, "Towards a Theory of Organizational Socialization."
[28] T. Burns and G. M. Stalker, *The Management of Innovation* (London: Tavistock, 1966).
[29] www.google.com, 2011.
[30] J. Pfeffer, *Organizations and Organizational Theory* (Boston: Pitman, 1982), pp. 147–162; J. Child, "Organizational Structure, Environment, and Performance: The Role of Strategic Choice," *Sociology* 6 (1972), 1–22.
[31] J. Pfeffer, *Organizations and Organizational Theory* (Boston: Pitman, 1982).
[32] P. R. Lawrence and J. W. Lorsch, *Organization and Environment* (Boston: Graduate School of Business Administration, Harvard University, 1967).
[33] Ibid.
[34] T. Burns and G. M. Stalker, *The Management of Innovation.*
[35] J. A. Courtright, G. T. Fairhurst, and L. E. Rogers, "Interaction Patterns in Organic and Mechanistic Systems," *Academy of Management Journal 32* (1989), 773–802.
[36] www.sony.com, press release, 2011.
[37] Ibid.

CHAPTER 5

Designing Organizational Structure: Authority and Control

Learning Objectives

To protect stakeholders' goals and interests, managers must continually analyze and redesign an organization's structure so that it most effectively controls people and other resources. In this chapter, the many crucial design choices involving the vertical dimension of organizational structure—the hierarchy of authority that an organization creates to control its members—is examined.

After reading this chapter you should be able to:

1. Explain why a hierarchy of authority emerges in an organization and the process of vertical differentiation.
2. Discuss the issues involved in designing a hierarchy to coordinate and motivate organizational behavior most effectively.
3. Understand the way in which the design challenges discussed in Chapter 4—such as centralization and standardization—provide methods of control that substitute for the direct, personal control that managers provide and affect the design of the organizational hierarchy.
4. Appreciate the principles of bureaucratic structure and explain their implications for the design of effective organizational hierarchies.
5. Explain why organizations are flattening their hierarchies and making more use of empowered teams of employees, both inside and across different functions.

Authority: How and Why Vertical Differentiation Occurs

A basic design challenge, identified in Chapter 4, is to decide how much authority to centralize at the top of the organizational hierarchy and how much authority to decentralize to middle and lower levels. (Recall from Chapter 2 that *authority* is the power to hold people accountable for their actions and to directly influence what they do and how they do it.) But what determines the shape of an organization's hierarchy, that is, the number of levels of authority within an organization? This question is important because the shape of an organization (evident in its organizational chart) determines how effectively the organization's decision-making and communication systems work. The decisions that managers make about the shape of the hierarchy, and the balance between centralized and decentralized decision making, establish the level of vertical differentiation in an organization.

The Emergence of the Hierarchy

An organization's hierarchy begins to emerge when managers find it more and more difficult to coordinate and motivate employees effectively.[1] As an organization grows, employees increase in number and begin to specialize, performing widely different kinds of tasks; the level of differentiation increases and this makes coordinating employees' activities more difficult.[2] Similarly, the division of labor and specialization produce motivational problems. When each employee performs only a small part of a total task, it is often difficult to determine how much he or she actually contributes to the task, and thus it is often difficult to evaluate each individual's performance. Moreover, if employees cooperate to achieve a goal it is often impossible to measure, evaluate, and reward them based on their individual performance level. For example, if two servers cooperate to serve tables, how does their boss know how much each contributed? If two chefs work together to cook a meal how is each person's individual impact on food quality to be measured and rewarded?[3]

An organization does two things to improve its ability to control—that is, coordinate and motivate—its members: (1) It increases the number of managers it uses to monitor, evaluate, and reward employees; and (2) it increases the number of levels in its managerial hierarchy so that the hierarchy of authority becomes taller over time.[4] Increasing both the number of managers and the levels of management increases vertical differentiation and gives the organization direct face-to-face control over its members—managers *personally* control their subordinates.

Direct supervision allows managers to shape and influence the behavior of subordinates as they work face to face in the pursuit of a company's goals. Direct supervision is a vital method of control because managers can continually question, probe, and consult with subordinates about problems or new issues they are facing to get a better understanding of the situation. It also ensures that subordinates are performing their work effectively and not hiding any information that could cause problems down the line. Personal control also creates greater opportunity for on-the-job task learning to occur and competences to develop, as well as greater opportunities to prevent free-riding or shirking.

Moreover, when managers personally supervise subordinates, they lead by example and in this way can help subordinates develop and increase their personal management skills. At GE, for example, considerable importance is given to each manager's responsibility to develop his or her subordinates and improve their chances of being promoted. The continual improvement of management skills at all levels inside GE is one of its core competences. Any manager who fails in this task is quickly rooted out and fired; those who mentor the lower-level managers most likely to succeed are promoted up the hierarchy. Thus personal supervision can be a very effective way of motivating employees and promoting behaviors that increase effectiveness. The personal authority relationship in an organization is perhaps the most significant or tangible one that creates and bonds people into an organization and determines how well they perform.

Tall organization
An organization in which the hierarchy has many levels relative to the size of the organization.

Size and Height Limitations

Figure 5.1 shows two organizations that have the same number of employees, but one has three levels in its hierarchy and the other has seven. An organization in which the hierarchy has many levels relative to the size of the organization is a **tall organization**. An organization

Figure 5.1 Flat and Tall Organizations

A tall organization has more hierarchical levels and more managers to direct and control employees' activities than does a flat organization with the same number of employees.

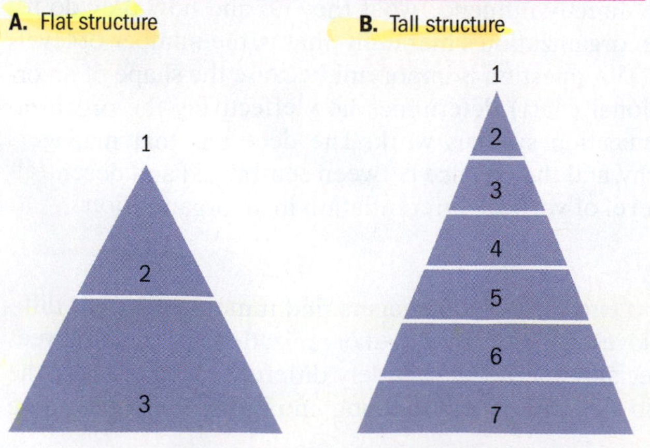

that has few levels in its hierarchy is a **flat organization**. The tall organization in Figure 5.1 has four more levels than the flat organization, and it uses many more managers to direct and control employee activities. Research evidence suggests that an organization with 3,000 employees is most likely to have seven levels in its hierarchy. Thus a 3,000-employee organization with only four levels in its hierarchy is considered flat, whereas one with nine levels is considered tall.

Flat organization
An organization that has few levels in its hierarchy relative to its size.

Figure 5.2 illustrates an interesting research finding concerning the relationship between organizational size (measured by number of employees) and the height of the vertical hierarchy. By the time an organization has grown to 1,000 members it is likely to have about four levels in its hierarchy: CEO, function or department heads, department supervisors, and employees. An organization that grows to 3,000 members is likely to have seven levels. After that size is reached, however, something striking happens: Organizations that employ 10,000 or even 100,000 employees typically do not have more than nine or ten levels in their hierarchy. Moreover, large organizations do not increase the numbers of managers at each level to compensate for this restriction in the number of levels in the hierarchy.[5] Thus most organizations have a pyramid-like structure and fewer and fewer managers at each level (see Figure 5.3A), rather than a bloated structure (Figure 5.3B) in which proportionally more managers at all levels control the activities of increasing numbers of members.

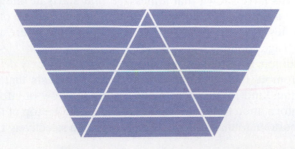

In fact, research suggests that the increase in the size of the managerial component in an organization is *less than proportional* to the increase in size of the organization as it grows.[6]

Figure 5.2 The Relationship between Organizational Size and Number of Hierarchical Levels

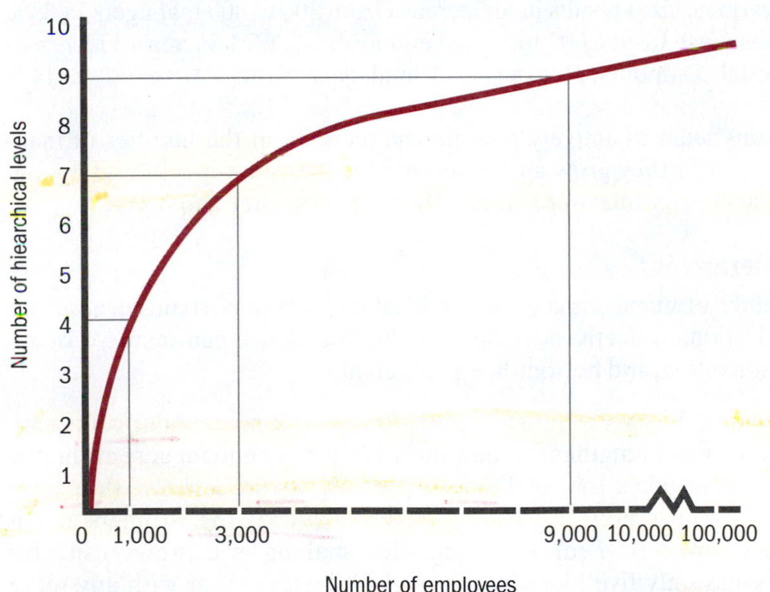

Figure 5.3 Types of Managerial Hierarchies

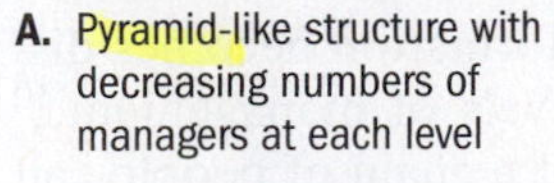

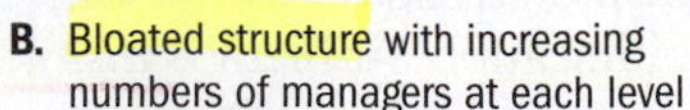

B. Bloated structure with increasing numbers of managers at each level

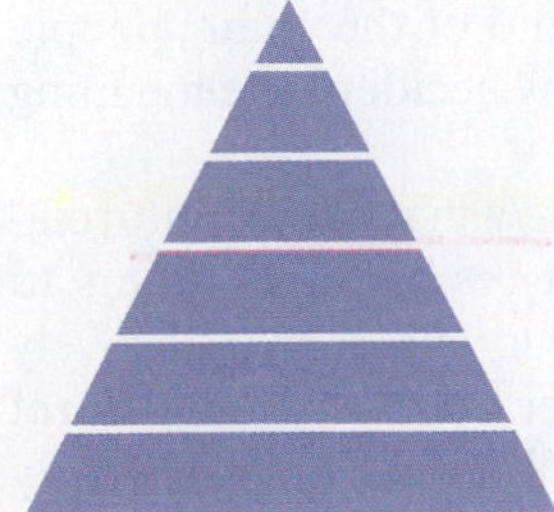

Figure 5.4 The Relationship between Organizational Size and the Size of the Managerial Component

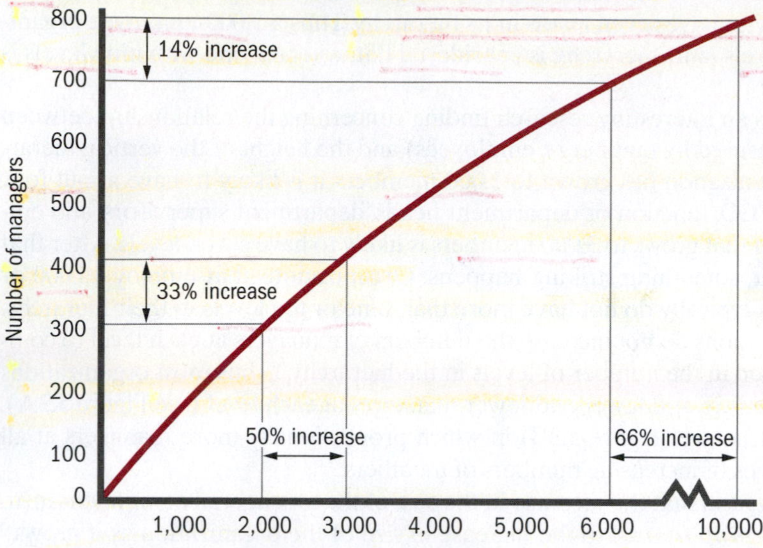

This phenomenon is illustrated in Figure 5.4. An increase from 2,000 to 3,000 employees (a 50% increase in organizational size) results in an increase from 300 to 400 managers (a 33% increase). However, an increase from 6,000 to 10,000 employees (a 66% increase) increases the size of the managerial component by only 100 managers (from 700 to 800, a 14% increase).

Why do organizations seem to actively restrain the increase in the number of managers and hierarchical levels as they grow and differentiate? The answer is that many significant problems arise as the organizational hierarchy becomes taller and taller.[7]

Problems with Tall Hierarchies

Choosing the right number of managers and hierarchical levels is important because this decision impacts organizational effectiveness. Specifically, this choice can increase or reduce communication, motivation, and bottom-line profitability.[8]

COMMUNICATION PROBLEMS Having too many hierarchical levels may hinder communication. As the chain of command lengthens, communication between managers at the top and bottom of the hierarchy takes longer. Decision making slows, and the slowdown hurts the performance of organizations that need to respond quickly to customers' needs or the actions of competitors.[9] At FedEx, fast decision making is a prerequisite for success, so the company has only five hierarchical levels; it believes that with any more levels the speed of communication and decision making would suffer. Similarly, when Liz Claiborne was designing the structure of her organization, she was careful to keep the hierarchy flat—four levels for 4,000 employees—to maximize the organization's ability to respond to quickly changing fashion trends.

Another significant communication problem is *distortion*. Information becomes distorted as it flows up and down the hierarchy through many levels of management.[10] Experiments have shown that a message that starts at one end of a chain of people can have quite a different meaning by the time it reaches the other end of the chain; people interpret messages according to their own needs and interests so by accident the meaning of the message changes.

In addition, managers up and down the hierarchy may *deliberately* manipulate information to promote their own interests. Research suggests that managers can lead others to make certain kinds of decisions by restricting the flow of information and/or by selectively feeding information to them.[11] When this happens, the top of the hierarchy may lose control over the bottom. Managers at low levels may also selectively transmit up the hierarchy only the information that serves their interests. A rational subordinate, for example, may decide to give a superior only information that makes him or her or the superior look good. Again, if this happens often, the top of the hierarchy may have little idea about or control over what is happening below, and the quality of decision making at all levels suffers.

Studies show that communication problems get progressively worse as the number of hierarchical levels increases. Thus managers are wise to try to limit and restrict the growth of the organizational hierarchy. When the number of levels surpasses seven or eight, communication problems can cause a breakdown in control and slow and unresponsive decision making. For example, DuPont, the company known for developing such products as nylon and Teflon, found its sales were slowing and it was experiencing increasing problems in developing new products in the 2000s.[12] Its CEO attributed these problems to an increase in the number of top levels of management that had taken place over time, which had slowed down recognition of and reaction to problems. So he decided to shake up top management. First, the topmost level of management—the executive committee, a group of former and current top executives who had been guiding DuPont for decades—was eliminated! Then began the elimination of levels of top management within the individual operating divisions. For example, in the huge Polymer Division, where nylon is made, one out of every four management jobs was cut. Where 11 levels of management were used to separate the top management team from a salesperson in the field, the number is now five.

The name of the game has been to flatten the structure so that the organization can be more responsive to customer needs and at the same time, the costs of operating DuPont's management hierarchy have been reduced by over $1 billion a year. Another example of how flattening the hierarchy can improve effectiveness is discussed in Organizational Insight 5.1.

Organizational Insight 5.1

Pfizer's New Energizing Hierarchy

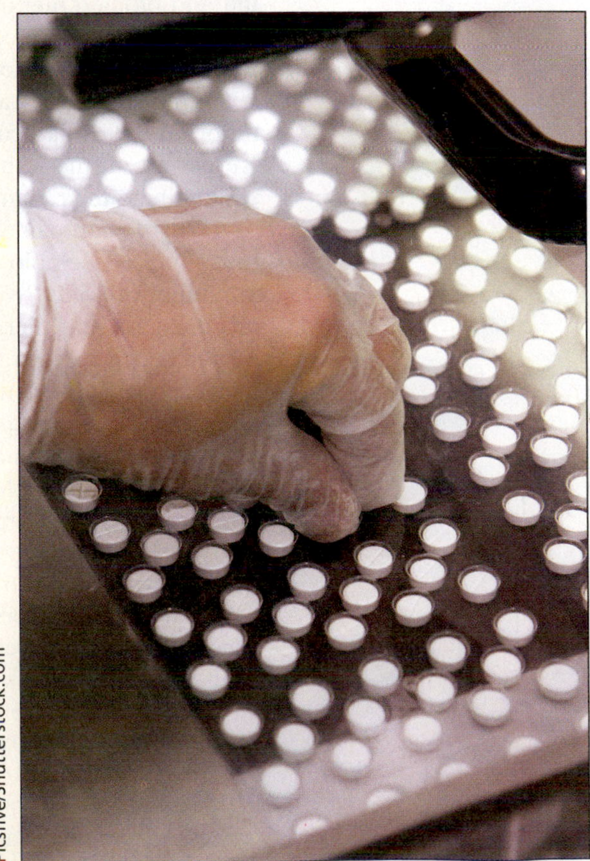
Picsfive/Shutterstock.com

Pfizer is the largest global pharmaceuticals company, with sales of almost $68 billion in 2010. In the past, Pfizer's researches have innovated some of the most successful and profitable drugs in the market, such as its leading cholesterol reducer Lipitor that earns $13 billion a year. In the 2000s, however, it ran into major roadblocks in innovating new blockbuster drugs. Although many of the drugs in its new product development seemed to be winners, when Pfizer's scientists tested them on groups of people, they failed to work as planned; this was a major crisis for Pfizer. Pfizer desperately needed to find ways to make its new product development pipeline work effectively, and one manager, Martin Mackay, believed he knew how to do it.

Mackay had watched how Pfizer's organizational structure had become taller and taller over time as a result of huge mergers with pharmaceuticals companies Warner Lambert and Pharmacia. After every merger, with more managers and levels in the hierarchy, there was a much greater need for committees to integrate across all their activities. Mackay felt that too many managers and committees had resulted in Pfizer's R&D function becoming bureaucratic, and scientists increasingly had to follow more and more rules and procedures to perform and report on their work. He planned to change this situation.

Mackay slashed the number of management layers between top managers and scientists from 14 to 7; he then abolished the scores of product development committees that he felt hampered not helped the process of transforming innovative ideas into blockbuster drugs. After streamlining the hierarchy of authority, he then focused his efforts on reducing the number of unnecessary bureaucratic rules scientists had to follow. He and his team examined every kind of report that scientists were supposed to make to report the results of their work for evaluation. He then proceeded to eliminate every kind of report he considered superfluous and that seemed to slow down the innovation process. For example, scientists had been in the habit of submitting quarterly and monthly reports to executives, explaining each drug's progress; Mackay told them to pick which one they wanted to keep and then the other would be eliminated.

So Mackay's goal is to move the company to more of an organic structure, which as you recall from Chapter 4 is flat, decentralized, and in which teams of scientists can collaborate to develop the norms and values that encourage innovation and entrepreneurship. Certainly Pfizer's scientists report that they felt "liberated" by the new structure and that drugs were moving faster along the pipeline. At the end of 2010, however, Mackay's success led him to be recruited by the giant European drug maker, AstraZeneca, where he now heads this company's global R&D research efforts.

MOTIVATION PROBLEMS As the number of levels in the hierarchy *increases*, the relative difference in the authority possessed by managers at each level *decreases*, as does their area of responsibility. A flat organization (see Figure 5.1) has fewer managers and hierarchical levels than a tall organization, so managers of a flat organization possess relatively more authority and responsibility than those of a tall organization. Many studies have shown that when more authority and responsibility is given to managers and employees, they are more motivated to perform their organizational roles, other things being equal. Thus motivation in an organization with a flat structure may be stronger than motivation in a tall organization. Also, when a hierarchy has many levels, it is easy for managers to pass the buck and evade responsibility by shifting this responsibility to the manager above them—actions that worsen the problem of slow decision making and poor communication.

BUREAUCRATIC COSTS Managers cost money. The greater the number of managers and hierarchical levels, the greater the bureaucratic costs—that is, the costs associated with running and operating an organization. The average middle manager costs an estimated $300,000 or more per year in salary, bonuses, benefits, and an office. Employing a thousand excess managers, therefore, costs an organization $300 million a year—an enormous sum that companies often belatedly recognize they do not need to pay. Because of the cost of a tall and bloated hierarchy, it is common, especially during a recession, for a company to announce it will reduce the number of levels in its hierarchy and lay off excess employees to reduce bureaucratic costs. In 2005, for example, Ford announced it would eliminate two levels in its hierarchy and lay off 600 managers, for a savings of $500 million. In 2008, Dell reported that it had cut 12,000 jobs for a savings of a billion dollars a year. HP, GM, and Xerox are some other large companies that have saved billions of dollars from streamlining their managerial hierarchies in the 2000s.

Why do companies suddenly perceive the need to reduce their workforce drastically, thus subjecting employees to the uncertainty and misery of the unemployment line with a minimum of notice? Why do companies not have more foresight and restrict the growth of managers and hierarchical levels to avoid large layoffs? Sometimes layoffs are unavoidable, as when a totally unexpected situation arises in the organization's environment: For example, innovation may render technology obsolete or uncompetitive, or an economic crisis brought about by events such as the subprime mortgage fiasco may abruptly reduce demand for an organization's products. Much of the time, however, dramatic changes in employment and structure are simply the result of bad management.

Managers of an organization that is doing well often do not recognize the need to control, prune, and manage the organization's hierarchy as the organization confronts new or changing situations. Or they may see the need but prefer to do little or nothing. As organizations grow, managers usually pay little attention to the hierarchy; their most pressing concern is to satisfy customer needs by bringing products or services to the market as quickly as possible. As a result, hierarchical levels multiply as new people are added without much thought about long-term consequences. When an organization matures, its structure is likely to be streamlined because, for example, two or more managerial positions may be combined into one and levels in the hierarchy are eliminated to improve decision making and reduce costs. The terms *restructuring* and *downsizing* are used to describe the  process by which managers streamline hierarchies and lay off managers and workers to reduce bureaucratic costs. This is discussed in detail in Chapter 10, where the issue of organizational change and redesign is the focus of analysis.

The Parkinson's Law Problem

While studying administrative processes in the British Navy, C. Northcote Parkinson, a former British civil servant, came upon some interesting statistics.[13] He discovered that from 1914 to 1928 the number of ships in operation in the British Navy decreased by 68%; but the number of dockyard officials responsible for maintaining the fleet had increased by 40% and the number of top navy officers in London—the officials responsible for managing the fleet—had increased by 79%! Why had this situation come about? Parkinson argued that growth in the number of managers and hierarchical levels is controlled by two principles: (1) "An official wants to multiply subordinates, not rivals," and (2) "Officials make work for one another."[14]

Managers value their rank, grade, or status in the hierarchy. The fewer managers at their hierarchical level and the greater the number of managers below them, the larger is their "empire" and the higher their status. Not surprisingly then, managers seek to increase the number of their subordinates. In turn, these subordinates realize the status advantages of having subordinates, so they try to increase the number of their subordinates, causing the hierarchy to become taller and taller. As the number of levels increases, managers must spend more of their time monitoring and controlling the actions and behaviors of their subordinates and thus create unnecessary work for themselves. More managers lead to more work—hence the British Navy results. Parkinson further contended that his principles apply to all organizational hierarchies if they are not controlled because managers in hierarchies make work for one another. "Work expands so as to fill the time available." That is Parkinson's law.

The Ideal Number of Hierarchical Levels: The Minimum Chain of Command

Managers should base the decision to employ an extra manager on the difference between the value added by the last manager employed and the cost of the last manager employed. However, as Parkinson noted, a person may have no second thoughts about spending the organization's money to improve his or her own position, status, and power. Well-managed organizations control this problem by simple rules—for example, "Any new recruitment has to be approved by the CEO"—which prompts upper-level managers to evaluate whether another lower-level manager or another hierarchical level is really necessary. An even more general principle for designing a hierarchy is the principle of minimum chain of command.

Principle of minimum chain of command
An organization should choose the minimum number of hierarchical levels consistent with its goals and the environment in which it operates.

According to the **principle of minimum chain of command,** an organization should choose the minimum number of hierarchical levels consistent with its goals and the environment in which it operates.[15] In other words, an organization should be kept as flat as possible, and top managers should be evaluated for their ability to monitor and control its activities with the fewest managers possible.

An organization with a flat structure will also experience fewer communication, motivation, and cost problems than a tall organization. The only reason why an organization should choose a tall structure over a flat structure is when it needs a high level of direct control and personal supervision over subordinates. Nuclear power plants, for example, typically have extremely tall hierarchies so that managers at all levels can maintain effective supervision of operations. Because any error could produce a disaster, managers continually oversee and crosscheck the work of managers below them to ensure rules and SOPs are followed accurately and consistently. Such supervision is vital when extraordinary events such as the earthquake and tsunami that swamped Japan's nuclear reactors in 2011 occur; however, stabilizing the reactor might take a decade, and the owner of the reactor was accused of not implementing new rules to build safety barriers to stop such storm surges—because such barriers cost billions of dollars.

In Chapter 9 we examine when factors such as technology and task characteristics make tall structures the preferred choice. Here, the issue is that organizations should strive to keep hierarchical levels to the minimum necessary to accomplish their mission. Organizational problems produced by factors such as Parkinson's law do not satisfy any stakeholder interest, for sooner or later they will be discovered by a new management team, which will purge the hierarchy to reduce excess managers. This has happened at many companies in the 2000s, such as IBM, GE, and Time Warner.

EMI, the British record company that launched the careers of the Beatles, Rolling Stones, and Garth Brooks, provides a good example of how to flatten an organization.[16] Although

EMI used to be the most profitable in the industry, its performance collapsed in the 2000s because it had come to be managed by a top-heavy team of overpaid executives who lacked the entrepreneurial ability either to recognize and promote new talent or to help their subordinates acquire that ability. A new CEO, Alain Levy, set out to shake up EMI's hierarchy and he fired almost 2,000 entrenched executives and eliminated three levels in the management hierarchy. Then his remaining managers were given a greater area of responsibility and he abolished the old reward system of guaranteed bonuses based on signing new talent. From then on, EMI managers were put on contracts and their performance bonuses were based on the future performance of the artists they signed up and promoted. Executives whose performance slips get shorter contracts; managers who can demonstrate a track record of success receive longer contracts, so to keep their jobs, managers must maintain high performance.[17] Bob Iger adopted a similar approach at Disney, as discussed in Organizational Insight 5.2.

Span of Control

Organizations that become too tall inevitably experience serious communications and coordination problems. Nevertheless, a growing organization must be able to monitor and control

Organizational Insight 5.2

Bob Iger Reshapes Walt Disney

Bob Iger took control of the troubled Walt Disney Company in 2006 after holding the position of COO under its autocratic CEO Michael Eisner. For several years Disney had been plagued by slow decision making and analysts claimed it had made many mistakes in putting its new strategies into action. Its Disney stores were losing money, its Internet properties were not getting many hits, and even its theme parks seemed to have lost their luster because only a small number of new rides or attractions had been introduced.

Iger believed that one of the main reasons for Disney's declining performance was that it had become too tall and bureaucratic and its top managers were following financial rules that did not lead to innovative strategies. So one of Iger's first moves to turn around its performance was to dismantle Disney's central strategic planning office. In this office several levels of managers were responsible for sifting through all the new ideas and innovations sent up by Disney's different business divisions, such as its theme parks and different movies studios. They then selected the best ones and presented them to the CEO for discussion and perhaps approval.

Iger saw the strategic planning office as a bureaucratic bottleneck that actually reduced the number of ideas coming from below and that often meant the right decisions were not being made at the top. So he decided to dissolve the office in 2008 and reassigned its managers back to their different business divisions.[18]

The result of cutting out an unnecessary layer in Disney's hierarchy was that its different business units were generating more new ideas by 2009. The level of innovation increased because managers are more willing to speak out and champion their ideas when they know they are dealing directly with the CEO and a top-management team searching for innovative new ways to improve performance, rather than a layer of strategic planning "bureaucrats" only concerned for the bottom line.[19] In 2009 Disney acquired Pixar, for example, and Iger created a partnership with Steve Jobs, Pixar's major owner, that has led to several joint initiatives. By 2011, Disney reported sharply higher operating profits despite the recession. Its decentralized management approach is helping it to invest resources in those products that will do the most to promote its growth, and allow it to remain the vacation place of choice, especially as the global economy recovers.[20]

Dan Bannister/Dorling Kindersley

Figure 5.5 Spans of Control

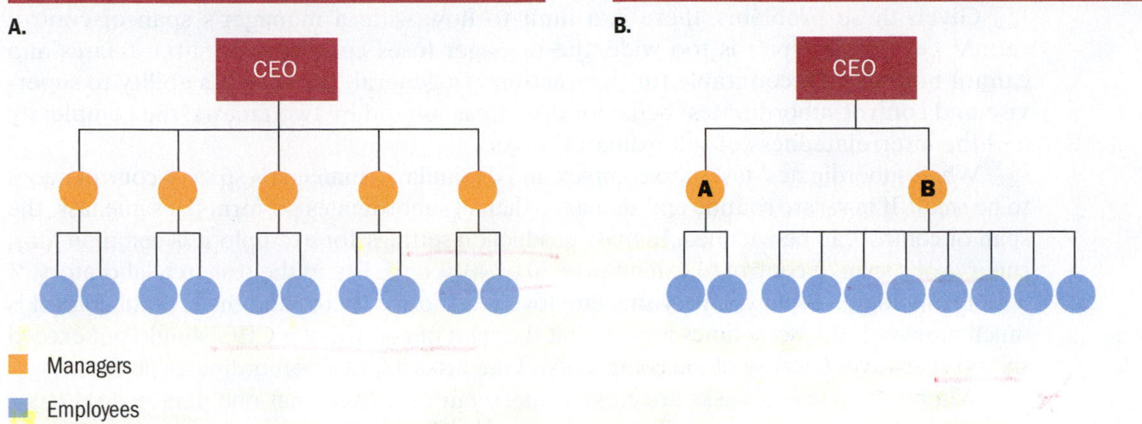

the activities of newly hired employees. How can an organization avoid becoming too tall yet maintain effective control of its workforce? One way is to increase its managers' **span of control**—the number of subordinates each manager directly manages.[21] If the span of control of each manager increases as the number of employees increases, then the number of managers or hierarchical levels does *not* increase in proportion to increases in the number of employees. Instead, each manager coordinates the work of more subordinates, and the organization substitutes an increase in the span of control for an increase in hierarchical levels.

Span of control
The number of subordinates a manager directly manages.

Figure 5.5 depicts two different spans of control. Figure 5.5A shows an organization with a CEO, five managers, and ten employees; each manager supervises two people. Figure 5.5B shows an organization with a CEO, two managers, and ten employees, but Manager A supervises two people, and Manager B supervises eight people. Why does Manager A's span of control extend over only two people and Manager B's extend over eight? Or, more generally, what determines the size *and* limit of a manager's span of control?

Perhaps the single most important factor limiting the managerial span of control is the inability to exercise adequate supervision over the activities of subordinates as they grow in number. Research has shown that an arithmetic increase in the number of subordinates is accompanied by an exponential increase in the number of subordinate relationships that a manager has to supervise.[22] Figure 5.6 illustrates this point.

The manager in Figure 5.6A has two subordinates and must manage three relationships: X, Y, and Z. The manager in Figure 5.6B has only one more subordinate than the manager in Figure 5.6A but must manage six relationships: X, Y, and Z, as well as U, V, and W. (The number of relationships is determined by the formula $n\,(n-1)/2$.) Thus a manager with eight subordinates has 28 relationships to manage. If managers lose control of their subordinates and

Figure 5.6 The Increasing Complexity of a Manager's Job as the Span of Control Increases

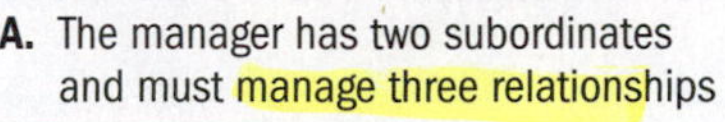

A. The manager has two subordinates and must manage three relationships

B. With the addition of just one more subordinate (for a total of three), the manager has six relationships to handle

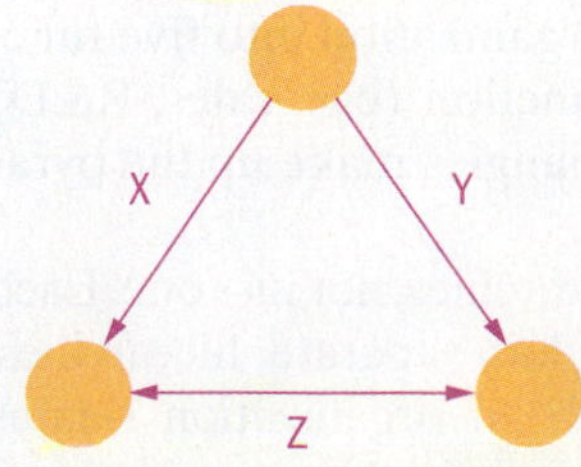

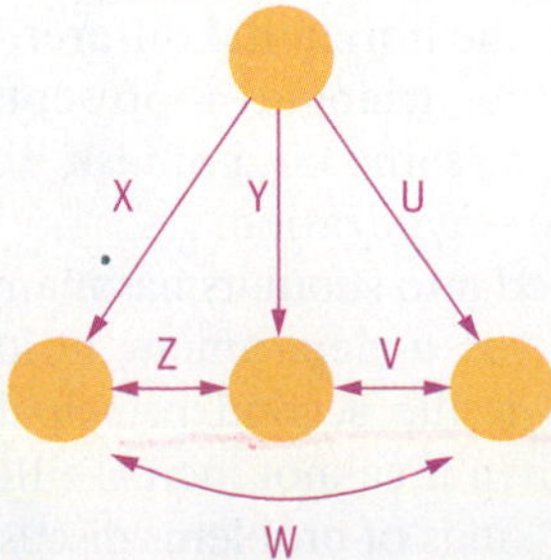

the relationships among them, subordinates have the opportunity to follow their own goals, to coast along on the performance of other group members, or to shirk their responsibilities.

Given these problems, there is a limit to how wide a manager's span of control should be.[23] If the span is too wide, the manager loses control over subordinates and cannot hold them accountable for their actions. In general, a manager's ability to supervise and control subordinates' behavior directly is limited by two factors: the complexity and the interrelatedness of subordinates' tasks.

When subordinates' tasks are complex and dissimilar, a manager's span of control needs to be small. If tasks are routine and similar so that all subordinates perform the same task, the span of control can be widened. In mass production settings, for example, it is common for a supervisor's span of control to extend over 30 or 40 people. But in the research laboratory of a biotechnology company, supervising employees is more difficult, and the span of control is much narrower. It is sometimes argued that the span of control of a CEO should not exceed six top executives because of the complexity of the tasks a CEO's subordinates perform.

When subordinates' tasks are closely interrelated, so that what one person does has a direct effect on what another person does, coordination and control are greater challenges for a manager. In Figure 5.6B, the interrelatedness of tasks means the manager has to manage relationships V, W, and Z. When subordinates' tasks are not closely interrelated, the horizontal relationships between subordinates become relatively unimportant (in Figure 5.6B, relationships V, W, and Z would be eliminated) and the manager's span of control can be dramatically increased.

Managers supervising subordinates who perform highly complex, interrelated tasks have a much narrower span of control than managers supervising workers who perform separate, relatively routine tasks (for this reason teams are used so widely as discussed in the next chapter). Indeed, the major reason organizations are normally pictured as pyramids is because the higher the level in the hierarchy, the more tasks become complex and interrelated, and so the span of control narrows to allow top managers to exert more control over their subordinates activities.

Design choices concerning the number of hierarchical levels and the span of control are major determinants of the shape of the organizational hierarchy. There are limits to how much an organization can increase the number of levels in the hierarchy, the number of managers, or the span of control, however. Even though a hierarchy of authority emerges to provide an organization with control over its activities, often if the structure becomes too tall or too top heavy with managers, or if managers become overloaded because they are supervising too many employees, an organization can lose control of its people and resources. How can an organization maintain adequate control over its work activities as it grows but avoid problems associated with a hierarchy that is too tall or a span of control that is too wide?

Control: Factors Affecting the Shape of the Hierarchy

When there are limits on the usefulness of direct, personal supervision by managers, organizations have to find other ways to control their activities. Typically, organizations first increase the level of horizontal differentiation (the second most important design choice) and then decide how to respond to the other design challenges discussed in Chapter 4. Keep in mind that successful organizational design requires managers to solve all these challenges *simultaneously* (see Figure 5.7).

Horizontal Differentiation

Horizontal differentiation leads to the emergence of specialized subunits—functions or divisions. Figure 5.8 shows the horizontal differentiation of an organization into five functions. Each of the five major triangles represents a specific function (e.g., sales, R&D) whose members perform the same kind of task. Together, the triangles make up the pyramid that depicts the whole organization.

An organization divided into subunits has many different hierarchies, not just one. Each distinct division, function, or a department inside a function has separate hierarchies. Horizontal differentiation is the second principal way in which an organization retains control over employees when it cannot increase the number of levels in the organizational hierarchy—because of the kinds of problems discussed earlier.

Figure 5.7 Factors Affecting the Shape of the Hierarchy

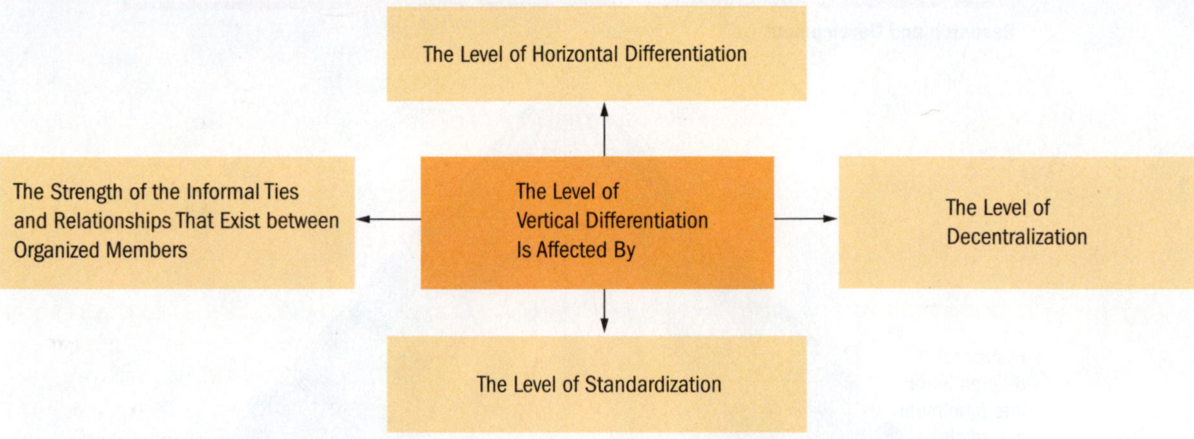

Figure 5.8 Horizontal Differentiation into Functional Hierarchies

The sales and R&D departments have three levels in their hierarchies; manufacturing has seven.

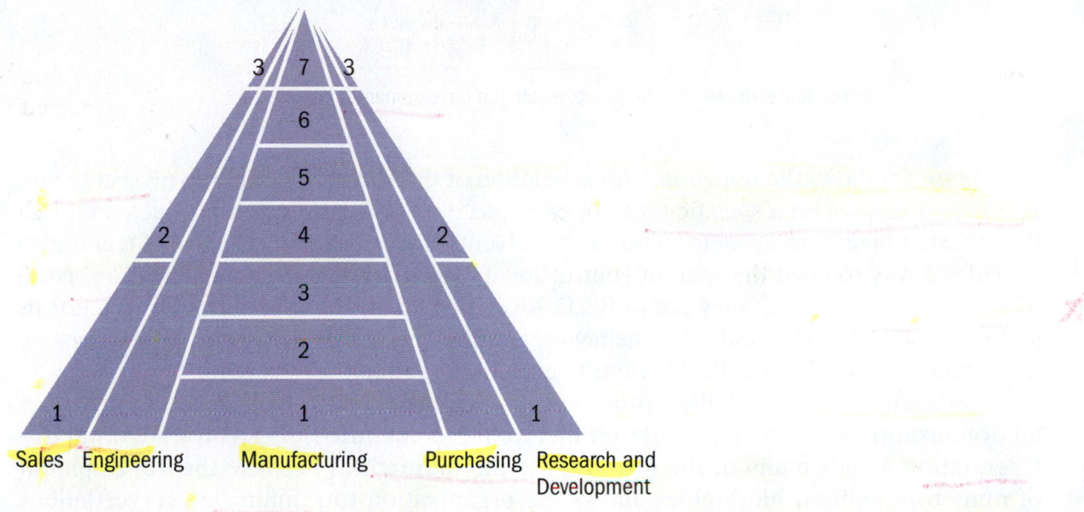

In Figure 5.8, the hierarchy of the manufacturing department has seven levels. The production manager, at level 7, reports to the CEO. In contrast, both the research and development and the sales functions have only three levels in their hierarchies. Why? Like the organization as a whole, each function also follows the principle of minimum chain of command when designing its hierarchy. Each function chooses the fewest number of hierarchical levels it needs to operate effectively and achieve its goals.[24] The manufacturing function typically has many levels because each manager at each level needs to exert tight control over their subordinates to keep production costs to a minimum. The sales department has fewer levels because supervisors use standardization, such as written reporting requirements and output controls that measure the amount salespeople sell, to monitor and control their behavior. Direct personal supervision is not required because managers can look at the numbers.

The R&D function also usually has few levels of managers, but for a different reason. Personal supervision on a continuing basis is superfluous in R&D: The tasks of scientists are complex and even if managers continually monitor researchers, they cannot evaluate how well they are performing because years may pass before significant research projects come to fruition. In an R&D context, control is generally achieved by scientists working in small teams, where they can monitor and learn from each other. This is why there is often another level of horizontal differentiation inside an organization—within a function or department, many kinds of task-oriented groups or teams are common.

Figure 5.9 Horizontal Differentiation within the R&D Functions

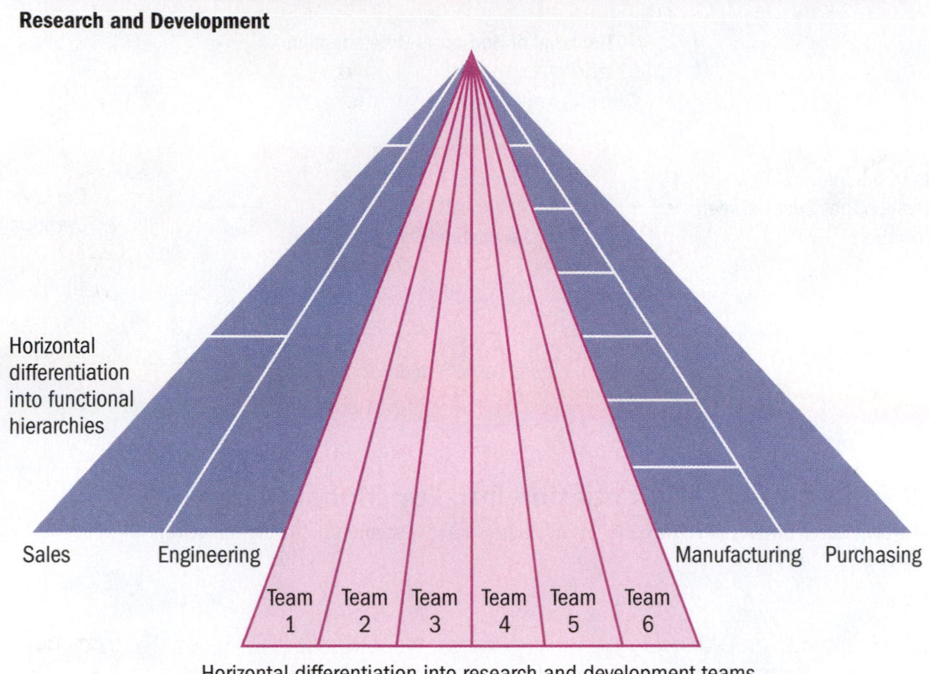

Figure 5.9 shows the horizontal differentiation of the R&D function into project teams. Each team focuses on a specific task, for example, developing different product, although the different teams are likely to share their problems and discoveries. The use of teams also provides a way to keep the span of control small, which is necessary when tasks are complex and interrelated—as they are in R&D. Moreover, in an R&D setting, informal norms and values develop to standardize behavior, and the "informal" organization becomes an important means of linking R&D teams to each other and to other functions.

Increasing horizontal differentiation thus increases vertical differentiation within an organization because many subunit hierarchies come into being. But horizontal differentiation avoids many of the problems of tall hierarchies because the development of numerous subunit hierarchies allows the organization to remain flat. Nevertheless, the problems associated with horizontal differentiation such as the development of divergent subunit orientations (see Chapter 4) can lead to additional coordination and motivation problems. Managers can control these problems by making wise choices concerning centralization, standardization, and the influence of the informal organization. (In Chapter 6 we discuss the coordination of activities between subunits.[25])

Centralization

As the hierarchy becomes taller and the number of managers increases, communication and coordination problems grow. Managers begin to spend more and more time monitoring and supervising their subordinates and less time planning and goal setting, and organizational effectiveness suffers. One solution to this problem is to decentralize authority because now less direct managerial supervision is needed. When authority is decentralized, the authority to make significant decisions is delegated to people throughout the hierarchy, not concentrated at the top. The delegation of authority to lower-level managers reduces the monitoring burden on top managers and reduces the need for "managers to monitor managers."

One organization that took steps to decentralize authority and flatten its structure because of declining performance was breakfast cereal maker Quaker Oats when it realized that competitors like Kraft and Heinz were forging ahead with new innovative product ideas and it was being left behind. Its then CEO, Robert Morrison, decided the problem was that the organization's structure put authority in the wrong place—with corporate managers above the level of the heads of its different food divisions, rather than with the heads of the food divisions themselves. So he took action. First, he eliminated the entire upper level of management—even though they were competent executives. Then he reorganized reporting relationships to decentralize authority to the division heads, who now reported directly to him, and he made them responsible for the food products under their control. As a result, he both flattened and decentralized control in the organization.

Coca-Cola Enterprises, the bottling arm of the soft-drink giant, faced a similar problem in the 2000s. Summerfield Johnston, who was then CEO, noted his company's inability to respond quickly to the changing needs of the different regions in which Coke is bottled. Johnston decided that centralized control (regional operations were controlled from the Atlanta head office) was hurting the bottling operations. Because of the long chain of command, many problems that the regions were experiencing were being dealt with slowly, and managers at the head office were often unaware of the problems that people faced on the front line. Johnston redesigned the management hierarchy. He fired over 100 managers at company headquarters and eliminated several levels in the hierarchy. He then decentralized control over operations to the vice presidents in charge of each of its 10 regional units, each of whom was given the responsibility to streamline regional operations and cut costs.[26]

Decentralization does not eliminate the need for many hierarchical levels in a large and complex organization. However, it enables even a relatively tall structure to be more flexible in its responses to changes in the external environment because it reduces the amount of direct supervision required.

Standardization

Managers can also gain control over employees by standardizing their behavior to make their actions predictable. The use of standardization reduces the need for personal control by managers and the need to add levels in the hierarchy because rules and SOPs *substitute* for direct supervision and face-to-face contact. Recall from Chapter 4 that managers standardize activities not only by creating detailed work rules but also by socializing employees into organizational norms and values. As subordinates' tasks become increasingly standardized and controlled by means of rules and norms, the amount of supervision required lessens, and a manager's span of control can be increased. Salespeople, for instance, are typically controlled by a combination of sales quotas that they are expected to achieve and written reports they are required to submit after calling on their clients. Managers do not need to monitor salespeople directly because they can evaluate their performance through those two standardized output controls. Standardization also allows upper-level managers to delegate responsibility more confidently when subordinates have clearly specified procedures to follow.

We have seen that an organization can control its members and their activities in different ways, ranging from personal control by managers in the hierarchy, to control through formalization and standardization, to informal control by means of norms and values. Structuring an organization to solve control problems requires decisions about all the different methods of control. The structure of every organization reflects the particular contingencies it faces, so every organization has a structure that is somewhat different. Nevertheless, some generalizations can be made about how organizations fashion a structure to control people and resources effectively.

First, managers increase the level of vertical differentiation, paying particular attention to keeping the organization as flat as possible and to maintaining an appropriate balance between centralization and decentralization. Second, they increase horizontal differentiation and thereby also increase vertical differentiation. Third, they decide how much they can use rules, SOPs, and norms to control activities. The more they can use them, the less they will need to rely on direct supervision from the managerial hierarchy, and the need for managers and for additional levels in the hierarchy will be reduced.

Organizational design is difficult because all these decisions affect one another and must be made simultaneously. For example, managers very often start out by designing an organic structure (see Chapter 4) with a flat hierarchy and rely on norms and values rather than on rules to control organizational activities. Very quickly, however, as the organization grows, they are forced to add levels to the hierarchy and to develop rules and SOPs to maintain control. Before managers realize it, their organization has a mechanistic structure, and they face a new set of control problems. Organizational structure evolves and has to be managed constantly if an organization is to maintain its competitive advantage.

Managerial Implications

Authority and Control

1. Managers must control the organizational hierarchy and make sure it matches the current needs of the organization. Periodically, managers should draw a new organizational chart of their organization or department and measure (a) the number of current employees, (b) the number of levels in the hierarchy, and (c) the size of the span of control of managers at different levels.
2. Using that information, managers should consider whether the hierarchy has grown too tall or too centralized. If they find the hierarchy has grown too tall, they should combine managerial positions and eliminate levels in the hierarchy by reassigning the responsibilities of the eliminated positions to managers in the level above or, preferably, by decentralizing the responsibilities to managers or employees in the levels below.
3. If managers find the hierarchy does not provide the control they need to maintain adequate supervision over people and resources, they should consider how to increase organizational control. They may need to add a level to the organizational hierarchy or, preferably, use an alternative means of control, such as increasing standardization or decentralization or making better use of the norms and values of the informal organization.
4. Managers should periodically meet in teams to consider how best to design and redesign the hierarchy so that it allows the organization to create the most value at the lowest operating cost.

The Principles of Bureaucracy

Around 1900, Max Weber (1864–1920), a German sociologist, developed principles for designing a hierarchy so it effectively allocates decision-making authority and control over resources.[27] Weber's interest was in identifying a system of organization or an organizational structure that could improve the way organizations operate—that is, increase the value they create and make them more effective.

Bureaucracy
A form of organizational structure in which people can be held accountable for their actions because they are required to act in accordance with rules and standard operating procedures.

A **bureaucracy** is a form of organizational structure in which people can be held accountable for their actions because they are required to act in accordance with well-specified and agreed-upon rules and standard operating procedures. Weber's bureaucratic organizing principles offer clear prescriptions for how to create and differentiate organizational structure so that task responsibility and decision-making authority are distributed in a way that maximizes organizational effectiveness. Because his work has been so influential in organizational design, it is useful to examine the six bureaucratic principles that, Weber argued, underlie effective organizational structure. Together these principles define a bureaucracy or bureaucratic structure (see Table 5.1).

Principle One: A bureaucracy is founded on the concept of rational-legal authority.

TABLE 5.1 The Principles of Bureaucratic Structure

Principle One: A bureaucracy is founded on the concept of rational-legal authority.

Principle Two: Organizational roles are held on the basis of technical competence.

Principle Three: A role's task responsibility and decision-making authority and its relationship to other roles should be clearly specified.

Principle Four: The organization of roles in a bureaucracy is such that each lower office in the hierarchy is under the control and supervision of a higher office.

Principle Five: Rules, standard operating procedures, and norms should be used to control the behavior and the relationship between roles in an organization.

Principle Six: Administrative acts, decisions, and rules should be formulated and put in writing.

Rational-legal authority is the authority a person possesses because of his or her position in an organization. In a bureaucracy, obedience is owed to a person not because of any personal qualities that he or she might possess (such as charisma, wealth, or social status) but because of the level of authority and responsibility associated with the organizational position the person occupies. Thus we obey a police officer not because he or she wears an impressive uniform and carries a gun but because that person holds the position of police officer, which brings with it certain powers, rights, and responsibilities that compel obedience. In theory, a bureaucracy is impersonal. People's attitudes and beliefs play no part in determining the way a bureaucracy operates. If people base decisions and orders on their personal preferences instead of on organizational goals, effectiveness suffers.

Rational-legal authority
The authority a person possesses because of his or her position in an organization.

Weber's first principle indicates that choices affecting the design of an organization's hierarchy should be based on the needs of the task, not on the needs of the person performing the task.[28] Thus subordinates obey the CEO because of the authority and power vested in the position, not because of the individual currently filling it. For a bureaucracy to be effective, however, the distinction between positions and the people who hold them must be clear: People are appointed to positions; they do not own them.

***Principle Two:* Organizational roles are held on the basis of technical competence, not because of social status, kinship, or heredity.**

In a well-designed hierarchy, people occupy roles because they can do the job, not because of who they are or who they know. Although this principle seems self-evident and the logical way to run an organization, it has often been ignored. Until 1850, for example, an officer's commission in the British Army could be bought by anybody who could afford the price. The higher the rank, the more the commission cost. As a result, most officers were rich aristocrats who had little or no formal army training, and many military disasters resulted from this system. Today, in many organizations and industries, so-called old-boy networks—personal contacts and relations—and not job-related skills influence the decision about who gets a job. The use of such criteria to fill organizational roles can be harmful to an organization because talented people get overlooked.

Picking the best person for the job seems an obvious principle to follow. In practice, however, following this principle is a difficult process that requires managers to view all potential candidates objectively. People must always remember that holding a role in an organization in a legal sense means their job is to use the organization's resources wisely for the benefit of all stakeholders, not just for personal gain.

Weber's first two principles establish the organizational role (and not the person in that role) as the basic component of bureaucratic structure. The next three principles specify how the process of differentiation should be controlled.

***Principle Three:* A role's task responsibility and decision-making authority and its relationship to other roles in the organization should be clearly specified.**

According to Weber's third principle, a clear and consistent pattern of vertical differentiation (decision-making authority) and horizontal differentiation (task responsibility) is the foundation for organizational effectiveness. When the limits of authority and control are specified for the various roles in an organization, the people in those roles know how much power they have to influence the behavior of others. Similarly, when the tasks associated with various roles are clearly specified, people in those roles clearly know what is expected of them. Thus, with those two aspects of a person's role in an organization clearly defined, a stable system emerges in which each person has a clear expectation and understanding of the rights and responsibilities attached to other organizational roles. In such a stable system all individuals know how much their supervisor can require of them and how much they can require of their subordinates. People also know how to deal with their peers—people who are at the same level in the organization as they are and over whom they have no authority, and vice versa.

Clear specification of roles avoids many problems that can arise when people interact. If, for example, some task responsibilities are assigned to more than one role, the people in those roles may have to fight over the same set of resources or claim responsibility for the same tasks. Is sales or marketing responsible for handling customer requests for information? Is the head of the army or the head of the air force responsible for invasive operations in enemy territory? The military is a vast bureaucracy in which the division of labor among the armed services is continually being negotiated to prevent such problems from emerging.

Role conflict
The state of opposition that occurs when two or more people have different views of what another person should do and, as a result, make conflicting demands on the person.

Role ambiguity
The uncertainty that occurs for a person whose tasks or authority are not clearly defined.

A clear pattern of vertical (authority) and horizontal (task) differentiation also cuts down on role conflict and role ambiguity.[29] **Role conflict** occurs when two or more people have different views of what another person should do and, as a result, make conflicting demands on the person. The person may be caught in the crossfire between two supervisors or the needs of two functional groups. **Role ambiguity** occurs when a person's tasks or authority are not clearly defined and the person becomes afraid to act on or take responsibility for anything. Clear descriptions of task and authority relationships solve conflict and ambiguity problems: When people know the dimensions of their position in the organization, they find it easier to take responsibility for their actions and to interact with one another.

Principle Four: The organization of roles in a bureaucracy is such that each lower office in the hierarchy is under the control and supervision of a higher office.

To control vertical authority relationships, the organization should be arranged hierarchically so people can recognize the chain of command.[30] The organization should delegate to each person holding a role the authority needed to make certain decisions and to use certain organizational resources. The organization can then hold the person in the role accountable for the use of those resources. The hierarchical pattern of vertical differentiation also makes clear that a person at a low level in the hierarchy can go to someone at a higher level to solve conflicts at the low level. In the U.S. court system, for example, participants in a court case can ask a higher court to review the decision of a lower court if they feel a bad decision was made. The right to appeal to a higher organizational level also needs to be specified in case a subordinate feels that his or her immediate superior has made a bad or unfair decision.

Principle Five: Rules, standard operating procedures, and norms should be used to control the behavior and the relationship among roles in an organization.

Rules and SOPs are formal written instructions that specify a series of actions to be taken to achieve a given end; for example, if A happens, then do B. Norms are unwritten standards or styles of behavior that govern how people act and lead people to behave in predictable ways. Rules, SOPs, and norms provide behavioral guidelines that can increase efficiency because they specify the best way to accomplish a task. Over time, these guidelines should change as improved ways of doing things are discovered. The goal is constant progress to meeting organizational goals.

Rules, SOPs, and norms clarify people's expectations about one another and prevent misunderstandings over responsibility or the use of power. Such guidelines can prevent a supervisor from arbitrarily increasing a subordinate's workload and prevent a subordinate from ignoring tasks that are a legitimate part of the job. A simple set of rules established by the supervisor of some custodial workers (Crew G) at a Texas A&M University building clearly established task responsibilities and clarified expectations (see Table 5.2).

Rules and norms enhance the integration and coordination of organizational roles at different levels and between different functions. Vertical and horizontal differentiation breaks the organization up into distinct roles that must be coordinated and integrated to accomplish organizational goals.[31] Rules and norms are important aspects of integration. They specify how roles interact, and they provide procedures that people should follow to jointly perform a task.[32] For example, a rule could stipulate that "Sales must give

TABLE 5.2 Crew G's Rules of Conduct

1. All employees must call their supervisor or leader before 5:55 A.M. to notify of absence or tardiness.
2. Disciplinary action will be issued to any employee who abuses sick leave policy.
3. Disciplinary action will be issued to any employee whose assigned area is not up to custodial standards.
4. If a door is locked when you go in to clean an office, it's your responsibility to lock it back up.
5. Name tags and uniforms must be worn daily.
6. Each employee is responsible for buffing hallways and offices. Hallways must be buffed weekly, offices periodically.
7. All equipment must be put in closets during 9:00 A.M. and 11 A.M. breaks.
8. Do not use the elevator to move trash or equipment from 8:50 to 9:05, 9:50 to 10:05, 11:50 to 12:05, or 1:50 to 2:05, to avoid breaks between classes.
9. Try to mop hallways when students are in classrooms, or mop floors as you go down to each office.
10. Closets must be kept clean, and all equipment must be clean and operative.
11. Each employee is expected to greet building occupants with "Good morning."
12. Always knock before entering offices and conference rooms.
13. Loud talking, profanity, and horseplay will not be tolerated inside buildings.
14. All custodial carts must be kept uniform and cleaned daily.
15. You must have excellent "public relations" with occupants at all times.

Your supervisor stands behind workers at all times when the employee is in the right and you are doing what you are supposed to. But when you are wrong, you are wrong. Let's try to work together to better Crew G because there are many outstanding employees in this crew.

production five days' notice of any changes in customer requirements." Or an informal norm could require underused servers to help those who have fallen behind in serving their customers. It is important never to underestimate the power of rules, as Organizational Insight 5.3 makes clear.

Alas, these moves came too late to save the chain; nothing kills a restaurant as much as a reputation for poor food quality. Customers tell their friends by word of mouth; the news spreads. The China Coast episode illustrates an important lesson in organizational design: Managers must have a structure planned, worked out, and tested before they embark on ambitious attempts at expansion. This is why today, before starting a chain of restaurants or any other kind of business, a prototype is created and tested at some typical location and all the bugs involved in operating the business are worked out, and rules and SOPs developed and codified in operations manuals before the concept is rolled out.

Principle Six: Administrative acts, decisions, and rules should be formulated and put in writing.

When rules and decisions are written down, they become official guides to the way the organization works. Thus, even when an employee leaves an organization, an indication of what that person did is part of the organization's written records. A bureaucratic structure provides an organization with memory, and it is the responsibility of its members to train their successors and ensure continuity in the organizational hierarchy. Written records also ensure that organizational history cannot be altered and that people can be held accountable for their decisions.

The Advantages of Bureaucracy

Almost every organization possesses some features of bureaucracy.[33] The primary advantage of a bureaucracy is that it lays out the ground rules for designing an organizational hierarchy that efficiently controls interactions between organizational levels.[34] Bureaucracy's

Organizational Insight 5.3

Never Underestimate the Power of Rules

General Mills, the cereal maker best known for Cheerios cereal and Yoplait yogurt, created two of the best-known restaurant chains in the United States—Red Lobster and the Olive Garden. Inspired by this success, its managers decided they could use the skills and experience they had gained from operating their growing restaurant chains to start a new chain specializing in Chinese food. Called China Coast, a prototype restaurant was opened in Orlando, Florida; customers were favorably impressed by the decor and by the food.

General Mills managers were excited by customers' positive response to the new restaurant and decided they would rapidly expand the chain. Operating at breakneck speed, managers opened 38 restaurants in nine states. With the restaurant chain in full swing, however, problems began to arise. Customers were no longer so enthusiastic about the quality of the food or the customer service, and sales volume fell off. What had gone wrong?

Apparently, in the attempt to open so many restaurants so quickly, managers lost control of quality. Chinese food is difficult to prepare properly, and employees require extensive training if they are to keep quality consistently high. Top managers had created a set of company-wide food-quality standards for restaurant managers to follow, but the restaurant managers failed to ensure that these output standards were met consistently. Moreover, there were customer complaints about the quality of service that had not been reported to managers at the Orlando prototype. While searching for reasons for the failure of the new restaurants to meet company standards, top managers discovered that the primary problem was that they had not put the right set of bureaucratic rules in place.

Restaurant managers had not received enough restaurant operations training. Top managers had not created enough rules and SOPs for restaurant managers either to follow or to teach to their employees—the cooks who actually prepared the food and the people who served it. Top managers decided that each restaurant manager should attend a four-month intensive training course during which he or she would be taught the rules to be followed when preparing and serving the food. The rules would be written down and formalized in an operations manual that managers would take back to their restaurants for reference when training employees.

To make sure that restaurant managers did indeed follow the rules to ensure high-quality food and customer service, General Mills's managers created a new layer of managers—regional managers whose responsibility was to supervise restaurant managers. Regional managers also were responsible for giving restaurant managers additional training as new dishes were introduced on the menu and for informing them of any changes in operating procedures that top managers had developed to improve the performance of individual restaurants.

clear specification of vertical authority and horizontal task relationships means there is no question about each person's role in the organization. Individuals can be held accountable for what they do, and such accountability reduces the transaction costs that arise when people must continually negotiate and define their organizational roles. Similarly, the specification of roles and the use of rules, SOPs, and norms to regulate how tasks are performed reduce the costs associated with monitoring the work of subordinates and increase integration within the organization. Finally, written rules regarding the reward and punishment of employees, such as rules for promotion and termination, reduce the costs of enforcement and evaluating employee performance.

Another advantage of bureaucracy is that it separates the position from the person. The fairness and equity of bureaucratic selection, evaluation, and reward systems encourage organizational members to advance the interests of all organizational stakeholders and meet organizational expectations.[35] Bureaucracy provides people with the opportunity to develop their skills and pass them on to their successors. In this way, a bureaucracy fosters differentiation, increases the organization's core competences, and improves its ability to compete in the marketplace against other organizations for scarce resources.[36] Bureaucracies provide the stability necessary for organizational members to take a long-run view of the organization and its relationship to its environment.

If a bureaucracy is based on such clear guidelines for allocating authority and control in an organization, why is bureaucracy considered a dirty word by some people, and why are terms like *bureaucrats* and *bureaucratic red tape* meant as insults? Why do bureaucratic structures generate such ill feeling?

One of the problems that emerges within a bureaucracy over time is that managers fail to control the development of the organizational hierarchy properly—in the manner advocated by Weber. As a result, these organizations often become very tall, centralized, and inflexible. Decision making slows down, the organization begins to stagnate, and bureaucratic costs increase because managers start to make work for each other.

Another problem with bureaucracy is that organizational members come to rely too much on rules and SOPs to make decisions, and this overreliance makes them unresponsive to the needs of customers and other stakeholders. Organizational members lose sight of the fact that their job is to create value for stakeholders. Instead, their chief goal is to follow rules and procedures and obey authority to protect their personal positions and interests.

Organizations that suffer from those problems are accused of being bureaucratic or of being run by bureaucrats. However, whenever we hear this claim, we must be careful to distinguish between the principles of bureaucracy and the people who manage bureaucratic organizations. Remember: There is nothing intrinsically bad or inefficient about a bureaucracy. When organizations become overly bureaucratic, the fault lies with the people who run them—with managers who prefer the pursuit of power and status to the pursuit of operating efficiency, who prefer to protect their careers rather than their organizations, and who prefer to use resources to benefit themselves rather than stakeholders. Indeed, one technique that can be used to mitigate these problems is management by objectives (MBO), although care has to taken to ensure that an MBO system is based on Weber's principles.

Management by Objectives

To provide a framework within which to evaluate subordinates' behavior and, in particular, to allow managers to monitor progress toward achieving goals, many organizations implement some version of **management by objectives (MBO),** a system of evaluating subordinates on their ability to achieve specific organizational goals or performance standards and to meet operating budgets. Most organizations make some use of MBO because it is pointless to establish goals and then fail to evaluate whether or not they are being achieved. MBO involves three specific steps:

Management by objectives (MBO) A system of evaluating subordinates on their ability to achieve specific organizational goals or performance standards and to meet operating budgets.

STEP 1 *Specific goals and objectives are established at each level of the organization.*

Management by objective starts when top managers establish overall organizational objectives, such as specific financial performance targets. Then objective setting cascades down throughout the organization as managers at the divisional and functional levels set their objectives to achieve corporate objectives. Finally, first-level managers and workers jointly set objectives that will contribute to achieving functional goals.

STEP 2 *Managers and their subordinates together determine the subordinates' goals.*

An important characteristic of management by objectives is its participatory nature. Managers at every level sit down with the subordinate managers who report directly to them and together they determine appropriate and feasible goals for the subordinate and bargain over the budget that the subordinate will need so as to achieve these goals. The participation of subordinates in the objective-setting process is a way of strengthening their commitment to achieving their goals and meeting their budgets. Another reason why it is so important for subordinates (both individuals and teams) to participate in goal setting is so they can tell managers what they think they can realistically achieve.

STEP 3 *Managers and their subordinates periodically review the subordinates' progress toward meeting goals.*

Once specific objectives have been agreed on for managers at each level, managers are accountable for meeting those objectives. Periodically, they sit down with their subordinates to evaluate their progress. Normally, salary raises and promotions are linked to the goal-setting process, and managers who achieve their goals receive greater rewards than those who fall short. (The issue of how to design reward systems to motivate managers and other organizational employees is discussed in Chapter 10.)

In the companies that have decentralized responsibility for the production of goods and services to teams, particularly cross-functional teams, management by objectives works somewhat differently. Managers ask each team to develop a set of goals and performance targets that the team hopes to achieve—goals consistent with organizational objectives. Managers then negotiate with each team to establish its final goals and the budget the team will need to achieve them. The reward system is linked to team performance, not to the performance of any one team member.

One company that has spent considerable time developing a formal MBO system is Zytec Corporation, a leading manufacturer of power supplies for computers and other electronic equipment. Each of Zytec's managers and workers participates in goal setting.

Managerial Implications

Using Bureaucracy to Benefit the Organization

1. If organizational hierarchies are to function effectively and the problems of overly bureaucratized organizations are to be avoided, both managers and employees must follow bureaucratic principles.
2. Both employees and managers should realize that they do not own their positions in an organization and it is their responsibility to use their authority and control over resources to benefit stakeholders and not themselves.
3. Managers should strive to make human resource decisions such as hiring, promoting, or rewarding employees as fair and equitable as possible. Managers should not let personalities or relationships influence their decisions, and employees should complain to managers when they feel their decisions are inappropriate.
4. Periodically, the members of a work group or function should meet to ensure that reporting relationships are clear and unambiguous and the rules that members are using to make decisions meet current needs.
5. Both managers and employees should adopt a questioning attitude toward the way the organization works to uncover the taken-for-granted assumptions and beliefs on which it operates. For example, to make sure they are not wasting organizational resources by performing unnecessary actions, they should always ask questions such as "Is that rule or SOP really necessary?" and "Who will read the report that I am writing?" An MBO system can also help managers evaluate the working of their hierarchy.

Top managers first establish cross-functional teams to create a five-year plan for the company and to set broad goals for each function. This plan is then reviewed by employees from all areas of the company. They evaluate the plan's feasibility and make suggestions about how to modify or improve it. Each function then uses the broad goals in the plan to set more specific goals for each manager and each team in the organization; these goals are reviewed with top managers. The MBO system at Zytec is organization-wide and fully participatory, and performance is reviewed both from an annual and a five-year time horizon. Zytec's MBO system has been very effective. Not only have organizational costs dropped dramatically, but the company also won the Baldrige Award for quality.

The Influence of the Informal Organization

The hierarchy of authority designed by management that allocates people and resources to organizational tasks and roles is a blueprint for how things are supposed to happen. However, at all levels in the organization, decision making and coordination frequently take place outside the formally designed channels as people interact informally on the job. Moreover, many of the rules and norms that employees use to perform their tasks emerge out of informal interactions between people and not from the formal blueprint and rules established by managers. Thus, while establishing a formal structure of interrelated roles, managers are also creating an informal social structure that affects behavior in ways that may be unintended. The importance of understanding the way in which the network of personal relationships that develop over time in an organization—the informal organization—affects the way the formal hierarchy works is illustrated in Organizational Insight 5.4.[37]

By reintroducing the plant's formal hierarchy of authority, the new management team totally changed the informal organization that had been governing the way workers thought they should act. The changes destroyed the norms that had made the plant work smoothly (although not from top management's perspective). The result of changing the informal organization, however, was lower productivity because of the strikes.

This example shows that managers need to consider the effects of the informal organization on individual and group behavior when they make any organizational

Organizational Insight 5.4

Wildcat Strikes in the Gypsum Plant

Gypsum is a mineral extracted from the ground, then crushed, refined, and compacted into wallboard. A gypsum mine and processing plant owned by the General Gypsum Company was located in a rural community, and farmers and laborers frequently supplemented their farm income by working in the plant.[38] The situation in the mine was stable, the management team had been in place for many years, and workers knew exactly what they had to do. Coordination in the plant took place through long-established informal routines that were taken for granted by management and workers alike. Workers did a fair day's work for a fair day's pay. For its part, management was very liberal. It allowed workers to take the inexpensive wallboard for their own personal use and overlooked absences from work, which were especially common during the harvest season.

The situation changed when the corporate office sent a new plant manager to take over the plant's operations and improve its productivity. When the new man arrived he was amazed by the situation. He could not understand how the previous manager had allowed workers to take wallboard, break work rules (such as those concerning absenteeism), and otherwise take advantage of the company. He decided that these practices had to stop, and he took steps to change the way the company was operated.

He began by reactivating the formal rules and procedures that, although they had always existed, had never been enforced by the previous management team. He reinstituted rules concerning absenteeism and punished workers who were excessively absent. He stopped the informal practice of allowing employees to take wallboard even though it cost only pennies, and he took formal steps to reestablish management's authority in the plant. In short, he reestablished the formal organizational structure—one that worked through the rigid hierarchy of authority and strictly enforced rules that no longer indulged the employees.

The results were immediate. The workforce walked out and, in a series of wildcat strikes, refused to return until the old system was restored. It made no difference to the workers that the formal rules and procedures had always been on the books. They were used to the old, informal routines and they wanted them back. Eventually, after prolonged negotiation about new work practices, the union and company reached an agreement that defined the relative spheres of authority of management and the union, and established a bureaucratic system for managing future disputes. When the new work routines were in place, the wildcat strikes ended.

changes. Altering the formal structure often disrupts the informal norms that make the organization work. Because an organization is a network of informal social relations, as well as a hierarchy of formal task and authority relations, managers must harness the power of the informal organization to help achieve organizational goals.

People in organizations go to enormous lengths to increase their status and prestige and always want others to know about and recognize their status. Every organization has an established informal organization that does not appear on any formal chart but is familiar to all employees. Much of what gets done in an organization gets done through the informal organization, in ways not revealed by the organizational chart. Managers need to consider carefully the implications of the interactions between the formal and informal hierarchies when changing the ways they motivate and coordinate employees.

The informal organization can actually enhance organizational performance. New approaches to organization design argue that managers need to tap into the power of the informal organization to increase motivation and provide informal avenues for employees to use to improve organizational performance. The formal hierarchical structure is the main mechanism of control, but managers should use the informal structure along with the formal one to allow people to work out solutions to their problems.

IT, Empowerment, and Self-Managed Teams

An important trend, which is accelerating as the result of advances in IT, is the increasing use of empowered workers, self-managed teams, cross-functional teams, and contingent or temporary workers. IT is making it much easier for managers to design a cost-effective structure and control system that gives them much more and much better information about subordinates' activities, assesses functional performance, and intervenes as necessary to better achieve organizational goals. IT, providing as it does a way of standardizing behavior through the use of a consistent, and often cross-functional, software platform, is an important means of controlling behavior. When all employees or functions use the same software platform to provide up-to-date information on their activities, this codifies and standardizes organizational knowledge and makes it easier to monitor progress toward goals. IT provides people at all levels in the hierarchy with more of the information and knowledge they need to perform their roles effectively. For example, employees are able easily to access information from other employees via cross-functional software systems that keep them all informed about changes in product design, engineering, manufacturing schedules, and marketing plans that will impact their activities. In this way, IT overlays and supports the structure of tasks and roles that is normally regarded as the "real" organizational structure.

Thus the increasing use of IT has led to a decentralization of authority in organizations and an increasing use of teams. As discussed earlier, decentralizing authority to lower-level employees and placing them in teams reduces the need for direct, personal supervision by managers, and organizations become flatter. **Empowerment** is the process of giving employees at all levels in an organization's hierarchy the authority to make important decisions and to be responsible for their outcomes. **Self-managed teams** are formal work groups consisting of people who are jointly responsible for ensuring that the team accomplishes its goals and who are empowered to lead themselves. **Cross-functional teams** are formal work groups of employees from across an organization's different functions that are empowered to direct and coordinate the value-creation activities necessary to complete different programs or projects.

Empowerment
The process of giving employees throughout an organization the authority to make important decisions and to be responsible for their outcomes.

Self-managed teams
Work groups consisting of people who are jointly responsible for ensuring that the team accomplishes its goals and who are empowered to lead themselves.

Cross-functional teams
Formal work groups of employees from across an organization's different functions that are empowered to direct and coordinate the value-creation activities necessary to complete different programs or projects.

The movement to flatten organizations by empowering workers in this way has increased steadily since the 1990s and has met with great success according to many stories in the popular press. However, whereas some commentators have forecasted the "end of hierarchy" and the emergence of new organizational forms based purely on lateral relations both inside and between functions, other commentators are not so sure. They argue that even a flat, team-based organization composed of empowered workers must have a hierarchy and some minimum set of rules and SOPs if the organization is to have sufficient control over its activities. Organizations sacrifice the advantages of bureaucratic structure only at their peril.[39] The challenge for managers is to combine the best aspects of both systems—of bureaucratic structure and empowered work groups. Essentially, what this comes down to is that managers must be sure they have the right blend of mechanistic and organic structure to meet the contingencies they face. Managers should use bureaucratic principles to build a mechanistic structure, and they should enhance the organization's ability to act in an organic way by empowering employees and making teams a principal way of increasing the level of integration in an organization.

Finally, as organizations have flattened their structures, there has been an increasing trend for companies to employ contingent workers to lower operating costs. **Contingent workers** are those who are employed for temporary periods by an organization and who receive no indirect benefits such as health insurance or pensions. Contingent workers may work by the day, week, or month performing some functional task, or they may contract with the organization for some fee to perform a specific service to the organization. Thus, for example, an organization may employ ten temporary accountants to "do the books" when it is time or it may contract with a software programmer to write some specialized software for a fixed fee.

Contingent workers
Workers who are employed for temporary periods by an organization and who receive no indirect benefits such as health insurance or pensions.

The advantages an organization obtains from contingent workers are that they cost less to employ because they receive no indirect benefits and they can be let go easily when their services are no longer needed. However, some disadvantages are also associated with contingent workers. First, coordination and motivation problems may arise because temporary workers may have less incentive to perform at a high level, given that there is no prospect for promotion or job security. Second, organizations must develop core competences in their functions to gain a competitive advantage, and it is unlikely that contingent workers will help them develop such competences because they do not remain with the organization very long and are not committed to it.

Nevertheless, it has been estimated that 20% of the U.S. workforce today consists of contingent workers, and this figure is expected to increase as managers work to find new ways to reduce bureaucratic costs. Indeed, one method that managers are already employing to keep their structures flat is the use of outsourcing and network structures, which are discussed in detail in the next chapter.

Summary

Stakeholder goals and objectives can be achieved only when organizational skills and capabilities are controlled through organizational structure. The activities of organizational members would be chaotic without a structure that assigns people to roles and directs the activities of people and functions.[40] This chapter has examined how organizations should design their hierarchy of authority and choose control systems that create an effective organizational structure. The shape of the hierarchy determines how decision making takes place. It also determines how motivated people will be to pursue organizational goals. Designing the hierarchy should be one of management's major tasks, but, as we have seen, it is a task that many organizations do not do well or fail to consider at all. Chapter 5 has made the following main points:

1. The height of an organization's structure is a function of the number of levels in the hierarchy, the span of control at each level, and the balance between centralization and decentralization of authority.
2. As an organization grows, the increase in the size of the managerial component is less than proportional to the increase in the size of the organization.
3. Problems with tall hierarchies include communication, motivation, and bureaucratic costs.
4. According to the principle of minimum chain of command, an organization should choose the minimum number of hierarchical levels consistent with the contingencies it faces.
5. The span of control is the number of subordinates a manager directly manages. The two main factors that affect the span of control are task complexity and task interrelatedness.
6. The shape of the hierarchy and the way it works are also affected by choices concerning horizontal differentiation, centralization versus decentralization, differentiation versus integration, standardization versus mutual adjustment, and the influence of the informal organization.
7. The six principles of bureaucratic theory specify the most effective way to design the hierarchy of authority in an organization.
8. Bureaucracy has several advantages. It is fair and equitable, and it can promote organizational effectiveness by improving organizational design. However, problems can arise if bureaucratic principles are not followed and if managers allow the organization to become too tall and centralized.
9. Managers need to recognize how the informal organization affects the way the formal hierarchy of authority works and make sure the two fit to enhance organizational performance.
10. To keep their organizations as flat as possible, managers are increasingly making use of IT and creating self-managed work teams of empowered workers and/or turning to contingent workers.

Discussion Questions

1. Choose a small organization in your city, such as a restaurant or school, and draw a chart showing its structure. Do you think the number of levels in its hierarchy and the span of control at each level are appropriate? Why or why not?
2. In what ways can the informal organization and the norms and values of its culture affect the shape of an organization?
3. What factors determine the appropriate authority and control structure in (a) a research and development laboratory, (b) a large department store, and (c) a small manufacturing company?
4. How can the principles of bureaucracy help managers design the organizational hierarchy?
5. When does bureaucracy become a problem in an organization? What can managers do to prevent bureaucratic problems from arising?

Organizational Theory in Action

Practicing Organizational Theory

How to Design a Hierarchy

Form groups of three to five people and discuss the following scenario:

You are the managers charged with reducing high operating costs. You have been instructed by the CEO to eliminate 25% of the company's managerial positions and then to reorganize the remaining positions so that the organization still exercises adequate supervision over its employees.

1. How would you go about analyzing the organizational hierarchy to decide which managerial positions should be cut first?
2. How will you be able to ensure adequate supervision with fewer managers?
3. What can you do to help make the downsizing process less painful for those who leave and for those who remain?

The Ethical Dimension #5

Suppose an organization is purging its top and middle managers. Some managers charged with deciding who to terminate might decide to keep the subordinates they like, and who are obedient to them, rather than the ones who are difficult or the best performers. They might decide to lay off the most highly paid subordinates even if they are high performers. Think of the ethics issues involved in designing a hierarchy and its effect on stakeholders.

1. What ethical rules should managers use when deciding who to terminate and when redesigning their hierarchy?
2. Some people argue that employees who have worked for an organization for many years have a claim on the organization at least as strong as its shareholders. What do you think of the ethics of this position: Can employees claim to "own" their jobs if they have contributed significantly to past success?

Making the Connection #5

Find an example of a company that recently changed its hierarchy of authority or its top-management team. What changes did it make? Why did it make them? What does it hope to accomplish as a result of them? What happened as a result of the changes?

Analyzing the Organization: Design Module #5

This module focuses on vertical differentiation and understanding the managerial hierarchy in your organization and the way the organization allocates decision-making authority.

Assignment

1. How many people does the organization employ?
2. How many levels are there in the organization's hierarchy?
3. Is the organization tall or flat? Does the organization experience any of the problems associated with tall hierarchies? Which ones?
4. What is the span of control of the CEO? Is this span appropriate, or is it too wide or too narrow?
5. How do centralization, standardization, and horizontal differentiation affect the shape of the organization?
6. Do you think your organization does a good or a poor job in managing its hierarchy of authority? Give reasons for your answer.

CASE FOR ANALYSIS

Ursula Burns Succeeds Anne Mulcahy as CEO of Xerox

In the early 2000s Xerox, the well-known copier company, was near bankruptcy because aggressive Japanese competitors were selling low-priced digital copiers that made Xerox's pioneering light-lens copying process obsolete. The result was plummeting sales as U.S. customers bought Japanese copiers and Xerox was losing billions of dollars. Xerox searched for a new CEO who had the management skills to revitalize the company's product line and the person chosen to lead the company's transformation was Anne Mulcahy, a 26-year Xerox veteran. Mulcahy had begun her career as a Xerox copier salesperson, transferred into human resource management, and then used her considerable leadership and communication skills to work her way up the company's hierarchy to become its president.

As the new CEO, the biggest organizational challenge Mulcahy faced was to find ways to reduce Xerox's high operating costs but, at the same time, find ways to develop innovative new lines of copiers. Specifically, she had to decide how to invest the company's research dollars to develop desperately needed new kinds of digital copiers that would attract customers back to the company and generate new revenues and profits. Simultaneously achieving both these objectives is one of the biggest challenges a manager can face, and how well she performed these tasks would determine Xerox's fate—indeed its very survival.[41]

To find a solution to this problem, Mulcahy, known as an unassuming person who as CEO prefers to stay in the background, focused her efforts on involving and listening to Xerox's managers, employees, and customers describe its problems. Mulcahy began a series of "town hall" meetings with Xerox employees, asked them for all kinds of creative input and their best efforts, but told them that tough times were ahead and that layoffs would be necessary. At the same time she emphasized that only their motivation to work hard and find ways to reduce costs and develop new products could save the company. To discover how the company should best invest its R&D budget, Mulcahy made reaching out to customers her other main priority. She insisted that managers and engineers at all levels should visit, meet, and talk to customers to uncover what they most wanted from new digital copiers—and from Xerox. During one of her initiatives, called "Focus 500," which required Xerox's top 200 managers to visit its top 500 customers, Mulcahy came to increasingly appreciate the skills of Ursula Burns, who had joined Xerox four years after her and was quickly establishing her own reputation as a manager who knew how to motivate and lead employees. Burns had started her career as a mechanical engineer and was now the top manager in charge of its manufacturing and supply chain activities—the main source of its high operating costs.

By listening closely to both employees and customers, Mulcahy, Burns, and Xerox's engineers gained insights that allowed them to transform the company's product line. Their goal was to spend Xerox's shrinking R&D funds to develop two new lines of digital copiers: a line of state-of-the-art digital color copying machines for use by large businesses, and a line of low-end copiers offering print quality, speed, and prices that even Japanese competitors could not match. To shrink costs Mulcahy was forced to flatten Xerox's management hierarchy and streamline its operating units that reduced the number of employees from 95,000 to 55,000 and cut 26% from corporate overhead. By 2008 it was clear that Mulcahy and her managers—in particular Ursula Burns, who was now Mulcahy's second in command—had devised a successful turnaround plan to save Xerox, and all its employees were committed to work together to continually improve its products and performance.

Continuing to work closely with customers, Mulcahy and Burns developed new strategies for Xerox based on improved products and services. In talking to Xerox customers, for example, it became clear they wanted a combination of copying software and hardware that would allow them to create highly customized documents for their own customers. Banks, retail stores, and small businesses needed personalized software to create individual client statements, for example. Mulcahy decided to grow the customized services side of Xerox's business to meet these specialized needs. She also decided to replicate Xerox's sales and customer service operations around the globe and customize them to the needs of customers in each country. The result was soaring profits.

In 2009 Mulcahy decided that her handpicked successor, Ursula Burns, should became its next CEO.[42] The move to transfer power from one woman CEO to another at the same company is exceptional, and Burns is also the first African-American woman to head a public company as large as Xerox. Within months of becoming CEO Burns announced a new major initiative to acquire Affiliated Computer Services for $6.4 billion so Xerox could increase its push to provide highly customized customer service. Burns said the acquisition would be a major game changer because it would triple Xerox's service revenue to over $10 billion and increase total company revenues to $22 billion. Also, $400 million in cost savings were expected. Xerox's shares have climbed 40% since Burns took over as CEO and in 2011 with Ursula Burns at the helm, Xerox's future looks bright indeed.

Questions for Discussion

1. In what ways can (a) flattening the hierarchy and (b) centralizing/decentralizing authority help an organization like Xerox to improve its performance?
2. What kinds of factors change the decision to centralize or decentralize authority over time in a fast-changing environment such as the digital document services industry?

References

1 J. R. Galbraith, *Designing Complex Organizations* (Reading, MA: Addison-Wesley, 1973).

2 P. R. Lawrence and J. W. Lorsch, *Organization and Environment* (Boston: Graduate School of Business Administration, Harvard University, 1967).

3 G. R. Jones, "Task Visibility, Free Riding, and Shirking: Explaining the Effect of Organization Structure on Employee Behavior," *Academy of Management Review* 4 (1984), 684–695.

4 P. M. Blau, "A Formal Theory of Differentiation in Organizations," *American Sociological Review* 35 (1970), 201–218.

5 J. Child, *Organization: A Guide for Managers and Administrators* (New York: Harper & Row, 1977), pp. 10–15; P. Blau, "A Formal Theory of Differentiation."

6 P. Blau, "A Formal Theory of Differentiation"; W. R. Scott, *Organizations: Rational, Natural, and Open Systems* (Englewood Cliffs, NJ: Prentice-Hall, 1981), pp. 235–240.

7 D. D. Baker and J. C. Cullen, "Administrative Reorganization and the Configurational Context: The Contingent Effects of Age, Size, and Changes in Size," *Academy of Management Journal* 36 (1993), 1251–1277.

8 P. M. Blau and R. A. Schoenherr, *The Structure of Organizations* (New York: Basic Books, 1971).

9 R. Carzo and J. N. Zanousas, "Effects of Flat and Tall Structure," *Administrative Science Quarterly* 14 (1969), 178–191; A. Gupta and V. Govindarajan, "Business Unit Strategy, Managerial Characteristics, and Business Unit Effectiveness at Strategy Implementation," *Academy of Management Journal* 27 (1984), 25–41.

10 D. Katz and R. L. Kahn, *The Social Psychology of Organizing* (New York: Wiley, 1966), p. 255.

11 A. M. Pettigrew, *The Politics of Organizational Decision Making* (London: Tavistock, 1973).

12 www.dupont.com, 2011.

13 C. N. Parkinson, *Parkinson's Law* (New York: Ballantine Books, 1964).

14 Ibid., p. 17.

15 See, for example, "Preparing the Company Organization Manual," *Studies in Personnel Policy*, no. 157 (New York: National Industrial Conference Board, 1957), p. 28.

16 www.emi.com, 2011.

17 C. Goldsmith and J. Ordonez, "Levy Jolts EMI: Can He Reform the Music Industry?" *Wall Street Journal*, September 6, 2002, pp. B1, B4.

18 J. McGregor, "The World's Most Innovative Companies," www.businessweek.com, May 4, 2007.

19 R. Nakashima, "Iger: Disney to Reap $1 Billion Online," www.yahoo.com, March 11, 2008.

20 www.disney.go.com, 2011.

21 V. A. Graicunas, "Relationships in Organizations," in L. Gulick and L. Urwick, eds., *Papers in the Science of Administration* (New York: Institute of Public Administration, 1937), pp. 181–185.

22 Ibid.

23 D. D. Van Fleet, "Span of Management Research and Issues," *Academy of Management Journal* 4 (1983), 546–552.

24 J. W. Lorsch and J. J. Morse, *Organizations and Their Members: A Contingency Approach* (New York: Harper & Row, 1974).

25 Lawrence and Lorsch, *Organization and Environment.*

26 W. Konrad, "The Bottleneck at Coca-Cola Enterprises," *Business Week*, September 14, 1992, pp. 28–30.

27 M. Weber, *From Max Weber: Essays in Sociology*, in H. H. Gerth and C. W. Mills, eds. (New York: Oxford University Press, 1946); M. Weber, *Economy and Society*, in G. Roth and C. Wittich, eds. (Berkeley: University of California Press, 1978).

28 C. Perrow, *Complex Organizations*, 2nd ed. (Glenview, IL: Scott, Foresman, 1979).

29 R. L. Kahn, D. M. Wolfe, R. P. Quinn, J. D. Snoek, and R. A. Rosenthal, *Organizational Stress: Studies in Role Conflict and Ambiguity* (New York: Wiley, 1964).

30 Weber, *From Max Weber*, p. 331.

31 Lawrence and Lorsch, *Organization and Environment:* J. R. Galbraith, *Organization Design* (Reading, MA: Addison-Wesley, 1977).

32 Lawrence and Lorsch, *Organization and Environment.*

33 Perrow, *Complex Organizations.*

34 G. R. Jones and C. W. L. Hill, "Transaction Cost Analysis of Strategy-Structure Choice," *Strategic Management Journal* 9 (1989), 159–172.

35 See Perrow, *Complex Organizations*, Ch. 1, for a detailed discussion of these issues.

36 P. S. Adler and B. Borys, "Two Types of Bureaucracy," *Administrative Science Quarterly* 41 (1996), 61–89.

37 A. W. Gouldner, *Wildcat Strike: A Study of Worker-Management Relationships* (New York: Harper & Row, 1954).

38 This is a pseudonym used by Gouldner. Ibid.

39 L. Donaldson, *Redeeming the Organization* (New York: Free Press, 1996).

40 Child, *Organization: A Guide for Managers and Administrators,* pp. 50–72.

41 www.xerox.com, 2011.

42 Ibid.

CHAPTER 6

Designing Organizational Structure: Specialization and Coordination

Learning Objectives

In this chapter the second principal issue in organizational design is addressed: how to group and coordinate tasks to create a division of labor that increases efficiency and effectiveness and increases organizational performance. The design challenge is to create the optimal pattern of vertical and horizontal relationships among roles, functions or departments, teams, and divisions that will enable an organization to best coordinate and motivate people and other resources to achieve its goals.

After studying this chapter you should be able to:

1. Explain why most organizations initially have a functional structure and why, over time, problems arise with this structure that require a change to a more complex structure.
2. Distinguish among three kinds of divisional structures (product, geographic, and market), describe how a divisional structure works, and explain why many organizations use this structure to coordinate organizational activities and increase their effectiveness.
3. Discuss how the matrix and product team structures differ, and why and when they are chosen to coordinate organizational activities.
4. Identify the unique properties of network structures and the conditions under which they are most likely to be selected as the design of choice.

Functional Structure

In Chapter 4, we noted that the tasks involved in running the B.A.R. and Grille became more numerous and more complex as the number of customers increased and the restaurant needed to serve more meals. At first, the owners, Bob and Amanda Richards, performed multiple roles, but as the business grew, they became overloaded and were forced to develop specialized roles and institute a division of labor. As Chapter 4 discusses, the assignment of one person to a role is the start of specialization and horizontal differentiation. As this process continues, the result is a **functional structure,** a design that groups people into separate functions or departments because they share common skills and expertise because they make use of the same resources. At the B.A.R. and Grille, servers and bussers were grouped into the dining room function, and chefs and kitchen staff were grouped into the kitchen function (see Figure 4.1). Similarly, research scientists at pharmaceutical companies like Pfizer and Amgen are grouped in specialized laboratories because they use the same skills and resources, and accountants are grouped in an accounting department.

Functional structure
A design that groups people together on the basis of their common expertise and experience or because they use the same resources.

Functional structure is the bedrock or foundation of horizontal differentiation. An organization groups different tasks into separate functions to increase the effectiveness with which it achieves its principal goal: providing customers with high-quality products at competitive prices.[1] As functions specialize, employees' skills and abilities improve and the core competences that give an organization a competitive advantage emerge. Different functions are formed as an organization responds to increasingly complex task requirements. The owner of a very small business, for example, might hire outside specialists to handle accounting and marketing. As an organization grows in size and complexity, however, it normally develops these functions internally because handling its own

Focus on New Information Technology

Amazon.com, Part 4

As we saw in Chapter 1, Jeff Bezos, the founder of Amazon.com, achieved phenomenal success with his concept for an online bookstore. In large part, his success has been due to the functional structure he created for his company that has allowed Amazon.com's proprietary Internet software to be used so effectively to link employees to customers (see Figure 6.1).

First, Bezos created Amazon.com's R&D department to continue to develop and improve the in-house software that he had initially developed for Internet-based retailing. Then, he established the information systems department to handle the day-to-day implementation of these systems and to manage the interface between the customer and the organization. Third, he created the materials management/logistics department to devise the most cost-efficient ways to obtain books from book publishers and distributors and to ship them quickly to customers. For example, the department developed new IT to ensure one-day shipping to customers. Next, as Amazon.com grew, he created a separate financial department and a strategic planning department to help chart the company's future. As we will see in later chapters, these departments have allowed Amazon to expand and provide many other kinds of products for its customers in the 2000s, such as electronics, housewares, food, and cloud computing services, and different departments have been created to manage each of these distinct product lines.

Figure 6.1 Functional Structure

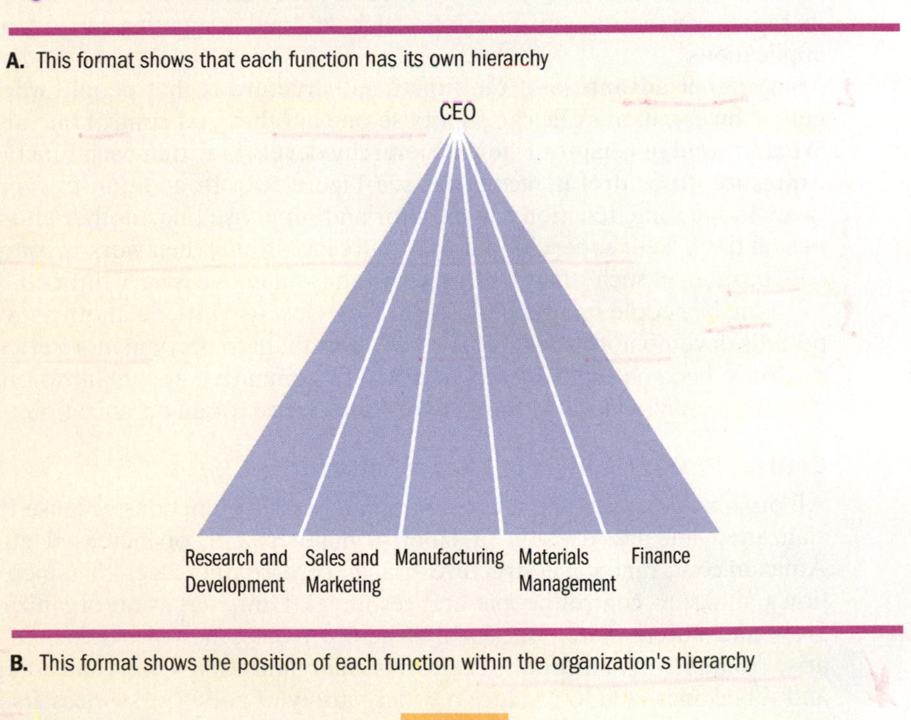

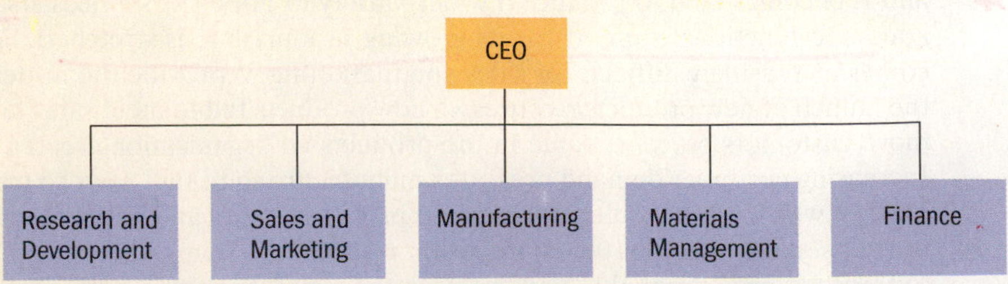

accounting and marketing activities becomes more efficient than hiring outside contractors. This is how organizations become more complex as they grow: They develop not only more functions but also more specialization within each function. (They also become vertically differentiated and develop a hierarchy of authority, as we saw in Chapter 5.) Focus on New Information Technology: Amazon.com, Part 4, provides an example of how the company used horizontal differentiation to develop a functional structure as it grew.

By focusing on the best way to divide into functions the total task facing the organization (the creation of valuable products for customers) and recruiting experienced functional managers from other organizations like Walmart to run them, Bezos created core competences that allowed his online bookstore to compete effectively with bricks-and-mortar bookstores. Many bookstores have disappeared because their small size did not allow them to differentiate and provide customers with the sheer range of books and convenient service that Amazon.com can. Amazon.com is able to do this because of the way it has developed a structure to manage its new information technology effectively.

Advantages of a Functional Structure

Functional structure develops first and foremost because it provides people with the opportunity to learn from one another and become more specialized and productive. When people with skills in common are assembled into a functional group, they can learn the most efficient techniques for performing a task, or the best way to solve problems, from one another. The most skilled employees are given responsibility to train new recruits, and they are the people who are promoted to become supervisors and managers. In this way an organization can increase its store of skills and abilities. For example, Google's value-creation ability is embedded in the skills of its employees and in the way it groups and organizes them to develop and utilize their skills. In 2010, Google's revenues exceeded $31 billion and it had 24,000 employees; by June 2011 it had added almost 3000 more employees to support its rapid growth into new businesses such as cloud computing services and mobile device applications.

Another advantage of the functional structure is that people who are grouped together by common skills can supervise one another and control one another's behavior. We discussed in Chapter 5 how a hierarchy develops within each function to allow an organization to control its activities (see Figure 5.8). In addition to functional managers, peers in the same function can monitor and supervise one another and keep work activities on track. Peer supervision is especially important when work is complex and relies on cooperation; in such situations, supervision from above is very difficult.

Finally, people in a function who work closely with one another over extended time periods develop norms and values that allow them to become more effective at what they do. They become team members who are committed to organizational activities. This commitment may develop into a core competence for an organization.

Control Problems in a Functional Structure

All organizations become divided into independent functions because this promotes specialization and the division of labor, a major source of increased effectiveness. As in Amazon.com, functional structure breeds core competences that increase an organization's ability to control people and resources. However, as an organization continues to grow and differentiate, functional structure creates new problems. Often the problems

arise from the organization's success: As an organization's skills and competences increase and it becomes able to produce a wider variety of goods or services, its ability to provide adequate functional support for its growing product line is stretched. For example, it becomes increasingly difficult for sales and marketing to provide the in-depth attention that the launch of new products requires, so new products fail to meet sales targets. Similarly, as more customers perceive value in the products an organization creates, demand goes up. Increasing customer demand pressures manufacturing to find ways to increase production quickly, which often results in decreased product quality and rising costs. In turn, the pressure of staying ahead of the competition places more demands on R&D and engineering to improve product quality and increase the range or sophistication of products, such as Apple's quest to offer a continuous flow of improved iPods and iPhones.

The problem facing a successful organization is how to keep control of increasingly complex activities as it grows and differentiates. As it produces more and more products, becomes geographically diverse, or faces increasing competition for customers, control problems impede managers' ability to coordinate organizational activities.[2]

COMMUNICATION PROBLEMS As more organizational functions develop, each with its own hierarchy, they become increasingly distant from one another. They develop different subunit orientations that cause communication problems.[3] For example, sales thinks the organization's main problem is the need to satisfy customer demands quickly to increase revenues; manufacturing thinks the main problem is to simplify products to reduce costs; and R&D thinks the biggest problem is to increase a product's technical sophistication. As a result of such differences in perception, communication problems develop that reduce the level of coordination and mutual adjustment among functions and make it more difficult for the organization to respond to customer and market demands. Thus, differentiation produces communication problems that companies try to solve, in part, by using more complex integrating mechanisms.

MEASUREMENT PROBLEMS To exercise control over a task or activity, there has to be a way to measure it; otherwise there is no benchmark to use to evaluate how task performance changes over time. However, as organizations grow and the number and complexity of their functions and products increases, the information needed to measure the contribution of any one function or product to overall profitability is often difficult to obtain. The reason for the difficulty is that the cost of *each* function's contribution to the development of *each* product becomes increasingly difficult to measure. For example, one or more products might actually be losing the company money, but managers are unaware of this because they cannot allocate functional costs to each individual product. Thus the organization is not making the most effective use of its resources.

LOCATION PROBLEMS As a company grows, it may need to set up shop and establish manufacturing or sales facilities in different geographic regions to serve customers better. Geographic spread can pose a control problem within a functional structure when centralized control from one geographic location prevents this from happening: Manufacturing, sales, and other support activities are not allowed to become responsive to the needs of each region. An organization with more than one location must develop a control and information system that can balance the need to centralize decision-making authority with the need to decentralize authority to regional operations. In fact, as Amazon.com expanded, it established five main U.S. distribution centers, located in Delaware, Nevada, Georgia, Kansas, and Kentucky.

CUSTOMER PROBLEMS As the range and quality of an organization's products increases, more and more customers are attracted to the organization and they have different kinds of needs. Servicing the needs of new kinds of customer groups and tailoring products to suit them are relatively difficult in a functional structure. Functions like production, marketing, and sales have little opportunity to specialize in the needs of a particular customer group; instead, they are responsible for servicing the complete product range. Thus in an organization with a functional structure, the ability to identify and satisfy customer needs may fall short, and sales opportunities are lost.

STRATEGIC PROBLEMS As an organization becomes more complex, top managers may be forced to spend so much time finding solutions to everyday coordination problems that they have no time to address the longer-term strategic problems facing the company. For example, they are likely to be so involved in solving communication and integration problems between functions that they have no time to plan for future product development. As a result, the organization loses direction.

Solving Control Problems in a Functional Structure

Sometimes managers can solve the control problems associated with a functional structure, such as poor communication between functions, by redesigning the functional structure to increase integration between functions (see Figure 6.2). For example, one ongoing

Figure 6.2 Improving Integration in a Functional Structure by Combining Sales and Marketing

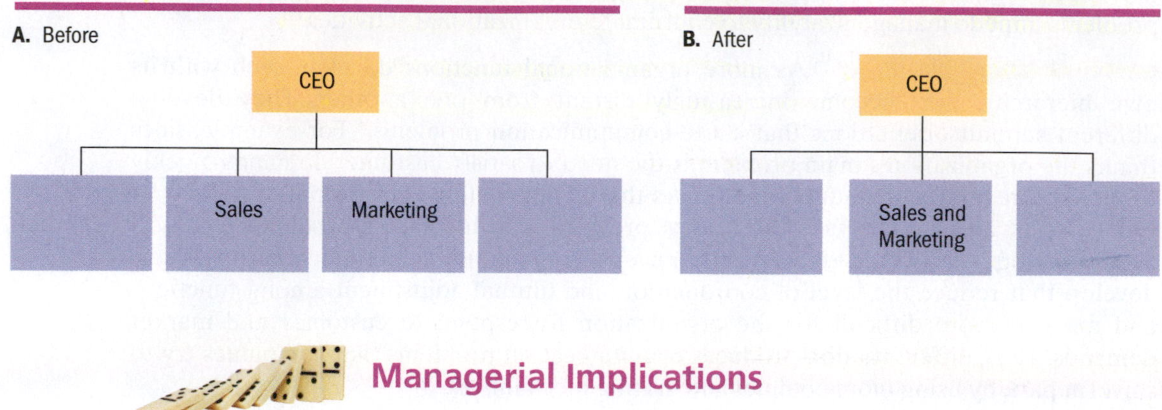

Managerial Implications

Functional Structure

1. For an entrepreneur starting a small business, or for a manager of a work group or department, creating the correct division of labor within a function and between functions is a vital design task.
2. To ensure that the division of labor is correct, list the various functions that currently exist in your organization, and itemize the tasks they perform.
3. Draw a diagram of task relationships both within and between functions, and evaluate to what degree your organization is obtaining the advantages of the functional structure (such as the development of new or improved skills) or experiencing the disadvantages of the functional structure (such as lack of integration between functions).
4. Experiment with different ways of altering the design of the functional structure to increase effectiveness—for example, by transferring task responsibilities from one function to another or by eliminating unnecessary roles.

organizational challenge is how to manage the relationship between sales and marketing. Figure 6.2A shows the traditional relationship between them: Each is a separate function with its own hierarchy. Many organizations have recognized the need to alter this design and have combined those activities into one function. Figure 6.2B shows that modification. Such changes to the functional structure increase control by increasing integration between functions.

From Functional Structure to Divisional Structure

If an organization (1) limits itself to producing a small number of similar products, (2) produces those products in one or a few locations, and (3) sells them to only one major type of customer, managers will be able to solve many of the control problems associated with a functional structure. As organizations grow over time, however, they begin to produce more and more products that are often very different from one another. For example, GE produces hundreds of different models of appliances, lightbulbs, turbine engines, and financial lending services. Moreover, when an organization increases the number and kinds of goods and services it produces, this also leads to an increase in the number and types of customers it has to serve, and to do this a company usually has to open up factories and offices at an increasing number of geographic locations.

When organizations grow in these ways, what is needed is a structure that will simultaneously (1) increase managers' control of its different individual subunits so that subunits can better meet product and customer needs, and (2) allow managers to control and integrate the operation of the whole company to ensure all its subunits are meeting organizational goals.

Managers regain control of their organizations when they decide to adopt a more complex structure, which is the result of three design choices:

1. ***An increase in vertical differentiation.*** To regain control, managers need to increase vertical differentiation. This typically involves (a) increasing the number of levels in the hierarchy; (b) deciding how much decision-making authority to centralize at the top of the organization; and (c) deciding how much to use rules, SOPs, and norms to standardize the behavior of low-level employees.
2. ***An increase in horizontal differentiation.*** To regain control, managers need to increase horizontal differentiation. This involves overlaying a functional grouping of activities with some other kind of subunit grouping—most often, self-contained product teams or product divisions that contain the functional resources needed to meet their goals.
3. ***An increase in integration.*** To regain control, managers need to increase integration between subunits. The higher the level of differentiation, the more complex the integrating mechanisms that managers need to use to control organizational activities. Recall from Chapter 4 that complex integrating mechanisms include task forces, teams, and integrating roles. Organizations need to increase integration between subunits to increase their ability to coordinate activities and motivate employees.

Figure 6.3 shows the way those three design choices increase differentiation and integration. The organization illustrated in Figure 6.3A has two levels in its hierarchy and three subunits, and the only integrating mechanism that it uses is the hierarchy of authority. Figure 6.3B shows the effects of growth and differentiation. To manage its more complex activities, the organization has developed three levels in its hierarchy and has eight subunits. Because of the increase in differentiation, it needed a greater degree of integration and thus created a series of task forces to control activities among subunits.

Figure 6.3 Differentiation and Integration: How Organizations Increase Control over Their Activities

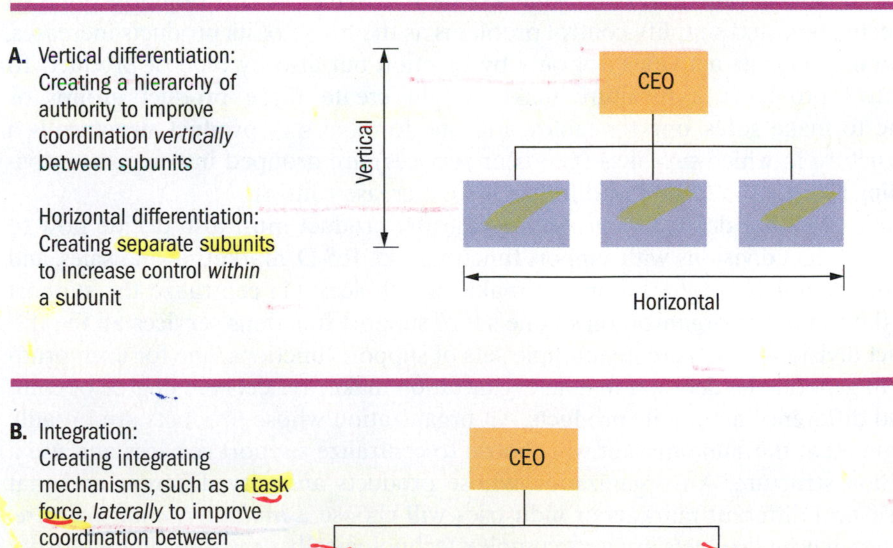

A. Vertical differentiation:
Creating a hierarchy of authority to improve coordination *vertically* between subunits
Horizontal differentiation:
Creating separate subunits to increase control *within* a subunit
Vertical
CEO
Horizontal

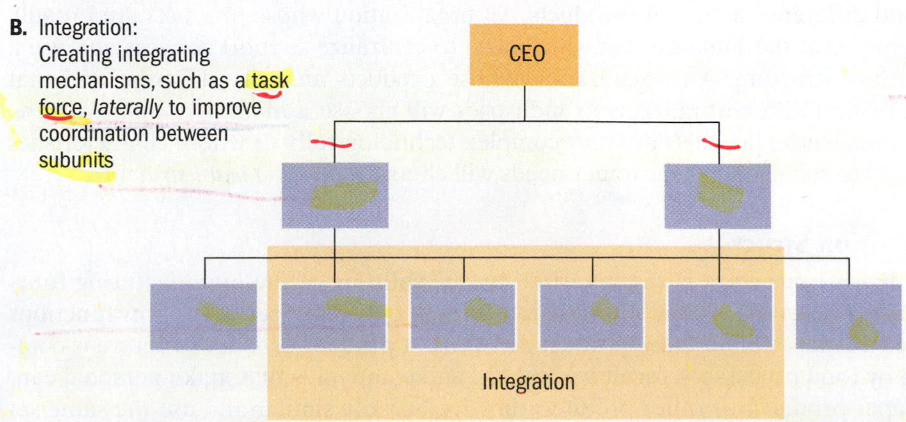

B. Integration:
Creating integrating mechanisms, such as a task force, *laterally* to improve coordination between subunits
CEO
Integration

All of the more complex organizational structures discussed in the remainder of this chapter come into being as a result of managers' design decisions about vertical differentiation, horizontal differentiation, and integration. The move to a complex structure normally involves changes in all three characteristics.

Moving to a Divisional Structure

Divisional structure
A structure in which functions are grouped together according to the specific demands of products, markets, or customers.

The structure that organizations most commonly adopt to solve the control problems that result from producing many different kinds of products in many different locations for many different types of customers is the divisional structure. A **divisional structure** groups functions according to the specific demands of *products, markets, or customers*. The goal behind the change to a divisional structure is to create smaller, more manageable subunits within an organization. The type of divisional structure managers select depends on the specific control problems discussed earlier that need to be solved.

If the control problem is due to the number and complexity of products, the organization divides its activities by product and uses a *product structure*. If the control problem is due to the number of locations in which the organization produces and sells its products, the organization divides its activities by region and uses a *geographic structure*. If the control problem is due to the need to service a large number of different customer groups, the organization divides its activities by customer group and uses a *market structure*.

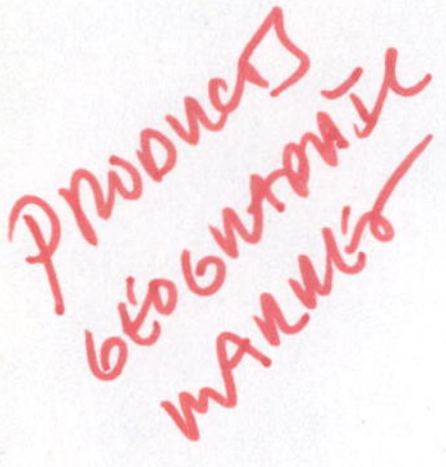

Next, we discuss these types of divisional structure, which are designed to solve specific control problems. Each type of divisional structure has greater vertical and horizontal differentiation than a functional structure and employs more complex integrating mechanisms.

Divisional Structure I: Three Kinds of Product Structure

Product structure
A divisional structure in which products (goods or services) are grouped into separate divisions, according to their similarities or differences.

As an organization increases the kinds of goods it manufactures or the services it provides, a functional structure becomes less effective at coordinating task activities. Imagine the coordination problems a furniture maker like IKEA would experience if it were to produce 100 styles of sofas, 150 styles of tables, and 200 styles of chairs in the same manufacturing unit. Gaining sufficient control over its value-creation activities would be impossible. To maintain effectiveness and simplify control problems as the range of its products increases, an organization groups its activities not only by function but also by type of product. To simplify control problems, a furniture maker might create three product groups or divisions: one to make sofas, one for tables, and one for chairs. A **product structure** is a divisional structure in which products (goods or services) are grouped into separate divisions, according to their similarities or differences, to increase control.

An organization that decides to group activities by product must also decide how to coordinate its product divisions with support functions like R&D, marketing and sales, and accounting. In general, an organization can make two choices: (1) centralize the support functions at the top of the organization so one set of support functions services all the different product divisions, or (2) create multiple sets of support functions, one for each product division. In general, the decision that an organization makes reflects the degree of complexity of and difference among its products. An organization whose products are broadly similar and aimed at the same market will choose to centralize support services and use a *product division* structure. An organization whose products are very different and that operates in several different markets or industries will choose a *multidivisional structure*. An organization whose products are very complex technologically or whose characteristics change rapidly to suit changing customer needs will choose a *product team structure*.

Product Division Structure

Product division structure
A divisional structure in which a centralized set of support functions services the needs of a number of different product lines.

A **product division structure** is characterized by the splitting of the manufacturing function into several different product lines or divisions; a centralized set of support functions then services the needs of *all* these product divisions. A product division structure is commonly used by food processors, furniture makers, and companies that make personal care products, paper products, or other products that are broadly similar and use the same set

Figure 6.4 Product Division Structure

Each product division manager (PDM) has responsibility for coordinating with each support function.

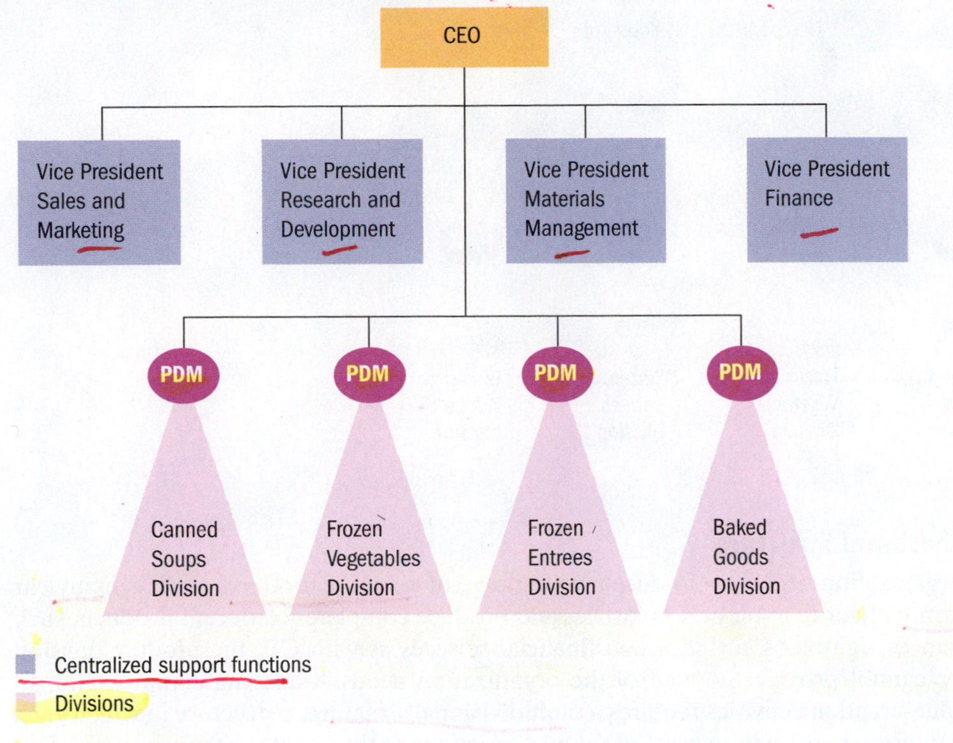

of support functions. Figure 6.4 shows a product division structure for a large food processor such as Heinz.

Because controlling the production of many different foods within the same manufacturing unit proved to be difficult and resulted in increasing costs, Heinz created separate product divisions that make frozen vegetables, frozen entrees, canned soups, and baked goods. This design decision increased horizontal differentiation within the organization, for each division is a separate manufacturing unit that has its own hierarchy headed by a product division manager. Each product division manager (PDM in Figure 6.4) is responsible for his or her division's product (manufacturing or service) activities. The product division manager also coordinates with the central support functions like marketing and materials management to make effective use of their skills and thus enhance product development. The role of product division manager adds a level to the hierarchy or authority and so also increases vertical differentiation in an organization.

Figure 6.4 shows that in a product division structure, support functions such as sales and marketing, R&D, materials management, and finance are centralized at the top of the organization. Each product division uses the services of the central support functions and does not have its own support functions. Creating separate support functions for each product division would be expensive, and the cost could be justified only if the needs of the different divisions were so *diverse* and *dissimilar* that different functional specialists were required for each type of product.

Each support function is divided into product-oriented teams of functional specialists who focus on the needs of one particular product division. Figure 6.5 shows the grouping of the R&D function into four teams, each of which focuses on a separate product division. This arrangement allows each team to specialize and become expert in managing the needs of its own product group. However, because all of the R&D teams belong to the same centralized function, they can share knowledge and information. The R&D team that focuses on frozen vegetables can share discoveries about new methods for quick-freezing vegetables with the R&D team for frozen entrees. Such sharing of skills and resources increases a function's ability to create value across product divisions.

Figure 6.5 The Assignment of Product-Oriented Functional Teams to Individual Divisions

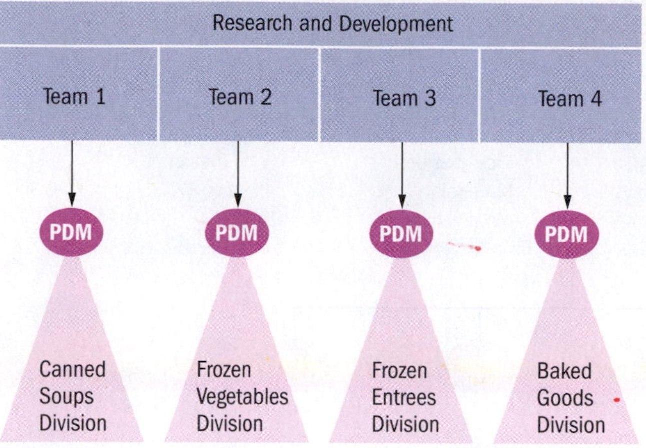

Multidivisional Structure

Multidivisional structure A structure in which support functions are placed in self-contained divisions.

As an organization begins to produce a wide range of complex products, such as many car or truck models, or to enter new industries and produce completely different products, such as appliances, lightbulbs, turbines, and financial services as with GE, the product division structure cannot provide the control the organization needs. Managing complex and diverse value-creation activities requires a **multidivisional structure,** a structure in which each product division is given its own set of support functions so they become *self-contained* divisions. Figure 6.6 depicts the multidivisional structure used by a large consumer products

Figure 6.6 Multidivisional Structure

Each division is independent and has its own set of support functions. The corporate headquarters staff oversees the activities of the divisional managers, and there are three levels of management: corporate, divisional, and functional.

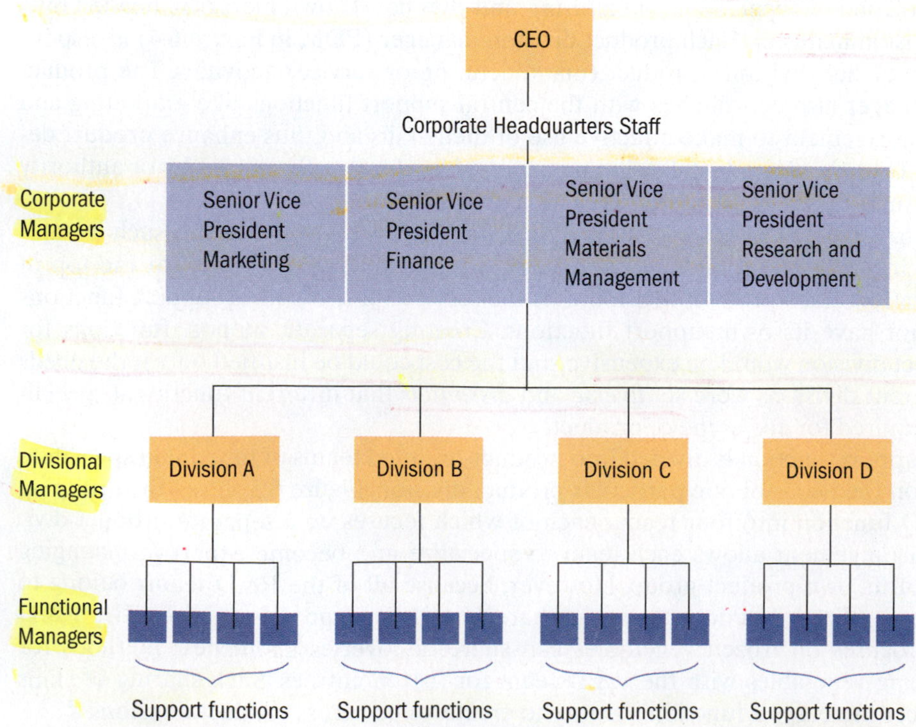

company. Four divisions are illustrated, although a company such as GE, IBM, Johnson & Johnson, or Matsushita might have 150 different operating divisions.

Compare the multidivisional structure shown in Figure 6.6 with the product division structure shown in Figure 6.4. A multidivisional structure has two innovations that overcome the control problems a company experiences with the product division structure when managers decide to produce a wider and wider range of different products in different industries.[4] The first innovation is the independence of each division. In a multidivisional structure, each division is independent and self-contained (in a product division structure, the divisions share the services of a set of centralized functions). When divisions are **self-contained,** each division has its own set of support functions and controls its own value-creation activities. Each division needs its own set of support functions because it is impossible for one centralized set of support functions to service the needs of totally different products—such as automobiles, computers, and consumer electronics. As a result, horizontal differentiation increases.

Self-contained division
A division that has its own set of support functions and controls its own value-creation activities.

The second innovation in a multidivisional structure is a new level of management, a **corporate headquarters staff,** composed of corporate managers who are responsible for overseeing the activities of the divisional managers heading up the different divisions.[5] The corporate headquarters staff is functionally organized, and one of the tasks of corporate managers is to coordinate the activities of the divisions. For example, managers at corporate headquarters can help the divisions share information and learn from one another so that divisional innovations can be quickly communicated throughout the organization. Recall from Chapter 4 that managers acting in that way are performing an *integrating role*.

Corporate headquarters staff
Corporate managers who are responsible for overseeing the activities of the divisional managers heading up the different divisions.

Because corporate managers now form an additional level in the hierarchy, vertical differentiation has increased, which provides more coordination and control. The heads of the divisions (divisional managers) link corporate headquarters and the divisions. Compared to a functional or a product division structure, a multidivisional structure provides additional differentiation and integration, which facilitate the control of more complex activities.

A corporate staff and self-contained divisions are two factors that distinguish a multidivisional structure from a product division structure. But there are other important differences between them. A product division structure can only be used to control the activities of a company that is operating in *one* business or industry. In contrast, a multidivisional structure is designed to allow a company to operate in many different businesses. Each division in a multidivisional structure is essentially a different business. Moreover, it is the responsibility of each divisional manager to design the divisional structure that best meets the needs of the products and customers of that division. Thus one or more of the independent divisions within a multidivisional structure could use a product division structure or any other structure to coordinate its activities. Figure 6.7 illustrates this diversity.

The multidivisional organization depicted in Figure 6.7 has three divisions, each with a different structure. The car-making division has a functional structure because it produces a small range of simple components. The PC division has a product division structure; each of its divisions develops a different kind of computer. The consumer electronics division has a matrix structure (which we discuss later in the chapter) because it has to respond quickly to customer needs. GE has over 150 different divisions. Its lightbulb division has a functional structure and its appliance division operates with a product division structure, but the whole GE empire is operated through a multidivisional structure.

Most Fortune 500 companies use a multidivisional structure because it allows them to grow and expand their operations while maintaining control over their activities. Only when an organization has a multidivisional structure does the management hierarchy expand to include the three main levels of management: corporate managers, who oversee the operations of *all* the divisions; divisional managers, who run the individual divisions; and functional managers, who are responsible for developing the organization's core competences. See Organizational Insight 6.1, which describes the history of GM's decision to move to a multidivisional structure, illustrates many of the issues and problems involved in operating a multidivisional structure, and reveals differences between it and a product division structure.

Figure 6.7 A Multidivisional Structure in Which Each Division Has a Different Structure

Organizational Insight 6.1

Creating GM'S Multidivisional Structure

William C. Durant formed the General Motors Company on September 16, 1908. Into it he brought about 25 different companies. Originally, each company retained its own operating identity, and the GM organization was simply a holding company, a central office surrounded by 25 satellites. When Alfred P. Sloan took over as president of GM in 1923, he inherited this collection of independently managed car companies, which made their own decisions, did their own R&D, and produced their own range of cars.

Ford, GM's main competitor, was organized very differently. From the beginning, Henry Ford had pursued the advantages of economies of scale and mass production and designed a mechanistic structure to achieve them. He created a highly centralized organization in which he had complete personal control over important decision making. To reduce costs, Ford at first produced only one vehicle, the Model T, and focused on finding ways to make the car more efficiently. Because of its organizational design, Ford's company was initially much more profitable than GM. The problem facing Sloan was to compete with Ford, not only in terms of making a successful product but also to improve GM's financial performance.

Confronted with Ford's success, Sloan must have been tempted to close several of GM's small operations and concentrate production in a few locations where the company could enjoy the benefits of cost savings from making fewer models and from economies of scale. For example, he could have chosen a product division structure, created three product divisions to manufacture three kinds of car, and centralized support functions such as marketing, R&D, and engineering to reduce costs. But Sloan recognized the advantages of developing the diverse sets of research, design, and marketing skills and competences present in the small car companies. He realized there was a great risk of losing this diversity of talent if he combined all these skills into one centrally located R&D department. Moreover, if the same set of support functions, such as engineering and design, worked for all of GM's divisions, there was a danger that all GM cars would begin to look alike. Nevertheless, Sloan also recognized the advantages of centralized control in achieving economies of scale, controlling costs, and providing for the development of a strategic plan for the company as a whole, rather than for each company separately.

So Sloan searched for an organizational structure that would allow him to achieve all these objectives simultaneously, and he found his answer in the multidivisional structure, which had been used successfully by DuPont Chemicals. In 1920, he instituted this change, noting that GM "needs to find a principle for coordination without losing the advantages of decentralization."[6]

All of GM's different car companies were placed in one of five self-contained operating divisions (Chevrolet, Pontiac, Oldsmobile, Buick, and Cadillac) with support services like sales, production, engineering, and finance. Each division became a profit center and was evaluated on its return on investment. Sloan was quite clear about the main advantage of linking decentralization to return on investment: It raised the visibility of each division's performance. And, Sloan observed, it (1) "increases the morale of the organization by placing each operation on its own foundation,... assuming its own responsibility and contributing its share to the final result"; (2) "develops statistics correctly reflecting... the true measure of efficiency"; and (3) "enables the corporation to direct the placing of additional capital where it will result in the greatest benefit to the corporation as a whole."[7]

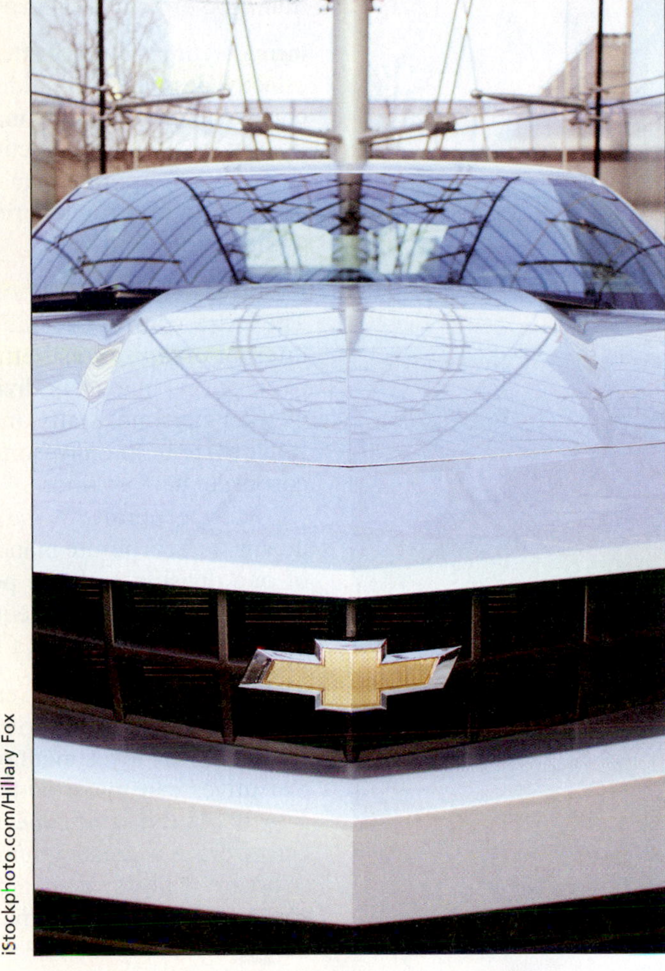
iStockphoto.com/Hillary Fox

Sloan recommended that transactions between divisions be set by a transfer pricing scheme based on cost plus some predetermined rate of return. However, to avoid protecting an inefficient high-cost internal supplier, he also recommended a number of steps involving analysis of the operations of outside competitors to determine the fair price. Sloan established a strong, professional, centralized headquarters management staff to perform such calculations. Corporate management's primary role was to audit divisional performance and to plan strategy for the total organization. Divisional managers were to be responsible for all product-related decisions.

In the 1980s, after fierce competition from the Japanese, GM took a hard look at its multidivisional structure. The duplication of R&D and engineering, and the purchasing of inputs by each division independently, were costing the company billions of extra dollars. In 1984, GM's five autonomous car divisions were combined into two groups: Chevrolet and Pontiac would concentrate on small cars; Buick, Oldsmobile, and Cadillac would focus on large cars.[8]

GM hoped that the reorganization would reduce costs and speed product development, but it was a disaster. With control of design and engineering more centralized at the group level, the cars of the different divisions started to look the same. Nobody could tell a Buick from a Cadillac or an Oldsmobile. Sales plummeted. Moreover, the reorganization did not speed decision making. It increased the number of levels in the hierarchy by introducing the group level into the organization. As a result, GM had 13 levels in its hierarchy, as compared with Toyota, for example, which had just 5. Once again the company was in trouble: Before the reorganization, it had been too decentralized; now it was too centralized. What to do?

Realizing its mistake, GM moved to return control over product design to the divisions while continuing to centralize high-cost functions like engineering and purchasing. This restructuring has had some success. Cadillac's management moved quickly to establish a new product identity and design new models. During the 1990s, GM reduced the number of different models it produced, and in 2004 it closed down its Oldsmobile division to reduce overhead costs.[9] However, it was not able to recover by 2008 and make the innovative cars U.S. customers want and, after the financial crisis of 2009, it was forced into bankruptcy. As we described in an earlier chapter, during its reorganization GM closed down its Saturn and Pontiac divisions and sold off its global car divisions to create a streamlined multidivisional structure that would allow it to make innovative cars and compete effectively on price. By 2011, the new GM reported that it was once again profitable and that its new models of cars were selling briskly because it had finally found ways to control its organizational structure effectively.[10]

As the GM story suggests, operating a multidivisional structure is no easy task—it is perhaps the biggest challenge that top managers face and the one that leads to a company's greatest successes or failures. Because the multidivisional structure is so widely used, we need to look closely at its advantages and disadvantages.

ADVANTAGES OF A MULTIDIVISIONAL STRUCTURE When the multidivisional structure is managed effectively, it provides a large, complex organization with several advantages.[11]

Increased Organizational Effectiveness A division of labor generally increases organizational effectiveness. In a multidivisional structure there is a clear division of labor between corporate and divisional managers. Divisional managers are responsible for the day-to-day operations of their respective divisions and for tailoring divisional activities to the needs of customers. Corporate managers are responsible for long-term planning for the corporation as a whole and for tailoring the mission of the divisions to suit the goals of the whole organization.

Increased Control Corporate managers monitor the performance of divisional managers. The extra control provided by the corporate office encourages the stronger pursuit of internal organizational efficiency by divisional managers. Knowing they have to answer to corporate managers, divisional managers may curb their inclination to increase the size of their personal staffs and thus increase their status and rein in costs. They may also think twice before investing in products that increase their status but do little to promote corporate performance.

More generally, as the GM example suggests, the creation of self-contained divisions means that corporate managers can develop control systems to compare the performance of one division with the performance of another by measuring profitability or product development time. Consequently, corporate managers are in a good position to intervene and take selective action to correct inefficiencies when they arise.

Profitable Growth When each division is its own profit center—that is, when its individual profitability can be clearly evaluated—corporate headquarters can identify the divisions in which an investment of capital will yield the highest returns.[12] Thus corporate executives can make better capital resource allocation decisions to promote corporate growth. At the same time, their role as monitor rather than as administrator means they can oversee a greater number of different businesses and activities. The multidivisional structure allows a company to grow without suffering from the problems of communication or information overload that can occur when the two roles are mixed, as they are in the functional structure.

Internal Labor Market The most able divisional managers are promoted to become corporate managers. Thus divisional managers have an incentive to perform well because superior performance results in promotion to high office. A large divisional company possesses an internal labor market, which increases managers' motivation to work to increase organizational effectiveness.

DISADVANTAGES OF A MULTIDIVISIONAL STRUCTURE Like other structures, certain problems can develop with multidivisional structures over time. Although good management can control most of the problems, it cannot eliminate them.

Managing the Corporate–Divisional Relationship The central management problem posed by a multidivisional structure is how much authority to centralize at the corporate level and how much authority to decentralize to the operating divisions. On one hand, each division is closest to its particular operating environment and is in the best position to develop plans to increase its own effectiveness, so decentralization is a logical choice. On the other hand, headquarters' role is to adopt the long-term view and to tailor divisional activities to the needs of the whole organization, so centralization has advantages too.

The balance between the two has to be managed all the time. Too much centralization of authority can straitjacket divisional managers, they lose control of decision making to headquarters managers who are far from the firing line, and the result can be poor performance. GM's attempt to centralize decision making to reduce costs was a disaster because all GM cars started to look the same. Too much decentralization, however, can result in giving divisional managers so much freedom that they slack off and fail to control their division's costs. The corporate–divisional relationship needs to be managed continually. Over time as the operating environment changes, the decision about which managerial activities to centralize and which to decentralize will change.

Coordination Problems between Divisions When a multidivisional structure is created, measures of effectiveness such as return on investment can be used to compare divisions' performance, and corporate headquarters can allocate capital to the divisions on the basis of their performance. One problem with this approach is that divisions may begin to compete for resources, and rivalry between them may prevent them from cooperating. Such rivalry can lower organizational performance when a company's effectiveness depends on the divisions' sharing of knowledge and information about innovations to enhance the performance of all divisions. It would be counterproductive, for example, if one of GM's divisions invented a new superefficient engine and refused to share the information with other divisions.

Transfer Pricing Problems between divisions often revolve around the **transfer price**—the price at which one division sells a product or information about innovations to another division. To maximize its own return on investment, one division will want a high transfer price, but that will penalize the other division, which is, after all, part of the same organization. Thus, as each division pursues its own goals, coordination problems inside the organization can emerge. The role of the corporate center is to manage such problems, as Sloan of GM noted. It is very important that a multidivisional organization establish integrating mechanisms that enable managers from different divisions to cooperate. Mechanisms like integrating roles and departments are important in promoting cooperation. The corporate office itself is a type of integrating department.

Transfer price
The price at which one division sells a product or information about innovations to another division.

Bureaucratic Costs Multidivisional structures are very expensive to operate. Each division has a full complement of support functions, including R&D. Thus there is extensive duplication of activities within the organization—plus there are the costs of corporate headquarters managers. The high costs of operating a multidivisional structure must continually be evaluated against the benefits the company obtains. And, if the benefits relative to the costs fall, the company should move to reduce the size of corporate headquarters, the number of divisions, or the costs of its support functions. It might be possible, for example, for an organization to change to a product division structure or to a product team structure (discussion follows) and service the needs of its different products through one set of centralized support functions.

Communication Problems Communication problems arise in tall hierarchies, particularly the distortion of information. These problems are common in multidivisional structures because they tend to be the tallest of all organizational structures. The gap between the corporate center and the divisions is especially large. The head of a division may deliberately disguise falling divisional performance to receive larger capital allocations; when a company has 200 divisions, such deception can be hard to detect. In addition, it may take so long for headquarters to make decisions and transmit them to divisions that responses to competitors are too slow. The more centralized an organization, the more of a problem communication will be.

Product Team Structure

In a product division structure, members of support functions such as marketing and R&D coordinate with the different divisions as their services are needed, but their main loyalty is to their function, not to the division. Increasingly, organizations are finding that the functional orientation of specialists is not in an organization's best interests because industry competition has become focused on the product. Today, it is especially important to customize products to suit customer needs while containing product development costs. Moreover, increased competition has made it important to reduce the time needed to bring a new product to market by speeding the product development process. One solution to this problem might be a multidivisional structure in which each division has its own set of support functions. But, as we just discussed, this structure is very expensive to operate, and communication problems between divisions can slow innovation and product development. Many companies, in their search for a new structure to solve these problems, have reengineered their divisional structures into a product team structure.

A product team structure is a cross between the product division structure, in which the support functions are centralized, and the multidivisional structure, in which

Figure 6.8 Product Team Structure

Each product team manager (PTM) supervises the activities associated with developing and manufacturing a product.

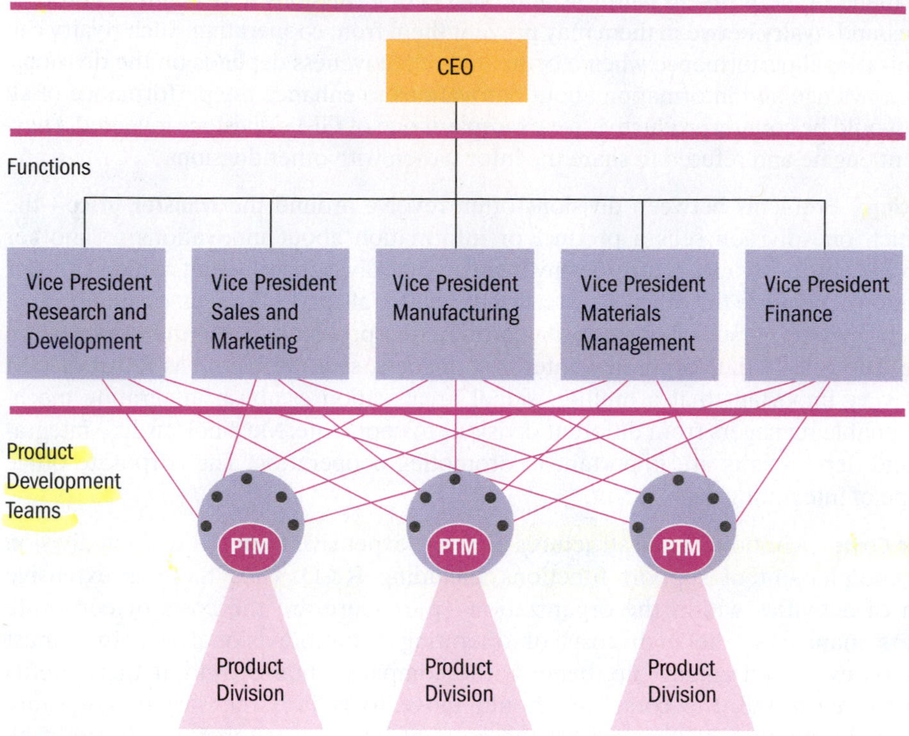

Product team structure A divisional structure in which specialists from the support functions are combined into product development teams that specialize in the needs of a particular kind of product.

each division has its own support functions. In a **product team structure,** specialists from the support functions are combined into product development teams that specialize in the needs of a particular kind of product (see Figure 6.8). Each team is, in effect, a self-contained division headed by a product team manager (PTM in Figure 6.8), who supervises the operational activities associated with developing and manufacturing the product. The product teams focus on the needs of one product (or client) or a few related products, and they owe their allegiance not to their functions but to the product team they join. The vice presidents of the functions, at the top of the organization, retain overall functional control, but decision-making authority for each product is decentralized to the team, and each team becomes responsible for the success of a project. Hallmark Cards has found this approach to coordinating functions and products to be an effective way to develop new products quickly.

In the past, Hallmark used a functional structure to coordinate its activities. A large number of artists, writers, lithographers, and designers working in different functional departments produced a huge array of greeting cards. The problems of coordinating the activities of 700 writers and artists across functional boundaries became so complex and difficult that it was taking Hallmark two years to develop a new card. To solve its product development problems, Hallmark reengineered to a product team structure. Artists and writers were formed into product teams around particular categories of greeting cards, such as Mother's Day cards, Christmas cards, and so on. With no differences in subunit orientation to impede the flow of information, mutual adjustment became much easier, and work was performed much more quickly. Product development time shrank from years to weeks.

A product team structure is more decentralized than a functional structure or a product division structure, and specialists in the various product teams are permitted to make on-the-spot decisions, particularly important in service organizations. The grouping into self-contained product teams increases integration because each team becomes responsible for all aspects of its operations. Through close collaboration, team members become intensely involved in all aspects of product development and in tailoring the product to its market. Moreover, the high level of integration produced by teams makes it possible to make decisions quickly and respond to fast-changing customer requirements.

The division of activities by product is the second most common method organizations use to group activities, after grouping them by function. Product structure increases horizontal differentiation and vertical differentiation (which separates managers into corporate-level, division-level, and function-level managers). In recent years, many large companies have moved from one type of product structure to another in an attempt to save money or make better use of their functional resources. Managers must continually evaluate how well their product structure is working because it has a direct impact on the effectiveness of their organization.

Divisional Structure II: Geographic Structure

Of the three types of product structure discussed earlier, the multidivisional structure is the one that large organizations most often use. It provides the extra control that is important when a company produces a wide array of complex products or services or enters new industries and needs to deal with different sets of stakeholders and competitive forces. However, when the control problems that companies experience are a function of geography, a **geographic divisional structure,** in which divisions are organized according to the requirements of the different locations in which an organization operates, is available.

Geographic divisional structure
A divisional structure in which divisions are organized according to the requirements of the different locations in which an organization operates.

As an organization grows, it often develops a national customer base. As it spreads into different regions of a country, it needs to adjust its structure to align its core competences with the needs of customers in different geographic regions. A geographic structure allows some functions to be centralized at one headquarters location and others to be decentralized to a regional level. For example, Crown Cork and Seal produces many of the thousands of cans used in canning soft drinks, vegetables, and fruits. Because cans are bulky objects that are expensive to transport, it makes sense to establish manufacturing plants in the different parts of the country where cans are most in demand. Also, there is a limit to how many cans it is possible for the company to produce efficiently at just one plant location; when economies of scale become exhausted at one location, it makes sense to establish another plant in a new location. So to keep costs to a minimum, Crown Cork and Seal operates several manufacturing plants in different regions of the United States and Canada. While each plant has its own purchasing, quality control, and sales departments, R&D and engineering are centralized at its headquarters location to minimize costs.

Neiman Marcus, the specialty department store, also has a geographic structure, but for a different reason. When Neiman Marcus operated only in Texas, a functional structure was all it required to coordinate its activities. But as it opened stores at selected sites across the United States, it confronted a dilemma: how to respond to the needs of well-off customers that differ region by region while achieving the cost advantages of central purchasing. Neiman Marcus's solution was to establish a geographic structure that groups stores by region (see Figure 6.9). Individual stores are under the direction of a regional office, which is responsible for coordinating the specific product needs of the stores in its region—for example, swimwear and sportswear in Los Angeles and hats, gloves, and down parkas in Chicago. The regional office feeds customer-specific requirements back to headquarters in Dallas, where centralized purchasing functions make decisions for the company as a whole.

Both Crown Cork and Seal and Neiman Marcus superimposed a geographic grouping over their basic functional grouping, thereby increasing horizontal differentiation. The creation of a new level in the hierarchy—regional managers—and the decentralization of control to regional hierarchies also increased vertical differentiation. The regional hierarchies provide more control than is possible with one centralized hierarchy and, in the cases of Crown Cork and Seal and Neiman Marcus, have increased effectiveness.

Figure 6.9 Geographic Structure

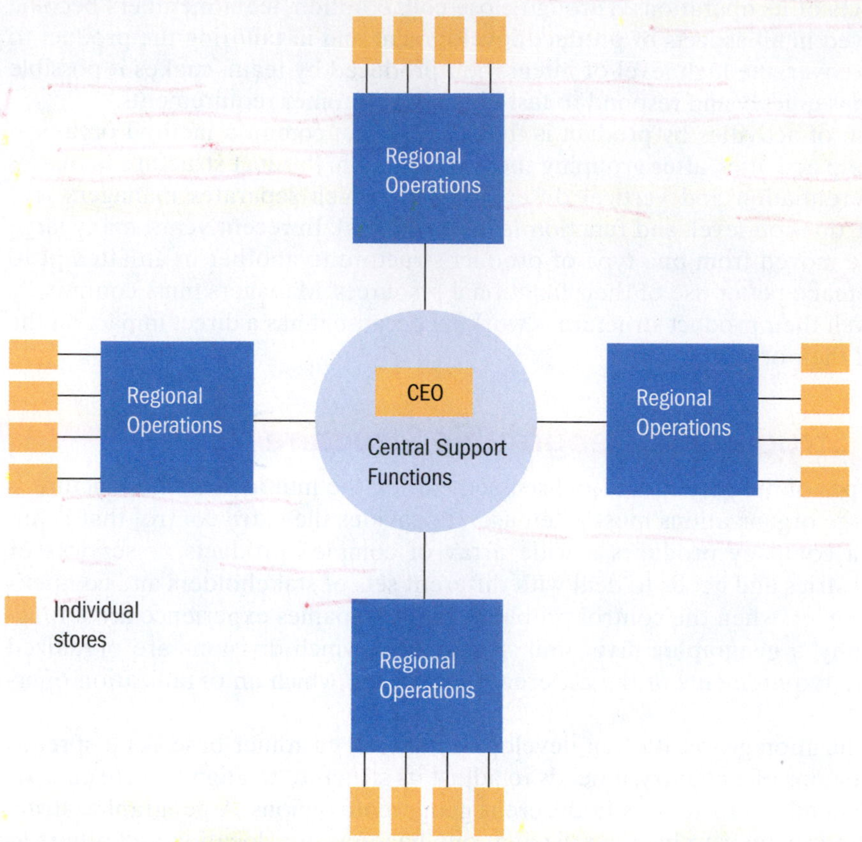

Divisional Structure III: Market Structure

The grouping of activities by product or geography makes the product or region the center of attention. In contrast, a market structure aligns functional skills and competences with the product needs of different customer groups. Marketing, not manufacturing, determines how managers decide how to group organizational activities into divisions. Figure 6.10 shows a market structure with divisions created to meet the needs of commercial, consumer, corporate, and government customers.

Each customer division has a different marketing focus, and the job of each division is to develop products to suit the needs of its specific customers. Each division makes use of centralized support functions. Engineering tailors products to suit the various needs of each division, and manufacturing follows each division's specifications. Because

Figure 6.10 Market Structure

Each division focuses on the needs of a distinct customer group.

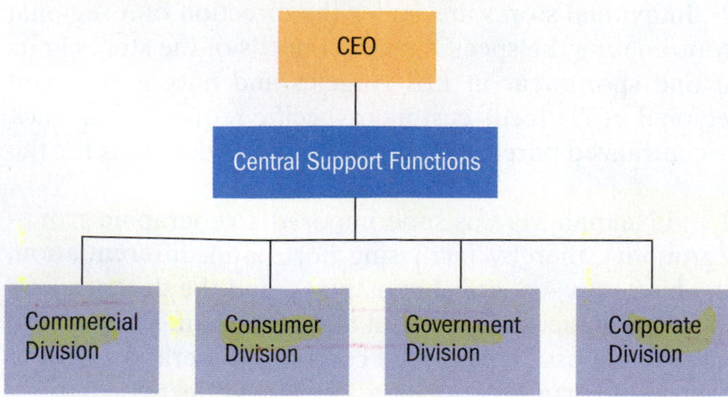

the market structure focuses the activities of the whole organization on the needs of the customer, the organization can quickly sense changes in its market and transfer skills and resources to satisfy the changing needs of this vital stakeholder group.

The way in which the Houston school district reorganized from a geographic to a market structure to increase its effectiveness is discussed in Organizational Insight 6.2.

Organizational Insight 6.2

Big Changes at the HISD

Like all organizations, state and city government agencies such as school districts may become too tall and bureaucratic over time and, as they grow, develop ineffective and inefficient organizational structures. This happened to the Houston Independent School District (HISD) when the explosive growth of the city during the last decades added over a million new students to school rolls. As Houston expanded many miles in every direction to become the fourth largest U.S. city, successive HISD superintendents adopted a geographic structure to coordinate and control all the teaching functions involved in creating high-performing elementary, middle, and high schools. The HISD eventually created five different geographic regions or regional school districts. And over time each regional district sought to control more of its own functional activities and became increasingly critical of HISD's central administration. The result was a slowdown in decision making, infighting between districts, an increasingly ineffectual team of district administrators, and falling student academic test scores across the city.

In 2010 a new HISD superintendent was appointed who, working on the suggestions of HISD's top managers, decided to reorganize HISD into a market structure. HISD's new organizational structure is now grouped by the needs of its customers—its students—and three "chief officers" oversee all of Houston's high schools, middle schools, and elementary schools, respectively. The focus will now be on the needs of its three types of students, not on the needs of the former five regional managers. Over 270 positions were eliminated in this restructuring, saving over $8 million per year, and many observers hope to see more cost savings ahead.

Many important support functions were recentralized to HISD's headquarters office to eliminate redundancies and reduce costs, including teacher professional development. Also, a new support function called school improvement was formed with managers charged to share ideas and information between schools and oversee their performance on many dimensions to improve service and student performance. HISD administrators also hope that eliminating the regional geographic structure will encourage schools to share best practices and cooperate so student education and test scores will improve over time.

By 2011 major cost savings had been achieved, but a huge budget deficit forced the HISD to close 12 middle and lower schools and relocate students to new schools in which class sizes would be higher. The result is a streamlined, better integrated divisional structure that HISD hopes will increase performance—student scores—in the years ahead but at a lower cost.

Managerial Implications

Changing Organizational Structure

1. As an organization grows, be sensitive to the need to change a functional structure to improve the control of organizational activities.
2. When the control problem is to manage the production of a wide range of products, consider using a form of divisional structure.
3. Use a product division structure if the organization's products are generally similar.
4. Move to a multidivisional structure if the organization produces a wide range of different or complex goods and services or operates in more than one business or industry.
5. When the control problem is to reduce product development time by increasing the integration between support functions, consider using a product team structure.
6. When the control problem is to customize products to the needs of customers in different geographic areas, consider using a geographic structure.
7. When the control problem is to coordinate the marketing of all of a company's products to several distinct groups of customers, use a market structure.
8. Always weigh the benefits that will arise from moving to a new structure (that is, the control problems that will be solved) against the costs that will arise from moving to the new structure (that is, the higher operating costs associated with managing a more complex structure) to see whether changing organizational structure will increase organizational effectiveness.

Matrix Structure

Matrix structure A structure in which people and resources are grouped in two ways simultaneously: by function and by project or product.

The search for better and faster ways to develop products and respond to customer needs has led some companies to choose a **matrix structure,** an organizational design that groups people and resources in two ways simultaneously: by function and by product.[13] A matrix structure is both similar to and different from a product team structure.

Before examining those differences, let's examine how a matrix structure works (see Figure 6.11). In the context of organizational design, a matrix is a rectangular grid that shows a *vertical* flow of *functional* responsibility and a *horizontal* flow of *product* responsibility. In Figure 6.11, the lines pointing down represent the grouping of tasks by function, and the lines pointing from left to right represent the grouping of tasks by product. An organization with a matrix structure is differentiated into whatever functions the organization needs to achieve its goals. The organization itself is very flat, having minimal hierarchical levels within each function and decentralized authority. Functional employees report to the heads of their respective functions (usually, functional vice presidents) but do not work under their direct supervision. Instead, the work of functional personnel is determined primarily by membership in one of several cross-functional product teams under the leadership of a product manager. The members of the team are called **two-boss employees** because they report to two superiors: the product team manager and the functional manager. The defining feature of a matrix structure is the fact that team members have two superiors.

Two-boss employees Employees who report to two superiors: the product team manager and the functional manager.

The team is both the basic building block of the matrix and the principal mechanism for coordination and integration. Role and authority relationships are deliberately left vague because the underlying assumption of matrix structure is that when team members

Figure 6.11 Matrix Structure

Team members are two-boss employees because they report to both the product team manager and the functional manager.

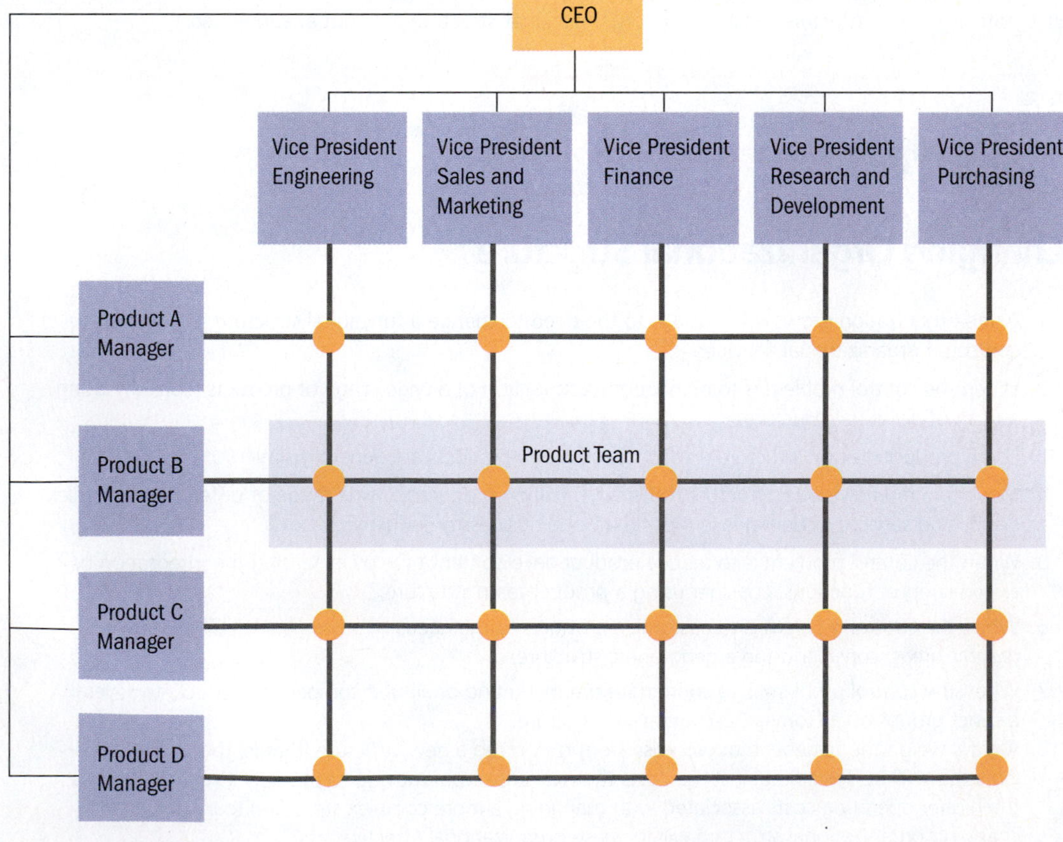

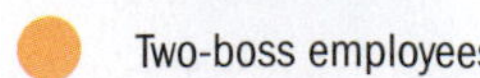

are given more responsibility than they have formal authority, they are forced to cooperate to get the job done. The matrix thus relies on minimal vertical control from the formal hierarchy and maximal horizontal control from the use of integrating mechanisms—teams—which promote mutual adjustment. Matrix structures are a principal form of organic structure (see Chapter 4).

Both matrix structure and product team structure make use of teams to coordinate activities, but they differ in two major respects. First, team members in a product team structure have only one boss: the product team manager. Team members in a matrix structure have two bosses—the product manager and the functional manager—and thus divided loyalty. They must juggle the conflicting demands of the function and the product. Second, in the matrix structure, team membership is not fixed. Team members move from team to team, to where their skills are most needed.

In theory, because of those two differences, the matrix structure should be more flexible than the product team structure, in which lines of authority and coordination are more stable. The matrix is deliberately designed to overcome differences in functional orientation and to force integration on its members. Does it work?

Advantages of a Matrix Structure

A matrix structure has four significant advantages over more traditional structures.[14] First, the use of cross-functional teams is designed to reduce functional barriers and overcome the problem of subunit orientation. With differentiation between functions kept to a minimum, integration becomes easier to achieve. In turn, the team structure facilitates adaptation and learning for the whole organization. The matrix's team system is designed to make the organization flexible and able to respond quickly to changing product and customer needs. Not surprisingly, matrix structures were first used in high-tech companies for which the ability to develop technologically advanced products quickly was the key to success. TRW Systems, a U.S. defense contractor, developed the matrix system to make the Atlas and Titan rockets that formed the U.S. space program in the 1960s.

A second advantage of the matrix structure is that it opens up communication between functional specialists and provides an opportunity for team members from different functions to learn from one another and develop their skills. Thus matrix structure facilitates technological progress because the interactions of different specialists produce the innovations that give a company its core competences.

Third, the matrix enables an organization to effectively use the skills of its specialized employees who move from product to product as needed. At the beginning of a project, for example, basic skills in R&D are needed, but after early innovation, the skills of engineers are needed to design and make the product. People move around the matrix to wherever they are most needed; team membership is constantly changing to suit the needs of the product.

Fourth, the dual functional and product focus promotes concern for both cost and quality. The primary goal of functional specialists is likely to be technical: producing the highest-quality, most innovative product possible (regardless of cost). In contrast, the primary goals of product managers are likely to concern cost and speed of development—doing whatever can be done given the amount of time and money available. This built-in focus on both quality and cost keeps the team on track and keeps technical possibilities in line with commercial realities.

Disadvantages of a Matrix Structure

In theory, the principles underlying matrix structures seem logical. In practice, however, many problems arise.[15] To identify the sources of these problems, consider what is missing in a matrix.

A matrix lacks the advantages of bureaucratic structure (discussed in Chapter 5). With a flat hierarchy and few rules and SOPs, the matrix lacks a control structure that allows employees to develop stable expectations of each other. In theory, team members continually negotiate with one another about role responsibilities, and the resulting give-and-take makes the organization flexible. In practice, many people do not like the role ambiguity and role conflict that matrix structures can produce. For example, the functional boss, focused on quality, and the product boss, focused on cost, often have different expectations of the team members. The result is role conflict. Team members become unsure of what to do, and a structure designed to promote flexibility may actually reduce it if team members become afraid to assume responsibility.

The lack of a clearly defined hierarchy of authority can also lead to conflict between functions and product teams over the use of resources. In theory, product managers are supposed to buy the services of the functional specialists on the team (say, for example, the services of ten engineers at $2,000 per day). In practice, however, cost and resource allocation becomes fuzzy as products exceed their budgets and specialists cannot overcome technical obstacles. Power struggles emerge between product and functional managers, and politicking takes place to gain the support of top management.

As this suggests, matrix structures have to be carefully managed to retain their flexibility. They do not automatically produce the high level of coordination that is claimed of them, and people who work in a matrix often complain about high levels of stress and uncertainty. Over time, people in a matrix structure are likely to experience a vacuum of authority and responsibility and move to create their own informal organization to provide them with some sense of structure and stability. Informal leaders emerge within teams. These people become increasingly recognized as experts or as great "team leaders." A status hierarchy emerges within teams. Team members often resist transfer to other teams in order to remain with their colleagues.

When top managers do not get the results they expect, they sometimes try to increase their control over the matrix and to increase their power over decision making. Slowly but surely, as people jockey for power and authority, a system that started out very flat and decentralized turns into a centralized, less flexible structure.

Matrix structures need to be managed carefully if their advantages are to outweigh their disadvantages. Matrix structures are not designed for use in everyday organizational situations, however. They are mainly appropriate when a high level of coordination between functional experts is needed because an organization must respond quickly to a changing environment. Given the problems associated with managing a complex matrix structure, many growing companies have chosen to overlay a functional structure or a product division structure with product teams rather than attempt to manage a full-fledged matrix. The use of IT greatly facilitates this process because it provides the extra integration needed to coordinate complex value-creation activities.

The Multidivisional Matrix Structure

Multidivisional structures allow an organization to coordinate activities effectively but are difficult to manage. Communication and coordination problems arise because of the high degree of differentiation within a multidivisional structure. Consequently, a company with several divisions needs to be sure it has sufficient integration mechanisms in place to handle its control needs. Sometimes the corporate center becomes very remote from divisional activities and is unable to play this important integrating role. When this happens, organizations sometimes introduce the matrix structure at the top of the organization and create a **multidivisional matrix structure,** which provides for more integration between corporate and divisional managers and between divisional managers. Figure 6.12 depicts this structure.

Multidivisional matrix structure
A structure that provides for more integration between corporate and divisional managers and between divisional managers.

As the figure shows, this structure allows senior vice presidents at the corporate center to send corporate-level specialists to each division, perform an in-depth evaluation of their performance, and to devise a functional action plan for each division. Divisional managers meet with corporate managers to exchange knowledge and information and to coordinate divisional activities. The multidivisional matrix structure makes it much easier for top managers from the divisions and corporate headquarters to cooperate and coordinate organizational activities jointly. Many large international companies that operate globally use this structure, as the example of Nestlé in Organizational Insight 6.3 illustrates.

Figure 6.12 Multidivisional Matrix Structure

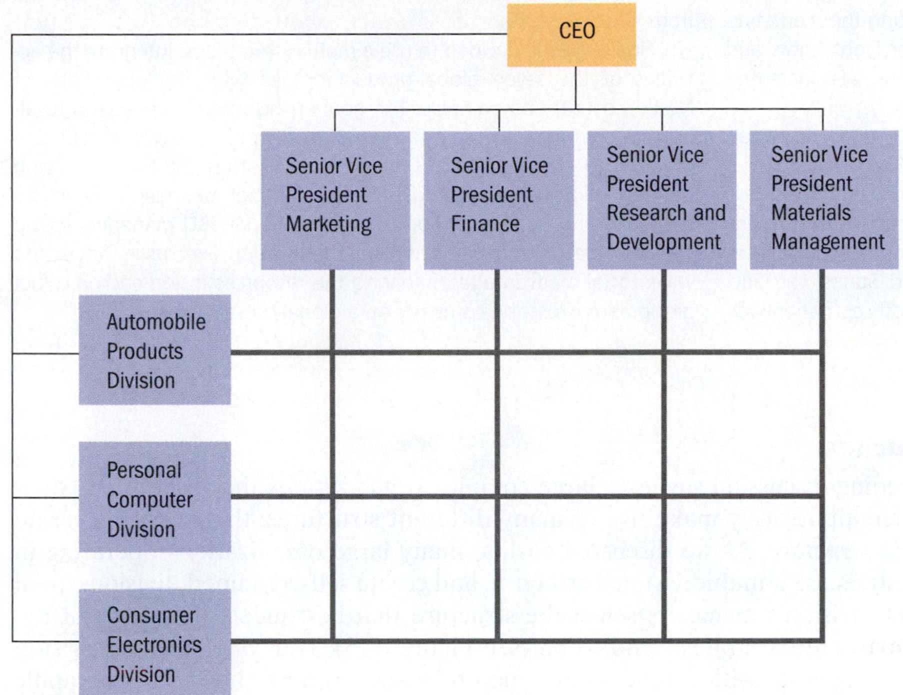

Organizational Insight 6.3

Nestlé's Global Matrix Structure

iStockphoto.com/Linda Steward

Nestlé, based in Vevey, Switzerland, is the world's largest food company, with global sales in excess of $80 billion in 2011. The company has been pursuing an ambitious program of global expansion by acquiring many famous companies, for example, Perrier, the French mineral water producer, and Rowntree, the British candy maker. In the United States, Nestlé bought Carnation, Stouffer Foods, Contadina, Ralston Purina, and Dreyer's Grand Ice Cream.

In the past, in each of the countries in which it operated, Nestlé allowed the managers of each of its product divisions (such as its Carnation division) to assume responsibility for making business decisions. For example, managers had the authority to make all product development, marketing, and manufacturing decisions. Nestlé's corporate managers at its Vevey headquarters made the broader acquisition, expansion, and resource allocation decisions such as how best to invest its capital. However, the size of the corporate staff in Vevey had increased dramatically to manage its rapid global expansion as it acquired more and more global food companies

By the end of the 1990s Nestlé's CEO realized the company had major problems because corporate managers had become remote from the divisional managers in its thousands of global operating divisions. Moreover, the way the company operated made it impossible to obtain the potential benefits from sharing its distinctive competences in food product development and marketing, both between divisions in a product group—for example the beverage group—and between product groups and world regions. Because each product group operated separately, corporate executives could not integrate product-group activities around the globe. To raise corporate performance, Nestlé's managers had to find a new way to organize its activities.

Its CEO decided to restructure Nestlé from the top down, creating seven global product groups, and giving the managers of each group the authority to oversee all the activities of the product divisions inside their group (for example, convenience food such as soup and frozen meals, beverages, and candy). Each global product group was to integrate the activities of the operating divisions in its group and transfer distinctive competences to create new kinds of food and beverage products to increase profitability. After the change, managers in the candy product group, for instance, began orchestrating the marketing and sale of Rowntree candy products, such as After Eight Mints and Smarties throughout Europe and the United States, and sales increased by 60%.

Nestlé then grouped all divisions within a country or world region into one national or regional strategic business unit (SBU) and created a team of SBU managers whose job was to help link and coordinate their activities and speed product development. When the different divisions inside each SBU started to share joint purchasing, marketing, and sales activities, major cost savings resulted. In the United States, the SBU management team reduced the number of sales offices nationwide from 115 to 22 and the number of suppliers of packaging materials from 43 to 3.

Finally, Nestlé decided to use a matrix structure to integrate the activities of the seven global-product groups with the operations of Nestlé's country-based SBUs. The goal of this matrix structure is to allow the company to obtain the benefits of learning how to create new products to satisfy customers in different countries and from achieving cost reductions by promoting higher cooperation between divisions inside each product group. For example, regional SBU managers spend considerable time in Vevey with product-group executives discussing ways to take advantage of sharing the resources inside each product group and across the company on a global basis.

Hybrid Structure

Hybrid structure
The structure of a large organization that has many divisions and simultaneously uses many different types of organizational structure.

As the preceding discussion suggests, large complex organizations that have many divisions often simultaneously make use of many different structures; that is, they operate with a **hybrid structure**. As we discussed earlier, many large organizations operating in several industries use a multidivisional structure and create self-contained divisions; then each product division's managers select the structure that best meets the needs of the particular environment, strategy, and so on (see Figure 6.13). Thus one product division may choose to operate with a functional structure, a second may choose a geographic structure, and a third may choose a product team structure because of the nature of the division's products or the desire to be more responsive to customers' needs.

Companies that operate only in one industry but choose to compete in different market segments of the industry also may use a hybrid structure. For example, Target uses a hybrid structure in the retail industry and groups its activities by type of market/customer segment and by geography.

As shown in Figure 6.13, Target operates its different store chains as four independent divisions in a market division structure. Its four market divisions are Mervyn's and Marshall Field's, which caters to the needs of affluent customers; Target Stores, which competes in the low-price segment; and target.direct, Target's Internet division, which manages online sales.[16]

Beneath this organizational layer is another layer of structure because both Target Stores and Marshall Field's operate with a geographic structure that groups stores by region. Individual stores are under the direction of a regional office, which coordinates the market needs of the stores in its region and responds to regional customer needs. The regional office feeds information back to divisional headquarters, where centralized merchandising functions make decisions for all Target or Marshall Field's stores.

Figure 6.13 Target's Hybrid Structure

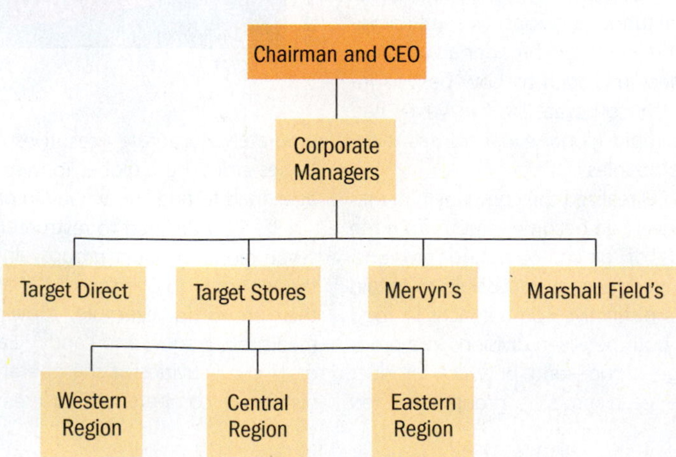

Organizational structure may thus be likened to the layers of an onion. The outer layer provides the overarching organizational framework—most commonly some form of product or market division structure—and each inner layer is the structure that each division selects for itself in response to the contingencies it faces—such as a geographic or product team structure. The ability to break a large organization into smaller units or divisions makes it much easier for managers to change structure when the need arises—for example, when a change in technology or an increase in competition in the environment necessitates a change from a functional to a product team structure.

Network Structure and the Boundaryless Organization

Another innovation in organizational design that swept across the world during the last decade is the use of network structures. Recall from Chapter 3 that a *network structure* is a cluster of different organizations whose actions are coordinated by contracts and agreements, rather than by a formal hierarchy of authority.[17] Very often one organization takes the lead in creating the network as it searches for a way to increase effectiveness; for example, a clothing manufacturer may search for ways to produce and market clothes more cheaply. Rather than manufacturing the clothes in its own factories, the company decides to outsource its manufacturing to a low-cost Asian company; it also forms an agreement with a large Madison Avenue advertising agency to design and implement its sales campaign. Recall also how *outsourcing* is moving a value-creation activity that was done *inside* an organization to the *outside*, where it is performed by another company.

Network structures often become very complex as a company forms agreements with a whole range of suppliers, manufacturers, and distributors to outsource many of the value-creation activities necessary to produce and market goods and services.[18] For example, Nike, the largest and most profitable sports shoe manufacturer in the world, has developed a very complex network structure to produce its shoes. At the center of the network is Nike's product design and research function located in Beaverton, Oregon, where Nike's designers pioneer new innovations in sports shoe design. Almost all the other functional specialisms that Nike needs to produce and market its shoes have been outsourced to companies around the world![19]

How does Nike manage the relationships among all the companies in its network? Principally by using modern IT (discussed in depth in Chapter 12). Nike's designers use computer-aided design (CAD) to design shoes, and all new product information, including manufacturing instructions, is stored electronically. When the designers have done their work, they relay all the blueprints for the new products electronically to Nike's network of suppliers and manufacturers in Southeast Asia.[20] For example, instructions for the design of a new sole may be sent to a supplier in Taiwan, and instructions for the leather uppers to a supplier in Malaysia. These suppliers then produce the shoe parts, which are then sent for final assembly to a manufacturer in China with whom Nike has established an alliance. From China these shoes are shipped to distributors throughout the world and are marketed in each country by an organization with which Nike has formed some form of alliance, such as a long-term contract.

Advantages of Network Structures

Why does Nike use a network structure to control the value-creation process rather than perform all the functional activities itself? Nike, and other organizations, can realize several advantages by using a network structure.

First, to the degree that an organization can find a network partner that can perform a specific functional activity reliably, and at a lower cost, production costs are reduced.[21] Almost all of Nike's manufacturing is done in Asia, for example, because wages in Southeast Asia are a fraction of what they are in the United States. Second, to the degree that an organization contracts with other organizations to perform specific value-creation activities, it avoids the high bureaucratic costs of operating a complex organizational structure. For example, the hierarchy can be kept as flat as possible and fewer managers are needed. Also, because Nike outsources many functional activities, it is able to stay small

and flexible. Control of the design process is decentralized to teams that are assigned to develop each of the new kinds of sports and leisure shoes for which Nike is well known.

Third, a network structure allows an organization to act in an organic way. If the environment changes, for example, and new opportunities become apparent, an organization can quickly alter its network in response. For example, it can sever the links to companies whose services it no longer needs and develop new linkages with companies that do have the skills it needs. An organization that performs all of its own functional activities would take a longer time to respond to the changes taking place. Fourth, if any of its network partners fail to perform up to Nike's standards, they can be replaced with new partners. Finally, a very important reason for the development of networks has been that organizations gain access to low-cost overseas sources of inputs and functional expertise, something crucial in today's changing global environment.

Disadvantages of Network Structures

Although the network structure has several advantages, it also has drawbacks in certain situations. To see what these are, imagine a high-tech company racing to bring to market proprietary hardware and software faster than its competitors. How easy would it be to outsource the functional activities necessary to ensure that the hardware and software are compatible and work with other companies' software? Not easy at all. Close interaction is needed between the hardware and software divisions, and between the different groups of hardware and software programmers responsible for designing the different parts of the system. A considerable level of mutual adjustment is needed to permit the groups to interact so that they can learn from one another and constantly improve the final product. Also, managers must be there to integrate the activities of the groups to make sure their activities mesh well. The coordination problems arising from having different companies perform different parts of the work process would be enormous. Moreover, there has to be considerable trust between the different groups so they are willing to share their ideas, which is necessary for successful new product development.

It is unlikely that a network structure would provide an organization with the ability to control such a complex value-creation process because managers lack the means to coordinate and motivate the various network partners effectively. First, it would be difficult to obtain the ongoing learning that builds core competences over time inside a company because separate companies have less incentive to make such an investment.[22] As a result, many opportunities to cut costs and increase quality would be lost. Second, if one of Nike's suppliers failed to perform well, Nike could easily replace it by forming a contract with another. But how easy is it to find reliable software companies that can both do the job and be trusted not to take proprietary information and use it themselves or give it to a company's competitors?

In general, the more complex the value-creation activities necessary to produce and market goods and services, the more problems are associated with using a network structure.[23] Like the other structures discussed in this chapter, network structures are appropriate in some situations and not in others.

The Boundaryless Organization

The ability of managers to develop a network structure to produce or provide the goods and services their customers want, rather than create a complex organizational structure to do so, has led many researchers and consultants to popularize the idea of the "boundaryless organization." The boundaryless organization is composed of people who are linked by computers, faxes, CAD systems, and video teleconferencing, and they may rarely or ever see one another face to face.[24] People come and go as their services are needed, much as in a matrix structure, but they are not formal members of an organization. They are independent functional experts who form an alliance with an organization, fulfill their contractual obligations, and then move on to the next project.

The use of outsourcing and the development of network organization are increasing rapidly as organizations recognize the many opportunities they offer to reduce costs and increase flexibility. Clearly, managers have to assess carefully the relative benefits of having their own organization perform a functional activity or make a particular input, versus forming an alliance with another organization to do so to increase organizational effectiveness. Designing organizational structure is becoming an increasingly complex management activity in today's changing world.

E-Commerce

E-commerce is trade that takes place between companies, and between companies and individual customers, using IT and the Internet. *Business-to-business (B2B) commerce* is trade that takes place between companies using IT and the Internet to link and coordinate the value chains of *different* companies (Figure 6.14). Companies use B2B commerce because it allows them to reduce their operating costs and may improve product quality. A main B2B network application is the *B2B marketplace,* an industry-specific trading network set up to connect buyers and sellers using the Internet. To participate in a B2B marketplace, companies agree to use the network software standard that allows them to search for and share information with each other. Then, companies can work together over time to find ways to reduce costs or improve quality.

E-commerce Trade that takes place between organizations, and between organizations and customers, using IT and the Internet.

Business-to-customer (B2C) commerce is trade that takes place between a company and its network of *individual customers* using IT and the Internet. When a company uses IT to connect directly to customers, they have increased control of their network. For example, they can handle their own marketing and distribution and do not need to use intermediaries like wholesalers and retailers. Dell, for example, was one of the first companies to create a B2C network that allowed it to sell directly to the customer and to customize its PCs to their needs. The use of online storefronts allows companies to provide customers with a much wider range of products and to give them much more information about these products in a very cost-effective way. This often allows them to attract more customers, and so a company's network strengthens over time. This is the goal of Dell and of course Amazon.com, which has opened over 50 different kinds of storefronts to be able to sell its millions of loyal customers a wider and wider range of products. Today, Amazon.com is working to expand its range of cloud-computing storefronts that will allow its customers to store their data, music, and videos on Amazon's servers and also to use the programs and computing power on its servers to process their data and satisfy their software needs. Creating this new form of cloud-based network structure is a major challenge for Amazon because competitors like Google, Apple, and Dell are also establishing their own virtual networks.

Figure 6.14 Types of E-Commerce

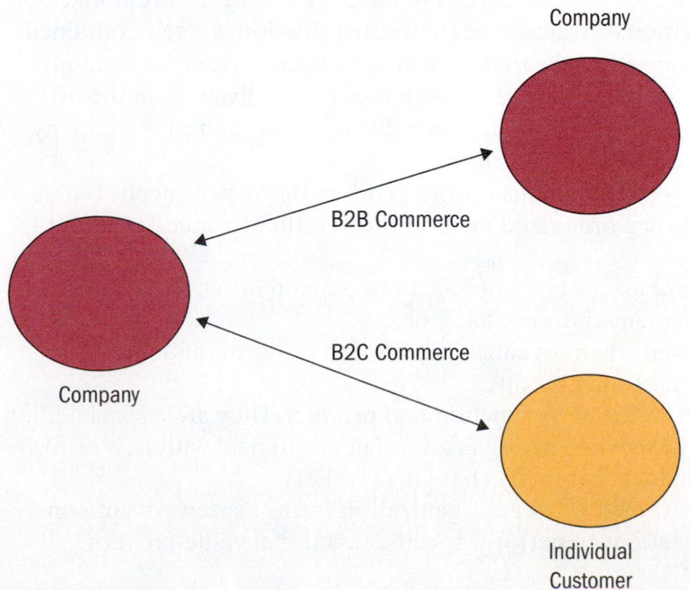

Summary

Designing organizational structure is a difficult and challenging task. Managers have to manage the vertical and horizontal dimensions of the structure continually and choose an appropriate allocation of authority and task responsibilities. As an organization grows and becomes more complex, changing its structure to respond to changing needs or contingencies becomes important.

Designing a structure that fits a company's needs is a major challenge. Each structure has advantages and disadvantages, and managers have to be ready and willing to redesign their organization to obtain the advantages and anticipate and minimize the problems of whichever structure they choose. An organization in control of its structure has an important competitive advantage over one that is not.

Many organizations ignore the coordination problems inherent in the organizing process. Too often, an organization waits until it is already in trouble (in decline) before attempting to deal with coordination and motivation problems. The characteristics of the top-management team are critical in this regard because they determine how decisions get made and how top managers perceive the problems the organization is experiencing. Chapter 6 has made the following main points:

1. A functional structure is a design that groups people because they have similar skills or use the same resources. Functional groups include finance, R&D, marketing, and engineering. All organizations begin as functional structures.
2. An organization needs to adopt a more complex structure when it starts to produce many products or when it confronts special needs, such as the need to produce new products quickly, to deal with different customer groups, or to handle growth into new regions.
3. The move to a more complex structure is based on three design choices: increasing vertical differentiation, increasing horizontal differentiation, and increasing integration.
4. Most organizations move from a functional structure to some kind of divisional structure: a product structure, a geographic structure, or a market structure.
5. The three kinds of product structure are product division structure, multidivisional structure, and product team structure.
6. Product division structure is used when an organization produces broadly similar products that use the same set of support functions.
7. Multidivisional structures are available to organizations that are growing rapidly and producing a wide variety of products or are entering totally different kinds of industries. In a multidivisional structure, each product division is a self-contained division with the operating structure that best suits its needs. A central headquarters staff is responsible for coordinating the activities of the divisions in the organization. When a lot of coordination between divisions is required, a company can use a multidivisional matrix structure.
8. Product team structures put the focus on the product being produced. Teams of functional specialists are organized around the product to speed product development.
9. Geographic structures are used when organizations expand into new areas or begin to manufacture in many different locations.
10. Market structures are used when organizations wish to group activities to focus on the needs of distinct customer groups.
11. Matrix structures group activities by function and product. They are a special kind of structure that is available when an organization needs to deal with new or technically sophisticated products in rapidly changing markets.
12. Network structures are formed when an organization forms agreements or contracts with other organizations to perform specific functional value-creation activities.

Discussion Questions

1. As organizations grow and differentiate, what problems can arise with a functional structure?
2. How do the product division structure and the multidivisional structure differ?
3. Why might an organization prefer to use a product team structure rather than a matrix structure?
4. What are the principal differences between a functional structure and a multidivisional structure? Why does a company change from a functional to a multidivisional structure?
5. What are the advantages and disadvantages associated with network structures?

Organizational Theory in Action

Practicing Organizational Theory

Which New Organizational Structure?

Break up into groups of three to five people, and discuss the following scenario:

You are a group of managers of a major soft-drinks company that is going head to head with Coca-Cola to increase market share. Your strategy is to increase your product range to offer a soft-drink bottled water in every segment of the market to attract customers, and to begin offering soft drinks and other beverage products tailored to the needs of customers in different regions of the country.

Currently you have a functional structure. What you are trying to work out now is how best to implement your strategy to launch your new products. To what kind of structure should you move?

1. Debate the pros and cons of the different possible organizational structures.
2. Which structure will allow you to best achieve your goal at (a) lowest cost; (b) give you most responsiveness to customers; or (c) both?

The Ethical Dimension #6

When organizations outsource their functional activities, they typically lay off many, if not most, of the employees who used to perform the functional task within the organization's boundary. Levi Strauss, for example, closed down its last U.S. plant in 2001; Dell Computer outsourced hundreds of its call center customer service jobs to India.

1. Does it make good business sense to outsource? What are the potential advantages and disadvantages?
2. Given these advantages and disadvantages, when, and under what conditions, is it ethical to outsource organizational activities, lay off workers, and send those jobs abroad?

Making the Connection #6

Find an example of a company that has changed its form of horizontal differentiation in some way. What did the company do? Why did it make the change? What does it hope to accomplish as a result of the change? What structure has it changed to?

Analyzing the Organization: Design Module #6

This module focuses on horizontal differentiation in your organization and on the structure the organization uses to coordinate its tasks and roles.

Assignment

1. What kind of structure (e.g., functional, product division, multidivisional) does your organization have? Draw a diagram showing its structure, and identify the major subunits or divisions in the organization.

2. Why does the company use this kind of structure? Provide a brief account of the advantages and disadvantages associated with this structure for your organization.
3. Is your organization experiencing any particular problems in managing its activities? Can you suggest a more appropriate structure that your company might adopt to solve these problems?

CASE FOR ANALYSIS

Liz Claiborne Refashions Its Structure

Liz Claiborne, like other well-known apparel makers, embarked on a major product expansion strategy in the 1990s when it acquired many smaller branded clothing and accessory companies and started many new brands of its own. The company's goal was to achieve greater operating efficiencies so that rising sales would also result in rising profits. By 2006, it had grown to 36 different brands, but although revenues had soared from $2 billion to over $5 billion, its profits had not kept pace. In fact, profits were falling because costs were rising as operational efficiency fell due to the enormous complexity and expense involved in managing so many brands.[25]

So Liz Claiborne recruited a new CEO, William McComb, to find a way to turn around the troubled company. Within months he decided to reverse course, shrink the company, and move to a new form of organizational structure that would once again allow it to grow—but this time with increasing profitability. CEO McComb's problem was to find a new organizational structure that would reduce the problems associated with managing its 36 different brands. He believed the company had developed a "culture of complexity" due to its rapid growth and overly complex organizational structure.

The company had created five different apparel divisions to manage its 36 brands; brands were grouped into different divisions according to the nature of the clothing or accessories they made. For example, luxury designer lines like Ellen Tracy were grouped into one division; clothes for working women such as its signature Liz Claiborne and Dana Buchman brands were in a second; trendy, hip clothing directed at young customers such as its Juicy Couture line were in a third division, and so on. A separate management team controlled each division, and each division performed all the functional activities like marketing and design needed to support its brands. The problem was that over time it had become increasingly difficult both to differentiate between apparel brands in each division as well as between the brands of different divisions because fashion styles change quickly in response to the demands of changing customer tastes. Also, costs were rising because of the duplication of activities between divisions, and increasing industry competition was resulting in new pressure to lower prices to retail stores to protect sales.

McComb decided it was necessary to streamline and change Liz Claiborne's organizational structure to meet the changing needs of customers and the increasing competition in retailing because of the growth of private-label brands. First, he decided that the company would either try to sell, license, or if necessary close down 16 of its 36 brands and focus on the remaining 20 that had the best chance of generating good profits in the future.[26] To better manage these 20 brands, he decided to change its organizational structure and to shrink from five different divisions to just two. This eliminated an entire level of top management, but it also allowed him to eliminate the duplication in marketing, distribution, and retail functions across the old five divisions and so would result in major cost savings.

The two remaining divisions are now its retail division called "direct brands" and its wholesale division called "partnered brands." Its new structure is intended to "bring focus, energy and clarity" to the way each division operates. The retail division, for example, is responsible for the brands that are sold primarily through Liz Claiborne's own retail store chains, such as its Kate Spade, Lucky Brand Jeans, and Juicy Couture chains. The goals of grouping together its fastest-growing brands is to allow divisional managers to make better marketing and distribution decisions to attract more customers. For example, Liz Claiborne plans to increase targeted marketing on direct labels to 3% to 5% of annual sales and to find ways to get new clothing designs more quickly to its store to compete with chains like Zara that are able to innovate new clothing collections almost every month. The company also plans to open 300 more stores in the next few years to add to its 433 specialty stores and 350 outlets stores.[27]

In contrast, the problem in the wholesale division, which sells branded apparel lines such as Liz Claiborne and Dana Buchman directly to department stores and other retailers, is to reduce costs to slow down the growing threat from private labels. For example, sales of Macy's private labels increased almost 10% during the 2000s. If managers of the wholesale division can find ways to improve operating efficiency, it can offer stores like Macy's lower prices for its clothing to encourage them to stick with its brands. Similarly, if the division's managers can find ways to reduce costs such as by turning inventory over more quickly, sharing marketing costs, and so forth, then even if the prices they can charge do fall, they can still increase profits. Wholesale managers are also partnering with department stores to develop exclusive lines of branded clothing so both parties benefit. For example, they reached an agreement with JCPenney to launch a line called Liz & Co. that will be sold only in its stores; so far sales have been good, and both partners have enjoyed higher profits.

Thus CEO McComb realized that to reduce complexity and allow each division to build the right merchandising culture, it was necessary to change Liz Claiborne's organizational structure. From grouping clothing products into divisions based on their quality or price, he changed to two market divisions where clothing brands are grouped according to the needs of each division's customers—either the people in its stores or the retail chains that buy its clothes to resell to individual customers. The real problem is that each division faces a quite different set of strategic and operational problems, and with its new structure managers in each division can now focus on solving the specific set of problems to achieve the best performance from their particular brands. In 2010, McComb's hope is that in the next decade the company's sales will grow rapidly, but this time its new structure will lead to higher efficiency and effectiveness and so rising profitability.

Discussion Questions

1. What were the problems with Liz Claiborne's old organizational structure?
2. How did McComb change Liz Claiborne's structure to improve its effectiveness? Go to the Web and find out how his design changes have worked.

References

1 J. Child, *Organization: A Guide for Managers and Administrators* (New York: Harper & Row, 1977); R. Duncan,"What Is the Right Organization Structure?" *Organization Dynamics* (Winter 1979): 59–80; J. R. Galbraith and R. K. Kazanjian, *Strategy Implementation: Structure, System, and Process,* 2nd ed. (St. Paul, MN: West, 1986).

2 O. E. Williamson, *Markets and Hierarchies: Analysis and Antitrust Implications* (New York: Free Press, 1975).

3 P. R. Lawrence and J. W. Lorsch, *Organization and Environment* (Boston: Graduate School of Business Administration, Harvard University, 1967).

4 A. D. Chandler, *Strategy and Structure* (Cambridge, MA: MIT Press, 1962); Williamson, *Markets and Hierarchies*.

5 Chandler, *Strategy and Structure*; B. R. Scott, *Stages of Development* (Cambridge, MA: Harvard Business School, 1971).

6 A. P. Sloan, *My Years at General Motors* (Garden City, NY: Doubleday, 1946), p. 46.

7 Ibid., p. 50.

8 A. Taylor, III, "Can GM Remodel Itself?" *Fortune* 13 (1992), pp. 26–34; W. Hampton and J. Norman, "General Motors: What Went Wrong?" *Business Week*, March 16, 1987, pp. 102–110.

9 "GM Will Match Japan Quality in 2–3 Years," www.yahoo.com, September 17, 2002.

10 www.gm.com, 2011.

11 C. W. L. Hill and G. R. Jones, *Strategic Management*, 7th ed. (Boston: Houghton Mifflin, 2007); G. R. Jones and C. W. L. Hill, "Transaction Cost Analysis of Strategy-Structure Choice," *Strategic Management Journal* 9 (1988), 159–172.

12 Sloan, *My Years at General Motors*.

13 S. M. Davis and P. R. Lawrence, *Matrix* (Reading, MA: Addison-Wesley, 1977); J. R. Galbraith, "Matrix Organization Designs: How to Combine Functional and Project Forms," *Business Horizons* 14 (1971), 29–40.

14 L. R. Burns, "Matrix Management in Hospitals: Testing Theories of Matrix Structure and Development," *Administrative Science Quarterly* 34 (1989), 349–368; Duncan, "What Is the Right Organization Structure?"

15 S. M. Davis and P. R. Lawrence, "Problems of Matrix Organization," *Harvard Business Review* (May–June 1978): 131–142; E. W. Larson and D. H. Gobelli, "Matrix Management: Contradictions and Insight," *California Management Review* (Summer 1987): 126–138.

16 www.target.com, 2011.

17 R. E. Miles and C. C. Snow, "Causes of Failure in Network Organizations," *California Management Review* (July 1992): 53–72.

18 W. Baker, "The Network Organization in Theory and Practice," in N. Nohria and R. Eccles, eds., *Networks and Organizations* (Boston: Harvard Business School, 1992), pp. 397–429.

19 www.nike.com, 2011.

20 G. S. Capowski, "Designing a Corporate Identity," *Management Review* (June 1993): 37–38.

21 J. Marcia, "Just Doing It," *Distribution* (January 1995): 36–40.

22 R. A. Bettis, S. P. Bradley, and G. Hamel, "Outsourcing and Industrial Decline," *Academy of Management Executive* (February 1992): 7–22.

23 C. C. Snow, R. E. Miles, and H. J. Coleman, Jr. "Managing 21st Century Network Organizations," *Organizational Dynamics* (Winter 1992): 5–20.

24 J. Fulk and G. Desanctis, "Electronic Communication and Changing Organizational Forms," *Organizational Science* 6 (1995), 337–349.

25 www.lizclaiborne.com, 2011.

26 R. Dodes, "Claiborne Seeks to Shed 16 Apparel Brands," www.businessweek.com, July 11, 2007.

27 www.lizclaiborne.com, 2011.

CHAPTER 7

Creating and Managing Organizational Culture

Learning Objectives

In this chapter, the concept of organizational culture is examined. Culture is discussed in terms of the values and norms that influence employees' behavior and bond them to the organization and determine how they perceive and interpret the environment and act in ways to give an organization a competitive advantage. The global dimension of culture is also examined, and the problems that organizations experience when they expand globally and encounter different kinds of values and norms is addressed.

After studying this chapter you should be able to:

1. Differentiate between values and norms, understand the way culture is shared by an organization's members, and why organizations have different types of culture.
2. Describe how individuals learn culture both formally (that is, the way an organization intends them to learn it) and informally (that is, by seeing what goes on in the organization).
3. Identify the four building blocks or foundations of an organization's culture that account for cultural differences among organizations.
4. Understand how an organization's culture, like its structure, can be designed or managed.
5. Discuss an important outcome of an organization's culture: its stance on corporate social responsibility.

What Is Organizational Culture?

Previous chapters have discussed how the most important function of organizational structure is to *control*—that is, coordinate and motivate—people within an organization. In Chapter 1, we defined **organizational culture** as the set of shared values and norms that control organizational members' interactions with each other and with suppliers, customers, and other people outside the organization. Just as an organization's structure is designed to achieve competitive advantage and promote stakeholder interests, an organization's culture can be used to increase organizational effectiveness.[1] This is because organizational culture controls the way members make decisions, the way they interpret and manage the organizational environment, what they do with information, and how they behave.[2] Culture thus affects an organization's performance and competitive position.

What are organizational values, and how do they affect behavior? **Values** are general criteria, standards, or guiding principles that people use to determine which types of behaviors, events, situations, and outcomes are desirable or undesirable. The two kinds of values are terminal and instrumental (see Figure 7.1).[3] A **terminal value** is a desired end state or outcome that people seek to achieve. Organizations might adopt any of the following as terminal values, that is, as guiding principles: excellence, responsibility, reliability, profitability, innovativeness, economy, morality, quality. Large insurance companies,

Organizational culture
The set of shared values and norms that control organizational members' interactions with each other and with people outside the organization.

Values
General criteria, standards, or guiding principles that people use to determine which types of behaviors, events, situations, and outcomes are desirable or undesirable.

Terminal value
A desired end state or outcome that people seek to achieve.

Figure 7.1 Terminal and Instrumental Values in an Organization's Culture

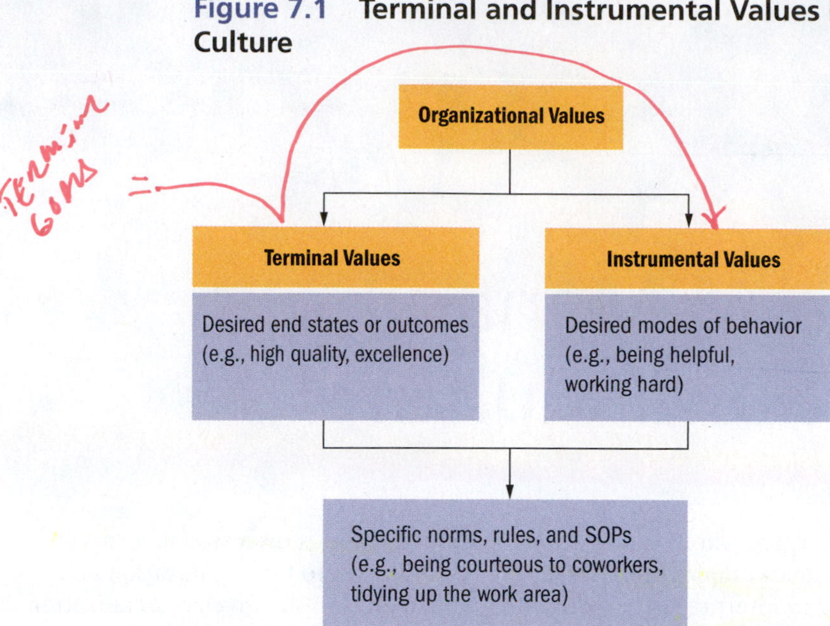

for example, may value excellence, but their terminal values are often stability and predictability because the company must be there to pay off policyholders' claims.

Instrumental value A desired mode of behavior.

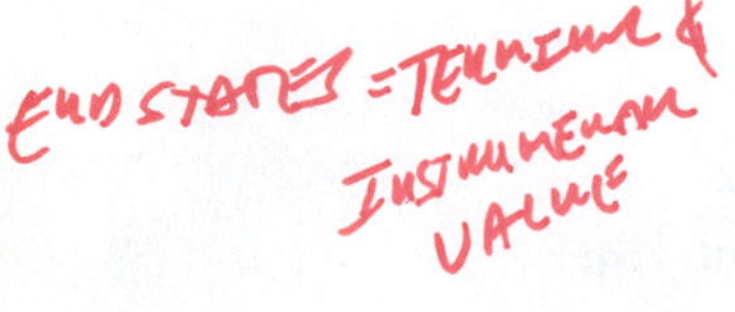

An **instrumental value** is a desired mode of behavior. Modes of behavior that organizations advocate include working hard, respecting traditions and authority, being conservative and cautious, being frugal, being creative and courageous, being honest, taking risks, and maintaining high standards.

An organization's culture thus consists of the end states that the organization seeks to achieve (its *terminal values*) and the modes of behavior the organization encourages (its *instrumental values*). Ideally, instrumental values help the organization achieve its terminal goals. Indeed, different organizations have different cultures because they possess different sets of terminal and instrumental values. For example, a computer software and hardware company like Google and Apple whose cultures emphasize the terminal value of innovativeness may attain this outcome through encouraging the development of instrumental values of being creative, taking risks, sharing new product ideas, and cooperating with other team members. That combination of terminal and instrumental values leads to an entrepreneurial culture. As Apple's CEO Steve Jobs commented, "You need a very product-oriented culture, even in a technology company. Lots of companies have tons of great engineers and smart people. But ultimately, there needs to be some gravitational force that pulls it all together."[4] That compelling force is provided by the type of control—the form of coordination and motivation—that results from an organization's culture.

In some organizations, however, values and norms that emphasize creative "out-of-the-box" thinking may be inappropriate. For example, a parcel delivery company like UPS or FedEx that desires stability and predictability to reduce costs may emphasize caution, attention to detail, speediness, and conformity to work rules and standard operating procedures (SOPs). The result will be a conservative culture—the gravitational force that guides UPS, as Organizational Insight 7.1 describes. FedEx has imitated UPS's approach. For example to save high-priced gasoline, FedEx uses a GPS positioning system to instruct its drivers on the most efficient ways to drive their routes. For example, they turn right at intersections when possible to reduce delivery time and distance; no doubt UPS uses a similar system.

Terminal values can often be found by studying an organization's mission statement and official goals, which tell organization members and other stakeholders what kinds of values and ethical standards it wishes its members to use in their decision making. So that members understand instrumental values—that is, the styles of behavior they are expected to follow as they pursue desired end states—an organization develops specific norms, rules, and SOPs that embody its instrumental values. In Chapter 4, we defined **norms** as standards or styles of behavior that are considered acceptable or typical for a group of people. The specific norms of being courteous and keeping the work area clean and safe, for example, will develop in an organization whose instrumental values include being helpful and working hard.

Norms
Standards or styles of behavior that are considered acceptable or typical for a group of people.

Organizational Insight 7.1

UPS Says There Is a Right Way to Deliver Parcels

United Parcel Service (UPS) controls more than three-fourths of the U.S. ground and air parcel service, delivering over 10 million packages a day in its fleet of 150,000 trucks.[5] It is also the most profitable company in its industry. UPS employs over 250,000 people, and since its founding as a bicycle messenger service in 1907 by James E. Casey, UPS has developed a culture that has been a model for competitors such as FedEx and the U.S. Postal Service.

From the beginning, Casey made efficiency, economy, and thrift the company's terminal values and loyalty, humility, discipline, dependability, and intense effort the key instrumental values that UPS employees should adopt. UPS has always gone to extraordinary lengths to develop and maintain these values and associated norms in its workforce, not least because UPS started out as an employee-owned company.

First, its operating systems from the top of the company down to its trucking operations are the subject of intense scrutiny by the company's 3,000 industrial engineers. These engineers are constantly on the lookout for ways to measure outputs and behaviors to improve efficiency; for example, they time every part of an employee's job. Truck drivers, for example, are instructed in extraordinary detail on how to perform their tasks: They must step from their truck with their right foot first, fold their money face up, carry packages under their left arm, walk at a pace of 3 feet per second, and slip the key ring holding their truck keys over their third finger.[6] Male employees are not allowed to have beards. All employees must be carefully groomed, and they are instructed on how to deal with customers. Drivers who perform below average receive visits from training supervisors who accompany them on their delivery routes and teach them how to raise their performance level. Not surprisingly, as a result of this intensive training and close behavior control, UPS employees internalize the company's strong norms about the appropriate ways to behave to help the organization achieve its values of economy and efficiency.

Its search to find the best set of output controls leads UPS to constantly develop and introduce the latest in IT into the company's operations, particularly its materials management operations. In fact, today UPS offers a consulting service to other companies in the area of global supply chain management. Its goal is to teach other companies how to pursue its values of efficiency and economy, values that the company has been pursuing for the last 100 years as a result of the values of its founder.

iStockphoto.com/Mark Jensen

Many of the most powerful and crucial values of an organization are not written down. They exist only in the shared norms, beliefs, assumptions, and ways of thinking and acting that people within an organization use to relate to each other and to outsiders and to analyze and deal with problems facing the organization. Members learn from one another how to interpret and respond to various situations in ways that are consistent with the organization's accepted values. Eventually, members choose and follow appropriate values without even realizing they are making a choice. Over time, they internalize the organization's values and the specific rules, norms, and SOPs that govern behavior; that is, organizational values become part of members' mindsets—people's own values systems—and affect their interpretation of a situation.[7] Once again, this is why the cultures of different companies can diverge so widely.

Organizational culture is based on relatively enduring values embodied in organizational norms, rules, SOPs, and goals. People in an organization draw on these cultural values when making decisions and acting upon them, and when dealing with ambiguity and uncertainty inside and outside the organization.[8] The values in an organization's culture are important shapers of members' behavior and responses to situations, and they increase the reliability of members' behavior.[9] In this context, *reliability* does not necessarily mean consistently obedient or passive behavior; it may also mean consistently innovative or creative behavior as in the case of Google and Apple, or consistently attentive, cautious, and speedy behavior as in the case of UPS or FedEx.[10] However, it can also mean totally unethical behavior.

Arthur Andersen, the disgraced, now-defunct accounting firm, was well known for its insistence that its employees abide by its rigid, constraining rules of behavior. Its employees had to wear dark blue suits, black shoes, and in some branches the managers insisted those shoes be the lace-up type or employees were told off. It also had in place an extensive and thorough MBO system and employees' performance was continually evaluated. Its values were based on obedience to company rules and norms, respect for partners, and the importance of following its well-established rules and SOPs. On the surface, the firm's demand that its employees follow its cultural values and norms would seem sound practice for a company whose business depends on the accurate measurement and accounting of the resources used by its clients. Accounting is a relatively precise science, and the last thing an accounting company needs is for its employees to practice "creative accounting."

Small wonder, then, that the business world was astounded in the early 2000s when it became clear that some of Arthur Andersen's most senior partners had been instructing their subordinates to overlook or ignore anomalies in its client books to obtain large consulting fees in order to maintain the clients' business, and to shred documents that revealed its unethical and illegal dealings with Enron before government regulators could examine them, which led to its collapse.

The paradox is that Arthur Andersen's values were so strong that they led subordinates to forget the "real" ethics of what they were doing and they followed its "distorted" ethics. Apparently, Arthur Andersen's culture was so strong it had an almost cult-like effect on its members, who were afraid to question what was going on because of the enormous status and power the partners wielded—and the threat of sanction if anyone disobeyed the rules.

Differences in Global Values and Norms

The values and norms of different countries also affect organizational culture. Indeed, differences between the cultures of different countries that arise because of differences in their national values and norms help reveal the powerful effect of organizational culture on behavior.[11] For example, today global outsourcing is a major organizing method that companies use to reduce costs, which obviously requires managers and employees in different countries to coordinate their actions. However, one recent study found that differences in culture are a major problem in getting coordination to work.

Cultural differences such as diverse communication styles, different approaches to completing tasks, different attitudes toward conflict, and different decision-making styles are major factors that hamper coordination in outsourcing relationships that require contact between people from different countries.

To get a feel for the effects of these differences in cultural values and norms on organizational behavior, consider what happened when a U.S. and a Mexican company attempted to cooperate in a joint venture. After much negotiation, Pittsburgh-based Corning Glass and Vitro, a Mexican glassmaking company, formed a joint venture to share technology and market one another's glass products throughout the United States and Mexico. They formed their alliance to take advantage of the opportunities presented by the North American Free Trade Agreement (NAFTA), which opened up the markets of both countries to one another's products. At the signing of the joint venture, both companies were enthusiastic about the prospects for their alliance. Managers in both companies claimed they had similar organizational cultures. Both companies had a top-management team that was still dominated by members of the founding families; both were global companies with broad product lines; and both had been successful in managing alliances with other companies in the past. Nevertheless, two years later Corning Glass terminated the joint venture and gave Vitro back the $150 million it had given Corning for access to Corning's technology.[12]

Why had the venture failed? The cultures and values of the two companies were so different that Corning managers and Vitro managers could not work together. Vitro, the Mexican company, did business the Mexican way, in accordance with values prevailing in Mexican culture. In Mexico, business is conducted at a slower pace than in the United States. Used to a protected market, Mexican companies are inclined to sit back and make their decisions in a "very genteel," consensual kind of way. Managers typically come to work at 9 A.M., spend two or more hours at lunch, often at home with their families, and then work late, often until 9 P.M. Mexican managers and their subordinates are also intensely loyal and respectful to their superiors; the corporate culture is based on paternalistic, hierarchical values; and most important decision making is centralized in a small team of top managers. This centralization slows decision making because middle managers may come up with a solution to a problem but will not take action without top-management approval. In Mexico, building relationships with new companies takes time and effort because trust develops slowly. Thus personal contacts that develop slowly between managers in different companies are an important prerequisite for doing business in Mexico.

Corning, the American company, did business the American way, in accordance with values prevailing in American culture. Managers in the United States take short lunch breaks or work through lunch so they can leave early in the evening. In many U.S. companies, decision-making authority is decentralized to lower-level managers, who make important decisions and commit their organization to certain courses of action. U.S. managers like to make decisions quickly and worry about the consequences later.

Aware of the differences in their approaches to doing business, managers from Corning and from Vitro tried to compromise and find a mutually acceptable working style. Managers from both companies agreed to take long working lunches together. Mexican managers agreed to forgo going home at lunchtime, and U.S. managers agreed to work a bit later at night so they could talk to Vitro's top managers and thus speed decision making. Over time, however, the differences in management style and approach to work became a source of frustration for managers from both companies. The slow pace of decision making was frustrating for Corning's managers. The pressure by Corning's managers to get everything done quickly was frustrating for Vitro's managers. Corning's managers working in Mexico discovered that the organizational cultures of Vitro and Corning were not so similar after all, and they decided to go home. Vitro's managers also realized it was pointless to prolong the venture when the differences were so great.

Corning and countless other U.S. companies that have entered into global agreements have found that doing business in any other country is different from doing business at home. U.S. managers living abroad should not expect to do business the U.S. way. Because values, norms, customs, and etiquette differ from one country to another, managers working abroad must learn to appreciate and respond to those differences.

Because many mergers fail due to the fact that differences between organizational cultures can be so great, companies that acquire other companies, even U.S. companies, such as Microsoft, Google, and Oracle, use seasoned teams of "merger culture" experts who take the steps necessary to blend the cultures of the merged companies. Likewise, some companies recognize beforehand that their cultures are so different that a merger would be impossible. For example, Microsoft contemplated merging with another leading global software company, German-based SAP. But after their top managers began negotiations, it became clear that despite the advantages of the merger, their two cultures were so different they could never successfully merge their skills and resources to create more value. Similarly, when Google sought to acquire Groupon in 2010 for $6 billion, Groupon's top managers decided they wanted to maintain their own culture and grow the company their own way, as we discussed in Chapter 1.

In sum, there are many ways in which culture can inspire and facilitate the intense kind of personal and team interactions that are necessary to develop organizational competences and obtain a competitive advantage. First, cultural values are important facilitators of mutual adjustment in an organization. When shared cultural values provide a common reference point, employees do not need to spend much time establishing rapport and overcoming differences in their perceptions of events. Cultural values can smooth interactions among organizational members. People who share an organization's values may come to identify strongly with the organization, and feelings of self-worth may flow from their membership in it.[13] Employees of companies like Google, Southwest Airlines, and Groupon, for example, seem to value their membership in the organization and are committed to it.

Second, organizational culture is a form of informal organization that facilitates the workings of the organizational structure. It is an important determinant of the way employees view their tasks and roles. It tells them, for example, if they should stay within established rules and procedures and simply obey orders or whether they are allowed to make suggestions to their superiors, find better or more creative ways of performing their roles, and feel free to demonstrate their competency without fear of reprisal from their peers or superiors.

This is not trivial. One of the most common complaints of employees and junior managers in organizations is that although they know certain tasks or roles could be accomplished better and should be performed in different ways, their organization's values and norms do not permit them to advise or question their superiors up the organizational hierarchy. They feel trapped, become unhappy, and often leave an organization, causing high turnover. To mitigate this problem, some companies like GE, Google, and Microsoft have open lines of communication to the CEO that bypass the immediate superior. These companies also go out of their way to develop values of equity and fairness that demonstrate their commitment to reward employees who work toward organizational goals, rather than behaving in their own self-interest. GE even has a name for the managers who are out for themselves—"Type 4" managers—and based on feedback from subordinates, these managers are routinely asked to leave to make room for those who can develop empowered, motivated subordinates. GE's work practices demonstrate its values to its members.

How Is an Organization's Culture Transmitted to Its Members?

The ability of an organization's culture to motivate employees and increase organizational effectiveness is directly related to the way in which members learn the organization's values. Organizational members learn pivotal values from an organization's formal socialization practices and from the stories, ceremonies, and organizational language that develop informally as an organization's culture matures.

Socialization and Socialization Tactics

Newcomers to an organization must learn the values and norms that guide its existing members' behavior and decision making.[14] Can they work from 10 A.M. to 7 P.M. instead of from 8 A.M. to 5 P.M.? Can they challenge the opinions of their peers and superiors or should they simply listen and remain silent? Newcomers are outsiders, and only when they have learned and internalized an organization's values and act in accordance with its rules and norms will they be accepted as insiders.

To learn an organization's culture, newcomers must obtain information about cultural values. They can learn values indirectly, by observing how existing members behave and inferring what behaviors are appropriate and inappropriate. From the organization's perspective, however, the indirect method is risky because newcomers might observe and learn habits that are *not* acceptable to the organization. From the organization's perspective, the most effective way for newcomers to learn appropriate values is through **socialization,** which, as we saw in Chapter 4, is the process by which members learn and internalize the norms of an organization's culture.

Socialization
The process by which members learn and internalize the values and norms of an organization's culture.

Van Maanen and Schein developed a model of socialization that suggests how organizations can structure the socialization experience so newcomers learn the values that the organization wants them to learn. In turn, these values influence the role orientation that the newcomers adopt.[15] **Role orientation** is the characteristic way in which newcomers respond to a situation: Do they react passively and obediently to commands and orders? Are they creative and innovative in searching for solutions to problems?

Role orientation
The characteristic way in which newcomers respond to a situation.

Van Maanen and Schein identified 12 socialization tactics that influence a newcomer's role orientation. The use of different sets of these tactics leads to two different role orientations: institutionalized and individualized (see Table 7.1).[16] An *institutionalized role orientation* results when individuals are taught to respond to a new context in the same way that existing organizational members respond to it. An institutionalized orientation encourages obedience and conformity to rules and norms. An *individualized role orientation* results when individuals are allowed and encouraged to be creative and to experiment with changing norms and values so an organization can better achieve its values.[17] The following list contrasts the tactics used to socialize newcomers to an institutionalized orientation with those tactics used to develop an individualized orientation.

1. ***Collective vs. Individual.*** Collective tactics provide newcomers with common learning experiences designed to produce a standardized response to a situation. With individual tactics, each newcomer's learning experiences are unique, and newcomers can learn new, appropriate responses for each situation.
2. ***Formal vs. Informal.*** Formal tactics segregate newcomers from existing organizational members during the learning process. With informal tactics, newcomers learn on the job, as members of a team.
3. ***Sequential vs. Random.*** Sequential tactics provide newcomers with explicit information about the sequence in which they will perform new activities or occupy new roles as they advance in an organization. With random tactics, training is based on the interests and needs of individual newcomers because there is no set sequence to the newcomers' progress in the organization.
4. ***Fixed vs. Variable.*** Fixed tactics give newcomers precise knowledge of the timetable associated with completing each stage in the learning process. Variable tactics provide no information about when newcomers will reach a certain stage in the learning process; once again, training depends on the needs and interests of the individual.

TABLE 7.1 How Socialization Tactics Shape Employees' Role Orientation

Tactics That Lead to an Institutionalized Orientation	Tactics That Lead to an Individualized Orientation
Collective	Individual
Formal	Informal
Sequential	Random
Fixed	Variable
Serial	Disjunctive
Divestiture	Investiture

Source: G. R. Jones, "Socialization Tactics, Self-Efficacy, and Newcomers' Adjustments to Organizations," *Academy of Management Review* 29 (1986); pp. 262–279.

5. ***Serial vs. Disjunctive.*** When serial tactics are employed, existing organizational members act as role models and mentors for newcomers. Disjunctive processes require newcomers to figure out and develop their own way of behaving; they are not told what to do.
6. ***Divestiture vs. Investiture.*** With divestiture, newcomers receive negative social support—that is, they are ignored or taunted—and existing organizational members withhold support until newcomers learn the ropes and conform to established norms. With investiture, newcomers immediately receive positive social support from other organizational members and are encouraged to be themselves.

When organizations combine the tactics listed in Table 7.1, some evidence indicates that they can influence an individual's role orientation.[18] Military-style socialization, for example, leads to an extremely institutionalized orientation. New soldiers are placed in platoons with other new recruits (*collective*); are segregated from existing organizational members (*formal*); go through preestablished drills and learning experiences (*sequential*); know exactly how long this will take them and what they have to do (*fixed*); have superior officers who are their role models (*serial*); and are treated with zero respect and tolerance until they have learned their duties and "gotten with the program" (*divestiture*). As a result, new recruits develop an institutionalized role orientation in which obedience and conformity to organizational norms and values are the signs of success. New members who cannot or will not perform according to these norms and values leave (or are asked to leave), so that by the end of the socialization process the people who stay are clones of existing organizational members.

No organization controls its members to the extent that the military does, but other organizations do use similar practices to socialize their members. Arthur Andersen, discussed earlier, had a very institutionalized program. Recruits were carefully selected for employment because they seemed to possess the values that Arthur Andersen's partners wanted—for example, hard working, cautious, obedient, and thorough. After they were hired, all new recruits attended a six-week course at its training center outside Chicago, where they were indoctrinated as a group into Arthur Andersen's way of doing business. In formal eight-hour-a-day classes, existing organizational members served as role models and told newcomers what was expected of them. Newcomers also learned informally over meals and during recreation what it meant to be working for Arthur Andersen. By the end of this socialization process, they had learned the values of the organization and the rules and norms that govern the way they are expected to behave when they represented Andersen's clients. This effort to create an institutionalized role orientation worked well until its unethical, greedy partners, seeking to maximize their returns at the expense of other stakeholders, took advantage of its strong culture to lead its employees astray.

Should an organization encourage an institutionalized role orientation in which newcomers accept the status quo and perform their jobs in keeping with the commands and orders they are given? Or should an organization encourage an individualized role orientation in which newcomers are allowed to develop creative and innovative responses to the jobs that the organization requires of them? The answer to this question depends on the organization's mission. A financial institution's credibility and reputation with clients depend on its integrity, so it wants to have control over what its employees do. It needs to adopt a strong socialization program that will reinforce its cultural values and standardize the way its employees perform their activities to develop a good reputation for honesty and reliability. So developing an institutionalized orientation is in the best interests of financial organizations such as Bank of America and insurance companies such as State Farm.

One danger of institutionalized socialization lies in the power it gives to those at the top of the organization to manipulate the situation. A second danger can lie in the sameness it may produce among members of an organization. If all employees have been socialized to share the same way of looking at the world, how will the organization be able to change and adapt when that world changes? When confronted with changes in the organizational environment (for example, a new product, a new competitor, or a change in customer demands), employees indoctrinated into old values will be unable to develop new values that might allow them to innovate. As a result, they—and thus the organization—cannot adapt and respond to the new conditions.

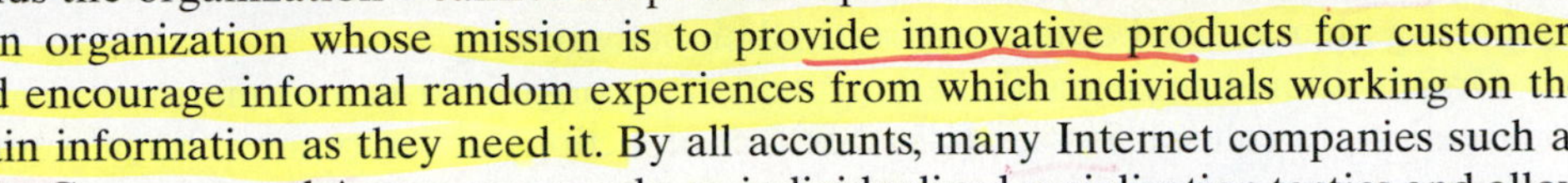

An organization whose mission is to provide innovative products for customers should encourage informal random experiences from which individuals working on the job gain information as they need it. By all accounts, many Internet companies such as Google, Groupon, and Amazon.com rely on individualized socialization tactics and allow members to develop skills in areas that capitalize on their abilities and interests.[19] These companies take this approach because their effectiveness depends not on standardizing individual behavior but on innovation and the ability of members to come up with new and improved solutions to Internet-related problems—such as Amazon.com's push in the 2000s to seek new ways to generate revenues to offset its rising operating costs. For example, it started a consultancy group to sell its IT skills to any interested organizations—something suggested by lower-level employees—and it is now moving quickly to take advantage of opportunities in cloud computing. In the 2010s it is using its strong values and norms to support its rapid entry into many new kinds of virtual markets to sell an increasing range of products. In every market, employees know how they should work to meet its goals because they are "Amazonians." In this way an organization's socialization practices not only help members learn the organization's cultural values and the rules and norms that govern behavior, but they also support the organization's mission by strengthening them over time.

Stories, Ceremonies, and Organizational Language

The cultural values of an organization are often evident in the stories, ceremonies, and language found in the organization.[20] At Southwest Airlines, for example, employees wearing costumes on Halloween, Friday cookouts with top managers, and managers periodically working with employees to perform basic organizational jobs all reinforce and communicate the company's collaborative culture to its members.

Organizations use several types of ceremonial rites to communicate cultural norms and values (see Table 7.2).[21] *Rites of passage* mark an individual's entry to, promotion in, and departure from the organization. The socialization programs used by the army, in colleges, and in companies like 3M and Microsoft, which recognize their most creative people with special job titles, plaques, and so on, are rites of passage; so too are the ways in which an organization grooms people for promotion or retirement. *Rites of integration*, such as shared announcements of organizational success, office parties, and company cookouts, build and reinforce common bonds between organizational members. *Rites of enhancement*, such as awards dinners, newspaper releases, and employee promotions, publicly recognize and reward employees' contributions.

Triad Systems, a computer company founded in Livermore, California, used many ceremonies to integrate and enhance its organizational culture. Every year in its annual trade show its managers gave out awards to recognize employees for excellent service. With much hoopla the *Grindstone Award* was awarded to "individuals who most consistently demonstrate initiative, focus, dedication, and persistence"; the *Innovator Award* to those who "conceive and carry out innovative ideas"; and the *Busting the Boundaries Award* to "those who work most effectively across departmental and divisional boundaries to accomplish their work."[22] The goal of Triad's awards ceremony is clear—to develop organizational folklore that supports work teams and builds a productive culture. Giving praise

TABLE 7.2 Organizational Rites

Type of Rite	Example of Rite	Purpose of Rite
Rite of passage	Induction and basic training	Learn and internalize norms and values
Rite of integration	Office Christmas party	Build common norms and values
Rite of enhancement	Presentation of annual award	Motivate commitment to norms and values

and recognition builds a community of employees who share similar values and promotes the development, across functional groups, of a common corporate language that bonds people together and so better coordinates their activities.

Organizational stories and the language of an organization are important media for communicating culture. Stories (whether fact or fiction) about organizational superstars provide important clues about cultural values and norms. Such stories can reveal the kinds of behaviors that the organization values and the kinds of practices the organization frowns on. Studying stories and language can reveal the values that guide behavior.[23] Because language is the principal medium of communication in organizations, the characteristic phrases that frame and describe events provide important clues about norms and values.

The concept of organizational language encompasses not only spoken language but how people dress, the offices they occupy, the company cars they drive, and how they formally address one another. In Google, Facebook, and many other high-tech organizations, casual dress is the norm, but in investment banks like Goldman Sachs, and luxury department stores like Neiman Marcus and Saks, expensive, well-tailored clothing is the order of the day.

Many organizations have technical languages that facilitate mutual adjustment between organizational members.[24] At 3M, inside entrepreneurs have to emphasize the relationship between their product and 3M's terminal values to push ideas through the product development committee. Because many 3M products are flat—such as sanding and grinding discs, Post-it notes, and thin plastics—the quality of flatness embodies 3M's terminal values, and flatness is often a winning theme in 3M's corporate language—it increases a new product's chance of getting funded. At Google, employees have developed a shorthand language of technical software phrases to describe company-specific communication problems. Technical languages are used by the military, by sports teams, in hospitals, and in many other specialized work contexts. Like socialization practices, organizational language, ceremonies, stories, and even detailed books of organization-specific rules help people learn the ropes and the organization's cultural values. Take the example of SiteROCK, profiled in Organizational Insight 7.2.

Organizational Insight 7.2

SiteROCK's Military Management Culture

The high-tech, dot-com culture is not usually associated with the values and norms that characterize the military. However, managers of the thousands of dot-coms that went belly up in the early 2000s might have benefited from some military-style disciplined values and norms. Indeed, a few dot-coms that survived the shakeout did so because their managers used military-style rules and SOPs to control their employees and ensure high performance. One of these companies is SiteROCK, based in Emeryville, California, whose COO, Dave Lilly, is a former nuclear submarine commander.

SiteROCK is in the business of hosting and managing the websites of other companies and keeping them up and running and error free. A customer's site that goes down or runs haywire is the major enemy. To maximize the performance of his employees and to increase their ability to respond to unexpected online events, Lilly decided he needed to develop an institutionalized role orientation and develop a comprehensive set of rules and standard operating procedures to cover all the major known problems.[25] Lilly insisted that every problem-solving procedure be written down and codified. SiteROCK now has over 30 thick binders listing all the processes and checklists that employees need to follow when an unexpected event happens. Their job is to try to solve the problem using these procedures.

Moreover, again drawing from his military experience, Lilly instituted a "two-man" norm: Whenever the unexpected happens, each employee must immediately tell a coworker and the two should attempt to solve the problem together. The goal is simple: Develop strong norms of cooperation to achieve the quick resolution of a complex issue. If the existing rules don't work, then employees must experiment, and when they find a solution, the solution is turned into a new rule to be included in the procedures book to aid the future decision making of all employees in the organization.

At SiteROCK, these written rules and SOPs have resulted in values that lead employees to achieve high levels of customer service. Because the goal is 100% reliability, detailed blueprints guide planning and decision making, not seat-of-the-pants problem solving, which might be brilliant 80% of the time but result in disaster the rest of the time. Before SiteROCK employees are allowed in the control room each day, they must read over the most important rules and SOPs. And at the end of a shift they spend 90 minutes doing paperwork that logs what they have done and states any new or improved rules that they have come up with. Clearly, SiteROCK has developed a company-specific testament that symbolizes to employees the need for sustained, cooperative effort.

Managerial Implications

Analyzing Organizational Culture

1. Study the culture of your organization, and identify the terminal and instrumental values on which it is based to assess how they affect organizational behavior.
2. Assess whether the goals, norms, and rules of your organization are effectively transmitting the values of the organizational culture to members. Identify areas for improvement.
3. Examine the methods your organization uses to socialize new members. Assess whether these socialization practices are effective in helping newcomers learn the organization's culture. Recommend ways to improve the process.
4. Try to develop organizational ceremonies to help employees learn cultural values, to enhance employee commitment, and to bond employees to the organization.

Finally, organizational symbols often convey an organization's cultural values to its members and to others outside the organization. In some organizations, for example, the size of people's offices, their location on the third floor or the thirty-third floor, or the luxury with which they are equipped are symbols that convey images about the values in an organization's culture. Is the organization hierarchical and status conscious, for example, or are informal, participative work relationships encouraged? In the 1990s, GM's executive suite on the top floor of their giant Detroit headquarters was isolated from the rest of the building and open only to top GM executives. A private corridor and stairway linked top managers' offices to the private elevators connected to their heated parking garage.

Sometimes, the very design of the building itself is a symbol of an organization's values. For example, Walt Disney hired famed Japanese architect Arata Isozaki to design the Team Disney Building, which houses Disney's "imagineering unit," in Orlando, Florida. This building's contemporary and unusual design featuring unusual shapes and bright colors conveys the importance of imagination and creativity to Walt Disney and to the people who work in it. Many organizations such as Google, Facebook, and Apple have followed this approach and designed futuristic office campuses to inform employees that their main task is to think ahead and predict changes in the organizational environment.

Where Does Organizational Culture Come From?

Now that you have seen what organizational culture is and how members learn and become part of an organization's culture, some difficult questions can be addressed: Where does organizational culture come from? Why do different companies have different cultures? Why might a culture that for many years helped an organization pursue its corporate mission suddenly harm the organization? Can culture be managed?

Organizational culture develops from the interaction of four factors: the personal and professional characteristics of people within the organization, organizational ethics, the property rights that the organization gives to employees, and the structure of the organization (see Figure 7.2). The interaction of these factors produces different cultures in different organizations and causes changes in culture over time. The way in which people's personal characteristics shape culture is discussed first.

Characteristics of People within the Organization

The ultimate source of organizational culture is the people who make up the organization. If you want to know why cultures differ, look at their members. Organizations A, B, and C develop distinctly different cultures because they attract, select, and retain people who have different values, personalities, and ethics.[26] People may be attracted to an

Figure 7.2 Where an Organization's Culture Comes From

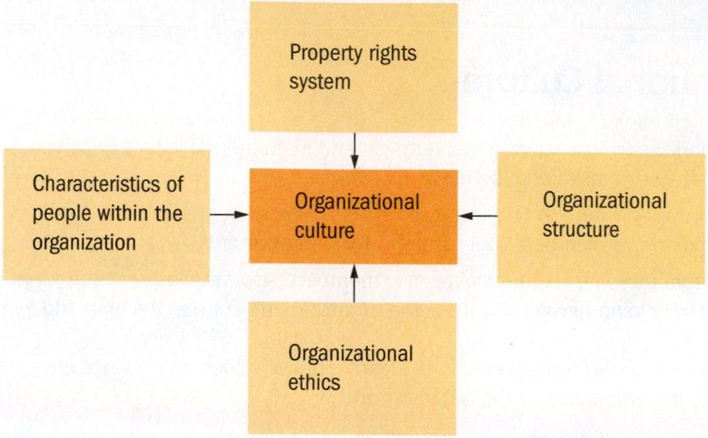

organization whose values match theirs; similarly, an organization selects people who share its values. Over time, people who do not fit in leave. The result is that people inside the organization become more and more similar, the values of the organization become more and more parochial, and the culture becomes more and more distinct from that of similar organizations.

The founder of an organization has a substantial influence on the organization's initial culture because of his or her personal values and beliefs.[27] Founders set the scene for the later development of a culture because they not only establish the new organization's values but hire its first members. Presumably, the people selected by the founder have values and interests similar to the founder's.[28] Over time, members buy into the founder's vision and perpetuate the founder's values in the organization.[29] An important implication of this "people make the place" view of organizational culture is that the culture of an organization can be strengthened and changed over time by the people who control and lead it.[30]

The growth of Google provides a good illustration of the important role a company's founders play in developing shared cultural values that establish a strong organizational culture.

Google was founded in 1995 when two Stanford graduate computer science students collaborated to develop a new kind of search engine technology. They understood the limitations of existing search engines and by 1998 they developed a superior engine that they felt was ready to go online. They raised $1 million from family, friends, and risk-taking "angel" investors to buy the hardware necessary to connect Google to the Internet.

At first, Google answered 10,000 inquiries a day, but in a few months it was answering 500,000, 3 million by the fall of 1999, 60 million by the fall of 2000, and in the spring of 2001 it reached 100 million per day. In the 2000s, Google has become the leading search engine, and it is one of the top five most used Internet companies. Rivals like Yahoo and Microsoft are working hard to catch up and beat Google at its own game.

Google's explosive growth is largely due to the culture or entrepreneurship and innovation its founders cultivated from the start. Although by 2011 Google had grown to over 26,000 employees worldwide, its founders claim that it still maintains a small company feel because its culture empowers its employees, which it calls staffers or "Googlers," to create the best software possible. Brin and Page created Google's entrepreneurial culture in several ways.

From the beginning, lacking space and seeking to keep operating costs low, Google staffers worked in "high-density clusters." Three or four employees, each equipped with a high-powered Linux workstation, shared a desk, couch, and chairs that were large rubber balls and worked together to improve its technology. Even when Google moved into more spacious surroundings at its "Googleplex" headquarters building, staffers continued to work in shared spaces. Google also designed its building so that staffers are constantly meeting one another in Google's funky lobby, in the Google Café where everyone eats together, in its state-of-the-art recreational facilities, and in its "snack rooms" equipped with bins packed with cereals, candy, yogurt, carrots, and of course make-your-own cappuccino. They also created many social gatherings of employees such as a TGIF open meeting and a twice-weekly outdoor roller hockey game where staffers are encouraged to bring down the founders.

All this attention to creating what just might be the "grooviest" company headquarters in the world did not come about by chance. Brin and Page knew that Google's most important strength would be its ability to attract the best software engineers in the world and then to motivate them to perform well. Common offices, lobbies, cafés, and so on bring staffers into close contact with one another, develop collegiality, and encourage them to share their new ideas with their colleagues and constantly improve its search engine technology and find new ways to grow the company—hence Google Chrome, Voice, Docs, and the many other applications it provides its users today. The freedom Google gives its staffers to pursue new ideas is a clear signal of its founders' desire to empower them to be innovative and to look off the beaten path for new ideas. Finally, recognizing that staffers who innovate important new software applications should be rewarded for their achievements, Google's founders also gave them stock in the company, which effectively makes staffers its owners as well.

Organizational Ethics

Many cultural values derive from the personality and beliefs of the founder and the top-management team and are in a sense out of the control of the organization. These values are what they are because of who the founder and top managers are. Google founder Larry Page, who became its CEO in 2011, is a workaholic who often works 14 hours a day. His terminal values for Google are excellence, innovation, and high quality and safety, and the instrumental values he advocates are hard work, creativity, and attention to detail. Page expects employees to put in long workdays because he requires this level of commitment from himself, and he expects them to do everything they can to promote innovation, quality, and safety because this is what he does. Employees who do not buy into these values leave Google, and those who remain are spurred by organizational norms to stay on the job, stick with the task, and go out of their way to help others solve problems that will help the organization.

An organization can, however, consciously and purposefully develop some cultural values to control members' behavior. Ethical values fall into this category. As discussed in Chapter 2, organizational ethics are the moral values, beliefs, and rules that establish the appropriate way for organizational members to deal with one another and with the organization's stakeholders (see Figure 7.3).

Figure 7.3 Factors Influencing the Development of Organizational Ethics

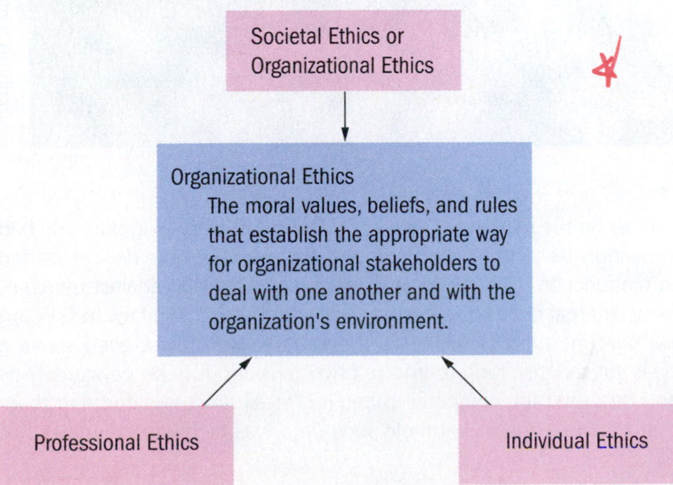

In developing cultural values, top managers must constantly make choices about the right or appropriate thing to do. IBM, Dell, or Sears, for example, might wonder whether they should develop procedural guidelines for giving advance notice to employees and middle managers about impending layoffs or store closings. In the past, companies have been reluctant to do so because they fear employee hostility and apathy. In 2010, Toyota and other car makers decided to recall several of its vehicles because problems with sticking brake pedals had caused wrecks that resulted in serious harm to passengers. Similarly, a company has to decide whether to allow its managers to pay bribes to government officials in foreign countries where such payoffs are an illegal yet accepted way of doing business. In such situations, managers deciding on a course of action have to balance the interests of the organization against the interests of other stakeholder groups.[31]

To make these decisions, managers rely on ethical instrumental values embodied in the organization's culture.[32] Such values outline the right and wrong ways to behave in a situation in which an action may help one person or stakeholder group, but hurt another.[33] Ethical values, and the rules and norms they embody, are an inseparable part of an organization's culture because they help shape the values that members use to manage situations and make decisions.

One of top management's main responsibilities is to ensure that organizational members obey the law. Indeed, in certain situations top managers can be held accountable for the conduct of their subordinates. One of the main ways in which top managers can ensure the legality of organizational behavior is to create an organizational culture that instills ethical instrumental values so that members reflexively deal with stakeholders in an ethical manner. Many organizations do act illegally, immorally, and unethically and take few steps to develop ethical values for their employees to follow. Organizational Insight 7.3 describes how Guidant put company interests above customers' health and above the law.

Organizational Insight 7.3

Has Guidant Solved Its Ethical Problems?

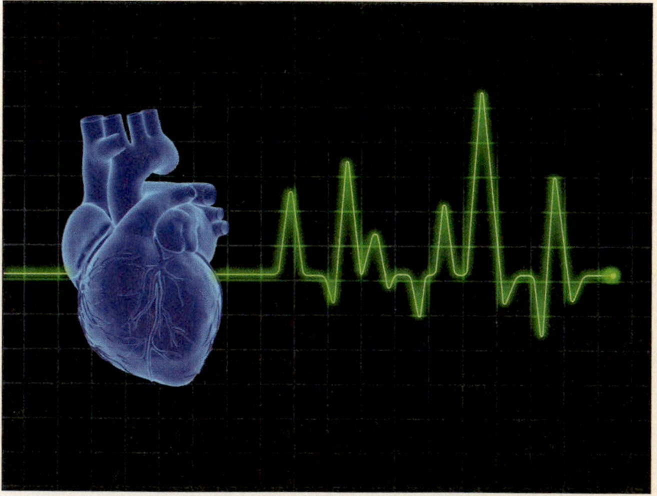

iStockphoto.com/Max Delson Martins Santos

In 2005, Guidant Corporation, a maker of medical cardiac devices, revealed that many of its defibrillators had an electrical defect that might cause them to fail when needed to interrupt an erratic and possibly fatal heart rhythm. Guidant was forced to recall more than 100,000 implantable heart devices, including three models of defibrillators with similar electrical flaws that were tied to at least seven patient deaths.

One of the most troubling aspects of the recall came into view when it was revealed that Guidant had known about the electrical problem for at least three years after two physicians in Minneapolis, Dr. Maron and Dr. Hauser, told the company about the problem. They urged Guidant to alert physicians about the device defect so they could check their patients and implant new models. Guidant made no effort to communicate the problem to physicians nationwide, or to the Food and Drug Administration (FDA), which has a clear procedure for when a company should make a legal written declaration about known problems with a medical product. When the company failed to act on their message and take their advice, the physicians contacted other physicians and the *New York Times*. The resulting story and outcry quickly forced Guidant to reveal the problem with its devices and communicate the problem to physicians nationwide.

In the ensuing investigation, a panel of medical experts came to the conclusion that Guidant had deliberately kept its faulty cardiac devices on the market without considering the medical impact and had knowingly failed to alert doctors and patients when the devices started to malfunction. Once legal proceedings were started against the company, internal documents further revealed that a consultant to Guidant had informed the company's top executives that he believed it had a clear ethical obligation to inform physicians about heart device defects and he urged the company to begin a recall process, informing them that their decision to withhold such data was highly questionable. He also noted that Guidant had a clear conflict of interest that would naturally lead it (and other companies) to disclose product failures only when necessary. So, if a tragedy occurred—which it did—Guidant's actions would be viewed in the worst possible light possible; it is always in a company's best interest to expose its dirty laundry.

This proved true when Guidant faced a product liability lawsuit filed in Texas by patients who received Guidant defibrillators and then faced a federal lawsuit in Minnesota that claimed the company had acted criminally when it knowingly sold potentially flawed defibrillators. Guidant had to pay hundreds of millions in damages to patients, and after intense negotiation with the Justice Department, it reached an agreement to plead guilty to two "misdemeanors" that related to problems concerning the completeness and accuracy of its filings with the FDA and to pay a $296 million fine—the largest ever imposed upon a medical device company.

In 2010, however, responding to ongoing criticism by the Minneapolis physicians who first revealed the problem that the fine was not enough to punish the company for its criminal actions, a federal judge in Minnesota rejected the plea agreement. The judge said that the deal did not hold Guidant sufficiently accountable for its criminal conduct in knowingly selling potentially flawed defibrillators and that prosecutors should have sought probation for Guidant and its new owner, Boston Scientific. Possible criminal charges against the executives who had orchestrated the cover-up were also suggested by some parties.

While on probation, the company would be required to take certain steps to ensure such unethical and illegal behavior did not happen again, such as by putting in place strict new ethical communication guidelines, an ethics ombudsman to take charge of the decision about when to communicate product defects, and charitable activities by Guidant to improve medical care among minority patients. The company announced it would support such steps and that by 2011 it would put in place the performance programs necessary to ensure its managers would never make such unethical and illegal decisions again.

Personal and professional ethics (see Chapter 2) also influence how a person will act in an organization, so an organization's culture is strongly affected by the people who are in a position to establish its ethical values. As we saw earlier, the founder and top managers of an organization play a particularly important role in establishing ethical norms and values—for better or worse. As an example of a worst-case scenario, consider the behavior of Beech-Nut's top managers in the early 1980s. Beech-Nut, the maker of baby foods, was in financial trouble as it strived to compete with Gerber, the market leader. To lower costs, Beech-Nut's top managers entered into an agreement with a low-cost supplier of apple juice concentrate to save the company over $250,000 a year.

Soon, one of Beech-Nut's food quality specialists became concerned about the concentrate that he believed was not made from apples alone but contained large quantities of corn syrup and cane sugar. He brought this information to the attention of top managers but, obsessed with the need to lower costs, they ignored it and the company continued to produce and sell its product as pure apple juice. Eventually, investigators from the U.S. Food and Drug Administration (FDA) confronted Beech-Nut's top managers with evidence that the concentrate was adulterated. The top managers issued denials and quickly shipped the remaining stock of apple juice to the market before their inventory could be seized.[34]

The specialist who had questioned the purity of the apple juice had resigned from Beech-Nut but decided to blow the whistle on the company. He told the FDA that top managers knew about the problem with the concentrate and eventually the company pleaded guilty to charges that it had deliberately sold adulterated juice. It was fined millions of dollars, its top managers were also found guilty and sentenced to prison terms, and consumer trust in Beech-Nut products plummeted, as did Beech-Nut stock. The company was taken over by Ralston Purina, which is today a division of Nestlé, a company well known for following the ethical values in its organizational mission and culture.

Property Rights

The values in an organization's culture reflect the ethics of individuals in the organization, of professional groups, and of the society in which the organization exists. The values in an organization's culture also stem from how the organization distributes **property rights**: the rights that an organization gives to its members to receive and use organizational resources.[35] Property rights define the rights and responsibilities of each inside stakeholder group and cause the development of different norms, values, and attitudes toward the organization. Table 7.3 identifies some of the property rights commonly given to managers and the workforce.

Property rights
The rights that an organization gives to its members to receive and use organizational resources.

TABLE 7.3 Common Property Rights Given to Managers and the Workforce

Managers' Rights	Workforce Rights
Golden parachutes	Notification of layoffs
Stock options	Severance payments
Large salaries	Lifetime employment
Control over organizational resources	Long-term employment
Decision making	Pension and benefits
	Employee stock ownership plans
	Participation in decision making

Shareholders have the strongest property rights of all stakeholder groups because they own the resources of the company and share in its profits. Top managers often have strong property rights because they are given large amounts of organizational resources, such as high salaries, the rights to large stock options, or golden parachutes, which guarantee them large sums of money if they are fired when their company is taken over. Top managers' rights to use organizational resources are reflected in their authority to make decisions and control organizational resources. Managers are usually given strong rights because if they do not share in the value that the organization creates, they are unlikely to be motivated to work hard on behalf of the organization and its other stakeholders.

An organization's workforce may be given strong property rights, such as a guarantee of lifetime employment and involvement in an employee stock ownership plan (ESOP) or in a profit-sharing plan. Most workers, however, are not given very strong property rights. Few are given lifetime employment or involved in ESOPs, though they may be guaranteed long-term employment or be eligible for bonuses. Often workers' property rights are simply the wages they earn and the health and pension benefits they receive. Workers' rights to use organizational resources are reflected in their responsibilities in the level of control they have over their tasks.

The distribution of property rights has a direct effect on the instrumental values that shape employee behavior and motivate organizational members.[36] Attempts to limit employees' benefits and reduce their rights to receive and use resources can often result in hostility and high turnover. However, establishing a company-wide stock option plan, as Google did, and encouraging employees to use organizational resources to find better ways of serving customers can foster commitment and loyalty, as at companies like Southwest Airlines and Microsoft.

The distribution of property rights to different stakeholders determines (1) how effective an organization is and (2) the culture that emerges in the organization. Different property rights systems promote the development of different cultures because they influence people's expectations about how people should behave and what they can expect from their actions. The power of property rights over people's expectations is apparent in a situation that occurred at Apple Computer in the 1990s—something that is hard to believe happened given its spectacular success today.

For its first ten years in operation, Apple had never had a layoff, and employees had come to take job security for granted as they worked hard to further the company's incredible early success. Although no written document promised job security, employees believed they were appreciated and possessed an implicit property right to their jobs. Imagine, then, what happened in 1991 when Apple announced the first layoffs in its history and several thousand middle- and lower-level personnel were terminated to reduce costs. Employees were dumbfounded: This was not how Apple treated its employees. They demonstrated outside Apple headquarters for several weeks. What effect did the layoff have on Apple's culture? It destroyed the belief that Apple valued its employees, and it destroyed an organizational culture in which employees had been motivated to put forth effort above and beyond their formal job descriptions. At Apple, employee loyalty turned into hostility. By 2011, after having received record salaries and bonuses, Apple once again has a committed workforce and hopefully will never again have to lay off employees.

Kodak, Dell, AT&T, and many other large companies that have recently laid off large numbers of employees are in the peculiar position of needing increased commitment from those who remain in order to turn their businesses around. Can they reasonably expect this? How can they encourage it? Perhaps they can give remaining employees property rights that will engender commitment to the organization. That task is the responsibility of top managers.

TOP MANAGEMENT AND PROPERTY RIGHTS Top managers are in a strong position to establish the terms of their own employment, their salary and benefits packages, and their termination and pension benefits. Top managers also determine the property rights received by others and thus determine what kind of culture will develop in an organization. The core competences of Apple and Google, for example, depend on their employees' skills and capabilities. To gain employee commitment, these organizations reward their functional experts highly and give them very strong property rights. Apple has a position called "Apple Fellow," which gives top programmers the right to work on any project in the corporation or start any new project that they find promising. Both corporations reward important employees with large stock options. Thousands of people who joined Microsoft in the 1970s and 1980s and Google in the 1990s and 2000s, for example, are today multimillionaires as a result of stock options they received in the past. It is not difficult to imagine how committed they are to the organization. Companies do not hand out stock options because they are generous, however; they do so because they want to encourage terminal values of excellence and innovation and instrumental values of creativity and hard work. And they also want to prevent their best people from leaving to found their own firms or go to work for their competitors! In 2010, Google increased the rewards of its employees by 10% across the board and handed out other bonuses to stop them from leaving and joining competitors like Facebook and Amazon.com.

Does giving stronger property rights to lower-level production line or staff workers produce a culture in which they are committed to the organization and motivated to perform highly? The introduction of an employee stock option plan at Bimba Manufacturing, which makes aluminum air cylinders in Monee, Illinois, had dramatic effects on employee behavior and the culture of the organization. Bimba's owner, Charles Bimba, decided to sell the company to its employees by establishing an ESOP. He kept 10% of the shares; the other 90% he sold to employees. Some of the employees' money came from an already existing profit-sharing plan; the rest was borrowed from a bank. Changes in the company since the ESOP was introduced have been dramatic, and the orientation of the workforce to the organization has totally changed.

Previously, the company had two groups of employees: managers who made the rules and workers who carried them out. Workers rarely made suggestions and generally just obeyed orders. Now, cross-functional teams composed of managers and workers meet regularly to discuss problems and find new ways to improve quality. These teams also meet regularly with customers to better meet their needs. Because of the incentives provided by the new ESOP, management and workers have developed new working relationships based on teamwork to achieve excellence and high quality. Each team hires its own members and spends considerable time socializing new employees in the new culture of the organization. The new cooperative spirit in the plant has forced managers to relearn their roles. They now listen to workers and act as advisers rather than superiors.

So far, changing the company's property rights system has paid off. In the 2000s Bimba has become an industry leader in providing pneumatic and hydraulic air cylinders; it has prospered and workers have repaid the loan they took out to finance the employee stock purchase. The ESOP totally changed Bimba's culture and the commitment of its workforce. In the words of one worker, it led to "an intense change in the way we look at our jobs."[37] Bimba's experience demonstrates how changing the property rights system can change organizational culture by changing the instrumental values that motivate and coordinate employees. The need for close supervision and the use of rigid rules and procedures to control behavior is no longer needed at Bimba because coordination is achieved by teams of employees who value cooperation and are motivated by the prospect of sharing in the profits created by the new work system.

CAN PROPERTY RIGHTS BE TOO STRONG? As the Bimba story suggests, the value and level of a person's behavior and performance are, in part, a consequence of the rights the person is given. Sometimes, however, employees can be given property rights that are so strong that the organization and its employees are actually harmed over time. A well-known example of this situation occurred at IBM in the 1990s. Over the years IBM developed a very conservative culture in which employees had strong rights, such as the implicit promise of lifetime employment. As a result, according to former CEO Lou Gerstner, IBM employees had become cautious and noninnovative. Gerstner claimed that the organization protected IBM employees so well that they had no motivation to perform, to take risks, or to rock the boat. He suggested that the property rights of IBM employees were too strong.

It is easy to understand how property rights can become too strong. Chapter 5 discussed how people in bureaucracies can come to believe they own their positions and the rights that go with them. When this happens, people take steps to protect their rights and resist attempts by others to wrest their rights away. The result is conflict, internal power struggles, and a loss of flexibility and innovation as the organization loses sight of its mission because its members are preoccupied with their own—not the organization's—interests. Property rights, therefore, must be assigned on the basis of performance and in a discriminating way. Managers must continually evaluate and address this difficult challenge.

Gerstner took steps to change IBM's property rights system and create an entrepreneurial culture by distributing rewards including salary and promotion based on performance and eliminated employees' expectations of lifetime employment. To create a certain kind of culture, an organization needs to create a certain kind of property rights system. In part, organizational culture reflects the values that emerge because of an organization's property rights system.

Organizational Structure

We have seen how the values that coordinate and motivate employees result from the organization's people, its ethics, and the distribution of property rights among various stakeholders. The fourth source of cultural values is organizational structure. Recall from Chapter 1 that *organizational structure* is the formal system of task and authority relationships that an organization establishes to control its activities. Because different structures give rise to different cultures, managers need to design a certain kind of organizational structure to create a certain kind of organizational culture. Mechanistic structures and organic structures, for example, give rise to totally different sets of cultural values. The values, rules, and norms in a mechanistic structure are different from those in an organic structure.

Recall from Chapter 4 that *mechanistic structures* are tall, highly centralized, and standardized, and *organic structures* are flat and decentralized and rely on mutual adjustment. In a tall, centralized organization, people have relatively little personal autonomy, and desirable behaviors include being cautious, obeying superior authority, and respecting traditions. Thus mechanistic structure is likely to give rise to a culture in which predictability and stability are desired end states. In a flat, decentralized structure, people have more freedom to choose and control their own activities, and desirable behaviors include being creative or courageous and taking risks. Thus an organic structure is likely to give rise to a culture in which innovation and flexibility are desired end states.

An organization's structure can promote cultural values that foster integration and coordination. Out of stable task and role relationships, for example, emerge shared norms and rules that help reduce communications problems, prevent the distortion of information, and speed the flow of information. Moreover, norms, values, and a common organizational language can improve the performance of teams and task forces. It is relatively easy for different functions to share information and trust one another when they share similar cultural values. One reason why product development time is short and the organization is flexible in product team structures and matrix structures is that the reliance on face-to-face contact between functional specialists in teams forces those teams quickly to develop shared values and common responses to problems.

Whether a company is centralized or decentralized also leads to the development of different kinds of cultural values. In some organizations, it is important that employees do not make decisions on their own and their actions be open to the scrutiny of superiors. In such cases, centralization can be used to create cultural values that reinforce obedience and accountability. For example, in nuclear power plants, values that promote stability, predictability, and obedience to superior authority are deliberately fostered to prevent disasters.[38] Through norms and rules, employees are taught the importance of behaving consistently and honestly, and they learn that sharing information with supervisors, especially information about mistakes or errors, is the only acceptable form of behavior.[39]

Conversely, by decentralizing authority, an organization can establish values that encourage and reward creativity or innovation. At 3M, employees are informally encouraged to spend 15% of their time working on personal projects. The founders of Hewlett-Packard established the "H-P Way," a decentralized approach to organizing that gives employees the right and obligation to access equipment and resources so they can be creative and conduct their own research informally, outside of their normal job responsibilities. In both these companies, the organizational structure produces cultural values that tell members it is all right to be innovative and to do things in their own way, as long as their actions are consistent with the good of the organization.

In sum, organizational structure affects the cultural values that guide organizational members as they perform their activities. In turn, culture improves the way structure coordinates and motivates organizational resources to help an organization achieve its goals. One source of a company's competitive advantage is its ability to design its structure and manage its culture so there is a good fit between the two. This gives rise to a core competence that is hard for other organizations to imitate. However, when companies fail to achieve a good fit, or when structural changes produce changes in cultural values, problems start to occur.

Can Organizational Culture Be Managed?

Managers interested in understanding the interplay between an organization's culture and the organization's effectiveness at creating value for stakeholders must take a hard look at all four of the factors that produce culture: the characteristics of organizational members (particularly the founder and top managers), organizational ethics, the property rights system, and organizational structure. To change a culture can be very difficult because those factors interact, and major alterations are often needed to change an organization's values.[40] To change its culture, an organization might need to redesign its structure and revise the property rights it uses to motivate and reward employees. The organization might also need to change its people, especially its top-management team. Keeping in mind the difficulty of managing organizational culture, let's look at how Microsoft's original culture evolved as a result of the interaction of the four factors.

First, Bill Gates's personal values and beliefs and his vision of what Microsoft could achieve from employees' creativity and hard work formed the core of Microsoft's culture, with its terminal values of excellence and innovation. After its initial success was established by its MS-DOS and Microsoft Word platforms, Microsoft began to attract the best software engineers in the world. Gates was therefore in a position to select those people who bought into his values and who could perform at the level that he and his managers required. Over time, norms based on the need for individual initiative (to enhance the instrumental values of creativity and risk taking) and for teamwork (to enhance cooperation) emerged, and Microsoft built one of the first campus-like headquarters complexes to promote the development of an informal atmosphere in which people could interact and develop strong working bonds.

Gates designed an organic structure for Microsoft and kept it as flat and decentralized as possible by using small teams to coordinate work activities. This design encourages risk taking and creativity. He also used a product team structure to reinforce a collaborative atmosphere and norms of "team spirit." Gates also established a culture for innovation by rewarding successful risk taking and creativity with strong property rights. Thousands of key employees received stock options, for example. Furthermore, Microsoft offered high-quality pensions and benefits and never had to lay off employees until the 2000s. Finally, the company has a history of behaving ethically toward its employees and customers (even if not toward its competitors). Microsoft's people, its structure, its property rights, and its ethics interact and fit together to make up Microsoft's culture.

Compare Microsoft's culture to the one Louis Gerstner, IBM's former CEO, had to change to turn around the failing company. IBM had a conservative, stable culture produced by property rights tied not to performance but to employee longevity in the organization, and a tall, centralized structure that promoted obedience and conformity. The people attracted to and retained by this IBM culture were those who liked working in a stable environment where they knew their place, who accepted the status quo, and who did not mind that the culture limited their opportunities to innovate or be creative. Although there was a match among the factors producing IBM's culture, the culture did not serve the company well. Because its cultural values emphasized stability, IBM was unable to adapt to changes in the environment, such as changes in technology and customer needs, and it almost failed in the early 1990s.

Can a company maintain a creative, entrepreneurial culture as it grows? Microsoft has not been able to maintain its dynamic and freewheeling culture as it has grown and has encountered many motivational and coordination problems. As a result, many analysts believe Microsoft has missed many opportunities, made many mistakes, and consequently has been overtaken by companies like Google and Facebook. However, by 2010 Google's rapid growth had also resulted in high employee turnover and its new CEO Larry Page, who took over in 2011, was having to work hard to maintain its entrepreneurial culture. In 2011, Microsoft also was striving to maintain its dominance in the PC software market and make advances into mobile computing and to prevent the development of inertia and complacency in the company.

To prevent an organization's culture from changing in ways that reduce effectiveness as the organization grows, top managers must continually redesign its structure to offset the control problems that occur with large size and complexity.[41] As just noted, these problems arise even within high-performing organizations such as Microsoft, Google, and Apple, which is why understanding organizational theory and design is such an important issue.

iStockphoto.com/Nancy Nehring

A company's culture can change over time as it grows. Despite its success, Google has had to work hard to maintain its entrepreneurial culture over the years.

Managerial Implications

Designing Organizational Culture

1. Try to identify the source of the values and norms of your organization's culture and analyze the relative effects of people, ethics, property rights, and structure on influencing organizational culture.
2. Use this analysis to produce an action plan for redesigning the culture of the organization to improve effectiveness.
3. Be sure that the action plan takes all four factors into consideration, because each one affects the others. Changing one factor alone may not be sufficient to change organizational culture.
4. Make the development of ethical organizational values one of your major priorities.

Social Responsibility

One very important consequence of the values and norms of its culture is an organization's stance with regard to social responsibility. The term *social responsibility* refers to a manager's duty or obligation to make decisions that nurture, protect, enhance, and promote the welfare and well-being of stakeholders and society as a whole. Many kinds of decisions signal an organization's interest in being socially responsible (see Table 7.4).

Approaches to Social Responsibility

The strength of an organization's commitment to social responsibility ranges from low to high (see Figure 7.4).[42] At the low end of the range is an **obstructionist approach.** Obstructionist managers choose not to behave in a socially responsible way. Instead, they behave unethically and illegally and do all they can to prevent knowledge of their behavior from reaching other organizational stakeholders and society at large. Managers at the Mansville Corporation adopted this approach when evidence that asbestos causes lung damage was uncovered. Managers at Beech-Nut who sought to hide evidence about the use of corn syrup in their apple juice also adopted this approach. The managers of all these organizations chose an obstructionist approach. The result was not only a loss of reputation but devastation for their organizations and for all stakeholders involved.

Obstructionist approach
The low end of the organization's commitment to social responsibility.

A **defensive approach** indicates at least a commitment to ethical behavior. Defensive managers stay within the law and abide strictly within legal requirements,

Defensive approach
An approach indicating a commitment to ethical behavior.

TABLE 7.4 Forms of Socially Responsible Behavior

Managers are being socially responsible and showing their support for their stakeholders when they:

- Provide severance payments to help laid-off workers make ends meet until they can find another job.
- Provide workers with opportunities to enhance their skills and acquire additional education so they can remain productive and do not become obsolete because of changes in technology.
- Allow employees to take time off when they need to and provide health-care and pension benefits for employees.
- Contribute to charities or support various civic-minded activities in the cities or towns in which they are located. (Target and Levi Strauss both contribute 5% of their profits to support schools, charities, the arts, and other good works.)
- Decide to keep open a factory whose closure would devastate the local community.
- Decide to keep a company's operations in the United States to protect the jobs of American workers rather than move abroad.
- Decide to spend money to improve a new factory so that it will not pollute the environment.
- Decline to invest in countries that have poor human rights records.
- Choose to help poor countries develop an economic base to improve living standards.

Figure 7.4 Approaches to Social Responsibility

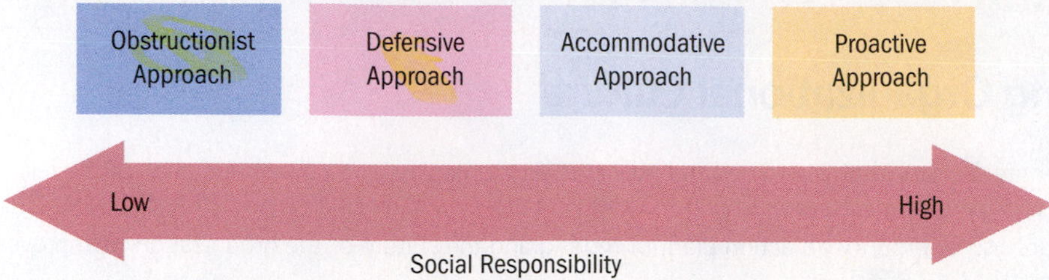

but they make no attempt to exercise social responsibility beyond what the law dictates. Managers adopting this approach do all they can to ensure that their employees behave legally and do not harm others. But when making ethical choices, these managers put the claims and interests of their shareholders first, at the expense of other stakeholders.

The very nature of a capitalist society—in which managers' primary responsibility is to the owners of the corporation, its shareholders—probably encourages the defensive response. Some economists believe that managers in a capitalistic society should always put stockholders' claims first, and if these choices are not acceptable to other members of society and are considered unethical, then society must pass laws and create rules and regulations to govern the choices managers make.[43] From a defensive perspective, it is not managers' responsibility to make socially responsible choices; their job is to abide by the rules that have been legally established. Thus defensive managers have little active interest in social responsibility.

Accommodative approach The acknowledgment of the need to support social responsibility.

An **accommodative approach** is an acknowledgment of the need to support social responsibility. Accommodative managers agree that organizational members ought to behave legally and ethically, and they try to balance the interests of different stakeholders against one another so the claims of stockholders are seen in relation to the claims of other stakeholders. Managers adopting this approach want to make choices that are reasonable in the eyes of society and want to do the right thing when called on to do so.

Proactive approach Managers who actively embrace the need to behave in socially responsible ways, go out of their way to learn about the needs of different stakeholder groups, and are willing to use organizational resources to promote the interests not only of stockholders but of the other stakeholders.

Managers taking a **proactive approach** actively embrace the need to behave in socially responsible ways, go out of their way to learn about the needs of different stakeholder groups, and are willing to use organizational resources to promote the interests not only of stockholders but of the other stakeholders. Such companies—HP, The Body Shop, McDonald's, Johnson & Johnson—are at the forefront of campaigns for causes such as a pollution-free environment, recycling and conservation of resources, minimizing or avoiding the use of animals in drug and cosmetic testing, and reducing crime, illiteracy, and poverty.

Why Be Socially Responsible?

Several advantages are argued to result when managers and organizations behave in a socially responsible manner. First, workers and society benefit directly because organizations (rather than the government) bear some of the costs of helping workers. Second, it has been said that if all organizations in a society were socially responsible, the quality of life as a whole would be higher. Indeed, several management experts have argued that the way organizations behave toward their employees determines many of a society's values and norms and the ethics of its citizens. It has been suggested that if all organizations adopted a caring approach and agreed their responsibility is to promote the interests of their employees, a climate of caring would pervade the wider society.[44] Experts point to Japan, Sweden, Germany, the Netherlands, and Switzerland as countries where organizations are very socially responsible and where, as a result, crime and unemployment rates are relatively low, the literacy rate is relatively high, and sociocultural values promote harmony between different groups of people. Other reasons for being socially responsible are that it is the right thing to do and companies that act responsibly toward their stakeholders benefit from increasing business and see their profits rise.[45]

Given these advantages, why would anyone quarrel over the pursuit of social responsibility by organizations and their managers? One issue that comes up is that although some stakeholders benefit from managers' commitment to social responsibility, other stakeholders, particularly shareholders, may think they are being harmed when organizational resources are used for socially responsible courses of action. Some people argue that business has only one kind of responsibility: to use its resources for activities that increase its profits and thus reward its stockholders.[46]

How should managers decide which social issues they will respond to and to what extent their organizations should trade profits for social gain? Obviously, illegal behavior should not be tolerated; all managers and workers should be alert to its occurrence and report it promptly. The term **whistle-blower** is used to refer to a person who reports illegal or unethical behavior and takes a stand against unscrupulous managers or other stakeholders who are pursuing their own ends.[47] Laws now exist to protect the interests of whistle-blowers, who risk their jobs and careers to reveal unethical behavior. In part, these laws were enacted because of the experiences of two engineers at Morton Thiokol who warned that the *Challenger* space shuttle's O-ring gaskets would be adversely affected by cold weather at launch.[48] Their warnings were ignored by everyone involved in the headlong rush to launch the shuttle. As a result, seven astronauts died when the *Challenger* exploded shortly after launch in January 1986. Although the actions of the engineers were applauded by the committee of inquiry, their subsequent careers suffered because managers at Morton Thiokol blamed them for damaging the company's reputation and harming its interests. A new set of rules designed to encourage employees to come forward and report unethical and illegal behavior is discussed in Organizational Insight 7.4.

Whistle-blowing
Informing (by an employee) an outside person or agency, such as a government agency or a newspaper or television reporter, about an organization's (its managers') illegal or immoral behavior.

Another way in which managers can ascertain whether they are acting socially responsibly is to apply ethical standards and values. Managers' own ethics influence their behavior, and their own values strongly influence whether they will take a proactive approach to social responsibility. An organization's code of ethics, usually printed in its annual reports and mission statements, also influences how conscientiously managers seek to support the interests of all their stakeholders. Some organizations, like Johnson & Johnson, view the company's code of ethics as the only policy to follow when an ethical dilemma is evident, and they allow this code to govern their choices. Other organizations pay lip service to the organization's ethical code and, as a result, managers facing a moral dilemma seek to protect their own interests first and worry later about how other stakeholders will be affected.[49] When such managers talk about protecting the organization, what they are really talking about is protecting their own interests: their jobs, bonuses, careers, and abilities to use organizational resources for their own ends.

Evidence suggests that managers who behave socially responsibly will, in the long run, most benefit all organizational stakeholders (including stockholders). It appears that socially responsible companies, in comparison with less responsible competitors, are less risky investments, tend to be somewhat more profitable, have a more loyal and committed workforce, and have better reputations, which encourage stakeholders (including customers and suppliers) to establish long-term business relationships with them.[50] Socially responsible companies are also sought out by communities, which encourage such organizations to locate in their cities and offer them incentives such as property-tax reductions and the construction of new roads and free utilities for their plants. Thus there are many reasons to believe that, over time, strong support of social responsibility confers the most benefits on organizational stakeholders (including stockholders) and on society at large.

Organizational Insight 7.4

New SEC Rules Offer Whistle-blowers Large Rewards

Gina Sanders/Shutterstock.com

In the 2000s, there have been many revelations of wrongdoing by financial executives, such as those that led to the subprime mortgage financial crisis, and about Ponzi schemes involving investment fund managers such as Bernie Madoff, who stole tens of millions from investors, and finally many cases of insider trading against such people as billionaire hedge fund manager Raj Rajaratnam, who in 2011 was convicted on all counts of illegally using inside information to make tens of millions in profit.

Given the increasing evidence of widespread fraud, and the increasing propensity of managers to behave unethically and eventually lead them to act illegally, the Securities and Exchange Commission (SEC) decided to approve regulations that would encourage whistle-blowers—other executives or subordinates who know about such activities—to come forward and report unethical and illegal actions to the SEC

In 2011, the SEC passed rules that would allow whistle-blowers who report corporate fraud or other misconduct to the government to gain up to 30% of the money recovered from the successful prosecution of illegal financial dealings by people or companies. The whistle-blower program was mandated by the financial overhaul law, the Dodd-Frank Act, passed in 2010. These rules were passed despite widespread opposition from large U.S. companies such as AT&T, FedEx, Google, and Target. These companies argued that whistle-blowers should first have to tell their companies about unethical or illegal actions by other managers that would allow them to correct problems before informing the SEC. However, supporters of whistle-blowers say requiring them to report wrongdoing first would discourage them because it makes them subject to punitive actions from their own companies, many of which have been known in the past to find ways to harm people who inform on their own organizations.

Nevertheless, the new rules state that even if employees report potential wrongdoing to their company, the SEC will officially designate them as whistle-blowers so that they are eligible for awards providing they give the SEC the same information within 120 days. They will even receive these rewards if they choose to remain with their organizations after providing such information. SEC Chairperson Mary Schapiro said, "Although companies' internal compliance programs play an extremely valuable role in preventing fraud, the new rules strike a balance between encouraging whistle-blowers to pursue internal compliance when appropriate and give them the option to go directly to the SEC. It is the whistle-blower who is in the best position to know which route is best to pursue."

Supporters of the new rules argue that whistle-blowers can be an effective line of defense against corporate wrongdoing, such as Bernard Madoff's multibillion-dollar fraud over nearly two decades that continued despite warnings the SEC received from at least two whistle-blowers. Under the new program, for example, if an insider at Goldman Sachs had given the SEC information leading to its $550 million civil fraud settlement with Goldman over its marketing of subprime mortgage securities, that person could have collected up to $165 million.

Clearly, the SEC's new rules for its whistle-blower program offer employees a powerful financial incentive to report potential misconduct in their companies directly to the government. The whistle-blower provision came on top of the requirements of the 2002 Sarbanes-Oxley Act, which mandated that organizations create effective internal compliance programs to learn about potential wrongdoing but which many companies have chosen to ignore.

Summary

Organizational culture exercises a potent form of control over the interactions of organizational members with each other and with outsiders. By supplying people with a toolbox of values, norms, and rules that tell them how to behave, organizational culture is instrumental in determining how they interpret and react to a situation. Thus an organization's culture can be a source of competitive advantage. Chapter 7 has made the following main points:

1. Organizational culture is a set of shared values that provide organizational members with a common understanding of how they should act in a situation.
2. There are two kinds of organizational values: terminal (a desired end state or outcome) and instrumental (a desired mode of behavior). Ideally, instrumental values help the organization to achieve its terminal goals.

3. Organizational culture affects organizational effectiveness because it can (a) provide an organization with a competitive advantage, (b) improve the way an organizational structure works, and (c) increase the motivation of employees to pursue organizational interests.
4. Culture is transmitted to an organization's members by means of (a) socialization and training programs and (b) stories, ceremonies, and language used by members of the organization.
5. Organizational culture develops from the interaction of (a) the characteristics of organization members, (b) organizational ethics, (c) the property rights distributed among the people in the organization, and (d) organizational structure.
6. Different organizational structures give rise to different patterns of interaction among people. These different patterns lead to the formation of different organizational cultures.
7. Social responsibility is an organization's moral responsibility to stakeholder groups affected by the organization's actions. There are four stances on social responsibility, and they have very different implications for organizational behavior.

Discussion Questions

1. What is the origin of organizational culture? Why do different organizations have different cultures?
2. How do newcomers learn the culture of an organization? How can an organization encourage newcomers to develop (a) an institutionalized role orientation and (b) an individualized role orientation?
3. In what ways can organizational culture increase organizational effectiveness? Why is it important to obtain the right fit between organizational structure and culture?
4. "An organization should always adopt a broad stance on social responsibility." Explain why you agree or disagree with this statement.

Organizational Theory in Action

Practicing Organizational Theory

Developing a Service Culture

Form groups of three to five people and discuss the following scenario:

You are the owner/managers of a new five-star resort hotel opening up on the white sand beaches of the western coast of Florida. For your venture to succeed, you need to make sure that hotel employees focus on providing customers with the highest-quality customer service possible. You are meeting to discuss how to create a culture that will promote such high-quality service, encourage employees to be committed to the hotel, and reduce the level of employee turnover and absenteeism, which are typically high in the hotel business.

1. What kinds of organizational values and norms encourage employees to behave in ways that lead to high-quality customer service?
2. Using the concepts discussed in this chapter (for example, people, property rights, and socialization), discuss how you will create a culture that promotes the learning of these customer service values and norms.
3. Which factor is the most important determinant of the kind of culture you expect to find in a five-star hotel?

The Ethical Dimension #7

The chapter discussed how Arthur Andersen's organizational culture had become so strong that some of its partners and their subordinates began to act unethically and pursue their own short-run interests at the expense of other stakeholders. Many employees knew they were doing wrong but were afraid to refuse to follow orders. At Beech-Nut, the company's ethical values completely broke down: Managers joked about harming stakeholders.

1. Why is it that an organization's values and norms can become too strong and lead to unethical behavior?
2. What steps can a company take to prevent this problem, to stop its values and norms from becoming so inwardly focused that managers and employees lose sight of their obligations to their stakeholders?

Making the Connection #7

Identify an organization that has been trying to change its culture. Describe the culture that it is trying to alter. Why is this culture no longer effective? How has the organization tried to bring about change? How successful has it been?

Analyzing the Organization: Design Module #7

In this module, you will analyze the culture of your organization, discuss the characteristic ways in which members act, and its stance on social responsibility.

Assignment

1. Do managers and employees use certain words and phrases to describe the behavior of people in the organization? Are any stories about events or people typically used to describe the way the organization works? (*Hint:* Look at the company's Web page.)
2. How does the organization socialize employees? Does it put them through formal training programs? What kind of programs are used, and what is their goal?
3. What beliefs and values seem to characterize the way people behave in the organization? How do they affect people's behavior?
4. Given the answers to the first three questions, how would you characterize the organization's culture and the way it benefits or harms the organization? How could the culture be improved?
5. Can you find a written statement of the organization's stance on social responsibility? Are there stories in the press about the company? If there are, what do they say?

CASE FOR ANALYSIS

A Tale of Two Cultures

In an attempt to give Southwest Airlines a competitive advantage based on low-cost, high-quality service, CEO Herb Kelleher developed terminal and instrumental values that made Southwest's culture the envy of its competitors. Southwest managers and employees alike are committed to the success of the organization and do all they can to help one another and to provide customers with excellent service (a terminal value). Four times a year, Southwest managers work as baggage handlers, ticket agents, and flight attendants so they get a feel for the problems facing other employees. An informal norm makes it possible for employees to gather with Kelleher every Friday at noon in the company's Dallas parking lot for a company cookout.

Southwest keeps the organization as flat and informal as possible, and managers encourage employees to be creative and to develop rules and norms to solve their own problems. To please customers, for example, employees dress up on special days like Halloween and Valentine's Day and wear "fun uniforms" every Friday. In addition, they try to develop innovative ways to improve customer service and satisfaction. All employees participate in a bonus system that bases rewards on company performance, and employees own over 22% of the airline's stock. The entrance hall at company headquarters at Love Field in Dallas is full of plaques earned by employees for their outstanding performance. Everybody in the organization cooperates to achieve Southwest's goal of providing low-cost, high-quality service.

The culture of excellence that Southwest has created seems to be working to its advantage. Southwest increased its operating routes and profits every year and is the most profitable airline flying today.

Contrast Southwest's CEO and culture with that of Value Line, Inc. Jean Buttner, publisher of the *Value Line Investment Survey,* fashioned a culture that the company's employees apparently hated. In her attempt to reduce costs and improve efficiency, she created instrumental values of frugality and economy that poisoned employees' attitudes toward the organization. Employees were told to sign in by 9 A.M. every day and sign out when leaving. If they faked their arrival or departure time, they could be terminated. Because at Value Line messy desks were regarded as signs of laziness or "unproductivity," Buttner required department managers to file a "clean surfaces report" every day, certifying that employees did tidy up their desks.[51] Salary increases were also kept as small as possible and the company's bonus and health plans were under tight rein.

How have these values paid off? Many highly trained professional workers left Value Line because of the hostile atmosphere produced by these "economical" values and by work rules that devalued employees. Also, this turnover generated discontent among the company's customers, who began to complain. So bad did feelings between employees and Buttner become that employees reportedly put up a notice on their bulletin board that criticized Buttner's management style and suggested that the company could use some new leadership. Buttner's response to this message from a significant stakeholder group was to remove the bulletin board. Clearly, at Value Line no culture of cooperation between managers and employees exists.

Discussion Questions

1. List the reasons why Southwest's and Value Line's cultures differ so sharply.
2. Could Value Line's next CEO copy Southwest's culture?

References

1 L. Smircich, "Concepts of Culture and Organizational Analysis." *Administrative Science Quarterly* 28 (1983), 339–358.

2 S. D. N. Cook and D. Yanow, "Culture and Organizational Learning," *Journal of Management Inquiry* 2 (1993), 373–390.

3 M. Rokeach, *The Nature of Human Values* (New York: Free Press, 1973).

4 P. Burrows, "The Seeds of Apple's Innovation," www.businessweek.com, October 24, 2004.

5 www.ups.com, 2011.

6 J. Van Maanen, "Police Socialization: A Longitudinal Examination of Job Attitudes in an Urban Police Department," *Administrative Science Quarterly* 20 (1975), 207–228.

7 P. L. Berger and T. Luckman, *The Social Construction of Reality* (Garden City, NY: Anchor Books, 1967).

8 J. P. Walsh and G. R. Ungson, "Organizational Memory," *Academy of Management Review* 1 (1991), 57–91.

9 K. E. Weick, "Organizational Culture as a Source of High Reliability," *California Management Review* 9 (1984), 653–669.

10 J. A. Chatman and S. G. Barsade, "Personality, Organizational Culture, and Cooperation: Evidence from a Business Simulation," *Administrative Science Theory* 40 (1995), 423–443.

11 E. H. Schein, "Culture: The Missing Concept in Organization Studies," *Administrative Science Quarterly* 41 (1996), 229–240.

12 www.corning.com, 2011.

13 A. Etzioni, *A Comparative Analysis of Organizations* (New York: Free Press, 1975).

14 G. R. Jones, "Psychological Orientation and the Process of Organizational Socialization: An Interactionist Perspective," *Academy of Management Review* 8 (1983), 464–474.

15 J. Van Maanen and E. H. Schein, "Towards a Theory of Organizational Socialization," in B. M. Staw, ed., *Research in Organizational Behavior,* vol. 1 (Greenwich, CT: JAI Press, 1979), pp. 209–264.

16 G. R. Jones, "Socialization Tactics, Self-Efficacy, and Newcomers' Adjustments to Organizations," *Academy of Management Review* 29 (1986), 262–279.

17 Ibid.

18 Ibid.

19 M. A. Cusumano and R. W. Selby, *Microsoft's Secrets* (New York: Free Press, 1995).

[20] H. M. Trice and J. M. Beyer, "Studying Organizational Culture Through Rites and Ceremonials," *Academy of Management Review* 9 (1984), 653–-669.

[21] H. M. Trice and J. M. Beyer, *The Cultures of Work Organizations* (Englewood Cliffs, NJ: Prentice Hall, 1993).

[22] M. Ramundo, "Service Awards Build Culture of Success," *Human Resources Magazine* (August 1992), 61–63.

[23] Trice and Beyer, "Studying Organizational Culture Through Rites and Ceremonials."

[24] A. M. Pettigrew, "On Studying Organizational Cultures," *Administrative Science Quarterly* 24 (1979), 570–582.

[25] B. Elgin, "Running the Tightest Ships on the Net," *Business Week*, January 29, 2001, pp. 125–126.

[26] B. Schneider, "The People Make the Place," *Personnel Psychology* 20 (1987), 437–453.

[27] E. H. Schein, "The Role of the Founder in Creating Organizational Culture," *Organizational Dynamics* 12 (1983), 13–28.

[28] J. M. George, "Personality, Affect, and Behavior in Groups," *Journal of Applied Psychology* 75 (1990), 107–116.

[29] E. Schein, *Organizational Culture and Leadership,* 2nd ed. (San Francisco: Jossey-Bass, 1992).

[30] George, "Personality, Affect, and Behavior in Groups"; D. Miller and J. M. Toulouse, "Chief Executive Personality and Corporate Strategy and Structure in Small Firms," *Management Science* 32 (1986), 1389–1409.

[31] R. E. Goodin, "How to Determine Who Should Get What," *Ethics* (July 1975): 310–321.

[32] T. M. Jones, "Ethical Decision Making by Individuals in Organizations: An Issue Contingent Model," *Academy of Management Review* 2 (1991), 366–395.

[33] T. L. Beauchamp and N. E. Bowie, eds., *Ethical Theory and Business* (Englewood Cliffs, NJ: Prentice-Hall, 1979); A. MacIntyre, *After Virtue* (South Bend, IN: University of Notre Dame Press, 1981).

[34] "What Led Beech-Nut Down the Road to Disgrace," *Business Week,* February 22, 1988, pp. 124–128; "Bad Apples in the Executive Suite," *Consumer Reports* (May 1989): 296; R. Johnson, "Ralston to Buy Beech-Nut, Gambling It Can Overcome Apple Juice Scandal," *Wall Street Journal,* September 18, 1989, p. B11.

[35] H. Demsetz, "Towards a Theory of Property Rights," *American Economic Review* 57 (1967), 347–359.

[36] G. R. Jones, "Transaction Costs, Property Rights, and Organizational Culture: An Exchange Perspective," *Administrative Science Quarterly* 28 (1983), 454–467.

[37] "ESOP Binges Change in Corporate Culture," *Employee Benefit Plan Review* (July 1992): 25–26.

[38] C. Perrow, *Normal Accidents* (New York: Basic Books, 1984).

[39] H. Mintzberg, *The Structuring of Organizational Structures* (Englewood Cliffs, NJ: Prentice-Hall, 1979).

[40] G. Kunda, *Engineering Culture* (Philadelphia: Temple University Press, 1992).

[41] J. P. Kotter and J. L. Heskett, *Corporate Culture and Performance* (New York: Free Press, 1992).

[42] E. Gatewood and A. B. Carroll, "The Anatomy of Corporate Social Response," *Business Horizons* (September-October 1981): 9–16.

[43] M. Friedman, "A Friedman Doctrine: The Social Responsibility of Business Is to Increase Its Profits," *New York Times Magazine,* September 13, 1970, p. 33.

[44] W. G. Ouchi, *Theory Z: How American Business Can Meet the Japanese Challenge* (Reading, MA: Addison-Wesley, 1981).

[45] J. B. McGuire, A. Sundgren, and T. Schneewis, "Corporate Social Responsibility and Firm Financial Performance," *Academy of Management Review* 31 (1988), 854–872.

[46] Friedman, "A Friedman Doctrine," pp. 32, 33, 122, 124, 126.

[47] J. B. Dozier and M. P. Miceli, "Potential Predictors of Whistleblowing: A Prosocial Perspective," *Academy of Management Review* 10 (1985), 823–836; J. P. Near and M. P. Miceli, "Retaliation Against Whistleblowers: Predictors and Effects," *Journal of Applied Psychology* 71 (1986), 137–145.

[48] "The Uncommon Good," *The Economist,* August 19, 1995, p. 55.

[49] Byrne, "The Best Laid Ethics Programs …," pp. 67–69.

[50] E. D. Bowman, "Corporate Social Responsibility and the Investor," *Journal of Contemporary Business* (Winter 1973): 49–58.

[51] A. Bianco, "Value Line: Too Lean, Too Mean," *Business Week,* March 16, 1992, pp. 104–106.

CHAPTER 8

Organizational Design and Strategy in a Changing Global Environment

Learning Objectives

Finding the right strategy to respond to changes taking place in the environment (such as changes in the needs of customers or actions of competitors overseas) is a complex issue facing managers. In a changing global environment it is easy to make mistakes, and managers must constantly monitor their strategies and structures to make sure they are working effectively both at home and abroad.

After reading this chapter you should be able to:

1. Identify the ways managers can use functional-level strategy to develop core competences that allow an organization to create value and give it a competitive advantage.
2. Explain how the way managers combine their organization's distinctive competences can create a successful business-level strategy that allows them to compete for scarce resources.
3. Differentiate among the corporate-level strategies companies can use to enter new domains where they can continue to grow and create value.
4. Appreciate the importance of linking strategy to structure and culture at each level—functional, business, and corporate—to increase the ability to create value.
5. Understand how global expansion strategies allow an organization to seek new opportunities to take advantage of its core competences to create value for stakeholders.

Strategy and the Environment

As we discussed in Chapter 1, an organization's **strategy** is a specific pattern of decisions and actions that managers take to use core competences to achieve a competitive advantage and outperform competitors.[1] An organization develops a strategy to increase the value it can create for its stakeholders. In this context, value is anything that satisfies the needs and desires of organizational stakeholders. Stockholders want a company to set goals and develop an action plan that maximizes the long-run profitability of the company and the value of their stock. Customers are likely to respond to a strategy based on the goal of offering high-quality products and services at appropriate prices.

Strategy
The specific pattern of decisions and actions that managers take to use core competences to achieve a competitive advantage and outperform competitors.

Through its strategy, an organization seeks to use and develop core competences to gain a competitive advantage so it can increase its share of scarce resources in its environment. Recall that **core competences** are skills and abilities in value-creation activities, such as manufacturing, marketing, or R&D that allow a company to achieve superior efficiency, quality, innovation, or customer responsiveness. An organization that possesses superior core competences can outperform its rivals. Organizational strategy allows an

Core competences
The skills and abilities in value-creation activities that allow a company to achieve superior efficiency, quality, innovation, or customer responsiveness.

organization to shape and manage its domain to exploit its existing core competences and develop new competences that make it a better competitor for resources.

McDonald's, for example, used its existing core competences in the production of fast food such as burgers and fries to provide fast food for the breakfast segment of the fast-food domain. By investing in food-testing facilities, McDonald's developed R&D competences that led to the development of breakfast items (such as the Egg McMuffin, burritos, and a variety of coffees and fruit drinks) that could be produced quickly. By using its existing core competences in new ways, and by developing new competences, McDonald's continuously creates new breakfast foods that contribute greatly to its revenues and profit. Similarly, Google developed its software engineering skills in search engine technology to expand its domain into email, document management, and mobile applications including instant purchase payment by smartphone in June 2011.

The more resources an organization can obtain from the environment, the better able it is to set ambitious long-term goals and then develop a strategy and invest resources to create core competences to allow it to achieve those goals. In turn, improved competences give an organization a competitive advantage, which allows the organization to attract new resources—for example, new customers, highly qualified employees, or new sources of financial support. Figure 8.1 shows this cyclical value-creation process.

Sources of Core Competences

The ability to develop a strategy that allows an organization to create value and outperform competitors is a function of an organization's core competences. The strength of its core competences is a product of the specialized resources and coordination abilities that it possesses and other organizations lack.[2]

Functional resources The skills possessed by an organization's functional personnel.

SPECIALIZED RESOURCES Two kinds of resources provide an organization with core competences that give it a competitive advantage: functional resources and organizational resources. **Functional resources** are the skills possessed by an organization's functional personnel. The skills embedded in Google's many different software engineering teams constitute its single biggest functional resource. The quality of 3M's many different R&D groups is the source of its continued growth. Procter & Gamble's expertise in new product development is its greatest functional resource.

To be a source of competitive advantage, however, it is not sufficient that an organization has high-quality functional resources; these resources must also be unique or special

Figure 8.1 The Value-Creation Cycle

Ample resources, a well-thought-out strategy, and distinctive competences give an organization a competitive advantage, which facilitates the acquisition of still more resources.

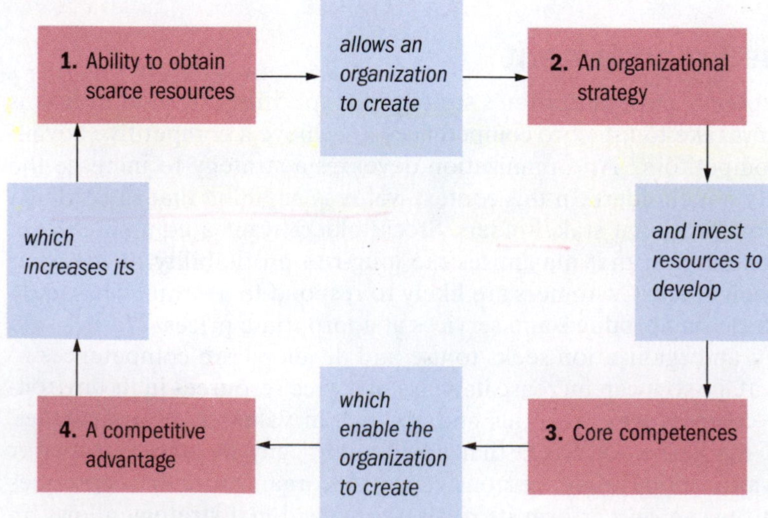

and difficult to imitate—to be *core competences*.[3] For example, Google's claim to uniqueness rests in the breadth and depth of the software talent it possesses. But suppose a rich competitor like Microsoft or Facebook comes along and tries to hire Google's best engineers, or DuPont lures away 3M's scientists. If that were to happen, those companies' claims to uniqueness would disappear (and top researchers do frequently move to other organizations). So to maintain its long-term competitive advantage, an organization needs to protect the source of its functional competences. That is why Google gives its best people strong property rights, including stock options that make them owners of the company, and why 3M is well known for its generous long-term employment policies.

Organizational resources are the company-specific skills and competence that give an organization a competitive advantage. They include the skills of a company's top-management team, the vision of its founder or CEO, and the possession of valuable and scarce resources such as land, capital reserves, and plant equipment. They also include intangibles such as a company's brand name and its corporate reputation.[4] Like functional resources, to provide a competitive advantage, organizational resources must be unique or difficult to imitate. When organizations can hire away one another's managers, or when any organization can buy the most advanced computer-controlled manufacturing technology from Hitachi or Caterpillar, organizational resources are not unique and do not give an organization a competitive advantage. However, brand names, like Coca-Cola and Toyota, and reputations, such as Google's and Microsoft's, are organizational resources that are unique and difficult to imitate. Obtaining those resources would entail buying the whole company, not just hiring away individual managers.

Organizational resources The attributes that give an organization a competitive advantage such as the skills of the top-management team or possession of valuable and scarce resources.

COORDINATION ABILITIES Another source of core competences is **coordination ability**, an organization's ability to coordinate its functional and organizational resources to create the most value. Effective coordination of resources (achieved through the control provided by organizational structure and culture) leads to a competitive advantage.[5] The control systems that an organization uses to coordinate and motivate people at the functional and organizational levels can be a core competence that contributes to the organization's overall competitive advantage. Similarly, the way an organization decides to centralize or decentralize authority or the way it develops and promotes shared cultural values increases its effectiveness and allows the organization to manage and protect its domain better than its competitors can protect theirs. Google and Microsoft design their structures and cultures around small teams to coordinate activities in a way that facilitates the rapid development and launch of new products.

Coordination ability An organization's ability to coordinate its functional and organizational resources to create maximal value.

An organization's ability to use its structure and culture to coordinate its activities is also important at the functional and organizational levels.[6] The way an organization coordinates people and resources within functions determines the strength of its core competences. For example, several organizations have access to fast-food production technology (a functional resource) similar to the advanced coffee machines that McDonald's uses, but none has been able to imitate the rules, SOPs, and norms that make its production operations so efficient. Competitors have been unable to duplicate the way McDonald's coordinates people and resources that enables it to produce its fast food so efficiently and reliably.

Similarly, at the organizational level, the ability to use structure and culture to coordinate and integrate activities across departments or divisions gives some organizations a core competence and thus a competitive advantage. For example, the success of 3M and Procter & Gamble can be explained in part by their ability to develop integrating mechanisms that allow their marketing, product development, and manufacturing departments to combine their skills to develop a constant stream of innovative products. Similarly, PepsiCo's success stems in part from its sharing of resources among its different divisions (Pepsi-Cola, Frito-Lay, and so on).

Although many functional and organizational resources are not unique and can be imitated, an organization's ability to coordinate and motivate its functions and departments is difficult to imitate. It might be possible to buy the functional expertise or technical knowledge of 3M or Google, but the purchase would not include access to the practices and methods that either organization uses to coordinate its resources. These intangible

Figure 8.2 The Creation of Value through Global Expansion

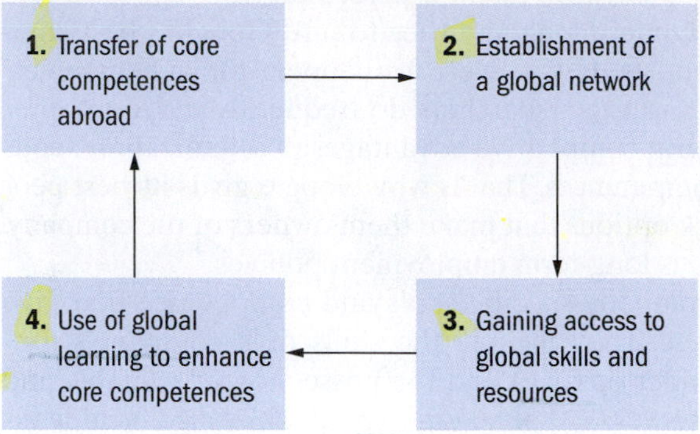

practices are embedded in the way people interact in an organization—in the way organizational structure and culture control behavior—and they make these companies more successful than their rivals.

Global Expansion and Core Competences

Expanding globally into overseas markets can be an important facilitator of the development of an organization's core competences. Figure 8.2 summarizes four ways in which global expansion allows an organization to create value for its stakeholders.

TRANSFERRING CORE COMPETENCES ABROAD Value creation at the global level begins when an organization transfers a core competence in one or more of its functions to an overseas market to produce cheaper or improved products that will give the organization a low-cost or differentiation advantage over its competitors in that market. For example, Microsoft, with its competence in the production of technologically advanced software, takes this differentiation advantage and produces software tailored to the needs of consumers in different countries. As a result of the transfer of its core competences abroad, over 60% of Microsoft's revenue comes from overseas sales.

ESTABLISHING A GLOBAL NETWORK Generally, when an organization decides to transfer its competences abroad, it locates its value-creation activities in countries where economic, political, and cultural conditions are likely to enhance its low-cost or differentiation advantage. It then establishes a global network—sets of task and reporting relationships among managers, functions, and divisions that link an organization's value-creation activities around the world. To lower costs, an organization may locate its value-creation functions in the countries in which production costs—the costs of raw materials, unskilled or skilled labor, land, and taxes—are lowest. To lower costs, a video game company like Nintendo or Sony may perform its assembly operations in one country and its design operations in another, have its headquarters in a third country, and buy its inputs and raw materials from still other countries. To link these far-flung activities, the organization creates a global network.

GAINING ACCESS TO GLOBAL RESOURCES AND SKILLS An organization with a global network has access to resources and skills throughout the world. Because each country has unique economic, political, and cultural conditions, different countries have different resources and skills that give them a competitive advantage. So, for example, a U.S. organization is likely to benefit from establishing itself in countries with low-cost or differentiation core competences so that it can gain access to and learn how to develop these competences. If organizations in one country have an R&D competence, it would pay a U.S. company to establish operations in that country to gain access to the competence. Japan, for example, still leads the world in lean manufacturing based on its efficient and high-quality production skills, and U.S. companies such as Xerox, Ford, and Caterpillar established operating divisions in Japan to learn these skills.

USING GLOBAL LEARNING TO ENHANCE CORE COMPETENCES Organizations set up their global operating network to gain access to knowledge that will allow them to improve their core competences. The access to global resources and skills that a global network provides allows an organization to find new ways to improve its effectiveness. After an organization learns a new functional skill in one country, for example, it can transfer it to its domestic base to enhance its core competences. It can then transfer its enhanced competences to all of its overseas operations to increase its competitive advantage abroad. For example, after World War II, the founders of Toyota, Panasonic, and other Japanese companies came to the United States to learn American production and marketing methods, which they then took back to Japan. The engineers who founded Toyota studied GM's and Ford's production techniques and took what they had learned back to Japan, where they improved on it and adapted it to the Japanese environment. As a result, Japanese companies obtained a competitive advantage over U.S. companies.

Of course, certain dangers are associated with outsourcing important functional competences to companies abroad. First, a company risks losing control of its core skills and technology by sharing it with a partner company abroad; and if its partner then works to improve on these skills, it may become a strong competitor in the future. Second, and related, if a company outsources a functional activity, it will no longer be investing resources to improve its skills in that activity—so it is giving away a potential source of future competitive advantage. For these reasons, organizations need to consider carefully which skills and competences they should nurture and protect and which they should allow other companies to perform for them to reduce their costs.

Four Levels of Strategy

An organization should match its strategy and structure so it can create value from its functional and organizational resources. But where is an organization's strategy created, and by whom? Strategy is formulated at four organizational levels—functional, business, corporate, and global—by the managers at each level. An organization's ability to create value at one level is an indication of its ability to manage the value-creation process at the other levels.

Functional-level strategy is a plan of action to strengthen an organization's functional and organizational resources, as well as its coordination abilities, to create core competences.[7] 3M and HP, for example, invest heavily to improve their skills in R&D and product design, and P&G and Coca-Cola invest heavily to devise innovative approaches to marketing.

Functional-level strategy
A plan of action to strengthen an organization's functional and organizational resources, as well as its coordination abilities, in order to create core competences.

To strengthen their technical and human resources, functional managers train and develop subordinates to ensure the organization has skills that match or exceed the skills of its competitors. Another part of the functional managers' job is to scan and manage the environment surrounding their particular function to ensure that they, and managers at all levels, understand changes that may affect the way the organization operates.

R&D functional managers, for example, need to understand the techniques and products of their rivals. R&D functional managers at car companies routinely buy competitors' cars and strip them down to their component parts to study the technology and design that went into their manufacture. Taking this information, they can imitate the best aspects of competitors' products. It is also the job of R&D experts to scan other industries to find innovations that may help their company. Innovations in the computer software and microchip industries, for example, are important in product development in the car industry. If all of the functional managers in an organization monitor their respective functional environments and develop their functional resources and abilities, the organization will be better able to manage the uncertainty of its environment.[8]

Business-level strategy is a plan to use and combine an organization's functional core competences to position it so it has a competitive advantage in its domain or segment of its industry.[9] Mercedes-Benz takes its skills in R&D and positions itself in the luxury segment of the car market where it competes with Lexus and BMW. Coca-Cola uses its marketing skills to defend its niche against PepsiCo—an ongoing battle.

Business-level strategy
A plan to combine functional core competences in order to position the organization so that it has a competitive advantage in its domain.

Business-level strategy is the responsibility of the top-management team (the CEO and vice presidents in charge of the various functions). Their job is to decide how to position the organization to compete for resources in its environment. CBS, NBC, and ABC, for example, compete with Fox, CNN, and HBO and hundreds of other TV channels to attract viewers (customers). Programming is the key variable that these companies can manipulate. They rely on functional experts in their news, documentary, comedy, and soap opera departments (among others) to scan the environment and identify future viewing trends so they can commission programs that will give them a competitive advantage. Because all of the TV networks are doing this and trying to outguess their rivals, programming is a complex and uncertain process.

Corporate-level strategy A plan to use and develop core competences so that the organization can not only protect and enlarge its existing domain but can also expand into new domains.

Corporate-level strategy is a plan to use and develop core competences so the organization not only can protect and enlarge its existing domain but can also expand into new domains.[10] Mercedes-Benz used its competences in R&D and product development to enter the household products and aerospace industries. Coca-Cola took its marketing skills and applied them globally in the soft-drinks industry.

Corporate-level strategy is the responsibility of corporate-level managers—the top-management team of a multibusiness organization. Their responsibility is to take the value-creation skills present in an organization's divisions and combine them to improve the competitive position of each division and of the organization as a whole. Corporate strategists strive to find ways to merge and use the resources of every division to create more value than could be obtained if each division operated alone and independently. For example, Honda took its strengths in engine production developed first in its motorbike and car divisions and then applied them to produce high-quality engines for products such as jet skis, pressure washers, and lawn mowers.

Global expansion strategy A plan that involves choosing the best strategy to expand into overseas markets to obtain scarce resources and develop core competences as discussed above.

Finally, **global expansion strategy** involves choosing the best strategy to expand into overseas markets to obtain scarce resources and develop core competences as discussed earlier. How does strategy at each level advance the goal of creating value? Organizational Insight 8.1 describes how Samsung used these strategies to create value; then we discuss each level of strategy and its effects on organizational design in the remainder of this chapter.

Organizational Insight 8.1

Samsung's Success Is Based on Many Strategies

In the 2000s, Samsung Electronics, based in Seoul, Korea, became the second-most profitable global technology company after Microsoft.[11] Samsung accomplished this when its pioneering CEO Lee Kun Hee decided to develop and build functional competences first in low-cost manufacturing, second in R&D, and then into the production of new products to compete globally. Samsung competes principally in the global consumer electronics industry. In the 1990s, its engineers studied how the Japanese companies Sony and Panasonic innovated new products. Then, its engineers copied Japanese technology and used their manufacturing skills to make low-priced versions of the products that they could sell at lower prices than the Japanese.

pcruciatti/Shutterstock.com

Samsung then decided to use its new competences to enter and compete in the mobile phone industry and develop a business-level strategy to make lower-cost phones than global giants Nokia and Motorola, and by 2011 it was the second biggest global competitor in this market. Samsung also entered the semiconductor industry in which it worked to make the lowest-cost memory chips; here too it used its functional skills to become the global cost leader by pursuing a low-cost strategy. The company also entered other digital-product markets such as cameras, printers, and storage devices, where it has rapidly gained market share because of its functional- and business-level strategies.

At the level of corporate strategy, Samsung's goals were to increase its profitability by creating value by transferring its competences in product development and manufacturing by entering new industries and producing new products. Its strategy was successful and profitable, but it was not playing in the same league as Sony, for example. Sony could charge premium prices for its leading electronics and continuously plow back profits into the R&D needed to make more advanced state-of-the-art electronics.

CEO Hee decided to adopt new strategies that would allow his company to compete head-to-head with Japanese and European electronics companies and make it a global technology leader. Samsung's goal was not to copy technology innovated by Sony, Matsushita, Phillips, and Nokia but for its engineers to develop the R&D skills necessary to rapidly innovate leading-edge technologies, such as LCD displays, to create products such as mobile computing devices more advanced than those of its competitors. Within a decade, Samsung became the leading supplier of advanced flash memory chips and LCD screens, premium-priced products that it sold to other global electronics makers, including Japanese flat-screen TV makers such as Sony![12] By 2010 Samsung had also become second in the market to Apple in terms of sales of smartphones and tablet computers, and it has become one of the most innovative electronics makers in the world.

Functional-Level Strategy

The strategic goal of each function is to create a core competence that gives the organization a competitive advantage. Earlier, we noted how McDonald's production and marketing functions give the organization unique core competences. No competitor can match the efficiency of McDonald's production process, and no competitor has developed the brand-name reputation that McDonald's enjoys.

An organization creates value by applying its functional skills and knowledge to inputs and transforming them into outputs of finished goods and services. To gain a competitive advantage, an organization must be able to perform functional activities (1) at a *lower cost* than that of its rivals so it can charge *lower prices* for its good and services; or (2) in a way that allows it to *differentiate* its products from those of its rivals, by giving them unique qualities that customers desire, so it can charge higher or *premium* prices.[13]

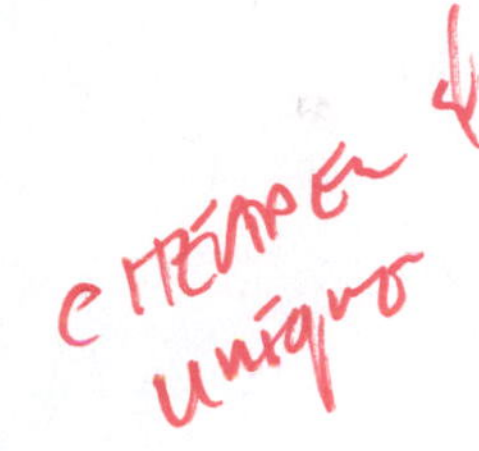

Strategies to Lower Costs or Differentiate Products

Any function that can lower the cost at which a product is produced or can differentiate a product adds value to the product and to the organization. Table 8.1 summarizes the ways in which different organizational functions can advance the goal of value creation.

The manufacturing function can lower the costs of production by pioneering the adoption of the most efficient production methods, such as computer-controlled flexible

TABLE 8.1 Low-Cost and Differentiation Advantages Resulting from Functional-Level Strategy

Value-Creating Function	Source of Low-Cost Advantage	Source of Differentiation Advantage
Manufacturing	• Development of skills in flexible manufacturing technology	• Increase in product quality and reliability
Human resource management	• Reduction of turnover and absenteeism	• Hiring of highly skilled personnel • Development of innovative training programs
Materials management	• Use of just-in-time inventory system/ computerized warehousing • Development of long-term relationships with suppliers and customers	• Use of company reputation and long-term relationships with suppliers and customers to provide high-quality inputs and efficient distribution and disposal of outputs
Sales and marketing	• Increased demand and lower production costs	• Targeting of customer groups • Tailoring products to customers • Promoting brand names
Research and development	• Improved efficiency of manufacturing technology	• Creation of new products • Improvement of existing products

manufacturing systems. Because manufacturing skills and competence can improve product quality and reliability, manufacturing can also contribute to product differentiation.[14] Toyota, for example, leads the world in lean manufacturing techniques, which both reduce production costs and increase quality by lowering the number of defects. Manufacturing thus gives Toyota vehicles a low-cost advantage and a differentiation advantage.

On the input side, the human resource management (HRM) function can lower costs by designing appropriate control and reward systems to increase employee motivation and reduce absenteeism and turnover.[15] HRM can contribute to differentiation by selecting and hiring high-quality employees and managers and by running innovative training programs. The use of employee stock ownership plans, the linking of pay to performance for different job categories, and the development of flexible work hours are all ways in which the HRM function can advance the cause of value creation. Xerox, Google, Nvidia, and other companies have developed sophisticated HRM systems for selecting and training their employees.

The role of materials management on both the input and the output sides is also crucial. Just-in-time inventory systems and computerized warehousing reduce the costs of carrying and shipping inventory. Purchasing managers' skills in developing long-term links with suppliers and distributors and in fostering an organization's reputation can lead to a low-cost or differentiation advantage.[16] Suppliers who trust an organization may offer more favorable payment terms or be more responsive to the organization when it needs more or different types of inputs in a hurry. The quality of a company–supplier relationship can also affect the quality of inputs. A supplier has more incentive to invest in specialized equipment to produce higher-quality inputs if it trusts the organization.[17] Highly skilled purchasing negotiators may also be able to strike good contract terms with suppliers.

VF Company, the clothes manufacturer that makes Lee and Wrangler jeans, has developed a low-cost core competence on the output side of the value-creation process. VF Company has a state-of-the-art inventory control system. A computer network links its manufacturing and distribution plants directly to its retail customers. When a Walmart customer buys a pair of VF jeans, for example, a record of the sale is transmitted electronically from Walmart to a VF warehouse, which restocks the retailer within five days. When a specified number of garments have been shipped from the VF warehouse, a reorder is automatically placed with the manufacturing plant. This system allows the VF organization to maintain a 95% in-stock rate (the industry average is 70%) and reduce lost sales for the retailer and manufacturer.

At the output end of the value-creation process, the expertise of sales and marketing contributes directly to a low-cost or differentiation advantage. A core competence in marketing can lower the cost of value-creation activities. Suppose a marketing department devises an online advertising campaign that significantly increases product sales and so the organization's market share steadily rises. When the organization expands production to meet increased customer demand, it will obtain manufacturing economies of scale and so production costs will fall. Panasonic and LG have a low-cost advantage because their marketing and sales efforts have developed global markets whose enormous size enables the companies to produce huge volumes of a product at lower and lower unit costs.

Marketing and sales help differentiate products because they tell customers about why one company's products are better than another's. They target customer groups and discover, analyze, and transmit to the product development and R&D departments the needs of customers so those functions can design new products to attract more customers.[18] A core competence in marketing can allow an organization quickly to discover and respond to customer needs. This speed gives the organization's products a differentiated appeal. Coca-Cola, Philip Morris, and Campbell's Soup are all known for innovative marketing that constantly promotes their brand names and protects their domains from competitors.

Research and development can also contribute significantly to an organization's value-creation activities.[19] R&D can reduce costs by developing cheaper ways of making a product. Skills in R&D have allowed Japanese companies to develop low-cost, flexible manufacturing techniques that Xerox, HP, and other U.S. manufacturers are copying. A core competence in R&D that results in the improvement of existing products or the creation of new products gives an organization a strong competitive advantage through differentiation. Intel's creation of faster and improved microchips is an example of incremental product improvement. Graphics chip technology developed by Nvidia and AMD is leading to ever more advanced graphics, gaming, video, and 3D movie capabilities on new generations of mobile computing devices. All makers of smartphones, laptops, tablets, and game consoles, and so on, rush to modify their products to use the new state-of-the-art chip; otherwise, they fear, their products are likely to lose their differentiated appeal.

Functional-Level Strategy and Structure

Every function in an organization can develop a core competence that allows an organization to perform value-creation activities at a cost lower than its rivals or that allows it to create clearly differentiated products, such as Google's. One goal of an organization is to provide its functions with the resources and the setting they need to develop superior skills and expertise. Thus organizational structure and culture are very important to the development of functional-level strategy. We first consider structure.

The strength of a function's core competence depends not only on its skills and resources, but also on its ability to coordinate the use of its resources. An organization's coordination abilities are, in turn, a product of its structure.[20] In Chapter 4, we discussed Lawrence and Lorsch's findings about how the degree of functional differentiation in the production, sales, and R&D departments within an organization, and the extent of integration among them directly affect organizational performance. In effective organizations, each of the three departments develops an orientation specific to its functional tasks and develops its own ways of responding to its particular functional environment.

According to contingency theory, an organization's design should permit each function to develop a structure that suits its human and technical resources. We continue to follow the contingency theory approach as we examine how to design a structure that allows the R&D, manufacturing, and sales functions to develop core competences.[21] Figure 8.3 summarizes the characteristics of structures that support the development of core competences by those three functions.

Successful innovation depends on the ability of R&D experts to apply their skills and knowledge in creative ways and to combine their activities with new technologies to produce superior differentiated products. The structure most conducive to the development of functional abilities in R&D is a flat decentralized structure in which mutual adjustment among teams is the main way of coordinating human and technical resources. This is the kind of setting that Google has developed. In such an organic structure, functional norms and values based on self-control and team control are likely to emerge, and a core competence in R&D is likely to emerge and strengthen over time.

What sort of structure supports the development of a core competence in production? Traditionally, the manufacturing function has used a tall hierarchy in which decision making is centralized and the speed of the production line controls the pace of work.[22] Standardization is achieved through the use of extensive rules and procedures, and the result of these design choices is a mechanistic structure. Has such a structure led to a core competence in manufacturing for U.S. companies? If we compare U.S. and Japanese manufacturing companies' competences today, we see that U.S. companies still lag behind, although they have made major advances in the last decade. What do the Japanese do differently? The manufacturing function in Japanese companies has always had a more organic structure than the manufacturing function in U.S. companies: It is flatter, more decentralized, and relies more on mutual adjustment.

A core competence based on coordination abilities in sales is another important source of competitive advantage that should be planned for in an organization's strategy. Typically, the sales function uses a flat, decentralized structure to coordinate its activities because incentive pay systems, rather than direct supervision by managers, are the primary control mechanism in sales settings.[23] Salespeople are generally paid on the basis of how much they sell, and information about customer needs and changing customer requirements is relayed

Figure 8.3 Structural Characteristics Associated with the Development of Core Competences in Production, Sales, and Research and Development

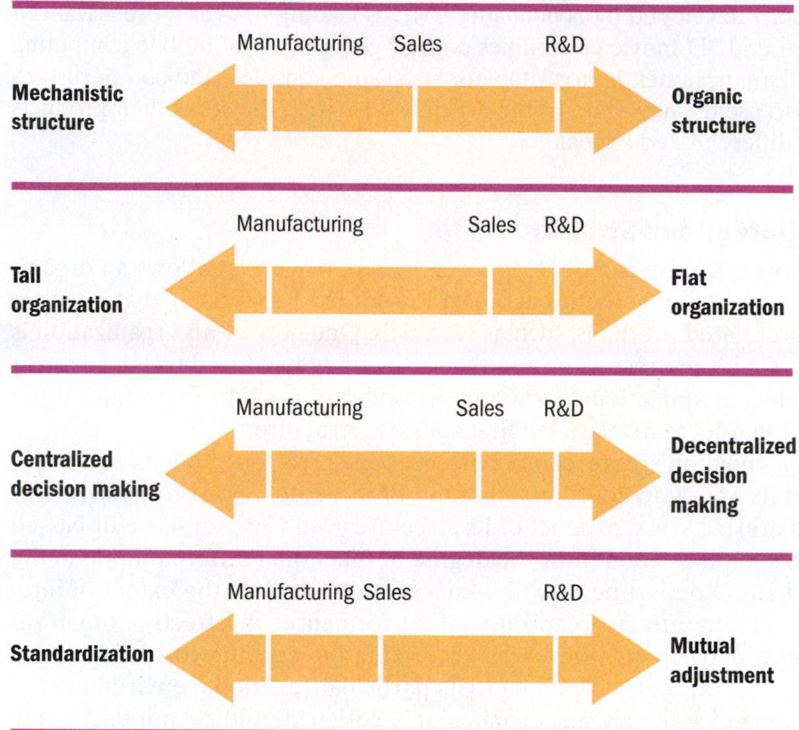

to the salespeople's superiors through a standardized reporting system. Because salespeople often work alone, mutual adjustment is relatively unimportant. Thus the structure of the sales function is likely to be relatively mechanistic, compared to that used by the R&D function, but not as mechanistic as that used by manufacturing.

In some sales settings, however, a differentiated appeal to customers is necessary. Luxury department stores such as Nordstrom and Neiman Marcus do not use incentive compensation. In such settings, the last thing the organization wants to do is encourage a standardized hard sell to customers. Instead, it wants salespeople to develop competence in a sales technique based on a courteous, personalized, customer-oriented approach.

The same strategic considerations shape the structure of other organizational functions—accounting, human resources, materials management, and so on. The coordination abilities of each function reflect the skill with which managers design the functional structure to suit the resources the function uses in its value-creation activities. The greater the organization's skills at coordinating functional resources, the stronger are the core competences the organization develops and the greater is its competitive advantage.

Functional-Level Strategy and Culture

The development of functional abilities that lead to core competences is also a result of the culture that emerges in a function or department. Recall from Chapter 7 that organizational culture is a set of shared values that organizational members use when they interact with one another and with other stakeholders. What is the importance of culture for a functional-level strategy? A competitor can easily imitate another organization's structure, but it is very difficult for a competitor to imitate another organization's culture, for culture is embedded in the day-to-day interactions of functional personnel. Culture is very difficult to control and manage, let alone imitate or copy, so a company that has an effective culture has an important source of competitive advantage.[24]

Managerial Implications

Functional-Level Strategy

1. As a member or manager of a function, identify the functional resources or coordination abilities that give your function a core competence. Having identified the sources of your function's core competence, establish a plan to improve or strengthen them, and create a set of goals to measure your progress.
2. Study your competitors and the methods and practices they use to control their functional activities. Pick your most effective competitor, study its methods, and use them as a benchmark for what you wish to achieve in your function.
3. Analyze the way your functional structure and culture affect functional resources and abilities. Experiment to see whether changing a component of structure or culture can enhance your function's core competence.

The reason is that the coordination abilities that stem from an organization's culture emerge gradually and are a product of many factors: an organization's property rights system, its structure, its ethics, and the characteristics of its top-management team. Because these factors can be combined in many different ways, reproducing another organization's culture is difficult.

To develop functional abilities and produce a core competence, it is necessary to choose the property rights, functional structure, and functional managers that seem most likely to enhance a function's coordination ability. We just saw that R&D uses a flat, decentralized structure and small teams to create norms and values that emphasize teamwork and cooperation. There are other ways in which an organization can build a culture to reinforce those norms and values. Employees can be given strong property rights, including job tenure and a share in the organizational profits; and an organization can recruit people who share its terminal values and socialize them to its functional instrumental values.[25] Apple and Google deliberately create an entrepreneurial culture by using small teams to socialize IT specialists to their instrumental values of hard work and cooperation; the same is true in biotech companies like Amgen and Genentech.

In sum, to create value at the functional level, the organizational strategy must allow and encourage each function to develop a core competence in lowering costs or differentiating its products from those of competitors. The sources of core competences lie in the resources an organization embeds in each function, and in the abilities of functional experts to take advantage of and coordinate those resources. To gain a competitive advantage, an organization needs to design its functional structure and culture to provide a setting in which core competences develop. The more a function's core competence is based on coordination abilities embedded in the way people in the organization interact, the more difficult it is for competing organizations to duplicate the core competence and the greater is the organization's competitive advantage.

Business-Level Strategy

The challenge of a business-level strategy is for an organization to take the core competences created by its functions and combine them to take advantage of opportunities in the environment to create value. Strategic managers at the business level select and manage the domain in which the organization uses its value-creation resources and coordination abilities to obtain a competitive advantage.[26] For example, core competences in three functions—production, marketing, and materials management—jointly give McDonald's a competitive advantage over rivals such as Burger King and

Wendy's. Obtaining a competitive advantage is important because, as we noted in Chapter 3, organizations in the same environment (e.g., fast food) are in competition for scarce resources—customers. Any organization that fails to devise a business-level strategy to attract customers is at a disadvantage vis-à-vis its rivals and in the long run is likely to fail. Thus the organization needs a business-level strategy that does both of the following: (1) selects the domain the organization will compete in and (2) positions the organization so it can use its resources and abilities to manage its specific and general environments in order to protect and enlarge that domain.

Strategies to Lower Costs or Differentiate Products

We have seen that the two basic ways in which an organization can create value are by reducing the cost of its value-creation activities and by performing those activities in a way that gives its products a differentiated appeal. Business-level strategy focuses on selecting the domain in which an organization can take advantage of its functional-level core competences. In the 2000s, for example, Chipotle has successfully chosen its domain—making high-quality customized burritos—and designed its materials management system to give it access to organic food products that it efficiently transforms in its restaurants into high-quality fast food. Its stock has soared in value because customers enjoy the way its resources create a tasty product they value.

Recall from Chapter 3 that the organizational domain is the range of goods and services that the organization produces to attract customers and other stakeholders. Once an organization has chosen its domain, it has two bases on which it can position itself to compete with its rivals. It can use its skills in low-cost value creation to produce for a customer group that wants low-priced goods and services. This plan is called a **low-cost business-level strategy**. Or it can use its skills at differentiation to produce for a customer group that wants and can afford differentiated products that command a high or premium price. This plan is called a **differentiation business-level strategy**.[27] Walmart and Target, for example, specialize in selling low-price clothing to customers who want or can afford to pay only a modest amount for their attire. Neiman Marcus and Saks Fifth Avenue specialize in selling high-priced clothing made by exclusive designers to wealthy customers who want prestige or status.

Low-cost business-level strategy
A plan whereby an organization produces low-priced goods and services for all customer groups.

Differentiation business-level strategy
A plan whereby an organization produces high-priced, quality products aimed at particular market segments.

Both Walmart and Neiman Marcus are in the retail clothing industry but have chosen different domains in which to compete. They have decided to sell different products to different groups of customers. In essence, Neiman Marcus and Saks have chosen a business-level strategy based on core competences in differentiation in order to charge a premium price, and Walmart and Target have chosen a business-level strategy based on core competences in low-cost value-creation activities in order to charge a low price.

To compete successfully, an organization must develop a low-cost or differentiation strategy to protect and enlarge its domain. An organization can also attempt to pursue both strategies *simultaneously* and produce differentiated products at low cost.[28] Doing so is extremely difficult and requires an exceptionally strong set of core competences. McDonald's is an organization that has successfully pursued both strategies simultaneously. McDonald's has developed a unique brand-name reputation by means of sophisticated marketing and has developed low-cost skills in its manufacturing and distribution functions. Moreover, McDonald's has used many of the interorganizational strategies discussed in Chapter 3 to pursue both strategies simultaneously. It has formed strategic alliances with suppliers and obtains bread, rolls, and restaurant fittings (tables, chairs, lights, and so on) from companies with which it has long-term contracts or in which it has a minority ownership interest. McDonald's uses franchising to maintain the reliability and efficiency of its retail outlets and owns many of the sources of its inputs, such as vast ranches in Brazil on which it raises large herds of cattle.

Over time, an organization has to change its business-level strategy to match changes in its environment. New technological developments, foreign competitors, and changes in customer needs and tastes may all affect the way an organization tries to compete for resources. Focus on New Information Technology: Amazon.com, Part 5 describes how changes in IT affected the company's choice of business-level strategy.

Focus on New Information Technology

Amazon.com, Part 5

Before the advent of online bookstores, competition among bookstores was limited at best. The market was essentially divided between two kinds of competitors: (1) large bookstore chains such as Barnes & Noble and Borders whose stores, often located in malls or large shopping strips, offered customers the latest lines of best-selling books and (2) independent bookstores, both those that are large and offer a huge selection of books to customers in major cities, and the small specialized bookstores found in most cities in the United States. The large bookstore chains used their huge purchasing power to negotiate low prices with book publishers, and they pursued a low-cost strategy, often offering price discounts. Bookstores that offered a large selection of books (compared to the chains) or that specialized in some way pursued a differentiation strategy. Thus the different kinds of bookstores were not in competition, and all were able to make comfortable profits.

Jeff Bezos's idea of using the Internet to sell books online made it possible to develop a *simultaneous* low-cost and differentiation strategy and thus outperform existing bookstore competitors. First, on the differentiation side, the ability of a computerized online catalog to both describe and make available to customers every book in the English language offered customers a selection that could not be rivaled even by the largest bookstores in cities like New York and San Francisco. Second, on the low-cost side, his use of IT technology to interface inexpensively with book publishers, distributors, and customers allowed him to offer these customers books at discounted prices, and to get them quickly to customers as well.

Small wonder, then, that this new low-cost/differentiation strategy gave Amazon.com a competitive advantage over its rivals. Many small and large stand-alone bookstores have exited the market; the large chains responded by opening up book superstores and by going online themselves. However, they have not repeated Amazon.com's success story; in fact, bookstore chain Borders went bankrupt in 2011 and Barnes & Noble was in big trouble. Why? Amazon.com has over 125 million customers in its database and over 65% of its business is from repeat customers.[29] In the 2010s its share price has once again soared to record highs because investors believe it has the core competences and business-level strategy that will continue to make it the online place to shop in the years ahead.

As Amazon.com's strategy suggests, organizations have to defend, protect, and continuously improve the sources of their competitive advantage if they are to control their environment successfully in the long run. Industry leaders such as Amazon, Google, Toyota, and McDonald's have so far sustained their competitive advantage by maintaining, improving, or rebuilding their functional-level resources and abilities. Amazon, for example, constantly updates its IT, such as its moves into eBooks using its Kindle reader, streaming video, and, most recently the remote storage of customers' library of music and videos on its cloud computing servers that allows them to access their library anywhere using any kind of electronic device. McDonald's was forced to find new ways to differentiate its fast-food offerings to compete against sandwich chains, salad bars, and coffee shops and has enjoyed remarkable success because it can offer customers similar kinds of products at a much lower cost.

Focus Strategy

Another business-level strategy is the focus strategy—specializing in one segment of a market and focusing all of the organization's resources on that segment.[30] KFC specializes in the chicken segment of the fast-food market; Tiffany specializes in the high-price luxury segment of the jewelry market; Rolls-Royce focuses on the highest price segment of the car market—a customized Rolls-Royce Phantom convertible costs over $500,000.

Business-Level Strategy and Structure

The value that an organization creates at the business level depends on its ability to use its core competences to gain a competitive advantage. This ability is a product of the way the organization designs its structure.[31] An organization pursuing a differentiation business-level strategy generally confronts design choices different from those faced by organizations pursuing a low-cost strategy. Figure 8.4 summarizes the differences.

The competitive strengths of an organization with a differentiation strategy come from functional skills that give the organization's products unique or state-of-the-art features that distinguish them from the products of competitors. An organization pursuing a differentiation strategy has to be able to develop products quickly because only if it gets its products to customers ahead of its competitors can it exploit its differentiation

Figure 8.4 Types of Business-Level Strategy

Strategy	Number of Market Segments Served: Many	Few
Low cost	●	
Focused low cost		●
Differentiation	●	
Focused differentiation		●

advantage. Close cooperation between functions is likely to be required to bring new products to market quickly. For example, R&D, marketing, manufacturing, and product development must be able to communicate easily and adjust their activities to one another smoothly to speed the development process. All these factors make it likely that an organization pursuing a differentiation strategy has an organic structure. An organic structure permits the development of a decentralized, cross-functional team approach to decision making, which is the key to speedy new product development.

A low-cost strategy is associated with the need for close control of functional activities to monitor and lower the costs of product development.[32] Manufacturing and materials management become the central functions for an organization pursuing a low-cost strategy. The other functions (R&D, marketing, and so on) tailor their skills to achieve the goal of producing a low-cost product. A speedy response to market changes is not vital to the competitive success of a low-cost organization. Often, because product development is so expensive, such an organization waits to develop a new or improved product until customers clearly demand it. The low-cost organization generally imitates the differentiator's product and always remains one step behind to keep costs low. Consequently, a mechanistic structure is often the most appropriate choice for an organization pursuing a low-cost strategy (see Figure 8.5). Centralized decision making allows the organization to

Figure 8.5 Characteristics of Organizational Structure Associated with Business-Level Differentiation and Low-Cost Strategies

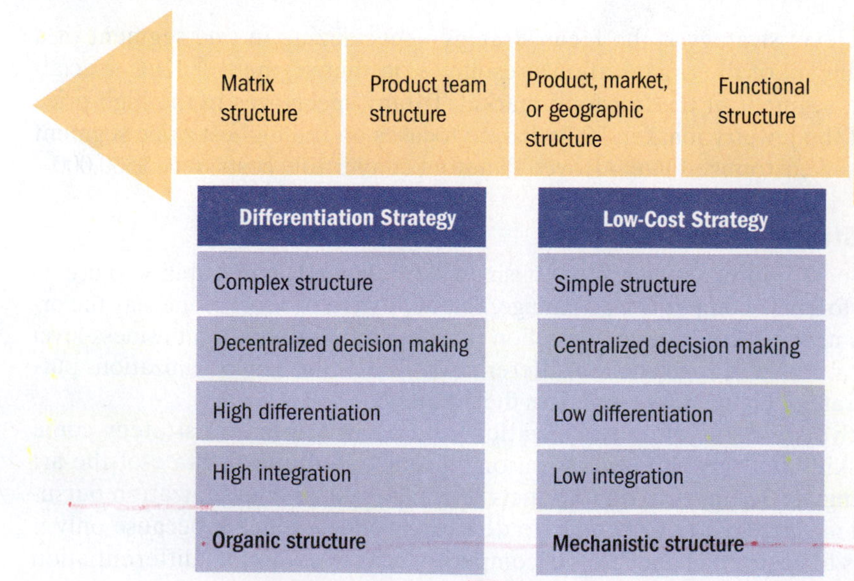

maintain close control over functional activities and thus over costs. Also, because there is no pressing need to respond quickly or innovatively, a mechanistic structure provides sufficient coordination to meet the demands of the competitive domain.

Further evidence for the match between differentiation strategy and organic structure, and the match between low-cost strategy and mechanistic structure, comes from contingency theory. Recall from Chapter 4 that contingency theory suggests that organizations in uncertain, rapidly changing environments require a greater degree of differentiation and integration than do organizations in more stable environments.[33] Because differentiators generally compete in a complex, uncertain environment where they need to react quickly to rivals' actions, and because low-cost companies usually compete in slow-moving environments, contingency theory suggests that effective differentiators will have greater differentiation and integration than low-cost companies have. Given that organizational structures with extensive differentiation and integration are costly to operate, contingency theory implies that low-cost companies should use the simplest structure possible because it will help to keep down the cost of value creation.[34]

In addition to examining the relationship between business-level strategy and organic and mechanistic structures, we can look at the relationship between strategy and the types of organizational structure discussed in Chapter 6: functional, divisional, and matrix structures. From a strategy perspective, three factors affect an organization's choice of a structure to create a competitive advantage for itself:

1. As an organization produces a wider range of products, it will need greater control over the development, marketing, and production of these products.
2. As an organization seeks to find new customer groups for its products, it will need a structure that allows it to serve the needs of its customers.
3. As the pace of new product development in an industry increases, an organization will need a structure that increases coordination among its functions.

Organizations following a low-cost strategy typically focus on producing one product or a few products to reduce costs. BIC Corporation, for example, produces only a few disposable razors for both men and women. A low-cost company does not face the problems of dealing with a wide range of products or with many customer groups. Moreover, low-cost companies are not leaders in product development. Because they are imitators, they do not have the problems of coordinating the activities of different functional groups. For all these reasons, low-cost companies generally adopt the simplest structure that is consistent with their strategy. Normally, a functional structure (one in which people are grouped by common skills or use of similar resources) is sufficient to coordinate the core competences of a low-cost organization.

By contrast, differentiators typically produce a wide range of products to suit the needs of different groups of customers. Also, to the degree that competition between differentiators is based on the development of new and innovative products (a situation found in the car and personal computer industries), differentiators need a structure that allows functional experts to cooperate so they can quickly develop and introduce new products. For these reasons, differentiators are likely to adopt a more complex structure. If the pressing need is to handle a wide range of products, a product structure (in which products are grouped into separate divisions served by the same set of support functions) is the appropriate choice. If handling different groups of customers is the key to success, a market structure or a geographic structure (in which functional activities are grouped to best meet the needs of different types of customers) will best fit the differentiator's needs. A product team structure or a matrix structure (in which product development is coordinated by teams of cross-functional specialists) can be adopted when rapid product development and speedy response to competitors are the keys to competitive advantage.

All of those structures can provide an organization with the ability to coordinate functional and organizational resources to create a core competence. Intel, the microchip maker, has decided that the only way to maintain its lead in the industry is to produce several generations of microchips at the same time. So it has established a product team structure in which teams of research and development specialists work side by side to plan the chips of the future.[35]

To summarize, an organization must match its business-level strategy to the organizational structure that allows the organization to use its functional and organizational resources to create a competitive advantage. A top-quality R&D department is useless unless an organization has a structure that coordinates R&D activities with a marketing department that can correctly forecast changes in customer needs and a product development department that can translate research and marketing findings into commercial products. Choosing the right structure has major payoffs for an organization by helping create a low-cost or differentiation advantage at the business level. As Organizational Insight 8.2 discusses, organizations sometimes lose control over their structures, and then they have to reorganize in radical ways to regain their competitive advantage.

Business-Level Strategy and Culture

Organizational culture is another major determinant of the ability to use functional and organizational resources effectively. The challenge at the business level is to develop organization-wide values, and specific norms and rules, all of which allow the organization to combine and use its functional resources to the best advantage. Over time, different functions may develop different subunit orientations, which impede communication and coordination. But if the various functions share values and norms, communication and coordination problems can be overcome. If managers in different functions can develop common ways of dealing with problems, an organization's competitive advantage will be enhanced.

How does the culture of a low-cost organization differ from that of a differentiator? Organizations pursuing a low-cost strategy must develop values of economy and frugality.[38] Frequently, specific norms and rules develop that reflect the organization's terminal and instrumental values. For example, when Ken Iverson was CEO of Nucor, a leading low-cost steel products maker, he operated the company in a frugal, careful way. Top managers at Nucor worked in small unpretentious corporate offices with few of the trappings of luxury. They drove their own cars to work, flew economy class, and on business trips shared rooms in hotels to reduce costs.

The functions within a low-cost organization are likely to develop goals that reflect the organization's values of economy. Marketing views its job as finding the most efficient ways of attracting customers. R&D sees its role as developing new products that offer the greatest potential return for the smallest investment of organizational resources.

In low-cost organizations, a common "language" and a code of behavior based on low-cost values develop. In a differentiator, by contrast, the need to be different from competitors and to develop innovative products puts product development or marketing at center stage. Values that promote innovation and responsiveness to customers, stories of products that became winners or of winning products that were not developed, and boosting the status of employees who create new products all make organizational members aware of the need to be the first or the best.[39] Cultural values of innovation, quality, excellence, and uniqueness help a differentiator implement its chosen strategy, and they become a source of competitive strength.

An insight into the way culture can influence a company's business-level strategy occurred when, after considerable negotiations, pharmaceutical company American Home Products (AHP) announced it would buy Monsanto, another large pharmaceutical and chemical company, for $33 billion. Analysts applauded the merger, believing it would provide important differentiation and low-cost advantages for the combined firm. Specifically, the merged companies would have a much broader product range, and the merger would eliminate expensive duplication of production facilities, leading to major cost savings.

Analysts were therefore shocked when the two companies later announced that the merger was off because it was not in the best interests of shareholders. Why? AHP has a culture characterized by a short-term focus on bottom-line profits. Its managers are cost conscious and only want to invest in products that have a short-term payoff. Monsanto, in contrast, has a long-term orientation. It is driven by a desire to produce innovative new products, many of which may not pay off except in the long run. Thus it has strong values

Organizational Insight 8.2

Why Companies Need to Change Their Global Structures and Strategies

Almond Chu © Dorling Kindersley

After a decade of profitable growth, Avon suddenly began to experience falling global sales in the mid-2000s both at home and in developing markets abroad.[36] After several months visiting the managers of its worldwide divisions, Andrea Jung, Avon's CEO, decided that Avon had lost the balance between centralization and decentralization of authority; managers abroad had gained so much authority to control operations in their respective countries and world regions that they had made decisions to benefit their own divisions, and these decisions had hurt the performance of the whole company. Specifically, Avon's operating costs were out of control, and it was losing both a low-cost and a differentiation advantage. Avon's country-level managers from Poland to Mexico ran their own factories, made their own product development decisions, and developed their own advertising campaigns. And these decisions were often based on poor marketing knowledge and with little concern for operating costs because their goal was to increase sales as fast as possible.

Also, when too much authority is decentralized to managers lower in an organization's hierarchy, these managers often recruit more and more managers to help them build their country "empires." The result was that Avon's global hierarchy had exploded—it had risen from 7 levels to 15 levels of managers in a decade as tens of thousands of extra managers were hired around the globe! Because Avon's profits were rising fast, Jung and her top management team had not paid enough attention to the way Avon's organizational structure was becoming taller and taller—and how this was taking away its competitive advantage.

In 2006, Jung woke up from this nightmare: She had to confront the need to lay off thousands of managers and restructure the hierarchy. She embarked on a program to take away the authority of Avon's country-level managers and to transfer authority to regional and corporate headquarters managers to streamline decision making and reduce costs. She cut out seven levels of management and laid off 25% of Avon's global managers in its 114 worldwide markets. Then, using teams of expert managers from corporate headquarters, she embarked on a detailed examination of all Avon's functional activities, country by country, to find out why its costs had risen so quickly and what could be done to bring them under control. The duplication of marketing efforts in countries around the world was one source of these high costs. In Mexico, one team found that country managers' desire to expand their empires led to the development of a staggering 13,000 different products! Not only had this caused product development costs to soar, it had led to major marketing problems, for how could Avon's Mexican sales reps learn about the differences among 13,000 products—and then find an easy way to tell customers about them?

In Avon's new structure the focus is now on centralizing all new major product development; Avon develops over 1,000 new products a year, but in the future although the input from different country managers would be used to customize products to country needs in terms of fragrance, packaging, and so on, R&D would be performed in the United States. Similarly, in the future the goal is to develop marketing campaigns targeted toward the average "global" customer but that can be easily customized to any country by using the appropriate language or changing the nationality of the models used to market the product, for example. Other initiatives have been to increase the money spent on global marketing, which had not kept pace with its rapid global expansion to increase differentiation and a major push to increase the number of Avon ladies in developing nations to attract more customers. By 2011, Avon recruited another 400,000 reps in China alone![37]

Country-level managers now are responsible for managing this army of Avon reps and for ensuring that marketing dollars are being directed toward the right channels for maximum impact. However, they no longer have any authority to engage in major product development or build new manufacturing capacity—or to hire new managers without the agreement of regional- or corporate-level managers. The balance of control has changed at Avon, and Jung and all her managers are now firmly focused on making operational decisions that lower its costs or increase its differentiation advantage in ways that serve the best interests of the whole company—and not just the country in which its cosmetics are sold.

Managerial Implications

Business-Level Strategy

1. Managers in each function should understand their function's contribution to the organization's low-cost advantage or differentiated appeal. Members of a function should examine their interactions with members of other functions to see if they can devise new ways of reducing costs or develop a differentiated appeal.
2. Managers should act like entrepreneurs and always be on the lookout for new opportunities to protect and enlarge the domain of their organization. They must continually experiment to see whether they can enlarge the existing organizational domain, find new uses for existing products, or develop new products to satisfy customer needs.
3. Managers must always evaluate whether the current organizational structure and culture are congruent with the organization's business-level strategy. If they are not, managers should move quickly to make changes that can improve their competitive position.

of innovation and excellence. Managers at these companies came to realize it was impossible to harmonize these different cultures and driving values. They foresaw that potential low cost and differentiation advantages might be wiped out by politics and infighting between managers of these two companies. It was just not worth the risk to go ahead with the merger.

An organizational culture that promotes norms and rules that increase effectiveness can be a major source of competitive advantage. In Chapter 7, we saw how organizations deliberately shape their culture to achieve their goals. Google and 3M, for example, promote innovation by establishing norms and rules that enable employees to move to positions where their talents are most valuable to the organization.

Recall, too, that organizational structures are chosen because of their effect on culture. Organic structures foster the development of cultural values of innovation and quality. In contrast, mechanistic structures foster economical values that focus attention on improving existing rules and SOPs, not finding new ones. Low-cost companies that seek to develop Japanese-style lean production systems will find a mechanistic structure useful because it focuses all efforts on improving existing work procedures.

In sum, organizational culture is another important factor shaping an organization's business-level strategy for improving its value-creation skills. As technology changes, as new products and markets come into being, and as the environment changes, an organization's culture likewise will change. Like organizational structure, the way in which organizational culture supports an organization's strategy for value creation can also be a source of competitive advantage. That is one reason why managers are increasingly trying to develop a strong global company culture to increase organizational effectiveness.

Corporate-Level Strategy

An organization that cannot create more value in its current domain often tries to find a new domain in which to compete for resources. Corporate-level strategy involves a search for new domains in which to exploit and defend an organization's ability to create value from the use of its low-cost or differentiation core competences.[40] Corporate-level strategy is a continuation of business-level strategy because the organization takes its existing core competences and applies them in new domains. If an organization takes marketing skills developed in one domain and applies them in a new domain, for example, it can create value in that new domain. When Philip Morris took marketing skills developed in the tobacco industry, applied them to Miller Brewing, and made Miller Lite the market leader, it created value for Miller's customers and for Philip Morris's shareholders. Now we look in detail at how vertical integration and diversification, two important corporate-level strategies, can help an organization create value.

Vertical Integration

Vertical integration A strategy in which an organization takes over and owns its suppliers (backward vertical integration) or its distributors (forward vertical integration).

An organization pursuing a strategy of **vertical integration** decides that it will establish—or take over and buy—operations to make some of its own inputs and become its own supplier (backward vertical integration) or dispose of or distribute its own outputs (forward vertical integration).[41] By doing so it now controls the production of some of its inputs or the disposal of its outputs (see Figure 8.6). As an illustration, Figure 8.7 shows a soft-drink company that enters new domains that overlap its core domain so it can use, enhance, or protect its low-cost or differentiation value-creation skills.

How does vertical integration allow an organization to use or enhance its core competences in value creation? An organization that supplies its own inputs and/or disposes of its own outputs may be able to keep for itself the profits previously earned by its independent suppliers and distributors. Moreover, production cost savings often arise when an organization owns its suppliers because, for example, inputs can now be designed so they can be assembled at a lower cost. Also, because it now controls the

Figure 8.6 Corporate-Level Strategies for Entering New Domains

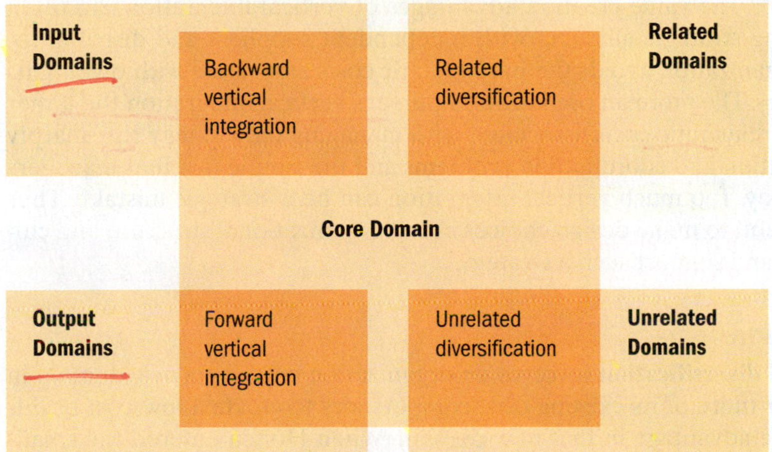

Figure 8.7 Soft-Drink Company's Corporate-Level Strategies for Entering New Domains

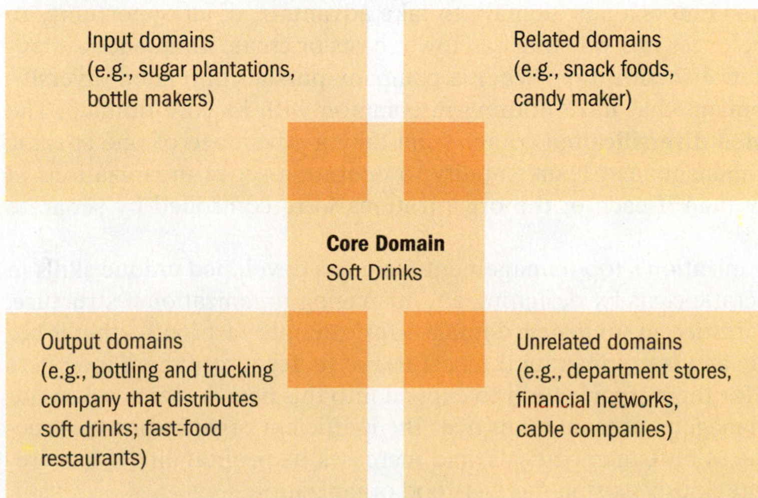

reliability and quality of inputs, this can save an organization a great deal of money if products eventually have to be repaired under guarantee.

An organization can call attention to its uniqueness by making its products different from those of its rivals. One way to do this is by making the inputs that make a product unique, that is, by using forward vertical integration. Coca-Cola, for example, has sole control over how the Coke formula is made, so Coca-Cola tastes like no other cola drink. Controlling inputs also helps the organization control quality, which confers uniqueness on a product. Rolls-Royce carefully tends the flocks of sheep from which it obtains the leather for its car upholstery: The sheep are kept in enclosures without barbed wire and are protected so the leather has no flaws and blemishes. Finally, taking over a supplier by vertical integration avoids problems that result when there are only a few suppliers in an industry who may try to take advantage of an organization by, for example, raising the prices of inputs or reducing their quality. Using backward vertical integration to control the way a product is distributed can also result in a low-cost or differentiation advantage. Radio Shack, for example, makes most of its own store brand products so it receives all the profit from both making and selling Radio Shack electronic merchandise—often at high prices.

Control of overlapping input and output domains enhances an organization's competitive advantage in its core domain and creates new opportunities for value creation. But an organization also needs to look at the bureaucratic costs associated with owning its suppliers and distributors.[42] An organization needs to evaluate whether minority ownership, strategic alliances, and other interorganizational strategies are viable alternatives to vertical integration.[43] The value-creation advantages of vertical integration can often be obtained by creating strategic alliances with independent suppliers and distributors, and by doing so an organization avoids the bureaucratic costs associated with owning its suppliers or distributors. The more an organization pursues vertical integration the larger it becomes, and the bureaucratic costs associated with managing the strategy rise sharply because of communication and coordination problems and the simple fact that managers are expensive to employ. Too much vertical integration can be a strategic mistake. Thus managers must be careful to make design choices about organizational structure and culture that will enhance and support such a strategy.

Related Diversification

Related diversification
The entry into a new domain that is related in some way to an organization's domain.

The strategy of **related diversification** involves an organization entering a *new* domain in which it can use one or more of its existing core competences to create a low-cost or differentiated competitive advantage in that new domain. When Honda entered the small-car and lawn-mower markets, for example, it entered new domains in which it could use its strong functional competences in engine design and manufacture that it had developed in its core domains, motorbikes and cars, to achieve a differentiation advantage.

Unrelated Diversification

Whenever an organization enters a new domain to take advantage of an opportunity to use any of its core competences in a way that can lower costs or create uniqueness, it creates value through related diversification. When a company pursues unrelated diversification, it enters new domains that have nothing in common with its core domain. The value created by **unrelated diversification** comes from taking advantage of one specific core competence: a top-management team's ability to operate a set of organizations in concert more effectively than if each of the organizations were controlled by separate top-management teams.[44]

Unrelated diversification
The entry into a new domain that is not related in any way to an organization's core domain.

Suppose a retail organization's top-management team has developed unique skills in economizing on bureaucratic costs by designing and managing organizational structure. If the team sees an organization in some new domain—for example, fast food—that is being managed inefficiently and is not making the best use of its resources, team members may see an opportunity for their organization to expand into this new domain and create value there. If the top-management team takes over the inefficient organization, restructures its operations, reduces bureaucratic costs, and increases its profitability, it has created value that did not previously exist in the fast-food organization.

An organization that takes over inefficient companies and restructures them to create value is pursuing a strategy of unrelated diversification. For example, companies like GE and United Technologies seek out underperforming companies and restructure them; they sell off unprofitable divisions and only keep those that can be reorganized to operate profitably. Indeed, designing an efficient organizational structure is an important part of unrelated diversification because companies that perform poorly often do so because they have high bureaucratic costs.

Corporate-Level Strategy and Structure

The appropriate organizational structure must be chosen at the corporate level to realize the value associated with vertical integration and related and unrelated diversification. In general, as we discussed in Chapter 6, for organizations operating in more than one domain, a multidivisional structure is the appropriate choice (see Figure 6.6). The use of self-contained operating divisions supported by a corporate headquarters staff provides the control the organization needs to coordinate resource transfers between divisions so core competences can be shared across the organization. There are a few variants of the multidivisional structure. Each is suited to realizing the benefits associated with either unrelated or related diversification.

CONGLOMERATE STRUCTURE AND UNRELATED DIVERSIFICATION Organizations that pursue a strategy of unrelated diversification attempt to create value by acquiring underperforming businesses, restructuring them, and then managing them more efficiently. This strategy frees corporate managers, the top management team of the parent organization, from day-to-day involvement in the running of its various divisions, that is, the companies the organization owns. After the restructuring, corporate management's only role is to monitor each division's performance and intervene to take selective action when necessary. Organizations with a strategy of unrelated diversification are likely to use a conglomerate structure.

As Figure 8.8 shows, in a **conglomerate structure,** each unrelated business is a self-contained division. Because there is no need to coordinate activities between divisions, only a small corporate headquarters staff is needed. Communication is from the top down and occurs most often on issues that concern bureaucratic costs, such as decisions about the level of financial expenditure necessary to pursue new value-creation opportunities. The conglomerate Hanson Trust, for example, operated with a corporate staff of only 120 people to oversee its more than 50 divisions; it operated primarily through rules

Conglomerate structure A structure in which each business is placed in a self-contained division and there is no contact between divisions.

Figure 8.8 Conglomerate Structure

A structure in which each business is placed in a self-contained division and there is no contact between divisions.

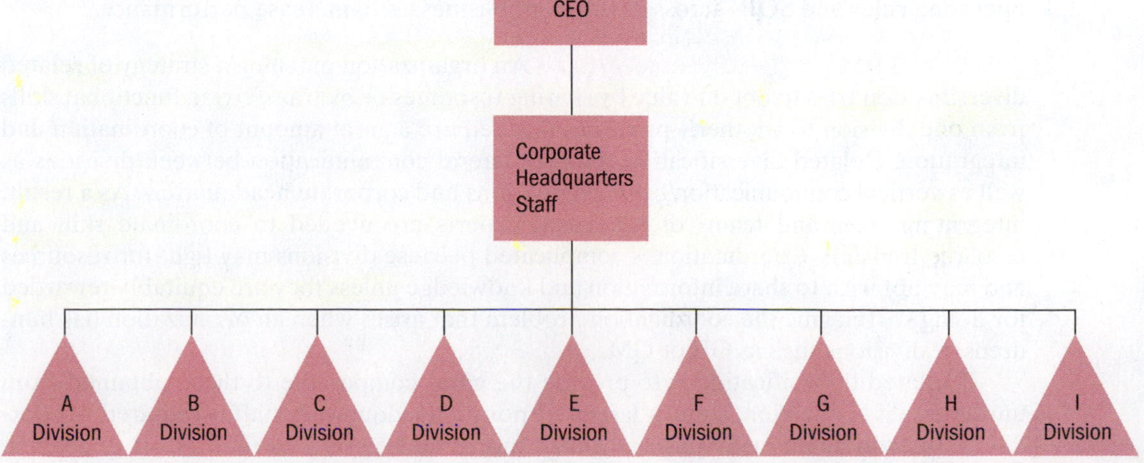

Organizational Insight 8.3

UTC Continuously Improves Operating Rules in Its Different Businesses

Vladislav Gajic/Shutterstock.com

United Technologies Corporation (UTC), based in Hartford, Connecticut, owns a wide variety of companies that operate in different businesses and industries. Some of the companies it owns are more well known than UTC itself, such as Sikorsky helicopters, the aircraft engine and component maker Pratt & Whitney, Otis elevators, Carrier air conditioning, and Chubb, the security and lock maker.[46]

In the 2000s, UTC has been one of the most profitable companies in the world and the reason, so its CEO George David claims, is its commitment to developing a program of innovative rules and operating processes to continuously increase quality. UTC's program originated when it had a major problem in its Otis elevator division, and David assigned one of its leading engineeers,Yuzuru Ito, to head a team of Otis engineers to find out why it performed so poorly. Under Ito's direction they created a set of "process" techniques that involve all employees—managers, designers, production workers—who had produced the elevator to analyze why the elevators were malfunctioning and then develop improved operating rules and procedures to solve the problem. This intensive study led to a total redesign of the elevator, and when their new and improved elevator was launched worldwide it met with great success.

After this success David decided the best way to increase UTC's profitability was to find ways to make the managers in all its diverse businesses focus on improving operating rules. He convinced Ito to take responsibility for championing the development of UTC's quality program, which is known as *Achieving Competitive Excellence,* or ACE. ACE is a set of rules and procedures used by employees from the shop floor to top managers to analyze systematically all aspects of the way a product is made to find ways to improve quality and reliability, to lower the costs of making the products, and especially to find new rules to make the next generation of a particular product perform better, in other words to encourage technological innovation.

David makes every employee in every function and at every level take responsibility for achieving the incremental, step-by-step gains from improved rules and procedures that can result in innovative products, built with ever-increasing quality and efficiency that can put a company on the path to dominating its industry. David calls these techniques "process disciplines," and he has used them to improve the performance of *all* UTC companies. In the decade since he took control, he has quadrupled UTC's earnings per share and its stock price has boomed and it has become one of the best-performing stocks in the 2010s.[47]

that controlled bureaucratic costs. Hanson Trust had a rule that required a corporate executive to approve any expenditure over $3,000.[45] Beyond this, it made little attempt to intervene in the affairs of the operating divisions. United Technologies, discussed in organizational Insight 10.3, offers an interesting example of how a company can develop operating rules and SOPs across its different businesses to increase performance.

STRUCTURES FOR RELATED DIVERSIFICATION An organization pursuing a strategy of related diversification tries to obtain value by sharing resources or by transferring functional skills from one division to another—processes that require a great amount of coordination and integration. Related diversification requires lateral communication between divisions as well as vertical communication between divisions and corporate headquarters. As a result, integrating roles and teams of functional experts are needed to coordinate skill and resource transfers. Coordination is complicated because divisions may fight for resources and may not wish to share information and knowledge unless they are equitably rewarded for doing so. Imagine the coordination problem that arises when an organization has hundreds of divisions such as GE or GM.

If related diversification is to provide the gains comparable to those obtained from unrelated diversification, a much larger corporate headquarters staff is required to coordinate interdivisional activities, and much more managerial time and effort is needed.

When the coordination problem becomes very severe, a multidivisional matrix structure is used to increase integration (see Figure 6.12). As we saw in Chapter 6, this structure provides the coordination between the divisions and corporate headquarters that allows for the transfer of skills and the sharing of resources around the organization. It gives top-level functional, divisional, and corporate managers the opportunity to meet in teams to plan the organization's future strategy.

The bureaucratic costs associated with managing related diversification (whether in a multidivisional structure or a matrix multidivisional structure) are much greater than those associated with vertical integration or unrelated diversification.[48] Considerably more communication and coordination are needed to create value from related diversification than from the other corporate-level strategies. Bureaucratic costs increase as the size of the corporate staff and the amount of time that both divisional and corporate managers spend in coordinating with other divisions increase. In contrast, the bureaucratic costs associated with unrelated diversification are likely to be low because there is no need to coordinate resource transfers between divisions—the divisions do not exchange anything.

Corporate-Level Strategy and Culture

Just as a move to a more appropriate organizational structure can reduce bureaucratic costs, so can a move to a more appropriate organizational culture. Cultural values and the common norms, rules, and goals that reflect those values can greatly facilitate the management of a corporate strategy. For example, Hanson Trust, which pursued a strategy of unrelated diversification, put most value on economy, cost cutting, and the efficient use of organizational resources. Divisional managers at Hanson Trust could not spend large amounts of money without the approval of corporate executives. Knowing that their performance was scrutinized closely, their actions were shaped by corporate values tied to bottom-line result.

By contrast, suppose an organization is pursuing a strategy of related diversification. What kinds of values, norms, and rules are most useful in managing the strategy? Because the creation of value from related diversification requires a large amount of coordination and integration, norms and values that emphasize cooperation between divisions are important. This type of culture lowers the costs of exchanging resources and is likely to feature a common corporate language that the various divisions can use in their dealings with one another. Each division will have its own culture, but the corporate culture can overcome differences in divisional orientation, just as at the business level an organization's culture can overcome differences in functional orientation.

At 3M and Procter & Gamble (P&G), for example, corporate values of innovation and entrepreneurship are passed on in the stories that organizational members use to frame significant corporate events. New employees are socialized to the innovative culture and learn the corporate language from their interactions with other employees. In choosing which divisional managers will be promoted to the corporate headquarters staff, 3M and P&G also send their members a clear message about the kinds of values and behaviors associated with career success—actions that lead to innovative new products.

Thus different cultures help organizations pursue different corporate-level strategies. An organization needs to create a culture that reinforces and builds on the strategy it pursues and the structure it adopts. In an organization that has a conglomerate structure, in which there is no connection between divisions, it would be pointless to develop a common corporate culture across divisions because the managers in the different divisions would not know one another. A multidivisional matrix structure, in contrast, does support the development of a cohesive corporate culture because it permits the rapid interchange of ideas and the transfer of norms and values around the organization. In sum, as we saw in Chapter 7, corporate culture is an important tool that organizations can use to coordinate and motivate employees.

As at the business level, the interorganizational strategies discussed in Chapter 3 are an important means of increasing the value an organization can create through its corporate strategy. Interorganizational strategies increase value by allowing the organization to avoid

Managerial Implications

Corporate-Level Strategy

1. To protect the organization's existing domains and to exploit the organization's core competences to create value for stakeholders, managers should carefully analyze the environment.
2. To distinguish between a value-creation opportunity and a value-losing opportunity, managers should carefully evaluate the benefits and costs associated with entering a new domain.
3. As part of this analysis, managers should weigh the benefits and costs of various strategies for entering the domain—for example, takeover of an existing company, versus establishing a new organization, versus using a strategic alliance such as a joint venture.
4. No matter which corporate strategy managers pursue, as the organization grows, managers must be careful to match their organization's structure and culture to the strategy they are pursuing.

the bureaucratic costs often associated with managing a new organization in a new domain. As the number of an organization's divisions increases, for example, the bureaucratic costs associated with managing interdivisional activities increase. Interorganizational strategies such as strategic alliances may allow an organization to obtain the gains from cooperation between divisions without experiencing the costs.

Suppose two organizations establish a joint venture to produce a range of products in a domain that is new to both of them. Each organization contributes a different skill or resource to the venture. One provides low-cost manufacturing skills; the other, differentiated R&D and marketing skills. By establishing the joint venture, they have avoided the bureaucratic costs that would be incurred if one organization took over the other or if either organization had to internally coordinate the new resource transfers necessary to make the new venture work. Similarly, the gains from vertical integration can often be realized through minority ownership or long-term contracts, which avoid the need to own the supplier or distributor. An organization that can use an interorganizational strategy to enter and compete in a new domain can often secure the benefits of the diversification and integration strategies without incurring bureaucratic costs.

Implementing Strategy across Countries

Global strategy can play a crucial role in strengthening a company's control over its environment. Companies can use four principal strategies as they begin to market their products and establish production facilities abroad: (1) a *multidomestic strategy*, oriented toward local responsiveness—a company decentralizes control to subsidiaries and divisions in each country in which it operates to produce and customize products to local markets; (2) an *international strategy*, based on R&D and marketing being centralized at home and all the other value-creation functions being decentralized to national units; (3) a *global strategy*, oriented toward cost reduction, with all the principal value-creation functions centralized at the lowest cost global location; and (4) a *transnational strategy*, focused so it can achieve both local responsiveness *and* cost reduction—some functions are centralized while others are decentralized at the global location best suited to achieving these objectives.

The need to coordinate and integrate global activities increases as a company moves from a multidomestic to an international to a global and then to a transnational strategy. For example, to obtain the benefits of pursuing a transnational strategy, a company must transfer its distinctive competences to the global location where they can create the most value and establish a global network to coordinate its divisions both at home and abroad. The objective of such coordination is to obtain the benefits from transferring or leveraging competences across a company's global divisions. Thus the bureaucratic costs incurred to solve communications and measurement problems that arise in managing transfers across countries to pursue a transnational strategy are much higher than those of pursuing the other strategies. The multidomestic strategy does not require coordination of activities on a global level because value-creation activities are handled locally, by country or world region. The international and global strategies fit between the other two strategies: Although products have to be sold and marketed globally, and hence global product transfers must be managed, there is less need to coordinate skill and resource transfers than for a transnational strategy.

The implication is that as companies change from a multidomestic to an international, global, or transnational strategy, they require a more complex structure, control system, and culture to coordinate the value-creation activities associated with implementing that strategy. In general, the choice of structure and control systems for managing a global business is a function of three factors:

1. The decision how to distribute and allocate responsibility and authority between managers at home and abroad so that effective control over a company's global operations is maintained
2. The selection of the organizational structure that groups divisions both at home and abroad in a way that allows the best use of resources and serves the needs of foreign customers most effectively
3. The selection of the right kinds of integration and control mechanisms and organizational culture to make the overall global structure function effectively

Table 8.2 summarizes the appropriate design choices for companies pursuing each of these strategies.

TABLE 8.2 Strategy-Structure Relationships in the International Environment

	Multidomestic Strategy	International Strategy	Global Strategy	Transnational Strategy
	Low ←	Need for Coordination		→ High
Vertical Differentiation Choices				
Levels in the hierarchy	Relatively flat	Relatively tall	Relatively tall	Relatively flat
Centralization of authority	Decentralized	Core competences centralized, others decentralized	Centralized	Simultaneously centralized and decentralized
Horizontal Differentiation	Global geographic structure	Global product group structure	Global product group structure	Global matrix or "matrix in the mind"
Integration				
Need for integrating mechanisms such as task forces and integrating roles	Low	Medium	Medium	High
Need for electronic integration and management networks	Medium	High	High	Very High
Need for integration by international organizational culture	Low	Medium	High	Very High
	Low ←	Bureaucratic Costs		→ High

Figure 8.9 Global Geographic Structure

Corporate Headquarters (located in Sweden)

Canadian Division | United States Division | British Division | French Division | Japanese Division | South American Division

Functional activities

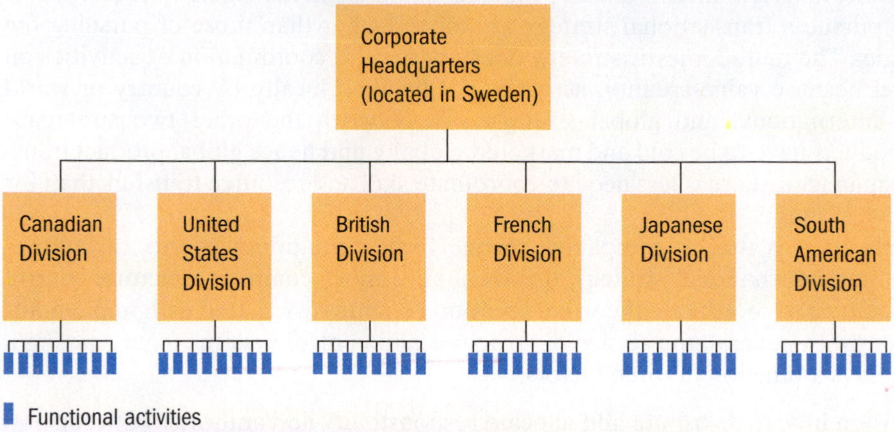

Implementing a Multidomestic Strategy

When a company pursues a multidomestic strategy, it generally operates with a global geographic structure (see Figure 8.9). When using this structure, a company duplicates all value-creation activities and establishes an overseas division in every country or world area in which it operates. Authority is then decentralized to managers in each overseas division, and they devise the appropriate strategy for responding to the needs of the local environment. Managers at global headquarters use market and output controls, such as return on investment, growth in market share, and operation costs, to evaluate the performance of overseas divisions. On the basis of such global comparisons, they can make decisions about capital allocation and orchestrate the transfer of new knowledge among divisions.

A company that makes and sells the same products in many different countries often groups its overseas divisions into world regions to simplify the coordination of products across countries. Europe might be one region, the Pacific Rim another, and the Middle East a third. Such grouping allows the same set of output and behavior controls to be applied across all divisions inside a region. Thus global companies can reduce communications and transfer problems because information can be transmitted more easily across countries with broadly similar cultures. For example, consumers' preferences regarding product design and marketing are likely to be more similar among countries in one world region than among countries in different world regions.

Because the overseas divisions themselves have little or no contact with others in different regions, no integrating mechanisms are needed. Nor does a global organizational culture develop because there are no transfers of skills or resources or transfer of personnel among managers from the various world regions. Historically, car companies such as GM, Volkswagen, and Ford used global-area structures to manage their overseas operations. Ford of Europe, for example, had little or no contact with its U.S. parent, and capital was the principal resource exchanged.

One problem with a global geographic structure and a multidomestic strategy is that the duplication of specialist activities across countries raises a company's overall cost structure. Moreover, the company is not taking advantage of opportunities to transfer, share, or leverage its competences and capabilities on a global basis: For example, it cannot apply the low-cost manufacturing expertise that has developed in one world region in another. Thus multidomestic companies lose the many benefits of operating globally.

Implementing International Strategy

A company pursuing an international strategy adopts a different route to global expansion. A company with many different products or businesses has the challenging problem of coordinating the flow of different products across different countries. To manage these

Figure 8.10 Global Product Group Structure

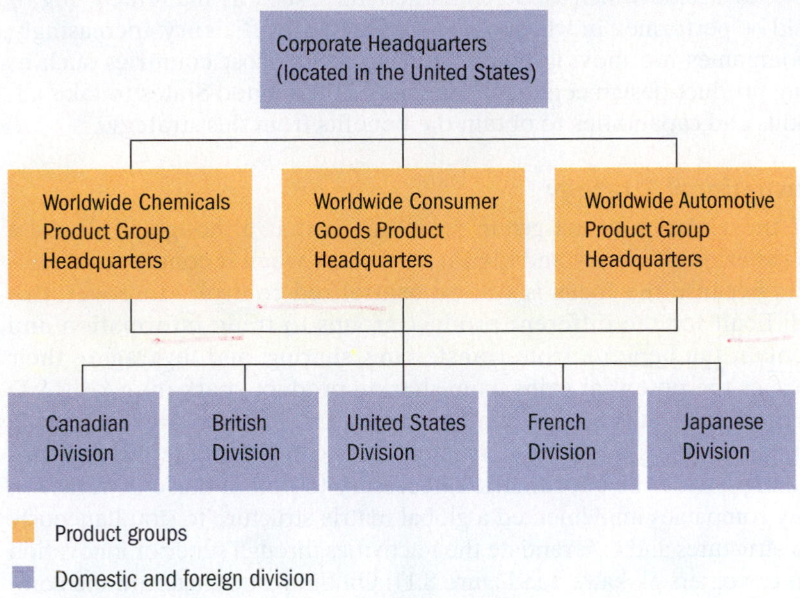

transfers, many companies use a global product group structure and create product group headquarters to coordinate the activities of both home and international divisions within each product group. Product group managers are responsible for organizing all aspects of value creation on a global level (see Figure 8.10).

This arrangement of tasks and roles reduces the transaction costs involved in managing handoffs across countries and world regions. However, managers abroad are essentially under the control of managers in the international divisions and if the number of levels of managers at the product group level becomes too great, corporate headquarters may lose control over company-wide decision making and product group and international division managers may compete for control of strategy making. The result is a loss of control, conflict, and a lack of cooperation. Many companies such as IBM and Citibank have experienced this problem. Very often, significant strategic control has been decentralized to overseas divisions. When cost pressures force corporate managers to reassess their strategy, and they decide to intervene, this frequently provokes resistance, much of it due to differences in culture—not just corporate, but country differences.

Implementing Global Strategy

When a company embarks on a global strategy today, it locates its manufacturing and other value chain activities at the global location that will allow it to increase efficiency and quality. In so doing, it has to solve the problems of coordinating and integrating its global activities. It has to find a structure that lowers the bureaucratic costs associated with resource transfers between corporate headquarters and its global divisions and provides the centralized control that a global strategy requires. The answer for many companies is also a global product group structure (see Figure 8.10).

Once again, the product groups coordinate the activities of home and overseas operations and decide where to locate the different functions at the optimal global location for performing that activity. For example, Philips has one worldwide product group responsible for coordinating the global R&D, manufacturing, marketing, and sales activities of the international divisions that make and sell its light bulbs. It has another worldwide group responsible for making and selling its medical equipment, and so on. The product group headquarters of its medical division and its R&D is located in Bothell, Washington. Manufacturing, however, is done in Taiwan, and the products are marketed and sold by each international division.

The product-group structure allows managers to decide how best to pursue a global strategy—for example, to decide which value-chain activities, such as manufacturing or product design, should be performed in which country to increase efficiency. Increasingly, U.S. and Japanese companies are moving manufacturing to low-cost countries such as China but establishing product-design centers in Europe or the United States to take advantage of foreign skills and capabilities to obtain the benefits from this strategy.

Implementing Transnational Strategy

The main failing of the global product-group structure is that although it allows a company to achieve superior efficiency and quality, it is weak when it comes to responsiveness to customers because the focus is still on centralized control. Moreover, this structure makes it difficult for the different product groups to trade information and knowledge and to obtain the benefits from transferring, sharing, and leveraging their competences. Sometimes the potential gains from sharing product, marketing, or R&D knowledge between product groups are high, but so too are the bureaucratic costs associated with achieving these gains. Is there a structure that can simultaneously economize on these costs and provide the coordination necessary to obtain these benefits?

In the 1990s, many companies implemented a global matrix structure to simultaneously lower their global cost structures and differentiate their activities through superior innovation and responsiveness to customers globally. See Figure 8.11: On the vertical axis are the company's overseas divisions in the various countries or world regions in which it operates. Managers at the regional or country level control local operations. On the horizontal axis are the company's corporate product groups, which provide specialist services such as R&D, product design, and marketing information to its overseas divisions, which are grouped by world region. These might be the chemicals, consumer goods, and automobile product groups. Through a system of output and behavior controls, they then report to corporate product group personnel back in the United States and ultimately to the CEO or president. The heads of the world regions or country managers are also responsible for working with U.S. product group managers to develop the control and reward systems that will promote the transfer, sharing, or leveraging of competences that will result in superior performance.

Figure 8.11 Global Matrix Structure

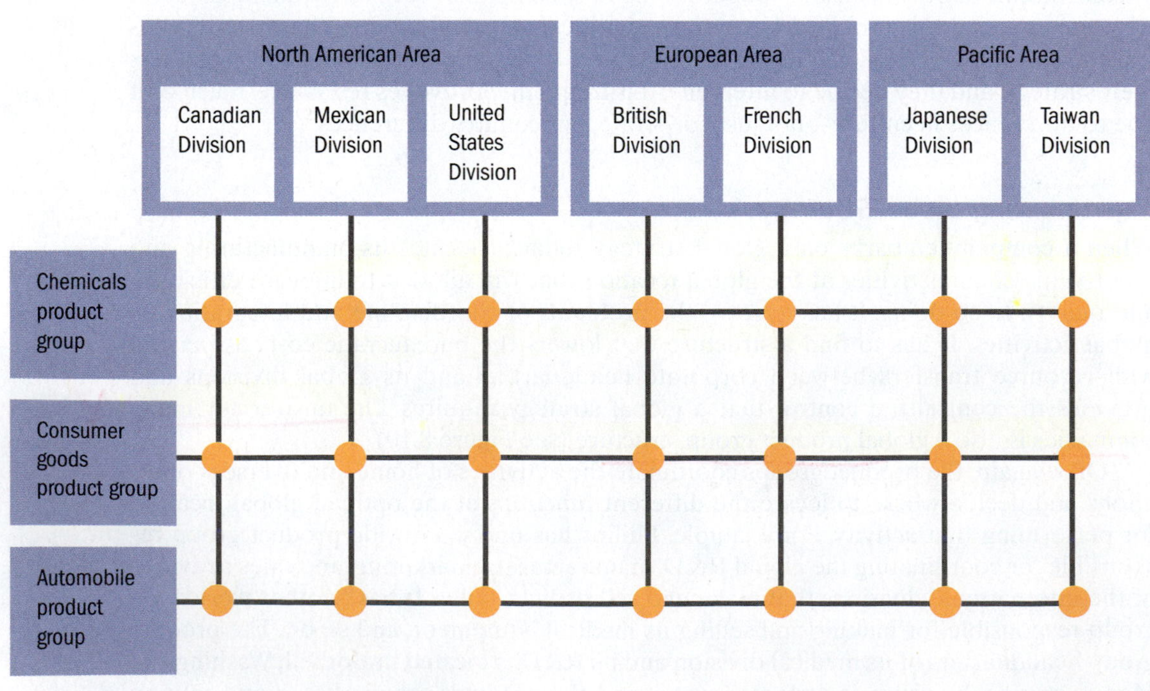

Implementing a matrix structure thus decentralizes control to overseas managers and provides them with considerable flexibility for managing local issues, but it can still give product and corporate managers in the United States the centralized control they need to coordinate company activities on a global level. The matrix structure can allow knowledge and experience to be transferred among geographic regions, among product groups, and among product groups and regions. Because it offers many opportunities for face-to-face contact between managers at home and abroad, the matrix facilitates the transmission of a company's norms and values and hence the development of a global corporate culture. This is especially important for a company with far-flung global operations for which lines of communication are longer. Club Med, for instance, uses a matrix to standardize high-quality customer service across its global vacation villages.

Summary

Organizational strategy is a plan of action that an organization undertakes to create value. Organizations that do not continually set ambitious new goals and try to find effective means of reaching those goals are likely to be threatened by younger, more agile competitors in search of ways to seize resources for themselves. Consequently, organizational members at all levels in the organization—functional, business, corporate, and global—must develop their value-creation skills and abilities. Managers must manage the interrelationship of strategy (at all levels), structure, and culture to maximize the organization's ability to manage, enhance, and protect its domain so it can create value to satisfy stakeholders. Chapter 8 has made the following main points:

1. The value that an organization creates by means of its strategy is a function of how the organization positions itself in its environment so it can use its core competences to compete for resources.
2. An organization's core competences are products of its functional and organizational resources and its coordination ability.
3. An organization must formulate strategy at four levels: functional, business, corporate, and global.
4. The goal of functional-level strategy is to create in each function a low-cost or differentiation competence that gives the organization a competitive advantage.
5. Functional structure and culture produce functional abilities that support the development of functional resources.
6. The goal of business-level strategy is to combine functional low-cost and differentiation competences to exploit opportunities in the organizational environment. Business-level strategy selects and manages the domain in which an organization uses its value-creation resources and coordination abilities.
7. The two main business-level strategies are low-cost business-level strategy and differentiation business-level strategy.
8. An organization chooses a structure and culture to develop coordination abilities that support its business-level strategy.
9. The goal of corporate-level strategy is to use and develop low-cost and differentiation competences so the organization can protect and enlarge its existing domain and expand into new ones.
10. Three main types of corporate-level strategy are vertical integration, related diversification, and unrelated diversification.
11. An appropriate corporate-level structure and culture can help reduce the bureaucratic costs of managing a strategy.
12. The four strategies that companies use to manage global expansion are a multidomestic strategy, an international strategy, a global strategy, and a transnational strategy. Each is associated with a different approach to value creation and a different set of organizational design problems.

Discussion Questions

1. How should an organization design its structure and culture to obtain a core competence in manufacturing and in research and development?
2. Pick an organization like a restaurant or a department store, and analyze how it might pursue a low-cost or a differentiation strategy.
3. What is the difference between a low-cost strategy and a differentiation strategy? How should a differentiated biotechnology organization and a low-cost fast-food organization design their structures and cultures to promote their respective competitive advantages?
4. Compare the competitive advantages enjoyed by a large restaurant chain, such as Steak and Ale or Red Lobster, and the sources of competitive advantages enjoyed by a small local restaurant.
5. Why would an organization choose a corporate-level strategy to expand its value-creation activities beyond its core domain? Discuss how an organization's structure and culture might change as the organization begins to enter new domains.
6. How and why do bureaucratic costs increase as a company goes from a multidomestic to an international to a global to a transnational strategy?

Organizational Theory in Action

Practicing Organizational Theory

What Kind of Supermarket?

Form groups of three to five people and discuss the following scenario:

You are a group of investors who are contemplating opening a new supermarket in your city. You are trying to decide what business-level strategy would provide your supermarket with a competitive advantage that would allow you to attract customers and outperform your prospective rivals.

1. List the supermarket chains in your city and identify their business-level strategies (for example, low cost, differentiation, or focus). Also, list any particular kinds of functional strengths or weaknesses that they might have (such as a great bakery or a lousy fish counter).
2. On the basis of this analysis, what type of business-level strategy do you think will best succeed in the local market? What will the specific elements of this strategy be? (For example: What kind of supermarket will it be? What kind of functional strengths will you try to develop? What kinds of customers will you aim for? What will you do to attract them?)

The Ethical Dimension #8

Bribery and corruption are common in some countries, and for people in those countries, they are a normal part of doing business. U.S. law bans any U.S. company from paying bribes to foreign officials or taking any steps to use illegal means to secure valuable foreign contracts or resources.

1. Why does the United States adopt this ethical and legal stance if people in the country accept bribery as the norm?
2. What could U.S. companies do to help reduce the incidence of bribery in these countries and promote ethical business practices?

Making the Connection #8

Find an example of an organization pursuing a business, corporate, or global expansion strategy. What kind of strategy is it pursuing? Why did it choose this strategy? How does the strategy create value? How does the strategy affect the organization's structure or culture?

Analyzing the Organization: Design Module #8

This module focuses on the kinds of goods and services that your organization produces, the markets it competes in, and the kinds of strategies it uses to create value for its stakeholders.

Assignment

This assignment asks you to explore how your company creates value through its strategy and structure for managing the environment.

1. Briefly describe your organization's domain—that is, the goods and services it produces and the customer groups it serves.
2. What core competences give the organization a competitive advantage? What are the organization's functional-level strategies?
3. What is your organization's principal business-level strategy: low cost or differentiation? How successfully is the organization pursuing this strategy? In what ways does it need to improve its core competences to improve its competitive position?
4. In what ways do your organization's structure and culture match its strategy? Is there a good match? In what ways could the match be improved? Is the organization experiencing any problems with its structure?
5. Is your organization operating in more than one domain? If it is, what corporate-level strategies is it pursuing? How is it creating value from these strategies? Is it successful?
6. What kind of strategy is your organization pursuing in the international environment? What kind of structure does your organization use to manage this strategy?

CASE FOR ANALYSIS

Schering-Plough Implements a New Global Strategy and Structure

One global company that found itself in trouble in the 2000s because of the way its structure and control systems were working was pharmaceutical maker Schering-Plough. In 2003, Schering was under pressures from many fronts. The Food and Drug Administration (FDA) was demanding a complete overhaul of its global manufacturing plants to increase and protect drug quality, and the patent on Claritin, its best-selling drug, was running out and it had few new products in the pipeline. Thus on both the quality and innovation dimensions, major sources of a differentiation advantage, the company's strategy was in trouble.

Schering-Plough's board of directors recruited Fred Hassan, a Pakistan-born Harvard MBA, to turn the company around. After meeting with hundreds of groups of managers and scientists, and visiting the company's operations around the globe, Hassan began to realize that the company's main problems stemmed from its global strategy and structure.[49]

Over time, the company had developed a multidomestic approach to planning its global value-chain activities and it had divided its activities up into world regions, where essentially each world region acted as the product group that made decisions inside its world region/group. The problem was that each of the heads of the regional groups had gained a near total control of their operations, so each world region was doing things such as manufacturing and marketing and sales in its own unique way. As a result, managers at corporate headquarters, and especially its top-management team, were not getting accurate information about the way each region, and especially the country operations within each region, were performing. And major drug quality problems had arisen because the corporate center didn't find out about the problems at the country level until a long time after they had occurred because of all the bureaucracy that had emerged at the level of the regional groups.

Schering only makes one major type of product—drugs—so Hassan decided it did not need separate worldwide product groups or separate regional groups. He decided to slash the number of levels in the company's global corporate hierarchy, eliminating all the layers between the country managers and himself. The heads of each international division now report directly to him or one of his top-management team members, so it is much easier to observe and evaluate their performance—and that of their divisions. It is also easier to standardize issues such as quality and sales practices around the world. He has also worked to expand the range of products each international division sells to achieve economies of scale. In 2007, for example, Hassan engaged in related diversification when he bought a major Dutch pharmaceutical company that is a leader in producing vaccines for animals and pets, as well as possessing a pipeline of potentially best-selling new drugs—it has five drugs in late trials, including an important new treatment for schizophrenia and bipolar disorder.

His new global organizational structure worked so well and sales and profits increased so much that by 2010 it was bought by and became part of Merck, one of its major competitors. Hassan is now the chairman of Bausch & Lomb, an optical products company, where he is applying the same kinds of organizational structure changes to help increase that company's global competitive position.[50]

Discussion Questions

1. What kinds of problems was Schering-Plough experiencing with its global strategy and structure?
2. How did Schering Plough change its global structure to solve these problems?

References

1 A. D. Chandler, *Strategy and Structure: Chapters in the History of the Industrial Enterprise* (Cambridge, MA: MIT Press, 1962).

2 C. W. L. Hill and G. R. Jones, *Strategic Management: An Integrated Approach*, 4th ed. (Boston: Houghton Mifflin, 2010).

3 M. E. Porter, *Competitive Strategy* (New York: Free Press, 1980).

4 K. Weigelt and C. Camerer, "Reputation and Corporate Strategy," *Strategic Management Journal*, *9* (1988), 443–454.

5 Hill and Jones, *Strategic Management*, Ch. 10.

6 R. R. Nelson and S. Winter, *An Evolutionary Theory of Economic Change* (Cambridge, MA: Harvard University Press, 1982).

7 M. E. Porter, *Competitive Advantage: Creating and Sustaining Superior Performance* (New York: Free Press, 1985).

8 R. W. Ruekert and O. C. Walker, "Interactions Between Marketing and R&D Departments in Implementing Different Business Strategies," *Strategic Management Journal*, *8* (1987), 233–248.

9 Porter, *Competitive Strategy.*

10 K. N. M. Dundas and P. R. Richardson, "Corporate Strategy and the Concept of Market Failure," *Strategic Management Journal* 1 (1980), 177–188.

11 www.samsung.com, 2011.

12 Ibid.

13 Porter, *Competitive Advantage.*

14 S. C. Wheelright, "Manufacturing Strategy: Defining the Missing Link," *Strategic Management Journal* 5 (1984), 77–91.

15 D. Ulrich, "Linking Strategic Planning and Human Resource Planning," in L. Fahey, ed., *The Strategic Planning Management Reader* (Englewood Cliffs, NJ: Prentice Hall, 1989), pp. 421–426.

16 E. S. Buffa, "Positioning the Production System—A Key Element in Manufacturing Strategy," in Fahey, *The Strategic Planning Management Reader*, pp. 387–395.

17 O. E. Williamson, *Markets and Hierarchies* (New York: Free Press, 1975).

18 R. M. Johnson, "Market Segmentation: A Strategic Management Tool," *Journal of Marketing Research* 8 (1971), 15– 23.

19 V. Scarpello, W. R. Boulton, and C. W. Hofer, "Reintegrating R&D into Business Strategy," *Journal of Business Strategy* 6 (1986), 49–56.

20 D. Miller, "Strategy Making and Structure: Analysis and Implications for Performance," *Academy of Management Journal* 30 (1987), 7–32.

21 P. R. Lawrence and J. W. Lorsch, *Organization and Environment* (Boston: Graduate School of Business Administration, Harvard University, 1967).

22 J. Woodward, *Industrial Organization: Theory and Practice* (London: Oxford University Press, 1965).
23 K. M. Eisenhardt, "Control: Organizational and Economic Approaches," *Management Science* 16 (1985), 134–138.
24 J. B. Barney, "Organization Culture: Can It Be a Source of Sustained Competitive Advantage?" *Academy of Management Review* 11 (1986), 791–800.
25 S. M. Oster, *Modern Competitive Analysis* (New York: Oxford University Press, 1990).
26 Porter, *Competitive Strategy*, Ch. 2.
27 Ibid.
28 R. E. White, "Generic Business Strategies, Organizational Context and Performance: An Empirical Investigation," *Strategic Management Journal* 7 (1986), 217–231; G. R. Jones and J. E. Butler, "Costs, Revenue, and Business-Level Strategy," *Academy of Management Review*, *13* (1988), 202–213.
29 www.amazon.com, 2011.
30 Porter, *Competitive Strategy*.
31 White, "Generic Business Strategies, Organizational Context and Performance"; D. Miller, "Configurations of Strategy and Structure," *Strategic Management Journal* 7 (1986), 223–249.
32 S. Kotha and D. Orne, "Generic Manufacturing Strategies: A Conceptual Synthesis," *Strategic Management Journal* 10 (1989), 211–231.
33 P. R. Lawrence and J. W. Lorsch, *Organization and Environment* (Cambridge, MA: Harvard University Press, 1967).
34 D. Miller, "Strategy Making and Structure: Analysis and Implications for Performance," *Academy of Management Journal* 30 (1987), 7–32.
35 A. Deutschman, "If They're Gaining on You, Innovate," *Fortune*, November 2, 1992, p. 86.
36 www.avon.com, 2011.
37 Ibid.
38 T. J. Peters and R. H. Waterman, Jr., *In Search of Excellence* (New York: Harper & Row, 1982).
39 E. Deal and A. A. Kennedy, *Corporate Cultures* (Reading, MA: Addison-Wesley, 1985).
40 M. E. Porter, "From Competitive Advantage to Competitive Strategy," *Harvard Business Review* (May–June 1987): 43–59.
41 Based on Chandler, *Strategy and Structure*.
42 Chandler, *Strategy and Structure*; J. Pfeffer and G. R. Salancik, *The External Control of Organizations* (New York: Harper & Row, 1978).
43 Williamson, *Markets and Hierarchies*; K. R. Harrigan, *Strategic Flexibility* (Lexington, MA: Lexington Books, 1985).
44 Porter, "From Competitive Advantage to Competitive Strategy."
45 C. W. L. Hill, "Hanson PLC," in C. W. L. Hill and G. R. Jones, *Strategic Management: An Integrated Approach*, 4th ed. (Boston: Houghton Mifflin, 1998), pp. 764–783.
46 www.utc.com, 2011.
47 Ibid.
48 G. R. Jones and C. W. L. Hill, "Transaction Cost Analysis of Strategy-Structure Choice," *Strategic Management Journal* 9 (1988), 159–172.
49 www.scheringplough.com, 2007–2009.
50 www.bausch&lomb.com, 2011.

CHAPTER 9

Organizational Design, Competences, and Technology

Learning Objectives

This chapter focuses on technology and examines how organizations use it to build competences and create value. Then it discusses why certain forms of organizational structures are suitable for different types of technology, just as earlier chapters used a similar contingency approach to examine why certain environments or strategies typically require the use of certain forms of structure.

After studying this chapter you should be able to:

1. Identify what technology is and how it relates to organizational effectiveness.
2. Differentiate among three different kinds of technology that create different competences.
3. Understand how each type of technology needs to be matched to a certain kind of organizational structure if an organization is to be effective.
4. Understand how technology affects organizational culture.
5. Appreciate how advances in technology, and new techniques for managing technology, are helping increase organizational effectiveness.

What Is Technology?

When we think of an organization, we are likely to think of it in terms of what it does. We think of manufacturing organizations like Whirlpool or Ford as places where people use their skills in combination with machinery and equipment to assemble inputs into appliances, cars, and other finished products. We view service organizations like hospitals and banks as places where people apply their skills in combination with machinery or equipment to make sick people well or to facilitate customers' financial transactions. In all manufacturing and service organizations, activities are performed to create value—that is, inputs are converted into goods and services that satisfy people's needs.

Technology
The combination of skills, knowledge, abilities, techniques, materials, machines, computers, tools, and other equipment that people use to convert or change raw materials into valuable goods and services.

Technology is the combination of skills, knowledge, abilities, techniques, materials, machines, computers, tools, and other equipment that people use to convert or change raw materials, problems, and new ideas into valuable goods and services. When people at Ford, the Mayo Clinic, H&R Block, and Google use their skills, knowledge, materials, machines, and so forth, to produce a finished car, a cured patient, a completed tax return, or a new online application, they are using technology to bring about change to something to add value to it.

Inside an organization, technology exists at three levels: individual, functional or departmental, and organizational. At the *individual* level, technology is the personal skills, knowledge, and competences that individual women and men possess. At the *functional* or *departmental* level, the procedures and techniques that groups work out to perform their work create competences that constitute technology. The interactions of the members of a surgical operating team, the cooperative efforts of scientists in a research and development laboratory, and techniques developed by assembly-line workers are all examples of competences and technology at the functional or departmental level.

The way an organization converts inputs into outputs is often used to characterize technology at the *organizational* level. **Mass production** is the organizational technology based on competences in using a standardized, progressive assembly process to manufacture goods. **Craftswork** is the technology that involves groups of skilled workers interacting closely and combining their skills to produce custom-designed products. The difference between these two forms of technology is clearly illustrated in Organizational Insight 9.1.

Mass production
The organizational technology that uses conveyor belts and a standardized, progressive assembly process to manufacture goods.

Craftswork
The technology that involves groups of skilled workers who interact closely to produce custom-designed products.

Organizational Insight 9.1

Progressive Manufacture at Ford

In 1913, Henry Ford opened the Highland Park plant to produce the Model T car. In doing so, he changed forever the way complex products like cars are made, and the new technology of "progressive manufacture" (Ford's term), or mass production, was born. Before Ford introduced mass production, most cars were manufactured by craftswork. A team of workers—a skilled mechanic and a few helpers—performed all the operations necessary to make the product. Individual craftsworkers in the automobile and other industries have the skills to deal with unexpected situations as they arise during the manufacturing process. They can modify misaligned parts so that they fit together snugly, and they can follow specifications and create small batches of a range of products. Because craftswork relies on workers' skills and expertise, it is a costly and slow method of manufacturing. In searching for new ways to improve the efficiency of manufacturing, Ford developed the process of progressive manufacture.

Ford outlined three principles of progressive manufacture:

1. Work should be delivered to the worker; the worker should not have to find the work.[1] At the Highland Park plant, a mechanized, moving conveyor belt brought cars to the workers. Workers did not move past a stationary line of cars under assembly.
2. Work should proceed in an orderly and specific sequence so each task builds on the task that precedes it. At Highland Park, the implementation of this idea fell to managers, who worked out the most efficient sequence of tasks and coordinated them with the speed of the conveyor belt.
3. Individual tasks should be broken down into their simplest components to increase specialization and create an efficient division of labor. The assembly of a taillight, for example, might be broken into two separate tasks to be performed all day long by two different workers. One person puts lightbulbs into a reflective panel; the other person screws a red lens onto the reflective panel.

As a result of this new work system, by 1914 Ford plants employed 15,000 workers but only 255 supervisors (not including top

Brian Delft © Dorling Kindersley

management) to oversee them. The ratio of workers to supervisors was 58 to 1. This very wide span of control was possible because the sequence and pacing of the work were not directed by the supervisors but were controlled by work programming and the speed of the production line.[2] The mass production system helped Ford control many workers with a relatively small number of supervisors, but it also created a tall hierarchy. The hierarchy at a typical Ford plant had six levels, reflecting the fact that management's major preoccupation was the vertical communication of information to top management, which controlled decision making for the whole plant.

The introduction of mass production technology to auto making was only one of Henry Ford's technological manufacturing innovations. Another was the use of interchangeable parts. When parts are interchangeable, the components from various suppliers fit together; they do not need to be altered to fit during the assembly process. With the old craftswork method of production, a high level of worker competence was needed to fit together the components provided by different manufacturers, which often differed in size or quality. Ford insisted that component manufacturers follow detailed specifications so that parts needed no remachining and his relatively unskilled work force would be able to assemble them easily. Eventually, the desire to control the quality of inputs led Ford to embark on a massive program of vertical integration. Ford mined iron ore in its mines in Upper Michigan and transported the ore in a fleet of Ford-owned barges to Ford's steel plants in Detroit, where it was smelted, rolled, and stamped into standard body parts.

As a result of these technological innovations in manufacturing, by the early 1920s Henry Ford's organization was making over two million cars a year. Because of his efficient manufacturing methods, Ford reduced the price of a car by two-thirds. This low-price advantage, in turn, created a mass market for his product.[3] Clearly, as measured by standards of technical efficiency and the ability to satisfy external stakeholders such as customers, Ford Motor was a very effective organization. Inside the factories, however, the picture was not so rosy.

Workers hated their work. Ford managers responded to their discontent with repressive supervision. Workers were watched constantly. They were not allowed to talk on the production line, and their behavior both in the plant and outside was closely monitored. (For example, they were not allowed to drink alcohol, even when they were not working.) Supervisors could instantly fire workers who disobeyed any rules. So repressive were conditions that by 1914 so many workers had been fired or had quit that 500 new workers had to be hired each day to keep the work force at 15,000.[4] Clearly, the new technology of mass production was imposing severe demands on individual workers.

Technology and Organizational Effectiveness

Recall from Chapter 1 that organizations take inputs from the environment and create value from the inputs by transforming them into outputs through conversion processes (see Figure 9.1). Although we usually think of technology only at the conversion stage, technology is present in all organizational activities: input, conversion, and output.[5]

At the *input* stage, technology—skills, procedures, techniques, and competences—allows each organizational function to handle relationships with outside stakeholders so that the organization can effectively manage its specific environment. The human resource function, for example, has techniques such as interviewing procedures and

Figure 9.1 Input, Conversion, and Output Processes

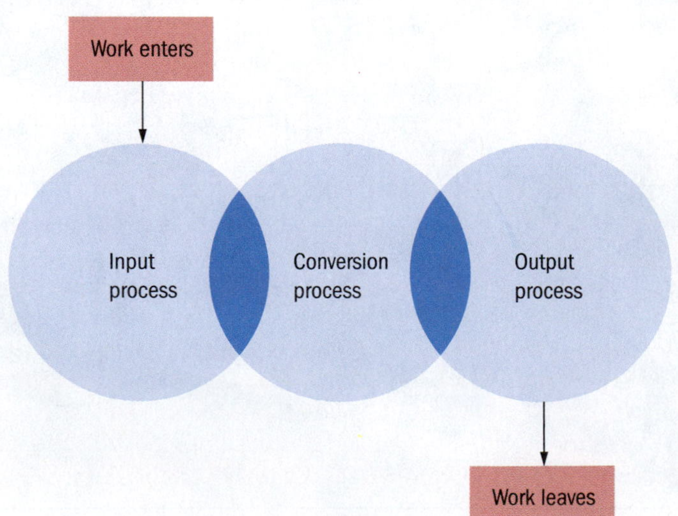

psychological testing that it uses to recruit and select qualified employees. The materials management function has developed competences in dealing with input suppliers, for negotiating favorable contract terms, and for obtaining low-cost, high-quality component parts. The finance department has techniques for obtaining capital at a cost favorable to the company.

At the *conversion stage*, technology—a combination of machines, techniques, and work procedures—transforms inputs into outputs. The best technology allows an organization to add the most value to its inputs at the least cost of organizational resources. Organizations often try to improve the efficiency of their conversion processes, and they can improve it by training employees in new time-management techniques and by allowing employees to devise better ways of performing their jobs.

At the *output stage*, technology allows an organization to effectively dispose of finished goods and services to external stakeholders. To be effective, an organization must possess competences in testing the quality of the finished product, in selling and marketing the product, and in managing after-sales service to customers.

The technology of an organization's input, conversion, and output processes is an important source of a company's competitive advantage. Why is Microsoft the most successful software company? Why is Toyota the highest-quality carmaker? Why is McDonald's the most efficient fast-food company? Why does Walmart consistently outperform Kmart and Sears? Each of these organizations excels in the development, management, and use of technology to create competences that lead to higher value for stakeholders.

Recall from Chapter 1 the three principal approaches to measuring and increasing organizational effectiveness (see Table 1.1). An organization taking the *external resource approach* uses technology to increase its ability to manage and control external stakeholders. Any new technological developments that allow an organization to improve its service to customers, such as the ability to customize products or to increase products' quality and reliability, increases the organization's effectiveness.

An organization taking the *internal systems approach* uses technology to increase the success of its attempts to innovate; to develop new products, services, and processes; and to reduce the time needed to bring new products to market. As we saw earlier, the introduction of mass production at the Highland Park plant allowed Henry Ford to make a new kind of product—a car for the mass market.

An organization taking the *technical approach* uses technology to improve efficiency and reduce costs while simultaneously enhancing the quality and reliability of its products. Ford increased his organization's effectiveness by organizing its functional resources to create better quality cars at a lower cost for both manufacturer and consumer.

Organizations use technology to become more efficient, more innovative, and better able to meet the needs and desires of stakeholders. Each department or function in an organization is responsible for building competences and developing technology that allows it to make a positive contribution to organizational performance. When an organization has technology that enables it to create value, it needs a structure that maximizes the effectiveness of the technology. Just as environmental characteristics require organizations to make certain organizational design choices, so do the characteristics of different technologies affect an organization's choice of structure.

In the next three sections we examine three theories of technology that are attempts to capture the way different departmental and organizational technologies work and affect organizational design. Note that these three theories are *complementary* in that each illuminates some aspects of technology that the others don't. All three theories are needed to understand the characteristics of different kinds of technologies. Managers, at all levels and in all functions, can use these theories to (1) choose the technology that will most effectively transform inputs into outputs and (2) design a structure that allows the organization to operate the technology effectively. Thus it is important for these managers to understand the concept of technical complexity, the underlying differences between routine and complex tasks, and the concept of task interdependence.

Technical Complexity: The Theory of Joan Woodward

Programmed technology
A technology in which the procedures for converting inputs into outputs can be specified in advance so that tasks can be standardized and the work process can be made predictable.

Technical complexity
A measure of the extent to which a production process can be programmed so that it can be controlled and made predictable.

Some kinds of technology are more complex and difficult to control than others because some are more difficult to program than others. Technology is said to be **programmed** when rules and SOPs for converting inputs into outputs can be specified in advance so that tasks can be standardized and the work process be made predictable. McDonald's uses a highly programmed technology to produce hamburgers and so does Ford to produce its vehicles, and they do so to control the quality of their outputs—hamburgers or cars. The more difficult it is to specify the process for converting inputs into outputs, the more difficult it is to control the production process and make it predictable.

According to one researcher, Joan Woodward, the **technical complexity** of a production process—that is, the extent to which it can be programmed so it can be controlled and made predictable—is the important dimension that differentiates technologies.[6] *High technical complexity* exists when conversion processes can be programmed in advance and fully automated. With full automation, work activities and the outputs that result from them are standardized and can be predicted accurately. *Low technical complexity* exists when conversion processes depend primarily on people and their skills and knowledge and not on machines. With increased human involvement and less reliance on machines, work activities cannot be programmed in advance, and results depend on the skills of the people involved.

The production of services, for example, typically relies much more on the knowledge and experience of employees who interact directly with customers to produce the final output than it relies on machines and other equipment. The labor-intensive nature of the production of services makes standardizing and programming work activities and controlling the work process especially difficult. When conversion processes depend primarily on the performance of people, rather than on machines, technical complexity is low, and the difficulty of maintaining high quality and consistency of production is great.

Joan Woodward identified ten levels of technical complexity, which she associated with three types of production technology: (1) small-batch and unit technology, (2) large-batch and mass production technology, and (3) continuous-process technology (see Figure 9.2).[7]

Small-Batch and Unit Technology

Organizations that employ small-batch and unit technology make one-of-a-kind customized products or small quantities of products. Examples of such organizations include a furniture maker that constructs furniture customized to the needs and tastes of specific clients, a printer that supplies the engraved wedding invitations that a particular couple desires, and teams of surgeons who work in specialized hospitals that provide a specific set of services such as eye or knee surgery. Small-batch and unit technology scores lowest on the dimension of technical complexity (see Figure 9.2) because any machines used during the conversion process are less important than people's skills and knowledge. People decide how and when to use machines, and the production operating process reflects their decisions about how to apply their knowledge. A custom furniture maker, for example, uses an array of tools—including lathes, hammers, planes, and saws—to transform boards into a cabinet. However, which tools are used and the order in which they are used depends on how the furniture maker chooses to build the cabinet. With small-batch and unit technology, the conversion process is flexible because the worker adapts techniques to suit the needs and requirements of individual customers.

The flexibility of small-batch technology gives an organization the capacity to produce a wide range of products that can be customized for individual customers. For example, high-fashion designers and makers of products like fine perfume, custom-built cars, and specialized furniture use small-batch technology. Small-batch technology allows a custom furniture maker, for example, to satisfy the customer's request for a certain style of table made from a certain kind of wood.

Figure 9.2 Technical Complexity and Three Types of Technology

Joan Woodward identified ten levels of technical complexity, which she associated with three types of production.

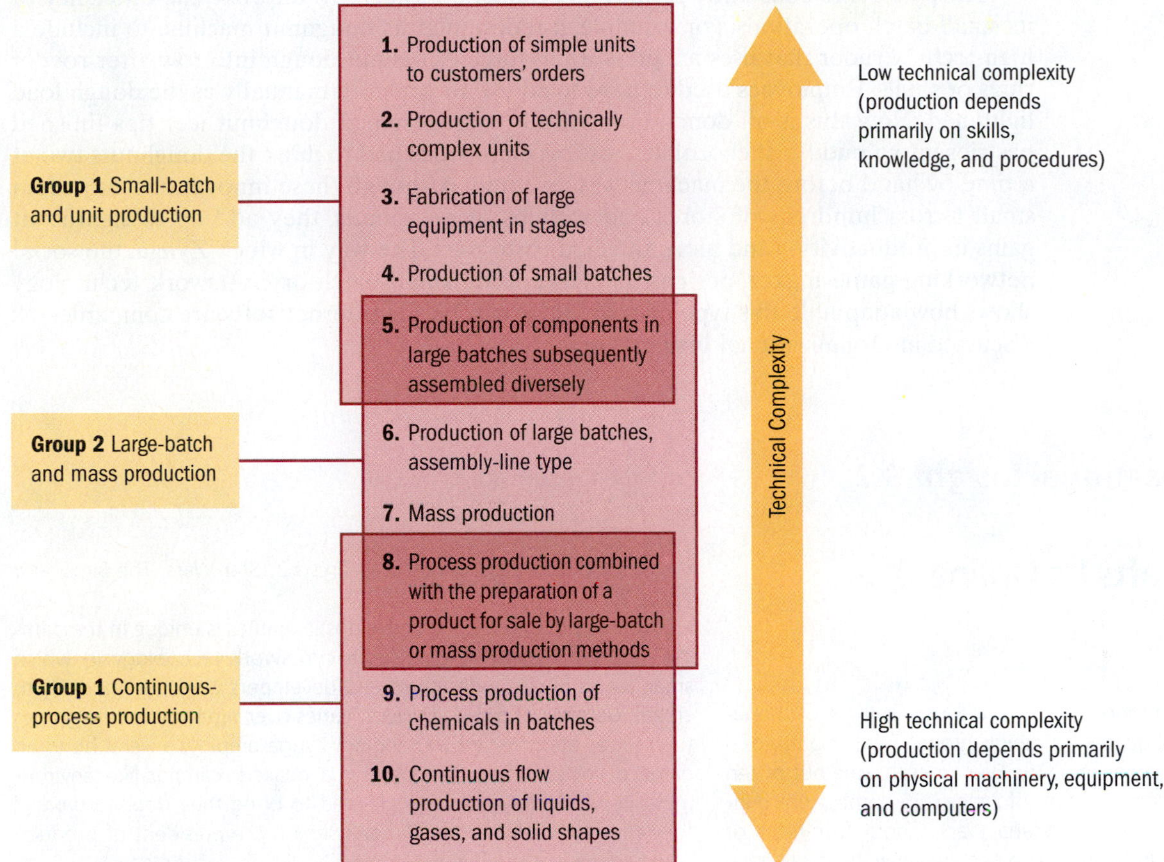

Source: Adapted from Joan Woodward, *"Management and Technology,"* London: Her Majesty's Stationery Office, 1958, p. 11. Reproduced with permission of the Controller of Her Britannic Majesty's Stationery Office on behalf of Parliament.

Small-batch technology is relatively expensive to operate because the work process is unpredictable and the production of customized made-to-order products makes advance programming of work activities difficult. However, flexibility and the ability to respond to a wide range of customer requests make this technology ideally suited to producing new or complex products. Google uses small-batch technology when it assigns a team of software engineers to work together to develop new software applications; so does a maker of doughnuts.

Founded in 1937 in Newington, Connecticut, Krispy Kreme is a leading specialty retailer of premium-quality yeast-raised doughnuts. Krispy Kreme's doughnuts have a broad customer following and command a premium price because of their unique taste and quality. The way it uses small-batch production to increase its operating efficiency and responsiveness to customers is instructive. Krispy Kreme calls its store production operations "doughnut theater" because its physical layout is designed so that customers can see and smell the doughnuts being made by its impressive company-built doughnut-making machines.

What are elements of its small-batch production methods? The story starts with the 65-year-old company's secret doughnut recipe that it keeps locked up in a vault. None of its franchisees know the recipe for making its dough, and Krispy Kreme sells the ready-made dough and other ingredients to its stores. Even the machines used to make the doughnuts are company designed and produced, so no doughnut maker can imitate its unique cooking methods and thus create a similar competing product.

The doughnut-making machines are designed to produce a wide variety of different kinds of doughnuts in small quantities, and each store makes and sells between 4,000 and 10,000 dozen doughnuts per day.

Krispy Kreme constantly refines its production system to improve the efficiency of its small-batch operations. For example, it redesigned its doughnut machine to include a high-tech extruder that uses air pressure to force doughnut dough into row after row of rings or shells. Employees used to have to adjust air pressure manually as the dough load lightened. Now this is all done automatically. A redesigned doughnut icer tips finished pastries into a puddle of chocolate frosting; employees had to dunk the doughnuts two at a time by hand before the machine was invented. Although these innovations may seem small, across hundreds of stores and millions of doughnuts, they add up to significant gains in productivity—and more satisfied customers. The way in which Zynga, the social networking game maker, designs its games using small-batch or craftswork technology shows how adaptable this type of technology can be for Internet software companies, as discussed in Organizational Insight 9.2.

Organizational Insight 9.2

How Zynga Crafts Its Online Social Games

Zynga Inc., based near Marina del Rey, California, is the most popular maker of online social games—a rapidly growing and highly competitive segment of the games industry. Every month, one out of ten users of the WWW plays one or more of Zynga's 55 games, which include FarmVille, Zynga Poker, and Mafia Wars. About four-fifths of the U.S. population—around 250 million people—play its games each month. In May 2011 Zynga rolled out its newest online game, Empires & Allies, that took the company into a new gaming arena, that of "action and strategy" games, which have been dominated by established global game developers like Electronic Arts (EA), some of whose blockbuster games include Crysis 2, Star Wars, The Sims, and Portal 2.

The way in which Zynga develops its games is unique in the gaming industry because it employs a craftswork technology in which small teams of game designers and developers work continuously to create, develop, and then perfect games over time so that the games themselves are constantly changing. Zynga employs several hundred game developers and designers in a relaxed, campus-like environment in which they are even allowed to bring their dogs to work if they choose. Mark Skaggs, Zynga's senior vice president of product, summed up the way the company's design technology works as "fast, light, and right."[8] Zynga's games take only a few weeks or months to design. Why? Because its teams of developers work in self-managed groups that have around 30 members. All the activities of each team member's performance, and the way they continuously

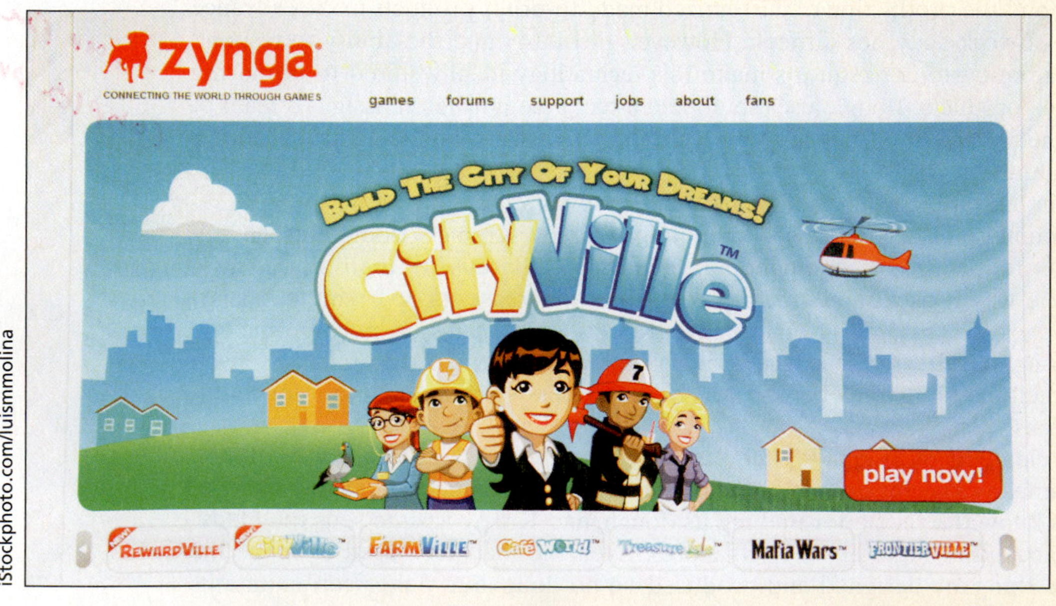

iStockphoto.com/luismmolina

make changes to a game, is immediately obvious to other team members because they are all linked through interactive realtime software that allows them to evaluate how the changes being made will affect the nature of the game. Team members can continuously approve, disapprove, or find ways to improve on the way a game's objectives and features are developing, to ensure the game will eventually appeal to Zynga's hundreds of millions of online users when it is released.

However, the other aspect of craftswork technology that works so well for Zynga lies in its competence to continue to customize and change every game it develops to better appeal to the likes and dislikes of its users—even *after* the game has been released online. Unlike more established game makers like EA, much of the game development that takes place after a Zynga game is released occurs as its designers work—often round-the-clock—to add content, correct errors, test new features, and constantly adjust the game based upon real-time feedback about how game players are "interacting" with it, and to find out what users enjoy the most. One of Zynga's unique competences is its ability to track the performance of each feature and design element of a game. By what it calls A/B testing, Zynga creates two different groups of online players—A and B—who act as guinea pigs as their responses to a game that has been modified or improved with new features are monitored. By counting how many players click on the new feature, Zynga knows if players like it and what they want, so its developers can continuously change the dynamics of the game to make it more satisfying to users.

The result is that its online games get better and better over time in the sense that they become more appealing to users. As Greg Black, Empires & Allies' lead game designer, says, "We can mine our users and see in real time what they like to do."[9] So, for example, while the first thousands of players of Empires & Allies were trying to work out how to play the game and conquer their rivals on their computer screens, the game's developers were watching their efforts and using their experiences to continually craft and improve the way the game is played to make it more exciting.

This amazing interactive approach to online game development is quite different from the technology used by game developers like EA, which may use hundreds of developers who take two years or more to finalize a new game before it is released for sale. EA, of course makes its money from the revenues earned on the sales of each game, which are often priced at $50–75, and a successful game can sell 50 million copies. In Zynga's model, however, all the online games are provided free of charge to hundreds of millions of online users. Online social games focus on the number of daily active users, which in Zynga's case is 50 million a day (it has an audience of 240 million players on Facebook alone). So, if only 2–5% of its players spend money on the extra game features that can be bought cheaply—often for nickels or dimes—with 50 million users a day Zynga is already obtaining revenues of over $200 million a year. And, the more games that Zynga can encourage users to play, the more money its earns! Small wonder that when the company announced a public offering of its shares in 2011, analysts estimated the company would be worth $20 billion!

Large-Batch and Mass Production Technology

To increase control over the work process and make it predictable, organizations try to increase their use of machines and equipment—that is, they try to increase the level of technical complexity and to increase their efficiency. Organizations that employ large-batch or mass production technology produce massive volumes of standardized products, such as cars, razor blades, aluminum cans, and soft drinks. Examples of such organizations include Ford, Gillette, Crown Cork and Seal, and Coca-Cola. With large-batch and mass production technology, machines control the work process. Their use allows tasks to be specified and programmed in advance. As a result, work activities are standardized, and the production process is highly controllable.[10] Instead of a team of craftsworkers making custom furniture piece by piece, for example, high-speed saws and lathes cut and shape boards into standardized components that are assembled into thousands of identical tables or chairs by unskilled workers on a production line, such as those produced in the factories of IKEA's global suppliers (see Closing Case, Chapter 3).

The control provided by large-batch and mass production technology allows an organization to save money on production and charge a lower price for its products. As Organizational Insight 9.1 describes, Henry Ford changed manufacturing history when he replaced small-batch production (the assembly of cars one by one by skilled workers) with mass production to manufacture the Model T. The use of a conveyor belt, standardized and interchangeable parts, and specialized progressive tasks made conversion processes at the Highland Park plant more efficient and productive. Production costs plummeted, and Ford was able to lower the cost of a Model T and create a mass market for his product. In a similar way, IKEA today also operates its own factories where its engineers specialize in finding ways to make furniture more efficiently; IKEA then transfers this knowledge to its global suppliers.[11]

Continuous-Process Technology

With continuous-process technology, technical complexity reaches its height (see Figure 9.2). Organizations that employ continuous-process technology include companies that make oil-based products and chemicals, such as Exxon, DuPont, and Dow, and brewing companies, such as Anheuser-Busch and Miller Brewing. In continuous-process production, the conversion process is almost entirely automated and mechanized; employees generally are not directly involved. Their role in production is to monitor the plant and its machinery and ensure its efficient operation.[12] The task of employees engaged in continuous-process production is primarily to manage exceptions in the work process, such as a machine breakdown or malfunctioning equipment.

The hallmark of continuous-process technology is the smoothness of its operation. Production continues with little variation in output and rarely stops. In an oil refinery, for example, crude oil brought continuously to the refinery by tankers flows through pipes to cracking towers, where its individual component chemicals are extracted and sent to other parts of the refinery for further refinement. Final products such as gasoline, fuel oil, benzene, and tar leave the plant in tankers to be shipped to customers. Workers in a refinery or in a chemical plant rarely see what they are producing. Production takes place through pipes and machines. Employees in a centralized control room monitor gauges and dials to ensure that the process functions smoothly, safely, and efficiently.

Continuous-process production tends to be more technically efficient than mass production because it is more mechanized and automated and thus is more predictable and easier to control. It is more cost efficient than both unit and mass production because labor costs are such a small proportion of its overall cost. When operated at full capacity, continuous-process technology has the lowest production costs.

Woodward noted that an organization usually seeks to increase its use of machines (if it is practical to do so) and move from small-batch to mass production to continuous-process production to reduce costs. There are, however, exceptions to this progression. For many organizational activities, the move to automate production is not possible or practical. Prototype development, basic research into new drugs or novel computer hardware or software applications, and the day-to-day operation of hospitals and schools, for example, are intrinsically unpredictable and thus would be impossible to program in advance using an automated machine. A pharmaceutical company cannot say, "Our research department will invent three new drugs—one for diabetes and two for high blood pressure—every six months." Such inventions are the result of trial and error and depend on the skills and knowledge of its researchers. Moreover, many customers are willing to pay high prices for custom-designed products that suit their individual tastes, such as custom-made suits, jewelry, or high-end gaming computers. Thus there is a market for the products of small-batch companies even though production costs are high.

Technical Complexity and Organizational Structure

One of Woodward's goals in classifying technologies according to their technical complexity was to discover whether an organization's technology affected the design of its structure. Specifically, she wanted to see whether effective organizations had structures that matched the needs of their technologies. A comparison of the structural characteristics of organizations pursuing each of the three types of technology revealed systematic differences in the technology–structure relationship.

On the basis of her findings, Woodward argued that each technology is associated with a different structure because each technology presents different control and coordination problems. Organizations with small-batch technology typically have three levels in their hierarchy; organizations with mass production technology, four levels; and organizations with continuous-process technology, six levels. As technical complexity increases, organizations become taller, and the span of control of the CEO widens. The span of control of first-line supervisors first expands and then narrows. It is relatively small with small-batch technology, widens greatly with mass production technology, and contracts dramatically with continuous-process technology. These findings result in the very differently shaped structures. Why does the nature of an organization's technology produce these results?

The main coordination problem associated with *small-batch technology* is the impossibility of programming conversion activities because production depends on the skills and experience of people working together. An organization that uses small-batch technology has to give people the freedom to make their own decisions so they can respond quickly and flexibly to the customer's requests and produce the exact product the customer wants. For this reason, such an organization has a relatively flat structure (three levels in the hierarchy), and decision making is decentralized to small teams where first-line supervisors have a relatively small span of control (23 employees). With small-batch technology, each supervisor and work group decides how to manage each decision as it occurs at each step of the input-conversion-output process. This type of decision making requires mutual adjustment—face-to-face communication with coworkers and often with customers. The most appropriate structure for unit and small-batch technology is an organic structure in which managers and employees work closely to coordinate their activities to meet changing work demands, which is a relatively flat structure.[13]

In an organization that uses *mass production technology*, the ability to program tasks in advance allows the organization to standardize the manufacturing process and make it predictable. The first-line supervisor's span of control increases to 48 because formalization through rules and procedures becomes the principal method of coordination. Decision making becomes centralized, and the hierarchy of authority becomes taller (four levels) as managers rely on vertical communication to control the work process. A *mechanistic structure* becomes the appropriate structure to control work activities in a mass production setting, and the organizational structure becomes taller and wider.

In an organization that uses *continuous-process technology*, tasks can be programmed in advance and the work process is predictable and controllable in a technical sense, but there is still the potential for a major systems breakdown. The principal control problem facing the organization is monitoring the production process to control and correct unforeseen events before they lead to disaster. The consequences of a faulty pipeline in an oil refinery or chemical plant, for example, are potentially disastrous. Accidents at a nuclear power plant, another user of continuous-process technology, can also have catastrophic effects, as accidents at Three Mile Island, Chernobyl, and most recently the meltdown at the Fukushima nuclear plant in Japan in 2011 following a disastrous tsunami have shown.

The need to constantly monitor the operating system, and to make sure that each employee conforms to accepted operating procedures, is the reason why continuous-process technology is associated with the tallest hierarchy of authority (six levels). Managers at all levels must closely monitor their subordinates' actions, and first-line supervisors have a narrow span of control, which creates a very tall, diamond-shaped hierarchy. Many supervisors are needed to supervise lower-level employees and to monitor and control sophisticated equipment. Because employees also work together as a team and jointly work out procedures for managing and reacting to unexpected situations, mutual adjustment becomes the primary means of coordination. Thus an *organic structure* is the appropriate structure for managing continuous-process technology because the potential for unpredictable events requires the capability to provide quick, flexible responses.

One researcher, Charles Perrow, argues that complex continuous-process technology such as the technology used in nuclear power plants is so complicated that it is uncontrollable.[14] Perrow acknowledges that control systems are designed with backup systems to handle problems as they arise and that backup systems exist to compensate for failed backup systems. He believes nevertheless that the number of unexpected events that can occur when technical complexity is very high (as it is in nuclear power plants) is so great that managers cannot react quickly enough to solve all the problems that might arise. Perrow argues that some continuous-process technology is so complex that no organizational structure can allow managers to safely operate it, no standard operating procedures can be devised to manage problems in advance, and no integrating mechanism used to promote mutual adjustments will be able to solve problems as they arise. One implication of Perrow's view is that nuclear power stations should be closed because they are too complex to operate safely. Other researchers, however, disagree, arguing that when the right balance of centralized and decentralized control is achieved, the technology can be operated safely. However, in 2011, after the catastrophe in Japan, Germany announced it would close all 22 of its nuclear power plants by 2022, and Japan was evaluating the safety of continuing to operate its other reactors in a country prone to earthquakes.

The Technological Imperative

Woodward's results strongly suggest that technology is a main factor that determines the design of organizational structure.[15] Her results imply that if a company operates with a certain technology, then it needs to adopt a certain kind of structure to be effective. If a company uses mass production technology, for example, then it should have a mechanistic structure with six levels in the hierarchy, a span of control of 1 to 48, and so on, to be effective. The argument that technology determines structure is known as the **technological imperative.**

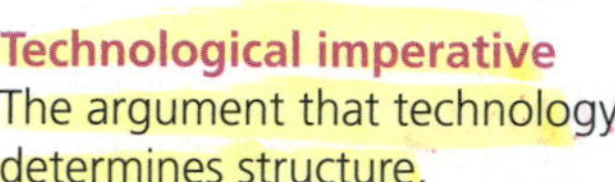

Technological imperative The argument that technology determines structure.

Other researchers also interested in the technology–structure relationship became concerned that Woodward's results may have been a consequence of the sample of companies she studied and may have overstated the importance of technology.[16] They point out that most of the companies that Woodward studied were relatively small (82% had fewer than 500 employees) and suggested that her sample may have biased her results. They acknowledge that technology may have a major impact on structure in a small manufacturing company because improving the efficiency of manufacturing may be management's major priority. But they suggested the structure of an organization that has 5,000 or 500,000 employees (such as Exxon or Walmart) is less likely to be determined primarily by the technology used to manufacture its various products.

In a series of studies known as the Aston Studies, researchers agreed that technology has some effect on organizational structure: The more an organization's technology is mechanized and automated, the more likely is the organization to have a highly centralized and standardized mechanistic structure. But, the Aston Studies concluded, organizational size is more important than technology in determining an organization's choice of structure.[17] We have seen in earlier chapters that as an organization grows and differentiates, control and coordination problems emerge that changes in the organization's structure must address. The Aston researchers argue that although technology may strongly affect the structure of small organizations, the structure adopted by large organizations may be a product of other factors that cause an organization to grow and differentiate.

We saw in Chapter 8 that organizational strategy and the decision to produce a wider range of products and enter new markets can cause an organization to grow and adopt a more complex structure. Thus the strategic choices that an organization—especially a large organization—makes about what products to make for which markets affect the design of an organization's structure as much as or more than the technology the organization uses to produce the outputs. For small organizations or for functions or departments within large organizations, the importance of technology as a predictor of structure may be more important than it is for large organizations.[18]

Routine Tasks and Complex Tasks: The Theory of Charles Perrow

To understand why some technologies are more complex (more unpredictable and difficult to control) than others, it is necessary to understand why the tasks associated with some technologies are more complex than the tasks associated with other technologies. What causes one task to be more difficult than another? Why, for example, do we normally think the task of serving hamburgers in a fast-food restaurant is more routine—that is, more predictable and controllable—than the task of programming a computer or performing brain surgery? If all the possible tasks that people perform are considered, what characteristics of these tasks lead us to believe that some are more complex than others? According to Charles Perrow, two dimensions underlie the difference between routine and nonroutine or complex tasks and technologies: task variability and task analyzability.[19]

Task Variability and Task Analyzability

Task variability is the number of exceptions—new or unexpected situations—that a person encounters while performing a task. Exceptions may occur at the input, conversion, or output stage. Task variability is high when a person can expect to encounter many new situations or problems when performing his or her task. In a hospital operating room during the course of surgery, for example, there is much opportunity for unexpected problems to develop. The patient's condition may be more serious than the doctors thought it was, or the surgeon may make a mistake. No matter what happens, the surgeon and the operating team must have the capacity to adjust quickly to new situations as they occur. Similarly, great variability in the quality of the raw materials makes it especially difficult to manage and maintain consistent quality during the conversion stage.

Task variability The number of exceptions—new or unexpected situations—that a person encounters while performing a task.

Task variability is low when a task is highly standardized or repetitious so a worker encounters the same situation time and time again.[20] In a fast-food restaurant, for example, the number of exceptions to a given task is limited. Each customer places a different order, but all customers must choose from the same limited menu, so employees rarely confront unexpected situations. In fact, the menu in a fast-food restaurant is designed for low task variability, which keeps costs down and efficiency up.

Task analyzability is the degree to which search and information-gathering activity is required to solve a problem. The more analyzable a task, the less search activity is needed; such tasks are routine because the information and procedures needed to complete it have been discovered, rules have been worked out and formalized, and the way to perform a task can be programmed in advance. For example, although a customer may select thousands of combinations of food from a menu at a fast-food restaurant, the order taker's task of fulfilling each customer's order is relatively easy. The problem of combining foods in a bag is easily analyzable: The order taker picks up the drink and puts it in the bag, then adds the fries, burger, and so on, folds down the top of the bag, and hands the bag to the customer. Little thought or judgment is needed to complete an order.

Task analyzability The degree to which search activity is needed to solve a problem.

Tasks are hard to analyze when they cannot be programmed—that is, when procedures for carrying them out and dealing with exceptions cannot be worked out in advance. If a person encounters an exception, the information needed to create the procedures for dealing with the problem must be actively sought. For example, a scientist trying to develop a new cancer-preventing drug that has no side effects or a software programmer working on a program to enable computers to understand the spoken word has to spend considerable time and effort collecting data and working out the procedures for solving problems. Often, the search for a solution ends in failure. People working on tasks with low analyzability have to draw on their knowledge and judgment to search for new information and procedures to solve problems. When a great deal of search activity is required to find a solution to a problem and procedures cannot be programmed in advance, tasks are complex and nonroutine.

Together, task analyzability and task variability explain why some tasks are more routine than others. The greater the number of exceptions that workers encounter in the work process, and the greater the amount of search behavior required to find a solution to each exception, the more complex and less routine are tasks. For tasks that are routine, there are, in Perrow's words, "well-established techniques which are sure to work and these are applied to essentially similar raw materials. That is, there is little uncertainty about methods and little variety or change in the task that must be performed."[21] For tasks that are complex, "there are few established techniques; there is little certainty about methods, or whether or not they will work. But it also means that there may be a great variety of different tasks to perform."[22]

Four Types of Technology

Perrow used task variability and task analyzability to differentiate among four types of technology: routine manufacturing, craftswork, engineering production, and nonroutine research.[23] Perrow's model makes it possible to categorize the technology of an organization and the technology of departments and functions inside an organization.

ROUTINE MANUFACTURING Routine manufacturing is characterized by low task variability and high task analyzability. Few exceptions are encountered in the work process, and when an exception does occur, little search behavior is required to deal with it. Mass production is representative of routine technology.

In mass production settings, tasks are broken down into simple steps to minimize the possibility that exceptions will occur, and inputs are standardized to minimize disruptions to the production process. There are standard procedures to follow if an exception or a problem presents itself. The low-cost advantages of mass production are obtained by making tasks low in variability and high in analyzability. One reason why McDonald's has lower costs than its competitors is that it continually streamlines its menu choices and standardizes its work activities to reduce task variability and increase task analyzability.

CRAFTSWORK With craft technology, task variability is low (only a narrow range of exceptions is encountered), and task analyzability is also low (a high level of search activity is needed to find a solution to problems). Employees in an organization using this kind of technology need to adapt existing procedures to new situations and find new techniques to handle existing problems more effectively. This technology was used to build early automobiles, as we saw earlier. Other examples of craftswork are the manufacture of specialized or customized products like furniture, clothing, and machinery, and trades such as carpentry and plumbing. The tasks that a plumber, for example, is called on to perform center on installing or repairing bathroom or kitchen plumbing. But because every house is different, a plumber needs to adapt the techniques of the craft to each situation and find a unique solution for each house.

ENGINEERING PRODUCTION With engineering production technology, task variability is high and task analyzability is high. The number or variety of exceptions that workers may encounter in the task is high, but finding a solution is relatively easy because well-understood standard procedures have been established to handle the exceptions. Because these procedures are often codified in technical formulas, tables, or manuals, solving a problem is often a matter of identifying and applying the right technique. Thus, in organizations that use engineering production technology, existing procedures are used to make many kinds of products. A manufacturing company may specialize in custom building machines such as drill presses or electric motors. A firm of architects may specialize in customizing apartment buildings to the needs of different builders. A civil engineering group may use its skills in constructing airports, dams, and hydroelectric projects to service the needs of clients throughout the world. Like craftswork, engineering production is a form of small-batch technology because people are primarily responsible for developing techniques to solve particular problems.

NONROUTINE RESEARCH Nonroutine research technology is characterized by high task variability and low task analyzability and is the most complex and least routine of the four technologies in Perrow's classification. Tasks are complex because not only is the number of unexpected situations large, but search activity is high. Each new situation creates a need to expend resources to deal with it.

High-tech research and development activities are examples of nonroutine research. For people working at the forefront of technical knowledge, there are no prepackaged solutions to problems. There may be a thousand well-defined steps to follow when building the perfect bridge (engineering production technology), but there are few well-defined steps to take to discover a vaccine for AIDS, and hundreds of teams of researchers are continuously experimenting to find the breakthrough that will lead to such a universal cure.

An organization's top-management team is another example of a group that uses research technology. The teams' responsibility is to chart the future path of the organization and make the resource decisions that will be needed to ensure its success five or ten years ahead. Managers make these decisions in a highly uncertain context; however, they never know how successful their choices will be. Planning and forecasting by top management, and other nonroutine research activities, are inherently risky and uncertain because the technology is difficult to manage.

Routine Technology and Organizational Structure

Just as the types of technology identified by Woodward have implications for an organization's structure, so do the types of technology in Perrow's model. Perrow and others have suggested that an organization should move from a mechanistic to an organic structure as tasks become more complex and less routine.[24] Table 9.1 summarizes this finding.

When technology is routine, employees perform clearly defined tasks according to well-established rules and procedures. The work process is programmed in advance and standardized. Because the work process is standardized in routine technology, employees need only learn the procedures for performing the task effectively. For example, McDonald's uses written rules and procedures to train new personnel so the behavior of all McDonald's employees is consistent and predictable. Each new employee learns the right way to greet customers, the appropriate way to fulfill customer orders, and the correct way to make Big Macs.

Because employee tasks can be standardized with routine technology, the organizational hierarchy is relatively tall and decision making is centralized. Management's responsibility is to supervise employees and to manage the few exceptions that may occur, such as a breakdown of the production line. Because tasks are routine, all important production decisions are made at the top of the production hierarchy and transmitted down the chain of command as orders to lower-level managers and workers. It has been suggested that organizations with routine technology, such as that found in mass production settings, deliberately "de-skill" tasks, meaning that they simplify jobs by using machines to perform complex tasks and by designing the work process to minimize the degree to which workers' initiative or judgment is required.[25]

If an organization makes these design choices, it is using a mechanistic structure to operate its routine technology. This certainly is the choice of huge global outsourcing

TABLE 9.1 Routine and Nonroutine Tasks and Organizational Design

Structural Characteristic	Nature of Technology	
	Routine Tasks	**Nonroutine Tasks**
Standardization	High	Low
Mutual adjustment	Low	High
Specialization	Individual	Joint
Formalization	High	Low
Hierarchy of authority	Tall	Flat
Decision-making authority	Centralized	Decentralized
Overall structure	Mechanistic	Organic

companies such as Foxconn and Flextronics, whose factories in China extend over thousands of acres. Flextronics' main plant in China, for example, employs over 40,000 workers who work in three shifts for six days a week to assemble flat-screen TVs, Blu-ray players, and so on. Control is rigid in these factories; workers are only motivated by the prospect of earning three times the normal wage for such work, but even this was not enough, as the experience of Foxconn discussed in Organizational Insight 9.3 describes.

The use of low-cost outsourcing by companies to make products is not the only way to remain competitive, however, and many companies have reevaluated the way they manufacture products. In Japan, in particular, the soaring value of the yen against the dollar put pressure on carmakers and electronics manufacturers to look for new ways to organize their production operations to lower costs. Innovative electronics products command high prices, and the need to ensure consistent high quality and protect their proprietary technology are important concerns of Japanese electronics makers. So, to keep the assembly of complex new products at home and reduce operating costs, Japanese companies have scrutinized every aspect of their operating technology to find ways to improve routine assembly-line production.

Traditionally, Japanese companies have used the straight or linear conveyor belt system that is often hundreds of feet long to mass produce identical products. When reexamining this system, Japanese production managers came to realize that a considerable amount of handling time is wasted as the product being assembled is passed from worker to worker, and that a line can only move as fast as the least capable worker. Moreover, this system is only efficient when large quantities of the same product are being produced. If

Organizational Insight 9.3

Honda, Apple, and Foxconn Have Mass Production Problems in China

In 2010, Honda's Beijing-based Chinese subsidiary announced that strikes at three different Honda-owned mass production vehicle assembly and parts production factories had arisen because, "Poor communication led to a great deal of discontent and eventually developed into a labor dispute. Our company will reflect deeply on this and strengthen communication with employees and build mutual trust."[26] The strikes shut down all of Honda's Chinese operations for many days. Honda is just one of many overseas companies with operations in China that have become used to dealing with uneducated, compliant Chinese workers willing to work for China's minimum wage of around $113 or 900 Yuan a week. Chinese factory workers employed by overseas companies like Honda, Toyota, and GM have raised little opposition to these companies' pay and labor practices—even though they are represented by government-sanctioned labor unions.

This all began to change during 2010, when rising prices and changing attitudes in China led Chinese workers to protest their harsh work conditions—monotonous jobs, long hours, and low pay. However, companies such as Honda, used to a compliant workforce, had not bothered to establish formal communication channels with workers that would allow them to gather information about workers' changing attitudes. Honda's Japanese managers ran the factories, its Chinese supervisors trained the workers to perform their jobs, and Honda's Japanese managers had no feeling for the attitudes of workers in its factories, hence their shock when Chinese employees went on strike.

Foxconn, a giant outsourcer owned by the Taiwanese company Hon Hai Precision Engineering, employs hundreds of thousands of workers in its Chinese factories and these workers had also been compliant for years. They performed repetitive assembly line work along fast-moving production lines often for 80 hours a week, after which they were allowed to eat in the company's canteens before returning to their dormitories. This all changed in 2010, when Foxconn found itself in the spotlight when its biggest factory in Shenzhen, which assembles Apple's iPhone, reported that over 11 workers had committed suicide by jumping off buildings in the past year. Because most workers are young, uneducated, and come from small farming communities, Foxconn had just taken advantage of workers' passivity and willingness to work at minimum wage. Indeed, Foxconn had steadily increased the number of hours workers were forced to work on assembly lines that moved at a rapid speed—a workweek of 80 hours performing the same repetitive task for $113 was common. U.S. companies such as Apple and Dell had sent inspectors to monitor factory conditions and had found many violations. However, once again, inspectors made no attempt to communicate directly with workers; they simply studied the companies' employment records.[27]

In any event, Honda, Foxconn, and many other foreign-owned companies have been forced to rapidly change their labor practices. In 2010, for example, Foxconn announced it would double the pay of its workers to make their work more palatable and Honda also agreed to increase the wages of its workers by over 60% and establish formal channels so managers can meet with union representatives regularly to find ways to improve work practices.[28] Problems of operating a mass production technology are likely to increase in the years ahead as companies in China find it harder to attract and keep workers who want better pay and working conditions.

customized products are what is needed, something increasingly common today, the production line is typically down while it is being retooled for the next product.

Recognizing these problems, production engineers searched for new ways to organize and control assembly-line layouts that could solve these problems. They began to experiment with layouts of various shapes, such as spirals, Ys, 6s, or even insects. At a Sony camcorder plant in Kohda, Japan, for example, Sony dismantled its previous assembly-line production system in which 50 workers worked sequentially to build a camcorder, and replaced it with a spiral arrangement in which four workers perform all the operations necessary to assemble the camcorder. Sony found this new way of organizing is 10% more efficient than the old system because it allows the most efficient assemblers to perform at a higher level.[29] Essentially, a craftswork-like organizing structure has replaced the mechanistic structure to achieve the advantages of flexibility at lower cost.

In the United States too, these new production layouts, normally referred to as *cell layouts,* have become increasingly common. It has been estimated that 40% of small companies and 70% of large companies have experimented with the new designs. Bayside Controls Inc., for example, a small gear-head manufacturer in Queens, New York, converted its 35-person assembly line into a four-cell design where seven to nine workers form a cell. The members of each cell perform all the operations involved in making the gear heads, such as measuring, cutting, and assembling the new gear heads. Bayside's managers say that the average production time necessary to make a gear has dropped to two days from six weeks, and it now makes 75 gear heads a day—up from 50 before the change—so costs have decreased significantly.[30] An additional advantage is that cell designs allow companies to be very responsive to the needs of individual customers, as this organizing approach permits the quick manufacture of small quantities of customized products.

Nonroutine Technology and Organizational Structure

Organizations operating a nonroutine technology face a different set of factors that affect the design of the organization.[31] As tasks become less routine and more complex, an organization has to develop a structure that allows employees to respond quickly to and manage an increase in the number and variety of exceptions and to develop new procedures to handle new problems.[32] As we saw in Chapter 4, an organic structure allows an organization to adapt rapidly to changing conditions. Organic structures are based on mutual adjustment between employees who work together, face to face, to develop procedures to find solutions to problems. Mutual adjustment through task forces and teams becomes especially important in facilitating communication and increasing integration between team members.

The more complex an organization's work processes, the more likely the organization is to have a relatively flat and decentralized structure that allows employees the authority and autonomy to cooperate to make decisions quickly and effectively.[33] The use of work groups and product teams to facilitate rapid adjustment and feedback among employees performing complex tasks is a key feature of such an organization.

The same design considerations are applicable at the departmental or functional level: To be effective, departments employing different technologies need different structures.[34] In general, departments performing nonroutine tasks are likely to have organic structures, and those performing routine tasks are likely to have mechanistic structures. An R&D department, for example, is typically organic, and decision making in it is usually decentralized; but the manufacturing and sales functions are usually mechanistic, and decision making within them tends to be centralized. The kind of technology employed at the departmental level determines the choice of structure.[35]

Task Interdependence: The Theory of James D. Thompson

Woodward focused on how an organization's technology affects its choice of structure. Perrow's model of technology focuses on the way in which the complexity of tasks affects organizational structure. Another view of technology, developed by James D. Thompson,

Task interdependence The manner in which different organizational tasks are related to one another.

focuses on the way in which **task interdependence,** the method used to relate or sequence different tasks to one another, affects an organization's technology and structure.[36] When task interdependence is low, people and departments are individually specialized—that is, they work separately and independently to achieve organizational goals. When task interdependence is high, people and departments are jointly specialized—that is, they depend on one another for supplying the inputs and resources they need to get the work done. Thompson identified three types of technology: mediating, long linked, and intensive (see Figure 9.3). Each of them is associated with a different form of task interdependence.

Mediating Technology and Pooled Interdependence

Mediating technology A technology characterized by a work process in which input, conversion, and output activities can be performed independently of one another.

Mediating technology is characterized by a work process in which input, conversion, and output activities can be performed independently of one another. Mediating technology is based on *pooled task interdependence*, which means that each part of the organization—whether a person, team, or department—contributes separately to the performance of the whole organization. With mediating technology, task interdependence is low because people do not directly rely on others to help them perform their tasks. As illustrated in Figure 9.3, each person or department—X, Y, and Z—performs a separate task. In a management consulting firm or hair salon, each consultant or hairdresser works independently to solve a client's problems. The success of the organization as a whole, however, depends on the collective efforts of everyone employed. The activities of a gymnastic team also illustrate pooled task interdependence. Each team member performs independently and can win or lose a particular event, but the collective score of the team members

Figure 9.3 Task Interdependence and Three Types of Technology

James D. Thompson's model of technology focuses on how the relationship among different organizational tasks affects an organization's technology and structure.

Type of technology	Form of task interdependence	Main type of coordination	Strategy for reducing uncertainty	Cost of coordination
Mediating	Pooled X Y Z *(e.g., piecework or franchise)*	Standardization	Increase in the number of customers served	Low
Long linked	Sequential X→Y→Z *(e.g., assembly-line or continuous-process plant)*	Planning and scheduling	Slack resources Vertical integration	Medium
Intensive	Reciprocal X↔Y↔Z *(e.g., general hospital or research and development laboratory)*	Mutual adjustment	Specialism of task activities	High

determines which team wins. Mediating technology has implications for organizational structure at both the departmental and the organizational level.

At the departmental level, piecework systems best characterize the way this technology operates. In a piecework system, each employee performs a task independently from other employees. In a machine shop, for example, every employee operates a lathe to produce bolts and is evaluated and rewarded on the basis of how many bolts each of them makes each week. The performance of the manufacturing department as a whole depends on each employee's level of performance, but their actions are not interdependent—one employee's actions do not affect the behavior of others. Similarly, the success of a sales department depends on how well each salesperson performs their activities independently. As a result, the use of a mediating technology to accomplish departmental or organizational activities makes it easy to monitor, control, and evaluate the performance of each individual because the output of each person is observable and the same standards can be used to evaluate each employee.[37]

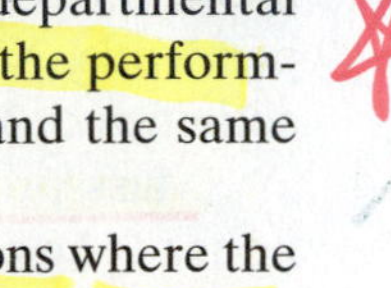

At the organizational level, mediating technology is found in organizations where the activities of different departments are performed separately and there is little need for integration between departments to accomplish organizational goals. In a bank, for example, the activities of the loan department and the checking account department are independent. The routines involved in lending money have no relation to the routines involved in receiving money—but the performance of the bank as a whole depends on how well each department does its job.[38]

Mediating technology at the organizational level is also found in organizations that use franchise arrangements to organize their businesses or that operate a chain of stores. For example, each McDonald's franchise or Walmart store operates essentially independently. The performance of one store does not affect another store, but together all stores determine the performance of the whole organization. One common strategy for improving organizational performance for an organization operating a mediating technology is to obtain more business from existing customers and attract new customers by increasing the number of products it offers. A fast-food chain can open a new restaurant or offer a wider menu; a retail organization can open a new store or expand the brands of clothing it sells; a bank can increase the number of financial services it offers customers to attract more business.

Over the past decades the use of mediating technology has been increasing because it is relatively inexpensive to operate and manage. Costs are low because organizational activities are controlled by standardization. Bureaucratic rules are used to specify how the activities of different departments should be coordinated, and SOPs control the way a department operates to ensure its activities are compatible with those of other departments. SOPs and advanced IT including electronic inventory control provide the coordination necessary to manage the business. Walmart, for example, coordinates its stores through advanced IT that provides store managers with realtime information about new product introductions, store deliveries, and changes in marketing and sales procedures.

As IT becomes more important in coordinating the activities of independent employees or departments, it becomes possible to use a mediating technology to coordinate more types of production activities. Network organizations, discussed in Chapter 6, are becoming more common as IT allows the different departments of an organization to operate separately and at different locations. Similarly, IT has spurred global outsourcing and today companies frequently contract with other companies to perform their value-creation activities (like production or marketing) for them because it is much easier to use mediating technology.

Recall from Chapter 3 how Nike contracts with manufacturers throughout the world to produce and distribute products to its customers on a global basis. Nike designs its shoes but then uses IT to contract its manufacturing, marketing, and other functional activities out to other organizations around the globe. Nike constantly monitors production and sales information from its network by means of a sophisticated global IT system to ensure its global network follows the rules and procedures that specify the required quality of input materials and the way its shoes should be manufactured to ensure the quality of the finished product.

Long-Linked Technology and Sequential Interdependence

Long-linked technology
A technology characterized by a work process in which input, conversion, and output activities must be performed in series.

Long-linked technology, the second type of technology that Thompson identified, is based on a work process where input, conversion, and output activities must be performed in series. Long-linked technology is based on *sequential task interdependence*, which means that the actions of one person or department directly affect the actions of another, so work cannot be successfully completed by allowing each person or department to operate independently. Figure 9.3 illustrates the dynamics of sequential interdependence. X's activities directly affect Y's ability to perform her task, and in turn the activities of Y directly affect Z's ability to perform.

Mass production technology is based on sequential task interdependence. The actions of the employee at the beginning of the production line determine how successfully the next employee can perform his task, and so forth on down the line. Because sequential interactions have to be carefully coordinated, long-linked technology requires more direct coordination than mediating technology. One result of sequential interdependence is that any error that occurs at the beginning of the production process becomes magnified at later stages. Sports activities like relay races or football, in which the performance of one person or group determines how well the next can perform, are based on sequential interdependence. In football, for example, the performance of the defensive line determines how well the offense can perform. If the defense is unable to secure the ball, the offense cannot perform its task: scoring touchdowns.

An organization with long-linked technology can respond in a variety of ways to the need to coordinate sequentially interdependent activities. The organization can program the conversion process to standardize the procedures used to transform inputs into outputs. The organization can also use planning and scheduling to manage linkages among input, conversion, and output processes. To reduce the need to coordinate these stages of production, an organization often creates **slack resources**—extra or surplus resources that enhance its organization's ability to deal with unexpected situations. For example, a mass production organization stockpiles inputs and holds inventories of component parts so the conversion process is not disrupted if there is a problem with suppliers. Similarly, an organization may stockpile finished products so it can respond quickly to an increase in customer demand without changing its established conversion processes. Another strategy to control the supply of inputs or distribution of outputs is *vertical integration*, which, as we saw in Chapter 8, involves a company taking over its suppliers or distributors to control the supply and quality of inputs.

Slack resources
Extra or surplus resources that enhance an organization's ability to deal with unexpected situations.

The need to manage the increased level of interdependence increases the coordination costs associated with long-linked technology. However, this type of technology can provide an organization with advantages stemming from specialization and the division of labor associated with sequential interdependence. Changing the method of production in a pin factory from a system where each worker produces a whole pin to a system where each worker is responsible for only one aspect of pin production, such as sharpening the pin, for example, can result in a major gain in productivity. Essentially, the factory moves from using a *mediating* technology, in which each worker performs all production tasks, to a *long-linked* technology, in which tasks become sequentially interdependent.

Tasks are routine in long-linked technology because sequential interdependence allows managers to simplify tasks so the variability of each worker's task is reduced and the analyzability of each task is increased. In mass production, for example, the coordination of tasks is achieved principally by the speed of the assembly line and by the way specialization and the division of labor are used to program tasks to increase production efficiency. This system, however, has two major disadvantages. Employees do not become highly skilled (they learn only a narrow range of simple tasks), and do not develop the ability to improve their skills because they must follow the specified procedures necessary to perform their specific task.

At the organizational level, sequential interdependence means that the outputs of one department become the inputs for another, and one department's performance determines how well another department performs. The performance of the manufacturing department depends on the ability of the materials management department to obtain adequate amounts of high-quality inputs in a timely manner. The ability of the sales function to sell finished products depends on the quality of the products coming out of the manufacturing department. Failure or poor performance at one stage has serious consequences for performance at the next stage and for the organization as a whole. The pressures of global competition are increasing the need for interdependence between departments and thus are increasing organizations' need to coordinate departmental activities. As we saw in Chapter 6, many organizations are moving toward the product team structure to increase interdepartmental coordination. This type of coordination encourages different departments to develop procedures that lead to greater production innovation and efficiency.

Intensive Technology and Reciprocal Interdependence

Intensive technology, the third type of technology Thompson identifies, is characterized by a work process where input, conversion, and output activities are inseparable. Intensive technology is based on *reciprocal task interdependence*, which means that the activities of all people and all departments fully depend on one another. Not only do X's actions affect what Y and Z can do, but the actions of Z also affect Y's and X's performance. The task relationships of X, Y, and Z are reciprocally interdependent (see Figure 9.3). Reciprocal interdependence makes it impossible to program in advance a sequence of tasks or procedures to solve a problem because, in Thompson's words, "the selection, combination, and order of [the tasks'] application are determined by *feedback from the object [problem] itself.*"[39] Thus the move to reciprocal interdependence and intensive technology has two effects: Technical complexity declines as the ability of managers to control and predict the work process lessens, and tasks become more complex and nonroutine.

Intensive technology A technology characterized by a work process in which input, conversion, and output activities are inseparable.

Hospitals are organizations that operate an intensive technology. A hospital's greatest source of uncertainty is the impossibility of predicting the types of problems for which patients (clients) will seek treatment. At any time, a general hospital has to have on hand the knowledge, machines, and services of specialist departments capable of solving a great variety of medical problems. For example, the hospital requires an emergency room, X-ray facilities, a testing laboratory, an operating room and staff, skilled nursing staff, doctors, and hospital wards. What is wrong with each patient determines the selection and combination of activities and technology to convert a hospital's inputs (sick people) into outputs (well people). The uncertainty of the input (patient) means that tasks cannot be programmed in advance—as they can be when interdependence is sequential.

Basketball, soccer, and rugby are other activities that depend on reciprocal interdependence. The current state of play determines the sequence of moves from one player to the next. The fast-moving action of these sports requires players to make judgments quickly and obtain feedback from the state of play before deciding what moves to make.

On a departmental level, R&D departments operate with an intensive technology, the sequence and content of their activities are determined by the problems the department is trying to solve—for example, a cure for lung cancer. R&D is so expensive because the unpredictability of the input-conversion-output process makes it impossible to specify in advance the skills and resources that will be needed to solve the problem at hand. A pharmaceutical company like Merck, for example, creates many different research and development teams. Every team is equipped with whatever functional resources it needs in the hope that at least one team will stumble onto the wonder drug that will justify the immense resource expenditures (each new drug costs over $500 million to develop).

The difficulty of specifying the sequencing of tasks that is characteristic of intensive technology makes necessary a high degree of coordination and makes intensive technology more expensive to manage than either mediating or long-linked technology. Mutual adjustment replaces programming and standardization as the principal method of coordination. Product team and matrix structures are suited to operating intensive technologies

because they provide the coordination and the decentralized control that allow departments to cooperate to solve problems. At Google and Accenture, for example, each company is organized into product teams so it can quickly move its specialists to the projects that seem most promising. Also, mutual adjustment and a flat structure allow an organization to quickly take advantage of new developments and areas for research that arise during the research process itself. Another way is to use self-managed teams, as Organizational Insight 9.4 illustrates.

Organizations do not voluntarily use intensive technology to achieve their goals because it is so expensive to operate. Like IBM and Accenture, they are forced to use it because of the nature of the products they choose to provide customers. Whenever possible, organizations attempt to reduce the task interdependence necessary to coordinate their activities and revert to a long-linked technology, which is more controllable and predictable. In recent years, for example, hospitals have attempted to control escalating management costs by using forecasting techniques to determine how many resources they

Organizational Insight 9.4

IBM and Accenture Use Technology to Create Virtual Organizations

Steven Newton/Shutterstock.com

Accenture, a global management consulting company, has been one of the pioneers in using IT to revolutionize its organizational structure. Its managing partners realized that since only its consultants in the field could diagnose and solve clients' problems, the company should design a structure that facilitates creative, on-the-spot decision making. To accomplish this, Accenture decided to replace its tall hierarchy of authority with a sophisticated IT system to create a virtual organization. First, it flattened the organizational hierarchy, eliminating many managerial levels, and set up a shared organization-wide IT system that provides each of Accenture's consultants with the information they need to solve clients' problems. If consultants still lack the specific knowledge needed to solve a problem, they can use the system to request expert help from Accenture's thousands of consultants around the globe.[40]

To implement the change, Accenture equipped all its consultants with state-of-the-art laptops and smartphones that can connect to its sophisticated corporate intranet and tap into Accenture's large information databases that contain volumes of potentially relevant information. The consultants can also communicate directly using their smartphones and use teleconferencing to help speed problem solving.[41] For example, if a project involves installing a particular kind of IT system, a consultant has quick access to consultants around the globe who have installed the system. Accenture has found that its virtual organization has increased the creativity of its consultants and enhanced their performance. By providing employees with more information and enabling them to confer with other people easily, electronic communication has made consultants more autonomous and willing to make their own decisions, which has led to high performance and made Accenture one of the best-known of all global consulting companies.

Similarly, IBM, which has been experiencing tough competition in the 2000s, has been searching for ways to better utilize its talented workforce to both lower costs and offer customers specialized kinds of services its competitors cannot. So IBM has also used IT to develop virtual teams of consultants to accomplish this.[42]

IBM has created "competency centers" around the globe that are staffed by consultants who share the same specific IT skill; its competency centers are located in the countries in which IBM has the most clients and does the most business. To use its consultants most effectively, IBM used its own IT expertise to develop sophisticated software that allows it to create self-managed teams composed of IBM consultants who have the optimum mix of skills to solve a client's particular problems. To form these teams, IBM's software engineers first analyze the skills and experience of its consultants and input the results into the software program. Then they analyze and code the nature of a client's specific problem and, using this information, IBM's program then matches each specific client problem to the skills of IBM's consultants and identifies a list of "best fit" employees. One of IBM's senior managers then narrows down this list and decides on the actual consultants who will form the self-managed team. Once selected, team members assemble as quickly as possible in the client's home country and go to work to develop the software necessary to solve and manage the client's problem. This new IT allows IBM to create an ever-changing set of global self-managed teams that form to solve the problems of IBM's global clients. In addition, because each team inputs knowledge about its activities into IBM's intranet, then as at Accenture, consultants and teams can learn from one another so that their problem-solving skills increase over time.

Managerial Implications

Analyzing Technology

1. Analyze an organization's or a department's input-conversion-output processes to identify the skills, knowledge, tools, and machinery that are central to the production of goods and services.
2. Analyze the level of technical complexity associated with the production of goods and services. Evaluate whether technical complexity can be increased to improve efficiency and reduce costs. For example, is an advanced computer system available? Are employees using up-to-date techniques and procedures?
3. Analyze the level of task variety and task analyzability associated with organizational and departmental tasks. Are there ways to reduce task variability or increase task analyzability to increase effectiveness? For example, can procedures be developed to make the work process more predictable and controllable?
4. Analyze the form of task interdependence inside a department and between departments. Evaluate whether the task interdependence being used results in the most effective way of producing goods or servicing the needs of customers. For example, would raising the level of coordination between departments improve efficiency?
5. After analyzing an organization's or a department's technology, analyze its structure, and evaluate the fit between technology and structure. Can the fit be improved? What costs and benefits are associated with changing the technology–structure relationship?

need to have on hand to meet customer (patient) demands. If, over a specified period, a hospital knows on average how many broken bones or cardiac arrests it can expect, it knows how many operating rooms it will need to have in readiness and how many doctors, nurses, and technicians to have on call to meet patient demand. This knowledge allows the hospital to control costs. Similarly, in R&D, an organization like Microsoft needs to develop decision-making rules that allow it to decide when to stop investing in a line of research that is showing little promise of success, and how to best allocate resources among projects to try to maximize potential returns from the investment—especially when aggressive competitors like Google and Facebook exist.

Another strategy that organizations can pursue to reduce the costs associated with intensive technology is **specialism,** producing only a narrow range of outputs. A hospital that specializes in the treatment of cancer or heart disease narrows the range of problems to which it is exposed and can target all its resources to solving those problems. It is the general hospital that faces the most uncertainty. Similarly, a pharmaceutical company typically restricts the areas in which it does research. A company may decide to focus on drugs that combat high blood pressure or diabetes or depression. This specialist strategy allows the organization to use its resources efficiently and reduces problems of coordination.[43]

Specialism
Producing only a narrow range of outputs.

From Mass Production to Advanced Manufacturing Technology

As discussed earlier, one of the most influential advances in technology in this century was the introduction of mass production technology by Henry Ford. To reduce costs, a mass production company must maximize the gains from economies of scale and from the division of labor associated with large-scale production. There are two ways to do this. One is by using dedicated machines and standardized work procedures. The other is by protecting the conversion process against production slowdowns or stoppages.

Traditional mass production is based on the use of **dedicated machines**—machines that can perform only one operation at a time, such as repeatedly cutting or drilling or stamping out a car body part.[44] To maximize volume and efficiency, a dedicated machine

Dedicated machines
Machines that can perform only one operation at a time, such as repeatedly cutting or drilling or stamping out a car body part.

produces a narrow range of products but does so cheaply. Thus this method of production has traditionally resulted in low production costs.

When the component being manufactured needs to be changed, a dedicated machine must be retooled—that is, fitted with new dies or jigs—before it can handle the change. When Ford retooled one of his plants to switch from the Model T to the Model A, he had to close the plant for over six months. Because retooling a dedicated machine can take days, during which no production is possible, long production runs are required for maximum efficiency and lowest costs. Thus, for example, Ford might make 50,000 right-side door panels in a single production run and stockpile them until they are needed because the money saved by using dedicated machines outweighs the combined costs of lost production and carrying the doors in inventory. In a similar way, both the use of a production line to assemble the final product and the employment of **fixed workers**—workers who perform standardized work procedures—increase an organization's control over the conversion process.

Fixed workers Workers who perform standardized work procedures increase an organization's control over the conversion process.

A mass production organization also attempts to reduce costs by protecting its conversion processes from the uncertainty that results from disruptions in the external environment.[45] Threats to the conversion process come from both the input and the output stages, but an organization can stockpile inputs and outputs to reduce these threats (see Figure 9.4A).

Figure 9.4 A. The Work Flow in Mass Production
B. The Work Flow with Advanced Manufacturing Technology

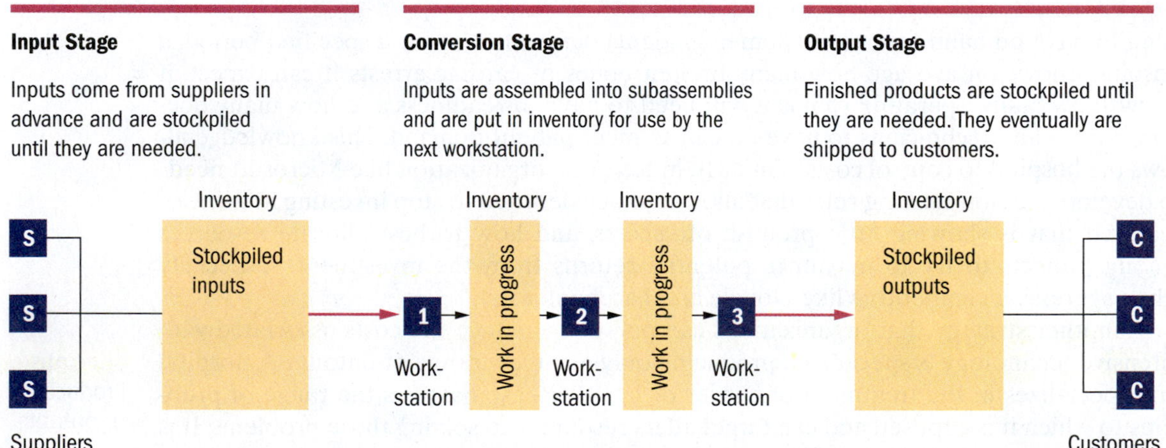
Input Stage
Inputs come from suppliers in advance and are stockpiled until they are needed.
Conversion Stage
Inputs are assembled into subassemblies and are put in inventory for use by the next workstation.
Output Stage
Finished products are stockpiled until they are needed. They eventually are shipped to customers.
Inventory
Inventory
Inventory
Inventory
S
S
S
Suppliers
Stockpiled inputs
1
Work-station
Work in progress
2
Work-station
Work in progress
3
Work-station
Stockpiled outputs
C
C
C
Customers

A. The Work Flow in Mass Production. Inventory is used to protect the conversion process and to prevent slowdowns or stoppages in production.

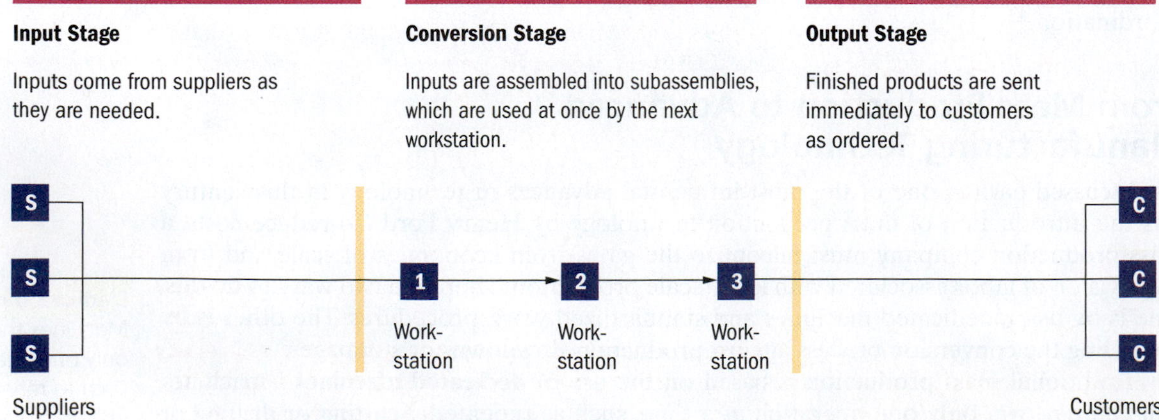
Input Stage
Inputs come from suppliers as they are needed.
Conversion Stage
Inputs are assembled into subassemblies, which are used at once by the next workstation.
Output Stage
Finished products are sent immediately to customers as ordered.
S
S
S
Suppliers
1
Work-station
2
Work-station
3
Work-station
C
C
C
Customers

B. The Work Flow with Advanced Manufacturing Technology. No inventory buffers are used between workstations.

At the input stage, an organization tries to control its access to inputs by keeping raw materials and semifinished components on hand to prevent shortages that would lead to a slowdown or break in production. The role of purchasing, for example, is to negotiate with suppliers contracts that guarantee the organization an adequate supply of inputs. At the output stage, an organization tries to control its ability to dispose of its outputs. It does so by stockpiling finished products so it can respond quickly to customer demands. An organization can also advertise heavily to maintain customer demand. In that case, the role of the sales department is to maintain demand for an organization's products so production does not need to slow down or stop because no one wants the organization's outputs. The high technical complexity, the routine nature of production tasks, and the sequential task interdependence characteristic of mass production all make an organization very inflexible. The term *fixed automation* is sometimes used to describe the traditional way of organizing production. The combination of dedicated machines (which perform only a narrow range of operations), fixed workers (who perform a narrow range of fixed tasks), and large stocks of inventory (which can be used to produce only one product or a few related products) makes it very expensive and difficult for an organization to begin to manufacture different kinds of products when customer preferences change.

Suppose an organization had a new technology that allowed it to make a wide range of products—products that could be customized to the needs of individual customers. This ability would increase demand for its products. If the new technology also allowed the organization to rapidly introduce new products that incorporated new features or the latest design trends, demand would increase even more. Finally, suppose the cost of producing this wide range of new customized products with the new technology was the same as, or only slightly more than, the cost of producing a narrow standardized product line. Clearly, the new technology would greatly increase organizational effectiveness and allow the organization to pursue both a low-cost and a differentiation strategy to attract customers by giving them advanced, high-quality, reliable products at low prices.[46]

What changes would an organization need to make to its technology to make it flexible enough to respond to customers while controlling costs? In the last 20 years, many new technological developments have allowed organizations to achieve these two goals. The new developments are sometimes called *flexible production, lean production,* or *computer-aided production*. Here we consider them to be components of advanced manufacturing technology.[47] **Advanced manufacturing technology** (AMT) consists of innovations in *materials technology* and in *knowledge technology* that change the work process of traditional mass production organizations.

Advanced manufacturing technology
Technology that consists of innovations in materials technology and in knowledge technology that change the work process of traditional mass production organizations.

Advanced Manufacturing Technology: Innovations in Materials Technology

Materials technology comprises machinery, other equipment, and computers. Innovations in materials technology are based on a new view of the linkages among input, conversion, and output activities.[48] Traditional mass production tries to protect the conversion process from disruptions at the input and output stages by using stockpiles of inventory as buffers to increase control and reduce uncertainty. With AMT, however, the organization actively seeks ways to increase its ability to integrate or coordinate the flow of resources among input, conversion, and output activities. AMT allows an organization to reduce uncertainty not by using inventory stockpiles but by developing the capacity to adjust and control its procedures quickly to eliminate the need for inventory at both the input and the output stages (see Figure 9.4B).[49] Several innovations in materials technology allow organizations to reduce the costs and speed the process of producing goods and services. Computer-aided design, computer-aided materials management, just-in-time inventory systems, and computer-integrated manufacturing affect one another and jointly improve organizational effectiveness. The first three are techniques for coordinating the input and conversion stages of production. The last one increases the technical complexity of the conversion stage.

Materials technology
Technology that comprises machinery, other equipment, and computers.

Computer-Aided Design

Mass production systems are set up to produce a large quantity of a few products. To some degree, this arrangement reflects the fact that a large part of the cost associated with mass production is incurred at the design stage.[50] In general, the more complex a product, the higher the design costs. The costs of designing a new car, for example, are enormous. Ford's recent world car, the Focus, cost over $5 billion to develop.

Computer-aided design (CAD)
An advanced manufacturing technique that greatly simplifies the design process.

Traditionally, the design of new parts involved the laborious construction of prototypes and scale models, a process akin to unit or small-batch production. **Computer-aided design (CAD)** is an advanced manufacturing technique that greatly simplifies the design process. CAD makes it possible to design a new component or microcircuit on a computer screen and then press a button, not to print out the plans for the part but to physically produce the part itself. Also, "printers" exist that squirt a stream of liquid metal or plastic droplets to create three-dimensional objects. Detailed prototypes can be sculpted according to the computer program and can be redesigned quickly if necessary. Thus, for example, an engineer at Ford who wants to see how a new gear will work in a transmission assembly can experiment quickly and cheaply to fine-tune the design of these inputs.[51]

Cutting the costs of product design by using CAD can contribute to both a low-cost and a differentiation advantage. Design advances that CAD makes possible can improve the efficiency of manufacturing. Well-designed components are easily fitted together into a subassembly, and well-designed subassemblies are easily fitted to other subassemblies. Improvements at the input design stage also make selling and servicing products easier at the output stage. The risk of later failure or of breakdown is reduced if potential problems have been eliminated at the design stage. Designing quality into a product up front improves competitive advantage and reduces costs. Toyota's core competence in product design, for example, evidenced by its relatively low recall rates, gives its cars a competitive advantage. Finally, CAD enhances flexibility because it reduces the difficulty and lowers the cost of customizing a product to satisfy particular customers. In essence, CAD brings to large-scale manufacturing one of the benefits of small-batch production-customized product design—but at far less cost. It also enhances an organization's ability to respond quickly to changes in its environment.[52]

Computer-Aided Materials Management

Computer-aided materials management (CAMM)
An advanced manufacturing technique that is used to manage the flow of raw materials and component parts into the conversation process, to develop master production schedules for manufacturing, and to control inventory.

Materials management, the management of the flow of resources into and out of the conversion process, is one of the most complex functional areas of an organization.[53] Computers are now the principal tool for processing the information that materials managers use for sound decision making, and computer-aided materials management is crucial to organizational effectiveness. **Computer-aided materials management (CAMM)** is an advanced manufacturing technique used to manage the flow of raw materials and component parts into the conversion process, to develop master production schedules for manufacturing, and to control inventory.[54] The difference between traditional materials management and the new computer-aided techniques is the difference between the so-called push and pull approaches to materials management.[55]

Traditional mass production uses the push approach. Materials are released from the input to the conversion stage when the production control system indicates that the conversion stage is ready to receive them. The inputs are pushed into the conversion process in accordance with a previously determined plan.

Computer-aided materials management makes possible the *pull* approach. The flow of input materials is governed by customer requests for supplies of the finished products, so the inputs are pulled into the conversion process in response to a pull from the output stage rather than a push from the input stage. Consider how VF Corporation, the manufacturer of Lee jeans, meets customer demand. As jeans sell out in stores, the stores issue requests by computer to Lee to manufacture different styles or sizes. Lee's manufacturing department then pulls in raw materials, such as cloth and thread, from suppliers as it needs them. If Lee were using the push approach, Lee would have a master plan that might say, "Make 30,000 pairs of style XYZ in May," and at the end of the summer 25,000 pairs might remain unsold in the warehouse because of lack of demand.

CAMM technology allows an organization to increase integration of its input, conversion, and output activities. The use of input and output inventories (see Figure 9.5) allows the activities of each stage of the mass production process to go on relatively independently. CAMM, however, tightly couples these activities. CAMM increases *task interdependence* because each stage must be ready to react quickly to demands from the other stages. CAMM increases technical complexity because it makes input, conversion, and output activities a continuous process, in effect creating a pipeline connecting raw materials to the customer. Because the high levels of task interdependence and technical complexity associated with CAMM require greater coordination, an organization may need to move toward an organic structure, which will provide the extra integration that is needed.

CAMM also helps an organization pursue a low-cost or differentiation strategy. The ability to control the flow of materials in the production process allows an organization to avoid the costs of carrying excess inventory and to be flexible enough to adjust to product or demand changes quickly and easily.

Just-in-Time Inventory Systems

Another advanced manufacturing technique for managing the flow of inputs into the organization is the just-in-time inventory system. Developed from the Japanese kanban system (a *kanban* is a card), a **just-in-time inventory (JIT) system** requires inputs and components needed for production to be delivered to the conversion process just as they are needed, neither earlier nor later, so input inventories can be kept to a minimum.[56] Components are kept in bins, and as they are used up, the empty bins are sent back to the supplier with a request on the bin's card (kanban) for more components. Computer-aided materials management is necessary for a JIT system to work effectively because CAMM provides computerized linkages with suppliers—linkages that facilitate the rapid transfer of information and coordination between an organization and its suppliers.

Just-in-time inventory (JIT) system A system that requires inputs and components needed for production to be delivered to the conversion process just as they are needed, neither earlier nor later, so that input inventories can be kept to a minimum.

In theory, a JIT system can extend beyond components to raw materials. A company may supply Ford or Toyota with taillight assemblies. The supplier itself, however, may assemble the taillights from individual parts (screws, plastic lenses, bulbs) provided by other manufacturers. Thus the supplier of the taillight assembly could also operate a JIT system with its suppliers, who in turn could operate JIT systems with their suppliers. Figure 9.5 illustrates a just-in-time inventory system that goes from the customer, to the store, and then back through the manufacturer to the original suppliers.

A JIT system increases task interdependence between stages in the production chain. Traditional mass production draws a boundary between the conversion stage and the input and output stages and sequences conversion activities only. JIT systems break down these barriers and make the whole value-creation process a single chain of sequential activities. Because organizational activities become a continuous process, technical complexity increases, in turn increasing the efficiency of the system.

At the same time, JIT systems bring flexibility to manufacturing. The ability to order components as they are needed allows an organization to widen the range of products it

Figure 9.5 Just-in-Time Inventory System

The system is activated by customers making purchases.

Customer buys product
Store orders more product from manufacturer
Manufacturer signals suppliers and makes product to meet store's order
Suppliers signal their suppliers and produce to meet manufacturer's order
Other Suppliers and so on...

makes and to customize products.[57] JIT systems thus allow a modern mass production organization because it is not tied to one product by large inventories to obtain the benefits of small-batch technology (flexibility and customization) with little loss of technical efficiency.

Like CAMM, JIT systems require an extra measure of coordination, and an organization may need to adopt new methods to manage this new technology. One of these, as we saw in Chapter 3, is to implement new strategies for managing relations with suppliers. Toyota, which owns a minority stake in its suppliers, periodically meets with its suppliers to keep them informed about new product developments. Toyota also works closely with its suppliers to reduce the costs and raise the quality of input components, and it shares the cost savings with them.[58] Because owning a supplier can increase costs, many organizations try to avoid the need to integrate vertically. Long-term contracts with suppliers can create cooperative working relationships that have long-term benefits for both parties.

In sum, just-in-time inventory systems, computer-aided materials management, and computer-aided design increase technical complexity and task interdependence and thus increase the degree to which a traditional mass production system operates like a continuous-process technology; they also increase efficiency and reduce production costs. The three advanced manufacturing techniques also give modern mass production the benefits of small-batch production: heightened flexibility and the ability to respond to customer needs and increased product quality. Together these techniques confer a low-cost and a differentiation advantage on an organization.

Now that we have looked at advanced techniques for coordinating the input and conversion stages, we can look at new developments inside the conversion stage. At the center of AMT's innovations of conversion processes is the creation of a system based on flexible workers and flexible machines.

Flexible Manufacturing Technology and Computer-Integrated Manufacturing

Flexible manufacturing technology
Technology that allows the production of many kinds of components at little or no extra cost on the same machine.

Traditional mass manufacturing technology uses dedicated machines, which perform only one operation at a time. **Flexible manufacturing technology,** by contrast, allows the production of many kinds of components at little or no extra cost on the same machine. Each machine in a flexible manufacturing system is able to perform a range of different operations, and the machines in sequence are able to vary their operations so a wide variety of different components can be produced. Flexible manufacturing technology combines the variety advantages of small-batch production with the low-cost advantages of continuous-process production. How is this achieved?

Computer-integrated manufacturing (CIM)
An advanced manufacturing technique that controls the changeover from one operation to another by means of the commands given to the machines through computer software.

In flexible manufacturing systems, the key factor that prevents the cost increases associated with changing operations is the use of a computer-controlled system to manage operations. **Computer-integrated manufacturing (CIM)** is an advanced manufacturing technique that controls the changeover from one operation to another by means of the commands given to the machines through computer software. A CIM system eliminates the need to retool machines physically. Within the system are a number of computer-controlled machines, each capable of automatically producing a range of components. They are controlled by a master computer, which schedules the movement of parts between machines in order to assemble different products from the various components that each machine makes.[59] Computer-integrated manufacturing depends on computers programmed to (1) feed the machines with components, (2) assemble the product from components and move it from one machine to another, and (3) unload the final product from the machine to the shipping area.

The use of robots is integral to CIM. A group of robots working in sequence is the AMT equivalent of a dedicated transfer machine. Each robot can be quickly programmed by software to perform different operations, and the costs of reprogramming robots are much lower than the costs associated with retooling dedicated transfer machines.

In sum, computer-integrated manufacturing, just-in-time inventory systems, computer-aided materials management, and computer-aided design give organizations the flexibility to make a variety of products, as well as different models of the same product, rapidly and cost effectively. They break down the traditional barriers separating the input, conversion, and output stages of production; as a result, input, conversion, and output activities merge into one another. These four innovations in materials technology decrease the need for costly inventory buffers to protect conversion processes from disruptions in the environment. In addition, they increase product reliability because they increase automation and technical complexity.

Summary

Technical complexity, the differences between routine and nonroutine tasks, and task interdependence jointly explain why some technologies are more complex and difficult to control than others and why organizations adopt different structures to operate their technology. In general, input, conversion, and output processes that depend primarily on people and departments cooperating and trading knowledge that is difficult to program into standard operating routines require the most coordination. An organization that needs extensive coordination and control to operate its technology also needs an organic structure to organize its tasks. Chapter 9 has made the following main points:

1. Technology is the combination of skills, knowledge, abilities, techniques, materials, machines, computers, tools, and other equipment that people use to convert raw materials into valuable goods and services.
2. Technology is involved in an organization's input, conversion, and output processes. An effective organization manages its technology to meet the needs of stakeholders, foster innovation, and increase operating efficiency.
3. Technical complexity is the extent to which a production process is controllable and predictable. According to Joan Woodward, technical complexity differentiates small-batch and unit production, large-batch and mass production, and continuous-process production.
4. Woodward argued that each technology is associated with a different organizational structure because each technology presents different control and coordination problems. In general, small-batch and continuous-process technologies are associated with an organic structure, and mass production is associated with a mechanistic structure.
5. The argument that technology determines structure is known as the technological imperative. According to the Aston Studies, however, organizational size is more important than technology in determining an organization's choice of structure.
6. According to Charles Perrow, two dimensions underlie the difference between routine and nonroutine tasks and technologies: task variability and task analyzability. The higher the level of task variability and the lower the level of task analyzability, the more complex and nonroutine are organizational tasks.
7. Using task variability and analyzability, Perrow described four types of technology: craftswork, nonroutine research, engineering production, and routine manufacturing.
8. The more routine the tasks, the more likely an organization is to use a mechanistic structure. The more complex the tasks, the more likely an organization is to use an organic structure.
9. James D. Thompson focused on the way in which task interdependence affects an organization's technology and structure. Task interdependence is the manner in which different organizational tasks are related to one another and the degree to which the performance of one person or department depends on and affects the performance of another.
10. Thompson identified three types of technology, which he associated with three forms of task interdependence: mediating technology and pooled interdependence; long-linked technology and sequential interdependence; and intensive technology and reciprocal interdependence.

11. The higher the level of task interdependence, the more likely an organization is to use mutual adjustment rather than standardization to coordinate work activities.
12. Advanced manufacturing technology consists of innovations in materials technology that change the work process of traditional mass production organizations. Innovations in materials technology include computer-aided design, computer-aided materials management, just-in-time inventory systems, flexible manufacturing technology, and computer-integrated manufacturing.

Discussion Questions

1. How can technology increase organizational effectiveness?
2. How does small-batch technology differ from mass production technology?
3. Why is technical complexity greatest with continuous-process technology? How does technical complexity affect organizational structure?
4. What makes some tasks more complex than others? Give an example of an organization that uses each of the four types of technology identified by Perrow.
5. What level of task interdependence is associated with the activities of (a) a large accounting firm, (b) a fast-food restaurant, and (c) a biotechnology company? What different kinds of structure are you likely to find in these organizations? Why?
6. Find an organization in your city, and analyze how its technology works. Use the concepts discussed in this chapter: technical complexity, nonroutine tasks, and task interdependence.
7. Discuss how AMT and innovations in materials technology and in knowledge technology have increased task interdependence and the technical complexity of the work process. How have these innovations changed the structure of organizations operating a mass production technology?

Organizational Theory in Action

Practicing Organizational Theory

Choosing a Technology

Form groups of three to five people and discuss the following scenario:

You are investors who are planning to open a large computer store in a big city on the West Coast. You plan to offer a complete range of computer hardware, ranging from UNIX-based workstations, to powerful PCs and laptop computers, to a full range of printers and scanners. In addition, you propose to offer a full range of software products, from office management systems to personal financial software and children's computer games. Your strategy is to be a one-stop shopping place where all kind of customers—from large companies to private individuals—can get everything they want from salespeople who can design a complete system to meet each customer's unique needs.

You are meeting to decide which kind of technology—which combination of skills, knowledge, techniques, and task relationships—will best allow you to achieve your goal.

1. Analyze the level of (a) technical complexity and (b) task variability and task analyzability associated with the kinds of tasks needed to achieve your strategy.
2. Given your answer to item 1, what kind of task interdependence between employees/departments will best allow you to pursue your strategy?
3. Based on this analysis, what kind of technology will you choose in your store, and what kind of structure and culture will you create to manage your technology most effectively?

The Ethical Dimension #9

The chapter discussed some of Henry Ford's strict labor practices that caused such high turnover. Workers were not allowed to talk on the production line, for example, and he employed detectives to spy on them when they were at home.

1. What limits should be placed on a company's right to monitor and control its employees from an ethical perspective?
2. What moral rules would you create to help managers decide when, and which actions and behaviors, they have a right to influence and control?

Making the Connection #9

Find an example of a company operating with one of the technologies identified in this chapter. Which technology is the company using? Why is the company using it? How does this technology affect the organization's structure?

Analyzing the Organization: Design Module #9

This module focuses on the technology your company uses to produce goods and services and the problems and issues associated with the use of this technology.

Assignment

Using the information at your disposal, and drawing inferences about your company's technology from the activities that your organization engages in, answer the following questions.

1. What kinds of goods or services does your organization produce? Are input, conversion, or output activities the source of greatest uncertainty for your organization?
2. What role does technology in the form of knowledge play in the production of the organization's goods or services?
3. What role does materials technology play in the production of the organization's goods and services?
4. What is the organization's level of technical complexity? Does the organization use a small-batch, mass production, or continuous-process technology?
5. Use the concepts of task variability and task analyzability to describe the complexity of your organization's activities. Which of the four types of technology identified by Perrow does your organization use?
6. What forms of task interdependence between people and between departments characterize your organization's work process? Which of the three types of technology identified by Thompson does your organization use?
7. The analysis you have done so far might lead you to expect your company to operate with a particular kind of structure. What kind? To what extent does your organization's structure seem to fit with the characteristics of the organization's technology? For example, is the structure organic or mechanistic?
8. Do you think your organization is operating its technology effectively? Do you see any ways in which it could improve its technical efficiency, innovativeness, or ability to respond to customers?

CASE FOR ANALYSIS

Microsoft Reorganizes to Speed Innovation

Microsoft, like other software makers, has been shocked by the increasing number of applications available on the Internet and not on the PC, many of which have been pioneered by Google and Yahoo! These include better and faster versions of Internet applications such as email, advanced specialized search engines, Internet phone services, imaging searching, and mapping such as Google's Earth. Rapid innovation is taking place in these and other areas, and the danger for Microsoft is that these online applications will make its vital Windows PC platform less useful and perhaps obsolete. If, in the future, people begin to use new kinds of online word processing and storage applications, then the only important PC software application will become operating system software. This would cause Microsoft's revenues and profits to plummet. So a major push is on at Microsoft to find ways to make its new software offerings work seamlessly with developing Internet-based service applications and its Windows platform so customers will remain loyal to its PC software.

To achieve this, Microsoft announced a major redesign of its organizational structure to focus on three major software and service products areas: Platform Products and Services, Business, and Entertainment & Services, each of which will be managed by its own new top management team. In doing this, Microsoft has created a new level in its hierarchy and has decentralized major decision-making responsibility to these managers. Inside each division, IT specialists will continue to work in small project teams.

Microsoft claims that the new structure will not only speed technological innovation in each division, but it will also create many synergies between the product divisions and foster collaboration and so improve product development across the organization. In essence, Microsoft is trying to make its structure more organic so it can better compete with nimble rivals like Google. As Microsoft's CEO Steve Ballmer commented, "Our goal in making these changes is to enable Microsoft to achieve greater agility in managing the incredible growth ahead and executing our software-based services strategy." Some analysts wonder, however, if adding a new level to the hierarchy will only create a new layer of bureaucracy that will further slow down decision making and allow Google to take an even greater lead in Internet services in the decade ahead.

Discussion Questions

1. Which of the following technology best characterizes the way Microsoft operates (a) craftswork, (b) engineering production, or (c) intensive technology?
2. In what ways does Microsoft hope its new way of organizing will help it to continually improve its competences and technology?

References

1 "Survey: The Endless Road," *Economist*, October 17, 1992, p. 4.
2 R. Edwards, *Contested Terrain: The Transformation of the Workplace in the Twentieth Century* (New York: Basic Books, 1979).
3 D. M. Rousseau, "Assessment of Technology in Organizations: Closed Versus Open Systems Approaches," *Academy of Management Review* 4 (1979), 531–542; W. R. Scott, Organizations: Rational, Natural, and Open Systems (Englewood Cliffs, NJ: Prentice-Hall, 1981).
4 H. Ford, "Progressive Manufacturing," *Encyclopedia Britannica,* 13th ed. (New York: Encyclopedia Co., 1926).
5 Edwards, *Contested Terrain*, p. 119.
6 J. Woodward, *Management and Technology* (London: Her Majesty's Stationery Office, 1958), p. 12.
7 Woodward, *Management and Technology*, p. 11.
8 www.zynga.com, 2011.
9 Ibid.
10 J. Woodward, *Industrial Organization: Theory and Practice* (London: Oxford University Press, 1965).
11 www.Ikea.com, 2011.
12 Woodward, *Industrial Organization.*
13 Woodward, *Management and Technology.*
14 C. Perrow, *Normal Accidents: Living with High-Risk Technologies* (New York: Basic Books, 1984).
15 E. Harvey, "Technology and the Structure of Organizations," *American Sociological Review* 33 (1968), 241–259; W. L. Zwerman, *New Perspectives on Organizational Effectiveness* (Westport, CT: Greenwood, 1970).
16 D. J. Hickson, D. S. Pugh, and D. C. Pheysey, "Operations Technology and Organizational Structure: An Empirical Reappraisal," *Administrative Science Quarterly* 14 (1969), 378–397; D. S. Pugh, "The Aston Program of Research: Retrospect and Prospect," in A. H. Van de Ven and W. F. Joyce, eds., *Perspectives on*

Organizational Design and Behavior (New York: Wiley, 1981), pp. 135–166; H. E. Aldrich, "Technology and Organizational Structure: A Reexamination of the Findings of the Aston Group," *Administrative Science Quarterly* 17 (1972), pp. 26–43.

17 J. Child and R. Mansfield, "Technology, Size and Organization Structure," *Sociology* 6 (1972), 369–393.

18 Hickson et al., "Operations Technology and Organizational Structure."

19 C. Perrow, *Organizational Analysis: A Sociological View* (Belmont, CA: Wadsworth, 1970).

20 Ibid.

21 Ibid., p. 21.

22 Ibid.

23 This section draws heavily on C. Perrow, "A Framework for the Comparative Analysis of Organizations," *American Sociological Review* 32 (1967), 194–208.

24 Perrow, *Organizational Analysis*; C. Gresov, "Exploring Fit and Misfit with Multiple Contingencies," *Administrative Science Quarterly* 34 (1989), 431–453.

25 Edwards, *Contested Terrain.*

26 www.honda,com, 2011.

27 www.apple.com, 2011.

28 www.foxconn.com, 2011.

29 M. Williams, "Back to the Past," *Wall Street Journal*, October 24, 1994, p. A1.

30 S. N. Mehta, "Cell Manufacturing Gains Acceptance at Smaller Plants," *Wall Street Journal*, September 15, 1994, p. B2.

31 J. Beyer and H. Trice, "A Re-Examination of the Relations Between Size and Various Components of Organizational Complexity," *Administrative Science Quarterly* 30 (1985), 462–481.

32 L. Argote, "Input Uncertainty and Organizational Coordination of Subunits," *Administrative Science Quarterly* 27 (1982), 420–434.

33 R. T. Keller, "Technology-Information Processing Fit and the Performance of R&D Project Groups: A Test of Contingency Theory," *Academy of Management Review* 37 (1994), 167–179.

34 C. Perrow, "Hospitals: Technology, Structure, and Goals," in J. March, ed., *The Handbook of Organizations* (Chicago: Rand McNally, 1965), pp. 910–971.

35 D. E. Comstock and W. R. Scott, "Technology and the Structure of Subunits," *Administrative Science Quarterly* 22 (1977), 177–202; A. H. Van de Ven and A. L. Delbecq, "A Task Contingent Model of Work Unit Structure," *Administrative Science Quarterly* 19 (1974), 183–197.

36 J. D. Thompson, *Organizations in Action* (New York: McGraw-Hill, 1967).

37 W. G. Ouchi, "The Relationship Between Organizational Structure and Organizational Control," *Administrative Science Quarterly* 22 (1977), 95–113.

38 Thompson, *Organizations in Action.*

39 Ibid., p. 17.

40 T. Davenport and L. Prusak, *Information Ecology.* (London: Oxford University Press, 1997).

41 www.accenture.com, 2011.

42 www.ibm.com, 2011.

43 Thompson, *Organizations in Action*; G. R. Jones, "Organization–Client Transactions and Organizational Governance Structures," *Academy of Management Journal* 30 (1987), 197–218.

44 C. Edquist and S. Jacobson, *Flexible Automation: The Global Diffusion of New Technology in the Engineering Industry* (London: Basil Blackwell, 1988).

45 Ibid.

46 M. Jelinek and J. D. Goldhar, "The Strategic Implications of the Factory of the Future," *Sloan Management Review*, *25* (1984), 29–37; G. I. Susman and J. W. Dean, "Strategic Use of Computer Integrated Manufacturing in the Emerging Competitive Environment," *Computer Integrated Manufacturing Systems* 2 (1989), 133–138.

47 C. A. Voss, *Managing Advanced Manufacturing Technology* (Bedford, England: IFS [Publications] Ltd., 1986).

48 Krafcik, "Triumph of the Lean Production System."

49 Ibid.; M. T. Sweeney, "Flexible Manufacturing Systems—Managing Their Integration," in Voss, *Managing Advanced Manufacturing Technology*, pp. 69–81.

50 D. E. Whitney, "Manufacturing by Design," *Harvard Business Review* (July–August 1988): 210–216.

[51] "Microtechnology, Dropping Out," *The Economist,* January 9, 1993, p. 75.

[52] F. M. Hull and P. D. Collins, "High Technology Batch Production Systems: Woodward's Missing Types," *Academy of Management Journal* 30 (1987), 786–797.

[53] R. H. Hayes and S. C. Wheelright, *Restoring Our Competitive Edge: Competing Through Manufacturing* (New York: Wiley, 1984).

[54] C. A. Voss, "Managing Manufacturing Technology," in R. Wild, ed., *International Handbook of Production and Operations Management* (London: Cassel, 1989), pp. 112–121.

[55] Ibid.

[56] S. M. Young, "A Framework for the Successful Adoption and Performance of Japanese Manufacturing Practices in the United States," *Academy of Management Review* 17 (1992), 677–700.

[57] A. Ansari and B. Modarress, *Just-in-Time Purchasing* (New York: Free Press, 1990).

[58] J. P. Womack, D. T. Jones, D. Roos, and D. Sammons, *The Machine That Changed the World* (New York: Macmillan, 1990).

[59] H. J. Warnecke and R. Steinhilper, "CIM, FMS, and Robots," in Wild, *International Handbook of Production and Operations Management*, pp. 146–173.

Part 3
Organizational Change

CHAPTER 10

Types and Forms of Organizational Change

Learning Objectives

Today, as never before, organizations are facing an environment that is changing rapidly, and the task facing managers is to help organizations respond and adjust to the changes taking place. This chapter discusses the various types of change that organizations must undergo and how organizations can manage the process of change to stay ahead in today's competitive environments.

After reading this chapter you should be able to:

1. Understand the relationship among organizational change, redesign, and organizational effectiveness.
2. Distinguish among the major forms or types of evolutionary and revolutionary change organizations must manage.
3. Recognize the problems inherent in managing change and the obstacles that must be overcome.
4. Describe the change process and understand the techniques that can be used to help an organization achieve its desired future state.

What Is Organizational Change?

Organizational change is the process by which organizations move from their current or present state to some desired future state to increase their effectiveness. The goal of planned organizational change is to find new or improved ways of using resources and capabilities to increase an organization's ability to create value and improve returns to its stakeholders.[1] An organization in decline may need to restructure its competences and resources to improve its fit with a changing environment. IBM, for example, experienced falling demand for its principal product, mainframe computers, in the 1990s. Its new CEO decided to refocus and build IBM's competences in providing IT consulting and services and in the 2000s IBM enjoyed a successful turnaround that by 2010 had made it a dominant competitor once again. Similarly, in the 2010s Ford has enjoyed a rebirth under CEO Alan Mulally, who totally changed the way the company operates by altering its structure and culture to meet the needs of a changing environment.

Organizational change
The process by which organizations move from their present state to some desired future state to increase their effectiveness.

Importantly, even thriving, high-performing organizations such as Google, Apple, and Facebook also need to continuously change the way they operate over time—often from week to week—to meet ongoing challenges. Managers must constantly search for better ways to use organizational resources to develop a flow of new and improved products or find new markets for their existing products. Competition in the smartphone and tablet computer markets changes all the time and managers and their organizations have to strive to stay one step ahead of their rivals—as Nokia and Research in Motion learned to their cost in 2011 as Apple became the leading smartphone company and its stock soared while theirs plunged. In the last decade, especially because of the recent recession, almost all Fortune 500 companies have restructured and changed to increase their effectiveness and ability to create value for customers.

Targets of Change

Planned organizational change is normally targeted at improving effectiveness at one or more of four different levels: human resources, functional resources, technological capabilities, and organizational capabilities.

HUMAN RESOURCES Human resources are an organization's most important asset. Ultimately, an organization's distinctive competences lie in the skills and abilities of its employees. Because these skills and abilities give an organization a competitive advantage, organizations must continually monitor their structures to find the most effective way of motivating and organizing human resources to acquire and use their skills. Typical kinds of change efforts directed at human resources include (1) a new investment in training and development activities so employees acquire new skills and abilities; (2) socializing employees into the organizational culture so they learn the new routines on which organizational performance depends; (3) changing organizational norms and values to motivate a multicultural and diverse workforce; (4) an ongoing examination of the way in which promotion and reward systems operate in a diverse workforce; and (5) changing the composition of the top-management team to improve organizational learning and decision making.

FUNCTIONAL RESOURCES As discussed in previous chapters, each organizational function needs to develop procedures that allow it to manage the particular environment it faces. As the environment changes, organizations often transfer resources to the functions where the most value can be created. Crucial functions grow in importance while those whose usefulness is declining shrink.

An organization can improve the value that its functions create by changing its structure, culture, and technology. The change from a functional to a product team structure, for example, may speed the new product development process. Alterations in functional structure can help provide a setting in which people are motivated to perform. The change from traditional mass production to a manufacturing operation based on self-managed work teams often allows companies to increase product quality and productivity if employees can share in the gains from the new work system.

TECHNOLOGICAL CAPABILITIES Technological capabilities give an organization an enormous capacity to change itself to exploit market opportunities. The ability to develop a constant stream of new products or to modify existing products so they continue to attract customers is one of an organization's core competences. Similarly, the ability to improve the way goods and services are produced to increase their quality and reliability is a crucial organizational capability. At the organizational level, an organization has to provide the context that allows it to translate its technological competences into value for its stakeholders. This task often involves the redesign of organizational activities. IBM, for example, changed its organizational structure to better capitalize on its new strengths in providing IT consulting. Previously, it had been unable to translate its technical capabilities into commercial opportunities because its structure was not focused on consulting but on making and selling computer hardware and software rather than providing advice.

ORGANIZATIONAL CAPABILITIES Through the design of organizational structure and culture, an organization can harness its human and functional resources to take advantage of technological opportunities. Organizational change often involves changing the relationships between people and functions to increase their ability to create value. Changes in structure and culture take place at all levels of the organization and include changing the routines an individual uses to greet customers, changing work group relationships, improving integration between divisions, and changing corporate culture by changing the top-management team.

These four levels at which change can take place are obviously interdependent; it is often impossible to change one without changing another. Suppose an organization invests resources and recruits a team of scientists who are experts in a new technology—for example, biotechnology. If successful, this human resource change will lead to the emergence of a new functional resource and a new technological capability. Top management will be forced to reevaluate its organizational structure and the way it integrates and coordinates its other functions to ensure that they support its new functional resources. Effectively utilizing the new resources may require a move to a product team structure. It may even require downsizing and the elimination of functions that are no longer central to the organization's mission.

Forces for and Resistance to Organizational Change

The organizational environment is constantly changing, and an organization must adapt to these changes to survive.[2] Figure 10.1 lists the most important forces for and impediments to change that confront an organization and its managers.

Forces for Change

Recall from Chapter 3 that many forces in the environment have an impact on an organization and that recognizing the nature of these forces is one of a manager's most important tasks.[3] If managers are slow to respond to competitive, economic, political, global, and other forces, the organization will lag behind its competitors and its effectiveness will be compromised (see Figure 10.1).

COMPETITIVE FORCES Organizations are constantly striving to achieve a competitive advantage.[4] Competition is a force for change because unless an organization matches or surpasses its competitors in efficiency, quality, or its capability to innovate new or improved goods or services, it will not survive.[5]

To lead on the dimensions of efficiency or quality, an organization must constantly adopt the latest technology as it becomes available. The adoption of new technology usually brings a change to task relationships as workers learn new skills or techniques to operate the new technology.[6] Later in this chapter we discuss total quality management and reengineering, two change strategies that organizations can use to achieve superior efficiency or quality.

Figure 10.1 Forces for and Resistances to Change

Forces for Change	Resistances to Change
Competitive Forces Economic Forces Political Forces Global Forces Demographic Forces Social Forces Ethical Forces	Organizational Level • Structure • Culture • Strategy Functional Level • Differences in Subunit Orientation • Power and Conflict Group Level • Norms • Cohesiveness • Groupthink Individual Level • Cognitive Biases • Uncertainty and Insecurity • Selective Perception and Retention • Habit

To lead on the dimension of innovation and obtain a technological advantage over competitors, a company must possess skills in managing the process of innovation, another source of change that we discuss later.

ECONOMIC, POLITICAL, AND GLOBAL FORCES Economic, political, and global forces continually affect organizations and compel them to change how and where they produce goods and services. Economic and political unions among countries are becoming an increasingly important force for change.[7] The North American Free Trade Agreement (NAFTA) paved the way for cooperation among Canada, the United States, and Mexico. The European Union (EU) includes over 27 members eager to take advantage of a large protected market. Japan and other fast-growing Asian countries such as China, recognizing that economic unions protect member nations and create barriers against foreign competitors, have moved to increase their operations in countries overseas. Japanese companies, for example, have opened thousands of manufacturing plants in the United States and Mexico, and in European countries such as Spain and the UK, so they can share in the advantages offered by NAFTA and the EU. Toyota, Honda, and Nissan have all opened large car plants in England to supply cars to EU member countries. No organization can afford to ignore the effects of global economic and political forces on its activities.[8]

Other global challenges facing organizations include the need to change an organizational structure to allow expansion into foreign markets, the need to adapt to a variety of national cultures, and the need to help expatriate managers adapt to the economic, political, and cultural values of the countries in which they are located.[9]

DEMOGRAPHIC AND SOCIAL FORCES Managing a diverse workforce is one of the biggest challenges to confront organizations in the 2000s.[10] Changes in the composition of the workforce and the increasing diversity of employees have presented organizations with many challenges and opportunities. Increasingly, changes in the demographic characteristics of the workforce have led managers to change their styles of managing all employees and to learn how to understand, supervise, and motivate diverse members effectively. Managers have had to abandon the stereotypes they unwittingly may have used in making promotion decisions, and they have had to accept the importance of equity in the recruitment and promotion of new hires, and acknowledge employees' desire for a lifestyle that strikes an acceptable balance between work and leisure. Many companies have helped their workers keep up with changing technology by providing support for advanced education and training. Increasingly, organizations are coming to realize that the ultimate source of competitive advantage and organizational effectiveness lies in fully utilizing the skills of their members, by, for example, empowering employees to make important and significant decisions.[11]

ETHICAL FORCES Just as it is important for an organization to take steps to change in response to changing demographic and social forces, it is also critical for an organization to take steps to promote ethical behavior in the face of increasing government, political, and social demands for more responsible and honest corporate behavior.[12] Many companies have created the position of ethics officer, a person to whom employees can report ethical lapses by an organization's managers or workers and can turn for advice on difficult ethical questions. Organizations are also trying to promote ethical behavior by giving employees more direct access to important decision makers and by protecting whistleblowers who turn the organization in when they perceive ethical problems with the way certain managers behave.

Many organizations need to make changes to allow managers and workers at all levels to report unethical behavior so an organization can move quickly to eliminate such behavior and protect the general interests of its members and customers.[13] Similarly, if organizations operate in countries that pay little attention to human rights or to the well-being of organizational members, they have to learn how to change these standards and to protect their overseas employees. Organizational Insight 10.1 describes how the way that roses are grown around the world has many ethical issues that U.S. customers need to be aware of.

From customer design preferences, to the issue of where clothes should be produced, to the question of whether economic or political unrest will affect the availability of raw

Organizational Insight 10.1

Everything Is *Not* Coming Up Roses

Every year on Valentine's Day tens of millions of roses are delivered to sweethearts and loved ones in the United States, and anyone who has bought roses knows that their price has been falling steadily. One of the main reasons for this is that rose growing is now concentrated in poorer countries in Central and South America. Rose growing has been a boon to poor countries where the extra income women earn can mean the difference between starvation or not for their families. Ecuador, for example, is the fourth biggest rose grower in the world, and the industry employs over 50,000 women who tend, pick, and package roses for above its national minimum wage. Most of these women are employed by Rosas del Ecuador, the company that controls the rose business in that country.

The hidden side of the global rose-growing business is that poorer countries tend to have lax or unenforced health and safety laws, something that lowers rose-growing costs in these countries. And, critics argue, many rose-growing companies and countries are not considering the well-being of their workers. For example, although the CEO of Rosas de Ecuador, Erwin Pazmino, denies that workers are subjected to unsafe conditions, almost 60% of his workers have reported blurred vision, nausea, headaches, asthma, and other symptoms of pesticide poisoning.[14] Workers labor in hot, poorly ventilated greenhouses in which roses have been sprayed with pesticides and herbicides. Safety equipment such as masks and ventilators is scarce and the long hours women work adds to chemical overexposure. If workers complain, they may be fired and blacklisted, which makes it hard for them to find other jobs. So, to protect their families' well-being, workers rarely complain and thus their health remains at risk.

Clearly, rose buyers worldwide need to be aware of these working conditions when deciding to buy roses, just as buyers of inexpensive clothing and footwear became concerned in the last few decades when they found out about the sweatshop conditions in which garment and shoe workers labored. Companies like Nike and Walmart have made major efforts to stop sweatshop practices, and today employ hundreds of inspectors who police the factories overseas that make the products they sell. As companies increasingly outsource the manufacturing of all kinds of products from socks to iPhones to countries with low labor costs such as China, Malaysia, and Vietnam, the behavior of the subcontractors in these countries has come under increasing scrutiny. Nike, Target, The Gap, Sony, and Mattel have all been forced to reevaluate the ethics of their labor practices and to promise to keep a constant watch on subcontractors in the future. A statement to this effect can be found on many of these companies' Web pages; see for example, Nike's (www.nikebiz.com) and The Gap's (www.thegap.com).[15] In a similar way, the main buyers and distributors of flowers for the U.S. market also began to consider the well-being of the workers who grow them and are lobbying for tighter controls over their working conditions.

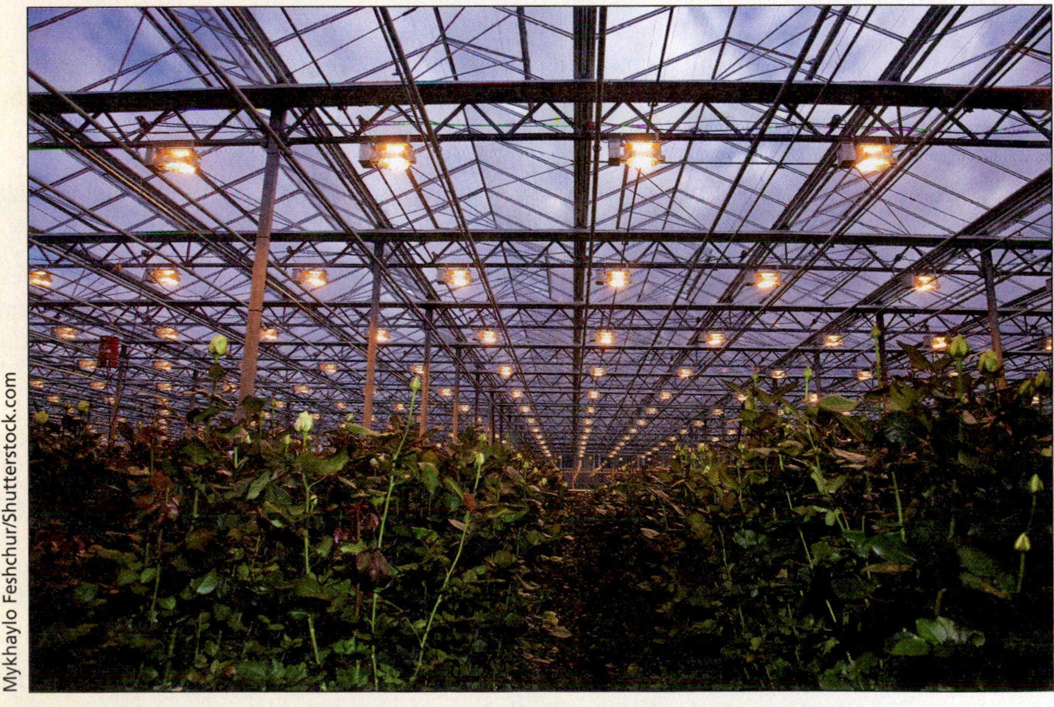

Mykhaylo Feshchur/Shutterstock.com

materials, and how to monitor the work conditions in which products are made overseas, the forces of change bombard organizations from all sides. Effective organizations are agile enough to adjust to these forces. But many forces internal to an organization make the organization resistant to change and thus threaten its effectiveness and survival.

Resistances to Change

In the last few years, many well-known companies such as Dell, Sony, and Nokia have seen their performance decline sharply as a result of increasing global competition. Why did these companies lose their effectiveness? The main explanation for such decline is almost always an organization's inability to change in response to changes in its environment because of *organizational inertia*, the tendency of an organization to resist change and maintain the status quo. Resistance to change lowers an organization's effectiveness and reduces its chances of survival.[16] Resistances or impediments to change that cause inertia are found at the organization, group, and individual levels[17] (see Figure 10.1).

Organization-Level Resistance to Change

Many forces inside an organization make it difficult for an organization to change in response to changing conditions in its environment.[18] The most powerful impediments to change include power and conflict, differences in functional orientation, mechanistic structure, and organizational culture.

POWER AND CONFLICT Change usually benefits some people, functions, or divisions at the expense of others. When change causes power struggles and organizational conflict, an organization is likely to resist it.[19] Suppose that a change in purchasing practices will help the management of materials to achieve its goal of reducing input costs but will harm manufacturing's ability to reduce manufacturing costs. Materials management will push for the change, but manufacturing will resist it. The conflict between the two functions will slow the process of change and perhaps prevent change from occurring at all. If powerful functions can prevent change, an organization will not change. In the old IBM, for example, managers of its mainframe computer division were the most powerful in the corporation, and to preserve their prestige and power they fought off attempts to redirect IBM's resources to produce the PCs that customers wanted—something that almost led to IBM's downfall.

DIFFERENCES IN FUNCTIONAL ORIENTATION Differences in functional orientation are another major impediment to change and a source of organizational inertia. Different functions and divisions often see the source of a problem differently because they see an issue or problem primarily from their own viewpoint. This tunnel vision increases organizational inertia because the organization must spend time and effort to secure agreement about the source of a problem before it can even consider how the organization needs to change to respond to the problem.

MECHANISTIC STRUCTURE Recall from Chapter 4 that a mechanistic structure is characterized by a tall hierarchy, centralized decision making, and the standardization of behavior through rules and procedures. By contrast, organic structures are flat and decentralized and rely on mutual adjustment between people to get the job done.[20] Which structure is likely to be more resistant to change?

Mechanistic structures are more resistant to change. People who work within a mechanistic structure are expected to act in certain ways and do not develop the capacity to adjust their behavior to changing conditions. The extensive use of mutual adjustment and decentralized authority in an organic structure fosters the development of skills that allow workers to be creative, responsive, and able to find solutions for new problems. A mechanistic structure typically develops as an organization grows and is a principal source of inertia, especially in large organizations.

ORGANIZATIONAL CULTURE The values and norms in an organization's culture can be another source of resistance to change. Just as role relationships result in a series of stable expectations between people, so values and norms cause people to behave in predictable ways. If organizational change disrupts taken-for-granted values and norms and forces people to change what they do and how they do it, an organization's culture will cause resistance to change. For example, many organizations develop conservative values that support the status quo and make managers reluctant to search for new ways to compete. As a result, if the environment changes and a company's products become obsolete, the

Organizational Insight 10.2

InBev Takes over Anheuser-Busch

Norbert Derec/Shutterstock.com

Anheuser-Busch, the giant U.S. brewer, has suffered from declining performance in the 2000s and its stock price has stagnated. Analysts claim that the major reason for this is poor management, which starts at the top: Its CEO, August Busch IV, is the fifth member of the Busch family to hold that position. Given its dominant position in the brewing industry, its managers have failed to make the major changes necessary to keep the company growing profitably. Its values and norms emphasize caution and prudence, and managers' main goal is to protect the company's U.S. market share, given that it makes satisfactory profits so no one wants to rock the boat, least of all its complacent board of directors that has never challenged its top-management team.

All this changed in 2008 when giant European brewer InBev, headquartered in Belgium, launched a hostile takeover attempt for Anheuser-Busch. proposing to buy it for $46.3 billion, a large premium over its then stock price. Within weeks, shocked Anheuser-Busch top managers announced that they had conducted a complete evaluation of the performance of its various business divisions and decided to make major changes to quickly improve its performance. To save a billion a year in operating costs, the changes they proposed included laying off over a thousand employees, forcing early retirement on a thousand more, closing down several old inefficient plants, buying back its stock, and raising the price of its beers.[21]

Analysts commented this was too little too late. Why hadn't its managers made these tough changes a long time ago? Now, the proposed changes simply revealed how poorly Anheuser-Busch was managed, and they doubted these moves would stop InBev's takeover attempt because it was likely a fresh management team, driven by a new set of performance-oriented values and norms. It would be able to overcome inertia in the brewing company and find billions more in cost savings—as well as ways to innovate new kinds of products. Analysts thought it was the right time to make a change at the top and to get rid of the incumbent top managers who simply used their power to protect their own positions and not to improve company effectiveness. By 2009, InBev had succeeded in its attempt to acquire Anheuser-Busch, and by 2011 it had been able to streamline the company and realize over $500 million in cost savings a year. Today it is a much more effective company.[22]

company has nothing to fall back on, and failure is likely.[23] Sometimes, values and norms are so strong that even when the environment is changing and it is clear that a new strategy needs to be adopted, managers cannot change because they are committed to the way they presently do business. Organizational Insight 10.2 illustrates what can happen to a company that suffers from this problem.

Group-Level Resistance to Change

Much of an organization's work is performed by groups, and several group characteristics can produce resistance to change. First, many groups develop strong informal norms that specify appropriate and inappropriate behaviors and govern the interactions between group members. Often, change alters task and role relationships in a group; when it does, it disrupts group norms and the informal expectations that group members have of one another. As a result, members of a group may resist change because a new set of norms must be developed to meet the needs of the new situation.

Group cohesiveness, the attractiveness of a group to its members, also affects group performance. Although some level of cohesiveness promotes group performance, too much cohesiveness may actually reduce performance because it stifles opportunities for the group to change and adapt. A highly cohesive group may resist attempts by management to change what it does or even who is a member of the group. Group members may unite to preserve the status quo and to protect their interests at the expense of other groups.

Groupthink is a pattern of faulty decision making that occurs in cohesive groups when members discount negative information in order to arrive at a unanimous agreement. Escalation of commitment worsens this situation because even when group members realize their decision is wrong, they continue to pursue it because they are committed to it. These group processes make changing a group's behavior very difficult. And the more important the group's activities are to the organization, the greater the impact of these processes on organizational performance.

Individual-Level Resistance to Change

There are also several reasons why individuals within an organization may be inclined to resist change.[24] First, people tend to resist change because they feel uncertain and insecure about what its outcome will be.[25] Workers might be given new tasks. Role relationships may be reorganized. Some workers might lose their jobs. Some people might benefit at the expense of others. Workers' resistance to the uncertainty and insecurity surrounding change can cause organizational inertia. Absenteeism and turnover may increase as change takes place, and workers may become uncooperative, attempt to delay or slow the change process, and otherwise passively resist the change in an attempt to quash it.

Moreover, there is a general tendency for people to selectively perceive information that is consistent with their existing views of their organizations. Thus, when change takes place, workers tend to focus only on how it will affect them or their function or division personally. If they perceive few benefits, they may reject the purpose behind the change. Not surprisingly, it can be difficult for an organization to develop a common platform to promote change across an organization and get people to see the need for change in the same way.

Habit, people's preference for familiar actions and events, is a further impediment to change. The difficulty of breaking bad habits and adopting new styles of behavior indicates how resistant habits are to change. Why are habits hard to break? Some researchers have suggested that people have a built-in tendency to return to their original behaviors, a tendency that stymies change.

Lewin's Force-Field Theory of Change

Force-field theory
A theory of organizational change that argues that two sets of opposing forces within an organization determine how change will take place.

A wide variety of forces make organizations resistant to change, and a wide variety of forces push organizations toward change. Researcher Kurt Lewin developed a theory about organizational change. According to his **force-field theory,** these two sets of forces are always in opposition in an organization.[26] When the forces are evenly balanced, the organization is in a state of inertia and does not change. To get an organization to change, managers must find a way to *increase* the forces for change, *reduce* resistance to change, or do *both* simultaneously. Any of these strategies will overcome inertia and cause an organization to change.

Figure 10.2 illustrates Lewin's theory. An organization at performance level P1 is in balance: Forces for change and resistance to change are equal. Management, however,

Figure 10.2 Lewin's Force-Field Theory of Change

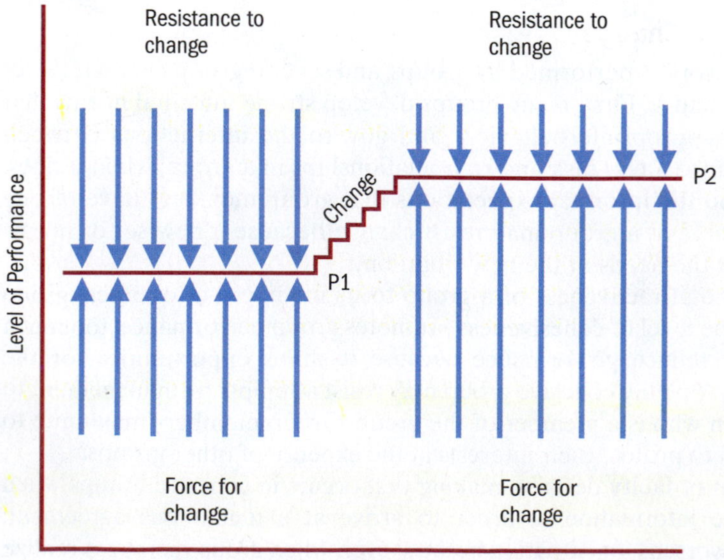

Managerial Implications

Forces for and Resistances to Change

1. Periodically analyze the organizational environment and identify forces for change.
2. Analyze how the change in response to these forces will affect people, functions, and divisions inside the organization.
3. Using this analysis, decide what type of change to pursue, and develop a plan to overcome possible resistance to change and to increase the forces for change.

decides that the organization should strive to achieve performance level P2. To get to level P2, managers must increase the forces for change (the increase is represented by the lengthening of the up arrows), reduce resistance to change (the reduction is represented by the shortening of the down arrows), or do both. If they pursue any of the three strategies successfully, the organization will change and reach performance level P2.

Before we examine in more detail the techniques that managers can use to overcome resistance and facilitate change, we need to look at the types of change they can implement to increase organizational effectiveness.

Evolutionary and Revolutionary Change in Organizations

Managers continually face choices about how best to respond to the forces for change. There are several types of change that managers can adopt to help their organizations achieve desired future states. In general, types of change fall into two broad categories: evolutionary change and revolutionary change.[27]

Evolutionary change is gradual, incremental, and narrowly focused. Evolutionary change involves not a drastic or sudden altering of the basic nature of an organization's strategy and structure but a constant attempt to improve, adapt, and adjust strategy and structure incrementally to accommodate to changes taking place in the environment.[28] Sociotechnical systems theory, total quality management, and the creation of empowered, flexible work groups are three instruments of evolutionary change that organizations use in their attempt to make incremental improvements in the way work gets done. Such improvements might be a better way to operate a technology or to organize the work process.

Evolutionary change Change that is gradual, incremental, and specifically focused.

Evolutionary change is accomplished gradually, incrementally. Some organizations, however, need to make major changes quickly. They do not want to take the time to set up and implement programs that foster evolutionary change or wait for the performance results that such programs can bring about. Faced with drastic, unexpected changes in the environment (for example, a new technological breakthrough) or with impending disaster resulting from years of inaction and neglect, an organization needs to act quickly and decisively. Revolutionary change is called for.

Revolutionary change is rapid, dramatic, and broadly focused. Revolutionary change involves a bold attempt to quickly find new ways to be effective. It is likely to result in a radical shift in ways of doing things, new goals, and a new structure. It has repercussions at all levels in the organization—corporate, divisional, functional, group, and individual. Reengineering, restructuring, and innovation are three important instruments of revolutionary change.

Revolutionary change Change that is sudden, drastic, and organization-wide.

Sociotechnical systems theory A theory that proposes the importance of changing role and task or technical relationships to increase organizational effectiveness.

Developments in Evolutionary Change: Sociotechnical Systems Theory

Sociotechnical systems theory was one of the first theories that proposed the importance of changing role and task or technical relationships to increase organizational effectiveness.[29] It emerged from a study of changing work practices in the British coal-mining industry.[30]

After World War II, new technology that changed work relationships between miners was introduced into the British mining industry. Before the war, coal mining was a small-batch or craft process. Teams of skilled miners dug coal from the coal face underground and performed all the other activities necessary to transport the coal to the surface. Work took place in a confined space where productivity depended on close cooperation between team members. Miners developed their own routines and norms to get the job done and provided one another with social support to help combat the stress of their dangerous and confining working conditions.

This method of coal mining, called the "hand got method," approximated small-batch technology (see Chapter 9). To increase efficiency, managers decided to replace it with the "long wall method." This method used a mechanized, mass production technology. Coal was now cut by miners using powered drills, and it was transported to the surface on conveyor belts. Tasks became more routine as the work process was programmed and standardized. On paper, the new technology promised impressive increases in mining efficiency, but after its introduction, efficiency rose slowly and absenteeism among miners, which had always been high, increased dramatically. Researchers were called in to figure out why the expected gains in efficiency had not occurred.

The researchers pointed out that to operate the new technology efficiently, management had changed the task and role relationships among the miners that had destroyed informal norms, damaged social support, disrupted long-established working relationships, and reduced group cohesiveness. To solve the problem, the researchers recommended linking the new technology with the old social system by recreating the old system of tasks and roles and by decentralizing authority to work groups. When management redesigned the production process in this way, productivity improved and absenteeism fell.

This study led to the development of sociotechnical systems theory, which argues that managers need to fit or "jointly optimize" the workings of an organization's technical and social systems—or, in terms of the present discussion, culture—to promote effectiveness.[31] A poor fit between an organization's technology and social system leads to failure, but a close fit leads to success. The lesson to take from sociotechnical systems theory is that when managers change task and role relationships, they must recognize the need to adjust the technical and social systems gradually so group norms and cohesiveness are not disrupted. By taking this gradual approach, an organization can avoid the group-level resistance to change that we discussed earlier in this chapter.

This pioneering study has been followed by many other studies that show the importance of the link between type of technology and cultural values and norms.[32] Managers need to be sensitive to the fact that the way they structure the work process affects the way people and groups behave. Compare the following two mass production settings, for example. In the first, managers routinize the technology, standardize the work process, and require workers to perform repetitive tasks as quickly as possible; workers are assigned to a place on the production line and are not allowed to move or switch jobs; and managers monitor workers closely and make all the decisions involving control of the work process. In the second, managers standardize the work process but encourage workers to find better ways to perform tasks; workers are allowed to switch jobs; and workers are formed into teams that are empowered to monitor and control important aspects of their own performance.

What differences in values and norms will emerge between these two types of sociotechnical systems? And what will be their effect on performance? Many researchers have argued that the more team-based system will promote the development of values and norms that will boost efficiency and product quality. Indeed, the goal of total quality management, the continuous improvement in product quality, draws heavily on the principles embedded in sociotechnical systems theory; so does the development of flexible workers and workgroups, both discussed next.

Total quality management (TQM)
A technique developed by W. Edwards Deming to continuously improve the effectiveness of flexible work teams.

Total Quality Management

Total quality management (TQM) is an ongoing and constant effort by all of an organization's functions to find new ways to improve the quality of the organization's goods and services.[33] In many companies, the initial decision to adopt a TQM approach signals a radical change in the way activities are organized. Once TQM is adopted by an organization, however, it leads to continuous, incremental change, and all functions are expected to cooperate with each other to improve quality.

First developed by a number of American business consultants such as W. Edwards Deming and Joseph Juran, total quality management was eagerly embraced by Japanese companies after World War II. For Japanese companies, with their tradition of long-term working relationships and cooperation between people and groups, the implementation of the new TQM system was an incremental step. Shop-floor workers in Japan, for example, had long been organized into **quality circles,** groups of workers who met regularly to discuss the way work is performed to find new ways to increase performance.[34] Changes frequently inspired by TQM include altering the design or type of machines used to assemble products and reorganizing the sequence of activities—either within or between functions—necessary to provide a service to a customer. As in sociotechnical systems theory, the emphasis in TQM is on the fit or match between technical and social systems.

Quality circles
Groups of workers who met regularly to discuss the way work is performed in order to find new ways to increase performance.

Changing cross-functional relationships to help improve quality is important in TQM. Poor quality often originates at crossover points or after handoffs when people turn over the work they are doing to people in different functions. The job of intermediate manufacturing, for example, is to assemble inputs that are put together into a final product. Coordinating the design of the various inputs so they fit together smoothly and operate effectively together is one area of TQM. Members of the different functions work together to find new ways to reduce the number of inputs needed or to suggest design improvements that will enable inputs to be assembled more easily and reliably. Such changes increase quality and lower costs. Note that the changes associated with TQM (as with sociotechnical systems theory) are changes in task, role, and group relationships. The results of TQM activities can be dramatic, as Citibank, a leading global financial institution, discovered when it began to use TQM to increase its responsiveness to customers.

Recognizing that customer loyalty determined the bank's future success, as the first step in its TQM effort Citibank focused on identifying the factors that dissatisfied its customers. When it analyzed customer complaints, managers found that most of them concerned the time it took to complete a customer's request, such as responding to an account problem or getting a loan. So Citibank's managers began to examine how they handled each kind of customer request. For each distinct kind of request, they formed a cross-functional team of people whose job was to break down a specific request into the steps between people and departments that were needed to complete the request and analyze them. These teams found that often many steps in the process were unnecessary and could be done away with by the use of the right information systems. They also found that very often delays occurred because employees simply did not know how to handle the request. They were not being given the right kind of training, and when they couldn't handle a request, they simply put it aside until a supervisor could deal with it.

So Citibank decided to implement an organization-wide TQM program. Managers and supervisors were charged with reducing the complexity of the work process and finding the most effective way to process a particular request, such as for a loan. They were also charged with training employees on how to answer each specific request. The results were remarkable. For example, in the loan department the TQM program reduced the number of handoffs necessary to process a request by 75%; average time taken to respond to a customer dropped from several hours to 30 minutes. Within one year, over 92,000 employees had been trained worldwide in the new TQM processes, and Citibank could easily measure TQM's effectiveness by the increased speed with which it was handling an increased volume of customer requests. Another example of how TQM works is described in Organizational Insight 10.3.

More and more companies are embracing the continuous, incremental type of change that results from the implementation of TQM programs. Many companies have found, however, that implementing a TQM program is not always easy because it requires workers and managers to adopt new ways of viewing their roles in an organization. Managers must be willing to decentralize control of decision making, empower workers, and assume the role of facilitator rather than supervisor. The "command and control" model gives way to an "advise and support" model. It is important that workers, as well as

Organizational Insight 10.3

Starwood's Uses TQM to Make Its Hotels More Effective

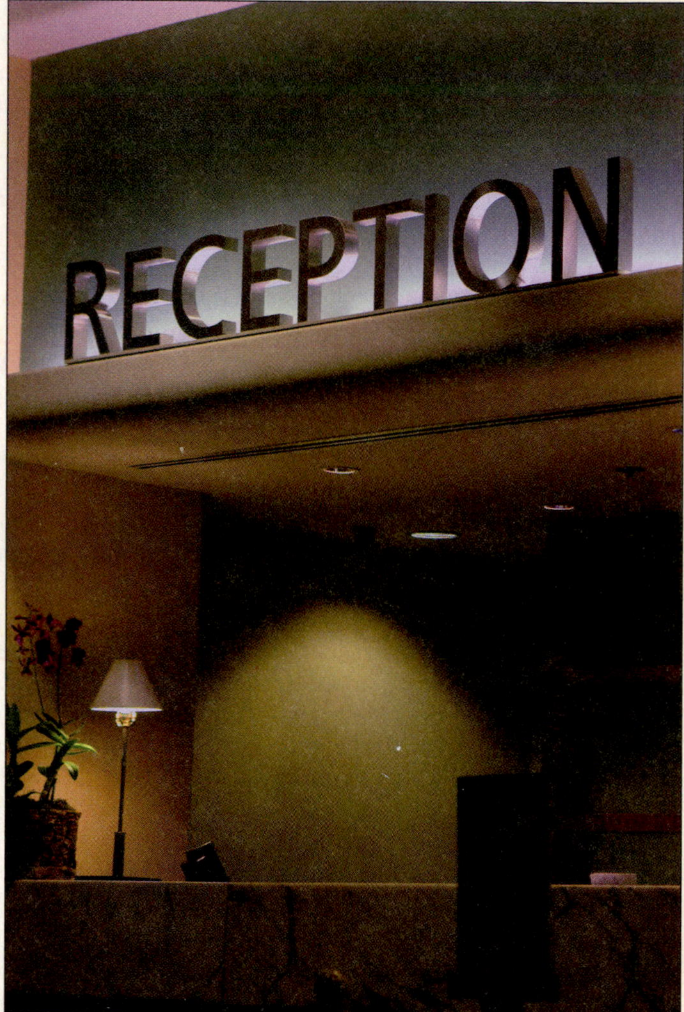

Mr Doomits/Shutterstock.com

Starwood's, based in White Plains, New York, is one of the largest global hotel chains and one of the most profitable: Its profit margins are nearly 15% higher than rivals like Hilton and Marriott. Why? Starwood's attributes a significant part of its high performance to its use of Six Sigma, a TQM technique that it began to use in the 2000s to improve the quality of service it provides its guests.[35]

The company's Six Sigma group is led by Brian Mayer, the vice president of "Six Sigma Operations Management & Room Support" and his father and grandfather both worked in the hospitality industry. Meyer, a Six Sigma expert, helped by a small group of other experts he recruited, implemented the TQM program in 2001. Since then they have trained 150 Starwood's employees as "black belts" and another 2,700 to be "green belts" in the practices of Six Sigma. Black belts are the lead change agents in each Starwood hotel who take responsibility for managing the change process to meet its main objectives—increasing quality customer service and responsiveness.[36] Green belts are the employees trained by Meyer's experts and each hotel's black belt to become the Six Sigma team in each hotel who work together to develop new ideas or programs that will improve customer responsiveness, and to find the work procedures and processes that will implement the new programs most effectively to improve customer service quality.

Almost all the new initiatives that have permeated across the thousands of individual hotels in the Starwood chain come from these Sigma Teams—whose work has raised the company's performance by hundreds of millions of dollars. For example, the "Unwind Program" was an initiative developed to cater to the interests of the 34% of hotel guests that a study found felt lonely and isolated in overnight hotels stays. Its purpose was to make guests feel at home so that they would become return customers. The chain's Six Sigma teams began brainstorming ideas for new kinds of activities and services that would encourage nightly guests to leave their rooms and gather in the lobby where they could meet and mingle with other guests and so feel more at home. They came up with hundreds of potential new programs. An initial concept was to offer guests short complimentary massages in the lobby that they hoped would then encourage them to book massage sessions that would boost hotel revenues. Teams at each hotel then dreamed up other programs that they felt would best meet guest needs. These ranged from fire dancing in hotels in Fiji to Chinese watercolor painting in its hotels in Beijing.[37] These ideas are shared across all the individual hotels in the chain using Starwood's proprietary "E-Tool," which contains thousands of successful projects that have worked—and the specific work procedures needed to perform them successfully.

In another major project, Starwood's managers were concerned about the number of injuries its hotel employees sustained during the course of their work, such as back-strain injuries common among the housekeepers who clean rooms. The black-green belt teams studied how housekeepers worked in the various hotels, and pooling their knowledge they realized that several changes could reduce injuries. For example, they found a large number of back strains occurred early in each housekeeper's shift because they were not "warmed up," so one central coordinating team developed a series of job-related stretching exercises. This team also looked at the cleaning tools being used, and after experimenting with different sizes and types found that curved, longer handled tools that required less bending and stretching could significantly help reduce injuries. To date the program has reduced the accident rate from 12 to 2 for every 200,000 work hours, a major achievement.

As Starwood's has found, having teams of Six Sigma specialists trained to always be on the alert for opportunities to improve the tens of thousands of different work procedures that go to create high-quality customers service pays off. For guests and employees the result is higher satisfaction and higher loyalty to the hotel chain, both in the form of repeat guest visits and in reduced employee turnover.

managers, share in the increased profits that successful TQM programs can provide. In Japan, for example, performance bonuses frequently account for 30% or more of workers' and managers' salaries, and salaries can fluctuate widely from year to year as a result of changes in organizational performance.

Resistance to the changes a TQM program requires can be serious unless management explicitly recognizes the many ways that TQM affects relationships between functions and even divisions. We discuss ways to deal with resistance to change at length later in this chapter.

Despite the success that organizations like Citibank, Harley-Davidson, and UTC have had with TQM, many other organizations have not obtained the increases in quality and reductions in cost that are often associated with TQM and have abandoned their TQM programs. Two reasons for a lack of success with TQM are underestimates of the degree of commitment from people at all levels in the organization necessary to implement a TQM program and the long time frame necessary for TQM efforts to succeed and show results. TQM is not a quick fix that can turn an organization around overnight. It is an evolutionary process that bears fruit only when it becomes a way of life in an organization.[38]

Flexible Workers and Flexible Work Teams

In many modern manufacturing settings, attention to the goals behind sociotechnical systems theory and TQM has led many organizations to embrace the concept of flexible workers and work teams as a way of changing employee attitudes and behaviors. First, employees need to acquire and develop the skills to perform any of the tasks necessary for assembling a range of finished products.[39] A worker first develops the skills needed to accomplish one work task and over time is trained to perform other tasks. Compensation is frequently tied to the number of different tasks that a person can perform. Each worker can substitute for any other worker. As the demand for components or finished products rises or falls, flexible workers can be transferred to the task most needed by the organization. As a result, the organization is able to respond quickly to changes in its environment. Performing more than one task also cuts down on repetition, boredom, and fatigue and raises workers' incentives to improve product quality. When workers learn one another's tasks, they also learn how the different tasks relate to one another. This understanding often leads to new ways of combining tasks or to the redesign of a product to make its manufacture more efficient and less costly.

To further speed the development of functional capabilities, flexible workers are then grouped into flexible work teams.[40] A **flexible work team** is a group of workers who assume responsibility for performing all the operations necessary for completing a specified stage in the manufacturing process. Production line workers who were previously responsible for only their own tasks are placed in groups and jointly assigned responsibility for one stage of the manufacturing process. At Ford plants, for example, one work team is responsible for assembling the car transmission and sending it to the body assembly area, where the body assembly team is responsible for fitting it to the car body. A flexible work team is self-managed: The team members jointly assign tasks and transfer workers from one task to another as necessary.

Flexible work team
A group of workers who assume responsibility for performing all the operations necessary for completing a specified stage in the manufacturing process.

Figure 10.3 illustrates the way in which flexible work teams perform their activities. Separate teams assemble different components and turn those components over to the final-product work team, which assembles the final product. Each team's activities are driven by demands that have their origins in customer demands for the final product. Thus each team has to adjust its activities to the pull coming from the output side of the production process. The experience of Plexus, discussed in Organizational Insight 10.4, illustrates many of the factors associated with the use of flexible work teams.

Developments in Revolutionary Change: Reengineering

The term "reengineering" has been used to refer to the process by which managers redesign how tasks are bundled into roles and functions to improve organizational effectiveness. In the words of Michael Hammer and J. Champy, who popularized the term, reengineering involves the "fundamental rethinking and radical redesign of business processes to achieve

Figure 10.3 The Use of Flexible Work Teams to Assemble Cars

Self-managed teams assemble brake systems, exhaust systems, and other components in accordance with the demands of the final-product team. Driven by customers demands, the final-product team assembles components to produce a car.

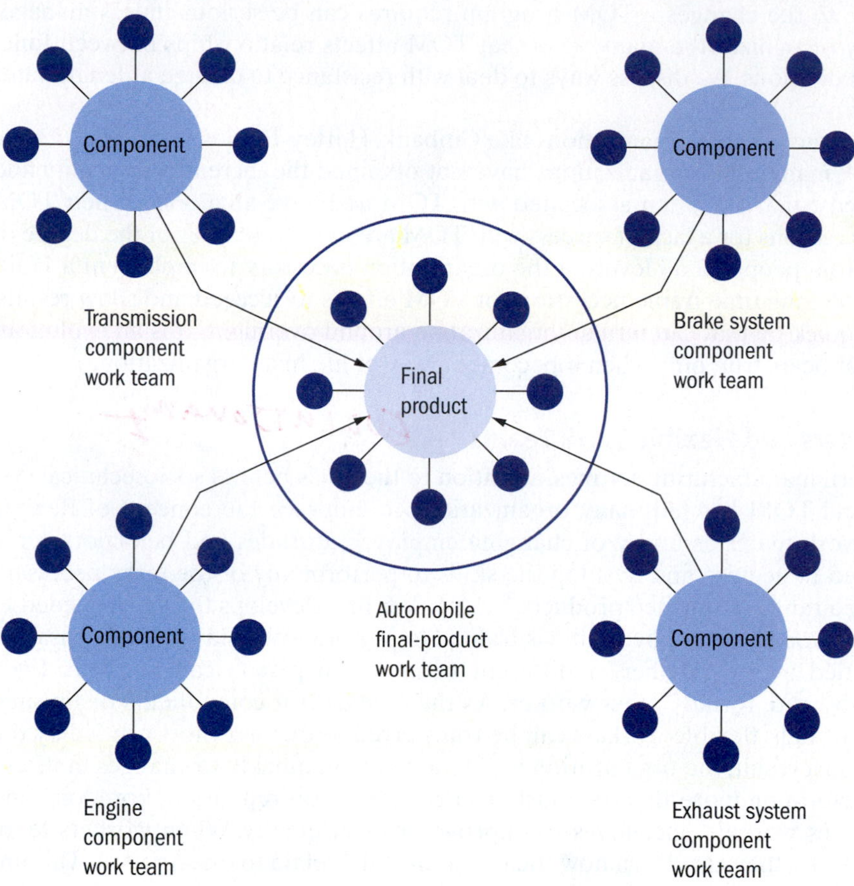

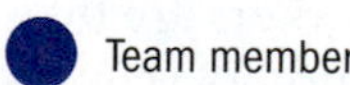

dramatic improvements in critical, contemporary measures of performance such as cost, quality, service, and speed.[43] Change resulting from reengineering requires managers to go back to the basics and pull apart each step in the work process to identify a better way to coordinate and integrate the activities necessary to provide customers with goods and services. Instead of focusing on an organization's *functions*, the managers of a reengineered organization focus on business *processes*. Processes, not organizations, are the object of reengineering. Companies do not reengineer their sales or manufacturing departments; they reengineer the work the people in those departments do.

As this definition suggests, an organization that undertakes reengineering must completely rethink how it goes about its business. Instead of focusing on an organization's functions in isolation from one another, managers make business processes the focus of attention. A **business process** is any activity (such as order processing, inventory control, or product design) that cuts across functional boundaries; it is the ability of people and groups to act in a cross-functional way that is the vital factor in determining how quickly goods and services are delivered to customers or that promotes high quality or low costs. Business processes involve activities across functions. Because reengineering focuses on business processes and not functions, an organization must rethink the way it approaches organizing its activities.

Business process
An activity that cuts across functional boundaries and is vital to the quick delivery of goods and services or that promotes high quality or low costs.

Organizations that take up reengineering deliberately ignore the existing arrangement of tasks, roles, and work activities. They start the reengineering process with the customer

Organizational Insight 10.4

Plexus Decides to Make Flexible Manufacturing Pay Off

In the United States, more than 2.3 million manufacturing jobs were lost to factories in low-cost countries abroad in 2003. While many large U.S. manufacturing companies have given up the battle, some companies like Plexus Corp., based in Neenah, Wisconsin, have been able to craft the decisions that have allowed them to survive and prosper in a low-cost manufacturing world.

Plexus started out making electronic circuit boards in the 1980s for IBM. In the 1990s, however, it saw the writing on the wall as more and more of its customers began to turn to manufacturers abroad to produce the components that go into their products, or even the whole product itself. The problem facing managers at Plexus was how to design a production system that could compete in a low-cost manufacturing world. U.S. companies cannot match the efficiency of foreign manufacturers in producing high volumes of a single product, such as millions of a particular circuit board used in a laptop computer. So Plexus's managers' decided to focus their efforts on developing a manufacturing technology, called "low-high," that could efficiently produce low volumes of many different kinds of products.

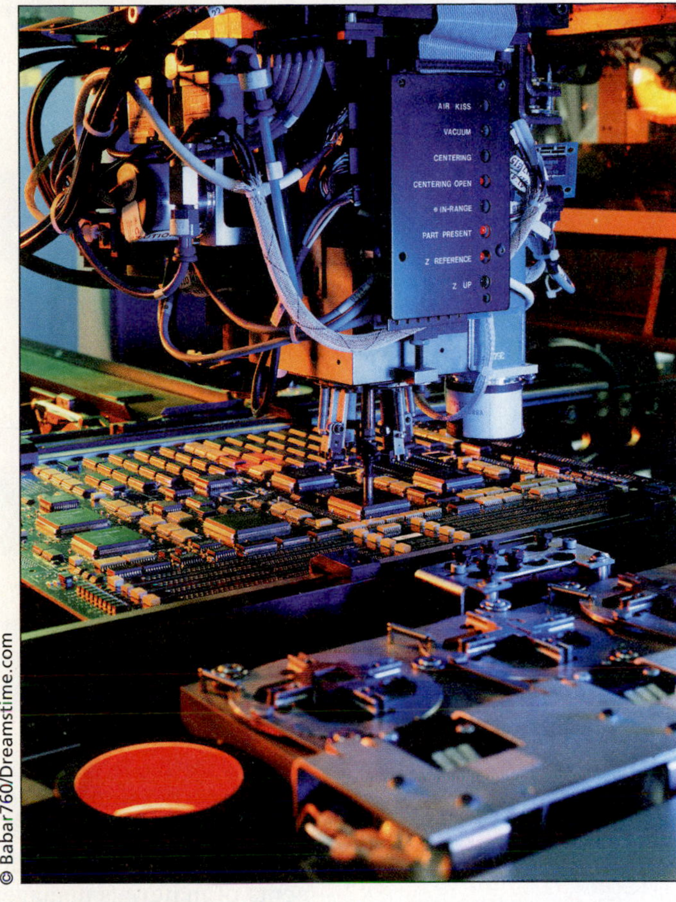

© Babar760/Dreamstime.com

Plexus's engineers worked as a team to design a manufacturing facility in which products would be manufactured in four separate "focused factories." The production line in each factory is designed to allow the operations involved in making each product to be performed separately, although operations still take place in sequence. Workers are cross-trained so they can perform any of the operations in each factory. So, when work slows down at any point in the production of a particular product, a worker further along the line can step back to help solve the problem that occurred at the earlier stage on the line.

These workers are organized into self-managed teams empowered to make all of the decisions necessary to make a particular product in one of the four factories. Since each product is different, these teams have to quickly make the decisions necessary to assemble them if they are to do so cost effectively. The ability of these teams to make rapid decisions is vital on a production line because time is money. Every minute a production line is idle adds hundreds or thousands of dollars to the cost of production. To keep costs down, employees have to be able to react to unexpected contingencies and make nonprogrammed decisions, unlike workers on a conventional production line who simply follow a set performance program.

Team decision making also comes into play when the line is changed over to make a different product. Since nothing is produced while this occurs, it is vital the changeover time be kept to a minimum. At Plexus, engineers and teams working together have reduced this time to as little as 30 minutes. Eighty percent of the time, the line is running and making products; it is idle only 20 percent of the time.[41] This incredible flexibility, developed by the members of the company working for years to improve the decisions involved in the changeover process, is the reason why Plexus is so efficient and can compete against low-cost manufacturers abroad. In fact, today, Plexus has about 400 workers, who can produce 2.5 times the product value that 800 workers could just a decade ago.

Quality is also one of the goals of the self-managed work teams. Employees know nothing is more important in the production of complex, low-volume products than a reputation for products that are reliable and have very low defect rates. By all accounts, both managers and workers are very proud of the way they have developed such an efficient operation. The emphasis at Plexus is on continuous learning to improve the decisions that go into the design of the production process.[42]

(not the product or service) and ask the question "How can I reorganize the way we do our work, our business processes, to provide the best quality, lowest cost goods and services to the customer?" Frequently when companies ask this question, they realize there are more effective ways of organizing their activities. For example, a business process that currently involves members of ten different functions working sequentially to provide goods and services might be performed by one or a few people at a fraction of the original cost, after reengineering.

Figure 10.4 Improving Integration in Functional Structure in Creating a Materials Management Function

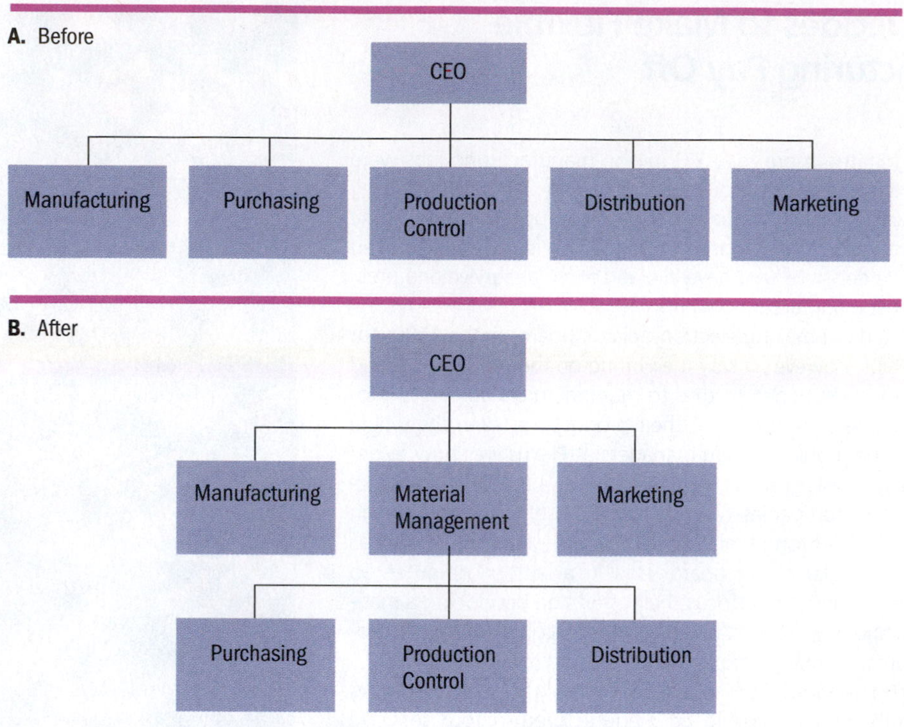

A good example of how to use reengineering to increase functional integration to increase control of activities comes from attempts to redesign the materials management function to improve its effectiveness (see Figure 10.4). In the past, the three main components of materials management—purchasing (responsible for obtaining inputs), production control (responsible for using inputs most efficiently), and distribution (responsible for disposing of the finished product)—were typically in separate functions and had little to do with one another. Figure 10.4A shows the traditional functional design. The problem with the traditional design is that when all aspects of materials management are separate functions, coordinating their activities is difficult. Each function has its own hierarchy, and there are problems in both vertical and horizontal communication. The structure shown in Figure 10.4A makes it difficult to process information quickly to secure cost savings. Computerized production and warehousing, for example, require the careful coordination of activities, but the traditional design of materials management activities does not provide enough control for this to be achieved.

Realizing this separation of activities has often slowed down production and raised costs, most organizations have moved to reengineer the materials management process. Today, most organizations put all three of the functional activities involved in the materials management process inside one function, as shown in Figure 10.4B. Now, one hierarchy of managers is responsible for all three aspects of materials management, and communication among those managers is easy because they are within the same function. Indeed, this redesign makes it much easier for companies to outsource their manufacturing and inventory control activities to specialist organizations such as Jabil Circuit, Flextronics, and UPS. Three guidelines for performing reengineering successfully are as follows:[44]

1. Organize around outcomes, not tasks. Where possible, organize work so one person or one function can perform all the activities necessary to complete the process, thus avoiding the need for transfers (and integration) between functions.
2. Have those who use the output of the process perform the process. Because the people who use the output of the process know best what they want, establish a system of rules and SOPs that will allow them to take control over it.

3. Decentralize decision making to the point where the decision is made. Allow the people on the spot to decide how best to respond to specific problems that arise.

Consider how Hallmark Cards—which is based in Kansas City, Missouri, and sells 55% of the 8 billion birthday, Christmas, and other kinds of cards sold each year in the United States—used reengineering to change its structure.[45] In the 1990s, Hallmark came under increasing attack from smaller and more agile competitors who pioneered new kinds of specialty greeting cards and sold them, often at discount prices, in supermarkets and discount stores. So, to keep Hallmark on top of its market, it hired a team of experts in reengineering to examine how things were currently being done at Hallmark, and then to determine what changes needed to be made to increase effectiveness.

First, these experts assigned 100 managers into 10 teams to analyze Hallmark's competitors, the changing nature of customer needs, the organizational structure the company was using to coordinate its activities, and the ways the company was developing, distributing, and marketing its cards—its basic business processes. What the teams found startled managers from the top down and showed the experts what kinds of change were needed.

Together, the experts and managers discovered that although Hallmark had the world's largest creative staff—over 700 artists and writers who design over 24,000 new cards each year—it was taking more than three years to get a new card to market. Once an artist designed a new card and a writer came up with an appropriate rhyme or message, it took an average of three years for the card to be produced, packaged, and shipped to retailers. Information on changing customer needs, a vital input into decisions about what cards should be designed, took many months to reach artists. That delay made it difficult for Hallmark to respond quickly to its competitors.

Using this new knowledge, the experts and team managers presented Hallmark's top management with 100 recommendations for changes that would allow the company to do its work more quickly and effectively. The recommendations called for a complete change in the way the company organized its basic business processes. Hallmark began by completely restructuring its activities. The organization had been using a functional structure. Artists worked separately from writers, and both artists and writers worked separately from materials management, printing, and manufacturing personnel. From the time a card went from the creative staff to the printing department, 25 handoffs (work exchanges between functions) were needed to produce the final product, and 90% of the time work was simply sitting in somebody's in- or out-basket. So Hallmark changed to a cross-functional team structure and members of different functions—artists, writers, editors, and so on—are now grouped into teams responsible for producing a specific kind of card, such as Christmas cards, get-well cards, or new lines of specialty cards.

To eliminate the need for handoffs between departments, each team is responsible for all aspects of the design process. To reduce the need for handoffs within a team, all team members work together from the beginning to plan the steps in the design process, and all are responsible for reviewing the success of their efforts. To help each team evaluate its efforts and to give each team the information it needs about customer desires, Hallmark introduced a computerized point-of-sales merchandising system in each of its Hallmark Card stores, so each team has instant feedback on what and how many kinds of cards are selling. The effects of these changes have been dramatic. Not only are cards introduced in less than a year, but some reach the market in a matter of months. Quality has increased as each team focuses on improving its cards and costs have fallen because of the efficiency of the new work system.

Reengineering and TQM are highly interrelated and complementary. After revolutionary reengineering has taken place and the question "What is the best way to provide customers with the goods or service they require?" has been answered, evolutionary TQM takes over with its focus on "How can we now continue to improve and refine the new process and find better ways of managing task and role relationships?" Successful organizations examine both questions simultaneously, and they continuously attempt to identify new and better processes for meeting the goals of increased efficiency, quality, and responsiveness to customers.

E-Engineering

The term *e-engineering* refers to companies' attempts to use all kinds of information systems to improve their performance. Previous chapters have provided many examples of how the use of Internet-based software systems can change the way a company's strategy and structure operates. New IT can be employed in all aspects of an organization's business and for all kinds of reasons. For example, Cypress Semiconductor's CEO, T. J. Rodgers, uses the company's online management information system to monitor his managers' activities continually and help him to keep the organizational hierarchy flat. Rodgers claims that he can review the goals of all his 1,500 managers in about four hours, and he does so each week. The importance of e-engineering is increasing as it changes the way a company organizes its value-creation functions and links them to improve its performance. We discuss this important issue at length in Chapters 12 and 13.

Restructuring

Restructuring and reengineering are also closely linked, for in practice the move to a more efficient organizational structure generally results in the layoff of employees, unless the organization is growing rapidly so employees can be transferred or absorbed elsewhere in the organization. It is for this reason that reengineering efforts are unpopular both among workers—who fear they will be reengineered out of a job—and among managers—who fear the loss of their authority and empires as new and more efficient ways of structuring task and role relationships are found.

Restructuring
A process by which managers change task and authority relationships and redesign organizational structure and culture to improve organizational effectiveness.

Nevertheless, **restructuring** refers to the process by which managers change task and authority relationships and redesign organizational structure and culture to improve organizational effectiveness. The move from a functional to some form of divisional structure, and the move from one divisional structure to another, represents one of the most common kinds of restructuring effort. As the environment changes, and as the organization's strategy changes, managers must analyze how well their structure now fits them. Frequently, they find there is a better way of grouping the products they now make to serve customer needs and move, for example, from one kind of product structure to another, for reasons outlined in Chapter 6.

Downsizing
The process by which managers streamline the organizational hierarchy and lay off managers and workers to reduce bureaucratic costs.

Another type of organizational restructuring that has become very common in recent years is **downsizing,** the process by which managers streamline the organizational hierarchy and lay off managers and workers to reduce bureaucratic costs. The size and scope of these recent restructuring and downsizing efforts has been enormous. It is estimated that in the last ten years, Fortune 500 companies have downsized so much that they now employ about 10% fewer managers than they used to. During the recent recession, companies laid off record numbers of employees as they restructured to reduce costs and improve efficiency.

The drive to reduce bureaucratic costs is often a response to increasing competitive pressures in the environment as companies fight to increase their performance and introduce new information technology.[46] For example, the wave of mergers and acquisitions that occurred in the 1990s in many industries such as telecommunications, banking, and defense has also resulted in downsizing because merged companies typically require fewer managers.

Often, after one industry company downsizes, other industry companies are forced to examine their own structures to search out inefficiencies; thus downsizing waves take place across companies in an industry. For example, Molson Breweries, the largest Canadian brewing company, announced it was slashing the size of its headquarters staff to reduce costs. Apparently, Molson's top managers had watched its main competitor, Labatt Breweries, reduce its headquarters staff to 110 and decided that Molson did not need the 200 headquarters staff it employed.[47]

Although there is no doubt that companies have realized considerable cost savings by downsizing and streamlining their hierarchies, some analysts are now wondering whether this process has gone far enough, or even too far.[48] There are increasing reports that the remaining managers in downsized organizations are working under severe stress, both because they fear they might be the next employees to be let go and because they are forced to do the work that was previously performed by the lost employees—work that often they cannot cope with.

Moreover, there are concerns that in pushing their downsizing efforts too far, organizations may be trading off short-term gains from cost savings for long-term losses because of lost opportunities. The argument is that organizations always need some level of "surplus" managers who have the time and energy to improve current operating methods and search the environment to find new opportunities for growth and expansion.[49] Downsized organizations lack the creative middle managers who perform this vital task, and this may hurt them in the future. Hence the terms *anorexic* or *hollow* are used to refer to organizations that downsized too much and have too few managers to help them grow when conditions change.

Although clearly disadvantages are associated with excessive downsizing, it remains true that many organizations became too tall and bloated because their past top-management teams failed to control the growth of their hierarchies and design their organizational structures appropriately. In such cases, managers are forced to restructure their organizations to remain competitive and even to survive. Organizations experiencing a rapid deterioration in performance frequently resort to eliminating divisions, departments, or levels in the hierarchy to lower operating costs. Change in the relationships between divisions or functions is a common outcome of restructuring.

Why does restructuring become necessary, and why may an organization need to downsize its operations? Sometimes, an unforeseen change in the environment occurs: Perhaps a shift in technology makes the company's products obsolete or a worldwide recession reduces demand for its products. Sometimes an organization has excess capacity because customers no longer want the goods and services it provides if they are outdated or offer poor value for money. Sometimes organizations downsize because they have grown too tall and bureaucratic and their operating costs have become much too high.

All too often, companies are forced to downsize and lay off employees because they have not continually monitored the way they operate—their basic business processes—and have not made the incremental changes to their strategies and structures that would have allowed them to contain costs and adjust to changing conditions. Paradoxically, because they have not paid attention to the need to reengineer themselves, they are forced into a position where restructuring becomes the only way they can survive and compete in an increasingly competitive environment.

Restructuring, like reengineering, TQM, and other change strategies, generates resistance to change. Often, the decision to downsize requires the establishment of new task and role relationships. Because this change may threaten the jobs of some workers, they resist the changes taking place. Many plans to introduce change, including restructuring, take a long time to implement and fail because of the high level of resistance that they encounter at all levels of the organization.

Innovation

Restructuring is often necessary because changes in technology make the technology an organization uses to produce goods and services, or the goods and services themselves, obsolete. For example, changes in technology have made computers much cheaper to manufacture and more powerful and have changed the type of computers customers want. If organizations are to avoid being left behind in the competitive race to produce new goods and services, they must take steps to introduce new products or develop new technologies to produce those products reliably and at low cost.

Innovation is the successful use of skills and resources to create new technologies or new goods and services so an organization can change and better respond to the needs of customers.[50] Innovation is one of the most difficult instruments of change to manage. Chapter 13 describes issues involved in managing innovation and in increasing the level of creativity and entrepreneurship inside an organization.

Innovation
The process by which organizations use their skills and resources to develop new goods and services or to develop new production and operating systems so they can better respond to the needs of their customers.

Managing Change: Action Research

No matter what type of evolutionary or revolutionary change an organization adopts, managers face the problem of getting the organization to change. Kurt Lewin, whose force-field theory argues that organizations are balanced between forces for change and

Figure 10.5 Lewin's Three-Step Change Process

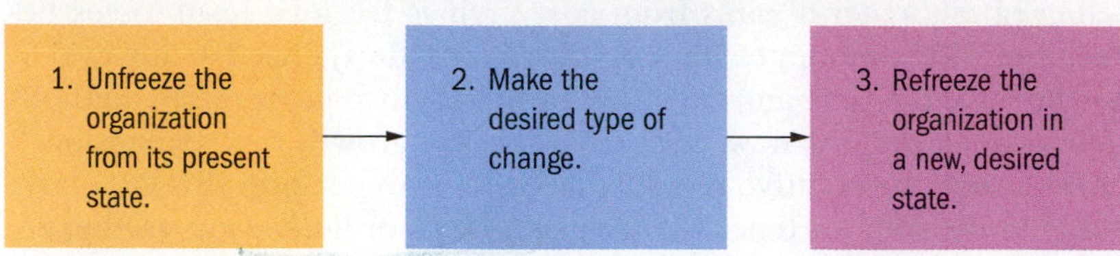
1. Unfreeze the organization from its present state.
2. Make the desired type of change.
3. Refreeze the organization in a new, desired state.

resistance to change, has a related perspective on how managers can bring change to their organization (see Figure 10.5).

In Lewin's view, implementing change is a three-step process: (1) unfreezing the organization from its present state, (2) making the change, and (3) refreezing the organization in the new, desired state so its members do not revert to their previous work attitudes and role behaviors.[51] Lewin warns that resistance to change will quickly cause an organization and its members to revert to their old ways of doing things unless the organization actively takes steps to refreeze the organization with the changes in place. It is not enough to make some changes in task and role relationships and expect the changes to be successful and to endure. To get an organization to remain in its new state, managers must actively manage the change process.

Action research
A strategy for generating and acquiring knowledge that managers can use to define an organization's desired future state and to plan a change program that allows the organization to reach that state.

Action research is a strategy for generating and acquiring knowledge that managers can use to define an organization's desired future state and to plan a change program that allows the organization to reach that state.[52] The techniques and practices of action research, developed by experts, help managers unfreeze an organization, move it to its new, desired position, and refreeze it so the benefits of the change are retained. Figure 10.6 identifies the main steps in action research.

Figure 10.6 Steps in Action Research

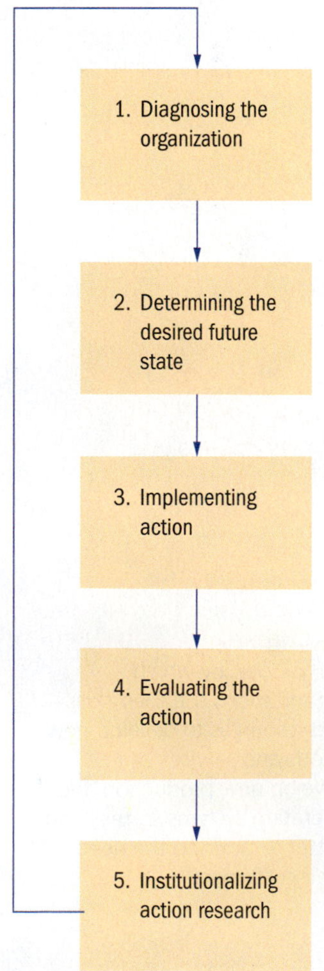
1. Diagnosing the organization
2. Determining the desired future state
3. Implementing action
4. Evaluating the action
5. Institutionalizing action research

Diagnosing the Organization

The first step in action research requires managers to recognize the existence of a problem that needs to be solved and acknowledge that some type of change is needed to solve it. In general, recognition of the need for change arises because somebody in the organization perceives a gap between desired performance and actual performance. Perhaps customer complaints about the quality of goods or services have increased. Perhaps profits have recently fallen or operating costs have been escalating. Perhaps turnover among managers or workers has been excessive. In the first stage of action research, managers need to analyze what is going on and why problems are occurring.

Diagnosing the organization can be a complex process. Like a doctor, managers have to distinguish between symptoms and causes. For example, there is little point in introducing new technology to reduce production costs if the problem is that demand is falling because customers do not like the design of the product. Managers have to carefully collect information about the organization to diagnose the problem correctly and get employees committed to the change process. At this early stage of action research, managers should collect information from people at all levels in the organization and from outsiders such as customers and suppliers. Questionnaire surveys given to employees, customers, and suppliers, and interviews with workers and managers at all levels, can provide information that is essential to a correct diagnosis of the organization's present state.

Determining the Desired Future State

After identification of the present state, the next step is to identify where the organization needs to be—its desired future state. This step also involves a difficult planning process as managers work out various alternative courses of action that could move the organization to where they would like it to be and determine what type of change to implement. Identifying the desired future state involves deciding what the organization's strategy and structure should be. Should the organization focus on reducing costs and increasing efficiency? Or are raising quality and responsiveness to customers the keys to future success? What is the best kind of organizational structure to adopt to realize organizational goals, a product structure or perhaps a cross-functional team structure?

Implementing Action

Implementing action is the third step of action research.[53] It is a three-step process. First, managers need to identify possible impediments to change that they will encounter as they go about making changes—impediments at the organization, group, and individual levels.[54] Suppose managers choose to reengineer the company from a functional to a cross-functional team structure to speed product development and reduce costs. They must anticipate the obstacles they will encounter when they unfreeze the organization and make the changes. Functional managers, for example, are likely to strongly resist efforts to change the company because the change will reduce their power and prestige in the organization. Similarly, members of each function who have grown accustomed to working with the same people and to stable task and role relationships will resist being assigned to a new team where tasks and roles have to be worked out again and new interpersonal relationships have to be learned.

The more revolutionary the change that is adopted, the greater the problem of implementing it. Managers need to find ways to minimize, control, and coopt resistance to change. They also need to devise strategies to bring organizational members on board and foster their commitment to the change process. Managers must also look to the future and seek ways to refreeze the changes that they have made so people cannot slide back into old behaviors.

The second step in implementing action is deciding who will be responsible for actually making the changes and controlling the change process. The choices are to employ **external change agents,** outside consultants who are experts in managing change; **internal change agents,** managers from within the organization who are knowledgeable about the situation; or some combination of both.[55]

External change agents Outside consultants who are experts in managing change.

Internal change agents Managers from within the organization who are knowledgeable about the situation to be changed.

The principal problem with using internal change agents is that other members of the organization may perceive them as being politically involved in the changes and biased toward certain groups. External change agents, in contrast, are likely to be perceived as less influenced by internal politics. Another reason for employing external change agents is that as outsiders they have a detached view of the organization's problems and can distinguish between the "forest and the trees." Insiders can be so involved in what is going on that they cannot see the true source of the problems. Management consultants from McKinsey & Co. are frequently brought in by large organizations to help the top-management team diagnose an organization's problems and suggest solutions. Many consultants specialize in certain types of organizational change, such as restructuring, reengineering, or implementing total quality management.

The third step in implementing action is deciding which specific change strategy will most effectively unfreeze, change, and refreeze the organization. Specific techniques for implementing change are discussed later in this chapter. The types of change that these techniques give rise to fall into two categories: top down and bottom up.[56]

Top-down change is implemented by managers at a high level in the organization. The result of radical organizational restructuring and reengineering is top-down change. Managers high up in the organization decide to make a change, realizing full well that it will reverberate at all organizational levels. The managers choose to manage and solve problems as they arise at the divisional, functional, or individual levels.

Top-down change Change implemented by managers at a high level in the organization.

Bottom-up change is implemented by employees at low levels in the organization and gradually rises until it is felt throughout the organization. When an organization wants to engage in bottom-up change, the first step in the action research process—diagnosing the organization—becomes pivotal in determining the success of the change. Managers involve employees at all levels in the change process, to obtain their input and to lessen their resistance. By reducing the uncertainty that employees experience, bottom-up change facilitates unfreezing and increases the likelihood that employees will retain the new behaviors they learn during the change process. Top-down change proceeds rapidly and forces employees to keep up with the pace of change, troubleshooting to solve problems as they arise.

Bottom-up change Change implemented by employees at low levels in the organization that gradually rises until it is felt throughout the organization.

In general, bottom-up change is easier to implement than top-down change because it provokes less resistance. Organizations that have the time to engage in bottom-up change are generally well-run organizations that pay attention to change, are used to change, and change often. Poorly run organizations, those that rarely change or postpone change until it is too late, are forced to engage in top-down restructuring simply to survive. This has happened to all the major airline companies and carmakers in the 2000s; to avoid bankruptcy they have moved to restructure and downsize and find ways to lower costs to compete with low-cost competitors.

Organizations that change the most are able to exploit the advantages of evolutionary bottom-up change because their managers are always open to the need for change and constantly use action research to find new and better ways to operate and increase effectiveness. Organizations in which change happens rarely are likely candidates for revolutionary top-down change. Because their managers do not use action research on a continuing basis, they attempt change so late that their only option is some massive restructuring or downsizing to turn their organization around.

Evaluating the Action

The fourth step in action research is evaluating the action that has been taken and assessing the degree to which the changes have accomplished the desired objectives. Armed with this evaluation, management decides whether more change is needed to reach the organization's desired future state or whether more effort is needed to refreeze the organization in its new state.[57]

The best way to evaluate the change process is to develop measures or criteria that allow managers to assess whether the organization has reached its desired objectives. When criteria developed at the beginning of action research are used consistently over time to evaluate the effects of the change process, managers have ample information to assess the impact of the changes they have made. They can compare costs before and after the change to see whether efficiency has increased. They can survey workers to see whether they are more satisfied with their jobs. They can survey customers to see whether they are more satisfied with the quality of the organization's products. As part of its TQM effort, managers at Citibank carefully surveyed their customers to make sure that service had improved, for example. That information helped them evaluate the success of their change effort.

Assessing the impact of change is especially difficult because the effects of change may emerge slowly. The action research process that we have been describing may take several years to complete. Typically, reengineering and restructuring take months or years, and total quality management, once under way, never stops. Consequently, managers need valid and reliable measures that they can use to evaluate performance. All too often poorly performing organizations fail to develop and consistently apply criteria that allow them to evaluate their performance. For those organizations, the pressure for change often comes from the outside as shareholders complain about poor profits, parents complain about their children's poor grades, or state inspectors find high rates of postsurgery infection in hospitals.

Institutionalizing Action Research

The need to manage change is so vital in today's quickly changing environment that organizations must institutionalize action research—that is, make it a required habit or a norm adopted by every member of an organization. The institutionalization of action research is as necessary at the top of the organization (where the top-management team plans the organization's future strategy) as it is on the shop floor (where workers meet in quality circles to find new ways to increase efficiency and quality). Because change is so difficult and requires so much thought and effort to implement, members at all levels of the organization must be rewarded for being part of successful change efforts. Top managers can be rewarded with stock options and bonus plans linked to organizational performance. Lower-level members can be rewarded through an employee stock ownership plan (ESOP) and by performance bonuses and pay linked to individual or group performance. Indeed, tangible, performance-related rewards help refreeze an organization in its new state because they help people learn and sustain desired behaviors.

Managerial Implications

Designing a Plan for Change

1. Develop criteria to evaluate whether change is necessary, and use these criteria systematically throughout the change process to assess progress toward the ideal future state.
2. After analyzing resistances to change, carefully design a plan that both reduces resistance to and facilitates change.
3. Recognize that change is easiest to manage when an organization and its members are used to change, and consider using a total quality management program as a way of keeping the organization attuned to the need for change.

Organizational Development

Organizational development (OD) is a series of techniques and methods that managers can use in their action research program to increase the adaptability of their organization.[58] In the words of organizational theorist Warren Bennis, OD refers to a "complex educational strategy intended to change beliefs, attitudes, values, and structure of organizations so that they can better adapt to new technologies, markets, and challenges and the dizzying rate of change itself."[59] The goal of OD is to improve organizational effectiveness and to help people in organizations reach their potential and realize their goals and objectives. As action research proceeds, managers need to continually unfreeze, change, and refreeze managers' and workers' attitudes and behaviors. Many OD techniques have been developed to help managers do this. We first look at OD techniques to help managers unfreeze an organization and overcome resistances to change. We then look at OD techniques to help managers change and refreeze an organization in its new, desired state.

Organizational development (OD)
A series of techniques and methods that managers can use in their action research program to increase the adaptability of their organization.

OD Techniques to Deal with Resistance to Change

Resistance to change occurs at all levels of an organization. It manifests itself as organizational politics and power struggles between individuals and groups, differing perceptions of the need for change, and so on. Tactics that managers can use to reduce resistance to change include education and communication, participation and empowerment, facilitation, bargaining and negotiation, manipulation, and coercion.[60]

EDUCATION AND COMMUNICATION One of the most important impediments to change is uncertainty about what is going to happen. Through education and communication, internal and external agents of change can provide organizational members with information about the change and how it will affect them. Change agents can communicate this information in formal group meetings, by memo, in one-on-one meetings, and, increasingly, through electronic means such as email and videoconferencing. Walmart, for example, has a state-of-the-art videoconferencing system. Managers at corporate headquarters put on presentations that are beamed to all Walmart stores so that both managers and workers are aware of the changes that will be taking place.

Even when plant closures or massive layoffs are planned, it is still best—from both an ethical and a change standpoint—to inform employees about what will happen to them as downsizing occurs. Many organizations fear that disgruntled employees may try to hurt the organization as it closes or sabotage the closing process. Most often, however, employees are cooperative until the end. As organizations become more and more aware of the benefits offered by incremental change, they are increasing communication with the workforce to gain workers' cooperation and to overcome their resistance to change.

PARTICIPATION AND EMPOWERMENT Inviting workers to participate in the change process is becoming a popular method of reducing resistance to change. Participation complements empowerment, increases workers' involvement in decision making, and gives them greater autonomy to change work procedures to improve organizational performance. In addition, to encourage workers to share their skills and talents, organizations are opening up their books to inform workers about the organization's financial condition. Some organizations use ESOPs to motivate and reward employees and to harness their commitment to change, such as Southwest Airlines and GE. Participation and empowerment are two key elements of most TQM programs.

When work-group members are empowered, workers often make many of the decisions and have a lot of the responsibility that used to be part of middle managers' jobs. As a result, one major change that has taken place in many organizations is the reduction in the number of middle managers. What do the remaining middle managers do when empowered work groups take on many of their former responsibilities? Essentially they serve as coaches, facilitators, teachers, and sponsors of the empowered groups. They are, in a sense, what some people call the "new non-manager managers."[61]

One of these new non-manager managers is 37-year-old Cindy Ransom, a middle manager in charge of a Clorox manufacturing plant in Fairfield, California, that employs around 100 workers. In the attempt to improve plant performance, Ransom decided to empower her subordinates by asking them to reorganize the entire plant. Teams of workers earning hourly wages were suddenly setting up training programs, drafting rules governing absenteeism, and redesigning the plant into five customer-focused business groups. Ransom intentionally chose not to interfere with what the workers were doing; her input consisted mainly of answering questions. Middle managers traditionally may have told workers what to do and how and when to do it, but managers of empowered work groups see it as their responsibility to ask the right questions and allow their work groups to decide on the answers.

Two years later, Ransom's plant showed the most improvement in performance in its division. What did Ransom do as workers started taking over many of the responsibilities and tasks she used to perform? She focused on identifying and satisfying the needs of Clorox's customers and suppliers, activities on which she had not spent much time in the past. All in all, empowerment has changed the nature of middle managers' jobs. They have lost some of their old responsibilities but have gained new ones.

FACILITATION Both managers and workers find change stressful because established task and role relationships alter as it takes place. There are several ways in which organizations can help their members to manage stress: providing them with training to help them learn how to perform new tasks, providing them with time off from work to recuperate from the stressful effects of change, or even giving senior members sabbaticals to allow them to recuperate and plan their future work activities. Companies such as Google and Apple, for example, give their most talented engineers time off from ordinary job assignments to think about ways to create new kinds of products.

Many companies employ psychologists and consultants who specialize in helping employees to handle the stress associated with change. During organizational restructuring, when large layoffs are common, many organizations employ consultants to help laid-off workers deal with the stress and uncertainty of being laid off and having to find new jobs. Some companies pay consultants to help their CEOs manage the responsibilities associated with their own jobs, including the act of laying off workers, which CEOs find particularly stressful, for they understand the impact that layoffs have on employees and their families.

BARGAINING AND NEGOTIATION Bargaining and negotiation are important tools that help managers manage conflict. Because change causes conflict, bargaining is an important tool in overcoming resistance to change. By using action research, managers can anticipate the effects of change on interpersonal and intergroup relationships. Managers can use this knowledge to help different people and groups negotiate their future tasks and roles and reach compromises that will lead them to accept change. Negotiation also helps individuals and groups understand how change will affect others so the organization as a whole can develop a common perspective on why change is taking place and why it is important.

When it is clear that change will help some individuals and groups at the expense of others, senior managers need to intervene in the bargaining process and manipulate the situation to secure the agreement, or at least the acceptance, of various people or groups to the results of the change process. As we discuss in Chapter 14, powerful managers have considerable ability to resist change, and in large organizations infighting among divisions can slow or halt the change process unless it is carefully managed. Politics and political tactics like co-optation and building alliances become important as ways of overcoming the opposition of powerful functions and divisions that feel threatened by the changes taking place.

COERCION The ultimate way to eliminate resistance to change is to coerce the key players into accepting change and threaten dire consequences if they choose to resist. Workers and managers at all levels can be threatened with reassignment, demotion, or even termination if they resist or threaten the change process. Top managers attempt to use the legitimate power at their disposal to quash resistance to change and to eliminate it. The advantage of coercion can be the speed at which change takes place. The disadvantage is that it can leave people angry and disenchanted and can make the refreezing process difficult.

Managers should not underestimate the level of resistance to change. Organizations work because they reduce uncertainty by means of predictable rules and routines that people can use to accomplish their tasks. Change wipes out the predictability of rules and routines and perhaps spells the end of the status and prestige that accompany some positions. It is not surprising that people resist change, which is why organizations, because they are collections of people, are so difficult to change.

OD Techniques to Promote Change

Many OD techniques are designed to make changes and to refreeze them. These techniques can be used at the individual, group, and organization levels. The choice of techniques is determined by the type of change. In general, the more revolutionary a change is, the more likely is an organization to use OD techniques at all three levels. Counseling, sensitivity training, and process consultation are OD techniques directed at changing the attitudes and behavior of individuals. Different techniques are effective at the group and organization levels.

COUNSELING, SENSITIVITY TRAINING, AND PROCESS CONSULTATION The personalities of individuals differ and these differences lead individuals to interpret and react to other people and events in a variety of ways. Even though personality cannot be changed significantly in the short run, people can be helped to understand that their own perceptions of a situation are not necessarily the correct or the only possible ones. People can also be helped to understand that they should learn to tolerate differences in perception and to embrace and accept human diversity. Counseling and sensitivity training are techniques that organizations can use to help individuals to understand the nature of their own and other people's personalities and to use that knowledge to improve their interactions with others.[62] The highly motivated, driven boss, for example, must learn that his or her subordinates are not disloyal, lazy, or afflicted with personality problems because they are content to go home at 5 o'clock and want unchallenging job assignments. Instead, they have their own set of work values, and they value their leisure time. Traditionally, one of OD's main efforts has been to improve the quality of the work life of organizational members and increase their well-being and satisfaction with the organization.

Organizational members who are perceived by their superiors or peers to have certain problems in appreciating the viewpoints of others or in dealing with certain types of organizational members are counseled by trained professionals such as psychologists. Through counseling they learn how to manage their interactions with other people in the organization more effectively.

Sensitivity training is an intense type of counseling.[63] Organizational members who are perceived as having problems in dealing with others meet in a group with a trained facilitator to learn more about how they and the other group members view the world.

Sensitivity training
An OD technique that consists of intense counseling in which group members, aided by a facilitator, learn how others perceive them and may learn how to deal more sensitively with others.

Group members are encouraged to be forthright about how they view themselves and other group members, and through discussion they learn the degree to which others perceive them in similar or different ways. Through examining the source of differences in perception, members of the group may reach a better understanding of the way others perceive them and may learn how to deal more sensitively with others.

Participation in sensitivity training is a very intense experience because a person's innermost thoughts and feelings are brought to light and dissected in public. This process makes many people very uncomfortable, so certain ethical issues may be raised by an organization's decision to send "difficult" members for sensitivity training in the hope that they will learn more about themselves.

Process consultation
An OD technique in which a facilitator works closely with a manager on the job to help the manager improve his or her interactions with other group members.

Is a manager too directive, too demanding, or too suspicious of subordinates? Does a manager deliberately deprive subordinates of information to keep them dependent? **Process consultation** provides answers to such questions. Process consultation bears a resemblance to both counseling and sensitivity training.[64] A trained process consultant, or facilitator, works closely with a manager on the job to help the manager improve his or her interaction with other group members. The outside consultant acts as a sounding board so the manager can gain a better idea about what is going on in the group setting and can discover the interpersonal dynamics that are determining the quality of work relationships within the group.

Process consultation, sensitivity training, and counseling are just three of the many OD techniques that have been developed to help individuals learn to change their attitudes and behavior so they can function effectively both as individuals and as organizational members. It is common for many large organizations to provide their higher level managers with a yearly budget to be spent on individual development efforts such as these, or on more conventional knowledge-gaining events such as executive education programs.

Team building
An OD technique in which a facilitator first observes the interactions of group members and then helps them become aware of ways to improve their work interactions.

TEAM BUILDING AND INTERGROUP TRAINING To manage change within a group or between groups, change agents can employ three different kinds of OD techniques. **Team building,** a common method of improving relationships within a group, is similar to process consultation except that all the members of a group participate together to try to improve their work interactions.[65] For example, group members discuss with a change agent who is a trained group facilitator the quality of the interpersonal relationships between team members and between the members and their supervisor. The goal of team building is to improve the way group members work together—to improve group processes to achieve process gains and reduce process losses that are occurring because of shirking and free-riding. Team building does *not* focus on what the group is trying to achieve.

Team building is important when reengineering reorganizes the way people from different functions work together. When new groups are formed, team building can help group members quickly establish task and role relationships so that they can work together effectively. Team building facilitates the development of functional group norms and values and helps members develop a common approach to solving problems.

The change agent begins the team-building process by watching group members interact and identifying the way the group currently works. Then the change agent talks with some or all of the group members one on one to get a sense of the problems that the group is experiencing or just to identify where the group process could be improved. In a subsequent team-building session that normally takes place at a location away from the normal work context, the change agent discusses with group members the observations he or she has made and asks for their views on the issues brought to their attention. Through this discussion, team members ideally develop a new appreciation about the forces that have been affecting their behavior. Group members may form small task forces to suggest ways of improving group process or to discuss specific ways of handling the problems that have been arising. The goal is to establish a platform from which group members themselves, with no input from the change agent, can make continuous improvements in the way the group functions.

Intergroup training
An OD technique that uses team building to improve the work interactions of different functions or divisions.

Intergroup training takes team building one step further and uses it to improve the ways different functions or divisions work together. Its goal is to improve organizational performance by focusing on a function's or division's joint activities and output. Given that cross-functional coordination is especially important in reengineering and total quality management, intergroup training is an important OD technique that organizations can exploit to implement change.

A popular form of intergroup training is called **organizational mirroring,** an OD technique designed to improve the effectiveness of interdependent groups.[66] Suppose that two groups are in conflict or simply need to learn more about each other and one of the groups calls in a consultant to improve intergroup cooperation. The consultant begins by interviewing members of both groups to understand how each group views the other and to uncover possible problems the groups are having with each other. The groups are then brought together in a training session, and the consultant tells them the goal of the session is to explore perceptions and relations in order to improve work relationships. Then, with the consultant leading the discussion, one group describes its perceptions of what is happening and its problems with the other group while the other group sits and listens. Then the consultant reverses the situation—hence the term *organizational mirroring*—and the group that was listening takes its turn discussing its perceptions of what is happening and its problems while the other group listens.

Organizational mirroring An OD technique in which a facilitator helps two interdependent groups explore their perceptions and relations in order to improve their work interactions.

As a result of that initial discussion, each group appreciates the other's perspective. The next step is for members of both groups to form task forces to discuss ways of dealing with the issues or problems that have surfaced. The goal is to develop action plans that can be used to guide future intergroup relations and provide a basis for follow-up. The change agent guiding this training session needs to be skilled in intergroup relations because both groups are discussing sensitive issues. If the process is not managed well, intergroup relations can be further weakened by this OD technique.

TOTAL ORGANIZATIONAL INTERVENTIONS A variety of OD techniques can be used at the organization level to promote organization-wide change. One is the **organizational confrontation meeting.**[67] At this meeting, all of the managers of an organization meet to confront the issue of whether the organization is effectively meeting its goals. At the first stage of the process, again with facilitation by a change agent, top management invites free and open discussion of the organization's situation. Then the consultant divides the managers into groups of seven or eight, ensuring that the groups are as heterogeneous as possible and no bosses and subordinates are members of the same group (so as to encourage free and frank discussion). The small groups report their findings to the total group, and the sorts of problems confronting the organization are categorized. Top management uses this statement of the issues to set organizational priorities and plan group action. Task forces are formed from the small groups to take responsibility for working on the problems identified, and each group reports back to top management on progress that has been made. The result of this process is likely to be changes in the organization's structure and operating procedures. Restructuring, reengineering, and total quality management often originate in organization-wide OD interventions that reveal the kinds of problems an organization needs to solve.

Organizational confrontation meeting An OD technique that brings together all of the managers of an organization at a meeting to confront the issue of whether the organization is meeting its goals effectively.

Summary

Organizational change is an ongoing process with important implications for organizational effectiveness. An organization and its members must be constantly on the alert for changes from within the organization and from the outside environment, and they must learn how to adjust to change quickly and effectively. Often, the revolutionary types of change that result from restructuring and reengineering are necessary only because an organization and its managers ignored or were unaware of changes in the environment and did not make incremental changes as needed. The more an organization changes, the easier and more effective the change process becomes. Developing and managing a plan for change are vital to an organization's success. Chapter 10 has made the following major points:

1. Organizational change is the movement of an organization away from its present state and toward some future state to increase its effectiveness. Forces for organizational change include competitive forces; economic, political, and

global forces; demographic and social forces; and ethical forces. Organizations are often reluctant to change because resistance to change at the organization, group, and individual levels has given rise to organizational inertia.

2. Sources of organization-level resistance to change include power and conflict, differences in functional orientation, mechanistic structure, and organizational culture. Sources of group-level resistance to change include group norms, group cohesiveness, and groupthink and escalation of commitment. Sources of individual-level resistance to change include uncertainty and insecurity, selective perception and retention, and habit.
3. According to Lewin's force-field theory of change, organizations are balanced between forces pushing for change and forces resistant to change. To get an organization to change, managers must find a way to increase the forces for change, reduce resistance to change, or do both simultaneously.
4. Types of change fall into two broad categories: evolutionary and revolutionary. The main instruments of evolutionary change are sociotechnical systems theory, total quality management, and the development of flexible workers and work teams. The main instruments of revolutionary change are reengineering, restructuring, and innovation.
5. Action research is a strategy that managers can use to plan the change process. The main steps in action research are (a) diagnosis and analysis of the organization, (b) determining the desired future state, (c) implementing action, (d) evaluating the action, and (e) institutionalizing action research.
6. Organizational development (OD) is a series of techniques and methods to increase the adaptability of organizations. OD techniques can be used to overcome resistance to change and to help the organization to change itself.
7. OD techniques for dealing with resistance to change include education and communication, participation and empowerment, facilitation, bargaining and negotiation, manipulation, and coercion.
8. OD techniques for promoting change include, at the individual level, counseling, sensitivity training, and process consultation; at the group level, team building and intergroup training; and at the organizational level, organizational confrontation meetings.

Discussion Questions

1. How do evolutionary change and revolutionary change differ?
2. What is a business process, and why is reengineering a popular instrument of change today?
3. Why is restructuring sometimes necessary for reengineering to take place?
4. What are the main steps in action research?
5. What is organizational development, and what is its goal?

Organizational Theory in Action

Practicing Organizational Theory

Managing Change

Break up into groups of three to five people and discuss the following scenario:

You are a group of top managers of one of the Big Three carmakers. Your company has been experiencing increased competition from other carmakers whose innovations in car design and manufacturing methods have allowed them to produce cars that are higher in quality and lower in cost than yours. You have been charged with preparing a plan to change the company's structure to allow you to compete better, and you have decided on two main changes. First, you plan to reengineer the company and move from a multidivisional structure (in which each division produces its own range of cars) to one in which cross-functional product teams become responsible for developing new car models that will be sold by all the divisions. Second, you have decided to implement a total quality management program to raise quality and decentralize decision making authority to the teams and make them responsible for achieving higher quality and lower costs. Thus the changes will disrupt role relationships at both the divisional and functional levels.

1. Discuss the nature of the obstacles at the divisional, functional, and individual level that you will encounter in implementing this new structure. Which do you think will be the most important obstacles to overcome?
2. Discuss some ways you can overcome obstacles to change to help your organization move to its desired future state.

Making the Connection #10

Find an example of a company that has recently gone through a major change. What type of change was it? Why did the organization make the change, and what does it hope to achieve from it?

The Ethical Dimension #10

Imagine you are managers responsible for reengineering an organization into cross-functional teams that will result in the layoff of over 30% of employees.

1. Discuss the resistance to change at the organization and individual levels that you will likely encounter.
2. How will you manage the change process to behave ethically to those employees who will be terminated, and to those who will be reassigned to new jobs and face a new organizational culture?

Analyzing the Organization: Design Module #10

This module focuses on the extent to which your organization has been involved in major change efforts recently and on its approach to promoting innovation.

1. Does *revolutionary* or *evolutionary* best describe the changes that have been taking place in your organization?
2. In what types of change (such as restructuring) has your organization been most involved? How successful have these change efforts been?
3. With the information that you have at your disposal, discuss (a) the forces for change, (b) obstacles to change, and (c) the strategy for change your organization has adopted.

CASE FOR ANALYSIS

Nike Learns How to Change

Nike, headquartered in Beaverton, Oregon, is the biggest sports shoemaker in the world. Throughout the 1990s it seemed that its founder and CEO, Phil Knight, and his teams of shoe designers could do no wrong; all their innovative design decisions led to the global acceptance of Nike's shoes and record sales and profits for the company. As time went by, however, and its fortune soared, some strange dynamics occurred. The company's managers and designers became convinced they "knew best" what customers wanted, and that their decisions about how to change and improve Nike's future shoes would be enthusiastically received by customers.

But things were changing in the sport-shoe environment. New competitors had entered the market and they began to offer alternative kinds of sports shoes—shoes targeted at specific market segments like skateboarders, soccer players, or power walkers. Nike had no shoes in these market segments. Moreover, Nike also failed to notice that sports shoes were evolving into performance shoes for more everyday uses such as walking or backpacking. It also failed to take note of consumers' increasing preferences for dark blue and black shoes that wore well in cities and that could double as work and walking shoes.

In the 2000s Nike's sales and profits fell sharply as many of its new lines of sports shoes were *not* well received by customers, and CEO Phil Knight knew he had to find a way to turn his company around. Realizing that his designers were starting to make poor decisions, he brought in managers from outside the company to change the way decisions were made. An executive who was brought in to lead the outdoor products division advised Knight to take over and purchase small specialized companies, such as North Face, to quickly widen Nike's product line. But Nike's other managers and designers resisted this idea, believing that they could still make the best decisions. With sales still slumping, it became obvious that Nike would have to take over specialist shoe companies to grow successfully. One of the first of its acquisitions was Cole Haan, the luxury shoemaker, and Nike's designers proceeded to revitalize its line of shoes by using their skills to make them more comfortable. Then, realizing it had to get into small markets, in the 2000s, Nike bought other small companies such as Hurley, the skate and surfboard apparel maker.

To try to overcome its past errors in its decision making, however, Knight decided on a new way to design shoes for specialized niche markets, like the skateboarding, golf, and soccer markets. Henceforth, rather than having Nike's designers all grouped together in one large design department, they would be split up into different teams. Each team would focus on developing unique products to match the needs of customers in its assigned market segment. The skate team, for example, was set up as a separate and independent unit, and its designers and marketing experts were charged to develop a unique line of shoes for the sport. Similarly, because of poor sales, Nike separated golf products from the rest of the company and created an independent unit to develop new golf shoes, clubs, and other golfing products.

Nike was attempting to demolish the old companywide mindset that had resulted in its past decision-making errors that led to the wrong kinds of changes. With many different teams, each working on different lines of shoes and other products, Nike was hoping to build diversity into its decision making and create teams of experts who were attuned to changing customer needs in their segments of the sports product market. Nike's new approach to decision making worked; most of its new shoes are now leaders in their market segments and its sales and profits have soared in the 2010s as a result of the way it has changed the way it makes decisions. Nike learned from its mistakes and Knight continues to promote organizational learning—the process of helping the members of an organization to "think outside the box" and be willing to experiment, take risks, and make change possible.[68]

Discussion Questions

1. How did Nike change the way it made decisions and introduce new products?
2. In what ways could Nike use the change techniques discussed in this chapter to find ways to improve its effectiveness and competitive advantage?

References

1 M. Beer, *Organizational Change and Development* (Santa Monica, CA: Goodyear, 1980); J. I. Porras and R. C. Silvers, "Organization Development and Transformation," *Annual Review of Psychology* 42 (1991), 51–78.

2 C. Argyris, R. Putnam, and D. M. Smith, *Action Science* (San Francisco: Jossey-Bass, 1985).

3 R. M. Kanter, *The Change Masters: Innovation for Productivity in the American Corporation* (New York: Simon & Schuster, 1984).

4 C. W. L. Hill and G. R. Jones, *Strategic Management: An Integrated Approach*, 3rd ed. (Boston: Houghton Mifflin, 2011).

5 Ibid.

6 G. R. Jones, *Organizational Theory: Text and Cases* (Reading, MA: Addison-Wesley, 2010).

7 C. W. L. Hill, *International Business* (Chicago: Irwin, 2009).

8 C. A. Bartlett and S. Ghoshal, *Managing Across Borders* (Boston: Harvard Business School Press, 1989).

9 C. K. Prahalad and Y. L. Doz, *The Multinational Mission: Balancing Local Demands and Global Vision* (New York: Free Press, 1987).

10 D. Jamieson and J. O'Mara, *Managing Workforce 2000: Gaining a Diversity Advantage* (San Francisco: Jossey-Bass, 1991).

11 S. E. Jackson and Associates, *Diversity in the Workplace: Human Resource Initiatives* (New York: Guilford Press, 1992).

12 W. H. Shaw and V. Barry, *Moral Issues in Business*, 6th ed. (Belmont, CA: Wadsworth, 1995).

13 T. Donaldson, *Corporations and Morality* (Englewood Cliffs, NJ: Prentice Hall, 1982).

14 Bohr, J. "Deadly Roses," *The Battalion,* February 13 (2006): 3.

15 www.nikebiz.com 2011; www.thegap.com, 2011.

16 M. Hannan and J. Freeman, "Structural Inertia and Organizational Change," *American Sociological Review*, 49 (1989), 149–164.

17 L. E. Greiner, "Evolution and Revolution as Organizations Grow," *Harvard Business Review* (July–August 1972): 37–46.

18 R. M. Kanter, *When Giants Learn to Dance: Mastering the Challenges of Strategy* (New York: Simon & Schuster, 1989).

19 J. P. Kotter and L. A. Schlesinger, "Choosing Strategies for Change," *Harvard Business Review* (March–April 1979): 106–114.

20 T. Burns and G. M. Stalker, *The Management of Innovation* (London: Tavistock, 1961).

21 www.anheuser-busch.com, 2011.

22 www.inbev.com, 2011.

23 P. R. Lawrence and J. W. Lorsch, *Organization and Environment* (Boston: Harvard Business School Press, 1972).

24 R. Likert, *The Human Organization* (New York: McGraw-Hill, 1967).

25 C. Argyris, *Personality and Organization* (New York: Harper & Row, 1957).

26 This section draws heavily on K. Lewin, *Field-Theory in Social Science* (New York: Harper & Row, 1951).

27 D. Miller, "Evolution and Revolution: A Quantum View of Structural Change in Organizations," *Journal of Management Studies* 19 (1982), pp. 11–151; D. Miller, "Momentum and Revolution in Organizational Adaptation," *Academy of Management Journal* 2 (1980), 591–614.

28 C. E. Lindblom, "The Science of Muddling Through," *Public Administration Review*, *19* (1959), 79–88; P. C. Nystrom and W. H. Starbuck, "To Avoid Organizational Crises, Unlearn," *Organizational Dynamics*, *12* (1984), 53–65.

29 E. L. Trist, G. Higgins, H. Murray, and A. G. Pollock, *Organizational Choice* (London: Tavistock, 1965); J. C. Taylor, "The Human Side of Work: The Socio-Technical Approach to Work Design," *Personnel Review* 4 (1975), pp. 17–22.

30 E. L. Trist and K. W. Bamforth, "Some Social and Psychological Consequences of the Long Wall Method of Coal Mining," *Human Relations* 4 (1951), 3–38; F. E. Emery and E. L. Trist, "Socio-Technical Systems" (London: Proceedings of the 6th Annual International Meeting of the Institute of Management Sciences, 1965), pp. 92–93.

31 E. L. Trist, G. Higgins, H. Murray, and A. G. Pollock, *Organizational Choice* (London: Tavistock, 1965); J. C. Taylor, "The Human Side of Work: The Socio-Technical Approach to Work Design," *Personnel Review* 4 (1975), 17–22.

32 For a review, see D. R. Denison, "What Is the Difference Between Organizational Culture and Organizational Climate? A Native's Point of View on a Decade of Paradigm Wars," *Academy of Management Review* 21 (1996), 619–654.

33 W. Edwards Deming, *Out of the Crisis* (Cambridge, MA: MIT Press, 1989); M. Walton, *The Deming Management Method* (New York: Perigee Books, 1990).

34 J. McHugh and B. Dale, "Quality Circles," in R. Wild, ed., *International Handbook of Production and Operations Research* (London: Cassel, 1989).

35 www.starwood.com, 2011.

36 S. E. Ante, "Six Sigma Kick-Starts Starwood," www.businessweek.com, August 30, 2007.

37 Ibid.

38 S. M. Young, "A Framework for the Successful Adoption and Performance of Japanese Manufacturing Techniques in the U.S.," *Academy of Management Review* 17 (1992), 677–700.

39 Young, "A Framework for the Successful Adoption and Performance of Japanese Manufacturing Practices in the U.S."

40 R. Parthasarthy and S. P. Sethi, "The Impact of Flexible Automation on Business Strategy and Organizational Structure," *Academy of Management Review* 17 (1992), 86–111; Voss, "Managing Manufacturing Technology."

41 W. M. Bulkeley, "Plexus Strategy: Smaller Runs of More Things," *Wall Street Journal*, October 8, 2003, B1, B.12.

42 www.plexus.com, 2011.

43 M. Hammer and J. Champy, *Reengineering the Corporation* (New York: HarperCollins, 1993).

44 M. Hammer, "Reengineering Work: Don't Automate, Obliterate," *Harvard Business Review* (July–August 1990): 104–112.

45 "Facts About Hallmark," www.hallmark.com, 2011.

46 S. J. Freeman and K. S. Cameron, "Organizational Downsizing: A Convergence and Reorientation Framework," *Organizational Science* 4 (1993), 10–29.

47 P. Brent, "3 Molson Executives Ousted in Decentralization Move," *Financial Post-Toronto,* December 20, 1995, p. 3.

48 R. L. DeWitt, "The Structural Consequences of Downsizing," *Organizational Science* 4 (1993), pp. 30–40.

49 "The Salaryman Rides Again," *The Economist*, December 4, 1995, p. 64.

50 Jones, *Organizational Theory*; R. A. Burgelman and M. A. Maidique, *Strategic Management of Technology and Innovation* (Homewood, IL: Irwin, 1988).

51 Lewin, *Field-Theory in Social Science*, pp. 172–174.

52 This section draws heavily on P. A. Clark, *Action Research and Organizational Change* (New York: Harper & Row, 1972); L. Brown, "Research Action: Organizational Feedback, Understanding and Change," *Journal of Applied Behavioral Research* 8 (1972), 697–711; N. Margulies and A. P. Raia, eds., *Conceptual Foundations of Organizational Development* (New York: McGraw-Hill, 1978).

53 W. L. French and C. H. Bell, *Organizational Development* (Englewood Cliffs, NJ: Prentice Hall, 1990).

54 L. Coch and J. R. P. French, "Overcoming Resistance to Change," *Human Relations* 1 (1948), 512–532.

55 French and Bell, *Organizational Development.*

56 Ibid.

57 W. L. French, "A Checklist for Organizing and Implementing an OD Effort," in W. L. French, C. H. Bell, and R. A. Zawacki, eds., *Organizational Development and Transformation* (Homewood, IL: Irwin, 1994), pp. 484–495.

58 Kotter et al., *Organization*, p. 487.

59 W. G. Bennis, *Organizational Development: Its Nature, Origins, and Perspectives* (Reading, MA: Addison-Wesley, 1969).

60 Kotter and Schlesinger, "Choosing Strategies for Change."

61 B. Dumaine, "The New Non-Manager Managers," *Fortune*, February 22, 1993, pp. 80–84.

62 E. H. Schein, *Organizational Psychology* (Englewood Cliffs, NJ: Prentice Hall, 1980).

63 R. T. Golembiewski, "The Laboratory Approach to Organization Change: Schema of a Method," in Margulies and Raia, eds., *Conceptual Foundations of Organizational Development*, pp. 198–212; J. Kelley "Organizational Development Through Structured Sensitivity Training," Ibid., pp. 213–228.

64 E. H. Schein, *Process Consultation* (Reading, MA: Addison-Wesley, 1969).

65 M. Sashkin and W. Warner Burke, "Organization Development in the 1980s," *Journal of Management* 13 (1987), pp. 393–417; D. Eden, "Team Development: Quasi-Experimental Confirmation Among Combat Companies," *Group and Organization Studies* 5 (1986), 133–146; K. P. DeMeuse and S. J. Liebowitz, "An Empirical Analysis of Team Building Research," *Group and Organization Studies* 6 (1981), pp. 357–378.

66 French and Bell, *Organization Development.*

67 R. Beckhard, "The Confrontation Meeting," *Harvard Business Review* (March–April 1967): 159–165.

68 www.nike.com, 2011.

CHAPTER 11

Organizational Transformations: Birth, Growth, Decline, and Death

Learning Objectives

Organizations that successfully carve out a niche in their environments so that they can attract resources (such as customers) face a series of problems in their struggle for growth and survival. This chapter examines the organizational change and transformation problems that occur over the life cycle of an organization. Entrepreneurs and managers who understand the forces that lead to the birth of organizations, that influence how they grow and mature over time, and that eventually may cause their decline and death will be able to change their organization's strategy and structure to increase its effectiveness and chances of survival.

After reading this chapter you should be able to:

1. Appreciate the problems involved in surviving the perils of organizational birth and what actions founders can take to help their new organizations survive.
2. Describe the typical problems that arise as an organization grows and matures, and how an organization must change if it is to survive and prosper.
3. Discuss why organizational decline occurs, identify the stages of decline, and describe how managers can work to prevent the failure and even the death or dissolution of an organization.

The Organizational Life Cycle

Why do some organizations survive and prosper while others fail and die? Why do some organizations have the ability to manage their strategies, structures, and cultures to gain access to environmental resources while others fail at this task? To answer these questions, researchers suggest we need to understand the dynamics that affect organizations as they seek a satisfactory fit with their environment.[1] It is commonly believed that organizations experience a predictable sequence of stages of growth and change over time: the **organizational life cycle.**

Organizational life cycle A sequence of stages of growth and development through which organizations may pass.

The four principal stages of the organizational life cycle are birth, growth, decline, and death (see Figure 11.1).[2] Organizations pass through these stages at different rates, and some do not experience every stage. Moreover, some companies go directly from birth to death without enjoying any growth if they do not attract customers or resources. Some organizations spend a long time in the growth stage, and many researchers have identified various substages of growth through which an organization must navigate. There are also substages of decline. Some organizations in decline take corrective action, change quickly, and turn themselves around.

The way an organization can change in response to the problems it confronts determines whether and when it will go on to the next stage in the life cycle and survive and prosper or fail and die. Each stage is examined in detail here.

Figure 11.1 A Model of the Organizational Life Cycle

Organizations pass through these four stages at different rates, and some do not experience every stage.

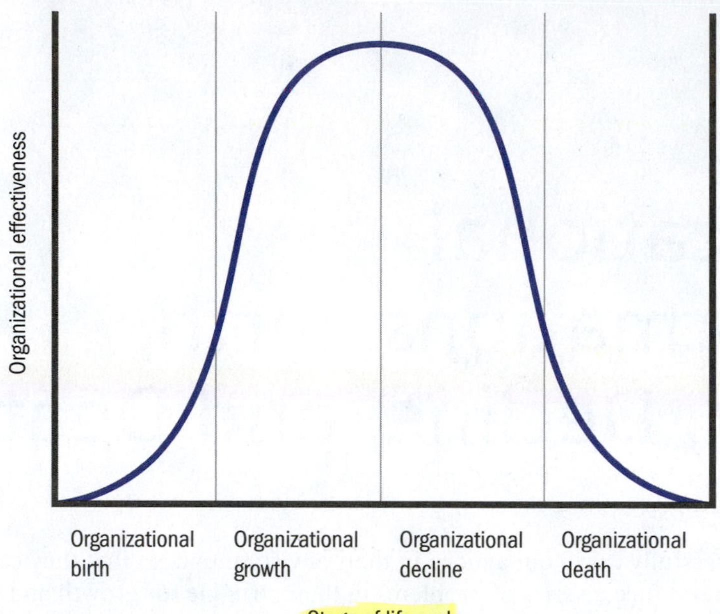

Organizational Birth

Entrepreneurs
People who recognize and take advantage of opportunities to use their skills and competences to create value.

Organizations are born when people called **entrepreneurs** recognize and take advantage of opportunities to use their skills and competences to utilize resources in new ways to create value.[3] Michael Dell found a new way to market low-priced computers to customers: mail order. Liz Claiborne took advantage of a growing niche in the women's clothing market—business attire for women. Dell and Claiborne saw an opportunity to create value (for computer users and businesswomen), and they both seized the opportunity to found an organization that could produce lower priced products—PCs and business attire—than the competition.

Organizational birth
The founding of an organization: a dangerous life cycle stage associated with the greatest chance of failure.

Liability of newness
The dangers associated with being the first in a new environment.

Organizational birth, the founding of an organization, is a dangerous stage of the life cycle and associated with the greatest chance of failure. The failure rate is high because new organizations experience the **liability of newness**—the dangers associated with being the first to operate in a new environment.[4] This liability is great for several reasons.

Entrepreneurship is an inherently risky process. Because entrepreneurs undertake *new* ventures, there is no way to predict or guarantee success.[5] Entrepreneurs bear this uncertainty because they stand to earn potentially enormous returns if their businesses take off. Much of the time, however, entrepreneurs make mistakes in judgment or planning, and the result is organizational death.[6]

A new organization is fragile because it lacks a formal structure to give its value-creation processes and actions reliability and stability. At first, all its activities are performed by trial and error; organizational structure emerges gradually as decisions are made about what roles, rules, and SOPs should be implemented. Eventually, for example, it may become clear that one manager should handle money coming in from customers (accounts receivable), another should control money being paid out to suppliers (accounts payable), and another should obtain new accounts. But at first, in a new organization, the structure is in the mind of the founder; it is not formalized in a chart or a set of rules. The structure is flexible and responsive, allowing the organization to adapt and continually improve its routines to meet the needs of its environment.

A flexible structure can be an advantage when it allows the organization to change and take advantage of new opportunities, but it can also be a disadvantage. A formal structure provides stability and certainty by serving as the organization's memory.

Structure specifies an organization's activities and the procedures for getting them done. If such procedures are not written down, a new organization can literally forget the skills and procedures that made it successful. A formal structure provides an organization with a firm foundation from which to improve on existing procedures and develop new ones.[7]

Another reason why organizational birth is a dangerous stage is that conditions in the environment may be hostile to a new organization. Resources, for example, may be scarce or difficult to obtain because many established organizations are competing for them.

Developing a Plan for a New Business

One way in which entrepreneurs can address all these issues is through the crafting of a business plan that outlines how they plan to compete in the environment. Table 11.1 lists the steps in the development of a business plan.

Planning for a new business begins when an entrepreneur notices an opportunity to develop a new or improved good or service for the whole market or for a specific market niche. For example, an entrepreneur might notice an opportunity in the fast-food market to provide customers with healthful fast food, such as rotisserie chicken served with fresh vegetables or burritos made with organic ingredients. This is what the founders of the Boston Market and Chipotle restaurant chains did.

The next step is to test the feasibility of the new product idea. The entrepreneur conducts as thorough a strategic planning exercise as possible, using SWOT analysis, the analysis of organizational strengths and weaknesses and environmental opportunities and threats. Potential threats might be that KFC will decide to imitate the idea and offer its customers rotisserie chicken, which KFC did after Boston Market identified the new market niche. The entrepreneur should conduct a thorough analysis of the external environment (see Chapter 3) to test the potential of a new product idea and must be willing to abandon an idea if it seems likely that the threats and risks may overwhelm the opportunities and returns. Entrepreneurship is always a very risky process, and many entrepreneurs become so committed to their new ideas that they ignore or discount the potential threats and forge ahead—only to lose their shirts.

If the environmental analysis suggests that the product idea is feasible, the next step is to examine the strengths and weaknesses of the idea. At this stage the main strength is the resources possessed by the entrepreneur. Does the entrepreneur have access to an adequate source of funds? Does the entrepreneur have any experience in the fast-food industry, such as managing a restaurant? To identify weaknesses, the entrepreneur needs to assess how many and what kind of resources will be necessary to establish a viable new

TABLE 11.1 Developing a Business Plan

1. Notice a product opportunity, and develop a basic business idea
   - Goods/services
   - Customers/markets
2. Conduct a strategic (SWOT) analysis
   - Identify opportunities
   - Identify threats
   - Identify strengths
   - Identify weaknesses
3. Decide whether the business opportunity is feasible
4. Prepare a detailed business plan
   - Statement of mission, goals, and financial objectives
   - Statement of strategic objectives
   - List of necessary resources
   - Organizational timeline of events

* HOSTILE TO NEW ORGANIZATIONS

venture—such as a chain of burrito restaurants. Analysis might reveal that the new product idea will not generate an adequate return on investment. Or it might reveal that the entrepreneur needs to find partners to help provide the resources needed to open a chain on a sufficient scale to generate a high enough return on investment.

After conducting a thorough SWOT analysis, if the entrepreneur decides that the new product idea is feasible, the hard work begins: developing the actual business plan that will be used to attract investors or funds from banks. Included in the business plan should be the same basic elements as in the product development plan: (1) a statement of the organization's mission, goals, and financial objectives; (2) a statement of the organization's strategic objectives, including an analysis of the product's market potential, based on the SWOT analysis that has already been conducted; (3) a list of all the functional and organizational resources that will be required to implement the new product idea successfully, including a list of technological, financial, and human resource requirements; and (4) a timeline that contains specific milestones for the entrepreneur and others to use to measure the progress of the venture, such as target dates for the final design and the opening of the first restaurant.

Many entrepreneurs do not have the luxury of having a team of cross-functional managers to help develop a detailed business plan. This obviously is true for solo ventures. One reason why franchising has become so popular is that potential entrepreneurs can purchase and draw on the business plan and experience of an already existing company, thereby reducing the risks associated with opening a new business.

In sum, entrepreneurs have a number of significant challenges to confront and conquer if they are to be successful. It is not uncommon for an entrepreneur to fail repeatedly before he or she finds a venture that proves successful. It also is not uncommon for an entrepreneur who establishes a successful new company to sell it in order to move on to new ventures that promise new risks and returns. An example of just such a entrepreneur is Wayne Huizenga, who bought many small waste disposal companies to create the giant WMX waste disposal company, which he eventually sold. A few years later Huizenga took control of Blockbuster Video and, by opening and buying other video store chains, turned Blockbuster Video into the biggest video chain in the United States, only to sell it in 1994. A historical example of an entrepreneur who transformed the steel industry is presented in Organizational Insight 11.1.

Organizational Insight 11.1

Andrew Carnegie and Entrepreneurship

Andrew Carnegie was born in Scotland in 1835; he was the son of a master hand-loom weaver who, at that time, employed four apprentices to weave fine linen tablecloths.[8] His family was well-to-do, yet ten years later they were living in poverty. Why? Advances in weaving technology had led to the invention of steam-powered weaving looms that could produce large quantities of cotton cloth at a much lower price than was possible through hand-loom weaving. Hand-loom weavers could not compete at these low prices and Carnegie's father was put out of business. In 1848, his family, like hundreds of thousands of other families in Europe at this time, decided to emigrate to the United States to find work and survive.

The Carnegies settled near Pittsburgh, where they had relatives, and the father continued to weave tablecloths and sell them door to door, making around $6 dollars a week. His mother, who had come from a family of cobblers, took in shoes for repair and made around $4 a week. Carnegie found a job as a "bobbin boy," replacing spools of thread on power looms in a textile factory; he took home $1.20 for a 60-hour week.

Once his employer found out he could read and write, a rare skill at this time, he became a bookkeeper for the factory. In his spare time he became a telegraph messenger and learned telegraphy. He began to deliver telegrams to Tom Scott, a top manager at the Pennsylvania Railroad, who came to appreciate Carnegie's drive and talents. Scott made him his personal telegrapher for the astonishing sum of $35 a week. Carnegie was now 17. Only seven years later, when he was 24, he was promoted to Scott's job, as superintendent of the Western Division of the railroad. At 30, he was offered the top job of superintendent of the whole railroad! Carnegie had other ambitions, however. During his time at the railroad he had invested cleverly in railroad stock and was now a wealthy man, with an income of $48,000 a year, of which only $2,800 came from his railroad salary.

While a manager at the railroad, Carnegie had made his name by continually finding ways to use resources more productively to reduce costs and increase profitability. His company's stock price had shot up—which explains why he was offered the railroad's top job. Carnegie saw

Wade H. Massie/Shutterstock.com

an opportunity to apply his cost-cutting skills in the backward steel industry. Carnegie had noticed U.S. railroads' growing demand for steel as they built new U.S. railways rapidly in the 1860s. At that time, steel was made using small-batch production, an expensive, labor-intensive process we discussed in Chapter 9, and the steel produced cost $135 a ton.[9]

In searching for ways to reduce the steel-making costs, Carnegie was struck by the fact that many different companies performed each of the different operations necessary to convert iron ore into finished steel products. One company smelted iron ore into "pig iron"; another company then transported the pig iron to other companies that rolled the pig iron into bars or slabs. Many other companies then bought these bars and slabs and made them into finished products such as steel rails, nails, wire, and so on. Intermediaries who bought the products of one company and then sold them to another connected the activities of these different companies. The many exchanges, or "handoffs," involved in converting iron ore into finished products greatly increased operating costs. At each stage of the production process steel had to be shipped to the next company and reheated to allow it to become soft enough to work on. Moreover, these intermediaries were earning large profits for providing this service, which also raised the cost of the finished products.

Carnegie also noticed that the steel produced by British steel mills was of a higher quality than the steel made in U.S. mills. The British had made major advances in steel-making technology, and U.S. railroads preferred to buy their steel rails. Carnegie made frequent trips to Britain to sell U.S. railroad stock. On one trip he saw a demonstration of Sir Henry Bessemer's new "hot blasting" method for making steel. Bessemer's famous process made it possible to produce great quantities of higher-quality steel continuously, as a process, not in small batches. Carnegie instantly realized the enormous cost-saving potential of the new technology. He rushed to become the first steel maker in the United States to adopt it.[10]

Carnegie sold all his stocks and invested his capital to create the Carnegie Steel Company, which was the first low-cost Bessemer steel-making plant in the United States. Determined to retain the profit that intermediaries were making in his business, he also decided his company would perform all the steel-making operations necessary to convert iron ore into finished products. For example, he constructed rolling mills to make steel rails next to his blast furnace so that iron ore could be converted into finished steel products in one continuous process.

Carnegie's innovations led to a dramatic fall in steel-making costs and revolutionized the U.S. steel industry. His new production methods reduced the price of U.S. steel from $135 a ton to $121, yet his company was enormously profitable, with a profit margin between 35% and 50%. Most of his competitors could not compete with his low prices and were driven out of business. He plowed back all his profits into building his steel business and constructed many new low-cost steel plants. By 1900, his company became the leading U.S. steel maker, and he was one of the richest men in the world.

A Population Ecology Model of Organizational Birth

The way in which Carnegie transformed the U.S. steel industry is a story about how and why the number and nature of companies in an industry changes over time. **Population ecology theory** seeks to explain the factors that affect the rate at which new organizations are born (and die) in a population of existing organizations.[11] A **population of organizations** comprises the organizations that are competing for the *same* set of resources in the environment. All the fast-food restaurants in Houston, Texas, constitute a population of restaurants that compete to obtain environmental resources in the form of dollars that people are willing to spend on to obtain food conveniently. Apple, Dell, HP, Lenovo, Acer, and the other PC companies constitute a population of organizations that are seeking to attract environmental resources in the form of dollars that consumers are willing to spend on personal computing. Different organizations within a population may choose to focus on different **environmental niches,** or particular sets of resources or skills. Today, as mobile computing devices become more possible, all these companies are competing against the

Population ecology theory
A theory that seeks to explain the factors that affect the rate at which new organizations are born (and die) in a population of existing organizations.

Population of organizations
The organizations that are competing for the same set of resources in the environment.

Environmental niches
Particular sets of resources.

leader, Apple, that was dominating the market in 2011 with its iPhone and iPad devices. To fight back, Nokia teamed with Microsoft to offer new mobile devices based on the Windows 8 operating system, and other companies have teamed with Google to develop mobile devices based on software platforms such as Android and Gingerbread.

Number of Births

Population density
The number of organizations that can compete for the same resources in a particular environment.

According to population ecology theory, the availability of resources determines the number of organizations in a population. The amount of resources in an environment limits **population density**—the number of organizations that can compete for the same resources in a particular environment.[12] Population ecology theorists assume that growth in the number of organizational births in a new environment is rapid at first as organizations are founded to take advantage of new environmental resources, such as dollars that people are willing to spend on mobile personal computing (see Figure 11.2).[13]

Two factors account for the rapid birthrate. The first is that as new organizations are founded, there is an increase in the knowledge and skills available to generate similar new organizations—such as companies that are eager to adopt Google's free mobile software platforms. Also, many new organizations are founded by entrepreneurs who leave existing companies to set up their own companies using the competences they have learned by working in those companies. Many new companies have been founded by people who left pioneering organizations such as Xerox, Microsoft, IBM, and Google. For example, eBay was founded by Pierre Omidyar, who left Microsoft to use his skills to develop its auction software platform.

The second factor accounting for the rapid birthrate in a new environment is that when a new kind of organization is founded and survives, it provides a role model. The success of the new organization makes it easier for entrepreneurs to found similar new organizations because success confers legitimacy, which will attract stakeholders. Fast-food restaurants, for example, were a relatively untested kind of organization until McDonald's proved their ability to attract resources in the form of customers. Entrepreneurs watched McDonald's create and succeed in the U.S. fast-food market and then imitated McDonald's by founding similar companies, such as Burger King and Wendy's. McDonald's became a U.S. institution, gave the population of fast-food organizations legitimacy, and allowed them to attract stakeholders such as customers, employees, and investors. Today, fast food is taken for granted in most countries around the world, especially China, where rising wages are allowing its one billion citizens to enjoy fast food, especially fried chicken from KFC. Similarly,

Figure 11.2 Organizational Birthrates over Time

According to population ecology theory, the rate of birth in a new environment increases rapidly at first and then tapers off as resources become less plentiful and competition increases.

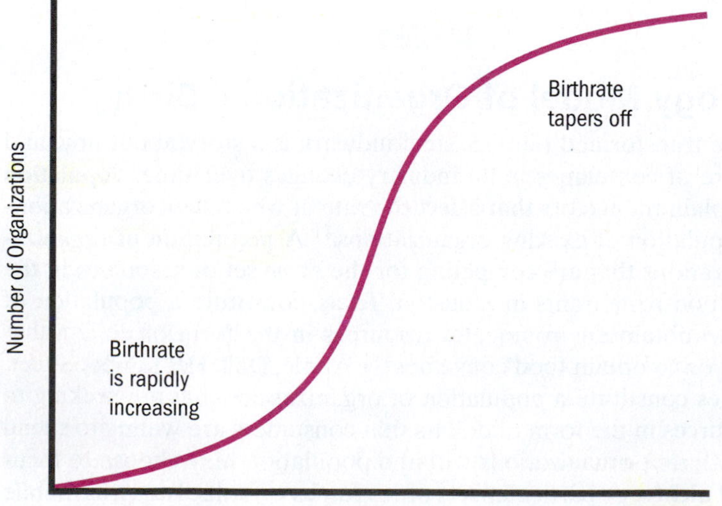

Groupon, the leader in the online deals that pioneered selling discounted services and goods, spawned imitators such as LivingSocial and is facing growing competition from companies such as Facebook and Google.

Once an environment is populated with a number of successful organizations, the organizational birthrate tapers off (see the S-shaped curve in Figure 11.2).[14] Two factors work to decrease the rate at which organizations are founded. First, births taper off as the availability of resources in the environment for late entrants diminishes.[15] Companies that start first, like McDonald's or Groupon, have a competitive edge over later entrants because of first-mover advantages. **First-mover advantages** are the benefits an organization derives from being an early entrant into a new environment. They include customer loyalty, a recognized brand name, and the best locations for new businesses like restaurants. Latecomers enter an environment that is partially depleted of the resources that they need to grow. Investors, for example, become increasingly reluctant to lend money to new startups because their chances of survival in an already competitive environment are poor unless they can somehow discover and find a way to attract resources. Similarly, the best managers and workers prefer to work in organizations that have established reputations and offer secure employment opportunities.

First-mover advantages The benefits an organization derives from being an early entrant into a new environment.

The second factor that decreases the birthrate is the difficulty of competing with existing organizations for resources.[16] Potential entrepreneurs are discouraged from entering an industry or market because they understand that the larger the number of companies already competing for resources, the more difficult and expensive the resources will be to obtain. To obtain new customers, new companies may need to overspend on advertising or innovation, or they may need to reduce their prices too much. Moreover, existing companies may band together and make it very hard for new companies to enter the market. They may engage in collusion, agreeing (illegally) to set their prices at artificially low levels to drive new rivals out of an industry, or they may erect barriers to entry by investing heavily in advertising so it is very expensive for new companies to enter the market.

Survival Strategies

Population ecologists have identified two sets of strategies that organizations can use to gain access to resources and enhance their chances of survival in the environment: (1) r-strategy versus K-strategy and (2) specialist strategy versus generalist strategy.

R-STRATEGY VERSUS K-STRATEGY Organizations that follow an **r-strategy** are founded early in a new environment—they are early entrants. Organizations that follow a **K-strategy** are founded late—they are late entrants.[17] The advantage of an r-strategy is that an organization obtains first-mover advantages and has first pick of the resources in the environment. As a result, the organization is usually able to grow rapidly and develop skills and procedures that increase its chance of surviving and prospering. Organizations that follow a K-strategy are usually established in other environments and wait to enter a new environment until the uncertainty in that environment is reduced and the correct way to compete is apparent. For example, Samsung, HTC, and Motorola did not enter the smartphone industry until Apple demonstrated the huge global market potential for smartphones and their applications. Sometimes these organizations then take the skills they have established in other environments and use them to develop effective products that allow them to compete with organizations following the r-strategy. In 2011, for example, Apple claimed Samsung's new smartphones and tablets were simply imitations of its own mobile devices, and Apple sued Samsung, which countersued, and a battle was raging between them.

r-strategy A strategy of entering a new environment early.

K-strategy A strategy of entering an environment late, after other organizations have tested the water.

The difference between r-strategy and K-strategy is evident in the situation that emerged in the PC environment. In 1977, Apple Computer founded the PC market when it developed the Apple I. Other small companies quickly followed Apple's lead. Each of them pursued an r-strategy and developed their own unique PCs. Many of these companies were successful in attracting resources, and the population of PC companies grew quickly. IBM, the dominant seller of mainframe computers, realized the huge potential resources of the PC market. It adopted a K-strategy and moved to develop its own PC (based on Microsoft's MS-DOS operating system), which it introduced in 1981. IBM's ability to put its massive competences to work in the new environment and to take

advantage of its brand name allowed IBM to become the dominant competitor. As MS-DOS became the industry standard, IBM drove most of the smaller r-strategists out of the PC market. Apple survived IBM's challenge by focusing its competences on satisfying the PC needs of academic and publishing customers. Then Steve Jobs returned and revolutionized the company, giving it a new "rebirth," and by 2011 Apple had become the most valuable global high tech company and Jobs was declared "CEO of the Decade."

Specialists
Organizations that concentrate their skills to pursue a narrow range of resources in a single niche.

Generalist
Organizations that spread their skills thinly to compete for a broad range of resources in many niches.

SPECIALIST STRATEGY VERSUS GENERALIST STRATEGY The difference between a specialist and a generalist strategy is defined by the number of environmental niches—or sets of different resources (customers)—for which an organization competes. Specialist organizations (or **specialists**) concentrate their competences and skills to compete for resources in a single niche—for example, smartphones. Generalist organizations (or **generalists**) use their well-developed competences to compete for resources in many or all niches in an environment—for example, smartphones, inexpensive cellphones, landline phones, netbooks, tablets, and so on.[18]

By focusing their activities in one niche, specialists are often able to develop core competences that allow them to outperform generalists in that niche. Specialists, for example, may be able to offer customers much better service than the service offered by generalists or, because they invest all their resources in a narrow range of products, they may be able to develop superior products. Nvidia, the leader in graphics chips, for example, invests all its resources to produce these state-of-the-art chips and does not invest resources to compete with Intel or AMD in making microprocessors or memory chips.

Generalists can often outcompete specialists when there is considerable uncertainty in the environment and when resources are changing so that niches emerge and disappear continually. Generalists can survive in an uncertain environment because they have spread their resources over many niches. If one niche disappears they still have others in which to operate. If a specialist's niche disappears, however, there is a much higher chance of organizational failure and death. In 2011 Nvidia was under increasing pressure as demand for desktop PCs and graphic chips fell sharply and its future now depends on the success of its Tegra mobile graphics chip.

Specialists and generalists normally coexist in many environments because generalists create the conditions that allow specialists to operate successfully.[19] Large department stores, for example, stock many different types of clothing but are only able to stock a limited amount of each type, for example, evening wear or sportswear. Given that customers often want more choices in clothing, specialty clothing stores that are able to offer an extensive selection of one type of clothing—for example, evening wear—can be successful, especially because they can charge a premium price for their selection of unique clothes. This is the opportunity for the entrepreneur even when there are powerful generalists around.

The Process of Natural Selection

The two sets of strategies—specialist versus generalist and r versus K—give rise to four strategies that organizations can pursue: r-specialist, r-generalist, K-specialist, and K-generalist (see Figure 11.3).[20]

Early in an environment, as a niche develops and new resources become available, new organizations are likely to be r-specialists—organizations that move quickly to focus on serving the needs of particular customer groups. Many new organizations grow and prosper, as did Apple. As they grow, they often become generalists and compete in new niches. While this is happening, however, K-generalists (usually the divisions or subsidiaries of large companies like IBM or GE) move into the market and threaten the weakest r-specialist organizations. Eventually, the strongest r-specialists, r-generalists, and K-generalists dominate the environment by serving multiple market segments and by pursuing a low-cost or differentiation strategy. Large companies, having chosen the K-generalist strategy, often create niches for new firms to enter the market, so K-specialists are founded to exploit the new market segments. In this way, generalists and specialists can coexist in an environment because they are *competing for different sets of resources*.

The early beginnings of the car industry provide a good example of this organizational birth process. The first car companies (such as Packard and Dusenberg) were small

Figure 11.3 Strategies for Competing in the Resource Environment

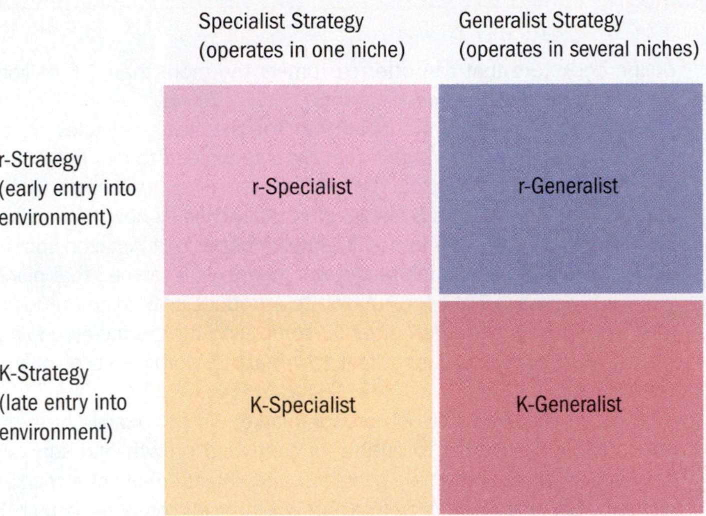

crafts operations that produced high-priced cars for small market segments. These companies were the original r-specialists. Then Henry Ford realized the potential for establishing a mass market via mass production, and he decided to pursue a K-generalist strategy by producing a low-priced standardized car for the mass market. Meanwhile, at GM, Alfred Sloan was rapidly developing a K-generalist strategy based on differentiation. He positioned GM's different car divisions to serve the whole range of market segments, from low-price Chevrolets to high-price Cadillacs. The low price and high variety of car models now available soon put many of the small r-specialists out of business. GM and Ford, together with Chrysler, proceeded to dominate the environment. Many new small companies pursuing K-specialist strategies then emerged to serve specialist segments that these companies had left open. Luxury-car manufacturers like Cord and Packard produced high-priced vehicles and prospered for a while, and overseas carmakers such as Rolls-Royce, Mercedes-Benz, and Bugatti were popular among the rich.

In the 1970s, Japanese companies like Toyota, Nissan, and Honda entered the U.S. market with a K-specialist strategy, producing cars much smaller than the vehicles that the Big Three were making. The popularity of these new cars quickly gave the Japanese companies access to the resources they needed to allow them to switch to a K-generalist strategy, and they began to directly threaten the Big Three. Thus, over time, new generations of organizations are born to take advantage of changes in the distribution of resources and the appearance of new niches.

New organizations continually emerge to take advantage of new opportunities. The driving force behind the population ecology model of organizational birth is **natural selection,** the process that ensures the survival of the organizations that have the skills and abilities that best fit with the environment.[21] Over time, weaker organizations, such as those with old-fashioned or outdated skills and competences or those that cannot adapt their operating structure to fit with changes in the environment, are selected out of the environment and die. New kinds of organizations emerge and survive if they can stake a claim to an environmental niche. In the car industry, Ford was a more efficient competitor than the craft shops, which declined and died because they lost their niche to Ford. In turn, Japanese companies, which continued to innovate and develop new skills, entered the U.S. car market. When customers selected Japanese cars because they wanted smaller, better quality vehicles, U.S. carmakers were forced to imitate their Japanese competitors in order to survive.

Natural selection The process that ensures the survival of the organizations that have the skills and abilities that best fit with the environment.

Natural selection is a competitive process. New organizations survive if they can develop skills that allow them to fit with and exploit their environment. Entrepreneurship is the process of developing new capabilities that allow organizations to take advantage of new niches or find new ways to serve existing niches more efficiently. Entrepreneurship,

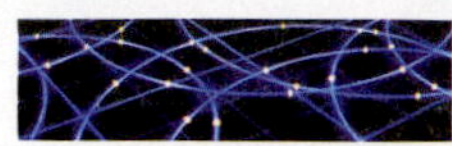

Focus on New Information Technology

Amazon.com, Part 6

Jeff Bezos was the first entrepreneur both to realize that the Internet could be used effectively to sell books and to act on the opportunity by establishing Amazon.com. As such he gave his company a first-mover advantage over rivals, which has been an important component of its strong position in the marketplace. Being early, Amazon.com was able to capture customer attention, and keep their loyalty—in 2011 65% of its business is repeat business. Moreover, Amazon.com's very success has made it difficult for new competitors to enter the market, and the birthrate into the industry has tapered off substantially.

First, new "unknown" competitors face the major hurdle of attracting customers to their websites rather than to Amazon.com's website. Second, even "known" competitors such as Barnes & Noble and Borders, which imitated Amazon's strategy and developed their own online bookstores, faced the problem of luring away Amazon's customer base and securing their position. Being late entrants, these organizations essentially followed a K-strategy, whereas Amazon.com followed an r-strategy. This delay in going online has cost them dearly in the current highly competitive environment, Barnes & Noble is struggling, and Border's went bankrupt in 2011, and all its stores were shut down.

Indeed, the process of natural selection has been operating in the book-selling industry in a major way because, as discussed in earlier chapters, thousands of small, specialized bookstores have closed their doors. Even large bricks-and-mortar bookstores that may carry hundreds of thousands of books have been unable to compete with an online bookstore that can offer customers the more than 1.5 million books in print at large price discounts.

In 2011, Amazon announced that for the first time sales of its heavily discounted online books that users download to its Kindle mobile reading devices outsold "paper" books. Amazon.com and its largest competitor Barnes & Noble, which launched its new Nook color book reader in 2011, are locked in a fierce battle, but Amazon.com is still winning the online book-selling war. However, it seemed that plans were in progress in 2011 for Amazon to introduce its own color Kindle as the popularity of all kinds of tablet computing devices increased and Apple's iPod became a new threat to Amazon's dominance of online book sales.

Even its success in the online book market did not provide Amazon with sufficient resources to ensure its continued growth and survival, however, and it has become a generalist and entered many new market niches by opening online storefronts in which it can compete profitably. As previously discussed, it started to sell more and more varieties of product and moved from being a specialist online bookstore to a generalist online retailer.[22] The changes to its strategy and structure not only have allowed it to survive—it has prospered as its profitability increased throughout the 2010s and its future looks rosy indeed. Borders' and Barnes & Noble's struggle makes it likely that Amazon will have less competition in the book market in the future. Similarly, in electronics, Circuit City went bankrupt in 2009. And Best Buy, the biggest bricks-and-mortar electronics retailer, is also struggling to compete against Amazon, which has been gaining market share in the electronics market as well. Small wonder that Amazon's stock price rose to a record high in 2011.

---

an ongoing process, leads to a continuous cycle of organizational birth as new organizations are founded to compete for resources in an environment, as Focus on New Information Technology: Amazon.com, Part 6 discusses.

The Institutional Theory of Organizational Growth

If an organization survives the birth stage of the organizational life cycle, what factors affect its search for a fit with the environment? Organizations seek to change themselves to obtain control over scarce resources and reduce uncertainty. They can increase their control over resources by growing and becoming larger.

Organizational growth The life cycle stage in which organizations develop value creation skills and competences that allow them to acquire additional resources.

Organizational growth is the life cycle stage in which organizations develop value-creation skills and competences that allow them to acquire additional resources. Growth allows an organization to increase its division of labor and specialization and thus develop a competitive advantage. An organization that is able to acquire resources is likely to generate surplus resources that allow it to grow further. Over time, organizations thus transform themselves: They become something very different than they were when they started. Microsoft took the resources that it obtained from its popular MS-DOS system, for example, and used them to employ more computer programmers, who developed new software applications to bring in additional resources. In this way, Microsoft grew from strength to strength and transformed itself into a software company that competes in almost all segments of the market. In 2011, facing strong competition from Google and Apple, it was striving to become a dominant player in mobile computing devices, hence its acquisition of Skype, the online communication service provider, for $8.5 billion and its alliance with Nokia that will use the Windows platform in its future mobile devices. Although sheer size can increase an organization's chances of stability and survival,

Microsoft and other companies should not pursue growth as an end in itself. Growth should be the by-product of an organization's ability to develop core competences that satisfy the needs of its stakeholders and so provide access to scarce resources.[23] **Institutional theory** studies how organizations can increase their ability to grow and survive in a competitive environment by becoming *legitimate*, that is, accepted, reliable, and accountable, in the eyes of their stakeholders.

Institutional theory
A theory that studies how organizations can increase their ability to grow and survive in a competitive environment by satisfying their stakeholders.

New organizations suffer from the liability of newness, and many die if they cannot develop the competences needed to attract customers and obtain scarce resources. To increase their survival chances as they grow, organizations must become acceptable and legitimate in the eyes of their stakeholders, and they do this by satisfying the latter's needs. Institutional theory argues that it is as important to study how organizations develop skills that increase their legitimacy to stakeholders as it is to study how they develop skills and competences that increase their operational efficiency. Institutional theory also argues that to increase their chances of survival, new organizations adopt many of the rules and codes of conduct found in the institutional environment surrounding them.[24]

The **institutional environment** is the set of values and norms that govern the behavior of a population of organizations. For example, the institutional environment of the insurance industry comprises strict rules and procedures about what insurance companies can and cannot do and penalties and actions to be taken against those that break those rules. Insurance companies that follow legal rules and codes of conduct are considered trustworthy, and therefore legitimate, by stakeholders, such as customers, employees, and any group that controls the supply of scarce resources.[25] As a result they are considered to be legitimate and are able to attract resources and improve their chances of survival. So the best way for a new organization to gain and strengthen its legitimacy is to imitate the goals, structure, and culture of successful organizations in its population.[26]

Institutional environment
The set of values and norms in an environment that govern the behavior of a population of organizations.

Organizational Isomorphism

As organizations grow, they may copy one another's strategies, structures, and cultures and try to adopt certain behaviors because they believe doing so will increase their chances of survival. As a result, **organizational isomorphism**—the process by which organizations in a population become more alike or similar—increases. Three processes that explain why organizations become more alike have been identified: coercive, mimetic, and normative isomorphism.[27]

Organizational isomorphism
The similarity among organizations in a population.

COERCIVE ISOMORPHISM Isomorphism is said to be *coercive* when an organization adopts certain kinds of values and norms because it is pressured to by other organizations or by society in general. For example, an organization that increasingly depends on other organizations will tend to adopt their values and norms so it will become increasingly similar to them. For example, the previous chapter discusses how the general public has put pressure on Nike, Walmart, Apple, and other organizations to boycott goods made by children in developing countries and how these companies have responded by creating uniform codes of supplier conduct. Coercive isomorphism also results when organizations are forced to adopt nondiscriminatory equitable hiring practices because they are mandated by law.

MIMETIC ISOMORPHISM Isomorphism is *mimetic* when organizations intentionally imitate and copy one another to increase their legitimacy. A new organization is especially likely to imitate the structure and processes of successful organizations when the environment is highly uncertain and so it needs to search for a structure, strategy, culture, and technology that will increase its chance of survival.[28] Because of mimetic isomorphism, a population of similar organizations, such as fast food restaurants, will increasingly come to resemble one another along the lines suggested by the S-shaped curve in Figure 11.2.

McDonald's was the first organization to operate a national chain of fast-food restaurants. Ray Kroc, the entrepreneur who orchestrated its growth, developed rules and procedures that were easy to replicate in every McDonald's restaurant. Standardization allowed the individual restaurants within the McDonald's organization to imitate one another, so that each reached its high-efficiency standards. Entrepreneurs who later entered the fast-food environment studied why McDonald's was so successful and then imitated the techniques and procedures that McDonald's had developed. Thus fast-food customers expect certain standards of quality, speed, and cleanliness, and they expect to clear their own tables. Retail stores also imitated one another in devising their codes of ethical conduct so that no particular retailer could be singled out as being unresponsive.

Although imitating the most successful organizations in a population increases their chances for survival and success, there is a limit to how much a new organization should seek to imitate existing ones. The first organization in an industry gains a first-mover advantage; if later arrivals model themselves too closely on the first mover, there might be no reason for customers to try them out. Each new organization must develop some unique competences to differentiate itself and define the niche where it has access to most resources. Chipotle's claim to fame is that it can provide customers with a customized, organic burrito, unlike Taco Bell, whose burrito is very standardized, and although Chipotle's burrito is more expensive, the chain has enjoyed explosive growth in the 2000s.

NORMATIVE ISOMORPHISM Isomorphism is *normative* when organizations come to resemble one another over time because they indirectly adopt the norms and values of other organizations in the environment. Organizations can acquire norms and values in a circuitous, even "viral" way for several reasons. Managers and employees frequently move from one organization to another and bring with them the norms and values of their former employers. Most companies in an industry recruit their managers from other companies in the same industry, for example. So AT&T recruits managers from Verizon and T-Mobile, and Dell recruits managers from PC and high-tech companies that have been experiencing similar kinds of operating problems. Organizations also indirectly acquire specific sets of values and norms through membership in industry, trade, and professional associations. Through meetings, personal contacts, and publications, these associations promote specific ideas and norms to their members. Because of this indirect influence, organizations within an industry come to develop a similar view of the world.

Disadvantages of Isomorphism

Although organizational isomorphism can help new and growing organizations develop stability and legitimacy, it has some disadvantages.[29] The ways organizations have learned to operate may become outdated, inertia sets in, and the result is low effectiveness. Also, the pressure to imitate competitors and beat them at their own game may reduce the incentive to experiment so that the level of innovation declines. For many decades, for example, the Big Three U.S. carmakers were happy to imitate one another and compete to make the best full-size fuel-inefficient cars. Innovations to reduce the costs of making a car or to improve efficiency and quality significantly were few and slow in coming because no U.S. company saw a reason to take the lead. Only the entry of new high-quality, low-cost global carmakers into the U.S. market showed U.S. carmakers how uncompetitive they had become and that new kinds of vehicles and better ways to make them should be developed as quickly as possible.

Greiner's Model of Organizational Growth

Institutional theory is one way to look at how the need to achieve legitimacy leads a growing organization to change its structure, strategy, and culture and imitate those of successful organizations. If organizations do model themselves on one another in this way, it follows that both the imitators and the imitated encounter similar kinds of strategic and structural problems as they grow over the life cycle.

One of the best-known life cycle models of organizational growth is Greiner's model (see Figure 11.4). He proposes that an organization passes through five sequential growth stages during the course of its evolution, and that at each stage a specific organizational design problem causes a crisis that must be solved if a company is not to fall into a chasm and so becomes unable to advance from one stage to the next.[30] Companies that fall into the chasm fail and die; companies that have skills in organizational design use them to cross the chasm and then they can proceed to the next stage of organizational growth.

Figure 11.4 Greiner's Model of Organizational Growth

Each stage that Greiner identified ends with a crisis that must be resolved before the organization can advance to the next stage.

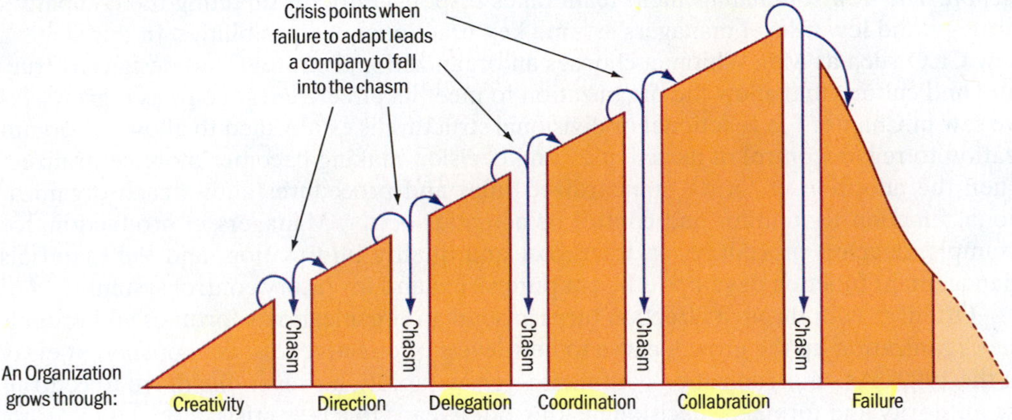

Stage 1: Growth through Creativity

Greiner calls the first stage in the life cycle the growth through creativity stage. In this stage (which includes the birth of the organization), entrepreneurs develop the skills and abilities to create and introduce new products for new market niches. As entrepreneurs create completely new procedures and learn to improve them, a great deal of organizational learning occurs. They learn which products and procedures work best, for example, and how to continuously improve them so they can continue to grow and obtain more resources. In this stage, innovation and entrepreneurship go hand in hand as an organization's founders work long hours to develop and sell their new products with the hope of being rewarded by future profits. As noted earlier, eBay was founded by Pierre Omidyar, the former Microsoft software engineer who designed a new online auction platform and then obtained the financing needed to bring it online on a shoestring budget. In the creativity stage, the norms and values of the organization's culture, rather than the hierarchy and organizational structure, control people's behavior.

Once a new organization is up and running, a series of internal forces begin to change the entrepreneurial process. As the organization grows, the founding entrepreneurs confront the task of having to manage the organization, and they discover that management is a very different process from entrepreneurship. Management involves using organizational resources to achieve organizational goals effectively. Thus, for example, in its manufacturing operations, management is confronted with the problem of making the production process more efficient. Early in the life of a new company, however, management is not likely to pay much attention to efficiency goals. Entrepreneurs are so involved in getting the organization off the ground that they forget the need to manage organizational resources efficiently. Similarly, they are so involved in providing customers with high-quality products that they ignore the costs involved. Thus, after securing a niche, the founding entrepreneurs are faced with the task of developing the functional competences necessary to allow their organization to grow effectively, a task to which they are often not really suited and for which they lack the necessary skills.

CRISIS OF LEADERSHIP Frequently, when an entrepreneur takes control of the management of the organization, significant problems arise that eventually lead to a *crisis of leadership*. eBay founder Pierre Omidyar, for example, had created the software platform that made it the dominant player in the online auction market. But to attract outside funding, investors demanded that eBay be managed by an experienced CEO who had the proven skills to manage a growing company. They recruited Meg Whitman, who had experience in high-tech startups, and she orchestrated its growth into the powerhouse it has become. Very often, investors realize that the founding entrepreneur is not the best person to manage a growing company because he or she lacks the organizational skills to develop the right strategy and structure to cross the chasm.

Stage 2: Growth through Direction

The crisis of leadership ends with the recruitment of a strong top-management team to lead the organization through the next stage of organizational growth: *growth through direction.* The new top-management team takes responsibility for directing the company's strategy, and lower-level managers assume key functional responsibilities. In this stage, a new CEO such as Meg Whitman chooses an organizational strategy and designs a structure and culture that allow the organization to meet its effectiveness goals as it grows. As we saw in Chapter 6, a functional or divisional structure is established to allow the organization to regain control of its activities, and decision making becomes more centralized. Then the adoption of formal standardized rules and procedures allows each organizational function to monitor and control its activities better. Managers in production, for example, develop procedures to track cost and quality information, and the materials management function develops efficient purchasing and inventory control systems.

Often, growth through direction turns around an organization's fortunes and propels the organization up the growth curve to new levels of effectiveness, as happened at eBay in the 1990s. As an organization continues to grow rapidly, however, the move to centralize authority and formalize decision making often leads to a new crisis.

CRISIS OF AUTONOMY With professional managers now running the show, many organizations experience a *crisis of autonomy*, which arises because the organization's creative people in departments such as R&D, product engineering, and marketing become frustrated by their lack of control over new product development and innovation. The structure designed by top managers and imposed on the organization centralizes decision making and limits the freedom to experiment, take risks, and be internal entrepreneurs. Thus the increased level of bureaucracy that comes in the growth-through-direction stage lowers entrepreneurial motivation. For instance, top-management approval may be needed to start new projects, and successful performance at low levels of the hierarchy may go unnoticed or at least unrewarded as the organization searches for ways to reduce costs. Entrepreneurs and managers in functional areas such as R&D begin to feel frustrated when their performance goes unrecognized and when top managers fail to act on their recommendations to innovate. Employees and managers feel lost in the growing organizational bureaucracy and become more and more frustrated with their lack of autonomy.

This situation occurred in eBay during the mid-2000s. When its rapid growth but deteriorating performance led its top managers to choose new ways to raise revenues that would raise its profits, it led to a revolt among eBay sellers, who saw more and more of their profit going to eBay. The level of innovation in eBay fell and Meg Whitman resigned in 2008 and was replaced by a new CEO, John Donahoe, who has worked hard to bring about new growth by finding new ways to attract buyers and sellers—and to lower selling costs. Once again, Amazon.com's online fixed-price retail platform has become a major competitor to eBay's auction platform, however, and hurt its performance.

What happens if the crisis of autonomy is not resolved? Internal entrepreneurs are likely to leave the organization and a company falls into the chasm. In high-tech industries, entrepreneurs often cite frustration with bureaucracy as one of the main reasons they leave one company to start their own.[31] In the 2000s, for example, many of Microsoft's top software engineers jumped ship and deserted the company for Google because they felt their efforts were not being rewarded; now in the 2010s Google is experiencing the same problem. The departure of an organization's entrepreneurs not only reduces its ability to innovate but also creates new competitors in the industry. By not resolving the crisis of autonomy, an organization creates a major problem for itself and limits its ability to grow and prosper.[32]

Stage 3: Growth through Delegation

To solve the crisis of autonomy, organizations must delegate authority to lower-level managers in all functions and divisions and link their increased control over organizational activities to a reward structure that recognizes their contributions. Thus, for example, managers and employees may receive bonuses and stock options that are directly linked to their performance. In essence, *growth through delegation* allows the organization to strike a balance between recruiting experienced managers to improve performance and the need to provide room for entrepreneurship so that the organization can innovate and find new ways to reduce costs or improve its products. Jen-Hsun Huang, CEO of Nvidia, the leading graphics chip company, delegates authority to small teams and creates a setting in which members can act entrepreneurially and control their own development activities. Huang also rewards these team members with stock options, and the most successful team members become highly visible stars in the organization. At the same time, however, Huang and his top-management team control the meshing of the activities of different teams to execute the company's long-term strategy. Indeed, Huang designed Nvidia's structure to avoid the crisis of autonomy, and the organization has profited from his foresight.

Thus, in the growth-through-delegation stage, more autonomy and responsibility are given to managers at all levels and functions. Moving to a product team structure or a multidivisional structure, for example, is one way in which an organization can respond to the need to delegate authority. These structures can reduce the time needed to get new products to market, improve strategic decision making, and motivate product or divisional managers to penetrate markets and respond faster to customer needs. At this stage in organizational growth, top managers intervene in decision making only when necessary. Growth through delegation allows each department or division to expand to meet its own needs and goals, and organizational growth often proceeds at a rapid pace. Once again, however, the organization's very success brings on another crisis: Explosive growth can cause top managers to feel that they have lost control of the company as a whole.

CRISIS OF CONTROL When top managers compete with functional managers or corporate-level managers compete with divisional managers for control of organizational resources, the result is a *crisis of control*. The need to resolve the crisis of autonomy by delegating authority to lower-level managers increases their power and control of organizational resources. Lower-level managers like this extra power because it is associated with prestige and access to valued rewards. If managers use this power over resources to pursue their own goals at the expense of organizational goals, the organization becomes less effective. Thus power struggles over resources can emerge between top and lower-level managers. Sometimes during this power struggle, top management tries to recentralize decision making and take back control over organizational activities. However, this action is doomed to failure because it brings back the crisis of autonomy and so an organization falls into the chasm. How does the organization solve the crisis of control so that it can prevent this and continue to grow?

Stage 4: Growth through Coordination

To resolve the crisis of control, as we saw in Chapter 4, an organization must find the right balance between centralized control from the top of the organization and decentralized control at the functional or divisional level. Top management takes on the role of coordinating different divisions and motivating divisional managers to take a company-wide perspective. In many organizations, for example, divisions can cooperate and share resources in order to create new products and processes that benefit the organization as a whole. In Chapter 8, we saw how this kind of coordination is very important for companies pursuing a strategy of related diversification. If companies are growing internationally, coordination is even more important. Top functional managers and corporate headquarters staff must create the "matrix in the mind" that facilitates international cooperation between divisions and countries.

At the same time, corporate management must use its expertise to monitor and oversee divisional activities to ensure that divisions efficiently use their resources, and it must initiate company-wide programs to review the performance of the various divisions. To motivate managers and align their goals with those of the organization, organizations often create an internal labor market in which the best divisional managers are rewarded with promotion to the top ranks of the organization while the most successful functional-level managers gain control over the divisions. If not managed correctly, all this coordination and the complex structures to handle it will bring about yet another crisis.

CRISIS BY RED TAPE

CRISIS OF RED TAPE Achieving growth through coordination is a complex process that has to be managed continuously if organizations are to be successful. When organizations fail to manage this process, they are plunged into a *crisis of red tape*. The number of rules and procedures increases, but this increased bureaucracy does little to increase organizational effectiveness and is likely to reduce it by stifling entrepreneurship and other productive activity. The organization becomes overly bureaucratic and relies too much on the formal organization and not enough on the informal organization to coordinate its activities. How can an organization cut itself free of all the confining red tape so that it can once again function effectively and avoid failure and the fall into the chasm?

Stage 5: Growth through Collaboration

In Greiner's model, *growth through collaboration* becomes the way to solve the crisis of red tape and push the organization up the growth curve. Growth through collaboration emphasizes "greater spontaneity in management action through teams and the skillful confrontation of interpersonal differences. Social control and self-discipline take over from formal control."[33] For organizations at this stage of the growth cycle, Greiner advocates the use of the product team and matrix structures which, as we discussed in Chapter 6, many large companies use to improve their ability to respond to customer needs and introduce new products quickly. Developing the interpersonal linkages that underlie the "matrix in the mind" for managing global linkages is also a part of the collaborative strategy. Collaboration makes an organization more organic by making greater use of mutual adjustment and less use of standardization.

Changing from a mechanistic to an organic structure as an organization grows is a difficult task fraught with problems; hence, many companies do fall into the chasm. Although Xerox and Chrysler moved to a product team structure to streamline their decision making, this change was not made until *after* both companies had experienced huge problems with their structures—problems that increased costs, reduced product quality, and severely reduced their effectiveness. Indeed, both companies came close to bankruptcy.

Managerial Implications

Organizational Birth and Growth

1. Analyze the resources available in an environment to determine whether a niche to be exploited exists.
2. If a niche is discovered, analyze how the population of organizations currently in the environment will compete with you for the resources in the niche.
3. Develop the competences necessary to pursue a specialist strategy in order to attract resources in the niche.
4. Carefully analyze the institutional environment to learn the values and norms that govern the behavior of organizations in the environment. Imitate the qualities and actions of successful organizations, but be careful to differentiate your product from theirs to increase the returns from your specialist strategy.
5. If your organization survives the birth stage, recognize that it will encounter a series of problems as it grows and differentiates.
6. Recognize the importance of creating an effective top-management team and of delegating authority to professional managers in order to build a stable platform for future growth.
7. Then, following principles outlined in earlier chapters, manage the process of organizational design to meet each growth crisis as it emerges. Establish an appropriate balance between centralizing and decentralizing authority, for example, and between standardization and mutual adjustment.

Organizational Decline and Death

Greiner's growth model shows organizations as continuing to grow through collaboration until they encounter some new, unnamed crisis. But, for many organizations, the next stage in the life cycle is not continued growth but organizational decline, as shown by the direction of the dashed line in Figure 11.4. Indeed, Greiner's model suggests that if an organization cannot solve the particular crisis associated with a growth stage, by changing its strategy or structure, this will result in organizational decline.

Organizational decline is the life cycle stage that an organization enters when it fails to "anticipate, recognize, avoid, neutralize, or adapt to external or internal pressures that threaten [its] long-term survival."[34] The liability of newness, for example, threatens young organizations, and the failure to develop a stable structure can cause early decline and failure. Similarly, in Greiner's model, the failure to adapt strategy and structure to match a changing environment can result in crisis and failure. Regardless of whether decline sets in at the birth or the growth stage, the result is a decrease in an organization's ability to obtain resources from its stakeholders.[35] A declining company may be unable to attract financial resources from banks, customers, or human resources because the best managers or employees prefer to work for the most successful organizations.

Organizational decline
The life cycle stage that an organization enters when it fails to anticipate, recognize, avoid, neutralize, or adapt to external or internal pressures that threaten its long-term survival.

Decline sometimes occurs because organizations grow too fast or too much.[36] The experience of IBM, GM, and Sony suggests that organizations tend to grow past the point that maximizes their effectiveness. Figure 11.5 illustrates the relationship between organizational size and organizational effectiveness. The figure shows that organizational effectiveness is highest at point A, where effectiveness E_1 is associated with organizational size S_1. If an organization grows past this point—for example, to point S_2—effectiveness falls to E_2, and the organization ends up at point B.

Effectiveness and Profitability

An important method stakeholders such as managers and investors employ to assess organizational effectiveness is to compare how well one company in an industry is performing relative to others by measuring its profitability relative to theirs. In evaluating organizational effectiveness, it is crucial to understand the difference between a company *making a profit* and *being profitable*, that is, a company's *profitability*.

Profit is simply the total or absolute monetary difference between a company's sales revenues and operating costs; if its sales are $10 million and costs are $8 million, it has

Figure 11.5 The Relationship between Organizational Size and Organizational Effectiveness

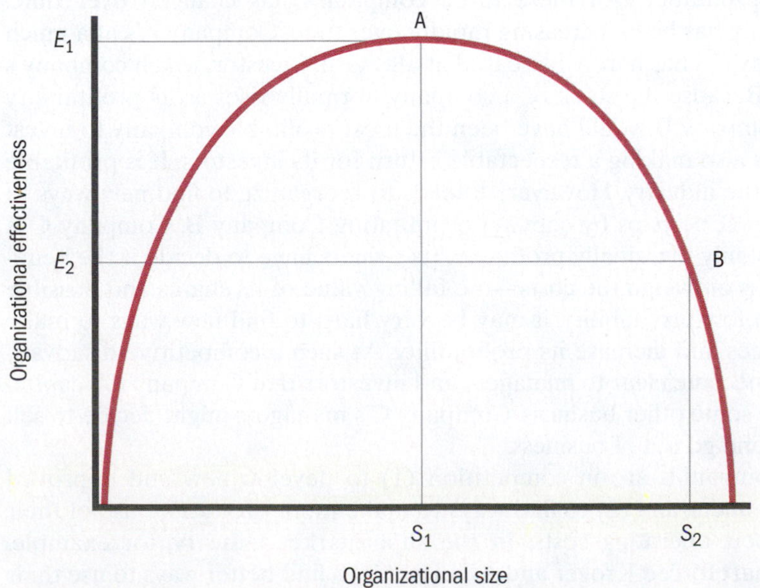

Profitability
A measurement of how well a company is making use of resources relative to its competitors.

made a profit of $2 million. **Profitability** measures how well a company is making use of its resources by investing them in ways that create goods and services that it can sell at prices that generate the most profit.

The important difference between them is that the size of the profit that a company makes in one year says little about how well its managers are making use of resources and its ability to generate future profits. In the car industry, for example, in good economic times, companies like Ford, GM, and Toyota may make billions of dollars of profit each year, but this tells us little about their relative profitability—which company is most effective now and will be in the future. Profitability, in contrast, gives managers and investors much more information to assess how well one company is performing against others in its industry. To see why this is so, consider the following example.

Imagine there are three large companies in an industry and each pursues a different business model. Company A decides to make and sell a no-frills low-priced product; Company B offers customers a state-of-the-art high-priced product; Company C decides to offer a midpriced product targeted at the average customer. The company that has invested its capital in such a way that (1) it is making the most productive use of its resources (which leads to low operating costs) *and* (2) has created a product that customers are clamoring to buy even at a premium price (which leads to high sales revenues) will have the highest profitability.

Suppose, for example, that Company A makes a profit of $50 million, B makes $25 million, and Company C makes $10 million. Does this mean Company A has outperformed Company B and C and is generating most returns for its stockholders? To answer this question, we need to calculate their relative profitability. Determining profitability is a two-step process. First, it is necessary to compute a company's profit, which is the difference between sales revenues and operating costs. Second, it is necessary to divide that profit by the total amount of capital invested in productive resources—property, plant, equipment, inventories, and other assets—to make and sell the product. Now we know how much capital each company has invested to generate that profit.

Suppose we find out that Company A has made $50 million profit on $500 million of invested capital, Company B has made $25 million on $100 million of invested capital, and Company C has made $10 million on $300 million. Company A's profitability is 10%, Company B's is 25%, and Company C's is 3%. *Company B is generating profit at two and a half times the rate of A, whereas C is only marginally profitable.* Company B has done the most to create value for stakeholders because its higher level of profitability will have increased the demand for and price of its stock. The importance of considering the relative profitability of companies, rather than differences in their total profit, is clear.

As noted earlier, company profitability is usually considered over time because it is seen as an indicator of a company's ability to generate future profit and capital. Figure 11.6 depicts how the profitability of these three companies has changed over time. Company B's profitability has been increasing rapidly over time, Company A's at a much lower rate, and Company C's has hardly increased at all. As an investor, which company's stock would you buy? Because the stock of a company normally rises as its profitability rises and vice versa, Company B would have been the most profitable company to invest in by far. Company A is also making a respectable return for its investors: It is profitable and holding its own in the industry. However, it needs to reorganize to find new ways to compete with Company B, perhaps by copying or imitating Company B. Company C is making a profit but it is only marginally profitable. Its owners have to decide if the benefits of staying in business outweigh the costs—the falling value of its shares and possible future losses. With such low profitability, it may be very hard to find new ways to make better use of its resources and increase its profitability. At such a competitive disadvantage, however, it might become clear to managers and investors that Company C's capital would be better used in some other business. Company C's managers might decide to sell their company's assets and go out of business.

In any industry, companies are in competition (1) to develop new and improved products to attract customers, and (2) to find ways to make more productive use of their resources to reduce their operating costs. In the supermarket industry, for example, competition from Walmart forced Kroger and Albertson's to find better ways to use their

Figure 11.6 Differences in Profitability

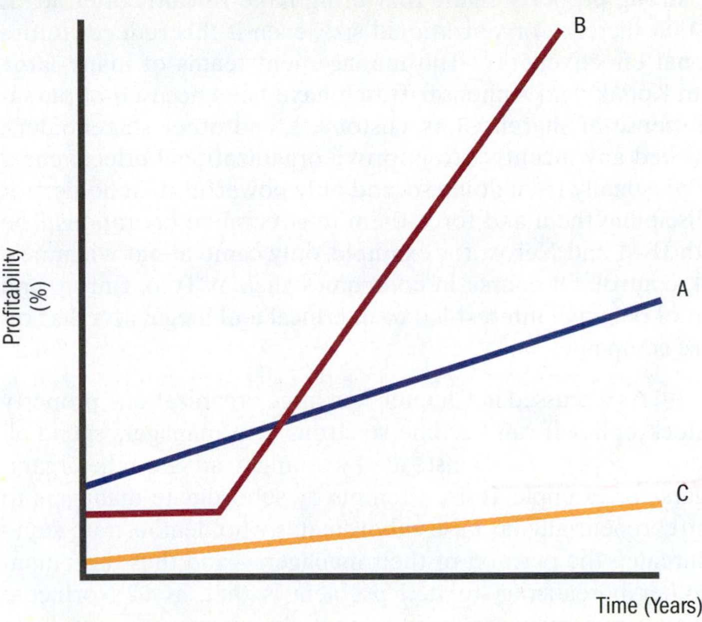

resources to maintain and increase profitability. Kroger, for example, invested its capital to build attractive new stores and install new kinds of IT to allow it to lower its operating costs. Its profit and stock price reached a record level in 2008. Albertson's has not done so well. It continued to decline and was bought by private investors who have been busy selling off thousands of its stores in different regions so it seems likely that the company will soon disappear and die.

Greiner's model assumes that managers have the ability to identify and solve organizational crises and so can restore company profitability if its performance begins to fall. In today's highly competitive global environment, there are many external and internal forces outside managers' control that prevent a turnaround and so profitability continues to fall. Two factors that often lead to continuing decline and loss in effectiveness are organizational inertia and environmental changes.

Organizational Inertia

An organization may find it difficult to adapt to changes occurring in the environment because of **organizational inertia**—the forces inside an organization that make it resistant to change. Although Greiner and other adaptation theorists believe organizations do have the ability to change and adapt to new conditions in their environments, population ecology theorists are more pessimistic. They believe that organizations are subject to considerable inertia and do not have the ability to quickly or easily change their strategy or structure to avoid decline. Some factors that cause inertia were discussed in the previous chapter. Three more are risk aversion, the desire to maximize rewards, and an overly bureaucratic culture. When these factors operate together, the problems facing managers are greatly compounded.

Organizational inertia Forces inside an organization that make it resistant to change.

RISK AVERSION As organizations grow, managers often become risk averse—that is, they become unwilling to bear the uncertainty associated with entrepreneurial activities.[37] They prefer to protect the status quo and keep things the way they are, so over time an organization becomes increasingly difficult to change. Risk aversion may set in for several reasons. Managers' overriding concern may be to protect their power and status so they pursue safe courses of action and choose inexpensive projects. Then, if the projects fail, no major damage will have been done. Often, managers try to maximize the chance of success by pursuing new projects similar to those that have already brought the organization success.

THE DESIRE TO MAXIMIZE REWARDS Research suggests that managers' desire for prestige, job security, power, and the strong property rights that bring large rewards often leads them to focus on strategies that increase organizational size, even if this reduces future profitability and organizational effectiveness.[38] The management teams of many large companies such as Goodyear, Kodak, and Anheuser-Busch have been accused of pursuing their own goals at the expense of shareholders, customers, and other stakeholders. Those management teams lacked any incentive to improve organizational effectiveness because they would not gain personally from doing so, and only powerful stakeholders or the threat of takeover can discipline them and force them to streamline operations. The turnarounds achieved at both IBM and Xerox, for example, only came about when new top management teams took control. Of course in companies such as Tyco, Enron, and Arthur Andersen, the pursuit of personal interest led to unethical and illegal acts that resulted in the downfall of these companies.

OVERLY BUREAUCRATIC CULTURE As discussed in Chapter 7, in large organizations, property rights (such as salaries and stock options) can become so strong that managers spend all their time protecting their specific property rights instead of working to advance the organization's interests. Top managers, for example, resist attempts by subordinate managers to take the initiative and act entrepreneurially because subordinates who demonstrate superior skills and abilities may threaten the position of their managers—and thus their managers' property rights.[39] Another bureaucracy-related problem is that, as C. Northcote Parkinson pointed out, in a bureaucracy, managers want to multiply subordinates, not rivals. So to protect their positions, managers limit the autonomy of their subordinates. One way of limiting autonomy is to establish a tall hierarchy so that subordinates have less authority and their behavior can be closely scrutinized. Another way is to develop a bureaucratic culture that emphasizes keeping the status quo and the need for maintaining conformity to organizational procedures. Such a culture might be desirable in the armed forces, but it is not beneficial to a large company fighting for survival in an uncertain environment.

Although the behavior of managers is sometimes a major cause of organizational inertia and decline, it is important to realize that managers may not be deliberately trying to hurt the organization. Bureaucratization and risk aversion may creep up on organizations unexpectedly.

Changes in the Environment

Environmental changes that affect an organization's ability to obtain scarce resources may lead to organizational decline. The major sources of uncertainty in the environment are complexity, the number of different forces that an organization has to manage; dynamism, the degree to which the environment is changing; and richness, the amount of resources available in the environment (see Figure 3.2). The greater the uncertainty in the environment, the more likely that some organizations in a population, especially organizations affected by inertia, will go into decline.

Sometimes the niche that an organization occupies erodes, and managers no longer have the incentive or ability to change strategy to improve the organization's access to resources. That is what happened to AOL and Yahoo! as the demand for new kinds of online applications such as social networking became so popular and users switched to Facebook. Sometimes the environment becomes poorer, and increased competition for resources threatens existing organizations that have not been managing their growth very effectively. For example, rising gas prices have harmed global carmakers that cannot offer price-conscious customers a range of small hybrid or electric fuel-efficient cars. In fact, rising fuel prices are an example of an "environmental jolt," a major change in the environment that precipitates an immediate crisis.[40] Just as global carmakers have been jolted by soaring fuel prices in the 2010s, so such prices have caused life-threatening problems for large U.S. airlines such as Delta and United Continental. Airlines have responded by massive downsizing that has involved the layoff of thousands of employees and the reduction in the number of flights as they shrink their route structure.

Obviously, the combination of an uncertain, changing environment with organizational inertia makes it difficult for managers to anticipate the need for change. It also hampers and limits their ability to adopt new strategies and structures that will allow an organization to adapt to the changing environment. In Chapter 12, we examine how organizations can promote organizational learning, a process that facilitates change and overcomes inertia. Here we discuss a model that charts the main stages of the decline process, just as Greiner's model charted the main stages of the growth process.

Weitzel and Jonsson's Model of Organizational Decline

Organizational decline occurs by degrees. Weitzel and Jonsson have identified five stages of decline.[41] At each stage except the dissolution stage, if managers do take prompt action they can reverse the decline.

STAGE 1: BLINDED In the blinded stage, the first decline stage identified by Weitzel and Jonsson, organizations are unable to recognize the internal or external forces and problems that threaten their long-term survival. The most common reason for this blindness is that organizations do not have in place the monitoring and information systems they need to measure organizational effectiveness and to identify sources of organizational inertia. Internal signals that indicate potential problems are an excessive number of personnel, a slowdown in decision making, a rise in conflict between functions or divisions, and a fall in profits.

At this stage, remedial action to gain access to good information and effective top managers who are able to react quickly and put in place the right strategies and structures can stop the decline and put the organization back on its growth path. Thus to avoid decline in the first place, managers must be able to monitor internal and external factors continuously, so they have the information to take timely corrective action.

STAGE 2: INACTION If an organization does not realize it is in trouble in the blinded stage, its decline advances to the inaction stage. In this stage, despite clear signs of deteriorating performance such as falling sales or profits, top managers make little attempt to correct problems. This failure to act may be because managers are misinterpreting available information. Managers might decide that their problems are owing to a short-term environmental change that the organization can weather, whereas in reality there has been an environmental jolt—a shift in consumer demand from pickups and SUVs to small fuel-efficient cars, for example. Inaction may also occur because managers are focused on the pursuit of goals that benefit them in the short run, even though in the long run this will hurt other stakeholders. Organizational inertia will also slow down managers' response to the situation. Management may follow tried-and-true approaches to solve the organization's problems—approaches that may be inappropriate given the shift in the environment.[42]

As the inaction stage progresses, the gap between acceptable performance and actual performance increases. Now, prompt wide-ranging action by managers is vital to reverse the decline. Managers must take major steps to stop decline, such as by downsizing and laying off employees or by scaling back the scope of their operations. Often a major reorganization and change to a new form of structure is necessary to overcome the inertia that has developed as the organization has become large and complex.

STAGE 3: FAULTY ACTION If managers fail to halt decline at the inaction stage, the organization moves into the faulty action stage. Problems continue to multiply despite corrective action. Managers may have made the wrong decisions because of conflict in the top-management team, or they may have changed too little too late because they feared that a major reorganization might do more harm than good. Often managers fear that radical change may threaten the way the organization operates and put the organization at risk.[43] For example, because of organizational inertia, Kodak's last five CEOs were either unable or unwilling to make the radical structural and strategic changes necessary to turn the company around. Only after Antonio Perez, its present CEO, took over has Kodak committed itself to the competitive reality of digital imaging and slashed its workforce and facilities. By then, however, Kodak was in stage 4, the crisis stage. Very often, an organization reaches the faulty-action stage because managers become overly committed to their present strategy and structure and fear changing them even though they are clearly not working to halt the decline. The incredible turnaround orchestrated by Carlos Ghosn at Nissan is discussed in Organizational Insight 11.2.

Organizational Insight 11.2

Carlos Ghosn Shakes Up Nissan

In 1999, Japanese carmaker Nissan was in big trouble: Its performance was rapidly declining. No longer profitable, its debt had soared to over $19 billion, and its market share both at home and in the vital U.S. market was dropping fast. In decline, it welcomed an offer by Renault, the French carmaker, to buy a controlling interest in its operations for $5.4 billion and to pump in money to turn around its performance. Nissan immediately dispatched Carlos Ghosn, an expert in managing turnarounds, to take control of the company. Ghosn had fixed Michelin's U.S. division by ruthless cost cutting. He was then recruited as Renault's COO to turn around that company and cut $4 billion in annual expenses. Now he was poised to do the same at Nissan.

Ghosn was one of the first non-Japanese CEOs of a major Japanese company. His appointment generated considerable resistance from Nissan's Japanese managers, who did not want a foreigner in charge, especially one who seemed likely to shake up the company. Ghosn quickly saw that the problem was that Nissan used 24 different car platforms to produce its cars, which required it to operate with too many expensive factories. Ghosn knew that to reduce costs it would be necessary to close down five factories and eliminate a dozen car platforms to wipe out $5 billion in operating costs. However, this was Japan, where lifetime employment is still widespread, and such a move would shock the company's employees. So operating in great secrecy to push his restructuring through, he waited to tell Nissan's board of directors about his plant-closing plans until the night before his public announcement. He also told them that if they did not back his decision, he would close down seven factories instead.[44]

iStockphoto.com/joel-t

The stunned Japanese gave in, but a public outcry took place in Japan as a foreign CEO proposed to break long-held Japanese norms. Ghosn was forced to travel with a bodyguard as he went on a tour of inspection of all Nissan's Japanese facilities, in part to share his views on how Nissan must change in the future. He made clear to Nissan's employees that his strategy was not just cost cutting. He also told Nissan engineers and managers that he was going to change Nissan's culture and thus the way they worked. Japanese companies are notoriously bureaucratic and hierarchical. They operate with conservative, cautious values that make subordinates reluctant to make suggestions to their superiors. Top managers are always jockeying to protect their turf—hence the 24 different product platforms—and change is always slow and incremental.

Ghosn destroyed these values by creating strict performance targets for managers, based on reducing costs and introducing innovative new vehicles, which could only be reached if managers reengineered the way the company worked. In particular, its engineers, designers, and other functional experts were instructed to be bold in their approach to new vehicle design and production. He created autonomous product teams empowered to make radical changes to vehicle design; he decentralized control, and the top managers who resisted were retired or moved around. Moreover, he insisted that Nissan's engineers and functional experts cooperate with those from Renault, both to speed innovation and share resources and to transform Nissan's values and norms. His goal quite simply was to transform the company and change the way it operated. One result is that today Nissan operates with only ten global platforms.[45]

Ghosn succeeded. Nissan, which also owns Infinity, has introduced a whole stream of futuristic vehicles in the 2000s that have received rave reviews and resulted in soaring sales. Today, Nissan is highly profitable, and in Japan Ghosn became a famous celebrity, even a national hero. He is revered as one foreigner who could show the Japanese how things could be done better. In 2005, Ghosn's success led to his appointment as the CEO of Renault. In 2011, he and the Renault-Nissan board still meet once a month to make the medium- and long-range decisions presented to them by a score of cross-company teams determined to keep the company at the forefront of the ongoing changes in carmaking such as the move to more fuel efficient, safer kinds of vehicles.

STAGE 4: CRISIS By the time the crisis stage has arrived, only radical top-down changes to an organization's strategy and structure can stop a company's rapid decline and increase its chances of survival. An organization in the crisis stage has reached a critical point in its history, and the only chance of recovery is a major reorganization that will very likely change the very nature of its culture forever. If no action has been taken before an organization reaches stage 4, change becomes even more difficult, and the chances of success decline because stakeholders have begun to dissolve their relationships with the organization.[46] The best managers may already have left because of fighting in the top-management team. Investors may be unwilling to risk lending their money to the organization. Suppliers may be reluctant to send the inputs the organization needs because they are worried about getting paid. Very often by the crisis stage only a new top-management team can turn a company around. To overcome inertia, an organization needs new ideas so it can adapt and change in response to new conditions in the environment.[47]

STAGE 5: DISSOLUTION When an organization reaches the dissolution stage, it cannot recover, and decline is irreversible. At this point, the organization has lost the support of its stakeholders, and its access to resources shrivels as its reputation and markets disappear. Perhaps Sharper Image has reached this point. If new leaders have been selected, they are likely to lack the organizational resources to institute a successful turnaround and develop new routines. The organization probably has no choice but to divest its remaining resources or liquidate its assets and enter into final bankruptcy proceedings. In either case, it moves into dissolution, and organizational death is the outcome.

As organizational death occurs, people's attachment to the organization changes. They realize the end is coming and that their attachment to the organization is only temporary.[48] The announcement of organizational death signals to people that efforts to prevent decline have failed and further actions by participants are futile. As the disbanding process begins, the organization severs its links to its stakeholders and transfers its resources to other organizations. Inside the organization, formal closing or parting ceremonies serve as a way of severing members' ties to the organization and focusing members on their new roles outside the organization.

The need to manage organizational decline is as great as the need to manage organizational growth. In fact, the processes of growth and decline are closely related to one another: The symptoms of decline often signal that a new path must be taken if an organization is once again to grow successfully. As many large organizations have found, the solution to their problem may be to shrink and downsize and focus their resources on a narrower range of products and markets. If an organization cannot adapt to a changing environment, it generally faces organizational death.

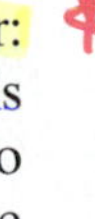

Managerial Implications

Organizational Decline

1. To prevent the onset of organizational decline, continually analyze the organization's structure to pinpoint any sources of inertia that may have emerged as your organization has grown and differentiated.
2. Continually analyze the environment, and the niche or niches that your organization occupies, to identify changes in the amount or distribution of resources.
3. Recognize that because you are a part of the organization, it may be difficult for you to identify internal or external problems. Call on other managers, members of the board of directors, and outside consultants to analyze the organization's current situation or stage of decline.
4. If you are the founder of the business, always keep in mind that you have a duty to your stakeholders to maximize the chances of your organization's survival and success. Be prepared to step aside and relinquish control if new leadership is required.

Summary

Organizations have a life cycle consisting of four stages: birth, growth, decline, and death. They pass through these stages at different rates, and some do not experience every stage. To survive and prosper, organizations have to change in response to various internal and external forces. An organization must make changes to its structure and culture at critical points in its life cycle. If successfully managed, an organization continues to grow and differentiate. An organization must adapt to an uncertain and changing environment and overcome the organizational inertia that constantly threatens its ability to adapt to environmental changes. The fate of organizations that fail to meet these challenges is death. Their place is taken by new organizations, and a new cycle of birth and death begins. Chapter 11 has made the following main points:

1. Organizations pass through a series of stages as they grow and evolve. The four stages of the organizational life cycle are birth, growth, decline, and death.
2. Organizations are born when entrepreneurs use their skills and competences to create value. Organizational birth is associated with the liability of newness. Organizational birth is a dangerous stage because entrepreneurship is a risky process, organizational procedures are new and undeveloped, and the environment may be hostile.
3. Population ecology theory states that organizational birthrates in a new environment are very high at first but taper off as the number of successful organizations in a population increases.
4. The number of organizations in a population is determined by the amount of resources available in the environment.
5. Population ecologists have identified two sets of strategies that organizations can use to gain access to resources and to enhance their chances of survival: r-strategy versus K-strategy (r = early entry; K = late entry) and specialist strategy versus generalist strategy.
6. The driving force behind the population ecology model is natural selection, the process that ensures the survival of the organizations that have the skills and abilities that best fit with the environment.
7. As organizations grow, they increase their division of labor and specialization and develop the skills that give them a competitive advantage, which allows them to gain access to scarce resources.
8. Institutional theory argues that organizations adopt many of their routines from the institutional environment surrounding them to increase their legitimacy and chances of survival. Stakeholders tend to favor organizations that they consider trustworthy and legitimate.
9. A new organization can enhance its legitimacy by choosing the goals, structure, and culture that are used by other successful organizations in its populations. Similarity among organizations is the result of coercive, mimetic, and normative isomorphism.
10. According to Greiner's five-stage model of organizational growth, organizations experience growth through (a) creativity, (b) direction, (c) delegation, (d) coordination, and (e) collaboration. Each growth stage ends in a crisis that must be solved by making the appropriate changes if the organization is to advance successfully to the next stage and continue to grow.
11. If organizations fail to manage the growth process effectively, the result is organizational decline, the stage an organization enters when it fails to anticipate, recognize, or adapt to external or internal pressures that threaten its survival.
12. Factors that can precipitate organizational decline include organizational inertia and changes in the environment.
13. Organizational decline occurs by degrees. Weitzel and Jonsson have identified five stages of decline: (a) blinded, (b) inaction, (c) faulty action, (d) crisis, and (e) dissolution. Managers can turn the organization around at every stage except the dissolution stage.

14. Organizational death occurs when an organization divests its remaining resources or liquidates its assets. As the disbanding process begins, the organization severs its links to its stakeholders and transfers its resources to other organizations.

Discussion Questions

1. What factors influence the number of organizations that are founded in a population? How can pursuing a specialist strategy increase a company's chances of survival?
2. How does r-strategy differ from K-strategy? How does a specialist strategy differ from a generalist strategy? Use companies in the fast-food industry to provide an example of each strategy.
3. Why do organizations grow? What major crisis is an organization likely to encounter as it grows?
4. Why do organizations decline? What steps can top management take to halt decline and restore organizational growth?
5. What is organizational inertia? List some sources of inertia in a company like IBM or GM.
6. Choose an organization or business in your city that has recently closed, and analyze why it failed. Could the organization have been turned around? Why or why not?

Organizational Theory in Action

Practicing Organizational Theory

Growing Pains

Form groups of three to five people and discuss the following scenario:

You are the top managers of a rapidly growing company that has been having great success in developing websites for large Fortune 500 companies. Currently, you employ over 150 highly skilled and qualified programmers, and to date you have operated with a loose, organic operating structure that has given them considerable autonomy. Although this has worked, you are now experiencing problems. Performance is dropping because your company is fragmenting into different self-contained teams that are not cooperating and not learning from one another. You have decided that somehow you need to become more bureaucratic or mechanistic, but you recognize and wish to keep all the advantages of your organic operating approach. You are meeting to discuss how to make this transition.

1. What kind of crisis are you experiencing according to Greiner's model?
2. What kind of changes will you make to your operating structure to solve this crisis, and what will be the problems associated with implementing these changes?

Making the Connection #11

Find an example of an organization that is experiencing a crisis of growth or an organization that is trying to manage decline. What stage of the life cycle is the organization in? What factors contributed to its growth crisis? What factors led to its decline? What problems is the organization experiencing? How is top management trying to solve the problems?

The Ethical Dimension #11

Managers have many opportunities to pursue their own interests, and as discussed earlier, they can use their power to take advantage of their subordinates, limit their freedom, and even steal their ideas. At the same time, managers may have a natural tendency to become risk averse.

1. What kind of ethical code should an organization create to try to prevent the selfish managerial behaviors that can contribute to inertia?
2. How can an organization use ethics to encourage managers to maintain a risk-taking attitude that benefits all stakeholders?

Analyzing the Organization: Design Module #11

This module focuses on the way your organization is managing (a) the dynamics associated with the life cycle stage that it is in and (b) the problems it has experienced as it evolved.

Assignment

Using the information at your disposal, answer the following questions.

1. When was your organization founded? Who founded it? What opportunity was it founded to exploit?
2. How rapid was the growth of your organization, and what problems did it experience as it grew? Describe its passage through the growth stages outlined in Greiner's model. How did managers deal with the crisis that it encountered as it grew?
3. What stage of the organizational life cycle is your organization in now? What internal and external problems is it currently encountering? How are managers trying to solve these problems?
4. Has your organization ever shown any symptoms of decline? How quickly were managers in the organization able to respond to the problem of decline? What changes did they make? Did they turn the organization around?

CASE FOR ANALYSIS

Cisco Systems Develops a Collaborative Approach to Organizing

Cisco Systems is famous for developing the routers and switches on which the Internet is built. In 2010 Cisco still made most of its $10 billion yearly revenue by selling its Internet routers and switches to large companies and Internet service providers (ISPs). But the boom years of Internet building that allowed Cisco to make enormous profits are over. And its CEO John Chambers, who has led the company from the beginning, has had to reexamine his organizing approach in order to improve the way his company's different teams and divisions work together.

Chambers admits that until the mid-2000s he had a "control and command" approach to organizing. He and the company's ten top corporate managers would work together to plan the company's new product development strategies; they then sent their orders down the hierarchy to team and divisional managers who worked to implement these strategies. Top managers monitored how fast these new products were developed and how well they sold and intervened as necessary to take corrective action. Chambers and Cisco's approach was largely mechanistic.

Chambers was forced to reevaluate his approach when Cisco's market value shrunk by $400 billion after the dot.com crisis. Given that the Internet was now established, how could he develop the new products to allow his company to keep on growing? After listening to his top managers he realized he needed Cisco's organizing approach and he developed a "collaborative approach," meaning that he and his top managers now focus on listening carefully to the ideas of lower-level managers and involve them in top level decision making. In other words, the goal of Cisco's new collaborative approach is to move toward a more organic structure that will allow Cisco's different teams and divisions to plan long-term strategies and work together to achieve them so that new product developments and technology are shared across the organization.

To facilitate collaboration, Chambers created cross-functional teams of managers from its different divisions who were charged to work together to develop promising new kinds of products. Within a year, 15% of his top managers who could not handle its new organic approach left the company. At the same time Chambers insisted that cross-functional teams set measurable goals such as time required for product development, and time to bring the product to market, to force them to think about short-term goals as well as long-term goals and speed product development. The top managers of its divisions who used to compete for power and resources now share responsibility for one another's success in the new collaborative, organic approach—their collective goal is to get more products to market faster. Cisco's network of cross-functional councils, boards, and groups that are empowered to launch new businesses has reduced the time needed to plan successful new product launches from years to months. Chambers believes Cisco's new organic approach will allow it to develop the new products that will make Cisco the global leader in both communications technology and Internet-linked IT hardware in the 2010s as it finds ways to bring innovative products to the market more quickly than its competitors.

Discussion Questions

1. How has Cisco changed its structure and control systems?
2. Relate Cisco's changes to its control and evaluation systems to the stages of growth in Greiner's model.
3. Go online and investigate how Cisco's new approach has worked. How is it continuing to change its structure and control systems to solve its ongoing problems?

References

1 R. E. Quinn and K. Cameron, "Organizational Life Cycles and Shifting Criteria of Effectiveness: Some Preliminary Evidence," *Management Science* 29 (1983), 33–51.

2 I. Adizes, "Organizational Passages: Diagnosing and Treating Life Cycle Problems of Organizations," *Organizational Dynamics* 8 (1979), pp. 3–25; D. Miller and P. Freisen, "Archetypes of Organizational Transitions," *Administrative Science Quarterly* 25 (1980), 268–299.

3 F. H. Knight, *Risk, Uncertainty, and Profit* (Boston: Houghton Mifflin, 1921); I. M. Kirzner, *Competition and Entrepreneurship* (Chicago: University of Chicago Press, 1973).

4 A. Stinchcombe, "Social Structure and Organizations," in J. G. March, ed., *Handbook of Organizations* (Chicago: Rand McNally, 1965), pp. 142–193.

5 J. A. Schumpeter, *The Theory of Economic Development* (Cambridge, MA: Harvard University Press, 1934).

6 H. Aldrich, *Organizations and Environments* (Englewood Cliffs, NJ: Prentice Hall, 1979).

7 R. R. Nelson and S. Winter, *An Evolutionary Theory of Economic Change* (Cambridge, MA: Harvard University Press, 1982).

8 www.u-s-history.com/Andrew Carnegie.

9 http://andrewcarnegie.tripod.com/, "History of Andrew Carnegie."

10 www.ussteel.com, 2011.

11 M. T. Hannan and J. H. Freeman, *Organizational Ecology* (Cambridge, MA: Harvard University Press, 1989).

12 G. R. Carroll, "Organizational Ecology," *Annual Review of Sociology*, 10 (1984), 71–93; G. R. Carroll and M. Hannan, "On Using Institutional Theory in Studying Organizational Populations," *American Sociological Review* 54 (1989), 545–548.

13 Aldrich, *Organizations and Environments.*

14 J. Delacroix and G. R. Carroll, "Organizational Foundings: An Ecological Study of the Newspaper Industries of Argentina and Ireland," *Administrative Science Quarterly* 28 (1983), 274–291; Carroll and Hannan, "On Using Institutional Theory in Studying Organizational Populations."

15 Ibid.

16 M. T. Hannan and J. H. Freeman, "The Ecology of Organizational Foundings: American Labor Unions, 1836–1975." *American Journal of Sociology* 92 (1987), 910–943.

17 J. Brittain and J. Freeman, "Organizational Proliferation and Density Dependent Selection," in J. Kimberly and R. Miles, eds., *Organizational Life Cycles* (San Francisco: Jossey-Bass, 1980), pp. 291–338; Hannan and Freeman, *Organizational Ecology.*

18 G. R. Carroll, "The Specialist Strategy," *California Management Review* 3 (1992), pp. 126–137; G. R. Carroll, "Concentration and Specialization: Dynamics of Niche Width in Populations of Organizations," *American Journal of Sociology* 90 (1985), 1262–1283.
19 Carroll, "Concentration and Specialization."
20 M. Lambkin and G. Day, "Evolutionary Processes in Competitive Markets," *Journal of Marketing* 53 (1989), 4–20; W. Boeker, "Organizational Origins: Entrepreneurial and Environmental Imprinting at the Time of Founding," in G. R. Carroll, *Ecological Models of Organization* (Cambridge, MA: Ballinger, 1987), pp. 33–51.
21 Aldrich, *Organizations and Environments,* p. 27.
22 See www.amazon.com, 2011.
23 J. Pfeffer and G. R. Salancik, *The External Control of Organizations* (New York: Harper & Row, 1978).
24 J. Meyer and B. Rowan, "Institutionalized Organizations: Formal Structure as Myth and Ceremony," *American Journal of Sociology* 83 (1977), 340–363; B. E. Ashforth and B. W. Gibbs, "The Double Edge of Organizational Legitimation," *Organization Science* 1 (1990), 177–194.
25 L. G. Zucker, "Institutional Theories of Organization," *Annual Review of Sociology* 13 (1987), 443–464.
26 B. Rowan, "Organizational Structure and the Institutional Environment: The Case of Public Schools," *Administrative Science Quarterly* 27 (1982), 259–279; P. S. Tolbert and L. G. Zucker, "Institutional Sources of Change in the Formal Structure of Organizations: The Diffusion of Civil Service Reform, 1880–1935," *Administrative Science Quarterly* 28 (1983), 22–38.
27 P. DiMaggio and W. Powell, "The Iron Cage Revisited: Institutional Isomorphism and Collective Rationality in Organizational Fields," *American Sociological Review* 48 (1983), 147–160.
28 J. Galaskiewicz and S. Wasserman, "Mimetic Processes Within an Interorganizational Field: An Empirical Test," *American Sociological Review* 48 (1983), 454–479.
29 Ashforth and Gibbs, "The Double Edge of Organizational Legitimation."
30 This section draws heavily on L. E. Greiner, "Evolution and Revolution as Organizations Grow," *Harvard Business Review* (July–August 1972): 37–46.
31 A. C. Cooper, "Entrepreneurship and High Technology," in D. L. Sexton and R. W. Smilor, eds., *The Art and Science of Entrepreneurship* (Cambridge, MA: Ballinger, 1986), pp. 153–168; J. R. Thorne and J. G. Ball, "Entrepreneurs and Their Companies," in K. H. Vesper, ed., *Frontiers of Entrepreneurial Research* (Wellesley, MA: Center for Entrepreneurial Studies, Babson College, 1981), pp. 65–83.
32 G. R. Jones and J. E. Butler, "Managing Internal Corporate Entrepreneurship: An Agency Theory Perspective," *Journal of Management* 18 (1992), pp. 733–749.
33 Greiner, "Evolution and Revolution as Organizations Grow," p. 43.
34 W. Weitzel and E. Jonsson, "Decline in Organizations: A Literature Integration and Extension," *Administrative Science Quarterly* 34 (1989), 91–109.
35 K. S. Cameron, M. U. Kim, and D. A. Whetten, "Organizational Effects of Decline and Turbulence," *Administrative Science Quarterly* 32 (1987), 222–240; K. S. Cameron, D. A. Whetten, and M. U. Kim, "Organizational Dysfunctions of Decline," *Academy of Management Journal* 30 (1987), pp. 126–138.
36 G. R. Jones, R. Kosnik, and J. M. George, "Internationalization and the Firm's Growth Path: On the Psychology of Organizational Contracting," in R. W. Woodman and W. A. Pasemore, eds., *Research in Organizational Change and Development* (Greenwich, CT: JAI Press, 1993).
37 A. D. Chandler, *The Visible Hand* (Cambridge, MA: Belknap Press, 1977); H. Mintzberg and J. A. Waters, "Tracking Strategy in an Entrepreneurial Firm," *Academy of Management Journal* 25 (1982), 465–499; J. Stopford and L. T. Wells, *Managing the Multinational Enterprise* (London: Longman, 1972).
38 A. A. Berle and C. Means, *The Modern Corporation and Private Property* (New York: Macmillan, 1932); K. Williamson, "Profit, Growth, and Sales Maximization," *Economica* 34 (1966), 1–16.
39 R. M. Kanter, *When Giants Learn to Dance: Mastering the Challenges of Strategy* (New York: Simon & Schuster, 1989).
40 A. Meyer, "Adapting to Environmental Jolts," *Administrative Science Quarterly* 27 (1982), 515–537.
41 Weitzel and Jonsson, "Decline in Organizations."

42 W. H. Starbuck, A. Greve, and B. L. T. Hedberg, "Responding to Crisis," in C. F. Smart and W. T. Stansbury, eds., *Studies in Crisis Management* (Toronto: Butterworth, 1978), pp. 111–136.

43 M. Hannan and J. Freeman, "Structural Inertia and Organizational Change," *American Sociological Review* 49 (1984), pp. 149–164. D. Miller, "Evolution and Revolution: A Quantum View of Structural Change in Organizations," *Journal of Management Studies* 19 (1982), 131–151.

44 www.businessweek.com, October 4, 2004, "Nissan's New Boss."

45 www.nissan.com, 2011.

46 Weitzel and Jonsson, "Decline in Organizations," p. 105.

47 B. L. T. Hedberg, P. C. Nystrom, and W. H. Starbuck, "Camping on Seesaws, Prescriptions for a Self-Designing Organization," *Administrative Science Quarterly* 21 (1976), 31–65; M. L. Tushman, W. H. Newman, and E. Romanelli, "Convergence and Upheaval: Managing the Steady Pace of Organizational Evolution," *California Management Review* 29 (1986), 29–44.

48 R. I. Sutton, "The Process of Organizational Death," *Administrative Science Quarterly* 32 (1987), 542–569.

CHAPTER 12

Decision Making, Learning, Knowledge Management, and Information Technology

Learning Objectives

Decision making results in choices that determine the way an organization operates and how it changes or transforms itself over time. Organizations must continually improve the way decisions are made so managers and employees can learn new, more effective ways to act inside the organization and respond to a changing environment.

By the end of this chapter you should be able to:

1. Differentiate among several models of decision making that describe how managers make decisions.
2. Describe the nature of organizational learning and the different levels at which learning occurs.
3. Explain how organizations can use knowledge management and information technology to promote organizational learning and improve the quality of their decision making.
4. Identify the factors, such as the operation of cognitive biases, that reduce the level of organizational learning and result in poor decision making.
5. Discuss some techniques that managers can use to overcome these cognitive biases and thus open the organization up to new learning.

Organizational Decision Making

In previous chapters, we discussed how managers design a structure and a culture that match the organization's environment, choose a technology to convert inputs into outputs, and choose a strategy to guide the use of organizational skills and resources to create value. In making these choices, managers are making *decisions*; indeed, everything that goes on in an organization involves a decision of some kind. Clearly, an organization is not only a value-creation machine, it is also a decision-making machine. At every level and in every subunit, employees' jobs involve making decisions—and the quality of decision making determines how much value they create.

Organizational decision making
The process of responding to a problem by searching for and selecting a solution or course of action that will create value for organizational stakeholders.

Programmed decisions
Decisions that are repetitive and routine.

Organizational decision making is the process of responding to a problem by searching for and selecting a solution or course of action that will create the most value for organizational stakeholders. Whether the problem is to find the best inputs, to decide on the right way to provide a service to customers, or to figure out how to deal with an aggressive competitor, in each case managers must decide what to do. To make the best choices, managers must make two kinds of decisions: programmed and nonprogrammed.

Programmed decision making involves selecting the most effective—easy, repetitive, and routine—operating procedures to handle an organization's ongoing value-creation activities.[1] Typically, the routines and procedures that result in the most efficient way of operating are formalized in advance in an organization's written rules and standard operating procedures (SOPs) and are present in the values and norms of its culture.

Nonprogrammed decision making involves managers making the most effective—creative, novel, and unstructured—decisions that allow an organization to find solutions to changing and uncertain conditions. No rules, routines, or SOPs can be developed to handle nonroutine problems in advance because they are unique or unexpected. So solutions often have to be found after new problems have arisen.[2]

Nonprogrammed decisions Decisions that are novel and unstructured.

Nonprogrammed decision making requires much more search for information—and active cooperation between managers, functions, and divisions—to find solutions than does programmed decision making. This is because in making unprogrammed decisions it is impossible to know in advance if these decisions are the right ones—unlike with programmed decisions that are based on the results of past experience and so managers can normally continually improve on routines and procedures over time.

For example, R&D is based on nonprogrammed decision making by scientists and engineers who must continually experiment to find a solution to a problem and often fail in the attempt. Similarly, the creation of an organization's strategy involves nonprogrammed decision making by managers who cooperate to find the best way to use an organization's skills and resources to create value—but they never know if they have made the best decision in advance.

So, nonprogrammed decision making forces managers to rely on judgment, intuition, and creativity to solve organizational problems; they cannot rely on rules and SOPs to provide nonprogrammed solutions. *Nonprogrammed decisions* lead to the creation of a new set of rules and procedures and then organizational members can improve the *programmed* decisions they use to increase organizational effectiveness (for example, by implementing TQM or changing task and role relationships).

All organizations must have the capability to make both programmed and nonprogrammed decisions. Programmed decision making allows an organization to increase its efficiency and reduce the costs of making goods and services; it provides stability and increases predictability. Nonprogrammed decision making allows an organization to change and find new ways to adapt to and take advantage of its environment, such as the way Apple first developed the iPod, then used its new skills to develop the iPhone and then the iPad. In the next section, we examine several models of organizational decision making.

Models of Organizational Decision Making

In the past, organizational decision making was portrayed as a rational process in which all-knowing managers make decisions that allow organizations to adjust perfectly to the environment in which they operate.[3] Today, we recognize that decision making is an inherently uncertain process in which managers grope for solutions that may or may not lead to outcomes favorable to organizational stakeholders.

The Rational Model

According to the *rational model*, decision making is a straightforward three-stage process (see Figure 12.1).[4] At stage 1, managers identify problems that need to be solved. Managers of an effective organization, for example, analyze all aspects of their organization's specific

Figure 12.1 The Rational Model of Decision Making

This model ignores the uncertainty that typically plagues decision making.

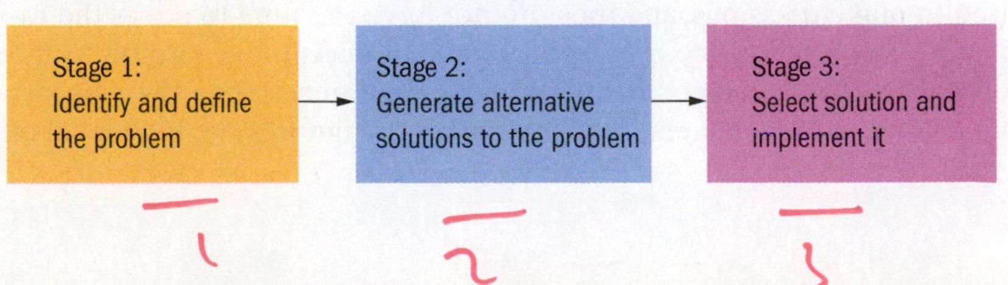
Stage 1:
Identify and define the problem
Stage 2:
Generate alternative solutions to the problem
Stage 3:
Select solution and implement it

and general environments to identify conditions or problems that call for new action. To achieve a good fit between an organization and its environment, they must recognize the opportunities or threats it presents. At stage 2, managers seek to design and develop a series of alternative courses of action to solve the problems they have identified. They study ways to take advantage of the organization's specific competences to respond to opportunities and threats. At stage 3, managers compare the likely consequences of each alternative and decide which course of action offers the best solution to the problem they identified in stage 1.

Under what "ideal" circumstances can managers be sure they have made a decision that will maximize stakeholders' satisfaction? The ideal situation is one in which there is no uncertainty: Managers know *all* the courses of action open to them. They know the exact effects of all alternatives on stakeholders' interests. They are able to use the same set of objective criteria to evaluate each alternative. And they use the same decision rules to rank each alternative and thus can make the one best or right decision—the decision that will maximize the return to organizational stakeholders.[5] Do such conditions exist? If they did, managers could always make decisions that would perfectly position their organizations in the environment to acquire new resources and make the best use of existing resources.

This ideal state is the situation assumed by the rational model of organizational decision making. The rational model ignores the ambiguity, uncertainty, and chaos that typically plague decision making. Researchers have criticized as unrealistic or simplistic three assumptions underlying the rational model: (1) the assumption that decision makers have all the information they need, (2) the assumption that decision makers have the ability to make the best decisions, and (3) the assumption that decision makers agree about what needs to be done.

INFORMATION AND UNCERTAINTY The assumption that managers are aware of all alternative courses of action and their consequences is unrealistic. For this assumption to be valid, managers would have access to all the information necessary to make the best decision, could collect information about every possible situation the organization might encounter, and would possess accurate knowledge about how likely it is that each situation would occur.[6]

The assumption that it is possible to collect all the information needed to make the best decision is unrealistic.[7] Because the environment is inherently uncertain, every alternative course of action and its consequences cannot be known. Furthermore, even if it were possible to collect information to eliminate all uncertainty, the costs of doing so would be as great as, or greater than, any potential profit the organization could make from selecting the best alternative. Thus nothing would be gained from the information.[8]

Suppose a fast-food company thinks that some new kind of sandwich has the potential to attract large numbers of new customers. According to the rational model, to identify the right kind of sandwich, the company would do extensive market research, test different kinds of sandwiches with different groups of customers, and evaluate all alternatives. The cost of adequately testing *every* alternative for *all* possible different groups of customers would be so high, it would swallow up any profit the new sandwich would generate from increased sales. The rational model ignores the fact that organizational decision making *always* takes place in the midst of uncertainty, which poses both an opportunity and a threat for an organization.

MANAGERIAL ABILITIES The rational model assumes that managers possess the intellectual capability not only to evaluate all the possible alternative choices but also to select the optimum solution. In reality, managers have only a limited ability to process the information required to make decisions, and most do not have the time to act as the rational model demands.[9] The intelligence required to make a decision according to the rational model would exceed a manager's mental abilities and necessitate the employment of an enormous number of managers. The rational model ignores the high level of managerial costs.

PREFERENCES AND VALUES The rational model assumes that different managers have the same preferences and values and will use the same rules to decide on the best alternative. The model also assumes that managers agree about what are the most important organizational goals. These "agreement assumptions" are unrealistic.[10] In Chapter 4, we discussed how managers in different functions are likely to have different subunit orientations that lead them to make decisions that favor their own interests over those of other functions, other stakeholders, or the organization as a whole.

To sum up, the rational model of decision making is unrealistic because it rests on assumptions that ignore the information and managerial problems associated with decision making. The Carnegie model and other newer models take these problems into consideration and provide a more accurate picture of how organizational decision making takes place.

The Carnegie Model

In an attempt to better describe the realities of the decision-making process, researchers introduced a new set of assumptions that have come to be called the Carnegie model of decision making.[11] Table 12.1 summarizes the differences between the Carnegie and the rational models of decision making. The Carnegie model recognizes the effects of "satisficing," bounded rationality, and organizational coalitions.

SATISFICING In an attempt to explain how organizations avoid the costs of obtaining information, the Carnegie model suggests that managers engage in **satisficing,** limited information searches to identify problems and alternative solutions.[12] Instead of searching for all possible solutions to a problem, as the rational model suggests, managers resort to satisficing. That is, to save time and cost, they choose a set of problem-specific criteria or measures they will use to evaluate a range of possible solutions.[13] They then work together to develop several best alternative solutions and select the one that best satisfies the criteria they have previously chosen. Thus satisficing involves a much less costly information search and puts far less of a burden on managers than does the rational model.

Satisficing
Limited information searches to identify problems and alternative solutions.

BOUNDED RATIONALITY The rational model assumes that managers possess the intellectual ability to evaluate all possible alternatives. The Carnegie model assumes that managers' ability is restricted by **bounded rationality,** meaning they only have limited capacity to process information about alternatives. But even though they only have limited information-processing capacity, managers can improve their decision making by sharpening their analytical skills.[14] Managers can also make use of technology like computers to improve their decision-making skills.[15] Thus bounded rationality in no way implies lack of ability or motivation. The Carnegie model recognizes that decision making is subjective and that decision-making quality depends on managers' prior experience, knowledge, beliefs, and intuition.

Bounded rationality
A limited capacity to process information.

TABLE 12.1 Differences between the Rational and the Carnegie Models of Decision Making

Rational Model	Carnegie Model
Information is available	Limited information is available
Decision making is costless	Decision making is costly (e.g., managerial costs, information costs)
Decision making is "value free"	Decision making is affected by the preferences and values of decision makers
The full range of possible alternatives is generated	A limited range of alternatives is generated
Solution is chosen by unanimous agreement	Solution is chosen by compromise, bargaining, and accommodation between organizational coalitions
Solution chosen is best for the organization	Solution chosen is satisfactory for the organization

ORGANIZATIONAL COALITIONS The rational model ignores the variation in managers' preferences and values and assumes different managers will evaluate different alternatives in the same way. The Carnegie model, in contrast, explicitly recognizes that the preferences and values of managers differ and that disagreement and conflict between different managers is inevitable.[16] The Carnegie model views an organization as a coalition of different interests, in which decision making takes place by compromise, bargaining, and negotiation between managers from different functions and areas of the organization. Any solution chosen must be approved by the *dominant coalition*, the collection of managers or stakeholders who have the power to decide which solution is chosen and can commit resources to implement it.[17] Over time, as the interests and preferences of managers change, so the makeup of the dominant coalition changes and so does decision making. The Carnegie model recognizes that decision making is not a rational "neutral" process driven by objective decision rules, but a subjective process in which managers formulate decision rules that allow them to achieve their personal goals and interests.

To sum up, the Carnegie model recognizes that decision making takes place in an uncertain environment where information is often incomplete and ambiguous. It also recognizes that decisions are made by people who are limited by bounded rationality, who satisfice, and who form coalitions to pursue their own interests. The Carnegie model offers a more accurate description of how decision making takes place in an organization than does the rational model. Yet Carnegie-style decision making is rational because managers act intentionally to find the best solution to reach their desired goal, despite uncertainty and disagreement over goals. In Organizational Insight 12.1, the response of GE to the question of whether it should continue to make its own appliances, such as washing machines, buy them from other companies—or even stay in the appliance business—illustrates decision making in accordance with the Carnegie model.

Organizational Insight 12.1

Should GE Make or Buy Appliances?

In the 1990s, GE faced a major decision. GE's appliance division, maker of well-known products such as dishwashers, ranges, refrigerators, and washing machines, was experiencing declining profitability. Its technologically outdated washing machine operations contributed significantly to this loss, and GE had to evaluate two alternative courses of action: Should GE spend $70 million and make a major investment in new technology to bring the washing machine operations up to date so GE could compete into the next century, or should GE close down its own washing machine operations and buy washing machines from another manufacturer that it would sell under its own brand name?

To evaluate each alternative, GE's managers had to decide which one would result in the best long-term outcome. They used criteria such as manufacturing costs, quality, and product development costs to evaluate each alternative. One of the factors that GE was most concerned about was whether the unions in its Appliance Park operations would agree to flexible work arrangements that would reduce labor costs. At the same time, managers talked to companies like Maytag and Whirlpool to determine what it would cost GE to have them make a washing machine according to GE specifications.[18]

If GE could buy another manufacturer's washing machine for less than it would pay to make its own, then it seemed to make sense to choose the less costly alternative. However, GE's managers had to evaluate the effects of other factors. For example, if GE stopped making washing machines, it would lose a core competence in washing machine production that it would be unable to recover. Suppose the company that GE chose to make its GE machines deliberately made inferior machines that were lower in quality than the machines it produced for itself? Then GE would be at the mercy of its supplier. Or suppose the unions reneged on the contract and refused to cooperate after GE had made the investment in modernizing the washing machine plant? The situation was further complicated by appliance division managers who were lobbying for the investment because it would protect their jobs and the jobs of 15,000 workers. The division managers championed the advantages of the investment for improving the competitive advantage of the division. Corporate managers, however, had to evaluate the potential return of the investment to the entire organization.

Because of uncertainty, GE's managers had a very difficult time evaluating the pros and cons of each alternative; they could not accurately predict the consequences of any decision they made. In the end they decided that GE should make the investment and continue to produce its own washing machines. New lines of modern washing machines were introduced throughout the 2000s. GE tripled the amount it spends on R&D to produce appliances that never break down and which "delight" its customers.[19] By the mid-2000s, GE's appliance division was once again profitable and it was making innovative new products such as front-loading, water-saving washing machines and energy-efficient appliances.

But in 2008, GE's top managers had to debate a new alternative because the company as a whole was now experiencing declining profitability. Analysts claimed the reason was that GE was operating in too many different industries (it has 150 different product divisions) and that it needed to sell off those divisions that had the poorest future prospects. The alternative on the table was that GE should get out of the appliance business, sell it to the highest bidder, and then invest the money to improve the competences of its other divisions.

Just as managers had debated the question of whether to make or buy washing machines, now they had to go through a new round of decision making and debate whether to keep or sell the appliance division. As before, using a set of relevant criteria, they made the choice, and in the spring of 2008, they put the division up for sale. LG, the Korean appliance maker, expressed strong interest in the appliance division, as did other global companies, but by 2009 it was clear that GE had much more to gain by investing in the division than selling it. GE announced a major new investment plan for its appliance division; in the future GE would make quality products that could equal any of its global competitors.[20] By 2011 the appliance division was churning out a new array of advanced appliances, such as its induction heat ranges and gas tankless water heaters that were earning rave reviews, so it seemed that its recent decision making was starting to pay off.[21]

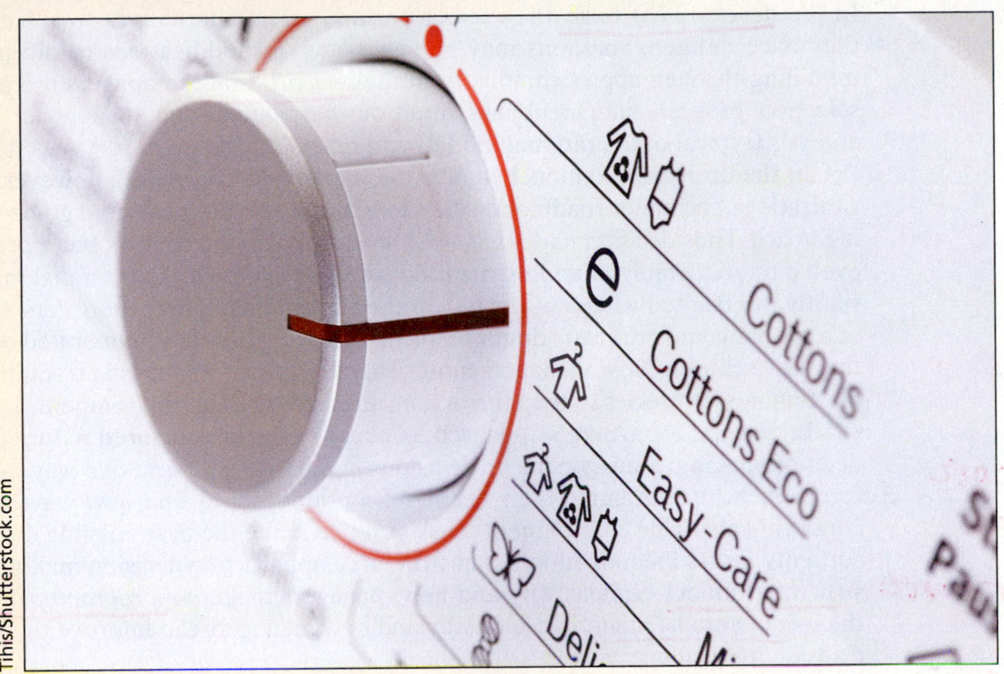

Tihis/Shutterstock.com

The Incrementalist Model

In the Carnegie model, satisficing and bounded rationality curb the number and complexity of alternatives that can be selected for analysis. According to the *incrementalist model* of organizational decision making, when selecting a set of new alternative courses of action, managers tend to choose those that are only slightly, or incrementally, different from those used in the past, thus lessening their chances of making a mistake.[22] Often called the science of "muddling through," the incrementalist model implies that managers rarely make major decisions that are radically different from decisions they have made before.[23] Instead, they correct or avoid mistakes through a succession of incremental changes, which eventually may lead to a completely new course of action. During the muddling-through process, organizational goals and the courses of action for achieving them may change, but they change very slowly so that corrective action can be taken if things start to go wrong.

The incrementalist model is very different from the rational model. According to the rational model, all-knowing decision makers weigh every possible alternative course of action and choose the best solution. According to the incrementalist model, managers, limited by lack of information and lack of foresight, move cautiously one step at a time to limit their chances of being wrong.

The Unstructured Model

The incrementalist approach works best in a relatively stable environment where managers can accurately predict movements and trends and so make the incremental decisions that will lead to higher effectiveness. In an environment that changes suddenly or abruptly, an incrementalist approach would prevent managers from changing quickly enough to meet new conditions and so cause the organization to go into decline. The *unstructured model* of decision making, developed by Henry Mintzberg and his colleagues, describes how decision making takes place when uncertainty is high.[24]

The unstructured model recognizes that decision making takes place in a series of small, incremental steps that collectively have a major effect on organizational effectiveness over time. Incremental decisions are made within an overall decision-making framework consisting of three stages—identification, development, and selection—that are similar to the stages shown in Figure 12.1. In the *identification* stage, managers develop routines to recognize problems and to understand what is happening to the organization. In the *development* stage, they search for and select alternatives to solve the problems they have defined. Solutions may be new plans or modifications of old plans, as in the muddling-through approach. Finally, in the *selection* stage, managers use an incremental selection process—judgment and intuition, bargaining, and to a lesser extent formal analysis (typical of the rational model)—to reach a final decision.[25]

In the unstructured model (unlike the incrementalist model), however, whenever organizations encounter roadblocks, they rethink their alternatives and go back to the drawing board. Thus decision making is not a linear, sequential process but a process that may evolve unpredictably in an unstructured way. For example, decision making may be constantly interrupted when uncertainty in the environment alters managers' interpretations of a problem and thus casts doubt on the alternatives they have generated or the solutions they have chosen. Now, managers must generate new alternatives and solutions, for example, find new strategies to help the organization adapt to its environment.

In essence, Mintzberg's approach emphasizes the unstructured nature of incremental decision making: Managers make decisions in a haphazard, intuitive way, and uncertainty forces them to reexamine their decisions continuously to find new ways to behave in a constantly changing environment. They strive to make the best possible decisions, but uncertainty forces them to adopt an unstructured approach to decision making. Thus the unstructured model explains why and how managers make *nonprogrammed* decisions, and the incrementalist model explains why and how managers can improve their *programmed* decision making over time.

The Garbage-Can Model

The view of decision making as an unstructured process is taken to its extreme in the *garbage-can model* of organizational decision making.[26] This model turns the decision-making process around and argues that managers are as likely to start decision making from the *solution side* as from the *problem side*. In other words, decision makers may propose solutions to problems that do not exist; they create a problem they can solve with solutions that are already available.

Garbage-can decision making arises in the following way: An organization has a set of solutions deriving from its competences and skills with which it can solve certain problems—for example, how to attract new customers, how to lower production costs, or how to innovate products quickly. Possessing these organizational competences, managers seek ways to use them and so they create problems—or decision-making opportunities—for them to solve. Suppose a company has skills in making custom-designed furniture. The head of the marketing department persuades the company president that the organization should take advantage of these skills by expanding internationally. Thus a new problem—how to manage international expansion—is created because of the existence of a solution—the ability to make superior custom-designed furniture.

While an organization's managers must tackle new problems of their own making, at the same time they must also generate alternatives and find solutions to problems that have arisen because of shifts in the environment or strains and stresses that stem from the way it operates. To further complicate decision making, different coalitions of managers may champion different alternatives and compete for resources to implement their own chosen solutions. Thus decision making becomes like a "garbage can" in which problems, solutions, and the preferences of different managers and coalitions all mix and contend with one another for organizational attention and action. In this situation, an organization becomes an "organized anarchy" in which the decision about which alternative to select depends on which manager or coalition has the most influence or power to sway other decision makers at that moment.[27] Chance, luck, and timing also come into play in determining which alternative is selected. Often, the problem that is currently generating the most uncertainty for the organization is the one that has the best chance of being acted on, and this may change from week to week. Decision making becomes fluid, unpredictable, and even contradictory as the preferences and priorities of decision makers change.

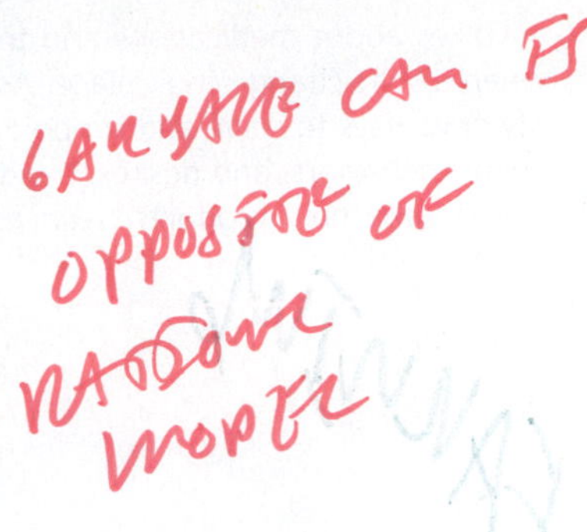

The garbage-can approach to organizational decision making is clearly the opposite of the approach described by the rational model. Instead of benefiting from the wisdom of all-knowing managers who can generate all possible solutions and unanimously agree on the best one so decisions can be programmed over time, in reality managers are forced to make unprogrammed decisions in an unstructured, garbage-can-like way to deal with the uncertainty that surrounds them.

The way in which IDEO helps organizations to "think out of the box" is instructive in this regard, as discussed in Organizational Insight 12.2.

Organizational Insight 12.2

IDEO Helps Organizations to "Learn How to Learn"

IDEO, founded in 1991 by David Kelly and Bill Moggridge, both well-known design engineers, has a mission to help organizations and their members "think out of the box." That is, to work in ways that help them develop the skills or what IDEO calls "creative confidence" to recognize and act on new opportunities and then respond to them by creating new and improved products that better meet their needs. IDEO offers companies seminars in which their managers, engineers, marketers, and so on can learn the techniques necessary to keep their companies on the cutting edge, or as IDEO puts it, to "Enable organizations to change their cultures and build the capabilities required to sustain innovation."[28] For example, IDEO invented the unfocused group technique in which all the side comments made by focus group members to one another are recorded to find out what was "not said" in focused group meetings. IDEO also practices "skilled brainstorming" in which it teaches teams of employees from client organizations how to conduct brainstorming sessions that promote creative solutions. Its recommendations include go for quantity (of new ideas), encourage wild ideas, and defer judgment.[29]

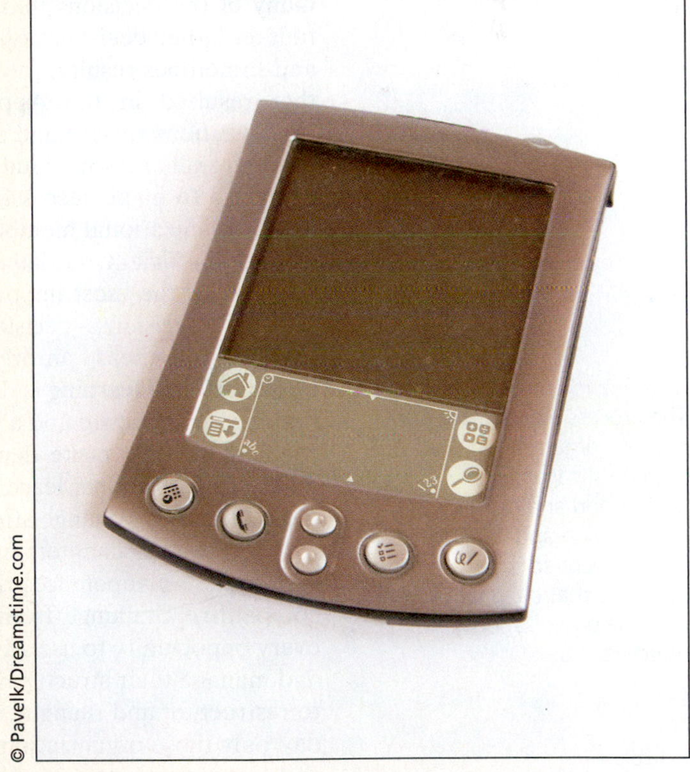

© Pavelk/Dreamstime.com

IDEO's goal is to improve a company's ability to innovate by helping them to learn how make better decisions, the decisions that result in blockbuster new products or ways to improve customer service and better satisfy customer needs (that IDEO believes often go unrecognized). So another method it uses to help organizations learn how to learn is to help them identify what customers really want—needs they may not even be aware of. Examples of products that IDEO designed that accomplished this include Apple's computer mouse, the "stand up" toothpaste tube, and the original Palm handheld organizer. To identify customer needs, IDEO uses the "deep dive" method; its employees—designers, anthropologists, marketing, and engineering researchers spend days or weeks shadowing and observing people focused on a certain task or event.[30] For example, the stand up toothpaste tube was developed by asking families what they most disliked about the "toothbrushing" experience and by observing their bathrooms. One complaint was crumpled toothpaste tubes that leak their contents over the bathroom sink, creating a soggy mess. In a hospital project, IDEOs researchers worked with hospital personnel to observe the problems that occurred when one nursing shift transferred control to another shift and how these problems affected nurses and patients. By studying shift changes for several days, 24 hours a day, the researchers were able to identify previously unrecognized problems. They then developed new software that provided better information that reduced the number of mistakes about medications and treatments and better patient care when a shift change took place. As IDEO puts it, we work to "identify new ways to serve and support people by uncovering their latent needs, behaviors, and desires," and then it works with companies to develop the new products, services, media, and even office spaces and cubicles that improve their well-being.[31] Clearly, the process of "learning to learn" using brainstorming and other methods to identify new opportunities and problems can help organizations make better decisions—the kind of decisions that result in long-term success.

LEARNING

In summary, decision making determines the way an organization operates. At the core of every organization is a set of decision-making rules and routines that bring stability and allow the organization to reproduce its activities, core competences, and structure over time. These routines provide the organization with a memory and provide managers with programmed solutions to problems, which in turn increase organizational effectiveness.[32] However, as we saw in Chapter 11, routines also can give rise to inertia. If an organization gets in a rut and managers cannot make the decisions that allow it to change and adapt to its environment, it may fail and die. To prevent this from happening, managers need to encourage organizational learning.

The Nature of Organizational Learning

Because decision making takes place in an uncertain environment, it is not surprising that many of the decisions that managers and organizations make are mistakes and end in failure. Other decisions, of course, allow the organization to adapt to the environment and sometimes result in outcomes that exceed managers' wildest dreams—such as those that resulted in the Apple iPod or Research in Motion's Blackberry cellphone. Organizations survive and prosper when managers make the right decisions—sometimes through skill and sound judgment, but sometimes through chance and good luck. If managers are to make successful decisions over time, they must put in place a system that helps organizational members improve their ability to learn new adaptive behaviors and unlearn inefficient, outdated ones.

One of the most important processes that helps managers to make better nonprogrammed decisions—decisions that allow them to adapt to, modify, and change the environment to increase an organization's chances of survival—is organizational learning.[33] **Organizational learning** is the process through which managers seek to improve organization members' desire and ability to understand and manage the organization and its environment so they make decisions that continuously raise organizational effectiveness.[34] Today, organizational learning is a vital process for organizations to manage because of the rapid pace of change affecting every organization.

Organizational learning
The process managers use to improve organization members' capacity to understand and manage the organization and its environment so they can make decisions that continuously increase organizational effectiveness.

As previous chapters have discussed, managers must strive to develop new and improved core competences that can give them a competitive advantage and fight off the competitive challenge from low-cost overseas competitors. To do this, they search for every opportunity to use advanced materials technology and IT to pursue their strategies and manage their structures more effectively. Indeed, the need for managers continually to restructure and reengineer their organizations is motivated by the realization that today, only those organizations that learn new ways to operate more efficiently will survive and prosper. Consequently, managers must understand how organizational learning occurs and the factors that can promote and impede it.

Types of Organizational Learning

James March has proposed that two principal types of organizational learning strategies can be pursued: exploration and exploitation.[35] **Exploration** involves organizational members searching for and experimenting with new kinds or forms of organizational activities and procedures to increase effectiveness. Learning that involves exploration might involve finding new ways to manage the environment—such as experimenting with the use of strategic alliances and network organizations—or inventing new kinds of organizational structures for managing organizational resources—such as product team structures and cross-functional teams.

Exploration
Organizational members' search for and experimentation with new kinds or forms of organizational activities and procedures.

Exploitation involves organizational members learning ways to refine and improve existing organizational activities and procedures to increase effectiveness. Learning that involves exploitation might involve implementing a total quality management program to promote the continuous refinement of existing operating procedures, or developing an improved set of rules to perform specific kinds of functional activities more effectively. Exploration is therefore a more radical learning strategy than exploitation, although both must be used together to increase organizational effectiveness.[36]

Exploitation
Organizational members' learning of ways to refine and improve existing organizational activities and procedures.

A **learning organization** is an organization that purposefully designs and constructs its structure, culture, and strategy so as to enhance and maximize the potential for organizational learning (explorative and exploitative) to take place.[37] How do managers create a learning organization, one capable of allowing its members to appreciate and respond quickly to changes taking place around it? By increasing the ability of employees, at every level in the organization, to question and analyze the way an organization currently performs its activities and to experiment with new ways to change them to increase effectiveness.

Learning organization
An organization that purposefully designs and constructs its structure, culture, and strategy so as to enhance and maximize the potential for organizational learning to take place.

Levels of Organizational Learning

To create a learning organization, managers need to encourage learning at four levels: individual, group, organizational, and interorganizational[38] (Figure 12.2). Some principles for creating a work setting at each level that encourages learning have been developed by Peter Senge and are discussed next.[39]

INDIVIDUAL At the individual level, managers need to do all they can to facilitate the learning of new skills, rules, norms, and values so individuals can increase their own personal abilities and, in doing so, help build an organization's core competences. Senge has argued that for organizational learning to occur, each of its members needs to develop a sense of *personal mastery*, by which he means that organizations should empower all employees and allow them to experiment and create and explore what they want. Google, for example, allows its employees to spend 30% of their time on projects of their own choosing to free them to "think out of the box."[40] The goal is to give employees the opportunity to develop an intense appreciation for their work that will translate into new distinctive competence for the organization, as it has for Google where employees suggested new applications such as Google Gadgets.

To help them achieve personal mastery, and to give employees a deeper understanding of what is involved in performing a particular activity, organizations need to encourage employees to develop and use complex *mental models* that challenge them to find

Figure 12.2 Levels of Organizational Learning

To create a learning organization, managers must use systems thinking and recognize the effects of one level of learning on another.

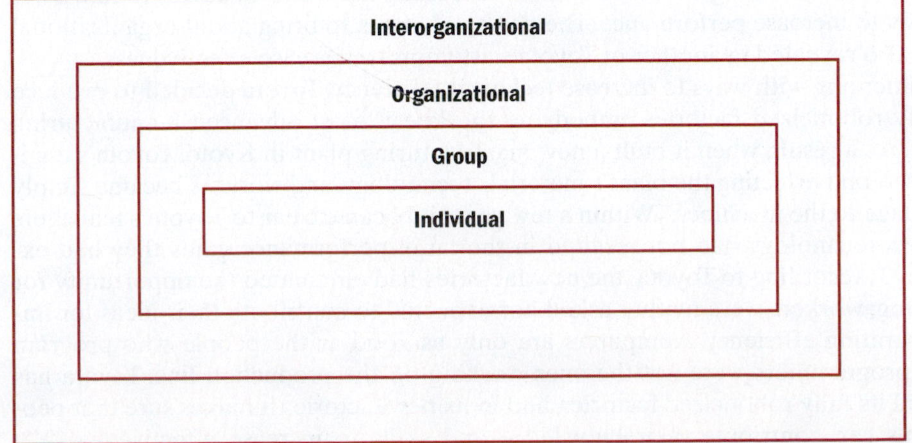

new or better ways of performing a task. To give an analogy, a person might mow the lawn once a week and treat this as a chore that has to be done. However, suppose the person decides to study how the grass grows and to experiment with cutting the grass to different heights and using different fertilizers and watering patterns. Through this study, he or she notices that cutting the grass to a certain height and using specific combinations of fertilizer and water promote thicker growth and fewer weeds, resulting in a better-looking lawn that needs less mowing. What has been a chore may become a hobby, and the personal mastery achieved from the new way of looking at the task may become a source of deep personal satisfaction. This is the message behind Senge's first principle for developing a learning organization: Organizations must encourage each individual member to develop a similar commitment and attachment to their job so they will develop a taste for experimenting and risk taking.[41]

A learning organization can encourage employees to form complex mental models and develop a sense of personal mastery by providing them with the opportunity to assume more responsibility for their decisions. This can be done in a variety of different ways. Employees might be cross-trained so they can perform many different tasks, and the knowledge that they gain may give them new insight into how to improve work procedures. Or perhaps a work procedure that was performed by several different workers can be redesigned or reengineered so only one worker, aided by advanced IT, is needed to perform the procedure. Again, the result may be an increase in the level of organizational learning as the worker finds new ways to get the job done. Recall that one of the aims of reengineering is fundamentally to rethink basic business processes. Reengineering is about promoting organizational learning.

GROUP At the group level, managers need to encourage learning by promoting the use of various kinds of groups—such as self-managed or cross-functional teams—so that employees can share or pool their skills and abilities to solve problems. Groups provide a setting for synergy to develop-—the idea that the whole is much more than the sum of its parts—which can enhance performance. In terms of Thompson's model of task interdependence discussed in Chapter 9, for example, the move from a pooled, to a sequential, to a reciprocal form of task interdependence increases the potential for synergy and group-level learning to develop because there is more opportunity for group members to interact and learn from one another over time. "Group routines" and "shared pools of collective meaning" that enhance group effectiveness may develop from such group interactions.[42] Senge refers to this kind of learning as *team learning* and argues that team learning is even more important than individual learning in promoting organizational learning because most important decisions are made in subunits such as groups, functions, and divisions.

The ability of teams to bring about organizational learning was unmistakable when Toyota revolutionized the work process in the former GM factory discussed in Organizational Insight 6.1. Large performance gains were achieved in the factory when Toyota's managers created work teams and empowered team members to take over the responsibility for measuring, monitoring, and controlling their own behavior to find ways continuously to increase performance. The power of teams to bring about organizational learning is also revealed in another of Toyota's attempts to increase effectiveness.

Experimenting with ways to increase technical efficiency, Toyota decided to produce cars in fully roboticized factories embodying the latest, most advanced manufacturing technology. As a result, when it built a new manufacturing plant in Kyoto, Toyota's engineers focused on perfecting the plant's materials technology, and workers became simply an "appendage to the machines." Within a few years it became clear to Toyota's managers that the new technology had not resulted in the large performance gains they had expected. Why? According to Toyota, the new factories had eliminated the opportunity for team learning; workers were neither asked nor expected to contribute their ideas for improving operating efficiency. Computers are only as good as the people who program them, and programmers were not the ones working on the production line. Toyota has since junked its fully roboticized factories, and in its new factories it makes sure that people in teams can contribute their knowledge and skills to increase effectiveness. Yet

Toyota is the first to admit it is not perfect and that it is constantly trying to learn and improve, as Organizational Insight 12.3 suggests.

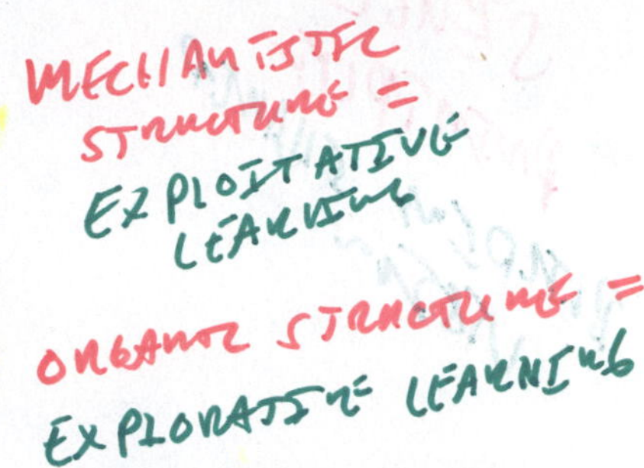

ORGANIZATION At the organizational level, managers can promote learning through the way they create its structure and culture. An organization's structure can be designed to inhibit or facilitate communication and cooperation between functions or divisions, for example, and so affects their ability to learn from each other. Similarly, mechanistic and organic structures encourage different approaches to learning. The design of a mechanistic structure facilitates exploitative learning; the design of an organic structure facilitates explorative learning. Indeed, organizations need to strike a balance between a mechanistic and an organic structure to take advantage of both types of learning.

Organizational Insight 12.3

Toyota Is a Learning Organization

Although Toyota is regarded as a world leader in total quality management and continually strives to learn better ways to perform its activities, it would be a mistake to believe its record is perfect—or anything close to it. Over the years it has made many mistakes and errors as it seeks to learn new and better ways to improve its functional activities and increase innovation, quality, and operating efficiency. The issue, however, is that Toyota always seeks to learn from its mistakes and it keeps tackling a problem until it finds a solution.

Boykov/Shutterstock.com

On the innovation front, for example, Toyota's Japanese engineers have often failed to understand the needs of its global customers because they did not listen to and learn from their managers, employees, and customers overseas. As a result, the first generation of many of its new vehicles such as pickup trucks, minivans, and SUVs were flops. For example, its first pickup truck was too small for the U.S. market, its first minivan was clumsy compared to Chrysler's, and its first SUV was underpowered and lacked the comfort and features of competitors such as Ford and Land Rover. Over time, Toyota's engineers have learned from their mistakes, and today, using the skills of its U.S. and European designers, its new generations of pickup trucks, minivans, and SUVs have become the market leaders.[43]

On the quality front, for which it is best known, it has also made many mistakes. On several occasions its engineers designed parts such as air conditioning and brake systems that proved defective and led to many recalls. But they have learned from their mistakes and most problems have been corrected. Even so, it was only in 2007 that Toyota realized it could find even more ways to improve quality if it started to collect repair information on what kinds of repair problems its vehicles suffered *after* their warranty had expired. If it had taken such a long-term view earlier, its engineers could have focused their attention on the specific problems that led to poor parts quality.[44]

On the efficiency front, cars have become more difficult to assemble because both components and work processes have become more complex. Although the world leader in the mid-2000s, Toyota, which has been rapidly expanding around the globe, found the number of recalls increasing. Since 2004, for example, Toyota has recalled 9.3 million vehicles in the United States and Japan—almost three times the previous rate. The reason for this problem was that in its concern to grow, managers had failed to increase the amount of work training employees receive to allow them to make its increasingly complex vehicles.[45] To solve this problem Toyota has delayed the introduction of some of its new models by several months while it trains its workforce in the many intricate procedures that must be followed to achieve the high quality it demands. Indeed, to allow it to regain its high-quality standards, it opened "global production centers," learning centers, in Kentucky, England, and Thailand to permit its engineers to train production supervisors in the advanced techniques, such as welding and painting, needed to maintain state-of-the-art production quality.

In 2007, Toyota's president, Katsuaki Watanabe, publicly apologized for these increasing errors and affirmed that Toyota was now back on the right track—even though it is almost always on top of the quality list of the best global carmaker.[46] Then, in 2009 Toyota once again experienced a major crisis as problems with the design of its vehicles' braking systems were reported to have led to unexpected acceleration that resulted in vehicle wrecks and deaths. Toyota became embroiled in lawsuits that have cost it billions of dollars and sales plunged, but its top managers are making sure every employee in the company now understands the importance of being open and willing to report mistakes or errors. In June 2011, Toyota recalled over 50,000 U.S. vehicles even though only one had reported a steering problem. Even the best companies have to strive to learn how to maintain—let alone exceed—their high standards and too keep learning.

Cultural values and norms are also an important influence on learning at the organizational level. Another of Senge's principles for designing a learning organization emphasizes the importance of *building shared vision*, by which he means creating an ongoing mental model that all organizational members can use to frame problems or opportunities and that binds them to an organization. At the heart of this vision is likely to be the set of terminal and instrumental values and norms that guide the way employees interact and so which affect how they learn from one another. Thus yet another important aspect of organizational culture is its ability to promote or inhibit organizational learning and change.

Adaptive cultures Cultures that value innovation and encourage and reward experimentation and risk taking by middle and lower-level managers.

Inert cultures Cultures that are cautious and conservative and do not encourage risk taking by middle and lower-level managers.

Indeed, in a study of 207 companies, John Kotter and James Heskett distinguished between adaptive cultures and inert cultures in terms of their ability to facilitate organizational learning.[47] **Adaptive cultures** are those that value innovation and encourage and reward experimenting and risk taking by middle and lower-level managers. **Inert cultures** are those that are cautious and conservative, do not value middle and lower-level managers taking such action, and, indeed, may actively discourage such behavior. According to Kotter and Heskett, organizational learning is higher in organizations with adaptive cultures because managers can quickly introduce changes in the way the organization operates that allow the organization to adapt to changes occurring in the environment. This does not occur in organizations with inert cultures. As a result, organizations with adaptive cultures are more likely to survive in a changing environment and should have higher performance than organizations with inert cultures—exactly what Kotter and Heskett found.

INTERORGANIZATIONAL Organizational structure and culture not only establish the shared vision or framework of common assumptions that guide learning inside an organization, they also determine how learning occurs at the interorganizational level. Organizations with organic, adaptive cultures, for example, are more likely to actively seek out new ways to manage linkages with other organizations, whereas mechanistic, inert cultures are slower to recognize and to take advantage of new linkage mechanisms, often preferring to go it alone.

In general, interorganizational learning is important because organizations can improve their effectiveness by imitating each other's distinctive competences. The previous chapter discusses how mimetic, coercive, and normative processes encourage organizations to learn from one another to increase their legitimacy, but this can also increase their effectiveness. In the car industry, for example, Japanese carmakers came to the United States after World War II to learn U.S. manufacturing methods and took this knowledge back to Japan where they improved on it. This process was then reversed in the 1980s when struggling U.S. carmakers went to Japan to learn about the advances that Japanese carmakers had pioneered, took this knowledge back to the United States, and improved on it.

Similarly, organizations can encourage explorative and exploitative learning by cooperating with their suppliers and distributors to find new and improved ways of handling inputs and outputs. Enterprise-wide IT systems, business-to-business networks, strategic alliances, and network organizations are important vehicles for increasing the speed at which new learning takes place because they open up the organization to the environment and give organizational members new opportunities to experiment and find new ways to increase effectiveness.

In fact, Senge's fifth principle of organizational learning, *systems thinking*, is that to create a learning organization, managers must recognize the effects of one level of learning on the others. For example, there is little point in creating teams to facilitate team learning if an organization does not also take steps to give employees the freedom to develop a sense of personal mastery. Similarly, the nature of interorganizational learning is likely to be affected by the kind of learning going on at the organization and group levels.

By encouraging and promoting organizational learning at all four levels—that is, by looking at organizational learning as a system—managers can create a learning organization that allows an organization to respond quickly to changes in the environment. Managers need to promote both explorative and exploitative learning and then use this learning in ways that will promote organizational effectiveness. In the next section an important technique for promoting organizational learning, knowledge management, is discussed. Then the many factors that may impede learning are examined.

Knowledge Management and Information Technology

As we have seen in previous chapters, new IT has had a major impact on the way an organization operates. IT-enabled organizational structure allows for new kinds of task and role relationships among electronically connected people that promote superior communication and coordination. One type of IT-enabled organizational relationship that has important implications for both organizational learning and decision making is **knowledge management,** the sharing and integrating of expertise within and between functions and divisions through real-time, interconnected IT.[48]

Knowledge management
A type of IT-enabled organizational relationship that has important implications for both organizational learning and decision making.

To understand the importance of knowledge management, consider how Accenture developed a knowledge management system to improve the ability of its consultants to acquire the vital new knowledge that allows them better to serve the needs of their clients. Accenture, the largest global management consulting company, has been a pioneer in using IT to revolutionize its business practices. As it grew to employ over 100,000 employees in more than 50 countries, it realized a new way to organize and control its army of global consultants was needed. Because only each of its consultants in the field could diagnose and solve client problems, however, Accenture realized the need for a control system that facilitates creative, on-the-spot, decentralized decision making. Moreover, to increase effectiveness, Accenture also needed to find a way to allow consultants to share each other's firsthand knowledge and expertise, which, after all, is the source of its competitive advantage.

To accomplish both these goals, Accenture decided to create a knowledge management system and substitute direct control by managers with control through a sophisticated in-house IT system.[49] First, they restructured the managerial hierarchy, eliminating many levels of managers. Then they went about setting up an organization-wide information management system to allow consultants to make their own decisions while providing them with access to an expert knowledge system that provided advice when they needed to solve client problems.[50]

The change process began by equipping every consultant with a state-of-the-art laptop computer. Using sophisticated in-house IT, each consultant was linked to all of the company's other consultants and became a member of a specific group that specialized in the needs of a particular kind of client, such as consumer product firms or brokerage companies. The group therefore possessed collective expert knowledge about a particular kind of client. To find a solution to a problem, the members of a specific group could email others in the group working at different client sites to see if they had faced similar client problems.

If group members still couldn't solve the problem, consultants communicated with members of other groups by tapping into Accenture's company-wide knowledge management database containing volumes of potentially relevant information. In this way different groups could share state-of-the-art business practices because it was likely another group had encountered the same problem in a different context and thus a solution did exist. Consultants who found clues using the electronic knowledge management system then communicated directly with consultants in other groups through a combination of phone, voice mail, email, and videoconferencing to gain access to the most current information being gathered and applied at existing client sites.[51] By using these resources, consultants kept abreast of the innovative practices within their own firm and within client firms. Remember that Accenture's consulting contracts with individual clients run into the millions of dollars; the enhancement in learning gained through an electronic knowledge management system is vital.

Accenture has found that its knowledge management system, by flattening its structure, decentralizing authority, and enlarging and enriching roles, has increased its consultants' creativity and performance. By providing employees with more information to make a decision and enabling them to coordinate easily with other people, IT has given consultants much more freedom to make decisions. And senior managers can easily manage what their consultants do by monitoring their progress electronically and taking corrective action as necessary. The result is that in 2011 Accenture was the biggest and most profitable global IT consulting company.[52]

As the example of Accenture suggests, one important benefit from using a knowledge management system is the development of synergies between people and groups that may result in competitive advantage in the form of product or service differentiation. Unlike more rigid bureaucratic organizing methods, IT-enabled organizations can respond more quickly to changing environmental conditions such as increased global competition.

What kind of knowledge management system should managers design for their organizations? Is the same kind of system suitable for all kinds of organizations? Or would we expect organizations with a more mechanistic or organic orientation to develop and adopt different kinds of systems?

KNOWLEDGE MANAGEMENT: CODIFICATION VERSUS PERSONALIZATION One solution to this question is that organizations should choose between a codification or personalization approach to creating an IT-based knowledge management system.[53] With a *codification approach*, knowledge is carefully collected, analyzed, and stored in databases where it can be retrieved easily by users who input organization-specific commands and keywords. Essentially, a codification approach results in collection of standardized organization best practices, rules, and SOPs that can be drawn on by anyone who needs them. It is a form of bureaucratic control that can result in major gains in technical efficiency and allow an organization better to manage its environment. For example, in 2011 Dell announced it would start to use an advanced in-house codification approach to manage its service and support activities with its business customers in an alliance with SAP. All of its business customers will have access to Dell's knowledge management system, which using SAP's software will give them realtime access to solutions to any software or database management problems. The system will also give them instant access to Dell's global online consultants who can help customers solve ongoing problems and ensure the safety and integrity of their company's databases—something increasingly important because Dell intends to become a leader in low-cost cloud computing.

A codification approach, however, is only suitable when the product or service being provided is itself quite standardized so best practices can continually be discovered and entered into the knowledge management system to be used by others in the organization. It works best when the different functions in the organization are able to provide standardized information—about changing customer demands or product specifications, for example—that provides vital input to other functions so the level of mutual adjustment and learning between functions increases, resulting in major gains in effectiveness. In this sense, a knowledge management system allows an organization with a more mechanistic structure to react in a more "organic" fashion, albeit the flexibility is provided by new, sophisticated IT protocols based on the codification of standardized organizational knowledge.

By contrast, a *personalization approach* to knowledge management is pursued when an organization needs to provide customized products or solutions to clients, when technology is changing rapidly, and when employees rely much more on know-how, insight, and judgment to make decisions. In these cases, it is very difficult (often impossible) to write down or even verbalize a course of action that leads to a solution. Often, the solution results from mutual adjustment between people and groups when intensive technology, discussed in Chapter 9, is employed.

In a personalization approach, information systems are designed to show employees who in the organization might possess the knowledge they might need or who might have confronted a similar problem in the past. In a consulting company such as Accenture, for example, individual consultants will write up synopses of the ways they have solved client problems, and the nature of these problems, so others in the organization can gain a sense of what they are doing. Working in teams, consultants can also spread their knowledge across the organization, often globally, and IT is used to facilitate direct interactions between people and the exchange of know-how by informing employees about upcoming seminars and visiting internal experts, for example.

Over time, as an organization like Accenture confronts more examples of a similar type of problem, consultants can increasingly codify this informal know-how into best practices that can be shared more widely throughout the organization. An organization's information system plays an especially crucial role, for competitive success depends on the speed with which it can provide clients with a state-of-the-art solution to their problems. And given that software is advancing all the time, such solutions change continually. An organization's ability to provide a quick, customized solution, and to translate this rapidly into best practices, often depends on the degree to which it is *specialized*—for example, by industry or product or service—and therefore deals with a narrower and deeper range of problems. That is why so many small specialized software and consulting computer companies exist.

Knowledge management is therefore an important tool for increasing the level of integration inside an organization, among people, functions, and even divisions. In the 2000s, many companies have moved to develop knowledge management systems to speed learning and decision making, and for many of them, it has resulted in success. It is important to remember, however, that knowledge management is expensive; people must be employed to help codify knowledge and disseminate it throughout the organization. Today, so much information is available to managers through IT that they can be swamped in it, and the process of discovering best practices and solutions requires a lot of search and judgment in its own right. Companies like HP, TI, and Oracle have saved hundreds of millions of dollars by implementing knowledge management systems; they also are spending hundreds of millions to maintain these systems. Organizations must always compare the benefits and costs of using IT and knowledge management to facilitate learning.

Factors Affecting Organizational Learning

Whereas knowledge management can enhance organizational learning, several factors may *reduce* the level of learning over time. A model developed by Paul C. Nystrom and William H. Starbuck illustrates how problems may arise that prevent an organization from learning and adapting to its environment and so result in an organizational crisis, a situation that seriously threatens an organization's survival.[54]

According to Nystrom and Starbuck, as organizations learn to make decisions they develop rules and SOPs that facilitate programmed decision making. If an organization achieves success by using its SOPs, this success may lead to complacency and deter managers from searching for and learning from new experiences![55] Thus past (successful) learning may inhibit new learning and lead to organizational inertia. In essence, if programmed decision making drives out nonprogrammed decision making, the level of organizational learning falls. Blindness and rigidity in organizational decision making may then set in and lead to a full-blown crisis.

Managers often discount warnings that problems are impending and do not perceive that crises are developing. Even if they notice, the source of the problems is often attributed to temporary disturbances in the environment. So managers implement "weathering-the-storm strategies," they postpone investments, downsize the workforce, and centralize decision making and reduce autonomy at lower levels in the organization. Managers adopt this incrementalist approach to decision making because sticking to what they know is much safer than setting off in new directions where consequences are unknown. Managers continue to rely on the information obtained from their existing operating routines to solve problems—information that does not reveal the real nature of the problems they are experiencing.

Another reason why past learning inhibits new learning is that managers' mindsets or cognitive structures shape their perception and interpretation of problems and solutions. A **cognitive structure** is the system of interrelated beliefs, preferences, expectations, and values that a person uses to define problems and events.[56] In an organization, cognitive structures reveal themselves in plans, goals, stories, myths, and jargon. Cognitive structures shape the way top managers make decisions—and determine the degree to which forces in the environment are perceived as opportunities and threats. Often top managers cling to outdated ideas and use inappropriate cognitive structures to interpret events and problems—something that leads to faulty learning. To explain why, it is necessary to

Cognitive structure The system of interrelated beliefs, preferences, expectations, and values a person uses to define problems and events.

examine some factors that distort managers' perceptions and flaw organizational learning and decision making.

Organizational Learning and Cognitive Structures

As noted earlier, cognitive structures are the systems of beliefs, preferences, and values that develop over time and predetermine managers' response to and interpretations of a situation. When managers confront a problem, their cognitive structures shape their interpretation of the information at hand; that is, the way managers view a situation is shaped by their prior experience and customary ways of thinking.[57] That view, however, might be distorted or wrong because of the operation of cognitive biases.

Types of Cognitive Biases

Cognitive biases
Factors that systematically bias cognitive structures and affect organizational learning and decision making.

Several factors may lead managers to develop a cognitive structure that causes them to misperceive and misinterpret information. These factors are called **cognitive biases** because they systematically bias managerial decision making and so lead to poor organizational learning and decision making (see Figure 12.3). Cognitive dissonance, illusion of control, and several other cognitive biases that influence organizational learning and decision making are discussed next.[58]

Cognitive Dissonance

Cognitive dissonance
The state of discomfort or anxiety a person feels when there is an inconsistency between his or her beliefs and actions.

Cognitive dissonance is the state of discomfort or anxiety that a person feels when there is an inconsistency between his or her beliefs and actions. According to cognitive dissonance theory, decision makers try to maintain consistency between their images of themselves, their attitudes, and their decisions.[59] Managers seek or interpret information that confirms and reinforces their beliefs, and they ignore information that does not. Managers also tend to seek information that is only incrementally different from the information they already possess and therefore supports their established position.

Cognitive dissonance theory explains why managers tend to misinterpret the real threats facing an organization and attempt to muddle through even when it is clear to many observers that the organization is in crisis. The desire to reduce cognitive dissonance pushes managers to adopt flawed solutions.

Figure 12.3 The Distortion of Organizational Decision Making by Cognitive Biases

Cognitive dissonance and other cognitive biases affect managers' information-processing abilities and distort managers' interpretation of a problem.

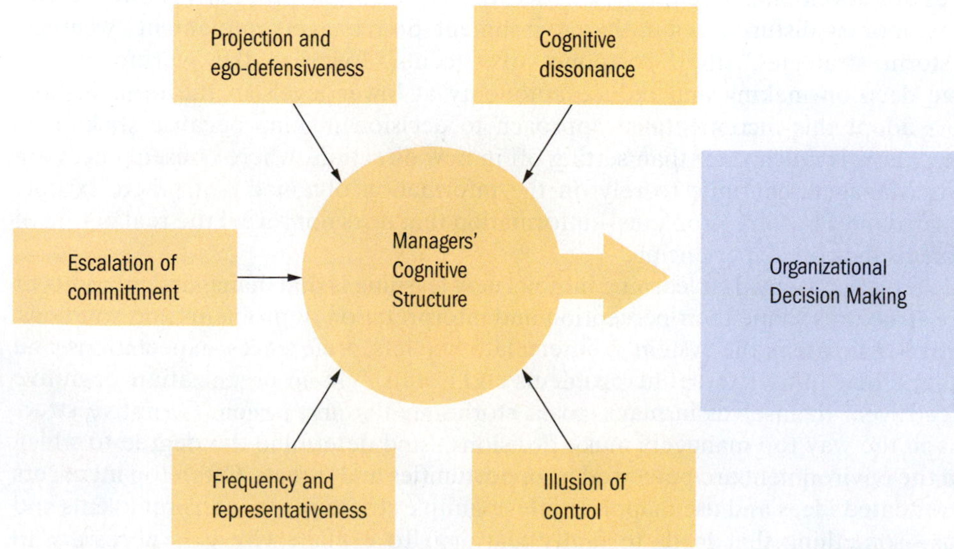

Illusion of Control

Some people, like entrepreneurs, seem able to bear high levels of uncertainty; others prefer the security associated with working in established organizations. Regardless of one's tolerance for ambiguity, however, uncertainty is very stressful. When an organization's environment or future is uncertain, managers do not know whether they have made the right choices, and considerable organizational resources are often at stake. Managers can reduce the degree to which they fear uncertainty by strengthening their perception that they have the personal abilities to control the situation.[60] However, the more managers perceive they can control a situation, the more likely is the cognitive bias known as illusion of control to arise.

Illusion of control is a cognitive bias that leads managers to overestimate the extent to which they can control a situation because they have the skills and abilities needed to manage uncertainty and complexity.[61] In uncertain situations in which their ability and competence are really being tested, managers may develop irrational beliefs about their personal ability to manage uncertainty. They may, for example, overestimate their skills to enter new industries and embark on a huge acquisition program. Soon, however, they encounter problems and realize they lack the ability to manage the more complex organization effectively, but it is too late.

Illusion of control
A cognitive bias that causes managers to overestimate the extent to which the outcomes of an action are under their personal control.

Frequently, when top managers lose control they move to centralize more authority, in the mistaken belief that this will give them greater control and allow them to solve their problems. But because their perception of control is an illusion, the organizational crisis deepens. It is not uncommon for a strong CEO or the members of an entrenched top-management team to develop the illusion that only they have the ability to manage the uncertainty facing the organization and to lead the organization to success—even when it is in crisis.

Frequency and Representativeness

Frequency and representativeness are tendencies that often lead managers to misinterpret information.[62] **Frequency** is a cognitive bias that deceives people into assuming that extreme instances of a phenomenon are more prevalent than they really are. Suppose purchasing managers have had a particularly bad experience with a supplier that has been shipping them large quantities of defective goods. Because of severe manufacturing problems caused by the defective parts, the managers decide to sever relations with that supplier. The frequency bias may cause them to become very fearful of relying on other suppliers for their inputs. They may instead decide to integrate their operations vertically so they control their inputs, even though vertical integration will increase costs. Although there is no rational reason to believe a new supplier will be as bad as, or worse than, the rejected supplier, the managers jump to an expensive solution to avoid the risk, and faulty learning has occurred.

Frequency
A cognitive bias that deceives people into assuming that extreme instances of a phenomenon are more prevalent than they really are.

Representativeness is a cognitive bias that leads managers to form judgments based on small and unrepresentative samples. Exposure to a couple of unreliable suppliers, for example, prompts managers to generalize and believe that all suppliers are untrustworthy and unreliable, again leading to faulty learning.

Representativeness
A cognitive bias that leads managers to form judgments based on small and unrepresentative samples.

Frequency and representative biases can also work in the opposite direction. A company that has great success with a new product may come to believe this product is the wave of the future and devote all its resources to developing a new product line for which there actually is little demand. FedEx, for example, believed that the demand for international express delivery would increase dramatically as companies became increasingly global. It came to this conclusion because it had been receiving more and more requests for international delivery. FedEx thus decided to invest a huge amount of resources to buy and operate a global fleet of planes and overseas facilities to handle worldwide express delivery. The decision was a disaster. The volume of express packages shipped to Europe turned out to be only half of that shipped in the United States, and the cost of operating the new global structure was enormous. After major losses, FedEx decided to form strategic alliances with foreign delivery companies to deliver the mail (rather than go it alone), and this new strategy has been successful. As this example shows, a bad decision can be made because top managers overgeneralize from a limited range of knowledge and experience.

Projection and Ego-Defensiveness

Projection
A cognitive bias that allows managers to justify and reinforce their own preferences and values by attributing them to others.

Projection is a cognitive bias that allows managers to justify and reinforce their own preferences and values by attributing them to others.[63] Suppose a top-management team is dominated by managers who are threatened by a deteriorating economic situation and doubt their ability to manage it. Feeling threatened and powerless, the team may accuse other lower-level managers of being unable to control the situation or of lacking the ability or desire to do so. Thus top managers project their own feelings of helplessness onto others and blame them. Obviously, when projection starts to operate, it can become self-reinforcing: Everybody blames everybody else, and the culture of the organization deteriorates.

Ego-defensiveness
A cognitive bias that leads managers to interpret events in such a way that their actions appear in the most favorable light.

Ego-defensiveness also affects the way managers interpret what is happening in the organization. **Ego-defensiveness** is a cognitive bias that leads managers to interpret events in such a way that their actions appear in the most favorable light. If an organization is employing more and more managers but profitability is not increasing, managers may emphasize that they are positioning the organization for future growth by putting in place the infrastructure to support future development. Ego-defensiveness results in little organizational learning, and faulty decision making ultimately leads to a manager's replacement or an organization's failure.

Escalation of Commitment

The bias toward escalation of commitment is another powerful cause of flawed learning and faulty decision making.[64] According to the Carnegie model of decision making, managers generate a limited number of alternative courses of action, from which they choose one that they hope will lead to a satisfactory (if not optimum) outcome. But what happens if they choose the wrong course of action and experience a negative outcome, such as when FedEx found itself losing enormous amounts of money as a result of its international express delivery venture? A logical response to a negative outcome would be a reevaluation of the course of action. Research, however, indicates that managers who have made an investment in a mistake tend to persist in the same behavior and increase their commitment to it, even though it is leading to poor returns and organizational ineffectiveness.

Escalation of commitment
A cognitive bias that leads managers to remain committed to a losing course of action and refuse to admit they have made a mistake.

Escalation of commitment is a cognitive bias that leads managers to remain committed to a losing course of action and to refuse to admit they have made a mistake, perhaps because of ego-defensiveness or because they are gripped by the illusion of control. In later decision making, they try to correct and improve on their prior (bad) decision rather than acknowledge that they have made a mistake and turn to a different course of action. At FedEx, for example, the CEO realized the error and quickly moved to redeploy resources to make the international express delivery venture viable, and he succeeded. The bias toward escalation of commitment is clearly reinforced by an incrementalist approach to decision making. Managers prefer to modify existing decisions to make them fit better with new conditions rather than to work out new solutions. Although this method of decision making may work in stable environments, it is disastrous when technology or competition is rapidly changing.

The net effect of all of the cognitive biases is that managers lose their ability to see new problems or situations clearly and to devise new responses to new challenges—and the level of learning falls. The flawed decision making that results from these biases hampers an organization's ability to adapt and modify its environment. By hampering organizational learning, biased decision making threatens an organization's ability to grow and survive. What can an organization do to develop a less incremental and more unstructured approach to decision making? How can managers be encouraged to be receptive to learning new solutions and to challenging the assumptions they use to make decisions?[65] Research has suggested several ways to increase organizational learning and promote organizational change.

Improving Decision Making and Learning

Organizational inertia and cognitive biases make it difficult to maintain the quality of organizational decision making and promote organizational learning over time. How can managers avoid using inappropriate routines, beliefs, and values to interpret and solve problems? Organizations can use several means to overcome the effect of cognitive biases and promote learning and change: implement strategies for organizational learning, increase the breadth and diversity of the top-management team, use devil's advocacy and dialectical inquiry, use game theory, and develop a collateral organizational structure.

Strategies for Organizational Learning

Managers must continuously unlearn old ideas and test their decision-making skills to confront errors in their beliefs and perceptions. Three ways in which they can unlearn old ideas (and learn new ones) are by listening to dissenters, by converting events into learning opportunities, and by experimenting.[66]

LISTENING TO DISSENTERS To improve the quality of decision making, top managers can choose to surround themselves with people who hold different and often opposing points of view. By doing so they can collect new information to evaluate new alternatives generated by dissenters and so find the best solution. Unfortunately, research shows that many top managers do not listen to their subordinates and surround themselves with flatterers who distort the information they provide, enhancing good news and suppressing the bad.[67] Moreover, because of bounded rationality, managers may be reluctant to encourage dissent because dissent will increase the amount of information they have to process—and this is a burdensome, stressful activity.

CONVERTING EVENTS INTO LEARNING OPPORTUNITIES Nystrom and Starbuck discuss one unidentified company that appointed a "Vice President for Revolutions," whose job was to step in every four years and shake up the organization by transferring managers and reassigning responsibilities so that old taken-for-granted routines were reexamined and people could bring new points of view to various situations. It did not make much difference what specific changes were made. The objective was to make them large enough so people were forced to make new interpretations of situations. After each shakeup, productivity increased for two years and then declined for the next two, until the organization was shaken up again.[68]

In general, an organization needs to redesign its structure and culture—in ways discussed in previous chapters—to motivate managers to find better ways to respond to a situation. TQM is based on the idea of having employees continuously examine their tasks to discover whether improvements that increase quality and productivity can be made. Also, different kinds of organizational structure and culture, for example, mechanistic or organic structures, can encourage or discourage organizational learning. An interesting study conducted in California of hospitals that experienced an environmental jolt caused by a doctor's strike shows the influence of organizational structure in decision making. The study found that responses by hospitals to this crisis were strongly influenced by the way in which each hospital typically made decisions in uncertain situations.[69] Hospitals that had organic structures characterized by decentralized decision making and frequently redesigned their structures were accustomed to both learning and unlearning. As a result, these hospitals dealt with the strike much better than did hospitals with centralized, mechanistic structures and a formalized, programmed approach to decision making.

EXPERIMENTING To encourage explorative learning, organizations must encourage experimenting, the process of generating new alternatives and testing the validity of old ones. Experimenting can be used to improve both incremental and garbage-can decision-making processes. To test new ways of behaving, such as new ways to serve customers or to manufacture a product, managers can run experiments that deviate only slightly from what the organization is currently doing. Or, taking a garbage-can approach, managers can brainstorm and come up with new solutions that surprise even themselves. Managers who are willing to experiment avoid overcommitment to previously worked-out solutions, reduce the likelihood of misinterpreting a situation, and can learn from their mistakes and failures. Today, using IT is a vital part of learning how to experiment to improve performance, as Organizational Insight 12.4 suggests.

Using Game Theory

As we have already discussed, organizations are in a constant competitive struggle with rivals in their industry to secure scarce resources. In understanding the dynamics of decision making between competitors in the environment, a useful tool that can help managers improve decision making and enhance learning is *game theory,* in which interactions between organizations are viewed as a competitive game. If companies understand the nature of the competitive game they are playing, they can make often make better decisions that increase the likelihood of their obtaining scarce resources.[70]

From a game theory perspective, companies in an industry can be viewed as players that are all simultaneously making choices about which decisions to make that will maximize their effectiveness. The problem that managers face is the potential effectiveness of each decision they make, for example of which competitive strategy they select is not some "fixed or stable amount." What value they will get from making a certain choice—the payoff—will vary depending on the strategies that rivals also select. There are two

Organizational Insight 12.4

Using IT to Improve Customer Service

Today, more and more potential buyers are taking advantage of the limitless information they can find on the WWW to learn about different products and become informed customers. Buyers can go online and search for information and reviews about the different qualities of competing products at shopping websites. They can then go to websites that specialize in providing up-to-date information about the current prices being charged for these products by different bricks-and-mortar (B&M) and online retailers. The availability of so much information online poses major challenges for retailers, especially B&M retailers, because their sales reps are now dealing with highly informed customers. And the ability to complete a sale often depends on a sales rep's ability to offer some kind of extra product information or assistance compared to an online retailer.

A main challenge confronting managers of B&M retailers is to find ways to use IT to improve the quality of the shopping experience, especially to better train their employees to provide higher-quality customer service. In the past, for example, one of the attractions of shopping at exclusive high-priced department stores was that their salespeople had great knowledge of the products they sold and would go to great lengths to satisfy customers. For example, sales reps would know which branch to phone to locate the right size of a dress or a comforter that a client wanted but was not in stock and how to have the item shipped overnight. But today customers often have learned more than employees about competing products because they use the Web to gather information. They assume employees have learned to use the Web to gain real-time information about the products they sell.

In reality, many retail stores have not kept up with the need to use IT to help their employees learn about the products they sell so that they can provide better customer service. Nor have they thought about how they can improve employee training to give them the knowledge and information they need to help customers learn about these products. The result has been falling store performance and the loss of customers to online stores. So how does a B&M retailer catch up by using advanced retailing IT to help salespeople learn how to better serve customers? The main way B&M companies can better compete with online retailers is to make better use of their employees—especially to train employees so they have more information at their disposal than IT-savvy customers. Also, to train them to provide other kinds of services that online stores cannot, for example, how to provide personalized in-store service and to offer customers profitable extra services such as home setup, service, and repair.

Best Buy, for example, decided it would retrain 30% of its top salespeople so they would not only possess detailed information about the products in their own store department, for example, PCs or flat-screen TVs, but also about how to match products across departments, for example, to help customers decide which printer is best for a PC that has a certain kind of graphics card. The goal is to provide customers with the "extra" or additional kinds of information that make a difference and so encourages them to make their purchases in B&M stores as well as to believe it is worth their while to come back in the future.

Indeed, another advantage of investing in high-quality customer service is that research has found that using IT to bring customers into the store, either to pick up products or to gain better advice, is a major source of extra sales. Why? Customer reps are trained to inform customers about the accessories that will help them better enjoy their purchases (e.g., type of protective case for laptop or newest video games for a game console). And, in B&M stores that offer a wide array of products such as Best Buy or Walmart, customers often explore its different departments and make extra purchases—like a pack of $10 energy-efficient light bulbs or a $2,000 high-definition TV. These extra purchases contribute significantly to a store's performance. Walmart, for example, developed an online link to a B&M store program in select stores in 2007 and found it increased the number of customers by 20% and that they spent an extra $60 during their pickup visit!

basic types of games: sequential move games and simultaneous move games. In a *sequential move game*, such as chess, players move in turn, and one player can select a strategy to pursue after considering its rival's choice of strategies. In a *simultaneous move game*, the players act at the same time, in ignorance of their rival's current actions.

In the environment, both sequential and simultaneous move games are commonplace as managers compete for scarce resources. Indeed, game theory is particularly useful in analyzing situations where a company is competing against a limited number of rivals in its domain and they are highly interdependent—something very common in most environments. In such a setting, the value that can be created by making a certain choice—for example, to pursue a low-cost or differentiation strategy—depends critically on the strategies pursued by rivals. The basic principles that underlie game theory can be useful in determining which choices to make and strategies to select to manage the environment.

A fundamental premise of game theory is that when making decisions, managers need to think in two related ways. First, they need to look forward, think ahead, and anticipate how rivals will respond to whatever might be their competitive moves. Second, managers need to reason backward to determine which moves their company should pursue today given their assessment of how their rivals will respond to various future moves. If managers do both these things, they should be able to make the decision that will lead to the best choice—to make the move that will lead to the greatest potential returns. This cardinal principle of game theory is known as *look forward and reason back:* To understand its importance, consider this scenario.

UPS and FedEx, which specialize in the next-day delivery of packages, dominate the U.S. air express industry. They have very high costs because they need to invest in a nationwide capital-intensive network of aircraft, trucks, and package-sorting facilities. For these companies, the key to increasing their effectiveness is to attract more customers, growing volume so they can reduce the average cost of transporting each package. Suppose a manager at UPS calculates that if UPS cuts prices for their next-day delivery service by 10%, the volume of packages they ship will grow by over 25%, and so will UPS's total revenues and profits. Is this a smart choice? The answer depends on whether the manager has remembered to look forward and reason back and think through how FedEx would respond to UPS's price cuts.

Because UPS and FedEx are competing directly against each other, their choices are interdependent. If UPS cuts prices, FedEx will lose market share, its volume of shipments will decline, and its profits will suffer. FedEx is unlikely to accept this. Rather, if UPS cuts prices by 10%, FedEx is likely to follow, make the same choice, and cut its prices by 10% to hold on to its customers. The net result is that the average level of prices in the industry will fall by 10%, as will revenues, and both players will see their profits decline and the environment will become poorer. To avoid this situation, and make better decisions, managers need always to look forward and reason back—an important principle of learning.

Decision trees can be used to help in the process of looking forward and reasoning back. Figure 12.4 maps out the decision tree for the simple game just analyzed from the perspective of UPS. (Note that this is a sequential move game.) UPS moves first, and then FedEx must decide how to respond. Here you see that UPS has to choose between two strategies, cutting prices by 10% or leaving them unchanged. If it leaves prices unchanged, it will continue to earn its current level of profitability, which is $100 million. If it cuts prices by 10%, one of two things can happen: FedEx matches the price cut, or FedEx leaves its prices unchanged. If FedEx matches UPS's price cut (FedEx decides to fight a price war), profits are competed away and UPS's profit will be $0. If FedEx does not respond, however, and leaves its prices unaltered, UPS will gain market share and its profits will rise to $300 million. So the best pricing strategy for UPS to pursue depends on its assessment of FedEx's likely response.

Note that Figure 12.4 assigns probabilities to the different responses from FedEx. Specifically there is a 75% chance that FedEx will match UPS's price cut and a 25% chance that it will do nothing. These probabilities come from each company's assessment of the other's likely decision based on their past history of making decisions in the environment—from looking at the history of FedEx's responses to UPS's price moves and vice versa. Although both sets of managers cannot calculate exactly what the profit

Figure 12.4 A Decision Tree for UPS's Pricing Strategy

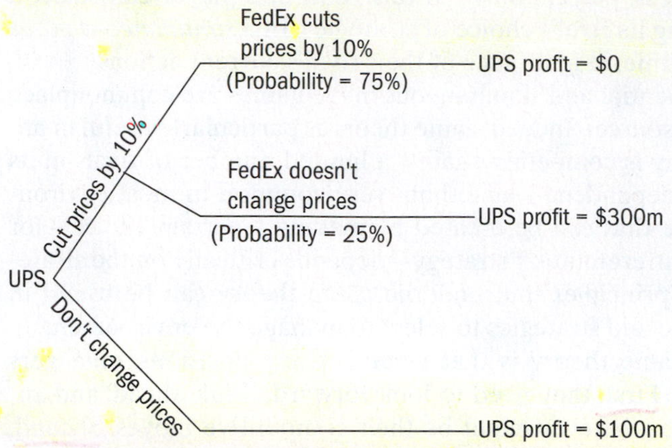

impact and probabilities would be, they make an informed decision by collecting information and devoting resources to learning about their rivals and about the environment. This illustrates a second basic principle of game theory: Know thy rivals! To improve learning, managers must put themselves in the position of a rival to answer the question of how that rival is likely to act in a particular situation. If a company's managers are to be effective at looking forward and reasoning back, they must have a good understanding of what their rival is likely to do under different scenarios, and they need to be able to extrapolate their rival's future behavior based on this understanding.

Nature of the Top-Management Team

The way the top-management team is constructed and the type of people who are on it affect the level of organizational learning.[71] There are various ways to construct a top-management team, and each has different implications for the processing of information, organizational learning, and the quality of decision making.[72] Figure 12.5 shows two top-management configurations, each of which has different implications for the level of learning taking place. In the wheel configuration, organizational learning is decreased because managers from the different functions report separately to the CEO. Rather than coordinate their own actions as a team, they send all information to the CEO, who processes this information, arrives at a decision, and communicates the decision back to the top managers. Research suggests that the wheel works best when problems are simple and require minimal coordination among top team members.[73] When problems are complex and nonprogrammed decision making is required, the wheel configuration slows organizational learning because all coordination takes place through the CEO.

Figure 12.5 Types of Top-Management Teams

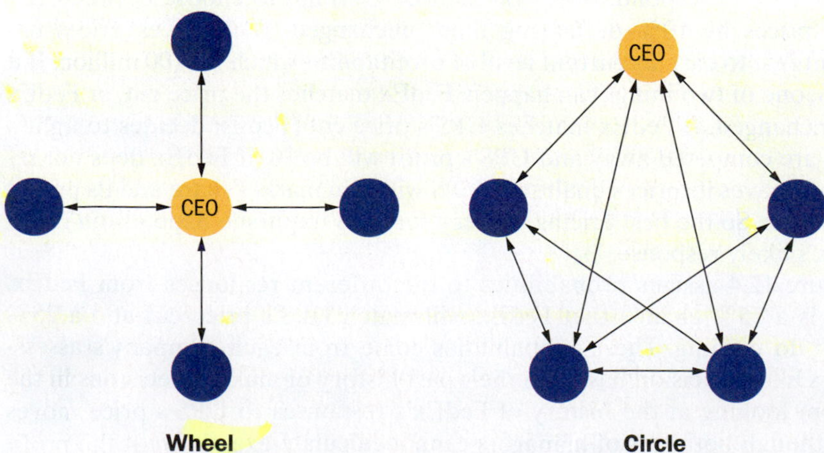

In the circle configuration, top managers from different functions interact with one another and with the CEO. That is, they function as a team, which promotes team and organizational learning. Research has suggested that the circle works best for complex problems requiring coordination among group members to arrive at a solution. The circle design solves complex problems much more quickly than the wheel arrangement: Communication around the circle takes less time because there is more opportunity for team and organization learning between all top managers.[74]

The level and quality of organizational learning and decision making by the top-management team is also a function of the personal characteristics and backgrounds of team members.[75] An organization that draws its top-management team from many different industries and different functional backgrounds can promote organizational learning and decision making. Diversity in the top-management team also exposes managers to the implications and consequences of many alternative courses of action. Such exposure may cause managers to examine their own expectations and assumptions more closely.

It has been found that the most learning takes place when there is considerable heterogeneity among team members and when managers from different functions have an opportunity to express their views. When managers bring different information and viewpoints to bear on a problem, the organization can avoid **groupthink,** the conformity that emerges when like-minded people reinforce one another's tendencies to interpret events and information in similar ways.[76] It has also been found that top-management teams function most effectively when their membership is stable and there is not too much entry into or departure from the team.[77] When team membership is stable, group cohesiveness increases and promotes communication among members and improved decision making.[78]

Groupthink
The conformity that emerges when like-minded people reinforce one another's tendencies to interpret events and information in similar ways.

Designing and managing the top-management team to promote organizational learning is a vital task for a CEO.[79] Often, an organization picks as CEO the person who has the functional and managerial background needed to deal with the most pressing issues facing the organization. Caterpillar, PepsiCo, Ford, and Walmart are some of the many companies that have chosen CEOs from managers who have had extensive experience in international business because their major problems center on the challenge of global expansion and competition.[80] Sometimes the only way to promote organizational learning is to change the CEO or the top-management team. Removing and changing top managers can be the quickest way to erase organizational memory and thus poor programmed decision making, allowing an organization to develop successful new routines.

Devil's Advocacy and Dialectical Inquiry

A **devil's advocate** is the person willing to stand up and question the beliefs of more powerful people, resist influence attempts, and work to convince others that new ideas or plans may be flawed or wrong and harmful. Devil's advocacy and a related technique, dialectical inquiry, are ways of overcoming cognitive biases and promoting organizational learning.[81] Figure 12.6 shows how these strategies differ from one another and from the rational approach to decision making. The goal of both is to improve decision making.

Devil's advocate
A person who is responsible for critiquing ongoing organizational learning.

An organization that uses devil's advocacy institutionalizes dissent by assigning a manager or management team the role of devil's advocate. The devil's advocate is responsible for critiquing ongoing organizational learning and for questioning the assumptions the top-management team uses in the decision-making process. 3M makes excellent use of devil's advocacy. At 3M, product managers submit proposals for a new product to a product development committee composed of top managers. The committee acts as devil's advocate. It critiques the proposal and challenges assumptions (such as the estimated size of the market for the product or its cost of manufacturing) to improve the plan and verify its commercial viability. 3M directly attributes its product development successes to the use of devil's advocacy.

An organization that uses dialectical inquiry creates teams of decision makers. Each team is instructed to generate and evaluate alternative scenarios and courses of action and then recommend the best one. After hearing each team's alternatives, all of the teams and the organization's top managers sit down together to cull the best parts of each plan and synthesize a final plan that offers the best chance of success.

Figure 12.6 How Devil's Advocacy and Dialectical Inquiry Alter the Rational Approach to Decision Making

Devil's advocacy and dialectical inquiry improve decision making by making managers aware of several possible solutions to a problem and by encouraging the analysis of the pros and cons of each proposed solution before a final decision is made.

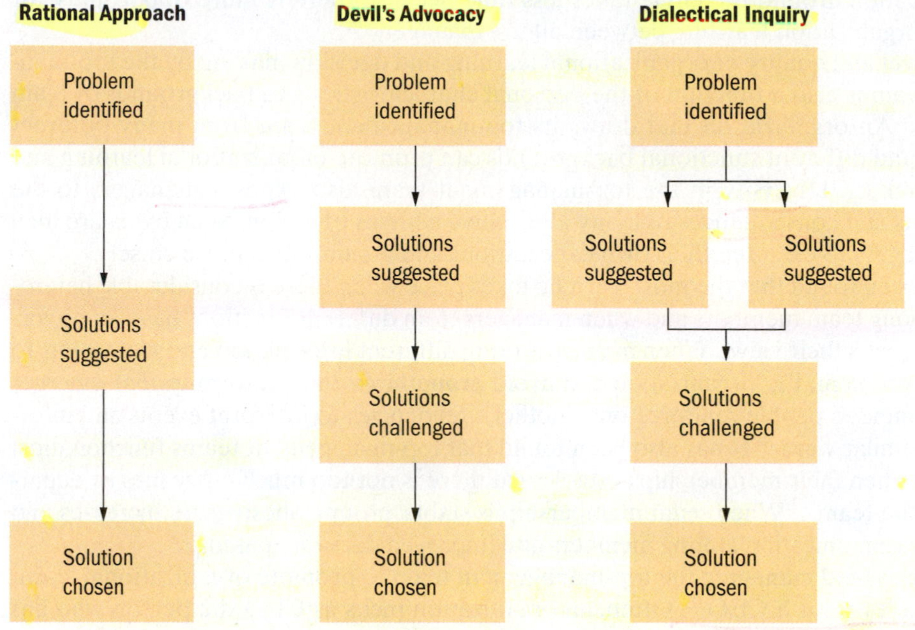

Collateral Organizational Structure

Finally, an organization can attempt to improve learning and decision making by establishing a *collateral organizational structure*—that is, an informal organization of managers set up parallel to the formal organizational structure to "shadow" the decision making and actions of managers in the formal organization.[82] Managers in the formal structure know that their decisions are being evaluated by others and become used to examining the assumptions that they use to test alternatives and arrive at a solution. An organization establishes a collateral structure to improve the organization's ability to learn and adjust to new situations, and to enhance its ability to make decisions in an unstructured way. A collateral organizational structure allows an organization to maintain its capacity for change at the same time it maintains its stability.

Managerial Implications

Decision Making and Learning

1. Try to guard against blindness and rigidity in decision making, be on the lookout for new problems, and be open to new solutions.
2. Develop a questioning attitude, and never discount warnings that problems are impending.
3. Analyze the cognitive structures through which you and your subunit define problems. Question whether these beliefs or values reflect the realities of the situation.
4. Examine your decision making to determine whether cognitive biases are affecting the quality of your decisions.
5. To protect the quality of your decision making, develop strategies to enhance organizational learning. For example, listen to your opponents, experiment with new solutions, encourage diversity, and use dialectical inquiry.

Summary

The problems that many established companies encounter are a warning about the need to encourage organizational learning so organizations have the ability to continuously adapt to and modify their environments. Strategy and structure are the tools that an organization uses to fashion its future; the decisions about strategy and structure that an organization makes now will determine its fate years from now. Too often, managers view strategy and structure as unchangeable and not as factors to be experimented with and altered to move the organization forward. When strategy and structure are viewed as something to be protected at all costs, they can become a source of organizational inertia that may bring an organization to its knees. Managers need to understand how an organization's current strategy and structure can constrain organizational learning, and they need to prevent the emergence of cognitive biases that reduce learning and distort the decision-making process. Chapter 12 has made the following main points:

1. Organizational decision making is the process of responding to a problem by searching for and selecting a solution or course of action that will create value for organizational stakeholders.
2. Managers make two basic types of decisions: programmed and nonprogrammed. Programmed decisions provide an organization with stability and increase efficiency. Nonprogrammed decisions allow an organization to adapt to changes in its environment and find solutions to new problems.
3. The rational model of decision making outlines how decision making takes place when there is no uncertainty. It ignores the effects of information costs and managerial costs.
4. Newer models of decision making recognize the effects of uncertainty, information, bounded rationality, satisficing, and bargaining by coalitions on the decision-making process. The Carnegie, incrementalist, unstructured, and garbage-can models provide a more realistic picture of how organizational decision making takes place.
5. Organizational learning is the process through which managers seek to improve organization members' desire and ability to understand and manage the organization and its environment so they can make decisions that continuously raise organizational effectiveness. There are two main kinds of learning—explorative and exploitative—and both are necessary to raise the quality of decision making.
6. The routines and procedures that an organization uses to make programmed decisions can cause organizational inertia. When programmed decision making drives out nonprogrammed decision making, the level of organizational learning drops. To encourage organizational learning, managers can act at the individual, group, organizational, and interorganizational levels.
7. Information technology and knowledge management systems can be developed to improve decision making and enhance organizational learning. The two main approaches to knowledge management are codification and personalization.
8. Cognitive structures (sets of interrelated beliefs, preferences, expectations, and values) affect the way managers interpret the problems facing an organization and shape the way they make decisions.
9. Cognitive biases may distort the way managers process information and make decisions. Common cognitive biases include cognitive dissonance, the illusion of control, frequency and representativeness, projection and ego-defensiveness, and escalation of commitment.
10. An organization can counter the effect of cognitive biases and raise the level of learning and decision making in several ways. It can implement strategies for organizational learning, use game theory, increase the breadth and diversity of the top-management team, use devil's advocacy and dialectical inquiry to evaluate proposed solutions, and develop a collateral organizational structure.

Discussion Questions

1. What are the critical differences between the rational and the Carnegie approaches to decision making? What are the critical differences between the incrementalist and the garbage-can models? Which models best describe how decision making takes place in (a) a fast-food restaurant and (b) the research and development laboratory of a major drug company?
2. What is organizational learning? In what ways can managers promote the development of organizational learning by acting at various levels in the organization? By using knowledge management?
3. How can knowledge management promote organizational learning? What determines which kind of knowledge management system a company should adopt?
4. How do cognitive biases affect organizational learning and the quality of decision making? What can be done to reduce their negative impact?

Organizational Theory in Action

Practicing Organizational Theory

Store Learning

Form groups of three to five people and discuss the following scenario:

You are a group of top managers of a major clothing store who are facing a crisis. Your establishment has been the leading clothing store in your city for the last 15 years. In the last three years, however, two other major clothing store chains have opened up in your city, and they have steadily been luring away your customers—your sales are down 30%. To find out why, you have been surveying some of your former customers and have learned that they perceive, for whatever reason, that your store is just not keeping up with changing fashion trends and new forms of customer service. In examining the way your store operates, you have come to realize that over time the ten buyers who purchase the clothing and accessories for your store have been buying increasingly from the same set of clothing suppliers, and they have become reluctant to try new ones. Moreover, your salespeople rarely, if ever, make suggestions for changing the way your store operates. Your goal is to shake up store employees and turn around store performance.

1. Devise a program to increase the level of organizational learning.
2. In what specific ways can you promote the level of learning at all levels?

Making the Connection #12

Find an example of an organization that has been using information technology to change the way it makes decisions or increase its level of learning. Why is the organization making these changes? What is it doing to stimulate new learning?

The Ethical Dimension #12

Managers' desire or willingness to act ethically and make ethical decisions can be affected by any cognitive biases that are operating in a particular context.

1. Discuss how the various cognitive biases can lead managers to behave unethically. Do you see any theme or pattern in how these biases operate on ethics?
2. Which kinds of techniques or tools discussed in this chapter, for example, a knowledge management system, can be best used to combat the problem of cognitive biases?

Analyzing the Organization: Design Module #12

This module focuses on organizational decision making and learning and on the way your company has changed its strategy and structure over time.

Assignment

1. Given the pattern of changes your organization has made to its strategy and structure over time, which of the decision-making models best characterizes the way it makes decisions?
2. At what hierarchical level does responsibility for nonprogrammed decision making seem to lie in your organization? What problems do you see with the way your company makes decisions?
3. Characterize your organization's ability to learn over time. Evaluate its capacity to adapt itself to and modify the environment.
4. Can you pinpoint any cognitive biases that may have affected the way managers made decisions or influenced their choice of strategy or structure? What was the effect of these cognitive biases?

CASE FOR ANALYSIS

How Mattel's Barbie Lost the War against the Bratz Doll

The rapid pace at which the world is changing is forcing strategic managers at all kinds of companies to speed up their decision making; otherwise they get left behind by agile competitors who respond faster to changing customer fads and fashions. Nowhere is this truer than in the global toy industry, in which vicious combat rages in the doll business, worth over $10 billion a year in sales. The largest global toy company, Mattel, has earned tens of billions of dollars from the world's best-selling doll, Barbie, since it introduced her over 50 years ago.[83] Mothers who played with the original dolls bought them for their daughters, and granddaughters, and Barbie became an American icon. However, Barbie's advantage as best-selling global doll led Mattel's managers to make major strategic errors in the 2000s.

Barbie and all Barbie accessories have accounted for about 50% of Mattel's toy sales since the 1990s, so protecting this star product was crucial. The Barbie doll was created in the 1960s when most women were homemakers; her voluptuous shape was a response to a dated view of what the "ideal" woman should look like. Barbie's continuing success, however, led Mattel's CEO Bob Eckert and his top managers to underestimate how much the world had altered. Changing cultural views about the role of girls, women, sex, marriage, and women working in the last decades shifted the tastes of doll buyers. But Mattel's managers continued to bet on Barbie's eternal appeal and collectively bought into an "If it's not broken don't fix it" approach. In fact, given that Barbie was the best-selling doll, they thought it might be dangerous to change her appearance; customers might not like the product development changes and stop buying the doll. Mattel's top managers decided not to rock the boat; they left the brand and business model unchanged and focused their efforts on developing new digital toys.

As a result, Mattel was unprepared when a challenge came along in the form of a new kind of doll, the Bratz doll, introduced by MGA Entertainment. Many competitors to Barbie had emerged over the years because the doll business is so profitable, but no other doll had matched Barbie's appeal to young girls (or their mothers). The marketers and designers behind the Bratz line of dolls had spent a lot of time to discover what the new generation of girls, especially those aged 7–11, wanted from a doll, however. It turned out that the Bratz dolls they designed met the desires of these girls. Bratz dolls have larger heads and oversized eyes, wear lots of makeup and short dresses, and are multicultural to give each doll "personality and attitude."[84] The dolls were designed to appeal to a new generation of girls brought up in a fast-changing fashion, music, and television market. The Bratz dolls met the untapped needs of "tween" girls, and the new line took off. MGA quickly licensed the rights to make and sell the dolls to toy companies overseas, and Bratz became a serious competitor to Barbie.

Mattel was in trouble. Its strategic managers had to change its business model and strategies and bring Barbie up to date; Mattel's designers must have been wishing they had been adventurous and made more radical changes earlier when they did not need to change. However, they decided to change Barbie's extreme shape; they killed off her old-time boyfriend Ken and replaced him with Blaine, an Aussie surfer.[85] They also recognized they had waited much too long to introduce new lines of dolls to meet the changed needs of tweens and older girls in the 2000s. They rushed out the "My Scene" and "Flava" lines of dolls that were obvious imitations of Bratz dolls, but they both flopped. And the decisions they made to change Barbie—her figure, looks, clothing, and boyfriends—came too late, and sales of Barbie dolls continued to fall.

By 2006, sales of the Barbie collection had dropped by 30%, which was critical to Mattel because its profits and stock price hinged on Barbie's success—and they both plunged. Analysts argued that Mattel had not paid enough attention to its customers' changing needs or moved quickly to introduce the new and improved products necessary to keep a company on top of its market. Mattel brought back Ken, but then in a sign of its mounting problems, Mattel's lawyers sued MGA Entertainment, arguing that the Bratz dolls' copyright rightfully belonged to them. Mattel complained that the head designer of Bratz was a Mattel employee when he made the initial drawings for the dolls and that Mattel had applied for copyright protection on a number of early Bratz drawings. Mattel claimed that MGA hired key Mattel employees away from the firm and these employees stole sensitive sales information and transferred it to MGA.

In 2008 a judge ruled in Mattel's favor and ordered MGA to stop using the Bratz name, and a jury awarded Mattel $100 million in damages. After an appeal, in 2009 a federal judge upheld the verdict and ruled that the Bratz doll is Mattel property and that MGA could sell the doll only until the end of 2009. In 2010 the companies were locked in a bitter dispute: Mattel wanted the rights to produce and sell the Bratz doll line, but MGA's founder was still trying to protect the profits made from the Bratz dolls' success. Meanwhile stores stopped selling the Bratz doll, Mattel revitalized its line of Barbie dolls, and its CEO exultantly declared that "Barbie is back" as increased doll sales helped raise the company's profits by 86% in the spring of 2010.[86]

Imagine then, how Mattel's managers reacted to the decision of the federal appeals court in July 2010 when it threw out the previous court decision and ruled that MGA Entertainment did have the right to make and sell the Bratz doll because their looks and image were not subject to existing copyright law! The rights to the Bratz doll were given back to MGA, and MGA is currently suing Mattel for major damages that have cost it hundreds of millions in profits.

Discussion Questions

1. Why were Mattel's managers so slow to change their decision making about the design of the Barbie doll over time? What kinds of cognitive errors may have contributed to this?
2. What kinds of factors affected the way managers at both Mattel and MGA made their decisions over time during their battle over control for the Bratz dolls?

References

1 H. A. Simon, *The New Science of Management Decision* (New York: Harper & Row, 1960), p. 206.
2 Ibid.
3 S. Keiser and L. Sproull, "Managerial Response to Changing Environments: Perspectives on Sensing from Social Cognition," *Administrative Science Quarterly* 27 (1982), 548–570; G. T. Allison, *The Essence of Decision* (Boston: Little, Brown, 1971).
4 Simon, *The New Science of Management Decision.*
5 H. A. Simon, *Administrative Behavior* (New York: Macmillan, 1945).
6 Ibid.; J. G. March and H. A. Simon, *Organizations* (New York: Wiley, 1958).
7 J. G. March, "Decision Making Perspective," in A. Van De Venn and W. Joyce, eds., *Perspectives on Organizational Design and Behavior* (New York: Wiley, 1981), pp. 205–252.
8 J. G. March, "Bounded Rationality, Ambiguity, and the Engineering of Choice," *Bell Journal of Economics* 9 (1978), 587–608.
9 Simon, *Administrative Behavior.*
10 R. M. Cyert and J. G. March, *A Behavioral Theory of the Firm* (Englewood Cliffs, NJ: Prentice Hall, 1963).
11 P. D. Larkey and L. S. Sproull, *Advances in Information Processing in Organizations*, vol. 1 (Greenwich, CT: JAI Press, 1984), pp. 1–8.
12 March and Simon, *Organizations.*

13 H. A. Simon, *Models of Man* (New York: Wiley, 1957); A. Grandori, "A Prescriptive Contingency View of Organizational Decision Making," *Administrative Science Quarterly* 29 (1984), 192–209.
14 Simon, *The New Science of Management Decision.*
15 H. A. Simon, "Making Management Decisions: The Role of Intuition and Emotion," *Academy of Management Executives* 1 (1987), 57–64.
16 Cyert and March, *A Behavioral Theory of the Firm.*
17 Ibid.
18 Z. Schiller, "GE's Appliance Park: Rewire, or Pull the Plug?" *Business Week*, February 8, 1993, p. 30.
19 J. Ward, "GE Center Makes Things Fail So It Can Make Them Better," *Courier Journal*, September 12, 1999, p. 1.
20 www.geappliances.com, 2011.
21 www.consumerreports.com, July 2011.
22 C. E. Lindblom, "The Science of Muddling Through," *Public Administration Review* 19 (1959), 79–88.
23 Ibid., p. 83.
24 H. Mintzberg, D. Raisinghani, and A. Theoret, "The Structure of Unstructured Decision Making," *Administrative Science Quarterly* 21 (1976), 246–275.
25 Ibid., p. 257.
26 M. D. Cohen, J. G. March, and J. P. Olsen, "A Garbage Can Model of Organizational Choice," *Administrative Science Quarterly* 17 (1972), 1–25.
27 Ibid.
28 www.ideo.com, 2011.
29 J. Hyatt, "Engineering Inspiration," *Newsweek*, June 14, 2010, p. 44.
30 L. Chamberlain, "Going Off the Beaten Path for New Design Ideas." *New York Times,* March 12, 2006, p.28.
31 www.ideo.com, 2011.
32 G. P. Huber, "Organizational Learning: The Contributing Processes and the Literature," *Organizational Science* 2 (1991), 88–115.
33 B. Hedberg, "How Organizations Learn and Unlearn," in W. H. Starbuck and P. C. Nystrom, eds., *Handbook of Organizational Design*, vol. 1 (New York: Oxford University Press, 1981), pp. 1–27.
34 P. M. Senge, *The Fifth Discipline: The Art and Practice of the Learning Organization* (New York: Doubleday, 1990).
35 J. G. March, "Exploration and Exploitation in Organizational Learning," *Organizational Science* 2 (1991), 71–87.
36 T. K. Lant and S. J. Mezias, "An Organizational Learning Model of Convergence and Reorientation," *Organizational Science* 5 (1992), 47–71.
37 M. Dodgson, "Organizational Learning: A Review of Some Literatures," *Organizational Studies* 14 (1993), 375–394.
38 A. S. Miner and S. J. Mezias, "Ugly Duckling No More: Pasts and Futures of Organizational Learning Research," *Organizational Science* 7 (1990), 88–99.
39 P. Senge, *The Fifth Discipline: The Art and Practice of the Learning Organization* (New York: Doubleday, 1990).
40 www.google.com, 2011.
41 P. Senge, "The Leader's New Work: Building Learning Organizations," *Sloan Management Review* (Fall 1990): 7–23.
42 Miner and Mezias, "Ugly Ducking No More."
43 www.toyotausa.com, 2011.
44 I. Rowley, "Even Toyota Isn't Perfect," www.businessweek.com, January 22, 2007.
45 "Toyota Blames Rapid Growth for Quality Problems," www.iht.com, March 13, 2008.
46 I. Rowley, "Katsuaki Watanabe: Fighting to Stay Humble," www.businessweek.com, March 5, 2007.
47 J. P. Kotter and J. L. Heskett, *Corporate Culture and Performance* (New York: Free Press, 1992).
48 Ibid.
49 www.accenture.com, 2011.
50 T. Davenport and L. Prusak, *Information Ecology* (New York: Oxford University Press, 1997).
51 www.accenture.com, 2011.
52 Ibid.

53 M.T. Hansen, N. Nohria, and T. Tierney, "What's Your Strategy for Managing Knowledge?" *Harvard Business Review* (March–April 1999): 3–19.

54 P. C. Nystrom and W. H. Starbuck, "To Avoid Organizational Crises, Unlearn," *Organizational Dynamics* 12 (1984), 53–65.

55 Y. Dror, "Muddling Through—Science or Inertia?" *Public Administration Review* 24 (1964), 103–117.

56 Nystrom and Starbuck, "To Avoid Organizational Crises, Unlearn."

57 S. T. Fiske and S. E. Taylor, *Social Cognition* (Reading, MA: Addison-Wesley, 1984).

58 See G. R. Jones, R. Kosnik, and J. M. George, "Internalization and the Firm's Growth Path: On the Psychology of Organizational Contracting," in R. W. Woodman and W. A. Pasemore, eds., *Research in Organizational Change and Development,* vol. 7 (Greenwich, CT: JAI Press, 1993), pp. 105–135, for an account of the biases as they operate during organizational growth and decline.

59 L. Festinger, *A Theory of Cognitive Dissonance* (Stanford, CA: Stanford University Press, 1957); E. Aaronson, "The Theory of Cognitive Dissonance: A Current Perspective," in L. Berkowitz, ed., *Advances in Experimental Social Psychology*, vol. 4 (New York: Academic Press, 1969), pp. 1–34.

60 J. R. Averill, "Personal Control over Aversive Stimuli and Its Relationship to Stress," *Psychological Bulletin* 80 (1973), 286–303.

61 E. J. Langer, "The Illusion of Control," *Journal of Personality and Social Psychology* 32 (1975), 311–328.

62 A. Tversky and D. Kahneman, "Judgment Under Uncertainty: Heuristics and Biases," *Science* 185 (1974), 1124–1131.

63 R. De Board, *The Psychoanalysis of Organizations* (London: Tavistock, 1978).

64 B. M. Staw, "The Escalation of Commitment to a Course of Action," *Academy of Management Review* 6 (1978), 577–587; B. M. Staw and J. Ross, "Commitment to a Policy Decision: A Multi-Theoretical Perspective," *Administrative Science Quarterly* 23 (1978), 40–64.

65 Nystrom and Starbuck, "To Avoid Organizational Crises, Unlearn."

66 Ibid.

67 L. Porter and K. Roberts, "Communication in Organizations," in M. Dunnette, ed., *Handbook of Industrial and Organizational Psychology* (Chicago: Rand McNally, 1976).

68 Nystrom and Starbuck, "To Avoid Organizational Crises, Unlearn."

69 A. D. Meyer, "Adapting to Environmental Jolts," *Administrative Science Quarterly* 27 (1982), 515–537; A. D. Meyer, "How Ideologies Supplant Formal Structures and Shape Responses to Environments," *Journal of Management Studies* 7 (1982), 31–53.

70 For a basic introduction to game theory, see A. K. Dixit and B. J. Nalebuff, *Thinking Strategically* (London: WW Norton, 1991). Also see A. M. Brandenburger and B. J. Nalebuff, "The Right Game: Using Game Theory to Shape Strategy," *Harvard Business Review* (July–August 1995): 59–71; and D. M. Kreps, *Game Theory and Economic Modeling* (Oxford, UK: Oxford University Press, 1990).

71 D. C. Hambrick, *The Executive Effect: Concepts and Methods for Studying Top Managers* (Greenwich, CT: JAI Press, 1988).

72 D. G. Ancona, "Top-Management Teams: Preparing for the Revolution," in J. S. Carroll, ed., *Applied Social Psychology and Organizational Settings* (Hillsdale, NJ: Lawrence Erlbaum Associates, 1990).

73 M. Shaw, "Communications Networks," in L. Berkowitz, ed., *Advances in Experimental Social Psychology*, vol. 1 (New York: Academic Press, 1964).

74 Ibid.

75 S. Finkelstein and D. C. Hambrick, "Top-Management Team Tenure and Organizational Outcomes: The Moderating Role of Managerial Discretion," *Administrative Science Quarterly* 35 (1990), 484–503.

76 I. L. Janis, *Victims of Groupthink*, 2nd ed. (Boston: Houghton Mifflin, 1982).

77 K. M. Eisenhardt and C. B. Schoonhoven, "Organizational Growth: Linking Founding Team, Strategy, Environment, and Growth Among U.S. Semiconductor Ventures, 1978–1988," *Administrative Science Quarterly* 35 (1990), 504–529; L. Keck and M. L. Tushman, "Environmental and Organizational Context and Executive Team Structure," *Academy of Management Journal* 36 (1993), 1314–1344.

78 A. J. Lott and B. E. Lott, "Group Cohesiveness and Interpersonal Attraction: A Review of Relationships with Antecedent and Consequent Variables," *Psychological Bulletin* 14 (1965), 259–309.

79 D. L. Helmich and W. B. Brown, "Successor Type and Organizational Change in the Corporate Enterprise," *Administrative Science Quarterly* 17 (1972), 371–381; D. C. Hambrick and P. A. Mason, "Upper Echelons: The Organization as a Reflection of Its Top Managers," *Academy of Management Journal* 9 (1984), 193–206.

80 R. F. Vancil, *Passing the Baton* (Boston: Harvard Business School Press, 1987).

81 C. Schwenk, "Cognitive Simplification Processes in Strategic Decision Making," *Strategic Management Journal* 5 (1984), 111–128.

82 D. Rubenstein and R. W. Woodman, "Spiderman and the Burma Raiders: Collateral Organization Theory in Practice," *Journal of Applied Behavioral Science* 20 (1984), 1–21; G. R. Bushe and A. B. Shani, *Parallel Learning Structures: Increasing Innovations in Bureaucracies* (Reading, MA: Addison-Wesley, 1991).

83 www.mattel.com, 2011.

84 "Doll Wars," *Business Life*, May 2005, 40–42.

85 www.mattel.com, 2011.

86 Ibid.

CHAPTER 13

Innovation, Intrapreneurship, and Creativity

Learning Objectives

As Chapter 10 noted, innovation is one of the most important types of organizational change because it results in a continuing stream of new and improved goods and services that create value for customers and profit for a company. Indeed, one important way of assessing organizational effectiveness is the rate or speed at which a company can bring new products to market; a second is the ability to create novel products that become an instant success such as Nintendo's Wii. Both these types of innovation ensure high performance, but they depend on the level of intrapreneurship and creativity inside an organization.

After studying this chapter you should be able to:

1. Describe how innovation and technological change affect each other.
2. Discuss the relationship among innovation, intrapreneurship, and creativity.
3. Understand the many steps involved in creating an organizational setting that fosters innovation and creativity.
4. Identify the ways in which information technology can be used to foster creativity and to speed innovation and new product development.

Innovation and Technological Change

Innovation
The process by which organizations use their skills and resources to develop new goods and services or to develop new production and operating systems so that they can better respond to the needs of their customers.

Innovation is the process by which organizations use their resources and competences to develop new and improved products or to find better ways to make these new products and thus increase their effectiveness.[1] Innovation can result in spectacular success for an organization. Apple changed the computing industry when it introduced the first PC, Honda transformed the motorcycle market when it introduced its new small 50cc models, Mary Kay changed the way cosmetics are sold when she introduced at-home cosmetics parties and a personalized style of selling, and when Toyota developed lean manufacturing it revolutionized carmaking.

Although innovation brings about change, it is also associated with a high level of risk because the outcome of research and development (R&D) is often uncertain.[2] It has been estimated that only 12% to 20% of R&D projects result in products that get to market; the rest are failures.[3] Thus although innovation can lead to change of the sort that organizations want—the introduction of profitable new technologies and products—it can also lead to the kind of change they want to avoid: technologies that are inefficient and products that customers don't want. (The way in which organizations can manage the innovation process to increase the chance of successful learning taking place is discussed in detail later in the chapter.)

Two Types of Innovation

In Chapter 9, *technology* is defined as the skills, knowledge, experience, tools, machines, and computers used in the design, production, and distribution of goods and services. Advances in technology are at the heart of the innovation process and today the world is experiencing an unprecedented level of technological change.[4] In general, the two principal types of technological change are quantum change and incremental change.

Quantum technological change refers to a fundamental shift in technology that revolutionizes products or the way in which they are produced. Examples of quantum changes in technology include the development of the first PCs, which revolutionized the computer industry; the development of biotechnology that has revolutionized the treatment of illness by replacing conventional pharmaceutical compounds with genetically engineered medicines; and the emergence of advanced computer software that permits social networking, payments through smartphone, and mobile game playing. New products or operating systems that incorporate a quantum technological improvement are referred to as **quantum innovations**. The introduction in 1971 of Intel's 4004 microprocessor, the first "computer on a chip" ever produced, is an example of a quantum product innovation. Quantum innovations are likely to cause major changes in an environment and to increase uncertainty because they force organizations to change the way they operate—as we have discussed in earlier chapters.

Quantum technological change
A fundamental shift in technology that revolutionizes products or the way they are produced.

Quantum innovations
New products or operating systems that incorporate quantum technological improvements.

Incremental technological change refers to the improvements that are continuously made to particular technologies over time, and **incremental innovations** refer to the superior products or operating systems that incorporate and benefit from those refinements. For example, since 1971, Intel has continuously improved its original 4004 microprocessor, introducing advanced chips such as the Pentium and its Sandy Bridge chips in 2011. Similarly, flexible manufacturing, robots, advanced management software solutions, and TQM are examples of incremental innovations. All these incremental technological changes have dramatically improved the performance, quality, and safety of all kinds of products—and reduced their cost—such as the new mobile computing devices and fuel efficient vehicles currently being introduced.

Incremental technological change
Technological change that represents a refinement of some base technology.

Incremental innovations
Products or operating systems that incorporate refinements of some base technology.

As one might expect, quantum innovations are relatively uncommon. As Philip Anderson and Michael Tushman note, "At rare and irregular intervals in every industry, innovations appear that command a decisive cost or quality advantage and that strike not at the margins of the profits and the outputs of existing firms, but at their foundations and their very lives."[5] Anderson and Tushman call these kinds of quantum innovations "technological discontinuities," and in their model of innovation, a technological discontinuity sets off an era of ferment. At the beginning, intense competition between companies in an industry arises to develop the design that will become the dominant model for others to copy—just as Intel's most advanced chips are the dominant design in the microprocessor industry and Apple's iPhone and iPad have become the dominant design for a new generation of mobile computing devices.

After the dominant design emerges, the next period of the technology cycle involves an era of incremental change and innovation during which companies work on and improve a specific technology. Competition to improve a technology in order to offer customers a better product, that is, incremental product innovation, is the type of innovation pursued by most organizations. For example, every time a carmaker redesigns and introduces the new version of one of its cars, it is engaged in incremental product innovation, but this is nevertheless a very competitive process. By 2011, for example, global carmakers had all recognized the growing popularity of fuel efficient vehicles and were competing to offer customers new kinds of hybrid or electric vehicles.

The innovations that result from quantum and incremental technological change are all around us. The increasing use of microprocessors used in all kinds of consumer products, cloud computing services that allow users to access their data, music, video remotely through the Internet using new kinds of mobile computing devices, ever-improving flat-screen TVs and gaming consoles, and the genetically engineered medicines produced by biotechnology either did not exist a few decades ago or were considered prohibitively expensive products. Today, these products are taken for granted and are continuously being improved as companies fight for competitive advantage—and indeed to survive. By 2011, for example, leading mobile phone makers like Nokia and Research in Motion found themselves under intense pressure from companies like Apple and Samsung that had forged ahead to develop new smartphone and tablet computer technology that allowed them to leapfrog over their rivals—and their stock price soared as a result.

Technological change is thus both an opportunity and a threat—it is both creative and destructive.[6] It helps create new product innovations that pioneering companies can take advantage of, but at the same time, these innovations reduce or eliminate demand for the products made by established but less innovative organizations. For example, the development of the iPod and iPhone by Apple destroyed demand for older products such as the Sony Walkman and Motorola Razr—and the profitability of these companies has plunged as a result.

Protecting Innovation through Property Rights

When a company's managers use its resources in an enterprising way, the result is a stream of innovations that create new and improved products and increase its effectiveness. Companies must invest enormous amounts of money in R&D to develop innovative new products, however. Intel spent over $13 billion on R&D in 2011, for example, and it is also expensive to build new manufacturing facilities to make advanced products—a new chip-making factory costs Intel from $3 to $5 billion to build, for example.

It would hardly be fair or equitable if, after a company spends billions of dollars on these activities, a competitor could just come along, piggyback on the company's innovations, and start to produce a copycat product. If this were easy to do, few companies would make the investment necessary to develop new products. Technological progress would plunge and a society's standard of living would advance little over time.

As Chapter 6 discusses, *property rights* give people and organizations the right to own and control productive resources and to profit from them. To motivate entrepreneurs and companies to take risks and invest in new ventures whose payoff is unknown, laws are enacted to protect the profits that result from successful efforts to innovate or create new products. Individual inventors and companies are given the legal property rights to own and protect their creations by the granting of patents, copyrights, and trademarks.

Patents give their owners the property right to use, control, license, and otherwise profit from their creation—a new product such as a door handle, machine, or new drug—for a period of 20 years from the date the patent is issued by the U.S. Patent Office. In other words, patents confer a monopoly right on their owner—the individual inventor or company that has pioneered and paid for the research that led to the new product. One of the most profitable kinds of patents are those obtained by pharmaceutical companies that develop new drugs that better treat some illness or disease. Merck, the company that developed Prozac and Viagra, made hundreds of billions from the sale of these drugs, for example. But once a patent has expired any company can manufacture a copy of the original drug, a generic drug, which is then sold for a fraction of the price of the patented drug, so the huge profits of the company that invented the drug disappear.

Copyrights also confer a monopoly right on their owner. They are typically granted to people who create intellectual property, such as written or visual works—books, videogames, poems, and songs produced by authors, software engineers, poets, and musicians. If they wish, the owners of the copyright can sell it to other people or companies—such as when a movie company buys the rights to turn a new book into a movie from its author. Copyrights last for much longer periods than patents, often the lifetime of the work's creator and beyond.

Currently, laws governing the length of copyrights are changing. Support is growing for the idea that copyrights to works should be granted for much shorter periods, perhaps for just 20 years or the life of their creator. Once a copyright expires, intellectual property enters the public domain and becomes a public good, meaning that anyone is free to make use of it at no cost. Today, tens of thousands of out-of-copyright books are available on websites such as Amazon.com and www.gutenberg.org.

To increase the benefits from their creations, innovators of new products and services are also given the legal right to the trademarks that they use to identify their products to customers. Trademarks are property rights to the name of a product (such as Nescafé or Ivory Soap), any symbols or logos associated with it, and the company that produces it (such as Nestlé or Procter & Gamble). Trademarks give their owner the sole legal right to use these names or symbols and control the use to which they are put—for example—advertising a product, in perpetuity.

Because people and companies have to invest their creativity, time, and money to obtain copyrights and trademarks to develop a brand name, it is only fair to allow them to benefit from the "identity" of their creations. Thus J. K. Rowling, the creator of Harry Potter, holds the copyrights to her books, and she and her publishing company own the trademarks associated with the Harry Potter brand name. Nobody can issue Harry Potter toys or clothing without paying a licensing fee to them because they own the trademark, just as no company has the right to use another company's patent unless it pays to use it—as long as the patent is in force.

Protecting property and resources of all kinds is one of the principal purposes of the law. The issue of who holds the rights to written resources in the digital age became a hotly debated topic in 2005 when Google announced its intention to scan millions of books in major world libraries and then make them available free over the Web to users throughout the world. Google quickly found itself embroiled in lawsuits with publishing companies that claimed it is violating their copyrights to these works. How long an author, artist, or company should be able to claim copyright over their intellectual property is an issue that the courts have to resolve. Organizational Insight 13.1 profiles the way the Rolling Stones developed a set of entrepreneurial skills to take advantage of their brand name and copyrights that has made them the wealthiest rock band in the world.

Organizational Insight 13.1

The Rolling Stones Are Not Gathering Moss

Marius Wigen/Shutterstock.com

The Rolling Stones have been one of the world's leading rock bands since the early 1960s when they burst into the music scene as the "bad boys" of rock and roll. As with most rock groups in those early days, they were an unproven product with no track record. Desperate to sign recording contracts, the Stones, like most early rock bands, were in a weak bargaining position when dealing with record companies such as Decca, the company they initially signed with. As a result, despite their enormous initial success, they received a relatively small percentage of the profits their best-selling records generated. Later, after these contracts expired and because they were now world famous, the Rolling Stones were able to renegotiate contracts with record companies on their own terms. They also used their fame to find new avenues for entrepreneurship.

Since 1989, the Stones, under the leadership of Mick Jagger, the CEO of Rolling Stones Inc., have based their business model on finding ways to use their product—their unique music and rock persona—to generate profit. Since 1989 the Stones have earned more than $2 billion in revenues; about $700 million has come from royalties earned on the sales of their records and songs. But the incredible success of their world tours generated the remaining $1.3 billion from the ticket sales, merchandising, and company sponsorship money associated with their tours. The way the Stones orchestrate their world tours shows how entrepreneurial they are.

It all began with the Steel Wheels tour in 1989, when for the first time the Stones, working with a Canadian promoter named Michael Cohl, took total control over all aspects of their tour. Before this, the Stones, like most rock bands, put together a schedule of cities to tour. They would then contact well-known promoters in those cities to take responsibility for staging the concert and the sales of tickets; the Stones then received a percentage of total concert revenues. With this business model the promoters were taking away over 60% of total revenues. Cohl proposed a new model in which he would assume responsibility for all 40 concert venues on the Steel Wheels Tour and guarantee to pay the Stones $1 million per concert, a much higher amount than they had ever received before. Cohl felt he could do this because his approach cut out the profits earned by the promoters; he also would be able to negotiate merchandising contracts to promote Stones T-shirts, posters, and so on, and to get corporate sponsorship for the tour.

After they had played the first several venues, it became clear to Cohl that he was losing money on each one. To make the tour a success they would *all* have to find new ways to cut costs and increase revenues. From this point on the Stones became directly involved in every decision concerning staging, music, advertising and promotion, and even the price of concert tickets, which have shot up in every tour since Steel Wheels. The Stones, and particularly Jagger, faced a huge task to learn how to improve the concert tour business model, but they persevered and step by step have continued to refine and develop their approach in every subsequent tour. In the end, the Steel Wheels tour made over $260 million and the Stones made far more than the $40 million they were promised. In later tours, from "Packing Them In" to the "Voodoo Tour" in 1995 and the "Licks" 2003 tour, world revenues from concerts surged, with tickets selling at face price for up to $350.

When Mick Jagger and Keith Richards, who are both now in their late 60s, were asked how long they planned to go on touring, their answer was "until we drop." The Stones reinvent themselves on every tour as creative artists, and performing at the level expected of them calls for a new burst of enterprise every time they get on the stage and give their billions of loyal fans the show they expect. In 2011, a new Stones 50-year anniversary "farewell' tour was in the works; whether this tour will go ahead in 2012 is not clear as Richards and Jagger began yet another personal squabble. Clearly, being innovative in the rock music business is never easy—it is very hard work.

Innovation, Intrapreneurship, and Creativity

Intrapreneurs
Entrepreneurs inside an organization who are responsible for the success or failure of a project.

The leaders of innovation and new product development in established organizations are **intrapreneurs,** employees who notice opportunities for either quantum or incremental product improvements and are responsible for managing the product development process to obtain them. Many managers, scientists, or researchers employed by existing companies engage in intrapreneurial activity. But people like Amazon.com's Jeff Bezos or Liz Claiborne who start new business ventures and found organizations are entrepreneurs. They assume the risks and receive many of the returns associated with the new business venture.[7]

There is an interesting relationship between entrepreneurs and intrapreneurs. Many intrapreneurs become dissatisfied when the organization they work for decides neither to support their creative new product ideas nor to fund development efforts that the intrapreneurs think will succeed. What do intrapreneurs do who feel that they are getting nowhere? They often decide to leave the organization and start their own organization to take advantage of their new product ideas. In other words, intrapreneurs become entrepreneurs and found their own organizations that may compete with the organizations they left.

Many of the world's most successful organizations have been started by frustrated intrapreneurs who became entrepreneurs. William Hewlett and David Packard left Fairchild Semiconductor, an early industry leader, because managers of that company would not support their computing ideas. Their company, now HP, soon outperformed Fairchild. Compaq Computer was founded by Rod Canion, who left Texas Instruments (TI) when managers there would not support his idea that TI should develop its own PC. HP eventually bought Compaq in 2001 to compete with Dell and this merger helped lead to Dell's current problems, although by 2011 both companies were suffering from competition from Apple, which had hired away many managers from both these companies. To prevent the departure of talented people, organizations need to take steps to promote internal entrepreneurship. (We discuss how to promote successful entrepreneurship in both new and existing organizations later in the chapter.)

Creativity
Ideas going beyond the current boundaries, whether those boundaries are based on technology, knowledge, social norms, or beliefs.

All innovation begins with creative ideas. It is important to realize, however, that creative ideas are not just those that lead to major new inventions or achievements: Creative ideas are any that take existing practices a step farther than the norm. **Creativity** is nothing more than going beyond the current boundaries, whether those boundaries are technology, knowledge, social norms, or beliefs.[8] Deciding that PCs do not have to be beige and can be blue, pink, or even made of clear plastic is a creative idea, just as putting together the first PC was a creative idea. Although the latter may be more memorable, and made Apple founders Steve Jobs and Stephen Wozniak famous, the millions of small creative ideas and actions that have gone into improving PCs since then are nevertheless highly significant and valuable. And Michael Dell's creative idea of selling PCs over the phone, although not in the same league as making the first PC, nevertheless led to his fame as an innovator.

From this perspective, most people have been and will be creative in their normal endeavors. Thus, employees must grasp the fact that their input, suggestions, and ideas are valuable and organizations should take steps to acknowledge how important these ideas are. Organizations can do this by promoting innovative values and norms in their organizational cultures and reinforce them by providing financial rewards for good ideas—as many organizations do. In 2011, Google's new CEO Larry Page decided to link employee bonuses and financial rewards to their ability to help the company succeed in its efforts to become a major player in social networking and so compete with Facebook.

Creativity is not just making new things; it is also combining and synthesizing two or more previously unrelated facts or ideas and making something new or different out of them. It is also modifying something to give it a new use or to make it perform better. Synthesis and modification are much more common than creation, and this is why incremental innovation is more common than radical innovation. As Anderson puts it, "We forget that moving a desk so that work flows smoother is also creativity. It's modification. And creativity also blooms when we redesign a job description so that related tasks are given to the same person. That's synthesis. It's even creativity when we cut our losses on a worthless industrial adhesive by slapping it on the back of our secretary's note pad . . . that bit of creation is the 3M 'Post-it' notes but nothing is going to make your firm creative unless you first help individuals to unlock their willingness to try."[9]

As Nonaka puts it, the process of innovation and creating new knowledge depends on the ability of managers to tap into the tacit, hidden, subjective insights, intuitions, and hunches of people everywhere in an organization.[10] The source can be a brilliant researcher's insight, a middle manager's intuition about changing market trends, or a shop floor worker's tacit knowledge built up by intense involvement in the work process over a number of years. The issue is to transform personal knowledge into organizational knowledge that results in new products. This can be complicated because such tacit knowledge is often difficult to verbalize; it is know-how accumulated by experience and tough to articulate in rules, formulas, or principles.

To obtain such tacit knowledge it is necessary to learn through observation, imitation, or modeling. Also, over time, through team interactions, team members learn how to share their knowledge, and team routines and "recipes" develop that are specific to a group and to an organization that lead to innovative kinds of behaviors. Some of these can be written down, though many are present only in the interactions between team members—in their knowledge of each other. Note too that from such interactions additional tacit knowledge may be created so that organizational knowledge builds up, spills over, and increases throughout an organization.[11]

A **knowledge-creating organization** is one in which such innovation is going on at all hierarchical levels and across all functions and divisions. Different teams meet to share their growing information and insights, so as knowledge is shared throughout the organization, new heights of innovation can be reached. Team leaders, as middle managers, then have to confront the task of translating creative new ideas into the stream of products that customers will buy. It is at this point that the issue of how to create and design an organizational setting to promote creativity and innovation becomes crucial. And designing a setting to encourage creativity is as much a form of innovation as the design of the new products that are created within it.

Knowledge-creating organization
An organization where innovation is going on at all levels and in all areas.

Entrepreneurship as "Creative Destruction"

The widespread technological changes brought about by increasing global competition that generate new innovations are often referred to as the process of "creative destruction." This process leads older, less-forward looking companies to become uncompetitive or even driven out of business by new, more innovative ones. No one foresaw how much the rapid advances made by Apple in mobile computing would hurt Nokia and Research in Motion, the leaders for a decade, by 2011. This is "creative" because companies—old ones like Apple or new ones like HTC—can use new global and technological opportunities to make better products or lower the costs of making existing products. Established companies that fail to invest in the "right" new technologies—the ones that provide customers with the most value—can find themselves at such a competitive disadvantage that they are driven out of business unless they can adapt quickly. New startups become the companies that will lead the industries of the future unless "older" competitors can find ways to fight back. Will Microsoft ever be able to meet the challenge from Google because it does not control the online search and advertising business? Will Google find that it will lose its leading position to Facebook because it does not control the social networking market? In the last decades, the emergence of new industries—such as digital communication, biotechnology, robotics, fuel cells, and online retailing and gaming—have created massive disruptions in the business world.

The industrial revolution is another example of how the process of creative destruction works. The old agricultural age, where wealth depended on land and physical labor, gave way to the age of steam-powered machinery and transportation. The new industrialists who used their capital to create new low-cost industries destroyed the old craft guilds. The information technology age represents the latest wave of major technological change in which all kinds of businesses must invest in IT to avoid being left behind by entrepreneurial companies that make such investments first—and then are able to forge ahead.

Innovation and the Product Life Cycle

When technology is changing, organizational survival requires that managers quickly adopt new technologies to innovate new products. Managers who do not do so soon find that they have no market for their existing products—and destroy their organization's future. Sony, for example, long the leader with its Walkman, suddenly lost its leading position in the music player business when Apple came along with its iPod player. But the "ancient" Rolling Stones release new records and tour often to keep their product current and fashionable.

Product life cycle
The changes in demand for a product that occur over time.

The rate of technological change in an industry—and particularly the length of the product life cycle—determines how important it is for managers to innovate. The **product life cycle** reflects the changes in demand for a product that occur over time.[12] Demand for the most successful, innovative, new products passes through four stages: the embryonic stage, growth, maturity, and decline. In the *embryonic stage* a product has yet to gain widespread acceptance; customers are unsure what the technology embedded in the product has to offer them, so there is little demand for it. If customers decide the technology is valuable and offers them a "value proposition," demand for the product takes off, and the product enters its growth stage.

In the *growth stage* many consumers are entering the market and buying the product for the first time; demand increases rapidly. Mobile computing devices are currently in this stage. Apple's high-tech mobile devices have spurred most global mobile computing companies to introduce their own products based on similar technologies. The growth stage ends and the *mature stage* begins when market demand peaks because most customers have already bought the product (relatively few first-time buyers are left). At this stage, demand is typically replacement demand because incremental innovation has resulted in a new generation of products that have better features—so customers junk the old ones such as out-of-date cellphones or bulky CRT monitors and TVs and go for high-definition flat-screen LCD TVs. The *decline stage* follows the mature stage if and when demand for a product falls because quantum technological change results in the emergence of a superior alternative product and a product becomes technologically obsolete—the iPod replaced the Walkman, for example.

RATE OF TECHNOLOGICAL CHANGE As this discussion suggests, the most important determinant of the length of a product's life cycle is the rate of technological change.[13] Figure 13.1 illustrates the relationship between the rate of technological change and the length of product life cycles. In some industries—such as PCs, semiconductors, and online books and music—technological change is rapid and product life cycles are very short. For example, technological change is so rapid in laptops that a new model becomes outdated only several months after its introduction.

In other industries the product life cycle is somewhat longer. In the car industry, for example, the average product life cycle is three to five years. The life cycle of a car is short because technological change produces a continual stream of incremental innovations in

Figure 13.1 Technological Change and Length of the Product Life Cycle

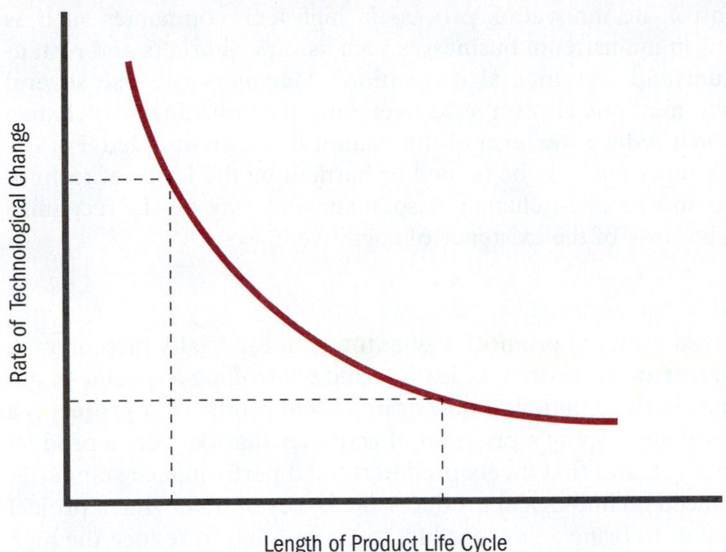

car design, such as the introduction of GPS positioning systems, advanced microcontrollers, plastic body parts, and more energy-efficient engines. In contrast, in industries where the pace of technological change is slower, product life cycles tend to be much longer. In steel or electricity, for example, changes in technology take longer to be introduced, and products such as steel girders and electrical cable can remain in the mature stage indefinitely.

ROLE OF FADS AND FASHION Fads and fashion are also an important determinant of the length of the product life cycle.[14] Today, customers have a major impact on the kinds of technological change that organizations pursue. The WWW and the massive flow of information that takes place quickly through websites such as Facebook and Twitter makes it apparent to customers which kinds of new products are in vogue. So organizations are increasingly watching the changing needs of customers—their fads and fashions—and investing resources to develop new technologies and products that will meet those needs. Few new car buyers today will buy a car introduced even a few years ago that is likely to be technologically outmoded, especially given the new kinds of styles and features the most recent cars possess. Similarly, in the restaurant business, customer demand for certain kinds of food changes rapidly so that the Cajun or Southwest cuisine popular one year may be history the next as Caribbean fare becomes the food of choice. McDonald's learned this lesson the hard way when tastes changed for fast food, but it has been able to respond successfully by innovating new kinds of fast foods and drinks. Fashion considerations are even more important, where at the upper end of the cosmetics and clothing business the last season's hit clothing line or perfume is passé by the next season. Thus today product life cycles may last no more than months, and only those companies that have the technological capability to respond fast—by developing new lines of clothing, perfumes, or mobile computing devices—will perform well.

The faster technology changes a product's life cycle, the more important it is to innovate products quickly and on a continuing basis. In industries where product life cycles are very short, managers must continually develop new or improved technologies or their growth and even their survival is threatened. The PC company that cannot develop new and improved models of ever-thinner, more powerful laptops and tablets within months to compete with those of Apple will soon find itself in trouble—something that has happened to Dell and Sony. The fashion house that fails to develop a new line of clothing for every season cannot succeed, nor can the small restaurant, club, or bar that fails to notice changing fads and fashions. So the problem facing organizations is how best to promote creativity, innovation, and intrapreneurship.

Managing the Innovation Process

How should managers control the innovation process in high-tech companies such as Amazon.com and Google or in mainstream businesses such as supermarkets and restaurants to raise both quantum and incremental innovation? Managers can use several related methods. These same methods also serve to overcome the resistances to change discussed in Chapter 10, which reduce the level of innovation if left unattended. For example, different divisions or functions may be helped or harmed by the kinds of technological change taking place and so resist change. Also, managers may fail to recognize new product opportunities because of the existence of cognitive biases.

Project Management

Project management The process of leading and controlling a project so it results in the creation of effective new or improved products.

Project A subunit whose goal centers on developing the products or service on time, within budget, and in conformance with predetermined performance specifications.

One technique that has proved useful at promoting quantum, but especially incremental, innovation is **project management,** the process of leading and controlling a specific ongoing work program so it results in the creation of new or improved products. A **project** is a subunit whose goal centers on developing a program of activities that delivers a product or service on time, within budget, and that meets predetermined performance standards. In the race to produce advanced technological products, the issues of managing a project both to reduce the time it takes to bring a new product to market and to reduce the high costs of innovation are becoming increasingly important. So it is useful to examine the role of project managers in effective new product development.

Effective project management begins with a clearly articulated plan that takes a product from its concept phase, to its initial test phase, to the modification phase, and to the final manufacturing or—in the case of services—setup phase. The concept phase typically involves the most work and cost of all these phases because the task facing the product development team, led by the project manager, is to use the latest research developments to create new products.

How does a project manager's job differ from that of a typical manager in an organization? First, a project manager is managing a higher proportion of highly skilled and educated professionals. Typically, many scientists and engineers of all kinds work on a project. A major project design choice involves the decision of how much authority should be decentralized to professional employees to make them responsible for their actions. Each team member's creative efforts must be harmonized with the needs of the project team as a whole, and with criteria such as a project's costs and time frame. However, the uncertainty surrounding a project and the fact that unexpected problems, delays, and breakthroughs are typically encountered often makes it difficult to determine when a project will be completed. The process of balancing team members' creative efforts with cost and time considerations is the most difficult task project managers (PMs) face.

The past experience and intuition of successful PMs allows them to judge how well or poorly progress is being made toward a successful outcome. Balancing the conflicting demands of performance, budget, and time schedule, and resolving the conflicts among them is a difficult process, especially as projects often are ongoing for one to three years or longer. One of the hardest tasks of a PM is to maintain the momentum of the project when team members such as engineers or designers find it difficult to solve specific problems or keep within the budget and a project threatens to flounder. Overcoming inertia, suggesting possible solutions, brainstorming, and providing encouragement and positive feedback are an essential part of the PM's job. But scientists and engineers can be perfectionists whose only goal is to increase the product's performance, and the PM must keep the goals of time and cost in mind. Engineers must be convinced that the search for a "perfect" product will turn out to be a disaster if it results in one that is so expensive that customers do not wish to buy it. Sony, for example, engineered laptops as thin as the ones Apple makes today a decade ago but they cost $4000 dollars and customers were not willing to pay such a high price.

It is the ability to think ahead and conduct effective advance planning that is often key to a PM's success. Based on their past experience, successful PMs know what typical problems arise, and they know how to organize and control employees to solve them. So when a crisis occurs, as it often does, resources can be quickly mobilized to confront and solve it.

Another important aspect of the advanced planning PMs conduct involves deciding how to respond to top managers who are continually evaluating the performance of a project—searching for signs of success or failure, for example. The ability to "sell" and champion their ideas and project is a never-ending task for PMs. Later, we discuss how PMs must be product champions, the people who believe in a project and are committed to its success; if they cannot show their enthusiasm, other managers are unlikely to show support for it. The ability to explain the nature of a new project clearly, and to crystallize its meaning and importance, are major determinants of a PM's ability to obtain funding for a project, and to gain additional funding for a project behind schedule to help ensure the survival of a project. Many projects are terminated abruptly because top managers lose faith in the PM and the project team.

PMs commonly employ quantitative modeling to conduct effective advanced planning, to uncover potential bottlenecks, and to help speed progress toward successful completion of a project. Such modeling allows PMs to develop "What if?" scenarios and to experiment with finding new and better ways of performing the sequential, and parallel, steps involved in reaching the final product.

One common modeling approach is to develop a *PERT/CAM network* or *GANTT chart*, which are essentially flowcharts of a project that can be built with many proprietary software packages (such as those of Microsoft).[15] These software packages focus on (1) modeling the sequences of actions necessary to reach a project's goal, and (2) relating these actions to cost and time criteria, such as the per-week cost of the scientists and engineers employed in the project, to (3) sort out and define the optimal path for reaching the goal. Once the PM has chosen a particular path to follow, these programs provide ongoing feedback on project performance that can be used to assess current project performance.

One of the first, and simplest, of these modeling techniques, the *critical path method* (CPM), captures the essence of what these models try to achieve. The goal of CPM is to determine (1) which particular tasks or activities of the many that have to be performed are critical in their effect on project time and cost and thus (2) to determine how to sequence or schedule critical tasks so a project can meet a target date at a minimum cost. Finding the critical path thus provides an optimal solution to the needs of a particular project. The flowchart in Figure 13.2 illustrates the critical tasks involved in building a house.

The optimal sequencing of tasks that have to be performed to reach the completed product is often worked out by a team, which experiments with different possible sequences. In this simple example of building a house, the most efficient sequencing of steps can be easily discovered. For many more complex projects, however, the analysis of these steps constitutes an important learning tool; many unforeseen interactions between these steps can be uncovered by a careful analysis. Attention is then paid to how to shorten the path—how to reorganize or combine tasks to cut time and cost and improve performance. Frequently, a team experiments by building prototypes of a new facility's layout or task structure if how to make a product or provide a service is the key issue.

Note the link to reengineering an organization, discussed in Chapter 10, where the move to combine the activities of different specialists or functions and focus on business processes, not activities, is also a way of shortening the critical path. PERT/CRM software packages permit the user to examine and compare many different kinds of configurations to find the best path to job completion. Modern IT systems that use computer-aided design (CAD), discussed in Chapter 9, can completely change task sequencing, especially when other types of organizing such as flexible work teams, product teams, and network structures are included in the project management process.

Indeed, such developments have made the job of the project manager increasingly prominent in many organizations. Successful PMs are often those who rise to more general management positions because they have demonstrated their competency in understanding how to design organizational structure and IT systems to facilitate the development of innovative products. Project management is often a prerequisite for promotion to top-management positions today.

Figure 13.2 CPM Project Design

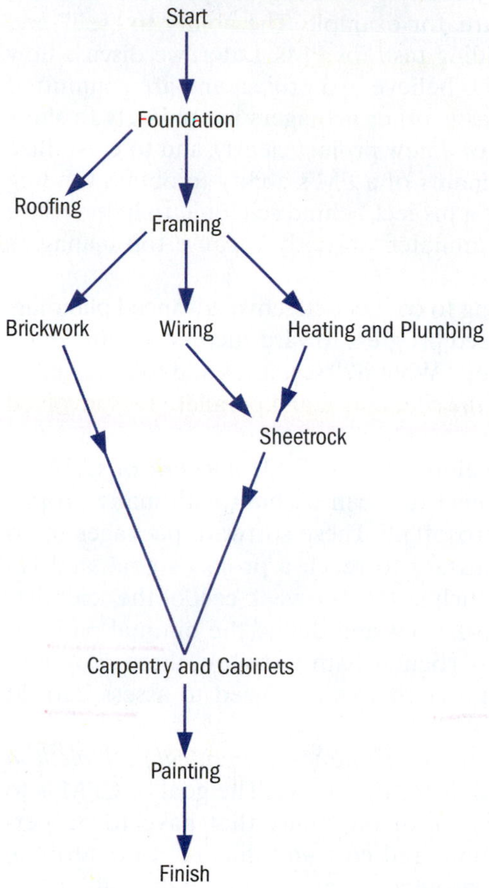

Stage-Gate Development Funnel

One of the mistakes that top managers often make as they control the innovation process is to fund too many development projects simultaneously. The result is that limited human, functional, and financial resources are spread too thinly over too many different projects. As a consequence, no single project or PM is given the resources necessary for a project to succeed, and the level of innovation falls.

Given the nature of this problem, it is necessary for managers to develop a structured process for evaluating different new product development proposals and deciding which to support. A common solution to this problem is to implement a stage-gate development funnel[16] (Figure 13.3). The purpose of a *stage-gate funnel* is to establish a structured and coherent innovation process that both improves control over the product development effort and forces managers to make choices among competing new product development projects so resources are not spread too thinly over too many projects.

Initially, the funnel has a wide mouth (stage 1) to promote innovation and encourage as many new product ideas as possible from both new and established project managers. Companies establish a wide mouth by creating incentives for employees to come up with new product ideas. Some organizations run "bright ideas" programs, which reward prospective project managers for submitting new product ideas that eventually make it through the development process. They also allow scientists and engineers to spend a certain percentage of work time on projects of their own choosing. For example, HP and 3M allow research scientists to spend 15% of their time on their own projects; Google allows them to spend 20%. (Typically, a person who submits a new idea that is approved will become the project manager who takes charge of a new project.)

New product ideas are submitted as brief written proposals for a cross-functional team of managers to evaluate. At gate 1, each product development proposal is reviewed in terms of its fit with the goals and strategies of the organization and chance of success in the market.

Figure 13.3 A Stage-Gate Development Funnel

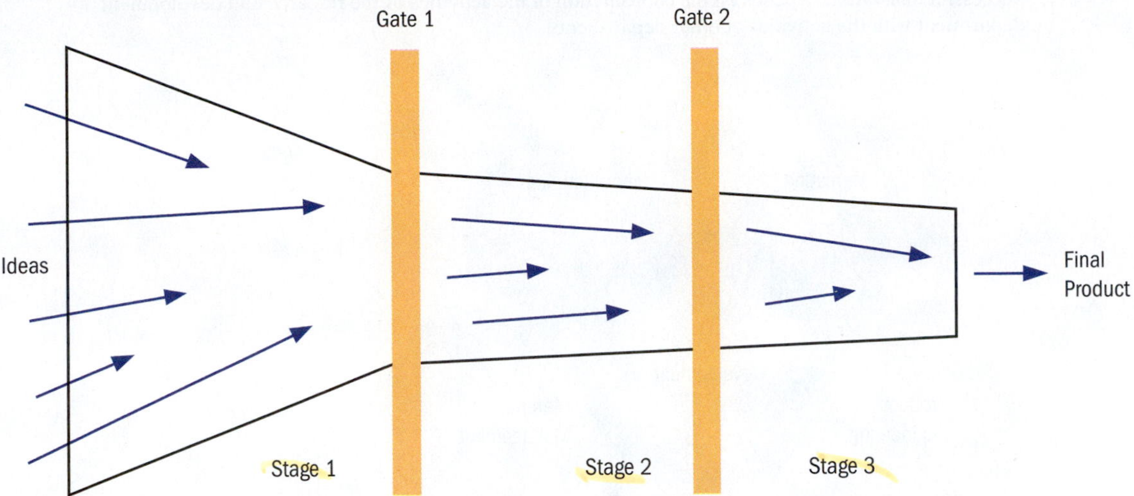

Proposals that meet these criteria are passed on to stage 2, and the rest are rejected (although the door is often left open to reconsider a proposal that has merit at a later date).

In stage 2, the prospective project manager must draft a detailed new product development plan that contains the detailed information that will allow the team of judges to decide whether or not to approve the idea and allow the new project managers to go ahead and pursue a full-blown product development effort. Included in the new product development plan should be factors such as strategic and financial objectives, an analysis of market potential, a list of desired product features, a list of technological requirements, a list of financial and human resource requirements, a detailed development budget, and a timeline that contains specific milestones (for example, dates for prototype completion and final launch). The managers who have judged and supported the project often help the new project manager improve the plan, for example, by developing a more detailed timeline or by meeting customers to learn how to tailor the new product to best meet their needs.

Once completed, the plan is reviewed by a senior management committee at gate 2. Here the review focuses on a detailed look at the new product development plan and considers whether the proposal is attractive, given its market potential, and viable, given the technological, financial, and human requirements of actually developing the product. This review is made in light of all other product development efforts being undertaken by the organization. At gate 2, projects are either rejected, sent back for revision, or allowed to proceed to the development phase (stage 3).

The stage 3 development effort can last anywhere from six months to ten years, depending on the industry and product type. For example, today many electronics products have development cycles of only six months; it takes only two to three years to develop a new car, about five years to develop a new jet aircraft, but seven or more years to develop a new medical drug.

Using Cross-Functional Teams and a Product Team Structure

As just noted, establishing cross-functional teams is a critical element in any structured new product development effort.[17] Although successful innovation begins in the R&D function, the way the activities of the R&D department are coordinated with the activities of other functions is crucial.[18] Figure 13.4 identifies the many functions necessary for successful innovation. In addition to R&D, they include engineering, materials management, manufacturing, and marketing.

Because those different groups usually have different orientations and attitudes, coordinating their activities is difficult. The link between R&D and engineering, for example, is vital to convert successful research into a product that can be designed and made efficiently. R&D scientists, however, may complain that the potential of "their" new

Figure 13.4 Innovation as a Cross-Functional Activity

Successful innovation depends on the coordination of the activities of the research and development department with the activities of other departments.

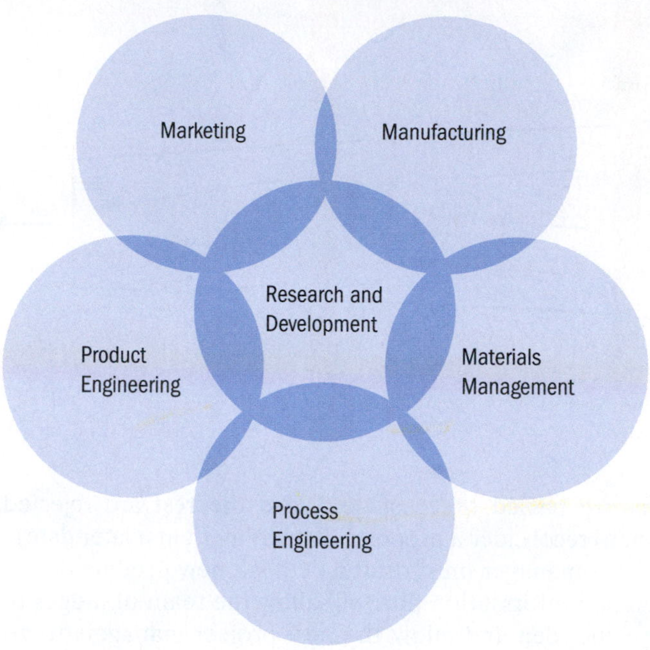

product is being sacrificed if the engineers tinker with its design to make production easy or cheap. In turn, engineering may feel that R&D is too emotionally committed to the product and has lost sight of the market in its pursuit of technical excellence.

Both R&D and engineering also need to coordinate with manufacturing to ensure the new product can be made cost effectively and reliably. A link with marketing will ensure the product possesses the features and qualities that customers need and want. Also, it confirms that R&D resources are not being spent to create or improve a product that customers do not want. Selected members of marketing, R&D, engineering, and manufacturing must be assigned to be core members of successful new product development teams to promote successful new product development. The term *core members* refers to the small group of functional experts who bear primary responsibility for the product development effort. In addition to core members, many other experts may work on the project as the need arises. But the core members stay with the project from inception to completion of the development effort: They "own it." To ensure core members are not distracted, they are usually assigned to only one development project at a time. If a new product development project is particularly important, core members may be removed from their regular functional role and assigned to work on the project full time.

Many organizations have been unable to manage the functional linkages necessary for successful product innovation because they have not adopted the appropriate organizational structure. In Chapter 6, we discussed the various types of structure that organizations can use to operate effectively when uncertainty is high. Two of them, product team structure and matrix structure, are especially suitable for managing innovation in high-tech organizations. Both of these structures focus on creating cross-functional teams to pursue new product development from the research concept stage, through the engineering design and manufacturing stages, to marketing and sales. These structures allow each function to develop an understanding of the problems and interests of the other functions, and they reduce communication problems. Decentralizing authority to the team also forces team members to cooperate and develop a shared understanding of the project.

Even though a product team structure facilitates innovation and the new product development process, it is often not sufficient to solve the coordination problem. Many organizations use additional integrating mechanisms to facilitate innovation: team leaders and project champions, "skunk works," new venture divisions, and joint ventures.

Team Leadership

Although establishment of a cross-functional product development team may be a necessary condition for successful innovation, it is not a sufficient condition. If a cross-functional team is to succeed, it must have the right kind of leadership, and it must be managed effectively.[19]

One important consideration is to have team leaders who can rise above their functional background and take a cross-functional view. Another issue is how much power and authority should be given to the team leader. Here a distinction can be made between lightweight and heavyweight team leaders.[20] A *lightweight team leader* is a mid-level functional manager who has lower status than the head of a functional department. The lightweight team leader is not given control over human, financial, and functional resources. Not a true project manager, this leader remains under the control of a functional department head. If the lightweight leader wants access to resources, he or she must pursue the heads of functional departments to obtain them. This arrangement weakens the power and authority of team leaders because they come to depend on the goodwill of the heads of functional departments. The result can be limited cross-functional coordination. Still, this arrangement might be appropriate in those cases when minor modifications of an existing product are all that is required.

A *heavyweight team leader* is a true project manager who has higher status within the organization. The heavyweight team leader is given primary control over key human, technological, and financial resources for the duration of the project. This allows the heavyweight leader to lay first claim to key resources and, if necessary, to override the wishes of the heads of the functions. For example, the heavyweight leader may be able to insist that a certain marketing or engineering manager be assigned full time to the project, even if the heads of the engineering and marketing departments are against this. Greater power gives the heavyweight team leader more ability to assemble a cross-functional team with the skills needed to develop a successful new product.[21]

Heavyweight team leaders often function as product champions, the people who take ownership of the project, solve problems as they occur, smooth over disputes between team members, and provide leadership to the team. Sometimes the product champion is not formally appointed but emerges informally during the innovation process. Organizational Insight 13.2 discusses how important the product champion role can be.

Organizational Insight 13.2

Championing the Mustang

Natalja/Shutterstock.com

Don Frey, an R&D engineer, was a product champion at Ford Motor Company. At Ford's R&D laboratories, Frey was assigned to projects that seemed new and interesting, but he never got to talk to customers and never got involved in operational decision making about what to offer the customer and how much new developments would cost. As a result, for many years, he and other R&D engineers worked on products that never got to market. Frustrated by the lack of payoff from his work, Frey began to question the utility of a corporate R&D laboratory that was so far removed from operations and the market. In 1957, he moved from R&D to head the passenger car design department, where he would be closer to market operations. In this new position, Frey was much closer to the customer and directed the energies of his department to producing innovations that customers wanted and were willing to pay for.

Frey soon concluded that in the automobile business, the best R&D is incremental: Year by year a car was improved to meet customer demands. He also saw how important it is to use customer complaints as a guide for investing R&D resources to get the most benefit. Equipped with this new perspective on innovation, he was made a member of Ford's top planning committee in 1961, and he became interested in developing a new car for the emerging "sporty car segment."

Frey and his staff saw the possibility of designing a car for this segment, and they began championing the development of a product. Ford, however, had just lost a fortune on the Edsel and was reluctant to start a new car. Because there was no corporate support for Frey's ideas, all of the early engineering and styling of what became the Mustang were carried out with bootleg funds—funds earmarked for other projects. By 1962, Frey and his team had produced the first working prototype of the Mustang and believed they had a winner. Top management in general and Henry Ford II in particular were not impressed and offered no support, still fearing the new car might turn out to be another Edsel.

Luckily for the Mustang team, Lee Iacocca became vice president and general manager of Ford in 1962, and he bought into the Mustang concept. Believing the Mustang would be a huge success, Iacocca risked his reputation to convince top management to back the idea. In the fall of 1962, after much pressure, funds to produce the car were allocated. With Frey as product champion, the Mustang was completed from approval to market in only 18 months. When the Mustang was introduced in 1964, it was an instant success, and over 400,000 Mustangs were sold.

Frey went on to champion other innovations in Ford vehicles, such as disc brakes and radial tires. Reflecting on his experiences as a product champion, he offered some coaching tips for future product champions: Innovation can start anywhere and from small beginnings, and product champions must be prepared to use all the skill they have to pull people and resources together and to resist top managers and financial experts who use numbers to kill new ideas.[22] As Frey's experience suggests, innovation is a risky business, and product champions have to go out on a limb to take on the disbelievers.

Skunk Works and New Venture Divisions

A *skunk works* is a task force, a temporary team that is created to expedite new product design and to promote innovation by coordinating the activities of functional groups.[23] The task force consists of members of the R&D, engineering, manufacturing, and marketing functions who are assigned to a separate facility, at a location isolated from the rest of the organization. This independent "autonomous" setting gives skunk works members the opportunity to engage in the intensive face-to-face interactions necessary for successful innovation. As a team, skunk works members "own the problem": They are the intrapreneurs responsible for the project's success or failure. Thus a skunk works is an island of innovation; it provides a large organization with a small-organization-type setting in which skunk works members have the opportunity and motivation to bring a new product to market quickly. Ford's original Mustang was developed in a skunks works setting by Don Frey, for example.

HP, 3M, and other organizations have also recognized the advantages of a small-organization atmosphere for fostering intrapreneurship. When potentially successful new product ideas are discovered by their R&D functions, these organizations create a *new venture division*, a self-contained, independent division given the resources to develop a complete set of value-creating functions to manage a project from beginning to end.[24] Unlike a skunk works, which is dissolved when the product is brought to market, a new venture division assumes full responsibility for the commercialization of the product. Heavyweight project members become the heads of the division's functions and assume responsibility for managing the functional structure created to bring the new product to market.

Establishing the balance of control between a new venture division and corporate headquarters can become a problem. As the new division demands more and more resources to fulfill its mission, corporate managers may become concerned about whether the project will be successful. If corporate managers start to intervene in the division's activities and its managers feel their judgment and autonomy is being threatened, the entrepreneurial spirit inside the new venture division may decline.

In contrast, major problems can arise if the parent organization establishes too many independent new venture divisions in the desperate attempt to spur innovation. One problem is the major expense this involves, which can quickly drive up operating costs. A second problem is that the new divisions may use their autonomy to pursue their own goals, regardless of whether or not these conflict with the goals of the whole organization. Finally, managing new venture divisions is a difficult process that requires considerable organizational skill. Managers must create the right kind of organizational structure if they are to be successful; utilizing the right kinds of IT systems is also vital; this important issue is discussed later in the chapter.

Joint Ventures

Joint ventures between two or more organizations, discussed in Chapter 3, are another important means of managing high-tech innovation. A joint venture allows organizations to combine their skills and technologies and pool their resources to embark on risky R&D projects. A joint venture is similar to a new venture division in that a new organization is created in which people can work out new procedures that lead to success. When both companies share revenues, risks, and costs, it often can result in the development of a stream of profitable new products. Joint ventures can also cause problems, however, if the venture partners begin to come into conflict over future development plans. This often happens when, over time, the venture begins to favor one partner over than another. Given this possibility, many joint venture agreements have clauses allowing one partner to buy the other out, or giving one partner 51% ownership of the venture, to ensure that the gains from future innovation can be achieved.

Creating a Culture for Innovation

Organizational culture also plays a major role in shaping and promoting innovation. Values and norms can reinforce the entrepreneurial spirit and allow an organization to respond quickly and creatively to a changing environment. Three factors that shape organizational culture and the degree to which its values and norms emphasize innovation are organizational structure, people, and property rights (see Figure 7.2).

ORGANIZATIONAL STRUCTURE Because organizational structure influences the way people behave, creating the right setting is important to fostering an intrapreneurial culture. Several factors can stunt innovation and reduce the ability of an organization to introduce new products as it grows.

Increasing organizational size may slow innovation. As organizations grow, decision making slows down. Decisions have to be made through established channels in a lengthy hierarchy, and a thriving bureaucracy stifles the entrepreneurial spirit. As an organization becomes more bureaucratic, people become more conservative and risk averse, and the creative people most able and willing to take risks and innovate become discouraged and may leave the organization.

As organizations age, they tend to become less flexible and innovative and so may fail to notice new opportunities to develop new products.[25] As Rosabeth Moss Kanter notes, this occurs because of "the inability of many traditional mature firms to anticipate the need for productive change and their resistance to ideas advanced by creative people."[26] In addition, it is difficult for people to remain entrepreneurial throughout their careers. Thus as organizations and their members age, there may be an inherent tendency for both to become more conservative.

With organizational growth comes complexity and an increase in vertical and horizontal differentiation that may hurt innovation. An increase in hierarchical levels makes it hard for employee intrapreneurs to exercise meaningful authority over projects. They may be under the constant scrutiny of superiors who insist on signing off on all decisions involving a project. Similarly, when the skills and knowledge needed for innovation are spread across too many functions, it is difficult for a project manager or product champion to obtain and coordinate the resources vital to bring a project to fruition.[27]

To promote innovation, organizations need to adopt a structure that can overcome those problems. Organic structures based on norms and values that emphasize lateral communication and cross-functional cooperation tend to promote innovation. Matrix and product team structures possess these organic qualities and provide autonomy for intrapreneurs to act decisively. In addition, organizations can give their members wide latitude to act outside formal task definitions and to work on projects where they think they can make a contribution. Apple and Microsoft confer on their top "thinkers" the title "research fellow" and give them the autonomy and resources to decide how to put their skills to best use, for example.

PEOPLE The culture of innovation in high-tech organizations is fostered by the characteristics of employees themselves. In many research settings, people cooperate so closely on product development that they become increasingly similar to one another. They buy into the same set of organizational norms and values and thus are able to communicate well with each other. In turn, organizational members select new members who buy into the same set of values, so that over time a recognizable set of values and norms that creates a culture that promotes creativity, cooperation, and the voluntary sharing of new ideas emerges. However, an organization needs to guard against groupthink and prevent team members from suffering from the kinds of cognitive biases discussed in Chapter 12—lest they lose sight of new or emerging trends in the industry. Microsoft's programmers, for example, fixated on improving its Windows software applications and ignored signs that customers wanted better ways to search the Web to quickly find more relevant and accurate information—so Google became the search leader. To maintain a capacity to innovate successfully, organizations must strive to maintain diversity in their skilled employees and allow them to follow divergent paths. The uncertainty associated with innovation makes it important for employees to be adaptable and open to new ideas. One way to encourage flexibility and open-mindedness is to recruit people who are committed to innovation but who travel along different pathways to achieve it. This is what 3M seems to do, as described in Organizational Insight 13.3.

Organizational Insight 13.3

Fostering Innovation at 3M

photosync/Shutterstock.com

3M is one of the most successful innovators of new products in the world. 3M uses many different technologies to innovate thousands of new and improved products for companies and individual consumers each year. To encourage successful new product development, 3M has set a challenging stretch goal that 30% of its revenues should be earned from new products developed in the last three years. This goal encourages its employees to act as entrepreneurs and to search out new opportunities to create products that customers will value and buy.

Sometimes, the process of developing new products at 3M begins with finding a technology to make a product that will better meet an existing customer need. In 1904, for example, 3M's engineers developed a new technology that allowed them to bond grit to paper, and the result was a blockbuster product—the first sandpaper. 3M developed this technology because it knew from watching its customers there was a large unmet need and thus potential market for an inexpensive, easy-to-use abrasive.

In many cases, it is more difficult for a company to discover customer needs—or even to discover potential uses for a new product. The way another 3M product, Scotch masking tape, was developed illustrates this. The story of Scotch tape begins when Dick Drew, a 3M scientist, visited an auto body shop in St. Paul, Minnesota, to test a new kind of sandpaper he was developing. Two-tone cars were popular then, and Drew watched as paint shop employees improvised a method to keep one color of paint from being over sprayed onto the other. They used a paint shield made up of a combination of heavy adhesive tape and butcher paper. Very often, as they pulled their shield off when the paint was dry, it took the other color paint with it. Employees joked with Drew that it would be a good idea if 3M could develop a product that made their job easier.[28]

Drew realized what was needed was a tape with a *weaker* glue or adhesive that would not pull the paint off. He went back to his lab to develop such a glue and, after many attempts, used it to develop the first masking tape. Paint shop employees now had a way to detach butcher paper from a car and achieve a first-class paint job. Once the success of the new product was proved, Drew began to think about other uses for masking tape. It soon became clear that the common need for a reliable way to seal, wrap, package, or attach something meant that the uses for masking tape were endless. Drew continued his research, and in 1930 he invented clear cellophane tape to meet many of these other kinds of customer needs.

Managerial Implications

Innovation

1. Research and development activities must be integrated with the activities of the other functions if the innovation process is to be successful.
2. Employees must be given autonomy and encouraged to use organizational resources to facilitate the continuous development of new products and processes.
3. Project managers, a stage-gate product development funnel, cross-functional teams, appropriate team leadership, a skunk works, and new venture divisions should be created to provide a setting that encourages entrepreneurship.
4. Top management must create a culture that supports innovation and recognizes and rewards the contributions of organizational members—for example, by linking rewards directly to performance.

PROPERTY RIGHTS The uncertainty associated with innovation makes it difficult for managers to evaluate the performance of highly skilled employees in R&D, marketing, and so on. Managers cannot simply observe highly skilled employees to determine how well they are performing. Often their performance can be evaluated only over a long time—perhaps years. Moreover, innovation is a complex, intensive process that demands skills and abilities inherent in competent employees, not in the organization. If one of these employees comes up with a new idea, it is relatively easy to take it and establish a new venture to take advantage of it. Indeed, much technological innovation occurs in new organizations founded by scientists who have left large organizations to branch out on their own. Given these issues, strong property rights are needed to align the interests of talented employees with those of their organization.[29]

An organization can create career paths for its highly skilled employees and project managers and demonstrate that success is closely linked to future promotion and rewards. Career paths can be established inside an organization that allow talented people to rise to the top. Inside the R&D function, for example, successful scientists can be groomed to manage future R&D projects. After some years in R&D, however, scientists might move to take control of manufacturing operations or to assume other functional or corporate responsibilities.

Strong property rights can also be created if an organization links effective individual and group performance to substantial organizational rewards or inducements. Innovative employees should receive bonuses and stock options proportional to the increase in profitability that can be attributed to their efforts. Making employees owners in the organization will discourage them from leaving and provide them with a strong incentive to perform well. Many successful high-techs such as Google, Merck, and Apple do this; and thousands of the current employees of Google and Apple are millionaires as a result of the decision to give stock options to employees.

By focusing on property rights, people, and structure, an organization can create a culture in which norms and values foster innovation and the search for excellence in new product development.

Information efficiencies
The cost and time savings that occur when IT allows individual employees to perform their current tasks at a higher level, assume additional tasks, and expand their roles in the organization due to advances in the ability to gather and analyze data.

Innovation and Information Technology

Previous chapters discussed how IT can raise organizational effectiveness, particularly by reducing operating costs. Why? Because of **information efficiencies,** the cost and time savings that occur when IT allows individual employees to perform their current tasks at a higher level, assume additional tasks, and expand their roles in the organization owing to advances in the ability to gather and analyze data.[30] The ability of IT to enhance a person's task knowledge and technical skills is also an important input into the innovation process, however. In fact, IT facilitates the innovation process because it promotes creativity in many ways and affects many aspects of the process of bringing new problem-solving ideas into use.

First, IT facilitates creativity by improving the initial base of knowledge to draw from when employees engage in problem solving and decision making. To the degree that IT creates a larger and richer pool of codified knowledge for any given employee to draw from, and allows these employees to work together, innovative potential is increased. Examples of knowledge codification from using knowledge management were discussed in Chapter 12. For example, at large consultancy firms like Accenture and McKinsey & Co., groups of experienced consultants assemble knowledge online from every level of the firm, then use in-house IT to disseminate information to consultants throughout the organization—information that would otherwise not have been available to them.

Knowledge or information availability alone will not lead to innovation; it is the ability to *creatively use* knowledge that is the key to promoting innovation and creating competitive advantage.[31] In 1990, Prahalad and Hamel, for example, suggested it is not the level of knowledge a firm possesses that leads to innovation and competitive advantage, but the velocity with which it is circulated in the firm.[32] Organizations must take steps to ensure that they use knowledge to develop distinctive competences at both the individual and functional levels, particularly between functions.

Similarly, a reshuffling of tasks likely will occur as new IT systems increase the ability of people or subunits to acquire and process information. This leads to many more opportunities for creatively combining, modifying, and synthesizing information leading to the incremental innovations discussed earlier. For example, what before might have been a task that requires the inputs of three different people or subunits becomes a task that one individual or function can perform more creatively and effectively because IT helps increase both the amount and quality of information that can be adequately processed. IT also facilitates cross-functional and divisional communication and coordination that can promote the sharing of tacit knowledge between people and groups, leading to increased organizational knowledge.

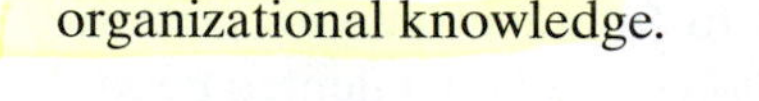

Innovation and Information Synergies

In fact, one of the most important performance gains that result from IT occur when two or more individuals or subunits pool their resources and cooperate and collaborate across role or subunit boundaries, creating **information synergies**. Information synergies occur when IT allows individuals or subunits to adjust their actions or behaviors to the needs of the other individuals or subunits on an ongoing basis and achieve gains from team-based cooperation.

Information synergies
The knowledge building created when two or more individuals or subunits pool their resources and cooperate and collaborate across role or subunit boundaries.

IT changes organizational forms and promotes creativity and innovation inside both network and virtual organizational forms. IT-enabled virtual forms composed of electronically connected people or firms facilitate knowledge sharing and innovation. Compared to face-to-face communication, for example, the use of electronic communication has increased the amount of communication within the organization. IT's ability to link and enable employees within and between functions and divisions—whether through database repositories, teleconferencing, or electronic mail—helps lead to information synergies. The application of IT promotes cross-functional work flows, makes critical information more accessible and transparent to employees, and increases the incidence of problem solving leading to innovation.[33]

The downside to linking employees must be noted as well. It is possible that not only the amount of good advice information seekers receive will increase—bad advice may increase as well. However, many firms work to ensure the reliability of information received via electronically weak ties by forming online communities where collections of experienced employees within a given area can be located (e.g., a software developers' forum, a sales force intranet, a manufacturing discussion group). Developing a knowledge management system also helps to ensure high-quality information and advice, given when requested.

IT also allows for an increase in **boundary-spanning activity**—interacting with individuals and groups outside the organization to obtain valuable information and knowledge from the environment—that helps promote innovation. IT allows an employee to search for and absorb new knowledge that is relevant to a problem at hand.[34] For example, in complex organizations, employees working on one task or project may wish to obtain useful knowledge residing in other operating units, but the employees may not know whether or not this knowledge exists and where it might reside. IT, through knowledge management systems, allows employees to search their network for information.

Boundary-spanning activity The interactions of people and groups across the organizational boundary to obtain valuable information and knowledge from the environment to help promote innovation.

IT has many other useful properties that can promote incremental and quantum technological change. IT allows researchers and planners to communicate more easily and less expensively across time and geographic location; to communicate more rapidly and with greater precision to targeted groups; to more selectively control access and participation in a communication event or network; to more rapidly and selectively access information created outside the organization; to more rapidly and accurately combine and reconfigure information; and to more concisely store and quickly use experts' judgments and decision models. All these qualities can enhance creativity and make project management more effective. Amazon.com is a company using IT to make creative decisions and broaden its product line, becoming a consultant itself and selling its own creative ideas (see Focus on New Information Technology, Part 7).

IT and Organizational Structure and Culture

IT also affects the innovation process through its many effects on organizational structure. Specialization typically leads to the development of subunit orientations that reduce the ability of employees to understand the wider context within which they are contributing their skills and expertise. IT can mitigate this tendency by providing greater

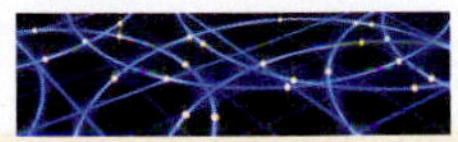

Focus on New Information Technology

Amazon.com, Part 7

Jeff Bezos's use of the Internet to sell books can probably be regarded as a quantum innovation in this industry. However, innovation at Amazon.com has not stopped there. Bezos and his top-management team have engaged in a series of incremental innovations to grow and expand Amazon's core competences as an online retailer.[35]

Although Bezos initially chose to focus on selling books, he soon realized that Amazon's information technology could be used to sell other kinds of products. He began to search for products that could be sold profitably over the Internet. First, he chose CDs, then when DVDs became popular Amazon began to sell them. Today, Amazon also has online storefronts offering music and video downloads of all kinds and gives its customers the opportunity to store their purchases online through its expansion into cloud computing services. All these new goods and services reflect its desire to offer the widest range of products possible to attract customers, and especially to encourage repeat business so that it can continue its mission to become the biggest global book, music, and video store.

In other ventures Amazon has opened a holiday gift store to entice customers to send gifts as well as books and DVDs as presents, offered a gift-wrapping service, and launched a free electronic greeting card service to announce the arrival of the Amazon gift. Today, it has over 40 different product storefronts.

Bezos has moved aggressively to use Amazon's developing expertise in virtual storefront retailing to offer a consulting service to organizations that wish to develop their own customer-friendly storefront that has made Amazon so popular. As discussed in previous chapters, it has also used its IT competences to widen its product line, and to keep its line up to date with regard to the ongoing changes in electronics and digital technology that are constantly altering the mix of products it offers in its virtual store.

As a result of these incremental innovations to Amazon's business, Bezos has transformed his company from "online book seller" to "leading Internet product provider." The company's share price has soared in the 2010s as Amazon has become the most profitable online retailer, and investors believe the company has the skills and competences to retain—and strengthen—its dominant position. The fact that it has overtaken eBay in recent years to become the online retail storefront of choice also suggests that its next challenge will be to take on Walmart as it expands its storefronts to offer customers more products and services, including the delivery of thousands of different kinds of food products, flowers, toiletries, and other kinds of basic consumer goods.

information access to specialists through such technologies as email, corporate intranets, access to the Internet, and so on.

To speed innovation, many organizations have begun to move decision making lower in the organization to take advantage of specialized workers who possess more accurate and timely local information. IT helps this process in two ways. First, IT gives lower-level employees more detailed and current knowledge of consumer and market trends and opportunities. For example, IT in customer support centers directed at solving customer problems via the Internet has become a widespread means of increasing effectiveness. Second, IT can produce information synergies because it facilitates increased communication and coordination between decentralized decision makers and top managers. Now, as decision-making authority moves lower in the hierarchy, it may become better aligned.[36]

Third, IT means that fewer levels of managers are needed to handle problem solving and decision making, which results in a flatter organization. In addition, because IT provides lower-level employees with more freedom to coordinate their actions, information synergies may emerge as employees experiment and find better ways of performing their tasks.

IT can also promote innovation through its effects on organizational culture. IT facilitates the sharing of beliefs, values, and norms because it allows for the quick transmission of rich, detailed information between people and subunits. IT thus can enhance the motivational effects of cultural values supportive of innovation. Using IT, an organization can make available to employees a slew of supportive messages and statements, often contained in an organization's mission statement, corporate goals, operating procedures, and so on. Email, voice mail, and intranets, for example, provide mechanisms for transferring and disseminating information about the organization to employees and can help promote the cultural shared norms, values, and expectations that can facilitate innovation.

Summary

Managing the process of innovation and change to enhance organizational effectiveness is a central challenge facing managers and organizations today. An increasing rate of technological change and an increase in global competition are two forces that are putting enormous pressure on organizations to find new and better ways of organizing their activities to increase their ability to innovate and create value. Chapter 13 has made the following major points:

1. Innovation is the development of new products or new production and operating systems (including new forms of organizational structures).
2. There are two types of innovation: quantum innovations, which are the result of quantum shifts in technology, and incremental innovations, which result from the refinements to an existing technology. Technological change that results in quantum innovations can create opportunities for an organization to introduce new products, but it can also be a threat because it can increase the level of competition.
3. Innovation, intrapreneurship, and creativity are closely related concepts, and each is vital to build a knowledge-creating organization.
4. Managers can use a number of techniques to help promote innovation. These include project management, using a stage-gate development funnel, using cross-functional teams and a product team structure, establishing strong team leadership, making use of skunk works and new venture divisions, and creating a culture for innovation.

5. IT creates information efficiencies and information synergies and thus is an important tool for promoting creativity and innovation, especially through its effects on organizational design, structure, and culture.

Discussion Questions

1. What is the relationship between quantum and incremental technological change?
2. What is the relationship among creativity, intrapreneurship, and innovation?
3. What is project management? How should managers decide which projects to pursue?
4. What steps would you take to create (a) a structure and (b) a culture congenial to innovation in a high-tech organization?
5. What are information synergies and in what ways can they enhance innovation?

Organizational Theory in Action

Practicing Organizational Theory

Managing Innovation

Break up into groups of three to five people and discuss the following scenario:

You are the top managers in charge of a chain of stores selling high-quality, high-priced men's and women's clothing. Store sales are flat, and you are increasingly concerned that the clothing your stores offer to customers is failing to satisfy changing customer needs. You think that the purchasing managers are failing to spot changing fads and fashions in time, and you believe store management is not doing enough to communicate to purchasing managers what customers are demanding. You want to revitalize your organization's product development process, which, in the case of your stores, means designing, selecting, and stocking the products that customers want.

1. Using the chapter material, outline the way you will create a program to increase creativity and intrapreneurship at the store and corporate level. For example, how will you encourage input from employees and customers, and who will be responsible for managing the program?
2. How will you make use of IT and organizational structure to facilitate the innovation process?

The Ethical Dimension #13

Some intrapreneurs make discoveries that earn millions or even billions of dollars of product sales for the companies they work for, but because this was not provided for in their employment contracts, they do not share in these profits. Other intrapreneurs make discoveries in the course of their work but do not share this information with their companies. They leave their organizations and found their own to exploit this knowledge.

1. Think about the ethical issues involved in each of these scenarios. Is it ethical either for the organization or the individual to act in this way?
2. Is there a way of solving the ethical dilemma posed in each of these cases?

Making the Connection #13

Find an example of an organization that has been trying to promote its level of innovation. What kind of innovation is it principally trying to promote? How is it attempting to do so? What has been its success so far?

Analyzing the Organization: Design Module #13

This model focuses on the extent to which your organization has been involved in efforts to promote innovation.

1. With the information that you have at your disposal, discuss (a) the forces for change, and (b) obstacles to change in your company.
2. With what kind of innovation (quantum or incremental) has your organization been most involved?
3. In what ways, if any, has your organization sought to manage the innovation process and alter its structure or culture to increase its capacity to develop new products or services?

CASE FOR ANALYSIS

Rising, Then Falling Innovation at Dell

Dell the PC maker, started by Michael Dell in his University of Texas dorm room, was one of the great success stories of the 1990s and early 2000s. Between the mid 1990s and 2007 Dell grew at an astonishing rate and was far more profitable than competing PC makers. However, from 2007 onward Dell's profitability declined, while several of its competitors, including most notably Apple and HP, improved their performance. Why did Dell's performance start to erode after 2007 and what actions is Dell taking to arrest the decline in its performance?

Dell's competence was based on selling PCs direct to customers and cutting out wholesalers and retailers so that it could give part of the value created back to customers in the form of lower prices that led to higher sales. Moreover, Dell's website allowed customers to mix and match product features such as microprocessors, memory, monitors, internal hard drives, DVD drives, keyboard and mouse format, and so on to customize their own computer system. The ability to customize orders kept customers coming back to Dell.

Another reason for Dell's rapid growth was the way it found innovative ways to manage its supply chain to minimize the costs of holding inventory. Once again Dell took advantage of the WWW to feed real-time information about changes in its demand for inputs to its suppliers so they could alter their production of components to match Dell's needs in the next weeks. Also, Dell's suppliers used this information to adjust their own production schedules to obtain the gains from just-in-time production, which also allowed Dell to drive down costs and prices.

What happened to Dell in the latter half of the 2000s that has helped lead to its current declining performance? First, a large proportion of Dell's sales came from business customers and during the 2008–2009 recession demand from business slumped. Second, during the 2000s HP had also learned how to outsource PC making to reduce costs and it was also able to sell business customers a bundle that included not just PCs, but also advanced servers, storage devices, network equipment, and the consulting services that helped businesses install, manage, and service this equipment. Dell lacked the competences in research and development needed to compete with HP and Apple. And, to increase demand for its PCs it was now forced to sell through regular bricks-and-mortar retailers like Walmart and Best Buy, which lowered its performance and profits. Finally, Apple was gaining market share from Dell by differentiating its products through their performance, design, and ease of use, and it created the impression that PCs from rivals such as Dell and HP were just old fashioned. From being the leader, Dell is now playing catch up in the industry and it is struggling to find innovative ways to turn around its performance as its profits continue to decline.

Questions for Discussion

1. What were the keys to Dell's success as it grew? How did entrepreneurship help the company grow?
2. Why has innovation at Dell been falling in recent years? Search the WWW for information that discusses how Michael Dell is making innovative changes to strategy and structure to turn around his company's performance.

References

1 R. A. Burgelman and M. A. Maidique, *Strategic Management of Technology and Innovation* (Homewood, IL: Irwin, 1988).

2 G. R. Jones and J. E. Butler, "Managing Internal Corporate Entrepreneurship: An Agency Theory Perspective," *Journal of Management* 18 (1992), 733–749.

3 E. Mansfield, J. Rapaport, J. Schnee, S. Wagner, and M. Hamburger, *Research and Innovation in the Modern Corporation* (New York: Norton, 1971).

4 R. D'Aveni, *Hyper-Competition* (New York: Free Press, 1994).

5 P. Anderson and Michael L. Tushman, "Technological Discontinuities and Dominant Designs: A Cyclical Model of Technological Change," *Administrative Science Quarterly* 35 (1990), 604–633; quoting J. Schumpeter, *Capitalism, Socialism, and Democracy* (New York: Harper Brothers, 1942).

6 The concept of creative destruction goes back to the classic work of J. A. Schumpeter; Ibid.

7 T. Lonier, "Some Insights and Statistics on Working Solo" (www.workingsolo.com).

8 J. V. Anderson, "Weirder than Fiction: The Reality and Myth of Creativity," *Academy of Management Executive* 6 (1992), 40–43.

9 Ibid, p. 43.

10 I. Nonaka, "The Knowledge Creating Company," *Harvard Business Review* (November–December 1991): 1–9.

11 Ibid.

12 V. P. Buell, *Marketing Management* (New York: McGraw-Hill, 1985).

13 See M. M. J. Berry and J. H. Taggart, "Managing Technology and Innovation: A Review," *R & D Management* 24 (1994), 341–353; and Clark and Wheelwright, *Managing New Product and Process Development*.

14 E. Abrahamson, "Managerial Fads and Fashions: The Diffusion and Rejection of Innovations," *Academy of Management Review* 16 (1991), 586–612.

15 http://www.microsoft.com/mspress/books/sampchap/ 4652a.asp?.

16 K. B. Clark and S. C. Wheelwright, *Managing New Product and Process Development* (New York: Free Press, 1993).

17 A. Griffin and J. R. Hauser, "Patterns of Communication among Marketing, Engineering, and Manufacturing," *Management Science* 38 (1992), 360–373; and R. K. Moenaert, W. E. Sounder, A. D. Meyer, and D. Deschoolmeester, "R&D-Marketing Integration Mechanisms, Communication Flows, and Innovation Success," *Journal of Production and Innovation Management* 11 (1994), pp. 31–45.

18 R. A. Burgelman and M. A. Maidique, *Strategic Management of Technology and Innovation*.

19 G. Barczak and D. Wileman, "Leadership Differences in New Product Development Teams," *Journal of Product Innovation Management* 6 (1989), 259–267; E. F. McDonough and G. Barczak, "Speeding Up New Product Development: The Effects of Leadership Style and Source of Technology," *Journal of Product Innovation Management* 8 (1991), pp. 203–211; and K. B. Clark and T. Fujimoto, "The Power of Product Integrity," *Harvard Business Review* (November–December 1990): 107–119.

20 K. B. Clark and S. C. Wheelwright, *Managing New Product and Process Development* (New York: Free Press, 1993).

21 Ibid.

22 D. Frey, "Learning the Ropes: My Life as a Product Champion," *Harvard Business Review* (September–October 1991): 46–56.

23 M. A. Maidique and R. H. Hayes, "The Art of High Technology Management," *Sloan Management Review* (Winter 1984): 18–31.

24 R. A. Burgelman, "Designs for Corporate Entrepreneurship in Established Firms," *California Management Review* 26 (1984), 154–166.

25 H. Mintzberg and J. A. Waters, "Tracking Strategy in an Entrepreneurial Firm," *Academy of Management Journal* 25 (1982), pp. 465–499; P. Strebel, "Organizing for Innovation over an Industry Life Cycle," *Strategic Management Journal* 8 (1987), 117–124.

26 R. M. Kanter, *The Change Masters* (New York: Simon & Schuster, 1983).

27 G. R. Jones and J. E. Butler, "Managing Internal Corporate Entrepreneurship: An Agency Theory Perspective," *Journal of Management* 18 (1992), 733–749.

28 Ibid.
29 www.3M.com, 2011.
30 T. Dewett and G. R. Jones, "The Role of Information Technology in the Organization: A Review, Model, and Assessment," *Journal of Management* 27 (2001), 313–346.
31 B. Leavy, "The Concept of Learning in the Strategy Field: Review and Outlook," *Management Learning* 29 (1998), pp. 447–466.
32 C.K. Prahalad and G. Hamel, "The Core Competency of the Corporation," *Harvard Business Review* (May–June 1990): 43–59.
33 J. F. Rockart and D. DeLong, *Executive Support Systems: The Emergence of Top Management Computer Use* (Burr Ridge, IL: Dow-Jones Irwin); J. F. Rockart, and J. E. Short, "IT and the 1990s: Managing Organizational Interdependencies," *Sloan Management Review* 30 (1989), 17–33.
34 M. T. Hanson, "The Search Transfer Problem: The Role of Weak Ties in Sharing Knowledge Across Organizational Subunits," *Administrative Science Quarterly* 44 (1999), 82–111.
35 www.amazon.com, 2011.
36 Dewett, T. and Jones, G.R. "The Role of Information Technology in the Organization: A Review, Model, and Assessment, *Journal of Management* 27 (2001), 313–346.

CHAPTER 14

Managing Conflict, Power, and Politics

Learning Objectives

This chapter focuses on the social and interpersonal processes that affect the way managers make decisions and the way organizations change and adapt to their environments. Specifically, it examines the causes, nature, and consequences of organizational conflict, power, and politics.

After studying this chapter you should be able to:

1. Describe the nature of organizational conflict, its sources, and the way it arises between stakeholders and subunits.
2. Identify the mechanisms by which managers and stakeholders can obtain power and use that power to influence decision making and resolve conflict in their favor.
3. Explain how and why individuals and subunits engage in organizational politics to enhance their control over decision making and obtain the power that allows them to influence the change process in their favor.
4. Appreciate the importance of managing an organization's power structure to overcome organizational inertia and to bring about the type of change that promotes performance.

What Is Organizational Conflict?

As noted in Chapter 2, an organization consists of different groups of stakeholders, each of which contributes something valuable to an organization in return for rewards. Stakeholders cooperate with one another to contribute jointly the resources an organization needs to produce goods and services. At the same time, however, stakeholders compete with one another for the resources the organization generates from these joint activities.[1] To produce goods and services, an organization needs the skills and abilities of managers and employees, the capital provided by shareholders, and the inputs provided by suppliers. Inside and outside stakeholders, such as employees, management, and shareholders, however, compete over their share of the rewards and resources that the organization generates.

To grow, change, and survive, an organization must manage both cooperation and competition among stakeholders. As Figure 14.1 suggests, each stakeholder group has its own goals and interests, which overlap somewhat with those of other groups because all stakeholders have a common interest in the survival of the organization. But stakeholders' goals and interests are not identical, and conflict arises when one group pursues its own interests at the expense of other groups. **Organizational conflict** is the clash that occurs when the goal-directed behavior of one group blocks or thwarts the goals of another.

Organizational conflict
The clash that occurs when the goal-directed behavior of one group blocks or thwarts the goals of another.

Because the goals, preferences, and interests of stakeholder groups differ, conflict is inevitable in organizations.[2] Although conflict is often perceived negatively, research suggests that some conflict is good for an organization and can improve organizational

Figure 14.1 Cooperation and Competition among Organizational Stakeholders

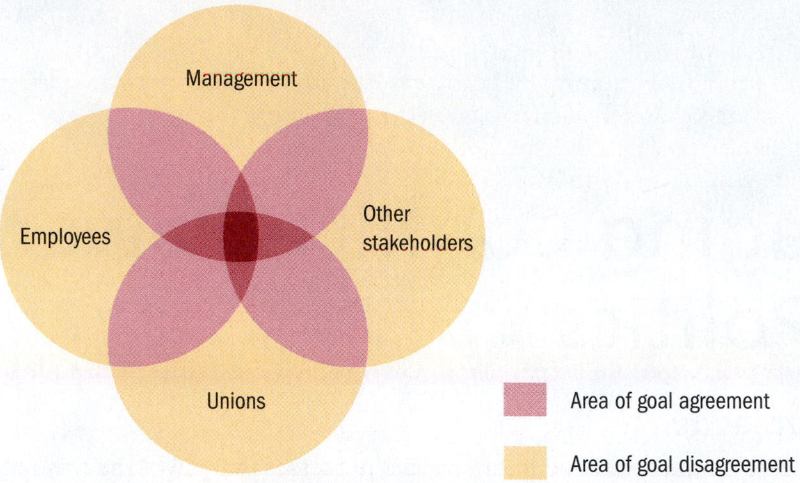

effectiveness. Beyond some point (point A in Figure 14.2), however, extreme conflict between stakeholders can hurt organizational performance.[3]

Why is some conflict good for an organization? Conflict can be beneficial because it can overcome organizational inertia and lead to organizational learning and change. When conflict within an organization or conflict between an organization and elements in its environment arises, the organization and its managers must reevaluate their view of the world. As we saw in Chapter 12, conflict between different managers or between different stakeholder groups can improve decision making and organizational learning by revealing new ways of looking at a problem or the false or erroneous assumptions that distort decision making. For example, conflict at AT&T between the board of directors and top managers about the slow pace at which the company was being restructured led to the appointment of a new CEO and top-management team. The new CEO, Randall Stephenson, has made many radical changes to the way the company operates and has taken major risks, including his 2011 decision to acquire T-Mobile for $39 billion.

Figure 14.2 The Relationship between Conflict and Organizational Effectiveness

Research suggests that there is an optimal level of conflict within an organization. Beyond that point (point A), conflict is likely to be harmful.

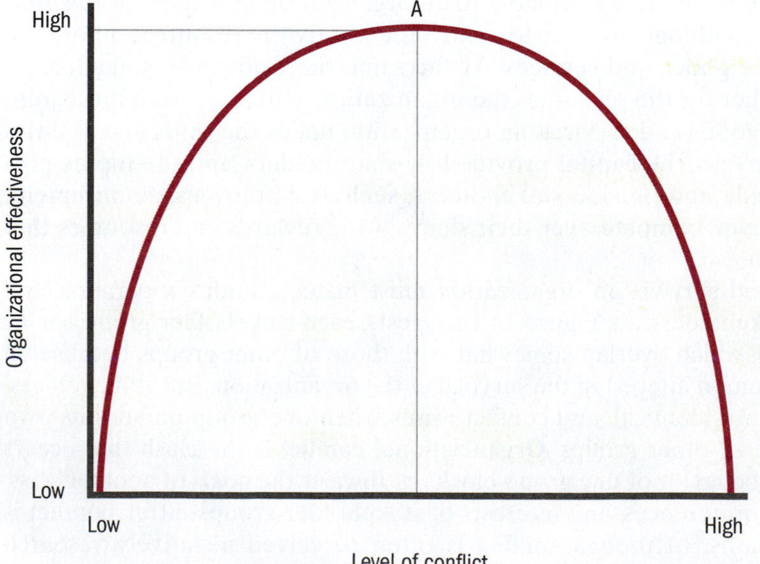

If the attempted acquisition fails for antitrust reasons, AT&T will have to pay T-Mobile $6 billion! Similarly, conflict between Ford's new CEO and top divisional managers resulted in a major change in organizational focus that produced major improvements in the carmaker's performance by 2011.

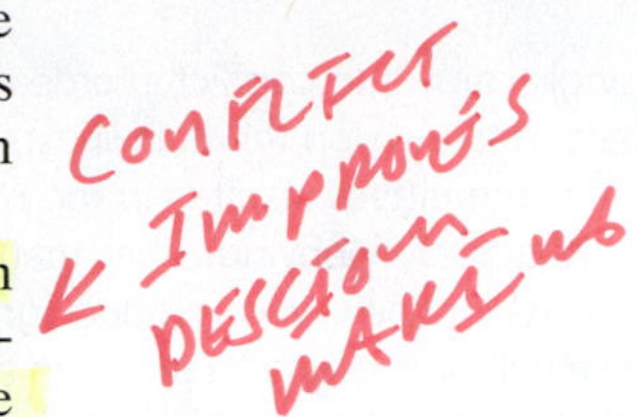

The conflict that arises when different groups perceive the organization's problems in different ways and are willing to act on their beliefs is a built-in defense against the organizational inertia produced by a top-management team whose members have the same vision of the world. In short, conflict can improve decision making and allow an organization to better change and adapt to its environment.[4]

Beyond a certain point, however, conflict stops being a force for good and becomes a cause of organizational decline. Suppose, for example, conflict between managers (or between other stakeholders) becomes chronic, so that managers cannot agree about organizational priorities or about how best to allocate resources to meet organizational needs. In this situation, managers spend all their time bargaining and fighting, and the organization gets so bogged down in the process of decision making that organizational change is slow in coming. Innovation, of course, is more or less impossible in such a setting. In a somewhat vicious cycle, the slow and ponderous decision making characteristic of organizations in decline leads to even greater conflict because the consequences of failure are so great. An organization in trouble spends a lot of time making decisions—time that it cannot afford because it needs to adapt quickly to turn itself around. Thus, although some conflict can jolt an organization out of inertia, too much conflict can cause organizational inertia: As different groups fight for their own positions and interests, they fail to arrive at consensus, and the organization drifts along; failure to change makes the organization go from bad to worse.[5]

Many analysts claim that both AT&T and Ford faced this difficult situation. Top managers knew they had to make radical changes to their organization's strategy and structure, but they could not do so because different groups of top managers lobbied for their own interests and for cutbacks to fall on other divisions. Conflict between divisions and the constant fight to protect each division's interests resulted in a slow rate of change and worsened the situation. In both companies, the boards of directors removed the CEO and brought in newcomers who they hoped would overcome opposition to change and develop a strategy that would promote organizational interests, not just the interests of a particular group. The way in which John Mackay achieved this at Pfizer illustrates these issues, as discussed in Organizational Insight 14.1

Organizational Insight 14.1

How Martin Mackay Controlled Conflict at Pfizer

Pfizer is the largest global pharmaceuticals company, with sales of almost $50 billion in 2011. Its research scientists have innovated some of the most successful and profitable drugs in the world, such as the first cholesterol reducer, Lipitor, that used to earn Pfizer $13 billion a year.[6] In the 2000s, however, Pfizer encountered major problems in its attempt to innovate new blockbuster drugs, while its blockbuster drugs like Lipitor lost their patent protection. Pfizer desperately needed to find ways to make its product development pipeline work. And one manager, Martin Mackay, believed he knew how to do it.

When Pfizer's longtime R&D chief retired, Mackay, his deputy, made it clear to CEO Jeffrey Kindler that he wanted the job. Kindler made it equally clear he thought the company could use some new talent and fresh ideas to solve its problems. Mackay realized he had to quickly come up with a convincing plan to change the way Pfizer's scientists worked to develop new drugs to gain Kindler's support and get the top job. So Mackay created a detailed plan for changing the way its thousands of researchers made decisions to make sure the company's resources, its talent and funds, would be put to their best use. After Kindler reviewed the plan, he was so impressed he promoted Mackay to the top R&D position. What was Mackay's plan?

As Pfizer had grown over time as a result of mergers with other large pharmaceutical companies, Mackay noted how decision-making problems and conflict between the managers of Pfizer's different drug divisions had increased. As it grew, Pfizer's organizational structure had become taller and taller and the size of its headquarters staff grew. With more managers and levels in the hierarchy there was a greater need for committees to integrate across their activities. However, in these meetings different groups of managers fought to promote the development of the drugs they had the most interest in and they increasingly came into conflict in order to ensure they got the resources they needed to develop them. In short, Mackay felt that too many managers and committees resulted in too much conflict between managers who were actively lobbying other managers and the CEO to promote the interests of their own product groups—and the company's performance was suffering as a result. In addition, although Pfizer success depended on innovation, this growing conflict had resulted in Pfizer developing a bureaucratic culture that reduced the quality of decision making, making it more difficult to identify promising new drugs.

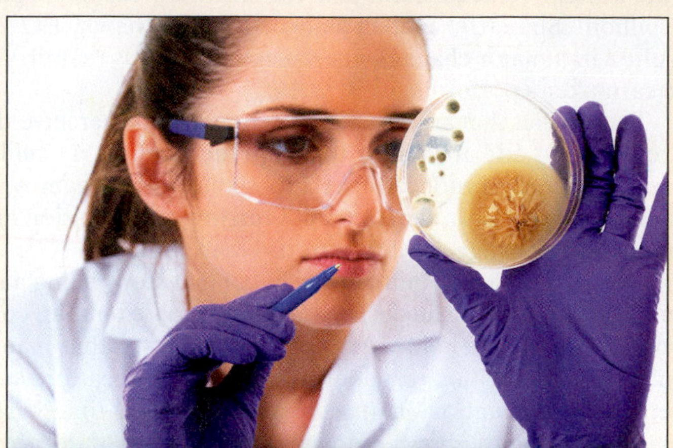
Michal Kowalski/Shutterstock.com

Mackay's bold plan to get rid of this increasing conflict involved slashing the number of management layers between top managers and scientists from 14 to 7, which resulted in the layoff of thousands of Pfizer's managers. He also abolished the scores of product development committees whose wrangling he believed was slowing down the process of transforming innovative ideas into blockbuster drugs. After streamlining the hierarchy he focused on reducing the number of bureaucratic rules scientists had to follow, many of which were unnecessary and had promoted conflict. He and his team eliminated every kind of written report that was slowing down the innovation process. For example, scientists had been in the habit of submitting quarterly and monthly reports to top managers explaining each drug's progress; Mackay told them to pick which one they wanted to keep, and the other would be eliminated.

As you can imagine, Mackay's efforts caused enormous upheaval in the company as managers fought to keep their positions and scientists fought to protect the drugs they had in development. However, Mackay was resolute and pushed his agenda through with the support of the CEO who defended his efforts to create a new R&D product development process that empowered Pfizer's scientists and promoted innovation and entrepreneurship. Pfizer's scientists reported that they felt "liberated" by the new work system, and the level of conflict fell and new drugs started to move faster along the pipeline. By 2011, Pfizer had won FDA approval for a major new antibacterial drug, and several potential new blockbuster drugs in its pipeline were on track.[7] However, Mackay left Pfizer to join AstraZeneca in 2011 as its new head of drug product development when Pfizer passed him over and appointed an outside manager as CEO.

On balance, then, organizations need to be open to conflict, to recognize the way it both helps managers to identify problems and promotes the generation of alternative solutions that improve decision making. Conflict can promote organizational learning. However, to take advantage of the value-creating aspects of conflict and avoid its dysfunctional effects, managers must learn how to control it. Louis R. Pondy developed a useful model of organizational conflict. Pondy first identifies the sources of conflict and then examines the stages of a typical conflict episode.[8] His model provides many clues about how to control and manage conflict in an organization.

Pondy's Model of Organizational Conflict

Pondy views conflict as a process that consists of five sequential episodes or stages, summarized in Figure 14.3. No matter how or why conflict arises, managers can use Pondy's model to interpret and analyze a conflict situation and take action to resolve it—for example, by redesigning the organization's structure.

Stage 1: Latent Conflict

In the first stage of Pondy's model, *latent conflict*, no outright conflict exists; however, the potential for conflict to arise is present, although latent, because of the way an organization operates. According to Pondy, all organizational conflict arises because vertical and horizontal differentiation lead to the establishment of different organizational subunits with different goals and often different perceptions of how best to realize those goals. In business enterprises, for example, managers in different functions or divisions can generally agree about the organization's central goal, which is to maximize its ability to create value in the long run. But they may have different ideas about how to achieve this goal: Should the organization invest resources in manufacturing to lower costs or in R&D to develop new products? Five potential sources of conflict between

Figure 14.3 Pondy's Model of Organizational Conflict

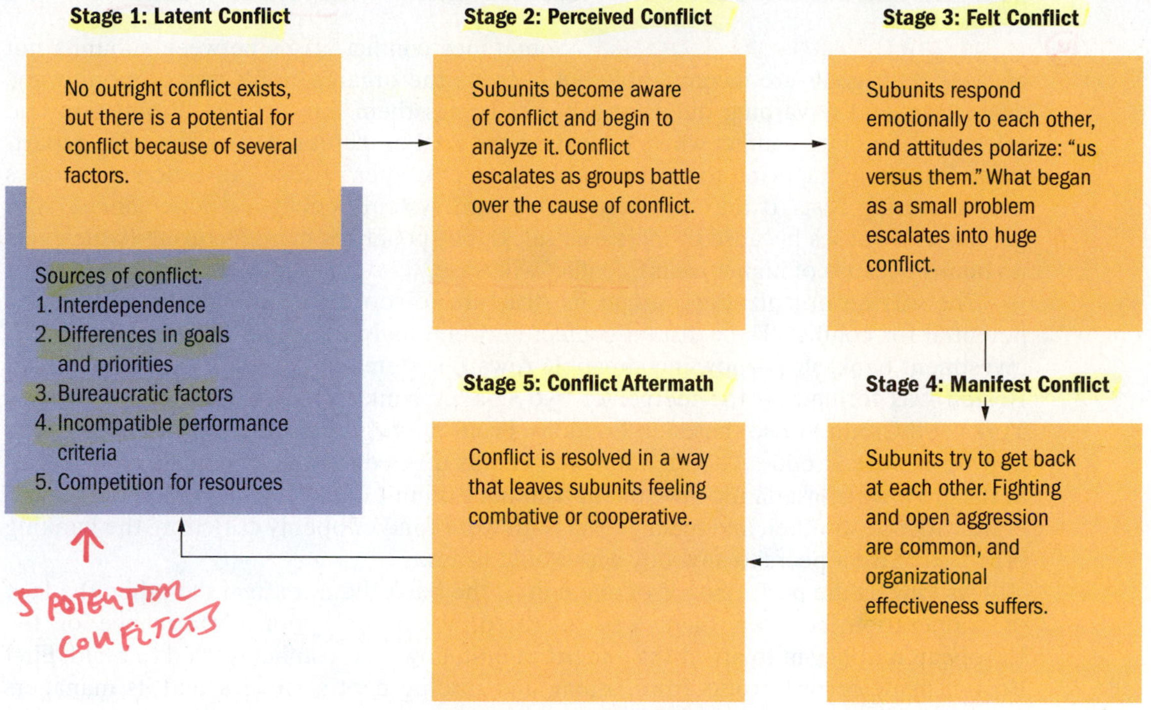
Stage 1: Latent Conflict
No outright conflict exists, but there is a potential for conflict because of several factors.
Sources of conflict:
1. Interdependence
2. Differences in goals and priorities
3. Bureaucratic factors
4. Incompatible performance criteria
5. Competition for resources
Stage 2: Perceived Conflict
Subunits become aware of conflict and begin to analyze it. Conflict escalates as groups battle over the cause of conflict.
Stage 3: Felt Conflict
Subunits respond emotionally to each other, and attitudes polarize: "us versus them." What began as a small problem escalates into huge conflict.
Stage 4: Manifest Conflict
Subunits try to get back at each other. Fighting and open aggression are common, and organizational effectiveness suffers.
Stage 5: Conflict Aftermath
Conflict is resolved in a way that leaves subunits feeling combative or cooperative.

subunits can be identified: subunits' interdependence, subunits' differing goals, bureaucratic factors, incompatible performance criteria, and competition for resources.[9]

INTERDEPENDENCE As organizations differentiate, each subunit develops a desire for autonomy and begins to pursue goals and interests that it values over the goals of other subunits or of the organization as a whole. Because the activities of different subunits are interdependent, subunits' desire for autonomy leads to conflict between groups. Eventually, each subunit's desire for autonomy comes into conflict with the organization's desire for coordination.

In terms of Thompson's model of technology, discussed in Chapter 9, the move from pooled to sequential to reciprocal task interdependence between people or subunits increases the degree to which the actions of one subunit directly affect the actions of others.[10] When task interdependence is high, conflict is likely to occur at the individual, functional, and divisional levels. If it were not for interdependence, there would be no potential for conflict to occur among organizational subunits or stakeholders.[11]

DIFFERENCES IN GOALS AND PRIORITIES Differences in subunit orientation affect the way each function or division views the world and cause each subunit to pursue different goals that are often inconsistent or incompatible. Once goals become incompatible, the potential for conflict arises because the goals of one subunit may thwart the ability of another to achieve its goals. As we discussed in Chapter 12, top managers often have different goals and priorities that may cause conflict in the decision-making process.

BUREAUCRATIC FACTORS The way in which task relationships develop in organizations can also be a potential source of conflict. Over time, conflict can occur because of status inconsistencies between different groups in the organization's bureaucracy. A classic type of bureaucratic conflict occurs between staff and line functions.[12] A *line function* is directly involved in the production of the organization's products. In a manufacturing company, manufacturing is the line function; in a hospital, doctors are the line function; and in a university, professors are the line function. *Staff functions* advise and support the line function and include functions such as R&D, accounting, and purchasing. In many organizations, people in line functions come to view themselves as *the* critical organizational resource and people in staff functions as secondary players. Acting on this belief, the line function constantly uses its supposedly lofty status as the producer of goods and services to justify putting its interests ahead of the other functions' interests. The result is conflict.[13]

INCOMPATIBLE PERFORMANCE CRITERIA Sometimes conflict arises between subunits not because their goals are incompatible but because the organization's way of monitoring, evaluating, and rewarding different subunits brings them into conflict. Production and sales can come into conflict when, to achieve the goal of increased sales, the sales department asks manufacturing to respond quickly to customer orders—an action that raises manufacturing costs. If the organization's reward system benefits sales personnel (who get higher bonuses because of increased sales), but penalizes manufacturing (which gets no bonus because of higher costs), conflict will arise.

The way an organization designs its structure to coordinate subunits can affect the potential for conflict. The constant conflict between divisions at CS First Boston, a U.S. investment bank, shows how incompatible reward systems can produce conflict. CS First Boston was formed by the merger of two smaller banks: First Boston (based in New York) and Crédit Suisse (based in London). From the beginning, the two divisions of the new bank were at odds. Although the merger was formed to take advantage of synergies in the growing transatlantic investment banking business, the divisions could never cooperate with one another, and managers in both were fond of openly criticizing the banking practices of their peers to anybody who would listen.

As long as the performance of one unit of the bank did not affect the other, the lack of cooperation between them was tolerated. When the poor performance of the European unit began to affect the American unit, however, conflict started to build. First Boston made record profits from issuing and trading debt securities, and its managers were expecting hefty bonuses. However, those bonuses were not paid. Why? The London arm of the organization had incurred huge losses, and although the losses were not the fault of the Boston-based bank, the company's top managers decided not to pay bonuses to their U.S. employees because of the losses from Europe.

As you can imagine, this inequitable decision, punishing U.S. employees for an outcome that they could not control, led to considerable conflict within the organization. Relations between the U.S. and European arms of the bank became even more strained; the divisions began fighting with top management. And, when employees decided that the situation would not change in the near term, they began to leave CS First Boston in droves. Many senior managers left for competitors, such as Merrill Lynch and Goldman Sachs.[14] Clearly, redesigning the reward system so it does not promote conflict between divisions should be one of a company's management's major priorities.

COMPETITION FOR SCARCE RESOURCES Conflict would never be a problem if there was always an abundance of resources for subunits to use. When resources are scarce, as they always are, choices about resource allocation have to be made, and subunits have to compete for their share.[15] Divisions fight to increase their share of funding because the more funds they can obtain and invest, the faster they can grow. Similarly, at the functional level there can be conflict over the amount of funds to allocate to sales, or to manufacturing, or to R&D to meet organizational objectives. Thus, to increase access to resources, functions promote their interests and importance often at one another's expense.

Together, these five factors have the potential to cause a significant level of conflict in an organization. At stage 1, however, the conflict is latent. The potential for conflict exists, but conflict has not yet surfaced. In complex organizations with high levels of differentiation and integration, the potential for conflict is especially great. The subunits are highly interdependent and have different goals and complicated reward systems, and the competition among them for organizational resources is intense. Managing organizational conflict to allocate resources to where they can produce the most value in the long run is very difficult.

Stage 2: Perceived Conflict

The second stage of Pondy's model, *perceived conflict*, begins when a subunit or stakeholder group perceives that its goals are being thwarted by the actions of another group. In this stage, each subunit begins to define why the conflict is emerging and to analyze the events that have led up to it. Each group searches for the origin of the conflict and constructs a scenario that accounts for the problems it is experiencing with other subunits. The manufacturing function, for example, may suddenly realize that the cause of many of its production problems is defective inputs. When production managers investigate, they discover that materials management always buys inputs from the lowest-cost sources of supply and makes no attempt to develop the kind of long-term relationships with suppliers that can raise the quality and reliability of inputs. Materials management reduces input costs and improves this function's bottom line, but it raises manufacturing costs and worsens that function's bottom line. Not surprisingly, manufacturing perceives materials management as thwarting its goals and interests.

Normally at this point the conflict escalates as the different subunits or stakeholders start to battle over the cause of the problem. To get materials management to change its purchasing practices, manufacturing complains about materials management to the CEO and whoever else will listen. Materials management is likely to dispute the charge that its purchase of low-cost inputs leads to inferior quality. Instead, it attributes the problem to manufacturing's failure to provide employees with sufficient training to operate new technology and dumps responsibility for the quality problems back in manufacturing's lap. Even though both functions share the goal of superior product quality, they attribute the poor quality to very different causes.

Stage 3: Felt Conflict

At the *felt conflict* stage, subunits in conflict quickly develop an emotional response toward one another. Typically, each subunit closes ranks and develops a polarized us-versus-them mentality that puts the blame for the conflict squarely on the other subunit. As conflict escalates, cooperation between subunits falls, and so does organizational effectiveness. It is difficult to speed new product development, for example, if R&D, materials management, and manufacturing are fighting over quality and final product specifications.

As the different subunits in conflict battle and argue their point of view, the conflict escalates. The original problem may be relatively minor, but if nothing is done to solve it, the small problem will escalate into a huge conflict that becomes increasingly difficult to manage. If the conflict is not resolved now, it quickly reaches the next stage.

Stage 4: Manifest Conflict

In the *manifest conflict* stage of Pondy's model, one subunit gets back at another subunit by attempting to thwart its goals. Manifest conflict can take many forms. Open aggression between people and groups is common. There are many stories and myths in organizations about boardroom fights in which managers actually come to blows as they seek to promote their interests. Infighting in the top-management team is very common as managers seek to promote their own careers at the expense of others. When Lee Iacocca was at Ford, for example, and Henry Ford II decided to bring in the head of GM as the new Ford CEO, Iacocca engineered his downfall within one year to promote his own rise to the top. Eventually, Iacocca lost the battle when Henry Ford forced Iacocca out because he feared Iacocca would usurp his power. A very different situation to that occurred in 2006 when Ford's then CEO, William Clay Ford, decided he could not solve the conflict between Ford's top managers and recruited Alan Mulally to become its new CEO—and he has orchestrated a dramatic turnaround in the company's performance.

A very effective form of manifest conflict is passive aggression—frustrating the goals of the opposition by doing nothing. Suppose there is a history of conflict between sales and production. One day, sales desperately needs a rush order for an important client. What might the manager of production do? One strategy is to agree informally to the sales department's request but then do nothing. When the head of sales comes banging on the door, the production manager says innocently, "Oh, you meant last Friday. I thought you meant *this* Friday." Organizational Insight 14.2 illustrates the damaging effects of manifest conflict between a company and its suppliers.

Organizational Insight 14.2

Manifest Conflict Erupts between eBay and Its Sellers

goldenangel/Shutterstock.com

Since its founding in 1995, eBay has always cultivated good relationships with the millions of sellers that advertise their goods for sale on its website. Over time, however, to increase its revenues and profits, eBay has steadily increased the fees it charges sellers to list their products on its sites, to insert photographs, to use its PayPal online payment service, and so on. Although this caused some grumbling among sellers because it reduced their profit margins, eBay increasingly engaged in extensive advertising that attracted millions more buyers to use its website, so sellers received better prices and thus their total profits also increased. As a result they remained largely satisfied with eBay's fee structure.

This all changed when a new CEO, John Donahoe, took over from eBay's long-time CEO, Meg Whitman, who had built the company into a dot-com giant. By 2008, eBay's revenues and profits had not increased fast enough to keep its investors happy and its stock price had plunged. To increase performance, one of Donohue's first moves was to announce a major overhaul of eBay's fee structure and feedback policy.[16] eBay's new fee structure would reduce upfront listing costs but increase back-end commissions on completed sales and payments. For small sellers who already had thin profit margins, these fee hikes were painful. In addition, in the future, eBay announced, it would block sellers from leaving negative feedback about buyers—feedback such as buyers didn't pay for the goods they purchased or took too long to do so. The feedback system that eBay had originally developed has been a major source of its success because it allows buyers to know they are dealing with reputable sellers and vice versa. All sellers and buyers have feedback scores that provide them with a reputation as good—or bad—people to do business with, and hence these scores reduce the risks involved in online transactions. Donohue claimed this change was to improve the buyer's experience because many buyers had complained that if they left negative feedback for a seller, the seller would then leave negative feedback for the buyer.

Together, however, throughout 2009 these changes resulted in a blaze of conflict between eBay and its millions of sellers who perceived they were being harmed by these changes, that they had lost their prestige and standing at eBay, and their bad feelings resulted in a revolt. Blogs and forums across the Internet were filled with messages expressing felt conflict, claiming that eBay had abandoned its smaller sellers and was pushing them out of business in favor of high-volume "powersellers" who contributed more to eBay's profits. eBay and Donohue received millions of hostile emails, and sellers threatened to move their business elsewhere, such as onto Amazon.com and Yahoo!, which were both trying to break into eBay's market. Sellers even organized a one-week boycott of eBay during which they expressed their dismay and hostility.by listing no items with the company. Many sellers did shut down their eBay online storefronts and move to Amazon.com, which claimed in 2011 that its network of sites had overtaken eBay in monthly unique viewers or "hits" for the first time.

The bottom line was that the level of perceived and felt conflict between eBay and its buyers had dramatically escalated and eBay's reputation with sellers was suffering. One survey found that while over 50% of buyers thought Amazon.com was an excellent sales channel, only 23% regarded eBay as being excellent. In essence, the bitter feelings produced by the changes that eBay had made were likely to result in increasing long-run conflict that would hurt its future performance. Realizing his changes had backfired, Donohue reversed course and eliminated several of eBay's fee increases and revamped its feedback system so that buyers and sellers can now respond to one another's comments in a fairer way.

These moves did improve and smooth over the bad feeling between sellers and eBay, but the old "community relationship" it had enjoyed with buyers in its early years largely disappeared. As this example suggests, finding ways to avoid conflict—such by testing the waters in advance and asking sellers for their reactions to fee and feedback changes—could have avoided many of the problems that arose. By 2010, eBay's turnaround plan was showing signs of success as its sales and profits increased—but Amazon.com had become the online retail portal of choice.

In general, as the example of eBay suggests, once conflict is manifest, organizational effectiveness suffers because coordination and integration between managers and subunits break down. Managers need to do all they can to prevent conflict from reaching the manifest stage, for two reasons: because of the breakdown in communication that is likely to occur and because of the aftermath of conflict.

Stage 5: Conflict Aftermath

Sooner or later, organizational conflict is resolved in some way, often by the decision of some senior manager. And sooner or later, if the sources of the conflict have not been resolved, the disputes and problems that caused the conflict arise again in another context. What happens when the conflict reappears depends on how it was resolved the first time. Suppose that sales comes to production with a new request. How are sales and production likely to behave? They probably will be combative and suspicious of each other and will find it hard to agree on anything. But suppose that sales and production had been able to solve their earlier dispute amicably and reached an agreement about the need to respond flexibly to the needs of important customers. The next time sales comes along with a special request, how is production likely to react? The production manager will probably have a cooperative attitude, and both parties will be able to sit down and work out a joint plan that suits the needs of both functions.

Every episode of conflict leaves a *conflict aftermath* that affects the way both parties perceive and react to future episodes. If a conflict is resolved before it gets to the manifest conflict stage, then the aftermath will promote good future working relationships. If conflict is not resolved until late in the process, or is not resolved at all, the aftermath will sour future working relationships, and the organizational culture is poisoned by permanently uncooperative relationships.

Managing Conflict: Conflict Resolution Strategies

Because organizational conflict can rapidly escalate and sour an organization's culture, managing organizational conflict is an important priority.[17] An organization must balance the need to have some "good" conflict (which overcomes inertia and allows new organizational learning) with the need to prevent "good" conflict from escalating into "bad conflict" (which causes a breakdown in coordination and integration between functions and divisions). In this section, we look at a few conflict resolution strategies designed to help organizations manage organizational conflict. Later in the chapter, we look at organizational politics as another way of managing organizational conflict when the stakes are high and when divisions and functions can obtain power to influence organizational outcomes, such as decisions about how to change or restructure an organization, in their favor.

The method an organization chooses to manage conflict depends on the source of the problem. Two common strategies managers use to resolve conflict involve: (1) changing an organization's structure to reduce or eliminate the cause of the conflict, or (2) trying to change the attitudes of individuals or replacing the individuals themselves.[18]

Acting at the Level of Structure

Because task interdependence and differences in goals are two major sources of conflict, altering the level of differentiation and integration to change task relationships is one way to resolve conflict. An organization might change from a functional structure to a product division structure to remove a source of conflict between manufacturing managers who are unable to control the overhead costs associated with different kinds of products. Moving to a product structure makes it much easier to assign overhead costs to different product lines. Similarly, if product managers are finding it difficult to convince departments to cooperate to speed product development, the move to a product team structure, in which different functional managers are assigned permanently to a product line, will remove the source of the problem.

If divisions are battling over resources, corporate managers can increase the number of integrating roles in the organization and assign top managers the responsibility for solving conflicts between divisions and for improving the structure of working relationships.[19] In general, increasing the level of integration is one major way in which organizations can manage the problem of differences in subunit goals. To resolve potential conflict situations, organizations can increase their use of liaison roles, task forces, teams, and integrating mechanisms (see Figure 4.5).

Another way to manage conflict is to make sure the design of an organization's hierarchy of authority is in line with its current needs. As an organization grows and differentiates, the chain of command lengthens, and the organization is likely to lose control of its hierarchy. This loss of control can be a major source of conflict because people have the responsibility to make decisions but lack the authority to do so because a manager above them must sign off on every move they make. Flattening the hierarchy, so that authority relationships are clearly defined, and decentralizing authority can remove a major source of organizational conflict. One source of such conflict occurs when two or more people, departments, or divisions compete for the same set of resources. This situation is likely to be disastrous because decision making is impossible when different people claim the right to control the same resources. For this reason, the military and some other organizations have established very clear lines of authority; there is no ambiguity about who reports to whom and who has control of what resources.

Good organizational design should result in the creation of an organizational structure that minimizes the potential for organizational conflict. However, because of inertia, many organizations fail to manage their structures and change them to suit the needs of a changing environment. As a result, conflict increases and organizational effectiveness falls.

Acting at the Level of Attitudes and Individuals

Differences in goals and in beliefs about the best way to achieve organizational goals are inevitable because of differences between functions and divisions. One way to harness conflict between subunits and prevent the polarization of attitudes that results during the stage of felt conflict in Pondy's model is to set up a procedural system that allows parties in conflict to air their grievances and hear other groups' points of view. Committees or teams, for example, can provide a forum in which subunits in dispute can meet face to face and negotiate directly with one another. In this way, subunits can clarify the assumptions they are using to frame the problem, and they can develop an understanding of one another's motives. Very often the use of a procedural system reveals that the issue in dispute is much smaller than was previously thought and that the positions of the parties are more similar than anyone had realized.

A procedural system is especially important in managing industrial conflicts between managers and unions. When a union exists, formal procedures govern the resolution of disputes to ensure the issue receives a fair hearing. Indeed, an important component of bargaining in labor disputes is *attitudinal structuring*—a process designed to influence the attitudes of the opposing party and to encourage the perception that both parties are on the same side and want to solve a dispute amicably.[20] Thus strikes become the last resort in a long process of negotiation.

An organization often engages a *third-party negotiator* to moderate a dispute between subunits or stakeholders.[21] The third-party negotiator can be a senior manager who occupies an integrating role or an outside consultant employed because of expertise in solving organizational disputes. The negotiator's role is to prevent the polarization of attitudes that occurs during the felt-conflict stage and thus prevent the escalation to manifest conflict. Negotiators are skilled in managing organizational conflict so as to allow new learning to take place. Often, the negotiator supports the weaker party in the dispute to make sure that both sides of the argument get heard.

Another way of managing conflict through attitude change is by the exchange and rotation of people between subunits to encourage groups to learn each others' points of view. This practice is widespread in Japan. Japanese organizations continually rotate people from function to function so they can understand the problems and issues facing the organization as a whole.[22]

When attitudes are difficult to change because they have developed over a long period of time, the only way to resolve a conflict may be to change the people involved. This can be done by permanently transferring employees to other parts of the organization, promoting them, or firing them. We have already seen that top-management teams are often replaced to overcome inertia and change organizational attitudes. Analysts attribute a large part of the conflict at CS First Boston to the attitudes of a few key top managers who had to be removed.

An organization's CEO is an important influence on attitudes in a conflict. The CEO personifies the values and culture of the organization, and the way the CEO acts affects the attitudes of other managers directly. As head of the organization, the CEO also has the ultimate power to resolve conflict between subunits. A strong CEO actively

Managerial Implications

Conflict

1. Analyze the organizational structure to identify potential sources of conflict.
2. Change or redesign the organizational structure to eliminate the potential for conflict whenever possible.
3. If conflict cannot be eliminated, be prepared to intervene quickly and early in the conflict to find a solution.
4. Choose a way of managing the conflict that matches the source of the conflict.
5. Always try to achieve a good conflict aftermath so that cooperative attitudes can be maintained in the organization over time.

manages organizational conflict and opens up a debate, allowing each group to express its views. The strong CEO can then use his or her power to build a consensus for a resolution and decision and can motivate subunits to cooperate to achieve organizational goals. In contrast, a weak CEO can actually increase organizational conflict. When a CEO fails to manage the bargaining and negotiation process between subunits, the strongest subunits (those with the most power) are encouraged or allowed to fight for their goals at the expense of other subunits. A weak CEO produces a power vacuum at the top of the organization, enabling the strongest members of the organization to compete for control. As consensus is lost and infighting becomes the order of the day, conflict becomes destructive.

What Is Organizational Power?

The presence of a strong CEO is important in managing organizational conflict. Indeed, the relative power of the CEO, the board of directors, and other top managers is important in understanding how and why organizations change and restructure themselves and why this benefits some people and subunits more than others. To understand how and why organizational conflict is resolved in favor of different subunits and stakeholders, we need to look closely at the issue of power.

What is power, and what is its role in organizational conflict? According to most researchers, **organizational power** is the mechanism through which conflict gets resolved. It can be defined as the ability of one person or group to overcome resistance by others to achieve a desired objective or result.[23] More specifically, organizational power is the ability of A to cause B to do something that B would not otherwise have done.[24] Thus, when power is used to resolve conflict, the element of coercion exists. Actors with power can bring about outcomes they desire over the opposition of other actors.

Organizational power The ability of one person or group to overcome resistance by others to resolve conflict and achieve a desired objective or result.

The possession of power is an important determinant of the kind of decisions that will be selected to resolve a conflict—for example, decisions about how to allocate resources or assign responsibility between managers and subunits.[25] When decisions are made through bargaining between organizational coalitions, the relative power of the various coalitions to influence decision making determines how conflicts get resolved and which subunits will benefit or suffer.

Thus conflict and power are intimately related. Conflict arises because although different managers or subunits must cooperate to achieve organizational goals, at the same time they are in competition for organizational resources and have different goals and priorities. When a situation arises that causes these groups to fight for resources or they strive to pursue their own interests, conflict emerges. When the issue is sufficiently important, individuals and groups use their power to influence decision making and obtain outcomes that favor them.

Sources of Organizational Power

If people, functions, and divisions engage in activities to gain power within an organization, where do they get it from? What gives one person or group the power to influence, shape, or control the behavior of others? To answer these questions, we must recognize the sources of power in an organization. Figure 14.4 identifies seven of them; we examine them next.

Authority

Authority, power that is legitimized by the legal and cultural foundations on which an organization is based, is the ultimate source of power in an organization.[26] The power of the president of the United States, for example, is based on the U.S. Constitution, which specifies the rights and obligations of the president and the conditions under which that person can seek or be removed from office. In a similar way, authority in an organization derives from the organization's legal charter, which allows shareholders, through the board of directors, to grant a CEO the formal power, or authority, to use organizational resources to create value for shareholders. In turn, the CEO has the right to grant authority to other top managers in the organization, and they have the right to confer it on their subordinates.

People who join an organization accept the legal right of the organization to control their behavior. In exercising authority, a manager exercises a legal right to control resources, including human resources. The way in which authority is distributed depends on the organizational setting. As discussed in Chapter 5, in organizations that are centralized, authority is retained by top managers. In organizations that are decentralized, authority is delegated to those lower in the hierarchy, who are then held responsible for the way they use organizational resources. When authority is centralized, there is generally less scope for people to engage in behaviors aimed at gaining power. Because top managers keep power among themselves, it is difficult for coalitions to form.

In such centralized organizations, however, a culture often develops in which people become afraid to take responsibility for decisions or to initiate new action for fear they will overstep their authority and be censured by top management. Instead, subordinates compete to ingratiate themselves with top managers in the hope of receiving favor. Thus the effectiveness of decision making in a centralized organization is reduced if managers surround themselves with yes people, and few important decisions get made. However, sometimes a subordinate who is active or competitive can indirectly take away a superior's authority by gradually assuming more and more of the supervisor's duties and responsibilities. The result, over time, is that even though the superior has legitimate authority, the subordinate has the real power. Superiors who are aware that this indirect seizure of authority can happen may take steps to prevent it. They may make a point of exercising their authority to show

Figure 14.4 Sources of Organizational Power

All functions and divisions gain power from one or more of these sources.

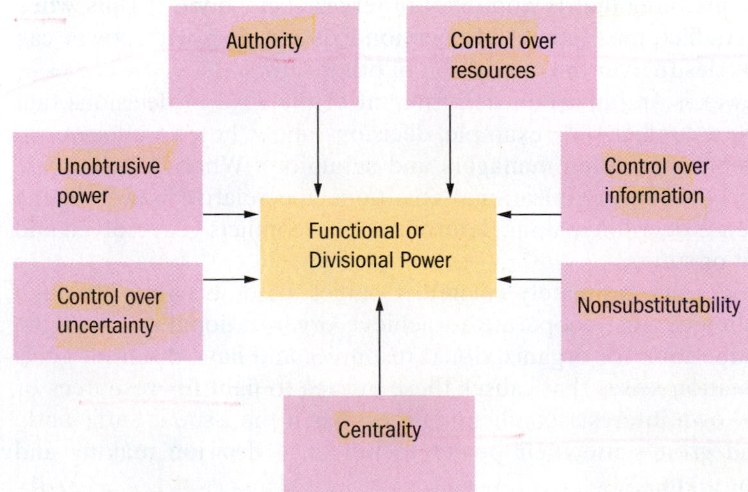

subordinates that they possess it, or they may insist on the display of certain rituals or symbols of their power—such as a big office and a personal secretary.

One of the classic ways in which superiors hold on to power is by restricting the information they give to subordinates to make a decision. If a manager gives out too much information, the subordinate will know as much as the manager does, and power over the subordinate will be lost. As a result of this fear, managers hoard information and do not share it with subordinates. However, if managers withhold too much and subordinates cannot make decisions, managers are likely to become overburdened, and the quality of decision making in the organization declines.

Managers have to realize there is a difference between the decentralization of authority and the loss of authority: Decentralizing authority to a subordinate does not necessarily reduce a manager's authority because the manager continues to bear the responsibility for whatever decisions the subordinate makes. Thus, when subordinates make decisions that have important consequences, the responsibility and authority of the superior also increase. If subordinates fail, however, the manager also bears the consequences. If the failure is big enough, the decision to decentralize can result in the loss of power—that is, the loss of the official position that carries the authority in the organization.

As noted elsewhere, *empowerment* is the deliberate decentralization of authority to encourage subordinates to assume responsibility for organizational activities.[27] The goal of empowerment is to give subordinates wide latitude to make decisions and thus motivate them to make the best use of their skills to create value. In an organization that decentralizes authority and empowers employees, all organizational members can gain authority as the organization prospers and attracts more resources. Employees who assume more authority and responsibility often demand more rights from the organization, such as higher salaries, increased job security, or bonuses tied to organizational performance.

Empowerment is also important at the corporate-divisional level. As we have seen, in some organizations the corporate center is reluctant to delegate authority to the divisional level and prefers to centralize decision making. The problem with this choice is that divisional managers become afraid to experiment and to initiate new action even though they are close to a problem and have more information and knowledge about it than corporate managers have. Thus divisions become unable to devise strategies that allow them to capitalize on opportunities in the environment, and both divisional and organizational performance suffer. For this reason, most CEOs deliberately empower divisional managers and make them responsible for their divisions' ultimate success in the marketplace. It is impossible to manage large complex companies unless managers at the divisional level and below have the authority and responsibility to innovate and make decisions. In most large companies the primary role of corporate managers is to make resource allocation decisions that maximize the amount of value the whole organization can create, and then monitor the performance of each division to ensure they make the best use of the resources they have been allocated.

Control over Resources

Power is not a fixed quantity. Managers who make decisions and perform actions that benefit the organization, such as making changes that raise performance, can increase their power. Just as an organization's power grows if it is able to obtain control of more and more resources in its environment, so power within an organization comes from the ability to control resources.[28] To survive, organizations require resources such as capital, human skills, raw materials, and customers. If a resource is particularly critical for an organization, the manager or subunit that has control over that resource has a good deal of power. At a company like Merck, for example, the R&D skills and knowledge necessary to develop new drugs are a critical resource. Given this fact, who has the most power at Merck? The answer is senior scientists because they possess the knowledge on which the success of the organization depends. Similarly, at companies that rely heavily on the success of their marketing efforts, like Coca-Cola or McDonald's, the marketing department has considerable power because it is the department that can attract customers—the critical scarce resource.

In a way, money or capital is the ultimate organizational resource because money buys other resources. This explains the ultimate power of top managers; legally they control the way the organization allocates its money and financial resources. Just as the ability to allocate financial resources is a major source of power, so too is the ability to *generate* financial resources.[29] The power of top managers at Merck rests in their ability to allocate R&D funds to various projects. Its scientists, however, are the people who invent the drugs that generate the company's future revenues on which its future success depends, and so their ability to generate resources gives them supreme power in the organization. In a multidivisional company, the product divisions that generate the most customer revenues have the most power. In a university setting, the most powerful departments are ones like engineering, chemistry, and agriculture because they generate millions of dollars in sponsored research. At many schools, athletics programs and alumni groups have considerable power because of their ability to generate revenues.

Control over Information

Information is also a very important and scarce organizational resource. Access to strategic information and the control of the information flow to, from, and between subunits are sources of considerable power in organizational decision making.[30] It is possible to shape the views of other people or subunits by carefully tailoring the information they receive. Andrew Pettigrew, in a study of the decision to buy a certain kind of computer system at a department store, showed how Jim Kenny, the head of management services, was able to influence the behavior of other senior managers by controlling the flow of information to them. Kenny was able to act as a "gatekeeper." Pettigrew observed, "By sitting at the junction of the communications channels between his subordinates, the manufacturers, and the board, Kenny was able to exert biases in favor of his own demands and at the same time feed the board negative information about the demands of his opponents."[31] Even in the face of strong opposition by other managers, Kenny was able to push through changes that resolved the conflict in his favor because he controlled the information used to evaluate alternatives. In conflict situations, top managers may deliberately manipulate other managers by supplying them with information that causes them to make bad decisions. In any future contest for power in the organization, these managers then lose out to managers with better performance records.[32]

The control of information is the source of the power of many people or subunits in specialized roles.[33] The power of doctors in a hospital or mechanics in a garage stems from their ability to control specific knowledge and information. People who consult an expert have to take that person's word on trust or else get a second opinion. Similarly, functions may have power because they control the information and knowledge necessary to solve organizational problems. Researcher Michael Crozier found that maintenance engineers in the French tobacco-processing plants he was investigating enjoyed an inordinate amount of power despite their low status in the organizational hierarchy.[34] The reason for their power was that the company's performance depended on the smooth running of its routine mass production technology; the major performance threat was machine breakdown. The maintenance engineers were the only people who knew how to repair the machines, and they used their knowledge to develop a considerable power base in the organization. Moreover, they jealously guarded their knowledge, refusing to write down repair procedures or share them with others, realizing if they did so they would undermine the source of their own power.

All subunits possess some expert information and knowledge, but the functions or divisions that control critical information have the most. As a result, they are able to influence decision-making outcomes and bring about change that favors their interests, but there is no guarantee that such change will benefit the whole organization. This is the problem that arises when managers and subunits use their power to influence the organizational change process: how to ensure change will increase rather than reduce organizational performance.

Nonsubstitutability

If no one else can perform the tasks that a person or subunit performs, that person or subunit is nonsubstitutable. Only it can provide the resources that other subunits or the organization requires. The maintenance engineers at the French tobacco plant had made themselves nonsubstitutable: Only they could reduce the major uncertainty facing the plant—machine breakdown. As a result of their nonsubstitutability, they exerted considerable power.[35]

Centrality

As we saw earlier, Jim Kenny had power because he could control information flows and was central to the decision-making process. In his role as manager of information services, he controlled the information that could reduce the uncertainty other managers experienced about existing accounts or future orders. Similarly, the people and subunits that control the flow of resources through an organization's production system are most central and have the ability to reduce the uncertainty facing other subunits.[36] The way in which two judges were able to control information to their own advantage because of their centrality and use it to act in unethical and illegal ways is described in Organizational Insight 14.3.

Organizational Insight 14.3

How Judges Can Use Their Central Positions to Corrupt the Court System

David E Waid/Shutterstock.com

Court judges at the federal, state, or county level are expected to possess the highest ethical standards and abide by the rule of law; they are the top managers who are at the center of the court and legal system and possess tremendous authority over prosecuting and defending lawyers and their clients. Why should ordinary citizens believe that their individual rights will be upheld fairly and that they are protected by the legal system if they cannot trust powerful judges? Imagine then, the shock citizens of Luzerne County in the heart of Pennsylvania's struggling coal country experienced in 2009 when an FBI investigation revealed that two respected county judges, Mark Ciavarella and Michael Conahan, had conspired to use their power to control the prosecution and sentencing of juveniles for personal gain.[37]

The way these judges controlled the county's judicial organization for this unethical and illegal purpose was revealed when investigators found that the number of youths entering detention in Luzerne County was two to three times higher than in similar counties—and these teens were being jailed for trivial violations. A boy who shoplifted a $4 bottle of nutmeg was jailed, for example, and so was the boy with him, who was charged with conspiracy to shoplift because he was just physically present. A girl who created a MySpace page that taunted her school administrator was also incarcerated.

Judges Ciavarella and Conahan's plan to subvert the court's organization and control system worked as follows. At that time Conahan controlled the county court and its budget, and Ciavarella controlled sentencing in the juvenile court. As the top managers of the court system, they were largely unsupervised and at the center of the flow of information between the different officials involved in legal process, prosecutors, defense attorneys, prison officers, and so on. Over time, they worked together to shut down the old county-run juvenile detention center by refusing to send teens there and cutting off its funding. Meanwhile they started their own privately owned detention center built by the judges' corrupt associates, to replace the county facility. Then the judges contracted with the county to pay $58 million to use their detention center for 10 years. The judges admitted they took "at least" $2.6 million in payoffs from their private youth detention center and tried to hide this dishonest income by creating false income tax records.

Most of the teens sentenced were on trial for minor first offenses, and their time in court to defend themselves often lasted for only minutes. Most were unrepresented because their parents were told it was "unnecessary" to have a lawyer; as a consequence one boy remained locked up for over two years and another boy committed suicide while in jail. The Pennsylvania Supreme Court has expunged the records of over 2,000 youths who were sent into detention by Ciavarella because of his unethical behavior.

In 2009 these corrupt ex-justices agreed to a plea bargain, stating that they would spend seven years in jail and pay back millions of dollars.[38] This plea bargain collapsed when the presiding judge decided it was too lenient, and in spring 2011 they still faced 64 charges that could lead them to spend decades in jail as a result of the way they abused their powerful positions at the center of the court system. In fact, in August 2011 Ciavarella, then 61, was given a 28-year jail sentence—which effectively amounts to a life sentence—because he abused his authority to harm the lives of so many teens.

Often, an organization's strategy is a crucial determinant of which subunit is central in an organization. In a company like Coca-Cola, which is driven by marketing, other subunits—product development, manufacturing, sales—depend on the information collected by the marketing department. The marketing department is central because it supplies a resource that all the other functions need: knowledge about customers and their future needs. R&D is not central at Coca-Cola because it responds to the needs of other functions—for example, to the marketing function's decision that the company should release 19 new "freestyle" flavors in 2011 to mark its 125th anniversary. In a biotechnology company like Amgen, whose success depends on successful R&D that results in a pipeline of new drugs, R&D becomes the central function, and marketing shapes its behavior to suit the needs of R&D.

Control over Uncertainty

A subunit that can directly control and reduce the main sources of uncertainty or contingencies facing an organization has significant power.[39] The R&D function in a biotechnology organization is powerful because the major source of uncertainty is whether the organization can discover safe new drugs. In a hospital, doctors have power because only they have the ability to diagnose and treat patient problems, the main source of uncertainty for a hospital.

Over time, as the contingencies facing an organization change, the power of the subunits that can respond to them increases while the power of the subunits that find their services no longer so valuable falls.[40] In business organizations after World War II, for example, the main source of uncertainty was the need to manufacture products fast enough to meet the demand for consumer goods that had built up during the war years. Manufacturing became the most important subunit during the postwar period, and many CEOs came from the manufacturing department. Then, during the 1960s, when companies were able to produce more than enough to meet customer needs, the main contingency became the need to find ways to sell more of their products, and marketing rose in prominence. With the 1970s came recession and companies diversified to compete in new industries, so finance became the most powerful organizational function. Today, given the rapid pace of change, the power of subunits rises and falls as their ability to cope with specific organizational contingencies changes.

Unobtrusive Power: Controlling the Premises of Decision Making

Another important source of power stems from the power of the *dominant coalition*, the set of managers who form a "partnership" and use their combined power secretively to influence the decision-making process in ways that favor their interests. Using their combined power, in a conflict situation, the dominant coalition often prevails over powerful individual managers or weaker coalitions. So when managers of different subunits have similar goals and interests, they often join in a coalition to increase their power to achieve their goal. Acting in concert, the dominant coalition can often use its power subtly to control the premises behind decision making. This is called *unobtrusive power* because other managers are generally not aware that the coalition is shaping their perceptions or interpretations of a situation.[41]

The power of a coalition lies in its ability to control the assumptions, goals, norms, or values that managers use to judge alternative solutions to a problem. As a result of unobtrusive power, many alternatives that some parties in a conflict might like to evaluate are ruled out because they do not fit with the ruling coalition's interests. Thus, even before a particular problem or issue enters the decision-making process, the coalition in power has ensured that the decision eventually made to solve the problem will support its interests.

An example will clarify how unobtrusive power works. Managers can increase profits in two basic ways: by expanding sales revenues or by decreasing operating costs. If managers from sales, marketing, and R&D form the dominant coalition, then the option of investing resources in cost-cutting new technologies receives little attention. Decision making will focus on how the organization should invest its resources in increasing its sales force or marketing budget or R&D expenditures to increase sales. Conversely, if production, materials management, and accounting form the dominant coalition, decision making revolves around how to invest resources in new advanced materials and information technology to better monitor and reduce operating costs, alternatives such as hiring more salespeople will receive little consideration.

A specific coalition's ability to resolve conflict in its favor depends on its ability to control the balance of power in the organization. Organizational power is a dynamic concept, and organizational strategy can change quickly if the balance of power shifts from one coalition to another.[42]

Using Power: Organizational Politics

Given the many advantages that accrue to managers who use power to bring about change that resolves conflicts in their favor, it is not surprising that managers want to acquire as much power as they can and then use it to get what they want. **Organizational politics** comprises, in the words of Jeffrey Pfeffer, "activities taken within organizations to acquire, develop, and use power and other resources to obtain one's preferred outcomes in a situation in which there is uncertainty or disagreement about choices."[43] To manage the change process to get conflicts resolved in their favor, individuals, subunits, and coalitions often engage in political activity and behavior to enhance the power and influence they have. Even if organizational members or subunits have no personal desire to play politics, they still must understand how politics operates because sooner or later they will come up against a master player of the political game. In such situations, apolitical managers (those who do not engage in politics) get all the tedious assignments or the responsibility for projects that do little to enhance their career prospects. Astute political managers get the visible and important projects that bring them into contact with powerful managers and allow them to build their own power base, which they can use to enhance their chances of promotion.

Organizational politics Activities taken within organizations to acquire, develop, and use power and other resources to obtain one's preferred outcomes in a situation in which there is uncertainty or disagreement about choices.

Tactics for Playing Politics

To understand the political component of organizational life, we need to examine the tactics and strategies that individuals and subunits use to increase their chances of winning the political game. The reward for success is change that gives them a greater share of organizational resources—authority, money, status, and so on. Individuals and subunits can use many political tactics to obtain the power they need to achieve their goals and objectives.

BECOMING INDISPENSABLE One prime political tactic that an individual or subunit can use to increase power is to become indispensable to the organization. Indispensability can be achieved by an increase in nonsubstitutability or an increase in centrality.

BECOMING NONSUBSTITUTABLE Wily managers deliberately engage in behaviors and actions that make them nonsubstitutable.[44] They may develop specialized organizational skills, such as knowledge of computers, that allow them to solve problems for other managers. They may specialize in an area of increasing concern to the organization—such as international trade regulations, pollution control, or health and safety—so they eventually are in a position to control a crucial contingency facing the organization. Nonsubstitutable managers and subunits need to be called in to solve specific problems as they arise, and their ability to come up with solutions increases their status and prestige.

BECOMING CENTRAL Managers can also make themselves indispensable if they focus their efforts on becoming more central in the decision-making process. They may deliberately accept responsibilities that bring them into contact with many functions or with many managers so they can enhance their personal reputation and that of their function. By becoming central they may also enhance their ability to obtain information they can use to make themselves and their functions nonsubstitutable. By being able to reduce the uncertainty experienced by others—for example, by supplying critical information or by helping out on rush projects—they make others dependent on them. Then, in return for their help, they can request favors (such as access to privileged information) from other people and groups and feed this information to other managers, who in turn become obligated to them and who share even more information. Following this process, politically astute managers cultivate both people and information and build a personal network of contacts in an organization that they can use to pursue personal goals, such as promotion, and functional goals, such as increasing its share of scarce resources.

ASSOCIATING WITH POWERFUL MANAGERS Another way to obtain power is by attaching oneself to powerful managers who are clearly on their way to the top. By supporting a powerful manager and making oneself indispensable to that person, it is possible to rise up the organizational ladder with that person. Top managers often become mentors to aspiring lower-level managers because planning for the managerial succession is an important organizational task of top managers.[45] CEOs promote their friends, not their enemies. Managers who have taken the initiative to develop skills that make them stand out from the crowd and who are central and nonsubstitutable have the best chance of being selected as protégés by powerful managers who are seeking people to groom as their successors.

To identify the powerful people in an organization, it is necessary to develop skills in sensing who has power. A politically savvy manager figures out the key people to cultivate and the best ways to get their attention. Indicators of power include an individual's personal reputation and ability to (1) influence organizational decision-making outcomes, (2) control significant organizational resources, and (3) display symbols of prestige and status such as access to the corporate jet or limousine.[46]

A secondary way to form an attachment with powerful people is to take advantage of common ties such as graduation from the same school or university or similarity in socioeconomic background. Recall from Chapter 7 on organizational culture that top managers typically select as associates or successors other managers who are like themselves. They do so because they believe that shared norms and values are evidence of reliability or trustworthiness. Not surprisingly, then, it is not uncommon for managers to go to considerable lengths to look and behave like their superiors and to imitate or copy the habits or preferences of a senior person. Imitation has been called the sincerest form of flattery, and flattery is never wasted on those in power. The more powerful the person, the more he or she is likely to appreciate it.

BUILDING AND MANAGING COALITIONS Forming a coalition of managers around an issue that is important to them all is a political tactic managers can use to obtain the power needed to resolve a conflict in their favor. Coalitions are often built around a trade-off: A supports B on an issue of interest to B in return for B supporting A on an issue of interest to A. Coalitions can be built through many levels in an organization, between various functions or divisions, and between important external or internal stakeholders. It is very important, for example, for top-level managers to build personal relationships with powerful shareholders or with members of the board of directors. Many of the most intense political contests occur at this level because the stakes are so high. The CEO needs the support of the board in any contest with members of the top-management team. Without it, the CEO's days are numbered. At The Gap, Paul Pressler lost the support of the board once it was clear his efforts to turn around the declining clothing company had failed. Glen Murphy became its new CEO in 2009 and with the help of talented clothing designers had orchestrated a turnaround at the company by 2011.

Building alliances with important customers is another valuable tactic, as is developing long-term relationships with the officers of the banks and other financial institutions from which a company obtains its capital. The more external linkages top managers can develop, the more chips they have to put on the table when the political game gets rough. Similarly, the ability to forge inside alliances with the managers of the most important subunits provides aspiring top managers with a power base they can use to promote their personal agendas. In the game of organizational politics, having a lot of friends greatly enhances one's claim to power in the organization.

Skills in coalition building are important to success in organizational politics because the interests of parties to a coalition change frequently as the environment changes. To maintain agreement among coalition members requires skillful negotiation and management.

Cooptation is a particularly important tool in coalition management. Recall from Chapter 3 that cooptation is a strategy that allows one subunit to overcome the opposition of a second subunit by involving it in decision making and rewarding cooperation. Giving an opponent a place on an important committee or an important managerial role in solving organizational problems makes the opponent part of the coalition, with rights to share in the rewards from the outcome of the political decision-making process.

ABILITY TO MANIPULATE DECISION MAKING One of the most important political tactics a manager can use to influence the politics of decision making is to develop the personal ability to utilize power to manipulate decision making. Possessing and using power (as a result of increasing indispensability, associating with powerful people, and knowing how to build and manage coalitions) is only the first skill needed to play politics. Knowing how and when to use power effectively is equally important. As we saw earlier, the use of power to influence decision making is most effective when power is unobtrusive. If other managers and coalitions become aware that active manipulation is taking place, they are likely to oppose the interests of the coalition doing the manipulating—or at least to insist that any decisions made also favor their interests. This is the thought behind the notion that a person who uses power loses it: Once the opposition realizes a manager is using power to further personal interests, opponents start to lobby for their own interests and protect their claims to the resource at stake.

Two tactics for controlling the decision-making process so the use of power seems to be legitimate—that is, in the organization's interests and not manipulation in the pursuit of self-interest—are controlling the agenda and bringing in an outside expert.[47]

CONTROLLING THE AGENDA Managers and coalitions like to be on committees so they can control the agenda or business decisions of the committee. By controlling the agenda, they are able to control the issues and problems that important decision makers will consider—such as how and when to change an organization's strategy and structure. Thus a coalition of powerful managers can prevent consideration of any issue they do not support by not putting it on the agenda. In this way conflict remains either latent or in the felt stage because the opposition does not get the chance to air its view on problems or solutions. The ability to control the agenda is similar to the ability to control the premises of decision making. Both tactics limit the alternatives considered in the decision-making process.

BRINGING IN AN OUTSIDE EXPERT When a major conflict exists, such as when top managers must decide how to change or restructure an organization, all managers and coalitions know that individuals and groups are fighting for their interests and perhaps for their political survival. Every subunit manager wants the axe to fall on other subunits and wants to try to benefit from whatever change takes place. Self-interested managers and coalitions, knowing that their preferred solution will be perceived by other subunits as politically motivated, are eager to legitimize their position, and so they often bring in an outside expert who is considered neutral. Then the supposedly objective views of the expert are used to support the position of the coalition in power.

In some cases, however, the experts are not neutral at all but have been coached by the coalition in power and know exactly what the coalition's view is so they can develop a favorable scenario. When this scenario is presented to the groups in conflict, the "objectivity" of the expert's plan is used to sway decision making in favor of the coalition in power. The opposition is outgunned and accepts the inevitable.

In sum, individuals, managers, subunits, and coalitions can use many tactics to obtain power and play organizational politics. The success of attempts to influence and control decision making to resolve conflicts in a certain way depends on individuals' ability to learn the political ropes and hone their political skills.

The Costs and Benefits of Organizational Politics

Organizational politics is an integral part of decision making in an organization. Coalitions form to control the premises behind decision making, to lobby for their interests, to control the path of organizational change, and to resolve organizational conflict in their own favor. Because the stakes are high—the control of scarce resources like promotions and budgets—politics is a very active force in most organizations. When we look to see what changes an organization makes to its strategy or structure, we need to recognize the role that politics plays in these choices. It can improve the choices and decisions that an organization makes, but it can also produce problems and promote conflict if it is not managed skillfully. If, for example, different coalitions continually fight about resource allocation decisions, more time is likely to be spent in making decisions than in implementing the decisions that are made. As a result, organizational effectiveness suffers.

To manage organizational politics and gain its benefits, an organization must establish a balance of power in which alternative views and solutions can be offered and considered by all parties and dissenting views can be heard (see Figure 14.5). It is also important for the balance of power to shift over time, toward the party that can best manage the uncertainty and contingencies facing the organization. An organization that confers power on those who can promote the changes that will help it the most can take advantage of the political process to improve the quality of organizational decision making. By allowing managers to use their power to advance their future objectives, and to form coalitions that compete for support for their agendas, an organization can improve the quality of decision making by encouraging useful and productive debate about alternatives. Thus politics can improve organizational effectiveness if it results in change that allocates resources to where they can produce more value.

An organization's ability to obtain the benefits of politics depends on the assumption that power flows to those who can be of most help to the organization. This assumption means that unsuccessful managers lose power to successful managers and there is a constant movement of power in the organization as an individual's or a group's power ebbs and flows. Suppose, however, that the top-management team in power becomes entrenched and is able to defend its power and property rights against its opponents even though the performance of the organization is faltering. Suppose a top-management team has institutionalized its power by occupying all important roles on organizational committees and by carefully selecting supporters for top organizational roles. Suppose the CEO is also the chair of the board and so can dominate the board of directors. In this situation, top management can use its power to fend off shareholders' attempts to restructure the organization to make better use of organizational resources. Similarly, top management, far from encouraging dissent among promising middle managers, might deny them promotion or decision-making power. By doing this, top management encourages the departure of those who threaten top management's dominant position. In this situation, the power that the top-management team has obtained as a result of its ability to control the distribution of property rights threatens organizational performance and survival.[48] Power holders are notoriously reluctant to give up the positions that give them the right to allocate resources and enrich themselves. CEOs, in particular, rarely give up

Figure 14.5 Maintaining a Balance of Power

A. Power Balance. Decisions result from bargaining between subunits, which improves the quality of organizational decision making.

B. Power Imbalance. Decisions are made in the interests of one subunit. As a result, the quality of decision making may decline.

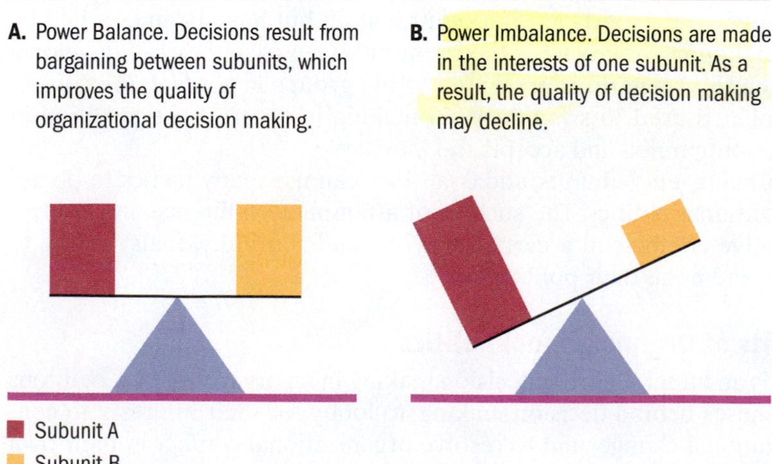

Organizational Insight 14.4

CIC's Managers Fight for Control

CIC Inc. was founded by two partners, David Hickson and Glenn S. Collins III, in College Station, Texas. Each founder took a 50–50 stake in the small business. CIC's strategy was to maintain and service high-tech equipment like CT scanners, X-rays, and lasers in hospitals and universities across the United States. Hickson's and Collins's new venture proved very successful, business increased very rapidly, and by 2000 the company had over 200 employees. CIC upgraded its service program so that all maintenance transactions could be handled electronically over the Internet using the company's in-house software programs. Since CIC's new Internet service could save hospitals up to 20% in maintenance costs, the savings would amount to millions of dollars a year. Hospitals flocked to join the program, and CIC's future looked bright indeed.

Imagine then what happened when Hickson, who had been on vacation with his family, returned to College Station to find that in his absence Collins had staged a coup. Hickson found he had been replaced as president by a CIC manager who was one of Collins's closest friends, that CIC managers and workers who were loyal to Hickson had been fired, and that all the keys and security codes to CIC buildings had been changed. Hickson immediately sought and obtained a legal restraining order from a judge that allowed him back into the company and that gave him the ability to reinstate fired employees. The judge also issued an order preventing the two men from taking any actions that were not part of their normal job duties.

Apparently this extraordinary situation had occurred because the two owners had quarreled bitterly about the future direction of the company and the personal relationship between them had deteriorated quickly. Since they were equal partners, neither had power over the other to resolve the conflict and so the conflict between them had grown worse over time. Different factions had formed in the organization, with some CIC managers giving their loyalty to Collins and others to Hickson.

In the months following this episode, it became clear that the two men would be unable to resolve the conflicts and problems between them. The only solution to the conflict seemed to be for one partner to buy out the other and they each searched for bank financing to buy the whole company. Finally, it was announced that Hickson had purchased Collins's share of CIC; however, the antagonism between the two men was not resolved.[49] After leaving CIC, Collins immediately announced that he would use the money from his share of CIC to start another company that would essentially provide the same kind of service as CIC!

their positions voluntarily, and sometimes will go any lengths to retain their power, as Organizational Insight 14.4 suggests.

When the balance of power between stakeholders or subunits does not force the allocation of resources to where they can best create value, organizational effectiveness suffers. When powerful managers can suppress the views of those who oppose their interests, debate becomes restricted, checks and balances fade, bad conflict increases, and organizational inertia increases. Today, after the increasing scandals in organizations such as Merrill Lynch, Johnson & Johnson, Goldman Sachs, and so on, there is increasing support for measures that would increase the power of stakeholders to remove inefficient top-management teams and CEOs who pay themselves exorbitant salaries that often are not tied to organizational performance. Thus, ultimately, whether power and politics benefit or harm an organization is a function of the balance of power among organizational stakeholders.

Managerial Implications

Power and Politics

1. Recognize that politics is a fact of organizational life, and develop the skills to understand how politics shapes organizational decision making.
2. Develop a personal power base to influence decision making, and use it to prevent political managers or groups from pursuing their interests at the expense of organizational interests.
3. To obtain power, try to associate with powerful managers and find a powerful mentor, make yourself central and nonsubstitutable, develop personal skills so you can reduce uncertainty for other subunits or for the organization, seek membership on committees that will give you access to information, and obtain control of organizational resources.
4. Seek to maintain a power balance between individuals or subunits in an organization to preserve the quality of organizational decision making.

Summary

Managing conflict, power, and politics is one of an organization's major priorities because these factors determine which decisions the organization makes and therefore, ultimately, its survival. Chapter 14 has made the following main points:

1. Organizational conflict is the clash that arises when the goal-directed behavior of one group blocks or thwarts the goals of another.
2. Conflict can be functional if it overcomes organizational inertia and brings about change. However, too high a level of conflict can reduce the level of coordination and integration between people and subunits and reduce organizational effectiveness.
3. The five stages of Pondy's model of organizational conflict are latent conflict, perceived conflict, felt conflict, manifest conflict, and the conflict aftermath.
4. The five sources of conflict between subunits are interdependence, differences in goals and priorities, bureaucratic factors, incompatible performance criteria, and competition for scarce resources.
5. Conflict resolution strategies are used to manage organizational conflict and to prevent it from becoming destructive. Two important strategies are acting at the level of structure to change task relationships and acting at the level of attitudes and individuals to change the attitudes of the parties or the parties themselves.
6. Organizational power is the ability of one actor or stakeholder to overcome resistance by other actors and achieve a desired objective or result.
7. The main sources of power available to managers and subunits are authority, control over resources, control over information, nonsubstitutability, centrality, control over uncertainty or contingencies, and unobtrusive power.
8. Organizational politics comprises activities carried out within organizations to acquire, develop, and use power and other resources to obtain one's preferred outcomes.
9. Tactics that individuals and subunits can use to play politics include increasing indispensability, associating with powerful managers, building and managing coalitions, controlling the agenda, and bringing in an outside expert.
10. Using power to play organizational politics can improve the quality of decision making if the people who have the power are those who can best serve the needs of the organization. However, if top managers have the ability to control and hoard power and entrench themselves in the organization, the interests of other organizational stakeholders may be jeopardized as decisions are made to serve top management's personal interests. Thus there needs to be a balance of power between organizational stakeholders.

Discussion Questions

1. Why and under what conditions can conflict be good or bad for an organization? Would you expect a higher level of conflict in a mechanistic or an organic structure? Why?
2. You have been appointed to manage a large R&D laboratory. You find a high level of conflict between scientists in the unit. Why might this conflict be arising? How will you try to resolve it?
3. Why is it important to maintain a balance of power between different groups of organizational stakeholders?
4. What is unobtrusive power? Why is it so important?
5. How can the design of the organization's structure and culture give some subunits more power than others?
6. Discuss how you, as manager of the R&D function in a cosmetic products company, might try to increase your power and the power of your subunit to control more resources in a battle with marketing and manufacturing.

Organizational Theory in Action

Practicing Organizational Theory

Managing Conflict

Form groups of three to five people and discuss the following scenario:

You are a group of top managers of a large well-established pharmaceutical company that has made its name by pioneering innovative new drugs. Intense competition from other companies in the pharmaceutical industry, plus increasing government pressure to reduce the price of drugs, has put pressure on you to find ways to reduce costs and speed product development. In addition, the emergence of large health maintenance organizations (HMOs) and other large buyers of drugs has made marketing drugs much more difficult, and marketing managers are demanding an increased say in which drugs should be developed and when. To respond to these pressures, you have decided to create cross-functional teams composed of people from R&D, marketing, finance, and top management to evaluate the potential of new drug products and to decide if they should be pursued.

1. How will the change in structure affect the relative power of the different functions?
2. How likely is conflict to occur because of these changes, and what will be the source of the conflict?
3. What can you do to help manage the conflict process to make the new operating system work as you hope it will?

The Ethical Dimension #14

The behavior of WorldCom's top managers and members of its board of directors is said to be quite common in many U.S. companies today. CEOs have considerable power to appoint board members, and the members of a company's compensation and stock option committee have wide latitude to reward the CEO and other top managers as they see fit.

1. Is it ethical for CEOs to be able to appoint the directors who will be evaluating their performance and determining their compensation?
2. What kinds of ethical rules should be developed to ensure that abuses of power and political plays such as those that occurred at WorldCom can be prevented in the future?

Making the Connection #14

Find an example of a conflict occurring between the managers, or between the managers and other stakeholders, of a company. What is the source of the conflict? How are managers using their power to influence the decision-making process?

Analyzing the Organization: Design Module #14

This module focuses on conflict, power, and politics in your organization.

Assignment

1. What do you think are the likely sources of conflict that may arise in your organization? Is there a history of conflict between managers or between stakeholders?
2. Analyze the sources of power of the principal subunits, functions, or divisions in the organization. Which is the most central subunit? Which is the most nonsubstitutable subunit? Which one controls the most resources? Which one handles the main contingencies facing the organization?
3. Which subunit is the most powerful? Identify any ways in which the subunit has been able to influence decision making in its favor.
4. To what degree are the organization's strategic and operational decisions affected by conflict and politics?

CASE FOR ANALYSIS

Politics at Walt Disney

In the early 2000s, Walt Disney CEO Michael Eisner came under increasing criticism for the company's falling performance and for the way that he had centralized decision making so that all important decisions affecting the company had to have his approval. He began to lose the support of the board of directors, especially of Roy Disney, who as a member of the founding family commanded a great deal of support. However, the majority of Disney's board of directors had been handpicked by Eisner, and he was able to control the agenda until the company began to incur major losses in the mid 2000s. Poor performance weakened Eisner's position, but so did his personal relationship with Steve Jobs, who was the CEO and major owner of Pixar, the company that had made most of Disney's recent blockbuster movies such as *Toy Story*, *Cars*, and so on.

After Jobs threatened to find a new distributor for Pixar's movies when its contract with Disney expired in 2007 because of the personal antagonism between himself and Eisner, Disney's board decided to act. Eisner was encouraged to become chair of Disney and to allow his handpicked successor, Bob Iger, assume control of the company as its CEO. Iger owed his rapid rise at Disney to his personal relationship with Eisner, who had been his mentor and loyal follower. Iger had always suggested new ways to improve Disney's performance but had never confronted Eisner—always a dangerous thing to do if a manager wants to become the next CEO!

Once Iger became CEO in 2006, pressure was applied to Eisner, who soon decided to resign as Disney's chair; then Iger negotiated the purchase of Pixar by Disney that resulted in Steve Jobs becoming its biggest stockholder. Disney was still performing poorly, but now that Iger was in total control and no longer under the influence of Michael Eisner, he adopted a plan to change the way Disney operated.

As COO of Disney under CEO Michael Eisner, Iger recognized that Disney was plagued by slow decision making that had led to many mistakes in putting its new strategies into action. Its Disney stores were losing money; its Internet properties were flops; and even its theme parks seemed to have lost their luster as few new rides or attractions were introduced. Iger believed one of the main reasons for Disney's declining performance was that it had become too tall and bureaucratic under Iger, and its top managers were following financial rules that did not lead to innovative strategies.

One of Iger's first moves to turn around Disney's performance was to dismantle its central "strategic planning office," which was composed of several levels of top managers who were responsible for sifting through all the new ideas and innovations sent up by Disney's different business divisions, for example, its theme parks, movies, and gaming divisions. After a lengthy decision-making process, they then decided which proposals should be presented to Eisner.

Iger saw the strategic planning office as a bureaucratic bottleneck that reduced the number of ideas coming from below; he dissolved the office, reassigned the best managers back to their different business units, and retired the rest.[50] The result of cutting out these unnecessary layers in Disney's hierarchy has been that more new ideas are generated by its different business units and the level of innovation has increased. Divisional managers are more willing to speak out and champion their ideas when they know they are dealing directly with CEO Iger and not with an office of bureaucrats concerned only with the bottom line.[51] Disney's performance has improved steadily under Iger; in 2010, it announced much improved revenues and profits and a new venture—Disney acquired Marvel, the company that owned the rights to such characters as Spider-Man, X-Men, and the Hulk—so many new kinds of rides and movies may be expected in the future.[52] In 2011, it announced new agreements with Apple and other companies such as Google and Amazon to stream its huge video library to customers online and to make them available for download using cloud computing so that users can access them using any mobile computing device.

Discussion Questions

1. What are the various sources of conflict and politics that have plagued Walt Disney in the past?
2. Discuss how Iger used different conflict resolution and political strategies to solve these conflicts to make better use the company's resources.

References

1 T. Burns, "Micropolitics: Mechanism of Institutional Change," *Administrative Science Quarterly* 6 (1961), 257–281.

2 J. G. March, "The Business Firm as a Coalition," *Journal of Politics* 24 (1962), 662–678.

3 L. Coser, *The Functions of Social Conflict* (New York: Free Press, 1956); S. P. Robbins, *Managing Organizational Conflict: A Non-Traditional Approach* (Englewood Cliffs, NJ: Prentice Hall, 1974).

4 J. McCann and J. R. Galbraith, "Interdepartmental Relationships," in P. C. Nystrom and W. H. Starbuck, eds., *Handbook of Organizational Design*, vol. 2 (New York: Oxford University Press, 1981), pp. 60–84.

5 A. C. Amason, "Distinguishing the Effects of Functional and Dysfunctional Conflict and Strategic Decision Making: Resolving a Paradox for Top Management Teams," *Academy of Management Review* 39 (1996), pp. 121–148.

6 www.pfizer.com, 2011.

7 Ibid.

8 The following discussion draws heavily on these sources: L. R. Pondy, "Organizational Conflict: Concepts and Models," *Administrative Science Quarterly* 2 (1967), pp. 296–320; and R. E. Walton and J. M. Dutton, "The Management of Interdepartmental Conflict: A Model and Review," *Administrative Science Quarterly* 14 (1969), 62–73.

9 J. D. Thompson, "Organizational Management of Conflict," *Administrative Science Quarterly* 4 (1960), 389–409; and K Thomas, "Conflict and Conflict Management," in M. D. Dunnette, ed., *The Handbook of Industrial and Organizational Psychology* (Chicago: Rand McNally, 1976).

10 J. D. Thompson, *Organizations in Action* (New York: McGraw-Hill, 1967).

11 J. A. Litterer, "Conflict in Organizations: A Reexamination," *Academy of Management Journal* 9 (1966), 178–186.

12 M. Dalton, "Conflicts Between Staff and Line Managerial Officers," *American Sociological Review* 15 (1950), 342–351.

13 P. R. Lawrence and J. R. Lorsch, *Organization and Environment* (Homewood, IL: Irwin, 1967).

14 "CS First Boston: All Together Now?" *The Economist*, April 10, 1993, p. 90.

15 Coser, *The Functions of Social Conflict*.

16 eBay.com, 2011.

17 R. H. Miles, *Macro Organizational Behavior* (Santa Monica, CA: Goodyear, 1980).

18 This discussion draws heavily on E. H. Nielsen, "Understanding and Managing Intergroup Conflict," in P. R. Lawrence, L. B. Barnes, and J. W. Lorsch, *Organizational Behavior and Administration* (Homewood, IL: Irwin, 1976).

19 Lawrence and Lorsch, *Organization and Environment*.

20 R. E. Walton and R. B. McKersie, *A Behavioral Theory of Labor Negotiations: An Analysis of a Social Interaction System* (New York: McGraw-Hill, 1965).

21 R. E. Walton, "Third-Party Roles in Interdepartmental Conflict," *Industrial Relations* 7 (1967), 29–43.

22 W. G. Ouchi, *Theory Z: How American Business Can Meet the Japanese Challenge* (Reading, MA: Addison-Wesley, 1981).

23 R. M. Emerson, "Power-Dependence Relations," *American Sociological Review* 27 (1962), 31–41; and J. Pfeffer, *Power in Organizations* (Boston: Pitman, 1981).

24 R. A. Dahl, "The Concept of Power," *Behavioral Science* 2 (1957), 210–215.

25 M. Gargiulo, "Two-Step Leverage: Managing Constraint in Organizational Politics," *Administrative Science Quarterly* 38 (1993), 1–19.

26 M. Weber, *The Theory of Social and Economic Organization* (New York: Free Press, 1947).

27 J. A. Conger and R. N. Kanungo, "The Empowerment Process: Integrating Theory and Practice," *Academy of Management Review* 13 (1988), 471–481.

28 G. R. Salancik and J. Pfeffer, "The Bases and Uses of Power in Organizational Decision Making," *Administrative Science Quarterly* 19 (1974), 453–473; J. Pfeffer and G. R. Salancik, *The External Control of Organizations: A Resource Dependence View* (New York: Harper & Row, 1978).

29 Salancik and Pfeffer, "The Bases and Uses of Power in Organizational Decision Making."

30 A. M. Pettigrew, "Information Control as a Power Resource," *Sociology* 6 (1972), 187–204.

31 A. M. Pettigrew, *The Politics of Organizational Decision Making* (London: Tavistock, 1973), p. 191.

32 C. Perrow, *Organizational Analysis: A Sociological View* (Belmont, CA: Wadsworth, 1970).

33 D. Mechanic, "Sources of Power of Lower-Level Participants in Complex Organizations," *Administrative Science Quarterly* 7 (1962), 349–364.

34 M. Crozier, *The Bureaucratic Phenomenon* (Chicago: University of Chicago Press, 1964).

35 D. J. Hickson, C. R. Hinings, C. A. Lee, R. E. Schneck, and J. M. Pennings, "A Strategic Contingencies Theory of Intraorganizational Power," *Administrative Science Quarterly* 16 (1971), 216–227.

36 Ibid.

37 D. Janoski, Conohan, Ciavarella Face New Charges, www.thetimestribune.com, September 10, 2009.

38 D. Janoski, Conohan, Ciavarella Deny New Charges, www.thetimestribune.com, September 15, 2009.

39 Ibid.

40 Pfeffer, *Power in Organizations*, Ch. 3.

41 S. Lukes, *Power: A Radical View* (London: MacMillan, 1974).

42 Pfeffer, *Power in Organizations*, pp. 115–121.

43 Ibid., p. 7.

44 Hickson, Hinings, Lee, Schneck, and Pennings, "A Strategic Contingencies Theory of Intraorganizational Power."

45 E. E. Jennings, *The Mobile Manager* (New York: McGraw-Hill, 1967).

46 J. R. P. French, Jr., and B. Raven, "The Bases of Social Power," in D. Cartwright and A. F. Zander, eds., *Group Dynamics* (Evanston, IL: Row Peterson, 1960), pp. 607–623.

47 This discussion draws heavily on J. Pfeffer, *Power in Organizations*, Ch. 5.

48 O. E. Williamson and W. G. Ouchi, "The Markets and Hierarchies Program of Research: Origins, Implications, Prospects," in A. E. Van De Ven and W. F. Joyce, eds., *New Perspectives on Organizational Design and Behavior* (New York: Wiley, 1981), pp. 347–406.

49 B. Fannin, "CIC Workers Ask Judge to Void Noncompliance Pact." *The Eagle*, October 23, 1997. p. 1.

50 J. McGregor, "The World's Most Innovative Companies," www.businessweek.com, May 4, 2007.

51 www.waltdisney, 2011.

52 Ibid.

Supplemental Case Map

Title	Source	Description
Continental Can Company of Canada, Ltd. • Vertical vs. horizontal differentiation • Standardization • Formal vs. informal organization	Harvard Business School # 478-017	Grouping and coordinating tasks; proper organizational design, core competences, and competitive advantage; types and uses of structures
Comcast New England: A Journey of Organizational Transformation	Harvard Business School # 908405-PDF-ENG	This case describes how Comcast's New England Region general manager transformed a low commitment and performance organization. The focus is on strategy, structure, and human resources.
Importance of Structure and Process to Strategy Implementation	Harvard Business School # BH114-PDF-ENG	The study shows how overall firm performance is influenced by how well a firm's business strategy is matched to its organizational structure and the behavioral norms of its employees.
Corning, Inc., Consumer Products Group	Darden # UV0360-PDF-ENG	Corning, Inc., is faced with a decision about what to do with one of its three business segments. The focus is on structure, core competences, and organizational flexibility in a mass production environment.
TRW Systems Group (A and B Condensed) • Organizational design choices • Power	Harvard Business School # 476-117	Using organizational theory concepts to analyze an organization; choices leading to organic structure; the contingency approach to management; cross-functional teams
Organization Design: Fashion or Fit?	Harvard Business School # 81106-PDF-ENG	The case relates organizational structure to situational variables and how to diagnose the problems of organizational design.
Dansk Designs Ltd.	Harvard Business School # 371288-PDF-ENG	Past growth and anticipated future expansion make organizational changes necessary to enter a new product era. Overseas operations, design changes, supplier relations, quality control, marketing strategy, and competition all have impact on the structure.
Texana Petroleum Corporation • Relationship between strategy and structure • Multidivisional structure	Harvard Business School # 413-056	Politics, conflicts; matching strategy and structure; advantages of multidivisional structure
Asea Brown Boveri (Condensed)	Harvard Business School # 199027-PDF-ENG	The case describes a restructuring of operations and a change in organizational cultures for competitive success.

(*Continued*)

Title	Source	Description
Three Roads to Innovation. Interactions among • People • Property rights • Structures • Ethics	Journal of Business Strategy. Sept/Oct 1990, pp. 18–21. Reprinted with permission of Faulkner & Gray, Inc., II Penn Plaza New York, NY 10001.	The case is an introductory one showing how promoting and maintaining a culture of innovation can result in rapid product development.
Reckitt Benckiser: Fast and Focused Innovation	Harvard Business School # 311116-PDF-ENG	The case discusses how a large consumer products goods company uses levers for innovation; high-performance culture; and high impact, grassroots product development.
Mars, Incorporated: Building an Innovation System	Harvard Business School # IMD703-PDF-ENG	The case addresses the following questions: What is innovation? How do you build a culture of innovation within the organization? How do you engage employees in the innovation agenda?
Applied Research Technologies, Inc.: Global Innovation's Challenges (Brief Case)	Harvard Business School # 4168-PDF-ENG	The case covers a company that has used best practices in creating a culture of institutionalized entrepreneurship and encouragement of innovation as an ongoing competitive advantage. Students are asked to consider the structures, systems, cultures, and management practices that allow for global innovation.
Leading Innovation at Kelvingrove (A)	Harvard Business School # UV3916-PDF-ENG	The case explores the leadership story of director Mark O'Neill as he oversees a major innovation initiative at Kelvingrove, Scotland's most visited museum. The "A" case describes his background, philosophy, and the actions he takes over a period of more than a decade to win the support of both staff and funders for the innovation.
Beijing EAPs Consulting Inc.	Harvard Business School # 909C05-PDF-ENG	Beijing EAPs Consulting Inc. (BEC) is a rapidly growing consulting company whose number of employees has increased from six to 16 in just one year. Collaboration between projects and department managers is not very smooth.
Merloni Group	Harvard Business School # 383152-PDF-ENG	The general manager of the recently established French subsidiary of an Italian appliance company is in conflict with headquarters. A change in organization structure is being debated.

Case Studies

CASE 1

United Products, Inc.

Jeffrey C. Shuman

Having just returned from lunch, George Brown, president of United Products, Inc., was sitting in his office thinking about his upcoming winter vacation—in a few days, he and his family would be leaving from Boston to spend three weeks skiing on Europe's finest slopes. His daydreaming was interrupted by a telephone call from Hank Stevens, UPI's general manager. Mr. Stevens wanted to know if their two o'clock meeting was still on. The meeting had been scheduled to review actions UPI could take in light of the company's sluggish sales and the currently depressed national economy. In addition, Brown and Stevens were to go over the financial results for the company's recently completed fiscal year—they had just been received from UPI's auditors. Although it had not been a bad year, results were not as good as expected, and this, in conjunction with the economic situation, had prompted Mr. Brown to reappraise the plans he had for the company for the upcoming year.

Company History

United Products, Inc., established in 1941, was engaged in the sales and service of basic supply items for shipping and receiving, production and packaging, research and development, and office and warehouse departments. Mr. Brown's father, the founder of the company, recognized the tax advantages in establishing separate businesses rather than trying to consolidate all of his operations in one large organization. Accordingly, over the years, the elder Mr. Brown had created new companies and either closed down or sold off older companies as business conditions seemed to warrant. As of the mid-1960s, his holdings consisted of a chain of four related sales distribution companies covering the geographic area from Chicago eastward.

In 1967, feeling it was time to step aside and turn over active control of the business to his sons, the elder Mr. Brown recapitalized and restructured his companies, merging some and disposing of others. When the restructuring process was completed, he had set up two major companies. United Products, Inc., was to be run by his youngest son, George Brown, with its headquarters in Massachusetts, while his other son, Richard Brown, was to operate United Products Southeast, Inc., headquartered in Florida.

Although the Brown brothers occasionally worked together and were on each other's board of directors, the two companies operated on their own. As George Brown explained, "Since we are brothers, we often get together and discuss business, but the two are separate companies and each files its own tax return."

During 1972, United Products moved into new facilities in Woburn, Massachusetts. From this location it was thought that the company would be able to serve its entire New England market area effectively. "Our abilities and our desires to expand and improve our overall operation will be enhanced in the new specially designed structure containing our offices, repair facilities, and warehouse," is how George Brown viewed the role of the new facilities. Concurrent with the move, the company segmented the more than 3,500 different items it carried into eight major product categories:

1. **Stapling machines.** Manual and powered wire stitchers, carton stitchers, nailers, hammers, and tackers
2. **Staples.** All sizes and types (steel, bronze, monel, stainless steel, aluminum, brass, etc.) to fit almost all makes of equipment
3. **Stenciling equipment and supplies.** Featuring Marsh hand and electric machines, stencil brushes, boards, and inks

Jeffrey C. Shuman, Ph.D., Associate Professor of Management, Bentley College, Waltham, MA. Reprinted with permission.

4. Gummed tape machines. Hand and electric, featuring Marsh, Derby, and Counterboy equipment
5. Industrial tapes. Specializing in strapping, masking, cellophane, electrical, cloth, nylon, and waterproof tapes made by 3M, Mystik, Behr Manning, and Dymo
6. Gluing machines. Hand and electric
7. Work gloves. All sizes and types (cotton, leather, neoprene, nylon, rubber, asbestos, and so on)
8. Marking and labeling equipment

In a flyer mailed to United Products' 6,000 accounts announcing the move to its new facilities, the company talked about its growth in this fashion:

> Here we grow again—thanks to you—our many long-time valued customers....
>
> Time and circumstances have decreed another United Products transPLANT—this time, to an unpolluted garden-type industrial area, ideally located for an ever-increasing list of our customers. Now, in the new 28,000-square-foot plant with enlarged offices and warehouse, we at UNITED PRODUCTS reach the peak of efficiency in offering our customers the combined benefits of maximum inventories, accelerated deliveries, and better repair services.

By 1974, the company had grown to a point where sales were $3.5 million (double that of four years earlier) and 34 people were employed. Results for 1973 compared to 1972 showed a sales increase of 22 percent and a 40 percent gain in profits. Exhibit 1 contains selected financial figures for 1971, 1972, and 1973, in addition to the fiscal 1973 balance sheet.

Competition

George Brown indicated that UPI does not have clearly defined rivals against whom it competes head on with respect to all of its 3,500-plus items:

> It is hard to get figures on competition, since we compete with no one company directly. Different distributors carry lines that compete with various of our product lines, but there is no one company that competes against us across our full range of products.

On a regular basis, Mr. Brown receives Dun & Bradstreet's Business Information Reports on specific firms with which he competes. Mr. Brown feels that since the rival firms are, like his own firm, privately held, the financial figures reported are easily manipulated and therefore are not a sound basis on which to devise strategies and plans. Exhibit 2 contains comparative financial figures for two competing companies, and Exhibit 3 contains D&B's description of their operations, along with D&B's comments about two other firms operating in UPI's New England market area.

Management Philosophy

When Mr. Brown took over UPI in 1967 at the age of 24, he set a personal goal of becoming financially secure and developing a highly profitable business. With the rapid growth of the company, he soon realized his goal of financial independence and in so doing began to lose interest in the company. "I became a rich person at age 28 and had

EXHIBIT 1 Selected Financial Information, United Products, Inc.

	11/30/71	11/30/72	11/30/73
Current assets	$ 862,783	$ 689,024	$ 937,793
Other assets	204,566	774,571	750,646
Current liabilities	381,465	223,004	342,939
Net worth	685,884	750,446	873,954
Sales	n.a.*	2,830,000	3,450,000

Statement of financial condition, November 30, 1973:

Cash on hand	$ 46,961	Accounts payable	$ 321,885
Accounts receivable	535,714	Notes payable	20,993
Merchandise in inventory	352,136		
Prepaid insurance, interest, taxes	2,980		
Current assets	$ 937,791	Current liabilities	$ 342,878
Fixtures and equipment	$ 42,891	Retained earnings	$ 471,655
Motor vehicles	49,037	Capital stock	519,800
Land and buildings	658,768	Surplus	354,154
Total assets	$ 1,688,487	Total liabilities	$ 1,688,487

*n.a.: Not available.

EXHIBIT 2 **Financial Information on Rival Firms**

East Coast Supply Co., Inc.—Sales $1 Million

	Fiscal December 31, 1971	Fiscal December 31, 1972	Fiscal December 31, 1973
Current assets	$ 88,555	$ 132,354	$ 163,953
Other assets	16,082	18,045	27,422
Current liabilities	41,472	47,606	74,582
Net worth	63,165	102,793	116,793

Statement of financial condition, December 31, 1973:

Cash	$ 42,948	Accounts payable	$ 39,195
Accounts receivable	86,123	Notes payable	27,588
Merchandise in inventory	34,882	Taxes	7,799
Current assets	$ 163,953	Current liabilities	$ 74,582
Fixtures and equipment	$ 15,211	Capital stock	$ 10,000
Deposits	12,211	Retained earnings	106,793
Total assets	$ 191,375	Total liabilities and net worth	191,375

Atlantic Paper Products, Inc.—Sales $6 Million

	June 30, 1970	June 30, 1971	June 30, 1972
Current assets	$ 884,746	$1,243,259	$1,484,450
Other assets	93,755	101,974	107,001
Current liabilities	574,855	520,572	1,120,036
Net worth	403,646	439,677	471,415
Long-term debt	0	384,984	

few friends with equal wealth who were my age. The business no longer presented a challenge and I was unhappy with the way things were going."

After taking a 10-month "mental vacation" from the business, George Brown felt he was ready to return to work. He had concluded that one way of proving himself to himself and satisfying his ego would be to make the company as profitable as possible. However, according to Mr. Brown, "The company can only grow at approximately 20 percent per year, since this is the amount of energy I am willing to commit to the business."

In 1974, at age 31, Mr. Brown described his philosophical outlook as "very conservative" and surmised that he ran UPI in much the same way as his 65-year-old father would have. In describing his managerial philosophy and some of the operating policies he had established, he said:

> I am very concerned about making UPI a nice place to work. I have to enjoy what I'm doing and have fun at it at the same time. I cannot make any more money, since I'm putting away as much money as I can. The government won't allow me to make more money, since I already take the maximum amount.
>
> I like to feel comfortable, and if we grow too quickly, it could get out of hand. I realize that the business won't grow to its potential, but why should I put more into it?... The company could grow, but why grow? Why is progress good? You have to pay for everything in life, and I'm not willing to work harder....
>
> Another thing... I am a scrupulously honest businessman, and it is very hard to grow large if you're honest. There are many deals that I could get into that would make UPI a lot of money, but I'm too moral a person to get involved....
>
> To me, happiness is being satisfied with what you have. I've got my wife, children, and health. Why risk these for something I don't need? I don't have the desire to make money, because I didn't come from a poor family; I'm not hungry.
>
> I have never liked the feeling of owing anything to anyone. If you can't afford to buy something, then don't. I don't like to borrow any money and I don't like the company to borrow any. All of our bills are paid within 15 days. I suppose I've constrained the business as a result of this feeling, but it's my business. The company can only afford to pay for a 20 percent growth rate, so that's all we'll grow.

EXHIBIT 3 Descriptions of Major Competitors

East Coast Supply Co., Inc.
Manufacturers and distributes pressure-sensitive tapes to industrial users throughout New England area on 1/10 net 30-day terms. Thirty-four employed including the officers, 33 here. Location: Rents 15,000 square feet on first floor of two-story building in good repair. Premises are orderly. Nonseasonal business. Branches are located at 80 Olife Street, New Haven, Connecticut, and 86 Weybosset Street, Providence, Rhode Island.
Atlantic Paper Products, Inc.
Wholesales paper products, pressure-sensitive tapes, paper specialties, twines, and other merchandise of this type. Sales to industrial accounts and commercial users on 1/10 net 30-day terms. There are about 1,000 accounts in eastern Massachusetts, and sales are fairly steady throughout the year. Employs 60, including officers. Location: Rents 130,000 square feet of floor space in a six-story brick, mill-type building in a commercial area on a principal street. Premises orderly.
The Johnson Sales Co.
Wholesales shipping room supplies, including staplings and packing devices, marking and stencil equipment. Sells to industrial and commercial accounts throughout the New England area. Seasons are steady. Terms are 1/10 net 30 days. Number of accounts not learned; 15 are employed including the owner. Location: Rents the first floor of a two-story yellow brick building in good condition. Housekeeping is good.
Big City Staple Corp.
Wholesales industrial staples, with sales to 2,000 industrial and commercial firms, on 1/10 net 30-day terms. Territory mainly New Jersey. Employs ten including the officers. Seasons steady and competition active. Location: Rents 5,000 square feet in one-story cinder block and brick structure in good condition; premises in neat order. Located on well-traveled street in a commercial area.

Organizational Structure

Upon returning to the company from his "mental vacation" in 1971, George Brown realigned UPI's organizational structure as shown in Exhibit 4. (The company does not have a formal organizational chart; this one is drawn from the case researcher's notes.) With respect to the way his company was organized, he remarked:

> We have to have it on a functional basis now. We are also trying something new for us by moving to the general manager concept. In the past when I was away, there was no one with complete authority; now my general manager is in charge in my absence.

In discussing the new structuring of the organization, Mr. Brown was quick to point out that the company had not established formalized job descriptions. "Job descriptions are not worth anything. My people wear too many hats, and besides, we're too small to put it in writing." At present the company employs 34 people, including Mr. Brown.

Mr. Brown is quick to point out that he has never had a personnel problem. "All my people enjoy working here." He believes that "nobody should work for nothing" and has therefore established a personal goal of seeing to it that no one employed by UPI makes less than $10,000 per year. Mr. Brown commented on his attitude toward his employees:

> The men might complain about the amount of responsibility placed on them, but I think it's good for them. It helps them develop to their potential. I'm a nice guy who is interested in all of my people. I feel a strong social obligation to my employees and have developed very close relationships with all of them. My door is always open to them no matter what the problem may be.
>
> I make it a policy never to yell at anyone in public; it's not good for morale. Maybe it's part of my conservative philosophy, but I want everyone to call me Mr. Brown, not George. I think it's good for people to have a Mr. Brown. Although I want to run a nice friendly business, I have learned that it's hard to be real friends with an employee. You can only go so far. Employers and employees cannot mix socially; it just doesn't work out over the long run.
>
> This is not your normal business. I am very approachable; I don't demand much and I allow an easy, open dialogue with my employees. Seldom do I take any punitive action. I'm just not a hard-driving tough guy.... I'm an easygoing guy.

EXHIBIT 4 UPI Organization Chart, December 1974

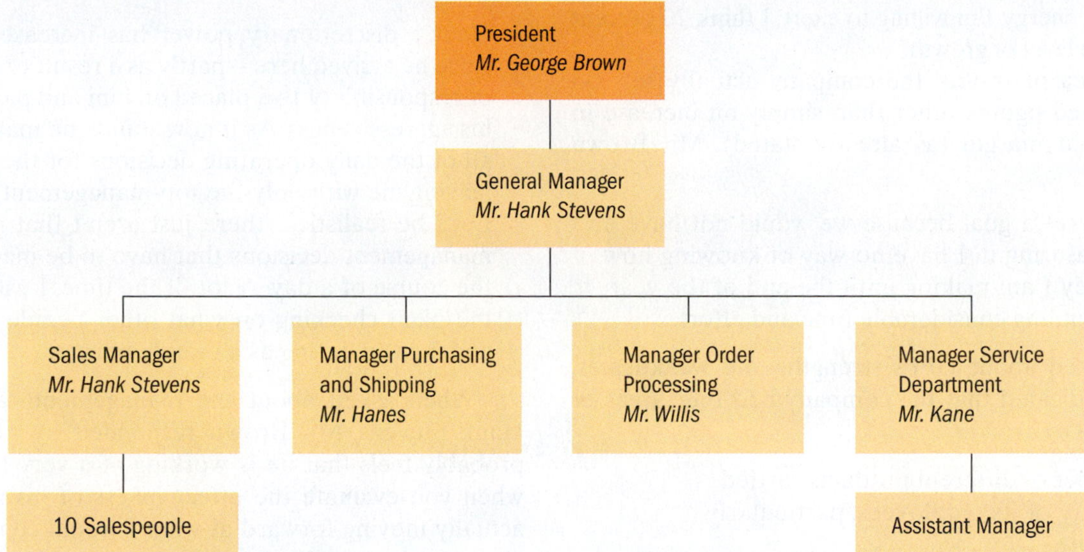

It would take much of the enjoyment out of the business for me to come in here and run this place like a machine.[1]

I find it hard to motivate the company's salespeople. Since we have so much trouble finding good, capable people, I'm not likely to fire any that I have. This situation makes it hard for me to put pressure on them to produce.

The bonus system, if you want to call it that, is, I guess, what you'd call very arbitrary. I have not set up specific sales quotas, or targeted goals for my inside people, so, as a result, I base my bonus decisions on my assessment of how well I feel an employee performed during the past year.

Recently, I've given some thought to selling the company. I could probably get around \$3–\$4 million for it. If I did that, I'm not sure what I would do with my time. Besides my family and UPI, there is not much that I am interested in. A couple of years ago, when I took my extended vacation, I got bored and couldn't wait to get back to the company.

UPI's Planning Process

George Brown claims to be a firm believer in planning. "I find myself spending more and more time planning for the company. Currently, I'm averaging about 50 percent of my time and I see this increasing." As he described it, the planning process at United Products is really a very loose system:

We have no set way as to how we do the planning. Basically, the process is directed at ways of increasing the profitability of the company. I look at the salespeople's performance on a weekly and monthly basis and use this information in the development of the plans. Since we have a very informal planning process, we only forecast out one year at most. The company's plans are reevaluated each month and, if necessary, new plans are set. Only on rare occasions have we ever planned beyond one year. However, I think the current economic and political situation may force us to develop plans that cover a two-year period.

I am familiar with commonly accepted theory about planning systems, but I do not feel it is necessary for UPI to institute, in a formal manner, any of those I've read about. We perform many of the activities advocated in the planning models, but we do them in a relaxed, casual fashion. For example, I am a member of many organizations connected with my business and receive industry newsletters on a regular basis. In addition, I receive input from friends and business associates both inside and outside my line of business. Since we do not have a formal process, planning tends to be a continuous process at UPI.

Although goals are not formally developed and written down, Mr. Brown said he established targets for the company to achieve in the areas of sales, profits, and organizational climate:

1. Increase sales volume by 20 percent per year.
2. Increase gross profit margin 0.5 to 1 percent per year.
3. Make UPI a friendly place to work.

Mr. Brown feels that the company has been able to grow at about 20 percent a year in the past and should be able to realize that level in the future. In addition, he believes that

[1]When the case researcher arrived at the plant one afternoon, he observed Mr. Brown running around the office deeply involved in a water fight with one of his office girls. By the way, he lost.

sales growth is a necessary evil: "Those companies that don't grow are swallowed up by the competition, and besides, given the amount of energy I'm willing to exert, I think 20 percent is a reasonable level of growth."

In the area of profits, the company actually sets no specific targeted figures other than simply an increase in the gross profit margin (as already stated). Mr. Brown observed:

> We do not set a goal because we would not have a way of measuring it. I have no way of knowing how much money I am making until the end of the year, without spending considerable time and effort.

When asked about UPI's strengths and weaknesses, Mr. Brown indicated that the company had four areas of strength:

1. The number of different products carried.
2. The quality of its employees, particularly salespeople.
3. The absence of any debt.
4. Purchasing capabilities.

The major weakness he viewed was an inability to get and train new personnel—primarily in the area of sales.

Sales Force

UPI's salespeople are not assigned a sales quota for the year, but rather are evaluated based on Mr. Brown's assessment of the particular salesperson's territory and initiative. He feels his salespeople make more than those of his competitors. Several of UPI's 10 salespeople have earned as much as $40,000 in a single year. All salespeople are compensated on a straight, sliding-scale, commission basis calculated as follows:

8 percent for the first $180,000 in sales
7 percent for the next $60,000
6 percent for the next $60,000
5 percent for all sales over $300,000

Mr. Brown is pleased with the sales success of his company and feels that United Products' greatest strength is its ability to "sell anything to anybody." Still, he perceives UPI's main problem as finding good salespeople. "There just aren't good salespeople around and this is a problem because salespeople are the lifeblood of our business."

UPI's Management Team

At the time of the company's reorganization, Hank Stevens was brought in as general manager and assistant to the president. Over the past several years, Mr. Stevens's areas of responsibility have grown to an extent where they now comprise approximately 80 percent of the activities that were formerly done by Mr. Brown. As a result, George Brown sometimes finds himself with little to do and often works only five hours per day. As he described it:

> Hank's discretionary power has increased steadily since he arrived here—partly as a result of the extent of responsibility I've placed on him and partly due to his aggressiveness. As it now stands, he makes almost all of the daily operating decisions for the company, leaving me with only the top-management decisions. Let's be realistic... there just aren't that many top-management decisions that have to be made here in the course of a day. A lot of the time, I walk around the plant checking on what other people are doing and, I guess, acting as a morale booster.

When asked about the management capabilities of Hank Stevens, Mr. Brown responded by saying, "Hank probably feels that he is working at a very fast pace, but when you evaluate the effectiveness of his actions, he is actually moving forward at what I would consider to be a very slow pace. However, everything else considered, Hank is the best of what is around. I guess if I could find a really good sales manager, I would add him to the company and relieve Hank of that area of responsibility."

Hank Stevens

Hank Stevens, 32, joined UPI at the time of the reorganization in 1970 after having graduated from a local university with a B.S. in economics. As general manager, Mr. Stevens's responsibilities include planning, purchasing, and sales management, as well as involvement in other decisions that affect UPI's policies. Mr. Stevens feels that he has been fortunate in that "ever since I came to UPI, I've reported to the president and in essence have had everyone else reporting to me."

When asked about the goals of UPI, Mr. Stevens responded, "As I see it, we have goals in three major areas: profitability, sales level, and personal relationships." In discussing his own personal goals, Hank explained that he hoped the organization would grow and that, as a result, he would be able to grow along with it. Since Mr. Stevens works so closely with Mr. Brown, he has given considerable thought to his boss's business philosophy:

> I feel that George's business philosophy is unique. I guess the best way to describe it is to say that above all he is a businessman. Also, he has very high moral values and as a result of that he is extremely honest and would never cheat anybody. Actually, the company would probably look better financially if it was run by someone who didn't operate with the same values as George.

When asked about the sales force at UPI, Mr. Stevens commented, "When a new salesman starts with the company, he does so with full salary. After a period of about two years, we change him over to a commission basis." As has always been the case, UPI concentrated its sales efforts on large customers. Mr. Stevens noted that "on the average the company processes approximately 105 orders per day, with an average dollar value per order of roughly $132. It's not that we won't write small orders, we just don't solicit business from small accounts. It just makes more sense to concentrate on the larger accounts."

Jim Hanes

Jim Hanes, 24, has been with UPI for over six years and during that time has worked his way up from assistant service manager to his current position as the number three man in the company—manager of purchasing and shipping. Jim is responsible for the front office, repair work, and the warehouse. He feels that his reporting responsibility is approximately 60 percent to Mr. Stevens and 40 percent to Mr. Brown. "Since I have responsibility for all merchandise entering and leaving the company, I get involved with both Hank and George, and therefore I guess I report to both of them."

In talking about where he would go from his present position, he explained:

> I guess the next step is for me to become a salesman so that I can broaden my background and move up in the company. However I am a little worried; I don't think the salespeople in our company are given the right sales training. As the system works now, a new salesman is assigned to work with an experienced salesperson for about six weeks—after which time he is given his own territory. Perhaps if our sales manager had had more experience as a salesman, he would handle the training differently.

In commenting on his understanding of Mr. Brown's philosophy, Jim summed up his position: "George is a very open person. I think he is too honest for a businessman. He certainly gives his people responsibility. He gives you the ball and lets you run with it. I don't think enough planning is done at UPI. At most, it appears that we look ahead one year, and even then what plans are developed are kept very flexible."

UPI's Corporate Strategy

When asked about UPI's current strategy, Mr. Brown responded that "the company is presently a distributor in the industrial packaging equipment, shipping supplies, and heavy-duty stapling equipment business. In the past when we've wanted to grow, we have either added new lines of merchandise or added more salespeople, or both. For example, this past year I got the idea to create what I call a contract sales department. It is a simple concept. I took one man, put him in an office with a telephone and a listing of the Fortune top 1,000 companies, and told him to call and get new business. You would be surprised at how easy it was to pick up new accounts."

Mr. Stevens looks at UPI as being in the distribution and shipping of packaging supplies business. "In order for UPI to reach the goals that have been set, we have to sell more products. That is, we can grow by adding new salespeople, adding more product lines, purchasing more effectively, and undertaking more aggressive sales promotion."

Mr. Brown believes that UPI should try to maximize the profit on every item sold. To do this the company tries to set its prices at a level that is approximately 10 percent above the competition. Mr. Brown explained his pricing philosophy:

> I don't understand why people are afraid to raise prices. If you increase the price, you will pick up more business and make more money. That allows you to keep the volume low and still make more money. In addition, although the customer may pay more, he gets more. The higher price allows me to provide top-notch service to all my customers.

In his view, UPI is an innovative company. "Until very recently we were always innovating with new products and new applications. Now I think it's again time that we started to look for additional new and exciting products."

Brown was aware that UPI's strategic emphasis on service, together with his business philosophy, had resulted in UPI's organization being larger than it had to be, given the level of business. Mr. Brown explained the reasoning behind this condition. "I know the organization is bigger than it has to be. We could probably handle three times the present volume of business with our present staff and facility. I think it's because of my conservative attitude: I've always wanted the organization to stay a step ahead of what is really needed. I feel comfortable with a built-in backup system and therefore I am willing to pay for it."

In December 1974, Mr. Brown talked optimistically about the future. He felt that sales should reach the $6–$7 million range by 1978. "Looked at in another way, we should be able to grow at 20–25 percent per year without any particular effort." He went on to say:

> I want to grow and therefore I am making a concerted effort. I am constantly looking for possible merger avenues or expansion possibilities. I do not want to expand geographically. I would rather control that market area we are now in.
>
> I recently sent a letter to all competitors in New England offering to buy them out. Believe it or not, no one responded.
>
> I do not see any problems in the future. The history has been good; therefore, why won't it continue to be?
>
> Growth is easy. All I have to do is pick up a new line and I've automatically increased sales and profits. Basically we are distributors, and we operate as middlemen between the manufacturers and users. In light of what has been happening in the market, I feel that supply and demand will continue to be a problem. Therefore, I am giving serious thought to integrating vertically and becoming a manufacturer. This will guarantee our supply.[2]

[2]Refer to Exhibit 5, which contains minutes of a United Products sales meeting held at the end of 1973.

EXHIBIT 5 Minutes of UPI's Sales Meeting, December 5, 1973

Mr. Brown presided at the meeting. His opening remarks highlighted the extraordinary times our country and our company are going through as far as the general economy and the energy crisis are concerned, and the extraordinary effects of these unusual crises on people and businesses, including our company and our sources of supply.

He thanked all present for the many thoughtful, considered, and excellent suggestions that they had offered in writing as to how the salespeople and their company might best handle the gasoline crisis without incurring an undue loss of sales and profits, and still maintain the high standards of service to which UNITED PRODUCTS' thousands of satisfied customers are accustomed.

The whole situation, according to Mr. Brown, boils down to a question of supply and prices. Mr. Brown reported that on his recent trip to the Orient, there were very few companies that wanted to sell their merchandise to us—rather, THEY WANTED TO BUY FROM US MANY OF THE ITEMS WE NORMALLY BUY FROM FOREIGN COMPANIES, i.e., carton-closing staples, tape, gloves, et cetera... and at inflated prices!!! The Tokyo, Japan, market is so great that they are using up everything they can produce—and the steel companies would rather make flat steel than the steel rods that are used for making staples. A very serious problem exists, as a result, in the carton-closing staple field not only in Japan, but also in Europe and America.

Mr. Brown advised that every year the company's costs of operating increase just as each individual's cost of living goes up and up yearly. Additional personnel, increased group and auto insurance premiums, increased Social Security payments, new office equipment and supplies, new catalogues, "Beeper system" for more salespeople—all of these costs accumulate and result in large expenditures of money. Manufacturers cover their increased operating costs by pricing their products higher—but to date, UNITED PRODUCTS has never put into their prices the increased costs resulting from increased operating expenses. Last year, the 3 percent increase that the company needed then was put into effect by many of you. HOWEVER, in order for the company to realize that additional profit, this 3 percent price increase had to be put into effect ACROSS THE BOARD... all customers... all items!

That Did Not Happen!!!

Mr. Brown advised that UNITED PRODUCTS got LAMBASTED when all of the sources of supply started to increase their prices. When SPOTNAILS, for example, went up 10 percent, the salespeople only increased their prices 7 percent. We did *not get the 3 percent price increase above the manufacturers' price increase*—and we needed it then and need it even more NOW.

Eliminating the possibility of cutting commissions, there are three possible solutions for the problem and how to get this much needed and ABSOLUTELY IMPERATIVE additional 3 percent PRICE INCREASE ACROSS THE BOARD to cover the constantly growing operating costs for running a successful, progressive-minded and growing business whose high standards of service and performance are highly regarded by customers and sources of supply alike, namely:

a. A 3 percent increase on all items to all customers across the board
b. A surcharge on all invoices or decrease in discounts allowed off LIST
c. A GCI charge (government cost increase) on all invoices

Considerable discussion regarding these three possibilities resulted in the following conclusions concerning the best method for obtaining this special 3 percent ACROSS THE BOARD PRICE INCREASE, as follows:

a. A new PRICE BOOK should be issued with all new prices to reflect not only the manufacturers' new increased prices, but in addition the 3 percent UNITED PRODUCTS PRICE INCREASE. All of the salespeople agreed that it would be easier to effect the additional 3 percent price increase if the 3 percent was "built in" on their price book sheets.
b. This new PRICE BOOK will be set up in such a way that prices will be stipulated according to quantity of item purchased . . . with no variances allowed. WITH NO EXCEPTIONS, the price of any item will depend on the quantity a customer buys.
c. Some items will continue to be handled on a discount basis—but lower discounts in order to ascertain that UNITED PRODUCTS is getting its 3 percent price increase.
d. Until these new PRICE BOOKS are issued, all salespeople were instructed to proceed IMMEDIATELY to effect these 3 percent price increases.

Ten New Accounts Contest

Seven of our ten salespeople won a calculator as a result of opening up 10 new accounts each... a total of 70 NEW ACCOUNTS for our company!!! However, both Mr. Brown and Mr. Stevens confessed that the dollar volume amount stipulated in the contest had been set ridiculously low, as a "feeler" to determine the success and effectiveness of such a contest. All the salespeople voiced their approval of all of the contests offered to them—and agreed that they had enjoyed many excellent opportunities of increasing their personal exchequers.

New Customer Letters

Mr. Brown again reminded all present that we have an excellent printed letter, which is available for sending to every new customer—and urged all to take advantage of this service by the office personnel by clearly indicating on their sales and order slips "NEW CUSTOMER." The procedure is but another step towards our goal of becoming more and more professional in our approach with our customers.

EXHIBIT 5 ***Continued***

New Catalogues

Mr. Brown advised that by the first of the new year, hopefully, all our hard-cover catalogues with their new divider breakdowns will be ready for hand-delivering to large accounts. These catalogues cost the company over $5 and should only be distributed by hand to those customers who can and will make intelligent and effective use of them.

Excessive Issuance of Credits

As a result of a detailed study made by Mr. Brown of the nature and reasons for the ever-increasing number of credits being issued, he instructed all of the salespeople to follow these procedures when requesting the issuing of CREDITS:

a. Issue the CREDIT at the right time.

b. Do not sell an item where it is not needed.

c. NEVER PUT "NO COMMENT" for the reason why merchandise is being returned. EVERY CREDIT MUST HAVE A REASON FOR ITS ISSUANCE.

The ever-increasing number of CREDITS being issued is extremely costly to the company: (1) new merchandise comes back 90-plus days after it has been billed, and frequently, if not always, is returned by the customer FREIGHT COLLECT: (2) CREDIT 9-part forms, postage for mailing, and extra work for both the Bookkeeping and Billing and Order Processing Departments mean higher expenses for the Company. More intelligent, considered and selective selling, plus greater care on the part of the Order Processing personnel, according to Mr. Brown, could easily eliminate a large percentage of these CREDITS.

Actually, I don't want to do the manufacturing. I think it would be better if I bought the manufacturing equipment and then had someone else use it to make my products.

The Future

Nevertheless, after reviewing with his accountant the results for the just-completed fiscal year, Mr. Brown was concerned about UPI's future course. "I know changes have to be made for next year as a result of this year, but I'm not sure what they should be." Mr. Brown continued:

> I think this next year is going to be a real bad year. Prices will probably fall like a rock from the levels they reached during 1974 and as a result those items that would have been profitable for the company aren't going to be, and we have much too large an inventory as it is. It isn't easy to take away customers from the competition. As a result of this, I feel we have to step up our efforts to get new lines and new accounts. Recently, I've given some thought to laying off one or two people for economic reasons, but I'm not sure. I will probably give raises to all employees even though it's not a good business decision, but it's an ingrained part of my business philosophy.

When asked if he had informed his employees of his concern about the future, Mr. Brown referred to the minutes of a sales meeting that had been held in November 1974:

> . . . Mr. Brown then presided at the meeting, and announced that Al King had won the coveted "Salesman of the Month" award. This was a "first" for our Al, and well deserved for his outstanding sales results in October. Congratulations and applause were extended to him by all present. The balance of the meeting was then spent in a lengthy, detailed discussion, led by Mr. George Brown, of the general, overall picture of what the future portends in the sales area as a result of the current inflationary, recessionary, and complex competitive conditions prevailing in the economy.

The gist of the entire discussion can be best summarized as follows:

1. Everyone present must recognize the very real difficulties that lie ahead in these precarious economic times.
2. The only steps available to the salespeople and to the company for survival during the rough period ahead are as follows:
   a. Minimize contacts with existing accounts.
   b. Spend the majority of time developing new accounts on the less competitive products, and selling new products to established accounts.
3. Concentrate on and promote our new items.
4. Mr. Brown and inside management are making and will continue to make every concerted effort to find new products and new lines for the coming year.

In preparation for his meeting with Hank Stevens, Mr. Brown had drawn up a list of activities to which Hank should address himself while running UPI during George's upcoming vacation. Mr. Brown believed that upon his return from Europe his activities at UPI would be increasing as a result of the problems caused by the uncertain economic conditions. The first item on the list was a possible redefinition of UPI's marketing strategy. Mr. Brown now believed that UPI would have to be much more liberal with respect to new products considered for sale. "I'm not saying we are going to get into the consumer goods business, but I think we need to give consideration to handling consumer products that require no service and that carry a high-profit-margin factor for the company."

As he sat at his desk thinking about possible changes he could make in UPI's planning process, Mr. Brown was convinced that if he hadn't done some planning in the past, the situation would be more drastic than it was. Yet at the same time, he wasn't sure that a more structured and formalized planning process would put UPI in any better position to face the more difficult times that he saw ahead.

CASE 2

The Paradoxical Twins: Acme and Omega Electronics

John F. Veiga

Part I

In 1955, Technological Products of Erie, Pennsylvania, was bought out by a Cleveland manufacturer. The Cleveland firm had no interest in the electronics division of Technological Products and subsequently sold to different investors two plants that manufactured printed circuit boards. One of the plants, located in nearby Waterford, Pennsylvania, was renamed Acme Electronics, and the other plant, within the city limits of Erie, was renamed Omega Electronics, Inc. Acme retained its original management and upgraded its general manager to president. Omega hired a new president, who had been a director of a large electronics research laboratory, and upgraded several of the existing personnel within the plant.

Acme and Omega often competed for the same contracts. As subcontractors, both firms benefited from the electronics boom of the early 1960s and both looked forward to future growth and expansion. Acme had annual sales of $10 million and employed 550 people. Omega had annual sales of $8 million and employed 480 people. Acme was consistently more effective than Omega and regularly achieved greater net profits, much to the chagrin of Omega's management.

Inside Acme

The president of Acme, John Tyler, credited his firm's greater effectiveness to his managers' abilities to run a "tight ship." He explained that he had retained the basic structure developed by Technological Products because it was most efficient for high-volume manufacture of printed circuits and their subsequent assembly. Tyler was confident that had the demand not been so great, its competitor would not have survived. "In fact," he said, "we have been able to beat Omega regularly for the most profitable contracts, thereby increasing our profits." Acme's basic organization structure is shown in Exhibit 1. People were generally satisfied with their work at Acme; however, some of the managers voiced the desire to have a little more latitude in their jobs. One manager characterized the president as a "one-man band." He said, "While I respect John's ability, there are times when I wish I had a little more information about what is going on."

Inside Omega

Omega's president, Jim Rawls, did not believe in organization charts. He felt that his organization had departments similar to Acme's, but he thought the plant was small enough that things such as organization charts just put artificial barriers between specialists who should be working together. Written memos were not allowed, since, as Jim expressed it, "the plant is small enough that if people want to communicate, they can just drop by and talk things over." Other members of Omega complained that too much time was wasted "filling in" people who could not contribute to the problem solving. As the head of the mechanical engineering department expressed it, "Jim spends too much of his time and mine making sure everyone understands what we're doing and listening to suggestions." A newer member of the industrial engineering department said, "When I first got here, I wasn't sure what I was supposed to do. One day I worked with some mechanical engineers and the next day I helped the shipping department design some packing cartons. The first months on the job were hectic, but at least I got a real feel for what makes Omega tick." Most decisions of any significance were made by the management team at Omega.

Part II

In 1966, the integrated circuits began to cut deeply into the demand for printed circuit boards. The integrated circuits (ICs), or "chips," were the first step into microminiaturization in the electronics industry. Because the manufacturing process for ICs was a closely guarded secret, both Acme and Omega realized the potential threat

This case was developed from material gathered from the two firms by Dr. John F. Veiga. All names and places have been disguised.

EXHIBIT 1 Acme Electronics Organization Chart

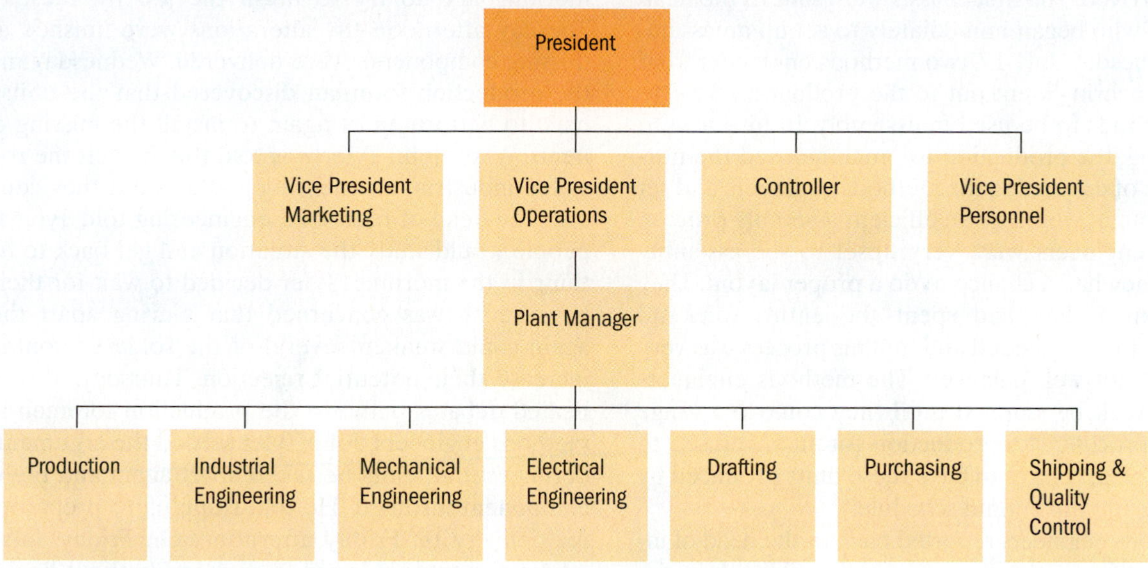

to their futures and both began to seek new customers aggressively. In July 1966, one of the major photocopy manufacturers was looking for a subcontractor to assemble the memory unit for its new experimental copier. The projected contract for the job was estimated to be $5–$7 million in annual sales. Both Acme and Omega were geographically close to this manufacturer and both had submitted highly competitive bids for the production of 100 prototypes. Acme's bid was slightly lower than Omega's; however, both firms were asked to produce 100 units. The photocopy manufacturer told both firms that speed was critical because their president had boasted to other manufacturers that they would have a finished copier available by Christmas. This boast, much to the designer's dismay, required pressure on all subcontractors to begin prototype production before final design of the copier was complete. This meant that Acme and Omega would have at most two weeks to produce the prototypes or delay the final copier production.

Part III

Inside Acme

As soon as John Tyler was given the blueprints (Monday, July 11, 1966), he sent a memo to the purchasing department requesting them to move forward on the purchase of all necessary materials. At the same time, he sent the blueprints to the drafting department and asked that they prepare manufacturing prints. The industrial engineering department was told to begin methods design work for use by the production department foremen. Tyler also sent a memo to all department heads and executives indicating the critical time constraints of this job and how he expected everyone to perform as efficiently as they had in the past. On Wednesday, July 13, purchasing discovered that a particular component used in the memory unit could not be purchased or shipped for two weeks because the manufacturer had shut down for summer vacations. The head of purchasing was not overly concerned by this obstacle, because he knew that Omega would face the same problem. He advised Tyler of this predicament, who in turn decided that Acme would build the memory unit except for the one component and then add that component in two weeks. Industrial engineering was told to build this constraint into their assembly methods. On Friday, July 15, industrial engineering notified Tyler that the missing component would substantially increase the assembly time if it was not available from the start of assembly. Mr. Tyler, anxious to get started, said that he would live with that problem and gave the signal to go forward on the assembly plans. Mechanical engineering received manufacturing prints on Tuesday, July 12, and evaluated their capabilities for making the chassis required for the memory unit. Because their procedure for prototypes was to get estimates from outside vendors on all sheet metal work before they authorized in-house personnel to do the job, the head of mechanical engineering sent a memo to the head of drafting requesting that vendor prints be drawn up on the chassis and that these prints then be forwarded to purchasing, which would obtain vendor bids. On Friday, July 15, Mr. Tyler called the head of mechanical engineering and asked for a progress report on the chassis. He was advised that mechanical engineering was waiting for vendor estimates before they moved forward.

Mr. Tyler was shocked by the lack of progress and demanded that mechanical engineering begin building those "damn chassis." On Monday, July 18, Mr. Tyler received word from the shipping department that most of the components had arrived. The first chassis were sent to the head of production, who began immediately to set up an assembly area. On Tuesday, July 19, two methods engineers from industrial engineering went out to the production floor to set up the methods to be used in assembly. In his haste to get things going, the production foreman ignored the normal procedure of contacting the methods engineers and set up what he thought would be an efficient assembly process. The methods engineers were very upset to see assembly begin before they had a chance to do a proper layout. They told the foreman they had spent the entire weekend analyzing the motions needed and that his process was very inefficient and not well balanced. The methods engineers ordered that work be stopped until they could rearrange the assembly process. The production foreman refused to stop work. He said, "I have to have these units produced by Friday and already I'm behind schedule."

The methods engineers reported back to the head of industrial engineering, who immediately complained to the plant manager. The plant manager sided with the production foreman and said, "John Tyler wants these units by Friday. Don't bother me with methods details now. Once we get the prototypes out and go into full production, then your boys can do their thing." As the head of industrial engineering got off the phone with the plant manager, he turned to his subordinates and said, "If my boss doesn't think our output is needed, to hell with him! You fellows must have other jobs to worry about, forget this one." As the two methods engineers left the head industrial engineer's office, one of them said to the other, "Just wait until they try to install those missing components. Without our methods, they'll have to tear down the units almost completely."

On Thursday, July 21, the final units were being assembled, although the process was delayed several times as production waited for chassis from mechanical engineering to be completed. On Friday, July 22, the last units were finished while John Tyler paced around the plant. Late that afternoon, Tyler received a phone call from the head designer of the photocopier manufacturer, who told Tyler that he had received a call on Wednesday from Jim Rawls of Omega. He explained that Rawls's boys had found an error in the design of the connector cable and had taken corrective action on their prototypes. He told Tyler that he checked out the design error and that Omega was right. Tyler, a bit overwhelmed by this information, told the designer that he had all of the memory units ready for shipment and that as soon as they received the missing component, on Monday or Tuesday, they would be able to deliver the final units. The designer explained that the design error would be rectified in a new blueprint he was sending over by messenger and that he would hold Acme to the delivery date on Tuesday.

When the blueprint arrived, Tyler called the production foreman in to assess the damages. The alterations in the design would call for total disassembly and the unsoldering of several connections. Tyler told the foreman to put extra people on the alterations first thing on Monday morning and to try to finish the job by Tuesday. Late Tuesday afternoon the alterations were finished and the missing components were delivered. Wednesday morning, the production foreman discovered that the units would have to be torn apart again to install the missing components. When John Tyler was told this, he "hit the roof." He called industrial engineering and asked if they could help out. The head of industrial engineering told Tyler that his people would study the situation and get back to him first thing in the morning. Tyler decided to wait for their study because he was concerned that tearing apart the units again could weaken several of the soldered contacts and increase their potential rejection. Thursday, after several heated debates between the production foreman and the methods engineers, John Tyler settled the argument by ordering that all units be taken apart again and the missing component installed. He told shipping to prepare cartons for delivery on Friday afternoon. On Friday, July 29, 50 prototypes were shipped from Acme without final inspection. John Tyler was concerned about his firm's reputation, so he waived the final inspection after he personally tested one unit and found it operational. On Tuesday, August 2, Acme shipped the last 50 units.

Inside Omega

Jim Rawls called a meeting on Friday, July 8, that included department heads to tell them about the potential contract they were to receive. He told them that as soon as he received the blueprints, work could begin. On Monday, July 11, the prints arrived and again the department heads met to discuss the project. At the end of the meeting, drafting had agreed to prepare manufacturing prints while industrial engineering and production would begin methods design. On Wednesday, July 13, at a progress report session, purchasing indicated a particular component would not be available for two weeks, when the manufacturer reopened from summer vacation shutdown. The head of electrical engineering suggested using a possible substitute component, which was made in Japan, containing all of the necessary characteristics. The head of industrial engineering promised to have the methods engineers study the assembly methods to see if the unit could be produced in such a way that the missing component could be installed last.

The head of mechanical engineering raised the concern that the chassis would be an obstacle if they waited for vendor estimates and he advised the group that his people would begin production even though it might cost more. On Friday, July 15, at a progress report session, industrial engineering reported that the missing component would increase the assembly time substantially. The head of electrical engineering offered to have one of his engineers examine the missing component specifications and said he was confident that the Japanese component would work. At the end of the meeting, purchasing was told to order the Japanese components.

On Monday, July 18, a methods engineer and the production foreman formulated the assembly plans, and production was set to begin on Tuesday morning. On Monday afternoon, people from mechanical engineering, electrical engineering, production, and industrial engineering got together to produce a prototype just to ensure that there would be no snags in production. While they were building the unit, they discovered an error in the connector cable design. All of the engineers agreed, after checking and rechecking the blueprints, that the cable was erroneously designed. People from mechanical engineering and electrical engineering spent Monday night redesigning the cable and on Tuesday morning, the drafting department finalized the changes in the manufacturing prints. On Tuesday morning, Jim Rawls was a bit apprehensive about the design changes and decided to get formal approval. Rawls received word on Wednesday from the head designer of the photocopier firm that he could proceed with the design changes as discussed on the phone. On Friday, July 22, the final units were inspected by quality control and were then shipped.

Part IV: Retrospect

Ten of Acme's final memory units were ultimately defective, while all of Omega's units passed the photocopier firm's tests. The photocopier firm was disappointed with Acme's delivery delay and incurred further delays in repairing the defective Acme units. However, rather than give the entire contract to one firm, the final contract was split between Acme and Omega, with two directives added: (1) Maintain zero defects and (2) reduce final cost. In 1967, through extensive cost-cutting efforts, Acme reduced its unit cost by 20 percent and was ultimately awarded the total contract.

CASE 3

How SAP's Business Model and Strategies Made It the Global Business Software Leader

This case was prepared by Gareth R. Jones, Texas A&M University.

In 1972, after the project they were working on for IBM's German subsidiary was abandoned, five German IBM computer analysts left the company and founded Systems Applications and Products in Data Processing, known today as SAP. These analysts had been involved in the provisional design of a software program that would allow information about cross-functional and cross-divisional financial transactions in a company's value chain to be coordinated and processed centrally—resulting in enormous savings in time and expense. They observed that other software companies were also developing software designed to integrate across value chain activities and subunits. Using borrowed money and equipment, the five analysts worked day and night to create an accounting software platform that could integrate across all the parts of an entire corporation. In 1973, SAP unveiled an instantaneous accounting transaction processing program called R/1, one of the earliest examples of what is now called an enterprise resource planning (ERP) system.

Today, ERP is an industry term for the multimodule applications software that allows a company to manage the set of activities and transactions necessary to manage the business processes for moving a product from the input stage, along the value chain, to the final customer. As such, ERP systems can recognize, monitor, measure, and evaluate all the transactions involved in business processes such as product planning, the purchasing of inputs from suppliers, the manufacturing process, inventory and order processing, and customer service itself. Essentially, a fully developed ERP system provides a company with a standardized information technology (IT) platform that provides managers with complete information about all aspects of its business processes and cost structure across all functions and divisions. This allows managers at all levels to (1) continually search for ways to perform these processes more efficiently and lower its cost structure, and (2) improve and service its products and raise their value to customers. For example, ERP systems provide information that allows for the redesign of products to better match customer needs and that result in superior responsiveness to customers.

To give one example, Nestlé installed SAP's newest ERP software across its more than 150 U.S. food divisions in the 2000s. Using its new IT platform, corporate managers discovered that each division was paying a different price for the same flavoring—vanilla. The same small set of vanilla suppliers was charging each individual division as much as they could get, so different divisions paid prices that varied widely depending on their bargaining power with the supplier. Before the SAP system was installed, corporate managers had no idea this was happening because their old IT system could not compare and measure the same transaction—purchasing vanilla—across divisions. SAP's standardized cross-company software platform revealed this problem, and hundreds of thousands of dollars in cost savings were achieved by solving this one transaction difficulty alone. This is why ERP systems can save large companies hundreds of millions and billions of dollars over time and explains why SAP's ERP became so popular.

Focus on Large Multinationals

Indeed, SAP focused its R/1 software on the largest multinational companies with revenues of at least $2.5 billion at first because they would reap the biggest cost savings. Although relatively few in number, these companies—mostly large global product manufacturers—stood to gain the most benefit from ERP, and they were willing to pay SAP a premium price for its product. Its focus on this influential niche of companies helped SAP develop a global base of leading companies. Its goal, as it had been from the beginning, was to create the global industry standard for ERP by providing the best business applications software infrastructure. And it succeeded—in 2011 it still has the largest installed base of the world's most well-known companies.

ERP and Consulting

In its first years, SAP not only developed ERP software, but it also used its own internal consultants to install it physically onsite at its customers' corporate IT centers, manufacturing operations, and so on. Determined to increase its customer base quickly, however, SAP switched strategies in the 1980s. It decided to focus primarily on the development of its ERP software and to outsource, to external consultants, more and more of the highly complex implementation consulting services needed to install and service its software onsite in a particular company. It formed a series of strategic alliances with major global consulting companies such as IBM, Accenture, and Cap Gemini to install its R/1 system in its growing base of global customers.

ERP installation is a long and complicated process. A company cannot simply adapt its information systems to fit SAP's software; it must use external consultants to rework the way it performs its value chain activities so that its business processes—and the IT system that measures and evaluates these business processes—become compatible with SAP's software. SAP's claim to fame was based on the fact that by modeling its business processes on its ERP platform, which contains the solutions needed to achieve best industry practices across its operations, a large company could expect a substantial increase, often 10% or more in performance. However, the more a particular company's managers wanted to customize the SAP platform so it fit their own internal business processes, the more difficult and expensive the implementation process became—and the harder it becomes for companies to realize the potential gains from cost savings and value added to the product by SAP's software.

SAP's outsourcing consulting strategy allowed it to penetrate global markets quickly and eliminated the huge capital investment required to employ the thousands of consultants needed to provide this service on a global basis. On the other hand, for consulting companies, the installation of SAP's popular software became a major money-spinner and they earned billions by learning how to install its ERP system. Consequently, SAP did not enjoy the huge revenue streams associated with providing software consulting services, such as the design, installation, and maintenance of an ERP platform on an ongoing basis. It earned only a small amount of revenue by training external consultants in the intricacies of how to install, customize, and maintain its ERP systems in its customer base. This was a major error because revenues from consulting over time are often as great as that those that can be earned from selling complex software applications. By focusing on ERP software development, not only did SAP forfeit high consulting profits, it also became dependent on consulting companies that now became the experts in the installation/customization arena—such as Accenture and IBM.

The Changing Global Landscape

This decision had unfortunate long-term consequences because SAP began to lose firsthand knowledge of its customers' emerging problems and an understanding of the changing needs of its customers. Something especially important as growing global competition, outsourcing, and the increasing use of the Internet to facilitate cross-company commerce became major competitive factors changing the ERP industry and software applications market. For a company whose goal was to provide a standardized platform across functions and divisions, this outsourcing consulting strategy seemed like a major error to many analysts. SAP's failure to work quickly to expand its own consulting operations to run parallel with those of external consultants, rather than providing a training service to these consultants to keep them informed about its constantly changing ERP software, left the door open for IBM and Accenture to dominate the software consulting industry, which they still do today.

To some degree, its decision to focus on software development and outsource more than 80% of installation was a consequence of its German founders' "engineering" mindset. Founded by computer program engineers, SAP's culture was built on values and norms that emphasized technical innovation, and the development of leading-edge ERP software algorithms and best practices. SAP's managers poured most of its profits into research and development (R&D) to fund new projects that would increase its ERP platform's capabilities; they had little desire to spend money on developing its consulting services. Essentially, SAP became a *product-focused* not a customer-focused company since it believed R&D would produce the technical advances that would be the source of its competitive advantage and allow it to charge its customers a premium price for its ERP platform. By 1990 SAP spent more than 30% of gross sales on R&D.

Global Sales and Marketing Problems

SAP's top managers focus on developing its technical competence had another unfortunate consequence. They underestimated the enormous problems involved in developing and implementing its global marketing and sales competency to increase its large customer base—and to attract new kinds of customers, especially smaller companies. The need to build an efficient global structure and control system to manage its own operations effectively was largely ignored because managers believed the ERP platform would sell itself! Indeed, SAP's focus on R&D and its neglect of its other functions made its sales, marketing, and internal consultants and training experts feel as if they were second-class citizens, despite the fact that they brought in new business and were the people responsible maintaining good relationships with SAP's growing customer base.

The classic problem of managing a growing business from the entrepreneurial to the professional management phase was emerging in SAP and its revenues and profits were slowing as a result. SAP's top managers were not experienced business managers who understood the problems of implementing a rapidly growing company's strategy on a global basis; the need to develop a sound corporate infrastructure was being shoved aside—something that has cost it billions of dollars in lost profits over the decades.

The Second Generation R/2 ERP Platform

In 1981, SAP introduced its second-generation ERP software, R/2. Not only did it contain many more value chain/business process software modules, but it also linked its ERP software seamlessly to the existing or legacy databases and communication systems used on a company's mainframe computers. This allowed for greater connectivity and ease of use of ERP throughout a company at all levels and across all subunits. The R/1 platform had been largely a cross-organizational accounting/financial software module; the new software modules could handle procurement, product development, and inventory and order tracking. Of course, these additional components had to be compatible with one another so that they could be seamlessly integrated onsite, at a customer's operations, and with its existing or legacy IT system.

SAP did not develop its own database management software package; its system was designed to be compatible with Oracle's database management software, the global leader in this segment of the software applications industry. Once again, this was to have repercussions later, when Oracle began to rapidly develop its own ERP software platform during the 2000s, essentially moving from database software into ERP, and other kinds of business software applications. As part of its push to make its R/2 software the global industry standard for the next decades, SAP also developed new "middleware" software that basically allows the hardware and software made by different global computer companies to work seamlessly together on any particular company's IT system. This is also an industry Oracle competes in.

Recognizing that the way value chain activities and business processes are performed differs *from industry to industry* because of differences in manufacturing and other business processes, SAP also spent a lot of time and money customizing its basic ERP platform to accommodate the needs of companies in different kinds of industries. Increasingly, over time, ERP companies recognized that their long-term competitive advantage depended upon them being able to provide the ERP software solutions customized by industry to perform most effectively. Its push to become the ERP leader across industries, across all large global companies, and across all value chain business processes required a huge R&D investment.

SAP Becomes a Global Leader

In 1988, SAP went public on the Frankfurt stock exchange to raise the necessary cash to fund its growing global operations, and by 1990 it became a global leader of business applications software as its market capitalization soared. SAP now dominated ERP software sales in the high-tech and electronics, engineering and construction, consumer products, chemical, and retail industries. Its product was increasingly being recognized as superior to the other ERP software being developed by companies such as PeopleSoft, S. D. Edwards, and Oracle. The main reason for SAP's increasing competitive advantage was that it was the only company that could offer a potential customer a broad, standardized, state-of-the-art solution that spanned a wide variety of value chain activities spread around the globe. By contrast, its competitors, like PeopleSoft, offered more-focused solutions aimed at one business process, such as human resources management.

SAP Introduces the R/3 Solution

SAP's continuing massive investment in developing new ERP software resulted in the introduction of its R/3, or third-generation, ERP solution in 1992. Essentially, the R/3 platform expanded on its previous solutions; it offered seamless, real-time integration for over 80% of a company's business processes. It had also embedded in the platform hundreds and then thousands of industry best practice solutions, or templates, that customers could use to improve their operations and processes. The R/3 system was initially composed of seven different modules corresponding to the most common business processes: production planning, materials management, financial accounting, asset management, human resources management, project systems, and sales and distribution. R/3 was designed to meet the diverse demands of its previous global clients. It could operate in multiple languages, convert exchange rates, and so on, on a real-time basis.

By the 1990s, however, as it now dominated the ERP market for large companies, SAP realized that for its sales to expand quickly it also needed to address the needs of small and medium-sized businesses (SMBs). Recognizing the huge potential revenues to be earned from SMB customers, SAP's engineers designed the R/3 platform so it could also be configured for smaller customers as well as customized to suit the needs of a broader range of industries in which they competed. Furthermore, SAP designed R/3 to be "open architecturally," meaning that using its middleware the R/3 could operate with whatever kind of computer hardware or software (the legacy system) an SMB was presently using.

Finally, in response to customer concerns that SAP's standardized system meant huge implementation problems in changing their business processes to match SAP's standardized solution, SAP introduced some limited customization opportunity into its software. Using specialized software from other companies, SAP claimed that up to 20% of R/3 could now be customized to work with the company's existing operating methods and thus would reduce the problems of learning and implementing the new system. However, the costs of doing this were extremely high and became a huge generator of fees for consulting companies. SAP used a variable-fee licensing system for its R/3 system; the cost to the customer was based on the number of users within a company, on the number of different R/3 modules that were installed, and on the degree to which users utilized these modules in the business planning process.

SAP's R/3 far outperformed its competitors' products in a technical sense and once again allowed it to charge a premium price for its new software. Believing that competitors would take at least two years to catch up, SAP's goal was to get its current customers to switch to its new product and then rapidly build its customer base to penetrate the growing ERP market. In doing so, it was also seeking to establish R/3 as the new ERP market standard in order to lock in customers before competitors could offer viable alternatives. This strategy was vital to its future success because, given the way an ERP system changes the nature of a customer's business processes once it is installed and running, there are high switching costs involved in moving to another ERP product, costs that customers want to avoid.

SAP's Growing Global Implementation Problems

R/3's growing popularity led SAP to decentralize more and more control of the marketing, sale, and installation of its software on a global basis to its overseas subsidiaries. While its R&D and software development remained centralized in Germany, it began to open wholly owned subsidiaries in most major country's markets. By 1995, it had eighteen national subsidiaries; today, it has over fifty. In 1995, SAP established a U.S. subsidiary to drive sales in the huge and most profitable market—the U.S. market. Its German top managers set the subsidiary a goal of achieving $1 billion in revenues within five years. To implement this aggressive growth strategy, and given that R/3 software needs to be installed and customized to suit the needs of particular companies and industries, several different regional SAP divisions were created to manage the needs of companies and industries in different U.S. regions. Also, the regional divisions became responsible for training an army of both internal and external consultants on how to install and customize the R/3 software. For every internal lead SAP consultant, there were soon about nine to ten external consultants working with SAP's customers to install and modify the software—which again boosted IBM and Accenture's profits.

Problems with Its U.S. Operations

The problems with its policy of decentralization soon caught up with SAP, however. Because SAP was growing so fast, and demand for its product was increasing so rapidly, it was hard to provide the thorough training consultants needed to perform the installation of its software. Often, once SAP had trained an internal consultant, that consultant would leave to join the company for which he or she was performing the work or even to start an industry-specific SAP consulting practice! The result that SAP customers' needs were being poorly served and the number of complaints about the cost and difficulty of installing its ERP software were increasing. Since large external consulting companies made their money based on the time it took their consultants to install a particular SAP system, many customers complained that consultants were deliberately taking too long to implement the new software to maximize their earnings, and were even pushing inappropriate or unnecessary R/3 modules. For example, Chevron spent over $100 million and two years installing and getting its R/3 system operating effectively. In one well-publicized case, FoxMeyer Drug blamed SAP software for the supply chain problems that led to its bankruptcy and the company's major creditors sued SAP, alleging that the company had promised R/3 would do more than it could. SAP responded that the problem was not the software but the way the company had installed it, but SAP's reputation was harmed nevertheless.

SAP's policy of decentralization was also somewhat paradoxical because the company's mission was to supply software that linked functions and divisions rather than separated them, and the characteristic problems of too much decentralization of authority soon became evident throughout SAP. In its U.S. subsidiary, each regional SAP division started developing its own procedures for pricing SAP software, offering discounts, dealing with customer complaints, and even rewarding its employees and consultants. There was a total lack of standardization and integration inside SAP America and indeed between SAP's many foreign subsidiaries and their headquarters in Germany. This meant that little learning was taking place between divisions or consultants, there was no monitoring or coordination mechanism in place to share SAP's *own* best practices between its consultants and divisions, and organizing by region in the United States was doing little to build core competences. For example, analysts were asking, "If R/3 has to be customized to suit the needs of a particular industry, why didn't SAP use a market structure and divide its activities by the needs of customers based in different industries?" These problems slowed down the process of implementing SAP software and prevented quick and effective responses to the needs of potential customers.

SAP's R/3 was also criticized as being too standardized because it forced all companies to adapt to what SAP had decided were best industry practices. When consultants reconfigured the software to suit a particular company's needs, this process often took a long time and sometimes the system did not perform as well as had been expected. Many companies felt that the software should be configured to suit their business processes and not the other way around, but again SAP argued that such a setup would not lead to an optimal outcome. For example, SAP's retail R/3 system could not handle Home Depot's policy of allowing each of its stores to order directly from suppliers, based upon centrally negotiated contracts between Home Depot and those suppliers. SAP's customers also found that supporting their new ERP platform was expensive and that ongoing support cost three to five times as much as the actual purchase of the software, although the benefits they received from its R/3 system usually exceeded these costs substantially.

The Changing Industry Environment

Although the United States had become SAP's biggest market, the explosive growth in demand for SAP's software had begun to slacken by 1995. Competitors such as Oracle, Baan, PeopleSoft, and Marcum were catching up technically, often because they were focusing their resources on the needs of one or a few industries or on a particular kind of ERP module (for example, PeopleSoft's focus on the human resources management module). Indeed SAP had to play catch-up in the HRM area and develop its own to offer a full suite of integrated business solutions. Oracle, the second largest software maker after Microsoft, was becoming a particular threat as it expanded its ERP offerings outward from its leading database knowledge systems and began to offer more and more of an Internet-based ERP platform. As new aggressive competitors emerged and changed the environment, SAP found it needed to change as well.

Competitors were increasing their market share by exploiting weaknesses in SAP's software. They began to offer SAP's existing and potential customers ERP modules that could be customized more easily to their situation and that were less expensive than SAP's. SAP's managers were forced to reevaluate their business model, and their strategies and the ways in which they implemented them.

New Implementation Problems

To a large degree, SAP's decision to decentralize control of its marketing, sales, and installation to its subsidiaries was due to the way the company had operated from its beginnings. Its German founders had emphasized the importance of excellence in innovation as the root value of its culture, and SAP's culture was often described as "organized chaos." Its top managers had operated from the beginning by creating as flat a hierarchy as possible to create an internal environment where people could take risks and try new ideas of their own choosing. If mistakes occurred or projects didn't work out, employees were given the freedom to try a different approach. Hard work, teamwork, openness, and speed were the norms of their culture. Required meetings were rare and offices were frequently empty because most of the employees were concentrating on research and development. The pressure was on software developers to create superior products. In fact, the company was proud of the fact that it was product driven, not service oriented. It wanted to be the world's leading innovator of software, not a service company that installed it.

Increasing competition led SAP's managers to realize that they were not capitalizing on its main strength—its human resources. In 1997, it established a human resources management (HRM) department and gave it the responsibility to build a more formal organizational structure. Previously it had outsourced its own HRM. HRM managers started to develop job descriptions and job titles, and put in place a career structure that would motivate employees and keep them loyal to the company. They also put in place a reward system, which included stock options, to increase the loyalty of their technicians, who were being attracted away by competitors or were starting their own businesses because SAP did not then offer a future: a career path. For example, SAP sued Siebel Systems, a niche rival in the customer relationship software business, in 2000 for enticing twelve of its senior employees, who it said took trade secrets with them. SAP's top managers realized that they had to plan long term, and that innovation by itself was not enough to make SAP a dominant global company with a sustainable competitive advantage.

At the same time that it started to operate more formally, it also became more centralized to encourage organizational learning and to promote the sharing of its own best implementation practices across divisions and subsidiaries. Its goal was to standardize the way each subsidiary or division operated across the company, thus making it easier to transfer people and knowledge where they were needed most. Not only would this facilitate cooperation, it would also reduce overhead costs, which were spiraling because of the need to recruit trained personnel as the company grew quickly and the need to alter and adapt its software to suit changing industry conditions. For example, increasing customer demands for additional customization of its software made it imperative that different teams of engineers pool their knowledge to reduce development costs, and that consultants should not only share their best practices but also cooperate with engineers so that the latter could understand the problems facing customers in the field.

The need to adopt a more standardized and hierarchical approach was also being driven by SAP's growing recognition that it needed more of the stream of income it could get from both the training and installation sector of the software business. It began to increase the number of its consultants. By having them work with its software developers, they became the acknowledged experts and leaders when it came to specific software installations and could command a high price. SAP also developed a large global training function to provide the extensive ERP training that consultants needed and charged both individuals and consulting companies high fees for attending these courses so that they would be able to work with the SAP platform. SAP's U.S. subsidiary also moved from a regional to a more market-based focus by re-aligning its divisions, not by geography, but by their focus on a particular sector or industry, for example, chemicals, electronics, pharmaceuticals, consumer products, and engineering.

Once again, however, the lines of authority between the new industry divisions and the software development, sales, installation, and training functions were not worked out well enough and the hoped-for gains from increased coordination and cooperation were slow to be realized. Globally, too, SAP was still highly decentralized and remained a product-focused company, thus allowing its subsidiaries to form their own sales, training, and installation policies. Its subsidiaries continued to form strategic alliances with global consulting companies, allowing them to obtain the majority of revenues from servicing SAP's growing base of R/3 installations. SAP's top managers, with their engineering mindset, did not appreciate the difficulties involved in changing a company's structure and culture, either at the subsidiary or the global level. They were disappointed in the slow pace of change because their cost structure remained high, although their revenues were increasing.

New Strategic Problems

By the mid-1990s, despite its problems in implementing its strategy, SAP was the clear market leader in the ERP software industry and the fourth largest global software company because of its recognized competences in the production of state-of-the-art ERP software. Several emerging problems posed major threats to its business model, however. First, it was becoming increasingly obvious that the development of the Internet and broadband technology would become important forces in shaping a company's business model and processes in the future. SAP's R/3 systems were specifically designed to integrate information about all of a company's value chain activities, across its functions and divisions, and to provide real-time feedback on its ongoing performance. However, ERP systems focused principally on a company's internal business processes; they were not designed to focus and provide feedback on cross-company and industry-level transactions and processes on a real-time basis. The Internet was changing the way in which companies viewed their boundaries; the emergence of global e-commerce and online cross-company transactions was changing the nature of a company's business processes both at the input and output sides.

At the input side, the Internet was changing the way a company managed its relationships with its parts and raw materials suppliers. Internet-based commerce offered the opportunity of locating new, low-cost suppliers. Developing Web software was also making it much easier for a company to cooperate and work with suppliers and manufacturing companies and to outsource activities to specialists who could perform the activities at lower cost. A company that previously made its own inputs or manufactured its own products could now outsource these value chain activities, which changed the nature of the ERP systems it needed to manage such transactions. In general, the changing nature of transactions across the company's boundaries could affect its ERP system in thousands of ways. Companies like Commerce One and Ariba, which offered this supply-chain management (SCM) software, were growing rapidly and posing a major threat to SAP's "closed" ERP software.

At the output side, the emergence of the Internet also radically altered the relationship between a company and its customers. Not only did the Internet make possible new ways to sell to wholesalers, its largest customers, or directly to individual customers, it also changed the whole nature of the company–customer interface. For example, using new customer relationship management (CRM) software from software developers like Siebel Systems, a company could offer its customers access to much more information about its products so that customers could make more-informed purchase decisions. A company could also understand customers' changing needs so it could develop improved or advanced products to meet those needs; and a company could offer a whole new way to manage after-sales service and help solve customers' problems with learning about, operating, and even repairing their new purchases. The CRM market was starting to boom.

In essence the Internet was changing both industry- and company-level business processes and providing companies and whole industries with many more avenues for altering their business processes at a company or industry level, so that they could lower their cost structure or increasingly differentiate their products. Clearly, the hundreds of industry best practices that SAP had embedded in its R/3 software would become outdated and redundant as e-commerce increased in scope and depth and offered improved industry solutions. SAP's R/3 system would become a dinosaur within a decade unless it could move quickly to develop or obtain competences in the software skills needed to develop Web-based software.

These developments posed a severe shock to SAP's management, who had been proud of the fact that, until now, SAP had developed all its software internally. They were not alone in their predicament. The largest software companies, Microsoft and Oracle, had been caught unaware by the quickly growing implications of Web-based computing. The introduction of Netscape's Web browser had led to a collapse in Microsoft's stock price because investors saw Web-based computing, not PC-based computing, as the choice of the future. SAP's stock price also began to reflect the beliefs of many people that expensive, rigid, standardized ERP systems would not become the software choice as the Web developed. One source of SAP's competitive advantage was based on the high switching costs of moving from one ERP platform to another. However, if new Web-based platforms allowed both internal and external integration of a company's business processes, and new platforms could be customized more easily to answer a particular company's needs, these switching costs might disappear. SAP was at a critical point in its development.

The other side of the equation was that the emergence of new Web-based software technology allowed hundreds of new software industry start-ups, founded by technical experts as qualified as those at SAP and Microsoft, to enter the industry and compete for the wide-open Web computing market. The race was on to determine which standards would apply in the new Web computing arena and who would control them. The large software makers like Microsoft, Oracle, IBM, SAP, Netscape, Sun Microsystems, and Computer Associates had to decide how to compete in this totally changed industry environment. Most of their customers, companies large and small, were still watching developments before deciding how and where to commit their IT budgets. Hundreds of billions of dollars in future software sales were at stake, and it was not clear which company had the competitive advantage in this changing environment.

Rivalry among major software makers in the new Web-based software market became intense. Rivalry between the major players and new players, like Netscape, Siebel Systems, Marcum, I2 Technology, and SSA, also intensified. The major software makers, each of which was a market leader in one or more segments of the software industry, such as SAP in ERP, Microsoft in PC software, and Oracle in database management software, sought to showcase their strengths to make their software compatible with Web-based technology. Thus, Microsoft strove to develop its Windows NT network-based platform and its Internet Explorer Web browser to compete with Netscape's Internet browser and Sun Microsystems's open-standard Java Web software programming language, which was compatible with any company's proprietary software, unlike Microsoft's NT.

SAP also had to deal with competition from large and small software companies that were breaking into the new Web-based ERP environment. In 1995, SAP teamed with Microsoft, Netscape, and Sun Microsystems to make its R/3 software Internet-compatible with any of their competing systems. Within one year, it introduced its R/3 Release 3.1 Internet-compatible system, which was most easily configured, however, when using Sun's Java Web-programming language. SAP raised new funds on the stock market to undertake new rounds of the huge investment necessary to keep its Web-based R/3 system up to date with the dramatic innovations in Web software development and to broaden its product range to offer new, continually emerging Web-based applications—for example, applications such as the corporate intranets, business-to-business (B2B) and business-to customer (B2C) networks, website development and hosting, security and systems management, and streaming audio and video teleconferencing.

Because SAP had no developed competence in Web software development, its competitors started to catch up. Oracle emerged as its major competitor; it had taken its core database management software used by thousands of large companies and overlaid it with Web-based operating and applications software. Oracle could now offer its huge customer base a growing suite of Web software, all seamlessly integrated. The suite of software also allowed it to perform Internet-based ERP value chain business processes. While Oracle's system was nowhere near as comprehensive as SAP's R/3 system, it allowed for cross-industry networking at both the input and output sides, it was cheaper and easier to implement quickly, and it was easier to customize to the needs of a particular customer. Oracle began to take market share away from SAP.

New companies like Siebel Systems, Commerce One, Ariba, and Marcum, which began as niche players in some software applications such as SCM, CRM, intranet, or website development and hosting, also began to build and expand their product offerings so that they now possessed ERP modules that competed with some of SAP's most lucrative R/3 modules. Commerce One and Ariba, for example, emerged as the main players in the rapidly expanding B2B industry SCM market. B2B is an industry-level ERP solution that creates an organized market and thus brings together industry buyers and suppliers electronically and provides the software to write and enforce contracts for the future development and supply of an industry's inputs. Although these niche players could not provide the full range of services that SAP could provide, they became increasingly able to offer attractive alternatives to customers seeking specific aspects of an ERP system. Also, companies like Siebel, Marcum, and I2 claimed that they had the ability to customize their low-price systems, and prices for ERP systems began to fall.

In the new software environment, SAP's large customers started to purchase software on a "best of breed" basis, meaning that customers purchased the best software applications for their specific needs from different, leading-edge companies rather than purchasing all of their software products from one company as a package—such as SAP offered. Sun began to promote a free Java computer language as the industry "open architecture" standard, which meant that as long as each company used Java to craft its specific Web-based software programs, they would all work seamlessly together and there would no longer be an advantage to using a single dominant platform like Microsoft's Windows or SAP's R/3. Sun was and is trying to break Microsoft's hold over the operating system industry standard, Windows. Sun wanted each company's software to succeed because it was "best of breed," not because it locked customers in and created enormous switching costs for them should they contemplate a move to a competitor's product.

All these different factors caused enormous problems for SAP's top managers. What strategies should they use to protect their competitive position? Should they forge ahead with offering their customers a broad, proprietary, Web-based ERP solution and try to lock them in and continue to charge a premium price? Should they move to an open standard and make their R/3 ERP Internet-enabled modules compatible with solutions from other companies, and indeed forge alliances with those companies to ensure that their software operated seamlessly together? Since SAP's managers still believed they had the best ERP software and the capabilities to lead in the Web software arena, was this the best long-run competitive solution? Should SAP focus on making its ERP software more customizable to its customers' needs and make it easier for them to buy selected modules to reduce the cost of SAP software? This alternative might also make it easier for them to develop ERP modules that could be scaled back to suit the needs of medium and small firms, which increasingly were becoming the targets of its new software competitors. Once these new firms got toeholds in the market, it would then be a matter of time before they improved their products and began to compete for SAP's installed customer base. SAP realized that it had to refocus its business model, especially because rivals were rapidly buying niche players and, at the same time, filling gaps in their product lines to be able to compete with SAP.

Protecting Its Competitive Position

In 1997, SAP sought a quick fix to its problems by releasing new R/3 solutions for ERP Internet-enabled SCM and CRM solutions, which converted its internal ERP system into an externally based network platform. SCM, now known as the "back end" of the business, integrates the business processes necessary to manage the flow of goods, from the raw material stage to the finished product. SCM programs forecast future needs, and plan and manage a company's operations, especially its manufacturing operations. CRM, known as the "front-end" of the business, provides companies with solutions and support for business processes directed at improving sales, marketing, customer service, and field service operations. CRM programs are rapidly growing in popularity because they lead to better customer retention and satisfaction and higher revenues. In 1998, SAP followed with industry solution maps, business technology maps, and service maps, all of which were aimed at making its R/3 system dynamic and responsive to changes in industry conditions.

Also in 1998, recognizing that its future rested on its ability to protect its share of the U.S. market, SAP listed itself on the New York Stock Exchange and began to expand the scope of its U.S. operations, both to encourage internal "organic growth," meaning growth through internal new venturing, and to allow it to develop a U.S. top management team that could develop the strategies and business model necessary to allow it to respond to the growing competition it was facing. As with all growing businesses, the need to manage the fit between its strategy and structure had become its major priority—SAP's R&D culture was hurting it in its battle with agile competitors and had to be changed.

References

www.sap.com, 1988–1999.

SAP Annual Reports and 10K Reports, 1989–1999.

SAP 10K Reports, 1989–2000.

CASE 4
The Scaffold Plank Incident

Stewart C. Malone and Brad Brown

What had started as a typically slow February day in the lumber business had turned into a moral dilemma. With 12 inches of snow covering the ground, construction (and lumber shipments) had ground to a halt and on the 26th of the month, the company was still $5,000 below break-even point. In the three years since he had been in the business, Bob Hopkins knew that a losing February was nothing unusual, but the country seemed to be headed for a recession, and as usual, housing starts were leading the way into the abyss.

Bob had gone to work for a commercial bank immediately after college but soon found the bureaucracy to be overwhelming and his career progress appeared to be written in stone. At the same time he was considering changing jobs, one of his customers, John White, offered him a job at White Lumber Company. The job was as a "trader," a position that involved both buying and selling lumber. The compensation was incentive-based and there was no cap on how much a trader could earn. White Lumber, although small in size, was one of the bank's best accounts. John White was not only a director of the bank but one of the community's leading citizens.

It was a little after 8:00 A.M. when Bob received a call from Stan Parrish, the lumber buyer at Quality Lumber. Quality was one of White Lumber's best retail dealer accounts, and Bob and Stan had established a good relationship.

"Bob, I need a price and availability on 600 pieces of 3 × 12 Doug fir-rough-sawn—2 & better grade—16-feet long," said Stan, after exchanging the usual pleasantries.

"No problem, Stan. We could have those ready for pickup tomorrow and the price would be $470 per thousand board feet."

"The price sounds good, Bob. I'll probably be getting back to you this afternoon with a firm order," Stan replied.

Bob poured a third cup of coffee and mentally congratulated himself. Not bad, he thought—a two-truck order and a price that guaranteed full margin. It was only a half-hour later that Mike Fayerweather, his partner, asked Bob if he had gotten any inquiries on a truck of 16-foot scaffold plank. As Bob said he hadn't, alarm bells began to go off in his brain. While Stan had not said anything about scaffold plank, the similarities between the inquiries seemed to be more than coincidence.

While almost all lumber undergoes some sort of grading, the grading rules on scaffold plank were unusually restrictive. Scaffold planks are the wooden planks that are suspended between metal supports, often many stories above the ground. When you see painters and window-washers six stories in the air, they generally are standing on scaffold plank. The lumber had to be free of most of the natural defects found in ordinary construction lumber and had to have unusually high strength in flexing. Most people would not be able to tell certified scaffold plank from ordinary lumber, but it was covered by its own rules in the grading book, and if you were working 10 stories above the ground, you definitely wanted to have certified scaffold plank underneath you. White Lumber did not carry scaffold plank, but its rough 3×12s certainly would fool all but the expertly trained eye.

At lunch, Bob discussed his concerns about the inquiry with Mike.

"Look, Bob, I just don't see where we have a problem. Stan didn't specify scaffold plank, and you didn't quote him on scaffold plank," observed Mike. "We aren't even certain that the order is for the same material."

"I know all that, Mike," said Bob, "but we both know that four inquiries with the same tally is just too big a coincidence, and three of those inquiries were for Paragraph 171 scaffold plank. It seems reasonable to assume that Stan's quotation is for the same stuff."

"Well, it's obvious that our construction lumber is a good deal cheaper than the certified plank. If Stan is quoting based on our 2 & better grade and the rest of his competition is quoting on scaffold plank, then he will certainly win the job," Mike said.

"Maybe I should call Stan back and get more information on the specifications of the job. It may turn out that this isn't scaffold plank job, and all of these problems will just disappear."

The waitress slipped the check between the two lumbermen. "Well, that might not be such a great idea, Bob. First, Stan may be a little ticked off if you were suggesting he might be doing something unethical. It could blow the relations between our companies. Second, suppose he does say that the material is going to be used for scaffolding. We would no longer be able to say we didn't know what it was going to be used for, and our best legal defense is out the window. I'd advise against calling him."

Bob thought about discussing the situation with John White, but White was out of town. Also, White prided himself on giving his traders a great deal of autonomy. Going

This case was prepared by Stewart C. Malone and Brad Brown, University of Virginia. This case was prepared as a basis for class discussion rather than to illustrate either effective or ineffective handling of administrative situations.

to White too often for answers to questions was perceived as showing a lack of initiative and responsibility.

Against Mike's earlier warnings, Bob called Stan after lunch and discovered to his dismay that the material was going to be used as scaffold plank.

"Listen, Bob, I've been trying to sell this account for three months and this is the first inquiry that I've had a chance on. This is really important to me personally and to my superiors here at Quality. With this sale, we could land this account."

"But, Stan, we both know that our material doesn't meet the specs for scaffold plank."

"I know, I know," said Stan, "but I'm not selling it to the customer as scaffold plank. It's just regular construction lumber as far as we are both concerned. That's how I've sold it, and that's what will show on the invoices. We're completely protected. Now just between you and me, the foreman on the job winked at me and told me it was going to be scaffolding, but they're interested in keeping their costs down too. Also, they need this lumber by Friday, and there just isn't any scaffold plank in the local market."

"It just doesn't seem right to me," replied Bob.

"Look, I don't particularly like it, either. The actual specifications call for 2-inch thick material, but since it isn't actually scaffold plank, I'm going to order 3-inch planks. That is an extra inch of strength, and we both know that the load factors given in the engineering tables are too conservative to begin with. There's no chance that the material could fail in use. I happen to know that Haney Lumber is quoting a non-scaffold grade in a 2-inch material. If we don't grab this, someone else will and the material will be a lot worse than what we are going to supply."

When Bob continued to express hesitation, Stan said "I won't hear about the status of the order until tomorrow, but we both know that your material will do this job OK—scaffold plank or not. The next year or two in this business are going to be lean for everyone, and our job—yours and mine—is putting lumber on job sites, not debating how many angels can dance on the head of a pin. Now if Quality can't count on you doing your job as a supplier, there are plenty of other wholesalers calling here every day who want our business. You better decide if you are going to be one of the survivors or not! I'll talk to you in the morning, Bob."

The next morning, Bob found a note on his desk telling him to see John White ASAP. Bob entered John's oak-paneled office and described the conversation with Stan yesterday. John slid a company sales order across the desk, and Bob saw it was a sales order for the 3×12s to Quality Lumber. In the space for the salesman's name, Bob saw that John had filled in "Bob Hopkins." Barely able to control his anger, Bob said, "I don't want anything to do with this order. I thought White Lumber was an ethical company, and here we are doing the same thing that all the fly-by-nighters do," sputtered Bob in concluding his argument.

John White looked at Bob and calmly puffed on his pipe. "The first thing you better do, Bob, is to calm down and put away your righteous superiority for a moment. You can't make or understand a good decision when you are as lathered up as you are. You are beginning to sound like a religious nut. What makes you think that you have the monopoly on ethical behavior? You've been out of college for four or five years, while I've been making these decisions for 40 years. If you go into the industry or the community and compare your reputation with mine, you'll find out that you aren't even in the same league."

Bob knew John White was right. He had, perhaps, overstated his case, and in doing so, sounded like a zealot. When he relaxed and felt as though he was once again capable of rational thought, he said, "We both know that this lumber is going to be used for a purpose for which it is probably not suitable. Granted, there is only a very small chance that it will fail, but I don't see how we can take that chance."

"Look, Bob, I've been in this business for a long time, and I've seen practices that would curl your hair. Undershipping (shipping 290 pieces when the order calls for 300), shipping material a grade below what was ordered, bribing building inspectors and receiving clerks, and so on. We don't do those things at my company."

"Don't we have a responsibility to our customers, though?" asked Bob.

"Of course we do, Bob, but we aren't policemen, either. Our job is to sell lumber that is up to specification. I can't and won't be responsible for how the lumber is used after it leaves our yard. Between the forest and the final user, lumber may pass through a dozen transactions before it reaches the ultimate user. If we are to assume responsibility for every one of those transactions, we would probably have time to sell about four boards a year. We have to assume, just like every other business, that our suppliers and our customers are knowledgeable and will also act ethically. But whether they do or don't, it is not possible for us to be their keepers."

Bob interjected, "But we have reason to believe that this material will be used as scaffolding. I think we have an obligation to follow up on that information.

"Hold on, just a second, Bob. I told you once we are not the police. We don't even know who the final user is, so how are we going to follow up on this? If Stan is jerking us around, he certainly won't tell us. And even if we did know, what would we do? If we are going to do this consistently, that means we would have to ask every customer who the final end user is. Most of our customers would interpret that as us trying to bypass them in the distribution channel. They won't tell us, and I can't blame them. If we carry your argument to its final conclusion, we'll have to start taking depositions on every invoice we sell.

"In the Quality Lumber instance, we are selling material to the customer as specified by the customer, Stan at Quality Lumber. The invoice will be marked. 'This material is not suitable for use as scaffold plank.' Although I'm not a lawyer, I believe that we have fulfilled our legal obligation. We have a signed purchase order and are supplying lumber that meets the specifications. I know we have followed the practices that are customary in the industry. Finally, I believe that our material will be better than anything else that could conceivably go on the job. Right now, there is no 2-inch dense 171 scaffold plank in this market, so it is not as though a better grade could be supplied in the time allotted. I would argue that we are ethically obligated to supply this lumber. If anyone is ethically at fault, it is probably the purchasing agent who specified a material that is not available."

When Bob still appeared to be unconvinced, John White asked him, "What about the other people here at the company? You're acting as though you are the only person who has a stake in this. It may be easy for you to turn this order down—you've got a college degree and a lot of career options. But I have to worry about all of the people at this company. Steve out there on the forklift never finished high school. He's worked here thirty years and if he loses this job, he'll probably never find another one. Janet over in bookkeeping has a disabled husband. While I can't afford to pay her very much, our health insurance plan keeps their family together. With the bills her husband accumulates in a year, she could never get him on another group insurance plan if she lost this job.

"Bob, I'm not saying that we should do anything and then try to justify it, but business ethics in the real world is not the same thing you studied in the classroom. There it is easy to say, 'Oh, there is an ethical problem here. We better not do that.' In the classroom, you have nothing to lose by taking the morally superior ground. Out here, companies close, people lose their jobs, lives can be destroyed. To always say, 'No, we won't do that' is no better than having no ethics at all. Ethics involves making tough choices, weighing costs and benefits. There are no hard-and-fast answers in these cases. We just have to approach each situation individually."

As Bob left John's office, he was more confused than ever. When he first entered his office, he had every intention of quitting in moral indignation, but John's arguments had made a lot of sense to him, and he both trusted and respected John. After all, John White had a great deal more experience than he did and was highly respected in both the community and the lumber industry. Yet he was still uncomfortable with the decision. Was selling lumber to Quality merely a necessary adjustment of his ivory tower ethics to the real world of business? Or was it the first fork in the road to a destination he did not want to reach?

CASE 5

Beer and Wine Industries: Bartles & Jaymes

Per V. Jenster

At the end of 1986, Bartles & Jaymes conquered the number one position in the wine cooler industry after coming in second to California Coolers since this product hit the consumer goods market. Going into 1987, Bartles & Jaymes and its corporate parent, Ernest & Julio Gallo Winery, were faced with the task of maintaining this market position and increasing sales of its newest product—the wine cooler.

History of the Firm

Ernest and Julio Gallo Winery, the world's largest, began in 1933 at a tragic point in the brothers' lives. They had just inherited their father Joseph's vineyard after he shot his wife, reportedly chased Ernest and Julio with a shotgun, and committed suicide. Suddenly they were faced with operating the vineyard where they grew up and had gone to work upon completing their education (high school for Julio and junior college for Ernest). The business of growing grapes was all they knew. Joseph Gallo, an immigrant from Italy, came to Modesto, California, and began his small grape-producing company. The fledgling company survived Prohibition due to the fact that the government allowed wine production for medicinal and religious use. The Depression dealt the small company a somewhat more devastating blow. It was at this company low point that Joseph decided on such a dramatic solution to his problems. Though he may have solved his problems, Joseph left his relatively young sons a burden of responsibility and decision making. Shortly after their parents' deaths, Prohibition was repealed and the brothers decided to move from grape growing to wine producing. With two pamphlets on wine making from the local public library and less that $6,000 in hand, the ambitious Gallos began their empire.

Gallo's climb to its dominant position in the wine industry (see Exhibit 1) began slowly. In the 1930s and 1940s, Ernest developed his acute marketing sense and Julio cultivated and refined his wine-making expertise. Initially they

Professor Per V. Jenster. IMD, Lausanne, Switzerland. Reprinted with permission. The author gratefully acknowledges the assistance of students Morlon Bell, Michele Goggins, and Mary Kay, as well as the support provided by the McIntire Foundation.

EXHIBIT 1 1985 Share of U.S. Wine Market

E. & J. Gallo Winery	26.1%
Seagram & Sons	8.3
Canandaigua Wine	5.4
Brown-Forman	5.1
National Distillers	4.0
Heublein	3.7
Imports	23.4
All others	24.0

Source: From *Advertising Age*, March 24, 1986. Reprinted with permission of Crain Communications Inc.

sold their product in bulk to bottlers on the East Coast, but in 1938 they decided it would be more profitable to bottle the wine under a Gallo label. In the 1950s, Gallo greatly increased its success with a high-alcohol, low-price product called Thunderbird. This product became exceptionally popular on skid rows and increased Gallo's profitability, but it may have done irreparable damage by saddling Gallo with a "gutter" image. In the 1960s and early 1970s, Gallo's image, not sales, was further tarnished by the "pop-wine" craze of which it was a leader with such products as Boone's Farm and Spanada wines. In the mid-1970s, Ernest Gallo became conscious of and concerned about the fact that even though it had formidable sales, it also had a "brownbag," jug-wine image. At that time, the company decided to attempt to upgrade its image and at the same time maintain its market share and sales. As part of this attempt, it began to produce premium table wines such as Zinfandel, Sauvignon Blanc, Ruby Cabernet, and French Colombard. This push to improve its image continued to be a dominating theme for Gallo.

As Gallo grew, it not only developed its wine sales but became extensively vertically integrated. It had divisions in virtually every step of the wine-producing process. The brothers owned one of the largest intrastate trucking companies in California, which was used to haul wine, grapes, raw materials, sand, lime, etc. Gallo was the only wine producer that made its own bottles, and its Midcal Aluminum Company supplied it with screw tops. Unlike most other wine producers, Gallo took an active role in the marketing of its products. Typical wineries would turn their products over to independent distributors who represented several producers and expected the distributor to get the product to the consumer. These distributors, on the other hand, felt their job consisted of taking orders and making deliveries. Gallo owned many of its distributors, and the independent distributors it used had to be willing to submit to Gallo's regimentation. Gallo was known to "encourage" its independent distributors to exclusively distribute Gallo products. Ten years ago, the Federal Trade Commission took offense at this, charging Gallo with unfair competition and forcing Gallo to sign a consent order. In 1984, the FTC removed the order due to the fact that the wine industry had become more competitive.

In its 50-year history, Gallo developed an extensive product line. It had products geared toward the low-priced, jug-wine market (Carlo Rossi, Chablis Blanc, etc.). It also had a replete category of premium wines, selling more than any competitor, but growth in this market was limited due to the fact that Gallo did not have snob appeal. In 1984, Gallo entered the wine cooler category (a carbonated drink with half white wine and half citrus juice) with its Bartles & Jaymes wine cooler. Gallo followed the lead of such industry innovators as California Cooler, Sun Country Coolers, etc., which fit well with its strategy of building market share through skillful marketing and sales, but not introducing inventive new products. Bartles & Jaymes was marketed in 12-ounce green bottles similar to those used for Michelob beer and aimed at a more sophisticated consumer than its competitors. To help promote this upgraded image, Gallo tried to distance itself from Bartles & Jaymes, and many consumers did not know that Gallo wine was used to make the coolers. In the summer of 1986, Bartles & Jaymes took over the number one position in the wine cooler market with a share of 22.1 percent.

With that initial $6,000, some ingenuity, a little luck, and a lot of spunk, the Gallo brothers built the world's preeminent wine dynasty. Because Gallo was a private, tightly held company, there was no public financial data, but it was estimated that it had annual sales of $1 billion and yearly earnings of $50 million. In comparison, Joe E. Seagram and Sons, the second largest winery, had revenues of $350 million and lost money on its best-selling table wines in 1985.

Background on Key Executives

E. & J. Gallo was a private company owned and operated by the Gallo brothers, Ernest and Julio. Julio, the 77-year-old president of the firm, and Ernest, chairman of the board at 78, ran their company in a very dichotomous manner. Julio was in charge of producing the wine and Ernest marketed and distributed it. They operated in their separate worlds and often did not have daily contact. It seemed to be a game—Julio trying to produce more than Ernest could sell and Ernest trying to sell more than Julio could produce. But the game apparently worked and provided the company with good returns.

Julio, the more easygoing of the two, described himself as a "farmer at heart." He spent much of his time in the fields and overseeing the wine making. Though definitely not a pushover, Julio was not the hard-core, intense businessman that his brother Ernest was. Ernest ruled over the company and usually made the final decisions. He was characterized as being polite, but blunt. He could not bear to relinquish power and control, and it was at his insistence that everything about the operation of the firm was kept secret. He could be a very demanding, driving boss, and when asked about the secret to Gallo's success, he remarked it was a "constant striving for perfection in every aspect of our business."

A looming concern, though not openly addressed or dealt with at Gallo, was the brothers' advancing age. Julio seemed to be training and grooming his son, Robert, and his son-in-law, James Coleman, in his area of expertise. Ernest, on the other hand, had no heir apparent. Two of his sons, David and Joseph, worked with him, but neither was viewed as having the ability to take over their father's job. Joseph was felt to give uneven decisions, and David was described as "occasionally bizarre." The firm had many intelligent, able, top-level executives, but they had no power to make decisions and predominantly strove to please Ernest. The deaths of Ernest and Julio, which were inevitable, could prove to be devastating for the firm.

Internal Operations

Because Gallo was so tightly held and secretive, it was hard to determine how and why things were done the way they were—maybe only Ernest knew. A few loyal senior managers ran the divisions of the vertically integrated firm and reported to Ernest. He had a hand in all major decisions and procedures and went so far as to help write a 300-page, very detailed training manual for sales representatives. Gallo was so secretive that at times even its own employees did not know what was happening. According to Diana Kelleher, former marketing manager at Gallo, "I never saw a profit-and-loss statement; Ernest wouldn't tell anyone the cost of raw materials, overhead, or packaging."

Industry History and Analysis

It would be difficult to pinpoint exactly when the wine cooler industry emerged. Three separate events were cited to mark the beginning of this prosperous industry. In 1977, Joseph Bianchi, owner of Bianchi Vineyards, observed people at a summer party mixing Seven-Up with wine. In 1981, Thomas Steid, owner of Canada Dry/Graf's Bottling Company, formulated his own wine cooler recipe. The event that was commonly viewed as the beginning of this industry stemmed from the concoction of Michael M. Crete and R. Stuart Bewley produced by California Cooler.

Crete and Bewley's drink was initially served in 1972, to their friends. Little did they know that this new refresher would be a huge success a decade later. Batches of white wine and fruit juice were mixed in a beer barrel and served from a plastic hose. Labels were stuck on by hand and an average workday consisted of bottling 100 to 150 cases. As this product was marketed in the early 1980s, sales began to increase steadily. This campaign spurred national attention toward the new market.

At the point of the cooler's entry, other sectors of the beverage industry were experiencing declining sales. The wine industry had experienced declining table wine sales for two years in a row at the beginning of the 1980s. Likewise, the beer industry was faced with declining sales. It was costing both industries more in advertising to keep their regular customers. Several factors caused such a response in the consumer market. First, drunken driving laws and the crackdown on drinking that they spurred led to more awareness about the negative effects of alcohol. Public interest groups such as MADD (Mothers Against Drunk Driving) played a key role in changing the consumer's perceptions of drinking. Second, there was growing concern for fitness. As the health-conscious consumers grew in number, the tendency to indulge in alcoholic beverages declined. Third, the raising of the legal drinking age presented obstacles to increasing sales. Since younger adults consumed a significant percentage of the alcohol sold, the change in age cut out some sales originally anticipated by beer and wine producers. Fourth, the lobbying to remove liquor advertising from television showed wineries and breweries as the villains in society.

In view of societal factors, a method was needed to help the alcohol industries survive. Thus, an alternative to beer and wine appeared to be the solution in the eyes of Crete and Bewley. They saw the potential and seized the opportunity to capitalize on the venture. To achieve a successful outcome, however, the product had to be positioned properly. The wine cooler was a fruity-tasting, slightly cloudy beverage made from chablis, blended citrus-pineapple juice, fructose, and a slight amount of carbonation. Its targeted consumers were young adults from legal drinking age to 34 years old, both male and female. The cooler was marketed in the same manner as beer, particularly its "coldbox," refrigerator bottling. It was to be less of an elitist drink than wine. It contained more alcohol than beer but less alcohol than wine.

For the wine cooler industry to succeed, several characteristics had to be present. Taste was an important factor to provide a basis for differentiation between products. Points of difference were sought to make individual brands stand out, by varying fruit flavors, packaging, or advertising techniques. Another major characteristic was merchandising, which was relevant to the success of any consumer market. In the wine industry particularly, price was the key to merchandising. It could be extremely difficult for competitors to come up with original ideas to differentiate their product, so most relied on price to help them capture a reasonable percentage of the market.

Several viewpoints have been given about wine coolers. The single-service focus was the major thrust of the cooler's marketing plan. It could be carried easily (exactly like beer) and did not concentrate heavily on the jug mentality of wineries. Coolers also cut across beverage boundaries by "touting the fizz of soft drinks, the popularity of white wine, the freshness of citrus juice, plus a bit of fructose to satisfy the sweet tooth." The cooler fit the desires of the current pluralistic consumer society. It was viewed as "wine for the common man" because it appealed to the beer drinker who wanted a little more alcohol, the wine drinker who wanted a little less, the calorie- and taste-conscious, and the first-time wine drinkers put off by the snobbery of the wine elite. The marketing module appeared to contain all the elements of success—"a firm product identity; a well-defined package and price image; a powerful distribution channel that stressed cold-box merchandising to capitalize on its 'cool' perception and enhance its full price and profit positioning; and advertising that communicated a refreshing message to the public." This segment showed second-generation development. Three trends were cited in the existing industry. One trend focused on the low alcohol content of approximately 6 percent. This aspect was probably influenced by the anti–drunk driving campaigns. Sales of coolers were said to have been spurred by this concern. Another trend was geared toward its thirst-quenching characteristic. Its refreshing health perspective was the focus of the last trend. Coolers were professed to be healthful since they contained half citrus juice.

The wine cooler industry appeared particularly attractive because the product offered high margins and a low base with no capital requirements. It generated better gross dollar margins than beer or wine. The expected annual growth rate was projected to be 13 percent until 1993. The expected growth rate in 1986 was 69 percent. Cooler sales were estimated to account for 17 percent to 20 percent of total wine sales in 1986 as compared to only 1 percent in 1984.

In 1986, the cooler industry was faced with various trends in the beverage world. First, it was reported that Americans were drinking more soft drinks (April 1986). The alcohol industry was still faced with overall declines, but the wine industry was better situated than the beer industry due to the success of the wine cooler. It was predicted that the wine cooler industry would soon be viewed separately from the wine industry. The second area of concern involved the steadily increasing cost of competing. The fight for wholesale and retail distribution was intensifying. This led marketers to cut prices to acquire more shelf space and visibility. Also, coupons were used to increase distribution. As of August 1986, the dollar level was low and the investment spending was high.

The wine cooler industry consisted of approximately forty producers and 154 individual labels during the summer of 1986. Because of the high barriers to entry competition from other segments, particularly the breweries and wineries, competition did not appear to be substantial. Since the beer and wine markets were mature, the success achieved in the wine cooler industry caused them to take a second look at this area for potential profits. Even though breweries and wineries experienced decreasing sales, only a small portion was attributed to the boom in the wine cooler industry. The soft-drink industry, on the other hand, proved to be a minor problem for coolers due to increased consumption by consumers. The effect of the competition was not significantly shown in the sales figures for coolers, but the potential loomed in the background. Experts raised questions concerning cooler sales. Declines were predicted based on a speculated consumer interest in a variety of flavored drinks. Were coolers a fad or a new and growing industry?

Competition

When California Cooler began peddling its wine cooler, the competition was sparse and far from formidable. Initially, the cost of entry into the new market was relatively low. But by the first quarter of 1986, the world's largest winery, brewery, and distillery were all vying for the top spot and all three were holding fat bankrolls. The cost of entry into the market had risen to $10 million just for advertising. Cooler marketers and industry observers were confident this category would continue to grow steadily for the next few years. It was estimated that 60 to 65 million cases of coolers—including malt-based coolers—would have been sold by the end of 1987, up from 41 million cases in 1985. In 1987, more than 150 kinds of wine coolers were competing with the top seven coolers, which controlled about 90 percent of the market—E. & J. Gallo Winery's Bartles & Jaymes, Brown-Forman Corporation's California Cooler, Canandaigua Wine Company's Sun Country, Joseph Victori Wines' Calvin Cooler, Stroh Brewery Company's malt-based White Mountain cooler, and Joe E. Seagram and Sons' Premium and Golden coolers. (See Exhibit 2.)

Bartles & Jaymes

By October 1986, Gallo's Bartles & Jaymes wine cooler was the largest-selling cooler in the nation, with a 22.1 percent market share. Its standing was quite remarkable in light of Bartles & Jaymes' relatively narrow product line. Gallo

EXHIBIT 2 Top 10 Cooler Brands' Share of the Market

	1986*	1985
1. Bartles & Jaymes	22.1%	17.5%
2. California Cooler	18.0	26.8
3. Sun Country	13.1	11.7
4. White Mountain	12.4	7.5
5. Calvin Cooler	8.3	6.5
6. Seagram's Golden	6.9	—
7. Seagram's Premium	5.5	9.3
8. Dewey Stevens	2.8	—
9. 20/20	2.5	3.7
10. La Croix	1.5	1.9

Source: From Impact Databank, 1986. Reprinted by permission of M. Shanken Communications, Inc.

*Estimate.

EXHIBIT 3 1986 Advertising Budgets

Bartles & Jaymes	$30,000,000
Seagram's	30,000,000
California Cooler	25,000,000
Dewey Stevens	20,000,000
Sun Country	20,000,000
White Mountain	12,000,000
Calvin Cooler	10,000,000

Source: From *Advertising Age*, March 24, 1986. Reprinted with permission of Crain Communications, Inc.

produced only one flavor of wine cooler (6 percent alcohol). This clear, less sweet cooler came in sleek 12-ounce green bottles like those of imported beers and was available in the standard four-pack.

Two key factors, advertising and distribution, differentiated the industry leader from its competitors. In 1986, Gallo budgeted $30 million for advertising expenditures for Bartles & Jaymes (see Exhibit 3). The majority of this money was spent on an ad campaign in which Gallo chose to distance its cooler from the parent corporation by creating fictional proprietors named Frank Bartles and Ed Jaymes, who sat on their front porch while Frank delivered low-key, comical monologues about the product. An advertiser with the Bartles & Jaymes campaign said, "Most of the competition was using youthful music and showing young people doing all the predictable things. We thought that if we got into all those clichés, we'd get lost." This was all part of a cold, hard-edged effort on Gallo's part to maintain a sense of warm, down-home, folksy legitimacy around the TV spots that obviously had many Americans believing there really was a Frank Bartles and an Ed Jaymes.

Some observers, including a few of Gallo's competitors, were not as amused by Gallo's marketing strategy as most of America seemed to be. Tom Gibbs, director of marketing for California Coolers, saw the ads as downright deceptive. "Yuppies are not Gallo drinkers, so they (Gallo) have tried to disassociate their names from this market." Mr. Gibbs said the public did not know Frank and Ed were not on the level and believed consumers would turn away from the product if they knew the truth. He claimed his company had done interviews after which people quit drinking Bartles & Jaymes once they learned it was a Gallo product—a name, he says, "people equate with jug wines."

Jon Fredrikson, an industry analyst with San Francisco-based wine industry consultants Gomberg, Fredrikson & Associates, said the public might react negatively if the truth got out on a widespread basis, but added that wasn't likely.

Aileen Fredrikson, also with Gomberg, said the campaign had the dual effect of helping beer drinkers relate to the wine cooler market. "Young people can always be convinced to try something once," she said, "but this may be a way to get hard-core beer drinkers to try it, since it's two good ole boys selling it."

The channel of distribution chosen by Gallo was the second key factor in differentiating Bartles & Jaymes from its competitors. Unlike other wine cooler producers who distributed their products through beer distributors, Bartles & Jaymes used Gallo's extensive wine distributorship. Ernest Gallo handpicked each of these distributors and then planned strategies with them down to the last detail, analyzing traffic patterns in every store in the district and the number of Gallo cases each should stock. Ernest Gallo encouraged distributors to hire a separate sales force to sell his products alone. He also tried to persuade distributors to sell his wine exclusively.

California Cooler

Stuart Bewley and Michael Crete were partners who founded California Cooler Company, Stockton, California, just five years ago. The two childhood friends created the product when they started filling washtubs at beach parties with their special mixture—half white wine and half citrus juice. In September 1985, Brown-Forman, a Louisville-based distiller, bought out the segment leader California Cooler for $63 million in cash plus millions more in incentive payments based on future sales.

California Coolers contained 6 percent alcohol and came in a variety of flavors including tropical, orange, and the original citrus flavor. Crucial to California Cooler's initial success was that it was marketed more as a beer than as a wine. From the beginning, Crete and Bewley wanted a quality package, and from their beer-drinking days, they felt nothing beat a Heineken bottle. So they packaged California Cooler in a green-tinged, twist-top, short-neck bottle, added a gold foil top, and sold it in four-packs for under $4. This, they figured, might draw some beer drinkers. Subsequently, to counter competition, California Cooler introduced several new packages, including 2-liter bottles, 198-milliliter bottles, and, in some areas, quarter and half barrels.

In another important step, they left the natural fruit pulp in the bottle and stressed it on the label. California Cooler was thus further removed from the clear, sipping wine category. California Cooler hoped to get the younger, natural-thinking consumers. The product was positioned as an informal, mainstream American drink, targeted toward males and females from 18 to 35 years of age.

Once the company broke even in early 1983, the cofounders began looking for an advertising agency to help broaden sales from its northern California base. Its only advertising up until that point was a spot radio jingle sung to the tune of the Beach Boys' hit "California Girls." The new advertising campaign positioned California Cooler not as a beer, not as a wine, but "beyond ordinary refreshment."

These ads were funny put downs by outsiders who were slightly envious of the hot tubs, health food fetishes, and all-around casual lifestyles of Californians—including their namesake drink, California Cooler. Other ads featured young people and 1960s rock 'n roll. Brown-Forman Corporation spent over $20 million on this ad campaign in 1986, yet still lost its top standing to Bartles & Jaymes. In 1986, California Cooler had an 18.0 percent market share, down from 26.8 percent in 1985 (see Exhibit 2).

Unlike Bartles & Jaymes, California Coolers were distributed by beer distributors, not wine wholesalers. The founders of California Cooler wanted their cooler to be in the "cold box" or refrigerator of a sales account. They felt the movement in beverages was out of the cold box, not the racks. Beer distributors were chosen because they typically had more accounts than their wine counterparts; beer distributors carried fewer products compared to the huge portfolios of wine wholesalers; and as "good ole boys," beer distributors represented their informal product better. More recently, though, to counter Gallo's tremendous distribution strength, California Cooler tried to take advantage of Brown-Forman's distribution muscle—it handled the popular Jack Daniels whiskey—and worked at broadening the overall market for coolers.

Sun Country

Sun Country coolers, produced by Canandaigua Wine, were the third-largest-selling wine coolers, with a 13.1 percent market share. Sun Country coolers were very similar to California Coolers: Both contained 6 percent alcohol; both retained the fruit pulp, which gave them a cloudy appearance; both were available in citrus, tropical, and orange flavors; and both were packaged in green bottles and sold in convenient four-packs or 2-liter bottles.

To help differentiate their product, Canandaigua expanded Sun Country's product line to include two new flavors, cherry and peach. They also pumped up advertising with a $25 million budget and celebrity spokespeople, including Charo, Cathy Lee Crosby, and The Four Tops. The ads targeted both men and women between the ages of 21 and 34.

Canandaigua also hoped to capitalize on exports of Sun Country, already available in Canada, Japan, South Africa, and the United Kingdom. As of 1986, about 600,000 of 10 million cases were exported.

White Mountain

Recognizing the appeal of wine coolers, several brewers entered the market with malt-based products. As of 1986, only Stroh's White Mountain cooler showed any real success and significant sales. White Mountain cooler had a market share of 12.4 percent, up from 7.5 percent in 1985. The majority of its sales came from states where it had a tax and distribution advantage over wine coolers. Several states like Pennsylvania, White Mountain's leading market, barred the sale of wine-based products in supermarkets and other food stores.

White Mountain cooler bore a closer resemblance to beer than to wine. It was derived from malt, but unless the consumers looked closely at the label or the advertising they wouldn't know it, and that was how the brewer wanted it. Rather than attempt to create a market for a subcategory of malt-based coolers, which could be misconstrued as a flavored beer, the brewers simply sold their products as "coolers," taking advantage of the imagery of the wine-based products. White Mountain's label said it was an "alcohol beverage with natural fruit juices" and 5 percent alcohol content by weight.

White Mountain cooler was packaged in 12-ounce bottles and sold in six-packs like beer. Stroh's had over a $12 million ad budget behind White Mountain, targeting mainly 21- to 40-year-olds. Stroh's also distributed its cooler through its existing beer distributors.

Seagram

Joe E. Seagram & Sons produced both Seagram's Premium and Seagram's Golden wine coolers. Combined, these two coolers made up 12.4 percent of the market. Seagram's coolers were a clear liquid, not cloudy like those of Sun Country and California Cooler. They came in 12-ounce glass bottles and were available in four-packs. Unlike the industry leaders, Bartles & Jaymes and California Cooler, which contained 6 percent alcohol, Seagram's coolers had just 4 percent alcohol. The Premium cooler came in a variety of flavors, including citrus, peach, wild berry, and apple cranberry.

Seagram's original ads for the Premium cooler were fast-paced scenes of young people playing outdoor sports, with energetic background music. The cooler ad was intentionally like a beer commercial because Seagram's was aiming its product at beer drinkers and encouraging them to switch. Though men consumed 80 percent of the beer sold, they tended to be skeptical of coolers. But since women consumed almost four times as much beer as wine, Seagram's hoped that women who switched would encourage men to join them.

The citrus-based Premium wine cooler did not receive the market leverage observers had expected. As a result, the company then backed Golden wine coolers, a new line, with a $25 million ad campaign. The campaign starred "Moonlighting" star Bruce Willis, who played the same roguish character he portrayed on the hit ABC-TV series. These ads were once again targeted toward women between the ages of 21 and 35.

Seagram's also introduced a new product into the market—Seagram's Golden Spirits. It was the first line of spirit-based drinks modeled after the wine cooler. It was sold in four-packs of 375-milliliter bottles that closely resembled the Golden wine cooler. The line's four flavors—Mandarin Vodka, Peach Melba Rum, Spiced Canadian (whiskey) and Sunfruit Gin—each contained 5.1 percent alcohol. These flavors were proprietary; consumers could not replicate them in their homes.

The spirit coolers were expected to appeal more to men and to an older audience than wine coolers did. "They're positioned somewhat more serious," said Thomas McInerney, executive VP-marketing, Seagram Distillers. "They are not being given the beach-party image of wine coolers."

Calvin

Calvin Cooler, produced by New York based Joseph Victori Wines, was the fifth-largest-selling cooler. The company broke into early dominance in New York City, thanks to a state law that allowed only New York state liquor products to be sold in grocery stores, when its cooler hit the market in 1984. As of 1986, Calvin Cooler had an 8.3 percent market share and distributed nearly 6 million cases to every state but South Dakota.

However, the cooler still sat behind competitors with stronger distribution channels and two or three times Calvin's $10 million ad budget.

Calvin coolers came in a full line of flavors, including raspberry, one of its most popular flavors. The product was available in both four-packs and 2-liter bottles.

Dewey Stevens

Dewey Stevens Premium Light, produced by Anheuser-Busch, was the first product of its kind. The wine cooler was sold in four-packs of 12-ounce bottles, each containing 4 percent alcohol and only 135 calories. Most wine coolers contained 5 percent to 6 percent alcohol and more than 200 calories. Dewey Stevens contained no artificial sweeteners; Anheuser-Busch cut the calories by cutting its wine content and adding water.

The ad campaign for the cooler made an appeal to active, young women and placed emphasis on the product's lower calorie content.

Selected References

William Dunn, "Coolers Add Fizz to Flat Wine Market," *American Demographics* (March 1986), pp. 19–20.

Scott Hume, "Drop in Consumption a Sour Note for Industries," *Advertising Age*, April 7, 1986, p. 23.

J. D. Stacy, "The Wine Cooler Phenomenon," *Beverage World* (December 1984), pp. 49–50.

Patricia Winters, "Predict Big Chill for Wine Coolers," *Advertising Age*, August 11, 1986.

CASE 6

Bennett's Machine Shop, Inc.

Arthur Sharplin

"This won't even be a one-page month," said Pat Bennett. "Worst month we've ever had." Pat was the owner of Bennett's Machine Shop, an automotive engine rebuilder in Lake Charles, Louisiana. He went on to explain what he meant by a "one-page month": "We write each engine job order on one line of a 32-line yellow legal pad. Last year, we figured out that a break-even point was about 60 engines a month. If we have three pages in a month, we have really made some money. A single page? We should have gone fishing."

Bennett's engine sales for July 1987 were $57,000, down from $80,000 to $90,000 a year earlier. Pat said, "We install about 40 percent of the engines we rebuild, at about $1,250 a shot. The carryouts average about $750. So I don't expect sales in August to even reach $30,000."

Pat saw his problem as "too little sales to support the overhead cost." He said, "Because of this, we have a day-to-day cash flow problem." After receiving his July financial statement from the accountant, Pat had laid off all the office help (a secretary/bookkeeper and a clerk/parts runner). Pat had released four mechanics and a helper earlier in the year.

Pat himself had been spending most of his time on a tool modification and sharpening contract with Boeing of Louisiana, Inc. (BLI). Bennett's had begun doing this work in February 1987, shortly after Boeing opened its new Louisiana facility, where Air Force KC-135 tankers (a variation of the Boeing 707) were reworked. In July, Boeing had begun returning Bennett's invoices, with a rubber-stamped note that they exceeded the $75,000 contract amount. By mid-August, unpaid billings to Boeing totaled over $60,000. Pat said, "I've cut about everything I can cut and sold about as much as I can sell. I even took out a second mortgage on my condo. If Boeing doesn't pay pretty soon, or a miracle doesn't happen in the machine shop, we're going to be history." The appendix contains excerpts from an interview with Pat Bennett conducted in mid-September 1987.

Company Background

In 1972, Pat Bennett earned a bachelor of science degree in mechanical engineering at McNeese University in Lake Charles. Recalling his senior year, Pat said, "I knew then I would not stick with my engineering career. Besides going through just a real burnout, I already had this machine shop idea. There were just three automotive machine shops in Lake Charles. And all the operators were in their late 50s. I knew there would be an excellent opportunity for a new shop in just a few years."

After graduation, Pat took a job with a chemical plant contractor as a designer/draftsman. The contract was completed in six months and Pat's employer offered him a chance to move to St. Louis. Instead, he quit and hired on at a local Cities Service plant as a "field engineer." Since all he actually did at the plant was drafting, Pat felt he had been misled. He stuck out his one-year contract—all except the last four hours. Pat said, "On the 365th day when the boss went to lunch, I said 'good-bye' to the man sitting beside me, took just the drafting equipment I could hold in my hand, and walked out the back door." Pat's impetuosity cost him the one week of vacation pay he had accumulated.

For the next year (1974–75), Pat commuted sixty miles to Beaumont, Texas, where he worked for Stubbs-Overbeck, Inc., a petroleum refinery engineering firm. According to Pat, this was "my first real engineering job." He explained:

> My first day on the job, they fired the civil engineer. I was sitting there feeling inadequate, worrying what my assignment would be and if I would remember how to do it. I heard the office manager ask two other guys, "Who are we going to get to run the theodolite (a sophisticated surveying instrument) so the design crew can get going?" I got their attention and timidly said, "I know how to run a theodolite." They questioned why a mechanical engineer would know how to do that. I told them I had worked for a civil engineer while in college.

At about the same time, Pat bought a boring bar (a tool used to recondition cylinders in engine blocks) from a farmer for $50. He also sold his wife's washer and dryer for $100 to get the down payment on a valve grinding machine, the other piece of equipment required for the most rudimentary engine rebuilder. At night and on weekends. Pat rebuilt engines in a six-by-eight-foot shack next to the trailer house where he lived with his wife, Cheryl. Customers gave Pat money to buy parts, and he charged them only for his labor.

Pat told of his big entrepreneurial decision:

> I worked 10 hours in Beaumont and drove an hour each way in addition to the time I spent doing engines. The drive just got too dangerous. I was sleepy most of the time and kept dozing at the wheel. Finally, one morning on the way to work I almost ran off the road. I had to pull over and sleep and didn't get to work until 9:30. When I got home that evening, Cheryl and I talked it over and decided I should quit my job and try the machine shop business full-time.

Pat rented a small Quonset hut as his first shop, paying the owner $75 for the month he used it. Then he moved to a stall in a service station about a block from the trailer park. There, his rent was one-third of all labor charges. The service station owner made additional profit on engine parts. Pat said, "I could not get any discount on parts. I had no business license. We did not even have a name. But the fellow who ran the service station bought parts at jobber prices."

Near the end of 1975, a local garage owner asked Pat if he would split the rent on a larger building the garage owner was considering. Pat would pay $150 of the $400 monthly rent. Pat agreed, and the arrangement lasted about two years. During that time Pat hired a helper (a pre-med student) and bought a cylinder head grinder and two other specialized machines (all on credit).

In 1977, Pat incorporated his business as Bennett's Machine Shop, Inc. and moved it to a rented building on Prien Lake Road, a busy commercial street. Sales and profits continued to expand through 1979, when his landlady, whom Pat had nicknamed "The Iron Maiden," ordered him to move because of the growing pile of used engines and parts next to the shop building. The shop flooded frequently anyway, and the fire department had complained about the oily rinse water Bennett's discharged into the city storm drains. Pat said, "I told the Iron Maiden that this was about as clean as it was going to get and made plans to move."

"I arranged to borrow $80,000 from Gulf National Bank," said Pat, adding, "I found a two-acre lot on the old Chennault air base for $57,000. I built a 4,000-square-foot building with the other $23,000 plus $3,000 I had saved." Bennett's Machine Shop moved to the new location in December 1979.

Pat said, "The first year we really had any extra money was 1981. We bought 11 pieces of property. We put 20 percent down on all of it and borrowed the rest, about $80,000." That year and the next, Pat added 6,000 square feet to the machine shop and built another shop building, all without borrowing. In 1981, Bennett's began to do "over-the-fender" work for the first time, installing engines and some minor general repair work. At about this time, Pat and Cheryl bought a "real house" in nearby Westlake and moved from their mobile home. By 1985, Pat had bought a new condominium in Lake Charles and a 38-foot cabin cruiser. Cheryl was using the Westlake home as a cat sanctuary, and the 60 cats she had taken in required much of her time. Pat had collected 22 "muscle cars" and his personal car was a 1984 Jaguar XJS coupe.

"Then we made our big blunder," said Pat. "I thought it was time to open a new location, not to rebuild engines, but to install them. We bought the back half of an old

Dodge dealership on Ryan Street [about three miles from Bennett's Machine Shop]. A Firestone tire store was in the front. Cheryl often reminds me how stupid it was to think I could run the business long-distance."

Pat opened the new shop as Lake Charles Motor Exchange, Inc. He assigned four of his people there. He said, "For 14 months, I pumped money into the new operation." Pat closed the Ryan Street location and sold the facility—he said at a $25,000 profit—in March 1986. "I never realized how personalized the business was," said Pat. He added, "By the way, we proved it again this summer, while I was fooling with Boeing. Things really got out of hand."

Operations

In late 1987, Bennett's Machine Shop was involved in three types of work: engine rebuilding, "over-the-fender" work, and tool sharpening and modification (the Boeing contract). Exhibit 1 shows the layout of Bennett's facilities.

Engine Rebuilding

Rebuilding engines is highly technical work. "The heart of it," said Pat, "is don't let the customer talk you into skipping the machine work. You've got to start with an empty, bare block." An actual case will illustrate the steps involved.

EXHIBIT 1 Layout of Bennett's Facilities

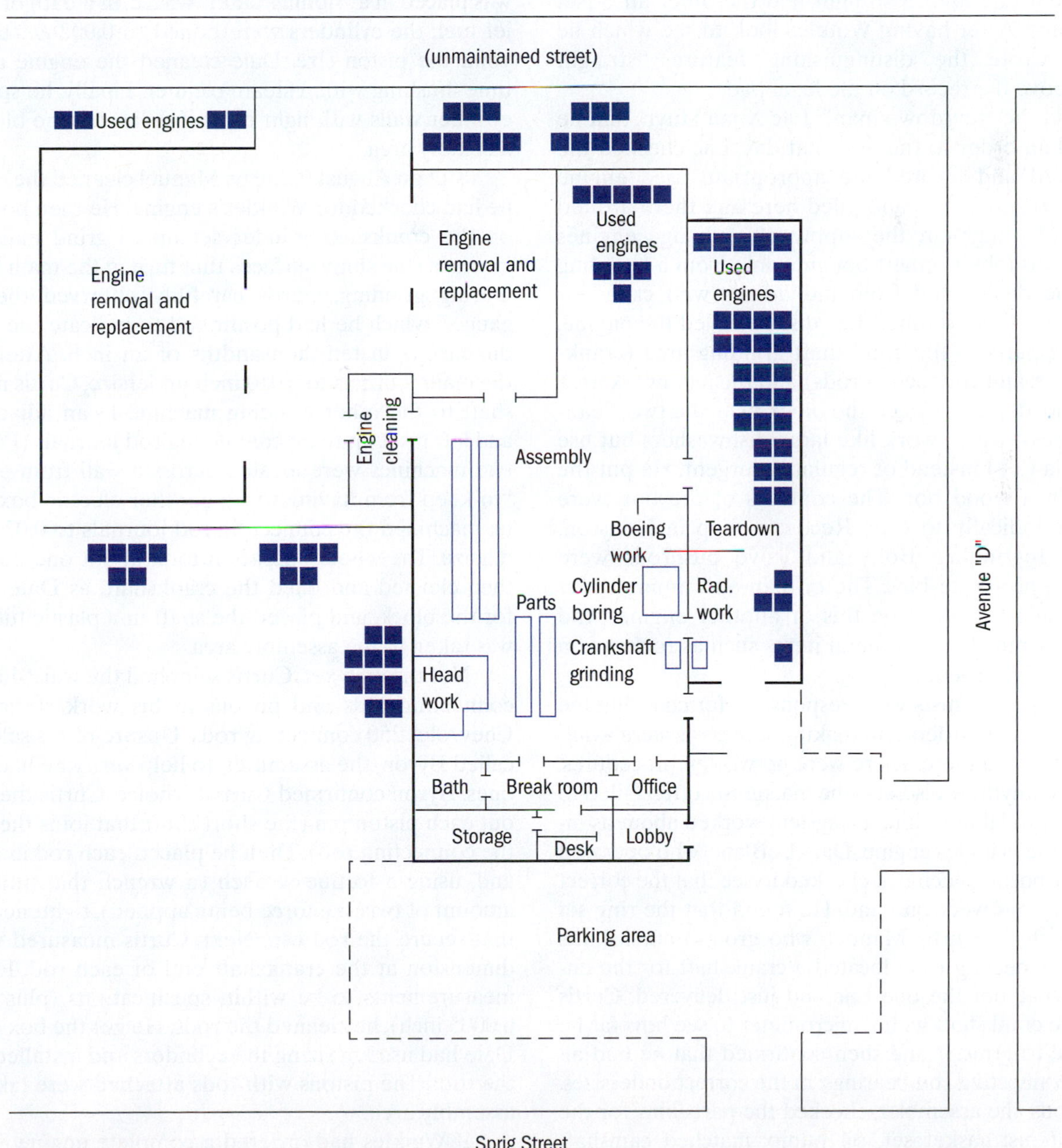

On August 9, 1987, Thomas Winkles, maintenance manager for a local dry cleaning firm and a personal friend of Pat's, ordered a "1974 250 Chevy short block." (A "short block" is a basic engine core, without the cylinder head, oil pan, oil pump, and several other parts that can be reused. These accounted for about 20 percent of the engines Bennett sold.) Pat felt Winkles was qualified to install the engine. "Otherwise," Pat said, "I would have questioned the customer to make sure the job could be done right. Replacing an engine is major surgery. It must not be done by amateurs."

Pat recorded the order on the yellow legal pad mentioned earlier and checked the Four-Star Engine Catalog (published by a national engine rebuilder) for casting numbers of 250-cubic-inch 1974 Chevrolet engines. He found there were two. Notes Pat had made in the catalog revealed that one used a straight and the other an offset starter motor. After having Winkles look to see which he had, Pat wrote the distinguishing feature, "straight starter," above the record on the legal pad.

Pat told the "teardown man," Lac Xuan Huyn, that he had added an order to the list. That day, Lac checked the order record and located the appropriate used engine among the several thousand piled here and there around the shop. (To augment the supply of exchange engines from previous jobs, Bennett bought some from a traveling used-engine dealer and from individuals who called or came by from time to time.) Lac disassembled the engine, distributing parts to the crankshaft grinding area (crankshaft, pistons, and connecting rods) and the headwork area (cylinder heads). Lac placed the block near the two cleaning machines—which work like large dishwashers but use caustic soda (lye) instead of regular detergent. He put the camshaft in a wood box. The contents of the box were shipped periodically to Cam-Recon, a shop in Houston, Texas, for regrinding. Bolts and valve pushrods were placed in appropriate bins. The oil pan and timing cover were set aside for reuse on this or another engine. And certain parts, mostly sheet metal items such as rocker-arm covers, were discarded.

Bennett's machinists were responsible for checking the legal pad record of orders and making sure parts were available for jobs listed there. There were no written procedures, about this or anything else, and the machinists often failed to verify parts availability. Still, the system worked about as intended for the Winkles engine. Dale LeBlanc, who operated the cylinder boring machines, checked to see that the correct pistons and rings were on hand. He found that the ring set was not in stock. Curtis Manuel, who ground crankshafts and sized connecting rods, located a crankshaft for the engine—as usual, not the one Lac had just delivered. Curtis checked the crankshaft with a micrometer to see how far he would have to grind it and then confirmed that he had all main and connecting rod bearings, in the correct undersizes. Byron Woods, the assembler, checked the parts bins for the following items: gasket set, oil pump, matched camshaft and crankshaft gears, camshaft, camshaft bearings, and valve lifters. No gasket set was in stock. Dale and Byron, separately, called a Bennett's supplier in Houston and ordered needed parts, confirming that parts would arrive by bus or UPS the next day.

Dale washed the engine block in one of the cleaning machines. He then took the block to the cylinder boring area and "magnafluxed" it. This involves sprinkling iron filings over unmachined surfaces and placing a large electromagnet at strategic points. Any crack would have been indicated by a string of concentrated iron filings. None existed. Dale selected a box of six 0.030-inch oversize 250 Chevrolet pistons. After measuring one of the pistons with a micrometer, he proceeded to bore the cylinders, to 0.001 inch larger than the piston size, manually checking cylinder diameters with a hand-held "bore gauge" after each cut. He visually inspected each cylinder for cracks. Then the block was placed in a "honing tank," where, in a bath of number 2 jet fuel, the cylinders were honed to 0.002–0.003 inch beyond the piston size. Dale cleaned the engine again, this time finishing with a steam cleaner. Finally, he sprayed the cylinder walls with light oil and delivered the block to the assembly area.

Still on August 9, Curtis Manuel cleaned the crankshaft he had checked for Winkles's engine. He then positioned it on the crankshaft grinder set up to grind main bearing journals (the shiny surfaces that turn in the main bearings). During grinding, Curtis carefully observed the "Arnold gauge," which he had positioned to indicate the undersize dimension, in ten-thousandths of an inch. After grinding the main journals to 0.010 inch undersize, Curtis moved the shaft to the other grinding machine in an adjacent room and left it set up to do connecting rod journals (Pat said the two machines were located across a wall from each other "to keep from having to rig another electric box"). There, he machined the connecting rod journals to 0.020 inch undersize. The whole operation took about one hour. Curtis then cleaned and oiled the crankshaft, as Dale had done for the block, and placed the shaft in a plastic tube. It, too, was taken to the assembly area.

Not through yet, Curtis searched the waist-high pile of connecting rods and pistons at his work station for six Chevrolet 250 connecting rods. Unsure of his selection, he called Byron, the assembler, to help verify he had the right ones. Byron confirmed Curtis's choice. Curtis then pressed out each piston pin (the short shaft that joins the piston to the connecting rod). Then he placed each rod in a rod vise and, using a torque wrench (a wrench that indicates the amount of twisting force being applied), tightened the nuts that secure the rod cap. Next, Curtis measured the inside dimension at the crankshaft end of each rod. Finding all measurements to be within specifications (plus or minus 0.0005 inch), he cleaned the rods. He got the box of pistons Dale had used in sizing the cylinders and installed them on the rods. The pistons with rods attached were taken to the assembly area.

If Winkles had ordered a complete engine, instead of just a short block, Scott McConathy or Martin Simmons, the machinists who recondition cylinder heads, would have been involved. Reconditioning a cylinder head mainly consists of resizing the valve guides, grinding valves and valve seats, and regrinding the cylinder head surface. After these operations, the cylinder head is cleaned, reassembled, and painted.

At about 3:00 P.M., Byron finished his previous job and began assembling the Winkles engine. He visually checked each cylinder for cracks. Then he painted the surfaces of the block that would be exposed to oil with "Cast Blast," a grey paint that seals cast iron surfaces and minimizes sludge buildup. Byron also painted the exterior surfaces of the block the appropriate original color. Next, he installed the plugs in the block, which seal holes required for certain casting and machining operations. After that, he manually installed the piston rings on the pistons. Byron then installed the major parts in the block—bearings, camshaft, crankshaft, and pistons—tightening all bolts to specified tightness and checking each part for free movement. Finally, he performed a careful inspection of the entire engine, recording the results on a specially designed form—kiddingly referred to as "the birth certificate."

The finished short block was placed in a bag and banded to a small pallet. The next day, Thomas Winkles picked up his new engine. A few days later, he dropped his old one by Bennett's.

Over-the-Fender Work

Over-the-fender work at Bennett's mainly involved removing and replacing engines. Of course, this often required replacing water hoses, V-belts, and other items that were worn or damaged at the time of the engine job. The engine warranty (12,000 miles or six months) was conditioned upon an exhaust gas analysis, which often revealed the need for carburetor work. Radiator disassembly and cleaning were also required as a condition of warranty, even for carryout engines. In addition to work related to engine replacement, Bennett's accepted general automobile repair work, such as carburetor rebuilding and air-conditioning component replacement.

Unlike the machinists already discussed, the mechanics furnished their own hand tools. Bennett's provided testing equipment, hoists, a pressurized air system, floor jacks and stands, hydraulic lifts, and cleaning equipment. Each mechanic had a separate work stall.

"We had a terrible, terrible parts situation," said Pat. "The situation was so out of control, I was actually looking at parts purchases as overhead and not as a profit producer. Items were either not getting on the tickets, or not getting on the cars." To solve this, Pat assigned one mechanic, his best, as checker, to make sure every part put on each car was on the respective invoice. He also closed all charge accounts with parts suppliers, requiring mechanics to come to Pat or his shop coordinator, Jack Beard, to get a check for any parts purchase. "Now we've got some control over it," said Pat.

Bennett's kept an inventory of common engine filters, ignition components, vacuum hoses and fittings, and nuts and bolts. Mechanics were required to order and pick up other required parts. Pat said, "We don't stock any radiator hoses, belts, or water pumps because there are just too many different ones."

Richard Hardesty, one of the mechanics Pat had laid off in July, leased one of the company's three buildings and the equipment in it to do general automotive repair, engine installations, and exhaust system repairs. Pat explained, "Our whole objective was to get the payroll down. Payroll taxes are a burden. And the $675 lease payment will come in handy. I was able to rent the building to Richard so cheaply because we don't owe anything on it."

Tool Sharpening and Modification

Boeing's operations in Lake Charles involved a great deal of drilling and reaming, especially of rivet holes in the skins of the KC-135s. Many screwed fasteners required countersunk holes to preserve a flush exterior surface. The thousands of drill bits, reamers, and countersinks used by Boeing required frequent modifications and/or sharpening. There were also numerous occasions when specialized tools such as reamer extensions had to be made, modified, or repaired. When Boeing had trouble locating a local supplier for these services, Pat Bennett volunteered to do the work and negotiated a single-source supply contract with Boeing procurement.

Gearing up to do this highly technical work consumed most of Pat's energy and time from February to August 1987. A 1,000-square-foot area of the machine shop building was enclosed and modified to house the tool work. A large horizontal lathe, a cylindrical grinder, two form-relief grinders, two tool and cutter grinders, and a drill bit sharpening machine were purchased and installed in the temperature-controlled enclosure. To find these machines, Pat traveled to Wichita, Cincinnati, Dallas, and Houston.

Boeing was on an extremely tight schedule on its own contract with the air force and there were frequent emergencies, often involving innovative solutions to unique problems. For example, Pat stayed up all night one night sharpening and resharpening a special cobalt drill bit then being used to drill through a titanium alloy engine mount. Much experimentation was required on this and other jobs, and Pat worked many nights and weekends to solve problems.

Generally, Pat Bennett picked up the tools to be modified at the Boeing plant, a few hundred yards from the machine shop, and returned them there. Because of a Boeing procedure, the tools only needing sharpening were picked up at a Boeing warehouse at the Lake Charles Port, four miles away. Each batch of tools to be serviced was accompanied by a work order providing instructions for the work to be done. For nonstandard modifications, Pat frequently had to call or visit the supervisor who wrote the order and get clarification of the instructions.

Five machinists, three on days and two on evenings, were hired to do the Boeing work. Two only sharpened drill bits, while the others did the work on countersinks, reamers, and special tools. James Smith, the machinist Pat charged with quality control for the Boeing contract, did most of the particularly innovative operations. For example, James designed and made a number of torque wrench extensions that allowed tightening nuts that were not directly accessible.

Pat personally trained the machinists to do the repetitive operations. "The most difficult operation to perfect," said Pat, "was grinding the flutes of a piloted reamer so that they would cut. We were finally able to do it on a German form-relief grinder. Everything on it was written in German. We couldn't read any of the buttons except the one which said 'halt.'" The machine came to be used solely for grinding the cutting edges on piloted reamers. A large magnifying glass was installed so the machinist could see the tiny flutes. With his left hand, the machinist would orient one of the six flutes on a reamer. Then, with his right hand, he would move the grinding head into the reamer flute and back, grinding the tiny cutting edge at precisely ten degrees. This was repeated on each of the six flutes. Because of the exactness required, the grinding wheel had to be reshaped daily with a diamond "dresser."

Drill bit sharpening is a fairly standard operation, although the Boeing specification added some complexity. Bennett's drill bit sharpening machine was hardly state-of-the-art, requiring several manual manipulations of each bit sharpened. Still, sharpening each bit took only about 45 seconds.

The two-way form-relief grinder used to sharpen countersinks was almost completely automatic. Once the machinist oriented a countersink to be ground, the machine did the rest. This took about four minutes per countersink.

A great deal of skill was required to set up each of the operations described and especially to do the custom tool making. But, according to Pat, a person of average dexterity could learn any of the repetitive jobs in a day or two.

Personnel

In late 1987, Bennett's employed 16 people in addition to Pat and Jack Beard, the shop coordinator. There were five machinists and a radiator repairman in the automotive machine shop, five mechanics in the service department, and five machinists in the tool grinding shop.

Jack Beard had been with Bennett's four years. He was about 29 years old. A hard worker, Jack often spent 10 hours a day at the shop, including every Saturday—except during hunting season, when Jack and Byron, an assembler, alternated Saturdays. On a weekend in August, Jack rebuilt the engine in a Chevrolet Citation he had just bought. The following Monday, he told Pat, "I can see how they have such a hard time getting any motors built. There is only one air hose, tools are scattered everywhere, and the place is filthy dirty."

Pat observed that Jack was right. He had tried several ways to get the workers to keep the shop clean, at one point assigning each person "just one little area" to clean. "Nothing worked," said Pat, "so that morning I just pulled the main breaker. When everything shut down and the men came to see why, I told them I would restore the power when the shop was clean." Pat said two of the "main culprits" came in to punch in on the time clock—they were on piece rates—so they would be paid for doing the cleaning. Pat objected to paying them "for cleaning up a mess they had a big part in creating," and they both quit. Asked how he replaced the men, Pat replied, "They weren't worth replacing."

The automotive machinists, Lac, Dale, Curtis, Scott, Martin, and Byron, were mentioned earlier. None had been automotive machinists when Bennett hired them, although Curtis had taken a regular machinist course at a local trade school. Lance Hammack, the radiator repairman, also learned his trade at Bennett's. He had been a welder. "It is much easier to teach a person a new trade than to get a person who already knows a trade to change bad work habits," said Pat.

Lac, a Vietnamese, was hired in 1985. Pat said, "He had to bring an interpreter to apply for the job, he could speak so little English. But his attitude—he just seemed so eager. He learned very rapidly. Meticulous. Pays attention to detail. Terribly dependable. I don't know that he ever missed a day—never even asks for time off."

Dale, Curtis, Martin, and Lance had all been with Bennett's less than six months. Dale had been a construction worker before Pat hired him. "Couldn't even read a micrometer," said Pat. "He had some kind of hangup about reading the dial. I got him a micrometer with a digital readout and three days later he was operating the cylinder boring machine." Curtis knew how to run a lathe when he was hired. "So we put him on our crankshaft grinder," said Pat. (The two machines have similarities but are far from identical.) Martin had been a paint and body technician before Pat hired him. "He turns out the prettiest paint jobs on cylinder heads you ever saw," Pat kidded. Martin worked most Saturdays, in addition to full days during the week. Radiator work was not a full-time job at Bennett's, so Lance helped out in the office, drove the delivery truck, and did other tasks.

Scott and Byron had been hired about four years earlier, Scott right out of high school, Byron off the unemployment line. According to Pat, Scott had a strong interest in cars. "He was easy to train, always thinking," said Pat. "I could just give him a few pointers and he would go with it. He is very thorough. I don't have to check anything he tells me. He doesn't mind staying late during the week, but he likes his Saturdays off." Pat said that Scott did almost all the "really difficult head jobs—the overhead cams, heads that need new valve seats." Byron, young and unskilled, had started doing engine "teardowns." "Most machinists are too proud to do that," said Pat. "They think that is the low-class job in the shop.

Byron was so easygoing. There was nothing he wouldn't try to learn if you needed him to do it."

Next Byron had mastered the cylinder-boring machine. Pat told how Byron got his next job: "I was grinding the crankshafts at that time. You should have seen me—an Extendaphone on my belt and a Sony Walkman under by shirt. People thought the Walkman was part of the machine. But I was grooving, listening to ''50s' music while I watched the cranks go round and round." Pat's wife, Cheryl, was "acting secretary" (the regular secretary had left due to illness) at the time. She quit after Pat threw a can of blue engine paint at her, so he had to take over the office. Another man, later fired for suspected theft, took over the boring machine, and Byron moved to the crankshaft grinder, relieving Pat. "That was a major accomplishment for Byron," Pat said. "He had never even run a lathe." Byron stayed with that job until March 1987, when he started assembling engines.

The five mechanics were Ronnie Smith, Tim "Tamale" Authemont, Kenneth Thornton, Clyde Brown, and Kevin "Goat" Gauthreaux. Ronnie, in his fourth year at Bennett's, was responsible for inspecting and test driving every vehicle repaired, regardless of who did the work. He also did mechanic work himself—all the carburetor work, certain diesel-to-gasoline conversions, and most of the computer checks. But Ronnie refused to do engine replacements in front-wheel-drive cars. Tim was a helper, supervised and paid by Ronnie. Tim had been with Bennett's over two years, but had worked as Ronnie's helper only about six months.

Kenneth Thornton was the longest-tenured employee Pat had, having hired on eight years earlier, when the shop was on Prien Lake Road. He did most of the engine replacements on front-wheel-drive cars, certain diesel-to-gasoline conversions, and regular repair work.

Clyde and Kevin had worked at Bennett's only a couple of months. Both did all kinds of engine replacements as well as a wide range of other mechanic work. Both were in their early thirties, married, with children. Pat said, "I am really impressed with their attitudes. Unlike many mechanics, they are not afraid of this new generation of cars—mostly transverse-engined, fuel-injected, and computer-controlled."

The machinists who did the tool work were James Smith (Ronnie's brother), James McManus, Craig McMichael, John Shearer, and Billy Lambert. James Smith had worked on and off for Bennett's for about five years, doing various construction jobs. He had hired on full-time in March 1987. Pat said, "In the early weeks of the Boeing job, I was running that German form-relief grinder while James was building the room around me." As the Boeing work had begun to increase, Pat taught James to run the grinder. Pat said, "I would run it on the weekends, he'd do it during the week." James had paid his own way to go with Pat and locate other machines to buy.

James McManus and Billy worked evenings. Craig and John worked days. James and Craig did reamers and countersinks. Billy and John sharpened drill bits. All four were in their early 20s. Pat recruited James and Craig through Sowela Tech, a local vo-tech school, and James continued as a co-op student there. John's father, who worked at the Boeing port warehouse, had recommended his unemployed son to Pat one day as Pat picked up an order; John had later recommended Billy.

The automotive machinists, except for Curtis (who operated the crankshaft grinder), were paid on a piece-rate basis, so much for each type of operation and each model of engine. Each had an established hourly rate as well, which was applied to other than normally assigned work. Curtis was paid on an hourly basis.

The mechanics were paid a combination of piece rates, commissions, and hourly rates. Piece rates applied to engine replacements. Most other automotive work was done on a commission basis—each mechanic got one-half of all labor charges that mechanic generated. Hourly rates were paid for warranty work that was not the mechanic's fault. Pat said, "We don't do like the dealerships and guarantee the mechanics a weekly minimum."

The machinists who did the tool grinding were all paid by the hour. At first, Pat set the machinists' wages according to the Boeing pay scale. But when Boeing tried to hire some of his people, he hiked the rate by about 40 percent. "I pay James Smith more than the rest," said Pat, "but he and I have an agreement that he doesn't get any overtime pay when he works over 40 hours."

Jack Beard, the shop coordinator, and Lance Hammack, the radiator repairman, were also paid by the hour.

Bennett's provided limited fringe benefits. There was a group health plan, paid entirely by the employees. Several chose not to participate. Each employee received six paid holidays each year (after a 90-day waiting period) and a one-week paid vacation each year after the first. Bennett's paid all uniform costs per employee over one dollar a day, although workers were not required to wear them. "I also let the men work on their personal and family cars in the shop after hours and on weekends," said Pat.

Marketing

Exhibit 2 provides demographic and economic data for Bennett's market area.

Sprig Street, where Bennett's was located, was "off the beaten path and far from the business district," according to Pat. He said, "The best thing about the location is it's one block outside the city limits. No one bothers us out here, no matter how messy it gets." It was messy. Except for concrete areas, grass and weeds were everywhere. Piles of greasy used engines were here and there—even next to the street behind the facility. Inside the machine shop building, half the space was occupied by stacks—no, piles—of engines and useless remnants of others long deceased. Individual blocks, heads, and other parts, as well as several derelict cars, littered the property, especially

EXHIBIT 2 Geographic and Demographic Data

	Lake Charles	Calcasieu Parish (County)	Southwest Louisiana*	State of Louisiana	United States
Population, 7/80	77,400	167,223	259,809	4,206,000	226,546,000
Per capita income, 1985	$10,183	$10,224	$8,806	$10,741	$12,772
Change in *real* per capita income, 1980–85 (percent change for period)	1.2	1.3	1.6	2.3	2.8
Work force employed in manufacturing, 3/87 (percent)	7.4	17.3	16.2	11.2	18.8
Work force employed in construction, 3/87 (percent)	8.7	9.4	9.0	6.2	3.0
Land area (square miles)	27	1,082	5,083	44,521	3,539,289

*Southwest Louisiana Parishes–Allen, Beauregard, Calcasieu, Cameron, and Jefferson Davis.

around the edges of driveways and other concrete areas. Everywhere there was grease and oil. Two large pitch-coated septic tanks and a stack of rusting metal shelves added confusion. A dingy, although lighted, 3-by-4-foot sign near the lobby and office area announced "Bennett's Machine Shop—Engine Rebuilding."

Thirty-second television spots featuring Pat Bennett ran throughout the year at a cost of about $350 per month. A feature article written by Pat appeared in the American Press, the local paper, once a month, at a cost of $114 per month. Once a year, when business was slow, a Bennett's supplement would be distributed with the 48,000-circulation newspaper. The cost was $1,600 for each distribution. The supplement offered discounts, good for two months with presentation of the flyer, on reconditioned engines—$50 on carryouts, $100 on installations. "The first time we did this, two years ago," said Pat, "we had to shut down and just answer the phones and take orders for two days. We sold 28 engines, almost a whole page, that time."

A form letter was sent to engine customers, thanking them for the business and asking for referrals to other prospective customers. Once a year, during the local festival called "Contraband Days," Bennett's subscribed to a radio advertising special. A 30-second spot was run 60 times during a 10-day period at a cost of $450. Pat said, "I've never seen a sale directly related to radio advertising. We did it one time, and they hounded us the next year till I agreed to do it."

Bennett's major competitors for engine sales were Dimick Supply Company, 100,000 Auto Parts, and Hi-Lo Auto Parts. None of these did installations and all bought their engines from large remanufacturers. No local automobile service shop other than Bennett's specialized in rebuilt engines, although most bought and installed them from time to time. Periodically, Pat Bennett checked the prices competitors charged for engines, often by simply calling and asking. He also kept current catalogs and price sheets for the engine remanufacturers who supplied Bennett's competitors. "We get their catalogs because we're a jobber," Pat said, "and sometimes we sell truck engines we buy from others—because the risk is so high if a truck engine fails."

Asked where he set his prices relative to the competition, Pat replied, "We make sure we're a little under everybody except Hi-Lo. They sell almost nothing but short blocks remanufactured in Texas. They are ridiculously low."

Pat said the quality of all the engines was about the same. "But if you have a problem with a Four-Star or a Roadrunner (the brands sold by Bennett's competitors) you bought from, say, Dimick," Pat said, "you have to take it out and wait for them to send it back to Texas. And they normally don't help you with labor." In contrast, he said, a Bennett's customer who has problems "can just bring the car to my front gate, and it's taken care of—if it's within warranty and hasn't been overheated or run out of oil." Pat complained, "Carryout customers will go to somebody else if there is just a $20 difference. It bothers me that customers will bring us their car if anything goes wrong, expecting us to fix it free. They wouldn't think of doing this at Hi-Lo or Dimick." He explained that parts-and-labor warranties, in general, only apply to situations where the labor is supplied by the vendor. "Sometimes." said Pat, "a customer will even call me for advice about some trouble with an engine he bought from a parts house. I tell him to call the parts house."

Mechanic labor at Bennett's was based on the time estimates in the Chilton Flat-Rate Manual (a book that gives estimated times to do all kinds of repair operations for most automobiles and light trucks), priced at $30 per hour. Most good mechanics can beat the flat-rate times significantly, more so on some types of work than on others. Bennett's priced most parts, other than engines, at locally competitive retail. The local parts houses gave Bennett's a 20 percent discount off retail. "List" prices, usually about 40 percent above retail, are shown on parts house invoices. Pat said, "If we think the list price is fair and the customer is unlikely to check with a parts house, we often use list instead of retail."

For the Boeing work, prices were set according to contract. Drill bit sharpening was at so much per item. The other operations were done by the hour. At first, Boeing allowed Bennett's to charge very profitable prices. After the work had totaled about $137,000, Boeing audited Bennett's costs and revised the prices downward, by more than 50 percent. The audit was conducted by Boeing's vendor cost analysis (VCA) group and involved many lengthy meetings with four different teams of auditors. In fact, Bennett's initial contract was apparently so remunerative that Boeing assigned a "security investigator" who asked many questions implying possible collusion between Pat and various Boeing officials.

Boeing held up payment on past invoices while pressure was exerted on Bennett's to reprice previously submitted invoices at the VCA-determined rates. Pat refused to do that and successfully insisted that the invoices be paid as submitted. Pat did decide to accept the VCA prices during month-to-month renewals of the contract, while Boeing made plans to let the work out for bids. Meanwhile, Pat was trying to decide how to bid the work. He was making money at the new rates. Profits on the earlier contract had more than paid for all his machines. So he was tempted to bid even a little below the VCA numbers. But he knew Boeing was having trouble finding other vendors with even minimal competence to do the work. And he had served Boeing faithfully, and at great cost to his other business, for several difficult months.

Finance

Exhibits 3 and 4 give financial summaries for Bennett's Machine Shop, Inc. For 10 years. Pat Bennett had employed a local accounting firm, Management Services, Inc., to keep financial records, prepare financial statements and sales and income tax returns, submit business license applications, and so forth. During the 1987 tax season, Bennett's was not able to get Management Services to prepare the usual monthly profit and loss statements. Pat explained, "They said they couldn't get to it. So I changed to a real CPA firm in the Lakeside Plaza Building—and that was worse. This guy had less time than Management Services did for us. When he finally, after 60 days, got the first month done, he asked me to come in at nine o'clock one day. I got there at 9:15, and nobody except the secretary was at work. I passed him on the sidewalk with his briefcase and his three-piece suit. That's the last time I saw him."

After firing his new accountant. Pat talked with Dorothy McConathy, who had been assigned his work at Management Services, and asked whom he could get to do his bookkeeping. Pat said, "Dorothy had already told her boss she was going to quit when she got one more account on the side. She already had two, so she agreed to keep my books and gave Management Services notice."

After buying the boring bar when he first started rebuilding engines in 1972, Pat never directly contributed any more equity funds to the business. Equipment vendors furnished financing for most of the machines Pat bought. When Pat started to buy a used crankshaft grinder, which he found at a shop in Plaquemines Parish, he approached the bank that handled his checking account. Pat had taken out a few small personal loans at the bank, but the loan officer who had approved them was gone at the time. The bank president refused to loan Pat the $6,400 he needed to buy the machine.

"I got my little file from him and went over to the new American Bank of Commerce," said Pat. "There, I was a total stranger, but I got the loan." Three years later, Pat needed the $80,000 loan to buy the Chennault property. "American Bank of Commerce wouldn't make a decision," said Pat, "so I went back to Gulf National. My friend Lloyd Rion, the loan officer who was gone that day three years earlier, was there. He gave me the money, and I moved our checking account back." The loan was a 10-year, fixed-rate loan at 10 percent interest.

From 1980 to 1985, Pat took out several 90-day loans to make additions to the shop facilities. The bank allowed him to roll the loans over once. "Those were super productive years. We never had any money problems." said Pat.

When Pat bought the Ryan Street shop in 1985, which he sold 14 months later, the seller financed the whole $180,000, for 10 years at 10–14 percent variable rate. "That's when our trouble started," said Pat. "We loaded up the company with operating loans—a $25,000 three-year loan, a $24,000 five-year loan, and another three-year loan for $12,000, all from Calcasieu Marine Bank. I also let the work force run up to 22 people. It was a real runaway situation."

Pat described 1986 as "one helluva bad year." "That's when we could have used some input from the bookkeeper," said Pat. "I didn't realize that payroll and the taxes related to it were having such a devastating effect. We had almost the same sales as in 1984. Just the increase in payroll-based taxes was $70,000. What really ticked me off was that I had to figure this out and show him (the bookkeeper)." Pat had to refinance the 10-year loan on the Chennault property. "I put off laying off the extra people from January to August," said Pat. "That cost me another $40,000 and made me have to redo the loan." Bennett's showed a $12,000 profit in November that year. Pat said, "It was our first three-page month in a long time. I was scared to death. If we had not made a profit with that kind of sales, I didn't

EXHIBIT 3 Bennett's Machine Shop, Inc., Income Statements

	Fiscal Year 1985*	Fiscal Year 1986*	Fiscal Year 1987*	4 Mos. 1988**
Revenue				
Automotive	926,243	1,091,890	971,950	140,131
Aircraft Tool	0	0	13,318	140,679
Total revenue	926,243	1,091,890	985,268	280,810
Expenses				
Direct costs				
Materials	456,828	570,372	504,811	64,939
Labor	248,833	316,164	271,858	53,693
Freight	0	0	0	1,031
Total direct costs	705,661	886,536	776,669	119,663
Gross profit	220,582	205,354	208,599	161,147
G & A expenses				
Advertising	10,697	15,831	17,828	1,193
Depreciation	33,550	42,240	29,220	7,359
Equipment leasing	5,680	950	1,657	0
Insurance	23,100	39,298	35,528	11,359
Interest	22,060	24,044	26,504	8,841
Miscellaneous	4,867	7,205	7,020	4,438
Office labor	6,815	11,420	13,300	3,961
Office supplies	5,883	7,015	6,458	2,129
Professional fees	3,696	8,373	6,622	1,175
Taxes	5,623	4,852	5,926	245
Utilities and telephone	15,871	30,767	27,933	8,830
Total G & A expenses	137,842	191,995	177,996	49,530
Net Income	82,740	13,359	30,603	111,617
Withdrawals***	(61,500)	(53,389)	(70,755)	(17,109)
Earnings reinvested	21,240	(40,030)	(40,152)	94,508

*Fiscal years end April 30 of years shown.

**May–August 1988.

***Includes funds to pay income taxes. The corporation is taxed as a partnership/proprietorship under Subchapter 5 of the Internal Revenue Code.

know what else to do." On the way to a New Year's Eve party. Pat made himself a promise: "I will not go through another year like that." A friend asked, "What are you going to do to prevent that—as if you have some control over it?" "I'm going to work my tail off," Pat replied.

The machinery to do the Boeing work was all financed with $37,000 in 90-day notes at Calcasieu Marine. There were no other financial crises until August, when Boeing was holding up payment and engine sales collapsed. Pat was able to sell enough assets to meet the payroll and pay oper-

EXHIBIT 4 Bennett's Machine Shop, Inc., Balance Sheets, April 30

	1985	1986	1987	1988*
Assets				
Current assets				
Cash	11,698	1,206	3,475	5,385
A/R, trade	0	1,255	16,662	65,436
N/R, stkhdr.	0	22,568	22,568	22,569
Inventory	37,548	45,436	45,436	45,436
Total c/a	49,246	70,465	88,141	138,826
Fixed assets				
Furniture & equip.	205,292	165,886	193,432	212,209
Buildings	305,657	155,657	155,657	155,657
Total depr.	510,949	321,543	349,089	367,866
Less accu. depr.	(133,559)	(134,067)	(143,834)	(155,081)
Net depr. assets	377,390	187,476	205,255	212,785
Land	126,418	90,000	90,000	90,000
Total fixed assets	503,808	277,476	295,255	302,785
Other assets				
Deposits	492	342	342	342
Total assets	553,546	348,283	383,738	441,953
Liabilities and Capital				
Current liabilities				
A/P, trade & other	12,727	25,062	29,407	31,242
N/P, current	103,160	16,385	60,299	57,775
Accrued payroll, taxes, interest	0	0	3,223	1,571
Total c/1	115,887	41,447	92,929	90,588
Long-term liabilities				
Notes payable	266,720	175,897	200,052	166,099
Stockholders' equity				
Common stock	10,000	10,000	10,000	10,000
Retained earnings	160,939	120,909	80,757	175,265
Total capital	170,939	130,909	90,757	185,265
Total liabilities and capital	553,546	348,253	383,738	441,952

*August 31, 1988.

ating expenses, but he was unable to pay maturing loans. So Pat mortgaged his condominium and consolidated the three term loans into one $45,000 five-year mortgage. Boeing paid its account up to date in early September, and Pat paid off the $37,000 in 90-day notes.

Until 1987, all the loans mentioned above were in Pat's and Cheryl's personal names, although entered on the company books and sometimes secured by company assets. The $45,000 mortgage loan from Calcasieu Marine was put in the company name, "So we could deduct the interest under the new tax law," according to Pat. But Pat and Cheryl had to personally endorse the note and sign continuing guaranty agreements with the bank.

Appendix: Excerpts from Interview with Pat Bennett

Q: What is your main objective for this year?

A: I guess the goal we're all in business for is to make it profitable, and it hasn't been for the past two years. We've had a real bad downward trend. We might not make a real big profit this year, but I hope we can stop the downward trend and turn it around. That would be a major accomplishment.

Q: What about the longer term?

A: I would like the business to be successful to the point that I would have some freedom to do some of the things I want to do. Travel some, sports in the winter—before I get decrepit. Until recently, I dreamed of having a nicer shop near the downtown area, but that seems out the window now.

Q: Can you be a little more specific about what the business would have to do to satisfy you?

A: If we got back to where net profit, including my total compensation, was $70,000–$100,000 a year—and we've been there—I would think that was okay.

Q: Do you mean in 10 years? Twenty years?

A: I'm not really that patient a person. I mean in the next two to three years. That is very obtainable.

Q: Do you think about 25 years from now, when you will be almost 65?

A: No.

Q: Do you feel responsible to make the business support anyone else but you and Cheryl, in the long or short term?

A: Sure, I probably have more loyalty to some of those guys than I should.

Q: Which ones? Or do you mean all of the workers?

A: I mean as a whole. My dad was a union man his entire life. We grew up with the idea that the company had to provide benefits—medical care, retirement, vacations, days off. Retirement is a big thing Dad always talked about. He always talked about the days before Roosevelt, when there wasn't any Social Security, not much to look forward to.

Q: Do the workers look out for your interests?

A: Sometimes I think they do. But on days like today I wonder.

Q: What happened today?

A: Everybody screwed up. Lac has trouble ordering anybody to do anything. Someday he's got to learn he isn't "one of the gang" anymore. Dale loaded the wrong engine on a customer truck. Lance spent the whole day chasing his tail, pretending to go get parts. One of my good customers asked for his car at 1:00—and it wasn't out until 4:00. Know what I'm going to do? I'm moving my desk right out to the middle of the shop, right by the boring bars. They'll be nervous with me watching every move. But I'm going to get this mess under control. [Within three weeks. Pat had built a six-by-eight-foot office in the center of the shop near the assembly area. It had one-way windows so that Pat could observe the machinists but could not be seen by them.]

Q: What major changes in the business do you foresee?

A: More diversity. Wait! I mean more diversification. We've had all the diversity we can stand.

Q: What do you mean by diversification?

A: There still are several areas of the engine business that are untouched in Lake Charles. I just did a catalog so we'll be ready to do the parts house business. The closest production shops are in Baton Rouge and Houston, both over two hours away. We've got the whole west side of the state. And the crack repair business, cylinder head cracks mainly, is just untapped. I visited a big diesel shop in Houston that does this. The whole system, really nothing more than a big fire-bricked oven, would cost only a couple of thousand dollars. This is an especially good business with today's thin-wall castings on engines. There are tremendous numbers of heads thrown away. A plain old six-cylinder Chevrolet head is $400 new, bare. I also think we have a good opportunity in the aircraft industry—the tool work, a heat-treating facility. And Boeing is about to certify us for "level II" work, allowing us to make parts which stay on the plane. No more gravy train—we'll have to bid everything. Level II will also let us bid on the work for the big Strategic Petroleum Reserve. They have to send their work 80 miles to New Iberia.

CASE 7
Southwest Airlines

For more than three years, seemingly endless rounds of litigation had thwarted the plan to launch a new Texas airline, to be known as Southwest Airlines. The Texas Aeronautics Commission approved the application in 1968, but legal challenges by incumbent airlines facing new competition for the first time in decades stretched the proceedings all the way to the Texas Supreme Court, which unanimously ruled in Southwest's favor on May 13, 1970.

When the U.S. Supreme Court upheld the Texas court ruling in December, Southwest's founders believed the courtroom battles lay behind them. However, the delays and litigation nearly wrecked Southwest's finances. The company had long since exhausted its original $543,000 in capital, but was able to continue the litigation only because its attorney, determined not to lose, agreed to absorb the legal costs himself.

The lawyer was Herb Kelleher, a transplanted New Jersey native who came to San Antonio to practice law. Kelleher had first been introduced to the idea of creating a new airline by his client, Rollin King, who had an idea that a commercial airline serving Texas's three largest markets might be able to make money. To illustrate his idea, King drew a triangle on a cocktail napkin, with the corners representing the Texas cities of Dallas, Houston, and San Antonio. Initially, Kelleher was skeptical, but as the discussion progressed, so did his interest. By one account, Kelleher's ultimate resolve was cemented with the words, "Rollin, you're crazy. Let's do it." Kelleher agreed to do the initial legal work for a 25 percent discount, but he wound up doing much of the work for free.

In exploring the feasibility of the project, Kelleher's research turned up some intriguing aspects of King's seemingly outlandish idea. Kelleher knew that the Civil Aeronautics Board, the federal regulatory body that had jurisdiction over the airlines, had not authorized the creation of a new major airline since before World War II. Indeed, the major function of the CAB was to prevent competition. But the CAB's jurisdiction extended only to interstate airlines—those with routes extending across state lines. By flying only within the state of Texas, Southwest might be able to avoid CAB jurisdiction.

In fact, a precedent existed. In California, Pacific Southwest Airlines (PSA) had flown for years as an intrastate airline. By avoiding the suffocating regulation of the CAB, PSA was able to offer low fares and frequent flights and had achieved great popularity with its customers. With the stimulus of competition, the California airline market had become the most highly developed in the world. Why couldn't Texas support the same kind of service?

On the competitive front, King and Kelleher were familiar with the sorry state of air service in Texas. Fares were high, flights were often late, and schedules frequently were dictated by the availability of aircraft after flying more lucrative, longer-haul flights where the CAB-regulated airlines made their real money. Short-haul, intrastate service was merely an afterthought, existing primarily as a tail-end segment of a longer flight coming in from New York or Minneapolis, for example.

Kelleher concluded that Texas was ripe for an airline that would focus on the intrastate passenger, offering good, reliable service at a reduced fare and on a schedule designed to meet the needs of local travelers rather than passengers coming in from far-off points.

After three years of litigation, Southwest still had no airplanes, no management team, no employees, and no money. But when the U.S. Supreme Court ruled in its favor, the founders quickly went to work and hired M. Lamar Muse as Southwest's president in January 1971. Muse was a wily veteran of the airline business, trained as an accountant, but possessed the brash and daring temperament of an entrepreneur.

With the certificate from the Texas Aeronautics Commission as Southwest's only valuable asset and its bank account down to $142, Muse somehow managed to raise $1.25 million through the sale of promissory notes. For his management team, Muse put together a group of industry veterans, most of whom had either retired from or been cut loose by old-line airlines. Muse is reported to have claimed that all the top people he hired had been fired by other airlines. "I figured the other airlines were doing such a lousy job that anybody they fired had to be pretty good."

As luck would have it, a slow market caused Boeing to have three new 737–200 aircraft sitting on the tarmac. Southwest recognized the 737 as the perfect aircraft for the mission it had in mind. The 737's modern, fuel-efficient, twin engine configuration would allow highly reliable, efficient, and economical operation in Texas' short-haul intrastate markets. Boeing executives accommodated the cash-strapped Texans by agreeing to finance 90 percent of the cost of the new planes—unheard-of terms for such desirable aircraft.

With airplanes secured and crews hired, Southwest's long-awaited inaugural flight finally seemed at hand. But the entrenched airlines hadn't quit. First, they asked

Southwest Airlines. Spirit, June, 1996. Reprinted courtesy of Southwest Airlines Spirit.

the CAB to exercise its jurisdiction to block the new competition in Texas. The CAB declined to interfere, throwing out the complaints by Braniff and Texas International on June 16, 1971—just two days before Southwest's first scheduled flight. Within hours, lawyers for Braniff and Texas International won a restraining order from a friendly district judge in Austin, banning Southwest from beginning service.

Southwest's leaders were simultaneously outraged and crestfallen. For more than three years, they had fought and won the legal battles. Now, on the eve of seeing their dream come to fruition, they faced the prospect of starting all over.

Kelleher, having left his San Antonio law office without a toothbrush or change of clothes, was in Dallas when he heard of the Austin judge's restraining order. An already rumpled-looking Kelleher headed to Austin, hitching a ride on a proving flight of one of Southwest's new and brightly painted red, orange, and desert-gold 737s. In Austin, Kelleher located Texas Supreme Court Justice Tom Reavely, the man who had written the court's unanimous 1970 opinion authorizing Southwest to fly. Kelleher persuaded Reavely to convene an extraordinary session of the Supreme Court the next day.

Kelleher worked through the night to prepare his papers and arguments for the court. The next day, June 17, 1971, sleepless and wearing the same well-worn suit, he appeared before the full Supreme Court, asking again that Southwest be allowed to take flight.

Finally, the phone in Muse's office rang. It was Kelleher. The Supreme Court not only had heard the arguments, it already had ruled. The district court's restraining order was thrown out. Southwest was free to start service the next day.

"What do I do if the sheriff shows up tomorrow with another restraining order?" Muse asked.

"Leave tire tracks on his back," Kelleher replied.

As 1973 began, Southwest had operated for a year and a half without approaching profitability. Start-up capital, including proceeds of a 1971 stock offering, was almost depleted. A fourth aircraft had been acquired, but it had to be sold to raise cash. Almost miraculously, the schedule had been maintained when Southwest employees, under the leadership of vice president Bill Franklin, invented the "10-minute turnaround," enabling a plane to be fully unloaded and reloaded in 10 minutes at the gate. With the increased productivity from the 10-minute turnaround, Southwest's management found that three planes could do the work of four. Thus was borne one of the precepts of Southwest's success—a plane doesn't make money sitting on the ground.

Still, cash was dwindling, and profitability remained a mere dream. The Dallas–Houston run was doing okay, but loads on the Dallas–San Antonio route were poor, draining the airline of its remaining cash. Muse decided to try a bold move. On January 22, 1973, he cut fares in half, to $13, on the Dallas–San Antonio route—every seat, every flight, no restrictions. What followed was one of the most widely reported and publicly watched conflicts in the history of the airline industry.

Braniff struck back, running full-page ads announcing a "Get Acquainted" fare of $13 between Dallas and Houston. Braniff's plan meant that Southwest would surely go broke if it matched the $13 fare between Dallas and Houston, Southwest's only profitable route.

Southwest's leaders frantically searched for a response. Even if they had known at the time that Braniff and Texas International ultimately would be convicted of federal criminal antitrust violations for their tactics, it would have provided little solace. The judicial system's ultimate judgment was years away. Insolvency was only days away.

The spark of inspiration that saved Southwest from certain liquidation finally came. The airline would give anybody who paid the full $26 fare a bottle of premium liquor—Chivas Regal, Crown Royal, or Smirnoff. But passengers could pay the $13 fare if they preferred.

Southwest vice president Franklin was dispatched to get a truckload of liquor delivered to the airport. To accommodate nondrinkers, Southwest vice president Jess Coker located a stash of leather ice buckets that hadn't sold well at Christmas and bought thousands of them. Somebody asked if it would be legal. Muse said to let Kelleher take care of that.

Muse then decided to write his company's reply to Braniff, which would be carried in Southwest's own full-page ads. After Kelleher removed the profanities and polished up Muse's initial draft, the ad ran under the headline "Nobody's going to shoot Southwest out of the sky for a lousy $13."

Suddenly, public attention was riveted on the air war over Texas. It became front-page news, the lead story on television and radio. For two months, Southwest was the largest liquor distributor in Texas. It was a defining moment, one in which people decided their allegiances for a lifetime.

The overwhelming response to Southwest's underdog crusade produced the first quarterly profit in the company's history and made 1973 Southwest's first profitable year.

"Tell the mayor that Southwest Airlines will be the best partner the city of Chicago ever had," Kelleher is saying into the telephone. It is November 1991, and Kelleher's face betrays a hint of tension and excitement as he makes his pitch to one of the mayor's closest advisers. For years, Southwest's efforts to expand in Chicago were stymied because of the unavailability of gate facilities at Midway Airport.

Southwest had grown beyond its Texas roots. With the passage of the federal Airline Deregulation Act of 1978, the end of the CAB's stranglehold on competition in interstate markets was assured. Southwest promptly became an interstate airline, flying first from Houston to New Orleans in January 1979. Although expansion out of Dallas's Love Field was limited by a 1979 congressional enactment known as the Wright Amendment, named for then-Congressman Jim Wright, who represented Fort Worth and sought to protect the growth of Dallas-Fort Worth International Airport, Southwest nonetheless found abundant opportunities for expansion outside Texas.

Kelleher had moved from the role of lawyer to executive, first becoming acting president in 1978 when Muse resigned after a disagreement with the board of directors, and then becoming full-time president and chief executive officer in September 1981 when Howard Putnam resigned to become president of Braniff. Expansion in the West had proved highly successful, although not free of competitive challenges. Using Phoenix as the major base for its westward push, Southwest penetrated most of the major markets in California and the southwestern United States during the eighties and early nineties.

But Chicago had been a particularly frustrating situation. Although Southwest offered 43 flights out of its four overcrowded gates, the demand existed for many more flights, to more destinations. Southwest could not expand to meet the demand because all remaining gates were leased—mostly to hometown favorite Midway Airlines. However, rumors now were swirling that Midway Airlines was about to shut down. Southwest had attempted to obtain leases on some of the gates in return for a cash payment and/or loan that might allow Midway Airlines to remain open. But Midway had transferred leases on all the gates to Northwest Airlines, in anticipation of an acquisition of the entire airline by Northwest. When Northwest announced on November 13, 1991, that it was abandoning plans to acquire the airline, Midway barely had enough cash to finish out the day.

Kelleher desperately wanted access to the Midway gates, which would now sit empty if Midway Airlines shut down. Although the lease belonged to Northwest, Jim Parker, Southwest's creative General Counsel, knew of a loophole—the city retained the right to permit another airline to use the gates any time they were not being used by the primary tenant. If Midway shut down that night, as seemed likely, Parker reasoned there was no way Northwest could occupy all of Midway's gates by the next day. Kelleher arranged a 9 o'clock meeting the next morning in Chicago between Southwest's representatives and top advisers to Mayor Richard M. Daley.

When Southwest's delegation arrived at their Chicago hotel at 1:00 A.M., live TV reports from Midway Airport were confirming the shutdown of Midway Airlines. While Southwest's lawyers planned their strategy that night, the airline's Facilities and Technical Services departments swung into action, diverting deliveries and pulling computer equipment, backwall signage, podium inserts, and hold-room chairs from other cities throughout the system, and shipped them to Chicago. Everyone knew that time was of the essence.

The entire city of Chicago was concerned about the shutdown of Midway Airlines. Not only were 4,300 employees thrown out of work, but serious concern existed about the future of Midway Airport itself, a longtime economic engine of the south side of Chicago. When Southwest's representatives met with the city's leaders at 9:00 A.M., they told the mayor's aides that Southwest Airlines was prepared to spend at least $20 million for the development and promotion of the airport and commit to a program of substantial expansion at Midway Airport if the city would exercise its authority to assure Southwest access to the facilities necessary to effect its growth plan. Negotiations continued throughout the day, as Southwest lawyers pointed to the airline's financial stability, record of developing underutilized airports, outstanding record of customer satisfaction, excellent employee relations, and commitment to community involvement as reasons why the city should choose Southwest over any competitor as its partner for the redevelopment of Midway Airport.

The people of Chicago didn't know much about Southwest Airlines, but apparently they were impressed. At mid-afternoon, the mayor's press aide entered the negotiating room and asked, "You guys have a deal yet? The mayor is having a press conference at 3:30." A letter of agreement and press release were quickly hammered out, and the deal was done.

Taking a side trip on his way into the press conference, Parker called Calvin Phillips, his contact from the Facilities Department, who had arrived in Chicago along with a dedicated band of volunteers from the Technical Services Department.

"Where's the equipment?" Parker hurriedly inquired.

"It's in Chicago, in a warehouse near the airport."

"We have a letter of agreement. Let's go."

"What if somebody from the department of aviation or Northwest tries to stop us?"

"Tell them to talk to the mayor," Parker replied.

When Mayor Daley announced Southwest Airlines as Chicago's new partner for the redevelopment of Midway Airport, a reporter inquired when he could expect to see some sign of Southwest's growth at the airport. A Southwest spokesman stepped forward, "If you go to the airport, you can see it right now." Daley beamed as reporters scurried for the door to head to the airport. News reports that night were filled with pictures of Midway Airport in transition, with Southwest workers toiling through the night to install Southwest signage and equipment at gate after gate.

A meeting was arranged the next day between representatives of Southwest and Northwest, the titular leaseholder.

"How far have your troops advanced?" the Northwest representative asked.

"I think they stopped at the edge of the A Concourse," Parker replied.

A deal ultimately was negotiated, whereby Northwest relinquished its claim to the former Midway Airlines gates and the city of Chicago entered into a direct lease with Southwest, assuring Southwest's ability to expand in Chicago and the Midwest.

Kelleher sits in his windowless office, contemplating his company's upcoming expansion into Florida. It is January 1996, and Southwest Airlines is approaching the twenty-fifth anniversary of that day in 1971 when Kelleher told Muse to leave tire tracks on the sheriff's back, if necessary.

Southwest's fleet has grown from three 737–200s to more than 220 modern Boeing 737 aircraft. So strong is Southwest's loyalty to the 737 that it is the only major U.S. airline with an all-Boeing fleet. The little airline that had to ask for 90 percent financing from Boeing in 1971 has served as the launch customer for three new models of the 737: the 737–300, now the workhorse of the fleet, the 737–500, and the upcoming 737–700, which will be delivered in 1997.

Since recording its first profit in 1973, Southwest is about to report its 23rd consecutive year of profitability. The halls and walls of Southwest's headquarters are filled with mementos of employee celebrations and accomplishments. The "Triple Crown" trophy sits proudly in the lobby, commemorating Southwest's unparalleled record of having the best on-time performance record, fewest mishandled bags, and fewest customer complaints, according to U.S. Department of Transportation consumer reports for four consecutive years. Southwest has become so successful that a 1993 U.S. Department of Transportation study described Southwest Airlines as "the principal driving force behind dramatic fundamental changes" in the U.S. airline industry.

The walls also include mementos of other innumerable achievements—the 1993 book by Robert Levering and Milton Moskowitz naming Southwest Airlines one of the 10 best companies to work for in America; the Air Transport World designation of Southwest as "Airline of the Year" for 1991; the *Condé Nast Traveler* magazine recognition of Southwest as the safest airline in the world for its accident-free history; the 1994 *Fortune* magazine cover with a zany picture of Kelleher and the caption, "Is Herb Kelleher America's Best CEO?"

But Kelleher is intense, uncharacteristically humorless, as he contemplates his company's upcoming expansion into Florida, a market he has coveted for more than a decade. He knows the competition will be intense, and his mind flashes back to past battles. Florida in 1996 bears striking similarities to California in 1989. Air fares are high, intrastate service poor, and the geography of the state lends itself to a need for high-frequency, low-fare, reliable air service between major metropolitan areas. In California, Southwest's one-time role model, PSA, and its in-state competitor, Air Cal, long ago lost their way and were swallowed up by megacarriers who cared little for short-haul intrastate markets, leaving a vacuum that Southwest gladly filled. Southwest's friendly low-fare service was quickly embraced by Californians with such enthusiasm that Southwest soon carried a majority of California's intrastate passengers.

The West Coast had become intensely competitive, however. United, the largest airline in the world, targeted Southwest as an unwanted intruder, and articulated a goal of eliminating, or at least slowing, Southwest's expansion. To this end, United created its own "airline within an airline," designed to offer low fares and fly largely in markets served by Southwest. In anticipation of the massive resources that could be thrown into the battle by United, an airline many times Southwest's size, Southwest had acquired Salt Lake City–based Morris Air, and launched a major expansion of its own into the Northwest.

After 15 months of competition, though, Southwest seemed to be at least holding its own. Despite a huge influx of new competitive service, Southwest's California traffic was actually up. United officials were no longer maintaining even a pretense that the effort to erode Southwest's base of loyal customers had been successful. To the contrary, Southwest was about to report its most profitable year ever.

Suddenly, a Southwest executive interrupts Kelleher's concentration. "Herb, you're not going to believe what one of our customers just told us."

"What?"

"Guess what happens if you pick up your phone and call 1-800-SOUTHWEST?"

"You mean 1-800-1 FLY SWA. That's our reservations number."

"I know, But guess what happens if you call 1-800-SOUTHWEST?"

Kelleher walks over to his telephone and dutifully dials the number. The answer comes after four rings.

"Shuttle by United reservations. This is Todd."

"What?" Kelleher exclaims in dismay.

"May I help you?"

"Uh. No, thanks."

After a moment of stunned silence, Kelleher explodes in laughter. The world's largest airline has been reduced to impersonating Southwest in an attempt to hold onto its West Coast passengers. An exquisite look of satisfaction settles over Kelleher's face as the laughter subsides.

A moment later, the look of intensity is back.

"Let's talk about Florida."

CASE 8
The Rise and Fall of Eastman Kodak: How Long Will It Survive Beyond 2011?

This case was prepared by Gareth R. Jones, Texas A&M University.

In 2011, Antonio Perez, CEO of the Eastman Kodak Co., was reflecting on his company's current situation. Since he had become CEO in 2005 and launched his strategy to make Kodak a leader in the consumer and business imaging markets, progress had been slow. His efforts to cut costs while investing heavily to develop new digital products had resulted in Kodak losing money in most of the previous years, and Kodak had already cut its profit estimates for 2011.

After spending billions of dollars to create the digital competences necessary to give Kodak a competitive advantage, and after cutting tens of thousands of jobs, the company's future was still in doubt. Could Kodak survive given the fact its digital rivals were continually introducing new and improved products that made its own look out of date? Was Kodak's new digital business model really working and did it have the digital products in place to rebuild its profitability and fulfill its "You press the button, we do the rest" promise? Or, after ten years of declining sales and profits, was the company on the verge of bankruptcy in the face of intense global competition on all product fronts?

Kodak's History

Eastman Kodak Co. was incorporated in New Jersey on October 24, 1901, as successor to the Eastman Dry Plate Co., the business originally established by George Eastman in September 1880. The Dry Plate Co. had been formed to develop a dry photographic plate that was more portable and easier to use than other plates in the rapidly developing photography field. To mass-produce the dry plates uniformly, Eastman patented a plate-coating machine and began to manufacture the plates commercially. Eastman's continuing interest in the infant photographic industry led to his development in 1884 of silver halide paper-based photographic roll film. Eastman capped this invention with his introduction of the first portable camera in 1888. This camera used his own patented film, which was developed using his own proprietary method. Thus Eastman had gained control of all the stages of the photographic process. His breakthroughs made possible the development of photography as a mass leisure activity. The popularity of the "recorded images" business was immediate, and sales boomed. Eastman's inventions revolutionized the photographic industry, and his company was uniquely placed to lead the world in the development of photographic technology.

From the beginning, Kodak focused on four primary objectives to guide the growth of its business: (1) mass production to lower production costs, (2) maintaining the lead in technological developments, (3) extensive product advertising, and (4) the development of a multinational business to exploit the world market. Although common now, those goals were revolutionary at the time. In due course, Kodak's yellow boxes could be found in every country in the world. Preeminent in world markets, Kodak operated research, manufacturing, and distribution networks throughout Europe and the rest of the world. Kodak's leadership in the development of advanced color film for simple, easy-to-use cameras and in quality film processing was maintained by constant research and development in its many research laboratories. Its huge volume of production allowed it to obtain economies of scale. Kodak was also its own supplier of the plastics and chemicals needed to produce film, and it made most of the component parts for its cameras.

Kodak became one of the most profitable American corporations, and its return on shareholders' equity averaged 18% for many years. To maintain its competitive advantage, it continued to invest heavily in research and development in silver halide photography, remaining principally in the photographic business. In this business, as the company used its resources to expand sales and become a global business, the name *Kodak* became a household word signifying unmatched quality. By 1990, approximately 40% of Kodak's revenues came from sales outside the United States.

Starting in the early 1970s, however, and especially in the 1980s, Kodak ran into major problems, reflected in the drop in return on equity. Its preeminence was being increasingly threatened as the photographic industry and the industry competition changed. Major innovations were taking place within the photography business, and new methods of recording images and memories beyond silver halide technology, most noticeably digital imaging, were emerging.

Increasing Competition

In the 1970s Kodak began to face an uncertain environment in all its product markets. First, the color film and paper market from which Kodak made 75% of its profits experienced growing competition from Japanese companies, led by Fuji Photo Film Co. Fuji invested in huge, low-cost manufacturing plants, using the latest technology to mass-produce film in large volume. Fuji's low production costs and aggressive, competitive price cutting squeezed Kodak's profit margin. Finding no apparent differences in quality and obtaining more vivid colors with the Japanese product, consumers began to switch to the cheaper Japanese film, and this shift drastically reduced Kodak's market share.

Besides greater industry competition, another liability for Kodak was that it had done little internally to improve productivity to counteract rising costs. Supremacy in the marketplace had made Kodak complacent, and it had been slow to introduce productivity and quality improvements. Furthermore, Kodak (unlike Fuji in Japan) produced film in many different countries in the world rather than in a single country, and this also gave Kodak a cost disadvantage. Thus the combination of Fuji's efficient production and Kodak's own management style allowed the Japanese to become the cost leaders—to charge lower prices and still maintain profit margins.

Another blow on the camera front came when Kodak lost its patent suit with Polaroid Corp. Kodak had forgone the instant photography business in the 1940s when it turned down Edwin Land's offer to develop his instant photography process. Polaroid developed it, and instant photography was wildly successful, capturing a significant share of the photographic market. In response, Kodak set out in the 1960s to develop its own instant camera to compete with Polaroid's. According to testimony in the patent trial, Kodak spent $94 million perfecting its system, only to scrub it when Polaroid introduced the new SX-70 camera in 1972. Kodak then rushed to produce a competing instant camera, hoping to capitalize on the $6.5 billion in sales of instant cameras. However, a federal judge ordered Kodak out of the instant photography business for violating seven of Polaroid's patents in its rush to produce an instant camera. The cost to Kodak for closing its instant photography operation and exchanging the 16.5 million cameras sold to consumers was over $800 million. By 1985 Kodak reported that it had exited the industry at a cost of $494 million; however, in 1991 Kodak also agreed to pay Polaroid $925 million to settle out of court a suit that Polaroid had brought against Kodak for patent infringement.

On its third product front, photographic processing, Kodak also experienced problems. It faced stiff competition from foreign manufacturers of photographic paper and from new competitors in the film-processing market. Increasingly, film processors were turning to cheaper sources of paper to reduce the costs of film processing. Once again the Japanese had developed cheaper sources of paper and were eroding Kodak's market share. At the same time, many new independent film-processing companies had emerged and were printing film at far lower rates than Kodak's own official developers. These independent laboratories had opened to serve the needs of drugstores and supermarkets, and many of them offered twenty-four-hour service. They used the less expensive paper to maintain their cost advantage and were willing to accept lower profit margins in return for a higher volume of sales. As a result, Kodak lost markets for its chemical and paper products—products that had contributed significantly to its revenues and profits. The photographic industry surrounding Kodak had changed dramatically. Competition had increased in all product areas, and Kodak, while still the largest producer, faced increasing threats to its profitability as it was forced to reduce prices to match the competition.

The Emergence of Digital Imaging

Another major problem that Kodak had to confront was not because of increased competition in its *existing* product markets but because of the emergence of *new* industries that provided alternative means of producing and recording images. The introduction of videotape recorders, and later video cameras, gave consumers an alternative way to use their dollars to produce images, particularly moving images. Video basically destroyed the old, film-based home movie business on which Kodak had a virtual monopoly. After Sony's introduction of the Betamax machine in 1975 the video industry grew into a multibillion-dollar business. VCRs and first 16mm and then compact 8mm video cameras became increasingly hot-selling items as their prices fell with the growth in demand and the standardization of technology. Then the later introduction of laser disks, compact disks, and, in the 1990s, DVDs were also significant developments. The vast amount of data that can be recorded on these disks gave them a great advantage in reproducing images through electronic means.

It was increasingly apparent that the whole nature of the imaging and recording process was changing from chemical methods of reproduction to electronic, digital methods. Kodak's managers should have perceived this transformation to digital-based methods as a disruptive technology because its technical preeminence was based on silver halide photography. However, as is always the case with such technologies, the real threat lies in the future. These changes in the competitive environment caused enormous difficulties for Kodak. Between 1972 and 1982, profit margins from sales declined from 16% to 10%. Kodak's glossy image lost its luster. It was in this declining situation that Colby Chandler took over as chairman in July 1983.

Kodak's New Strategy

Chandler saw the need for dramatic changes in Kodak's businesses and quickly pioneered four changes in strategy: (1) he strove to increase Kodak's control of its existing chemical-based imaging businesses; (2) he aimed to make Kodak the leader in electronic imaging; (3) he spearheaded attempts by Kodak to diversify into new businesses to increase profitability; and (4) he began on major efforts to reduce costs and improve productivity. To achieve the first three objectives, he began a huge program of acquisitions, realizing that Kodak did not have the time to venture new activities internally. Because Kodak was cash rich (it was one of the richest global companies) and had low debt, financing these acquisitions was easy.

For the next six years, Chandler acquired businesses in four main areas. By 1989 Kodak had been restructured into four main operating groups: imaging, information systems, health, and chemicals. At its annual meeting in 1988 Chandler announced that with the recent acquisition of Sterling Drug for $5 billion the company had achieved its objective: "With a sharp focus on these four sectors, we are serving diversified markets from a unified base of science and manufacturing technology. The logical synergy of the Kodak growth strategy means that we are neither diversified as a conglomerate nor a company with a one-product family."

The way these operating groups developed under Chandler's leadership is described in the following text.

The Imaging Group

Imaging comprised Kodak's original businesses, including consumer products, motion picture and audiovisual products, photo finishing, and consumer electronics. The unit was charged with strengthening Kodak's position in its existing businesses. Kodak's strategy in its photographic imaging business has been to fill gaps in its product line by introducing new products either made by Kodak or bought from Japanese manufacturers and sold under the Kodak name. For example, to maintain market share in the camera business Kodak introduced a new line of disk cameras to replace the Instamatic lines. Kodak also bought a minority stake and entered into a joint venture with Chinon of Japan to produce a range of 35mm automatic film cameras that would be sold under the Kodak name. This arrangement would capitalize on Kodak's strong brand image and give Kodak a presence in this market to maintain its camera and film sales. Kodak sold 500,000 cameras and gained 15% of the declining film camera market. In addition, Kodak invested heavily in developing new and advanced film such as a new range of "DX" coded film to match the new 35mm camera market that possesses the vivid color qualities of Fuji film. Kodak had not developed vivid film color earlier because of its belief that consumers wanted "realistic" color—its managers were still fixated on improving core declining film business.

Kodak also made major moves to solidify its hold on the film-processing market. It attempted to stem the inflow of foreign low-cost photographic paper by gaining control over the processing market. In 1986 it acquired Fox Photo Inc. for $96 million and became the largest national wholesale photograph finisher. In 1987 it acquired the American Photographic Group and in 1989 it solidified its hold on the photo-finishing market by forming a joint venture, Qualex, with the photo-finishing operations of Fuqua industries. These acquisitions provided Kodak with a large, captive customer for its chemical and paper products as well as control over the photofinishing market. Also, in 1986 Kodak introduced new improved one-hour film-processing labs to compete with other photographic developers. To accompany the new labs, Kodak popularized the Kodak "Color Watch" system that requires these labs to use only Kodak paper and chemicals. Kodak's strategy was to stem the flow of business to one-hour mini-labs and also establish the industry standard for quality processing. It succeeded, but the pace of change to the digital world was accelerating and by the end of the 1980s, given the soaring popularity of digital PCs, Kodak's managers should have recognized they were on the wrong track.

Kodak's rapidly declining profitability forced it to engage in a massive internal cost-cutting effort to improve the efficiency of the photographic products group. Beginning in 1984 it introduced more and more stringent efficiency targets aimed at reducing waste while increasing productivity. In 1986, it established a baseline for measuring the total cost of waste incurred in the manufacture of film and paper throughout its worldwide operations. By 1987 it had cut that waste by 15%, and by 1989 it announced total cost savings worth $500 million annually. This was peanuts given the rapidly changing competitive situation—Kodak's managers did not want to shrink their large, bureaucratic company that had become conservative and paternalistic over time. As a result, Kodak's profits dropped dramatically in 1989 as all film makers woke up to the new competitive reality and Polaroid and Fuji also aggressively tried to capture market share by engaging in price cutting and increased advertising to increase market share. The result was even further major declines in profitability. These rising expenditures offset most of the benefits of Kodak's cost-cutting effort and there was little prospect of increasing profitability because Kodak's core photographic imaging business was in decline—Kodak already had 80% of the market; it was tied to the fortunes of one industry. This fact, plus the increasing use and growing applications of digital imaging techniques, led to Chandler's second strategic thrust: an immediate policy of acquisition and diversification into new industries, including the electronic imaging business with the stated goal of being "first in film imaging and digital. He thought the two could still co-exist. He could not understand that digital imaging was a disruptive technology.

The Information Systems Group

In 1988 Sony introduced a digital electronic camera that could take still pictures and then transmit them back to a television screen. This was an obvious signal that the threat to Kodak from new digital imaging techniques was going to accelerate. However, at that time the pictures taken with video film could not match the quality achieved with chemical reproduction but technology always advances, and the introduction of CDs was also a sign that new forms of digital storage media were on the horizon—the silver halide film media was already out of date as declining sales showed. For Kodak to survive in the imaging business its managers woke up to the fact that it required expertise in a broad range of new technologies to satisfy customers' recording and imaging needs—they began to see the threat posed by the disruptive technology. Kodak's managers saw in all its film markets different types of digital products were emerging as strong competitors. For example, electronic imaging had become important in the medical sciences and in all business, technical, and research applications driven by introduction of ever more powerful servers and PCs.

However, Kodak's managers did not choose to focus on imaging products and markets close to "photographs." For example, Kodak could have bought Sony or Apple. Instead, they began to target any kind of imaging applications in communications, computer science, and so on, that they believed would be important in digital imaging markets of the future. Since Kodak had *no* expertise in digital imaging, its managers decided to acquire companies they perceived did have these skills and then market these companies' products under its own famous brand name—for example, a Kodak electronic publishing system for business documents, and a Kodak imaging record keeping system.

Kodak thus began its disastrous strategy of acquisitions and joint ventures that wasted much of its huge retained earnings in new imagining technologies that its managers hoped, somehow, would increase its future profitability. In the new information systems group, acquisitions included Atex Inc., Eikonix Corp., and Disconix Inc. Atex made newspaper and magazine electronic publishing and text-editing systems for newspapers and magazines worldwide as well as to government agencies and law firms. Eikonix Corp. was a leader in the design, development, and production of precision digital imaging systems. Further growth within the information systems group came with the development of the Ektaprint line of copier-duplicators that did achieve some success in the competitive high-volume segment of the copier market. In 1988, Kodak made another major move into the copier service business when it purchased IBM's copier service business and announced that it would market copiers manufactured by IBM as well as its own Ektaprint copiers. But these copiers were not based on digital imaging—even though they used digital technology they were still based on chemical ink. With these moves, Kodak extended its activities into the electronic areas of artificial intelligence, computer systems, consumer electronics, peripherals, telecommunications, and test and measuring equipment. Kodak was hoping to gain a strong foothold in these new businesses to make up for losses in its traditional business, but it was still not trying to streamline and shrink its core business to reduce its cost structure fast enough, and obviously these acquisitions raised its cost structure.

In addition, top managers, now terrified by how far Kodak was behind, decided to purchase imaging companies that made products as diverse as computer workstations and floppy disks! Kodak aggressively acquired any IT companies that might fill in its product lines and obtain technical expertise in digital technology that might help it in its core imaging business. After taking more than a decade to make its first four acquisitions, Kodak completed seven acquisitions in 1985 and more than ten in 1986. Among the 1985 acquisitions was Verbatim Corp., a major producer of floppy disks. This acquisition made Kodak one of the three big producers in the floppy disk industry—an industry in which it had no expertise.

In entering office information systems, Kodak entered new markets where it faced strong competition from established companies such as IBM, Apple, and Sun. The Verbatim acquisition brought Kodak into direct competition with 3M. Entering the copier market brought Kodak into direct competition with Japanese firms such as Canon that was the leader in marketing advanced, new, low-cost copiers—and Canon still is today.

In brief, Kodak was entering new businesses where it had little expertise, where it was unfamiliar with the competitive forces, and where there was already strong competition. Soon, Kodak was forced to retreat from many of these markets. In 1990, it announced that it would sell Verbatim to Mitsubishi. (Japanese investors immediately criticized Mitsubishi for buying a company with an old, outdated product line!) Kodak was forced to withdraw from many other areas of business simply by selling assets, closing operations, and taking write-offs such as its nondigital videocassette operations. The fast-declining performance of its information systems group, which Kodak attributed to increased competition and delays in bringing out new products, reduced earnings from operations from a profit of $311 million in 1988 to a loss of $360 million in 1989. This was a major wake-up call to investors, who now realized that Kodak's top managers had no viable business model for the company and were simply wasting its capital.

The Health Group

Kodak's interest in health products emerged from its involvement in the design and production of film for medical and dental X-rays. The growth of digital imaging in medical sciences seemed another opportunity for Kodak to apply its "skills" in new markets, and it began to develop such products as Kodak Ektachem—clinical blood analyzers. It developed other products—Ektascan laser imaging films, printers, and accessories—for improving the display, storage, processing, and retrieval of diagnostic images. This seemed more related to its core business imaging mission.

However, Kodak did not confine its interests in medical and health markets to imaging-based products. In 1984, it established within the health group a life sciences division to develop and commercialize new products deriving from Kodak's distinctive competences in its still profitable chemical division. Kodak had about 500,000 chemical formulations on which it could base new products, and top managers decided that they could use these resources to enter newly developing biotechnology market and grow its "life sciences" division, which soon engaged in joint ventures with major biotechnology companies such as Amgen and Immunex. However, these advances into biotechnology proved highly expensive and again Kodak had no expertise in this complex industry! Soon even its own managers realized this, and in 1988 Kodak quietly exited the industry. What remained of the life sciences division was then folded into the health group in 1988, when Chandler completed Kodak's biggest and most useless acquisition, the purchase of Sterling Drug, for more than $5 billion.

The Sterling acquisition once again had no relevance to Kodak's business model. Sterling Drug was a global maker of prescription drugs, over-the-counter medicine, and consumer products with familiar brand names such as Bayer aspirin, Phillips' Milk of Magnesia, and Panadol. Chandler thought this merger would allow Kodak to become a major player in the pharmaceuticals industry. With this acquisition, Kodak's health group became pharmaceutically oriented, its mission being to develop a full pipeline of major prescription drugs and a world-class portfolio of over-the-counter medicine—something that is an enormously complex, uncertain, and expensive process. Analysts immediately questioned the acquisition because once again Chandler was taking Kodak into a new industry where competition was intense and was consolidating because of the massive costs of drug development. Some analysts claimed that the acquisition was aimed at deterring a possible takeover of Kodak—because it was still cash rich and its capital was being wasted. The acquisition of Sterling also resulted in a major decline in profits in 1989; this was growth without profitability.

The Chemical Division

Established almost a hundred years ago to be the high-quality supplier of raw materials for Kodak's film and processing businesses, the Eastman Chemical division was responsible for developing many of the chemicals and plastics that made Kodak the leader in silver-halide film making. The chemical division was also a major supplier of chemicals, fibers, and plastics to thousands of customers worldwide and Kodak had benefited from the profits from its plastic material and resins unit because of the success of Kodak PET (polyethylene terephthalate), today the major polymer used in soft-drink bottles.

However, in its chemical division Kodak also ran into the same kinds of problems experienced by its other operating groups. There is intense competition in the plastics industry, not only from U.S. firms like DuPont but also from large Japanese and European companies. In specialty plastics and PET, for example, increased competition forced Kodak to reduce prices by 5% and this also led to the plunge in its earnings in 1989. The chemical division, however, had excellent resources and competences—but not now that they were still controlled by a declining film giant.

Kodak's Failing Business Model Results in Massive Cost Cutting

With the huge profit reversal in 1989 after all the years of acquisition and "internal development," analysts were questioning the existence of the "logical synergy," or economies of scope that Chandler claimed for Kodak's new acquisitions. Certainly, Kodak had new sources of revenue—but was this profitable growth? Was Kodak positioned to compete successfully in the future? What were the synergies that Chandler was talking about and wasn't any increase in profit due to its attempts to reduce costs?

Indeed, as Chandler made his acquisitions he also realized the increasing need to change Kodak's management style and organizational structure to reduce costs and allow it to respond more quickly to changes in the competitive environment. Because of its dominance in the industry, in the past, Kodak had not worried about outside competition. As a result, the organizational culture at Kodak emphasized traditional, conservative values rather than entrepreneurial values. Kodak was often described as a conservative, plodding monolith because all decision making had been centralized at the top of the organization among a clique of senior managers. Furthermore, the company had been operating along functional lines. Research, production, and sales and marketing had operated separately in different units at corporate headquarters and dispersed to many different global locations. Kodak's different product groups also operated separately. The result of these factors was a lack of communication and slow, inflexible decision making that led to delays in making new product decisions. When the company attempted to transfer resources between product groups, conflict often resulted, and the separate functional operations also led to poor product group relations, for managers protected their own turf at the expense of corporate goals. Moreover, there was a lack of attention to the bottom line, and management failed to institute measures to control waste.

Another factor encouraging Kodak's conservative orientation was its promotion policy. Seniority and loyalty to "mother Kodak" counted nearly as much as ability when it came to promotions. Only twelve presidents had led the company since its beginnings in the 1880s. Long after George Eastman's suicide in 1932, the company followed his cautious ways: "If George didn't do it, his successors didn't either."

Kodak's technical orientation also contributed to its problems. Traditionally, its engineers and scientists had dominated decision making, and marketing had been neglected. The engineers and scientists were perfectionists who spent enormous amounts of time developing, analyzing, testing, assessing, and retesting new products. Little time, however, was spent determining whether the products satisfied consumer needs. As a result of this technical orientation, management passed up the invention of xerography, leaving the new technology to be developed by a small Rochester, New York, firm named Haloid Co—later Xerox. Similarly, Kodak had passed up the instant camera business.

With its monopoly in the photographic film and paper industry gone, Kodak was in trouble. Chandler had to alter Kodak's management orientation. He began with some radical changes in the company's culture and structure. Forced to cut costs, Chandler began a massive downsizing of the work force to eliminate the fat that had accumulated during Kodak's prosperous past. Kodak's policy of lifetime employment was swept out the door when declining profitability led to continuing employee layoffs and cost reductions. Between 1985 and 1990 Kodak laid off over 10,000 of its former 136,000 employees, less than 10% of its workforce and a tiny percentage that would do nothing to prevent its declining performance. Kodak was now a company that had come unstuck; it could not recognize that it had lost its competitive advantage and that all its new strategies were just accelerating its decline. It was burning money but its top managers did not want to damage the company or its employees. It was obviously a dinosaur.

Every move top managers made failed. Kodak attempted to create a structure and culture to encourage internal venturing. It formed a "venture board" to help underwrite projects imitating 3M and created an "office of submitted ideas" to screen projects. Kodak's attempts at new venturing were unsuccessful; of the fourteen ventures that Kodak created six were shut down, three were sold, and four were merged into other divisions. One reason was Kodak's management style, which also affected its new businesses. Kodak's top managers never gave operating executives real authority or abandoned the centralized, conservative approach of the past. Kodak also reorganized its worldwide facilities to increase productivity and lower costs, For example, Kodak streamlined European production by closing duplicate manufacturing facilities and centralizing production and marketing operations and in doing so thousands more employees were laid off.

George Fisher Tries to Change Kodak

Chandler retired as CEO in 1989 and was replaced by his COO, Kay Whitmore, another Kodak veteran. As Kodak's performance continued to plunge, Whitmore hired new top managers from outside Kodak to help restructure the company. When they proposed selling off Kodak's new acquisitions and laying off tens of thousands more employees to reduce costs, Whitmore resisted; he too was entrenched in the old Kodak culture. Kodak's board of directors ousted Whitmore as CEO and in 1993 George Fisher left his job as CEO of Motorola to become Kodak's new CEO. At Motorola, he had been credited with leading that company into the digital age.

Fisher's strategy was to reverse Chandler's diversification into any industry outside digital imaging and to strengthen its competences in this industry. Given that Kodak had spent so much money on making useless acquisitions, and the company was now burdened with huge debt from its acquisitions and because of falling profits, Fisher's solution was dramatic. Strategizing about Kodak's four business groups, Fisher decided that the over-the-counter drugs component of the health products group was reducing Kodak's profitability and he decided to divest it and use the proceeds to pay off debt. Soon, all that was left of this group was the health imaging business. Fisher also decided that the chemicals division, despite its expertise in the invention and manufacture of chemicals, no longer fitted with his new digital strategy. Kodak would now buy its chemicals in the open market and in 1995 he spun the chemicals division off and gave each Kodak shareholder a share in the new company. This was a very profitable move for shareholders who kept their shares in Eastman Chemicals—its price has soared.

The information systems group with its diverse businesses was a more difficult challenge. Which new businesses would promote Kodak's new digital strategy, and which did not and should be sold off? Fisher decided Kodak should focus on building its strengths in document imaging and focus on photocopiers, business imaging, and inkjet printers and exited all its business that did not fit this theme.

After two years Fisher had reduced Kodak's debt by $7 billion and boosted Kodak's stock price. Fisher still had to confront the problems inside Kodak's core photographic imaging group and here the solution was neither easy nor quick. Kodak was still plagued by high operating costs that were over 27% of annual revenue, and Fisher knew he needed to reduce these costs by half to compete effectively in the digital world. Kodak's workforce had shrunk by 40,000 to 95,000 by 1993 and the only means to quickly slash costs was to implement more layoffs and close down its operations. However, Kodak's top managers fought him all the way because they wanted to keep their power, arguing that it was better to find ways to raise revenue that lay off a loyal workforce to reduce costs.

Kodak put off the need to take the hard steps necessary to reduce operating costs by billions. At the same time, top managers were urging Fisher to invest billions of its declining capital in R&D to build competences in digital imaging. Kodak still had no particular competence in making either digital cameras or the software necessary to allow them to operate efficiently. Over the next five years Kodak spent over four billion dollars on digital projects, but new digital products were slow to come online and its competitors were drawing ahead because they had the first-mover advantage. Also, in the 1990s consumers were slow to embrace digital photography because early cameras were expensive, bulky, and complicated to use and printing digital photographs was also expensive. By 1997 Kodak's digital business was still losing over $100 million a year and Japanese companies were coming out with the first compact, easy-to-use digital cameras. To make things worse, Kodak's share of the film market was falling as price wars broke out to protect market share and its revenues continued to plunge.

To speed product development, Fisher reorganized Kodak's product divisions into fourteen autonomous business units based on serving the needs of distinct groups of customers, such as those for its health products or commercial products. The idea was to decentralize decision making and put managers closer to their major customers and so escape Kodak's suffocating centralized style of decision making. Fisher also changed the top managers in charge of the film and camera units but he did not bring in many outsiders to spearhead the new digital efforts—Kodak's top managers prevented him. However, the creation of these 14 business units also meant that operating costs soared because each unit had its own complement of functions; thus sales forces and so on were duplicated.

The bottom line was that Fisher was making little progress and was in a weak position and pressured by powerful top managers, backed by Kodak's directors. Daniel A. Carp, a Kodak veteran, was named Kodak's president and COO, meaning that he was Fisher's heir apparent as Kodak's CEO. Carp had spearheaded the global consolidation of its operations and its entry into major new international markets such as China. He was widely credited with having had a major impact on Kodak's attempts to fight Fuji on a global level and help it to maintain its market share. Henceforth, Kodak's digital and applied imaging, business imaging, and equipment manufacturing—almost all its major operating groups—would now report to Carp.

However, Kodak's revenues and profits continued to decline throughout the 1990s and into the 2000s as it steadily lost market share in its core film business to Fuji and to new cheap generic film makers. Prices and profits plunged, and so did its market share—down over 25% in the last decade to 66% of the U.S. market, meaning the loss of billions in annual revenues. Meanwhile, the quality of the pictures taken by digital cameras was advancing rapidly as more and more pixels were being crammed into them. And the price of basic digital cameras was falling rapidly because of huge economies of scale in global production by companies such as Sony and Canon. Finally, the digital photography market was taking off, but could Kodak meet the challenge?

The answer was no. Kodak had effectively taken control of Japanese camera manufacturer Chinon to make its advanced digital cameras and scanners and Kodak continued to introduce low-priced digital cameras—but it was just one more company in a highly competitive market now dominated by Sony and Canon. Kodak also bought online companies that offered digital processing service over the Internet and began offering Kodak-branded digital picture-maker kiosks in stores where customers could edit and print out their digital images. Although Kodak was making some progress in its digital mission—its digital cameras, digital kiosks, and online photofinishing operations were being increasingly used by customers—it was being left behind by agile competitors. In 1999 Carp replaced Fisher as CEO to head Kodak's fight to develop the digital skills that would lead to innovative new products in all its major businesses. In 1999, its health imaging group announced the then fastest digital image management system for echocardiography labs. It also entered the digital radiography market with three state-of-the-art digital systems for capturing X-ray images. Its document imaging group announced several new electronic document management systems. It also teamed up with inkjet maker Lexmark to introduce the stand-alone Kodak Personal Picture Maker by Lexmark, which could print color photos from both compact flash cards and SmartMedia. Its commercial and government systems group announced advanced new high-powered digital cameras for uses such as in space and in the military.

With these developments, Kodak's net earnings increased between 1998 and 2000, and its stock price rose. However, one reason for the increase in profits was that the devastating price war with Fuji ended in 1999 as both companies realized it simply reduced both their profits. The main reason was simply the fact that the stock market soared in the late 1990s and Kodak's stock price increased with it—for no good reason. Kodak was still not introducing the new digital imaging products it needed to drive its future profitability. Also, Carp made no major efforts to reduce costs in its film products division, where the powerful managers who had backed Carp to become CEO made sure he did nothing to threaten their interests. It was the same old story, a rising cost structure and declining revenues and profits.

Kodak in the 2000s

Rapidly advancing digital technology and the emergence of ever more powerful, easy-to-use digital imaging devices increasingly began to punish Kodak in the 2000s. In the consumer imaging group, for example, Kodak launched a new camera, the EasyShare, in 2001. Over 4 million digital cameras were sold in 2000 and over 6 million in 2001. However, given the huge R&D costs to develop its new products, and intense competition from Japanese companies like Sony and Canon, Kodak could not make any money from its digital cameras because profit margins were razor thin. Moreover, every time it sold a digital camera, it reduced demand for its high-margin film products that really had been the source of its incredible profitability in the past. Kodak was being forced to cannibalize a profitable product (film) for an unprofitable one (digital imaging). Kodak was now a dinosaur in the new digital world and its stock collapsed in 2000 and 2001, falling from $80 to $60 to around $30. Investors now saw the writing on the wall as its profitability plunged.

Carp argued that Kodak would make more money in the future from sales of the highly profitable photographic paper necessary to print these images and from its photofinishing operations. However, consumers were not printing out many of the photographs they took, preferring to save most in digital form and display them on their PCs and then on the rapidly emerging digital photo frames market that basically made film-based photograph albums obsolete. Revenues would not increase from sales of film or paper. Similarly, the photofinishing market was declining and its own Qualex and Fox photo finishing chains were forced into bankruptcy.

Kodak was also faring badly in the important health imaging market, where its state-of-the-art imaging products were expected to boost its profitability. However, competition increased when health care providers demanded lower prices from imaging suppliers and Kodak was forced to slash its prices to win contracts with other large health care providers. So intense was competition that in 2001 sales of laser printers and health-related imagining products, which make up Kodak's second biggest business, fell 7% and profit fell 30%, causing Kodak's stock price to plunge. Also, in 2001 Carp announced another major reorganization of Kodak's businesses to give it a sharper focus on its products and customers. Kodak would create four distinct product groups: the film group, which now contained all its silver halide activities; consumer digital imaging; health imaging; and its commercial imaging group, which continued to develop its business imaging and printing applications. Nevertheless, revenues plunged from $19 billion in 2001 to only $13 billion by 2002 and its profits disappeared.

Analysts wondered if Carp was doing any better than Fisher and if real change was taking place. Now Carp was forced to cut jobs, and by 2003 its workforce was down to 78,000—still far too high a number given its declining performance. Carp was still trying to avoid the massive downsizing that was still needed to take place to make Kodak a viable company because its entrenched, inbred, and unresponsive top managers frustrated real efforts to reduce costs and streamline operations. Despite all the advances it had made in developing its digital skills, Kodak's high operating costs combined with its declining revenues were driving the company further down the road to bankruptcy. Would even layoffs or reorganization be enough to turn Kodak's performance around at this point?

The year 2002 proved to be a turning point in the photographic imaging business as sales of digital cameras and other products began to soar at a far faster pace than had been expected. The result for Kodak's film business was disastrous because sales of Kodak film started to fall sharply and so too did demand for its paper—people printed only a small fraction of the pictures they took. From 2003 to 2005 this trend accelerated, as it has ever since. Digital cameras became the camera of choice for photographers worldwide and Kodak's film and paper revenues sank. Kodak had become unprofitable, which was somewhat ironic given that Kodak's line of EasyShare digital cameras had become one of the best-selling cameras and Kodak was the number two global seller with about 18% of the market. However, profit margins on digital products were razor thin because of intense competition from companies such as Canon, Olympus, and Nikon. Profits earned in digital imaging were not enough to offset the plunging profits in its core film and paper making divisions.

The Decline and Fall of Kodak's Core Film Business

In 2004 Carp announced Kodak's cash-cow film business was in "irreversible decline" and that Kodak would stop investing in its core film business and pour all its resources into developing new digital products, such as new digital cameras and accessories to improve its competitive position and profit margins. To protect its competence in digital imaging, it bought the remaining 44% of Chinon, its Japanese division that designed and made its digital cameras. Kodak began a major push to develop new state-of-the-art digital cameras and to develop new skills in inkjet printing to create digital photo printing systems so its users could directly print from its cameras—and achieve economies of scope. Also, Carp announced that Kodak would invest to grow its digital health imaging business that had gained market share, and it would launch a new initiative to make advanced digital products for the commercial printing industry.

Analysts and investors reacted badly to this news. Xerox had tried to enter the digital printer business years before with no success against HP, the market leader. Moreover, they wondered how new revenues from digital products could ever make up for the loss of Kodak's film and paper revenues. Carp also announced that to fund this new strategy, Kodak would reduce its hefty dividend by 72% from $1.80 to .50 a share, which would immediately raise $1.3 billion to invest in digital products. Investors had no faith in Carp's new plan, and Kodak's stock plunged to $22, its lowest price in decades. Kodak's top management came under intense criticism for not reducing its cost structure, and Kodak's stock price continued to fall as it became clear its new strategy would do little to raise its falling revenues. This might be the beginning of Kodak's end.

In 2004 Carp finally announced what the company should have done 10 years before. Kodak would cut its workforce by over 20% by 2007; another 15,000 employees would lose their jobs, saving a billion dollars a year in operating costs. Jobs would be lost in film manufacturing, at the support and corporate levels, and from global downsizing as Kodak reduced its total facilities worldwide by one-third and continued to close its out-of-date photo-finishing labs that served retailers. This news sent Kodak's share price up by 20% to over $30. But it was now too late for Kodak to build the competences that might have offered it a chance to rebuild its presence as a digital imaging company. There were too many agile competitors and digital technology was changing too fast for the company to respond—at least under Carp's leadership.

Antonio Perez Takes Control of Kodak

It had become clear that Carp would not radically restructure Kodak's operations and bring it back to profitability. Kodak's board of directors decided to hire Antonio Perez, a former HP printing executive, as its new president and COO, to take charge of the reorganization effort. Perez now made the hard choices about which divisions Kodak would close and announced the termination of thousands of more managers and employees. Carp resigned and Perez's restructuring efforts were rewarded by his appointment as Kodak's new CEO. He was now in charge of implementing the downsized, streamlined company's new digital imaging strategy. Perez announced a major three-year restructuring plan in 2004 to continue to 2007 to try to make Kodak a leader in digital imaging.

On the cost side, Perez announced that Kodak needed "to install a new, lower-cost business model consistent with the realities of a digital business. The reality of digital businesses is thinner margins—we must continue to move to the business model appropriate for that reality." His main objectives were to reduce operating facilities by 33%, divest redundant operations, and reduce its workforce by another 20%. In 2004 Kodak ended all its traditional camera and film activities except for advanced 35mm film. It allowed Vivitar to make film cameras using its name, but in 2007 that agreement ended. Kodak also implemented SAP's ERP system to link all segments of its value chain activities together and to its suppliers to reduce costs after benchmarking its competitors showed it had a much higher cost of goods sold. Using ERP, Kodak's goal was to reduce costs from 19% to 14% by 2007 and so increase profit margins.

From 2004 to 2007 Perez laid off 25,000 more employees, shut down and sold operating units, and moved to a more centralized structure. All four heads of Kodak's main operating groups report directly to Perez. In 2006 Kodak also signed a deal with Flextronics, a Singapore-based outsourcing company to make its cameras and ink-jet printers that allowed it to close its own manufacturing operations. The costs of this transformation were huge. Kodak lost $900 million in 2004, $1.1 billion in 2005, and $1.6 billion in 2006. Because of its transformation, and the high costs involved in terminating employees while investing in new digital technology, its 2006 ROIC was a negative 20%, compared to its main digital rival, Canon, which enjoyed a positive 14% ROIC!

Kodak's Increasing Problems, 2007

Kodak's revenues and profits were falling fast but in its three main digital business groups—consumer imaging, business graphics, and health imaging—Perez continued his push to develop innovative new products. The goals was to reduce costs in its declining film division, which still enjoyed much higher profit margins than its digital business groups! Kodak had to increase profit margins in all its digital divisions if it was to survive.

The Medical Imaging Group

By 2006 the costs of research and marketing digital products in its consumer and commercial units was putting intense pressure on the company's resources—and Kodak still had to invest large amounts of capital to develop a lasting competitive advantage in its medical imaging unit. Here too in the 2000s, Kodak had made many strategic acquisitions to strengthen its competitive advantage in several areas of medical imaging such as digital mammography and advanced X-rays. It had developed one of the top five medical imaging groups in the world. However, in May 2006 Kodak put its medical imaging unit up for sale. It realized that this unit required too much future investment in its own right if it was to succeed, and its consumer and commercial groups were not providing the profits necessary to fund this investment. In addition, although the medical unit accounted for nearly one-fifth of Kodak's overall sales in 2005, its operating profit plunged 21% as profit margins fell because of increased competition from major rivals such as GE. In 2007 Kodak announced that it had sold its medical imaging unit to the Onex Corp., Canada's biggest buyout firm, for $2.35 billion. By selling its health imaging unit, Kodak cut another 27,000 jobs and its global workforce was now under 50,000 from a peak of 145,300 in 1988. Once again Perez said, "We now plan to focus our attention on the significant digital growth opportunities within our businesses in consumer and professional imaging and graphic communications."

Developments in the Consumer Imaging Group

In the consumer group, improving its digital imaging products and services was still the heart of Perez's business model for Kodak; he was determined to make Kodak the leader in digital processing and printing. Perez focused on developing improved digital cameras, ink-jet printers, and photofinishing software and services.

ADVANCED DIGITAL CAMERAS Perez pushed designers to continuously innovate new and improved models several times a year to increase profit margins and keep its lead over competitors. It was the market leader in the United States by 2005 in digital camera sales, and sales and revenues increased sharply. However, by 2006 Kodak's prospects deteriorated as the growth in sales of its digital cameras came to a standstill because of increasing price competition. Now many new companies like Samsung were making digital cameras that had become a commodity product, and profit margins plunged for all digital camera makers. Nevertheless, in 2006, the company brought out new digital camera products such as its first dual-lens camera, and cameras with Wi-Fi that could connect wirelessly to PCs to download and print photographs, and it used these innovations once again to raise prices. Kodak also entered the growing digital photo frame market in 2007, introducing four new EasyShare-branded models in sizes from 8 to 11 inches, some of which included multiple memory card slots and even Wi-Fi capability to connect with Kodak's cameras.

Since 2007, however, Kodak has been forced to cut the prices of its digital cameras to compete with Canon and Sony. U.S. customers had lost faith that its EasyShare models offered the best value and so Kodak's profits from the sales of its cameras continued to decline. At the same time, increasing digital camera sales led to a major decline in sales of its film products. In 1999, Kodak announced that it was ending production of its consumer film products and its "yellow boxes" disappeared from sight as it sought to cut costs. In sum, its camera business offered little prospect of being able to raise its future profitability.

NEW INKJET PRINTERS A major change in strategy occurred when Perez launched a major advertising campaign to launch its new Kodak EasyShare all-in-one inkjet printers. This new line of color digital printers used an advanced Kodak ink that would provide brighter pictures that would keep their clarity for decades. Apparently Perez, who had been in charge of HP's printer business before he left Kodak, had all along made the development of digital printers a major part of his turnaround strategy—even though profit margins were shrinking on these products as well. However, Perez's printer strategy is based upon charging a higher price for the printer than competitors like HP and Lexmark, but then charging a much lower price for the ink cartridge to attract a bigger market share—a razor and razor blades strategy. Black ink cartridges will cost $9.99 and color $14.99, which will average out to about 10 cents a print—far lower than the 20 to 25 cents per print using an HP printer. Perez believed this would attract the large market segment that still wants to print out large numbers of photographs and so would make this product a multibillion-dollar revenue generator in the future. Perez announced he expected inkjet printing to result in double-digit increases in profit within three years.

Kodak's new printers did attract a lot of customers who were alienated by the high costs of ink cartridges. However, as online photo processing and storage solutions became more and more popular, and new mobile devices made it increasingly easy to access photos from the Net—on iPods, iPads, and smartphones in general—users had less and less incentive to burden themselves with paper-based photo albums. Nevertheless, its new printers did help increase revenues and profits, although they never achieved the gains Perez anticipated. In 2009 it announced its new line of ESP all-in-one digital printers that still used all its EasyShare technology to help users print and share their photographs. Kodak's new printers were popular and helped to increase revenues and profits. For example, in 2010–2011 sales increased by over 40% but this was still not enough to make up for declines in revenues elsewhere in digital imaging.

DIGITAL PHOTOFINISHING Another part of Perez's consumer strategy was to invest in developing both online and physical "digital kiosks," channels to allow customers to download, process, print, and store their photographs using its EasyShare software. Kodak's EasyShare Internet service allows customers to download their images to its online website, Kodak Gallery, and receive back both printed photographs and the images on a CD.

In a major effort to develop an empire of digital processing kiosks, Kodak began to rapidly install them in stores, pharmacies, and other outlets as fast as possible, especially because they used its inks and paper. It configured these kiosks to give customers total control over which pictures to develop at what quantity, quality, and size. Kodak and Wal-Mart signed an alliance to put 2,000 kiosks into 1,000 Walmart stores and by 2006 Kodak had over 65,000 kiosks. However, this was an expensive business to operate and profit margins were razor thin as competition increased.

These moves proved popular because it was easy to use and photofinishing revenues increased as it built a base of 30 million customers. But profit margins were slim because competition increased and many other free online programs were being introduced, such as Google's Picasa. Between July 2010 and 2011 profits dropped from $36 million to $2 million and did nothing to help Kodak's bottom line.

Kodak also made major attempts to penetrate the mobile imaging market because of the huge growth in the use of cameras in mobile phones in the 2000s. The Kodak Mobile Imaging Service offers camera phone users several options to view, order, and share prints of all the digital photos on their phones. Users can upload and store pictures from their cameras in their personal Kodak gallery accounts; then after editing using Kodak's free EasyShare software they can send their favorite photos back to their mobile phones or wirelessly link to its picture kiosks to arrange to print the best photographs. Kodak also joined up with social media sites like Facebook and Picasa, now linked to Google+, to easily download photos to members of their social community. And of course it has developed applications for the Apple iOS, Blackberry OS, and Android OS mobile operating systems to make it easy for users to connect their Kodak EasyShare pictures to whatever kinds of mobile computing devices they are using. Kodak benefits from revenues received when mobile customers take advantage of its processing and printing services while they upload and share photographs; for example, any user can request a paper copy or an enlargement of a particular photograph or a series of photos contained in an album. Kodak kiosks also allow users to upload pictures wirelessly through Bluetooth; customers can beam photos right to the kiosk from mobile device to get Kodak prints and more.

One problem, however, was that increasing sales of powerful cameras in smartphones led to a major decline in the number of customers who intended to upgrade to a more advanced digital camera—smartphones were cannibalizing sales of digital cameras. In addition, this has not proved to be an important source of additional revenues; its greater market share has not translated into higher profits. By 2010 there was intense competition in all areas of the digital imaging and information markets, including PCs, smartphones, MP3 players, and gaming consoles, as more and more people gravitated online and became used to the Web as the place to process and store their documents in whatever form—written, graphic, photographic, video, music, or movies. Although Kodak had achieved a presence in the consumer digital imaging and storage market segment, it still could not generate the profits needed to offset its losses resulting from the rapid decline of its cash-cow film business, and in its other business areas.

In fact, in July 2011 Kodak announced major falls in profits and sales across many of its product groups. Sales of cameras were down by 8% and revenues from its photofinishing operations were down 14%. Sales of ink and inkjet printers had increased by over 40%, a bright spot, but nevertheless overall sales had decreased by 10% compared to the previous year, and the group had lost $92 million.

The Graphic Communications Group

Although its consumer digital business is its most visible business group, by 2007 Perez had recognized that its graphic communications group that dealt with business customers also offered an opportunity to grow revenues and profits if it could develop distinctive competences. Profit margins are much higher in commercial imaging and packaging because the users of these products are companies with large budgets. The five main customer groups served by this group are commercial printers, in-plant printers, data centers, digital service providers, and packaging companies. For each of these segments, Kodak developed a suite of digital products and services that offered customers a single end-to-end solution to deliver the products and services they need to compete in their business. Kodak was able to develop this end-to-end solution because of its acquisition of specialist digital printing companies such as KPG, CREO, Versamark, and Express. From each acquisition Kodak gained access to more products and more customers along with more services and solutions to offer them. Perez claimed that no other competitor could offer the same breadth of products and solutions that it offers. Kodak's product line includes image scanners and document management systems, and the industry's leading portfolio of digital proofing solutions and state-of-the-art color packaging solutions that can be customized to the needs of different customers, whether they need cardboard boxes or rigid or flexible cardboard or plastic packaging.

Following his decision to make Kodak a major competitor in consumer ink-jet printing, by 2009, with his HP printing background, Perez also decided to make it a major player in commercial printing as well, bringing it into direct competition with HP, Xerox, and Canon. Kodak had developed an award-winning wide-format inkjet printing process, including the most robust toner-based platforms for four-color and monochrome printing. Kodak also claimed to have the leading continuous inkjet technology for high-speed, high-volume printing, as well as imprinting capabilities that can be combined with traditional offset printing for those customers still in the process of making the transition to digital printing.

At the same time, Perez decided to invest resources to improve Kodak's packaging solutions to utilize its expertise in color processing, and he made packing another avenue to increase revenues and profits. Kodak announced in July 2011 that second-quarter sales from this group were $685 million, similar to the previous year. However, this group also lost $45 million, compared to $17 million in the same quarter the year before because of the enormous development and marketing costs necessary to support growth in its commercial inkjet operations.

Will Kodak Survive?

In January 2009 Kodak posted a $137 million loss and announced plans to cut 4500 jobs, which brought its workforce down to about 18,000. In June 2009 it announced it would retire its Kodachrome film—the main source of its incredible past financial success. In fact, its losses have been increasing in the last five years, but the extent of these losses has been disguised because of the way the company has sold many of its assets to reduce its losses and has engaged in patent battles. For example, in 2007 it sold its Light Management Film Group to Rohm & Hass, and in 2009 it sold its Organic Light-Emitting Diode (OLED) business unit to LG Electronics. Both were advanced LED flatscreen technologies that it could no longer afford to invest in—but this brought in a few hundred million dollars.

Then, to find new sources of revenue to offset losses, Kodak launched a series of lawsuits against other electronics companies, claiming that they had infringed on its huge library of digital patents that it has generated over the years. In 2008 Kodak selected its first targets, Samsung and LG, which it claimed had used its technology in the cameras in their mobile phones. A U.S. judge decided in 2009 that these companies had infringed on its patents but they decided not to appeal. Kodak announced it would settle out of court and develop cross-license agreements with these companies; it is estimated that Kodak received over $900 million from these settlements.

Emboldened by its success, Kodak decided to take on Apple and Research in Motion (RIM) in March 2010. The Kodak complaint, filed with the U.S. International Trade Commission (ITC), claimed that Apple's iPhone and RIM's camera-enabled BlackBerrys infringe on a Kodak patent that covers technology related to a method for previewing images. At the end of March the ITC ruled in favor of Kodak, which seemed to have won its patent dispute with Apple and RIM, a victory that might provide it with $1 billion in new licensing revenue. Overnight Kodak's stock soared by 25%. Then Apple filed a countersuit, and in April 2011 it sold its Microfilm Unit to raise the millions needed to fund its lawsuits. In June 2011 the ITC, under a new judge, issued a mixed ruling and announced the final decision would not be made until August 2011—and Kodak's stock plunged 25%.

Perez claimed he would use the proceeds from intellectual property licensing to continue to invest in the company's now core growth businesses—inkjet printing, packaging and software, and services—in order to counter falling revenue from camera film. However, since 2007 Kodak's stock has plunged from $24 to around $2.50 in July 2011. It seems that Perez's strategies have done little or nothing to turn around Kodak, whose market value was only around $650 million in July 2011. Some analysts claimed the only reason the company had not been acquired for this low price was that it had $2.6 billion in unfunded pension obligations because of its huge layoffs over the last decade. Given that it had less than $900 million in cash in 2011, many wondered how long the company would be able to survive—and what would push it into bankruptcy.

References

www.kodak.com, Annual reports, 1980–2010.

www.kodak.com, 10K reports, 1980-2011.

CASE 9

Philips NV

Charles W. L. Hill

Established in 1891, the Dutch company Philips NV is one of the world's largest electronics enterprises. Its businesses are grouped into four main divisions: lighting, consumer electronics, professional products (computers, telecommunications, and medical equipment), and components (including chips). In each of these areas it ranks alongside the likes of Matsushita, General Electric, Sony, and Siemens as a global competitor. In the late 1980s, the company had several hundred subsidiaries in 60 countries, it operated manufacturing plants in more than 40 countries, it employed approximately 300,000 people, and it manufactured thousands of different products. However, despite its global reach by 1990, Philips was a company in deep trouble. After a decade of deteriorating performance, in 1990 Philips lost $2.2 billion on revenues of $28 billion. A major reason seems to have been the inability of Philips to adapt to the changing competitive conditions in the global electronics industry during the 1970s and 1980s.

Philips' Traditional Organization

To trace the roots of Philips' current troubles, one has to go back to World War II. Until then, the foreign activities of Philips had been run out of its head office in Eindhoven. However, during World War II the Netherlands was occupied by Germany. Cut off from their home base, Philips' various national organizations began to operate independently. In essence, each major national organization developed into a self-contained company with its own manufacturing, marketing, and R&D functions.

Following the war, top management felt that the company could be most successfully rebuilt through its national organizations. There were several reasons for this belief. First, high trade barriers made it logical that self-contained national organizations be established in each major national market. Second, it was felt that strong national organizations would allow Philips to be responsive to local demands in each country in which it competed. And third, given the substantial autonomy that the various national organizations had gained during the war, top management felt that reestablishing centralized control might prove difficult and yield few benefits.

At the same time, top management felt the need for some centralized control over product policy and R&D in order to achieve some coordination between national organizations. Its response was to create a number of worldwide product divisions (of which there were fourteen by the mid-1980s). In theory, basic R&D and product development policy were the responsibilities of the product divisions, whereas the national organizations were responsible for day-to-day operations in a particular country. Product strategy in a given country was meant to be determined jointly by consultation between the responsible

Charles W. L. Hill, University of Washington. Reprinted with permission.

national organization and the product divisions. It was the national organizations that implemented strategy.

Another major feature of Philips' organization was the duumvirate form of management. In most national organizations, top-management responsibilities and authority were shared by two managers—one responsible for "commercial affairs" and another responsible for "technical activities." This form of management had its origins in the company's founders—Anton and Gerard Philips. Anton was a salesman and Gerard an engineer. Throughout the company there seemed to be a vigorous, informal competition between technical and sales managers, with each attempting to outperform the other. Anton once noted:

> The technical management and the sales management competed to outperform each other. Production tried to produce so much that sales would not be able to get rid of it; sales tried to sell so much that the factory would not be able to keep up. [Aguilar and Yoshino, 1987]

The top decision-making and policy-making body in the company was a 10-person board of management. While board members all shared general management responsibility, they typically maintained a special interest in one of the functional areas of the company (for example, R&D, manufacturing, marketing). Traditionally, most of the members of the management board were Dutch and had come up through the Eindhoven bureaucracy, although most had extensive foreign postings, often as a top manager in one of the company's national organizations.

Environmental Change

From the 1960s onward, a number of significant changes took place in Philips' competitive environment that were to profoundly affect the company. First, due to the efforts of the General Agreement on Tariffs and Trade (GATT), trade barriers fell worldwide. In addition in Philips' home base, Europe, the emergence of the European Economic Community, of which the Netherlands was an early member, led to a further reduction in trade barriers between the countries of Western Europe.

Second, during the 1960s and 1970s a number of new competitors emerged in Japan. Taking advantage of the success of GATT in lowering trade barriers, the Japanese companies produced most of their output at home and then exported to the rest of the world. The resulting economies of scale allowed them to drive down unit costs below those achieved by Western competitors such as Philips that manufactured in multiple locations. This significantly increased competitive pressures in most of the business areas where Philips competed.

Third, due to technological changes, the cost of R&D and manufacturing increased rapidly. The introduction of transistors and then integrated circuits called for significant capital expenditures in production facilities—often running into hundreds of millions of dollars. To realize scale economies, substantial levels of output had to be achieved. Moreover, the pace of technological change was declining and product life cycles were shortening. This gave companies in the electronics industry less time to recoup their capital investments before new-generation products came along.

Finally, as the world moved from a series of fragmented national markets toward a single global market, uniform global standards for electronic equipment were beginning to emerge. This standardization showed itself most clearly in the videocassette recorder business, where three standards initially battled for dominance—the Betamax standard produced by Sony, the VHS standard produced by Matsushita, and the V2000 standard produced by Philips. The VHS standard was the one most widely accepted by consumers, and the others were eventually abandoned. For Philips and Sony, both of which had invested substantially in their own standard, this was a significant defeat. Philips's attempt to establish its V2000 format as an industry standard was effectively killed off by the decision of its own North American national organization, over the objections of Eindhoven, to manufacture according to the VHS standard.

Organizational and Strategic Change

By the early 1980s Philips realized that, if it was to survive, it would have to restructure its business radically. Its cost structure was high due to the amount of duplication across national organizations, particularly in the area of manufacturing. Moreover, as the V2000 incident demonstrated, the company's attempts to compete effectively were being hindered by the strength and autonomy of its national organizations.

The first attempt at change came in 1982 when Wisse Dekker was appointed CEO. Dekker quickly pushed for manufacturing rationalization, creating international production centers that served a number of national organizations and closing many small inefficient plants. He also pushed Philips to enter into more collaborative arrangements with other electronics firms in order to share the costs and risks of developing new products. In addition, Dekker accelerated a trend that had already begun within the company to move away from the dual leadership arrangement within national organizations (commercial and technical), replacing this arrangement with a single general manager. Furthermore, Dekker tried to "tilt" Philips' matrix away from national organizations by creating a corporate council where the heads of product divisions would join the heads of the national organizations to discuss issues of importance to both. At the same time, he gave the product divisions more responsibility to determine companywide research and manufacturing activities.

In 1986, Dekker was succeeded by Cor van de Klugt. One of van de Klugt's first actions was to specify that profitability was to be the central criterion for evaluating performance within Philips. The product divisions were given primary responsibility for achieving profits. This was followed in late 1986 by his termination of the U.S. Philips trust, which had been given control of Philips's North American operations during World War II and which still maintained control as of 1986. By terminating the trust, van de Klugt in theory reestablished Eindhoven's control over the North American subsidiary. Then, in May 1987, van de Klugt announced a major restructuring of Philips. He designated four product divisions—lighting, consumer electronics, components, and telecommunications and data systems—as "core divisions," the implication being that other activities would be sold off. At the same time he reduced the size of the management board. Its policy-making responsibility was devolved to a new group management committee, comprising the remaining board members plus the heads of the core product divisions. No heads of national organizations were appointed to this body, thereby further tilting power within Philips away from the national organizations toward the product divisions.

Despite these changes, Philips' competitive position continued to deteriorate. Many outside observers attributed this slide to the dead hand of the huge head office bureaucracy at Eindhoven (which comprised more than 3,000 people in 1989). They argued that while van de Klugt had changed the organizational chart, much of this change was superficial. Real power, they argued, still lay with the Eindhoven bureaucracy and their allies in the national organizations. In support of this view, they pointed out that since 1986 Philips' work force had declined by less than 10 percent, instead of the 30 percent reduction that many analysts were calling for.

Alarmed by a 1989 loss of $1.06 billion, the board forced van de Klugt to resign in May 1990. He was replaced by Jan Timmer. Timmer quickly announced that he would cut Philips's worldwide work force by 10,000, to 283,000, and launch a $1.4 billion restructuring. Investors were unimpressed—most of them thought that the company needed to lose 40,000–50,000 jobs—and reacted by knocking the share price down by 7 percent. Since then, however, Timmer had made some progress. In mid-1991, he sold off Philips's minicomputer division—which at the time was losing $1 million per day—to Digital Equipment. He also announced plans to reduce costs by $1.2 billion by cutting the work force by 55,000. In addition, he entered into a strategic alliance with Matsushita, the Japanese electronic giant, to manufacture and market the Digital Compact Cassette (DCC). Developed by Philips and due to be introduced in late 1992, the DCC reproduces the sound of a compact disc on a tape. The DCC's great selling point is that buyers will be able to play their old analog tape cassettes on the new system. The DCC's chief rival is a portable compact disc system from Sony called Mini-Disk. Many observers see a replay of the classic battle between the VHS and Betamax video recorder standards in the coming battle between the DCC and the Mini-Disk. If the DCC wins, it could be the remaking of Philips.

References

Aguilar, F. J., and M. Y. Yoshino. "The Philips Group: 1987." Harvard Business School, Case #388–050.

Anonymous. "Philips Fights the Flab." *The Economist*, April 7, 1992, pp. 73–74.

Bartlett, C. A., and S. Ghoshal. *Managing Across Borders: The Transnational Solution.* Boston, Mass.: Harvard Business School Press, 1989.

Kapstein, J., and J. Levine. "A Would-Be World Beater Takes a Beating." *Business Week*, July 16, 1990, pp. 41–42.

Levine, J. "Philips's Big Gamble." *Business Week*, August 5, 1991, pp. 34–36.

CASE 10

"Ramrod" Stockwell

Charles Perrow

The Benson Metal Company employs about 1,500 people, is listed on the stock exchange, and has been in existence for many decades. It makes a variety of metals that are purchased by manufacturers or specialized metal firms. It is one of the five or six leading firms in the specialty steel industry. This industry produces steels in fairly small quantities with a variety of characteristics. Orders tend to be in terms of pounds rather than tons, although a 1,000-pound order is not unusual. For some of the steels, 100 pounds is an average order.

The technology for producing specialty steels in the firm is fairly well established, but there is still a good deal of guesswork, skill, and even some "black magic" involved. Small changes are made in the ingredients going into the melting process, often amounting to the addition of a tiny bit of expensive alloying material in order to produce varieties of specialty steels. Competitors can analyze one another's products and generally produce the same product without too much difficulty, although there are some secrets. There are also important variations stemming from the type of equipment used to melt, cog, roll, and finish the steel.

In the period that we are considering, the Benson Company and some of its competitors were steadily moving into more sophisticated and technically more difficult steels, largely for the aerospace industry. The aerospace products were far more difficult to make, required more research skills and metallurgical analysis, and required more "delicate" handling in all stages of production, even though the same basic equipment was involved. Furthermore, they were marketed in a different fashion. They were produced to the specifications of government subcontractors, and government inspectors were often in the plant to watch all stages of production. One firm might be able to produce a particular kind of steel that another firm could not produce even though it had tried. These steels were considerably more expensive than the specialty steels, and failures to meet specifications resulted in more substantial losses for the company. At the time of the study about 20 percent of the cash value output was in aerospace metals.

The chairman, Fred Benson, had been president (managing director) of the company for two decades before moving up to this position. He is an elderly man but has a strong will and is much revered in the company for having built it up to its present size and influence. The president, Tom Hollis, has been in office for about four years; he was formerly the sales director and has worked closely with Fred Benson over many years. Hollis has three or four years to go before expected retirement. His assistant, Joe Craig, had been a sales manager in one of the smaller offices. It is the custom of this firm to pick promising people from middle-management and put them in the "assistant-to" position for perhaps a year to groom them for higher offices in their division. For some time these people had come from sales, and they generally went back as managers of large districts, from whence they might be promoted to a sales manager position in the main office.

Dick Benson, the executive vice president (roughly, general manager), is the son of Fred Benson. He is generally regarded as being willing, fairly competent, and decent, but weak and still much under his father's thumb. Traditionally, the executive vice president became president. Dick is not thought to be up to that job, but it is believed that he will get it anyway.

Ramsey Stockwell, vice president of production, had come into the organization as an experienced engineer about six years before. He rose rather rapidly to his present position. Rob Bronson, vice president of sales, succeeded Dick Benson after Benson had a rather short term as vice president of sales. Alan Carswell, the vice president of research, has a doctorate in metallurgy and some patents in his name, but he is not considered an aggressive researcher or an aggressive in-fighter in the company.

The Problem

When the research team studied Benson Metal, there were the usual problems of competition and pricecutting, the difficulties with the new aerospace metals, and inadequate plant facilities for a growing industry and company. However, the problem that particularly interests us here concerned the vice president of production, Ramsey Stockwell. He was regarded as a very competent production man. His loyalty to the company was unquestioned. He managed to keep outdated facilities operating and still had been able to push through the construction of quite modern facilities in the finishing phases of the production process. But he was in trouble with his own staff and with other divisions of the company, principally sales.

It was widely noted that Stockwell failed to delegate authority to his subordinates. A steady stream of people came into his office asking for permission for this and that or bringing questions to him. People who took some action on their own could be bawled out unmercifully at times. At other times they were left on their own because of the heavy demands on Stockwell's time, given his frequent attention to details in some matters, particularly those concerning schedules and priorities. He "contracted" the lines of authority by giving orders directly to a manager or even to a head foreman rather than by working through the intermediate levels. This violated the chain of command, left managers uninformed, and reduced their authority. It was sometimes noted that he had good men under him but did not always let them do their jobs.

The key group of production men rarely met in a group unless it was to be bawled out by Stockwell. Coordinating committees and the like existed mainly on paper.

More serious perhaps than this was the relationship to sales. Rob Bronson was widely regarded as an extremely bright, capable, likable, and up-and-coming manager. The sales division performed like a well-oiled machine but also had the enthusiasm and flashes of brilliance that indicated considerable adaptability. Morale was high, and identification with the company was complete. However, sales personnel found it quite difficult to get reliable information from production as to delivery dates or even what stage in the process a product was in.

Through long tradition, they were able to get special orders thrust into the work flow when they wanted to, but they often could not find out what this was going to do to normal orders, or even how disruptive this might be. The reason was that Stockwell would not allow production people to give any but the most routine information to sales personnel. In fact, because of the high centralization of authority and information in production, production personnel often did not know themselves. "Ramrod" Stockwell knew, and the only way to get information out of him was to go up the sales line to Rob Bronson. The vice president of sales could get the information from the vice president of production.

But Bronson had more troubles than just not wanting to waste his time by calling Stockwell about status reports. At the weekly top-management meeting, which involved all personnel from the vice presidential level and above, and frequently a few from below that level, Bronson would continually ask Stockwell whether something or other could be done. Stockwell always said that he thought it could be. He could not be pressed for any better estimations, and he rarely admitted that a job was, in fact, not possible. Even queries from President Tom Hollis could not evoke accurate forecasts from Stockwell. Consequently, planning on the part of sales and other divisions was difficult, and failures on the part of production were many because it always vaguely promised so much. Stockwell was willing to try anything, and worked his head off at it, but the rest of the group knew that many of these attempts would fail.

While the men under Stockwell resented the way he took over their jobs at times and the lack of information available to them about other aspects of production, they were loyal to him. They admired his ability and they knew that he fought off the continual pressure of sales to slip in special orders, change schedules, or blame production for rejects. "Sales gets all the glory here" said one. "At the semiannual company meeting last week, the chairman of the board and the managing director of the company couldn't compliment sales enough for their good work, but there was only the stock 'well done' for production; 'well done given the trying circumstances.' Hell, Sales is what is trying us." The annual reports over the years credited sales for the good years and referred to equipment failures, crowded or poor production facilities, and the like in bad years. But it was also true that problems still remained even after Stockwell finally managed to pry some new production facilities out of the board of directors.

Stockwell was also isolated socially from the right group of top personnel: He tended to work later than most, had rougher manners, was less concerned with cultural activities, and rarely played golf. He occasionally relaxed with the manager of aerospace sales, who, incidentally, was the only high-level sales person who tended to defend Stockwell. "Ramrod's a rough diamond; I don't know that we ought to try to polish him," he sometimes said.

But polishing was in the minds of many. "Great production man—amazing when he gets out of that mill. But he doesn't know how to handle people. He won't delegate; he won't tell us when he is in trouble with something; he builds a fence around his men, preventing easy exchange," said the president. "Bullheaded as hell—he was good a few years ago, but I would never give him the job again," said the chairman of the board. He disagreed with the president that Stockwell could change. "You can't change people's personalities, least of all production men." "He's in a tough position," said the vice president of sales, "and he has to be able to get his men to work with him, not against him, and we all have to work together in today's market. I just wish he would not be so uptight."

A year or so before, the president had approached Stockwell about taking a couple of weeks off and joining a leadership training session. Stockwell would have nothing to do with it and was offended. The president waited a few months, then announced that he had arranged for the personnel manager and each of the directors to attend successive four-day T-group sessions run by a well-known organization. This had been agreed on at one of the directors' meetings, though no one had taken it very seriously. One by one, the directors came back with marked enthusiasm for the program. "It's almost as if they had our company in mind when they designed it," said one. Some started having evening and weekend sessions with their staff, occasionally using the personnel manager, who had had more experience with this than the others. Stockwell was scheduled to be the last one to attend the four-day session, but he canceled at the last minute—there were too many crises in the plant, he said, to go off that time. In fact, several had developed over the previous few weeks.

That did it, as far as the other vice presidents were concerned. They got together themselves, then with the president and executive vice president, and said that they had to get to the bottom of the problem. A top-level group session should be held to discuss the tensions that were accumulating. The friction between production and sales was spilling over into other areas as well, and the morale of management in general was suffering. They acknowledged that they put a lot of pressure on production, and were probably at fault in this or that matter, and thus a session would do all the directors good, not just Stockwell. The president hesitated. Stockwell, he felt, would just ride it out. Besides, he added, the "Old Man" (chairman of the board) was skeptical of such techniques. The executive vice president was quite unenthusiastic. It was remarked later that Stockwell had never recognized his official authority, and thus young Dick feared any open confrontation.

But events overtook the plan of the vice president. A first-class crisis had developed involving a major order for their oldest and best customer, and an emergency top-management meeting was called, which included several of their subordinates. Three in particular were involved: Joe Craig, assistant to the president, who knows well the problems at the plant in his role as troubleshooter for the managing director; Sandy Falk, vice president of personnel, who is sophisticated about leadership training programs and in a position to watch a good bit of the bickering at the middle and lower levels between sales and production; Bill Bletchford, manager of finishing, who is loyal to Stockwell and who has the most modern-equipped phase of the production process and the most to do with sales. It was in his department that the jam had occurred, due to some massive scheduling changes at the rolling phase and to the failure of key equipment.

In the meeting, the ground is gone over thoroughly. With their backs to the wall, the two production men, behaving somewhat uncharacteristically in an open meeting, charge sales with devious tactics for introducing special orders and for acting on partial and misinterpreted information from a foreman. Joe Craig knows, and admits, that the specialty A sales manager made promises to the customer without checking with the vice president of sales, who could have checked with Stockwell. "He was right," said Vice President Bronson, "I can't spend all my time calling Ramsey about status reports; if Harrison can't find out from production on an official basis, he has to do the best he can." Ramsey Stockwell, after his forceful outburst about misleading information through devious tactics, falls into a hardened silence, answering only direct questions, and then briefly. The manager of finishing and the specialty A sales manager start working on each other. Sandy Falk, of personnel, knows they have been enemies for years, so he intervenes as best he can. The vice president of research, Carswell, a reflective man, often worried about elusive dimensions of company problems, then calls a halt with the following speech:

> You're all wrong and you're all right. I have heard bits and pieces of this fracas a hundred times over the last two or three years, and it gets worse each year. The facts of this damn case don't matter unless all you want is to score points with your opponents. What is wrong is something with the whole team here. I don't know what it is, but I know that we have to radically rethink our relations with one another. Three years ago this kind of thing rarely happened; now it is starting to happen all the time. And it is a time when we can't afford it. There is no more growth in our bread-and-butter line, specialty steels. The money, and the growth, is in aerospace; we all know that. Without aerospace we will just stand still. Maybe that's part of it. But maybe Ramsey's part of it too; this crisis is over specialty steel, and more of them seem to concern that than aerospace, so it can't be the product shift or that only. Some part of it has to be people, and you're on the hot seat, Ramsey.

Carswell let that sink in, then went on.

> Or maybe it's something more than even these.... It is not being pulled together at the top, or maybe, the old way of pulling it together won't work anymore. I'm talking about you, Tom [Hollis], as well as Fred [Benson, the chairman of the board, who did not attend these meetings] and Dick [the executive vice president, and heir apparent]. I don't know what it is, here are Ramsey and Rob at loggerheads; neither of them are fools, and both of them are working their heads off. Maybe the problem is above their level.

There is a long silence. Assume you break the silence with your own analysis. What would that be?

Company Index

ABC, 212
Accenture, 260, 347–348, 384, 432
Acer, 69, 309
Acme Electronics, 428–431
Affiliated Computer Services, 145
Airbus Industries, 6
Air Cal, 462
Air France, 19
AirTran, 19
Albertson's, 322–323
Alcoa, 10, 69, 76
Altavista, 25
Amazon.com, 3–4, 11, 13, 20, 54, 68, 108, 149–151, 173, 187, 195, 218–219, 314, 370, 385, 398, 414
AMD, 42, 215
American Airlines, 67
American Bank of Commerce, 455
American Home Products (AHP), 222, 224
American Photographic Group, 465
Amgen, 2, 105–106, 406, 467
Anheuser-Busch, 248, 279, 324, 444, 445, 447
AOL, 13, 42, 324
Apple Computer, 2, 9–13, 17, 24, 41, 61, 77, 102, 106, 111, 118, 150, 173, 180, 182, 189, 194–195, 198, 213, 217, 254, 273, 296, 309–312, 314–315, 335, 341, 343, 366, 367–368, 370, 372, 374, 381, 383, 388, 414, 466, 472, 474
Applied Research Technologies, Inc., 418
Ariba, 436, 438
ARM, 9
Arthur Andersen, 182, 186, 203–204, 324
Asea Brown Boveri, 417
AstraZeneca, 394
Atex Inc., 466
Atlantic Paper Products, Inc., 422
AT&T, 6, 73–74, 76, 195, 202, 316, 392–393
Avon, 223

Baan, 435
Bang & Olufsen, 78
Bank of America, 38–39, 43, 78–79, 186
B.A.R. and Grille, 92–97, 103, 148
Barnes & Noble, 68, 314
Bartles & Jaymes, 441–442, 444–446
Bausch & Lomb, 238
Bayside Controls Inc., 255
Bechtel Corp., 73
Becton Dickinson, 99–100, 105–106
Beech-Nut, 193, 199, 204
Behr Manning, 420
Beijing EAPs Consulting Inc., 418
Ben & Jerry's, 59–60
Bennett's Machine Shop, Inc., 447–458
Benson Metal Company, 476–479
Best Buy, 354, 388
Bianchi Vineyards, 443
BIC Corporation, 221
Big City Staple Corp., 422
Bimba Manufacturing, 195–196
Blackberry, 11, 17, 62, 472
Blockbuster Video, 2, 17, 308
BMW, 61, 72, 211
Body Shop, 46, 200
Boeing Corporation, 18, 33, 63, 81, 459, 462
Boeing of Louisiana, Inc. (BLI), 447, 449, 451–453, 455, 457
Borders, 68, 314
Boston Market, 307
BP, 33–34
Braniff, 460–461
Bristol-Myers-Squibb, 68
Broadcom, 20
Brown-Forman Corporation, 442, 444–446
Bugatti, 313
Burger King, 5, 56, 59–61, 84, 217–218, 310

Calcasieu Marine Bank, 455–457
California Cooler Company, 445–446
Calvin Cooler, 444–445, 447
Campbell's Soup, 59, 214
Cam-Recon, 450
Canada Dry/Graf's Bottling Company, 443
Canadaigua Wine, 442
Canandaigua Wine, 444–445
Canandaigua Wine Company, 444, 446
Canon, 466, 469–470, 472–473
Cap Gemini, 432
Carnation, 169
Carnegie Steel Company, 309
Carrier, 228
Caterpillar, 209–210, 357
CBS, 2, 212
Chevron, 434
China Coast, 137–138
Chinon, 465, 469–470
Chipotle, 218, 307, 316
Chrysler, 66–67, 313, 320, 345
Chubb, 228
Chunghwa, 77
CIC Inc., 411
Cisco Systems, 330–331
Citibank, 233, 294
Clorox, 296
Club Med, 235
CNN, 212
Coca-Cola, 9, 76, 133, 175, 209, 211–212, 214, 226, 247, 403, 406
Cole Haan, 302
Columbia/HCA hospital chain, 36–37
Comcast, 17, 417
Commerce One, 436, 438
Compaq Computer, 370
Computer Associates, 20, 38–39, 437
Contadina, 169
Continental Airlines, 10
Continental Can Company of Canada, Ltd., 417
Cord, 313
Corning Glass, 183
Corning Inc, 417
Costco, 70, 77
Countrywide Mortgage, 79
Crédit Suisse, 396
CREO, 473
Crown Cork & Seal, 69, 163, 247
CS First Boston, 396, 400
Cypress Semiconductor, 290

Dansk Designs Ltd., 417
DeBeers, 72
Delco, 84
Dell Computer Corp., 13, 33, 69, 71, 77, 85, 102, 106, 126, 173, 175, 192, 195, 254, 278, 306, 309, 316, 348, 370, 373, 388
Delta Airlines, 67, 324
Dimick Supply Company, 454
Disconix Inc., 466
Dow, 248
Dreyer's Grand Ice Cream, 169
Dun & Bradstreet, 420
DuPont, 102, 125, 159, 209, 248, 467
Dusenberg, 312
Dymo, 420

East Coast Supply Co., Inc., 422
Eastman Chemicals, 467–468
Eastman Dry Plate Co., 463
Eastman Kodak Co., 463–474
eBay, 13, 310, 317–318, 398
Eikonix Corp., 466
Ekco Group, 83
Electronic Arts, 246
EMI, 127–128
Enron, 20, 29, 35, 182, 324
Ernest & Julio Gallo Winery, 441–446
Express, 473
Exxon, 248, 250

Facebook.com, 2, 9, 13, 104–105, 111–112, 188–189, 195, 198, 209, 261, 273, 311, 324, 371–373, 472
Fairchild Semiconductor, 370
FedEx, 19, 20, 106–107, 124, 180, 182, 202, 351, 352, 355, 356
FedEx Kinko's, 1–2
Fiat, 61
Fidelity, 29
First Global Xpress, 19–20
Flextronics, 254, 288, 471
Ford Motor Company, 6, 14–15, 39–40, 41, 59–60, 61, 65–67, 78, 108, 148, 185, 210, 211, 232, 240, 241–242, 247, 262, 264, 265, 273, 313, 322, 345, 357, 379–380, 393, 397
Fox, 212
Foxconn, 254
FoxMeyer Drug, 434
Fox Photo Inc., 465, 470
Fuji Bank, 74–75
Fuji Photo Film Co., 464–465, 469
The Gap, 277, 408

Gap Inc., 2
Genentech, 2
General Dynamics, 53, 81
General Electric (GE), 4, 34, 39, 63, 79, 95, 122, 127, 152, 157, 184, 227–228, 296, 312, 338–339, 471, 474
General Gypsum Company, 141
General Mills, 61, 138
General Motors (GM), 4–6, 24, 42, 59, 61, 63–67, 79, 82–84, 126, 157–161, 189, 228, 232, 254, 313, 321–322, 344
Gillette, 46, 247
Goldman Sachs, 188, 396, 411
Gomberg, Fredrikson & Associates, 445
Goodyear, 324
Google, 2, 7, 9, 13, 17, 62, 79, 104–105, 111–112, 150, 173, 180, 182–184, 187–191, 194–195, 198, 202, 208–209, 214–215, 217, 219, 224, 240, 245, 260–261, 269–270, 273, 296, 310–311, 314, 318, 343, 369, 371–372, 383, 414, 472
Groupon, 12–13, 78, 184, 187, 311
GrouponLive, 78
Guidant, 192–193
Gulf National, 455

Halliburton, 34
Hallmark Cards, 163, 289
Haloid Co, 468
Hanson Trust, 227–229
Harley-Davidson, 185
HBO, 212
Heineken, 445
Heinz, 59, 132, 155
Heublein, 442
Hewlett Packard (HP), 38–39, 71, 85, 106, 126, 197, 200, 211, 215, 309, 349, 370, 376, 388, 470–473
Hi-Lo Auto Parts, 454
Hilton, 284
Hitachi, 209
Home Depot, 435
Honda, 6, 61, 65, 67, 176, 254, 313, 366
Hon Hai Precision Engineering, 254
Hoover, 59
Howard Johnson's, 59–60
H&R Block, 240
HTC, 311, 371
I2 Technology, 437

IBM, 2, 4, 6, 12, 24, 42, 59, 79, 81–82, 85, 102, 108, 111, 127, 157, 192, 196, 198, 233, 260, 273, 276, 278, 287, 310–312, 321, 324, 431–432, 437
IDEO, 341–342
IKEA, 88–89, 154, 247
IMB, 466
Immunex, 467
InBev, 279
Industrial Light & Magic Group, 102
Infeon, 77
Intel, 7, 9, 17, 42, 69, 367–368
iTunes, 11

J. B. Hunt Transport, 73
Jabil Circuit, 288
JCPenney, 48, 177
JetBlue, 19
Joe E. Seagram and Sons, 442, 444, 446
Johnson & Johnson, 157, 200–201, 411
The Johnson Sales Co., 422
Joseph Victori Wines, 444, 447
Juicy Couture, 176

Kate Spade, 176
Kellogg, 31, 61, 73
Kelvingrove, 418
KFC, 5, 307, 310
Kmart, 48, 83, 243
Kodak, 14–15, 79, 82, 195, 324–325
KPG, 473
Kraft Foods, 132
Krispy Kreme, 245–246
Kroger, 26, 70, 322–323

Labatt Breweries, 290
Lake Charles Motor Exchange, Inc., 449
Land Rover, 345
LEG, 473
Lenovo, 69, 309
Levi Strauss, 63, 103, 105, 107–108, 175, 199
Lexmark, 469, 472
Lexus, 211
LG Electronics, 77, 118, 214, 473
Li & Fung, 85
Live Nation Entertainment, 78
LivingSocial, 311
Liz Claiborne, 124, 176–177, 306
L.L. Bean, 47
Lotus, 7
LucasArts, 101–102

Lucky Brand Jeans, 176
Lundberg Family Farms, 64

Macy's, 176–177
Management Services, 455
Mansville Corporation, 199
Marcum, 435, 437, 438
Marriott, 284
Mars, Incorporated, 418
Marshall Field's, 170
Mary Kay, 366
Matsushita, 157, 213, 474–475
Mattel Inc., 277, 361–362
Mayo Clinic, 240
Maytag, 338
McDonald's, 4–5, 60–61, 63, 66, 76, 84, 200, 208–209, 213, 217–219, 243, 252, 253, 257, 310–311, 315–316, 373, 403
McKinsey & Co., 293, 384
Mercedes-Benz, 211, 212, 313
Merck, 68, 238, 259, 368, 383, 403, 404
Merloni Group, 418
Merrill Lynch, 43, 79, 396, 411
Mervyns, 170
MGA Entertainment, 361–362
Michelin, 326
Michelob, 442
Microsoft, 2, 7, 9, 10, 12, 41, 62, 72–73, 79, 102, 105, 183–184, 187, 190, 194, 195, 197–198, 209–210, 243, 261, 269–270, 310, 314, 315, 317, 318, 372, 375, 381, 435, 437, 438
Midcal Aluminum Company, 442
Midway Airlines, 461
Miller Brewing, 224, 248
Mitsubishi, 466
Molson Breweries, 290
Monsanto, 222
Morris Air, 462
Morton Thiokol, 201
Motorola, 77, 212, 311, 368, 468
Mystik, 420

NationsBank, 78–79
NBC, 212
Neiman Marcus, 163–164, 188, 216, 218
Nestlé, 31, 99, 168–170, 193, 368, 431
Netflix, 17, 39, 111
Netscape, 437
NEXT, 10
Nike, 73, 85, 171–172, 257, 277, 301–302, 315
Nikon, 470
Nintendo, 118
Nippon Restaurant Enterprise Co., 64
Nissan, 74, 276, 313, 325–326
Nokia, 61–62, 72–73, 79, 212–213, 273, 278, 310, 314, 367, 371
Nordstrom, 216
North Face, 302
Northwest Airlines, 461–462
Novell, 7
Nucor, 10, 222
Nvidia, 69, 72, 214–215, 312, 319

OAO Sollers, 78
Olympus, 470
Omega Electronics, Inc., 428–431
100,000 Auto Parts, 454
Onex Corp., 471
Oracle, 183–184, 349, 433, 435, 437
Otis, 228

Pacific Southwest Airlines (PSA), 459, 462
Packard, 312–313
Panasonic, 61, 78, 211–212, 214
Peanut Corporation of America, 31–32

Pennsylvania Railroad, 308–309
PeopleSoft, 433, 435
PepsiCo, 9, 76, 209, 211, 357
Perrier, 169
Peugeot, 61
Pfizer, 68, 125–126, 393–394
Pharmacia, 125
Philip Morris, 214, 224
Philips, 78, 233
Philips NV, 474–476
Phillips, 213
Picasa, 472
Pixar, 10, 17, 128, 414
Plexus Corp., 285, 287
The Point, 13
Polaroid Corp., 464–465
Pratt & Whitney, 228
Procter & Gamble, 24, 59, 95, 208–209, 211, 229, 368

Quaker Oats, 132–133
Qualex, 470

Radio Shack, 226
Ralston Purina, 169, 193
Reckitt Benckiser, 418
Red Lobster, 236
Reebok, 47
Renault, 326
Research in Motion, 273, 343, 367, 371, 474
Rohm & Hass, 473
Rolling Stones Inc., 369–370, 372
Rolls-Royce, 219, 226, 313
Rosas del Ecuador, 277
Rowntree, 169–170

S. D. Edwards, 433
Safeway, 26
Saks, 188, 218
Salomon Smith Barney, 43
Salvation Army, 4
Samsung, 9, 61, 62, 69, 77, 118–119, 212–213, 311, 367, 472–473
Santa Fe Pacific Corporation, 73
SAP, 184, 348, 431–438, 471
Schering-Plough, 237–238
Seagram and Sons, 442, 445
Seagram Distillers, 447
Sears, 2, 14–15, 192, 243
7-11, 26
Sharp, 77
Shell, 76
Siebel Systems, 436–438
Siemens, 474
Sikorsky, 228
SiteROCK, 188
Skype, 314
Smith Corona, 2
Sony, 61, 63, 78, 118–119, 212–213, 255, 277–278, 321, 368, 372–374, 466, 469, 474–476
Southwest Airlines, 18–19, 30–31, 77, 184, 187, 194, 204–205, 296, 459–462
Sprint, 76
SSA, 437
Starbucks, 4
Starwood, 284
State Farm, 186
Steak and Ale, 236
Sterling Drug, 465, 467
Stouffer Foods, 169
Stroh Brewery Company, 444, 446
Stubbs-Overbeck, Inc., 448
Subway, 61

Sun, 466
Sun Microsystems, 437

Taco Bell, 5, 56, 61, 316
Target, 2, 48, 77, 85, 170, 199, 202, 218, 277
Technological Products, 428
Texana Petroleum Corporation, 417
Texas Instruments, 370
Texas International, 460
3M, 187–188, 197, 209, 211, 224, 229, 371, 376, 382, 420, 468
TI, 349
TIAA/CREF, 29
Tiffany, 219
Timberland, 47
Time Warner, 41–42, 127
T-Mobile, 316, 392–393
Toyota, 5–6, 61, 65, 67, 74, 83, 159, 176, 209, 211, 214, 219, 243, 254, 265–266, 313, 322, 344–345, 366
Trader Joe's, 26
Transocean, 34
Triad Systems, 187–188
TRW Systems, 167
TRW Systems Group, 417
Tungsram, 79
Twitter, 104, 111–112, 373
Tyco, 29, 324

Union Pacific Railroad, 104–105
United Airlines, 462
United Continental, 324
United/Continental Airlines, 67
United Products, Inc., 419–428
United Technologies Corporation (UTC), 227–228
United Way of America, 34
UPS, 19–20, 106–107, 180–182, 288, 355–356
U.S. Steel, 15
UTC, 285

Value Line, Inc., 205
Verbatim Corp., 466
Verizon, 316
Versamark, 473
VF Company, 214
VF Corporation, 264–265
Virgin Atlantic, 19
Vitro, 183
Volkswagen, 10, 61, 232

Walmart, 2, 12, 48, 65, 70, 83, 99, 150, 214, 218, 243, 250, 257, 295, 315, 322, 354, 357, 388, 472
Walt Disney Company, 2, 10, 17, 38–39, 128, 189, 414
Warner Lambert, 125
Wendy's, 217–218, 310
Westland/Hallmark Meat Co., 56
Whirlpool, 101, 240, 338
White Lumber Company, 439–441
Whole Foods Market, 52–53
Willbros Group Inc., 73
WMX, 308
WordPerfect, 7
WorldCom, 35, 44

Xerox, 34, 126, 145–146, 210, 214–215, 310, 320, 324, 468, 470, 473

Yahoo!, 13, 25, 104–105, 190, 269, 324, 398

Zara, 176
Zynga, 246–247
Zytec Corporation, 139–140

Name Index

Allman, Jan, 15
Anderson, Philip, 367, 371
Authemont, Tim "Tamale," 453

Ballmer, Steve, 270
Bartles, Frank, 445
Bartz, Carol, 104–105
Beard, Jack, 451–453
Beaudo, Daren, 33
Bennett, Cheryl, 448–449, 453, 457–458
Bennett, Pat, 447–458
Bennis, Warren, 295
Benson, Dick, 477–478
Benson, Fred, 477, 479
Bewley, R. Stuart, 443, 445
Bezos, Jeffrey, 4, 68, 108, 149–150, 219, 314, 370, 385
Bimba, Charles, 195–196
Black, Greg, 247
Bletchford, Bill, 478
Bloomberg, Michael R., 49
Brin, Sergey, 7, 9, 111, 190–191
Bronson, Rob, 477–479
Brooks, Garth, 127
Brown, Brad, 439–441
Brown, Clyde, 453
Brown, George, 419–428
Brown, Richard, 419
Burns, Tom, 112, 114–116
Burns, Ursula, 145
Busch, August, IV, 279
Buttner, Jean, 205

Canion, Rod, 370
Carnegie, Andrew, 308–309
Carp, Daniel A., 469–471
Carswell, Alan, 477, 479
Casey, James E., 181
Chambers, John, 330–331
Champy, J., 285–286
Chandler, Colby, 464–465, 467–468
Chao, Elaine L., 34
Charo, 446
Cheema, Wasim Khalid, 49
Chua, Micheline, 102
Ciavarella, Mark, 405
Claiborne, Liz, 124, 306, 370
Cohl, Michael, 369
Coker, Jess, 460
Coleman, James, 443
Collins, Glenn S., III, 411
Conahan, Michael, 405
Coulombe, Joe, 26
Craig, Joe, 477–478
Crete, Michael M., 443, 445
Crosby, Cathy Lee, 446
Crozier, Michael, 404

Daley, Richard M., 461
David, George, 228
Dekker, Wisse, 475
Dell, Michael, 370, 388
Deming, W. Edwards, 283
Disney, Roy, 414
Donahoe, John, 318, 398
Drew, Dick, 382
Durant, William C., 158

Eastman, George, 463, 467
Ebbers, Bernie, 44–45
Eisner, Michael, 414

Falk, Sandy, 478, 479
Fayerweather, Mike, 439–440
Fisher, George, 468–469
Ford, Henry, 241–243, 247, 269, 313
Ford, Henry, III, 39–40
Ford, Henry II, 380, 397
Ford, William Clay, 397
Franklin, Bill, 460
Fredrikson, Aileen, 445
Fredrikson, Jon, 445
Frey, Don, 379–380

Gallo, David, 443
Gallo, Ernest, 441–443, 445
Gallo, Joseph (father of Ernest and Julio Gallo), 441
Gallo, Joseph (son of Julio Gallo), 443
Gallo, Julio, 441–443
Gates, Bill, 197–198
Gauthreaux, Kevin "Goat,", 453
Georger, Gloria, 15
Gerstner, Louis, 196, 198
Ghosn, Carlos, 325–326
Gibbs, Tom, 445
Greiner, L. E., 317, 320–321, 323
Gundotra, Vic, 112

Hamel, G., 384
Hammack, Lance, 453, 458
Hammer, Michael, 285–286
Hanes, Jim, 425
Hardesty, Richard, 451
Hassan, Fred, 237–238
Hee, Lee Hun, 212
Heskett, James, 346
Hewlett, William, 370
Hickson, David, 411
Hill, Charles W. L., 474–476
Hollis, Tom, 477–479
Hopkins, Bob, 439–441
Huang, Jen-Hsun, 319
Huizenga, Wayne, 308

Iacocca, Lee, 397
Iger, Bob, 128, 414
Iverson, Ken, 222

Jagger, Mick, 369–370
Jaymes, Ed, 445
Jenster, Per V., 441–447
Jobs, Steve, 10–11, 17, 41, 128, 180, 312, 370, 414
Johnston, Summerfield, 133
Jones, Gareth R., 185, 431–438, 463–474
Jonsson, E., 325, 328
Jung, Andrea, 223
Juran, Joseph, 283

Kamprad, Ingvar, 88–89
Kanter, Rosabeth Moss, 381
Kay, Mary, 366
Kelleher, Diana, 443
Kelleher, Herbert, 18, 30, 204, 459–462
Kelly, David, 341
Kenny, Jim, 404–405
Kindler, Jeffrey, 393
King, Al, 427
King, Rollin, 459
Knight, Phil, 302
Kotter, John P., 346
Kroc, Ray, 315

Lac Xuan Huyn, 450, 452, 458
Lambert, Billy, 453
Land, Edwin, 464
Lawrence, Paul R., 112–116, 215
LeBlanc, Dale, 450, 458
Levering, Robert, 462
Levy, Alain, 128
Lewin, Kurt, 280, 291–292, 300
Lorsch, Jay, 112–116, 215
Lucas, George, 102

Mackay, Martin, 125–126, 393–394
Mackey, John, 52–53
Madoff, Bernie, 202
Malone, Stewart C., 439–441
Manuel, Curtis, 450
March, James, 342
Mason, Andrew, 13
Mayer, Brian, 284
McComb, William, 176–177
McConathy, Dorothy, 455
McConathy, Scott, 450–452
McManus, James, 453
McMichael, Craig, 453
Mendell, Steven, 56
Mintzberg, Henry, 340
Moggridge, Bill, 341
Morrison, Robert, 132–133
Moskowitz, Milton, 462
Mulally, Alan, 40, 273
Mulcahy, Anne, 145
Murphy, Glen, 408
Muse, M. Lamar, 460, 462

Nasser, Jacques, 39
Nonaka, I., 371
Nystrom, Paul C., 349, 353

Omidyar, Pierre, 317

Packard, David, 370
Page, Larry, 7, 9, 17, 41, 111–112, 190–191, 198, 371
Parker, Jim, 461–462
Parkinson, C. Northcote, 127, 324
Parnell, Stewart, 31–32
Parrish, Stan, 439–440
Pazmino, Erwin, 277
Perez, Antonio, 325, 463, 471–474
Perrow, Charles, 249–253, 267, 269, 476–479
Pettigrew, Andrew, 404
Pfeffer, Jeffrey, 407
Phillips, Calvin, 461
Pondy, Louis R., 394, 396–397, 400
Potter, Harry, 369
Prahalad, C. K., 384
Pressler, Paul, 408
Putnam, Howard, 461

Rajaratham, Raj, 42, 202
Ransom, Cindy, 296
Rawls, Jim, 428, 430–431
Reavely, Tom, 460
Richards, Amanda, 92–97, 148
Richards, Bob, 92–97, 148
Richards, Keith, 370
Rion, Lloyd, 455
Rodgers, T. J., 290

Rowling, J. K., 369

Sant, Roger, 103
Schein, E. H., 185
Schmidt, Eric, 41
Scott, Tom, 308
Sculley, John, 10
Senge, Peter, 343, 346
Sharplin, Arthur, 447–458
Shearer, John, 453
Shuman, Jeffrey C., 419–428
Simmons, Martin, 450–452
Sinegal, James, 70
Skaggs, Mark, 246
Sloan, Alfred P., 158–159, 161
Smith, James, 452–453
Smith, Ronnie, 453
Stalker, G. M., 112, 114–116
Starbuck, William H., 249, 353
Steid, Thomas, 443
Stephenson, Randall, 392
Stevens, Hank, 424–425
Stockwell, Ramsey, 477–479
Stringer, Howard, 118–119

Thompson, James D., 255–256, 258, 269, 395
Thornton, Kenneth, 453
Timmer, Jan, 476
Tushman, Michael, 367
Tyler, John, 428–430, 429

van de Klugt, Cor, 475–476
Van Mannen, J., 185
Viega, John F., 428–431

Wang, Jerry, 104
Weber, Max, 134–135, 139
Weitzel, W., 325, 328
White, John, 439–441
Whitman, Meg, 317–318, 398
Whitmore, Kay, 468
Whitwam, David, 101
Willis, Bruce, 446
Winkles, Thomas, 450–451
Woods, Byron, 450–453
Woodward, Joan, 244–245, 248, 250, 253, 255, 267
Wozniak, Stephen, 10, 370
Wright, Jim, 461

Subject Index

Accommodative approach, 200
Acquisitions, 466
Action research, 292–294
Adaptive cultures, 346
Adaptive functions, 96
Advanced manufacturing technology (AMT), 261–267
Agency problem, 41
Agency theory perspective, 41–43
Agenda, control of, 409
Airline Deregulation Act, 460
Assets. *See* Specific assets
Aston Studies, 267, 350
Attitudes, organizational conflict and, 400–401
Attitudinal structuring, 400
Authority, 95
  See also Organizational authority
Autonomy, crisis of, 318

B2B marketplace, 173
Backward vertical integration, 225–226
Bargaining, in organizational change, 296–297
Birth. *See* Organizational birth
Blinded stage of organizational decline, 325
Bottom-up change, 293
Boundaryless organization, 172–173
Boundary-spanning activity, 385
Bounded rationality, 80–81, 337
Bricks-and-mortar retailers, 4, 150, 314
Building coalitions, 408–409
Bureaucracy
  advantages of, 137–139
  definition, 134
  management by objectives, 139–140
  organizational conflict and, 395–396
  principles of, 134–137
Bureaucratic costs
  internal transaction costs as, 82
  in multidivisional structure, 161
  organizational authority, 126
Bureaucratic culture, 324
Business-level strategy, 217
  culture and, 222–224
  definition, 211–212
  differentiation, 218
  focus strategy, 219
  low-cost, 218
  structure and, 219–222
Business model
  of Eastman Kodak, 467–468, 471
  of SAP, 432–433
Business plan development, 307–308
Business process, 286
Business-to-business (B2B) commerce, 173
Business-to-customer (B2C) commerce, 173

Capital keiretsu, 74
Career paths, 43
Carnegie model of organizational decision making, 337–338
Cartels, 77
Centrality, 405–408
Centralization, 436
  control and, 132–133
  decentralization, 103–106, 434–435, 469
  decentralization *versus*, 103–106
  failure from, 467–468
Ceremonies, 187–189
Chain of command, 39
  See also Minimum chain of command principle
Chair of the board, 37, 39
Change. *See* Organizational change
Change agent, 298–299
Chief executive officer (CEO), 39–44, 288
  in top-management team, 356–357
Chief operating officer (COO), 16, 40, 43
Child labor, 47–48
Coalitions
  building and managing, 408–409
  dominant, 406–407
  organizational, 338
Codification, 348–349
Coercion, in organizational change, 297
Coercive isomorphism, 315
Cognitive biases, 350
Cognitive dissonance, 350
Cognitive structure, 349–350
Collaboration, organizational growth through, 320
Collateral organizational structure, 358
Collective tactics, 185, 186
Collusion, 77
Commitment, escalation of, 352
Communication, organizational change and, 295
Communication problems
  in functional structure, 151
  in multidivisional structure, 161
  organizational authority, 124–125
Competing goals, 35–36
Competition
  Acme and Omega case, 428–429
  Bartles & Jaymes case, 444–447
  Eastman Kodak case, 464–467
  organizational stakeholders, 392
  for resources, 396
  SAP case, 435–438
  Southwest Airline case, 459–462
  UPI case, 420
Competitive advantage, 12–14
Competitive forces for change, 275–276
Competitive interdependencies, 71
Competitive resource interdependencies, 76–79
Complex tasks, 250–255
Computer-aided design (CAD), 264, 375
Computer-aided material management (CAMM), 264–265
Computer-aided production, 263
Computer-integrated manufacturing, 266–267
Conflict. *See* Organizational conflict
Conflict aftermath, 395, 398–399
Conflict resolution strategies, 399–401
Contingencies, 11–12
Contingency approach, 112
Contingent workers, 142
Continuous-process technology, 248
Contracts, long-term, 73
Contributions, 28–29
Control, 7, 10–11, 95
  Acme and Omega case, 428–429
  centralization and, 132–133
  crisis of, 319
  differentiation and, 153
  divisional structures and, 152–154
  ethical, 53
  in functional structure, 150–152
  hierarchy and, 130–134
  horizontal differentiation and, 130–132
  illusion of, 351
  information, 404
  in multidivisional structure, 160
  organizational roles and, 135
  organizational structure, 130–134
  over resources, 403–404
  over uncertainty, 406
  quality, 429–431, 439–441
  span of, 128–130
  standardization and, 133
Cooperation, among organizational stakeholders, 392
Cooptation, 72
Coordination, organizational growth through, 319–320
Coordination ability, 209–210
Copyrights, 368
Core competences, 12, 96
  differentiation and, 210
  functional-level strategy, 213–217
  global expansion and, 210–211
  sources of, 208–210
  strategy and, 207–213
Core members, 387
Corporate-divisional relationship, 160
Corporate-level strategy, 212, 224
  conglomerate structure, 227–228
  organizational culture and, 229–230
  organizational structure and, 227–229
  related diversification, 226
  related diversification structures, 228–229
  structure and, 227–229
  unrelated diversification, 226–227
  UPI case, 425–427
  vertical integration, 225–226
Corporate managers, 40
Cost reduction, functional-level strategies for, 213–215
Counseling, in organizational change, 297
Craftswork, 241, 252
Creativity
  innovation and, 370–373
  organizational growth through, 317
Crisis stage of organizational decline, 327
Critical path method (CPM), 375
Cross-functional teams, 377–378
Culture. *See* Organizational culture
Customer problems, in functional structure, 151
Customers, 30–31

Death. *See* Organizational decline and death
Decentralization, 434–435, 469
  centralization *versus*, 103–106
Decision making. *See* Organizational decision making
Decision tree, 356
Decline stage, of product life cycle, 372
Dedicated machines, 261–262
Defensive approach, 199, 200
Delegation, organizational growth through, 318–319
Demographic forces, 276
Departmental-level technology, 240–241
Design. *See* Organizational design
Devil's advocate, 357–358
Diagnosis, 292
Dialectical inquiry, 357–358
Differentiation, 98–99
  B.A.R and Grille, 92–97
  building blocks of, 95
  design challenge, 93
  differentiation at, 96–97
  divisional structures and, 153

Differentiation (*Continued*)
integration *versus*, 102–103
Lawrence and Lorsch on, 112–114
organizational insight, 94
organizational roles, 94–95
subunits, 95–96
vertical and horizontal, 97
Differentiation business-level strategy, 218
Direct contact, 100
Direction, organizational growth through, 318
Disjunctive tactics, 186
Dissenters, listening to, 353
Dissolution stage of organizational decline, 327
Distortion, 124
Diversity management, 14–16
Divestiture tactics, 186
Division, 95
self-contained, 96
Divisional managers, 41
Divisional structure
differentiation and, 153
geographical divisional structure, 163–164
market structure, 164–165
multidivisional structure, 156–161
product division structure, 154–156
product team structure, 161–163
Division of labor, 5, 92–93
Dominant coalition, 406–407
Downsizing, 126, 290
Dynamism. *See* Environmental dynamism

E-commerce, 173
Economic forces, 63, 276
Economies of scale, 6
Economies of scope, 6
Education, organizational change and, 295
E-engineering, 290
Efficiency, 14, 16
Ego-defensiveness, 352
Embryonic stage, of product life cycle, 372
Employees. *See* Workforce
Employee stock ownership plans (ESOPs), 194
Empowerment
authority and, 403
organizational development and, 295–296
organizational structure and, 141–142
Engineering production, 252
Enterprise resource planning (ERP), 431–438
Entrepreneurs, 306, 371–372
Entrepreneurship, 2
Environment, 59
institutional, 315
specific, 61–63
See also Global environment; Organizational environment
Environmental complexity, 66–67
Environmental dynamism, 67
Environmental forces, 64–65
Environmental niches, 309–310
Environmental richness, 67–68
Environmental uncertainty, 65–69, 80–81
Environment change, in Philips NV case, 475
Escalation of commitment, 352
Ethical culture, 53
Ethical dilemma, 43–44
Ethical forces, 64–65, 276–277
Ethical organizations, 52–54
Ethical structure, 53
Ethics
case study, 56, 439–441
individual, 48–49
justice model of, 46
law and, 44–45
moral rights model of, 46
organizational, 43–52
organizational stakeholders and, 45–47
organizational theory exercise, 55–56
personal, 51
professional, 48
reasons for, 49–51
societal, 47–48
sources of, 47–49
summary, 54
top management and, 43–52
top managers and, 43–52
utilitarian model of, 46
European Union (EU), 276
Evaluation of action, 294
Events, as learning opportunities, 353
Evolutionary change, 281
Experimenting, 353–354
Experts, organizational politics and, 409
Exploitation, 343
Exploration, 342
External change agents, 293
External resource approach, 17

Facilitation, in organizational change, 296
Fads, role of, 373
Fashion, role of, 373
Faulty action stage of organizational decline, 325–326
Feedback, 259
Felt conflict, 395, 397
Finance, in Bennett Machine Shop case, 455–458
Financial keiretsu, 73–74
First-mover advantages, 311
Fixed tactics, 185
Fixed workers, 262
Flat organization, 122–123
Flexible manufacturing technology, 266
Flexible production, 263
Flexible work teams, 285–286
Focus strategy, 219
Force-field theory, 280–281
Formalization, 106
Formal tactics, 185, 186
Frequency, 351–352
Function, 95
Functional-level strategy, 211, 213–217
Functional-level technology, 240–241
Functional managers, 41
Functional orientation differences, 278
Functional resources, 208–209, 274
Functional structure, 150–152

Game theory, 354–356
GANTT chart, 375
Garbage-can model of organizational decision making, 340–342
General environment, 63–65
Generalists, 312
General public, 34
Geographical divisional structure, 163–164
Global environment
case study, 88–89
information technology, 68
Nokia case, 62
organizational environment, 59–69
resource dependence theory, 69–79
SAP case, 432–433
summary, 86–87
transaction cost theory, 79–86
Global expansion strategy, 210–213, 434
Global forces, 276
Global matrix structure, 169–170
Global networks, 210–211
Global strategy, 474–476
Global supply chain management, 61, 85
Global values, 182–184
Goals. *See* Management by objectives; Organizational goals
Governance mechanisms, 42
Government, 32–33
Group level of organizational learning, 344–345
Group-level resistance to change, 279–280
Groupthink, 357
Growth. *See* Organizational growth
Growth stage, of product life cycle, 372

Habits, 280
Heavyweight team leaders, 379
Heredity, 135
Hierarchy, 97
of authority, 39, 99–100, 121–134
control and, 130–134
emergence of, 121–122
size and height limitations, 122–124
tall hierarchies problems, 124–126
See also Organizational authority
High technical complexity, 244
Horizontal differentiation, 97
control and, 130–132
diffentiation and, 99
organizational structure and, 130–132
strategy and, 231
Hospitals, doctors as stockholders in, 36–37
Human resource management (HRM), 214
Human resources, organizational change and, 274
Hybrid structure, 170–171

Identification stage of unstructured decision-making model, 340
Illusion of control, 351
Implementation of action, 293–294
Inaction stage of organizational decline, 325
Incremental innovations, 367
Incrementalist model of organizational decision making, 339
Incremental technological change, 367
Indispensability, 407
Individual ethics, 48–49
Individual level of organizational learning, 343–344
Individual-level resistance to change, 280
Individual-level technology, 240
Individual tactics, 185
Inducements, 28–29
Inert cultures, 346
Informal organization, 140–141
Informal tactics, 185
Information, 466
control over, 404
uncertainty and, 336
Information efficiencies, 383–384
Information synergies, 384–386
Information technology
empowerment, 141–142
global environment, 68
innovation and, 383–384
knowledge management and, 347–349
organizational culture, 385–386
organizational structure, 141–142, 385–386
Innovation, 14, 16, 291, 366
case study, 388
information synergies and, 384–386
information technology and, 383–384
intrapraneurship and creativity, 370–373
management of, 374–383
organizational theory exercise, 387–388
summary, 386–387
technological change and, 366–370
Inputs, 3–4, 240–241
Inside stakeholders, 28–30
Institutional environment, 315

Institutionalization of action research, 294
Institutional theory, 315
Instrumental value, 180
Integrating role, 102
Integration, 99
 differentiation *versus*, 102–103
 divisional structures and, 152, 153
 functional structures and, 151
 integrating mechanisms, 99–102
 Lawrence and Lorsch on, 112–114
 rites of, 187
 vertical, 225–226, 258
Intensive technology, 259
Interdependence, 395
Intergroup training, 298–299
Interlocking directorate, 72
Internal change agents, 293
Internal cost-cutting, 465
Internal labor market, 160
Internal systems approach, 17
Internal transaction costs, 82
Interorganizational level of organizational learning, 346
Interorganizational strategy
 resource dependence theory, 70–71
 transaction cost theory, 82–86
Intrapreneurs, 370
Intrapreneurship, 370–373
Investiture tactics, 186

Joint ventures, 75–76, 381
 strategy of, 466
Justice model of ethics, 46
Just-in-time inventory (JIT) system, 265–266

Keiretsu, 74–75
K-generalists, 312–313
Kinship, 135
Knowledge-creating organization, 371
Knowledge management, 347–349
K-specialists, 312–313
K-strategy, 311–312

Labor. *See* Division of labor; Workforce
Labor market, internal, 160
Language. *See* Organizational language
Large-batch and mass production technology, 247
Latent conflict, 394–396
Law
 ethics and, 44–45
 Southwest Airlines case and, 459–462
Leadership
 crisis of, 317
 team, 379–380
 top-management team, 40–41, 356–357
Lean production, 263
Learning. *See* Organizational learning
Learning organization, 343
Liability of newness, 306
Liaison roles, 100
Life cycle. *See* Organizational life cycle
Lightweight team leaders, 379
Line function, 395
Line role, 40
Linkage mechanisms, 71–73, 78, 81–82
Local communities, 33
Location problems, in functional structure, 151
Long-linked technology, 258
Long-term contracts, 73
Low-cost business-level strategy, 218
Low technical complexity, 244

Maintenance functions, 96
Management by objectives (MBO), 139–140
Management philosophy, of UPI, 420–421
Management team, in UPI, 424–425
Managerial abilities, 336
Managerial functions, 96
Managers, 30
 in Bartles & Jaymes case, 442–443
 differentiation *versus* integration, 102–103
 ethics and, 43–52
 management by objectives and, 139–140
 organizational authority and, 134, 140
 organizational effectiveness measurements by, 16–20
 organizational politics and, 408
 property rights and, 194
 rational model of organizational decision making and, 335–337
Managing coalitions, 408–409
Manifest conflict, 395, 397–398
Manufacturing, 252, 261–263
Manufacturing technology, 261–267
Marketing
 in Bennett Machine Shop case, 453–455
 SAP case, 433
Market structure, 164–165
Mass production, 241
 to advanced manufacturing technology, 261–263
Mastery, 343
Material management, 264–265
Materials technology, 263–267
Matrix structure, 166–171
Mature stage, of product life cycle, 372
Measurement problems, in functional structure, 151
Mechanistic structures, 110, 115–116, 196, 278
Mediating technology, 256–258
Mergers, 76, 78
Mimetic isomorphism, 315–316
Minimum chain of command principle, 127–128
Minority ownership, 74–75
Mission, 19–20
Moral hazard problem, 41–42
Moral rights model of ethics, 46
Motivation problems, 126
Multidivisional matrix structure, 168–170
Multidivisional structure, 156–159
 bureaucratic costs in, 161
 control in, 160
 profitability in, 160
Multidomestic strategy, 230, 232
Multinationals, 432
Mutual adjustment, 106, 108

Natural selection, 312–314
Negotiation, in organizational change, 296–297
Negotiator, third-party, 400
Networks, 73–74
Network structure, 171–172
New venture divisions, 380–381
Nonprogrammed decisions, 335
Nonroutine research, 252–253
Nonroutine technology, 255
Nonsubstitutability, 404–405, 407
Normative isomorphism, 316
Norms, 107, 181
 global values and, 182–184
 See also Organizational culture

Objectives. *See* Management by objectives
Obstructionist approach, 199, 200
Official goals, 19–20
Operations, in Bennett Machine Shop case, 449–452
Operative goals, 20
Opportunism, 81
Organic structures, 110–111, 115–116, 196
Organizational authority, 37–41, 95
 bureaucratic costs, 126
 case study, 477–479
 centralization *versus* decentralization, 103–106
 communication problems, 124–125
 empowerment and, 403
 hierarchy and control, 130–134
 hierarchy of authority, 39, 99–100, 121–134
 managerial implications, 134, 140
 minimum chain of command principle, 127–128
 organizational power and, 402–403
 in organizational structure, 121–130
 Parkinson's law problem, 127
 rational-legal authority, 134–135
 size and height limitations, 122–124
 span of control, 128–130
 summary, 143
Organizational birth, 306–314
Organizational capabilities, organizational change and, 274
Organizational change, 10–11, 22–23, 273
 action research, 291–295
 case study, 301–302
 coercion in, 297
 counseling in, 297
 evolutionary, 281–285
 forces for and resistance to, 275–281
 importance of, 11
 organizational culture and, 274, 278–279
 organizational development and, 295–299
 organizational theory exercise, 300–301
 in Philips NV case, 475–476
 revolutionary, 285–291
 Starwood case, 284
 summary, 299–300
 targets of, 274–275
Organizational coalitions, 338
Organizational conflict, 278, 393
 attitudes and, 400–401
 bureaucracy and, 395–396
 case study, 414
 conflict resolution strategies, 399–401
 felt conflict, 395, 397
 goals and, 395
 latent conflict, 394–396
 manifest conflict, 395, 397–398
 organizational effectiveness and, 391–392
 organizational structure and, 399–400
 organizational theory exercise, 413
 perceived conflict, 395–397
 Pondy's model of, 394–399
 role conflict, 136
 summary, 412
Organizational confrontation meeting, 299
Organizational culture, 9
 adaptive culture, 346
 bureaucratic, 324
 business-level strategy, 222–224
 case study, 204–205
 corporate-level strategy and, 229–230
 definition, 179–184
 ethical, 53
 inert culture, 346
 information technology, 385–386
 innovation and, 381–383
 management of, 197–199
 organizational change and, 274, 278–279
 organizational ethics in, 191–193
 organizational theory exercise, 203–204
 origins of, 189–197
 social responsibility, 199–202
 summary, 202–203
 transmission of, 184–189
 UPS case, 181

Organizational decision making, 334–335
  case study, 361–362
  improving, 353–358
  knowledge management and information technology, 347–349
  models of, 335–346
  organizational politics and, 409
  organizational power and, 406–407
  organizational theory exercise, 360–361
  summary, 359
Organizational decline and death, 321–327
Organizational design, 9–10, 14–16, 22
  case study, 118–119
  centralization and decentralization, 103–106
  contingency approach to, 112
  differentiation, 92–99
  differentiation and integration, 99–103
  integration, 99–103
  mechanistic and organic organizational structures, 109–116
  organizational theory exercise, 117–118
  poor, 14–16
  standardization and mutual adjustment, 106–109
  summary, 116
  Yahoo! case, 104–105
Organizational development (OD), 297–299
  empowerment and, 295–296
Organizational domain, 60
Organizational effectiveness
  case study, 26
  measurement of, 16–20
  in multidivisional structure, 160
  organizational conflict and, 391–392
  organizational decline and, 321–323
  organizational goals, 19–20
  organizational theory exercise, 24–25
  stakeholder goals and interests, 34–37
  summary, 23
  technology and, 242–243
Organizational environment, 3, 59–60
  case study, 88–89
  general environment, 63–65
  global environment, 59–69
  Lawrence and Lorsch on, 112–114
  management of, 6, 20–21
  managerial implications, 69
  organic *versus* mechanistic structures, 111–112
  organizational decline and, 324–325
  organizational theory exercise, 87–88
  resource dependence theory, 69–70
  specific environment, 61–63
  strategy and, 71–86, 207–213
  summary, 86–87
  transaction cost theory, 79–86
  uncertainty in, 65–69
Organizational ethics, 191–193
  See also Ethics
Organizational goals, 35–36
  management by objectives and, 139–140
  organizational conflict and, 395
Organizational growth, 314–320
Organizational inertia, 323–324
Organizational isomorphism, 315–316
Organizational language, 187–189
Organizational learning
  factors affecting, 349–352
  levels of, 343–346
  nature of, 342
  types of, 342–343
Organizational level of organizational learning, 345–346
Organizational life cycle, 305
  birth, 306–314
  case study, 330–331
  decline and death, 321–327
  growth, 314–320
  models of, 316–317, 325–327
  organizational theory exercise, 329–330
  summary, 328–329
Organizational mirroring, 299
Organizational politics, 407–411
Organizational power, 401
  organizational politics and, 407–411
  sources of, 402–407
Organizational resources, 209
Organizational rites, 187
Organizational roles, 94–95, 135–136, 185–186
Organizational stakeholders, 28
  cooperation and competition among, 392
  ethical organizations, 53–54
  ethics and, 45–47
  inside stakeholders, 28–30
  outside stakeholders, 30–34
  satisfying stakeholders' goals and interests, 34–37
Organizational structure, 8–9, 278–279, 381
  Acme and Omega case, 428–431
  Acme case, 428–430
  boundaryless organization, 172–173
  bureaucracy, principles of, 134–137
  business-level strategy and, 219–222
  case study, 145–146
  control, 130–134
  corporate-level strategy and, 227–229
  e-commerce, 173
  empowerment and well-managed teams, 141–142
  ethical, 53
  functional-level strategy and, 215–216
  functional structure, 148–152
  functional to divisional structure, 152–154
  horizontal differentiation and, 130–132
  IKEA case study, 88–89
  informal organization, 140–141
  information technology and, 141–142, 385–386
  matrix structure, 166–171
  mechanistic and organic organization, 109–116
  network structure, 171–172
  nonroutine technology and, 255
  organizational authority in, 121–130
  organizational conflict and, 399–400
  organizational culture and, 196–197
  organizational theory exercise, 144
  Philips NV case, 475–476
  product structure, 152–163
  routine technology and, 253–255
  summary, 174
  technical complexity and, 248–250
  UPI case, 422–423
  values and, 154, 156–157
Organizational theory, 8
Organizational theory exercise
  ethics, 55–56
  organizational change, 300–301
  organizational conflict, 413
  organizational culture, 203–204
  organizational decision making, 360–361
  organizational design, 117–118
  organizational effectiveness, 24–25
  organizational environment, 87–88
  organizational life cycle, 329–330
  organizational structure, 144
  strategy, 236–237
  technology, 268–269
Outside pressure, 51–52
Outside stakeholders, stakeholders and, 30–34
Outsourcing, 61, 85, 171
Parkinson's law problem, 127–128
Participation, in organizational change, 295–296
Patents, 368
People
  characteristics of, 189–191
  innovation and, 382
Perceived conflict, 395–397
Performance criteria, incompatible, 396
Personal ethics, 51
Personalization, 348–349
Personnel, in Bennett Machine Shop case, 452–453
PERT/CAM network, 375
Planning, 431–438
  UPI case, 423–424
Political forces, 64–65, 276
Politics. *See* Organizational politics
Pondy's model of organizational conflict, 394–399
Pooled interdependence, 256–258
Pooled task interdependence, 256
Population density, 310–311
Population ecology theory, 309
Population of organizations, 309
Power, 7, 278
  unobtrusive, 406–407
  See also Organizational power
Preferences in rational model of organizational decision making, 337
Principle of minimum chain of command, 127
Priorities, differences in, 395
Proactive approach, 200
Process consultation, 298
Product division structure, 154–156
Production functions, 96
Product life cycle, 372–373
Product team structure, 161–163, 377–378
Professional ethics, 48
Profitability
  internal cost-cutting for, 465
  in multidivisional structure, 160
  organizational decline and, 321–323
Programmed decisions, 334–335
Programmed technology, 244
Project, 374
Projection, 352
Project management, 374–376
Promotion tournaments, 42
Property rights, 193–196, 368–370, 383
Public. *See* General public

Quality circles, 283
Quality control, 429–431, 439–441
Quantum innovations, 367
Quantum technological change, 367

Random tactics, 185
Rational-legal authority, 134–135
Rational model of organizational decision making, 335–337
Reciprocal task interdependence, 259
Red tape, crisis of, 320
Reengineering, 285–290
Related diversification, 226
Representativeness, 351–352
Reputation, 71–72
Reputation effect, 50
Research
  action, 292–294
  nonroutine, 252–253
Resources, 17, 76–79, 431–438
  competition for, 396
  control over, 403–404
  functional, 208–209, 274

human, 214, 274
organizational, 209
slack, 258
Resource dependence theory, 69
competitive interdependencies management strategies, 76–79
Costco, 70
interorganizational management strategies, 70–71
managerial implications, 80
symbiotic interdependencies management strategies, 71–76
Restructuring, 126, 290–291
Revolutionary change, 281
Reward maximization, 324
Rewards allocation, 36–37
r-generalists, 312–313
Risk aversion, 323
Rites of enhancement, 187
Rites of integration, 187
Rites of passage, 187
Role ambiguity, 136
Role conflict, 136
Role orientation, 185–186
Routine manufacturing, 252
Routine technology, 253–255
r-specialists, 312–313
r-strategy, 311–312
Rules
ethical, 47, 49–51
written, 106–107

Sales, 433
UPI case, 424
Sarbanes-Oxley Act, 29–30, 43, 202
Satisficing, 337
Selection stage of unstructured decision making model, 340
Self-contained division, 96
Self-dealing, 42
Self-interest, 51
Self-managed teams, 141–142
Sensitivity training, 297–298
Sequential interdependence, 258–259
Sequential tactics, 185, 186
Sequential task interdependence, 258
Serial tactics, 186
Shareholders, 29–30
Skunk works, 380–381
Slack resources, 258
Small-batch and unit technology, 244–246
Social forces, 276
Socialization, 108, 184–187
Social responsibility, 199–202
Social status, 135
Societal ethics, 47–48
Sociotechnical systems theory, 281–282
Span of control, 128–130
Specialism, 261
Specialists, 312
Specialization, 5
Specific assets, 81
Specific environment, 61–63
Speed, 14
Staff function, 395
Staff role, 40
Stage-gate funnel, 376–377
Stakeholders. *See* Organizational stakeholders
Standardization, 106–109, 133
Standard operating procedures (SOPs), 106
Stock-based compensation, 42
Stories, 187–189
Strategic alliances, 72–73, 78
Strategic change, in Philips NV case, 475–476
Strategic problems, in functional structure, 151
Strategy, 12–14, 436–438
business-level, 211–212, 217–224
case study, 237–238
core competencies and, 207–213
corporate-level, 212, 224–230, 425–427
across countries, 230–235
Eastman Kodak case, 465–467
functional-level, 211, 213–217
global, 230, 233–234
global expansion, 212–213
horizontal differentiation and, 231
international, 230, 232–233
multidomestic, 230, 232
organizational environment and, 71–86, 207–213
organizational theory exercise, 236–237
summary, 235
transnational, 230, 234–235
UPI case, 425–427
Structure. *See* Organizational structure
Subunit orientation, 99
Subunits, 95–96
Suppliers, 32
Supply chain management. *See* Global supply chain management
Support functions, 95–96
Symbiotic interdependencies, 71
Symbiotic resource interdependencies, 71–76
Systems theory, sociotechnical, 281–282

Takeovers, 76
Tall hierarchies problems, 124–126
Tall organizations, 122–126
Task analyzability, 251
Task forces, 100–101
Task interdependence, 255–261
Tasks, routine and complex, 250–255
Task variability, 251–252
Teams, 101, 274
cross-functional, 377–378
flexible work, 285
heavyweight team leaders, 379
management, 424–425
product team structure, 161–163, 377–378
self-managed, 141–142
Top-management, 40–41, 356–357
Team building, 298
Team leadership, 379–380
Technical approach, 18–19
Technical complexity, 244–250
Technological capabilities, organizational change and, 274
Technological forces, 64
Technological imperative, 250
Technology, 240–241
advanced manufacturing technology, 261–267
case study, 269–270
Eastman Kodak case, 463–474
mass production, 261–263
organizational effectiveness and, 242–243
organizational theory exercise, 268–269
summary, 267–268
task interdependence, 255–261
tasks, routine and complex, 250–255
technical complexity, 244–250
Temporary workers. *See* Contingent workers
Terminal value, 179–181
Third-party linkage mechanism, 78
Third-party negotiator, 400
Top-down change, 293
Top management
ethics and, 43–52
property rights and, 194
Top-management team, 40–41, 356–357
Total quality management (TQM), 282–285
Trademarks, 368–369
Trade unions, 33
Transaction costs, 6–7, 50, 79
linkage mechanisms and, 81–82
sources of, 80–81
Transaction cost theory, 79–81
interorganizational strategy and, 82–86
Transfer price, 161
Trusteeship, 37, 38
Two-boss employees, 166

Uncertainty, 114
control over, 406
differentiation *versus* integration, 102–103
environmental, 65–69, 80–81
information and, 336
Unethical behavior, 51–52
Unions, 29, 33, 63, 276
Unit technology. *See* Small-batch and unit technology
Unobtrusive power, 406–407
Unrelated diversification, 226–227
Unstructured model of organizational decision making, 339–340
Utilitarian model of ethics, 46

Values, 179–181
global, 182–184
organizational structure and, 154, 156–157
rational model of organizational decision making and, 337
Value creation, 3–5
functional-level strategy, 208
global expansion strategy, 210
Value-creation cycle, 208
Variable tactics, 185
Vertical differentiation, 97
Vertical integration
corporate-level strategy, 225–226
distribution of outputs, 258

Whistle-blowing, 53, 193, 201, 202
Wildcat strikes, 141
Workers, contingent, 142
Workforce, 30
child labor, 47–48
property rights, 194
Work teams, 274
flexible, 285–286
Written rules, 106–107